W9-BXH-198

Handbook
of Studies on MEN &
MASCULINITIES

Handbook of Studies on MEN & MASCULINITIES

Editors

Michael S. Kimmel | Jeff Hearn | R.W. Connell

State University of
New York at Stony Brook

Swedish School of
Economics, Helsinki

University of Sydney

SAGE Publications
Thousand Oaks ■ London ■ New Delhi

For information:

Sage Publications, Inc.
2455 Teller Road
Thousand Oaks, California 91320
E-mail: order@sagepub.com

Sage Publications Ltd.
1 Oliver's Yard
55 City Road
London EC1Y 1SP
United Kingdom

Sage Publications India Pvt. Ltd.
B-42, Panchsheel Enclave
Post Box 4109
New Delhi 110 017 India

Printed in the United States of America

Library of Congress Cataloging-in-Publication Data

Handbook of studies on men and masculinities / edited by Michael S. Kimmel,
Jeff Hearn, and R.W. Connell.
    p. cm.
Includes bibliographical references and index.
ISBN 978-0-7619-2369-5 (cloth)
  1. Men—Social conditions. 2. Masculinity. 3. Sex role. I. Kimmel, Michael S.
II. Hearn, Jeff, 1947- III. Connell, R. W.
HQ1090.H33 2004
305.31—dc22   2004003826

This book is printed on acid-free paper.

09   10   11   12   10   9 8 7 6 5 4 3 2

Acquisitions Editor:	Jerry Westby
Editorial Assistant:	Vonessa Vondera
Production Editor:	Denise Santoyo
Copy Editors:	Katherine Chilton
	A. J. Sobczak
Typesetter:	C&M Digitals (P) Ltd.
Indexer:	Pamela Van Huss
Cover Designer:	Michelle Lee Kenny

Contents

1

INTRODUCTION

R. W. CONNELL

JEFF HEARN

MICHAEL S. KIMMEL

In recent decades, the study of gender has expanded rapidly and with it, studies of gender issues about men and masculinities. Interest in these questions has developed across the social sciences, the humanities, the biological sciences, and (to some extent) in other fields. This research interest reflects a growing public interest in men's and boys' identities, conduct, and problems, ranging from men's violence to boys' difficulties in school.

The field of gender research has mainly addressed questions about women and has mainly been developed by women. The impulse to develop gender studies has come mainly from contemporary feminism, and women have therefore mainly been the ones to make gender visible in contemporary scholarship and in public forums.

Revealing the dynamics of gender, however, also makes masculinity visible and problematizes the position of men. Both women and men have addressed this problem. Where men's outlooks and culturally defined characteristics were formerly the unexamined norm for science, citizenship, and religion, the specificity of different masculinities is now recognized, and their origins, structures, and dynamics are investigated. This investigation has now been active for more than 20 years and has produced a large and interesting body of research.

Monographs on masculinities appear in every social and behavioral science discipline and in every field of the humanities. As indicators of the active growth of this field, there are now several scholarly journals specifically devoted to it. The scholarly journal *Men and Masculinities,* published by Sage, is now in its seventh volume year. Other journals include *International Journal of Men's Health, Journal of Men's Studies, Psychology of Men and Masculinity, Working With Men,* and the now defunct *Masculinities* and *IASOM Bulletin.* Several publishers have launched book series devoted to studies of men and masculinities, including Beacon, Routledge, Unwin Hyman, and Zed. One of the first, and perhaps the most successful, series has been the Sage Series on Men and Masculinities, which included 15 independently edited thematic volumes published from 1992 to 2002. There are also a number of

Web-based and other bibliographic resources available, including *The Men's Bibliography*, constructed by Flood (2003), now in its 11th edition.

The global growth of research is shown by the fact that in the last 7 years, not just individual research reports but whole collections of research have been published in Australia (Tomsen & Donaldson, 2003), Brazil (Arilha, Unbehaum Ridenti, & Medrado, 1998), France (Welzer-Lang, 2000), the former Soviet countries (Novikova & Kambourov, 2003), Germany (*Multioptionale Männlichkeiten?*, 1998, Bosse & King, 2000), Japan (Louie & Low, 2003), Latin America as a whole (Olavarría & Moletto, 2002), the Middle East (Ghoussoub & Sinclair-Webb, 2000), New Zealand (Law, Campbell, & Dolan, 1999), the Nordic regions (Ervø & Johansson, 2003a, 2003b), the postcolonial world (Ouzgane & Coleman, 1998), and Southern Africa (Morrell, 2001a), in addition to the work published beginning in the late 1980s in the United Kingdom (Hearn & Morgan, 1990), Canada (Haddad, 1993; Kaufman, 1987), and the United States (Brod, 1987; Kimmel, 1987). In addition, several works have appeared on global perspectives more generally, in a series called Global Masculinities (Cleaver, 2002; Pease & Pringle, 2002). There are also a number of collective publications from the 10-country European Union (EU)–funded European Research Network on Men in Europe (see Chapter 9). The global perspective on research on men and masculinities is discussed in more detail below.

The research debate is closely paralleled by the global policy debate. Following the world conferences on women that began in 1975, there has been an increasing global debate on the implications of gender issues for men. Paragraph 3 of the Platform for Action, adopted at the 1995 Fourth World Conference on Women, said, "The Platform for Action emphasises that women share common concerns that can be addressed only by working together and in partnership with men towards the common goal of gender equality around the world" (United Nations, 2001, p. 17).

These issues are increasingly being taken up in the United Nations (UN), its various agencies, and other transgovernmental organizations and policy discussions. For example, the UN's Division for the Advancement of Women (2003) recently organized an online discussion forum and expert group meeting on "the role of men and boys in achieving gender equality" as part of its preparation for the 48th session of the Commission on the Status of Women, with the following comments:

> Over the last decade, there has been a growing interest in the role of men in promoting gender equality, in particular as the achievement of gender equality is now clearly seen as a societal responsibility that concerns and should fully engage men as well as women. The global commitment to gender equality in the Beijing Platform for Action and other major international conferences and summits, and in the existing international legal framework, including the Convention on the Elimination of All Forms of Discrimination against Women and ILO Conventions, have encouraged and accelerated efforts in this regard. To further develop efforts in this area, the United Nations Commission on the Status of Women (CSW) will consider the role of men and boys in achieving gender equality at its forty-eighth session in March 2004.

We believe this is a propitious moment to stand back from this developing field, summarize where we have got to, and think about future directions for the field. These are the tasks of this handbook. We hope to make current scholarship available to a new generation of researchers and students and to a wider audience concerned with policy and with practical or cultural issues about men, boys, and gender.

The authors of these chapters are among the best-known experts in their particular fields today. Many have themselves undertaken the path-breaking research that defined and energized a particular line of enquiry. Their command of the field and their ability to convey it in an accessible manner make each chapter both an authoritative review of current knowledge and a stimulus to further enquiry.

We have named the subject matter of the book "studies of men and masculinities." There is some debate about what to call this field of knowledge. Some scholars have called the field "men's studies" by analogy with (or reaction against) "women's studies," and this certainly reflects the origins of the field. Other scholars consider the symmetrical nomenclature misleading because of the asymmetry of gender relations that made the creation of "women's studies" a project of self-knowledge by a subordinated group. The editors of this volume fall into this latter camp and consider terms such as "studies of men and masculinities" and "critical studies on men" to more accurately reflect the nature of contemporary work, which is inspired by, but not simply parallel to, feminist research on women.

SOCIAL SCIENCE APPROACHES TO MEN AND MASCULINITIES

Although focused scholarship on men and masculinities has expanded in the humanities and to some extent in some of the natural and technological sciences, it is the social sciences that have produced the greatest amount of research on men and masculinities. Similarly, in this handbook, the contributions and almost all of the contributors can be located primarily within the social sciences, even though there are important debates from the humanities and, to a lesser extent, from the natural sciences that are taken up in some of the chapters. In particular, there is now a substantial development of studies on men and masculinities in literature, visual art, dance, music, and other cultural and aesthetic fields.

The view of social science here in the handbook is a broad one. It necessarily draws on a number of traditions. Although not wishing to play down debates and differences between traditions, this broad approach to men and masculinities in the handbook can be characterized in a number of ways:

- By a *specific,* rather than an implicit or incidental, *focus* on the topic of men and masculinities
- By taking account of *feminist, gay, and other critical gender scholarship*
- By recognizing men and masculinities as *explicitly gendered* rather than nongendered
- By understanding men and masculinities as *socially constructed, produced, and reproduced* rather than as somehow just "naturally" one way or another
- By seeing men and masculinities as *variable and changing* across time (history) and space (culture), within societies, and through life courses and biographies
- By emphasizing men's relations, albeit differentially, to *gendered power*

- By spanning both *the material and the discursive* in analysis
- By interrogating the *intersecting of the gender with other social divisions* in the construction of men and masculinities.

This last point may need a little more explanation. Although men and masculinities are the explicit focus and are understood as explicitly gendered, men and masculinities are not formed by gender alone. Men are not simply men or simply about gender, and the same applies to masculinities. Men and masculinities are shaped by differences of age, by class situation, by ethnicity and racialization, and so on. The gendering of men only exists in the intersections with other social divisions and social differences. Indeed, paradoxically, it might be argued that as studies of men and masculinities continue to deconstruct the gendering of men and masculinities and assumptions about them, other social divisions, such as age, class, and disability, come more to the fore and are seen as more important. In this sense, part of the long-term trajectory of gendered studies of men could, paradoxically, be the deconstruction of gender (Lorber, 1994, 2000).

The social science approaches to men and masculinities, both in this handbook and in the field more generally, are certainly diverse. They vary and range across different disciplines, theoretical perspectives, methodologies, conceptualizations, and positionings. These variations are thus relevant here in at least three ways: in terms of the varied and uneven development of the field of studies on men and masculinities, the range of material reviewed in the individual chapters of the handbook, and the range of authors and authorships of the chapters. We will now discuss these variations in a little more detail.

In the recent development of studies on men and masculinities, there have been significant developments in almost all the principal social science disciplines. Accordingly, the disciplines represented in this handbook include most of the social sciences: sociology, social psychology, political science, cultural studies, education, and social policy, as well as women's studies, gender studies, gay studies, and postcolonial studies. There are also major debates from psychology and history that are important influences in some chapters. In addition, significant subdisciplines include criminology; family studies; violence studies; studies of ethnicity, race, and (anti-) racism; and military studies. Many—perhaps most—of the contributions are multidisciplinary or interdisciplinary, but the most fully represented disciplinary approach in this handbook is sociological. Two major disciplines that are somewhat underrepresented here are economics and law, although economic and legal issues are discussed in some chapters. Of the largest and institutionally most developed social science disciplines, economics has probably been the most reluctant to contribute to studies on men and masculinities, even though economy and economic considerations are absolutely fundamental aspects of gender relations and the gendering of men and masculinities.

There are as many theoretical social science perspectives on men and masculinities as there are theoretical perspectives in the social sciences more generally. These include positivism, cultural relativism, psychoanalysis, interpretivism, critical theory, neomarxism, feminism (of various forms and kinds), poststructuralism, postmodernism, and postcolonialism. All of these and other theoretical perspectives have been influential in the development of studies on men and masculinities and are represented to varying degrees in the contributions here. Indeed, it could be argued that social theory questions have been rather prominent throughout the developments of the last 20 years or so (Brod & Kaufman, 1994; Hearn & Morgan, 1990). Additionally, nongendered traditions that are common within mainstream social theory need to be both drawn on and critiqued in terms of their implicit and explicit conceptualizations of gender, women, and men.

Similarly, we recognize the variety of methods and methodologies in studying men and masculinities. These include social surveys; statistical analyses; ethnographies; interviews; and qualitative, discursive, and deconstructive approaches. Furthermore, an explicitly gendered focus on men and masculinities can lead to the rethinking of how particular research methods are to be done. For example, Schwalbe and Wolkomir (2002) have recently set out some of the key issues to be borne in mind when conducting research interviews with men.

Another key issue has been the state of conceptualization. The concept of masculinities has been extremely important over the last 20 years in widening the analysis of men and masculinities within the gender order (Brod, 1987; Carrigan, Connell, & Lee, 1985; Connell, 1995). It has succeeded the concept of the "male sex role" and is generally preferred to, for example, manhood or manliness (we will return to this development in a little more detail in the next section). There is also a growing debate and critique around the concepts of masculinities and hegemonic masculinity from a variety of methodological positions, including the historical (MacInnes, 1998), materialist (Donaldson, 1993; Hearn, 1996, 2004; McMahon, 1993), and poststructuralist (Whitehead, 2002) perspectives.

Another very important source of variation is the positioning of the author in relation to the topic of men. This can be understood as a personal, epistemological, and geopolitical relation. Researchers and analysts, men and women, may position themselves discursively in relation to the object of research, the topic of men and masculinities, in a variety of ways—for example, in treating the topic nonproblematically (through taking for granted its absence or presence), through sympathetic alliance with those men studied or the contrary subversion of men, or with ambivalence, in terms of alterity (the recognition of various forms of otherness between and among men) or through a critical relation to men (Hearn, 1998). This is partly a matter of individual political choices and decisions in positioning, but increasingly the importance of the more structural, geopolitical positioning of commentators is being recognized. Postcolonial theory has shown that it matters whether the analysis of men is being conducted from within the West, the global South, the former Soviet territories, the Middle East, or elsewhere. In that way, history, geography, and global politics matter in epistemologies and ontologies in studying men.

Accordingly, it is to this increasingly global nature of the field of study of men and masculinities that we now turn in more substantive detail.

THE GLOBAL DEVELOPMENT OF MEN AND MASCULINITIES AS A RESEARCH FIELD

All human cultures have ways of accounting for the positions of women and men in society and have different ways of picturing the nature of men and the patterns of practice we call masculinities. Central Australian Aboriginal communities, for instance, have Dreaming stories of legendary heroes crossing, and creating, the land. Through these narratives, the rights and obligations of groups of men (and the different rights and obligations of groups of women) are taught and located in a specific landscape that is part of the web of obligations (Sutton, 1988). Neo-Confucian clan rules in late Qing-dynasty China also defined the obligations of men, but not in relation to landscapes. Rather, they offered abstract moral exhortation, advice about occupations (devaluing the military), a model of social hierarchy and personal character for men (emphasising restraint), and an idealized description of family life (Liu, 1975).

The distinctive combination of empirical description and secular explanation that we call social science took shape during the later 19th century, at the high tide of European imperialism. Gender issues were among its main concerns, and it is not surprising that its ideas of gender were influenced by imperialism. Stories from the colonial frontier were a major source of data for European and North American social scientists writing about sexuality, the family, and the social position of women and men. The very idea of "race," which became a key concept in Western culture at this time, embedded sexuality and gender relations. The emancipation of women was seen by many social scientists as a measure of social progress, and the supposed "backwardness" of the colonized became a public justification of colonial rule. There was, then, a global dimension in the Western social science of gender from its earliest stage (Connell, 2002).

However, the evolutionary framework was discarded in the early 20th century. The first steps toward the modern analysis of masculinity are found in the depth psychology pioneered in Austria by Freud and Adler. Psychoanalysis demonstrated that adult character was not predetermined by the body but was constructed, through emotional attachments to others, in a turbulent process of growth (see Connell, 1994). In the next generation, anthropologists such as Malinowski and Mead emphasised cultural differences in these processes and the importance of social structures and norms. By the mid-20th century, these ideas had crystallized into the concept of "sex roles."

Masculinity was then understood in psychology, sociology, and anthropology as an internalized role or identity, reflecting a particular (in practice often meaning United States or Western) culture's norms or values, acquired by social learning from agents of socialization such as family, school, and mass media.

Under the influence of women's liberation and gay liberation, the "male role" was subject to sharp criticism as oppressive and limiting (Pleck & Sawyer, 1974). The "question of men" was a significant item on feminist agendas (e.g., Friedman & Sarah, 1982). Hanmer (1990) lists 53 feminist publications "providing the ideas, the changed consciousness of women's lives and their relationship to men—all available by 1975" (pp. 39-41). Recent feminist initiatives have suggested various analyses of men and ways forward for men (see, e.g., Gardiner, 2001). In the United States, the idea of "men's studies" as an academic field emerged out of debates sparked by this critique (Massachussets Institute of Technology, 1979).

In the social sciences, the concept of a "male sex role" has become obsolete, rejected for its ethnocentrism, lack of power perspective, and incipient positivism (Brittan, 1989; Eichler, 1980; Kimmel, 1987). In its place, a broader social constructionist perspective that highlights issues of social power has emerged (Carrigan et al., 1985; Kaufman, 1987). In Anglophone social science, life history and ethnographic research provided close descriptions of multiple and internally complex masculinities (Mac an Ghaill, 1994; Messner, 1992; Segal, 1997). In European social science, pioneering survey research (Holter, 1989; Metz-Göckel & Müller, 1985) showed the diversity of men's life patterns within a persisting gender system. Conceptual work emphasised social structure as the context for the formation of particular masculinities (Connell, 1987; Hearn, 1987; Holter, 1997), with some recent authors emphasizing that masculinities are constructed within specific discourses (Petersen, 1998).

Historical research has traced the emergence of new masculinities and the institutions in which they arise. These have included both dominant (e.g., Davidoff & Hall, 1990; Hall, 1992; Hearn, 1992; Kimmel, 1997; Tosh, 1999; Tosh & Roper, 1991) and resistant (e.g., Kimmel & Mosmiller, 1992; Strauss, 1982) forms of masculinity at home, in work, and in political and cultural activities. Particularly important and interesting historical work has been done from gay history (Mort, 2000; Weeks, 1990) and from colonies of settlement such as New Zealand and Natal on schools and military forces (Morrell, 2001b; Phillips, 1987).

Research, however, is only one dimension of the new discussions of men and masculinities. In the rich countries, including Japan, Germany, and the United States, and in some less wealthy countries, including Mexico and Brazil, the late 1980s and 1990s saw rising media interest and public debate about boys and men. Mainly focused on social problems such as unemployment, educational failure, domestic violence, and family breakdown, but also discussing men's changing identities, these debates have different local emphases. In Australia, the strongest focus has been on problems of boys' education (Lingard & Douglas, 1999). In the United States, more attention has been given to interpersonal relationships and to ethnic differences (Kimmel & Messner, 2001). In Japan, there has been a specific challenge to the "salaryman" model of middle-class masculinity (see Chapter 8). In Scandinavia, there has been more focus on gender equity policies and men's responses to the changing position of women (Lundberg, 2001). In Latin America, especially in Mexico, public debate has addressed the broad cultural definition of masculinity in a long-standing discussion of "machismo," its roots in colonialism, and its effects on development (Adolph, 1971; see also Chapter 7).

In most of the developing world, these debates have not emerged, or have emerged only intermittently. In the context of mass poverty, the problems of economic and social development have had priority. However, questions about men and masculinities emerged in development studies in the 1990s, as feminist concerns about women in development led to discussion of "gender and development" and the specific economic and political interests of men (White, 2000). These debates also have different emphases in different regions. In Latin America, particular concerns arose about the effects of economic restructuring and with men's sexual behavior and role in reproduction, in the context of population control policies and sexual health issues, including HIV/AIDS prevention (Valdés & Olavarría, 1998; Viveros Vigoya, 1997). In Southern Africa, regional history has led debates on men and masculinities to have a distinctive focus on race relations and on violence, both domestic and communal (Morrell, 2001a). In the Eastern Mediterranean and Southwest Asia, the cultural analysis of masculinity has particularly concerned modernization and Islam, the legacy of colonialism, and the region's relationship with contemporary Western power (Ghoussoub & Sinclair-Webb, 2000).

By the late 1990s, the question of men and masculinity was also emerging in international forums, such as diplomacy and international relations (Zalewski & Parpart, 1998), the peacekeeping operations of the United Nations (Breines, Connell, & Eide, 2000), and international business (Hooper, 2000). Equally important, there is research and debate about the impact of globalization on local gender patterns: men's employment, definitions of masculinity, and men's sexuality (Altman, 2001).

The analysis of masculinities, men, and men's place in the gender order has thus become a worldwide undertaking, with many local differences of emphasis. Although most of the empirical research is still produced within the developed countries and is especially rich in the United States, global perspectives are now possible. New conceptual approaches are affecting the field, including poststructuralism from Europe (Wetherell & Edley, 1999) and postcolonial perspectives from the global South (Ouzgane & Coleman, 1998). It therefore seemed timely, two decades after the first statements of social constructionist perspectives on masculinity, to undertake an international survey of the field. Hence this handbook: an attempt to order the knowledge that has been produced, compare different regions of the world, and address emerging themes and arenas.

OVERVIEW OF THE BOOK

This book is divided into five sections. These sections help organize both the global and the local studies of men and masculinities. They center on several different themes that together compose the current understandings of men and masculinities and place the critical inquiries offered here in a more unified and coherent context.

We explore the construction of masculinities in four different frames: (a) the social organization of masculinities in their global and regional iterations; (b) the institutional reproduction and articulation of masculinities; (c) the ways in which masculinities are organized and practiced within a context of gender relations—that is, the ways in which interactions with other men and with women express, challenge, and reproduce gender inequalities; and (d) the ways in which individual men express and understand their gendered identities.

In organizing this book, we move from the larger global and institutional articulations of masculinities to the more intimate and personal expressions. We do this because, as sociologists, we believe that these institutional arenas and processes form the framework in which masculinities are experienced and expressed. Gender identity is more than a simple psychological property belonging to a person, something one "has" as a result of socialization and that one consequently inserts into all interactions. Gender identity is a constant process, always being reinvented and rearticulated in every setting, micro or macro. Gender identity is the codified aggregation of gendered interactions; its coherence depends on our understanding of those interactions.

Locating gender identity does not, however, make it a simple derivative of gendered institutions and gendered processes. Gender relations are constantly shifting; gender identities are always in motion, always dynamic. Such movement creates the seams by which political transformations may take place.

In the first part, "Theoretical Perspectives," the authors ground contemporary inquiries in the study of men and masculinities in the three theoretical traditions that seem to inform most social scientific thinking on the subject. Øystein Gullvåg Holter locates the social scientific inquiry at the intersection of several problematic concepts raised in the studies of social stratification and inequality: domination, patriarchy, and sexism. He focuses on the relationship between male dominance and patriarchal structures in society. Judith Kegan Gardiner and Tim Edwards anchor these inquiries to the theoretical perspectives most cognizant of gender, gender relations, the gender order, and the social construction of gender identity: feminist theory and queer theory. The former problematizes the dynamics of gender, as well

as the relationships between women and men, institutionally; the latter approaches the gender order through the problematization of sexuality and specifically, in this context, relationships among men.

Gardiner shows that feminist theories over the last 40 years have taken varied approaches to gender equality that are intertwined with their varied perspectives on men and masculinity: They endorse some aspects of traditional masculinity, critique some, and ignore others. Edwards explores and critiques the relationship between masculinity and homosexuality both theoretically, in the light of sexual politics and the rise of poststructural theory, and more politically.

The next part explores the shifting dynamic of global and local as the national settings in which masculinities are constructed. R. W. Connell explores the ways in which certain dominant versions of masculinities are rearticulated in the global arena as part of the larger project of globalization. The next four chapters detail the ways in which regional articulations in the constructions of masculinities rely on local cultural formations as well as on the collision of those local cultures with other national cultures or with larger transnational institutions, such as the global market. Robert Morrell and Sandra Swart examine how men in postcolonial contexts construct their masculinities. They note the salience of poverty and underscore, more broadly, the significance of context, as well as identifying some new approaches to understanding postcolonial masculinity. The chapter by Matthew Gutmann and Mara Viveros Vigoya and that by Futoshi Taga survey the variety of studies of men and masculinities in Latin America and East Asia, respectively, tracing the origins of the field, analyzing its accomplishments, and indicating areas for future research.

Finally, the chapter by the collaborators in the European Union's Social Problem of Men research project (Critical Research on Men in Europe [CROME]) indicates an effort to generate a comparative framework for understanding masculinities in the new Europe, one that remains sensitive to cultural differences among the many countries of that continent and to the ways in which all nations of the European Community are, to some extent, developing convergent definitions of gender.

The chapters in Part III explore intersectionality—the intersection of gender with the structural and institutional. David Morgan explains how different classes exhibit different forms of masculinities and the ways in which these both challenge and reproduce gender relations among men and between women and men. Ken Plummer poses similar questions around sexuality, and James Messerschmidt examines how the gendered practices of men and boys may result in crime. He outlines initial approaches to masculinities and crime in the early 1990s and critically scrutinizes several new directions in the criminological literature.

Masculinities do not exist in social and cultural vacuums but rather are constructed within specific institutional settings. Gender, in this sense, is as much a structure of relationships within institutions as it is a property of individual identity. Several other chapters in this section examine how masculinities shape, and are shaped by, the major institutions of modern society: the workplace (David Collinson and Jeff Hearn), the media (Jim McKay, Janine Mikosza, and Brett Hutchins), and education (Jon Swain).

Two additional chapters explore the construction of masculinities in families. William Marsiglio and Joseph Pleck explore a wide range of fatherhood scholarship from a gendered and critical perspective. They consider both how the style of men's fathering contributes to gendered social inequalities within and outside families and how men's participation in systems of gendered social relations—both between and within genders—shapes their fathering opportunities, attitudes, and behavior. Michele Adams and Scott Coltrane examine the intersection of family dynamics, paid work and housework, and child care.

The chapters in Part IV explore the ways in which men's practices shape masculinities, as well as assessing the impact of that construction on ourselves and others. Michael Messner traces the development of scholarship on men, masculinities, and sport. His chapter describes the contributions that this scholarship has made to the more general scholarly work on masculinities and bodies, health, and violence and closes by outlining new directions in work on men and sport—particularly studies that examine sport as an institutional and cultural context for relations between women and men and between various

groups of boys and men. Don Sabo outlines all the different epidemiological issues that certain constructions of masculinities provoke. He discusses the history and development of men's health studies, key theoretical models, and some of men's gender-specific health issues. Several male groups with unique health needs are identified and, finally, some global frameworks for understanding men's health are presented. Walter DeKeseredy and Martin Schwartz review and critique the sociological literature on the relationship between masculinities and variations in interpersonal violence across different social classes and racial or ethnic backgrounds. They pay special attention to violence against women in heterosexual relationships, homicide, and youth gang violence.

Among the most exciting developing areas in gender studies is the exploration of the making of the gendered body as a material object and the making of its cultural representations. In his chapter, Tom Gerschick examines the ways in which men with disabilities repair and restore potentially "damaged" masculinities and in the process create new sources of resistance to embodied notions of masculinity. He offers a critical review of the extant biographical, empirical, and theoretical literature on masculinities and the body, with particular attention to disability. The chapter summarizes and analyzes key questions, themes, and debates in this literature and concludes with suggestions for future research. Richard Ekins and Dave King take this one step further, examining the ways in which transgendered people throw open the question of how and whether gender identity inheres in a corporeal body, and, if it does, what happens to that identity when that body is transformed. They consider the interrelations between transgenderedness, masculinity, and femininity in terms of transgendering as a social process within which males "renounce" or "suspend" the masculinity that is expected of them and females (unexpectedly) embrace it. The chapter takes a historical and chronological approach, focuses on four very influential perspectives on the topic, and discusses their conceptions of and implications for masculinity (and usually of and for femininity, as well).

Finally, the chapters in Part V address the politicization of masculinity and the masculinity of politics. Joane Nagel examines the social, historical, and cultural spaces coinhabited by men and nations, by manhoods and nationhoods, and by masculinities and nationalisms. Michael Kimmel uses this gendered framework to explore the reactions and resistance among the groups of men who are the "losers" in the globalization project, specifically among the downwardly mobile lower middle classes of small farmers, artisans, and small shopkeepers. Paul Higate and John Hopton explore the intersections of war and the military with constructions of masculinity and the "gendered" nature of political and military institutions.

Shahin Gerami argues that a core component of the Islamic Revolution's ideology was reformulation of gender discourse around an Islamic hypermasculinity. This hypermasculinity promoted three ideals of manhood: mullahs, who are the interpreters of the Qur'an and Shari'at; martyrs, the young men who bide the dictates of the mullahs and sacrifice themselves for the republic; and ordinary men, who are perceived to have benefited from this hypermasculinity. Economic hardship and sociopolitical pressure assail all men. Additionally, they all pay for gender discrimination against women in general and women of their social group in particular.

Finally, Michael Flood provides a useful brief reminder that scholarly inquiries into gender are always in dialogue with political movements for gender equality.

The Future of the Field

It is impossible to predict the future of a research field accurately—if we could do that, the research would not need to be done. It may, however, be possible to identify emerging problems and approaches that are likely to be fruitful.

There is, first, the task of filling in the picture on a world scale. The social scientific record, as revealed even in the consciously international perspective of this handbook, is very uneven; research on men and masculinities is still mainly a First World enterprise. There is far more research in the United States than in any other country. There are major regions of the world where research even partly relevant to these questions is scarce—among them China, the Indian subcontinent, and Central and West Africa. To respond to this scarcity is not a matter of sending First World researchers out with existing paradigms. That has happened all too

often in the past, and it reproduces, in the realm of knowledge, the very relations of dominance and subordination that are part of the problem. It is a question of finding forms of cooperative research that use international resources (including existing knowledge) to generate new knowledge of local relevance.

Next, there are issues that seem to be growing in significance. The most obviously important is the relation of masculinities to those emerging dominant powers in the global capitalist economy, the transnational corporations. Organization research has already developed methods for studying men and masculinities in corporations (Collinson & Hearn, 1996; Ogasawara, 1998). It is not difficult to see how this approach could be applied to transnational operations, although again, it will call for some creative international cooperation.

There are other problems of which the significance has been known for some time but that have remained undeveloped. A notable example is the development of masculinities in the course of growing up. How children were "socialized" into gender was a major theme of "sex role" discussions, and when the male role literature went into a decline, this problem seems to have stagnated with it. All the sound and fury about boys' education has produced very little original research and no new developmental theorizing. However, a variety of approaches to development and social learning exist (ethnographic, psychoanalytic, cognitive) along with excellent models of fieldwork (e.g., Thorne, 1993).

Finally, there are new or underdeveloped perspectives that may give new insight even into well-researched issues. The possibilities of poststructuralist theory are now well discussed, although there are doubtless new applications to be found. However, the possibilities in postcolonial theory are still little explored (see Chapter 6), and they seem very relevant to the transformation of a research field historically centred in the First World. Economic analysis is also seriously underdeveloped. Most discussions of men and gender acknowledge the importance of power and also the importance of the world of work but do not carry them forward into analysis of a gendered economy. As Godenzi (2000) points out, economic inequality is crucial to understanding the link between masculinity and violence, and the same may be argued for other issues about masculinity.

A research agenda on these issues would certainly move our understanding of men and masculinities a long way forward. Nevertheless, understanding is mainly worth having if we can do something with it. Therefore the uses of knowledge, and the relationship between research and practice, must be key issues for the development of this field.

REFERENCES

Adolph, J. B. (1971). The South American macho: Mythos and mystique. *Impact of Science on Society, 21*(1), 83-92.

Altman, D. (2001). *Global sex.* Chicago: University of Chicago Press.

Arilha, M., Unbehaum Ridenti, S. G., & Medrado, B. (Eds.). (1998). *Homens e masculinidades: Outras palavras* [Men and masculinities: Other words]. Sao Paulo, Brasil: ECOS/Editora 34.

Bosse, H., & King, V. (Eds.). (2000). *Männlichkeitsentwurfe* [Models of masculinity]. Frankfurt, Germany: Campus Verlag.

Breines, I., Connell, R., & Eide, I. (Eds.). (2000). *Male roles, masculinities and violence: A culture of peace perspective.* Paris: UNESCO.

Brittan, A. (1989). *Masculinity and power.* Oxford, England: Blackwell.

Brod, H. (Ed.). (1987). *The making of masculinities.* London: Unwin Hyman.

Brod, H., & Kaufman, M. (Eds.). (1994). *Theorizing masculinities.* Thousand Oaks, CA: Sage.

Carrigan, T., Connell, R. W., & Lee, J. (1985). Toward a new sociology of masculinity. *Theory and Society, 14*(5), 551-604.

Cleaver, F. (Ed.). (2002). *Masculinities matter! Men, gender and development.* London: Zed.

Collinson, D. L., & Hearn, J. (Eds.). (1996). *Men as managers, managers as men: Critical perspectives on men, masculinities and managements.* London: Sage.

Connell, R. W. (1987). *Gender and power: Society, the person and sexual politics.* Cambridge, England: Polity Press.

Connell, R. W. (1994). Psychoanalysis on masculinity. In H. Brod & M. Kaufman (Eds.), *Theorizing masculinities* (pp. 11-38). Thousand Oaks, CA: Sage.

Connell, R. W. (1995). *Masculinities.* Cambridge, England: Polity Press.

Connell, R. W. (2002). *Gender.* Cambridge, England: Polity Press.

Davidoff, L., & Hall, C. (1990). *Family fortunes: Men and women of the English middle class 1780-1850.* Chicago: University of Chicago Press.

Division for the Advancement of Women, United Nations. (2003, September 24). *Aide-memoire for the expert group meeting on the role of men and boys in achieving gender equality.* Retrieved December 10, 2003, from http://www.un.org/womenwatch/daw/egm/men-boys2003/aide-memoire.html

Donaldson, M. (1993). What is hegemonic masculinity? *Theory and Society, 22*(5), 643-657.

Eichler, M. (1980). *The double standard: A feminist critique of feminist social science.* London: Croom Helm.

Ervø, S., & Johansson, T. (2003a). *Among men: Moulding masculinities* (Vol. 1). Aldershot, England: Ashgate.

Ervø, S., & Johansson, T. (2003b). *Bending bodies: Moulding masculinities* (Vol. 2). Aldershot, England: Ashgate.

Flood, M. (2003, May 30). *The men's bibliography: A comprehensive bibliography of writing on men, masculinities, gender, and sexualities.* Retrieved December 10, 2003, from http://www.xyonline.net/mensbiblio/

Friedman, S., & Sarah, E. (Eds.). (1982). *On the problem of men.* London: Women's Press.

Gardiner, J. K. (Ed.). (2001). *Masculinity studies and feminist theory.* New York: Columbia University Press.

Ghoussoub, M., & Sinclair-Webb, E. (2000). *Imagined masculinities: Male identity and culture in the modern Middle East.* London: Saqi Books.

Godenzi, A. (2000). Determinants of culture: Men and economic power. In I. Breines, R. Connell, & I. Eide (Eds.), *Male roles, masculinities and violence: A culture of peace perspective* (pp. 35-51). Paris: UNESCO.

Haddad, T. (Ed.). (1993). *Men and masculinities: A critical anthology.* Toronto: Canadian Scholars' Press.

Hall, C. (1992). *White, male and middle-class: Explorations in feminism and history.* New York: Routledge.

Hanmer, J. (1990). Men, power and the exploitation of women. In J. Hearn & D. Morgan (Eds.), *Men, masculinities and social theory* (pp. 21-42). London: Unwin Hyman/Routledge.

Hearn, J. (1987). *The gender of oppression: Men, masculinity and the critique of Marxism.* Brighton, England: Wheatsheaf.

Hearn, J. (1992). *Men in the public eye: The construction and deconstruction of public men and public patriarchies.* London: Routledge.

Hearn, J. (1996). "Is masculinity dead?" A critical account of the concepts of masculinity and masculinities. In M. Mac an Ghaill (Ed.), *Understanding masculinities: Social relations and cultural arenas* (pp. 202-217). Milton Keynes, PA: Open University Press.

Hearn, J. (1998). Theorizing men and men's theorizing: Men's discursive practices in theorizing men. *Theory and Society, 27*(6), 781-816.

Hearn, J. (2004). From hegemonic masculinity to the hegemony of men. *Feminist Theory, 5*(1), 97-120.

Hearn, J., & Morgan, D. (Eds.). (1990). *Men, masculinities and social theory*. London: Routledge.

Holter, Ø. G. (1989). *Menn* [Men]. Oslo, Norway: Aschehoug.

Holter, Ø. G. (1997). *Gender, patriarchy and capitalism: A social forms analysis*. Oslo, Norway: University of Oslo.

Hooper, C. (2000). Masculinities in transition: The case of globalization. In M. H. Marchand & A. S. Runyan (Eds.), *Gender and global restructuring: Sightings, sites and resistances* (pp. 59-73). London: Routledge.

Kaufman, M. (1987). *Beyond patriarchy: Essays by men on pleasure, power and patriarchy*. Toronto: Oxford University Press.

Kimmel, M. (Ed.). (1987). *Changing men: New directions in research on men and masculinity*. Newbury Park, CA: Sage.

Kimmel, M. (1997). *Manhood in America: A cultural history*. New York: Free Press.

Kimmel, M., & Messner, M. A. (Eds.). (2001). *Men's lives* (5th ed.). Boston: Allyn and Bacon.

Kimmel, M., & Mosmiller, T. (Eds.). (1992). *Against the tide: Pro-feminist men in the United States, 1779-1990. A documentary history*. Boston: Beacon.

Law, R., Campbell, H., & Dolan, J. (Eds.). (1999). *Masculinities in Aotearoa/New Zealand*. Palmerston North, New Zealand: Dunmore Press.

Lingard, B., & Douglas, P. (1999). *Men engaging feminisms: Pro-feminism, backlashes and schooling*. Buckingham, England: Open University Press.

Liu, H.-C. W. (1975). An analysis of Chinese clan rules: Confucian theories in action. In A. F. Wright (Ed.), *Confucianism and Chinese civilization* (pp. 16-49). Stanford, CA: Stanford University Press.

Lorber, J. (1994). *Paradoxes of gender*. New Haven, CT: Yale University Press.

Lorber, J. (2000). Using gender to undo gender. *Feminist Theory, 1*(1), 79-95.

Louie, K., & Low, M. (Eds.). (2003). *Asian masculinities: The meaning and practice of manhood in China and Japan*. London: RoutledgeCurzon.

Lundberg, C. (Ed.). (2001). Mannen. *Fronesis* (8, special issue).

Mac an Ghaill, M. (1994). *The making of men: Masculinities, sexualities and schooling*. Buckingham, England: Open University Press.

MacInnes, J. (1998). *The end of masculinity: The confusion of sexual genesis and sexual difference in modern society*. Buckingham, England: Open University Press.

Massachusetts Institute of Technology. (1979). *Men's studies bibliography* (4th ed.). Cambridge, MA: Human Studies Collection, Humanities Library, MIT.

McMahon, A. (1993). Male readings of feminist theory: The psychologization of sexual politics in the masculinity literature. *Theory and Society, 22*(5), 675-696.

Messerschmidt, J. W. (1993). *Masculinities and crime: Critique and reconceptualization of theory*. Lanham, MD: Rowman & Littlefield.

Messner, M. A. (1992). *Power at play: Sports and the problem of masculinity*. Boston: Beacon.

Metz-Göckel, S., & Müller, U. (1985). *Der Mann: Die BRIGITTE-Studie* [Man: The BRIGITTE study]. Hamburg, Germany: Beltz.

Morrell, R. (Ed.). (2001a). *Changing men in southern Africa*. London: Zed Books.

Morrell, R. (2001b). *From boys to gentlemen: Settler masculinity in colonial Natal, 1880-1920*. Pretoria, South Africa: UNISA Press.

Mort, F. (2000). *Dangerous sexualities: Medico-moral politics in England since 1830* (2nd ed.). London: Routledge.

Multioptionale Männlichkeiten? [Multi-option masculinities?]. (1998). *Widersprüche, 67* (Special issue).

Novikova, I., & Kambourov, D. (Eds.). (2003). *Men and masculinities in the former Soviet countries*. Helsinki, Finland: Kikimora, Aleksantteri Institute, University of Helsinki.

Ogasawara, Y. (1998). *Office ladies and salaried men: Power, gender, and work in Japanese companies*. Berkeley: University of California Press.

Olavarría, J., & Moletto, E. (2002). *Hombres: Identidad/es y sexualidad/es. III encuentros de estudios de masculinidades* [Men: Identity(ies) and sexuality(ies). Third conference on studies of masculinities]. Santiago, Chile: FLACSO-Chile.

Ouzgane, L., & Coleman, D. (1998). Postcolonial masculinities: Introduction. *Jouvert: A Journal of Postcolonial Studies, 2*(1). Retrieved December 10, 2003, from http://social.chass.ncsu.edu/jouvert/v2i1/con21.htm

Pease, B., & Pringle, K. (Eds.). (2002). *A man's world: Changing men's practices in a globalized world*. London: Zed Books.

Petersen, A. (1998). *Unmasking the masculine: "Men" and "Identity" in a sceptical age*. London: Sage.

Phillips, J. (1987). *A man's country? The image of the Pakeha male: A history*. Auckland, New Zealand: Penguin.

Pleck, J. H., & Sawyer, J. (Eds.). (1974). *Men and masculinity*. Englewood Cliffs, NJ: Prentice-Hall.

Schwalbe, M. L., & Wolkomir, M. (2002). Interviewing men. In J. F. Gubrium & J. A. Holstein (Eds.), *Handbook of interview research* (pp. 203-219). Thousand Oaks, CA: Sage.

Segal, L. (1997). *Slow motion: Changing masculinities, changing men* (2nd ed.). London: Virago.

Strauss, S. (1982). *Traitors to the masculine cause.* Westport, CT: Greenwood Press.

Sutton, P. (Ed.). (1988). *Dreamings: The art of Aboriginal Australia.* New York: Asia Society Galleries/George Braziller.

Thorne, B. (1993). *Gender play: Girls and boys in school.* New Brunswick, NJ: Rutgers University Press.

Tomsen, S., & Donaldson, M. (Eds.). (2003). *Male trouble: Looking at Australian masculinities.* Melbourne, Australia: Pluto.

Tosh, J. (1999). *A man's place: Masculinity and the middle-class home in Victorian England.* New Haven, CT: Yale University Press.

Tosh, J., & Roper, M. (Eds.). (1991). *Manful assertions: Masculinities in Britain since 1800.* London: Routledge.

United Nations. (2001). *Beijing declaration and platform for action.* New York: United Nations Department of Public Information.

Valdés, T., & Olavarría, J. (Eds.). (1998). *Masculinidades y equidad de género en América Latina* [Masculinities and gender equity in Latin America]. Santiago, Chile: FLACSO/ UNFPA.

Viveros Vigoya, M. (1997). Los estudios sobre lo masculino en América Latina: Una producción teórica emergente [Studies on the masculine in Latin America: An emerging conceptual development]. *Nómadas, 6,* 55-65.

Weeks, J. (1990). *Coming out: Homosexual politics in Britain, from the nineteenth century to the present* (Rev. ed.). London: Quartet.

Welzer-Lang, D. (Ed.). (2000). *Nouvelles approches des hommes et du masculin* [New approaches to men and the masculine]. Toulouse, France: Presses Universitaires du Mirail.

Wetherell, M., & Edley, N. (1999). Negotiating hegemonic masculinity: Imaginary positions and psycho-discursive practices. *Feminism and Psychology, 9*(3), 335-356.

White, S. C. (2000). "Did the earth move?" The hazards of bringing men and masculinities into gender and development. *IDS Bulletin, 31*(2), 33-41.

Whitehead, S. M. (2002). *Men and masculinities: Key themes and new directions.* Cambridge, England: Polity.

Zalewski, M., & Parpart, J. (Eds.). (1998). *The "man" question in international relations.* Boulder, CO: Westview Press.

Zulehner, P. M., & Volz, R. (1998). *Männer im Aufbruch: Wie Deutschlands Männer sich selbst und wie Frauen sie sehen* [Men awakening: How German men see themselves and how women see them]. Ostfildern, Germany: Schwabenverlag.

PART I

THEORETICAL PERSPECTIVES

2

SOCIAL THEORIES FOR RESEARCHING MEN AND MASCULINITIES

Direct Gender Hierarchy and Structural Inequality

ØYSTEIN GULLVÅG HOLTER

While men are frequently the agents of the oppression of women, and in many senses benefit from it, their interests in the gender order are not pregiven but constructed by and within it. Since in many ways men's human needs and capacities are not met within the gender orders of modern societies, they also have a latent "emancipatory interest" in their transformation.

—Caroline New (2001)

Men are encountering the shamefulness of being a man as such and at all. . . . I suggest that, where shame tends nowadays to be seen as a moral emotion, and to be discussed as an ethical problem, its reach is larger than this. I argue that shame is not only to be thought of as a moral prop or provocation, but as a condition of being, a life-form, even.

—S. Connor (2001)

This chapter addresses the implications of social theories used in researching men and masculinities. In particular, I focus on two types of social theories: what I will call *direct gender hierarchy* theories that emphasize the social primacy of male dominance, and *structural inequality* theories that are more concerned with the social structural relations of gender inequality. In the views and traditions described here, many of today's researchers would probably describe themselves as "social constructivists," or at least give a nod in this direction. Current direct gender hierarchy theories emphasizing the social primacy of male dominance differ from the sociobiological assumptions 20 years ago, and the same is the

15

case with structural inequality theories. There has been a similar type of movement in both traditions, away from sex-gender toward gender as a more purely social creation, including economic patterns, social sanctions, culture, psychology, and so on. However, structural gender equality theories have usually been further developed, and are more socially and sociologically insistent, with a wider and more historical view of social constructions.

Societal theories of gender and inequality can often be seen as "poststructuralist," although such a term is of questionable utility today. Good gender research and theory creation go beyond a static structure-actor division. Connecting society and the individual has been a major point for feminist research development as a whole. This has been especially evident in developments of *relational* feminism (in the Nordic region, see, e.g., Haavind, 1984, 1994)—an attempt to move from "statistical sex-related difference" to "everyday relationships." However, the common trend toward relational emphasis in the 1980s was interpreted in quite different ways, as can be seen in debates concerning the meaning of "sisterhood" (e.g., in France and the United States) or the "women-friendly welfare state" (Nordic region). Interpreted as women's micropolitics, relational emphasis had different and often inconsistent meanings in macro terms. These debates showed the dilemmas between a "market class" definition of women and the need to improve all women's rights.

Current gender equality theories retain elements of 1970s critical theory and power-patriarchy analysis, 1980s postmodernism, renewed social actor orientation, and other perspectives. Research on gender does not just challenge the division between masculine and feminine, it challenges the division between neutral and gendered. This is a major theoretical point, creating a need to extend gender research into wider areas of society and focus on indirect forms of structural inequality.

International work with emerging studies of men and masculinities confirms the importance of the social context for the kinds of views that are developed in research. As the editor of the *Newsletter of the International Association for Studies of Men* (IASOM) from 1993 to 2000, I received quite different contributions from different countries and regions. In some regions,

the process that Jalna Hanmer (1990) and David Collinson and Jeff Hearn (1994) have called "naming men as men" is still in a very early stage and is a controversial venture. The greater the research possibility—especially, the freedom for research to investigate the wider ground of patriarchy and inequality, rather than just the figure of gender—the further gender research is brought along from simply recognizing direct gender hierarchy to understanding structural inequality in society. In other words, the stronger the framework of equality, allowing research not just into gender and women but, even more controversially, men as gendered persons and the wider role of societal institutions, the better the chance of grounded theory in a positive sense. This includes important developments in studies on gender and men, such as going from a belief in fairly static types of men to understanding changes and new practices. Even in regions that are fairly advanced in terms of both economic development and gender equality politics (such as the Nordic region), however, patriarchal-critical views may be controversial, as they implicate not just "problem men" but also the problems of the powerful institutions of society.

In this chapter, I focus specifically on two social theory perspectives and their implications for research on men and masculinities: (a) a structural equality-inequality view of men and masculinities and (b) its relationship to a direct gender hierarchy or direct male dominance view. In Nordic research, these are often called *patriarchy* (i.e., society and social structures of oppression) and *male dominance* (i.e., men's use of power, also called gender-power), but as this contrast is not common in the English-language debate, I use the terms *indirect* and *direct gender hierarchy* here. Are these different terms for the same issues? Or do they in fact represent quite different perspectives, leading to different research priorities and concepts of change? If this is so, what are the connections between structural gender inequalities or patriarchal structures and direct gender hierarchy (usually meaning male dominance)?

My main point is to introduce some of the central elements in a structural inequality perspective and examine how they relate to the direct gender hierarchy approach. These elements include notions of gender inequality or patriarchal structure, gender reification and a dual-sphere economic analysis, concepts of patriarchalization and genderization, and models of change suggested by recent research. I also draw attention to Nordic region studies in which gender in/equality research traditions have been developed.

Before going further, it is necessary to note that the direct and indirect gender hierarchy views I describe are broad paradigmatic approaches, and elements of both may thus be found within the work of the particular theorists and researchers. There is an ambivalence, one might say, that characterizes the field as a whole. Although each perspective often implies the other, they also often point in quite different directions regarding the main problems and the main ways to solve them. The direct view highlights men's dominance and the implications of masculinities, whereas the indirect view is more concerned with men as part of society and the implications of societal change.

The remainder of the chapter is organized in the following manner: first, outlines are given of the direct gender hierarchy perspective and the indirect gender hierarchy perspective or structural inequality perspective, as I shall refer to it here; the direct gender hierarchy perspective is then critiqued; some applications of the structural inequality perspective are considered; and finally, implications of this perspective are provided, followed by some concluding remarks.

The Direct Gender Hierarchy Perspective

Current Research

In current research, the direct gender hierarchy model view is the most well-known and widespread perspective, typically emphasizing male dominance or men's dominance. The structural inequality perspective, or patriarchy-critical view, is far less well known. For example, the world's largest database of social science abstracts listed, as of 1995, 3,516 papers concerning *gender*, many of them discussing male dominance—but only 107 papers concerning *patriarchy* (Holter, 1998).

Scholarship on men and masculinities, especially critical scholarship, has been strongly influenced by notions of direct gender hierarchy, which usually invoke some notion of male dominance. The direct gender hierarchy perspective emphasizes the consequences of men's superior social position. It looks at the effects of gender discrimination with a view to the immediate causes, which can often be summarized as "men" or "male dominance." (A more general cause could be masculinity *in* men and women, but this is a social psychological area that lacks research today.) In the European context, this kind of theorizing has in turn led to a focus on the analysis of men and masculinities through the framework of gender equality and gender inequalities. Indeed, male or men's dominance clearly suggests a variety of forms of structural gender inequality. Similarly, the frame of structural gender inequality usually implies some notion of male (or men's, or some men's) dominance. Yet the links between the two are not well known in current research.

Is direct gender hierarchy a universal fact or a varying pattern? Is being a man the same as being in a powerful position? At the outset, this issue should be understood in its social and historical context. The direct gender hierarchy view has been a primary reaction to the "neutralizing" or "malestream" type of social science in which issues of gender and power have been ignored. It has often appeared as a spontaneous interpretation in areas like violence against women, where gender and power seem to be very closely linked.

The direct gender hierarchy view certainly has some empirical support in many areas, yet it is often more of an implicit notion than an explicit model or a systematic theory. It is implicit in that it corresponds to widely held social norms, cultural images, and behavioral patterns. The notion that men are the dominant ones does not need to be argued at length. Its tendency, when the larger silence of the main- or malestream is broken, is to picture women and men in a relationship between equal-women and unequal-men. The portrait of men and women often resembles Max Weber's notion of market class (Brudner & White, 1997, p. 162; Wright, 2000, p. 21). Men and women are competing groups with different chances in the market. Most researchers know that the picture is more complex, yet this form of appearance is understandable, given a historical period of increased gender equality. This is how the problem emerges—as a problem of men; men at large; and now, also, men circumscribed by women. The "woman question" turns around into a "man question." For example, "women are seen as 'parents' while men are seen as 'fathers'" (Bekkengen, 1999).

Even if power and masculinity are now often seen as "relational constructions" in male dominance or direct gender hierarchy research, there is a tendency to make masculinity static and solid. This is often connected to a view in which power stems from the "inner" workings of masculinity (or male nature, in traditional terms). "Masculine power is largely exercised through self-regulation and self-discipline—a process of 'identity work,'" it is argued in a recent masculinities theory overview (Whitehead & Barrett, 2001, p. 17). Men's privilege is a consequence of this self-discipline. By acting "in ways consistent with gender norms . . . they reproduce male domination and power differentials." This view is presented in general terms—men are "inculcated with dominant discourses." Masculinity is "unlikely ever to disappear" (p. 18). Or, as stated elsewhere in this volume, even if "'being a man' appears to be flexible and varied, it is then wrong to assume that this variation undermines male dominantion" (Brittan, 2001, p. 54). A view that holds true in some situations becomes the abstract rule. Social institutions and variation tend to disappear. This tendency can be found in applied areas also: for example, in violence research and the issue of whether all men are potentially violent (discussed later). Arguably, the link between masculinity and pride or shame rests on this overall equation of masculinity and power.

THE STRUCTURAL INEQUALITY PERSPECTIVE

An Underexplored Tradition

Notions of direct gender hierarchy, male (or men's) dominance, and structural gender equality and inequalities can thus be seen as interconnected. In this chapter, I focus primarily on the latter frame of reference; first, because this approach is still relatively rarely explored in an explicit way as a theoretical tradition in scholarship on men and masculinities; second,

because the gender equality and inequalities perspective has been especially significant in European contexts, especially German, Nordic, and United Kingdom contexts. In the Nordic case, it could be argued that this significance has been facilitated to some extent by the development of state politics concerning gender equality. This is particularly in terms of public governmental commitment to gender equality, even though a variety of gender inequalities continue, such as the gender wage gap, men's domination of business management, and men's violence toward women. On the other hand, it could be argued that state gender equality politics have tended to emphasize a liberal and limited view of gender equality.

The main theme in the structural equality perspective is overall discrimination or inequality in society and their causes, rather than direct gender hierarchy as such. This research can be critical in situations, positions, and institutions in a society or culture that hinders gender equality, whether the context is overtly "gendered" or not. It extends a view that was advanced in Nordic feminist sociology in the 1970s, in which gender was analyzed both as social differentiation and as social stratification and the use of class models was criticized (Holter, 1970, pp. 18, 225).

From a gender equality point of view, the international developments discussed here illustrate how the debate and research tend to start with the "figure" of direct gender hierarchy rather than the "ground" of structural inequality. The structures of structural inequality are often comparatively hidden and difficult to recognize, especially as they often appear to be gender neutral, although they are by no means neutral in their effects. The problems of the direct gender hierarchy approach can be summarized as a takeover of the traditional patriarchal view of men. Men are seen as the more important, more socially responsible persons, compared to women. Only now is this grand picture of men being seen as a negative rather than a positive factor.

In structural inequality research and studies of patriarchal societies, more complex theories have developed. Here, the discrimination of woman has been seen as a matter of society and of men's role in society, not of men as such (see, e.g., Holter, 1997, pp. 273-303). However, there are problems with these approaches also. Traditional views of society are likely to be taken on board, along with a tendency to downplay the existence of direct gender hierarchy patterns that cannot so easily be explained by gender inequality structures. There is a tendency for the structural background to become all and for the action-related figure to disappear.

Clearly, gender equalities and inequalities work in complex and contradictory ways. They can, indeed, even in a patriarchal and male-dominated society, at times work against the interests of men, individually and collectively, although at the same time the overriding pattern of structural inequality works in favor of men and against women.

Gender Equality Research

Let us turn to the societal developments and emerging traditions arising from gender equality research. In the next sections, I present some research examples and discuss the use of terms such as *patriarchy*. What is the new view of gender, when one starts from the equality-inequality dimension? I outline some patterns that have emerged in research, especially dual-sphere imbalance and gender reification connected to "horizontal" gender discrimination.

Some examples of gender-equal-status–oriented research and gender equality theory in the Nordic region can illustrate this development. In a study extending a relational view of gender, Harriet Holter, Hanne Haavind, and other authors (H. Holter, 1984) showed how patriarchal social patterns are reorganized and are changing over time. Anna Jonasdóttir (1991) contextualized structural inequality in economic terms, describing women as "love power" as well as "labor power" in the labor market. In Sylvia Walby's (1990) theory of patriarchy, the public phase of patriarchy is distinguished from the private. This theory has been influential in Nordic research, as elsewhere. (Walby's perspective has been further developed in studies of men, especially in the context of the United Kingdom; see Hearn, 1992). Øystein Gullvåg Holter and Helene Aarseth (1993) divided modern forms of patriarchy into three main frameworks and periods: paternalistic power, or "paternate," in early modernity; masculinistic power, or "masculinate," in the industrial age (much like Walby's two phases), and a third "androgynatic" form in a period with decreasing discrimination. Using literary sources, Jørgen

Lorentzen (1996) showed how masculinities changed in the onset of modernity and how caring was marginalized in the men's world. Claes Ekenstam (1993) discussed the embodiment of modern masculinity and the restrictions in men's emotional expressivity. Jorun Solheim (1998) developed relational analysis in a symbolic direction, focusing on the home as an extension of the feminine.

Structural Inequality and Patriarchy

As mentioned, the term patriarchy is rarely used in today's research; gender is the more frequently used term. The phrases gender equality and gender inequality are also more peripheral than one would expect. The lack of awareness surrounding patriarchy is not surprising. There are many reasons why gender is visible, or even supervisible or "hyperreal" (Baudrillard, 1993, p. 171), and patriarchy is obscure.

Formal or open patriarchy has been weakened and dissolved over the last centuries. There is some truth to the idea that it is no longer there. Its *effects* are still often there, however, so we should not take this too far. For example, the levels of gendered violence and rape remain higher than one would expect in a gender equality–oriented society. They display a deep gender-power connection.

Systematic gender-related discrimination still appears in many areas, whether we call it patriarchy, direct gender hierarchy, or inequality. The wording is not the main issue but rather the acknowledgment that all of society (and culture) is involved, not just some special "gendered zones." Research needs better concepts of gender discrimination.

Many operative patriarchal structures are difficult to perceive directly, although we witness their effects. Sometimes the tracks disappear. Examples include wage-work restructuring that devalues women and social competence and labor market regulations that work to the same effect (Hoel & Sørhaug, 1999; Holter, Karlsen, & Salomon, 1998). They usually have no explicit gendered message or reference, yet they dictate new conditions for men and women.

The key links of patriarchal structure still often seem to be covered by a veil of secrecy, an untouchable neutral and yet mostly male zone. Conversely, in areas where the effects of patriarchy seem fairly visible, such as with the persistent social problems of rape or battering, it is not so easy to tell the societal and cultural causes and the effects on society in general.

The term patriarchy is perhaps best dropped in favor of the phrase structural gender inequality. Yet we need a term that pinpoints the structural character of inequality and a recognition that structural gender inequality has survived, even if patriarchy in the literal sense (father-power) has not. Patriarchal structures may be reproduced through fatherhood or through other social institutions and patterns. What is specific to the terms patriarchy and patriarchal society, as distinct from an egalitarian society or from a society with some male power ("proto-patriarchy" has been used among historians, e.g., Bin-Nun, 1975), is the fairly *systematic, general* character of the oppression of women and the linked oppression of nonprivileged men within a given society and culture. A patriarchal society is one that displays two interlinked power structures, between and across the genders (Holter, 1997). Men and women are easy to distinguish. Patriarchal structures are comparatively hidden. They do not walk around with a sign saying "Hit me." Critical gender discourses need more awareness at this point.

A CRITIQUE OF THE DIRECT GENDER HIERARCHY PERSPECTIVE

Gender as a Compromise Formation

One way to align the two perspectives—direct gender hierarchy and structural inequality—goes back to early feminist sex role sociology, in which gender was seen as a mixed pattern, containing social differentiation as well as social stratification. True, gender differentiation is strongly influenced by stratification, but it cannot simply be reduced to stratification or the power dimension. Rather, the gender system is a *framework of meaning,* containing relations within which the sex of the person is made socially relevant. This framework concerns power but also many other issues. It is often more of an *adaptation* to power than it is power or powerlessness by itself. A gender system, in this view, is a *response* to a more or less patriarchal structure, and the two must be carefully distinguished. Gender is a compromise

formation; it is formed by power structures but also by other forces, such as the need for social recognition. In modern society, gender is a social psychological link between the individual and the collective.

From a sociological and historical perspective, the wider implications of the direct gender hierarchy view are often problematic. Obviously, notions of direct gender hierarchy are important in gender equality theory. Yet they cannot be treated as universals. Rather, it is the form of society—the existence of historical, changing forms of patriarchy or gender-unequal societal structures—that *creates* certain types of masculinities and the ways that power becomes linked to them. The reverse is not true. There is no abstraction called "men" that always shapes society and history. Still, there is evidence that is quite wide-ranging and robust of direct gender hierarchy that must be taken into account in any societal or historical argument regarding gender equality.

Concepts such as compensation and emulation are relevant in this area. Many studies have shown the importance of compensatory forms of masculinity. We can imagine a society in which only a minor section of men actually profit from patriarchal privileges, and yet many men participate in direct gender hierarchy. This is likely especially in contexts wherein the gender division is emphasized as a universal division, a matter of all individuals in society—as is the case in the modern age. In fact, the men at the top of the social hierarchy may use mainly gender-neutral ways to achieve their aims. For example, they may use their economic or political influence, and the men below will use what *they* have—namely, their gender. In other cases, nonprivileged men may emulate the gendered behavior of the dominant men. These themes have been central in masculinities theories, linked to the breadwinner type of gender contract. A third important approach concerns gender as reification, experienced as something pregiven, even before gender as performance. This is discussed further later on.

In these ways, we may explain the existence of direct gender hierarchy patterns even among men who objectively have little to gain by supporting patriarchal structures. We may also better understand why many revolts against traditional patriarchal structures have been accompanied by renewed "fratriarchy," or direct gender hierarchy. For example, the history of socialism (as well as the earlier history of bourgeois revolutions) has been full of comradely forms of neopatriarchal power, up to the "geriatric patriarchy" that came to dominate the former Eastern Bloc.

The idea that gender is a *system of meaning* that is distinguishable from patriarchy as a *structure of power* can be used to outline a critique of the current view of gender and power that is quite different from the usual complaint that it attacks men. On the contrary, it can be argued that the "attack" on men is taken too far only when society is left out of the picture. More precisely, structural inequality mechanisms that are *not* overtly gendered (not clearly a matter of direct gender hierarchy) tend to disappear from view.

Many of the current studies on masculinities concern areas where we find both explicitly gendered frameworks of meaning and structural patriarchal relations. Here, patriarchal dominance, defined as relations that *objectively* weaken women's position and create related forms of discrimination, is associated with subjective *gendered meaning*. In this perspective, patriarchal inequality and direct gender hierarchy may seem to be two terms for the same thing.

In this approach, however, other areas are easily overlooked or misinterpreted. The most serious case concerns an area of social patterns that objectively recreate gender inequality—yet not with much direct reference to sex or gender. It can be argued that this area represents a major blind spot in current gender studies—or at least, in the gender studies that take the reference to gender as their point of departure. Because patriarchy is not announced, it is assumed that it is not there. A major example, discussed later, is the relationship between "production" and "reproduction" in society. Economic or political forces that objectively place producers (mainly, men) ahead of reproducers (mainly, women) appear as gender neutral and are not adequately addressed.

Another mistake concerns the existence of gender as social differentiation, which tends to be interpreted as if social stratification (power) were also automatically of importance. But this may not be the case. Representative surveys on men and gender equality carried out in the Nordic region and elsewhere (e.g., Holter, 1989;

Jalmert, 1984; Zulehner & Volz, 1998) are warning lights in this respect. We should be very careful with arguments going directly from the meaning of gender or the form of masculinity in a given context to the actual power relations, including the degree of discrimination of women (and nonpowerful men), in that context. Gender and masculinity forms do have a relation to the degree (and form) of gender discrimination, but the relation tends to be more complex, thus supporting the compromise view.

At this point, the dynamic role of the gender system comes into view. Why do women—or nonprivileged men—often emphasize gender, even beyond the compensatory mechanisms discussed earlier? The historical dimension is important here. The modern gender system was created partly "from below," as a *response* to older patriarchal structures. True, it may recreate these structures, but it also has more democratic and dynamic elements. Therefore, women and nonprivileged men may emphasize gender as part of a way of overcoming traditional constrictions. Gender may become a means of self-realization (O. Holter, 1983). Through the gender system, gender meaning becomes *embodied*. Bodies become "sexed," with sex as "the sign on the body" (Søndergaard, 1996). This is obviously a field of tension; gendering is a process that occurs for a variety of reasons. One cannot simply assume that all cases of gender are cases of gender-power.

Two Dimensions

Distinguishing between gender as a system of meaning and patriarchy as a structure of power is still often a new idea in international research. Researchers are much more used to thinking in terms of a gender-power order. The arrangement can have various names, such as direct gender hierarchy or gender-power, but it is commonly seen as one unified system.

In the gender equality view presented here, instead, there are two quite different dimensions: equal status on the one hand and gender on the other. Gender relations, or the gender system, are seen as a partially independent and dynamic framework of meaning. It is slanted so that it seems to relate especially to women, children, and reproduction, but it concerns men and the sphere of production as much as women and the sphere of reproduction.

All societies have some element of gender organization, work division between the genders, and gender-linked norms and behaviors. This does *not* mean that all societies have the same major sphere divisioning, such as in the contemporary economy. It is more like a tendency in this direction—a bit of Talcott Parsons's (1964, pp. 130-133) complementary sex relation, but not the whole package; not the nuclear family, not the breadwinner contract, not the modern-democratic definition of the individual, not wage labor versus free time, and so on. When this minimal "sexed organization" overlaps with the organization of power and exploitation, more specific and expansive gender systems are created, such as the modern one (Holter, 1997; Holter & Aarseth, 1993).

The specificity and independent role of gender have varied. In some circumstances, gender is a fairly egalitarian differentiation system, and emerging direct gender hierarchy or protopatriarchy turns to age and seniority relations, rather than sex, to legitimize new conditions (as in early historical societies). In other contexts, gender divisions are important in society but still play a secondary role to patriarchy (e.g., the late Middle Ages). In a third type of setting, patriarchy has been partly dismantled, there is some gender equality development, and gender becomes a more independent social system. This characterizes modern society. Gender becomes more distinct from the patriarchal concept of the person, a more democratic venture and a more horizontal (but also wider) socioeconomic division.

In this situation, the gender system is not simply an echo of the structures of inequality. It develops its own dynamics, sometimes acting on its own, often with tension and conflict-filled relations to patriarchal structures. For example, "protest masculinity" is not just one of several masculinity forms. Protest, in some form, is a common element in modern masculinities, brought out in different ways. This type of model implies a mixed and conflict-filled gender-patriarchy relationship. Against this background, men's and women's gender positions and gender identities can be described as compromise formations, attempts to balance "life needs" and "power needs." Gender is mainly an adaptation to power, even if it has, in turn, power consequences and emerges as "gender-power" (Holter, 1997, pp. 195-241). The core idea of the model is to distinguish between patriarchal structure and gender system developments and then to look at the changing connections between the two.

The Gender-Power Dilemma

If all gender is power, if gender and structural inequality are mainly one and the same pattern, then the existence of gender warrants the conclusion that power is there too. If gender as power is "virtually universal" (Kimmel, 2000a, p. 53), we may assume, for example, that workplace discrimination is generally good for men (p. 190), or that men's violence against women "is restorative, a means to reclaim the power that he believes is rightfully his" (p. 262).

Yet the research often tells a different story. First, it discloses variation within as well as between the genders. Second, it shows an interplay between gender and power that the researchers do not yet fully understand. One cannot say that this dilemma is solved in any of the traditions and views presented here.

Let us first look at variation within the genders, especially among men. It has long been argued that direct gender hierarchy is primarily associated with the powerful positions among men. This has traditionally been a main thread of argument in direct gender hierarchy studies and also in the emerging field of studies of men or men's studies. It has roots in women's studies and in feminist portraits of patriarchy as a system of suppression of women and nondominant men. It can be found in the structural inequality tradition as well.

Yet some empirical material, some of it from key zones of evidence such as violence against women or prostitution, has made some researchers formulate the opposite rule, namely, that power over women is associated with *lack* of power in relation to other men. For example, men who buy women for sex have been seen as "losers in the male role" (Prieur & Taksdal, 1989). Patterns where masculinity could be seen as compensatory had already been identified by sex role theorists in the 1960s and earlier, partly based on psychodynamic theory. The "lack of power" kind of rule often rings true to researchers who have studied social stratification or power systems in other areas.

Although problems may be generated at the top of a power structure or hierarchy (or by the hierarchy as a whole, linked to circumstances at the top), they often become larger, or at least more negatively visible, further down ("beware of the little man" is folk wisdom at this point). Further, advanced power regimes usually have built-in mechanisms to minimize the cost of power by shifting it downward (Holter, 1997, pp. 396-404). The further down in the hierarchy, the higher may be the emphasis on the possibility to be "in on the deal" by using force downward. This can be seen as a main, traditional, patriarchal principle—"submit to your master, and you yourself will be a master" (Holter, 1989, p. 31). In the modern world, it is partly hidden by the market and democratic institutions. Yet authoritarian structures persevere through elements like bullying and victimization.

For such reasons, we might expect that lower status men are more involved in gender discrimination than upper status men. This is sometimes the case. For example, a 1988 Norwegian survey (Holter, 1989) of men and gender equality showed a higher level of domestic violence in the family of origin of working class men compared with other men (that is, in working class families in the 1950s and 1960s compared with other families). However, violence in the home seems more related across class to authoritarianism, according to qualitative research (e.g., Lundgren, 1985) as well as a German survey (Zulehner & Volz, 1998).

Based on democracy and work research, a third type of model comes into view. Here, it is not the top or bottom but the middle layers that face the biggest problems, precisely due to the problematical character of the contact and overall character of the system.

Together, the three models suggest a mixed picture. The empirical results confirm this. In time-use studies (e.g., Vaage, 2002) and in opinion surveys regarding gender equality, there is no consistent pattern that oppression of women is larger in one class or status group than in others. A "from the top" tendency can be found, but it is often counteracted by other tendencies.

Several gender equality surveys and many qualitative studies in the Nordic region make it possible to give some empirically based evaluation of these models. Education seems to have a slight positive effect on gender equality orientation and practices, with emphasis on orientation. There is an "in principle" gap (Jalmert, 1984)

between words and actions to which we shall return. Money, however, has no clear, consistent effect. Perhaps there is an "A curve," with some problems most typical in the mid- to high-income group, as if gender-power were a petit bourgeois syndrome, but this trend is neither strong nor clear. Other problems tend to heap up at the bottom, such as violence, although some of this is a reporting effect. Typically, different measures show different results, without a clear demarcation of "one type of man" in terms of class, social status, or job factors. Note that money does have an effect on men's wish to recreate a breadwinner type of gender contract, according to "marriage market" research. The (male) money–(female) beauty connection is still in force, even in proclaimed egalitarian circumstances (Holter, 1990b).

The mixed empirical picture shows that even if theories of masculinities (e.g., Carrigan, Connell, & Lee, 1985; Connell, 1995) are important for understanding the dynamics of the gender system, the link between the type of masculinity and the degree of inequality is less direct than is sometimes suggested. This strengthens the point made earlier, that gender and patriarchy are different (only partially overlapping) dimensions. Indeed, empirical findings have often led feminist researchers in the opposite direction, namely, that the men involved in problem areas such as prostitution or violence against women are simply "normal" men. They come from all groups or forms of masculinity.

In this view, it is "Mr. Typical" who beats or buys. The selection of the typical man may vary with country and culture, but the main trend is global. We are led back to the direct gender hierarchy model, where all men participate in the discrimination against women.

Still, this argument is often based on status- or class-related evidence, using indicators such as income or education, which is not the most relevant at this point. In fact, bringing it in can be seen as an example of how gender is unconsciously made into class. One argues as if gender could be derived from status or class. Yet the argument concerns gender, *not* class. We do not know whether the men involved in problem behaviors have been exposed to higher than normal levels of *structural inequality*—defined through measures such as the object status of women, victimization and bullying, aggression, violence, self-sacrifice, reification, and so on. From qualitative research, it seems likely (Holter, 1989). As these examples show, the gender-power dilemma is often a gender-power-class dilemma. Social status or class is a third party to the debate.

Locating Inequality Patterns

Some researchers have argued that repro-duction of children is the core of the gender order (for a recent example, see Connell, 2002, pp. 38, 54). In the 1970s debate, the family was often seen as the core arena of patriarchy. I think this is a mistake of figure and ground, as concerns today's society. We know that repro-duction often *appears* as the main zone of gender-power. But that, by no means, secures its position as a key element in structural inequality or patriarchy. We cannot judge by gender meaning or visibility but must look for the actual, objective effects. For example, we must analyze whether a wage policy actually increases the wage gap between men and women, and this question is quite distinct from the question of whether the process, negotia-tions, motives, and so on were *gendered* or not.

Gender equality and "genderedness" are two different dimensions. In much research, they have been confused. Therefore we should be extra careful with the empirical evidence. Mostly, we do not know which is which. A lot of economic and work research evidence speaks against the "family and children" version of patriarchy. Instead, research tells of families losing out in the adaptation to work life, of production sphere dominance and horizontal discrimination creating a major foundation for gender discrimination and gendered violence in the home as well as the job. Families and children are no longer the main context of patri-archy, even if male dominance and violence are still major problems in the domestic sphere. The institutions in this sphere are changing, with more mixed power regimes today. Families and children often come second, after the jobs have had their say. Work and family studies (Borchgrevink & Holter, 1995; Holter, 1990a) show that "being able to talk about job prob-lems" is one important issue in modern family life. "Being able to use my competence" is a main job satisfaction item. Family life is used to correct—and recreate—labor market imbalance.

"Greedy" wage work and production dominance in the domestic sphere tend to recreate social problems.

All this confirms Sylvia Walby's theory of a shift toward public patriarchy and Holter and Aarseth's (1993) analysis of the "late mas-culinate." A man today becomes a man through "the public eye" more than through his family status or particularistic relations (Hearn, 1992). Patriarchy has turned public and economic. Gender, to some extent, is a "functional equiv-alent" of patriarchy, to use Robert Merton's (1957, p. 52) term, yet it is more independent and dynamic and can also be an oppositional force. Reproduction and households remain two of the main contexts of inequality. Yet pro-duction may weigh more in the total picture. And the main point may be precisely the *con-nections* between work and family, masculine and feminine, neutral and gendered—not each on its own. A relational view is once more relevant. It seems that inequality or patriarchy is not mainly one type of structure, or a set of structures, but relations between structures. This, and not a specific zone or work area, is the "core."

APPLICATIONS OF THE STRUCTURAL INEQUALITY PERSPECTIVE

The Case of Caregiving Men

Men's position in female-associated work or in domestic labor is often interpreted dif-ferently in the two perspectives. In the direct gender hierarchy view, the same overall pattern of dominance can be found in these areas as can be found in others. This is shown, for example, by men's access to "glass escalator" mechanisms in female-typed jobs that lead men upward in the work hierarchy while the women stay below (Williams, 2000). In the structural inequality view, the changing societal posi-tioning of men and women is the main matter. The positions in each concrete arena may differ from the overall rule; all the more so, if they are linked to societal imbalances.

The secondary status of women's activity fields (mainly in the sphere of reproduction) does not always imply women's secondary status *within* these fields. On the contrary, recent studies show the importance of "hegemonic femininity" in an interplay with patriarchal tradition in, for example, studies of nursing (Bakken, 2001). Women often actively create gender segregation (Krøjer, 2003). Research shows Rosabeth Moss Kanter's (1977) minority logic coming into play when men are the small minority in gendered activity or work areas. The men are easily turned into stereotypical representatives of the "others," token contrast types, and they easily take on this behavior. Compensatory masculinity can be relevant in this terrain.

One study of an experiment with an all-men group of employees in a kindergarten, initiated by the woman leader of the kindergarten, found greater variance and role freedom among the men, that they more easily could take on "homely" activities, show feelings, and so on. Yet it also demonstrated that men in this situation distanced themselves from feminine standards, as if a symbolic mother were constantly looking over their shoulder (Bredesen, 2000). It has been argued that men in kindergartens experience a "centrifugal" process that leads them away from the caregiving, "feminine" core of the work (Baagøe Nielsen, 2003).

Men may be in a weak position in female-associated fields of work not because society has now reached a state of gender equality but because of persistent inequality that positions these fields below others and makes them into predominantly feminine domains. Therefore, men in caregiving roles or other female-associated areas may experience particular forms of gender discrimination (Forsèn, Gislason, Holter, & Rongevær, 2000; Holter, 2003).

In this perspective, the link between discrimination against women and discrimination against some men is emphasized. Inequality is seen as a varying relationship rather than a universal dividing line that creates two classlike gender categories. Like the burdens, the benefits of inequality are diverse and shifting. Although men benefit on the overall level, closer analyses show huge variation among men in regard to inequality. Women, also, are not always disadvantaged by gender segregation and inequality. Patterns that sustain segregation, or conversely promote equality and integration, can be found among both genders.

Direct gender hierarchy analyses mainly concern the power and benefits of an ongoing system of direct gender hierarchy comparable to an informal or latent "brotherhood." The main categories are *men* and *women*. Gender equality analysis, on the other hand, emphasizes the role of society and the position of both men and women in ways that decrease or increase gender equality. Here, the tendency is to place people into *more or less gender-equal* categories, with more women at the equal end of the scale, more men at the patriarchal end, and much mixture all along.

In this perspective, gender discrimination has a major element of positional discrimination. It hits people in specific positions, regardless of their gender. This may seem like a nicely detached sociological perspective. But something is missing. Can we really compare discrimination against some men in caregiving positions to the general discrimination against women? The problem is that gender discrimination *seems* to follow the person, or the sex of the person, regardless of situations or positions—*and* that this appearance becomes what Durkheim called a social fact, acting by itself (see Lukes, 1988, p. 14). Why does that happen? At that point, the notion of gender as a meaning system becomes too thin. It does not explain why these meanings are so closely connected to power. Instead, modern gender as a system of *reification* comes into view—a framework of a quite specific economic type, characteristically conceived as a universal fact. Women's and gender studies have discussed this in terms of alienation and sex objectification (see, e.g., Foreman, 1977; MacKinnon, 1983). It is probably often seen as a peripheral or irrelevant Marxist concept. Yet I think it is a key term for understanding modern gender. It creates a kind of absolutistic being that goes before "gender as performance" (Butler, 1990, 1998) and before various notions of gender as situated subjectivity. It is related to the dual sphere view of gender oppression (described later).

The Preference System

In the structural inequality view, current gender inequality can be described as a societal preference system that involves both genders. This system has economic, social, cultural, and psychological elements. It is linked to the breadwinner type of gender contract, that is, the man's primary provider position vis-à-vis the woman. Yet the preference system also appears in politics, law, and many other areas, generally pulling men and women in two different directions, rewarding gender segregation. So a preference system may seem "profitable" also for women, in the short run and the concrete situation, even if it sustains inequality in the longer run and works to the detriment of women in society as a whole (Holter, 2003).

In this case, as in others, inequality is seen as a pattern that partly runs across the gender division, not just between the genders. Even if men are more likely to be on the privileged side, there is significant variation. As mentioned, the principal analytical unit in this type of approach is not men or women as such but, rather, equal and unequal tendencies. Each tendency can be found within persons of each gender, in varying strengths, forms, and interrelations, depending on the wider social context. It is not surprising that *context* becomes a key word in this type of approach.

The Case of Violence

Men's violence against women is one important issue. If we use the conventional direct gender hierarchy view, in which gender and power are closely linked, we would expect that the type of man or the form of masculinity is a good predictor of the chance of violence. Because masculinity is deeply entangled with power, the relation should be a strong one. Yet that does not seem to hold true. Although there is an empirical connection, it does not seem very strong (as far as can be judged from representative surveys such as "Men in Norway 1988" [Holter, 1989] and "The Norwegian Man 1998" [Haugen, Hammer, & Helle, 1998]). The case is perhaps stronger in Germany, as reported by Zulehner and Volz (1998), but this may be a reporting or design effect. Qualitative researchers, therapists, and others give a mixed picture and often tell about "feminine" as well as "masculine" men who use violence. I mentioned the tendency in feminist research, which can be found in violence research also, to go the other way, toward arguments that *any* man can be violent, that violent men are of all types and come from all socioeconomic categories (Lundgren, Heimer, Westerstrand, & Kalliokoski, 2001).

This is not surprising, if gender is in fact more indirectly related to power than the mixed model assumes. So let us use the two-dimensional model instead. Here we would expect that the degree of inequality is a strong predictor of violence, but gender should be moderately or weakly related (expressing mixed relations and adaptations). The chance of male violence against women should be higher in imbalanced relationships and households than in more balanced ones. There is increasing empirical support for this, although the evidence has not been systematized. Household balance has a positive impact, reducing the level of violence against women (Walby, 2002). Qualitative studies indicate that the chance of violence is higher in contexts where the woman has few resources compared with the man.

Structural Discrimination

Gender equality research shows that gender discrimination is more than a personal, direct, or active relationship, such as a man's violent relation to a woman. There is also a more indirect component, which can be called *passive* gender discrimination (a term used in, e.g., the EU Amsterdam treaty) or *collective* discrimination. It clearly involves social circumstances, not just the relation or unit at hand (e.g., "bad family"). It consists of the wider, social causes of the discrimination.

The *wage gap* between men and women is an example of this sort of structure. It can change over time; structures are not fixed or static but are often slow moving. Here and now, the wage gap contributes to the social preference system, in which a man's time appears to be more valuable than a woman's. The gap in ownership, property, leading capital positions, and so on works the same way. The economy tells us that men have more value than women, even if politics says they should count for the same.

Premodern patriarchy was mainly a sociopolitical structure, underpinned by religion and the military. Modern patriarchy emerged through a "problem period" during which the emerging factory system attracted women before men. The nuclear family may not have been a major change in terms of household size, but it was a new type of *organization,* mainly structured on the need to provide new "producers of human personality" (Parsons, 1988, p. 126). This was principally different from both the aristocratic households of older Europe and the gender relations among working people, small farmers, and artisans. The institutions of the modern gender system, with a nuclear or breadwinner family system creating new "marriage market" arenas, evolved in the 20th century along with a new view of sexuality (Holter, 1983).

Most or all current gender equality theories share a critique of traditional wage-work-only definitions of work. Much research in the late 1970s and the 1980s showed how the wage-only view crashed with realities. This was shown by time-use studies and a lot of qualitative evidence. Wider, more realistic, and more relational concepts of work were needed.

Dual-sphere theory was one answer. It seems to have originated among many researchers, in slightly different terms and versions, around this time. The framework could also be called "work and family," with family and household seen as a workplace on its own. Studies (e.g., Berk, 1985) claimed that household work forms gender identity. The two spheres could be described as *production sphere* and *reproduction sphere,* production meaning the creation of things or nonhuman resources and reproduction the creation of human resources. The needs in this human-oriented work process, somewhat defensively called reproduction, could be described in terms of an "emancipatory minimum" (Fürst, 1994). Many studies showed that reproductive work was relational in tendency, having a socialization effect. One works one's way to gender.

Before we go on, a rather dramatic implication of this kind of analysis should be noted. In principle, if all producers work for a wage and the reproducers work for the producers (wage workers), the class of producers will "own" the class of reproducers. The reproducers will be individually dependent on the producers for their livelihood. It is no wonder that, from this perspective, the producer becomes socially enlarged and, in gender terms, that everything may seem to rest on "the man" or "male dominance." This extreme system has never fully existed (despite breadwinner ideology). The point, however, is that it exists as a background economic pattern strong enough to sustain a gender-power system. Even if women make their own wages, through paid reproduction work, their payments are deducted from the money (seemingly) brought in solely by the production sphere. Production is the place of profits. Reproduction is the place of costs. With this economic regime, the older patriarchal-political order became redundant (Holter, 1982).

Reification and the Deconstruction of Gender

This brings us to reification as a key issue of the modern gender system. We saw that, in the gender equality view, gender systems are formed and transformed according to shifting equality and to discrimination patterns in society and culture as a whole. In this sense, one can say that power frames our whole picture of gender difference (Kimmel, 2000a). Yet this is not just the power of men, or even mainly gender-power. Gender-power is after the fact. It is what happens *if* certain social conditions are at work. We need to know these wider conditions.

One approach in this direction starts with a key performance area and realization of gender; that is, the transactions and exchanges between two potential partners seeking a relationship or marriage, traditionally leading to the formation of a gender dyad or couple. In this *gender market analysis,* the gender market is defined as the nonmonetary exchange of future rights to a relationship or household partner. Each participant "offers" and "asks" for offers. Although the economic patterns are muted in terms of money—or precisely for that reason—they are clearly gendered, much more clearly than, for example, in the labor market (Holter, 1983).

Two levels of exchange are distinguished in this analysis. One level is individual—a level of exchange between men and women. Here, the exchange form varies between giving, sharing, and simple exchange. There is no consistent difference between women and men (in empirical terms, friends are often described as part of this category). On another level, however, the exchange is much more abstract. It is a gender-*making* relation, not just a playing out of something already there. It is a potential producer and reproducer who meet each other, creating the key gender relation through their meeting. A major point of the analysis is that the sex of the persons does not determine the outcome. Instead, it is the social form of the exchange— the way that the two main spheres of society are connected, through individual links—that makes the participants *appear as if* gender was already at hand. This creates the fetishism (ideological image of reification) in which it seems obvious that gender is always already there. It is not sex, or some combination of biology and early socialization, that creates a "she" that is body and beauty and a "he" as a more neutral and universal person. Rather, this is the outcome of the relationship between two spheres of society, expressed in a particular individualized form (Ø. Holter, 1984).

Studies of the gender market that use fairly openly gender-commercial arenas (such as contact advertising and public meeting places) as indicators of the wider social pattern show that the man is in a situation of "having" something in this relation, compared with the woman's "being" something. The relation does not work out in the same sense for him as for her; it does not mainly concern something embodied in him as a person. He "is" not; he "has." For example, she thinks of him as person who exhibits social control. This social control appears as something the man has, by making it; it is "self-made," in the market ideology. The woman, who is in the position of equivalent at this level of the exchange, functions as sex object and beauty subject. Her presence becomes strangely money-like (related to extended and total forms of exchange), as it functions not only as the scale of measurement of individual men's offers but also as the key investment capital to get a new reproduction-production unit going.

My own research on the gender market (mainly in the 1980s) was later criticized for being too "economistic" (Fürst, 1994) and also too victimizing of women. I did not accept the picture of women and use value (so-called "soft values") neatly divided from the harsh world of men and value ("hard values"). I find even less reason to do so today. The gender market turns our expectation around in regard to who is an economic object and who is not. This is related to the second critique, with which I mainly agree. Placing women in a passive victim status was a typical tendency in research from this period. If women are victimized as object beauty and body capital, they are also, for once, the leading market investors. Women's upward class mobility through marriage is part of this picture. At the abstract gender level, the woman comes into a social position that does not stem from her individuality or the individual level of the exchange and communication; a position and relation that, undoubtedly,

shows that gender has an economic element not just in prostitution, but in normal dating-like contact also (Holter, 1990b). Economic analysis of gender is still very much an underdeveloped field.

Abstract masculinity is a term for the "man = person who has" element, as opposed to "woman = person who is." In gender market analysis, if beauty is capital in women, the wage, and what it represents and can be converted to (means of reproduction), is capital in the men's world. In the market, it is the position as producer and wage earner that is tested through the equivalent.

In this analysis, the social constructions of masculinity and femininity originate in specific positions that have no direct relation to sex but are instead created by the sphere relationship of production and reproduction. Gender appears through reification as the individualized form of transaction between the two spheres.[1] In this perspective, it is not surprising that research generally shows that the gender market is a fairly gender-conservative place, where the successful breadwinner ideal is more operative than elsewhere in society. "He" is the one with the arm on which to lean. "She" is the one who leans. The phenomenology at this point is rich, as, for example, Erving Goffman (1977) noted. The market's high level of polarization shows that the logic of men being "not-women," which Nancy Chodorow (1978) and others attributed to early socialization, may be more operative in certain key phases later in life. The gender market can be seen as the "prestation stage" (Mauss, 1989) of the production-reproduction relationship, or it can be seen as the main gender contract. It is a stage of segregation.

Why does gender segregation increase as men and women negotiate private relationships? This seems to be caused partly by the dynamics of the market itself, but it may be mainly due to the connection between gender and class brought out in the gender market in terms of gendered attractiveness. It is in every participant's interest in terms of upward mobility to define gender commercially. Thereby, even the gender market, a free-floating institution compared with earlier systems of marriage alliances, betrays its partially patriarchal background. We do not have to assume that men (or the market as an institution) intend the actual result—women (and some men) as sex objects. Instead, this is the way the market works, due to the fact that it exists in a context of *partial* gender equality rather than pure free love. The inequality shows up in the market in the form of abstract masculinity or wage-earning capacity, on the one hand, and money-like embodied beauty, on the other.

The gender market forms part of the conditions of reproduction and gender relationships; that is, the actual couples or families. As symbol-oriented feminist researchers have pointed out, *beauty* translates into *cleanliness* and *reproduction*, including the woman-mother as a symbolic food figure (Borchgrevink & Solheim, 1988). Yet increasing expectations of gender equality have made the market patterns more problematic, along with other breadwinner-related structures. Research has shown a change from "naturalistic" to more "individualistic" gender images (Holter, 1990b). Abstract masculinity is linked to patterns such as "job magnetism" and the greater "social space" of the producer vis-à-vis the caregiver or reproducer (Holter & Aarseth, 1993). Gender patterns often express labor patterns and the ranking of labor in society. This is connected to the "meta-institutional" power of labor and capital in modern society (Postone, 1993).

New Gender Forms

So what could a new, reconstructed view of gender consist of?

Nordic research, especially in Sweden, has shown the importance of social sanctions for the formation of masculinity, especially the importance of "unmanliness" and the "fear of falling" (Ekenstam, Johansson, & Kuosmanen, 2001). This is connected to shame and authority, but the more precise background is not clear. Fear of falling, in this context, seems similar to Kimmel's concept of market-related anxiety. Gender market studies tell of men's fear of personal ruin, expressed in loneliness.

Diversity is one main part of the new gender picture. Sexuality, once seen as a historical constant, can now be approached as a modern form of intimacy, distinct from, for example, the eroticism of Antiquity or the Middle Ages, thanks to the research of Michel Foucault (1977), John Boswell (1980), and others. Men's emotional range and expressions that could be shown in public, such as crying, have varied much more than formerly believed.

The new or "diverse" gender is the gender that is still there when social asymmetry—rank, status, power, exploitation—is left out of the picture. It can scarcely help being somewhat ideal, today, yet its contours are becoming clearer. New, more egalitarian and diverse gender forms seem to be embodied and life oriented, rather than cognitive-rational and power or work oriented. Equality-oriented people do not refuse to be a man or a woman—the logical conclusion, if power is all there is to gender—yet they do not presume that gender is an eternal and massive dividing line, either. They want individual flexibility, which will allow them to create gender from that basis, gender in a form of their own choosing.

Direct gender hierarchy does not disappear, but it appears in a new light. To decrease and dissolve direct gender hierarchy, the broader structures that support it must be addressed. Gender-equal cooperation must be a clear goal rather than an exception in working life, politics, and the economy (Holter & Sørensen, 2003). Now, more diverse masculinities have a better chance. New cultural politics of masculinities need to be combined with structural reforms; that is, measures to balance the labor market, do away with breadwinner preference systems, and reduce overwork. This can be achieved by uniting different parties through common, long-term democratization interests.

IMPLICATIONS OF THE STRUCTURAL INEQUALITY PERSPECTIVE

Studies of Men

What do the discussion and examples given here say regarding research?

Although research developments in gender, women, and men's studies have strengthened social construction views of gender, biology is not necessarily thrown out. It reappears in a diverse gender that is more healthy and less apt to "soak up" patriarchal problems. A recent family study found that traditional gender roles are recreated in embodied forms in modern households. It is when the pressure of daily life rises that communication fails, typically with the women eventually expressing dissatisfaction (Lilleaas, 2003). This is not so much a result of cognitive or power-related strategies as of material fatigue.

Thirty years ago, as research into gender began, "sex" was the dominant concept. Biological sex was the factor that had to be weighed into the argument, usually in pronouncements like "gender is both biological and social." Today, biology is approached in different terms. The social (including cultural, economic, psychological, etc.) side of gender has been shown to be more varied and changing than formerly believed. The social is more like a metacode, shifting according to circumstances, not hard coded. By implication, it is more advanced in its relation to biology, too, as shown in the earlier example.

Talcott Parsons's (1964) notion of *gender complementarity,* formulated in the mid-20th century, is an example of the ideology of hard-coded gender. Parsons argued that men and women were best served in a "complementary" relationship, with the man as breadwinner and woman as homemaker. He argued that this was in keeping with their biological (sexual) natures. Later, Parsons's theory was developed in, for example, economy (Becker, 1981) but was largely dismissed as unrealistic in sociology due to rising democratic and feminist consciousness.

Today, many theorists would interpret Parsons's argument mainly as a reflection of modern gender ideology. Yet gender complementarity was an ongoing affair in society, a socially effective arrangement. Norms really did seem to materialize. Parsons's ideas were formed when the breadwinner ideal of the nuclear family ideal was still in its ascendancy. Later research found that, indeed, the provider pattern was (and still is) a core part of masculinity.

Parsons also, probably correctly, assumed a *tendency* toward sex complementarity in human societies generally. But like most sociologists of his time, he took the complementarity to be hard coded, a sign of nature represented by the body. We may note how gender as a relational concept emerged from older usage, in which it was considered to be situated inside women (women as "*the* sex"), appearing in terms such as "sex appeal" (Heath, 1982). Parsons thought that a complementarity principle could straightaway be derived from the modern context. Thereby, the nuclear family and breadwinner ideal of the mid-20th century became paradigmatic of human development.

Here, as in many other cases, not least in the vicinity of gender, the modern *abstraction*

turned out to be a poor guide to other periods or societies, the larger ground of true social science *generalization* (Holter, 1997). Today, historians and social researchers are becoming more aware that the modern "gender glasses" do not work well for understanding other societies or for in-depth analysis of modern society. Human beings are more than the gender attributed to them; they dynamically change gender and other parts of society and generally make trouble for abstractist or categorical theory (Connell, 1987). Some feminists saw this early on. "Women are not trying to prove the innate superiority of one sex to another. That would be repeating the male mistake," wrote Gloria Steinem (1974, p. 134).

The societal and cultural context is vitally important. Gender is not an isolated subject. Gender discrimination does not exist in the world alone, does not act as a social force in isolation, but mainly exists and is socially effective through its connection to other main forms of discrimination, including social status and race.

DEMOCRACY AND DEPATRIARCHALIZATION

Studies of gender in wars and conflict in modern society offer further proof, if we needed it, that modern society is still a partly patriarchal society. In wars, inequality structures often become sharp and clear, targeting nonprivileged men as well as women and children (Jones, 2002).

From the two-dimensional gender-patriarchy model, we would expect that the dynamics of depatriarchalization were connected to specific gendering processes, but in mixed and indirect ways, sometimes in conflict. This is in line with surveys and other studies from the research of recent decades. The model makes us expect that patriarchal forces often use gender system mechanisms in attempts to hinder equal status developments. There is evidence of this in many areas (e.g., in the use of gender stereotypes in the media).

The changes among men needed to create gender equality differ from the changes among women. In this respect, these changes are especially significant from a democratization point of view. Changes among men are important for reducing and dissolving authoritarian relations in society. Existing (but often hidden or subdued) power patterns and exploitative structures in family life, working life, and other areas can be addressed and reduced.

Further, depatriarchalization—for example, in policies such as gender mainstreaming for men—means democratization in terms of social class. This has not been achieved by most of the movement on the women's side—instead, the process has sometimes contributed to a popular stereotype of gender-equal status as a matter for career women only.

Democratization of class and status remains important in today's world, with its large economic differences. A more sharply differentiated class society created by globalization means greater social costs and problems unless countermeasures are applied. Depatriarchalization can be seen as a new approach to this policy area. It is different from a gender strategy of bringing men in as gendered persons, naming men as men, but also similar, as it has similar goals, such as creating new public spaces where problems like violence and rape are openly discussed. It specifically addresses men as "gender equality responsible" in their own right, as much as women, and sets cooperation between men and women as method as well as goal.

Because women's movements toward gender-equal status (taking greater part in traditional men's activities, etc.) have usually been upwardly mobile in social class terms, although men's have not, we should expect gender-related sanctions to be different. In general, we should be very careful with the idea that the two main positions in the gender system are mirror images of each other—polarized positions and similar. Asymmetry is a main part of the system, linked to the way it is integrated, through partial equality structures, with society at large. Although men participate in the equality-patriarchy power dimension as much as women, we should not assume that men are gendered in the same ways or even to the same extent that women are gendered. This is a matter of better study with clearer concepts.

Conclusion

In this chapter, I have discussed studies on men and masculinities from the point of view of

gender equality analysis and historical research on changing patriarchal societal structures. Without a compass, it is difficult to make a map, and using the result is apt to be misleading. Today's gender research offers parts of a map, but it is not well oriented. I regard gender equality as similar to the compass. Without a distinct understanding of equality, one that falls back into a patriarchal, reified gender discourse, the map will remain obscure. I describe a common discourse in gender studies and debate, constructed on the basis of the "men = patriarchy" or "masculinity = power" line of imagination, without any perceived need to consider the equality dimension. The map is all, the compass nothing. However, too much compass—or too structural a view—can also be a problem. I have argued against approaches in which direct gender hierarchy becomes the principal, theoretical guideline. This does not amount to an argument that direct gender hierarchy does not exist. On the contrary, my point is that more context- and process-oriented approaches, based on better gender equality analyses, are needed to better identify direct gender hierarchies—not just their existence, but also their causes, dynamics, and possibilities for reduction. Thus, even if radical approaches to direct gender hierarchy may seem most action oriented in the short run, I think the opposite is true in the longer run.

I have discussed masculinities as outcomes of gendering processes in conditions of uneven and partial gender-equal status. We cannot expect "new men" as passive outcomes of more postpatriarchal structures; men need to engage in these processes, and research must show the profit for men as well as women. There is a very gradual and quite uneven development toward increased equality. Men are increasingly apparent as social actors in this development, often through a connection of caring and caregiving. This is associated with children, women, and emerging diversity. These are the main areas for new studies, methods, and theory creation.

Note

1. The reification analysis builds on feminist analyses of alienation (e.g., Foreman, 1977); see further Holter (1997).

REFERENCES

Baagøe Nielsen, S. (2003). Vi trænger nye kræfter, sagde lederen—og ansatte en mand [We need new forces, the leader said—and recruited a man]. In K. Hjort & S. Baagøe Nielsen (Eds.), *Mænd og omsorg* [Men and caregiving] (pp. 136-163). København, Denmark: Hans Reitzels forlag.

Bakken, R. (2001). *Modermordet: Om sykepleie, kjønn og kultur* [Matricide: On nursing, gender and culture]. Oslo, Norway: Universitetsforlaget.

Baudrillard, J. (1993). *Symbolic exchange and death.* London: Sage.

Becker, G. S. (1981). *A treatise on marriage.* Cambridge, MA: Harvard University Press.

Bekkengen, L. (1999). Män som "pappor" och kvinnor som "föräldrar" [Men as "dads," women as "parents"]. *Kvinnovetenskapligt Tidsskrift, 1,* 33-48.

Berk, S. F. (1985). *The gender factory: The apportionment of work in American households.* New York: Kluwer Academic/Plenum.

Bin-Nun, S. (1975). *The Tawananna in the Hittite kingdom.* Heidelberg, Germany: Carl Winter.

Borchgrevink, T., & Holter, Ø. (Eds.). (1995). *Labour of love: Beyond the self-evidence of everyday life.* Aldershot, UK: Avebury.

Borchgrevink, T., & Solheim, J. (1988). En råtten tekst: Om kjønn, mat og fortolkning [A rotten text: On gender, food and interpretation]. *Sosiologi i dag, 1*(2).

Boswell, J. (1980). *Christianity, social tolerance and homosexuality.* Chicago: University of Chicago Press.

Bredesen, O. (2000). *Kule, analytiske og rå* [Cool, analytical, and raw]. Oslo, Norway: Hovedfagsoppgave sosiologi, Universitetet i Oslo.

Brittan, A. (2001). Masculinities and masculinism. In S. M. Whitehead & F. J. Barrett (Eds.), *The masculinities reader* (pp. 51-55). Cambridge, England: Polity Press.

Brudner, L. A., & White, D. R. (1997). Class, property, and structural endogamy: Visualizing networked histories. *Theory and Society, 26,* 161-208.

Butler, J. (1990). *Gender trouble: Feminism and the subversion of identity.* New York: Routledge.

Butler, J. (1998). How bodies come to matter: An interview by Irene Costa Meijer and Baukje Prins. *Signs, 23*(2), 275-286.

Carrigan, T., Connell, R. W., & Lee, J. (1985). Toward a new sociology of masculinity. *Theory and Society, 14*(5), 551-604.

Chodorow, N. (1978). *The reproduction of mothering.* Berkeley: University of California Press.

Collinson, D. L., & Hearn, J. (1994). Naming men as men: Implications for work, organizations and management. *Gender, Work and Organization, 1*(1), 2-22.

Connell, R. W. (1987). *Gender and power: Society, the person and sexual politics.* Cambridge, England: Polity Press.

Connell, R. W. (1995). *Masculinities.* Cambridge, England: Polity Press.

Connell, R. W. (2002). *Gender.* Cambridge, England: Polity Press.

Connor, S. (2001). The shame of being a man. *Textual Practice, 15*(2), 211-230.

Ekenstam, C. (1993). *Kroppens idehistoria: Disciplinering och karaktärsdaning i Sverige 1700-1950* [The history of ideas of the body: Discipline and character formation in Sweden, 1700-1950]. Hedemora, Sweden: Gidlunds.

Ekenstam, C., Johansson, T., & Kuosmanen, J. (2001). *Sprickor I fasaden: Manligheter i forandring* [Cracks in the facade: Masculinities in transition]. Stockholm, Sweden: Gidlunds.

Foreman, A. (1977). *Femininity as alienation.* London: Pluto Press.

Forsèn, R., Gislason, I., Holter, Ø. G., & Rongevær, Ø. (2000). *Kan menn? Menn og likestilling i arbeidslivet* [Can men? Men and gender equality in working life]. Copenhagen, Denmark: Nordic Council of Ministers.

Foucault, M. (1977). *The history of sexuality* (Vol. 1). Harmondsworth, England: Penguin.

Fürst, E. L'o. (1994). Mat: Et annet språk. En studie av rasjonalitet, kropp og kvinnelighet belyst med litterære tekster [Food: Another language. A study of rationality, the body, and femininity through literary texts] (ISO Rapport No. 7). Oslo, Norway: Universitetet i Oslo.

Goffman, E. (1977). The arrangement between the sexes. *Theory and Society, 4*(3), 301-331.

Haavind, H. (1984). Love and power in marriage. In H. Holter (Ed.), *Patriarchy in a welfare society.* Oslo, Norway: Universitetsforlaget.

Haavind, H. (1994). Kjønn i forandring: Som fenomen og som forståelsesmåte [Gender in transition: As phenomenon and interpretational framework]. *Tidsskrift for Norsk Psykologforening, 31,* 767-783.

Hanmer, J. (1990). Men, power and the exploitation of women. In J. Hearn & D. Morgan (Eds.), *Men, masculinities and social theory* (pp. 21-42). London: Routledge.

Haugen, T., Hammer, G., & Helle, M. (1998). *Den norske mannen 1998* [The Nordic man 1998]. Oslo, Norway: MMI Tabellrapport.

Hearn, J. (1992). *Men in the public eye: The construction and deconstruction of public men and public patriarchies.* London: Routledge.

Heath, S. (1982). *The sexual fix.* London: MacMillan.

Hoel, M., & Sørhaug, T. (1999). *Omstilling, ledelse og likestilling: Sluttrapport fra et bedriftsprosjekt* [Restructuring, leadership and gender equality:

Final report from an enterprise project]. Oslo, Norway: Institutt for samfunnsforskning.

Holter, H. (1970). *Sex roles and social structure.* Oslo, Norway: Universitetsforlaget.

Holter, H. (Ed.). (1984). *Patriarchy in a welfare society.* Oslo, Norway: Universitetsforlaget.

Holter, Ø. G. (1982). Det verdifulle patriarkatet [The valuable patriarchy]. In R. Haukaa, M. Hoel, & H. Haavind (Eds.), *Kvinneforskning: Et bidrag til samfunnsteori* [Women's studies: A contribution to social theory]. Oslo, Norway: Universitetsforlaget.

Holter, Ø. G. (1983). *Raggning, kärlek och kønnsmarknad* [Dating, love, and the gender market]. Stockholm, Sweden: Hammarstrøm & Åberg.

Holter, Ø. G. (1984). Gender as forms of value. In H. Holter (Ed.), *Patriarchy in a welfare society.* Oslo, Norway: Universitetsforlaget.

Holter, Ø. G. (1989). *Menn* [Men]. Oslo, Norway: Aschehoug.

Holter, Ø. G. (1990a). Arbeid og familie: En studie av teknologkulturen [Work and family: A study of technological culture]. Oslo, Norway: Universitetsforlaget.

Holter, Ø. G. (1990b). Kjærlighet i forandring: Endring i makevalg 1973-1985 [Love in change: Changes in mate selection 1973-1985]. *Tidsskrift for samfunnsforskning, 31*, 125-146.

Holter, Ø. G. (1997). *Gender, patriarchy and capitalism: A social forms analysis* (Doctoral dissertation, University of Oslo, 1997). Oslo, Norway: Work Research Institute.

Holter, Ø. G. (1998). Forskning om menn 1970-97: Bidrag til en oversikt [Research on men 1970-1997: Contribution to an overview]. In B. Westerberg (Ed.), *Han, hon, den, det: Om genus och køn* [He, she, it: On gender and sex]. Stockholm, Sweden: Ekerlids.

Holter, Ø. G. (2003). *Can men do it? Men and gender equality: The Nordic experience.* Copenhagen, Denmark: Nordic Council of Ministers.

Holter, Ø. G., & Aarseth, H. (1993). *Menns livssammenheng* [Men's life connection]. Oslo, Norway: Ad. Notam Gyldendal.

Holter, Ø. G., Karlsen, B., & Salomon, R. (1998). *Omstillinger I arbeidslivet* [Restructuring in working life]. Oslo, Norway: The Work Research Institute.

Holter, Ø., & Sørensen, B. A. (2003). Kjønnskulturer i arbeidslivet [Gender cultures in working life]. Oslo, Norway: The Work Research Institute.

Jalmert, L. (1984). *Den svenske mannen* [The Swedish man]. Stockholm, Sweden: Tiden.

Jonasdóttir, A. G. (1991). Love, power and political interest. Örebro, Sweden: University of Örebro.

Jones, A. (2002, May 31). *Gendercide and genocide.* Paper presented at the "Constructions of Men and Masculinities in Conflict and War" seminar of the Norwegian Network for Studies of Men and The Centre for Gender Equality, Oslo, Norway.

Kanter, R. M. (1977). Some effects of proportions in group life. *American Journal of Sociology, 82,* 965-990.

Kimmel, M. S. (2000a). *The gendered society.* Oxford, England: Oxford University Press.

Kimmel, M. S., with Aronsen, A. (Eds.). (2000b). *The gendered society reader.* Oxford, England: Oxford University Press.

Krøjer, J. (2003). Når Farmand kommer hjem [When Farmand comes home]. In K. Hjort & S. Baagøe Nielsen (Eds.), *Mænd og omsorg* [Men and caregiving] (pp. 72-89). København, Denmark: Hans Reitzels forlag.

Lilleaas, U.-B. (2003). Moderne par i gamle roller [Modern couples in old roles]. *Aftenposten.*

Lorentzen, J. (1996). *Mannlighetens muligheter: Om mannlig under, erfaring og etikk I det moderne gjennombrudds litteratur* [The possibilities of manhood: On masculine wonder, experience and ethics in the literature of the breakthrough of modernity]. Unpublished doctoral dissertation, University of Oslo, Norway.

Lukes, S. (1988). *Emile Durkheim: His life and work. A historical and critical study.* London: Penguin Books.

Lundgren, E. (1985). *I herrens vold* [In the hand of the Lord]. Oslo, Norway: J. W. Cappelens forlag.

Lundgren, E., Heimer, G., Westerstrand, J., & Kalliokoski, A.-M. (2001). *Slagen dam: Mans vold mot kvinnor i jamstallda Sverige. En omfångsundesøkning* [Men's violence against women in gender-equal Sweden: A prevalence study]. Stockholm, Sweden: Fritzes Offentlige.

MacKinnon, C. A. (1983). Feminism, Marxism, method and the state: Toward feminist jurisprudence. *Signs, 8*(4), 635-658.

Mauss, M. (1989). *The gift.* London: Routledge.

Merton, R. (1957). *Social theory and social structure* (Rev. ed.). Glencoe, IL: Free Press.

New, C. (2001). Oppressed and oppressors? The systematic mistreatment of men. *Sociology, 35,* 729-748.

Parsons, T. (1964). *Social structure and personality.* New York: Free Press.

Parsons, T. (1988). Sosiologiske essays (p. 126). Trans. by Dag Østerberg, Pax, Oslow.

Postone, M. (1993). *Time, labour and social domination: A reinterpretation of Marx's critical theory.* Cambridge, England: Cambridge University Press.

Prieur, A., & Taksdal, A. (1989). *Å sette pris på kvinner* [Pricing women]. Oslo, Norway: Pax.

Solheim, J. (1998). *Den åpne kroppen* [The open body]. Oslo, Norway: Pax.

Søndergaard, D. M. (1996). Tegnet på kroppen: Koder og konstruktioner blant unge voksne I Akademia

[The sign of the body: Codes and construction among young adults in academia]. København, Denmark: Museum Tusculanums forlag.

Steinem, G. (1974). The myth of masculine mystique. In J. H. Pleck & J. Sawyer (Eds.), *The forty-nine percent majority: The male sex role.* Englewood Cliffs, NJ: Prentice-Hall.

Vaage, O. F. (2002). *Til alle døgnets tider: Tidsbruk 1971-2000* [All through the day: Time use, 1971-2000]. Oslo, Norway: Statistisk Sentralbyrå.

Walby, S. (1990). *Theorizing patriarchy.* Oxford, England: Blackwell.

Walby, S. (2002). Reducing gendered violence. In M. Eriksson, A. Nenol, & M. M. Nilsen (Eds.), *Køn och våld I Norden* [Gender and violence in the Nordic countries] (TemaNord conference report No. 2002:545). Copenhagen, Denmark: Nordic Council of Ministers.

Whitehead, S. M., & Barrett, F. J. (2001). The sociology of masculinity. In S. M. Whitehead & F. J. Barrett (Eds.), *The masculinities reader* (pp. 1-26). Cambridge, England: Polity Press.

Williams, C. L. (2000). The glass escalator: The hidden advantages for men in "female" professions. In M. S. Kimmel with A. Aronsen (Eds.), *The gendered society reader* (pp. 294-310). Oxford, England: Oxford University Press.

Wright, E. O. (2000, September 21-24). *The shadow of exploitation in Weber's class analysis.* Paper presented at the International Symposium "Economy and Society: Max Weber in 2000," Madison, WI. Retrieved January 7, 2004, from http://www.ssc.wisc.edu/~wright/weber.pdf

Zulehner, P. M., & Volz, R. (Eds.). (1998). *Männer im Aufbruch: Wie Deutschlands Männer sich selbst und wie Frauen sie sehen. Ein Forschungsbereich* [Men in transition: How German men see themselves and how women see them. A research report]. Ostfildern, Germany: Schwabenverlag.

3

Men, Masculinities, and Feminist Theory

Judith Kegan Gardiner

"Is it true... that women in your society are treated exactly like men?" a doctor in Ursula LeGuin's (1974) science fiction novel, *The Dispossessed,* asks a visiting anarchist. The anarchist replies with a laugh, "That would be a waste of good equipment" (p. 16). Then he explains that in his society, "a person chooses work according to interest, talent, strength—what has the sex to do with that?" (p. 17). Published in 1974, at the height of the 20th-century American movement for women's liberation, LeGuin's fantasy attempts to visualize gender equality as a society without differences based on one's anatomical sex, but one, it turns out, that primarily takes the form of allowing women the occupational choices and sexual freedoms already common to men; men do a little child care and are otherwise unchanged. Feminist theories take a number of approaches to this slippery goal of gender equality that are intertwined with their varying perspectives on men and masculinity. They endorse some aspects of traditional masculinity, critique some, and ignore others, as they ask who will be equal to whom, in what respects, and with what results for male and female individuals and their societies.

The most important accomplishment of 20th-century feminist theory is the concept of gender as a social construction; that is, the idea that masculinity and femininity are loosely defined, historically variable, and interrelated social ascriptions to persons with certain kinds of bodies—not the natural, necessary, or ideal characteristics of people with similar genitals. This concept has altered long-standing assumptions about the inherent characteristics of men and women and also about the very division of people into the categories of "men" and "women." The traditional sexes are now seen as cultural groupings rather than as facts of nature based on a static division between two different kinds of people who have both opposed and complementary characteristics, desires, and interests. By seeking to understand the causes, means, and results of gendered inequality, feminist theories hope to develop effective ways to improve women's conditions, sometimes by making women more similar to men as they are now, sometimes by making men more similar to women as they are now, sometimes by validating women's traditional characteristics, sometimes by working toward the abolition or minimizing of the categories of gender altogether, but all simultaneously transforming ideologies and institutions, including the family, religion, corporations, and the state.

Some women living prior to organized movements for women's rights claimed that they were equal to men, as men described themselves; that men were not fully equal to the ideal of masculinity they themselves put forward; and that men and masculinity placed women and femininity in a subordinate position. With the resurgence of a movement for women's rights in the second half of the 20th century, varied theories developed to explain the causes of male domination, to correct erroneous assumptions about both women and men, and to imagine new kinds of men and of women in new circumstances. These theories charged that cultural ideologies favored men, that social institutions reflected these ideologies, and that men as a group benefited from the subordination of women as a group, despite the great disparities that existed in the advantages accruing to individual men or subgroups of men in relation to other men and to women. Thus men and masculinity play a crucial role in feminist theory, the body of thought that seeks to understand women's social situation and to articulate justice from a woman-centered perspective. Furthermore, feminist thinking has been fundamental to the formation of contemporary men's and masculinity studies as intellectual endeavors, academic subjects, and social movements. This chapter briefly sketches how men and masculinity figure in several strands of feminist theory. It looks at what the treatment of men and masculinity reveals about the gaps and assumptions in these theories. Focusing chiefly on a few key figures, it also indicates some advantages and future directions that these theories pose for masculinity studies.

Misogyny created feminist theory, and feminist theory has helped create masculinity. That is, cultural condemnation leveled against women by religious writers, philosophers, and popular discourses across centuries and cultures produced rebuttals by women and men. The first feminist theories were primarily defensive, and as they questioned men's appropriation to themselves of essential humanity, they charged that men, too, were embodied as a specific gender defined according to cultural ideals for people with similar bodies, characterized by certain psychological dispositions, and shaping social institutions to serve their interests. As women sought to be included in the rights and privileges of citizens, they questioned the gendered meanings of such ideals as liberty, fraternity, and equality and so initiated one continuing theme of feminist theorizing that has extended into masculinity studies as well.

Men's superiority to women is a tenet of the world's main monotheisms, although the major religions also include countervailing tendencies that value women's spiritual capacities and delimit male power and authority. The ancient Greek philosopher Aristotle portrayed women as naturally men's inferiors in terms of reason. In the long educational and philosophical tradition that venerated his authority, masculinity was thus rendered both invisible and normative: Masculinity was equated with the human rationality of men, and women were marked by sexuality, emotion, and their bodies. Champions of women repeatedly asked, if God and nature had made women so clearly inferior to men, why were such strong social inducements necessary to retain their subjugation?

In reaction to claims that women were irrational, weak, vicious, and sinful, the early defenders of women repeated a number of strategies. They claimed women were equal or superior to men, writing, for example, books about heroic, saintly, learned, and otherwise exemplary women. In another common strategy, they asserted equality less by raising the image of women than by lowering the image of men. They thereby launched an inquiry into the meaning of equality that continues to the present. Idealistic depictions of men as the embodiments of reason and humanity, they said, flew in the face of the evils men did: Men, too, were as embodied, irrational, and vicious as the misogynists claimed women were. Furthermore, men tyrannize over women rather than loving and protecting them as they claim to do. So the French medieval author Christine de Pizan (1405/1982) has her allegorical character Reason say "that these attacks on all women—when in fact there are so many excellent women—have never originated with me, Reason" but were occasioned rather by men's own vices, jealousies, and pride (p. 18). Margaret Cavendish (1985), a 17th-century English aristocrat, suggests that women rich enough not to depend on men financially "were mad to live with Men, who make the Female sex their slaves" (p. 89).

In the democratizing ferment of the French Revolution, Mary Wollstonecraft (1985) cried out for recognition of the common humanity of both sexes. Her "Vindication of the Rights of Woman" appealed to men to "generously snap our chains, and be content with rational fellowship instead of slavish obedience" (p. 431). When Abigail Adams (1994) wrote her husband John Adams, one of the founders of the American republic and later president of the United States, to "Remember the Ladies" in framing the new American state, she pleaded for gender equality under Enlightenment ideals of freedom: "Do not put such unlimited power into the hands of the Husbands. Remember all Men would be tyrants if they could" (p. 876). The pioneering American feminists at the Seneca Falls Women's Rights Convention of 1848 implicitly accepted the claims of men to both a rational and religious basis for citizenship when they attempted to add women to the language of the Declaration of Independence: "We hold these truths to be self-evident: that all men and women are created equal; that they are endowed by their Creator with certain inalienable rights. . . ." However, their statement immediately accused men of failing to uphold their own ideals: "The history of mankind is a history of repeated injuries and usurpations on the part of man toward woman" (Stanton, 1994, p. 1946). Furthermore, they said, "man" has withheld from women "rights which are given to the most ignorant and degraded men—both natives and foreigners" (p. 1947), a strategic attempt to divide the category of "man" by showing some women superior to groups of men whom other men also held in disrespect. Thus feminist efforts to achieve political and educational equality with men argued that at least some women already possessed equality in the qualities necessary for these privileges—immortal souls and educable human reason—but repeatedly oscillated between imitating and critiquing men. At least a few men agreed and even furthered these arguments. The liberal English philosopher John Stuart Mill (Mill & Mill, 1970), who developed his ideas about women in dialogue with his wife, Harriet Taylor, contended that an equal education for both sexes would disprove men's claims to superior intelligence.

Despite increasing numbers of women intellectuals, men continued to think of humanity as made in their image, according to French philosopher Simone de Beauvoir (1949/1968). Although they knew themselves as subjects capable of transcending their immediate experiences through reason and will, they treated Woman as their Other—mystery, complement, object of desire, creature of body and change. De Beauvoir's path-breaking book *The Second Sex* defended women's claims to full personhood and undercut men's pretensions to fulfill their own ideals. "It is clear that in dreaming of himself as donor, liberator, redeemer, man still desires the subjection of women," she writes (p. 172). She attacks the myths of masculine superiority and confirms masculine dualities that elevate mind over body by insisting that men, too, are creatures of bodily and sexual infirmity rather than disembodied minds: "Indeed no one is more arrogant toward women, more aggressive or scornful, than the man who is anxious about his virility" (p. xxv). In a current version of this critique, Rosi Braidotti (2002) alleges that "the price men pay for representing the universal is disembodiment, or loss of gendered specificity into the abstraction of phallic masculinity," and she suggests that men need "to get real" by recognizing their embodiment (p. 355). Exactly what this means and how both men and women, including those with physical and sensory disabilities, experience their embodiment is a fruitful topic in current feminist and masculinity studies (Hall, 2002).

Twentieth-century liberal feminism continued the tradition of seeking for women the privileges already enjoyed by men. Betty Friedan (1963) and the National Organization for Women (founded in 1966) believed that changing laws and educating people against erroneous prejudices would remedy gender discrimination, giving women equal opportunities with men to exercise individual choices in life. They sought gender equity through changes in law and childhood socialization. They lobbied for equal treatment of boys and girls in school and wrote children's books featuring cooperative boys as well as resourceful girls. They welcomed men into their organizations and encouraged women to enter previously male-dominated occupations. In all these endeavors, their critics alleged, they merely sought women's inclusion in current, male-dominated institutions, accepting a restrictively narrow model of equality without questioning the masculine norms that valorized abstract reason and law over the bodies and emotions they ruled. Current versions of liberal feminist theories, however, are more sophisticated in their analyses and offer to men's studies models for inquiries into the gendering of the law, the media, the state, and the professions; civil rights organizations open to male members with accessible goals for social reform; and ideals such as androgyny for combining traditionally masculine and feminine personality characteristics in individuals. There is still ample room for further studies in these areas; for example, concerning what fosters boys' and girls' best learning. Are girls still shortchanged by schools, especially in math and science, or are boys now suffering from a school system designed to keep good girls quiet and studious? The questions about which gender wins or loses by which kind of setting or practice are ripe for reframing while the idea of equality is still in contention in numerous societal and institutional settings.

Psychologist Eleanor Maccoby (1998) represents a recent version of this liberal view in encouraging individuality and freedom of choice for both sexes and allowing for a varied play of masculine and feminine difference across the life cycle. She sees youth "growing up apart" in groups segregated by sex and adults experiencing "convergence" in sex and work (p. 189). She describes greater divergence within each gender than between the two, notes contradictory components of both masculinity and femininity, and emphasizes that "sex-linked behavior turns out to be a pervasive function of the social context" more than of individual personality (p. 9). Other feminist theorists also seek to deflate gender dualism by viewing gender as developmental across the life course, so that, for example, masculinity might be defined by boys' development from childishness to maturity rather than by opposition to a denigrated femininity (Ehrenreich, 1983; Gardiner, 2002).

Another approach to disputing gender binaries and the equation of masculinity with human rationality lies through the psychoanalytic theories of Sigmund Freud and his French follower Jacques Lacan. Freud and Lacan (Gardiner, 1992) contradictorily asserted that all people were governed by irrational unconscious desires, thus unseating male claims to superior reason, and that men but not women had a privileged relationship to social power, which was visibly symbolized in the male anatomical part that men feared losing and women envied. Luce Irigiray (1985) reversed what she called the "phallogocentric" Freudian concept of women's "penis envy" as instead a defining characteristic of the masculine psyche: this alleged female envy "soothes the anguish man feels, Freud feels, about the coherence of his narcissistic construction and reassures him against what he calls castration anxiety" (p. 51). Thus Irigiray follows one feminist strategy in defining masculinity as a condition of lack, vulnerability, and weakness, in an ironic mirroring of Freudian versions of women's lacking genital equipment and defective moral development. American theorist Drucilla Cornell (1998) develops this Lacanian theory to argue that masculinity is not a transcendent human norm but is always imperiled by unconscious castration fears. The "bad news for the little boy" who identifies with the power of the idealized father, she says, is that "this fantasy leaves him in a constant state of anxiety and terror that what makes him a man can always be taken away from him" (p. 143). This insecurity then fuels men's fantasies of superiority to women but also provides them, she believes, with the motive for joining feminists in challenging the gender order and so freeing themselves from impossible standards of masculinity against which they will always fail. As with all uses of psychoanalytic theory, Cornell and Irigiray's feminist deployment leaves open the question of how much the Freudian or Lacanian framework distorts or prejudges issues of gender, sexuality, and sexual difference, both in individual human psychology and in cultural representations. Perhaps these very schema encourage the overestimation of the importance of sexual difference in psychic functioning, also minimizing the complexities of intrasexual relationships and of nonerotic bonds and antagonisms.

Rejecting psychoanalysis as the unscientific projection of male fantasies, contemporary feminist scientists join the feminist tradition of rationally disputing sexist claims that men are superior to women and different by nature as well as the claim that science itself is gender neutral (Collins, 1999; Fausto-Sterling, 1992). Susan Bordo (1999) describes the prevailing pervasiveness of androcentrism in science and in men's attitudes to nature: "The phallus stands, not for the superior fitness of an individual male over other men, but for *generic* male superiority—not only over females but also over other species" (p. 89). Although some conservative adaptations of evolutionary theory reinforce traditional gender roles, for example in explaining male aggression and promiscuity as optimizing reproductive success and so as predicted strategies for human survival, Darwinian feminist theorists dispute such ahistorical mythologizing. Instead, they emphasize the social construction of scientific categories, the reliance on gendered metaphors in science texts, and the sexism within science (Fausto-Sterling, 1992). They draw attention to the vast variety of primate as well as human societies and manifestations of gender and to the importance in the animal world of social systems over genetic programming. For instance, Barbara Smuts (1992) shows that female solidarity among primates decreases the prevalence of aggression by males against females. Thus a wide variety of feminist theorists disputes all definitions of masculinity that claim the natural superiority of men over women and other creatures. Further work will be developing the philosophy and sociology of science with respect to the gendering of nature and of contemporary scientific practices.

If one strand of feminist theory critiques the supposed rationality of masculinity, another characterizes masculinity as in itself harmful to women and other men. These are the theories most frequently characterized as male bashing, because they focus on male violence against women and on men's sexual objectification of women as the very definitions of masculinity. These theories seek gender equality by abolishing or dramatically transforming men and masculinity, although they may either extol or vilify the characteristics ascribed to traditional femininity.

Mocking male pretensions to power and authority, theologian Mary Daly (1987) rejected religions dependent on a Father God and sought to remake a new, nonpatriarchal language as a step toward defeating androcentrism. The puns and startling new word usages in her *Wickedary* associate masculinity not with power but with the follies and failures of men as individuals and of male-dominated institutions. Thus, for instance, she defines "male-function" as meaning "characteristically unreliable performance of phallic equipment. *Example:* the explosion of the space shuttle *Challenger*" or as an "archetypically endless ceremony or gathering of maledom. *Examples:* diplomatic functions, church functions, White House functions" (p. 209).

Legal theorist Catharine MacKinnon is the best-known exponent of a radical feminist viewpoint. Her theory posits male oppression of women as the first and most pervasive of all oppressions, the model for racism and class injustice and the structuring principle of all established institutions. She begins one book, for example, with this grim invitation to a female reader:

> Imagine that for hundreds of years your most formative traumas, your daily suffering and pain, the abuse you live through, the terror you live with, are unspeakable—not the basis of literature. You grow up with your father holding you down and covering your mouth so another man can make a horrible searing pain between your legs. When you are older, your husband ties you to the bed and drips hot wax on your nipples and brings in other men to watch and makes you smile through it. Your doctor will not give you drugs he has addicted you to unless you suck his penis. (MacKinnon, 1993, p. 3)

This passage constructs everywoman as eternally a victim, despite its invisible, authoritative female narrator. Its version of men and masculinity is horrifying, bizarre, and implicitly culture specific: Men are represented by a father who facilitates the rape of his daughter, a husband who flaunts his sexual sadism, and a dope-dealing doctor who forces fellatio on his patients.

MacKinnon (1987) makes gender dependent on sex and sex dependent on male force. Such social practices as pornography, rape, and prostitution institutionalize "the sexuality of male supremacy, which fuses the eroticization of dominance and submission with the social construction of male and female. Gender is sexual. Pornography constitutes the meaning of that sexuality" (p. 148). MacKinnon does not discuss the origin of this system, but her paradigm implies that men have always had the rapist mentality to desire forced heterosexual sex as well as the superior physical power to accomplish it. For her, masculinity defines men, rather than the reverse. "By men I mean the status of masculinity that is accorded to males," but not to those persons who are "defined as subordinated by force as women are" (p. 170). Men must work constantly to keep this masculine control and dominance in place, and the place of subordinated men, including gay men, is rendered ambiguous in this account.

Although male domination is universal, MacKinnon (1987) believes, it is also shaped by contemporary society: "women are the property that constitutes the personhood, the masculinity, of men under capitalism" (p. 159). Furthermore, in her view, the standards for all aspects of culture are masculine: "masculinity, the male standard for men" (p. 71), establishes patriarchal law and relegates women to the "private, moral, valued, subjective"; men, on the other hand, accrue to themselves the values of the "public, ethical, factual, objective" (p. 151). She claims that every quality that distinguishes men from women is affirmatively compensated by society:

> Men's physiology defines most sports, their needs define auto and health insurance coverage, their socially designed biographies define workplace expectations and successful career paths, their perspectives and concerns define quality in scholarship, their experiences and obsessions define merit, their objectification of life defines art, their military service defines citizenship, their presence defines family, their inability to get along with each other . . . defines history, their image defines God, and their genitals define sex. (MacKinnon, 1987, p. 36)

It is not merely the case that men make their behavior the norm for all people but that these norms are themselves harmful. Pornography impels male bodies to act, creating a total mind-body split that apparently constitutes masculinity but not femininity. For MacKinnon, the masculine has always defined humanity, but the masculine is inhumane. The ultimate solution to this grim paradox is the abolition of both masculinity and femininity; that is, the abolition of gender, although feminist-inspired laws, like those she and Andrea Dworkin proposed to outlaw pornography and sexual harassment, might help to identify and ameliorate such negative consequences of eroticized masculine dominance (MacKinnon, 1987, pp. 200-201).

Not only sexual violence but national and ethnic violence, as manifest in torture and war, provoke feminist theorizing about the relationship between masculinity and these predominantly male activities, with the goal of eliminating these horrors rather than of militarizing women. Sociologist Nancy Chodorow explores the links between masculinity, nationalism, and violence, attributing men's aggression more to cycles of humiliation and domination among older and younger men than, like MacKinnon, to men's sexual exploitation of women. She rejects the Freudian theory that all people are innately aggressive and instead sees aggression in both sexes as defending the self when it is endangered either by physical force or by humiliation and shame. However, she believes that men are more psychologically prone to respond to humiliation by violence against others than women are (Chodorow, 2002). Ecofeminist theorists also derive war from a "militarized 'cult of masculinity'" in which man conquers nature and defines national security as the protection of male privilege (Seager, 1999, p. 168). This "environmentally destructive ethos includes a cultivation of hypermasculinity, secrecy, fraternity, and an inflated sense of self-importance" (p. 169). At its most extreme, Joni Seager alleges, the "culture of nuclear destruction" is "a private men's club, within which masculinity is both an explicit sexualized expression and an implicitly taken-for-granted context" (p. 172). Thus, for ecofeminists and for many global feminists, a masculinity that validates competition among men and domination over women also imperils the planet. For some of these theorists, masculine attempts to dominate nature contrast with more feminist attitudes of attunement with nature. This masculine arrogance, they believe, leads to the extinction of species, the depletion of natural resources, war, and the destruction of ecosystems necessary for human survival.

These radical feminist theories attack masculinity rather than simply defending against sexist charges about women's inferiority. Their vision of masculinity can be violent and negative, void of any of the positive characteristics traditionally assigned to masculinity. Moreover, the superior force of disembodied reason sometimes seems appropriated in them to that of the female spokesperson for the voiceless and oppressed category of other women. Nevertheless, some male theorists agree with these radical feminist and ecofeminist positions. For John Stoltenberg (1989), the only ethical position for persons with penises is antimasculine feminism. Thus he encourages other male humans to join him in *Refusing to Be a Man*. Exaggerated as the claims of radical feminism may sometimes seem, it succeeded in breaking long-standing commonsense assumptions about the naturalness of heterosexual predation and the triviality of female complaints against male treatment of women in streets and offices. With its focus on the harms women experience, it articulated sexual harassment as a crime and sexual objectification as a pervasive component of gender inequality. Once stated, these perspectives made sense to some men as well, both with regard to relations with women and to relations among men. Men around the world work now with other men to reduce gendered violence through profeminist organizations such as the Global Network of Men and Mentors on Violence Prevention, as well as in environmental and peace organizations (Freedman, 2002, p. 287). Some men's studies already address men's bullying and harassment of other men in workplaces and schools. A question that is still open is the usefulness to men's theorizing of the model of harm developed by radical feminists. Aída Hurtado (1999), among others, critiques masculinist men's studies on the grounds that although they trumpet men's "wounds" from childhood, they leave white upper-class male privilege intact and unexamined. "The Western male intellectual tradition cannot theorize from a position of privilege," she claims, but, rather, only one of a "victimhood" that "leaves the status quo untouched" (p. 126). However, accurate assessments of men's self-perceptions and perceptions of others that avoid both justification and blaming may well be necessary to those designing psychological incentives for social change.

In contrast to radical feminist theories, many cultural feminist theories do not see male aggression and other traditionally gendered attributes as innate but rather as developed within individual psychologies by mother-dominated child rearing and other widespread social practices. Whereas sharply binary "dominance" theories such as MacKinnon's seem in danger of positing a masculinity that obliterates femininity, these "difference," "cultural feminist," or woman-centered theories validate women's traditional characteristics. Such theories tend to portray masculinity and femininity as complementary, with both containing good as well as bad traits. Psychologist Dorothy Dinnerstein (1976) argues that the universal female control of early child rearing explains both male dominance and misogyny, because all infants fear their mothers' life-giving or withholding powers and transfer these unconscious associations to other women. Chodorow (1978) also explains men's and women's disparate personality structures through psychological dispositions linked to female-dominated child rearing. Because boys, unlike girls, form their masculine gender identity not through direct imitation of the same-sex parent but through separation and contrast from their mothers, she hypothesizes, they develop a sense of self that is independent, autonomous, and individuated; conversely, girls' selves are more interdependent, nurturant, and empathic.

Rather than accepting male dominance as necessary to human society, Chodorow's popular theory of 1978 explains it through forms of child rearing that have been universal in the past but that modern technologies and social arrangements can now alter. Furthermore, she describes masculinity as so limiting for men's lives, rather than so enjoyably privileged, that men should also have incentives for change. If fathers take equal responsibility with mothers for early child care, she argues, gender inequality would disappear, women would be relieved of the unfair burdens of caregiving, and men would gain a satisfying intimacy with their children, women, and each other. Chodorow (1978) thinks "equal parenting" could bring all people "the positive capacities" now restricted to each sex separately, and both sexes would also be more flexible in their choice of sexual objects (p. 218). This optimistic theory about gender transformation requires dramatic changes in men's lifestyles as they assume heavy childcare responsibilities to produce more egalitarian personality structures in the future; women, on the other hand, will continue their current multitasking of work and family obligations. Current empirical studies in parenting show some changes in fathers' and mothers' tasks and commitments of time and emotion to their children. The effects on the parents, the children, and society at large await future investigation.

Unlike MacKinnon's and other radical feminist theories that simply posit a dominating masculinity as the origin of gender inequality, Chodorow's (1978) psychoanalytic theory explains masculinity as a defensive and compensatory formation in individual men's development. Identifying with their individual mothers, women become mothers in turn, but men become masculine by identifying with the male roles in society. "Masculine identification," she says, "is predominantly a gender role identification. By contrast, feminine identification is predominantly *parental*," based on a girl becoming like her mother, whereas being a father has been a minor part of most modern men's identity (p. 176). Thus gender is defined by men's difference from women in these theories but asymmetrically rather than in a relation of either simple opposition or negation. According to Chodorow, this leaves contemporary men confused about how to be masculine. She asserts that it is "crucial for everyone . . . to have a stable sexual identity. But until masculine identity does not depend on men's proving themselves, their *doing* will be a reaction to insecurity rather than a creative exercise of their humanity" (p. 44).

In her early discussions of masculine identity formation based on feminist object-relations psychology, Chodorow (1978) claimed that masculinity based on negation of the mother is a defensive construction likely to be rigid, formed on unrealistic stereotypes and narrow cultural norms, and disadvantageous to both the individual and the culture. However, her more recent defenses of heterosexuality as potentially as varied and exciting as the homosexualities lead her to embrace the view that all formations of unconscious desire have defensive, possibly even perverse components (Chodorow, 1994, 1999). Thus, if defensive personality structures can be as flexible, complex, and exciting as nondefensive ones, there is no longer a theoretical reason to polarize masculinity as formed negatively and defensively in contrast to a more positive femininity. Similarly, although feminist assessments of moral reasoning and "women's ways of knowing" initially appeared to polarize a rigid abstract masculinity against interdependent and interpersonal female styles, current theorists see these gendered styles as dependent on variable social contexts rather than as stable characteristics of individual personality (Belenky, Clinchy, Goldberger, & Tarule, 1986; Gilligan, 1982; Maccoby, 1998, pp. 198-199). This is a rich field for future research, especially in social contexts outside the college survey laboratory or therapist's consulting room.

Theories of gender complementarity based on the psychological asymmetries of child rearing are subject to the criticisms that they underestimate the effects of social dominance, historical and cultural differences, and differences among members of the same sex. However, their emphasis on the importance of fathering has found widespread acceptance among both masculinist and profeminist masculinity theorists (Gardiner, 2002). Profeminist scholars Michael Kimmel and Michael Kaufman (1995), for example, argue that manhood is dangerous when formed in flight from femininity. They cite Chodorow and Dinnerstein, among others, to claim that "men need to heal the mother wound, to close the gap between the mother who cared for us and the mother we have tried to leave behind" (p. 28). They contrast themselves with the masculinist men's movement of Robert Bly (1990), which urges men to "cut our psychic umbilical cord" with women rather than sharing with them in the labors of bringing up the next generation (p. 27).

If radical feminist theories sharply divide masculine power from feminine powerlessness and cultural feminist theories focus especially on psychological differences between men and women, other theories are more attentive to the myriad differences that divide men from other men and women from other women, as well as to the commonalities between the sexes and the relationships among the various categories of social inequality (Lorber, 1994; Maccoby, 1998). Feminists of color and many feminists influenced by Marxism emphasize the interconnectedness of gender with other social hierarchies, including nationality, ethnicity, social class, racialized identities, and sexualities. African American feminist theorist Patricia Hill Collins (1999) explains that the "construct of intersectionality references two types of relationships: the interconnectedness of ideas and the social structures in which they occur, and the intersecting hierarchies" of social power; "viewing gender within a logic of intersectionality redefines it as a constellation of ideas and social practices that are historically situated within and that mutually construct multiple systems of oppression" (p. 263). The categories these theorists describe are not additive but transformative, so that, for example, Chicano masculinities are not simply Anglo masculinities with a salsa beat or a dose of machismo but complex responses to Hispanic cultures, Catholic religion, dominant American middle-class white masculine assumptions, and the internal dynamics of Latino families (González, 1996). These multidimensional feminist theories allow for more theoretical nuance as well, as seen in Hurtado's (1999) "blasphemies," addressed to white feminism and positing, for example, white men's differential treatments of white women, who are needed to reproduce white children, and women of color, who become used rather as sexual and economic objects.

Black feminists have repeatedly sought to balance understanding of the particular oppressions experienced by women of color with sympathy toward the vicissitudes of men in their communities. They critically examine the difficulties that men of color face in achieving mainstream versions of masculinity and critique those forms of masculinity that depend on sexism and male supremacy. In addition, they join male black intellectuals in indicting the projections of endemic social problems such as male violence against women or substance abuse exclusively onto blacks. Both male and female theorists situate African American gender characteristics within the common history of U.S. racism and the legacy of slavery. In particular, they speak of the dispersal of families and cultures; the imposition of alien ideologies, physical hardship, and degrading servitude; and the denial of education, opportunity, sexual choice, and occupational mobility. Chattel slavery was literally dehumanizing, in that it did not recognize the human status of slaves in law or practice (Williams, 1991, pp. 216-236); infantilizing, in that it did not recognize the adult status of slaves but kept them as wards and dependents judged incapable of citizenship; and sometimes also emasculating, castration figuring prominently in the terrorist postbellum tortures of lynching (Ross, 2002). These discussions affirm the strength necessary to survive such conditions and the resulting cross-sex unity of African American communal experience, and at times they invoke the West African origins of many African American people or the small-town American black South as models for more ideal and harmonious societies than those of the contemporary capitalist West.

In response to some second-wave white feminists who drew analogies between the disadvantaged positions of women and African Americans, African American feminists published the pioneering text *All the Women Are White, All the Blacks Are Men, but Some of Us Are Brave: Black Women's Studies* (Hull, Scott, & Smith, 1982). African American feminist theorists repeatedly sought to balance sympathy and critique for African American men. Michelle Wallace (1990) began her book *Black Macho and the Myth of the Superwoman* (originally published in 1978) with the premise that African American men felt deprived of manhood by white supremacy, so that it was a revolutionary claim for human dignity, not a tautology, when striking male garbage workers mobilized by the Reverend Martin Luther King, Jr., wore signs saying, "I am a man" (p. 1). According to Wallace, African American men in the decade of the black power movement (1966-1977) came to believe that "manhood was essential to revolution" and that authority over women was a primary agenda for liberation (p. 17). Thus African American feminist discussions of masculinity were also discussion of the relationships between men and women within African American communities and of the relationships between these communities and the dominant white culture.

One prominent African American feminist theorist who has returned to these issues repeatedly over the decades is bell hooks. Writing in collaboration with minister and public intellectual Cornel West (1991), she bases her discussion and models her goal of an African American "beloved community" on "a vision of transformative redemptive love between Black women and men" (see the dedication). Portraying the ideal bonding between African American men and women not through sexual metaphors but as political friendship, hooks (1984) sees men as "comrades in struggle" (p. 67). She argues that the poor or working class man has been hurt—and sometimes hurts others—by being unable to live up to dominant definitions of masculinity because he does not have the privilege or power society has taught him "real men" should possess. Alienated, frustrated, pissed off, he may attack, abuse, and oppress an individual woman or women, but he is not reaping positive benefits from his support and perpetuation of sexist ideology [and so is] not exercising privilege. (hooks, 1984, p. 73)

Looking back to her childhood, hooks (1992) describes a harmonious African American community where "there was no monolithic standard of black masculinity" and many men, despite their difficulties in attaining breadwinner economic status, were "caring and giving" (p. 88). In recent years, however, she believes that media distortions confuse men and women, white people and people of color, with their "stereotypical, fantastical representations of black masculinity," and some African American male celebrities augment these distortions with swaggering, self-centered "dick thing" masculinity (p. 105). Although she thinks African American men "receive respect and admiration" from white as well as other African American men for flaunting their ostensible sexual prowess and domination of women, she sees these new ideals as spurious and harmful (p. 93). African American manhood should once again connote providing and protecting, she believes, rather than its current emphasis on men's "capacity to coerce, control, dominate" that has ruined relationships between sexes in the black community (p. 66). In contrast, hooks models a kind of feminism built on cooperation between men and women. "Revolutionary feminism is not anti-male," she claims, but rather seeks the full development of all individuals (p. 63). She thinks feminism can help both men and women attain the "capacity to be wholistic. . . . Rather than defining manhood in relation to sexuality, we would acknowledge it in relation to biology: boys become men, girls women, with the understanding that both categories are synonymous with selfhood" (p. 69). African American male theorists are responding to such feminist calls. Philip Brian Harper's (1996) book *Are We Not Men? Masculine Anxiety and the Problem of African-American Identity,* for example, addresses the varieties of African American male experience and the relationships between African American men and women. This is a

tense area in contemporary discourse but an essential one if there is to be research rather than mere rhetoric in the future.

Thus the theories of feminists of color expand the categories of gender analysis beyond a masculine-feminine binary, often looking to larger structures of oppression and social representations to explain tensions between African American men and women and inviting African American men to join in both theorizing and community building. However, the disparity of explanatory schemes among these various feminist theories may help indicate some of the gaps in each. If some white men who have not experienced racist oppression are sexist or violent toward women, this explanation is unlikely to be the whole story for African American men either. Conversely, if external economic and social pressures rather than innate aggression or gendered psychological identifications influence the expressions of masculinity in African American men, such causation is likely to be operative for other men as well. Currently, many studies are segregated less by gender than by academic discipline, whereas more interdisciplinary analyses of the effects of racism and sexism on the lives of all people are warranted.

Other U.S. theorists of color and global feminists currently join African American feminists in analyzing ways in which masculinity is constructed in specific historical and cultural contexts. For example, Anna Maria Alonso (1992) describes a Mexican construction of masculinity in which the independent peasant is fully masculine, in opposition to the wage worker, who is "both like a child and like a woman because he relies on others for his sustenance" (p. 414). Chandra Talpade Mohanty, Ann Russo, and Lourdes Torres (1991) show British imperial rule in India operating through "the ideological construction and consolidation of white masculinity as normative and the corresponding racialization and sexualization of colonized peoples" (p. 15). Chilla Bulbeck (1998), who describes global feminisms often overlooked by Anglo feminists, reports on changing categories of same-sex behavior and "third genders" around the world (p. 154). Evelyn Nakano Glenn (1999) traces the problematic effects of equating masculinity with independence in "the racialized gender construction of American citizenship" (p. 22), and Valentine Moghadam (1999) investigates the interconnections among huge military expenditures, deindustrialization, civil conflict, the rise of fundamentalist movements, and the consequent "reinstitutionalization of patriarchal gender relations" in the developing world (p. 132). Typical of this postmillennial perspective is Cherríe L. Moraga's (2002) inclusive definition of the concerns of women of color in terms affecting both men and women throughout the restructuring globe: She includes "immigrant rights, indigenous peoples' water and land rights, the prison industrial system, militarism, [and] reproductive rights."

Because these global and multicultural feminists all seek to make an impact on mixed-gender communities defined in opposition to the dominant white Western culture, they tend to adopt the position of collaborators in struggle with male colleagues from their constituencies, adding their methodological tools of intersectional analysis to antiracist and antiglobal organizing strategies. Their visions of equality look to a more inclusive and fairer future for both sexes throughout the world. As hooks (2000) wrote,

The only genuine hope of feminist liberation lies with a vision of social change that takes into consideration the ways interlocking systems of classism, racism, and sexism work to keep women exploited and oppressed [in relation to] a global white supremacist patriarchy [that] enslaves and/or subordinates masses of Third World women. (p. 109)

The gendered work of global systems and of various human ecologies will be important to future research agendas, as will such areas as the differential gendering and sexualization of new technologies.

As we have seen, many strands of feminist theory seek to make masculinity visible as a gender, rather than allowing it to retain the prestige of being equated with human rationality or the invisibility of being equated with economic or scientific law. Some of the feminist theories discussed here divide masculinity sharply from either a devalued traditional femininity of passivity and sexual objectification or from a revalued femininity of nurturance and empathy. Intersectional and multicultural feminist theories retain gender as a crucial element in the complex, changing, and interrelated social hierarchies they describe throughout the globe.

In contrast, some poststructuralist feminist theories, especially those claiming the rubric "queer," interrogate the very concept of gender as tied to specific kinds of human bodies. That is, they question the foundational categories of *men* and *women* altogether and may wish to eliminate or proliferate gender beyond the current male-female dichotomy.

Poststructuralist feminists tend to see gender as fluid, negotiable, and created through repeated performances rather than as fixed or innate. They believe their view is more liberating than the ideas of either traditionalists or other feminists. Although they do not claim that androgyny or gender convergence has already been achieved, their theories forecast a multiplicity of gendered possibilities for people rather than only two opposed conditions. In her highly influential book *Gender Trouble* (Butler, 1990), philosopher Judith Butler calls gender "a kind of persistent impersonation that passes as the real" (p. x). Her goal is not to make it more genuine but to convince others of its artificiality. "As a strategy to denaturalize and resignify bodily categories" in a less polarized manner, she proposes "a set of parodic practices based in a performative theory of gender acts that disrupt the categories of the body, sex, gender, and sexuality and occasion their subversive resignification and proliferation beyond the binary frame" of masculinity and femininity (p. xii). She often repeats her belief that to "denaturalize" is to rename in a way that is liberating and progressive. Part of moving "beyond the binary frame," in Butler's work, is her deemphasis on masculinity and femininity in favor of "gender," understood as potentially multiple and variable. Neither "masculinity" nor "femininity" appears in the index to *Gender Trouble,* although "bisexuality," "feminism," "phallogocentrism," and "sex/gender distinction" are all represented. Butler's work thus continues the feminist strategy of seeking liberation from traditional constraints by disputing the naturalness of gender altogether, but its distinctive contribution lies in the argument that institutionalized heterosexuality creates gender (Butler, 1997, p. 135). If it were not socially useful for there to be two sexes to marry one another and divide work and kinship, she claims, people would not need to be divided into the categories of men and women at all.

Butler's performative theory of gender has been enormously productive for the development of queer theory as a field and for the advancement of an antihomophobic political agenda in alliance with the movement for gay, lesbian, bigender, and transsexual rights (d'Emilio & Freedman, 1997). Many male queer theorists have analyzed abject and alternative masculinities among men in relation to hegemonic masculinities (Bersani, 1988; Thomas, 1996). Some female queer theorists, too, have focused specifically on alternative masculinities, especially as they are represented in the media. For example, film theorist Kaja Silverman (1992) argues for the progressive potential of nonphallic masculinities that avoid dominant masculinity's disavowal of powerlessness and instead "embrace castration, alterity, and specularity" (p. 3). Even more radically, other queer theorists embrace masculinity when its signs are manifest in female rather than male bodies. For example, sociologist Gayle Rubin (1992) argues that the lesbian categories of butch and femme compose an alternative gender system, not a simple imitation of the two conventional genders of male masculinity and female femininity. Although she admits that butch and femme are created within the environment of heterosexist society, she claims they refigure traditional gender in ways that may be either reactionary or liberating for the individuals involved and for society as a whole. She says that "like lesbianism itself, butch and femme are structured within dominant gender systems" and may either resist or uphold those systems but never completely escape them (p. 479). Thus butch is specifically lesbian masculinity, configured differently but always in relation to heterosexual men's masculinity, which is itself a complicated, changing, and sometimes self-contradictory social constellation. For some women, she says, feeling they had traits often ascribed to men, such as athleticism or aggression, seems to have impelled their butch identities; for others, sexual desire for other women implied to them their own masculinity. For yet other women, the primary impulse toward a butch identity seems to have been the feeling that they were inwardly or essentially a man. Ways of achieving congruence with that feeling include adopting men's masculine signifiers, such as a necktie or moustache, or, these days, a surgically transformed body.

Queer theorist Judith Halberstam (1998) catalogues varieties of masculinity in female bodies, what she calls "masculinity without men," including the androgyne, the tribade, the female husband, the stone butch, and the drag king. She concludes that "we are all transsexuals" and that "there are no transsexuals": Contemporary possibilities for surgical transformation of the body "threaten the binarism of homo/heterosexuality by performing and fictionalizing gender" (Halberstam, 1994, pp. 225-226). That is, with the categories of men and women unstable, people cannot be categorized by habitual sexual desire directed toward one or the other of two categories. Halberstam (1998) seeks an end to "compulsory gender binarism" and its replacement by more flexible, depathologized forms of "gender preference" (p. 27). Nor are masculine women the only ones with a vested interest in masculinities, as Eve Kosofsky Sedgwick (1995) notes. "As a woman, I am a consumer of masculinities, but I am not more so than men are; and, like men, I as a woman am also a producer of masculinities and a performer of them" (p. 13). Furthermore, Sedgwick claims that masculinity and femininity are not opposite ends of the same continuum but rather "orthogonal to each other"; that is, independent variables in "perpendicular dimensions" so that a person could be high or low in both scales at once (p. 15). This arena looks particularly fruitful for psychological studies in masculinity and queer theory as well as in feminist scholarship.

Although some contemporary feminists want to claim masculinity for women or multiply genders, other feminists strive to minimize gender polarization or to eliminate gender altogether. Psychologist Sandra Lipsitz Bem (1993) explains that she found the concepts of androgyny and of sexual orientation too limiting to fit her own needs and so came to think that "gender polarization, androcentrism, and biological essentialism" all reinforced male power and so distorted the possibilities for gender equality (p. viii). Sociologist Judith Lorber (1994) stresses the multiplicity of "gendered sexual statuses" that might be categorized by genitalia, object choice, appearance, gender display, kinds of relationship, relevant group affiliation, sexual practices, and self-identifications (pp. 58-59). Her fundamental goal is the abolition of gender by structuring equality so thoroughly into society that many forms of sexuality are recognized as equally valid and gender no longer organizes social life at all. This view takes the abolition of gender as the only way of eliminating gender inequality and as a positive goal in itself: "When the information about genitalia is as irrelevant as the color of the child's eyes . . . then and only then will women and men be socially interchangeable and really equal" (p. 302). Until then, of course, research that documents actual change in attitudes, behaviors, and institutions will be of special value.

Poststructuralist feminist and queer theories encourage the flexibility and variability of both identity and desire and the decoupling of gender identity and sexual preference. Although female theorists seem especially interested in female-embodied masculinities and sometimes warn their male colleagues about exclusive attention to male practices, queer theories generally are accommodating to male practitioners and disruptive of the heteronormativity that many feminists feel upholds male dominance. On the other hand, queer theorists pay little attention to some of the central concerns of other kinds of feminist theorizing: to parenting, for example, or citizenship, or the gendered politics of work, although both male and female queer theorists are now more frequently incorporating antiracist, global, and other multifactored perspectives into their analyses.

The movement for women's equality has been one of the most successful social movements of the past century, despite the varying oppressions still suffered by women around the globe. Feminist theories have been shaped by women's changing place in contemporary societies, and these theories have sometimes proved effective in changing both men's and women's consciousness and conditions. The widespread establishment of women's studies programs in colleges and universities, especially in the United States, has created a pool of practitioners of feminist theory and inspired the establishment of men's and masculinity studies as well (Boxer, 1998). Although masculinist men's movements sometimes decry feminism, generally men's studies treat feminism and feminist theory as scholarly big sisters, perhaps dull, dowdy, outmoded, or too restrictive, but nevertheless models to be followed and

bettered. Feminists ridicule masculinist men's studies and welcome profeminist efforts by men. American feminist journalist Gloria Steinem (1992) announces that "women want a men's movement" if that means men will "become more nurturing toward children, more able to talk about emotions," and less violent and controlling (p. v). English psychologist Lynne Segal (1990) regrets the "slow motion" of men toward gender equality and muses that the literature of masculinity "uncannily mirrors" its feminist forebears: it "focuses upon men's own experiences, generates evidence of men's gender-specific suffering and has given birth to a new field of enquiry, 'Men's Studies'" (2000, p. 160). At present, feminist theorists are citing masculinity scholars more frequently than previously, and vice versa. Feminist thinkers are benefiting from the theoretical insights and empirical findings of masculinity studies that concern the complex asymmetries, changing histories, local conditions, and institutional variances of gender in a wide variety of specific settings.

Current textbooks in women's and masculinity studies agree in their basic feminist premises, all describing hierarchies of dominance, relationally defined gender, and multiple and interactive axes of social oppression (Gardiner, 2003). In a rapidly changing world marked by contradictory forces of war, violence, disrupted ecologies and economies, fundamentalist backlash, enhanced opportunities for women, the feminization of poverty, the casualization of labor, the decline of traditional male wages, the objectification of male bodies, the recognition of more diverse sexualities, the reconfiguration of nationalities and ethnicities, the rise of liberating social movements, and what Donna Haraway (1989) calls the "the paradoxical intensification and erosion of gender itself" (p. 191), feminist theories continue to develop in conversation with men's and masculinity studies and other movements for social justice. They continue to seek an equality for men and women and for people around the globe at the highest level of human imagination and aspiration rather than the lowest common denominator. As Gloria Anzaldúa (2002) comments, "in this millennium we are called to renew and birth a more inclusive feminism, one committed to basic human rights, equality, respect for all people and creatures, and for the earth" (p. xxxix).

REFERENCES

Adams, A. (1994). Letter . . . 1776. In P. Lauter (Ed.), *The Heath anthology of American literature* (Vol. 1, 2nd ed., p. 876). Lexington, MA: D. C. Heath.

Alonso, A. M. (1992). Gender, power, and historical memory: Discourses of *Serrano* resistance. In J. Butler & J. W. Scott (Eds.), *Feminists theorize the political* (pp. 404-425). New York: Routledge.

Anzaldúa, G. (2002). Foreword, 2001. In C. Moraga & G. E. Anzaldúa (Eds.), *This bridge called my back: Writings by radical women of color* (pp. xxiv-xxxix). Berkeley, CA: Third Woman Press.

Beauvoir, S. de. (1968). *The second sex* (Ed. and Trans. H. M. Parshley). New York: Bantam Books. (Original work published 1949)

Belenky, M. F., Clinchy, B. M., Goldberger, N. R., & Tarule, J. M. (1986). *Women's ways of knowing: The development of self, voice, and mind*. New York: Basic Books.

Bem, S. L. (1993). *The lenses of gender: Transforming the debate on sexual inequality*. New Haven, CT: Yale University Press.

Bersani, L. (1988). Is the rectum a grave? In D. Crimp (Ed.), *AIDS: Cultural analysis/cultural activism* (pp. 197-222). Cambridge, MA: MIT Press.

Bly, R. (1990). *Iron John: A book about men*. Reading, MA: Addison-Wesley.

Bordo, S. (1999). *The male body: A new look at men in public and private*. New York: Farrar, Straus and Giroux.

Boxer, M. J. (1998). *When women ask the questions: Creating women's studies in America*. Baltimore: Johns Hopkins University Press.

Braidotti, R. (2002). Cyberfeminism with a difference. In C. L. Mui & J. S. Murphy (Eds.), *Gender struggles: Practical approaches to contemporary feminism* (pp. 347-357). Lanham, MD: Rowman & Littlefield.

Bulbeck, C. (1998). *Re-orienting Western feminisms: Women's diversity in a postcolonial world*. Cambridge, England: Cambridge University Press.

Butler, J. (1990). *Gender trouble: Feminism and the subversion of identity*. New York: Routledge.

Butler, J. (1997). *The psychic life of power: Theories in subjection*. Stanford, CA: Stanford University Press.

Cavendish, M. L. (1985). From *The Convent of Pleasure*. In M. Ferguson (Ed.), *First feminists: British women writers 1578-1799* (pp. 86-101). Bloomington: Indiana University Press.

Chodorow, N. J. (1978). *The reproduction of mothering: Psychoanalysis and the sociology of gender*. Berkeley: University of California Press.

Chodorow, N. J. (1994). *Femininities, masculinities, sexualities: Freud and beyond*. Lexington: University Press of Kentucky.

Chodorow, N. J. (1999). *The power of feelings*. New Haven, CT: Yale University Press.

Chodorow, N. J. (2002). The enemy outside: Thoughts on the psychodynamics of extreme violence with special attention to men and masculinity. In J. K. Gardiner (Ed.), *Masculinity studies and feminist theory: New directions* (pp. 235-260). New York: Columbia University Press.

Collins, P. H. (1999). Moving beyond gender: Intersectionality and scientific knowledge. In M. M. Ferree, J. Lorber, & B. B. Hess (Eds.), *Revisioning gender* (pp. 261-284). Thousand Oaks, CA: Sage.

Cornell, D. (1998). *At the heart of freedom: Feminism, sex, and equality*. Princeton, NJ: Princeton University Press.

Daly, M., with Caputi, J. (1987). *Websters' first new intergalactic wickedary of the English language*. Boston: Beacon Press.

d'Emilio, J., & Freedman, E. (1997). *Intimate matters: A history of sexuality in America*. Chicago: University of Chicago Press.

Dinnerstein, D. (1976). *The Mermaid and the minotaur: Sexual arrangements and human malaise*. New York: Harper and Row.

Ehrenreich, B. (1983). *The hearts of men: American dreams and the flight from commitment*. New York: Anchor.

Fausto-Sterling, A. (1992). *Myths of gender* (2nd ed.). New York: Basic Books.

Freedman, E. B. (2002). *No turning back: The history of feminism and the future of women*. New York: Ballantine Books.

Friedan, B. (1963). *The feminine mystique*. New York: Dell.

Gardiner, J. K. (1992, Winter). Psychoanalysis and feminism: An American humanist's view. *Signs, 17*, 437-454.

Gardiner, J. K. (2002). Theorizing age and gender: Bly's boys, feminism, and maturity masculinity. In J. K. Gardiner (Ed.), *Masculinity studies and feminist theory: New directions* (pp. 90-118). New York: Columbia University Press.

Gardiner, J. K. (2003, Winter). Gender and masculinity texts: Consensus and concerns for feminist classrooms. *NWSA Journal, 3*(14), 147-157.

Gilligan, C. (1982). *In a different voice: Psychological theory and women's development*. Cambridge, MA: Harvard University Press.

Glenn, E. N. (1999). The social construction and institutionaliztion of gender and race: An integrative framework. In M. M. Ferree, J. Lorber, & B. B. Hess (Eds.), *Revisioning gender* (pp. 3-43). Thousand Oaks, CA: Sage.

González, R. (Ed.). (1996). *Muy macho: Latino men confront their manhood.* New York: Anchor Doubleday.

Halberstam, J. (1994). F2M: The making of female masculinity. In L. Doan (Ed.), *The lesbian postmodern* (pp. 210-228). New York: Columbia University Press.

Halberstam, J. (1998). *Female masculinity.* Durham, NC: Duke University Press.

Hall, K. Q. (Ed.). (2002, Fall). Feminist disability studies [Special issue]. *NWSA Journal, 14*(3).

Haraway, D. (1989). A manifesto for cyborgs: Science, technology, and socialist feminism in the 1980s. In E. Weed (Ed.), *Coming to terms: Feminism, theory, politics* (pp. 173-204). New York: Routledge.

Harper, P. B. (1996). *Are we not men? Masculine anxiety and the problem of African-American identity.* New York: Oxford University Press.

hooks, b. (1984). *Feminist theory: From margin to center.* Boston: South End Press.

hooks, b. (1992). *Black looks: Race and representation.* Boston: South End Press.

hooks, b. (2000). *Where we stand: Class matters.* New York: Routledge.

hooks, b., & West, C. (1991). *Breaking bread: Insurgent black intellectual life.* Boston: South End Press.

Hull, G. T., Scott, P. B., & Smith, B. (1982). *All the women are white, all the blacks are men, but some of us are brave: Black women's studies.* Old Westbury, CT: Feminist Press.

Hurtado, A. (1999). *The color of privilege: Three blasphemies on race and feminism.* Ann Arbor: University of Michigan Press.

Irigiray, L. (1985). *Speculum of the other woman* (G. C. Gill, Trans.). Ithaca, NY: Cornell University Press.

Kimmel, M. S., & Kaufman, M. (1995). Weekend warriors: The new men's movement. In M. S. Kimmel (Ed.), *The politics of manhood: Profeminist men respond to the mythopoetic men's movement (and the mythopoetic leaders answer)* (pp. 16-43). Philadelphia: Temple University Press.

Kimmel, M. S., & Messner, M. A. (Eds.). (2000). *Men's lives* (5th ed.). Boston: Allyn and Bacon.

LeGuin, U. (1974). *The dispossessed.* New York: Harper Collins.

Lorber, J. (1994). *Paradoxes of gender.* New Haven, CT: Yale.

Maccoby, E. E. (1998). *The two sexes: Growing up apart, coming together.* Cambridge, MA: Belknap Press.

MacKinnon, C. (1987). *Feminism unmodified.* Cambridge, MA: Harvard University Press.

MacKinnon, C. (1993). *Only words.* Cambridge, MA: Harvard University Press.

Mill, J. S., & Mill, H. T. (1970). *Essays on sex equality* (A. S. Rossi, Ed.). Chicago: University of Chicago Press.

Moghadam, V. M. (1999). Gender and the global economy. In M. M. Ferree, J. Lorber, & B. B. Hess (Eds.), *Revisioning gender* (pp. 128-160). Thousand Oaks, CA: Sage.

Mohanty, C. T., Russo, A., & Torres, L. (Eds.). (1991). *Third World women and the politics of feminism.* Bloomington: Indiana University Press.

Moraga, C. L. (2002). From inside the First World: Foreword, 2001. In C. Moraga & G. E. Anzaldúa (Eds.), *This bridge called my back: Writings by radical women of color* (pp. xv-xxiii). Berkeley, CA: Third Woman Press.

Pizan, C. de. (1982). *The book of the city of ladies* (E. J. Richards, Trans.). New York: Quality Paperback Book Club. (Original work published 1405)

Ross, M. (2002). Race, rape, castration: Feminist theories of sexual violence and masculine strategies of black protest. In J. K. Gardiner (Ed.), *Masculinity studies and feminist theory: New directions* (pp. 305-343). New York: Columbia University Press.

Rubin, G. (1992). Of catamites and kings: Reflections on butch, gender, and boundaries. In J. Nestle (Ed.), *The persistent desire: A femme-butch reader* (pp. 466-482). Boston: Alyson.

Seager, J. (1999). Patriarchal vandalism: Militaries and the environment. In J. Silliman & Y. King (Eds.), *Dangerous intersections: Feminist perspectives on population, environment, and development* (pp. 163-188). Cambridge, MA: South End Press.

Sedgwick, E. K. (1995). Gosh, Boy George, you must be awfully secure in your masculinity! In M. Berger, B. Wallis, & S. Watson (Eds.), *Constructing masculinity* (pp. 11-20). New York: Routledge.

Segal, L. (1990). *Slow motion: Changing masculinities, changing men.* New Brunswick, NJ: Rutgers University Press.

Segal, L. (2000). *Why feminism?* New York: Columbia University Press.

Silverman, K. (1992). *Male subjectivity at the margins.* New York: Routledge.

Smuts, B. (1992). Male aggression against women: An evolutionary perspective. *Human Nature, 3,* 1-44.

Stanton, E. C. (1994). Declaration of sentiments. In P. Lauter (Ed.), *The Heath anthology of American literature* (Vol. 1, 2nd ed., pp. 1946-1948). Lexington, MA: D. C. Heath.

Steinem, G. (1992). Foreword. In K. L. Hagan (Ed.), *Women respond to the men's movement: A feminist collection* (pp. v-ix). New York: Pandora.

Stoltenberg, J. (1989). *Refusing to be a man: Essays on sex and justice.* Portland, OR: Breitenbush Books.

Thomas, C. (1996). *Male matters: Masculinity, anxiety, and the male body on the line.* Urbana and Chicago: University of Illinois Press.

Wallace, M. (1990). *Black macho and the myth of the superwoman* (Rev. ed.). London: Verso.

Williams, P. J. (1991). *The alchemy of race and rights.* Cambridge, MA: Harvard University Press.

Wollstonecraft, M. (1985). From *A vindication of the rights of woman.* In M. Ferguson (Ed.), *First feminists: British women writers 1578-1799* (pp. 422-431). Bloomington: Indiana University Press.

4

QUEERING THE PITCH?

Gay Masculinities

TIM EDWARDS

On the face of it, gay masculinities are a contradiction in terms: Gay negates masculine. The litany of terminology associated with homosexuality over the past century, let alone its representations (ranging from Quentin Crisp's *Naked Civil Servant* to *The Adventures of Priscilla, Queen of the Desert,* as well as a camp tradition of television stars from John Humphries in *Are You Being Served?* to Graham Norton's self-titled chat show), provide ample demonstration of the never-ending association of the homosexual with the effeminate: limp-wristed, shirt-lifting poofs, pansies, and queens.[1] Nonetheless, the defining feature of the gay man is that he loves or simply eroticizes men as opposed to women and therefore, in some sense, the masculine as opposed to the feminine. This factor was strongly reinforced in the 1970s when, in the wake of gay liberation, many gay men rejected the effeminate in favor of the hypermasculine, sexually driven machismo of "clone culture" (defined later). All of this leaves us with something of a conundrum, for if gay men are not real men at all, or if they are gender deviants whose relationship to masculinity is essentially one of *lack*, then how does this square with their attempts to reclaim the masculine, if only through desire?

It would seem that at the crux of this contradiction, and without necessarily invoking any specific psychoanalytic connotation, is the wider playing out of the relationship of desire and identification.[2] Within the heterosexual frame, this is, at least stereotypically, quite simple: The male, in identifying as masculine, learns to desire what he is not, on some level at least; namely, the female and the feminine. Yet, within the frame of the homosexual, this relationship is far more complex: The male, in possibly still identifying as masculine, but strongly undermined by stereotypes and attitudes to the contrary, desires what he perhaps still is or wants to be, which is also masculine. Or, to put it more simply, in relation to homosexuality, desire and identification become, if not the same, then certainly less distinct.

This sense of contradiction surrounding male homosexuality and masculinity would also seem to work on several strongly interrelated levels: first, and most personally, in relation to homosexual men themselves, who are caught up in still being men but also desiring them— which renders them somehow not men at all;

51

second, more socially, in relation to questions of representation and attitudes that often see gay men as either promiscuous perverts of some monstrous masculine sexuality or as effeminate queens whose only relationship to the masculine is a negative; and third, discursively and historically, possessing a sexuality that is somehow never simply just a matter of preference but a matter of gender and of definitions of normalcy and deviance.

Consequently, it is my primary intention in this chapter to expose, explore, and perhaps resolve some of these contradictions concerning homosexuality and masculinity that, when connected, constitute the complex phenomenon that is contemporary gay masculinity. As frequently noted, this invokes a focus on the politics as well as the theory of gender and sexuality, as the one has constantly informed the other and vice versa (Weeks, 1985). There are three key sections: first, a consideration of the history of homosexuality; second, a discussion of various academic and political perspectives taken from the successes and failures of gay liberation; and third, an evaluation of more recent theoretical attempts to resolve, or at least understand, the contradictions of masculinity and homosexuality.

THE HOMOSEXUAL TRIUMPHANT: HIS STORY OF HOMOSEXUALITY

It is now well-known, within more academic circles at least, that homosexuality is a culturally specific, modern, and Western phenomenon (Caplan, 1987; Greenberg, 1988; Katz, 1976; Plummer, 1981; Weeks, 1977). While same-sex desire is in all likelihood universal throughout time and space, the homosexual as a type of person is only a century or so old and only fully exists in a similar form within parts of the United States, Australasia, and Northern Europe, with variant forms elsewhere within the developed world and very little that is truly comparable anywhere else. What this assertion crucially rests on is the distinction of sexual acts and sexual identities—or, to put it more directly, homosexual sex alone does not a gay man make. This accounts, among other things, for the routine ability of a large number of men who have sex with men, in public toilets or elsewhere, not

to regard themselves as "gay" at all. It is also borne out in studies of sexual behavior that report very large discrepancies between the numbers of men who have had sexual experience with other men and the numbers of men who identify themselves as homosexual or gay, most famously in the Kinsey Report of the 1940s but reinforced in later research (Kinsey, Pomeroy, & Martin, 1948; Spada, 1979; Wellings, Field, Johnson, & Wadsworthy, 1994).

What this assertion also rests on is the logic of social construction. Social constructionist theory, in a variety of ways, seeks to demonstrate that sexuality, far from being biological, constant, or inevitable, is socially variable, contingent, and ambiguous. Fundamental in this was the now legendary work of anthropologist Margaret Mead in Samoa, in which she demonstrated, in some empirical detail, a variety of sexual practices and gendered identities that were often at significant variance from those in the West, as well as the wider sociological concern with the social rather than biological nature of human society (Cooley, 1902; Durkheim, 1951; Mead, 1977). More recently, social constructionist accounts of sexuality have gained significant impetus from the work of Michel Foucault. Foucault, in his pioneering *History of Sexuality* (1978), saw the homosexual as a specific type of person, "invented," as it were, through the work of a series of Northern European scientists of sex, or sexologists, in the late 19th century, including the Swiss doctor Karoly Benkert, who coined the term *homosexual*; Krafft-Ebing; and Magnus Hirschfeld, among others (Foucault, 1978, 1984a, 1984b). The assertion that the homosexual identity is a culturally specific phenomenon that varies in perception, practice, and outcome from time to time and place to place also strongly undermined the notion that the homosexual *identity* at least, if not same-sexual *activity*, is simply the result of some kind of behavioral, biological, or psychological essence. In addition, for Foucault this counteracted any notion of Victorian repression, and even sexual desire itself was constructed discursively through processes of medical, scientific, and psychiatric labeling, as well as other often state-driven attempts to set up and enforce the boundaries of sexual normalcy and sexual pathology. In conjunction with this, the rise of expertise *per se*, as part of what Foucault called "scientia sexualis," or an entire science of sex, further hammered home the conception of the homosexual as a type of person and homosexuality as a condition, a perception validated, reinforced, and perpetuated as sexual "truth."

This perspective has been adopted and elaborated throughout a variety of studies both historical and anthropological, as well as political and sociological. In relation to anthropology, Foucault's legacy has been used to illustrate the indeterminacy of sex, exposing a wide diversity of cultural attitudes and practices in relation to sexuality (see, for example, Caplan, 1987; Greenberg, 1988). More historically, Jeffrey Weeks (1977, 1981, 1985) in particular provided a thoroughgoing analysis of the twin motors of reform and regulation that were then seen to found and form the development of contemporary gay culture. Gay liberation was thus seen to be the culmination of much earlier movements toward reform dating back to the 19th century and the work of Edward Carpenter (1908), among others, as well as the increased visibility brought about by the trial of Oscar Wilde in the United Kingdom.[3] Politically, the same argument has been used to critique medical and psychological attempts to pathologize the homosexual and to develop a primarily utopian vision of a world in which erotic attachment is merely a matter of lifestyle or personal choice of no more concern than liking tea or coffee (Bristow & Wilson, 1993; Harwood et al., 1993; Walter, 1980). Sociologically, social constructionist theory has also come to inform a range of studies of gender and sexuality more widely. In particular, these include interactionist work, in which sexual identity is seen as form of self-constructed narrative, or storytelling; and feminist work, in which the logic of constructionism has clearly fueled the sense of the *un*naturalness of femininity in the wake of second-wave feminism and, more recently, the attempt to deconstruct the very category of woman (Plummer, 1984; Riley, 1988; Wittig, 1997). Ironically, one might also now conjecture that social constructionism has become adopted so routinely within the social sciences as to constitute a near "discourse" in itself.

That said, this particular history of homosexuality is not without critique, perhaps most tiresomely from variant forms of essentialism that never-endingly try to claim that homosexuality

is the result of some abnormality in hormones, the brain, or parental upbringing (see, for example, Le Vay, 1993). The problems of essentialism are now well established and are based on three central points: first, that claims made are of dubious reliability and validity in scientific terms, as they are often based on small samples, animals, or identical twins, from which wider generalizations are necessarily limited; second, that in reiterating the significance of the etiology of homosexuality, these claims have had the consequence, intended or not, of both marginalizing and pathologizing homosexuality through the lack of any comparable attention to heterosexuality; and third, that such claims undermine the capacity for change and absolve responsibility both personally and socially, leading to an "I/they can't help it" model of homosexuality.

The ambiguity of these claims more politically has not gone unnoticed where attempts have not only been made to pathologize homosexuality (through aversion therapy, for example) but to establish the rights of those with a gay biology through an appeal to civil liberties or a similar minority platform. Similarly, constructionist claims often champion homosexuality as an alternative lifestyle choice, yet these beliefs can also lead to fears of contagion, or gay sexuality "rubbing off," which often underpins much resistance to gay and lesbian parenting (Epstein, 1987, 1988; Evans, 1993). It is not my intention here, however, to evaluate these claims in detail or to fuel an already very old and tired debate between essentialists and constructionists.

I do, however, wish to raise several concerns in relation to the constructionist history of homosexuality as it is most commonly perceived, played out, and perpetuated within predominantly sexual-political understandings of sexuality. It is of critical importance here to note that I am *not* attempting to provide a critique of Foucault's work per se; rather, I am questioning some of the ways in which it has been adopted and applied elsewhere. I am thinking particularly of the work of various gay historians and the adoption of their work within some forms of socialist feminism, as well as some of its more contemporary and eclectic variants (Bristow & Wilson, 1993; Harwood et al., 1993; Patton, 1985; Segal, 1990; Weeks, 1985). Although varying significantly, all of these theorists cite Foucault as a major influence in adopting a politically informed perspective that is at pains to point out both that homosexuality is socially constructed and that gay liberation represented a high-water mark in wider movements toward greater social acceptance of sexual diversity. As I have already documented and critiqued these perspectives in detail elsewhere, I do not plan to do so again here (Edwards, 1994, 1998). However, it remains necessary to summarize some of the key problems: First, these perspectives often fail to problematize gay liberation sufficiently either theoretically or politically; second, to varying degrees, they present a view of sexual history that is insufficiently racialized or gendered; and third, they tend to lead to a form of triumphalism, a kind of "we've made it" perspective that offers few solutions to current problems other than to reiterate the joys of diversity and pluralism ad nauseam. The rest of this section will document some of these difficulties more fully, particularly as they pertain to the relationship of homosexuality and masculinity.

First, the history of homosexuality remains profoundly gendered. As I have argued elsewhere, gender and sexuality as practices, discourses, and indeed constructs are intricately linked, and it is often far more accurate to talk in terms of gendered sexualities and sexualized genders than of gender and sexuality as if they were two distinct categories (Edwards, 1990). In addition, the stigmatization of male homosexuality has much to do with gender. Gay men are often castigated as the wrong sort of men: too masculine, too promiscuous, too phallic, or too lacking in masculinity, somehow incompetent at it, or simply effeminate. Similar themes also emerge in relation to female homosexuality— lesbians become "butch diesel dykes" and masculinity in the wrong body or, conversely, some kind of feminine hormonal sexuality gone wild, "lipstick lesbians" who just can't help helping themselves to "a bit of the other." In sum, the gay man is often oppressed for being the wrong sort of man, and the lesbian is subordinated for being the wrong sort of woman.

What also comes into play here, however, is the sense in which the commonly played out history of homosexuality as socially constructed fails to recognize the significance of gender *even within in its own terms.* Some feminists have highlighted this gender absence as indicative of a deliberate attempt to suppress the importance of feminism, depoliticize academia, and indeed exclude women (Stanley, 1984). I would like to suggest that the issue here is perhaps wider and indeed more historical. Women's sexuality, particularly in any form autonomous from men's, has had a very long history of struggling to find voice in the face of often concerted attempts to silence it or even deny its existence. The comparative invisibility, even now, of lesbianism compared with the public spectacle, if not pariahlike, status of gay male sexuality, is testimony to this, as is the frequent desexualization of female homosexuality into mere "romantic friendship" (Faderman, 1981). Recent attempts to reclaim some sense of the sexuality of lesbianism either discursively, through reinventing the connotations of the identity of the dyke, or through representations of women as promiscuous sexual predators, for example in the work of photographer Della Grace, have often succeeded more in openly parodying gay male sexuality and less in finding an alternative voice for the women who wish to express their sexual desires for other women (Grace, 1993). It is, I think, clear, then, that this contemporary constructionist story of sexuality is indeed *his* story of *his* homosexuality, and it is not satisfactory as an explanation of, or even as an engagement with, its female equivalent. Strictly within that caveat, it *may* remain satisfactory as an understanding of the history of male homosexuality alone. However, as we shall see, several difficulties remain.

The gendering of this history of homosexuality does not end with the simple differentiation of its male and female variations. Far more significantly, the history of male homosexuality remains gendered per se. The most cursory glance through past forms of male same-sex sexuality reveals a very significantly varying, yet equally profoundly unending, connection with gender. Greco-Roman culture may show no appropriate parallel with contemporary understandings of gay male sexuality, yet it equally demonstrates its connection with questions of maleness and masculinity. Here, Spartan sexual relations were hardly formations of gay identity, yet they were importantly connected with initiations into socially prescribed patterns of manhood (Eglinton, 1971). Similarly, the molly houses of the Renaissance were in no way simple equivalents to contemporary gay male clubs, bars, or ghettos, yet they did perform the function of providing meeting places for perceived gender, as well as sexual, deviants (Bray, 1982). In addition, the sexology of the 19th century makes repeated reference to the connection of gender to male same-sex desire, whether as a third alternative or as an inversion (Carpenter, 1908). Equally, the clone culture of the 1970s was as much concerned to prove that gay men were men and not simply gay and, in attempting to reformulate the relationship between sexuality and masculinity, the connection remained. None of these historical moments is remotely the same or even easily comparable, but they do in very different ways repeatedly allude to the continued connection, and not separation, of "the love that dare not speak its name" with questions of masculinity.[4] To assert, then, that sexuality is a thing apart from gender for anything other than heuristic purposes is not only theoretically inadequate but empirically inaccurate and politically naïve.

It is perhaps the politics of this social constructionist history of homosexuality that are its weakest link. I have already noted its feminist limitations, and one could equally highlight its wholesale whitewashing of the issue of race, color, or ethnicity, as have Kobena Mercer and Isaac Julien (1988). However, what is perhaps most insidious here is the sense in which it fails to meet the needs or expectations of even privileged white gay men. As we shall see, sexism, racism, and ageism are but some of the "isms" thrown at gay male culture, but it is gay men themselves who often seem to lose out most and suffer most directly. As one disillusioned writer in the gay press recently pointed out

> It was the politics of visibility, but rather than create an image that was drawn from our inner selves, we appropriated a macho stance. For the first time, we congregated in defined gay spaces, but because our struggle was based on sexuality, the meeting points were based around sex. Despite gathering under the "gay" banner, our ghetto was very much homosexual. By looking like "real men" we made gay sex more acceptable but lost an opportunity to create a gay identity beyond the active sex object. (Miles, 2003, p. 34)

This may seem gloomy, but Miles is far from alone in his complaint that gay culture is a shallow, youth-dominated, image-, sex-, and body-obsessed world predicated upon self-loathing and leaving profoundly little room for

any alternative but to conform, pump iron, and deny one's emotional dissatisfactions, a feeling that arguably remains largely unchanged and undiminished since gay liberation. Indeed, given the media's increasing fuelling of gay, and perhaps all, culture as merely a matter of fashion, looks, and entertainment, the pressures are probably worse today. The commonly played out constructionist history of homosexuality has no answer to this. Within this perspective, the homosexual is not only triumphant academically as a socially constructed category but rather victorious socially, politically, and personally as an alternative way of life. In its never-ending emphasis on the power of coming out, in its championing of the hard-won benefits of gay liberation, and in its promotion of the politics of pluralism for sexual minorities, all that remains is to metaphorically, and perhaps literally, throw one's legs in the air and enjoy it. Such an account never even conceives of the question "and then what?," let alone offering any solution. It is to this question of the failings and problems of gay liberation that we now turn.

CLONE COMPLAINTS: THE PROBLEMS OF GAY LIBERATION

Gay liberation is problematic not least because liberation per se is problematic, both theoretically and politically. In theoretical terms, the notion of liberation tends to imply essentialism, and, in relation to sexuality, this is compounded by its conflation with the concept of repression and the assertion of some otherwise contained or constrained sexual desire. The difficulty here is not so much the charge of essentialism, which must remain in some senses merely a descriptive term, but the sense of confusion invoked concerning what exactly is being liberated: a sexual desire, a sexual identity, a sexual community, or all three? This is not to deny in the least that gay men still constitute a marginalized, stigmatized, and, on occasion, even demonized group, yet such an experience is perhaps more accurately understood as a problem of subordination, emancipation, or, indeed, oppression. The term *liberation* therefore remains rather inadequate in theoretical terms.

Nevertheless, it has remained the political incantation of the gay movement since the

Stonewall rebellion of 1969.[5] Given the aforementioned ambiguities of the terminology theoretically, it is worth trying to unpack a little of what is more politically meant by the term "gay liberation." On its most immediate level, gay liberation proclaimed the importance of coming out, which was seen to work on three interconnected levels: first, through accepting one's sexuality for oneself; second, in exploring it with others of similar orientation; and third, by telling the rest of the world with pride (Walter, 1980). Coming out is again ambiguous here, whether purely as a matter of personal choice or more widely as a form of political affirmation, as it retains the potential implication of freeing an essential and hidden, or simply inner and asocial, self. None of this, of course, affected the development of a thriving commercial culture of clubs, bars, cafes, and shops premised on a politics of increased visibility through coming out.

This sense of ambiguity, or even ambivalence, concerning gay liberation was, however, also illustrated more academically. Some of the earliest works on gay politics, particularly those of Hocquenghem (1972) and Mieli (1980), attributed a liberating force to gay desire in celebrating promiscuity, pushing the boundaries of decency, and, more generally, going against the mores of mainstream heterosexual society; others, particularly those of Altman (1971) and Weeks (1977), saw gay politics as a culturally specific phenomenon contingent on histories of movements toward reform and slowly shifting morals and values. It was not, perhaps, surprising, then, that much of this ambivalence should also be played out through a series of academic debates that followed the onset of gay liberation. These more theoretical debates were in themselves often founded on the political involvements of young writers and academics making their careers in colleges and universities. Most of these controversies centered in turn on various, and often violently opposed, perspectives of the development of commercial gay culture and the practices and attitudes of gay men, most notoriously those of the overtly sexualized and hypermasculine cruising clone.

The cruising gay clone has now become something of pariah, both within academic circles and more popular culture, pumped and inflated into near mythic status as *the* iconic symbol of gay liberation. With his sexuality blatantly displayed, literally bulging out of his plaid shirts, leather jackets, and button-fly jeans, and publicly paraded down the streets of many of the world's most major cities in celebration of his unconstrained promiscuous desire for more and more of precisely the same thing, namely those like himself, he became the emblem of the "sex" in homosexuality, or what Michael Bronski once called "sex incarnate" (Bronski, 1984). Proclaimed by some as the epitome of a guilt-free lifestyle of sexual liberation and castigated by others as the nadir of misogynist self-loathing, the cruising gay clone came, perhaps mistakenly, to represent gay sexuality in its entirety and divide politically motivated academia like an axe through an apple. More precisely, and as I have demonstrated elsewhere, what this entire uproar often centered on was the perceived relationship of the homosexual to the masculine (Edwards, 1994, 1998).

Following this, then, I wish to explore and expose this perception through a discussion of the various academic perspectives developed around the gay clone and gay liberation more widely. These include feminist work and men's analyses of masculinity, as well as gay and lesbian studies. A potential problem here is the tendency to perceive these debates as going on solely *between* these areas of study, when they have, in fact, been conducted as much, if not more, from *within* each of them. There is, then, no one feminist, no single gay, and no unitary male perspective on the conundrums posed by gay liberation or even the gay clone; yet, as I shall argue strongly, all of these perspectives are underpinned by a varyingly implicit, yet mostly assumed, perception of the relationship of the homosexual to the masculine.

It is perhaps proper to start with gay men's own perspectives of their liberation and the clone that some of them helped create. One of the earliest and most influential of these was a chapter by Gregg Blachford (1981) in Ken Plummer's (1981) path-breaking collection *The Making of the Modern Homosexual*, titled "Male Dominance and the Gay World." Relying heavily on a primarily Althusserian understanding of the role of subculture, Blachford perceived both reproduction and resistance to male domination in postliberation gay culture. Resistance was perceived to come through the lack of any *direct* connection of such styles and practices to any wider culture that simultaneously also informed its reproduction through its separation from it. To put it more simply, macho gay male culture neither fully resisted nor purely reproduced male domination by virtue of its strict containment *within* a subculture. A somewhat later and less academically informed argument was made by Jamie Gough (1989), who, although acknowledging the sexist implications of some contemporary gay culture, saw macho gay men as merely aping "real" masculinity. Joseph Bristow (1989), in a powerful polemic against lesbian accusations of homosexual misogyny, pushed this argument further, seeing the gay clone as contrived and playful, theatrical and fake, a *clone copy*. The comic effect of this was not lost on gay men themselves, who joked that any illusion of the clone's masculinity was lost as soon as he opened his mouth and started discussing art and interior design, and society at large bore witness to the disco group The Village People, who did a number of decidedly camp dance routines with the individual members dressed as a cowboy, a cop, a construction worker, and other stereotypical symbols of gay fantasy. From this perspective, then, masculinity and homosexuality were exposed as increasingly playful social constructions that had no intrinsic interaction or relationship.

Others, however, were less convinced of the frivolousness. In *Two Steps Forward, One Step Back*, John Shiers (1980) sounded a personal note of painful concern. In particular, this centered on his perception that gay men were still caught in the double bind and, indeed, double standards of heterosexual society so that, in trying to maintain more socialist or feminist convictions, gay men ran the risk of losing sight of their own, primarily sexual, cause. Consequently, when copying more traditional patterns of monogamous sexual practices with long-term partners in private, gay men risked little social opprobrium, but in publicly displaying a promiscuous desire for the masculine, they felt the full wrath of their stigma and heterosexual society's homophobia. Ultimately, then, gay men were in a no-win situation of being forced into a closet not of their own making and made into public pariahs when they broke its bounds. Rumbling under the surface here were increasing concerns relating to the potential pitfalls of the newly sexualized and, indeed, masculinized, dimensions of gay liberation.

At the same time, others still felt that gay male promiscuity could, or even should, be celebrated, a point put most forcibly in John Allen Lee's (1978) *Getting Sex: A New Approach—More Fun, Less Guilt*. Lee argued that gay men were quite simply better at "getting sex," having developed a highly sophisticated system of dress codes and visual cues to indicate sexual preference, as well as adapting a variety of formal and informal public contexts in which to practice sex and enjoy it. Evidence for this was provided in the literary and often autobiographical accounts of John Rechy (1977) and Edmund White (1986), as well as in various surveys of sexual behavior at the time (Jay & Young, 1979; Spada, 1979). Similarly, in *The Silent Community*, Edward Delph (1978) conducted an ethnographic study of men's sexual behavior with other men in public and semipublic places, such as parks, toilets, and saunas, and, in doing so, emphasized both the sophistication of this behavior and its silence.

What these studies also illustrated, however, was the connection of gay men's sexual practices with questions of masculinity, not only in reinforcing the stereotype that men are simply more promiscuous than women but the sense in which the clone donned a stereotypically masculine appearance and practiced a stereotypically masculine sexuality that was divorced from emotional commitment and intimacy, a form of sexual expression so minimal that even conversation could destroy it. This was, of course, precisely its appeal, the emotionally risk-free, pared-down, and butt-naked excitement: pure, exposed and throbbing—the cock stripped bare.

Others, though, found such sexual practices lacking, and complained that development of an increasingly body-conscious commercial scene and networks founded on the promotion of sex before, and often without, love were not for all— that, ultimately, they were another lesson in the continued alienation of homosexuality. Of fundamental importance in this was the articulation, or reworking, of the relationship of homosexuality and masculinity. Gay culture, in asserting that gay men could be real men too, although divorcing homosexuality from its more negative relationship to masculinity, also forced homosexuals together into a form of matrimony that was not necessarily happy. In particular, Michael Pollak (1985) saw the promiscuous cruising of the clone as a form of "internalized maximization of profits," or a performance-driven masculine sexuality wherein gay men notched up partners like cars off a production line. In short, the constraints of the closet were often swapped for the pressures of performance. Of importance in this was Pollak's historically focused analysis of the development of gay male culture alongside emergent forms of masculinity within industrial capitalism that were, in turn, founded on a form of rationalized self-alienation. In a more romantic vein, some also complained that the commercial gay world provided little emotional (although plenty of sexual) sustenance, a point made most strongly in the historically nuanced and erudite work of Barry Adam (1987) and echoed elsewhere (Dowsett, 1987). It reached its most extreme form in the novels and plays of Larry Kramer (1978, 1983, 1986), an AIDS activist in New York who once infamously accused gay men of quite literally "thinking with their cocks" and "fucking themselves to death."

What begins to emerge here is a bipolarized debate whereby the post–gay liberation gay man is *either* the emblem of a celebration of uninhibited sexual expression *or* simply the latest incarnation of sexual oppression. Although both perspectives in extremis remain problematic, it is the liberal, or perhaps liberationist, approach that is most in question. In denying that the development and form of gay culture had *any* connection with wider society other than to challenge it, or indeed with masculinity other than to celebrate it, gay liberationists also ran the risk of disowning all political responsibility, a problem highlighted by the feminist critique of gay sexuality—to which we now turn.

Of most direct significance here were the conflicts that soon developed between gay men and lesbians. In the first instance, gay liberation meant gay men and gay women, yet within a very few years, the two groups had suffered a very acrimonious divorce, and many lesbians found their interests better served within the women's movement. Most fundamentally, this centered on a profoundly differing set of needs and wants, or what Annabel Faraday (1981) once called the "polar experiences" of gay men and lesbians. Although gay men were often primarily concerned with sexual liberation in the face of continued public hostility and actually rising, rather than falling, criminal prosecutions, lesbians were finding that much of their own liberation depended on their gender rather than their sexuality. The women's movement,

in highlighting the role of heterosexuality in women's oppression, often offered very clear and direct support for lesbians with feminist or gender-oriented concerns. More problematically, gay men's economic power was increasingly overt and being channeled into the rapid expansion of a commercial gay scene of shops, bars, clubs, saunas, restaurants, and a whole host of other services from which lesbians felt increasingly excluded, a factor that rapidly turned into fierce accusations of sexism and misogyny. Liz Stanley (1982), for example, experienced considerable disillusionment in working with gay men politically, and Sheila Jeffreys (1990) argued similarly that gay liberation was merely another aspect of *men's* sexual liberation and *men's* sexual needs masqueraded as the permissive society. Conversely, some gay men increasingly complained that lesbians were often aggressive and moralizing in their lack of support for gay men's concerns, and lesbians could themselves perhaps be accused of being complicit in heterosexual homophobia. Joseph Bristow (1989) and Craig Owens (1987) argued strongly here that misogyny and homophobia were not opposed but two sides of the same coin of patriarchal and heterosexual dominance. This conflict rapidly became both overly polarized and problematic in itself, often diverting wider political energies into infighting. On a more positive note, lesbians and gay men later proved they were still able to work together successfully, for example, in opposition to Section 28, a government statute that attempts to outlaw the "promotion" of homosexuality and "pretend" families by local authorities in the United Kingdom.

Nevertheless, such conflict exposed a deeper divide within feminism in relation to questions of gender and sexuality, and feminist accounts of gay liberation were often confused and conflicting. Perhaps most influentially, Gayle Rubin (1984), in her article "Thinking Sex," argued strongly for an analysis of sexuality as a separate mechanism, or what she called a "vector of oppression," not simply dependent on, and indeed distinct from, the analysis of gender. Consequently, she documented "hierarchies of sexuality," through which heterosexuality, whether male or female, and particularly if marital, was still privileged over homosexuality, which was, in turn, less stigmatized if monogamous; promiscuity, prostitution, sadomasochism, and pedophilia were deemed the lowest or worst of all. This, in many ways, revolutionized, or at least counteracted, an increasingly vociferous North American view of sexuality as solely an extension of gender domination, theorized most fully in the work of Andrea Dworkin (1981) and Catharine MacKinnon (1987). The most fundamental thrust of this perspective was to perceive sexuality primarily as a form of power, most notoriously in relation to rape and pornography.

Without wishing to stir up an already overly whipped debate, the conflict that developed within feminism concerning sexuality also exposed a profoundly different, if not competing, set of feminist perspectives upon gay liberation. For Rubin, and indeed a variety of other feminist writers, including Pat Califia, Mary McIntosh, Lynne Segal (Califia, 1994; Segal & McIntosh, 1992), and Carole Vance (1984), gay men constituted a marginalized group with their own agenda; also, gay liberation, although far from unproblematic *for* women, was not necessarily *about* women (this remained primarily the responsibility of feminism). For Dworkin (1981) and MacKinnon (1987), as well as Sheila Jeffreys (1990) and others (Stanley, 1982), however, this separation was false. Gay liberation was indeed about gender oppression, and gay men were deeply bound up with the degradation of women and the feminine. The macho gay clone, in celebrating the male and masculine sexuality, was then engaged precisely in the annihilation of the female and feminine sexuality more widely.

What opened up rapidly here was the sense in which it was the relationship of gender and sexuality, here homosexuality and masculinity, that was at issue. The more liberal feminist approach, in successfully exposing the complexities of sexuality, also ran the risk of separating it entirely from gender, although more radical or revolutionary feminists, in asserting its very connectedness to gender, could lose sight of its specific significance. One potential solution to an often escalating and entrenched sense of conflict here emerged in the form of a more poststructural feminism, concerned precisely to undermine the binaries of gender and sexuality, which I consider in the next section.

Given the ongoing concern here with the connection, and not separation, of homosexuality and masculinity, the development of men's own critical studies of masculinity remains significant, if rather overshadowed. We are presented with something of a problem here: namely, the heterosexist bias of men's studies, a point put most forcibly by Carrigan, Connell, and Lee (1985) in "Toward a New Sociology of Masculinity." They argued that the emergent men's studies, particularly in the late 1970s, neither recognized the significance of gay liberation in attempting to undermine traditional masculinity nor the importance of heterosexuality in maintaining male domination, but paid mere lip service to gay men in token chapters and short passages in otherwise overwhelmingly white, middle class, heterosexual works and perspectives. This was more than partially explained as a result of the development of a new men's studies of masculinity *as a response to* second-wave feminism both personally and politically and partly as a necessary outcome to the limits of the functionalist sex-role theory that informed these studies and that could often only adapt to seeing masculinity as a singular, rather than pluralist, concept and practice (Kimmel, 1987).

One major exception to this, and a significant development in overcoming it, was the work of Carrigan and associates (1985) in formulating the notion of a hierarchy of masculinities. Connell (1987), in *Gender and Power,* extended this idea further and challenged the idea of a singular male sex role, arguing for a pluralistic and hierarchical notion of masculinities in which some forms were hegemonic and others subordinate. Thus, most obviously, black, gay, and working class masculinities were seen as subordinate to and, indeed, oppressed by white, heterosexual, and middle class masculinities that remained mostly dominant or hegemonic, although this was still contingent on changing social and political contexts. Consequently, men's studies of masculinity became increasingly complex and diverse in themselves, developing more sociostructural, philosophical, and even autobiographical dimensions in the work of Jeff Hearn (1987), Vic Seidler (1994), and David Morgan (1992), respectively.

Where did this leave the new critical studies of men and masculinity in relation to gay liberation? The answer is, in some senses, frustratingly, not very far forward. Following the arguments of radical feminism, John Stoltenberg (1989) made a blistering assault on the failures of gay liberation and made gay men out to be near traitors to the cause of gender politics; at the opposite extreme, Robert Bly (1990) and the New Men's Movement promoted a return to a traditional patriarchal order that was implicitly, if not explicitly, homophobic. Although less problematic politically, the vast majority of more contemporary men's studies of masculinity still remain overwhelmingly generalist in focus, often making merely fleeting mention of the specifics of gay masculinities.

One more thoroughgoing and empirically based work here is Connell's (1995) *Masculinities*. Following interviews with a small sample of gay men, Connell remained ambivalent concerning the impact of gay liberation on wider gender or masculinity politics. Although acknowledging the fundamental subversion of heterosexual object choice in the formation of gay identities, Connell reiterates the sense in which men's bodies also incorporate masculinity. In desiring them, gay men thus remain, in a sense, "very straight." The often criticized watering down of gay politics and its cooptation by consumer culture also adds to the sense in which the position of gay men, for Connell, remains contradictory in terms of gender politics. Here, then, gay men's identification *as* men may be problematic, but their desire *for* men limits their commitment to sexual politics. We are, then, back to where we started: the relationship between desire and identification in relation to homosexuality and masculinity. The question precisely, then, is one of how to go forward.

FROM HOMOSEXUAL TO HOMOSOCIAL: THE POSTSTRUCTURAL SOLUTION

Poststructural theory is often as amorphous as it is diffuse and as ill defined as it is wide ranging. It is not my intention, then, to discuss what now constitutes an entire canon of poststructural and postmodern theory or the cultural studies and queer politics that it often informs. In relation to gender and sexuality more specifically, however, poststructural theory perhaps most fundamentally provides a critique of identity politics and, indeed, identity per se (Nicholson & Seidman, 1995). First, individual and group identities are perceived as equally semantically and socially dynamic, open, plural, conflicting, or contingent rather than fixed, closed, unitary, consensual, or set. Thus, the position of a young

gay black lawyer, for example, is quite simply *un*categoric. Second, identity politics more theoretically are argued to have had the consequence, intended or unintended, of reinforcing rather than challenging the binaries of black-white, man-woman, straight-gay. And third, more politically, identity politics are perceived to tend to undermine any wider political platform on which to challenge conservatism or minority oppression, due to their tendency to reinforce differences and divisions within and across different groups. The previous section demonstrated this itself by illustrating the degree of conflict aroused, and often unresolved, around gay masculinities. Poststructural theory clearly provides an effective critique of this, yet the question remains as to the efficacy of its solutions.

In this next section, I wish initially to focus on the work of Eve Kosofsky Sedgwick and Judith Butler as two of the most eminent and influential poststructural theorists in relation to gender and sexuality. In addition, I will also consider more recent attempts to apply their work more directly to the question of gay masculinities. It is necessary in the first instance to explicate this work in some detail to see more precisely where it leads us prior to examining its wider implications. In doing so, I hope to show how poststructural theory adds to our understanding of the problematic nature of the relationship between desire and identification that underpins the position of gay masculinities. I will also seek to expose some of the difficulties that tend to ensue from this perspective.

In *Between Men*, Sedgwick (1985) started to forge a major reconsideration of the role and nature of homosexuality through an analysis of its representation across a range of North American, British, and other European literature. In particular, she constructed a new concept of homosociality to describe the range of affective relationships between men that exist on a continuum from the unemotional to the fully homosexual. As a result, although perhaps inadvertently, she drew a parallel with Adrienne Rich's (1984) influential notion of the lesbian continuum used to describe relationships between women. The main thrust of Sedgwick's analysis was, however, to interrogate the relationship of the homosexual and the masculine and, in particular, to expose the extent to which the two concepts are interdependent. Her discussion was also historically focused, seeing the homosexual identity as interdependent with emergent forms of masculinity throughout the 19th century. This, then, led to a series of highly sophisticated textual analyses of a selection of literary works from the mid-18th century through to the mid-19th century, from which Sedgwick then extrapolated a complex map of developments in the gendered nature of male relationships. As an analysis within the discipline of literary criticism per se, this was sophisticated and, indeed, often quite dazzling, yet it remained problematic, not least because of the exposition of a series of social and political developments from an analysis of primarily elite cultural texts.

Sedgwick (1990) then extended her analysis of the role of the homosexual in *Epistemology of the Closet*. Following on from Foucault, she sought to deconstruct the category of the homosexual and, more important, the entire divisive system of sexual categorization. The initial aim of her analysis was to undermine the persistence of "the homosexual" as a defining category that simultaneously creates the closet from which the homosexual had to endlessly "come out." The difficulty here is that the closet remains not merely a semantic construction but an institutionally supported social reality premised on wider processes of stigma and ostracism. To put it more simply, the discursive closet would not matter were it not for the negative consequences that may, and often do, ensue in coming out from the more social closet. However, the cut of Sedgwick's work was as much to address the semiotic question of the relationship of reader and text, as exemplified in her final chapter on Proust, as it was to address the question of homosexual oppression.

Sedgwick's work also echoed that of Dennis Altman (1971) in *Homosexual: Oppression and Liberation,* in which he foretold that the end of homosexual oppression would also entail the end of the homosexual identity. What was also implicit in Altman's predicament was, however, the perceived *necessity* of the homosexual identity if the social and, indeed, ontological, assumption of heterosexuality were to be opposed. Ironically, although recent decades have witnessed an ever-strengthening "discourse of homosexuality" centered on increasing visibility and opposition to older negative definitions and stereotypes, discussion of heterosexuality has, for the most part, tended to remain overshadowed, and it is difficult to see how Sedgwick's reverse policy of "*un*speaking" the homosexual can undermine this discursive privileging of the heterosexual, let alone make the quantum jump into heterosexual social and political dominance. The end of the homosexual does not, then, necessarily entail the end of the heterosexual, and the project remains, ironically, to remove heterosexuality from the sanctity of its discursive closet.

In later work, Sedgwick (1995) forged a further disjuncture between sex and gender, here masculinity and homosexuality, as two concepts she perceived as not *necessarily* in any way directly related. In sum, masculinity does not necessarily relate to men, or men only, and Sedgwick returns to an understanding of gender centered on androgyny, as explored previously by Sandra Bem (1974), whereby some men and women have more, or less, masculinity and, indeed, femininity. This would seem not only to implode gender dualisms but to throw up another question entirely, namely the extent to which masculinity has anything to do with men, gay or straight, at all.

A similar problem underpinned Judith Butler's (1990) attempt to implode the dualisms of gendered identity in *Gender Trouble*. Butler sought, in the first instance, to undermine the fundamental necessity of the category of "woman" and asserted instead that a feminist politics must produce a radical critique of the politics of identity per se. On top of this, via a series of psychoanalytic investigations, she sought to demonstrate the mutual dependence and contradictions of the categories of sex and gender as wholly artificial and unnatural constructions that exist primarily at the level of repeated performance. Consequently, she perceived gender as only truly existing through continuous processes of acting, speaking, and doing. In addition, at least by implication, the bottom line of Butler's argument would seem, like Sedgwick's, to be that the feminine has little to do with the female and femininity little to do with women.

There was, however, an added dimension here, for gender is performed according to social sanctions and mores that can, and do, lead to what Butler (1990) calls "punishments," on a number of levels, from social ostracism to legal control. Nevertheless, the thrust of her analysis was that gender primarily exists at the level of discourse. Thus, although its documentation of the power relations of discourse were important, Butler's work ran the risk of missing an analysis of power as an institutionally coercive, politically sanctioned, and socially practiced series of mechanisms of oppression. In addition, it is this tension of the structural and the textual that often still lurks in the controversy surrounding Butler's arguments concerning the role of drag, defined as an overall gender performance and not merely a camp minority practice, in demonstrating the artificiality and fantasy that surrounds gender categories. Nevertheless, the concept of performance remains an important one that opens up potentially radical political solutions to overly entrenched understandings, and indeed practices, of gender, leading to Butler wrestling with some of the political implications in later work (Butler, 1993).

How, though, does such a perspective work in relation to questions of masculinity and homosexuality? In following Freud, Butler (1995) argues that masculine identification depends on a prior formation of sexual orientation and, in particular, a rejection of homosexuality. As a result, masculinity fundamentally and psychologically depends on the disavowal not only of femininity but of homosexuality, and, in doing so, is predicated upon a lack, or absence, rather than a given, or presence. The problem, then, becomes a near algebraic one: Masculinity as a positive identification depends on a double, not single, negative dissociation. The additional, and profoundly psychological, difficulty here is that the loss of homosexuality is never avowed and therefore cannot be mourned. Butler's argument depends on Freud's analysis of polymorphous perversity, whereby the infant experiences—and gains from—both homosexual and heterosexual attachment but to successfully form a gender identity must suffer a loss, a loss, moreover, that cannot be affirmed. The double problem that then ensues for the male infant is that neither the attachment to another male nor its loss can be recognized, leading to the impossibility of *either* affirming *or* mourning homosexuality. This also has wider social implications, reflected in the lack of recognition of gay male relationships and the intensity of difficulties involved in their loss, for whatever reason. Thus, more particularly, the AIDS epidemic is seen to expose the anguish of gay men's grief as a difficulty in mourning per se. In sum, male homosexual attachment is put onto the never-never: never having lost and never having loved.

The mention of AIDS at this juncture is not coincidental, and the conjunction of the rise of the epidemic with the simultaneous development and application of more poststructural theory to questions of sexuality is not insignificant. When AIDS was first recognized in the early 1980s, predominantly in the gay communities of the United States and as a sexually transmitted disease that continued to affect the gay male population disproportionately in Western societies, it was quickly perceived as a symbolic phenomenon as much as, if not more than, a medical condition. To put it more simply, AIDS was rapidly presented and understood as a morally loaded disease of *lifestyle*. At the epicenter of this, once again, were the sexual activities of the promiscuous gay clone and, indeed, 1970s gay culture more generally. The moral outrage, homophobic vitriol, and backlash that took place against the gay community, particularly through the tabloid media, who often presented AIDS as the "gay plague," is now well documented, particularly in the work of Simon Watney (1987) in the United Kingdom and Randy Shilts (1987) in the United States. It was not, perhaps, surprising, then, that gay studies often went on the defensive and further invoked the logic of constructionism and the discursive legacy of Foucault to prove that AIDS had no intrinsic connection with gay sexuality other than one of creating illness and stigmatization (see, for example, Altman, 1986; Crimp, 1988; Patton, 1985).

However, this defensiveness had the effect, intended or not, of overriding an intriguing dimension raised by the epidemic of masculinity's connection with sexuality, particularly in relation to gay male sexuality. To put it directly, AIDS, in threatening the very life, let alone style, of promiscuous gay male sexuality in the 1970s, opened up the question of just what having lots of sex meant to gay men and where their identities might end up without it. The fundamental dependence of gay male identity and, indeed, masculinity more widely on sexuality and particularly sex per se was raised within more social psychological circles, particularly in the work of Person (1980) and Kimmel (1994), as well as my own (Edwards, 1992), yet it was never fully raised within gay studies and quickly turned into an often media-driven and pejorative question of "sex addiction." In a sense, then, AIDS triangulated the relationship of gender, sexuality, and identity more strongly, although often the issue was only forced through an individual, but also collective, experience of grief.

This important, if rather painful, line of argument was pursued to some extent by Leo Bersani (1988, 1995), who sought to connect a personal question of mourning, particularly in the wake of the AIDS epidemic, to a political question of militancy. The overall thrust of his analysis was to seek to marry, rather than divorce, the intensely individual, psychological, and sexual with the social, external, and pedagogic. At the center of this logic was, once again, the promiscuous sexuality of the cruising gay clone. In the first instance, Bersani rejected the argument that the rise of a gay hypermasculinity was necessarily about subversion play or parody, arguing that sexual desire remained, in essence, a serious business that could potentially reinforce patriarchal or conservative politics as much as it could undermine them. Thus, a homosexual, or even sexual, love of rough trade and uniforms did not make that love radical. As a result, gay men were, and are, in the uneasy situation of potentially desiring, and perhaps even sleeping with, their enemies. This is an argument that could easily be used to bolster some more simplistic and homophobic dimensions of feminism, as outlined previously, yet, precisely because Bersani, like Butler, invokes psychoanalytic theory, the issue becomes inverted, and gay men's desire for the masculine remains not only to be problematized, but also to be *celebrated*, precisely for its constant invoking of the disavowed, male, sexual object.

Where, though, does this leave our analysis of the relationship of homosexuality and masculinity? By way of concluding this section, I would like to consider the work of Bech as perhaps the most complete attempt to document the more contemporary nature of the relationship of masculinity and homosexuality. In *When Men Meet*, Bech (1997) starts by critiquing social constructionism for its lack of explanatory power and then moves on to examine, pivotally, what he calls absent homosexuality. This is, in essence, a reworking of Sedgwick's notion of "homosociality," in which masculinity is seen quite literally to depend on both the permanent presence and,

indeed, the absence of homosexuality. To put it more simply, relations between men, both past and present, are characterized by the constant possibility of, and quite simultaneously the equally continuous prohibition of, homosexuality. Thus homosexuality per se works as a primarily invisible mechanism in the maintenance of masculinity. For example, the homosexuality of movies is demonstrated through the explicit lack or absence of portrayals of homosexuality, a point echoed elsewhere (Kirkham & Thumin, 1993; Simpson, 1994). Thus Bech starts to demonstrate the crucial extent to which homosexual identity depends even more fundamentally on masculinity than heterosexuality. This is intriguing, but it leads him into an equally constant overplaying of the significance of certain stereotypes of homosexuality; namely, that homosexuality is all about furtive glances and even more furtive sexual practices and is usually conducted in cities. Quite where this leaves the monogamous practices of the suburban and rural homosexual is anyone's guess. Despite this, Bech's reworking of the relationship of homosexuality and masculinity retains an untapped potential. In particular, it starts to tip into an analysis of visual culture and the ways in which the male, and the masculine, have increasingly become both the object as well as the subject of the gaze; for example, in relation to contemporary patterns of sexual objectification, advertising, and the world of fashion. This forms what he calls a "telemediated" society, or visual and media culture that simultaneously emphasizes processes of aestheticization as well as sexualization and in which relations between men become, almost by quirk, absent of absent homosexuality. It is important to note that this would seem to start to extend Sedgwick's more historical and textual analysis of homosociality toward an understanding of more contemporary and applied discussion developments concerning masculinity, yet Bech's analysis in the final instance is left hanging and inconclusive. Also implicit and problematic here is Bech's invocation of the increasing globalization of gay sexuality, given the rising significance of the Internet and international travel and of sexual practices generally that not only informs the development of the AIDS epidemic and sex trafficking but also, according to Dennis Altman (2001) at least, begins to scramble the very certainties of gay identity, both theoretically and politically, as gay identity becomes at once both globalized and localized.

To summarize, these applications of post-structural theory have reworked understandings of the relationship of homosexuality and masculinity, in terms of sexuality and gender, as follows: Successful heterosexual and masculine identification psychologically and socially depend on the repudiation of *both* femininity and homosexuality. Gay male sexuality offers a potentially, though not necessarily, radical challenge to both psychological and social sexual and gender order. In addition, this necessary repudiation poses a series of difficulties for gay men themselves, whose relationships and even losses are not avowed or recognized and whose desires have the potential to work against them as much as with them. In sum, the relationship between desire and identification, which I have argued to be at the core of the problem raised by identity politics, is both explored and explicated beyond a sense of simple contradiction to become something which, in a sense, cuts both ways. In this scheme of things, then, gay men are neither more nor less "masculine" or misogynist than straight men but located in an awkward, and perhaps even dialectical, relation to gender both psychologically and socially.

Having said this, I should further note that a number of significant difficulties remain both theoretically and politically. Perhaps the most fundamental of these is the relationship of such psychoanalytically or textually centered theory to social or even cultural practice. Although some extrapolation of social and cultural implications from such work is perhaps easily accepted as simply common sense, wider aspects and questions, including the issue of social and cultural change, are in no way straightforwardly "read off" from the use of psychoanalytic, literary, or textual analysis. Without wishing to imply any form of return to positivism, the sense of distance involved is often further reinforced through the lack of empirically centered research or evidence that might otherwise help to fill the gap exposed between theory and practice.

A second and equally difficult problem concerns the question of values. Identity politics, for all its faults in setting up overly polarized and often divisive contests, not only used but rather developed, intentionally or not, a system of value. In relation to our discussion here, masculinity became problematized in value terms as

something that was not neutral and that also had an impact on such phenomena as institutional power relations and violent crime. Some of this impact at least is potentially lost in overdivorcing the analysis of masculinity from men.

Third, although masculinity remains a social construct that has no *necessary*, in the intrinsic sense, connection with men, it is clearly incorrect to state that it has *no* relationship to men *at all* or that this is not qualitatively different from its relationship to women. Furthermore, this also may undermine the sense in which masculinity itself can become problematized for both men and women. To put it more simply, if men and masculinity are not one and the same, then they may remain related, and in separating them, one should not disconnect them entirely.

More important, the tendency to separate analysis and theory from questions of practice and politics also has the tendency to lead, potentially at least, to a neglect of the fundamental ways in which patriarchy and masculinity are reinforced and perpetuated through institutions both formal and informal and, perhaps most important of all, the resistance to change that may come from individual men and women. What this begins to expose in more directly political terms is a problem of both relativism and liberalism. Masculinity, although clearly a lot more "open" than once conceived, is, equally clearly, also not an entirely mutable phenomenon that is "up for grabs"; some forms of "performing" and "doing" masculinity remain more, or less, problematic than others.

Where, though, does this leave us in relation to gay men and gay masculinities? Poststructural theory would seem to offer more theoretical solutions to the conundrums posed by identity politics, yet it equally tends to elide discussion of its applications and implications in practice. In sum, the difficulty remains more political. Despite this, there seems little reason to presume that these questions could not be addressed more fully. More significantly, and perhaps ironically, this seems to depend on undermining rather than reinforcing the sense of separation that has developed between so-called old guard identity politics and avant garde poststructural or queer theory and politics (Seidman, 1995). The continuing logic of social constructionism is critical here, and the questions and the problems involved, if not necessarily the answers, would seem to remain the same.

Conclusions: Queering the Pitch?

At this final juncture, it is, I think, worth returning to some fundamental questions in relation to gay men. First and foremost, gay men are not simply the same as other men, for if they were, their gayness would neither matter nor even register as significant. Clearly, being gay does still matter, even within the liberal and open spaces of advanced Western industrial societies, let alone within the confines of conservatism, moralism, or fundamentalism past or present. Second, gay men remain a stigmatized and marginalized minority whose gains, and these are still significant, are perilous. There is as yet nothing approaching full legal or statutory equality for gay men or lesbians and very little antidiscriminatory legislation or protection. As such, their progress and position remain very open to regression and undermining on many fronts. The AIDS epidemic exemplifies this in many ways and exposes not only the resistance of gay and lesbian communities but also their vulnerability. Third, gay men remain men, with all the perhaps increasingly precarious privileges and benefits that maleness bestows on them. Although these may be both perilous and uncertain, gay men remain related to masculinity, and they cannot and, indeed, should not be understood as separated from it. Fourth, and more theoretically, it remains important to recognize the contingent and changing nature of, as well as the diversity and plurality of, masculinities and homosexualities. A fifth and utterly fundamental point, then, is that gay men do not constitute a homogeneous group, or even a unified category, and their position varies significantly according to such factors as social class, geography, race, or ethnicity, let alone individual politics, practices, or preferences. Whether or not, then, gay masculinity queers the pitch of sexual politics depends on a whole host of other micro and macro individual and social factors. Consequently, there is no easy answer, and accusations of gay male misogyny are no more, and no less, valid than endorsements of the gay male relationship to more feminist agendas. An added difficulty here is that the endless questioning and indeed "queering" of gay men's pitch is somewhat misplaced on an oppressed minority and is, perhaps, even a form of heterosexism in itself. What *does* remain more certain, then, is the need to address far more

than previously an entirely different question of *hetero*sexual men's relationship to their *hetero*sexuality, not just to their masculinity—for them to queer their own pitch.

Notes

1. I refer here to Quentin Crisp's now legendary memoir-cum-novel *The Naked Civil Servant* (Crisp, 1968), later dramatized by the BBC and starring John Hurt in the title role, and Stephan Elliott's 1994 movie *The Adventures of Priscilla, Queen of the Desert*, each of which in different ways celebrated effeminate and cross-dressing homosexuality with a vengeance.

2. See Freud (1977).

3. Carpenter campaigned vigorously for legal reform following the criminalization of homosexual acts, if not homosexuality itself, under the Labouchère Amendment of 1885 in the United Kingdom; however, the subsequent trial and imprisonment of Oscar Wilde achieved an unprecedented level of visibility for homosexuality and perhaps some wider ambivalence, if not sympathy, toward it. The more-or-less simultaneous categorization and criminalization of homosexuality, coupled with the rapid formation of movements toward reform, constitute a conjunction of factors studied most fully in the work of Jeffrey Weeks (1977).

4. It is interesting that this phrase comes from the poem *Two Loves* by Oscar Wilde's lover, Lord Alfred Douglas, yet gained a Wildean flourish when Wilde later quoted it in his own defense at his trial.

5. The Stonewall Inn, a gay pub in New York, was subject to frequent raids by the police in the 1960s. On June 27, 1969, the clientele fought back, and so, legend has it, gay liberation began.

References

Adam, B. D. (1987). *The rise of a gay and lesbian movement*. Boston: Twayne.

Altman, D. (1971). *Homosexual: Oppression and liberation*. Sydney, Australia: Angus & Robertson.

Altman, D. (1986). *AIDS and the new puritanism*. London: Pluto Press.

Altman, D. (2001). *Global sex*. Chicago: University of Chicago Press.

Bech, H. (1997). *When men meet: Homosexuality and modernity*. Cambridge, England: Polity.

Bem, S. (1974). The measurement of psychological androgyny. *Journal of Consulting and Clinical Psychology, 42*, 155-162.

Bersani, L. (1988). *Is the rectum a grave?* In D. Crimp (Ed.), *AIDS: Cultural analysis, cultural activism.* London: MIT Press.

Bersani, L. (1995). Loving men. In M. Berger, B. Wallis, & S. Watson (Eds.), *Constructing masculinity.* London: Routledge.

Blachford, G. (1981). Male dominance and the gay world. In K. Plummer (Ed.), *The making of the modern homosexual.* London: Hutchinson.

Bly, R. (1990). *Iron John.* New York: Addison-Wesley.

Bray, A. (1982). *Homosexuality in Renaissance England.* London: Gay Men's Press.

Bristow, J. (1989). Homophobia/misogyny: Sexual fears, sexual definitions. In S. Shepherd & M. Wallis (Eds.), *Coming on strong: Gay politics and culture.* London: Unwin Hyman.

Bristow, J., & Wilson, A. (Eds.). (1993). *Activating theory: Lesbian, gay, bisexual politics.* London: Lawrence & Wishart.

Bronski, M. (1984). *Culture clash: The making of a gay sensibility.* Boston: South End Press.

Butler, J. (1990). *Gender trouble: Feminism and the subversion of identity.* London: Routledge.

Butler, J. (1993). *Bodies that matter: On the discursive limits of sex.* London: Routledge.

Butler, J. (1995). Melancholy gender/refused identification. In M. Berger, B. Wallis, & S. Watson (Eds.), *Constructing masculinity.* London: Routledge.

Califia, P. (1994). *Public sex: The culture of radical sex.* San Francisco: Cleiss Press.

Caplan, P. (Ed.). (1987). *The cultural construction of sexuality.* London: Tavistock.

Carpenter, E. (1908). *The intermediate sex: A study of some transitional types of men.* London: Mitchell Kennedy.

Carrigan, T., Connell, R. W., & Lee, J. (1985). Toward a new sociology of masculinity. *Theory and Society, 14,* 551-604.

Connell, R. W. (1987). *Gender and power.* Cambridge, England: Polity.

Connell, R. W. (1995). *Masculinities.* Cambridge, England: Polity.

Cooley, C. H. (1902). *Human nature and the social order.* New York: Scribner's.

Crimp, D. (Ed.). (1988). *AIDS: Cultural analysis, cultural activism.* London: MIT Press.

Crisp, Q. (1968). *The naked civil servant.* Glasgow: Collins.

Delph, E. W. (1978). *The silent community: Public sexual encounters.* Beverly Hills, CA: Sage.

Dowsett, G. (1987). Queer fears and gay examples. *New Internationalist, 175,* 10-12.

Durkheim, E. (1951). *Suicide: A study in sociology.* Glencoe, IL: Free Press.

Dworkin, A. (1981). *Pornography: On men possessing women.* London: Women's Press.

Edwards, T. (1990). Beyond sex and gender: Masculinity, homosexuality and social theory. In J. Hearn & D. Morgan (Eds.), *Men, masculinities and social theory.* London: Unwin Hyman.

Edwards, T. (1992). The AIDS dialectics: Awareness, identity, death and sexual politics. In K. Plummer (Ed.), *Modern homosexualities: Fragments of lesbian and gay experience.* London: Routledge.

Edwards, T. (1994). *Erotic and politics: Gay male sexuality, masculinity and feminism.* London: Routledge.

Edwards, T. (1998). Queer fears: Against the cultural turn. *Sexualities, 1*(4), 471-484.

Eglinton, J. Z. (1971). *Greek love.* London: Neville Spearman.

Epstein, S. (1987). Gay politics, ethnic identity: The limits of social constructionism. *Socialist Review, 17,* 9-54.

Epstein, S. (1988). Nature vs. nurture and the politics of AIDS organising. *Out/Look, 1*(3), 46-50.

Evans, D. (1993). *Sexual citizenship: The material construction of sexualities.* London: Routledge.

Faderman, L. (1981). *Surpassing the love of men: Romantic friendship and love between women from the renaissance to the present.* New York: William Morrow.

Faraday, A. (1981). Liberating lesbian research. In K. Plummer (Ed.), *The making of the modern homosexual.* London: Hutchinson.

Foucault, M. (1978). *The history of sexuality: Vol. 1. An introduction.* London: Penguin.

Foucault, M. (1984a). *The history of sexuality: Vol. 2. The use of pleasure.* London: Penguin.

Foucault, M. (1984b). *The history of sexuality: Vol. 3. The care of the self.* London: Penguin.

Freud, S. (1977). *On sexuality: Three essays on the theory of sexuality and other works.* London: Penguin.

Gough, J. (1989). Theories of sexual identity and the masculinization of the gay man. In S. Shepherd & M. Wallis (Eds.), *Coming on strong: Gay politics and culture.* London: Unwin Hyman.

Grace, D. (1993). Dynamics of desire. In V. Harwood, D. Oswell, K. Parkinson, & A. Ward (Eds.), *Pleasure principles: Politics, sexuality, and ethics.* London: Lawrence & Wishart.

Greenberg, D. F. (1988). *The construction of homosexuality.* London: University of Chicago Press.

Harwood, V., et al. (Eds.). (1993). *Pleasure principles: Politics, sexuality, and ethics.* London: Lawrence & Wishart.

Hearn, J. (1987). *The gender of oppression: Men, masculinity and the critique of Marxism.* Brighton, England: Wheatsheaf.

Hocquenghem, G. (1972). *Homosexual desire.* London: Allison & Busby.

Jay, K., & Young, A. (1979). *The gay report.* New York: Summit Books.

Jeffreys, S. (1990). *Anticlimax: Feminist perspectives on the sexual revolution.* London: Women's Press.

Katz, J. (1976). *Gay American history: Lesbians and gay men in the USA.* New York: Thomas Y. Crowell.

Kimmel, M. S. (Ed.). (1987). *Changing men: New directions in research on men and masculinity.* London: Sage.

Kimmel, M. S. (1994). Masculinity as homophobia: Fear, shame, and silence in the construction of gender identity. In H. Brod & M. Kauffman (Eds.), *Theorizing masculinities.* London: Sage.

Kinsey, A. F., Pomeroy, W. B., & Martin, C. E. (1948). *Sexual behavior in the human male.* Philadelphia: W. B. Saunders.

Kirkham, P., & Thumin, J. (Eds.). (1993). *You Tarzan: Masculinity, movies and men.* London: Lawrence & Wishart.

Kramer, L. (1978). *Faggots.* London: Methuen.

Kramer, L. (1983). 1,112 and counting. *New York Native, 59,* 14-27.

Kramer, L. (1986). *The normal heart.* London: Methuen.

Lee, J. A. (1978). *Getting sex: A new approach—more fun, less guilt.* Toronto, Ontario: Mission Book.

Le Vay, S. (1993). *The sexual brain.* London: MIT Press.

MacKinnon, C. A. (1987). *Feminism unmodified: Discourses on life and law.* Cambridge, MA: Harvard University Press.

Mead, M. (1977). *Sex and temperament in three primitive societies.* London: Routledge & Kegan Paul.

Mercer, K., & Julien, I. (1988). Race, sexual politics and black masculinity: A dossier. In R. Chapman & J. Rutherford (Eds.), *Male order: Unwrapping masculinity.* London: Lawrence & Wishart.

Mieli, M. (1980). *Homosexuality and liberation: Elements of a gay critique.* London: Gay Men's Press.

Miles, M. (2003). Ghetto culture. *Axm, 6*(1), 32-34.

Morgan, D. (1992). *Discovering men.* London: Routledge.

Nicholson, L., & Seidman, S. (Eds.). (1995). *Social postmodernism: Beyond identity politics.* Cambridge, England: Cambridge University Press.

Owens, C. (1987). Outlaws: Gay men in feminism. In A. Jardine & P. Smith (Eds.), *Men in feminism.* London: Methuen.

Patton, C. (1985). *Sex and germs: The politics of AIDS.* London: South End Press.

Person, E. S. (1980). Sexuality as the mainstay of identity: Psychoanalytic perspectives. *Signs, 5*(4), 605-630.

Plummer, K. (Ed.). (1981), *The making of the modern homosexual.* London: Hutchinson.

Plummer, K. (1984). *Telling sexual stories: Power, change and social worlds.* London: Routledge.

Pollak, M. (1985). Male homosexuality, or happiness in the ghetto. In P. Aries & A. Bejin (Eds.), *Western sexuality: Practice and precept in past and present times.* Oxford: Basil Blackwell.

Rechy, J. (1977). *The sexual outlaw: A documentary.* London: W. H. Allen.

Rich, A. (1984). Compulsory heterosexuality and lesbian existence. In A. B. Snitow, C. Stansell, & S. Thompson (Eds.), *Desire: The politics of sexuality.* London: Virago.

Riley, D. (1988). *Am I that name? Feminism and the category of "women" in history.* New York: Macmillan.

Rubin, G. (1984). Thinking sex: Notes for a radical theory of the politics of sexuality. In C. S. Vance (Ed.), *Pleasure and danger: Exploring female sexuality.* London: Routledge & Kegan Paul.

Sedgwick, E. K. (1985). *Between men: English literature and male homosexual desire.* New York: Columbia Press.

Sedgwick, E. K. (1990). *Epistemology of the closet.* Berkeley: University of California Press.

Sedgwick, E. K. (1995). *"Gosh, Boy George, you must be awfully secure in your masculinity!"* In M. Berger, B. Wallis, & S. Watson (Eds.), *Constructing masculinity.* London: Routledge.

Segal, L. (1990). *Slow motion: Changing masculinities, changing men.* London: Virago.

Segal, L., & McIntosh, M. (Eds.). (1992). *Sex exposed: Sexuality and the pornography debate.* London: Virago.

Seidler, V. J. (1994). *Unreasonable men: Masculinity and social theory.* London: Routledge.

Seidman, S. (1995). Deconstructing queer theory, or the under-theorization of the social and ethical. In L. Nicholson & S. Seidman (Eds.), *Social postmodernism: Beyond identity politics.* Cambridge, England: Cambridge University Press.

Shiers, J. (1980). Two steps forward, one step back. In Gay Left Collective (Ed.), *Homosexuality: Power and politics.* London: Allison & Busby.

Shilts, R. (1987). *And the band played on: Politics, people, and the AIDS epidemic.* London: Penguin.

Simpson, M. (1994). *Male impersonators: Men performing masculinity.* London: Routledge.

Spada, J. (1979). *The Spada report.* New York: Signet.

Stanley, L. (1982). Male needs: The problems and problems of working with gay men. In S. Friedman & E. Sarah (Eds.), *On the* problem of men: Two feminist conferences. London: Women's Press.

Stanley, L. (1984). Whales and minnows: Some sexual theorists and their followers and how they contribute to making feminism invisible. *Women's Studies International Forum, 7*(1), 53-62.

Stoltenberg, J. (1989). *Refusing to be a man: Essays on sex and justice.* Portland, OR: Breitenbush Books.

Vance, C. S. (Ed.). (1984). *Pleasure and danger: Exploring female sexuality.* London: Routledge & Kegan Paul.

Walter, A. (Ed.). (1980). *Come together: The years of gay liberation (1970-73).* London: Gay Men's Press.

Watney, S. (1987). *Policing desire: Pornography, AIDS and the media.* London: Comedia.

Weeks, J. (1977). *Coming out: Homosexual politics in Britain from the nineteenth century to the present.* London: Quartet.

Weeks, J. (1981). *Sex, politics and society: The regulation of sexuality since 1800.* London: Longman.

Weeks, J. (1985). *Sexuality and its discontents: Meanings, myths and modern sexualities.* London: Routledge & Kegan Paul.

Wellings, K., Field, J., Johnson, A. M., & Wadsworth, J. (1994). *Sexual behaviour in Britain: The National Survey of Sexual Attitudes and Lifestyles.* London: Penguin.

White, E. (1986). *States of desire: Travels in gay America.* London: Picador.

Wittig, M. (1997). One is not born a woman. In S. Kemp & J. Squires (Eds.), *Feminisms.* Oxford: Oxford University Press.

PART II

GLOBAL AND REGIONAL PATTERNS

5

GLOBALIZATION, IMPERIALISM, AND MASCULINITIES

R. W. CONNELL

THE NEED FOR A GLOBAL PERSPECTIVE IN STUDIES OF MEN AND MASCULINITY

Recent research on the social construction of masculinity has been very diverse in subject matter and social location, but it has had a characteristic focus and style. Its main focus has been the making of masculinity in a particular milieu or moment, whether a professional sports career in the United States (Messner, 1992), a group of colonial schools in South Africa (Morrell, 2001b), drinking groups in Australian bars (Tomsen, 1997), a working class suburb in Brazil (Fonseca, 2001), or the marriage plans of young middle class men in urban Japan (Taga, 2001). The characteristic research style has been ethnographic, making use of participant observation, open-ended interviewing, documentary and discourse analysis. The primary research task has been to give close descriptions of processes and outcomes in the local site.

This ethnographic moment brought a much-needed gust of realism to discussions of men and masculinity. The concrete detail in such

studies corrected the abstractions of "sex role" theory, previously the main framework for social-scientific work on masculinity. Ethnographic research also challenged the ways of talking about men that had become predominant in Western popular culture: biological essentialism, religious revivalism, and the mystical generalities of the mythopoetic movement.

Nevertheless, it has always been recognized that some issues go beyond the local. Even the religious and mythopoetic men's movements can only be understood by considering the upheaval in gender relations that has produced a whole spectrum of agendas for remaking masculinity (Messner, 1997). Historical studies of public images and debates about masculinity, such as Phillips (1987) on New Zealand, Sinha (1995) on India, and Kimmel (1996) on the United States, have been able to trace such cultural processes over time and show the significance of a broader historical context for local constructions of masculinity.

As I have previously argued (Connell, 1998), this logic should be taken further. Global history

Author's note: I am grateful for the generous assistance of John Fisher in the preparation of this chapter, and for advice from colleagues, especially James Messerschmidt and my coeditors, which has helped to improve it.

and contemporary globalization must be part of our understanding of masculinities. Locally situated lives are (and were) powerfully influenced by geopolitical struggles, Western imperial expansion and colonial empires, global markets, multinational corporations, labor migration, and transnational media.

A number of arguments now converge to emphasize this. Gittings (1996) and colleagues have shown the extent to which constructions of masculinity in a First World country, in this case Britain, are based in the history of empire. Nagel (1998) shows the interweaving of masculinities with the construction of nationality and thus with the dynamics of war. Hooper (1998) shows the connection of masculinities to the system of international relations and the processes of globalization. Ouzgane and Coleman (1998) argue for the importance of postcolonial studies for understanding the cultural dynamics of contemporary masculinities. Though most research on masculinities has been done in cities, most of the world's population is rural, so Campbell and Bell's (2000) argument for giving attention to rural masculinities is also important.

To understand local masculinities, then, we must think globally. But how? In this chapter, I offer a framework for thinking about masculinities as a feature of world society and for thinking about men's gender practices in terms of global structures. The first step is to characterize the global gender order. We need to distinguish between two contexts of masculinity formation: local gender orders and transnational arenas. The next step is to consider the impact of globalization on men's bodies. I then examine, in turn, the impact of globalization on masculinities in local gender orders and the masculinities constructed in transnational arenas. Finally I consider the pattern of masculinity politics in the global gender order as a whole.

The World Gender Order as Context of Men's Lives

Masculinities do not first exist and then come into contact with femininities. Masculinities and femininities are produced together in the process that constitutes a gender order. Accordingly, to understand masculinities on a world scale, we must first develop a concept of the globalization of gender.

This is difficult, because the very conception is counterintuitive. We are so accustomed to thinking of gender as the attribute of an individual, even an unusually intimate attribute of the individual, that it requires a considerable wrench to think of gender on the vast scale of global society. As Smith (1998) argues for the study of international politics, the key is to shift the focus from individual-level gender differences to "the patterns of socially constructed gender relations." If we recognize that very large scale institutions, such as the state and corporations, are gendered (Hearn & Parkin, 2001), and if we recognize that international relations, international trade, and global markets are inherently an arena of gender politics (Enloe, 1990), then we can recognize the existence of a world gender order. The world gender order can be defined as the structure of relationships that interconnect the gender regimes of institutions, and the gender orders of local societies, on a world scale (Connell, 2002).

This gender order is an aspect of a larger reality: global society. Accordingly, the analysis of the world gender order must start with the broad features of contemporary globalization and its historical predecessor, European imperialism. By *imperialism*, I mean the systems of direct colonial rule and indirect economic domination that spread across the globe from the early 16th to the mid-20th centuries. By *globalization*, I mean the current pattern of world integration via global markets, transnational corporations, and electronic media under the political hegemony of the United States.

How to understand global society is much debated. Current media talk about globalization pictures a homogenizing process sweeping across the world, driven by new technologies and producing vast unfettered global markets, world music, global advertising, and world news, in which all the world's people participate on equal terms. As Hirst and Thompson (1996) show, the global economy is highly unequal, and the degree of homogenization is often greatly exaggerated. Bauman (1998), too, emphasizes that globalization produces social and cultural division as much as it produces homogeneity.

Globalization is best understood as centering on a set of linked economic changes characteristic of the current stage of capitalism. The main changes are the expansion of worldwide markets, the restructuring of local economies under the pressure of the world economy, and the creation of new economic institutions. Multinational corporations based in the three economic great powers (the United States, the European Union, and Japan) are the major economic actors, alongside financial markets that have risen to an unprecedented scale and power. The rise of these economic forces has been accompanied by political change—the dominance of neoliberalism, or market ideology, and the decline of the welfare state in the West and communist centralism in the East.

Globalization also involves a powerful process of cultural change. Western cultural forms and ideologies circulate, local cultures change in response, and the dominant culture itself changes in an immense dialectic. Some homogenization results as local cultures are destroyed or weakened. But new forms appear—hybrid and "creole" identities and cultural expressions. All these processes are uneven in their impact and articulate with each other in different ways in different parts of the world (Lechner & Boli, 2000).

The historical processes that produced global society were, from the start, gendered. Colonial conquest and settlement were carried out by gender-segregated forces. In the stabilization of colonial societies, new gender divisions of labor were produced in plantation economies and colonial cities, and gender ideologies were linked with racial hierarchies and the cultural defense of empire. The growth of a postcolonial world economy has seen gender divisions of labor installed on a massive scale in the "global factory" (Fuentes & Ehrenreich, 1983), as well as the spread of gendered violence alongside Western military technology (Breines, Gierycz, & Reardon, 1999).

The links that constitute a global gender order seem to be of two basic types. The first is interaction between existing gender orders. Imperial conquest, neocolonialism, and the current world systems of power, investment, trade, and communication have brought very diverse societies in contact with each other. The gender orders of those societies have consequently been brought into contact with each other.

This has often been a violent and disruptive process. Local gender arrangements were reshaped by conquest and sexual exploitation, imported epidemics, missionary intervention, slavery, indentured labor, migration, and resettlement. The process of economic development and the institutions of development aid continue to bring the gender politics of rich countries into relation with those of the "underdeveloped." This creates complex problems of gender equity, especially around recent attempts to extend the scope of "women and development" programs by bringing men more explicitly into gender issues (White, 2000).

The gender patterns resulting from these interactions are the first level of a global gender order. They are local patterns but carry the impress of the forces that make a global society. A striking example is provided by Morrell's (2001a) analysis of the situation of men in contemporary South Africa. The transition from apartheid—itself a violent but doomed attempt to perpetuate colonial race relations—has created an extraordinary social landscape. In a context of reintegration into the global polity and economy, rising unemployment, continuing violence, and a growing HIV/AIDS epidemic, there are attempts to reconstitute rival patriarchies in different ethnic groups, which clash with agendas for the modernization of masculinity, the impact of feminism, and the new government's "human rights" discourse.

The second type of link that constitutes a world gender order is the creation of new "spaces" and arenas beyond individual countries and regions. The most important seem to be those I list here.

• *Transnational and multinational corporations.* Corporations operating in global markets are now the largest business organizations on the planet. The biggest ones, in industries such as oil, car manufacturing, computers, and telecommunications, have resources amounting to hundreds of billions of dollars and employ hundreds of thousands of people. They typically have a strong gender division of labor, and, as Wajcman's (1999) study of British-based multinationals indicates, a strongly masculinized management culture.

• *The international state.* The institutions of diplomacy and war, the principal means by which sovereign states have related to each other, are heavily masculinized. Zalewski and

Parpart (1998) aptly call this *The "Man" Question in International Relations*. United Nations agencies, the European Union, and a range of other international agencies and agreements have been set up to transcend these old and dubious arrangements. They regulate gender issues globally through, for instance, development aid, education, human rights, and labor conventions. They, too, are gendered, mainly run by men although with more cultural complexity than multinational corporations (Gierycz, 1999).

- *International media.* Multinational media corporations circulate film, video, music, and news on a very large scale. There are also more decentralized media (post, telegraph, telephone, fax, the Internet, the Web) and their supporting industries. All contain gender arrangements and circulate gender meanings. Cunneen and Stubbs (2000), for instance, document the use of Internet sites to commodify Filipina women in an international trade in wives and sexual partners for First World men.

- *Global markets.* It is important to distinguish markets themselves from the individual corporations that operate in them. International markets—capital, commodity, service, and labor markets—have an increasing reach into local economies. They are often strongly gender structured; an example is the international market in domestic labor (Chang & Ling, 2000). International labor markets are now (with the political triumph of neoliberalism) very weakly regulated, apart from border controls reinforced by political panics in First World countries about illegal immigrants.

The net result of these two forms of linkage is a partially integrated, highly unequal, and turbulent set of gender relations, with global reach but uneven impact. This is the context in which we must now think about the construction and enactment of masculinities.

THE MASCULINITIES OF TRANSNATIONAL ARENAS

We should not expect the structure of gender relations in transnational or global arenas simply to mirror patterns known in local arenas. The interaction of many local gender orders multiplies the forms of masculinity present in the global gender order. At the same time, the creation of institutions and communications that operate across regions and continents also creates the possibility of patterns of masculinity that are, to some degree, standardized across localities. I call such masculinities "globalizing" rather than "global" to emphasize the *process*—and the fact that it is often incomplete. It is among globalizing masculinities, rather than narrowly within the metropole,[1] that we are likely to find candidates for hegemony in the world gender order.

I will start with a sketch of major forms of globalizing masculinity in the historical development of global society and then focus on patterns in the contemporary postcolonial world.

Conquest, Settlement, and Empire. The creation of the imperial social order involved peculiar conditions for the gender practices of men. Colonial conquest itself was mainly carried out by segregated groups of men—soldiers, sailors, traders, administrators, and a good many who were all these by turn. They were drawn from the more segregated occupations and milieux in the metropole, and it is likely that those men drawn into colonization were the more rootless.

Certainly the process of conquest could produce frontier masculinities that combined the occupational culture of these groups with an unusual level of violence and egocentric individualism. The political history of empire is full of evidence of the tenuous control over the frontier exercised by the state, from the Spanish monarchs unable to rein in the conquistadors to the governors in Capetown unable to hold back the Boers. Other forms of control were similarly weakened. Extensive sexual exploitation of indigenous women was a common feature of colonial conquest.

In certain circumstances, frontier masculinities might be reproduced as a local cultural tradition long after the frontier had passed. Examples are the gauchos of southern South America, the cowboys of the western United States, and the bush workers of outback Australia (Lake, 1986). However, conquest and exploitation were generally succeeded by some degree of settlement. Sex ratios in the colonizing population changed as women arrived and locally born generations followed, and a shift back toward the family patterns of the metropole was probable. The construction of an orderly settler masculinity might even be a goal of state policy, as in late 19th century New Zealand (Phillips, 1987).

As Cain and Hopkins (1993) have shown for the British empire, the ruling group in the colonial world as a whole was an extension of the dominant class in the metropole, the landed gentry. The imperial state thus became a transnational arena for the production and circulation of masculinities based on gentry customs and ideology, although these were increasingly modified by military and bureaucratic needs. The narrow social life of the British ruling class in India, marked by gender and racial segregation and a striking lack of interest in local (or indeed any wider) culture, provides a well-documented case (Allen, 1975).

Conquest and settlement had the capacity to disrupt all the structures of indigenous society, although the course of events in different regions varied widely (Bitterli, 1989). Indigenous gender orders were no exception, and their disruption doubtless made it more feasible for indigenous men to be drawn into the masculinizing practices and hierarchies of colonial society. The imperial social order created a scale of masculinities as it created a scale of communities and races. The colonizers distinguished "more manly" from "less manly" groups among their subjects. A well-known suburb of Sydney in Australia is still named Manly because the first British governor was impressed by the bearing of some Aboriginal men he saw there. In British India, Bengali men were supposed by the colonizers to be effeminate, but Pathans and Sikhs were regarded as strong and warlike. Similar distinctions were made by the colonizers in South Africa between "Hottentots" and Zulus and, in North America, between (for example) Iroquois, Sioux, and Cheyenne on one side and peaceable tribes such as the Hopi on the other.

The deepening ideology of gender difference in European culture provided general symbols of superiority and inferiority in the empire. Within the imperial "poetics of war" (MacDonald, 1994), the conqueror was virile and the colonized were dirty, sexualized, and effeminate or childlike. In many colonial situations, including Zimbabwe, indigenous men were called "boys" by the colonizers (Shire, 1994). Sinha's (1995) study of the language of

political controversy in India in the 1880s and 1890s shows how the images of "manly Englishman" and "effeminate Bengali" were deployed to uphold colonial privilege and to contain movements for change. In the late 19th century, racial barriers in colonial societies were hardening rather than weakening, and gender ideology tended to fuse with racism in forms that the 20th century never untangled.

The imperial state, and imperial trade and communications, as a transnational arena, affected gender relations among the ruling group. Colonial households with a large supply of indigenous domestic servants changed the position of wives, who became more leisured and managerial—as shown in Bulbeck's (1992) study of Australian women in Papua New Guinea. Empire figured prominently as a source of imagery for the remaking of masculinity in Britain—in the Boy Scouts (as noted later) and in the cult of Lawrence of Arabia (Dawson, 1991). Frontier masculinity played a similar role in the United States, through such media as the Hollywood western. As Mellen's (1978) study of masculinity in American films cautions, the reduction of masculine heroism to a test of physical prowess was a gradual development. Early Hollywood had a wider array of heroes and masculinities.

Imperial power was met, from the start, by resistance. Anticolonial struggles have continued to the present day, usually classified as "terrorism" by the colonial or neocolonial powers. This struggle has itself functioned as an arena of gender formation, as in the case of Palestinian resistance to Israel. Dine (1994) traces some of the cultural consequences of the Algerian anticolonial struggle for the French colonizers. One was the creation of hypermasculine heroes out of the "paras" (French paratroopers), but another was the disillusion that could result from a contrasting image of the home society's corruption, or revulsion stemming from the torture and destruction that accompanied colonial war. The parallels with the U.S. experience in Vietnam and the British experience in India and east Africa are easy to see.

In South Africa, the armed struggle carried on by the "comrades," as the resistance fighters were called, on behalf of the African National Congress produced a generation of young men accustomed to violence and independent action and also lacking formal education and regular work experience (Xaba, 2001). The personal trauma involved in anticolonial struggles—small-scale, intimate warfare with a racial dimension, with communities all around and within reach of the weapons—should not be underestimated.

Postcolonial Situations and the Neoliberal New World Order. It follows from what has just been said that decolonization and transition to a postcolonial world are likely to involve problems about masculinity and violence. Xaba (2001) goes so far as to write of a confrontation between "struggle masculinity" and "post-struggle masculinity." In the new world, in which the African National Congress is the government, responsible for law and order, the "young lions" of the resistance movement are marginalized. Other men have the advantage in the new racially integrated labor markets and public sector. The former "comrades" continue to be targeted by police; some become criminalized and violent and are, in turn, targeted by vigilante actions responding to rapes, robberies, and killings. In the worst cases, a spiral of community violence results.

In cases where decolonization has been accomplished with less violence, the integration of men into subordinate positions in the global economy goes ahead more smoothly. The postcolonial state may appropriate colonial models of masculinity for the project of nation building, as Lee Kuan Yew did in Singapore (Holden, 1998). National liberation movements often recruited women; indeed, they often depended heavily on women's activism. The same movements in power have celebrated male "founding fathers" and have had a very ambiguous relation with women's liberation (Mies, 1986).

With the collapse of Soviet communism, the decline of postcolonial socialism, and the ascendance of the new right in Europe and North America, world politics is more and more organized around the needs of transnational capital and the creation of global markets. To the extent that the identification of men with the world of work is established, the global capitalist economy becomes the key arena for the making of masculinities.

Winter and Robert (1980) pointed out some of the consequences, especially the centrality of instrumental reason associated with the technical organization of work. The spread of the market itself is important. In market exchange, the rational calculation of self-interest is the key to action. Men's predominance in capitalist markets then underpins two cultural contrasts: between rational man and irrational woman and between "modern" and "traditional" masculinities.

Both managerial and working class masculinities are affected. The *sarariiman* ("salaryman," or company man) embodied a rational calculation of self-interest in the new industrial economy of Japan. Moodie's (1994) study of South African gold miners shows how, as the workforce became detached from the homestead economy and more completely proletarianized, gender practices and gender ideas also changed—toward a sharper separation of masculinity from femininity. It is important to recognize that capitalist modernization may *increase* gender distinctions. Parallel examples can be found in the metropole (Cockburn, 1983).

The neoliberal agenda has little to say, explicitly, about gender. The new right speaks a gender-neutral language of "markets," "individuals," and "choice." But the world in which neoliberalism is ascendant is still a gendered world, and neoliberalism has an implicit gender politics. The "individual" of market theory has the attributes and interests of a male entrepreneur. The new right's attack on the welfare state generally weakens the position of women, who are more dependent on nonmarket incomes. Deregulation of the economy, in a corporate world, places strategic power in the hands of particular groups of men—managers and entrepreneurs.

Wajcman's (1999) study of multinational corporations based in the United Kingdom shows that even where women have entered management, they have had to do so on men's terms, conforming to the masculinized culture and practices of the managerial elite. In short, as Wajcman puts it, they have to "manage like a man." Research in the corporate world in the United States (Glass Ceiling Commission, 1995) shows a similar picture.

It is not surprising that the restoration of capitalism in Eastern Europe and the former Soviet Union has been accompanied by a reassertion of dominating masculinities and, in some situations, a sharp worsening in the social position of women (Novikova, 2000).

It seems particularly important, then, to examine the masculinity associated with those who control the dominant institutions of the world economy: the capitalists and business executives who operate in global markets and the political executives who interact (and in many contexts merge) with them. I call this "transnational business masculinity."

International businessmen are not readily available for ethnographic study, but some sources of evidence exist: management literature, business journalism, corporate self-promotion, and studies of local business elites. These sources give suggestive but partly contradictory indications. Donaldson's (1998) study of "the masculinity of the hegemonic," based on biographical sources about the very rich, emphasizes emotional isolation and a deliberate toughening of boys in the course of growing up: the development of a sense of social distance and material abundance combined with a sense of entitlement and superiority. Hooper's (2000) study of the language and imagery of masculinity in *The Economist* in the 1990s, a business journal closely aligned with neoliberalism, shows a distinct break from old-style patriarchal business masculinity, although the new pattern includes many remnants of colonialist attitudes toward the developing world. *The Economist* associates with the global a technocratic, new-frontier imagery and, in the context of restructuring, emphasizes a cooperative, teamwork-based style of management.

A study of recent management textbooks by Gee, Hull, and Lankshear (1996) gives a rather more individualistic picture. The executive in "fast capitalism" is represented as a person with very conditional loyalties, even to the corporation. The occupational world reflected here is characterized by a limited technical rationality, sharply graded hierarchies of rewards, and sudden career shifts or transfers between corporations. Wajcman's (1999) survey indicates a rather more stable managerial world that is closer to traditional bourgeois masculinity and marked by long hours of work and both dependence on, and marginalization of, a domestic world run by wives.

The divergences among these pictures partly reflect differences within the international capitalist class (e.g., between big owners and professional managers) and partly differences between the sources (magazines and textbooks might be expected to exaggerate novelty). Nevertheless, there seem to be further reasons

for recognizing change, especially in relation to the embodiment of masculinity. There are signs of an increasingly libertarian sexuality, with a tendency to commodify relations with women. Hotels catering to businessmen in most parts of the world now routinely offer pornographic videos, and in some parts of the world there is a well-developed prostitution industry catering to international businessmen.

Current business masculinity does not require direct bodily force any more than the older bourgeois masculinity did. But corporations increasingly use the exemplary bodies of elite sportsmen in their marketing strategies, and "corporate boxes" at professional sporting events are now a common setting for business entertaining, deal making, and networking. Periodicals addressed to business audiences (such as the in-flight magazines of international airlines) seem to be giving increased attention to fitness, sport, and appearance. It would seem that the deliberate cultivation of the body has become a significant practice helping to define contemporary business masculinity.

THE LOCAL RECONSTRUCTION OF MASCULINITIES UNDER GLOBALIZATION

Under the pressure of global markets and media, but also as a result of active local desire to participate in the global economy and global culture, pressures for change are set up in the local gender order. This may, and often does, lead to some reconstruction of masculinities, in a process different from the construction of masculinities in global arenas just discussed. I will explore the local transformation processes in this section.

Three preliminary points are important. First, reconstruction is not the work of men alone. As Fonseca (2001) and others have emphasized, women are active in the shaping of masculinities. Second, any reconstruction is likely to be uneven. Taga's (2001) case studies of young Japanese middle class men show the point very clearly. Under cultural pressure from women to move away from "traditional" Japanese patriarchal masculinity, four contrasting patterns of response emerge, ranging from rejection of change to transformation of identity. Third, reconstruction does not start from the same point. There is no cross-cultural equivalence in conceptions of masculinity; indeed, some cultures may not have such a concept at all. But a certain common ground is created by processes of globalization.

An important reason for the unevenness of change is the internal complexity of gender relations. At least four substructures in gender relations can be identified (Connell, 2002). I will examine the reconstruction of masculinities in relation to each of these substructures in turn.

The Division of Labor. It is characteristic of modernity that the world of "work" is culturally defined as men's realm. In most parts of the world, men do have a significantly higher labor force participation rate than women. West Africa and the former Soviet countries are the main exceptions. Fuller (2001), interviewing Peruvian men in three cities, found that work is the main basis of adult masculine standing and self-respect. A man who cannot hold a regular job is felt not to have arrived at full adult masculinity. In this, the Peruvian respondents are articulating ideas found in many parts of the world.

In fact, women collectively do as much work as men, often more. It is the type of work, and the social relations in which it occurs, that matter in regard to gender. As Holter (2003) argues, the structural distinction between the household (as a domain of gift exchange) and the commodity economy (where labor is sold and paid for) is a basis of the modern European gender system. This distinction has been exported into colonial and neocolonial economies, restructuring local production systems to produce a male wage-worker and female domestic-worker couple (Mies, 1986). This has generally produced (or reinforced) an identification of masculinity with the public realm and production and femininity with domesticity and consumption.

The process need not produce a "housewife" in the Western suburban sense. Where the wage work involved migration to plantations or mines, women might take over homestead production (Moodie, 1994) or provide domestic service for groups of men rather than for an individual husband. The men's work, too, might take on a distinctive local configuration. The most famous example is the making of the *sarariiman* in Japanese economic development in the early 20th century (Kinmonth, 1981). This was a pattern of middle class masculinity adapted to a corporate power structure that demanded conformity and loyalty in exchange for security and high late-career rewards.

But if the world capitalist economy increasingly constructed men as wage earners and thus tended to reshape masculinity by linking gender identity with work, this same process made the new masculinities vulnerable. The global economy is turbulent, marked by economic downturns as well as booms, regional decline as well as regional growth. Mass unemployment will undermine masculinities identified with "work." This situation is now very common, as a result both of the decline of former industrial areas such as the industrial cities of northern England and of the rural-urban migration that has created huge underemployed workforces in cities like New Delhi, Sao Paulo, and Mexico City. A movement of women into employment will also undermine "work"-based masculinities. Such a movement is now happening worldwide as a result of women's emancipation, women's education, and the raw economic need of families unable to rely on a male wage.

The resulting challenges to masculinities have now been documented by researchers in a variety of settings: Corman, Luxton, Livingstone, and Seccombe (1993) in Canada; Connell (1995) in Australia; Gutmann (1996) in Mexico; and O'Donnell and Sharpe (2000) in Britain. We can reasonably regard this as one of the main dynamics of change in contemporary masculinities. Even the *sarariiman* is vulnerable. As the security provided by the Japanese corporate world declined in the 1990s, there began to be more anxiety, and more satire, about this pattern of masculinity. The new figure of the "salaryman escaping" has appeared in Japanese media discussions (Dasgupta, 2000).

Power Relations. The colonial and postcolonial world has tended to break down "purdah" systems of patriarchy that are based on the extreme subordination and isolation of women, in the name of modernization and women's rights (Kandiyoti, 1994). By and large, men have adjusted to this. There are exceptions: for instance, in the extremely disturbed conditions of Afghanistan in the 1990s there was a reimposition of severe controls on women by the Taliban regime. Broadly, however, the acceptance of the principle of women's presence in the public realm (the vote, the right to work, legal autonomy) is one of the most important and widespread of recent changes in gender ideology among men. A large-scale survey by Zulehner and Volz (1998) has shown that the rejection of patriarchal models of gender relations is particularly strong among the younger generation of German men, who favor either an egalitarian pattern or some compromise between the two. Anecdotal evidence suggests this generational difference can be found in other countries as well.

At the same time, the creation of a Westernized public realm has seen the installation of large-scale organizations such as state agencies and corporations. Men continue worldwide to hold the large majority of top positions in governments, corporations, courts, armies, churches, political parties, and professional associations (Connell, 2002).

Colonialism, decolonization, and globalization, however, have created many other situations where power is not firmly established and conflict and disorder prevail. Peteet (1994) documents one such case, the Palestinian *Intifada* against Israeli occupation. Here the violence of the occupation and the resistance have changed the conditions in which masculinity is constructed. Older men no longer have authority over the process; rather, leadership in the resistance is in the hands of young men. Boys and youth establish their identities and claims to leadership within the collectivity of young men. Beatings and imprisonment by the occupying forces become a rite of passage for Palestinian youth.

Violence has also been particularly important in the construction of masculinities in South Africa. The struggles around apartheid produced a militarized (and still heavily armed) society in which gun ownership and gun violence are widely associated with masculinity (Cock, 2001). Waetjen and Maré (2001) show how both real violence (assassinations and beatings of opponents) and the symbolism of violence (appeal to warrior traditions) are used by the neoconservative *Inkatha* movement in the creation of an ethnic-national identity for Zulu men.

We should bear in mind that the construction of masculinities in situations of conflict, although it may have spectacular public expressions (as it does in these cases), is still linked to patterns of gender relations in the private realm. Thus Peteet (1994) emphasizes the significance of Palestinian mothers in the *Intifada,* both in

witnessing and dampening violence. Holter (1996), in a striking reanalysis of an old discussion of fascism, shows how Norwegian men's propensity to adopt authoritarian stances is statistically linked to their childhood family experiences of having a dominating father, experiencing parental divorce, and being brought up by a lone mother. Again it seems likely that the connection shown between the changing dynamics of families, and processes in the public realm, is not confined to one country.

Emotional Relations. Patterns of emotional attachment, although often felt to be the most intimate and personal of all social relationships, are also subject to reconstruction by large-scale social forces. This may even be deliberate. Under colonialism, Christian missionaries have often intervened against indigenous sexual customs that contravene the missionary religion— especially indigenous homosexual and cross-gender practices and premarital heterosexual relationships. For instance, missionaries backed by the Spanish colonial authorities tried to stamp out the third-gender *berdache* tradition in North America (Williams, 1986).

In the postcolonial world, although missionary intervention continues, the more powerful influence seems to be commercial mass media. Multinational media corporations and local media imitating U.S. models circulate, on an enormous scale, narratives based on an ideology of romantic love and images based on Western models of attractiveness. This has been particularly well documented for femininity (e.g., Simpson, 1993), but of course the exaltation of heterosexual romantic love also has an impact on men. It shifts the process of forming relationships out of the arena of extended-family negotiations (so-called arranged marriages, which appear oppressive only from within the ideology of romantic love) into the arena of individual competition in a gender market (Holter, 1996). It is this, perhaps, that underlies the discontent with current masculinity among younger urban men in Chile. Valdés and Olavarría (1998) indicate that this does not involve a basic critique of the hegemonic model of masculinity but takes the form of a sense of imprisonment in unchanging family roles.

The realm of sexuality and emotional relationships may also be the site where larger changes or tensions are registered. Ghoussoub

(2000) points to such a process in Egypt, where rumors about impotence-causing chemicals, and a burst of popularity for medieval sex manuals, can be understood as signs of a larger cultural disturbance about masculinity. Ghoussoub notes that the recent increase in women's status in Arab societies has posed dilemmas for men whose identities are still based in traditional conceptions of gender.

There is unlikely to be a radical break in the pattern of emotional relations as a result of the impact of metropolitan or urban gender models. Research by Pearlman (1984) among the Mazatec people of Mexico points to a kind of coexistence. Young men who migrate to the city to work and then return to the Mazatec community bring with them urban models of masculine dominance that are at odds with the relatively egalitarian gender relations of this community, in which women pursue their own prestige and construct their own networks. The young men do not abandon either model; rather, they develop a practice that Pearlman calls "code switching," in which different patterns of masculinity are enacted with different audiences—older women versus other young men, for instance.

The recent research in metropolitan countries that considers hegemonic masculinity as a discursive practice (Wetherell & Edley, 1999) reveals a very similar process. This research shows that there are ways in which men are not permanently committed to a particular model of masculinity—contrary to what we assume on the basis of familiar models of "gender identity." Rather, men strategically adopt or distance themselves from the hegemonic model, depending on what they are trying to accomplish at the time.

A comparable complexity has emerged in research with men involved in homosexual relationships. Research in Brazil (Parker, 1985) encountered multiple patterns of sexual practice and social identity, actively negotiated and played with by those involved. Over time, an understanding of identity that centered on sexual practice (emphasizing the distinction between penetrating and being penetrated) has been displaced by a medico-legal model focused on the gender of one's partner (thus emphasizing the hetero-homo distinction). This in turn has been challenged by a consciously egalitarian "gay" identity. A North American style of gay

identity, as the main alternative to heterosexual masculinity, has now circulated globally. This process is widely criticized (often by homophobic politicians) as a form of cultural imperialism. But, as Altman (2001) observes, the "globalization of sexual identities" does not simply displace indigenous models. Rather, they interact in extremely complex ways, with many opportunities for code switching.

> The dutiful Confucian or Islamic Malaysian son one weekend might appear in drag at Blueboy, Kuala Lumpur's gay bar, the next—and who is to say which is "the real" person? Just as many Malaysians can move easily from one language to another, so most urban homosexuals can move from one style to another, from camping it up with full awareness of the latest fashion trends from Castro Street to playing the dutiful son at a family celebration. (Altman, 2001, p. 92)

Symbolization. Mass media, especially electronic media, in most parts of the world follow North American and European models and relay a great deal of metropolitan content. As noted, gender imagery is an important part of what is circulated. In counterpoint, "exotic" gender imagery has been used in marketing products from nonmetropolitan countries.

For instance, airline advertising by Singapore and Malaysia presents images of flight attendants as exotic, submissive women—a tactic based on the long-standing combination of the exotic and the erotic in the colonial imagination (Jolly, 1997). In the international sex trade, the same device of racialized gender stereotyping is used in marketing Asian women to North American and Australasian men (Cunneen & Stubbs, 2000). Lest this be thought a harmless fantasy, we should note that the rate of death by homicide among Filipino women in Australia—usually at the hands of non-Filipino men who have been their husbands or partners—is nearly six times higher than the "normal" rate of homicide in Australia.

The advent of metropolitan media, fashion, and ideologies creates many opportunities for creative cultural work. The keynote is the active appropriation and transformation of gender meanings. This can be highly self-conscious. A striking example is the marketing of a line of men's suits by the Japanese fashion firm Comme des Garçons under the catchphrase *Nihon no sebiro* (Japanese Saville Row). Like most Westernized businessmen's dress since the early 20th century, the actual cut of the clothes varied only a little from older models. But the advertising made an elaborate pitch to the "spiritual elite" among men, to the idea of a Japanese aesthetic, with overtones of imperial nostalgia and a distinctively Japanese fusion of tradition and modernity (Kondo, 1999).

Davis (1997) describes a very different reworking of these themes in the poor communities of the Torres Strait Islands, in the far north of Australia. Collapse of the regional maritime industry in the 1960s had thrown the men back into the community. One result was a revival of boys' initiation rituals, which had lapsed. These ceremonies had previously been secluded. They were now made public, although girls' ceremonies were not. The revival of "tradition" thus constructed the "modern" pattern of masculinity being identified with the public realm and femininity with the private. At the same time, the celebration of local heroes from regional border clashes was linked to the Australian nationalist-masculine cult of World War I Australian and New Zealand Army Corps (ANZAC) soldiers. The meaning of hero tales was thus shifted from teaching conflict resolution to emphasizing national identity. In both respects, the symbolic dimension of masculinity was reconstructed in ways that linked it to themes of masculinity and nationality in the dominant European-settler Australian society.

The Western symbolism of masculinity is not fixed either, and the dynamics of globalization are also in play in the metropole. As Messner (1993) has pointed out, it was an episode in the military stabilization of global order, the United States operations in Kuwait and Iraq in 1990 and 1991, that provided legitimation for public displays of emotion by powerful men. General Schwartzkopf was praised in the media for crying in public over his casualties. Niva (1998) agrees, going on to suggest that the symbolic "remasculinization" of American power after the defeat in Vietnam, modified by a cult of high-technology violence (the theme emphasized in media coverage of the war), and flavored by compassion and cultural sensitivity, has created a template of "new world order masculinity." But no such display of compassion or sensitivity accompanied the Western attack on Iraq in 2003. Either the shift was ephemeral or—more probably—the Bush government and its supporters simply drew on an alternative media imagery of power and toughness that had coexisted with the other.

MEN'S BODIES IN GLOBALIZATION PROCESSES

Because *globalization* refers to very large scale processes, it is important to recognize that the effects of these processes appear at the most intimate level. Men's bodies, not just broad masculine ideologies and institutions, are involved.

The global social order distributes and redistributes bodies through migration and through political controls over movement. The creation of empire itself involved migration, as groups of the conquerors settled in the new lands. In some cases mass migration followed, producing the settler colonialism of North America, Australasia, Algeria, and Siberia. In settler colonialism, elements of the gender order of Europe were reassembled in new territories. Studies of settler masculinities show, however, that this was selective and influenced by the local situation. Morrell (2001b) remarks on the production of a rugged, rather than cerebral, masculinity in the boys' schools of British colonists in Natal. This resonates with the construction of masculinity on the frontier of settlement in New Zealand (Phillips, 1987) and Australia (Lake, 1986).

Labor migration within the colonial system was a means by which existing gender practices were spread, but it was also a means by which they were reconstructed, as labor migration was a gendered process. Moodie's (1994) study of migrant labor in South African gold mines provides the classic analysis, tracing the reconstruction of men's gender practices in the space between capitalist mining and the pastoral homestead economy. Migration from the colonized world to the First World is also a mass process. Studies of the Mexican-origin population of the United States were among the earliest to explore the consequences of migration for masculinity (Baca Zinn, 1982) and have found an active renegotiation of gender relations. A traditionalist model of masculinity is reproduced, but with great variation according to class situation and the degree of ethnic exclusion being experienced. Poynting, Noble, and Tabar (1998), interviewing Lebanese male youth in Australia, similarly find contradictory gender consciousness and a strategic use of stereotypes in the face of racism. There is an assertion of dignity, but a masculine dignity, in a context that implies the subordination of women.

Men's bodies, of course, are capable of other practices besides labor. Violence is a relationship between bodies that has been of great importance in the history of masculinities and will be discussed further as we move on. Sexual practices are equally important. The process of economic development has for a long time been interwoven with population dynamics—both through "pronatalist" policies intended to build national strength and through population control policies intending to make possible a rising standard of living. As Figueroa-Perea and Rojas (1998) argue, although demography focuses on women as the unit of reproduction, the reproductive behavior of men is also a critical issue, especially where "fatherhood" is an important part of the cultural definition of masculinity. The population policies of the postcolonial state are thus likely to encounter, and may seek to change, some aspects of men's gendered definitions of their bodies.

The same is true of sexual health campaigns. It is now widely recognized that the shape and intensity of the HIV/AIDS epidemic is affected by economic circumstances, communications, and the pattern of gender relations. For instance, the high rates of HIV infection among contemporary South African gold miners are related to the construction of men's lives in an alienating and dangerous industry—a strong impulse to assert manhood, which in turn is understood as "going after women," and also a desire for intimate, "flesh-to-flesh" contact. "The very sense of masculinity that assists men in their day-to-day survival also serves to heighten their exposure to the risks of HIV infection" (Campbell, 2001, p. 282).

Bodies are never naked; they are always clothed with meaning. But the meanings may be reconstructed by imperialism and globalization. MacKenzie (1987) gives a historical example: the figure of the "imperial pioneer and hunter" in the Anglophone world of the late 19th century. Through the career of Baden-Powell, the founder of the Boy Scout movement, the colonial imagery of the outdoorsman was brought back to the metropole as an agenda for the education of boys. Through exemplary figures such as Theodore Roosevelt, it was fed into the repertoire of metropolitan politics. Viveros Vigoya's (2001) survey of Latin American research on masculinity gives a more current example: the changing definition of fatherhood. Contradictory situations are created when rising demands for men's involvement as fathers, in accordance with international trends, are confronted by growing autonomy on the part of women, also an international trend, or are blocked by economic dislocation resulting from the pressures of the global economy.

These relocations and reinterpretations of bodies create many possibilities for hybridization and change in gender imagery, sexuality, and other forms of practice. The movement is not always toward synthesis, however. The racial hierarchies of colonialism have been reasserted in new contexts, including the politics of the metropole. Ethnic and racial divisiveness has been growing in importance in recent years. As Klein (2000) argues in the case of Israel and Tillner (2000) in the case of Austria, this is a fruitful context for the production of masculinities oriented toward domination and violence.

MASCULINITY POLITICS ON A WORLD SCALE

The world gender order broadly privileges men over women. Although there are many local exceptions, there is a patriarchal dividend for men collectively, arising from higher incomes, higher labor force participation, unequal property ownership, and greater access to institutional power; there is also cultural and sexual privileging. This has been documented by international research on women's situation (Taylor, 1985; Valdés & Gomáriz, 1995), although its implications for men have mostly been ignored. The conditions thus exist for the production of a hegemonic masculinity on a world scale—that is to say, a dominant form of masculinity that embodies, organizes, and legitimates men's domination in the world gender order as a whole.

The inequalities of the world gender order, like the inequalities of local gender orders, produce resistance. The main pressure for change has come from an international feminist movement (Bulbeck, 1998). International cooperation among feminist groups goes back at least a century, although it is only in recent decades that a women's movement has established a strong presence in international forums. Mechanisms such as the 1979 Convention on the Elimination of all forms of Discrimination Against Women and the United Nations' Decade for Women (1975-1985) placed gender inequality on the diplomatic agenda. The follow-up 1995 Beijing Conference agreed on a detailed "Platform For Action," providing for international action on issues ranging from economic exclusion, women's health, and violence against women, to girls' education.

Equally important is the circulation of ideas, methods and examples of action. The presence of a worldwide feminist movement (however diverse and conflicted) and the undeniable fact of a worldwide debate about gender issues has intensified cultural pressure for change. In Japan, for instance, a range of women's organizations existed before 1970, but a new activism was sparked by the international women's liberation movement (Tanaka, 1977). This was reflected in genres such as girls' fiction and comic books with images of powerful women. Men, and men's cultural genres, gradually responded—sometimes with marked hostility. Ito (1992), tracing these changes, argues that established patterns of Japanese "men's culture" have collapsed, amid intensified debate about the situation of men. However, no new model of masculinity has become dominant.

With local variations, a similar course of events has occurred in many developed countries. Challenge and resistance, plus the disruptions involved in the creation of a world gender order, have meant many local instabilities in gender arrangements. These instabilities include the following:

- Contestation of all-male networks and sexist organizational culture as women move into political office, the bureaucracy, and higher education (Eisenstein, 1991)
- The disruption of sexual identities that produced "queer" politics and other challenges to gay identities in metropolitan countries (Seidman, 1996)
- The shifts in the urban intelligentsia that produced profeminist politics among heterosexual men (Pease, 1997)
- Media images of "the new sensitive man," the shoulder-padded businesswoman, and other icons of gender change

One response to such instabilities, on the part of groups whose power or identity is challenged, is to reaffirm local gender hierarchies. A masculine fundamentalism is, accordingly, an identifiable pattern in gender politics. Swart (2001) documents a striking case in South Africa, the paramilitary Afrikaner Weerstandsbeweging movement led by Eugene Terre Blanche, which attempts to mobilize Afrikaner men against the postapartheid regime. A cult of masculine toughness is interwoven with open racism; weapons are celebrated and women are explicitly excluded from authority. There are obvious similarities to the right-wing militia movement in the United States documented by Gibson (1994) and brought to world attention by the Oklahoma City bombing. Tillner (2000), discussing masculinity and racism in central Europe, notes evidence that it is not underprivileged youth specifically who are recruited to racism. Rather, it is young men oriented to dominance, an orientation that plays out in gender as well as race.

These fundamentalist reactions against gender change are spectacular but are not, I consider, the majority response among men. As noted earlier, there is considerable survey evidence of widespread acceptance of some measure of gender change (i.e., a swing of popular attitudes toward gender equality). This change of attitudes, however, need not result in much change of organizational practice. For instance, Fuller (2001) remarks that despite changes of opinion among Peruvian men,

> the realms in which masculine solidarity networks are constructed that guarantee access to networks of influence, alliances, and support are reproduced through a masculine culture of sports, alcohol consumption, visits to whorehouses, or stories about sexual conquests. These mechanisms assure a monopoly of, or, at least, differential access by men to the public sphere and are a key part of the system of power in which masculinity is forged. (p. 325)

I would argue that this practical recuperation of gender change is a more widespread, and more successful, form of reaction among men than masculine fundamentalism is. Such recuperation is supported by neoliberalism. The neoliberal agenda for the reform of national and international economies involves closing down historic possibilities for gender reform. It subverts the gender compromise represented by the metropolitan welfare state. It undermines the progressive-liberal agendas of sex role reform represented by affirmative action programs, antidiscrimination provisions, child-care services, and the like. Right-wing parties and governments have been persistently cutting such programs in the name of either individual liberties or global competitiveness. Through these means, the patriarchal dividend to men is defended or restored, without an explicit masculinity politics in the form of a mobilization of men.

Within the global arena of international relations, the international state, multinational corporations, and global markets, there is, nevertheless, a deployment of masculinities. Two models of the state of play in this arena have recently been offered.

In a previous paper (Connell, 1998), I proposed that the transnational business masculinity I have described here has achieved a position of hegemony. This has replaced older local models of bourgeois masculinity, which were more embedded in local organizations and local conservative cultures, in a process well described by Roper's (1994) study of British manufacturing managers. In global arenas, it has had only one major contender for hegemony in recent decades: the rigid, control-oriented masculinity of the military, with its variant in the militarized bureaucratic dictatorships of Stalinism. With the collapse of Stalinism and the end of the Cold War, the more flexible, calculating, egocentric masculinity of the new capitalist entrepreneur holds the world stage. The political leadership of the major powers, through such figures as Clinton, Schröder, and Blair, for a while conformed to this model of masculinity, working out a nonthreatening accommodation with feminism.

Transnational business masculinity, however, is not homogeneous. A Confucian variant, based in East Asia, has a stronger commitment to hierarchy and social consensus; a secularized "Christian" variant, based in North America, has more hedonism and individualism, as well as greater tolerance for social conflict. In certain arenas, there is already conflict between the business and political leaderships embodying these forms of masculinity. Such conflicts have arisen over "human rights" versus "Asian values" and over the extent of trade and investment liberalization.

Focusing more on international politics than on business, Hooper (1998) also suggests a pattern of hegemony in the masculinities of global arenas. A tough, power-oriented masculinity predominates in the arena of diplomacy, war, and power politics—distanced from the feminized world of domesticity but also distinguished from other masculinities, such as those of working class men, subordinated ethnic groups, wimps, and homosexuals. This is not just a matter of preexisting masculinity being expressed in international politics. Hooper argues that international politics is a primary site for the construction of masculinities; for instance, in war or through continuing security threats. Hooper further argues that recent globalization trends have "softened" hegemonic masculinity in several ways. Ties with the military have been loosened, with a world trend toward demilitarization—the total numbers of men in world armies have fallen significantly in the last 15 years. Men are now more often positioned as consumers, and contemporary management gives more emphasis to traditionally "feminine" qualities such as interpersonal skills and teamwork. Hooper also comments on the interplay of North American with Japanese corporate culture, noting some convergence and borrowing in both directions in the context of global restructuring.

Although the "softening" of hegemonic masculinity spoken of by Hooper (1998), Connell (1998), Niva (1998), and Messner (1993) is real enough, it does not mean the obliteration of "harder" masculinities. The election of George W. Bush to the U.S. presidency, the political aftermath of the attack on the World Trade Center in New York, and the remobilization of nationalism and military force in the United States culminating in the attack on Iraq in 2003 show that hard-line political leadership is still possible in the remaining superpower. It has never gone away in China. Bush's distinctive combination of U.S. nationalism, religiosity, support for corporate interests, and rejection of alternative points of view is not, perhaps, an easily exported model of masculinity. But local equivalents might be forged elsewhere.

If these are contenders for hegemony, they are not the only articulations of masculinity in global forums. The international circulation of gay identities, discussed earlier, is an important indication that nonhegemonic masculinities may operate in global arenas. They can find political expression, for instance, around human rights and AIDS prevention (Altman, 2001).

Another political alternative is provided by counterhegemonic movements opposed to the current world gender order and the groups dominant in it. They are sometimes associated with the promotion of "new masculinities," but they also address masculinity as an obstacle to the reform of gender relations. The largest and best known are the profeminist men's groups in the United States, with their umbrella group NOMAS (National Organization of Men Against Sexism), a group that has been active since the early 1980s (Cohen, 1991). More globally oriented is the "White Ribbon" campaign, originating in Canada as a remarkably successful mobilization to oppose men's violence against women, and now working internationally (Kaufman, 1999).

Such movements, groups, or reform agendas exist in many countries, including Germany ("Multioptionale Männlichkeiten?" 1998), Britain (Seidler, 1991), Australia (Pease, 1997), Mexico (Zingoni, 1998), Russia (Sinelnikov, 2000), India (Roy, 2003), and the Nordic countries (Oftung, 2000). The spectrum of issues they address is well illustrated by the conference of the Japanese men's movement in Kyoto in 1996. This conference included sessions on youth, gay issues, work, child rearing, bodies, and communications with women—as well as the globalization of the men's movement (Menzu Senta, 1997).

Most of these movements and groups are small, and some are short-lived. They have, however, been a presence in gender politics since the 1970s and have built up a body of experience and ideas. These are circulated internationally by translations and republications of writings, by traveling activists and researchers, and through intergovernmental agencies. Recently, some international agencies, including the Council of Europe (Ólafsdóttir, 2000), FLACSO (Valdés & Olavarría, 1998), and UNESCO (Breines, Connell, & Eide, 2000), sponsored the first conferences to discuss the implications for public policy of the new perspectives on masculinity. The role of men in achieving gender equality emerged as an issue in the Program for Action that emerged from the 1995 Beijing world conference on women, and a number of United Nations agencies are currently involved

with discussions and policy formation in this area (United Nations Division for the Advancement of Women, 2003). It seems that issues about changing men and masculinities have arrived on the international agenda.

CONCLUSION

The issues discussed in this chapter have only recently come into focus. The earliest discussion I know of masculinities and global change was in a special issue of the magazine *New Internationalist* in September 1987, and that was very exploratory (Brazier, 1987). Actual research on men and masculinities in transnational arenas is still rare. Most of the arguments in this chapter have been built up from indications in studies that have other primary concerns. Yet the issues discussed here seem of great importance. They bear on questions of peace and war, global inequalities and economic change, as well as change in intimate relationships and identities. I hope this tentative synthesis will help to stimulate research and debate.

NOTE

1. By *metropole* I mean the group of rich countries, mostly former imperial powers, that form the core of the world capitalist economy.

REFERENCES

Allen, C. (Ed.). (1975). *Plain tales from the Raj: Images of British India in the twentieth century.* London: Andre Deutsch.

Altman, D. (2001). *Global sex.* Chicago: University of Chicago Press.

Baca Zinn, M. (1982). Chicano men and masculinity. *Journal of Ethnic Studies, 10*(2), 31-44.

Bauman, Z. (1998). *Globalization: The human consequences.* Cambridge, England: Polity Press.

Bitterli, U. (1989). *Cultures in conflict: Encounters between European and non-European cultures, 1492-1800.* Stanford, CA: Stanford University Press.

Brazier, C. (Ed.). (1987, September). Birth of a new man: The politics of masculinity. *New Internationalist*, (175, Special issue).

Breines, I., Connell, R., & Eide, I. (Eds.). (2000). *Male roles, masculinities and violence: A culture of peace perspective.* Paris: UNESCO Publishing.

Breines, I., Gierycz, D., & Reardon, B. (Eds.). (1999). *Towards a women's agenda for a culture of peace.* Paris: UNESCO Publishing.

Bulbeck, C. (1992). *Australian women in Papua New Guinea: Colonial passages 1920-1960.* Cambridge, England: Cambridge University Press.

Bulbeck, C. (1998). *Re-orienting Western feminisms: Women's diversity in a postcolonial world.* Cambridge, England: Cambridge University Press.

Cain, P. J., & Hopkins, A. G. (1993). *British imperialism: Innovation and expansion, 1688-1914.* New York: Longman.

Campbell, C. (2001). "Going underground and going after women": Masculinity and HIV transmission amongst black workers on the gold mines. In R. Morrell (Ed.), *Changing men in Southern Africa* (pp. 275-286). Pietermaritzburg, South Africa: University of Natal Press.

Campbell, H., & Bell, M. M. (2000). The question of rural masculinities. *Rural Sociology, 65*(4), 532-546.

Chang, K. A., & Ling, L. H. M. (2000). Globalization and its intimate other: Filipina domestic workers in Hong Kong. In M. H. Marchand & A. S. Runyan (Eds.), *Gender and global restructuring* (pp. 27-43). London: Routledge.

Cock, J. (2001). Gun violence and masculinity in contemporary South Africa. In R. Morrell (Ed.), *Changing men in Southern Africa* (pp. 43-55). Pietermaritzburg, South Africa: University of Natal Press.

Cockburn, C. (1983). *Brothers: Male dominance and technological change.* London: Pluto.

Cohen, J. (1991, Winter/Spring). NOMAS: Challenging male supremacy. *Changing Men, 10,* 45-46.

Connell, R. W. (1995). *Masculinities.* Cambridge, England: Polity Press.

Connell, R. W. (1998). Masculinities and globalization. *Men and Masculinities, 1*(1), 3-23.

Connell, R. W. (2002). *Gender.* Cambridge, England: Polity Press.

Corman, J., Luxton, M., Livingstone, D. W., & Seccombe, W. (1993). *Recasting steel labour: The Stelco story.* Halifax, NS: Fernwood.

Cunneen, C., & Stubbs, J. (2000). Male violence, male fantasy and the commodification of women through the Internet. In *Domestic violence: Global responses* (pp. 5-28). Bicester, England: AB Academic.

Dasgupta, R. (2000). Performing masculinities? The "salaryman" at work and play. *Japanese Studies, 20*(2), 189-200.

Davis, R. (1997, June). *Engagement and transformation in Torres Strait Islander masculinity.* Paper presented at the "Masculinities: Renegotiating Genders" conference, University of Wollongong, Australia.

Dawson, G. (1991). The blond Bedouin: Lawrence of Arabia, imperial adventure and the imagining of English-British masculinity. In M. Roper & J. Tosh (Eds.), *Manful assertions: Masculinities in Britain since 1800* (pp. 113-144). London: Routledge.

Dine, P. (1994). *Images of the Algerian war: French fiction and film, 1954-1992.* Oxford, England: Clarendon Press.

Donaldson, M. (1998). Growing up very rich: The masculinity of the hegemonic. *Journal of Interdisciplinary Gender Studies, 3*(2), 95-112.

Eisenstein, H. (1991). *Gender shock: Practising feminism on two continents.* Sydney: Allen & Unwin.

Enloe, C. (1990). *Bananas, beaches and bases: Making feminist sense of international politics.* Berkeley: University of California Press.

Figueroa-Perea, J.-G., & Rojas, O. L. (1998, May). *Some characteristics of the reproductive process of males.* Paper presented at the seminar on "Men, Family Formation and Reproduction," Buenos Aires.

Fonseca, C. (2001). Philanderers, cuckolds, and wily women: A re-examination of gender relations in a Brazilian working-class neighbourhood. *Men and Masculinities, 3*(3), 261-277.

Fuentes, A., & Ehrenreich, B. (1983). *Women in the global factory.* Boston: South End Press.

Fuller, N. (2001). The social construction of gender identity among Peruvian men. *Men and Masculinities, 3*(3), 316-331.

Gee, J. P., Hull, G., & Lankshear, C. (1996). *The new work order: Behind the language of the new capitalism.* Sydney: Allen & Unwin.

Ghoussoub, M. (2000). Chewing gum, insatiable women and foreign enemies: Male fears and the Arab media. In M. Ghoussoub & E. Sinclair-Webb (Eds.), *Imagined masculinities* (pp. 227-235). London: Saqi Books.

Gibson, J. W. (1994). *Warrior dreams: Paramilitary culture in post-Vietnam America.* New York: Hill and Wang.

Gierycz, D. (1999). Women in decision-making: Can we change the status quo? In I. Breines, D. Gierycz, & B. Reardon (Eds.), *Towards a women's agenda for a culture of peace* (pp. 19-32). Paris: UNESCO.

Gittings, C. E. (Ed.). (1996). *Imperialism and gender: Constructions of masculinity.* Hebden Bridge, England: Dangaroo Press.

Glass Ceiling Commission. (1995). *Good for business: Making full use of the nation's human capital. The environmental scan.* Washington, DC: Author.

Gutmann, M. C. (1996). *The meanings of macho: Being a man in Mexico City.* Berkeley: University of California Press.

Hearn, J., & Parkin, W. (2001). *Gender, sexuality and violence in organizations.* London: Sage.

Hirst, P., & Thompson, G. (1996). *Globalization in question: The international economy and the possibilities of governance.* Cambridge, England: Polity Press.

Holden, p. (1998). The significance of uselessness: Resisting colonial masculinity in Philip Jeyaretnam's *Abraham's Promise. Jouvert,* 2(1). Retrieved December 22, 2003, from http://social.chass.ncsu.edu/jouvert/v2i1/Holden.htm

Holter, Ø. G. (1996). Authoritarianism and masculinity. *International Association for Studies of Men Newsletter,* 3(1), 18-35.

Holter, Ø. G. (2003). A theory of gender, patriarchy and capitalism. In S. Ervø & T. Johansson (Eds.), *Among men: Moulding masculinities* (Vol. 1, pp. 29-43). Aldershot, England: Ashgate.

Hooper, C. (1998). Masculinist practices and gender politics: The operation of multiple masculinities in international relations. In M. Zalewski & J. Parpart (Eds.), *The "man" question in international relations* (pp. 28-53). Boulder, CO: Westview.

Hooper, C. (2000). Masculinities in transition: The case of globalization. In M. H. Marchand & A. S. Runyan (Eds.), *Gender and global restructuring* (pp. 59-73). London: Routledge.

Ito, K. (1992). Cultural change and gender identity trends in the 1970s and 1980s. *International Journal of Japanese Sociology,* (1), 79-98.

Jolly, M. (1997). From Point Venus to Bali Ha'i: Eroticism and exoticism in representations of the Pacific. In L. Manderson & M. Jolly (Eds.), *Sites of desire, economies of pleasure* (pp. 99-122). Chicago: University of Chicago Press.

Kandiyoti, D. (1994). The paradoxes of masculinity: Some thoughts on segregated societies. In A. Cornwall & N. Lindisfarne (Eds.), *Dislocating masculinity: Comparative ethnographies* (pp. 197-213). London: Routledge.

Kaufman, M. (Ed.). (1999). Men and violence. *International Association for Studies of Men Newsletter,* 6(Special issue).

Kimmel, M. S. (1996). *Manhood in America: A cultural history.* New York: Free Press.

Kinmonth, E. H. (1981). *The self-made man in Meiji Japanese thought: From samurai to salary man.* Berkeley: University of California Press.

Klein, U. (2000). "Our best boys": The making of masculinity in Israeli society. In I. Breines, R. Connell, & I. Eide (Eds.), *Male roles, masculinities and violence: A culture of peace perspective* (pp. 163-179). Paris: UNESCO.

Kondo, D. (1999). Fabricating masculinity: Gender, race, and nation in a transnational frame. In C. Kaplan, N. Alarcón, & M. Moallam (Eds.), *Between woman and nation* (pp. 296-319). Durham, NC: Duke University Press.

Lake, M. (1986). The politics of respectability: Identifying the masculinist context. *Historical Studies,* 22(86), 116-131.

Lechner, F. J., & Boli, J. (Eds.). (2000). *The globalization reader.* Oxford, England: Blackwell.

MacDonald, R. H. (1994). *The language of empire: Myths and metaphors of popular imperialism, 1880-1918.* Manchester, England: Manchester University Press.

MacKenzie, J. M. (1987). The imperial pioneer and hunter and the British masculine stereotype in late Victorian and Edwardian times. In J. A. Mangan & J. Walvin (Eds.), *Manliness and morality* (pp. 176-198). Manchester, England: Manchester University Press.

Mellen, J. (1978). *Big bad wolves: Masculinity in the American film.* London: Elm Tree Books.

Menzu Senta [Men's Centre Japan]. (1997). *Otokotachi no watashisagashi* [How are men seeking their new selves?]. Kyoto, Japan: Kamogawa.

Messner, M. A. (1992). *Power at play: Sports and the problem of masculinity.* Boston: Beacon Press.

Messner, M. A. (1993). "Changing men" and feminist politics in the United States. *Theory and Society,* 22(5), 723-737.

Messner, M. A. (1997). *The politics of masculinities: Men in movements.* Thousand Oaks, CA: Sage.

Mies, M. (1986). *Patriarchy and accumulation on a world scale: Women in the international division of labour.* London: Zed.

Moodie, T. D. (1994). *Going for gold: Men, mines, and migration.* Johannesburg, South Africa: Witwatersrand University Press.

Morrell, R. (Ed.). (2001a). *Changing men in Southern Africa.* Pietermaritzburg, South Africa: University of Natal Press.

Morrell, R. (2001b). *From boys to gentlemen: Settler masculinity in colonial Natal.* Pretoria: University of South Africa Press.

Multioptionale Männlichkeiten? [Multi-option masculinities?]. (1998). *Widersprüche, 67* (Special issue).

Nagel, J. (1998). Masculinity and nationalism: Gender and sexuality in the making of nations. *Ethnic and Racial Studies, 21*(2), 242-269.

Niva, S. (1998). Tough and tender: New world order masculinity and the Gulf War. In M. Zalewski & J. Parpart (Eds.), *The "man" question in international relations* (pp. 109-128). Boulder, CO: Westview Press.

Novikova, I. (2000). Soviet and post-soviet masculinities: After men's wars in women's memories. In I. Breines, R. Connell, & I. Eide (Eds.), *Male roles, masculinities and violence: A culture of peace perspective* (pp. 117-129). Paris: UNESCO.

O'Donnell, M., & Sharpe, S. (2000). *Uncertain masculinities: Youth, ethnicity and class in contemporary Britain.* London: Routledge.

Oftung, K. (2000). Men and gender equality in the Nordic countries. In I. Breines, R. Connell, & I. Eide (Eds.), *Male roles, masculinities and violence: A culture of peace perspective* (pp. 143-162). Paris: UNESCO.

Ólafsdóttir, O. (2000). Statement. In I. Breines, R. Connell, & I. Eide (Eds.), *Male roles, masculinities and violence: A culture of peace perspective* (pp. 281-283). Paris: UNESCO.

Ouzgane, L., & Coleman, D. (1998). Postcolonial masculinities: Introduction. *Jouvert, 2*(1). Retrieved December 22, 2003, from http://social.chass.ncsu.edu/jouvert/v2i1/int21.htm.

Parker, R. (1985). Masculinity, femininity, and homosexuality: On the anthropological interpretation of sexual meanings in Brazil. *Journal of Homosexuality, 11*(3-4), 155-163.

Pearlman, C. L. (1984). Machismo, marianismo and change in indigenous Mexico: A case study from Oaxaca. *Quarterly Journal of Ideology, 8*(4), 53-59.

Pease, B. (1997). *Men and sexual politics: Towards a profeminist practice.* Adelaide, Australia: Dulwich Centre.

Peteet, J. (1994). Male gender and rituals of resistance in the Palestinian Intifada: A cultural politics of violence. *American Ethnologist, 21*(1), 31-49.

Phillips, J. (1987). *A man's country? The image of the Pakeha male: A history.* Auckland, New Zealand: Penguin.

Poynting, S., Noble, G., & Tabar, P. (1998). "If anyone called me a wog, they wouldn't be speaking to me alone": Protest masculinity and Lebanese youth in Western Sydney. *Journal of Interdisciplinary Gender Studies, 3*(2), 76-94.

Roper, M. (1994). *Masculinity and the British organization man since 1945.* Oxford, England: Oxford University Press.

Roy, R. (2003). *Exploring masculinities: A travelling seminar.* Unpublished manuscript, New Delhi.

Seidler, V. J. (1991). *Achilles heel reader: Men, sexual politics and socialism.* London: Routledge.

Seidman, S. (Ed.). (1996). *Queer theory/sociology.* Oxford, England: Blackwell.

Shire, C. (1994). Men don't go to the moon: Language, space and masculinities in Zimbabwe. In A. Cornwall & N. Lindisfarne (Eds.), *Dislocating masculinity* (pp. 147-158). London: Routledge.

Simpson, A. (1993). *Xuxa: The mega-marketing of gender, race and modernity.* Philadelphia: Temple University Press.

Sinelnikov, A. (2000). Masculinity à la Russe: Gender issues in the Russian Federation today. In I. Breines, R. Connell, & I. Eide (Eds.), *Male roles, masculinities and violence: A culture of peace perspective* (pp. 201-209). Paris: UNESCO.

Sinha, M. (1995). *Colonial masculinity: The "manly Englishman" and the "effeminate Bengali" in the late nineteenth century.* Manchester, England: Manchester University Press.

Smith, S. (1998). "Unacceptable conclusions" and the "man" question: Masculinity, gender, and international relations. In M. Zalewski & J. Parpart (Eds.), *The "man" question in international relations* (pp. 54-72). Boulder, CO: Westview Press.

Swart, S. (2001). "Man, gun and horse": Hard right Afrikaner masculine identity in post-apartheid South Africa. In R. Morrell (Ed.), *Changing men in Southern Africa* (pp. 75-89). Pietermaritzburg, South Africa: University of Natal Press.

Taga, F. (2001). *Dansei no jendâ keisei: "Otokorashisa" no yuragi no naka de* [The gender formation of men: Uncertain masculinity]. Tokyo: Tôyôkan Shuppan-sha.

Tanaka, K. (1977). *A short history of the women's movement in modern Japan* (3rd ed.). Tokyo: Femintern Press.

Taylor, D. (1985). Women: An analysis. In *Women: A world report* (pp. 1-98). London: Methuen.

Tillner, G. (2000). The identity of dominance: Masculinity and xenophobia. In I. Breines, R. Connell, & I. Eide (Eds.), *Male roles, masculinities and violence: A culture of peace perspective* (pp. 53-59). Paris: UNESCO.

Tomsen, S. (1997). A top night: Social protest, masculinity and the culture of drinking violence. *British Journal of Criminology, 37*(1), 90-103.

United Nations Division for the Advancement of Women. (2003, June 30–July 25). *The role of men and boys in achieving gender equality* (Online discussion). Retrieved December 22, 2003, from http://esaconf.un.org/~gender-equality-role-men-boys

Valdés, T., & Gomáriz, E. (1995). *Latin American women: Compared figures.* Santiago, Chile: Instituto de la Mujer and FLACSO.

Valdés, T., & Olavarría, J. (1998). Ser hombre en Santiago de Chile: A pesar de todo, un mismo modelo [To be a man in Santiago, Chile: Despite all, a model]. In T. Valdés & J. Olavarría (Eds.), *Masculinidades y equidad de género en América Latina* [Masculinities and gender equity in Latin America] (pp. 12-36). Santiago, Chile: FLACSO/UNFPA.

Viveros Vigoya, M. (2001). Contemporary Latin American perspectives on masculinity. *Men and Masculinities, 3*(3), 237-260.

Waetjen, T., & Maré, G. (2001). "Men amongst men": Masculinity and Zulu nationalism in the 1980s.

In R. Morrell (Ed.), *Changing men in Southern Africa* (pp. 195-206). Pietermaritzburg, South Africa: University of Natal Press.

Wajcman, J. (1999). *Managing like a man: Women and men in corporate management.* Sydney: Allen & Unwin.

Wetherell, M., & Edley, N. (1999). Negotiating hegemonic masculinity: Imaginary positions and psycho-discursive practices. *Feminism and Psychology, 9*(3), 335-356.

White, S. C. (2000). "Did the earth move?" The hazards of bringing men and masculinities into gender and development. *IDS Bulletin, 31*(2), 33-41.

Williams, W. L. (1986). *The spirit and the flesh: Sexual diversity in American Indian culture.* Boston: Beacon Press.

Winter, M. F., & Robert, E. R. (1980). Male dominance, late capitalism, and the growth of instrumental reason. *Berkeley Journal of Sociology, (24-25),* 249-280.

Xaba, T. (2001). Masculinity and its malcontents: The confrontation between "struggle masculinity" and "post-struggle masculinity" (1990-1997). In R. Morrell (Ed.), *Changing men in Southern Africa* (pp. 105-124). Pietermaritzburg, South Africa: University of Natal Press.

Zalewski, M., & Parpart, J. (Eds.). (1998). *The "man" question in international relations.* Boulder, CO: Westview Press.

Zingoni, E. L. (1998). Masculinidades y violencia desde un programa de acción en México [A Mexican program of action on masculinities and violence]. In T. Valdés & J. Olavarría (Eds.), Masculinidades y equidad de género en América Latina (pp. 130-136). Santiago, Chile: FLACSO/UNFPA.

Zulehner, P. M., & Volz, R. (1998). *Männer im Aufbruch: Wie Deutschlands Männer sich Selbst und wie Frauen Sie Sehen* [Men awakening: How German men see themselves and how women see them]. Ostfildern, Germany: Schwabenverlag.

6

MEN IN THE THIRD WORLD

Postcolonial Perspectives on Masculinity

ROBERT MORRELL

SANDRA SWART

This chapter examines men and masculinity in the postcolonial world, a world formerly controlled by European colonizers. It considers how men and masculinity have been analyzed using a number of different theories and literatures and suggests that the specific gender conditions of the postcolonial world require a flexible, yet syncretic, approach if their lives are to be understood and, more important, appreciated and improved.

Our starting point is that the world still bears the mark of colonialism. The World Bank, for example, divides the world into two economic categories: "more developed regions"—Europe, North America, Australia, New Zealand, and Japan—and "less developed regions"—the rest of the world. A further sub-category (a part of the less developed regions that includes the poorest countries of the world) is "Sub-Saharan Africa." There is still good reason to talk about the dichotomy between the metropole and the periphery and about

the developed and developing worlds. These concepts are crude, sometimes misleading, and often inaccurate. Yet they retain an undeniable truth. As a shorthand, for all its shortcomings, we shall in this chapter be using the term *Third World* to refer to the un- and underdeveloped regions concentrated in South America, Africa, and parts of Asia, an area often termed "the South" to distinguish its state from the industrialized and wealthy "North."

The differences between the First and Third Worlds can be found in the statistics shown in Table 6.1.

People in different parts of the world have hugely divergent experiences of life. We can make some generalizations that will underpin this study. Many babies never make it to their first birthdays, and those who achieve this live in poverty for much of their lives. Many will live in rural areas, with little access to the technology that people in the more developed world rely on. And the situation is getting worse: The share

Authors' note: We would like to thank R. W. Connell and Jeff Hearn for their helpful comments on this chapter.

Table 6.1   Differences Between the First and Third Worlds

	Births per 1000 of Population	Deaths per 1000 of Population	Infant Mortality Rate	Life Expectancy at Birth (Total)	Life Expectancy at Birth (Male)	Life Expectancy at Birth (Female)	Percentage of Urban Population
More developed	11	10	8	75	72	79	75
Less developed	25	8	61	64	63	66	40
Sub-Saharan Africa	41	15	94	51	49	52	30

SOURCE: Population Reference Bureau (2001a, p. 2).

of the poorest 20% of the world's population in the global economy in 1960 was 2.3%; in 1997 it was down to 1.1% (Heward, 1999, p. 9). Beyond this generalization, there are gender differentiations, which this chapter will explore.

The Third World is still portrayed in the mass media in ways that Edward Said (1978) explained in terms of the concept "orientalism." The (mostly) black people of the Third World were "othered." Despite the vigorous debates about such (mis)representation, the Third World is nonetheless represented as a combination of emaciated children, crying women, and men engaged in war. These gendered portrayals both reflect global disparities and gravely misrepresent them. In this chapter, we set out to see how these global inequalities can be understood in gendered terms. Following the main thrust of critical men's studies, we move beyond gendered essentialisms to examine how different masculinities are constructed and how men are positioned and act in the world. It is important from the outset to note that there has been little analysis of men and masculinity in the Third World. Anthropologists have left a rich description of the doings of men, although seldom have these been put into a conscious gender frame, and rarely have these scholars incorporated the history of colonial and postcolonial society into their ethnographic accounts (Finnström, 1997). Two works consciously working from a critical men's studies perspective provide exceptions to this generalization in South Africa (Morrell, 2001) and South America (Gutmann, 2001). It is surprising that the emergence of postcolonial theory, with a strong element of feminism in it, has done little to rectify this omission, although,

as we show in the third section of this chapter, the general approach has the potential both to focus theoretical light on men in the periphery and to prompt new angles of research into masculinity that give greater weight to alternative paradigms (particularly, indigenous knowledge systems).

SOME HISTORICAL AND THEORETICAL STARTING POINTS

Postcolonialism refers to the period after colonialism. Although the impact of colonialism is contested, we take it to refer to a phase in world history beginning in the early 16th century that eventually, by 1914, saw Europe hold sway over more than 85% of the rest of the globe.

Another meaning of colonialism refers to the political ideologies that legitimated the modern occupation and exploitation of already settled lands by external powers. For the indigenous populations, it meant the suppression of resistance, the imposition of alien laws, and the parasitic consumption of natural resources, including human labor.

Colonialism was a highly gendered process. In the first instance, it was driven by gendered metropolitan forces and reflected the gender order of the metropole. The economies of Europe from the 16th century onward were geared toward the colonies. The men who were engaged in conquest and those who were absorbed into industry producing and profiting from the subordination of large parts of the world, working and ruling classes together, were complicit in exploitative practices, the most brutal of which was the nearly three-century-long trans-Atlantic slave trade. Europe's Enlightenment ambitions, fused with its colonial past, were based on the power and symbolic potency of the nation-state. Today the process of the transnational economy spells the decline of nation-states as principals of economic and political organization. The decline of the nation-state and the end of colonialism also marks the concomitant historical crisis of the values it represented, chiefly masculine authority founded and embodied in the patriarchal family, compulsory heterosexuality, and the exchange of women—all articulated in the crucible of imperial masculinity.

As many have argued—from one of the first Africanist historians, Basil Davidson (1961), to the historian of the transatlantic diaspora and its cultural impact, Paul Gilroy (1993)—the slave trade changed the meaning of "race" and produced an equation of *black* with *inferiority*. Much of the research on race (Hoch, 1979; Staples, 1982; Stecopoulos & Uebel, 1997) is still trying to make sense of the way in which masculinities in the 20th century were shaped by the systematic elaboration of racist discourses. A derivative of recent theoretical advances has been to examine how the experience of race in the colonies (Stoler, 1989) influenced class relations and identities in the metropole (Hall, 1992) and how metropolitan ideas travelled into the periphery (Johnson, 2001). In *Imperial Leather,* Anne McClintock (1995) argues that to understand colonialism and postcolonialism, one must first recognize that race, gender, and class are not "distinct realms of experience, existing in splendid isolation from each other"; rather, they come into existence in relation to each other, albeit in conflictual ways. Others have argued before her that the Victorians connected race, class, and gender in ways that promoted imperialism abroad and classism at home, but McClintock argues that these connections proved crucial to the development of Western modernity. "Imperialism," she explains,

is not something that happened elsewhere—a disagreeable fact of history external to Western identity. Rather, imperialism and the invention of race were fundamental aspects of Western, industrial modernity. The invention of race in the urban metropoles . . . became central not only to the self-definition of the middle class but also to the

policing of the "dangerous classes": the working class, the Irish, Jews, prostitutes, feminists, gays and lesbians, criminals, the militant crowd and so on. At the same time, the cult of domesticity was not simply a trivial and fleeting irrelevance, belonging properly in the private, "natural" realm of the family. Rather, I argue that the cult of domesticity was a crucial, if concealed, dimension of male as well as female identities—shifting and unstable as these were. (McClintock, 1995, p. 5)

In his chapter in this volume, R. W. Connell (see Chapter 5) argues for the need to look beyond ethnography and local studies to comprehend how globalization is shaping gender power in the 21st century. In this chapter, we argue that a necessary complement to this approach is the need to recognize what anthropologists used to call "the Fourth World"—a world that policies of modernization did not touch, where life continued much as it had always done except that the ecological consequences of advanced industrialization were experienced catastrophically in climate change and attendant natural disasters. Added to this is the need to examine contexts wherein development has failed and people no longer believe in the promise of progress. In large parts of the world, people today are poorer than they were half a century ago. In most instances, the slide into poverty has not been linear but has been punctuated by moments of material improvement. There are few places in the world that still harbor the illusion that, in material terms at least, things will get better soon.

Globalization has been described as another form of colonialism or imperialism. It has not "corrected" the legacies of the uneven march of capitalism or the differential impacts of imperialism (Golding & Harris, 1997). Instead, globalization has fostered media and cultural imperialism. Information technologies have disseminated Hollywood images around the world, giving an illusion of a homogeneous global culture. This does not mean, as Anthony Appiah (1991) emphatically remarks, "that it is the culture of every person in the world" (p. 343). And, as Nyamnjoh contends, "globalization does not necessarily or even frequently imply homogenization or Americanization, [as] different societies tend to be quite creative in their appropriation or consumption of the materials of modernity" (Appadurai, 1996, p. 17; Gray, 1998). However, he concedes that the developing world continues to bear the brunt of the risk and volatility associated with the exploitation of information technologies and markets.

Before turning to the different literatures that bear on postcolonial men and masculinity, it is important to note that the term *postcolonial* refers inexactly to a political and geographical terrain. On occasion, the term includes countries that have yet to achieve independence, or people in the developed world who are minorities, or even independent colonies that now contend with "neocolonial" forms of subjugation through expanding global capitalism. In all of these ways, postcolonial, rather than indicating only a specific and materially historical event, seems to describe the second half of the 20th century in general as a period in the aftermath of the zenith of colonialism. Even more generically, postcolonial is used to denote a position against imperialism and Eurocentrism. Although technically postcolonial, Canada, the United States, and Australia, for example, are seldom analyzed in this paradigm (although, see, as a counter, Coleman, 1998). Western ways of knowledge production and propagation then become objects of scrutiny for those seeking alternative means of expression. The term thus yokes a diverse range of experiences, cultures, and problems.

ANALYZING POSTCOLONIALISM: THREE APPROACHES

This section examines three different literatures (postcolonial theory, writings on indigenous knowledge, and work on gender and development). All are, in one way or another, a response to postcolonialism. We start out by considering the reasons for the emergence of postcolonial theory and look at the intellectual and political climate that spawned it. We then show how this new theory attempts to offer an alternative reading of agency and subjectivity and, at the same time, tackles the issue of representation and power in the periphery.

The second body of writing makes a claim for the status of indigenous knowledge. This is a type of knowledge that is site specific and claims no universal validity. Historically, it predates colonialism. It has been attacked and marginalized by the processes of colonialism, yet seldom has it been totally destroyed. It

therefore belongs to and is possessed by indigenous, formerly colonized peoples. This type of knowledge offers different ways of understanding the world and making sense of life and death. Its assumptions are normally quite different from those seen in Western, subject-centered frames. For example, human existence is understood in terms of communal and environmental belonging rather than as something intrinsically related to the fact of an individual's birth.

The claims made on behalf of indigenous knowledge have been generated by postcolonial conditions and the perceived condescension of the First World for the Third. Objecting to the imperial gaze, Third World writers, instead of using the sophisticated theoretical tools of postmodernism, have trawled the past and interrogated cultural practices in the attempt to give indigenous knowledge appropriate status in the world. Indigenous knowledge claims autonomy and independence from metropolitan knowledge. It offers new ways of understanding the world that are sometimes at odds with Western ways. It is, to use current South African and pan-African terminology, an attempt at a renaissance—to recover "old" ways of understanding and to restore "old," lost, or forgotten ways of doing. As with postcolonial theory, one of the major concerns of indigenous knowledge is to reclaim agency and black (Third World) voices.

The third body of work (the gender and development literature) engages with postcolonialism in terms of ongoing inequality between the First and Third Worlds. It responds to the challenge that this poses for an international community formally committed to human rights and equality. This literature is not so much concerned with representation as with actually effecting improvement in material life. Contributors speak from both metropolitan and Third World contexts as they collectively try to find effective ways of reducing inequality and promoting growth. This literature has been much more sensitive to debates about gender and masculinity than the first two, partly because the language of the international community (especially agencies of the United Nations) has been particularly receptive to developments in gender theory and responsive to the suggestion that a gender (and latterly a masculinity) lens be used to assist the delivery of development projects.

Postcolonial Theory

Postcolonial theory is not a coherent body of writing or theorization. In fact, its realm is contested, and writers who ostensibly belong together as "postcolonial theorists" dispute its political mission and ambit. Its rise and entrenchment in academia may arguably be dated from the publication of Edward Said's influential critique of Western constructions of the Orient in his 1978 book, *Orientalism*. Its origins are diverse. It is easier to follow these if we recognize a basic split in postcolonial theory, one that Moore-Gilbert (1997) characterizes as postcolonial *theory* and postcolonial *criticism*. Postcolonial theory draws on postmodern theory to unpick the modernist project, exposing its twin nature: freedom, self-determination, reason—and yet also submission, marginalization, and inadequacy of the "other." Postcolonial theory is primarily associated with "the holy trinity" (Young, 1995, p. 165): Said, Homi Bhabha, and Gayatri Spivak. What unites them is their intellectual debt to postmodern writers, their focus on the importance of culture, and their political opposition to the cultural domination of the West. All three are based in prestigious Western universities, something that has made some critics skeptical of the sincerity of their work.

The originality of their work is best appreciated by contrasting it with the work of Marxist scholars like Andre Gunder Frank (1971, 1978) and Colin Leys who, in the 1960s and early 1970s, pointed out that political independence had not ended the domination of the former colonies by their metropolitan masters but had strengthened the dependence of the former on the latter. Here the analysis highlighted ongoing material inequality. Postcolonial theory focused on the role of culture in politics. The fact that the Orient was "othered" and subjected to a Western gaze by colonial writers had consequence for the inhabitants of the Third World. They were deprived of a voice. Postcolonial theorists developed theories of race and subjectivity that opened up a new terrain of study and offered new concepts with which to analyze. Possibly the most influential was the term *hybridity*—a term developed to try and capture the fluidity of postcolonial life and the postmodern insights into the multiple identities and subject positions available. Here the debt to postmodernism—the stress on conditionality and contingency and the suspicion of absolutes and progress—was very strong.

Postcolonial theorists, and Bhabha (1994) in particular, argue that colonial identities are always about agony and transition or flux. However, Bhabha does not accept a neat black-white division but subscribes to the idea of "messy" borders, "the tethered shadow of deferral and displacement" (cited in Loomba, 1998, p. 176). Where he detects the mimicry of white master by black subject, he argues that this actually undermines white hegemony and is therefore an anticolonial strategy. He further argues that the identity of both colonized and the colonizer are unstable and fraught. This is because of inherent instability and contradictions in the modernist project.

Postcolonial theory insists that everyone has some agency. This concept is both useful and inadequate. It is useful in the sense that it provides a constructive starting point in literary studies of representation and is very accepting of the idea of a fluid or "multiple" identity. This balances the more rigidly Marxian and structuralist perspectives, with their linear trajectories of class and power. However, postcolonial theory does not move the marginal to the center—it does not invert the historical hierarchy—it critiques the center from both the periphery and the metropolitan core (Hutcheon, 1992). Bhabha (1994), for example, says "there is no knowledge—political or otherwise—outside representation" (p. 23). Everything is thus analyzed in terms of linguistic interchange, offering vocabularies of subjectivity. What postcolonial theory often does not do is show how subjectivities are shaped by class, gender, and geospatial context.

The emancipatory claims of postcolonial theory are contested in another way. Aijaz Ahmad (1992, 1996) and Ania Loomba (1998), particularly, have objected to the marginalization of politics and the increasingly abstruse theoretical direction taken, as well as to the decreasing purchase of this theory on Third World realities: the truths of class, race, and gender inequality. Similar concerns have also been expressed in Third World contexts (Sole, 1994). Neil Lazarus (1999) has characterized postcolonial theory as "the idealist and dehistoricizing scholarship currently predominant in that field in general" (p. 1). It is not incidental that for these scholars, feminism and Marxism remain important in understanding the world and that for them, that which Lenin said many years ago remains true:

"Politics begin where the masses are; not where there are thousands, but where there are millions, that is where serious politics begins" (quoted in Carr, 1964, p. 50).

When it comes to gender, the impact of postcolonial theory has been disappointing (Moore-Gilbert, 1997, p. 168). Spivak's concern for Third World women, particularly their cultural position and representation, is universally acknowledged, but in the study of men and masculinity, the impact has been slight, limited to one particular work (Sinha, 1995). One possible explanation for this is identified by Connell:

> The domain of culture (all right, "discourse," I prefer the older language) is a major part of social reality. It defines memberships of categories, and it defines oppositions between categories; hence, the very category of gender is necessarily cultural (or constituted in discourse). But it is not constituted only in discourse. Gender relations also involve violence, which is not discourse; material inequality, which is not discourse; organizations such as firms, which are not discourse; structures such as markets, which are not discourse. So the analysis of the discursive constitution of masculinities, while often highly illuminating, can never be a complete, or even very adequate, analysis of masculinities. (Ouzgane & Coleman, 1998, point 21)

A second type of approach to the study of the postcolonial is "postcolonial criticism," which is described as a "more or less distinct set of reading practices" (Moore-Gilbert, 1997, p. 12), and which emerged within English language and cultural studies. The close examination of texts permitted a critique of colonial literary method and also focused attention on the representation of the racialized subject. Here it shared its field of study with postcolonial thought, although it was much more sensitive to the existence of indigenous critique. Among those whose writings have been acknowledged are the South African author of *Native Life in South Africa* and one of the founders in 1912 of the African National Congress, Sol Plaatje (Plaatje & Head, 1996); Black American civil rights activist, author of *Black Reconstruction*, and cofounder of the National Association for the Advancement of Colored People, W. E. B. du Bois (1934/2001); the Caribbean author of *The Black Jacobins* and theoretician of Marxism, cricket, and West Indian self-determination, C. L. R. James

(1938/1989); and the Martinique-born resident of Algeria who became famous as a revolutionary writer, the author of *Wretched of the Earth,* whose writings had profound influence on the radical movements in the 1960s in the United States and Europe, Frantz Fanon (1963/1986).

The willingness to search for and listen to alternative narratives (penned by those subordinated by colonialism) also made possible a trans-Atlantic conversation that fed into postcolonial debates and gave access to authors as diverse as Henry Louis Gates, an authority in African American identity studies who worked to include works by African Americans in the American literary rights movement in the 1960s; Walter Rodney, the radical Marxist from Guyana, killed by a car bomb in Georgetown in 1980; and Patricia Hill Collins (1990) and bell hooks, prominent black American academic feminists of the 1980s and 1990s.

Race and Gender: Black Men and Masculinity

Postcolonial theory draws attention to agency and is also powerfully subversive regarding essentialisms. It is predicated on the deconstruction of the "essential." Diana Fuss (1989) says,

> [Essentialism] is most commonly understood as a belief in the real, true essence of things, the invariable and fixed properties which define the "whatness" of a given entity. . . . Importantly, essentialism is typically defined in opposition to difference. . . . The opposition is a helpful one in that it reminds us that a complex system of cultural, social, psychical, and historical differences, and not a set of pre-existent human essences, position and constitute the subject. However, the binary articulation of essentialism and difference can also be restrictive, even obfuscating, in that it allows us to ignore or deny the differences within essentialism. (pp. xi-xii)

In the field of gender studies, reaction to essentialism can be seen in the acceptance of the concept of "masculinities" developed by, among others, the Australian gender theorist R. W. Connell in the 1980s and 1990s. Elsewhere in this volume, this development is exhaustively discussed, so we now move on to examine how the critique of essentialism has played out in the analysis of black men.

How are we to understand "black men"? This is not a question that has received the attention it deserves, as the focus of gender work in underdeveloped world contexts and in terms of race has been insistently on women. An ironic consequence has been to silence or to render black men invisible. For example, Heidi Mirza (1997) refers to "Black Feminism" as anything that is recognizably antiracist and postcolonial: "the political project has a single purpose: to excavate the silences and pathological appearances of a collectivity of women assigned to the 'other' and produced in gendered, sexualized, wholly racialised discourses" (pp. 20-21).

Black men need to be understood as "multidimensional social subject(s)" (Mac an Ghaill, 1996, p. 1). The masculinity of black men needs to be considered in the "ambivalent and contradictory sites of black identity and ethnicity and their complex interaction with state institutions and racial ideologies" (Marriott, 1996, p. 185). This involves highlighting the relationship between masculinity, sexuality, and power. One approach, which centralizes race, is suggested by Gayatri Chakravorty Spivak (1996), who guardedly suggests the path of "strategic essentialism." Trinh T. Minh-Ha (1995) personalizes the choices facing a post-colonial subject struggling with identity issues:

> Every path I/i take is edged with thorns. On the one hand, i play into the Savior's hands by concentrating on authenticity, for my attention is numbed by it and diverted from other important issues; on the other hand, i do feel the necessity to return to my so-called roots, since they are the fount of my strength, the guiding arrow to which i constantly refer before heading for a new direction. (p. 268)

The *black* man is faced with a choice and has to exercise his agency. Identity becomes a matter of choice, although it is a choice played out against the backdrop of environment and history.

Another approach is sociological—to examine collectivities of black men and the social constructions of masculinity. Black men and boys in the British schooling system develop subordinate masculinities that reflect their exclusion from hegemonic male power (Mac an Ghaill, 1996). There is a defensive aspect to this construction of masculinity that permits the creation of safe space (both emotional and spatial), but it also signals a defiance and

validates difference (Westwood, 1990). Elsewhere in the United States, a similar marginal position with regard to societal power has resulted in the construction of African American masculinities that are also subordinate to the hegemonic ideal. Such constructions include, among other things, the emphasis of physicality, a particular cultural style ("cool pose"), music (hip-hop and rap), and investment in sporting achievement. But there is a danger of essentializing black men by fixing and generalizing these choices to all black men (Majors, 1986; Staples, 1982). This has resulted in the stereotyping and demonizing of black men as either thugs or sportsmen (Jefferson, 1996; Ross, 1998).

The focus on race generally and black men in particular reflects a concern with politics and a desire for emancipation of the subject and the eradication of inequality. The foregrounding of the black subject (and race as analytical category) constitutes, according to Marriott (1996), "black political and cultural attempts to stabilize 'blackness'" and "a determined attempt to retain the position and influence of race authenticity over ethnicity, gender and class" (p. 198). This approach, with its emphasis on symbolism, subordination, and resistance, has given rise to many highly perceptive accounts of the experience of colonialism. In the South African context, this approach has been used to explain apparent mental illness as a form of resistance (Comaroff & Comaroff, 1987) and has thus steered analysis away from what some considered to be a unidimensional materialist register of racial oppression. In other Third World contexts, such as India, a similar approach to the understanding of oppression has been developed to demonstrate how identities shift and develop in the interstices of society to accommodate highly unequal gender relations. At the same time, transgressive and dissenting voices emerge to challenge the patriarchal discourses centered on the family, community, and nation (Rajan, 1999).

Nonetheless, the focus on race cannot just be about emancipation because black (just like other) men are in oppressive relations with women. The strained relationship between black women and men is carefully identified by bell hooks (1981, 1990). Compassionately, she observed, "Like black men, many black women believed black liberation could only be achieved by the formation of a strong black patriarchy" (hooks, 1981, p. 182). But she went on to point out that black men were also responsible for high levels of violence against women, as well as against other men, and cautioned against romanticizing either black men or women. Her subsequent work has been filled with hope, and she looks to self-reflective, politically conscious black men working with black women as a means of advancing an emancipatory project.

> We need to hear from black men who are interrogating sexism, who are striving to create different and oppositional views of masculinity. Their experience is the concrete practice that may influence others. Progressive black liberation struggle must take seriously feminist movements to end sexism and sexist oppression if we are to restore to ourselves, to future generations of black people, the sweet solidarity in struggle that has historically been a redemptive subversive challenge to white supremacist capitalist patriarchy. (hooks, 1990, p. 77)

In a similar vein in South Africa, Kopano Ratele (1998, 2001) has sought to combat black nationalist views that gloss over gender difference. Arguing against racial essentialism, he points out that misogyny is a deeply constitutive aspect of urban, emerging middle class, young, black men. For Ratele, black men have to face up to their masculinity if they want to live in harmonious relations with women and the broader society.

Admonitions about black men are not confined to heterosexual behavior. Jonathon Dollimore (1997) is critical of Frantz Fanon's homophobia, arguing that in Fanon's writing there are places where "homosexuality is itself demonised as both a cause and an effect of the demonising psychosexual organization of racism that Fanon elsewhere describes and analyses so compellingly" (p. 33). In attempting to explore "the racial distribution of guilt" that results from the psychic internalization and social perpetuation of discrimination between subordinated groups, Fanon (says Dollimore) deploys some "of the worst prejudices [about the sexuality of women and the heterosexuality of men] that psychoanalysis has been used to reinforce" (p. 32). Homophobia has become a feature of African nationalism, with leaders such as Robert Mugabe (Zimbabwe) and Sam Nujoma (Namibia) launching witch hunts against gays (Epprecht, 1998). Among students at a Zimbabwe training college, homophobia (rather than misogyny) is one of the defining features of an African nationalist hegemonic masculinity (Pattman, 2001).

Indigenous Knowledge

The second response to postcolonialism is presented here as an organic response of indigenous people struggling to be heard. In reality, the notion of indigenous people or knowledge itself runs the risk of essentializing and fixing. We refer to indigenous knowledge as a value system that predates colonialism and was integral to, and supportive of, precolonial societies and life. Such a value system was often the explicit target of early colonization, when missionaries sought to banish heathen beliefs and replace them with the English language, English customs, and the Christian Bible. Over centuries of colonialism, many of these value systems were eroded and disappeared. Their material and social forms were often the first to feel the effects of colonialism—buildings and space were regimented along colonial lines and families shaped to meet the requirements of the colonial and, later, capitalist economies. What was more tenacious were values and rituals concerning deep existential and philosophical questions such as "who am I?" and "what is the meaning of life?" Throughout the formerly colonized world, there has been a movement to recover this value system—in Australasia, in South America, and in Africa there are now established movements to retrieve traditions and to validate alternative ways of understanding.

This development makes sense when one considers Spivak's (1996) deep skepticism about the idea of "any easy or intrinsic fit between the aims and assumptions of First and Third World, or postcolonial, feminism." For Spivak, the ostensible emancipatory project of Marxism and Western feminism "runs the risk of exacerbating the problems of the Third World gendered subject" (Moore-Gilbert, 1997, p. 77). Other postcolonial writers have gone further. Adam and Tiffin (1990) argue that "Postmodernism . . . operates as a Euro-American western hegemony, whose global appropriation of time-and-place inevitably proscribes certain cultures as 'backward' and marginal while co-opting to itself certain of their 'cultural "raw" materials'" (quoted in Williams & Chrisman, 1993, p. 13).

On the other hand, the claim for indigenous knowledge can easily be used to justify tyranny and injustice on the basis that practices are drawn from "our culture." Indeed, the recent debate in South Africa about whether HIV causes AIDS has seen President Thabo Mbeki reject scientific evidence concerning this connection as Western arrogance and has linked his own position to a broader campaign for continental regeneration (called the African Renaissance), central to which is the restoration of indigenous knowledge to a position of respect and honor in politics and policy (Freedman, 1999; Makgoba, 1999; Mbeki, 1998; Msimang, 2000; Mulemfo, 2000).

Underpinning these weaknesses is the danger of romanticizing the past and underestimating the responses of indigenous peoples to colonialism, which altered their culture and left nothing the same. There is a constant temptation to construct an imaginary precolonial heaven to drive home the point of the disastrous consequences of colonialism (see Epprecht, 2001; Salo, 2001). In theoretical terms, indigenous knowledge runs the risk of trying to sit "outside" Western perspectives, a fruitless endeavor, according to all Foucauldian theory.

In Africa, the search for an independent voice and, implicitly, indigenous knowledge has long roots and was frequently intrinsic to anticolonial struggles. In historical literature, distinctions are often made between millenarian, backward-looking, traditionalist uprisings (which attempted to hold onto "the old ways") and modern, nationalist opposition to colonialism (which attempts to struggle for a share of colonialism's "gifts"— citizenship, employment on equal terms, access to land and public services, and so on). The defeat of first-wave anticolonial movements did not end the commitment to indigenous knowledge. V. Y. Mudimbe (1994) observes that there exists a "primary, popular interpretation of founding events of the culture and its historical becoming. . . . Silent but permanent, this discreet and, at the same time, systematic reference to a genesis marks the everyday practices of a community" (p. xiii).

The search for, and retrieval of, historical traditions has been taken up by Africanist scholars exploring questions of gender. An extreme example (Oyewumi, 1997) has cast doubt on the value of foundational feminist concepts and has asked: Is gender still an appropriate unit of analysis, or is it merely a colonial imposition with limited value? Should the concept of gender be expanded to focus on its relational component by examining African constructions of masculinities, as well as femininities? What categories of identity and personhood are more appropriate and germane to African societies?

The search for indigenous knowledge has often been accompanied by hostility toward Western feminism. Ifi Amadiume (1987), for example, attacks feminist work because of its binary use of the categories "man" and "woman" and its assumptions that men and women are different and that they therefore have fundamentally different interests. She rejects analysis that stresses the adversarial nature of gender relations. Along with others, she develops an alternative approach, which attempts to retrieve indigenous knowledge that challenges the universalist claims of Western thought. She describes gender fluidity and harmony (as opposed to fixed gender roles and gender conflict) in precolonial Igbo society (in present-day Nigeria). A similar argument is made for the Yoruba (Oyewumi, 1997). In this view, gender ceases to be the major category of analysis, becoming one of many. In this tradition, the consensual (rather than antagonistic) features of African gender relations are stressed. These writings analyze social life in ways that stress community not just in temporal but in spiritual ("ancestral") terms. In terms of these readings, gender is part of a variety of relational understandings that are subsumed under a general assumption about humanity. In this understanding, humanity is what is common among people and is what unites them. In some respects, this view is incommensurable with modern worldviews, which are distinguished by causal thinking, linear time, the idea of progress, the self as autonomous, the domination of nature, and representation as the way in which politics is conducted. A "traditional" worldview, on the other hand, has at its center a complex continuity with the past, with ancestors and spirits, and is distinguished by correlative thinking, cyclical time, the self as communal, the interdependence of people and nature, and the conduct of politics via participation.[1] The idea of adhesion, what makes people live together, is therefore the starting point. In the South African context, this can be seen in the concept of *ubuntu* (Broodryk, 1995; Mbigi, 1995).

Ubuntu literally means "peopleness" (humanity). It has recently become synonymous with a particular worldview. *Ubuntu* is a "prescription or set of values for a way of living your life as one person" (Johnson, 1997). The meaning of "being human" embraces values such as "universal brotherhood of Africans," "sharing," and "treating and respecting other people as human beings." Centrally, *ubuntu* is a notion of communal living in society. Being human cannot be divorced from being in society, and in this respect, it is fundamentally different from Western notions, in which gender identities and other group identities are acquired individually (Johnson, 1997; Makang, 1997). Gender is an important constituent of the reality, but in the long run historically, the vast scope of the past and the challenges of living join people (men and women) in the project of life. Individuals are the unit of analysis, but they are not self-standing, being rather part of a collectivity. One obvious problem with this approach, particularly in analyses of the Third World, is that it has frequently been used to disguise the exploitation of women in African society. By concentrating on racial and ethnic oppression primarily as a result of external forces, the internal forces of gender oppression have been concealed or ignored. In this sense, there is a real danger of focuses on *ubuntu* simply reflecting or reinforcing patriarchal discourses. In South Africa, the *ubuntu* approach has been used for a variety of purposes—party political, nationalist, and gendered (patriarchal).

Impetus has been given to indigenous knowledge approaches (labeled by Williams and Chrisman, 1993, as "nativism") by colonial legacies that still divide black and white women. In South Africa, for example, feminism and the goals of gender equality have been treated with suspicion and rejected outright by some black nationalists. Christine Qunta (1987) objected that feminism was a Western, white philosophy that was irrelevant to African conditions and was designed to sow discord among black people fighting for freedom. This objection was more subtlely made, and with greater sophistication, in the early 1990s as white feminists in the academy faced the wrath of black feminists "outside" (Hassim & Walker, 1992; Serothe, 1992).

Yet although nativist approaches correctly highlight the importance of race, alternative value systems, and global location, they can lose sight of enduring gender inequalities (Stichter & Parpart, 1988). Third World and African feminism provides a corrective to give the (black) female subaltern a voice and draws attention to the diversity of experiences among women (Mohanty, Russo, & Torres, 1991; Lewis, 2001). In the process, the focus also falls on the relationship of race to subordination and marginalization. Concerns about injustice and exploitation blend with those that focus on the condition of peoples in the developing (Third) world.

Development and Gender

Postcolonial contexts are, by definition, contexts that require or call out for development. Postcolonial can refer to countries as dissimilar as Canada and the Central African Republic. In this chapter, the development challenges of what we earlier called Third World or underdeveloped countries will be discussed.

The challenges of development in the Third World are vast and have become greater with globalization and the spread of free-market ideology. The gap between the First and Third Worlds is getting larger, but of equal concern is the growing stratification of Third World populations as the poor get poorer and a new middle class (often associated with the apparatuses of the state) gets richer. As feminists have remarked, this process has often hit women the hardest, producing the "feminization of poverty."

The challenges of development since the Cold War period have been experienced in many different ways. Starting with a modernization paradigm, the emphasis was on a gender-insensitive use of technology to solve the supposed failure of Third World countries to convert political independence into economic growth. The failure of this First World–sponsored approach caused a change of tack, and in the 1980s, the importance of gender was acknowledged with the introduction of what subsequently came to be termed "women in development." This approach introduced women as a central element into development policy and implementation. It was recognized that not only were women critical in reproduction issues (biological and social) but that they also did much of the work. Programs then began to focus on delivering development to women. It was recognized within a decade that this approach was flawed: It focused in a simplistic way on a set of agents (women) and ignored the context of relationships and power relations in which these women operated.

"Women in development" perspectives were part of, and contributed to, international work that focused on the subordinated position of women. Such work included, as a corrective, arguments about the hitherto neglected centrality of women in resisting globalization (and patriarchy) (Mohammed, 1998; Oduol & Kabira, 1995). In these analyses, masculinity was, for the most part, overlooked, and men all too often tacitly were regarded as obstacles to gender justice.

Thus it was that in the late 1980s and 1990s gender and development (GAD) perspectives emerged. It was now acknowledged that not all women suffered equally (that it was poor women who should be the main beneficiaries of development) and that gender inequalities required not just a liberal feminist ministering to "women" but a more sophisticated grappling with relationships that generated gender inequality. The new approach broadened the focus of development work so that even though women remained an important focus as the intended beneficiaries in the delivery of programs, it was now recognized that it was unhelpful to simply target them for "help." Attention had to be paid to context, and here the complexity of gender relations was acknowledged. Development could only be sustainable if gender inequalities were addressed. Projects designed to address this, however, soon found that attacking patriarchy head-on (and casting men as the enemy) was not a solution. Such projects divided communities and undermined the goals of development. It was in this context that, in the mid-1990s, a focus on men and masculinity emerged.

The introduction of masculinity into development debates was contested. The discussions within feminism concerning the political location and purpose of feminist men's involvement in gender-emancipatory projects were also played out in the development realm. The concerns were that so much development work had historically been directed at men that they should not be reinserted into a development agenda that was only beginning to redress the legacy of neglect of women. Would men once again dominate and pervert development for patriarchal purposes? A more recent query has been about the appropriation of gender into global governance discourses. With gender becoming mainstreamed, the concern has been raised that it also has become depoliticized, and women's interests have thus become decentered and subject to marginalization (Manicom, 2001).

Two influential special issues of development journals, edited by Caroline Sweetman (1997) and Andrea Cornwall and Sarah White (2000), have done much to clarify thinking and raise the critical issues of gender and development. Developments within the United Nations—for example, the work of the U.N. International Research and Training Institute for the Advancement of Women—have begun to insert masculinity perspectives into influential development agencies (Greig, Kimmel, & Lang, 2000).

There are two basic themes that emerge from these debates. The first concerns the politics of development and gender transformation. The key question here has been how GAD programs have actually affected gender relations and contributed to the reduction in gender inequality. Without wishing to impose a false uniformity on the debate, it would seem that a number of issues emerge. GAD has not yet fully acknowledged the importance of men in development work—men are ignored, or, as Andrea Cornwall (2000) puts it, "missing." Following from this observation, Sylvia Chant (2000) argues that GAD programs would be strengthened if they paid more attention to men and included masculinity work. She notes that such an approach could promote men working *together* with women. The importance of working with masculinity and the new acceptance that this is not a fixed gender identity also features powerfully in this work. Development initiatives should focus on men's self-image, their involvement in parenting and caring, reproductive health issues, and reducing violence (Engle, 1997; Falabella, 1997; Greene, 2000; Greig, 2000; Large, 1997). Reflecting initiatives elsewhere (for example, in refocusing domestic violence work from female victims onto male perpetrators), development agencies and governments have begun to include work with and on men in their programs.

The second issue that has been raised is that of the specificity of context and the appropriateness of the theoretical framework currently used. Sarah White (2000) has argued that the shift to work with men and masculinity is predicated on eurocentric conceptions of development and of gender. Here she has drawn on Third World feminism (itself connected to postcolonial theory) to urge a rethinking of development work in postcolonial contexts. She also begins to suggest that indigenous knowledge systems need to be taken into account in prosecuting a development agenda with gender results.

White's cautions draw on debates outlined earlier, about indigenous knowledge and postcolonial contexts. The concept of a "new man," developed first in socialist literature in the Soviet Union and Cuba and transformed by masculinity scholarship into the image of a woman-friendly man wholeheartedly committed to gender equity, is not appropriate to many Third World contexts when it is used as a model for change. The idea of the "new man" was really developed for Northern, white, middle class, urban men. It misses men in the Third World whose situations are different. This does not mean, however, that there is not something very important about developing new role models and visions for masculinity. The transformation of male roles and identities (which, in a theoretical sense, draws on the postcolonial theory described earlier) is a key part of development work. In the Caribbean, Niels Sampath (1997) shows how men are open to messages of transformation but will use local idiom to make sense of the possibilities and will attempt change within existing parameters rather than aspiring to externally prescribed norms. In Africa, the context for development work and the tenacity of indigenous value systems remain important factors.

> Traditional ordering of relations between genders and generations based on hierarchy and authority is now largely history, and more clearly so in towns than in the countryside. A moral ordering in this area survives, however, as social memory, as scattered practices, particularly important in relation to reproductive strategies, and most of all with poor urban youth, as an absence and a yearning. Poor families have less opportunities of substituting old orders with new ones, because of a situation of instability and lack of material and immaterial resources. . . . Generally speaking, modern socializing practices, such as we find them in poor sections of the cities, undertaken broadly by religious institutions, schools and

> nuclear family, have not filled the real or imagined void left by the breakdown of time-honoured ways. (Frederiksen, 2000, p. 221)

In the African context, the importance of indigenous knowledge and context is made abundantly clear in the work of Paul Dover (2001), an anthropologist whose work was conducted in rural Zambia in the 1990s. Dover locates his argument (specifically about reproductive health in Third World contexts) in a context in which development is seen to have failed. Zambia is a country where hope for an improvement in the material quality of life, carried by the copper boom of the 1960s, has evaporated. People have thus turned from the optimistic Western development discourses and have sought understanding of their lives in older, indigenous discourses. Colonialism was never able to eradicate these, but now they have greater visibility and acceptance. These discourses place cosmology at the center of a person's worldview. In terms of this perspective, the body and soul are not separate, and any problem has therefore to be tackled by ministering to both. Because cosmology is gendered and particular qualities are held to reside discretely in men and women, gender roles have a fixity that postcolonial theories are reluctant to grant them. But this does not mean they are fixed. Rather, it means that there are limits to change and that these are determined by the parameters of the indigenous belief system. In other words, Dover is not saying that men cannot change. He is not invoking primitivism or essentialism. He is arguing for the need to take full account not just of material circumstances (which so tragically speak of inequality), but of culture. In the next section, we return in more detail to the implications of these views and detail his arguments.

MEN AND MASCULINITIES IN A POSTCOLONIAL WORLD

It is undoubtedly the stuff of caricature, but there is also a great deal of truth in the observation that the Third World is characterized by poverty and subject to wars and violence. In 1999, Africa alone was the site of 16 armed conflicts, with 34% of countries hosting conflicts, making up 40% of global conflicts. Recent statistics show that since 1970, more than 30 wars have been fought in Africa. In 1996 alone, 14 of the 53 countries of Africa saw armed conflicts, accounting for more than half of all war-related deaths worldwide and resulting in more than 8 million refugees, returnees, and displaced persons (Diallo, 1998; King, 2001; Regehr, 1999). Some of these conflicts lasted for several decades (such as the one in the Sudan, often called a "forgotten conflict").

The relationship of poverty to war is complex. There is no doubt that wars produce poverty and that poverty creates conditions fertile for the prosecution of wars. As wars have historically been highly gendered—declared and fought primarily by men but with civilian (primarily women) casualties an increasingly prominent feature of modern wars—it is important that we now look at constructions of masculinity in the Third World.

Approximately 33% of the Third World's population is under 15 years old (Population Reference Bureau, 2001a). Most young people (about 85%) live in developing countries. Youth are numerically the largest and arguably the most significant political constituency. They are the group most subject to the scourges of unemployment, most vulnerable to AIDS, and most likely to be involved in wars. Media images in 1999 and 2000 brought this home to the world—boys as young as 10 years old recruited to fight and excited to commit brutalities that included large-scale amputations and systematic rapes (not infrequently of family members). More than 50 countries currently recruit child soldiers into the armed forces, and it is estimated that child soldiers are being used in more than 30 conflicts worldwide (Goodwin-Gill & Cohn, 1994; Peters & Richards, 1998).

There are dangers in focusing on wars and bloodshed because this can easily distract from other less dramatic but equally important developments. There is a similar danger in limiting discussion of violence to wars alone. Violence takes many forms, and these are by no means confined to theaters of war. The rest of this section, therefore, will examine men and masculinity in three contexts: poverty, violence, and AIDS.

Poverty, Work, Family, and Identity

The changing nature of work that has been a feature of globalization in the First World and the extension of under- and unemployment in the Third World (Rifkin, 1995) has profoundly affected masculinities. Modern masculinities are centrally constructed around work. The lack of work and engaging in labor which no longer has an associated status or meaning have produced a variety of responses from men. These have ranged from middle class men protesting inroads made into their privilege (Lemon, 1995; Swart, 1998), to older men striking out at younger pretenders to enforce the power of patriarchy, to the subordination of juniors (Campbell, 1992) to passivity by men in rural areas who no longer can support their families and thus no longer command respect (Silberschmidt, 1992).

There are two cases that we briefly want to discuss. The first concerns men in employment. In much of Africa, and particularly in the former settler colonies, African men have found jobs by migrating to the places of employment. This has not only given them access to money and the power that goes with it, it has placed them outside the power of traditional chiefs, whose authority rests on patronage and kinship. Globalization has meant that men who have managed to hold on to jobs have become "big men" (Dover, 2001). They are, relative to the unemployed, well off, although this should not divert attention from the fact that, relative to the bosses, they are poor, and they probably support a great many family members on their wages. In a recent examination of contemporary migrant labor in South Africa, Ben Carton (2001) has described how African men negotiate issues of identity in this context. He looks at a poverty-stricken area and witnesses the arrival of the young men from the city. Bumptious with the power of money, they bring their urban style into this rural context. They pay only some attention to the chiefs who notionally are in charge. The tempo of rural life picks up. There is carousing and celebrating, and then they leave and return to the cities, leaving the chiefs to reclaim their positions. What makes the story interesting is that the men in employment still acknowledge their rural origins. Even if they do not fully pay the respects expected, they acknowledge the position of the chiefs, although briefly usurping it. We see in their behavior the residue of tradition and the penumbra of indigenous knowledge. We see also how they negotiate different identities—urban and rural, modern and traditional—but at the center is the image of *adult male*. In another African context, Paul Dover (2001) identifies the different constituent components of manhood—a mature body, a wife and children, an education and labor, and the reciprocal expectation for *tsika*—respect and moral behavior (p. 156).

The second case is of those men who have failed to retain a grip on the labor market. The literature that correctly identifies the feminization of poverty unfortunately all too often neglects to examine the consequences of poverty on men. Most African men do not "have work" in the Western sense of the word (a job). This is not surprising given the shrinkage of the world of careers and jobs, which has been more severe on the periphery. There are many consequences of this; among the foremost are a rise in domestic violence, alcoholism, and suicide (Gemeda & Booji, 1998; Mayekiso, 1995).

Margrethe Silberschmidt, who conducted anthropological research in East Africa for 20 years, made it the focus of her work to examine the changing position of African men living in a rural community in Kenya. The story is of the impact of colonialism, of changes in the political economy and in local gender roles. The result is that men lose their status, power, and self-esteem, and there is heightened gender antagonism (Silberschmidt, 1992, 1999).

Colonialism came relatively late (in the second decade of the 20th century) to the Kisii district. It was not welcomed, and the area was among the slowest to embrace Christianity, schooling, and wage labor. The imposition of taxes forced men to seek work. This produced a major change in their societal roles. Before colonialism,

> manliness was based on a father's and a husband's dignity, reflected in respect from juniors in his family, his wives and most importantly, his own self-restraint. The male head of the household was its decision-maker and controller of its wealth. . . . As long as he lived, he was the only person who could officiate at sacrifices [to] the ancestors, whose goodwill controlled the health and fertility of the whole family. (Silberschmidt, 1999, p. 36)

The advent of migrant labor produced a change in the role of men—they became "breadwinners." While men remained in employment, this change did not cause social problems, but with the postindependence slump of the 1960s,

men no longer found work in the cities and returned to the rural areas. Here, cattle villages no longer existed (one of the effects of land loss and overcrowding). There was no alternative lifestyle to adopt, and men busied themselves with odd jobs and informal activity. They now earned very little, and what they did earn, they chose not to spend on their households but on alcohol and women.

The problem has three further dimensions. The economic position of women has not deteriorated as it has with men. Women remain involved in subsistence agriculture. However, households still need the involvement of all family members, and the refusal and failure of men to contribute has produced great tension. This is exacerbated by the lapsing of bridewealth payments and the decline in marriage rates. Men are no longer bound into families as they were in the past. They thus escape responsibility, but they also lose status, because being married remains an important part of manhood. Other aspects of masculinity that have their roots in the precolonial period and are still valued are in the following list of "what a respected and good man should do":

- [He] takes care of his family
- [He] educates his children and pays school fees
- His wife does not roam about
- He marries many wives and gets many children
- He is friendly and shows respect toward his people
- He assists his people when they have problems and gives good advice
- He is generous and does not quarrel
- He respects himself (Silberschmidt, 1999, p. 53)

Most men cannot live up to these ideals, and thus their self-esteem has dropped dramatically. One response has been a rise since the 1960s in assaults and rape of women. This response has drawn on an available gender dictionary. Traditional conceptions of manliness stress "men's 'role' as a warrior i.e. men in Kisii were defined by violent deeds" (Silberschmidt, 1999, p. 36) and include "command over women in all matters, and, in particular, sexual control" (p. 70).

Thus men in Kisii have an uneasy and antagonistic relationship with women as they try to control their fertility and women resist. The men have not responded to their problems by moving back into the family and becoming good fathers. They have sought solace in alcohol and love affairs. This is, however, not continentally or universally the case. Paul Dover's (2001) work shows that although men in Zambia seem distant and emotionally unengaged as fathers, in fact there is a widespread belief that it is best for a child to have a mother and a father. In this context, a father gives emotional succor to a child when the child is young and commands respect later on. The process of distancing that accompanies the aging of the child is not considered to be damaging but rather is an integral and important part of the whole process of parenting (Dover, 2001, p. 139).

With the decline of work, men have had opportunities to shape their gender identities in new ways. As indicated, the response has been varied, but the option of becoming more involved in family matters has remained. Such involvement can take many forms. In some cases, it can represent a reactive response to a loss of power and involve the assertion of the rights of the father within the family. In other circumstances, it can involve greater engagement with parenting. The place of the father is, of course, a key issue in meditations about a "crisis of masculinity." First World literature has debated the absent father ad nauseam. Some have identified him as the cause of the malaise of masculinity (Biddulph, 1997; Corneau, 1991). Others have argued that "absent fathers" are but one of a number of issues which need to be taken into account in understanding modern masculinities. In terms of this view, no special status should be given to "the father."

Increasingly, work set in rural African contexts reminds us of the tenacity of traditions (Dover, 2001; Heald, 1999; Moore, Sanders, & Kaare, 1999; Silberschmidt, 1999). Within these traditions, manhood, as a concept, is not questioned. Rather, it is the content of manhood and the way men exercise their powers that have become critical issues. In exploring this, Heald (1999), in her study of the Gisu of Uganda, argues that the discourse of masculinity and its power to set moral agendas is widely acknowledged but that "this is not necessarily in a way that is comfortable for men as the privileged gender" (p. 4).

But what of black youth, particularly in urban settings or where authority structures (the state, for example) have lost their strength, who have often claimed the status of manhood by defining themselves violently *against* their fathers and against authority (Carton, 2001; Everatt, 2000)? There is a continuum, from outright rejection of family and fathers to a difficult tension held by young men between independence and a residual connection (maintained in memory or in reality by occasional trips to family in rural areas) with family and fathers. For many Third World youth, two realities exist—an urban, modern reality and a premodernist and traditional reality. They exist side by side and can operate simultaneously (Niehaus, 2000). Thus we need to explore the backward and forward effects on identity, created, for example, by the Gisu circumcision ritual, which is specifically designed to make the boys "tough" and "fierce" (Heald, 1999, p. 28), and urban socialization processes, by which young urban boys are initiated into gang cultures that also stress violent behavior (Mager, 1998; Xaba, 2001).

Violence and Men

This section began by noting the prevalence of wars and societal violence, which prompts this question: Is violence a postcolonial problem?

Amina Mama (1997), Third World feminist, has argued that violence in the Third World is a direct legacy of colonialism. Although the connection between historical and contemporary violence is strong, it does not alone explain the current phenomenon. There is the temptation to excuse the Third World's violence by relating it causally to poverty, which in turn can be associated with colonialism. These factors are important, but it is important to note that most Third World inhabitants are not violent, and those who sometimes are are not violent most of the time. To examine men and violence, we need, in the first instance, to reject "Dark Continent" theories about this being a normal or natural condition. In the second instance, without denying the importance of these factors, we need to note that poverty does not cause violence. In the context of Central America, it has been noted that misogyny, rather than poverty, causes violence (Linkogle, 2001). This observation takes us directly to the issue of men and masculinity.

Although there can be little doubt that the arbitrary nature of the way in which colonial borders were established, colonial and imperial meddling in ethnic and regional politics, and subsequent international machinations and global politics have contributed to wars, in this subsection, we turn to look at the way in which constructions of masculinity have been implicated in less spectacular, if equally deadly, forms of interpersonal violence. To give some sense of this, here are some recent details from Zimbabwe. In 1993, domestic violence accounted for more than 60% of murder cases that went through the courts. Although wife battery is more common in rural areas, there are no accurate figures for the phenomenon there. In towns, wife battering occurred among about 25% of married women (Getecha & Chipika, 1995, pp. 120-124).

How can we make sense of this? As a starting point, we take Suezette Heald's (1999) anthropological study of the Gisu people in Uganda, which is unusual for its focus on men. She finds that manhood is synonymous with violence, but she does not stop there. "The attribution of violence is profoundly ambivalent. Might only sometimes equals right and, even when it does, its legitimacy and limits are open to question." She then examines

> the extreme way in which violent power is located in men, a source of their rights but also . . . a source of self-knowledge and responsibility. . . . Men fear their own violence, their own violent responses and the onus throughout, therefore, is upon self-control. The good man is one who is his own master, and can master himself well. (Heald, 1999, p. 4; see also Wardrop, 2001)

Trying, in the first instance, to make sense of Third World violence and, in the second instance, to help in reducing levels is only partially assisted by referring to the huge First World literature on families, youth, and violence (e.g., Hearn, 1998, 2001; Messerschmidt, 2000). As already indicated, it may make sense in certain contexts to promote men as fathers, but it makes less sense in societies in which the fathers (and other esteemed men, such as teachers) are among the major perpetrators of rape (Hallam, 1994; Jewkes & Abrahams, 2000; Jewkes, Levin, Mbananga, & Bradshaw, 2002).

To reflect on a postcolonial masculinity, we turn again to the work of Heald (1999) on the Gisu of Uganda in the late 20th century. She concludes,

> The Gisu imagining of their identity as male citizens is deeply "essentialist" and, while it might be

thought that the strength and formation of this male character has much to do with militaristic past, its continuing salience can just as easily be related to the very loss of a warrior role. No simple anachronism, it keeps it alive as a possibility and provides the discursive justification for male claims to status. And . . . this, in turn, creates its own characteristic moral dilemmas. (p. 165)

The warrior role of Gisu men is a deeply entrenched part of ethnic identity, which is itself an expression of autonomy, of resistance to colonialism and postcolonial forces that beat at the specificity of the local and penetrate it with global goods, messages, and technologies. To criticize the warrior image is to threaten Gisu life itself. And yet this does not give rise to a situation of unbridled violence. As Heald (1999) observes,

> Gisu ethics addresses the problem of social control through the necessity for self-control. Self-assertion as the right of all men is thus coupled with restraint as the mark of the social self. This gives a particular understanding of African selfhood in the context of male egalitarianism in which the use and control of force is at the disposal of all. (p. 3)

The critical issue for Gisu society is not whether men are violent but how they use this violence. This is not just a social issue; it is a profoundly spiritual one. One can see this most clearly in the circumcision ritual (*imbalu*), during which 17- to 25-year-old men are circumcised. If one is not circumcised, one is not a man. The process is highly ritualized, very painful and frightening. The young man must stand before a large group of people while the procedure is performed. He must show no sign of "fear, pain or reluctance. . . . Failure threatens on many counts. Most evidently in the display of cowardice or fear. . . . the whole of his adult life is also seen as dependent on *imbalu*" (Heald, 1999, pp. 50-51).

The ordeal needs and nurtures two things: strength (of both mind and body, although Gisu does not distinguish along such Cartesian lines) and violent emotional energy (*lirima*), which is needed and harnessed in the process. "A good man is one whose *lirima* is strictly under control" (Heald, 1999, p. 18). *Lirima* is a "basic fact of life" and is associated with men, not boys or women. "It is not something which can be tampered with or altered. It is inherent in the nature of men" (Heald, 1999, p. 19).

Through circumcision, all men become heroes. They are heroes because they have survived the ordeal with dignity. "Having faced 'death' he is deemed free from the fear of it and capable of taking responsibility for himself amongst other self-determining Gisu men. . . . It is thus, above all, a rite of emancipation from parental authority" (Heald, 1999, p. 52). Hereafter, a man is expected to marry, set up a household, and look after dependants. But the ritual is even more important, for, in proving their own manhood, the young men "are in effect proving the identity of all Gisu as men and validating the power of the tradition which unites them all. Caught by the ancestral power of circumcision, the boys, in effect, personify the power of the ancestors and the continuity of tradition" (Heald, 1999, p. 51).

So, for Heald, Gisu men *must* be violent to be men. Their violence is an affirmation of their collective being, a rejection of the modern, an affirmation of their past. Yet, and this is the key point, the violence is not unrestrained. It is not either "good" or "bad." Men have power and the obligation to use it wisely.

This is not necessarily in a way that is comfortable for men as the privileged gender. The attribution of violence is profoundly ambivalent. Might only sometimes equals right and, even when it does, its legitimacy and limits are open to question. As already implied, in the West, as the older codes of masculinity have come under threat, a crisis of masculinity is now more apparent than one involving women. (Heald, 1999, p. 4)

Violence, then, belongs to men, but it is the source of self-knowledge and responsibility. "Men fear their own violence, their own violent responses and the onus throughout, therefore, is upon self-control. The good man is one who is his own master, and can master himself well" (Heald, 1999, p. 4).

AIDS and Men

In 1999, worldwide, there were 33.6 million people living with AIDS: 16.4 million men, 14.8 million women, and 1.2 million children under 15 years (Whiteside & Sunter, 2000, p. 36). Although these figures are contested, there is

little doubt that what started out as a homosexual, white, Northern disease has become a heterosexual, black, Southern catastrophe. Sub-Saharan Africa is by far the worst affected. In 1999, there were nearly 24 million people living with HIV in this region. The area with the next most serious rate of infection was Latin America, with 1.3 million. The adult prevalence rate in Africa is 8%. The next highest is the Caribbean (1.96%). Australia and New Zealand have a rate of 0.1% (Whiteside & Sunter, 2000, p. 38). Of the world's HIV-infected people, 70% come from an area that contains only 10% of its population. In Sub-Saharan Africa, 55% of HIV-infected people are female.

In Africa, the disease is overwhelmingly spread via unprotected heterosexual acts. Many young Africans (15-19 years old)—many more than in the equivalent age-group in developed countries—have had sex. In most African countries, about 30% of boys are sexually experienced, whereas for girls, the rates vary from fewer than 10% in Senegal and Zimbabwe to more than 45% in the Côte d'Ivoire (Population Reference Bureau, 2001b). Despite the fact that boys are generally more sexually active than girls, it is the girls who, for reasons of biology and gender inequality, are more seriously affected by HIV/AIDS. In every country surveyed by the Population Reference Bureau, girls were two to three times more likely to be infected than boys (Population Reference Bureau, 2001b, p. 19).

Until recently, the focus of attention on AIDS was either on homosexual men or on women. It has only been since the late 1990s that researchers, policy workers, and AIDS activists have begun to call for the issue of heterosexual men to be involved. Mostly, these are calls for the involvement of men, recognizing that gender inequality is at the heart of the pandemic and that constructions of masculinity therefore need to be taken into account (Bujra, 2000; Foreman, 1999; Tallis, 2000).

Masculinity is constructed in many different ways. Two major concerns in AIDS scholarship are how sexuality is expressed and how this is linked to issues of gender power, especially in hyperheterosexuality contexts. Sexuality is most publicly on display as *hetero*sexuality. In Africa, this is partly an effect of high levels of homophobia and partly because in some contexts, homosexuality has no resonance in indigenous culture (Epprecht, 1998). This has not prevented, especially in South Africa, a strong gay movement from emerging (Gevisser & Cameron, 1994). As already indicated, gay men are no longer the most afflicted by AIDS, but in South Africa it has been gay men, by and large, who have led and propelled social movements around AIDS. Zackie Achmat, Simon Nkoli, and Edwin Cameron (Gevisser & Cameron, 1994, pp. 10-11), for example, declared their support for people living with AIDS while promoting messages of gay tolerance. Elsewhere in the Third World, in Brazil, for example, the gay world has also been thrust into the forefront by the pandemic, and, in the process, masculinities have publicly been problematized. The heterosexist norm has been shaken by AIDS (Parker, 1999).

And yet, in Africa, compulsory heterosexuality is a key feature of hegemonic masculinity. Numerous studies now testify to the importance among young and old men of having sex with women and having many female sexual partners. These preferences might not individually be problematical except for the insistence on penetrative sex (MacPhail & Campbell, 2000), the levels of force, and the disregard for safety that accompanies sexual transactions (Wood & Jewkes, 1997).

In three revealing studies in South Africa, the constructions of masculinity are revealed to be critical for the way in which pleasure is sought and obtained. Thokozani Xaba's (2001) study of cadres recently demobilized from the ANC's military units shows how their disillusionment with the new political order and their failure to find a place in the new South Africa drove them to crime, including armed robbery and rape. In another context, young black men in an impoverished township engage in a headlong pursuit of sex and girlfriends as they try to obtain status and self-esteem. But they are caught on the horns of a dilemma—if they all want lots of girlfriends, it will mean that they will compete with one another, and this produces homosocial tensions. These tensions are most often taken out on their sexual partners (who are assaulted), but at the same time, their predicament—no life trajectory out of intense poverty—reminds them that love is "dangerous" (Wood & Jewkes, 2001). Even among young, rising, middle class, urbanized African men, the importance of "having a girl" is central to constructions of masculinity. Although the levels of violence

associated with poorer and marginalized black men is not a feature in their relationships, the black *ouens* ("guys") are nevertheless heavily invested in the possession of women (Ratele, 2001). None of these men is concerned about inequalities in their relationships. The power of men over women is a foundation of their masculinity.

We now turn to an anthropological study that investigated HIV/AIDS in Zambia. Paul Dover (2001) starts with power—in Shona, *simba*. It can be understood as social as well as physical. It is an *amoral* force that can be tapped, although it resides, in bodily terms, in a *man's* body in terms of vitality and potency (p. 113). In Shona thought, power is at the center of religion. It is ambiguous and can be used for good and evil. Age and ancestors are venerated because social power is granted as one moves through the (social and age-structured) system. To use power for "fighting" leads to punishment by the ancestors and "failure" (p. 115). In this system, which is rather like that of feudal Europe, (male) chiefs do not only occupy secular positions of authority, they are also people with specific spiritual powers and alone officiate in rituals that confirm the ongoing importance of tradition, the spirits, and the ancestors. And yet, "as well as achieving community or lineage positions of power, male roles are bound up with modern ideals of being the 'head of household' bread-winner" (p. 120). Thus the modern and the traditional are fused.

In Zambia, power and gender are conceived in ways that do not fit snugly into Western modes of thought. In terms of understanding HIV/AIDS, the significant points are that body and mind-spirit are not separated and that to cure a body requires ministering to the whole person, also taking into account ancestral influence. *Simba* is a male attribute, and HIV symptoms and modes of transmission are understood and treated in gender-specific ways. Calls by government and health NGOs to use condoms as the main way of reducing HIV transmission have not been successful precisely because they do not take into account indigenous gendered understandings and are therefore resisted by men.

How does one acquire masculinity in Zambia? Dover (2001) identifies a life course similar to that described by Silberschmidt and Heald. "Becoming married and having children are [also] important markers of having achieved adulthood" (Dover, 2001, p. 136). As a boy matures physically,

> he will increasingly be expected to help his father and other kinsmen with male tasks. He also takes on less deferential body postures to older males. At the same time a male superiority is assumed even to his mother: he sits on the stool while she sits on the floor. (Dover, 2001, p. 136)

Men have the capacity for action and agency, which is captured in the saying, "Men's hearts are different because they accomplish what they desire, but women often fail!" This is translated into all areas of activity but specifically in regard to women. Men are seen as not being satisfied with what they have; women, by contrast, are held to be "easily satisfied" (Dover, 2001, p. 146). And yet, as both Chenjerai Shire (1994) and Dover point out, women are appreciated for their capacities and play a major part in the development of masculinity. Although they may not have *simba,* this does not mean that they are powerless.

In terms of AIDS, there is nothing intrinsic to the indigenous value system that promotes nonconsensual sex even though the inequalities in social power and material wealth provide reason to expect that women's voices, in the negotiation of sex, are not always heard or heeded.

As indicated earlier, the initial focus in the AIDS pandemic was not on heterosexual men, although this is changing. One of the major ways in which men are engaged in prevention campaigns is via sex education. Many of these international campaigns focus on the technology of sex (condoms) or on communication style. The transmission of information is often the central plan of programs (Varga, 2001). Dissatisfaction with these interventions, as well as a profound disillusionment with the idea of development and the promise of modernity, has produced a number of indigenous responses. In South Africa, the best known is "virginity testing" among Zulu speakers in KwaZulu-Natal. The initiative draws on an old practice conducted by women and bound up with bride-wealth practices. Young girls are physically inspected in public to see if the hymen is intact. Girls are given a certificate, which is synonymous with being HIV negative. In this process, old African women are resurrecting a role that has fallen into disuse and are asserting their power. What makes virginity testing problematic, however, is that it makes girls responsible for the spread of the disease—boys are not tested. The international focus on gender inequality and masculinity is thus left out (Leclerc-Madlala, 2001).

It is easy to condemn such local interventions on many grounds, including the violation of children's rights. Yet to do so runs the risk of negating indigenous knowledge and of preaching to the very people who are most affected and who, in these kinds of initiatives, are trying to regain control of their lives. Fortunately, there is evidence of sensitivity in many areas of gender work that suggests that in the response to AIDS, space will be made for indigenous knowledge and the people who are affected.

There are, of course, difficulties. To get men to change and be more responsive toward and respectful of women requires overcoming obstacles that are rooted in men's position and power in the spheres of production and social reproduction. Yet programs that work with men have been successful. In Jamaica, 50% of urban fathers reported changes in domestic roles, including significant involvement in family life (shopping, cooking, and cleaning). In Brazil, young men are far more flexible (than the men of the previous generation) in their role expectations and are much more willing to take on caring duties (Greig et al., 2000, p. 8).

For rural people who still revere "tradition," there are also possibilities. In Zambia, a program of "responsible patriarchy" has been disseminated by the church. This has been very popular but runs the risk of reestablishing male power in the home (Dover, 2001, p. 242; see also Schwalbe, 1996). It is important to remember that most African men are poor and not well educated in Western school terms. It is not easy to see how Connell's "patriarchal dividend" plays out in their lives. Yet, Paul Dover (2001) argues, "The roles of responsibility in hegemonic models of masculinity have many positive aspects, but a basic question is how to promote these without reproducing the underlying system of gender inequality" (p. 243). Turning from approaches stressing a "softer" masculinity that includes introspection and caring, Dover looks at the areas of joint interest between men and women for hope. Men and women pursue common community and political goals. They are also increasingly sharing tasks and responsibilities at the household level.

The explanation for these changes is that "women's and men's common interests are usually more important than other differences and working together gives better opportunities for achievements" (Dover, 2001, p. 244). This approach gets away from the binary, almost Manichean, view of women as victims and men as perpetrators and promotes an approach rooted in the material realities of the Third World and in local (indigenous) value systems as well.

CONCLUSION

Men in the postcolonial world face many challenges. Poverty, violence, and AIDS are among the most daunting. Yet, they do not face these challenges alone or without resources. Theoretical attention given to postcolonial situations shows that men already are responding creatively to their marginalization, not least by understanding what this marginalization means and how, historically, it has come about. The representation of black and postcolonial masculinity can now no longer be taken for granted as neutral. The way in which black men are positioned has become central to the ways in which we think about men in postcolonial contexts.

Postcolonial men use a variety of cultural resources to give their lives meaning and to shape their interaction with their social environment. Indigenous knowledge offers ways of understanding life in terms that are not derived from the metropole or necessarily mediated by the cultural effects of globalization. Such understanding can promote harmonious and communal living and, in this way, provide a buttress against the corrosive, individualizing imperatives of globalization.

Yet globalization undoubtedly affects the postcolonial world. It aggravates class divisions and deepens poverty. Fortunately, it also provides the possibility for new forms of collective action and politics (Hyslop, 1999). People in the Third World wrestling with the depredations of globalization have been able to take some comfort from the growth of the "third (service) sector," in which nongovernmental organizations (NGOs) have proved to be critical in fostering development. In many countries, NGOs have become the primary agents for the delivery of services. Growing sensitivity in the development sector to the importance of working with men and

masculinity and to the danger of ignoring local conditions and knowledge has provided some room for cautious optimism. Initiatives are bringing men and women together to build a new future. They are helping to shape fresh and innovative ways of "being a man."

NOTE

1. These ideas are drawn from seminars delivered by James Buchanan at the University of Natal, Durban, in March 1997.

REFERENCES

Adam, I., & Tiffin, H. (1990). *Past the last post: Theorizing post-colonialism and postmodernism.* Calgary, Alberta: University of Calgary Press.

Ahmad, A. (1992). *In theory: Classes, nations, literatures.* London: Verso.

Ahmad, A. (Ed.). (1996). *Lineages of the present.* New Delhi: Taluka.

Amadiume, I. (1987). *Male daughters, female husbands: Gender and sex in an African society.* London: Zed Press.

Appadurai, A. (1996). *Modernity at large: Cultural dimensions of globalisation.* Minneapolis: University of Minnesota Press.

Appiah, K. A. (1991). Is the post- in postmodernism the post- in postcolonial? *Critical Inquiry, 17*(2), 336-357.

Berger, R. (1992). Review of Adam, Ian, and Helen Tiffin, eds. *Past the last post: Theorizing postmodernism and post-colonialism.* Calgary: U Calgary P, 1990 [Book review]. *Postmodern Culture, 2*(2). Retrieved January 31, 2004, from http://muse.jhu.edu/journals/postmodern_culture/toc/pmc2.2.html

Bhabha, H. K. (1994). *The location of culture.* London: Routledge.

Biddulph, S. (1997). *Raising boys.* Sydney: Finch.

Broodryk, J. (1995). Is ubuntuism unique? In J. G. Malherbe (Ed.), *Decolonizing the mind* (pp. 31-37). Pretoria, South Africa: Research Unit for African Philosophy, UNISA.

Bujra, J. (2000). Targeting men for a change: AIDS discourse and activism in Africa. *Agenda,* 6-23.

Campbell, C. (1992). Learning to kill: Masculinity, the family and violence in Natal. *Journal of Southern African Studies, 18*(3), 614-628.

Carr, E. H. (1964). *What is history?* Harmondsworth, England: Penguin Books.

Carton, B. (2001). Locusts fall from the sky: Manhood and migrancy in KwaZulu. In R. Morrell (Ed.),

Changing men in Southern Africa (pp. 129-140). Pietermaritzburg, South Africa: University of Natal Press.

Chant, S. (2000). From "woman-blind" to "man-kind": Should men have more space in gender and development? *IDS Bulletin, 31*(2), 7-17.

Coleman, D. (1998). *Reading the post colonial male in new Canadian narratives.* Toronto, Ontario: University of Toronto Press.

Collins, P. H. (1990). *Black feminist thought: Knowledge, consciousness and the politics of empowerment.* Boston: Unwin Hyman.

Comaroff, J., & Comaroff, J. (1987). The madman and the migrant: Work and labor in the historical consciousness of a South African people. *American Ethnologist, 14*(2), 191-209.

Corneau, G. (1991). *Absent fathers, lost sons.* Boston: Shambhala.

Cornwall, A. (2000). Missing men? Reflections on men, masculinities and gender in GAD. *IDS Bulletin, 31*(2), 18-27.

Cornwall, A., & White, S. (Eds.). (2000). Men, masculinities and development: Politics, policies and practice. *IDS Bulletin, 31*(2), 60-67.

Davidson, B. (1961). *Black mother: Africa—the years of trial.* London: Gollancz.

Diallo, D. (1998, August). New images of Africa in the news. *Africa Recovery Online, 12*(1). Retrieved January 31, 2004, from http://www.un.org/ecosocdev/geninfo/afrec/vol12no1/baobab.htm

Dollimore, J. (1997). Desire and difference: Homosexuality, race and masculinity. In H. Stecopoulos & M. Uebel (Eds.), *Race and the subject of masculinities* (pp. 17-44). Durham, NC: Duke University Press.

Dover, P. (2001). *A man of power: Gender and HIV/AIDS in Zambia.* Unpublished doctoral thesis, Uppsala University, Sweden.

du Bois, W. E. B. (2001). *Black reconstruction: An essay toward a history of the part which black folk played in the attempt to reconstruct democracy in America, 1860.* Notre Dame, IN: University of Notre Dame Press. (Original work published 1934)

Engle, P. L. (1997). The role of men in families: Achieving gender equity and supporting children. *Gender and Development, 5*(2), 31-40.

Epprecht, M. (1998). The "unsaying" of indigenous homosexualities in Zimbabwe: Mapping a blindspot in an African masculinity. *Journal of Southern African Studies, 24*(4), 631-652.

Epprecht, M. (2001, January). An African feminism (Book review). H-SAfrica.

Everatt, D. (2000). From urban warriors to market segment? Youth in South Africa 1990-2000. *Development Update, 3*(2), 1-39.

Falabella, G. (1997). New masculinity: A different route. *Gender and Development, 5*(2), 62-64.

Fanon, F. (1986). *Wretched of the earth* (C. Farrington, Trans.). New York: Grove Press. (Original work published 1963)

Finnström, S. (1997). Post coloniality and the post colonial: Theories of the global and the local. *Working Papers in Cultural Anthropology, 7.*

Foreman, M. (1999). *AIDS and men: Taking risks or taking responsibility.* London: Zed Press.

Frank, A. G. (1971). *Capitalism and underdevelopment in Latin America.* London: Penguin Books.

Frank, A. G. (1978). *Dependent accumulation and underdevelopment.* London: Macmillan Press.

Frederiksen, B. F. (2000). Popular culture, gender relations and the democratization of everyday life in Kenya. *Journal of Southern African Studies, 26*(2), 209-222.

Freedman, M. (1999). *Renaissance dawning: South Africa—into the 21st century.* Rivonia, South Africa: Zebra.

Fuss, D. (1989). *Essentially speaking: Feminism, nature, and difference.* New York: Routledge.

Gemeda, A., & Booji, L. (1998). Violence against Oromo women by the dominant society and by members of the indigenous community. In A. van Achterberg (Ed.), *Out of the shadows: The first African indigenous women's conference* (pp. 83-85). Amsterdam: Netherlands Centre for Indigenous People.

Getecha, C., & Chipika, J. (Eds.). (1995). *Zimbabwe women's voices.* Harare: Zimbabwe Women's Resource Centre and Network.

Gevisser, M., & Cameron, E. (Eds.). (1994). *Defiant desire: Gay and lesbian lives in South Africa.* Johannesburg, South Africa: Ravan.

Gilroy, P. (1993). *The black Atlantic: Modernity and double consciousness.* Cambridge, MA: Harvard University Press.

Golding, P., & Harris, P. (Eds.). (1997). *Beyond cultural imperialism: Globalization, communication, and the new international order.* London: Sage

Goodwin-Gill, G., & Cohn, I. (1994). *Child soldiers: The role of children in armed conflicts.* Oxford, England: Clarendon Press.

Gray, J. (1998). *False dawn: The delusion of global capitalism.* London: Sage.

Greene, M. E. (2000). Changing women and avoiding men: Gender stereotypes and reproductive health programmes. *IDS Bulletin, 31*(2), 49-59.

Greig, A. (2000). The spectacle of men fighting. *IDS Bulletin, 31*(2), 28-32.

Greig, A., Kimmel, M., & Lang, J. (2000, May). *Men, masculinities and development: Broadening our work towards gender equality* [UNDP/GIDP No. 10]. New York: United Nations Development Program.

Gutmann, M. (2001). The vicissitudes of men and masculinities in Latin America. *Men and Masculinities, 3*(3), 235-236.

Hall, C. (1992). *White, male and middle-class: Explorations in feminism and history.* Cambridge, England: Polity Press.

Hallam, R. (1994). *Crimes without punishment: Sexual harassment and violence against female students in schools and universities in Africa.* London: African Rights.

Hassim, S., & Walker, C. (1992). Women's studies and the women's movement. *Transformation, 18/19.*

Heald, S. (1999). *Manhood and morality: Sex, violence and ritual in Gisu society.* New York: Routledge.

Hearn, J. (1998). *The violences of men.* Thousand Oaks, CA: Sage.

Hearn, J. (2001, September). Men stopping men's violence to women. *Development: The Journal of the Society for International Development, 44*(3), 85-89.

Heward, C. (1999). The new discourses of gender, education and development. In C. Heward & S. Bunwaree (Eds.), *Gender, education and development: Beyond access to empowerment* (pp. 1-14). London: Zed Books.

Hoch, P. (1979). *White hero, black beast: Racism, sexism and the mask of masculinity.* London: Pluto.

hooks, b. (1981). *Ain't I a woman: Black women and feminism.* Boston: South End Press.

hooks, b. (1990). *Yearning: Race, gender, and cultural politics.* Boston: South End Press.

Hutcheon, L. (1992). *A poetics of postmodernism.* London: Routledge.

Hyslop, J. (1999). *African democracy in the era of globalization.* Johannesburg, South Africa: University of the Witwatersrand Press.

James, C. L. R. (1989). *The black Jacobins: Toussaint L'Ouverture and the San Domingo revolution.* New York: Vintage Books. (Original work published 1938)

Jefferson, T. (1996). From "little fairy boy" to "the compleat destroyer": Subjectivity and transformation in the biography of Mike Tyson. In M. Mac an Ghaill (Ed.), *Understanding masculinities.* Milton Keynes, PA: Open University Press.

Jewkes, R., & Abrahams, N. (2000). *Violence against women in South Africa: Rape and sexual coercion.* Pretoria, South Africa: Medical Research Council.

Jewkes, R., Levin, J., Mbananga, N., & Bradshaw, D. (2002, January 26). Rape of girls in South Africa. *Lancet, 359,* 274-275.

Johnson, D. (1997). *Democracy and the law.* Cape Town, South Africa: Juta.

Johnson, D. (2001). Travellers' tales: Alternative traditions. *Wasafiri, 34.*

King, A. E. V. (2001, January 22). *Women and conflict management in Africa.* Retrieved January 31, 2004, from http://www.africaleadership.org/tuniskey.htm

Large, J. (1997). Disintegration conflicts and the restructuring of masculinity. *Gender and Development, 5*(2), 23-30.

Lazarus, N. (1999). *Nationalism and cultural practice in the postcolonial world.* Cambridge, England: Cambridge University Press.

Leclerc-Madlala, S. (2001). Virginity testing: Managing sexuality in a maturing HIV/AIDS epidemic. *Medical Anthropology Quarterly, 15*(4), 533.

Lemon, J. (1995). Masculinity in crisis? *Agenda, 24,* 61-71.

Lewis, D. (2001). African feminisms. *Agenda, 50,* 4-10.

Linkogle, S. (2001). Nicaraguan women in an age of globalization. In S. Rowbotham & S. Linkogle (Eds.), *Women resist globalization: Mobilizing for livelihoods and rights.* London: Zed Books.

Loomba, A. (1998). *Colonialism/postcolonialism.* London: Routledge.

Mac an Ghaill, M. (Ed.). (1996). *Understanding masculinities.* Milton Keynes, PA: Open University Press.

MacPhail, C., & Campbell, C. (2000). "I think condoms are good but, aai, I hate those things": Condom use among adolescents and young people in a southern African township. *Social Science and Medicine, 52,* 1613-1627.

Mager, A. (1998). Youth organisations and the construction of masculine identities in the Ciskei and Transkei, 1945-1960. *Journal of Southern African Studies, 24*(4), 653-668.

Mohammed, P. (1998). Towards indigenous feminist theorizing in the Caribbean. *Feminist Review, 59,* 6-33.

Majors, R. (1986). Cool pose: The proud signature of black survival. *Changing Men: Issues in Gender, Sex and Politics, 17,* 83-87.

Makang, J.-M. (1997). Of the good use of tradition: Keeping the critical perspective in African philosophy. In E. C. Eze (Ed.), *Post colonial African philosophy: A critical reader* (pp. 326-327). London: Blackwell.

Makgoba, M. W. (Ed.). (1999). *African renaissance: The new struggle.* Sandton, South Africa: Mafube.

Mama, A. (1997). Heroes and villains: Conceptualizing colonial and contemporary violence against women in Africa. In M. J. Alexander & C. T. Mohanty (Eds.), *Feminist genealogies, colonial legacies* (pp. 46-62). New York: Routledge.

Manicom, L. (2001). Globalizing "gender" in—or as—governance? Questioning the terms of local translations. *Agenda, 48,* 6-21.

Marriott, D. (1996). Reading black masculinities. In M. Mac an Ghaill (Ed.), *Understanding masculinities.* Milton Keynes, PA: Open University Press.

Mayekiso, T. V. (1995). Attitudes of black adolescents towards suicide. In L. Schleubusch (Ed.), *Suicidal behaviour 3* (Proceedings of the Third

Southern African Conference on Suicidology). Durban, South Africa: University of Natal Medical School.

Mbeki, T. (1998). *Africa: The time has come.* Cape Town, South Africa: Mafube.

Mbigi, L. (1995). *Ubuntu: A rainbow celebration of cultural diversity.* Pretoria, South Africa: Ubuntu School of Philosophy.

McClintock, A. (1995). *Imperial leather: Race, gender, and sexuality in the colonial context.* New York: Routledge.

Messerschmidt, J. (2000). Becoming "real men": Adolescent masculinity challenges and sexual violence. *Men and Masculinities, 2*(3), 286-307.

Minh-Ha, T. (1995). Writing post coloniality and feminism. In B. Ashcroft, G. Griffiths, & H. Tiffin (Eds.), *The post colonial studies reader* (pp. 264-268). London: Routledge.

Mirza, H. S. (Ed.). (1997). *Black British feminism.* New York: Routledge.

Mohanty, C., Russo, A., & Torres, L. (Eds.). (1991). *Third World women and the politics of feminism.* Bloomington: Indiana University Press.

Moore, H. L., Sanders, T., & Kaare, B. (Eds.). (1999). *Those who play with fire: Gender, fertility and transformation in East and Southern Africa.* London: Athlone Press.

Moore-Gilbert, B. (1997). *Postcolonial theory: Contexts, practices, politics.* London: Verso.

Morrell, R. (Ed.). (2001). *Changing men in Southern Africa.* Pietermaritzburg: University of Natal Press.

Msimang, S. (2000). African renaissance: Where are the women? *Agenda, 44,* 67-83.

Mudimbe, V. Y. (1994). *The idea of Africa.* Bloomington: Indiana University Press.

Mulemfo, M. M. (2000). *Thabo Mbeki and the African renaissance: The emergence of a new African leadership.* Pretoria, South Africa: Actua Press.

Niehaus, I. (2000). Towards a dubious liberation: Masculinity, sexuality and power in South African lowveld schools, 1953-1999. *Journal of Southern African Studies, 26*(3), 387-407.

Oduol, W., & Kabira, W. M. (1995). The mother of warriors and her daughters: The women's movement in Kenya. In A. Basu (Ed.), *The challenge of local feminisms: Women's movements in global perspective* (pp. 187-208). Boulder, CO: Westview Press.

Ouzgane, L., & Coleman, D. (1998). Cashing out the patriarchal dividends: An interview with R. W. Connell. *Jouvert, 2*(1). Retrieved December 27, 2003, from http://social.chass .ncsu.edu/jouvert/v2i1/Connell.htm

Oyewumi, O. (1997). *The invention of women: Making an African sense of Western gender discourses.* Minneapolis: University of Minnesota Press.

Parker, R. (1999). *Beneath the equator: Cultures of desire, male homosexuality, and emerging gay communities in Brazil.* New York: Routledge.

Pattman, R. (2001). "The beer drinkers say I had a nice prostitute, but the church goers talk about things spiritual": Learning to be a man at a teachers college in Zimbabwe. In R. Morrell (Ed.), *Changing men in Southern Africa* (pp. 225-238). Pietermaritzburg: University of Natal Press.

Peters, K., & Richards, P. (1998). Why we fight: Voices of youth combatants in Sierra Leone. *Africa, 68*(2), 183-210.

Plaatje, S. T., & Head, B. (1996). *Native life in South Africa.* Athens: Ohio University Press.

Population Reference Bureau. (2001a). *2001 world population data sheet.* Washington, DC: Author.

Population Reference Bureau. (2001b). *Youth in Sub-Saharan Africa: A chartbook on sexual experience and reproductive health.* Washington, DC: Author.

Qunta, C. (1987). *Women in Southern Africa.* Johannesburg, South Africa: Skotaville.

Rajan, R. S. (Ed.). (1999). *Signposts: Gender issues in post-independence India.* New Delhi: Kali for Women.

Ratele, K. (1998). The end of the black man. *Agenda, 37.*

Ratele, K. (2001). Between "ouens": Everyday makings of black masculinity. In R. Morrell (Ed.), *Changing men in southern Africa.* Pietermaritzburg, South Africa: University of Natal Press.

Regehr, E. (1999). Introduction. In *Project Ploughshares: Armed conflicts report 1999.* Retrieved January 31, 2004, from http://www .ploughshares.ca/content/ACR/ACR99.html

Rifkin, J. (2000). *The end of work: The decline of the global work-force and the dawn of the post-market era.* London: Penguin Books.

Ross, M. B. (1998). In search of black men's masculinities. *Feminist Studies, 24*(3), 599-626.

Said, E. (1978). *Orientalism.* New York: Pantheon.

Salo, E. (2001). Interview with Amina Mama: Talking about feminism in Africa. *Agenda, 50,* 58-63.

Sampath, N. (1997). "Crabs in a bucket": Re-forming male identities in Trinidad. *Gender and Development, 5*(2), 47-54.

Schwalbe, M. (1996). *Unlocking the iron cage: The men's movement, gender politics and American culture.* New York: Oxford University Press.

Serothe, P. (1992). Issues of race and power expressed during gender conferences in South Africa. *Agenda, 14,* 22-24.

Shire, C. (1994). Men don't go to the moon: Language, space and masculinities in Zimbabwe. In A. Cornwall & N. Lindisfarne (Eds.),

Dislocating masculinities: Comparative ethnographies (pp. 147-158). London: Routledge.

Silberschmidt, M. (1992). Have men become the weaker sex? Changing life situations in the Kisii district, Kenya. *Journal of Modern African Studies, 30*(2), 237-253.

Silberschmidt, M. (1999). *"Women forget that men are the masters": Gender antagonism and socioeconomic change in Kisii District, Kenya.* Copenhagen, Denmark: Nordiska Afrikainstitutet.

Sinha, M. (1995). *Colonial masculinity: The "manly Englishman" and the "effeminate Bengali" in the late nineteenth century.* Manchester, England: Manchester University Press.

Sole, K. (1994). Democratising culture and literature in a "New South Africa": Organisation and theory. *Current Writing, 6*(2), 1-37.

Spivak, G. (1996). "Women as theatre": United Nations Conference on Women, Beijing 1995. *Radical Philosophy, 75,* 2-4.

Staples, R. (1982). *Black masculinity: The black male's role in American society.* San Francisco: Black Scholar Press.

Stecopoulos, H., & Uebel, M. (Eds.). (1997). *Race and the subject of masculinities.* Durham, NC: Duke University Press.

Stichter, S. B., & Parpart, J. L. (Eds.). (1988). *Patriarchy and class: African women in the home and the workforce.* Boulder, CO: Westview Press.

Stoler, A. (1989). Making empire respectable: The politics of race and sexual morality in 20th-century colonial cultures. *American Ethnologist, 16,* 634-660.

Swart, S. (1998). A Boer and his gun and his wife are three things always together. *Journal of Southern African Studies, 24*(4), 737-752.

Sweetman, C. (Ed.). (1997). Men, masculinity, and development. *Gender and Development, 5*(2, Special issue).

Tallis, V. (2000). Gendering the response to HIV/AIDS: Challenging gender inequality. *Agenda, 44,* 58-66.

Varga, C. (2001). The forgotten fifty percent: A review of sexual and reproductive health research and programs focused on boys and young men in Sub-Saharan Africa. *African Journal of Reproductive Health, 5*(3), 175-195.

Wardrop, J. (2001). "Simply the best": Soweto flying squad, professional masculinities and the rejection of machismo. In R. Morrell (Ed.), *Changing men in Southern Africa* (pp. 255-270). Pietermaritzburg, South Africa: University of Natal Press.

Westwood, S. (1990). Racism, black masculinity and the politics of space. In J. Hearn & D. Morgan (Eds.), *Men, masculinities and social theory.* London: Unwin Hyman.

White, S. (2000). "Did the earth move?": The hazards of bringing men and masculinities into gender and development. *IDS Bulletin, 31*(2).

Whiteside, A., & Sunter, C. (2000). *The challenge for South Africa.* Johannesburg, South Africa: Human & Rousseau.

Williams, P., & Chrisman, L. (Eds.). (1993). *Colonial discourse and post colonial theory.* Harlow, England: Harvester Wheatsheaf.

Wood, K., & Jewkes, R. (1997). Violence, rape and sexual coercion: Everyday love in a South African township. *Gender and Development, 5*(2), 41-46.

Wood, K., & Jewkes, R. (2001). "Dangerous" love: Reflections on violence among Xhosa township youth. In R. Morrell (Ed.), *Changing Men in Southern Africa.* Pietermartizburg/London: University of Natal Press/Zed Books.

Xaba, T. (2001). Masculinity and its malcontents: The confrontation between "struggle masculinity" and "post struggle masculinity" (1990-1997). In R. Morrell (Ed.), *Changing men in Southern Africa.* Pietermaritzburg, South Africa: University of Natal Press.

Young, R. (1995). *Colonial desire: Hybridity in theory, culture, and race.* London: Routledge.

7

MASCULINITIES IN LATIN AMERICA

MATTHEW C. GUTMANN

MARA VIVEROS VIGOYA

BACKGROUND

The embryonic study of men and masculinities in Latin America has already made rich theoretical and empirical contributions to the field as a whole. Covering an area of several hundred million men and women within some two dozen countries and well over 100 language groups, scholarly research in the 1980s and 1990s on *hombres* and *homens* in the region emerged as a crucial component of gender studies as a whole.[1]

One of the outstanding features of scholarship on men and masculinities in Latin America stems from the fact that the field was initiated and developed by feminist women as an outgrowth of their previous work in the 1970s on women's oppression and feminist movements. Men's studies were envisioned from the beginning as a component part of gender studies and the struggle against gender inequalities overall. Thus, their origins stand somewhat in contrast to the study of men and masculinities in the Anglo-Saxon world, where it was far more a case of men studying other men—men like themselves in at least some respects. Indeed, to this day, feminist women continue to play a particularly prominent role in the study of men and masculinities in this region.

In addition to noting its origins in earlier feminist efforts, the study of masculinities in Latin America was born from practical efforts to understand and combat AIDS. In this respect, the study of AIDS illustrates another noteworthy characteristic of the study of masculinities in Latin America: its attention to social problems and their solutions. In line with scholarship more generally in the region, and at a time when class was no longer seen as a relevant distinction in other regions of the world—when, instead, issues of ethnicity, race, and sexual orientation received far more attention in scholarship of masculinities elsewhere—class inequalities have remained far more consistently embedded in the research of Latin American social scientists. Part of the reason for this undoubtedly relates to the fact that the process of modernization in Latin America has always been extremely uneven. The crises of the 1980s, for instance, were catastrophic for masses of people in Latin America, and governmental responses merely accentuated the differences between rich and poor, broadened unemployment among men, and forced women to find new ways of surviving in ever more precarious circumstances. As we will see, these crises also contributed to the transformation that some in the region termed "an erosion of machismo."

The ideology of *mestizaje,* racial and ethnic mixing, has been so strong historically in Latin America that the relevance of race and ethnicity for the study of masculinities in Latin America has not been recognized nearly as much as is necessary in the region. Historically, ethnicity has been understood in Latin America as a question of triethnic societies of Spanish, Indian, and Black peoples, which were somehow magically molded into a *mestizo* whole. Only in the final years of the 20th century did people in Latin America begin to talk seriously of multiculturalism and pluriethnicity.[2] Consequently, only a few studies of masculinities in Latin America to date have focused on Indian and black populations.

As is true for other parts of the world, there is a tendency in research on masculinities in Latin America to oversimplify supposed common traits found among men in the region as a whole and to equate manliness with particular national or regional qualities, as if distinctions among men within the region mattered little and as if women were not also active participants in the creation and transformation of cultural traits in general. The tension between generalizing for Latin American men overall and emphasizing cultural diversity between men continues to provoke debate and controversy. Similarly, the impact on the region of gender stereotypes about the region that emanate from elsewhere is a reflection of the conceptualization outside Latin America of a solitary Latin American mestizo male. Other men—for example, blacks, Indians, and men who have sex with other men—have been largely ignored or misrepresented.

Most of the initial studies of masculinities in Latin America have been conducted by anthropologists, historians, psychologists, sociologists, and researchers in public health. Although some disciplines and concentrations in particular areas and interests have been better represented than others in the field, feminist studies on the relationship of men to gender inequality and attention to AIDS and same-sex sex have been consistent concerns within the emerging scholarship on men and masculinities throughout Latin America. In the 1990s, several North Americans wrote outstanding ethnographies and histories in English of men and masculinities in Latin America. During the same period, there was a simultaneous "boom" in research on this subject written in Spanish and Portuguese in Latin America. But very few of these Spanish and Portuguese studies were translated into English, and for this reason, many English-only scholars have not had access to the investigations and conclusions of their Latin American colleagues. To be sure, more than a matter of translation is involved, because there are not only linguistic obstacles to collegial exchanges but a need to facilitate the ongoing process of learning from different conceptual frameworks, methodological styles, and research questions.

KEY THEORETICAL PERSPECTIVES

By the end of the 1980s in Latin America, the two theoretical paradigms that had been dominant in the 1970s—North American functionalism and Marxism—came under sharp critique. In their place, in distinct disciplines of the social sciences, renewed attention was paid to questions of daily life, emotions and feelings, and gender relations. As soon as the working class became less central, for example, the so-called new social movements (among them, the feminist movement) opened the way for new theoretical conceptions and new social concerns. Feminist women historians, anthropologists, and philosophers provided new theoretical and political frameworks; Joan Scott (1999) and Marta Lamas (1986, 1996) pointed to the ways power is articulated in gender relations; Henrietta Moore (1988) and Verena Stolcke (1992) underlined articulations between gender, class, race, ethnicity, culture, and history; and Gayle Rubin (1993) developed a widely used framework for understanding the relationship between gender and sexuality. The work of authors like Pierre Bourdieu, Anthony Giddens, and Norbert Elias also proved especially influential in Latin American studies of masculinity.

Bourdieu's (1990, 1998) discussion of Mediterranean beliefs organized around "the cult of virility," for instance, has been used to discuss more generally questions of male domination in relation to other forms of power inequalities. Research in Latin America on sexuality, love, the body, and personal negotiations that take place in intimate spaces has drawn on the work of Giddens (1991, 1992). Elias (e.g., 1994) has been employed to explore the relationship between broad social transformations and daily life with respect to power equilibriums. Although not focused on questions of gender, the work of Néstor García Canclini (e.g., 1995) on questions of "hybridity" (cultural mixing) is also worth mentioning for its general influence in understanding the particularities of modernity and masculinity in Latin America, although it must be added that this concept has been criticized when employed to promote a kind of "neo-exotic" Latin America in which hybridity is simply the source of pleasure, in contrast to a view of the region grounded in an understanding of the politically challenging and incompatible differences that exist there.

Theories of hegemonic and marginal masculinities by R. W. Connell (1987) and others have been adapted to specific local conditions in studies throughout the region (Viveros, Olavarría, & Fuller, 2001), and more recently, concepts developed in queer theory (e.g., Butler, 1993) have helped researchers frame certain aspects of their investigations relating to subordinate forms of masculinity (Fuller, 1997). Among the important studies of masculinity and the body in Latin America have been those by Jardim (1995), Leal (1995), and Viveros (1999). In his influential formulation linking questions of hegemonic masculinity with studies of the body, Benno de Keijzer (1998) advances the notion of "masculinity as a risk factor"; in the field of public health, for instance, issues of domestic violence, reproductive health, and alcoholism are directly traced by de Keijzer to hegemonic patterns of male embodiment.

KEY EMPIRICAL RESEARCH

Among the areas of research that have been developed in the study of masculinity in Latin America, some of the most promising have focused on questions of family divisions of labor, parenting, and housework; homosociality in friendship and social spaces; masculine identity construction; reproductive health issues concerning same-sex sex, active and passive sexuality, AIDS, and male reproductive rights; ethnicity and masculinity among indigenous, African Latino, and *mestizo* populations; class and work; and the infamous matter of machismo.

Fatherhood and Family

Santiago Bastos (1998) seeks to understand gender relations as they are manifested in internal dynamics of households in popular sectors in indigenous and nonindigenous households in the same working class neighborhoods of Guatemala City. Bastos examines the manner, often implicit, in which economic responsibility and domestic authority operate and proposes that we conceptualize the activities of heads of households as analytically discrete, in part normative and in part actual and practical. Elsewhere, Bastos (1999) explains certain ambiguous behavior by men in popular sectors through the "double system" of masculinity in relation to men's capacity to fulfill their roles as economic providers and men's need to present themselves as free from social ties, in particular those with women.

In their study on heads of households and fatherhood among popular sectors of the population of Medellín, Colombia, Marie Dominique de Suremain and Oscar Fernando Acevedo (1999) use a similar analytic perspective to show that, along with new social and parenting demands on fathers, the objective obstacles—unemployment and unstable employment, "displacements,"[3] marital separations, and women's adoption of new roles—impeding a positive realization of this paternal role have multiplied. As one of the few scholars to deal with the construction of masculinity in dominant social sectors in Latin America, Norma Fuller (1997, 2001) demonstrates that in the middle class, Peruvian men have not experienced significant changes as much as women, because the latter have entered spheres traditionally considered masculine and have in this way acquired new freedoms. Thus, if men have seen reason to question existing male models, it is due to the transformations undergone by women.

In *O Mito da Masculinidade,* Nolasco (1993) argues that paternity in Brazil represents the most conflictive dimension of masculine identity. Nolasco examines the father-son link to better understand what happens to men who attempt to create a sense of belonging and involve themselves with their own children more completely than did their own fathers. For Nolasco, fatherhood is a manner in which men insert themselves into society to fuse the processes of masculine identity construction with the authoritarian role that is performed by men.

Hernán Henao (1997) describes recent changes in the manner of being a father in Colombia. Drawing on a series of field studies in the Antioquia region of that country, Henao points out that the image of the traditional father has existed precisely because of the discourse promoted by mothers and priests. The traditional father has been "an unreachable being, one who disappears in everyday events." Today, on the contrary, fathers are men expected to interact more with family members and to enjoy their home environment, very different from the fathers of bygone times, when male roles and values were determined by men's lives outside the domestic sphere. As Henao suggests, these new demands on the father began taking shape in the 1960s, with the feminist movements at the time, and acquired a particular salience in the 1990s, when Colombian men began to become aware of the gender problem.

In his ethnographic study on changing gender relations in Mexico City, Matthew Gutmann (1996) explores themes associated with fatherhood, such as the precarious connection between masculine sexuality and reproductive imperatives; the importance of blood ties and their relation to abandonment and adoption; and popular concepts about family, adultery, and polygamy. For Gutmann, diverse paternal practices existing in Mexico reveal the ambiguous character of masculinity there. In this context, he argues that there exists no solitary model of Mexican masculinity against which men can compare themselves or be compared. The results of his research lead to an opposite conclusion: For many men, being a committed parent is a central characteristic of being a man. Further, Gutmann shows how the ideas and practices related to fatherhood are elaborated differently in a range of social classes. Thus, in popular classes with lower educational achievement and few economic resources, it is not rare for men to care for small children; in social sectors with more resources, on the other hand, maids and nannies assume the majority of child care.

Adolescent fatherhood has been largely ignored in examinations of fatherhood in Latin America. In a recent study on adolescent male fatherhood in Brazil, Jorge Luiz Cardoso (1998) points to a "wall of silence" erected by institutions, researchers, and individuals affected in Brazil. He suggests that even when an adolescent father tries to play an active role in rearing his son or daughter, social institutions may impede or deny him the right to take on this role. Cardoso's study concludes that by culturally attributing conception and child rearing to women alone, the widespread perception in Brazilian society that children belong exclusively to their mothers is perpetuated, and adolescent fathers continue to be regarded merely as sons and not as potential fathers.

These studies illustrate the contradictions of contemporary fatherhood in Latin America, the impact of socioeconomic and political changes on intrafamilial relations, the progressive deinstitutionalization of fathers' role—increasingly more independent of authority—and the growing importance of fatherhood for masculine life projects. As noted, many authors point to a great variability in the experience of fatherhood according to men's socioeconomic and ethnic-racial allegiances, their generation, their primary experiences, the specific moment of the life cycle in which they find themselves, and the sexes and ages of their children.

Homosociality

With respect to the expression of masculinity in public spaces, including symbolic spaces of power in which women have traditionally not been present, Marqués (1997) points out, "in earlier Western patriarchal societies, most social life took place in exclusively male spaces, so that homosociality was an inevitable fact" (p. 28). Denise Fagundes Jardim (1992) presents a similar reflection about the social construction of male identity among the working class in Porto Alegre, Brazil. In her description of the *butecos* (bars where working class men gather), Jardim shows how men in Porto Alegre appropriate this social space to construct masculine territories. In these transitional spaces between the public work space and the private space of family life, conversations about politics, sports, or business are privileged, and when someone touches on a topic about private life, it is discussed from an impersonal and coded perspective, with little direct reference to the personal lives of those gathered. In another article about the same topic, Jardim (1995) highlights the importance for men of being able to share moments with other men in which they can reflect on ideal masculine behavior. In particular, they seek to present themselves as workers and providers for their families and to contrast this image with the negative figure of the Brazilian *malandro* (vagabond).

In his article on sports in Brazil, Edison Luis Gastaldo (1995) describes male relationships within a martial arts academy, Full Contact, and analyzes the practices and representations of the body by one group of participants. According to Gastaldo, the men's discourse about the relation of their bodies to this sport is characterized by three traits in particular: the use of the body for sparring, the rejection of pain, and the acceptance of rules that control this martial art. The description and discourse analysis of the practitioners of this sport suggest that the emphasis placed on overcoming pain and exhaustion by submitting to a strict regimen is part of constructing a masculine form of perceiving and molding the body.

The work site is another location affected by gender relations, involving as it does differences and inequalities in jobs, income distribution, working conditions, and the classification of work as male or female. This is illustrated in a study by Virginia Guzmán and Patricia Portocarrero (1992) through analysis of the life histories of male and female workers in Lima, Peru. In particular, Guzmán and Portocarrero examine the value assigned to women's and men's work within factory work spaces and the ways in which gender and broader social identities are linked. The authors maintain that women's presence in factories is not entirely accepted and that the values most esteemed in this environment are those most associated with "virile" qualities such as strength, capacity for resistance, the possession of technical knowledge, and the exercise of power. They also point out that the factory is occupied materially and symbolically by men and that discourse in the union is also dominated by notions of dominant masculinity, clearly linked in turn to a conceptualization of public space and citizenship as male privileges.

As in other parts of the world, homophobia in Latin America is a widespread source of violence directed at men who are seen as in some sense effeminate or are believed to have sex with other men. Homophobia in Latin America can be approached narrowly, as applying only to the ideas and actions of heterosexuals against homosexuals, or it may be understood in a broader sense, as incorporating feelings of homosocial discomfort and engendered ideologies of domination and subordination. It is not surprising that the issue of homophobia is given more systematic attention in studies of subordinate masculine practices (e.g., homosexual, transvestite, cross-dressing, gay, drag queen) than are heterosexual men in Latin America. Just as surely, however, scholars whose research is more concerned with self-identified heterosexual men also address matters like homosocial desires, fears, experiences, and prejudices in relation to topics like male friendships and social spaces. In Quibdó, Colombia, for instance, Mara Viveros (2002) reports that male youth routinely use the epithet *maricas* (queers) when referring to other youth who have demonstrated a lack of *lealtad* (loyalty). As Viveros concludes, "To betray the group constitutes the worst crime and a youth who was accused of being a traitor was labeled a 'marica,' not for his sexual practices but because of his disloyalty" (p. 208).

Such studies highlight the importance that men ascribe to these spheres of masculine homosociality in Latin America, where the very competition among men allows them to validate their maleness. In a sense, one could say that encounters between adult men in these spaces mitigate the forces that drive the masculinity of young gang members. With modernity, there emerges a feminine presence in spaces that have been regarded as proverbially masculine, such as cafés, bars, places of recreation and sport, workshops, and factories. Despite the fact that there are multiple concepts of masculinity, and despite the recent increase in encounters between men and women in time and space, however, there has often, in Latin America, been a tendency to reproduce relations grounded in hegemonic masculinity; that is, to ignore or subordinate women.

Identity Construction

Two pioneering studies, largely exploratory in character, have faced the challenge of recognizing and analyzing what it means to be a man and the consequences of being a man within a Latin American context. Indeed, one of the principal themes analyzed is the construction of masculine identity. Among the first Latin American studies seeking to answer these questions was the work of Sócrates Nolasco (1993) and that of Rafael L. Ramírez (1993/1999).

In the first case, in a study of 25 middle class men between 25 and 35 years old, Nolasco (1993) analyzes the oppressive forms in which Brazilian men are traditionally socialized—their relation to work, themselves, partners, friends, and children—thereby questioning the social parameters through which to define what a man is. Nolasco proposes that in various countries, increasing numbers of men are seeking other paths, therapies, and communities that will allow them to discover another kind of subjectivity, one in which emotions are not classified according to a sexist referent and in which emotions are not regarded as something harmful and irrational. The stereotype of the macho male excludes such subjective dynamics, making individuals believe that men are made from a series of absolutes: They never cry, they must be the best, they must always compete, they must be strong, they must not get affectively involved, and they must never retreat.

In his study, Ramírez (1993/1999) explores the construction of masculinity in Puerto Rico. The study begins with a critique of how the term *machismo* has been used and continues with a description of diverse masculinities in distinct ethnographic contexts. Ramírez also insists that the dominant ideology of masculinity is reproduced among men in homosexual relations and concludes his study by suggesting the possibility of constructing a new masculine identity, one stripped of the power games and competition present in the traditional male role. Ramírez concludes that in Puerto Rico, "masculine identity is embodied in the genitals and is articulated with sexuality and power" (p. 48) and that "encounters between men are based on power, competition, and possible conflict" (p. 58).

In contrast to Ramírez (1993/1999) and others, such as Olavarría and Parrini (2000), Sócrates Nolasco (1993) attempts to distinguish his study from feminism, arguing that the organization of groups of men cannot be characterized as a political movement and that each of these movements has its own characteristics and dynamics. Nolasco also criticizes what he sees as the association made by early feminism between patriarchy and men and the representation of women as virtuous and men as fundamentally bad.

Reproductive Health and Sexuality

In recent years, men's role in reproduction has become an important focus of studies on masculinity in Latin America (see, for example, Lerner, 1998). Scholars began by questioning the exclusive emphasis on women in reproductive health research, seeking instead to examine men's influence on women's health and on reproductive decisions in general (Tolbert, Morris, & Romero, 1994). Important studies, such as those of Juan Guillermo Figueroa (1998) in Mexico, Hernando Salcedo (1995) and Viveros and Gómez (1998) in Colombia, and Tolbert, Morris, and Romero (1994) in Latin America overall, have attempted to fill this void. Figueroa (1998), for example, seeks to conceptualize the ways in which Latin American scholars, educators, and activists have interpreted reproductive health in the male sphere and to analyze how men may be "located" within reproductive health processes. A particular theme discussed by Salcedo (1995) and Tolbert et al. (1994) has been the way in which gender relations overall affect decisions made in relation to abortion. Viveros and Gómez (1998) discuss male sterilization in Colombia as a contraceptive decision taken in a specific social context that defines and limits men's contraceptive options, models of masculinity, and the meanings of fatherhood and sexuality.

To incorporate men more explicitly in reproductive health research, Figueroa (1998) uses aspects of traditional demographic analysis linked to fertility to identify more comprehensive indicators of individual experiences involved in fertility and the reproductive process overall. Subsequently, Figueroa argues that by ignoring existing power relations between men and women, the medicalization of fertility can tend to endorse existing and exclusive "gender specialization." Men are, in effect, treated as agents who *can* impede or facilitate the regulation of fertility but are, ultimately, *incapable* of regulating it. He concludes by proposing several analytical and methodological strategies to uncover the presence of men in the reproductive health sphere.

In their research, Tolbert et al. (1994) discuss the relationship between gender relations and decisions to have abortions by couples in

Colombia, Peru, Mexico, and elsewhere. In particular, they note that couples whose relationships were characterized by a greater gender equality were more candid in their negotiations about abortion. In a similar fashion, based on 72 formal interviews with Colombian men who wrestled over abortion decisions, Salcedo (1995) analyzes the relationship between masculinity and abortion, including masculine representations of sexuality, reproductive life, and feelings of desire. Salcedo evaluates men's first reproductive event as a male rite of passage, discusses men's tendency to separate reproductive and sexual desires, and examines the relation between men's desire for heirs and women's own affective lives. Salcedo concludes by calling on men to participate more in reproductive decisions and to seek alternative ways of thinking about fatherhood.

In his study of 300 Uruguayan men, Gomensoro (1995) comes to similar conclusions. His findings show that men may change some opinions about family, couples, sexuality, and some of their social roles but that they often preserve a deeper set of "existential infrastructures." For this reason, relationships between couples and families are paradoxically more conflictive than ever before. In response to this crisis, he proposes a "new masculine condition." de Keijzer (1998) links masculine socialization to certain forms of intrafamilial violence, abuse, and sexual punishment; to the limited use of birth control and participation during pregnancy; and to the principal causes of male mortality. He (1998) conceives of "masculinity as a risk factor" in three arenas: men's relationships with women, with other men, and with themselves. In each arena, he explains how hegemonic masculinity has a notably harmful impact on men's health.

A common denominator in each of these studies is to reveal men's involvement in a realm traditionally assigned to women—the reproduction of the species—and to study male behavior and attitudes in sexual and reproductive health separately and from male points of view in various cultural contexts in Latin America. Although it has generally been argued that masculine sexuality is characterized by its separation from reproduction, these studies show how, by questioning the relationship between masculine identity and values associated with sexuality, male participation in different reproductive events (e.g., birth control, abortion, fatherhood,

sterilization) has been made problematic. At the same time, it is clear that a rift still exists between adoption of a modern discourse emphasizing male participation in reproductive decisions and the construction of new models of family life and gender relations on a more democratic and equal basis throughout the region.

Several studies (e.g., Cáceres, 1995; Serrano, 1994) point to the fact that adoption of traits or behaviors identified as masculine or feminine because they represent active or passive roles in sexual relations is independent of sexual orientation. Thus, many scholars have attempted to show that homosexual or heterosexual behavior is not necessarily linked to a differentiated sense of sexual identity (Parker, 1999). Writing in Colombia, José Fernando Serrano (1994) argues that homosexuality is a constructed category that refers to certain aspects of human life, that it involves more than sexual components, and that it carries with it certain implications for how life may be lived and a way of understanding and experiencing the world. Drawing on interviews with homosexual men from urban, middle class sectors in Colombia, Serrano determines that there exists no unitary homosexuality but rather a diversity of situations—multiple homosexual genders in which feminine and masculine components interact, varying according to individual lives. At the same time, through their practices, homosexual men in urban Colombia assign new meanings to categories and roles imposed by society, in this way resolving the tension between the identity socially suggested to them and the identities they develop and recreate.

In his article on health and bisexuality in Lima in the 1990s, Carlos Cáceres (1995) proposes a taxonomy of the range of experiences of homosexual men in Lima. The "characters" described by Cáceres are neither static nor clearly defined but rather in a process of appearance and disappearance. In this way, in working class sectors, for instance, one finds the "active" or *mostacero* bisexual man, who does not question his basic heterosexuality; the effeminate *marica* or *cabro*, who will not call himself a man; and the transvestite, who expresses himself through aggressively exaggerated feminine mannerisms. In middle class sectors, one finds the *entendido*, who participates in clandestine homosexual encounters, and the "married bisexual," the "bisexual gay," and the "gay," who participate fully in local homosexual culture and assume a macho style. Based on these characterizations, Cáceres proposes programs for AIDS prevention and sexual health that take into account the heterogeneity of sexual meanings.

Richard Parker (1999) is also interested in problems of sexual and reproductive health in relation to the development of sexual communities in Brazil and elsewhere in Latin America. Parker argues that some studies about gay communities in various developed countries point to an important correlation established between social development and support networks for gay communities and the resulting reduction of risk in sexual behavior. According to Parker, the absence of such structures in developing countries largely explains the limited behavioral changes in sexual matters in these regions. The spread of HIV/AIDS and the emergence of new homosexual communities, each with its own institutional structures and social representations, have called attention to specific social dynamics and economic and political processes found in sexual communities, particularly in developing countries, albeit within the context of an increasingly globalized system (see also Parker, 1994; Parker & Terto, 1998).

Based on the studies examined, we may conclude that the relationship between sexual behavior and gender identity in Latin America is a very complex one and that the way in which sexual identities are constructed in different cultural contexts depends to a large degree on the categories and classifications used in each culture to treat sexuality. The focus of these studies has evolved from concern with actual sexual behavior to explorations of the sociocultural conditions in which such behavior occurs and to the cultural norms that organize sexuality. How men and women in the region engage in verbal play with these corporal reference points, how they perform with more or less skill the gestures associated with masculinities and femininities, and how they defy concepts and practices prevalent in the worlds into which they were born are the subjects of Claudia Fonseca's (2001) examination of the discourse and substance of philandering in Porto Alegre, Brazil, and Xavier Andrade's (2001) look at political pornography in Guayaquil, Ecuador. From this point of view, local cultural categories and the classification schemes structuring and defining

sexual experience in different contexts have been increasingly emphasized, as it has become evident that categories such as homosexuality and heterosexuality do not reflect the diversity and complexity of the lived sexual experiences and that homosexual and heterosexual behavior have been disconnected from a distinct sense of gender identity.

Despite the work of gender studies to break with binary thinking, such models die slowly, and male-female divisions are still the foundation for much gender research in Latin America. A parallel model is found in some studies whose subject is same-sex sex among men, where rigid active-passive contrasts aim at explaining why active, penetrating men are not necessarily considered homosexual or gay by themselves or by others in society more broadly. As Richard Parker (1999) shows, although retaining useful elements, the active-passive taxonomy can miss as much as it captures with respect to changing norms and actual sexual practices (see also Lancaster, 1998; Núñez Noriega, 2001). With both so-called political passivity and sexual passivity there is evidently more at play than is perhaps immediately apparent; both forms of assumed passivity represent territories that remain to be more fully charted. Clearly, one obstacle that must be overcome in studying sexual passivity in Latin America is the notion that passivity is the mirror opposite of activity. Part of this conflation is confusion over power and control in sexual politics and choice. In her study of transvestites, queens, and machos in Mexico City, Annick Prieur (1998, p. 129) makes a similar point when she insists that, although her informants are victims of symbolic (and not so symbolic) violence, they are also in just as real a sense actors who *choose* certain elements of their lives; they are not simply the passive subjects of history.

Ethnicity and Race

In Latin American societies—multicultural, with a broad array of social classes—it has become necessary to think about the various ways in which masculine identities are constructed in various social sectors, ethnic groups, and sociocultural contexts. Although still too few in number, studies already conducted on ethnicity, race, and masculinity in Latin America have drawn important conclusions and indicate several new areas for future research. Work in Brazil by Ondina Fachel Leal (1992a, 1992b), for instance, considers the connection between cultural identity and gender identity. Drawing on her work on *gaúcho*[4] culture, Leal noted that gaúcho identity is strongly linked to masculine identity and described cultural expressions of the former such as myths, enchantments and seduction magic, verbal duels, and representations of death. Leal (1992a) looks at the meaning of masculine suicide in Rio Grande do Sul, the region where gaúcho culture is concentrated in Brazil, where suicide is a common practice and death represents a challenge and an opportunity for men to prove their masculinity.

Men in the Afro-Colombian population have been the focus of several studies. Joel Streicker (1995) analyzes the links established between class, race, and gender in daily life in the coastal city of Cartagena, Colombia. In particular, Streicker examines the interactions between these three categories in the everyday discourse of the residents of one barrio in Cartagena, claiming that the interdependence of race, class, and gender is related to the naturalization of difference and provides a powerful way of neutralizing social and individual subjectivities. The notion of masculinity is constructed not only in opposition to femininity but also in contrast to the masculinity of black men and rich men: The first group is considered dangerous and associated with what is animal; the second is perceived as more feminine because rich men are seen as more interested in themselves and more subject to restrictions imposed by their wives. From this perspective, Mara Viveros (1998, 1999) analyzes the representations of masculinity of a group of adult men from middle class sectors of Quibdó, the capital of the Chocó region of Colombia, where the largest percentage of the Afro-Colombian population lives. The author contends that sexual performance and a capacity for seduction and conquest are traits linked to black and masculine identities. Rather than confirming the racist stereotype that black men are obsessed with sex, this finding illustrates the overlap between gender and ethnic-racial identities. If one takes into account that identity is a relational construct, it is evident that Chocoan male masculinities have emerged in contrast to nonblack masculinities, because Chocoan men have in this manner used their corporeality in constructing their ethnic-racial identities as much as they have their gender identities. More recently, Fernando Urrea and Pedro Quintín (2001) have conducted important research among Afro-Colombian males younger than 25 years old in the city of Cali in the Pacific region of the country, seeking to understand the relationship between forms of sociability and conditions of socioracial exclusion there, as well as the production of subjectivities and identities among these young men.

Work by others, such as Santiago Bastos (1999) in Guatemala and Thomas Gregor (1985) in the Amazon region, represents pioneering explorations of the largely untapped topic of men and masculinity among indigenous peoples throughout the Americas. Taken as a whole, these initial forays into questions of ethnicity, race, and masculinity in Latin America demonstrate that just as it is important to recognize multiple masculinities across ethnic and racial lines, it is also necessary to understand that there is no essential black, *gaúcho,* or indigenous masculinity in Latin America.

Work

The connection between men's employment and their financial "maintenance" of a household and the connection between paid work and male identities is developed by numerous scholars, such as Agustín Escobar Latapí (2003), who looks at the impact of economic and social restructuring in Mexico on the lives of Mexican men in Monterrey, Guadalajara, and Mexico City in relation to their families, schooling, migration, and work. In Chile as elsewhere, as José Olavarría (2001) demonstrates, the industrial revolution separated the workplace from the home. This was particularly true in urban areas. Such a separation detached the place where people lived from sites where they produced. As the familial division of labor between wage-earning father-provider and domestic, child-rearing mother became general and routinized, men came to assume ever more patriarchal roles at the head of nuclear families; women took charge of few outside matters. Especially in the 20th century, this type of family became idealized by a large sector of the urban poor in Santiago as the normal and natural model. In fact, the existence and perpetuation of the patriarchal nuclear family was turned into an ideological truth through theories of sex-determined roles (see Chant, 2002b). Steve Stern (1995) shows, in his study of colonial Mexico, certain of the historical permutations that eventually led to a system in contemporary Mexico whereby remunerated labor was socially compulsory for men.

Machismo

Men in Mexico, Latin America, and indeed all Spanish-speaking countries have often been characterized as uniformly macho by anthropologists, other scholars, and journalists. Despite the fact that the terms *macho* and *machismo* have short histories as words, many writers from all over the world have seemed intent on discovering a ubiquitous, virulent, and "typically Latin" machismo among men from these areas. In the 1990s, there was a veritable boom in ethnographic and kindred work on machismo; for instance, the works of de Barbieri (1990), Parker (1991), Lancaster (1998), Limón (1994), Brusco (1995), Carrier (1995), Gutmann (1996), Mirandé (1997), Fuller (1998), and Ramírez (1993/1999).

The central claim of Brusco (1995), for example, is that evangelist Protestantism in Colombia has liberated women because it has "domesticated" men: Evangelist husbands and fathers eschew "public" machismo—drunkenness, violence, and adultery—and return to their family responsibilities. Ramírez (1993/1999) notes that the expression *machismo* is not used in the working class areas he studied in Puerto Rico, yet it is commonly employed in academic and feminist circles on the island. Lancaster (1992) reports that particular and unequal male-male sexual relations are what ultimately "grounds" the system of machismo in general in Nicaragua. Women may be ever present in men's lives, but they do not factor into the masculinity equation for basic bodily reasons.

In short, the word machismo has become a bellwether term in nearly all discussions of men and masculinities in Latin America. Although fewer scholars today argue that all Latin American men exhibit an obvious and identical machismo and that machismo, in the sense of sexism, is unique to Latin America, still, both popularly and in most scholarly literature, a tacit view that machismo is ubiquitous in the region

is alive and well. Without doubt, throughout the world today, machismo is a common expression for sexism, yet it is a term with a remarkably short history as a word, and its etymology derives as much from international political and social currents as from cultural artifacts peculiar to Latin America (see Gutmann, 1996).

CURRENT DEBATES AND CONTROVERSIES

Of the many specific topics of significant discussion and disagreement in the study of men and masculinities in Latin America at the beginning of the 21st century, we would highlight three. One, as indicated earlier, is the subject of same-sex sex. By the late 1990s, most scholars carefully avoided simplistic employment of the term "homosexual" to refer to men who have sex with other men in the region. Studies of Brazil and Mexico have been especially fruitful in developing these distinctions (for Brazil, see, for example, Beattie, 2001; Green, 2000; Kulick, 1998; and Parker, 1991, 1999; for Mexico, see Carrier, 1995; Hernández Cabrera, 2001; Higgins & Coen, 2000; Núñez Noriega, 1994, 2001; and Prieur, 1998).

Another topic of controversy in the region relates to understanding change and resilience; more specifically, how much men have changed in recent years. One area of research has been new forms of masculine domination and contradictions between modern discourses and so-called traditional practices. More generally, there has been considerable debate regarding diverse factors involved in change, such as political movements and modernization efforts with respect to education, reproductive health, and changing employment patterns.

Finally, it is important to note certain general differences evident in studies conducted *from* in contrast to those *about* Latin America. Scholars from Latin America often are especially concerned with developing and adapting theories for the complex conditions pertaining in different parts of their region, and they have shown themselves more reticent to adopt wholesale theories of, for example, hegemonic masculinity that initially emerged from distinct European and U.S. historical and cultural contexts. It goes without saying that sweeping generalizations about "Latin American men" or "Latin American machismo"—stereotypes, as often as not, grounded in the colonial imaginary and European notions of modernity—are encountered far more in studies written by scholars writing outside Latin America than in research performed by those writing from within the region.

FUTURE WORK

In the 1980s and 1990s, studies of "men-as-men" in Latin America developed in the wake of earlier feminist research by women and as an extension of these other studies. More than was true in the United States, studies of men-as-men in Latin America were usually framed by feminist theories of gender oppression, regardless of whether the primary focus was on heterosexual men or men who have sex with other men. That is, from the beginning, in studying men as engendered and engendering beings, in Latin America there was a more unambiguous adoption of critical feminist lenses for understanding men-as-men within general paradigms delineating power and inequality. The "me too-ism" that developed in parallel in certain wings of men's studies in North America and Europe has been far less influential in Latin America, although, to be sure, a translation into Spanish of Robert Bly's mythopoetic manifesto on Iron John, *Hombres de Hierro: Los ritos de iniciación masculina del Nuevo Hombre,* was quickly brought into print in 1992. Scholarship on men and masculinities in Latin America has been marked by feminist theoretical frameworks, and many women who have long been active in research and activism concerning women's oppression have been leaders in the emerging study of men and masculinities in the region.

With respect to announcements of the death of antiquated masculinity, one need not adopt the view that there is a New Man who has surfaced from the Argentine pampas to the shallows of the Rio Grande River, nor claim that challenges to men and masculinity are novel phenomena of our contemporary age, to recognize that men and women throughout Latin America have been grappling with what seem to many to be new ideas and relationships related to their masculine identities.

Despite differences of class, ethnic group, region, and generation, Latin America is still seen by many as constituting, in some palpable sense, a coherent area of historical and cultural commonalties with respect to certain aspects of gender and sexuality. That is, despite the real and unanimous acknowledgement of the profound impact of globalization on sexualities throughout Latin America, there is still simultaneously the deep-seated sense that these global influences were still filtered through particular, local, Latin American contexts. For this reason, to understand men and masculinities in the region, we are compelled to seek more than simply the Latin versions of global trends and transformations.

Although we find pan-Latin frameworks altogether inaccurate, we are compelled nonetheless to ask how sexualities in Latin America are part of global processes of change, those transformations under way in the late 20th century that carry profound implications for sexualities in the Latin Americas (see Olavarría, 2001; Parker, 1999).

Economically, these changes are evident in tracing the impact of neoliberal programs on reproductive health programs, the growing numbers of women working outside the home for money, and the expansion of international sex markets (see de Barbieri, 1990; García, 1994; Viveros, 1999). Politically, men and masculinities in Latin America have been affected regionally in dramatic ways by feminist projects and globally by urban movements for social services in which women have often played a significant role and in which men have been challenged by women's independence and initiative (see Chant & Gutmann, 2000; Fuller, 1997; Gutmann, 1997; Valdés, Benavente, & Cysling, 1999); by general trends toward democratization that have raised new issues of cultural citizenship, including issues concerning gender differences (see Gutmann, 2002; Viveros, 2001); and by AIDS activism in many countries of the region (see Parker & Cáceres, 1999).

Demographically, mass access to modern forms of contraception and the consequent fall in birth rates has tested gender and sexuality identities, behavior, and roles in intimate and associational ways (see Figueroa, 1998; Salcedo, 1995), and the fact that girls' attendance rates at school have risen more quickly than boys' has had obvious implications in numerous ways, including the training and qualifications of women and men for various sectors of employment. The shift from more uniformly differentiated divisions of household labor in the countryside to situations that have given rise to greater fluidity in gender employment patterns as a result of modernization and urbanization has, accordingly, had dramatic consequences for men and women as they have become more thoroughly incorporated into wage labor relations.

Research is needed in several areas relating to men and masculinity in Latin America. As mentioned, the relationship between ethnicity, race, and masculinity in the region is an important topic for future work. Another concerns various aspects of masculinity and violence, from state-sponsored wars to domestic abuse to questions of criminality. Despite recent work on reproductive health, additional studies on issues as diverse as AIDS and vasectomies are necessary, including further applications of de Keijzer's (1998) formulation regarding "masculinity as a risk factor." Although some histories of masculinity in Latin America have appeared in English (e.g., Beattie, 2001; Green, 2000; Stern, 1995), we need to better distinguish between more genuinely novel identities and social relations involving men and women and those sometimes too casually termed "traditional." More generally, there is some urgency in the need for gender analysis to be brought into areas of research involving men but in which men have not been treated as engendered and engendering beings, such as the displaced of Colombia, Mexican immigrants to the United States, and the political hierarchies throughout the continent.

ACKNOWLEDGMENTS

Throughout this chapter, we draw liberally from our other work on men and masculinity in Latin America. We would like to express our gratitude in particular for the opportunities we have had in recent years to participate in conferences and panels on various aspects of this theme—ranging from fatherhood to homosociality to reproductive health—in Bogotá, Cambridge, Cartagena, Chicago, Lima, Medellín, Porto Alegre, Providence, Rio de Janeiro, Salvador, and Santiago. On every occasion, we have learned from each other and from other colleagues about the specific meanings and realities of being a man historically and today in Latin America.

NOTES

1. For the sake of simplicity, in this chapter, *Latin America* refers to the peoples living in countries in the Western Hemisphere where the Spanish and Portuguese languages predominate, as well as to the 35 million Spanish-speaking people in the United States. For a recent, excellent survey of gender in the region, see Chant (2002a).

2. This new emphasis on multiculturalism is also reflected in changes made to several national constitutions in Latin America during this period in which nations were redefined as multiethnic and pluricultural.

3. "Displacements" refers to the more than one million people in Colombia who, in the 1990s, were forced to abandon their homes, fleeing violence perpetrated by one or another military group in that country.

4. The *gaúcho* is defined by the author as a rural cattle worker who lives in the pampas of southern Latin American.

REFERENCES

Andrade, X. (2001). Machismo and politics in Ecuador: The case of Pancho Jaime. *Men and Masculinities, 3*(3), 299-315.

Bastos, S. (1998). Desbordando patrones: El comportamiento doméstico de los hombres [Going beyond the standard: Domestic behavior of men]. *La Ventana, 7*, 166-224.

Bastos, S. (1999). Concepciones del hogar y ejercicio del poder: El caso de los mayas de ciudad de Guatemala. In M. González de la Rocha (Ed.), *Divergencias del modelo tradicional: Hogares de jefatura femenina en América Latina* (pp. 37-75). Mexico City: CIESAS/Plaza y Valdés.

Beattie, P. M. (2001). *The tribute of blood: Army, honor, race, and nation in Brazil, 1864-1945.* Durham, NC: Duke University Press.

Bly, R. (1992). *Hombres de hierro: Los ritos de iniciación masculina del Nuevo Hombre* [Men of iron: Masculine initiation rituals of the New Man]. Mexico City: Planeta.

Bourdieu, P. (1990). La domination masculine [Masculine domination]. *Actes de la Recherche en Sciences Sociales, 84*, 3-31.

Bourdieu, P. (1998). *La domination masculine* [Masculine domination]. Paris: Seuil.

Brusco, E. E. (1995). *The reformation of machismo: Evangelical conversion and gender in Colombia.* Austin: University of Texas Press.

Butler, J. (1993). *Bodies that matter: On the discursive limits of "sex."* New York: Routledge.

Cáceres, C. (1995). Bisexualidades masculinas en la Lima de los noventa: Consideraciones de salud sexual [Masculine bisexualities in Lima in the 1990s: Considerations of sexual health]. In L. Kogan (Ed.), *El amor y sus especies* [Love and the like] (pp. 39-57). Lima, Peru: Pontificia Universidad Católica del Perú.

Canclini, N. G. (1995). *Hybrid cultures: Strategies for entering and leaving modernity* (C. L. Chiappari & S. L. López, Trans.). Minneapolis: University of Minnesota Press.

Cardoso, J. L. (1998). Paternidade adolescente: Da investigaçao à intervençao [Adolescent paternity: From research to intervention]. In M. Arilha, S. Unbehaum, & B. Medrado (Eds.), *Homens e masculinidades: Outras palavras* [Further thoughts on men and masculinities] (pp. 185-215). Sao Paulo, Brazil: Ecos/ Editora 34.

Carrier, J. (1995). *De los otros: Intimacy and homosexuality among Mexican men*. New York: Columbia University Press.

Chant, S., with N. Craske. (2002a). *Gender in Latin America*. New Brunswick, NJ: Rutgers University Press.

Chant, S. (2002b). Researching gender, families and households in Latin America: From the 20th into the 21st century. *Bulletin of Latin American Research, 21*(4), 545-575.

Chant, S., & Gutmann, M. C. (2000). *Mainstreaming men into gender and development: Debates, reflections, and experiences*. Oxford, England: Oxfam.

Connell, R. W. (1987). *Gender and power: Society, the person, and sexual politics*. Stanford, CA: Stanford University Press.

de Barbieri, T. (1990). Sobre géneros, prácticas y valores: Notas acerca de posibles erosiones del machismo en México [On genders, practices, and values: Notes on the possible erosion of machismo in Mexico]. In J. M. Ramírez-Sáiz (Ed.), *Normas y prácticas morales y cívicas en la vida cotidiana* [Moral and civil norms and practices in everyday life] (pp. 83-105). Mexico City: Porrúa/UNAM.

de Keijzer, B. (1998). El varón como factor de riesgo [Man as a risk factor]. In B. Schmukler (Ed.), *Familias y relaciones de género en transformación: Cambios transcendentales en América Latina* [Transforming families and gender relations: Transcendent changes in Latin America]. Mexico City: Population Council/EDAMEX.

de Suremain, M. D., & Acevedo, O. F. (1999). Feminización de la pobreza y retroceso de la paternidad en sectores populares de Medellín [The feminization of poverty and setbacks in fathering in popular sectors of Medellín, Colombia]. *Cuadernos Familia Cultura y Sociedad, 3-4*, 123-133.

Elias, N. (1994). El cambiante equilibrio de poder entre los sexos. Estudio sociológico de un proceso: El caso de Antiguo Estado Romano [Change in the balance of power between the sexes. A sociological study of a process: The case of Ancient Rome]. In J. Varela (Ed.), *Conocimiento y poder* (pp. 121-167). Madrid: La Piqueta.

Figueroa, J. G. (1998). Algunos elementos para interpretar la presencia de los varones en los procesos de salud reproductiva [Some elements in the interpretation of the presence of men in the process of reproductive health]. *Revista de Cadernos de Saúde Pública, 14*(Suppl. 1), 87-96.

Fonseca, C. (2001). Philanderers, cuckolds, and wily women: A reexamination of gender relations in a Brazilian working-class neighborhood. *Men and Masculinities, 3*(3), 261-277.

Fuller, N. (1997). *Identidades masculinas: Varones de clase media en el Perú* [Male identities: Middle class men in Peru]. Lima: Fondo Editorial Pontificia Universidad Católica del Perú.

Fuller, N. (1998). Reflexiones sobre el machismo en América Latina [Reflections on machismo in Latin America]. In T. Valdés & J. Olavarría (Eds.), *Masculinidades y equidad de género en América Latina* [Masculinities and gender equity in Latin America] (pp. 258-266). Santiago, Chile: FLACSO/UNFPA.

Fuller, N. (2001). The social constitution of gender identity among Peruvian men. *Men and Masculinities, 3*(3), 316-331.

García, C. I. (1994). Los pirobos del Terraza: Interacción y discriminación sociales en un grupo de trabajadores sexuales [Young male prostitutes in the Terraza Center: Social interaction and discrimination among a group of sex workers]. Unpublished senior thesis, Universidad Nacional de Colombia, Bogotá.

Gastaldo, E. L. (1995). A forja do homem de ferro: A corporalidade nos esportes de combate [The forge of the iron man: Corporeality in combat sports]. In O. F. Leal (Ed.), *Corpo e significado* [Body and meaning] (pp. 207-225). Rio Grande do Sul, Brazil: Universidade Federal do Rio Grande do Sul.

Giddens, A. (1991). *Modernity and self-identity: Self and society in the late modern age*. Stanford, CA: Stanford University Press.

Giddens, A. (1992). *The transformation of intimacy: Sexuality, love, and eroticism in modern societies*. Stanford, CA: Stanford University Press.

Gomensoro, A. (1995). *La nueva condición del varón: Renacimiento o reciclaje?* [Men's new condition: Renaissance or recycling?]. Montevideo, Uruguay: Editorial Fin de Siglo.

Green, J. (2000). *Beyond Carnival: Male homosexuality in twentieth-century Brazil*. Chicago: University of Chicago Press.

Gregor, T. (1985). *Anxious pleasures: The sexual lives of an Amazonian people*. Chicago: University of Chicago Press.

Gutmann, M. C. (1996). *The meanings of macho: Being a man in Mexico City*. Berkeley: University of California Press.

Gutmann, M. C. (1997). The ethnographic (g)ambit: Women and the negotiation of masculinity in Mexico City. *American Ethnologist, 24*(4), 833-855.

Gutmann, M. C. (2002). *The romance of democracy: Compliant defiance in contemporary Mexico*. Berkeley: University of California Press.

Guzmán, V., & Portocarrero, P. (1992). *Construyendo diferencias* [Constructing differences]. Lima, Peru: Flora Tristán Ediciones.

Henao, H. (1997). Un hombre en casa: La imagen del padre de hoy. Papeles y valores que destacan 400 encuestados en Medellín [A man in the house: The image of the father today. Roles and values highlighted in a survey of 400 men in Medellín, Columbia]. *Nómadas, 6*, 115-124.

Hernández Cabrera, P. M., & Miguel, P. (2001). La construcción gay en un grupo gay de jóvenes de la Ciudad de México [The construction of gay identity in a group of young gay men in Mexico City]. *Desacatos, 6*, 63-96.

Higgins, M., & Coen, T. (2000). *Streets, bedrooms and patios: The ordinariness of diversity in urban Oaxaca: Ethnographic portraits of the urban poor, transvestites, discapacitados, and other popular cultures*. Austin: University of Texas Press.

Jardim, D. F. (1992). Espaço social e autosegregaçao entre homens: Gostos, sonoridades e masculinidades [Social space and self-segregation among men: Tastes, sounds, and masculinities]. *Cuadernos de Antropologia, 7*, 28-41.

Jardim, D. F. (1995). Performances, reproduçao e produçao dos corpos masculinos [Performances, reproduction, and production of male bodies]. In O. F. Leal (Ed.), *Corpo e Significado* [Body and meaning] (pp. 93-207). Rio Grande do Sul, Brazil: Universidade Federal do Rio Grande do Sul.

Kulick, D. (1998). *Travesti: Sex, gender, and culture among Brazilian transgendered prostitutes*. Chicago: University of Chicago Press.

Lamas, M. (1986). La antropología feminista y la categoría de género [Feminist anthropology and the category of gender]. *Nueva Antropología, 30*, 146-187.

Lamas, M. (Ed.). (1996). *El género: La construcción cultural de la diferencia sexual* [Gender: The cultural construction of sexual difference]. Mexico City: UNAM/Porrúa.

Lancaster, R. N. (1992). *Life is hard: Machismo, danger, and the intimacy of power in Nicaragua*. Berkeley: University of California Press.

Lancaster, R. (1998). Sexual positions: Caveats and second thoughts on "categories." *The Americas, 54*(1), 1-16.

Latapí, A. E. (2003). Men and their histories: Restructuring, gender inequality, and life transitions in urban Mexico. In M. C. Gutmann (Ed.), *Changing men and masculinities in Latin America* (pp. 84-114). Durham, NC: Duke University Press.

Leal, O. F. (1992a). O mito da Salamandra do Jarau: A constituiçao do sujeito masculino na cultura gaúcha [The myth of Salamandra do Jarau: Building the masculine subject in gaúcho culture]. *Cuadernos de Antropologia, 7*, 6-14.

Leal, O. F. (1992b). Suicidio, honra e masculinidade na cultura gaúcha [Suicide, honor, and masculinity in gaúcho culture]. *Cuadernos de Antropología, 6*, 7-21.

Leal, O. F. (Ed.). (1995). *Corpo e significado: Ensaios de antropologia social* [Body and meaning: Essays from social anthropology]. Porto Alegre, Brazil: Editora da Universidade.

Lerner, S. (Ed.). (1998). *Varones, sexualidad y reproducción* [Men, sexuality, and reproduction]. Mexico City: El Colegio de México.

Limón, J. (1994). *Dancing with the devil: Society and culture poetics in Mexican-American South Texas*. Madison: University of Wisconsin Press.

Marqués, J. V. (1997). Varón y patriarcado [Men and patriarchy]. In T. Valdés & J. Olavarría (Eds.), *Masculinidad/es: Poder y crisis* [Masculinity(ies): Power and crisis] (pp. 17-31). Santiago, Chile: ISIS Internacional/FLACSO.

Mirandé, A. (1997). *Hombres y machos: Masculinity and Latino culture*. Boulder, CO: Westview.

Moore, H. (1988). *Anthropology and feminism*. Minneapolis: University of Minnesota Press.

Nolasco, S. (1993). *O mito da masculinidade* [The myth of masculinity]. Rio de Janeiro: Editorial Rocco.

Núñez Noriega, G. (1994). *Sexo entre varones: Poder y resistencia en el campo sexual* [Sex between men: Power and resistence in sexual relations]. Mexico City: UNAM/Porrúa/El Colegio de Sonora.

Núñez Noriega, G. (2001). Reconociendo los placeres, descontruyendo las identidades: Antropología, patriarcado y homoerotismos en México [Recognizing pleasures, deconstructing identities: Anthropology, patriarchy, and homoeroticism in Mexico]. *Desacatos, 6*, 15-34.

Olavarría, J. (2001). Invisibilidad y poder: Varones de Santiago de Chile [Invisibility and power: Men of Santiago, Chile]. In *Hombres e identidades de género: Investigaciones desde América Latina* [Men and gender identities: Research from Latin America]. Bogotá: Universidad Nacional de Colombia.

Olavarría, J., & Parrini, R. (Eds.). (2000). *Masculinidad/es: Identidad, sexualidad y familia* [Masculinity(ies): Identity, sexuality, and family]. Santiago, Chile: FLACSO.

Parker, R. (1991). *Bodies, pleasures and passions: Sexual culture in contemporary Brazil.* Boston: Beacon Press.

Parker, R. (1994). *A construção da solidariedade: AIDS, sexualidade e política no Brasil* [The construction of solidarity: AIDS, sexuality, and politics in Brazil]. Rio de Janeiro: Relume-Dumará Editores.

Parker, R. (1999). *Beneath the equator: Cultures of desire, male homosexuality, and emerging gay communities in Brazil.* New York: Routledge.

Parker, R., & Cáceres, C. (1999). Alternative sexualities and changing sexual cultures among Latin American men. *Culture, Health and Sexuality, 1*(3), 201-206.

Parker, R., & Terto, V., Jr. (Eds.). (1998). *Entre homens: Homossexualidade e AIDS no Brasil* [Between men: Homosexuality and AIDS in Brazil]. Rio de Janeiro: Associação Brasilera Interdisciplinar de AIDS.

Prieur, A. (1998). *Mema's house, Mexico City: On transvestites, queens, and machos.* Chicago: University of Chicago Press.

Ramírez, R. (1999). *What it means to be a man: Reflections on Puerto Rican masculinity* (R. E. Casper, Trans.). New Brunswick, NJ: Rutgers University Press. (Original work published 1993)

Rubin, G. (1993). Thinking sex: Notes for a radical theory of the politics of sexuality. In H. Abelove, M. A. Barale, & D. M. Halperin (Eds.), *The lesbian and gay studies reader* (pp. 3-44). New York: Routledge.

Salcedo, H. (1995). *El aborto en Colombia: Exploración local de la experiencia masculina* [Abortion in Colombia: A local exploration of the masculine experience]. Bogotá: Universidad Externado de Colombia.

Scott, J. (1999). *Gender and the politics of history* (Rev. ed.). New York: Columbia University Press.

Serrano, J. F. (1994, March). *Diversidad cultural y homosexualidades* [Cultural diversity and homosexualities]. Paper presented at the Simposio Sexualidad y Construcción de Identidad de Género, VII Congreso de Antropología, Medellín, Colómbia.

Stern, S. J. (1995). *The secret history of gender: Women, men, and power in late colonial Mexico.* Chapel Hill: University of North Carolina Press.

Stolcke, V. (1992). ¿Es el sexo para el género como la raza para la etnicidad? [Is sex to gender as race is to ethnicity?]. *Cuadernos Inacabados, 8*, 87-111.

Streicker, J. (1995). Race, class and gender in Cartagena, Colombia. *American Ethnologist, 22*(1), 54-74.

Tolbert, K., Morris, K., & Romero, M. (1994, November). *Los hombres y el proceso de decisión respecto al aborto: Hacia un modelo de relaciones de género y aborto* [Men and the process of decision making regarding abortion:

A model of gender relationships and abortion]. Paper presented at the Simposio Sexualidad y Construcción de Identidad de Género, VII Congreso de Antropología, Medellín, Colombia.

Urrea, F., & Quintín, P. (2001, February). *Jóvenes negros de barriadas populares en Cali: Entre masculinidades hegemónicas y barriales* [Black youth in popular neighborhoods of Cali, Colombia: Between hegemonic and neighborhood masculinities]. Paper presented at the Terceiro Programa de Treinamiento em Pesquisa sobre Direitos Reprodutivos na América Latina e Caribe, Prodir, III, Homens-Masculinidades, Recife, Brazil.

Valdés, T., Benavente, M. C., & Cysling, J. (1999). *El poder en la pareja, la sexualidad y la reproducción: Mujeres de Santiago* [Power in couples, sexuality and reproduction: Women of Santiago]. Santiago, Chile: FLACSO.

Viveros, M. (1998, September). *Dionisios negros: Sexualidad, corporalidad y orden racial en Colombia* [Black Dionysus: Sexuality, corporeality, and racial order in Colombia]. Paper presented at the Latin American Studies Association congress, Chicago.

Viveros, M. (1999). Orden corporal y esterilización masculina [Corporeal orders and male sterilization]. In M. Viveros & G. Garay (Eds.), *Cuerpo, diferencias y desigualdades* [Body, differences, and inequalities] (pp. 164-184). Bogotá: Universidad Nacional de Colombia.

Viveros, M. (2001). Masculinidades. Diversidades regionales y cambios generacionales [Masculinities: Regional diversity and generational change]. In M. Viveros, N. Fuller, & J. Olavarría (Eds.), *Hombres e identidades de género: Investigaciones desde América Latina* [Men and gender identity: Research from Latin America] (pp. 35-153). Bogotá: CES, Universidad Nacional de Colombia.

Viveros, M. (2002). *De quebradores y cumplidores: Sobre hombres, masculinidades y relaciones de género en Colombia* [Rogues and reliable ones: On men, masculinities, and gender relations in Colombia]. Bogotá: CES, Universidad Nactional de Colombia.

Viveros, M., & Gómez, F. (1998). La elección de la esterilización masculina: Alianzas, arbitrajes y desencuentros conyugales [Choosing male sterilization: Alliances, bargains, and disagreements among couples]. In L. G. Arango (Ed.), *Mujeres, hombres y cambio social en Bogotá* [Women, men, and social change in Bogota] (pp. 85-133). Bogotá: Universidad Nacional de Colombia.

Viveros, M., Olavarría, J., & Fuller, N. (2001). *Hombres e identidades de género: Investigaciones desde América Latina* [Men and gender identity: Research from Latin America]. Bogotá: Universidad Nacional de Colombia.

8

EAST ASIAN MASCULINITIES

FUTOSHI TAGA

The recent expansion of research on men and masculinities is phenomenal. One after another, different aspects of the social construction of masculinity in various moments and milieus have been disclosed. Most of the research published in the English-speaking world, however, comes from within the Western world and from Western perspectives. Although it is important to consider the construction of masculinity in the worldwide context with the background of globalization (Connell, 2000), non-Western masculinities are likely to be distant from the concerns of international academic work, both in terms of the object of knowledge and the viewpoint. East Asia is no exception, even though it contains one of the three great economic powers in the world. Research on East Asian masculinities is small in quantity and is relatively unknown, compared with that on Western masculinities.

In this chapter, through a review of the main literature, both in English and Japanese, I will trace in outline the history of East Asian masculinities and present the main findings and the nature of the research in East Asia. To begin with, I will describe the characteristics of East Asian masculinities in premodern society and then discuss the impact of the foundation of the modern capitalist nation-state. Next I present the dominant forms of masculinities after World War II in each country and then discuss

issues concerning men and masculinities in contemporary East Asia. Finally, I introduce the current trend of research (especially in Japan) and consider the future of research on men and masculinities in East Asia.

PREMODERN SOCIETY

In premodern East Asia, although there was a definite distinction between men and women, and male dominance was notable (especially among the ruling class under the influence of Confucianism), a softness of manner and even homosexual behavior did not threaten a man's manliness. At the same time, there seems to have been diversity in the construction of masculinity according to class and region.

East Asia has many kinds of cultural and religious traditions. Confucianism, Buddhism, and Taoism have each had a great influence over a wide area. Relations among the three are ambivalent. On the one hand, each has regarded the others as heresy and disapproved of them. On the other hand, by gradual introduction of doctrine derived from the others, each has undergone significant changes over the centuries and has had much effect on the construction of masculinity (and femininity) up to the present.

In regard to the definition and symbolization of gender relations among the ruling class,

Confucianism has been the most influential of all. Confucianism is a series of ideas that originated in the instructions of an ancient Chinese great thinker, Confucius (551?–479 B.C.). His teachings and related texts became the core curriculum of Chinese education in the Han dynasty (206 B.C.–A.D. 220), after which Confucianism spread to other East Asian countries (Tu, 1998). One of the main characteristics of Confucianism is the definite distinction between the public (outer) space occupied by men and the domestic (inner) space occupied by women. These spaces were linked by a firm hierarchy of the sexes that was dominated by men. For example, *Li-chi,* one of the traditional Confucian textbooks, says that the woman must practice the art of "following"—following her father as a daughter, following her husband as a wife, and following her son as a mother.

In the period when China was divided between the northern dynasties and the southern dynasties (A.D. 220–589), against the background of the flourishing of Taoism and the consolidation of the philosophy of "greater vehicle" Buddhism, the influence of Confucianism was weakened. In the Sung period (960-1279), however, Confucian thought was restored as neo-Confucianism, which brought renewed emphasis on familial duty and moral asceticism. In the Choson dynasty of Korea (1392-1910), which was the most Confucianized of all dynasties in East Asian history, the continuation of the family lineage is one of the most important duties for *yangban* upper class. A woman who did not have a son was considered a nonperson (Cho, 1998). In Tokugawa Japan (1603-1867), neo-Confucianism was a fundamental basis of spirit and behavior for the samurai warrior class (De Vos, 1998). In China, neo-Confucianism reached its apex during the Ch'ing dynasty (1644-1912) (Tu, 1998).

At first glance, it seems that gender relations in East Asia were not much different from those of Western countries under the influence of Christianity. But we can see specific characteristics of the construction of traditional East Asian masculinities in regard to heroic images and male homosexual behavior. Louie and Edwards (1994) argue that, in Chinese cultural tradition (and probably also in other parts of Asia), concepts of manliness have been constructed around the intertwining of two ideals: *wen* (mental or civil ideals) and *wu* (physical or martial ideals). The balance between *wen* and *wu* and the notable presentation of both were supposed to lead to masculinity at its highest level. This is most obvious in Ruhlman's (1975) three types of hero, seen in Chinese popular fiction: scholar, swordsman, and prince. The scholar is the symbol of *wen* and the swordsman represents *wu.* The prince plays only a passive part but is skilled in choosing scholars and swordsmen who will enable him to fulfill his destiny. In other words, he sits between and above *wen* and *wu.* Significantly, in Chinese tradition generally, it has been considered that *wen* would be superior to *wu* and that scholars and officials would be more respected than soldiers. In addition, *wen* is closer to women than *wu,* in contrast with Western concepts. For example, as Louie and Edwards point out, although a romance of scholar and beauty is a common theme in Chinese fiction, the *wu* hero shows his strength and masculinity by *containing* his sexual and romantic desires.

The second distinctive characteristic of East Asian traditional masculinity is the tolerance of male homosexual relationships. According to Hinsch (1990), Chinese men were not divided into strict categories of "homosexuals" and "heterosexuals" and experienced a relaxed bisexuality, at least before the 20th century. Based on literary and historical documentation, Leupp (1995) argues that male homosexual behavior was celebrated rather than tolerated in premodern Japan. *Nanshoku* (male-to-male sex), which was one of the two subconcepts of *shikidô* (the way of sexual behaviors; the other subconcept being *joshoku,* male-to-female sex), began to spread within the Buddhist monastic community in the ninth century and permeated the samurai (warrior) class as well by the 12th century. *Nanshoku* did not necessarily contradict the Confucian code of Japanese feudal society. Because of men's bisexuality, homosexual behavior did not threaten the continuation of the family lineage, which was dependent on the birth of male offspring. The "high and low" structure in sexual relations between *nenja* (the lover, of elder or upper status) and *chigo* (the loved, of younger or lower status) was also concordant with this hierarchical social structure. According to Furukawa (1995), *nanshoku* was thought to bring masculinity to a man; *joshoku* was thought to make a man weak.

On the other hand, it is argued that, in the popular classes, more egalitarian gender relations were constructed compared with those in the ruling class. For example, Brugger (1971) argues that within the Chinese peasant family in precommunist traditional society, the roles of men and women were determined by economic necessity rather than by Confucian ideology. Certainly, a rough distinction would be seen between a woman as the domestic manager and a man as the breadwinner. However, at the lower social levels, the husband's power over his wife was not as strong as Confucian ideology prescribed because of the woman's participation in physical labor and the vague boundary between domestic management and breadwinning. Women as well as men are thought to have enjoyed sexual freedom outside marriage.

In addition to the difference by class, we may also see regional differences in gender patterns within each country. For example, Edo (today's Tokyo) in the Tokugawa period is characterized as a "masculine city" (Nishiyama, 1997). The population of Edo in the early 18th century was calculated to be around a million and was divided roughly equally between samurai and *chônin* (townspeople). Building the metropolis had required the influx of a great number of individuals with traditional skills and knowledge, ranging from craftsmen to scholars, most of whom were male. According to a census taken during the *Kyôhô* era (1716-1739), two thirds of the *chônin* population was male. As for the samurai class, present in large numbers because *daimyo* (provincial lords) were required to be in the capital, with vassals, in alternate years, the armed force was exclusively male. There were constant conflicts among the *chônin* over their rights and interests and also between the samurai and *chônin,* who managed to use the authority of the *bakufu* (feudal government) or their lord to gain advantage over competitors. Such demography and social structure formed an atmosphere in which justice usually meant violence.

THE IMPACT OF MODERNIZATION

Social conditions in East Asia experienced great changes in the latter half of the 19th century. Each country aimed to build a modern capitalist nation, introducing Western technology and political systems. Contrary to general assumptions, however, modernization reinforced and reconstructed gender division and hierarchy in East Asia rather than leading to liberation and equality between sexes.

Japan succeeded earliest in East Asia in the transformation into the modern nation-state. As in the birth of the modern European nations, only men were given citizenship rights, such as the vote and the right to own property. Women were not to win those rights until the end of World War II. Against a background of strong nationalism, the *ryôsai kenbo* (good wife, wise mother) ideology was formed through a reinterpretation of Confucian virtue. Although it legitimized the modern gender division of labor, this ideology ranked both sexes equal in the sense that women also contribute to the nation through the production of high-quality children. The formal curriculum of primary and secondary education was designed in the 1880s with that ideology in mind. Boys and girls were indoctrinated with the idea of different duties for men and women through moral education, and only girls were taught needlecraft and domestic science (Fukaya, 1966). A similar educational system for girls was introduced to Korea under imperial Japan's control in the early days of the 20th century (Sechiyama, 1996, p. 142).

In China, after the beginning of the 20th century, the disorganization of rural peasant communities and the increase of factory workers reinforced male power and the demarcation between the roles of breadwinner and domestic manager. Although the *Kuomintang* government legislated for equality of the sexes in the rights of property, inheritance, and divorce in 1931, these rights did not work in practice in districts controlled by traditional gentry. The recruitment of large numbers of men into the army during the Sino-Japanese War (1937-1945) and the Chinese Civil War (1945-1949) accelerated gender division (Brugger, 1971).

The influence of industrialization and militarization, interwoven with Western science and Christian ethics, produced changes in men's sexuality. As progressive scholars supported Western medical and psychological doctrines and Christian notions that the only purpose of sex was reproduction, the Chinese and the Japanese began to see homosexuality as pathological or criminal (Furukawa, 1995; Hinsch,

1990). Gradually, most Japanese men became careful neither to display homosexual behavior nor to realize their own homosexual desire. Watanabe and Iwata (1989) argue that, from the demographic viewpoint, such a change of sexuality was reasonable, especially in Japan, whose *fukoku kyôhei* (enrich the country and strengthen the military) policy encouraged having as many children as possible, to provide large-scale manpower to growing labor markets and military forces. The population of Japan, which was about 33 million in the 1870s, was already steadily increasing and reached about 55 million in 1920.

The conversion of masculinity in the context of modernization can be confirmed most remarkably in the portraits of the Japanese Meiji Emperor Mutsuhito (1868-1912) and his family (Osa, 1999). The emperor, who had been merely a noble and had little political power in the Tokugawa era, suddenly became a top manager of politics and the military of a modern nation-state because of the Meiji Restoration (1868). In that year, Mutsuhito looked androgynous in traditional Japanese clothes. It was more important for his appearance to display his nobility than his maleness. In the portrait of 1888, however, he was drawn in the style that gives dignity to European monarchs in the 19th century: sitting on a chair with a sword; wearing Western military ceremonial dress; with moustache, beard, and thick eyebrows. The emperor's masculinity was represented more clearly in relation to the empress and their children. Although female emperors had existed in the past, the Imperial Constitution of 1889 limited the succession explicitly to male descendants. Subsequently, the empress was located as support behind the emperor rather than represented as a political leader. In the newspaper images of the imperial family that were distributed as an appendix in 1905, we can clearly see the emperor's figure as husband and father.

We may find similar changes in the iconography of political power in the process of China's modernization. When Sun Yatsen declared the foundation of the Republic of China and took the temporary presidency in 1912, he was wearing modified Western dress. The last emperor of the Ch'ing dynasty, Puyi, was still wearing traditional hair style and dress in the picture taken that same year.

AFTER WORLD WAR II: SALARYMAN AND SOCIALISM

After World War II, each country in East Asia witnessed a different construction of masculinity according to the prevailing political-economic structure and the attitude toward Confucianism (Sechiyama, 1996; Shinozaki, 1995).

In Japan, after the defeat in the war, Confucianism was denied, at least officially, as a feudal idea. Democracy and modernization were encouraged under the guidance of the Allied Powers. During the period of economic growth starting in the 1950s, the *sarariiman* (derived from the neologism "salaryman," meaning a salaried, white-collar employee of private-sector organizations) became the hegemonic discourse of Japanese masculinity (Dasgupta, 2000).

This term has different connotations in different contexts. Within the job context, "salaryman" is one side of a dualistic gender discourse, the other side of which is the "office lady," a female employee who generally has no chance for promotion and mainly serves as an assistant for male employees (Ogasawara, 1998, p. 12). In the mirror of the office lady, the salaryman represents male privilege, dominance, and centrality in the company and the society. In the family context, the salaryman is one side of another duality in gender discourse. Here the opposite is *sengyô-shufu* (full-time housewife), whom, ideally, he is supposed to marry (Dasgupta, 2000). As the breadwinner, the salaryman husband was accustomed to demanding the services and attention of his indulgent wife in an authoritarian manner in what was referred to as *teishu kanpaku*. This pattern of relationship was considered normal until the 1970s (Salamon, 1975). Within this discourse, a salaryman represents not only the heterosexual but also the provider and dominator of woman. Further, Ueno (1995) points out that men's activities in Japanese industrial society have been expressed by terminology that has strong military connotations: for example, *kigyô-senshi* (corporate soldier) and *shijô-senryaku* (market strategy). Although the military has not represented a Japanese masculine ideal since the defeat in World War II, the military image has survived in the masculine field of the economic war.

Although the term *sarariiman,* with its implications of middle class, white-collar employees in a large company, is almost synonymous with masculinity in contemporary Japanese discourses, the majority of male workers do not fit with this image. More than half of all private sector male employees in the Japanese economy (excluding agriculture) were employed in *small* firms (fewer than 100 workers) in 1960, in 1980, and again in 2000. The percentage of white-collar workers (the total of professional and technical workers, managers, and officials; clerical and related workers; and sales workers, including self-employed and family workers) grew slowly over this period but had reached no more than 46% by 2000. Clearly, the classic salaryman was always in a minority.

We can get a glimpse of working class men's lives from ethnographic research. Most of those laborers who are paid daily lead a life that is far from both "the company" and "the marriage" indispensable to the image of the salaryman (Fowler, 1996; Gill, 1999). Many are single; live in cheap, poor-quality lodgings; and look for 1-day contract jobs every morning. Although the pay for day labor is not bad compared with that of the salaryman generally, the salary parity tends to disappear into a hedonistic lifestyle (mainly gambling and alcohol). Although the salaryman enjoys the seniority system, confidently expecting pay increases and promotion with increasing age, the day worker finds it more and more difficult to endure hard manual labor and eventually is thrown into unemployment. Roberson (1998), through participant observation research in a small company, argues that, unlike the stereotypical image of the salaryman who swears loyalty to his company under the life-long employment system, the workers in that small company create their identity more through leisure and relationships outside work rather than through work and the company.

Although there is a general lack of research, we can draw some limited conclusions about the construction of masculinities in the socialist states in this period. In China, the Maoist regime (beginning with the Socialist Revolution in 1949, through the Great Leap Forward in 1958-1959 and the Cultural Revolution that began in 1965, ending with Mao's death in 1976) provided conflicting social contexts for the construction of masculinities. First, there was a contradiction regarding gender between the Maoist regime's official policy and the actual power structure (Brugger, 1971; Sechiyama, 1996). On the one hand, the regime actually promoted more egalitarian gender relations. Women's status was improved not only economically but in the private arena through various policies, such as rural collectivization; the mobilization of women to the labor force; the revision of the Marriage Law, which legalized divorce; and the propaganda campaign for gender equality, which was represented by the unisexual "Mao jacket" and Mao's words "Women hold up half the sky." On the other hand, the political, economic, and military power was kept almost exclusively in the hands of men.

Second, as far as the ideal masculine image goes, there seemed to be a contradiction between the Confucian cultural tradition and Maoism. As related earlier, Chinese tradition has shown respect for the intellectual who exemplified *wen.* By contrast, Maoist policy regarded intellectuals with hostility and idealized violence and manual labor. We can find the images of heroic masculinity in the People's Liberation Army soldier and the manual worker painted on a campaign poster in 1971 (Honig, 2002).

Korea was divided into two countries in 1948. In the capitalist state of South Korea, rapid industrialization and urbanization from the 1960s increasingly conspired to place a man in the position of breadwinner. Like the Japanese salaryman, the Korean husband and father came to spend most of his time and energy on work and on his association with colleagues outside the house. The result was a "fatherless" complex where the wife and mother took over the role of head of the family (Lee, 1998).

Although the socialist nation of North Korea mobilized women into the labor force, it was different from postrevolutionary China with respect to the powerful influence of Confucianism (Sechiyama, 1996). Intellectuals were respected in North Korea. We can learn this from the symbol of the Korean Worker's Party, in which a pen (intellectual) is centrally located between a hammer (worker) and a sickle (farmer). Because of tendencies that retained the difference between men and women, gender equality had not been achieved as much as in China, and men participated less in housework, although women worked as hard as men.

Changing Masculinities in Recent Decades

The recent promotion of equality between the sexes on a global scale has had a great impact on the construction of masculinities in East Asia. In the capitalist nations of Japan and South Korea, the governmental policy of gender equality, the economic recession, and demographic change threatened the hegemonic form of masculinity that had been established after World War II. As a reaction to this situation, some men tried to redefine masculinity. In the People's Republic of China, in which the sociocultural distinction between the sexes had been the most revised in East Asia, gender relations are being reconstructed along with the introduction of the capitalist market economy. In the complex of conventional and alternative values, we can see the complicated conditions in which masculinities are constructed.

In Japan, a series of governmental policies aimed at gender equality undermined the legitimacy of male dominance and gender division of labor (Ôsawa, 2000). The symbolic event was the enactment of the Basic Law for the Gender-Equal Society in 1999. To promote equality between the sexes and to stop the birthrate decreasing, the government admitted men's parental leave by law in 1991. An official campaign also began to promote men's participation in child care. A poster and TV advertisement published by the Ministry of Health and Welfare became topical in 1999. In both, the husband of Japan's most popular female singer cradled his child, saying, "A man isn't called a father unless he takes part in raising his child." The Tokyo metropolitan government began to grope for ways in which a man could be independent of the company and strike a balance between work, family, and community (Metropolitan Tokyo Women's Foundation, 1998). These efforts had limited success. Despite the 1991 law, Japanese men rarely take parental leave. The reasons include insufficient pay guarantees and the resistance to a man's absence from the workplace for "private" reasons. For example, among government employees in 1998, of all men who were entitled to take parental leave, only 0.2% did so; the percentage among women was 86.2%.

Economic recession also delivered a blow to salaryman masculinity. The increasing number of suicides by men who experienced anxiety about work brought on by the continuing recession and the collapse of the old corporate safeguard system prompted a reappraisal of men's former working style (Fuyuno, 2001; Kashima, 1993). In 1997, when personnel downsizing went into full swing, the number of men's suicides per 100,000 population in Japan rose rapidly from 26 to 36.5 in 1 year; that of women rose from 11.9 to 14.7. In 1997, suicide motivated by economic or occupational problems made up 25% of all suicides among men, although it made up only 5% among women.

Analyzing the articles in postwar Japanese newspapers, Okamoto and Sasano (2001) traced a transition in images of the salaryman. The tendency to take the term *salaryman* for granted appeared at the beginning of the postwar economic boom in the 1950s. In the latter half of the 1960s, the post–oil crisis period, salarymen were expected to be good taxpayers, to be breadwinners, and to go straight home after work. The self-evident nature of the salaryman, however, came to be doubted in the latter half of the "bubble economy" period in the 1980s. The traditional images regarding salarymen have been marginalized in the 1990s.

Demographic changes have also had a strong impact on Japanese masculine identity. The Japanese enjoy the longest life span, on average, in the world. In 1955, the average life expectancy of Japanese men and women was about 63 and 67 years old, respectively. This became 71 and 76 in 1975 and 77 and 83 in 1995. This extension of the average life span brought to salarymen a new problem of "the second life" after retirement (K. Itô, 1996). The fast-growing elderly population has increased the numbers of men who must take care of aged parents or an elderly wife (Harris, Long, & Fujii, 1998).

In light of these social changes, negative images of the salaryman have come to the fore. "Sarariiman as beleaguered and routinized, forever cogs in someone else's wheel, are common images in the popular culture" (Allison, 1993, p. 1). Ogasawara (1998) found that female employees tended to resist control at work more than male employees, despite the inferiority of their place in the company system. The seeming lack of male resistance may be understood as the consequence of their personal assessment and identification with company and management goals. According to a case study of a Japanese security company by Shire (1999), male employees are encouraged to align their individual attitudes and behavior with company goals through company socialization, but the meaning of social adulthood for a female employee is related to future family roles. In Japan's salaryman culture, in contrast to Western counterparts, group acceptance and membership in successful groups are more respectable than a display of individual aggressiveness. *Karôshi* (death from overwork) is more a result of "hyperdevotion" to the company than a result of a "hypercompetitive" orientation (Kersten, 1996). Seeking after-work relaxation, salarymen often go out to hostess clubs where the hostesses "treat them like men" and make them feel important and privileged while drinking. However, such "masculine privilege depends on the ability and willingness of males to continue to work as productive and compliant workers" (Allison, 1993, p. 2). These observations indicate how pervasive and effective are corporate control mechanisms for male employees.

Likewise, in the home, the status of salarymen as husbands or fathers is increasingly ambivalent. Their *teishu kanpaku* behavior has increasingly been viewed as problematic and unsupportive (Salamon, 1975). Because of the surviving custom that husbands should hand their salary over to their wives, combined with the "fatherless household" syndrome similar to that in South Korea, a situation has developed in which more power in domestic management lies with the wife. As may be discerned from the popular saying that was prevalent in the 1980s—"It's important that husbands are healthy and not at home"—salaryman fathers tend to have only guest status in the family (Kersten, 1996).

In response to such trends, "men's movements" that question assumptions about masculinities began to spread in Japan (Ôyama & Ôtsuka, 1999). One group established the "Men's Center Japan" in Osaka in 1995 (Menzusentâ, 1996). *Otoko no Fesutibal* (men's festival), the national annual conference that aims at the solution of men's problems and serves as an interchange for men's groups, has been held since 1996. The workshops in this conference cover a lot of issues: men's sexuality, domestic violence, working life, communication between husband and wife, fatherhood, and so on (Menzusentâ, 1997). Although the majority of men's movements take a profeminist stance, an essentialist discourse, which advocates a clear distinction of paternity from maternity on the basis of Jungian psychology, is gaining popularity (Hayashi, 1996).

Men's movements are budding little by little in South Korea, as well. The main example is the "fathers' movement," which aims at good relations between a man and his wife and children. In 1997, this movement organized the National Organization of Fathers Club, in which about 70 groups joined, and established the Father Foundation as an NGO. With the recent recession, however, fathers are primarily expected not to be sacked rather than actually expected to be a "good father." In Japan, the 50-year-olds of the postwar baby boom generation are at the center of the men's movement, but in South Korea, the 30- and 40-year-olds who are the first nuclear family generation lead the men's movement. Also in South Korea, there are Christian men's movements, which work together with the U.S. Promise Keepers; men's movements for egalitarian culture; and telephone counseling for men (Chung, 2000).

Against the background of social changes in which traditional sexist ideology and egalitarian antisexist ideology coexist, more men are experiencing conflicts concerning gender and are being encouraged to cope with them. According to Soh (1993), men (and women) in South Korea, who are faced with contradictory dual gender role ideologies, organize their everyday life by compartmentalizing their interactional situations: public versus private and formal versus informal.

Japanese men's conflicts about gender are the subject of my recent research with young men of the middle class (Taga, 2001, 2003). This interview-based project explored the areas of life in which men experienced gender conflict, how they came up against it, and how they dealt with it. Some wondered how a husband should share paid work and housework with his wife, some questioned the validity of male dominance over women, and some were rethinking the "traditional" definition of masculinity. Some experienced conflict and were encouraged to rethink gender relations because they fell in love with a career-oriented girl. The ways they dealt with the conflicts are various. Some tried to suppress conflict concerning the definition of masculinity and to achieve a stable masculine identity, regarding the career as the most masculine practice. Some responded by converting sexist views to an antisexist perspective, preserving the partnership with a career-oriented girlfriend. Some tried to get over the conflicting situation by avoiding commitment to any ideologies concerning gender before marriage or getting a steady girlfriend. Others avoided conflicts by choosing as wife a woman who agreed with their sexist beliefs.

Although some subjects in the study were reappraising traditional masculinity, the meaning of "becoming a man" (*ichininmae ni naru*) for Japanese men seems to be fundamentally unchanged. Most took for granted that they would take a decent job and get married to a woman at some point in the future. Even a senior student who envied women for what he perceived to be their lack of need to find a career could not imagine a workless life in any realistic way. Among 21 subjects of that study who seemed to be heterosexual, only one student had no interest in getting married. One of two subjects who confided their homosexual orientation hoped to get married to a woman and to have children. Despite the recent climate in which books dealing seriously with homosexuality have been published both in academic (Vincent, Kazama, & Kawaguchi, 1997; Yajima, 1997) and nonacademic fields (S. Itô, 1996), and some kinds of *manga* (comics) glamorize male homosexuality (McLelland, 2000), nonheterosexuals still tend to be derided in everyday life.

In China, with the return of capitalism after Mao's death, arguments have been heard that encourage women to stay home. The growth of the private sector seems to cause a revival of the gender division of labor (Entwisle, Henderson, Short, Bouma, & Fengying, 1995). But the rate of men's participation in housework in China is still particularly high in comparison with other Asian countries (Sechiyama, 1996, p. 189).

Underlying views about masculinity, and their relation to the social conditions of each country, can be seen in preferences for a baby's sex. In China and South Korea, there is a strong preference for male babies, even now. According to statistics, the ratio of boys' births to girls' is about 116 to 100 in South Korea and 114 to 100 in China; the ratio in Japan and some Western countries is generally about 105 to 100, which may be the biological standard (Sômuchô-Tôkeikyoku, 2000). The continuity of the patrilineal family is still a very important principle for Korean life (Lee, 1998). In China, although the Confucian tradition has been denied officially, the idea that the male succeeds to the family name does not change easily. Having children, particularly boys, is also very important for the future labor force, as well as for security in old age for the farmer and the self-employed family under the imperfect social security system. The capacity to determine sex in utero resulted, under the "One Child Policy," in widespread abortion of female fetuses. On the other hand, a preference for girl babies has become stronger in Japan recently. It seems that more Japanese began to want their own daughter to look after them in their old age rather than a daughter-in-law (Wakabayashi, 1994).

RESEARCH ON MEN AND MASCULINITIES IN EAST ASIA

Judging from the limited literature in English and Japanese, Japan has made the greatest advances in research on men and masculinities in East Asia. Most of the research published in English reflects work done by Western researchers or by East Asian researchers who are studying in Western countries. In the Japanese literature, there is hardly any research on men and masculinities in Asian countries other than Japan. In South Korea, according to Chung (2000), men's studies were introduced in the official curriculum for the first time in Pusan University in 1998, but Korean men have paid less attention to the issue than Japanese so far. Therefore, in this section, I will focus on the trend of research on men and masculinities in Japan, referring to works not cited in the previous sections.

Although a large number of studies about sex roles had been done (Azuma & Suzuki, 1991; Shirakawa, Shiraishi, & Sukemune, 1992; Sugihara & Katsurada, 1999), there were few Japanese academic studies focusing on men and masculinities until the mid-1990s. There were, however, a few pioneering works.

In the 1980s, feminist researchers and women journalists who came under the influence of Japan's women's liberation movement in the 1970s began research on men and masculinities. To begin with, they translated into Japanese

Western literature such as *The Hazards of Being Male* (Goldberg, 1976) and *Dilemmas of Masculinity* (Komarovsky, 1976) and introduced the realities of men's lives in the United States (Shimomura, 1982) and Sweden (Jansson, 1987). Original studies appeared in the late 1980s. Kasuga (1989) is one of the most representative. Based on field observation and interviews in single-father circles, she pointed out the contradiction that patriarchal society created for single fathers. They were alienated from the supposed dominant position of men because of their parental role and by virtue of their singleness. In the mid-1990s, when Japan's representative feminists published the seven-volume collection *Feminism in Japan,* they included a volume of Japanese men's studies as an addendum (Inoue, Ueno, & Ehara, 1995). Although most of the essays in this volume were nonacademic, the various issues were covered: sexuality, family, labor, men's movements, and so on. All contributors were men who had experienced the impact of feminism.

A short time after the female pioneers, male researchers started their own research. Watanabe (1986) is the pioneering empirical work. Based on observations of transvestite circles and using psychoanalytic theory, he argued the necessity of men's liberation from the current repression and argued for *danseigaku* (men's studies) to complement *joseigaku* (women's studies). The same author also edited the first interdisciplinary anthology of men's studies, in which both men and women researchers contributed articles from the perspective of sociology, psychoanalysis, sexology, and anthropology (Watanabe, 1989).

The 1990s witnessed the burgeoning of Japanese men's studies. Kimio Itô is one of the leaders (Itô, 1993). It is said that he opened the first men's studies class in Japan at Kyoto University in 1992. After he published *Danseigaku Nyûmon* (Introduction to men's studies) explaining men's studies and issues about men for nonacademic readers (K. Itô, 1996), men's studies began to diffuse not only in academia but also within adult education. Texts also appeared discussing men's movements in the United States (Nakamura, 1996), reviewing the books about men and masculinities (Nakamura & Nakamura, 1997), and considering the history of Japanese men's movements (Ôyama & Ôtsuka, 1999). In 1998, a substantial men's

studies session was held for the first time at the conference of the Japan Sociological Society. The titles of the presentations were "An Analysis of Masculinities as an Arena and the Scope of Men's Studies" (Tadashi Nakamura); "Sociology of Gender Formation: Men's Studies Perspective" (Futoshi Taga); "The Invisibilized: Sport-Maladapted Men" (Takao Ôtsuka); "The Sexuality of Disabled Men and the Culture of Disability" (Tomoaki Kuramoto); and "On the History of the Men's Movement in Japan" (Haruhiko Ôyama).

This attention to the male gender awakened Japanese researchers' interest in the performance and plurality of masculinities and brought some unique approaches to the construction of nondominant forms of masculinity. Sunaga (1999), interviewing men who recognized themselves as *hage* (bald), argues that the interaction between a bald man and people who deride him contributes to the reproduction of the dominant images of masculinity. Most bald men thought that there was no way other than enduring and laughing along with the taunting, because if they tried to conceal their bald head or got angry with it, they would be seen as unmanly not only because they were bald but also because of their attitude. Another unique approach to Japanese marginal masculinity is Ukai's (1999) case study of "trainphiles," most of whom are men. Trainphile men tend to be ridiculed and thought alienated from company work, family, normal dress, and relationships with women. But they are very competitive in their own circles in relation to knowledge of trains and the collection of train-goods. Ukai suggests that they have retreated from the competition for hegemonic masculinity in the wider social context and are chasing it within a localized context. As related earlier, Taga (2001) shows that among middle class young men with similar living conditions, diverse masculine identities develop.

CONCLUSION

This chapter has presented, in a broad perspective, the main features of the construction of East Asian masculinities. Similarities and continuities may be observed to some degree against a background of cultural tradition, but masculinities have also displayed differences corresponding to the social milieu and the historical moment. I conclude this chapter by offering several suggestions for further development in this field.

First, the more the public interest in men's issues keeps growing in East Asia, the more research from a practical perspective will be required. On the one hand, we need to reinterpret women's issues as men's issues. For example, although most discussions about domestic violence and prostitution focus on women as the victims, we should also inquire why men batter women and why men buy the services of prostitutes. On the other hand, it is also important to explore the negative consequences of being masculine for men themselves. It was pointed out in the previous section that men's suicide and overwork (i.e., the behavior of "company-first men") are increasingly seen as problems in Japan. The social background of such men's behaviors, however, has not been explained sufficiently. English-speaking countries have made advances in research studies that illuminate men's motives for domestic violence and propose countermeasures (Dutton & Golant, 1995), that explain men's depression in relation to adherence to manliness (Real, 1998), and that propose antisexist programs for boys in school (Askew & Ross, 1988). We must examine the applicability of these findings to East Asian countries and develop programs suitable for the region. As one of the vanguard, a citizens' group in 1998 set out a program of violence prevention for men in Japan (Nakamura, 2001).

Second, we should promote research on the construction of East Asian masculinities in a comparative perspective. If the characteristics of a society are illuminated by comparison with other societies that seem similar (Sechiyama, 1996, p. 4), a comparison with other societies within East Asia is as important as comparisons with countries outside the region. The comparison between socialist societies (China and North Korea) and capitalist societies (Japan and South Korea) would be a typical approach. For example, the impact of the military on the construction of masculinity could be explored by comparison between South Korea, which practices conscription, and Japan, which has renounced war under the constitution created after World War II.

Finally, it is important to show the international audience East Asian realities from East Asian perspectives. It seems that Western perspectives and international statistics do not always mirror East Asian realities. As noted earlier, Louie and Edwards (1994) argue that the inappropriate application of Western paradigms of masculinity to Chinese men led to the notion that Chinese men are effeminate and "not quite real men." They propose an alternative paradigm of masculinity. Hoffman (1995) observes that in South Korea, despite the official ideology of gender difference, there exists an underlying cultural psychology that stresses a fundamental intimacy between men and women in which gender categories are blurred. Among older Japanese couples, the tendency of the wife to take the initiative with the family budget (Kersten, 1996) and the husband's emotional dependence on his wife (Salamon, 1975) implies a complexity in the power relations between men and women in East Asia that is not easily captured by superficial observation.

If the modernization of masculinity in global society means the Westernization of masculinity, we may get a hint for the deconstruction of masculinity (and femininity) from non-Western cultural traditions. Although the recent global movements for gender justice seem to offer some challenge to the hegemony of modern masculinity, they have not necessarily succeeded in offering an alternative vision that can take over from the current gender order. In creating an alternative vision of gender in global society, what East Asian experiences and perspectives can offer must be considered.

REFERENCES

Allison, A. (1993). Dominating men: Male dominance on company expense in a Japanese hostess club. *Genders, 16*, 1-16.

Askew, S., & Ross, C. (1988). *Boys don't cry: Boys and sexism in education.* Buckingham, England: Open University Press.

Azuma, K., & Suzuki, A. (1991). Seiyakuwari-taido-kenkyû no tenbô [Review of research on sex role attitudes]. *Sinrigaku Kenkyuu, 62*(4), 270-276.

Brugger, W. (1971). The male (and female) in Chinese society. *Impact of Science on Society, 21*(1), 5-19.

Cho, H. (1998). Male dominance and mother power: The two sides of Confucian patriarchy in Korea. In W. H. Slote & G. A. De Vos (Eds.),

Confucianism and the family (pp. 187-207). Albany: State University of New York.

Chung, C.-K. (2000). Kankoku ni okeru danseigaku to joseigaku [Men's studies and women's studies in South Korea]. In A. Fujitani & K. Itô (Eds.), *Jendâgaku wo manabu hitono tameni* [For students of gender studies] (pp. 75-90). Kyoto, Japan: Sekaishisô-sha.

Connell, R. W. (2000). *The men and the boys.* Sydney: Allen & Unwin.

Dasgupta, R. (2000). Performing masculinities? The "salaryman" at work and play. *Japanese Studies, 20*(2), 189-200.

De Vos, G. A. (1998). A Japanese legacy of Confucian thought. In W. H. Slote & G. A. De Vos (Eds.), *Confucianism and the family* (pp. 105-117). Albany: State University of New York.

Dutton, D. G., & Golant, S. K. (1995). *The batterer: A psychological profile.* New York: Basic Books.

Entwisle, B., Henderson, G. E., Short, S. E., Bouma, J., & Fengying, Z. (1995). Gender and family businesses in rural China. *American Sociological Review, 60,* 36-57.

Fowler, E. (1996). *San'ya blues: Laboring life in contemporary Tokyo.* New York: Cornell University Press.

Fukaya, M. (1966). *Rôsai-kenbo-shugi no kyôiku* [Education of "good wife, wise mother" ideology]. Tokyo: Reimei Shobô.

Furukawa, M. (1995). Dôseiaisha no shakaishi [The history of homosexuality]. In T. Inoue, C. Ueno, & Y. Ehara (Eds.), *Danseigaku* [Men's studies] (pp. 237-248). Tokyo: Iwanami Shoten.

Fuyuno, I. (2001). A silent epidemic. *Far Eastern Economic Review, 163*(39), 78-80.

Gill, T. (1999). Yoseba no otokotachi: Kaisha, kekkon nashi no seikatsu-sha [Men in *Yoseba:* Living without company and marriage]. In Y. Nishikawa & M. Ogino (Eds.), *Kyôdô-kenkyû dansei-ron* [Discussions about men: A collaboration] (pp. 17-43). Kyoto, Japan: Jinbun Shoin.

Goldberg, H. (1976). *The hazards of being male: Surviving the myth of masculine privilege.* New York: Sanford J. Greenburger.

Harris, P. B., Long, S. O., & Fujii, M. (1998). Men and elder care in Japan: A ripple of change. *Journal of Cross-Cultural Gerontology, 13,* 177-198.

Hayashi, M. (1996). *Fusei no fukken* [The restoration of paternity]. Tokyo: Chuôkôron-sha.

Hinsch, B. (1990). *Passions of the cut sleeve: Male homosexual tradition in China.* Berkeley: University of California Press.

Hoffman, D. M. (1995). Blurred genders: The cultural construction of male and female in South Korea. *Korean Studies, 19,* 112-138.

Honig, E. (2002). Maoist mappings of gender: Reassessing the Red Guards. In S. Brownell & J. N. Wasserstrom (Eds.), *Chinese femininities/*

Chinese masculinities: A reader (pp. 255-268). London: University of California Press.

Inoue, T., Ueno, C., & Ehara, Y. (Eds.). (1995). *Danseigaku* [Men's studies]. Tokyo: Iwanami Shoten.

Itô, K. (1993). *Otokorashisa no yukue* [Where are men going?]. Tokyo: Shin'yô-sha.

Itô, K. (1996). *Danseigaku nyuumon* [An introduction to men's studies]. Tokyo: Sakuhin-sha.

Itô, S. (1996). *Dôseiai no kiso-chishiki* [Basic knowledge of homosexuality]. Tokyo: Ayumi Shuppan.

Jansson, Y. (1987). *Otoko ga kawaru* [Changing men]. Tokyo: Yûhikaku.

Kashima, T. (1993). *Otoko no zahyôjiku: Kigyô kara katei shakai e* [The configuration of men: From business to home and society]. Tokyo: Iwanami Shoten.

Kasuga, K. (1989). *Fushikatei wo ikiru: Otoko to oya no aida* [The single father's family: Living as a man and a parent]. Tokyo: Keisô Shobô.

Kersten, J. (1996). Culture, masculinities and violence against women. *British Journal of Criminology, 36,* 381-395.

Komarovsky, M. (1976). *Dilemmas of masculinity: A study of college youth.* New York: W. W. Norton.

Lee, K. K. (1998). Confucian tradition in the contemporary Korean family. In W. H. Slote & G. A. De Vos (Eds.), *Confucianism and the family* (pp. 249-264). Albany: State University of New York.

Leupp, G. P. (1995). *Male colors: The construction of homosexuality in Tokugawa Japan.* Berkeley: University of California Press.

Louie, K., & Edwards, L. (1994). Chinese masculinity: Theorizing wen and wu. *East Asian History, 8,* 135-148.

McLelland, M. J. (2000). *Male homosexuality in modern Japan.* Richmond, VA: Curzon.

Menzusentâ. (1996). *Otokorashisa kara jibunrashisa e* [From manliness to selfness]. Kyoto, Japan: Kamogawa Shuppan.

Menzusentâ. (1997). *Otokotachi no watashisagashi* [How are men seeking their new selves?]. Kyoto, Japan: Kamogawa Shuppan.

Metropolitan Tokyo Women's Foundation. (1998). *Dansei no jiritsu to sono jôken wo meguru kenkyû: Dankai sedai wo chûshin ni* [A study on men's independence and its condition: Concerning the Baby-Boomers]. Tokyo: Author.

Nakamura, A., & Nakamura, T. (Eds.). (1997). *Otoko ga mietekuru jibunsagashi no hyakusatsu* [100 books for men's self-exploration]. Kyoto, Japan: Kamogawa Shuppan.

Nakamura, T. (1996). *Otokorashisa kara no jiyû* [Liberation from manliness]. Kyoto, Japan: Kamogawa Shuppan.

Nakamura, T. (2001). *Domesutikku baiorensu to kazoku no byôri* [Domestic violence and familial pathology]. Tokyo: Sakuhin-sha.

Nishiyama, M. (1997). *Edo culture: Daily life and diversions in urban Japan, 1600-1868* (G. Groemer, Ed. & Trans.). Honolulu: University of Hawaii Press.

Ogasawara, Y. (1998). *Office ladies and salaried men: Power, gender, and work in Japanese companies.* Berkeley: University of California Press.

Okamoto, T., & Sasano, E. (2001). Sengo Nihon no "sarariiman" hyôshô no henka [Changes in representations of "salarymen" in postwar Japanese newspapers]. *Shakaigaku Hyôron, 52*(1), 16-32.

Osa, S. (1999). Tenshi no jendâ: Kindai tennô-zô ni miru otokorasisa [Emperor's gender: Masculinity in the image of the modern emperor]. In Y. Nishikawa & M. Ogino (Eds.), *Kyôdô-kenkyû dansei-ron* [Discussions about men: A collaboration] (pp. 275-296). Kyoto, Japan: Jinbun Shoin.

Ôsawa, M. (2000, April). Government approaches to gender equality in the mid-1990s. *Social Science Japan Journal, 3*(1), 3-19.

Ôyama, H., & Ôtsuka, T. (1999). Nihon no danseiundô no ayumi 1: *Menzuribu* no tanjô [On the history of men's movements in Japan. Part 1: The birth of the *Menzuribu* movement]. *Nihon Jendâ Kenyû, 2*, 43-55.

Real, T. (1998). *I don't want to talk about it: Overcoming the secret legacy of male depression.* New York: Fireside.

Roberson, J. E. (1998). *Japanese working class lives: An ethnographical study of factory workers.* London: Routledge.

Ruhlmann, R. (1975). Traditional heroes in Chinese popular fiction. In A. F. Wright (Ed.), *Confucianism and Chinese civilization.* Stanford, CA: Stanford University Press.

Salamon, S. (1975). "Male chauvinism" as a manifestation of love in marriage. *Journal of Asian and African Studies, 10*(1-2), 20-31.

Sechiyama, K. (1996). *Higashi-ajia no kafuchô-sei* [Patriarchy in East Asia]. Tokyo: Keisô Shobô.

Shimomura, M. (1982). *Amerika no otokotachi wa ima* [The contemporary lives of American men]. Tokyo: Asahi Shinbun-sha.

Shinozaki, M. (1995). Higashi-ajia no kafuchô-sei kazoku no henyô to jizoku: Souru, Bankoku, Fukuoka, Pekin chôsa kara [The transformation and continuity of the East Asian patriarchal family: Research in Seoul, Bangkok, Fukuoka, and Beijing]. *Syakaibunseki, 22*, 71-85.

Shirakawa, Y., Shiraishi, T., & Sukemune, S. (1992). Current research on gender roles in Japan. *Psychologia, 35*(4), 193-200.

Shire, K. A. (1999). Socialization and work in Japan: The meaning of adulthood of men and women in a business context. *International Journal of Japanese Sociology, 8*, 77-92.

Soh, C.-H. S. (1993). Sexual equality, male superiority, and Korean woman in politics: Changing gender relations in a "patriarchal democracy." *Sex Roles, 28*(1/2), 73-89.

Sômuchô-Tôkeikyoku. (2000). *Sekai no tôkei* [World statistics]. Tokyo: Ôkura-shô Insatsu-kyoku.

Sugihara, Y., & Katsurada, E. (1999). Masculinity and femininity in Japanese culture: A pilot study. *Sex Roles, 40*(7/8), 635-646.

Sunaga, F. (1999). *Hage wo ikiru* [Getting through the hairlessness]. Tokyo: Keisô Shobô.

Taga, F. (2001). *Dansei no jendaa keisei* [The gender formation of men]. Tokyo: Tôyôkan Shuppan-sha.

Taga, F. (2003). Rethinking male socialization: Life histories of Japanese male youth. In K. Louie & M. Low (Eds.), *Asian masculinities: The meaning and practice of manhood in China and Japan* (pp. 137-154). London: RoutledgeCurzon.

Tu, W.-M. (1998). Confucius and Confucianism. In W. H. Slote & G. A. De Vos (Eds.), *Confucianism and the family* (pp. 3-36). Albany: State University of New York.

Ueno, C. (1995). *Kigyô senshitachi* [Corporate soldiers]. In T. Inoue, C. Ueno, & Y. Ehara (Eds.), *Danseigaku* [Men's studies] (pp. 215-216). Tokyo: Iwanami Shoten.

Ukai, M. (1999). Tetsudô mania no kôgengaku [Ethnography of the trainphile]. In Y. Nishikawa & M. Ogino (Eds.), *Kyôdô-kenkyû dansei-ron* [Discussions about men: A collaboration] (pp. 96-121). Kyoto, Japan: Jinbun Shoin.

Vincent, K., Kazama, T., & Kawaguchi, K. (1997). *Gei sutadîzu* [Gay studies]. Tokyo: Seidosha.

Wakabayashi, K. (1994). *Chûgoku jinkô-chôtaikoku no yukue* [China: The future of the superpopulated country]. Tokyo: Iwanami Shoten.

Watanabe, T. (1986). *Datsu-dansei no jidai: Andonojinasu wo mezasu bunmeigaku* [The age of demasculinization: The study of civilization toward androgyny]. Tokyo: Keisô Shobô.

Watanabe, T. (Ed.). (1989). *Danseigaku no chôsen: Y no higeki?* [The challenge of men's studies: The tragedy of Y?]. Tokyo: Shin'yô-sha.

Watanabe, T., & Iwata, J. (1989). *The love of the samurai: A thousand years of Japanese homosexuality* (D. R. Roberts, Trans.). London: Gay Men's Press.

Williams, W. L. (1994). Sexual variance in Asian cultures. *Amerasia Journal, 20*(3), 87-94.

Yajima, M. (Ed.). (1997). *Dansei dôseiaisha no raifu-hisutorî* [Life histories of male homosexuals]. Tokyo: Gakubun-sha.

9

MEN, MASCULINITIES, AND "EUROPE"

CRITICAL RESEARCH ON MEN IN EUROPE (CROME):
IRINA NOVIKOVA, KEITH PRINGLE, JEFF HEARN,
URSULA MUELLER, ELZBIETA OLEKSY, EMMI LATTU, JANNA CHERNOVA,
HARRY FERGUSON, ØYSTEIN GULLVÅG HOLTER, VOLDEMAR KOLGA,
EIVIND OLSVIK, TEEMU TALLBERG, AND CARMINE VENTIMIGLIA

In this chapter, we provide a broad view of the dynamic changes that seem to be occurring in Europe in relation to men and men's practices. This is an especially interesting and, from feminist and profeminist points of view, a rather anxious time to be surveying the European field. In particular, as we will demonstrate, the momentum of an enlarging European Union (EU) and of a broadening NATO alliance is pushing forward crucial changes of emphasis in dominant relations of power associated with issues of gender in both Eastern and Western parts of Europe—changes that generate oppressive and hegemonic forms of masculinities. Indeed, we will argue that the very project of creating and re-creating the idea and the practice of "Europe" is itself central to this process. Therefore, instead of providing a detailed survey of what is occurring with regard to men's practices in each European country, in the limited space available to us we have chosen to focus on the wider European canvas, a "bigger picture" that we believe has, to a considerable extent, been neglected in recent European writings on men and masculinities. At the same time, we seek to make links between these processes in Europe and even broader, more global, trends in relation to men's practices that have received some attention in recent years (Connell, 1998, 2002; Pease & Pringle, 2001; Pringle, 1998a, 1998b).

Given what has just been said, in a task such as ours, it is crucial to access a broad range of materials relating to men's practices across Europe. Consequently, among other sources, this chapter explicitly draws on the work carried

Authors' note: We are extremely grateful to all scholars from the countries of East-Central Europe, the Baltic regions, and Russia who have been helpful in providing information and critical insights for this chapter. We are, of course, well aware that we have not addressed the issues in such countries as Hungary, Slovenia, Yugoslavia, Ukraine, and Byelorussia. Other scholars would be welcome in this field.

out by a thematic research network titled "The Social Problem and Societal Problematisation of Men and Masculinities."[1] The central objective of the network (to which all the coauthors belong) is "to analyse men's practices, gender relations and policy responses to them in their social and cultural contexts, as both socially and culturally constructed and with real material forms, effects and outcomes for people's lives" (Hearn & Pringle, 2001). It therefore collates, assesses, and disseminates data on men and masculinities from across Europe from an explicitly critical, feminist, and profeminist perspective (Hearn et al., 2002; Pringle et al., 2001). The very formation and operation of the network for this purpose suggests some important issues central to our chapter. Consequently, we here consider the reasons for the network's existence, as well as some major conceptual and practical challenges it has faced in relation to the topic of men and Europe. Later we will discuss more broadly what we regard as the most critical of these issues.

One of the reasons for developing a European research network focused on the issue of men has been the gradually growing realization that men and masculinities are just as gendered as are women and femininities (Hearn et al., 2002). Gendering of men is both a matter of changing academic and political analyses of men in society and of contemporary changes in the form of men's own lives, experiences, and perceptions, which often develop counter to their earlier expectations and earlier generations of men. However, the network is also premised on the recognition that these gendering processes in relation to men often have a particular quality. Not only are men now increasingly recognized, albeit to varying extents, as gendered, but they, or, rather, some men, are also increasingly recognized as a gendered social problem in many European countries. This can apply in terms of men's violence to women and children, crime, drug and alcohol abuse, health problems, buying of sex, accidents, and so on—as well as, indeed, the denial of such problems as sexual violence. Such problematizations of men and constructions of men as gendered social problems in the European context apply in academic and political analysis and in men's own lives and experiences. They also exist more generally at the societal level, and in quite different ways in different societies. Although it may be expected that some more general problematization of men and masculinities may now be observable in many, perhaps most, European societies (for instance, in terms of media and public policy debates), the form this problematization takes is very different indeed from society to society.

Such an approach clearly leads to awkward questions about how one can actually speak of men and masculinities "in Europe" or provide a comparative analysis of men and masculinities across Europe. This awkwardness arises partly from the massive cultural variations in social contexts encountered across Europe, as well as from the fact that the issue of men and masculinities has been studied to very different extents and in very different ways across Europe (Hearn et al., 2002). However, the awkwardness also derives from the question of what we mean by *Europe*. Like, say, "Asia," the concept of "Europe" is a social construction. Moreover, that process of social construction has at least two aspects. The first aspect focuses on which geographical areas are deemed to be European as opposed to other—and by whom such definitions are set. The second aspect considers whether there are some countries deemed to be more European than others and, within specific countries, whether there are certain sections of society that are similarly deemed to be more or less European—and, once again, attention needs to be paid to who has the privilege of definition in such situations (Pringle, 1998a).

Issues of "being European" are of central concern for several reasons. First, the definitional processes involved are highly political, and, as we shall show, the relations of power associated with them are deeply gendered (Yuval-Davis, 1997). Second, these processes of definition have very material consequences for individuals, consequences that depend upon the individual's precise social location, one very important determinant of which is gender.

Moreover, for the last 45 years, but especially in the last 10 years, one particular institution that has become increasingly crucial in debates about what, who, and where is Europe and European and who, what, and where is more or less other is the European Union. The EU is an economic, social, and political union, initially of six countries in 1957, that has sought to increase the harmonization of economic and social policies across member states but still respect the principle of "subsidiarity" (decisions being made at the lowest appropriate level). The EU is premised on a "single market" among member states and on parliamentary democracy, albeit of different forms in the member states. Over the years, this has inevitably involved tensions between the push to economic and social convergence and the defence of national political interests. As it has expanded, these tensions have become more complex, although it is probably fair to say that the "strong agenda" toward greater unity has become more dominant in recent years.[2]

The current dynamics regarding men and masculinities between EU member states and those countries in Central and Eastern Europe generally labeled as other, many of whom are acceding to the EU, provide a clear illustration of the issues mentioned earlier. This is true in terms of the definitional processes concerning "otherness," the close associations of those definitional processes with gendered power relations, and the central implication of the EU project itself in those processes. In this chapter, we focus on these dynamics partly because we believe they tell us something very important about being a man and being a woman in Europe now. Thus, rather than producing some monolithic and (probably Western dominated) survey of men's practices across Europe, we examine patterns of hegemonic and nonhegemonic men's practices in terms of the processes by which the concept and the practice of Europe is currently being constructed.

The next section of the chapter considers the current dynamics concerning "masculinities" in some of the countries of Northern, Southern, and Western Europe—specifically, the countries of the European Union pre-2004 and nations already closely associated with the EU (for instance, Norway and Switzerland). What, in particular, are the trends regarding dominant and less dominant forms of masculinity there, and how far do such trends relate to the European Union project? The third section of the chapter considers the trends in some of the countries of Central and Eastern Europe and the impact of the European Union project on those trends.

NORTHERN, SOUTHERN, AND WESTERN EUROPE

In a chapter of this size, it is not possible to provide a comprehensive survey of men and masculinities in all of Northern, Southern, and Western Europe. Nor, from our perspective, would such a survey necessarily be useful. Indeed, many analyses of social phenomena in Europe concentrate on just those geographical segments and scarcely mention countries in the central or eastern parts of Europe; or, if they do mention the latter, these are frequently treated as a homogeneous bloc (Pringle, 1998a). This is one simple example of how hegemonic judgements are made about what constitutes Europe or which parts of Europe are deemed more (or less) worthy of attention or respect. It is important that we do not compound this tendency here, either by focusing disproportionately on those parts of Europe that hold relative dominance in a range of social and economic domains, including the academic, or by dismissing the individuality and complexity of countries in the central and eastern parts of Europe. Rather, our aim is, at least partially, to look critically at men's practices and masculinities in terms of the processes of the European Union project itself.

Moreover, in terms of the amount of critical academic and analytical material available, it would be easy to write a chapter on men in Europe that was dominated by the situation in Northern, Southern, and Western Europe. The extent of critical academic analysis on men and masculinities varies greatly across Northern, Southern, and Western Europe, both in terms of its overall content and in terms of which topics related to men's practices receive coverage and which do not (Hearn et al., 2002). Nevertheless, compared with the situation in central and eastern sectors of Europe, the North, South, and West have been the location for a massive proportion of the relevant academic material on men in Europe. In some countries, especially Germany, Norway, Sweden, and the United Kingdom, there is now some form of relatively established tradition of research on men, albeit of different orientations. In many countries, the situation is made complex by a difference between the amount of research that is relevant to the analysis of men and the extent to which that research is *specifically focused* on men. For example, in Finland and Italy, there is a considerable amount of relevant research, but most of it has not been constructed specifically in terms of a tradition of explicitly gendered research on men (Hearn et al., 2002).

Critical research on men's practices in Northern, Southern, and Western Europe on forms of masculinity formation in those regions highlights several significant patterns.[3] In terms of issues that concern home and work, recurring themes across nations include men's occupational, working, and wage advantages over women; gender segregation at work; and many men's close associations with paid work. In many countries, there are twin problems of the unemployment of some or many men in certain social categories along with work overload and long working hours for other men. These can especially be a problem for young men and young fathers, and they can affect both working class and middle class men, as, for example, during economic recession. Another recurring theme is men's benefit from avoidance of domestic responsibilities and the absence of fathers. In many countries, there is a general continuation of traditional "solutions" in domestic arrangements, but there is also growing recognition of the micropolitics of fatherhood, domestic responsibilities, and homework reconciliation, for at least some men. At the same time, there are counter and conflictual tendencies. On the one hand, there are increasing emphases on home, caring, and relationships. This may be linked to "family values," from either a politically right wing or gender-equal status perspective. On the other hand, there are tendencies toward more demanding and turbulent working life, through which men may be more absent.

As regards social exclusion, this can figure in the research literature in different ways, such as unemployment, ethnicity, and homosexuality, and with considerable variation between countries. The social exclusion of certain men links with unemployment of certain categories of men (such as those less educated, rural, ethnic minority, young, older), men's isolation within and separation from families, and associated social and health problems. These are clear issues throughout all countries. Globalizing processes may create new forms of work and marginalization. Some men find it difficult to accommodate to these changes in the labour market and changed family structure. Instead of going into the care sector or getting more education, some young men become marginalized from work and family life. It should also be noted that there is a lack of attention to men engaged in creating and *reproducing* social exclusion, for example, in regard to racism.

The recurring theme in the Western European literature on men's violence takes the form of the widespread nature of the problem of men's violence toward women, children, and other men, and in particular, the growing public awareness of men's violence against women. Men are overrepresented among those who use violence, especially heavy violence. This violence is also age related, with a weighting toward younger men.

Violence against women by known men is becoming recognized as a major social problem in most countries in Western Europe. The abusive behaviors perpetrated on victims include direct physical violence, isolation and control of movements, and abuse through the control of money. There has been much feminist research on women's experiences of violence from men and the policy and practical consequences of that violence, including those of state and welfare agencies, as well as some national representative surveys of women's experiences of violence. Gendered studies of men's violence toward women is a growing focus of research, as is professional intervention. Child abuse, including physical abuse, sexual abuse, and child neglect, is now being recognized as a prominent social problem in many countries. Both the gendered nature of these problems and how service responses are themselves gendered are beginning to receive more critical attention, in terms of both perpetrators and victims or survivors. There is some research on men's sexual abuse of children, but research on this is still underdeveloped in most countries. In some countries, sexual abuse cases remain largely hidden, as does men's sexual violence toward men.

In terms of health issues and men's practices, the major recurring themes are men's relatively low life expectancy, poor health, accidents, suicide, and morbidity. Some studies see traditional masculinity as hazardous to health. Men also constitute the majority of drug abusers and are far greater consumers of alcohol than women, although the gap may be decreasing among young people. It is surprising that there has been relatively little academic work on men's health from a gendered perspective in many countries. Socioeconomic factors, qualifications, social status, lifestyle, diet, smoking and drinking, hereditary factors, and occupational hazards can all be important, and they seem to be especially important for morbidity and mortality. Gender differences in health also arise from how certain work done by men is hazardous. Evidence suggests that generally men neglect their health and that for some men, at least, their "masculinity" is characterized by risk taking, an ignorance of the male body, and reluctance to seek medical intervention for suspected health problems. Risk taking is especially significant for younger men as regards smoking, alcohol, drug taking, unsafe sexual practices, and road accidents.

One particularly noteworthy pattern that cuts across issues of home and work, social exclusion, violence, and health is the different extents to which research in various countries has addressed one or both of two categories of men's practices: first, the problems some men create for women, children, other men, and themselves, and second, the problems some men have to endure as a result of patriarchal relations of power in society. For instance, to some extent, the focus of research in Finland tends to have been on the misfortune of some men in respect to issues such as mortality, unemployment, job insecurity, and alcohol and drug abuse. In Germany, too, in recent years, there has been a significant growth in studies of men who are said to represent disadvantaged groups in society (Hearn et al., 2002). Similarly (yet differently), considerable research in Norway has focused on the positive value of men as fathers and the various societal barriers that may be limiting their ability to fulfil that positive potential. By contrast, the emphasis of critical research on men in the United Kingdom has been much more on the problems some men may create for women, children, and (to perhaps a lesser extent) men, particularly in the form of violence (Hearn, 1998; Hearn et al., 2002; Pringle, 1995, 1998a).

Such differences of emphasis do not by any means simply represent differences in the actual size of social problems as far as we know them. For instance, the issue of men's violence toward women in Finland is a massive one socially (Heiskanen & Piispa, 1998), with levels of violence comparable to community-based studies in the United Kingdom (see, e.g., Mooney, 1993). However, this comparability between the two countries in the statistical size of the problem is not represented in the amount of critical scholarly activity devoted to the issue in Finland

and the United Kingdom, the attention accorded to it being far greater in the latter than in the former (see also Hearn, 2001). Exactly the same point could now be made in relation to Sweden, following the recent survey there of the experiences of 7,000 women (Lundgren, Heimer, Westerstrand, & Kalliokoski, 2001). That Swedish study also provided some significant evidence of high levels of child sexual abuse in Sweden committed primarily by men against children, another issue that has been prominently researched and addressed in the United Kingdom to a far greater extent than anywhere else in Northern, Southern, and Western Europe (Hearn et al., 2002; Pringle, 1998a). An even more recent qualitative study of the Swedish welfare system by one of the coauthors of this chapter (Pringle, 2002a) suggests that dominant discourses within the system routinely seek to downplay forms of oppression perpetrated by men upon women and children, especially where such forms of oppression are mainly perpetrated by men from within the white ethnic majority. That study also suggests a tendency within the Swedish research infrastructure to avoid topics or research methodologies that might bring such forms of oppression by men into clearer view. This state of affairs can once again be contrasted with that in the United Kingdom where such forms of oppression toward women and children are far more fully problematized publicly, professionally, and in terms of the research community. Moreover, an earlier qualitative research study of the Danish welfare system seems to suggest a pattern in Denmark similar to those described earlier for Finland and Sweden, compared with the United Kingdom (Pringle, 2002c; Pringle & Harder, 1999).

As a generalization, we may say that even though there are indications that men's violence is beginning to receive more attention as a whole, the bulk of critical research on masculinities in Northern, Southern, and Western Europe has focused considerably more on the problems that men endure than on the problems men create (Pringle, 1998a, 1998b, 2002b), with the United Kingdom and, to some extent, Germany (Hearn et al., 2002) being slight exceptions.

The division of research attention between the problems men endure and the problems men create is not tenable in scholarly terms. Instead, the frequent analytic unity of "the problems men endure" and "the problems men create" has to be recognized. For instance, one cannot adequately address the issue of men's health without in various ways considering the profound linkages between that subject and men's violence more broadly: for example, as regards accidents, mortality rates, drug and alcohol abuse, and inattention to self–health care (Hearn et al., 2002; Pringle et al., 2001). Similarly, one cannot adequately address either the issue of promoting men as carers or the issue of men's violence without a mutual consideration of the linkages between the two topics (Pringle, 1998b).

Europe and the EU

The implications of the current imbalance of research attention devoted to "the problems men endure" in the countries of Northern, Southern, and Western Europe should be considered more broadly. In many countries of Central and Eastern Europe, profound transformations in gendered power relations are occurring as a result of the social and economic upheavals since the late 1980s and due to the increasing links being forged with countries of the West. Moreover, a considerable number of these states are, at the time of writing (2003), themselves shortly due to accede to the EU within the next year. Interestingly, the EU's own research and policy approach to men's practices has largely mirrored the imbalance in the majority of the current 15 member states. The EU has tended to concern itself far more with issues such as reducing the limitations on men as carers, men's working conditions, and men's health rather than on topics such as men's violence toward women and children (Pringle, 1998a, 2002b). Although there are signs that some shift is beginning to occur in EU priorities, EU policy and research priorities overall remain tilted very much in favor of "the problems men endure." For instance, even the very considerable concern of the European Union with child prostitution and pornography and the sexual exploitation of children betrays this order of priorities. That concern has largely focused on the activities of EU citizens (mainly men) *outside* the territory of the EU—typically in parts of Central and Eastern Europe, South Asia, and East Asia (Pringle, 1998a, 2002b). This emphasis

has largely ignored the systematic abuse and exploitation of children *within* the confines of the EU itself. The development of EU policy on these issues as some of those countries in Central and Eastern Europe themselves become EU members is of considerable interest.

An obvious illustration of EU priorities in relation to men's practices is the trafficking of women. In recent years, this topic has been placed relatively high on the EU agenda, particularly in relation to women from the central and eastern parts of Europe. Although this may seem to contradict the previous argument, the context of the EU's interest in trafficking in fact supports that argument. EU interest has largely been framed in terms of the fight against crime associated with migration into the EU from outside its borders rather than arising primarily from concern with women's well-being (Pringle, 1998a, 2001). The emphasis of this EU anticrime initiative on cross-border trafficking seems to have largely ignored the male users of trafficked women—most of these users are, of course, citizens within existing EU member states. There are clearly a considerable number of these men, and it is their activities within the EU that fuel trafficking. This relative invisibility of users within the EU's approach to trafficking remains true despite the recent EU presidency of Sweden (Pringle, 2002b), the country that has led the way in antiprostitution policy in Europe by placing the emphasis of prosecution on the users rather than the women (Månsson, 2001). The focus of EU concern has not primarily been on its own citizens who create the trafficking problem; instead, the focus has been on external migrants and their countries of origin outside the EU, not least the Baltic states.

This outward focus, also observable in relation to the commercial sexual exploitation of children (Pringle, 2002b, 2002c), is a clear example of that hegemonic definition of "otherness" to which we alluded in the first section of this chapter. The commercial sexual exploitation of children and the trafficking of women are intensely gendered and are direct outcomes of practices associated with hegemonic forms of masculinity. In both cases, the reaction of the EU and most of its existing members has been to divert attention to the non-European sphere or to the citizens of allegedly problematic European nation-states currently outside the EU. The implications of this are that they are defined as less civilized, less "European" than the existing member states of the EU to whom they supposedly pose threats from outside. It is again interesting to consider (a) how EU policies and practices in relation to such gendered issues will develop when some of those stigmatized "others" become member states in the next year and (b) what messages regarding gender are already being received and constructed in those countries about to accede to the EU. In other words, how will gendered otherness be dealt with by both the existing EU members and the candidate states as they make the transition to membership?

The EU and its member states have conflated the issue of women trafficking with the broader subject of inward migration. The latter subject, along with the allied topic of racism, offers yet another example of the way in which power relations associated with hegemonic forms of masculinity are entering into the processes by which the idea and practice of *Europe* is being constructed. Racism, in one guise or another, seems to be very widespread in virtually all the countries of Europe. Social exclusion and processes of social marginalization are often defined (Hearn et al., 2002) and constituted (Pringle, 2002c; Pringle & Harder, 1999) differently in the various European countries. Nevertheless, very many of the national reports produced by the thematic research network partners acknowledge racism as a highly significant issue, even if its precise configuration varies from one cultural context to another. The issue of hegemonic masculinity is remarkably absent in debates about the dynamics of racism (Mueller, 2000) in Northern, Southern, and Western Europe (Hearn et al., 2002; Mueller, 2000; Pringle, 2002c). The relative silence about men's practices and racism in European academic and policy considerations seems particularly strange (Pringle, 2001).

Often central to the issue of racism in Europe and the issue of how EU member states treat migrants are questions about what Europe is, who is European, and who is "more European"— and who is, once again, "other"? Such questions may often be partly about whose masculinity is purer or more superior. Yet both the current member states of the EU and the European Commission itself have largely avoided confronting those highly gendered issues in their policies to combat racism and in addressing the

issue of migration. The part played by power relations associated with hegemonic forms of masculinity in the processes of "Europe creation" has been disguised and ignored. We need to ask ourselves what impact this state of affairs is having on conceptions and practices of gender across the countries within the central and eastern parts of Europe, many of which have been defined by the processes noted earlier as "other." This is especially the case given their growing economic, social, and cultural dependence on the states of Northern, Southern, and Western Europe, as well as the imminent prospect for some of the EU's membership.

This situation, whereby the states of Central and Eastern Europe are gravitating economically, socially, culturally, and politically toward their neighbors in the West, raises important issues about complex hegemonic and nonhegemonic forms of masculinity developing in both the (culturally) Western and Eastern segments of Europe and the complex relationships between those segments. One way of opening up some of those issues may be by considering models by which men's practices have been conceptualized transnationally. Transnational comparative analyses of men and masculinities are still relatively scarce. Significant exceptions to this include Connell (1991, 1998, 2002), Cornwall and Lindisfarne (1994), Hearn (1996), and Pease and Pringle (2001). This scarcity also applies to Europe. In fact, our survey here and some earlier articles produced from the outcomes of our network (e.g., Hearn & Pringle, 2001; Hearn et al., 2002; Pringle et al., 2001) represent considerable advances in this respect. As regards developing an initial analysis of the interactions between processes of masculinity formation in the Eastern and Western parts of Europe, Connell's model of changing historical forms of "globalizing masculinities" offers particular assistance (Connell, 1998). Although his thesis may be criticized for an overreliance on Western-oriented globalization theories (Pease & Pringle, 2001), there seems no reason to doubt his central contention about the ongoing development of a "global business masculinity." As he argues, certain hegemonic masculinities have now been globalized, with the making of masculinities shaped by global forces. Thus, to understand masculinities in specific local contexts, we need to think in global terms, at least to some extent (Pease & Pringle, 2001).

The main axes identified by Connell for this "global business masculinity" are the "metropolitan societies," particularly those of the North Atlantic such as North America and Western Europe (Connell, 1998). This concept has proved useful for analyzing some developments in Western Europe: for instance, the recent history of masculinity formation in Ireland (Ferguson, 2001). It may also be relevant to a range of broader issues in the northern, southern, and western parts of Europe. For example, there are the issues of growing job insecurity, more unemployment, and longer working hours (Hearn et al., 2002). Moreover, one highly underresearched issue across Europe is the topic of men in power (Hearn & Pringle, 2001; Hearn et al., 2002). It is true that dominant and diverse genderings of mainstream business and governmental organizations have been subject to research and analysis. Moreover, feminists and critical, feminist-influenced studies have spelled out the explicit and implicit genderings of business organizations and management (Acker, 1990; Collinson & Hearn, 1994, 1996; Ferguson, 1984; Hearn & Parkin, 1983, 1995; Mills & Tancred, 1992; Powell, 1988). Nevertheless, much research on gender relations in organizations has not considered the gendering of women and men in organizations with equal thoroughness. This is despite the fact that the explicit gendered focus on men and masculinities in organizations and management is important in several ways, including the analysis of national and transnational private and public sector managers and managements. This ongoing relative silence in itself attests to the critical importance of hegemonic forms of masculinity, not least those associated with global capital.

For present purposes, it may be useful to consider the concept of global business masculinity in relation to the European Union as a whole. On the one hand, if that concept is particularly consonant with a "neo-liberal" welfare model (Esping-Andersen, 1990, 1996), as it seems logical to assume, and if the European Commission espouses certain neoliberal approaches (as it often seems to do in prescribing budget stringency), then the economic and social profile of European Commission policies might be expected to promote global business masculinity. On the other hand, if we consider the European Commission's (1994) first White Chapter on Social Policy, *The Way Forward*, we find a rather confused and confusing mélange of statements. Many of these clearly do espouse a form of neoliberalism, as expected. However, more unexpectedly, a significant number of others apparently derive from a more socially responsible conservative corporatist or even social democratic ideology (Pringle, 1998a).

A similarly mixed picture emerges regarding mainstream EU policies toward Central and Eastern Europe. On the one hand, a heavily neoliberal agenda is often apparent. The criteria set by the EU for states hoping to accede to the EU have strong neoliberal overtones. This approach is similar to the often socially regressive criteria set by the EU, the World Bank, and the International Monetary Fund whereby some of the states of Central and Eastern Europe were given financial support in the 1990s (Pringle, 1998a). The message clearly being sent by the European Union and its member states to the central and eastern parts of Europe has been, and still is, that highly capitalist values (which we may regard as consonant with global business masculinity) are to be prized and promoted. What is the impact of such an approach on those countries in Central and Eastern Europe already seeking to cope with major social and economic transformations? In particular, what is the impact on gender relations, which have also been undergoing various forms of transformation in those countries? On the other hand, the European Union has placed policies in a central position that are clearly not consonant with the values of global business masculinity. An obvious example is the EU's emphasis on gender equality mainstreaming, which necessarily applies to acceding states as well as to existing members. What might be the complex consequences of such policies for gendered power relations in those acceding states?

In this section, we have reviewed various complex ways by which gendered power relations associated with dominant forms of masculinity are entering centrally into the hegemonic processes whereby the European Union, its member states, and associated countries are seeking to redefine "Europe" and what it is to be "European." Moreover, as we have also seen, the part played by gender relations within these processes has largely been kept invisible.

In the next section, we consider how gender relations within some of the countries in the central and eastern parts of Europe have been undergoing transformation arising from the social and economic changes occurring there since the late 1980s and the influence of trends in the northern, southern, and western parts of Europe, particularly via the activities of the EU and NATO.

THE COUNTRIES OF EAST-CENTRAL EUROPE, THE BALTIC REGIONS, AND THE NEW INDEPENDENT COMMONWEALTH

Gendered Transitions

The issues of men and masculinities in East-Central Europe, the Baltic states, and the countries of the Commonwealth of Independent States are to be contextualized within regional and national developments and the ways in which the gendering of cultures and nations have "organized" variable routes into modern formations of nation-state and citizenship. Most of the states and cultures of the region, together with their perceived European identity, have been historically shaped by forces of exclusion and marginalization as well as by shared peripherality between the German, Russian, British, Austro-Hungarian, and Ottoman empires. Gender, men, and women are themes that require a long-term comparative analysis of how cultural meanings of gender were constituted and stabilized in these specific settings. A related and fascinating issue is how meanings of gender framed individual experiences of men and women who have embodied "the historical structures of the masculine order in the forms of unconscious schemes of perception and appreciation" (Bourdieu, 2001, p. 4).

National histories of the region represent an extremely rich and yet unresearched potential archive in constructing gender orders so that there is a danger of simplification and generalization in an attempt to overview men's practices, research on men, and critical studies on men in the complexity of postsocialist political, economic, social, and cultural restructurings. As well as the many points of similarity, there are also critical points of deep and significant difference that constitute "what men really are" or rather—as history has intervened—"what men have become" (Blom, Hagemann, & Hall, 2002) and what "men of Europe" are becoming.

The breakdown of the socialist bloc in the past 10 years has brought a radical change in the development of Europe and, indeed, the whole world. It has also turned out to be an experience beyond its categorization as a "transitional" period to the world of capitalism and the free market. Most countries of the region have experienced the resurgence of a nationalism that has incorporated elements of an agrarian "return to tradition" (or "roots"), together with an urban populist perspective of the "return of the nation" and a "transitional" feedback in the shape of a "return to Europe." The reunification of the nation in the countries that received independence, reclaimed their political independence, or renationalized their postsocialist political spaces meant transforming trajectories of territorial imaginations of state and nation in the newly rebordered community and reunified identity of Europe.

The dissociation of the socialist economic and political system was seen as men's return from their "satellite" emasculation in the socialist hierarchy of political power to their traditional power positions in family and in society. As Zarana Papic (2000) points out,

> The most influential concept in post-communist state-building was the patriarchal nation-state concept, the ideology of state and ethnic nationalism based on patriarchal principles inevitably became the most dominant building force. Various forms of ethnic nationalism, national separatism, chauvinist and racist exclusion or marginalisation of old and new minority groups are, as a rule, closely connected with patriarchal, discriminatory and violent politics against women, and their civil and social rights, previously guaranteed under the old communist order.

Arguments that blame women's emancipation for social problems such as falling birth rates, "emasculation" of men, "selfishness" of women, and sexual depravity everywhere are not unique. There are precedents in European social history before World War II (Brittan, 1989; Segal, 1990). The difference is that we reproduce these "backlash" arguments in a new transitional situation, marked by an endless political crisis. Political effeminacy can be compensated for, in nationalist and religious fundamentalist moods, by media imagery of a "powerful politician" or a "strong businessman" (Novikova, 2000).

Ethnicization of political processes in postsocialist states, a shared regional characteristic, incorporated the politics of "gender restoration" (Eley, 1998). It has been somewhat similar to the arguments about motherhood in the welfare politics of welfare states during the interwar period when "maternalism was the medium of restabilization, of reestablishing women's place in the home—not as the foundation of female emancipation . . . but as the basis of gender restoration" (p. 514). This "gender restoration" as a backlash response to socialist "sex equality" projects in a national, regional, and European setting has been instrumentalized and deployed in several scripts—starting from economic shock therapy in Poland, combining with antiwomen social policies, and leading to the tragic Balkan decade. At the same time, various neoethnicity scripts of postsocialist nation rebuilding have been carving out the related legislation in national labor and family codes, thus reflecting a targeted, active reconstruction of men's social roles and representations, as well as images of masculinity.

Ethnicization of postsocialist national projects has been actively feeding into constructions of national hegemonic masculinity models, or the rise of masculinism (Watson, 1996). It formed the bedrock of "order" and "rationality" in reunifying political imaginations. In their turn, these have been bringing in resistant discourses of manhood, male roles, and male behavior in subordinated groups of populations (e.g., Latvian-Russian in Latvia, Rumanian-Hungarian in Rumania, Ukrainian versus Roma people in Ukraine) in the imminent presence of minority homelands over the border.

On the other hand, in the complexities of the transnational "east-east" divide, the political, economic, and military "completing of Europe" controversially urges the construction of the "bedrock" male identity in state- and nation-building projects. This transnational bedrocking process has actually exposed certain shared characteristics in the gender histories of nations and states, specifically, scenarios "with the doubled or contradictory temporal conception of the nation" (Wenk, 2000, p. 69). As Silke Wenk argues, following Anne McClintock, "on the one hand, the nation presents itself as a project of the future, and, on the other hand, as a project grounded in a mythically original past

as well" (Wenk, 2000, p. 69). Anne McClintock emphasizes that

> the temporal anomaly within nationalism— veering between a nostalgia for the past and the impatient, progressive sloughing off of the past—is typically resolved by figuring the contradiction in the representation of time as a natural division of gender. Women are represented as the atavistic and authentic body of national tradition, . . . embodying nationalism's conservative principle of continuity. (Wenk, 2000, p. 69)

Silke Wenk (2000) continues: "Men would then stand ultimately for the opposite, for progress and also for discontinuity. Nationalism's anomalous relation to time is thus managed as a natural relation to gender" (p. 69).

The explicit mobilization of masculine "bias" (Connell, 2002, pp. 58-59) in the political restructuring of the postsocialist "easts" of Europe, informed by the post–Berlin Wall reformation of strategic geoeconomic interests, explicitly gendered explosive "transitions" in existing concepts of gender stereotypes, images, roles, and values in the societies. The Balkan tragedy exposed violence as a transnational issue of violence across Europe—beyond the regional transparency of the extreme levels of men's violence against women and children and other men in situations of armed conflict. The exposure to forms of "gendercide"—either rape of "enemy" women or massive murder of battle-age "enemy" men—affected gender relations, systems, and traditions dramatically and structurally.

Somewhat similar syndromes are characteristic of warless countries of the region who are going through "peaceful" marketization of their economies. Zarana Papic (2003) writes,

> Although some post-communist states with a more or less ethnically "pure" population structure, like Poland, were not practising extreme ethnic violence, all of them violated women's essential human rights, above all the right to abortion, thus showing that the colonisation of women's bodies is central to post-communist processes of nation-building. Because men have gained decisive political and reproductive control over women, these societies are often labeled as "male democracies," or "new patriarchies." The absence of women from politics in post-communist transitions reveals the damaging effects of the patriarchal communist legacy, which gave women the right to work, education, divorce,

abortion, but prevented them from becoming active political subjects of their own destiny. Along with the nations' new legislatures becoming masculinised, Eastern European gender relations have become predominantly sexualised.

In Poland, for example, the research on unemployed men under 36 years old (performed from 1994 through 1996; Pielkowa, 1997, cited in Novikova, 2000) shows that "after they lost their jobs 40% of them reported the loss of family leadership which was taken over by their working wives. 23,4% of the unemployed husbands assumed household responsibilities and 3,8% took over the upbringing of children from their wives" (Oleksy, 2001). The loss of jobs also affected their lifestyles: Unemployed men spend most of their time watching sports on TV and playing cards with friends. Twenty-eight percent of these men perceived the change in family relations as negative after they had become unemployed; 32% reported the worsening of husband-wife relations (Oleksy, 2001). Clearly, the effects of men's unemployment bring us to address the issue of men's health.

In Lithuania, an ethnically heterogeneous and neighboring country of Poland, such factors as military conflicts in the Balkans and citizenship issues, as in Latvia and Estonia, have not arisen, and the "transitional" period has been considered as another instance of a "peaceful" scenario. Lithuania is the only country in the region with a law on equal opportunities for men and women and an ombudsman's office. However, the *Lithuanian Human Development Report 2000* points out,

> The demographic situation in Lithuania began to deteriorate in 1990. Since then the birth rate has been declining continuously, resulting in a negative natural increase in population even though mortality—after an increase in the first half of the decade—has decreased slightly in the past five years and in 1999 reached the same level as 1990. . . . Mortality among men of all age groups living in either rural or urban areas was 1.2-1.3 times higher than that of women. . . . People of working age accounted for 23.7% of the total mortality rate; 3.6 times more men from this age [group]. . . . Mortality among men of all age groups living in either rural or urban areas was 1.2-1.3 times higher than that of women. . . . men commit suicide far more often than women do (73.8 and 13.6 people per 100,000, respectively). The greatest difference between the suicide rates

of men and women is in rural areas, where men commit suicide seven times more often than women do. The proportion of young people who commit suicide remains high. . . . women in Lithuania live almost ten years longer than men on average. (Maniokas et al., 2000)

In Estonia, and more generally, in many other countries of East-Central Europe, "men's low life expectancy is a major health problem" (Kolga, 2001). Across the region, life expectancies of men have dropped, and the life-span gender gap varies from 10 to 15 years. There is an increase in coronary heart disease. Stress as a gender-related process and the cardiovascular heart disease epidemic among middle-aged men are again common features of dysfunctional social welfare, health care, and body politics. Cardiovascular mortality, chronic stress, and male suicide rates in former communist countries are 73 per 100,000 in Russia and Lithuania, 64 in Estonia, 59 in Latvia, 49 in Hungary (compared with 19 per 100,000 in the United States and an average of about 28 in Western Europe). In Poland, according to Oleksy (2001),

> The number of suicide attempts registered by the Militia in the 1980s went down from 4.7 thousand in 1980 to 3.7 thousand in 1989. . . . Men constituted ca. 79% of suicides then. The number of suicides increased greatly in the 1990s in comparison with the 1980s, and men were still more numerous in this population—81%. Public statistics for 1990 show that for every 100 thousand men there were 17 suicides and for every 100 thousand women there were 4 suicides, and in 1998 26 and 6, respectively. . . . The analysis of the data given in the report shows that there may exist interconnections among the four areas discussed, they are not, however, scientifically justified ([there are] no surveys in this area on a sample in [all of] Poland). Increasing unemployment, especially among men, may be connected with crime committed by men in Poland, also domestic violence, deterioration of the condition of health of Poles, an increase in suicide committed due to hardship following a job loss and inability to find new employment.

In Russia, as Janna Chernova (2001) argues, one of the probable explanations of the new rise in the death rate is massive stress caused by the macroeconomic instability that leads to uncertainty about the future of Russian society. This explanation is supported by two important facts:

First, the rise in the death rate at the beginning of the 1990s was not caused by children and old people; second, it was men who suffered the most. One of the primary reasons for these deaths was the rise in alcohol consumption in the beginning of the 1990s (compared with the low level reached at the time of the antialcoholic campaign of 1985-1988) (Chernova, 2001).

All these examples explicitly show how important it is to observe political, economic, and social developments from the point of view of men to integrate the gender analysis of the processes of men's social and cultural self-identifications in these developments. At the same time, data from several countries indicate that research and statistics are concentrated on men's misfortunes (somewhat similarly to pervasive themes in Finnish research) (Hearn et al., 2002). However, such studies are not based on gendered analyses of men's practices, values, roles, and so on. Such analyses should pursue the formation of specific multinodal identities of men as a gendered process reflected by the structuring of men's positions in labor markets (and their "shadow" aspects). The key questions here are how men see themselves and how the diversity of men's roles in this dispersed space is constructed in contrast to the essentialist notion of the nation-state that has excluded or marginalized them in the formal structures of national cultures.

Labor and Family

Family patterns and division of labor, as well as self-perceptions of men as agents of family and the private sphere, cannot escape deep, consequential transformations. One may assume that hegemonic masculinity in diverse national contexts is based on the role of a family man and breadwinner, and as such, dictates choices and the form of social welfare policies today. Moreover, the *Lithuanian Human Development Report 2000* (Maniokas et al., 2000) notes specifically that "the breadwinner is a farmer." However, for the families that have a "breadwinner with no income," the report points out, "These households have only 59% of the average household income. Social assistance benefits are the major source of the household's survival." This suggests a specific formation of a passive receiver-consumer model, or, in other words, a reobjectification process in which

charity, explicit or implicit, becomes a dominant feature in organizing the "citizen-consumer." Yuval-Davis (1997) argues that in this discourse, "Citizenship stops being a political discourse and becomes a voluntary involvement within civil society, in which the social rights of the poor, constructed as the passive citizens, would be transferred, at least partly, from entitlements into charities (p. 84).

Yuval-Davis (1997) emphasizes that

in the name of social cohesion, obligations are being shifted from the public sphere of tax-financed benefits and services to the private sphere of charity and voluntary services. And charity, usually, assumes the dependency and passivity of those given the charity. Rights become gifts and active citizenship assumes a top-down notion of citizenship. (p. 84)

This discourse implies the hegemony of an enterprise culture, either national or transnational, "with an economically successful middle class male head of a family" (Yuval-Davis, 1997, p. 84). This is particularly important to consider, for example, in such societies as Estonia, in which

the population is basically divided into two major classes: economically active and non-active population. The relation between these two classes depends from two main factors: economic situation and population age structure. As we see, more than half the population is economically inactive (713 000 persons are economically active and 390 000 are non-active persons). From the economically active population ca 10% is unemployed, and almost half (172 300) the economically nonactive people are retired, pensioners. The relation of self-employed and employees is now ca 1: 10. (Kolga, 2001)

The related question is how the forms of citizenship inspired with neoliberal economic politics transform the gender relations of men and women as well as relations between men in their private and public practices. With economic restructuring and the development of social forms of gender related to the nonmonetary economic sector, the deterioration of the former social welfare system brings the "welfare" function of women (taking care of children and the elderly) into the family. A woman takes back her "natural" functions in the family with the collapse of social care and health care. She also takes part in the nonmonetary productive part of a family, in addition to her monetary income, which is likely to be insufficient for the family's survival. In Latvia, for example, it is not unusual to have urban families involved in monetary sectors of the national economy spend large amounts of time in the countryside during planting, growing, and harvesting seasons, thus organizing their gendered time use accordingly. Postsocialist women may also be invited into the service sector of a transitional economy as an offshoot of their functions in the family. The postsocialist woman definitely experiences deprivileging moments differently from men, as she was brought up in the socialist (but still patriarchal) system and has now finally been "caught up" in the repatriarchalization of her society.

At the same time, in this variegated national and transnational context, the family is becoming a site of men's practices, roles, and values that seek new microsocial forms of gender contracts within the family itself. Voldemar Kolga (2001), for example, points out that in the 1990s, traditional families—couples (officially married or cohabiting) with children—still form the largest group, as in Estonia. However, he notes the growth of the number of childless couples (22% in Estonia, compared with 19% in the EU) as a sign of the new times.

In Russia, as Janna Chernova (2001) argues, the number of men is greater than the number of women in the cities when both are under 30 years old, and in the villages when both are under 50. She indicates that these tendencies have not resulted in an increase in marriages.

> Since 1994 the situation with the two most important marriage indexes has changed: the tendency of a decrease in the summarial marriage coefficient is still taking place but there is an increase in middle marriage age. The number of officially registered marriages decreases among younger generations. . . . Thus, the main tendency in the process of family forming is that young people of both sexes give up a traditional form of marriage more often, and its official registration, in particular. As results of different researches show, young people prefer living together as an alternative to official marriage. (Chernova, 2001)

In Poland, a comparative analysis of family type "shows that the number of single mothers and fathers rose together with the rise in population in the 1990s. In this group, both in 1988 and 1998, single fathers constituted ca. 11%, single mothers—89%" (Oleksy, 2001).

Polish researchers have represented further portrayals of men. For example, Kostyla and Socha (1998; cited in Oleksy, 2001) write about typical Polish young men of the 1990s who assist in the delivery of their children, take their children for walks, share household responsibilities with their wives, and cook for their women. They devote over 10 hours daily to professional activities, avoid medical doctors, eat unhealthy food, smoke cigarettes, and drink alcohol to overcome stress. And although Polish young men follow the European trend, playing squash and bicycling during the weekend, only 65 out of 100 will live to the age of retirement (65 years old in Poland). Moreover, men "constitute about 70% of drug abusers and they drink 3-4 times more alcohol than women. The rate of suicides shows a consistency which has been detected for many years—the relation between men who commit suicides and women who commit suicides is 3:1" (Oleksy, 2001).

These examples, whether from the Balkans or the Baltic regions, testify to the issues of men and masculinities in these regions as differentiated contextually. On the other hand, these examples, at least partially, expose some patriarchal processes, tendencies, and structures (Holter, 1997, p. 281) of men's individual and collective uses, practices, institutions, identifications, and values of masculinities. Governance, army, family, work, health care, and social security are regarded as highly risky and destructive forms of men's "gender privilege" (Greig, Kimmel, & Lang, 2000, p. 1) that need transformative change. The Balkan decade shows how an armed conflict brings in the essential meanings of gender as part of a nation's sense of continuity. The Lithuanian, Polish, Estonian, and Russian examples show a different and differentiated landscape of transition in which the naturalizing of gender has been taking place, with the aggressive entry of capitalism acting as a break to the former economic and political system by gender as its "evaluative code" (Holter, 1997, p. 65).

Transition Toward "Europe"

In this context, the process leading toward a unified Europe and its recentering strategies along the geopolitical axis West to East were articulated in the early 1990s (Modood & Werbner, 1997) as coming back to the "normal" and to civilization, or as a recivilizing process.

> Return to Europe! Every day the Polish press brings new articles about the conditions of our return to Europe. We are returning to Europe because we just had our first free elections. We are returning to Europe because we expect Poland to become a member of the Council of Europe. And yet we cannot return to Europe as long as our towns are dirty, our telephones dysfunctional, our political parties reactionary and parochial, and our mentalities sovietised. Europe is a measure, a purpose, a dream. (Jedlicki 1990, p. 6 cited in Kürti, 1997, p. 27)

Cultural and "civilizational" normalization rhetoric implicitly pulls in the rhetoric of difference between the European ("normal") self of the recovered nation and its "other," thus switching public visions of "East" from a communist virus to the alien and contaminating presence of "strangers inside" (Bauman, 1998), added to a long list of forms of postsocialist abjections.[4] The progressivist discourse of "the return to Europe" has been incorporated into reimaginations of national fraternal projects that ensure protection to economic power concentrated in the hands of men. This concentration of financial power and resources resulted from the economic discrimination against women and their alienation from political power in the socialist period. Another important factor was that the socialist period had blocked ways in which women's movements could have developed their autonomy, diversity, advocacy, and empowerment mechanisms, which were submerged under the populist and nationalist agendas of the 1990s.

In terms of Europe and, specifically, the European Union, the demand of the EU to harmonize national legislations of the accession countries with gender policies of the European Union does not "bypass" developmental connotations. The demand actually minimizes an important recognition that women's and men's economic and social situations in East-Central European countries radically worsened in the postsocialist liberalization of national markets. It vacuum cleaned the space of social policies rather successfully, having thrown out an unwanted baby together with the bathwater—the

opportunity for women's movements to carve themselves out of the democratic process of the late 1980s and early 1990s. The democratic process instrumentalized women's experiences of participating in environmental, popular mothers' movements by coopting them into the independence, reconstruction, and revival agendas.

At the same time, a complex relationship between local, traditional gender systems (themselves in transition) and the production of manhood in the socialist mythology of men's roles and hegemonic masculinities (themselves in crisis) was contested, reworked, and reaffirmed as a relationship between residual (traditional and socialist) and emergent (neoliberal) institutions, practices, and ideologies. Symptomatically, this is how Dimitar Kamburov, a profeminist researcher from Bulgaria, argues about men's issues in his country and culture: "A general understanding that males' positions are OK historically and socially in this region somehow cancels the very vision of issues like men and masculinities" (D. Kamburov, personal correspondence, April 26, 2001). He also emphasized that "the historical ambiguities, of men's position are in the social, cultural and everyday structure of Bulgarian, Southeast European and East European communitarian structure," and he indicated that this is the "problem of hidden matriarchy and men's fictive power and spurious authority in the region. The question of traditional labour distribution as an implicitly subversive agent of men's domination" is part of the same argument.

In Estonia, as Voldemar Kolga (2001) argues, the patriarchal structure of society has changed over time, but many attitudes and stereotypes treating men's central role as universal and natural have survived until today. "Men in Estonian society have traditionally been attributed the role of a leader, strong actor and punisher, while women have been viewed as caretakers, subordinates and those expressing compassion" (Kolga, 2001). At the same time, with economic restructuring, from 1995 onward, "the unemployment rate among men has been somewhat higher than among women. According to [a] 1997 labour survey, women's unemployment rate was 9.7% and men's 11.2%" (Kolga, 2001).

The return into "ethnic authenticity," into "normal statehood and nationhood" as the retrieval of "natural gender order" was traumatically compromised by the tsunami-like transformations in national labor markets, their transnationalization, and the political "re-Europeanization" of the region (marked as a West-East relationship). Mass media celebrated the survival of the "strongest." As a form of wishful thinking, they also fabricated the view of "successful" First World projects, such as the Nordic, American, West European, and Japanese, as normative (because economically successful) models of gender relations (Novikova, 2000). In this context, what Dimitar Kamburov underlines as a problem for men in the Balkan regions can be referred to as common to the east-central part of post–Berlin Wall Europe. As he writes,

> The advent of machismo as an overreaction to the new crisis of masculine positioning is related to the crisis of men's self-reflection as an outburst of the radical change of values of success and sense of life in the process of transition. (D. Kamburov, personal correspondence, April 24, 2001)

In Russia, however, there has developed a discourse, defined as "masculinity crisis," with major indicators of low life expectancy compared with women, self-destructive practices (e.g., so-called bad habits such as hard drinking and alchoholism, smoking, excessive eating), and high rates of morbidity and mortality that make it a "sad privilege" to be a man (Chernova, 2001). Demographic, health, and birth and death rate studies; new studies of men and violence; exclusion of some men's groups (homosexuals, for instance) from the field of the normative masculinity—all this led to the emergence of a peculiar "victimization theory." According to this theory, men are passive victims of their biological nature and structural (cultural) circumstances. In other words, men are represented in this theory as victims who can hardly be called "actively functioning" social agents of their own lives (Chernova, 2001). Finally, the rhetorical triumph of nationalists' "man as a victim" who is not responsible for the political, economic, and social malfunctioning in the (not uniquely) Russian context has been developing into a multifunctional instrument that can attack either "those emancipated women" in the past or "feminist (Western and rotten) spoils" in the present.

The victimization and infantilization of men became a topic in the Soviet territories at least 20 years ago, and (surprise!) the public discourse since then has similarly condemned women occupying men's places. Neither the Russian "masculinity crisis" nor the "Eastern male inferiority complex" (labeled as "men's effemi-nization," "men's emasculation," "men's infan-tilization") seem to be just national or regional symptoms of socially gendered transformations. A social and psychological crisis of masculinity is not the first attempt of its "justified" reaffir-mation in modern times. However, its postmod-ern manifestation is mobilized across Europe in an overall utterance of denouncement that speaks against epistemologically informed polit-ical and social practices that delegitimize the gender of hegemonic conceptualizations of "equality" and, at least in Eastern Europe, enjoy the steady cannibalization of gender equality packaged as sexual transgression and perversion.

Meanwhile, as Stephen Whitehead (2002) points out, in the West, men in crisis either should find their "authentic selves" outside of the stereotypical machismo that damages and imprisons them or reassess their mas-culinity by adopting roles that are "relevant to modern times." They might also "find their identity in fraternal projects and missions" to restore a "damaged inner psyche" that has been "damaged through consumerism and/or domestication" (p. 55). He then argues that

> the crisis of masculinity discourse suggests that the inability of many men to cope with the new expectations of women (feminism), combined with the demise of traditional work patterns and male roles, makes them especially vulnerable to engaging in forms of resistance that lead on to criminal behaviour. . . . In short, women's new-found expectations and achievements are a social problem, not a social good—not least because they serve to put those males who are seen as most likely to offend (working-class white and black youths) in an untenable situation whereby their "natural" masculine inclinations have no ready outlet. Thus the relation between feminism, male criminality and redundant and dysfunctional forms of masculinity is reified. (p. 53)

In different situations, however, either low professional competitiveness or the effects of economic restructuring on different social groups of men are easily transformed into mas-tering the public desire for narratives of violated maleness naturally embodied in men's practices as performances of dominant masculinity images: "Significantly, the male crisis discourse has seeped out of cultural discussion and is now increasingly being used to inform public policy" (Whitehead, 2002, p. 51), and this looks true of postsocialist policy developments as well.

In Latvia, for example, the new labor code has a clause on paternity leave as a right for the working father. On the one hand, it is an attempt to reclaim men as active fathers by practicing gender equality in the family and the labor market. However, contextually, this legislative measure addresses the issue of absence of fathers from their families—discursively constructed as "men's crisis" and "crisis of a Latvian family." Returning a father to a family has been a significant component of the "healthy normal nuclear family" discourse, against the reality of the single-parent (mainly single-mother) family. Another implication lies in the valorization of the private sphere by enhanced paternity rights, although there is not a parallel enhancement in terms of valorizing women's jobs in the labor market (at least in terms of their salaries). The "cultural image of the New Father" (Hondagneu-Sotelo & Messner, 1994, p. 206), accepted unproblematically, is not linked up with career and pay equity for women as "a structural precondition for the development of equality between husbands and wives in the family" (p. 205). Moreover, domesticity can become a territory for conservative familism to "conquer" in terms of expanding new gender privileges and disadvantages in family socialization patterns for children. The initiatives for changing a father's role in the family are not adequately accompanied by gender-informed educational reforms and creation of societal awareness about the plurality of family models and their social valorization beyond a "universal" nuclear, heterosexual, "normal" family.

One can also presume that reevaluation of a father's role in the family is negotiated in revising gender orders of welfare regimes across Europe; thus the private sphere is gradually completing the gendered power mapping of the private, but also the public. Family has been, increasingly, an extremely important social and economic agent in the transnational gendered economic circuit and a revised site of crumbling social policies, with the return of caring functions to the private domain. However, inviting a father's caring (apart from hidden social welfare restructuring) can fit "into a right-wing family values agenda, almost suggesting that children need fathers more than they need mothers (if not fathers, at least patriarchs)" (Aronson & Kimmel, 2001, p. 49). Let me dwell on this argument and add that professionalism remains a central value in the practice of masculinity, along with the appropriated (or "retrieved," or "returned") caring function of a father.

"Return to Europe," as the mainstream political and economic agenda of the countries included in the EU-accession cohort, is part of the globalization process. In these terms, militarization of Europe as part of global militarization is a "'technical modality' of connectivity" (Tomlinson, 1999, p. 4) in the package of processes that are rewriting the autonomy principles of the nation-state in its supranational and regional negotiations and involvements. The boundaries of regional military blocks are becoming actual borders of global mapping of power relations, within which, for any country to join the EU, the metonym of Europe, means to prove exactly that "I am not a stranger." It achieves this by diffusing angst to those either in their territories (diasporas, clefts in the Baltic regions, new vs. old in East-Central Europe) as extensions of strangers outside their countries or through Islamization of angst expressed in the works of theorists as a major trait of globalization. In this context, the outcome of this gendered social and economic process awaits research, with the focus on men's (and "new" minority or transnational men's) self-identifications and views about their situation in the 1990s, following the radical economic and political change in gender regimes. Its central questions should be (a) What is considered relevant in the self-articulation of cultural and social identities of men in minority, diasporic, and transnational communities? and (b) How do men consider the democratic management of their societies with regard to the specific problems of diversity and transformation?

"Completing Europe" is likely to remain a battlefield, an explicitly gendered project. That project may manifest itself either in rebuilding small nation-states and their armies or in constructing a new role of a future European soldier in high-tech, "remote-control" wars. The latter will be "an anonymous legionary supporting a European/international order in invisible and intangible wars, with invisible, media-defined enemies" (Novikova, 2000). Whatever language is used, militarization of the economy, accompanied with the European Monetary Union, betrays the two gendered dimensions of the nation-state, translated into a supranational formation—army and money—recarving new visions of hegemonic masculinities out of "soldiering and sea trading," the men's occupations that, as R. W. Connell argues, gave rise to early modern Europe as a gendered enterprise (Connell, 1987).

The globalized international market is another projection of the global "battlefield" within which postsocialist countries must elaborate their gendered projects and schemes of welfare regimes. The national economies have been structured and perceived so that the private sector is more "male" and the public sector concentrates men mainly in the upper echelons of power and salaries. The picture, however, is even more complicated by the presence of what is called an "informal economy" in all countries of the transitional belt. It definitely is another sphere of male dominance in regard to producing transnational, regional, national, and local hierarchies and patterns of men's social identities and representations.

As the past 15 years have shown, postsocialist societies have (possibly unknowingly) worked to restore a man-as-breadwinner model of family (variable) and related private-public divisions of gender roles. A man is defined in his social role and social identity of breadwinner as dominant, thus involving implicitly his control over income and possession. As such, this role is granted a social representation of hegemonic masculinity imageries. R. W. Connell (1987, 1995), however, argues about the historical production of contemporary Euro-American masculinities. The issue here is dominance-inequality as the dimension of social structures in dominated European countries whose gender relations have historically been part of European imperial configurations and very diverse men's practices, cultural forms and norms, and identifications. The "frontiers" of Europe offer new "Eastern" leverages for new policies for European and global coproduction of "a dominance-based masculinity" that R. W. Connell sees as operating in "a technocratic rather than confrontationist style" and, moreover, as "misogynist as before."

The misogyny is not a static phenomenon, and gender regimes on both national and supranational levels avoid confrontational politics by recruiting the "innocently" class-blind but "perfectly" gender-friendly language of negotiation, partnership, and cooperation. We are obviously dealing with forms of misogyny that work covertly in the space between politically correct legislations and destructive social and economic environments. In this, the notion of collectivity as providing values of gender equality is being devalued. The return of "biology" is bound up with high levels of violence against women and men, homosexuals, children, old people, and immigrants across Europe (burning of Turkish houses in Germany, murdering of an immigrant boy in Norway, harassment at a gay rally in Belgrade), which is what lies behind the discourse of multiculturalism across Europe. The skinhead actions in Russia and anti-Semitic outbursts across Europe in 2002 are symptoms of the processes in which the mosaic of "biology," "strongest," "authenticity," "enemy," and "order" is brewed into the Molotov cocktail legitimation of a reconstructing word (e.g., peacekeeping), as West-East European male "rationality" claims to progressively reproduce a new European social world and its gender order.

STUDIES ON MEN IN THE COUNTRIES OF EAST-CENTRAL EUROPE AND THE FORMER SOVIET UNION

At the same time, it is difficult to disagree with Elzbieta Oleksy (2001) that, due to little interest in "men's" issues in our countries, "it is difficult to talk about men's politics." In Poland, for example, there is only one organization that addresses men exclusively: the Association for the Defense of Fathers' Rights (*Stowarzyszenie Obrony Praw Ojca*).

Across the region, men are active in organizing gay groups; there are men who are interested in organizing fathers' groups (e.g., in Poland) and men's groups analogous to Robert Bly's mythopoetic trend. However, it is extremely difficult to collect information on men's groups and organizations across the region.

Academic communities of the regions and countries were exposed to women's studies in the early 1990s, when family and demographic sociologists were searching for promising areas of research that would open roads to the West.

Thus there was an attempt to translate women's studies in a way that was relevant to our environments, as something parallel to that which traditional women's research had been doing in Soviet socialist times. Gender studies were appropriated with less difficulty because the word *feminist* meant everything alien to the ideas and traditions of those nations in the process of self-reconstruction after regaining political independence from the USSR in 1991. Gender studies promised something that could more easily work with mainstream academia.

At the time of state and nation rebuilding, the power of the nation had to be in the hands of men. All problems related to men were labeled as men's crises because, according to widespread opinion, the Soviet socialist regimes had infantilized and feminized them in the ideology of sexual equality. The nationalist discourses of the early 1990s literally did not leave any room for forming influential and independent women's movements, and women's and gender studies centers were politically ghettoized in the academic communities.

Apart from societal transformations having brought new values and identities into gender relations, research on women had been active in the former socialist and Soviet academic institutions, as women had been viewed in terms of their productive as well as reproductive value in every nation. What research there was on men had "accompanied" the research on women. It was becoming of more importance in the 1980s, with demographic decline and growing alcoholic consumption, in particular in the regions of the USSR.

What Elzbieta Oleksy (2001) notes for Poland is also true for other countries: "masculinity as an independent research topic has enjoyed little if not marginal popularity among Polish authors." Iva Smidova (2002), a researcher from the Czech Republic, writes,

> In the Czech Republic, men have not been studied yet; the theme of masculinities is often considered as unproblematic, or "men's role" is only discussed under other branches of sociological inquiry—mainly research on family. Men (and women still) are an "exceptional" topic for the general public opinion; for they must understand and know "what is going on here." To question the everyday experience and (re)define it as problematic, to list men's problems and study them, or just deconstruct men's position and stereotypes of the "norm" and point to prejudices will be a delicate task. (p. 1; see also Smidova, 2003, 2004)

There, however, has emerged a new type of research on changes in men's practices and images (Smidova, 2002). Smidova points to an important, specific feature that might be attributed to the development of feminist and gender studies in other countries of East-Central Europe: a tendency in the Czech Republic to study women in relation to men and not to exclude men from feminist studies and research.

Issues of men's practices, values, and masculinity images have been among thematic interests for scholars in the Balkan countries such as Svetlana Slapsak (Slovenia), Rastko Mocnik (Slovenia), Marina Blagoevich (Yugoslavia), Zarana Papic (Yugoslavia), Tomislav Longinovich (Yugoslavia), and others. In the Baltic regions so far, several attempts to attract academic and public attention to men's issues were made at the Valmiera conference in 1998: Nordic men involved in men's studies organized a special workshop with a focus on men and violence and men and family roles.

Publications and translations of works about men and masculinities are gradually and steadily becoming part of our research horizon, as, for example, the collections on integrating post-socialist perspectives on men (Novikova & Kambourov, 2003), and on men and masculinities in Russia (Oushakine, 2002). The latter includes scholars who have done individual research on men's issues in politics, business, and culture in Russia and outside it. However, they are not united in networks, seminar programs, or team research projects. The academic settings are structured so that women researchers in gender, women's, and feminist studies remain in their peripheral spaces, with no potential for a career in mainstream academia. Thus women researchers practice a "borderland" strategy by combining research they are personally interested in with research that will be beneficial for their career. A man who would pursue the goal of making a career in the national academy certainly excludes the "feminized" periphery from his ambitions, apart from exceptional cases in which gender studies are used as a route for an academic jump into a Western program or institution.

There are no research projects on the issues identified in this chapter that have been conducted by scholars in the regions and countries we deal with here and, more specifically, by scholars from those regions and countries working in a concerted way. There is an obvious connection between the noticeable absence of such scholars among male academics engaged in critical and feminist research on men and masculinities and their marginal presence in mainstream academic research. This is not to assert that a particular experience is crucial to the research of particular issues. It is to say that the exclusion and marginalization of particular issues in politics and research explicitly tells us more about general moments in the gendered structuration of the region's democratic deficit.

CONCLUSION

As should be clear from our analysis in this chapter of the underlying (and often hidden) gender processes that permeate the current (re)creation of "Europe," the EU research network on men, from whose outcomes we have mainly drawn, represents a significant step in bringing together women and men researchers for the development of good quality European research on men in Europe. The research and network team has included scholars from Poland, Estonia, Russia, and Latvia and has provided an excellent opportunity for collaboration with and learning from the expertise of colleagues, as well as promoting comparative methodologies and disciplinary developments of men's research into national and regional settings. It is particularly important because the research network addresses men and masculinities in the four main aspects that have never found direct relevant research and policy statements in the East-Central European states, the Baltic states, and Russia. These aspects are men in relation to home and work, men in relation to social exclusion, men's violence, and men's health.

For the future, the outcomes of the network point to the urgent necessity for researchers to address all these aspects—most of all, in terms of which models of differential welfare regimes are being constructed in the countries of East-Central Europe, the Baltic states, and Russia. This is in the context of the EU's eastern enlargement and the demands of the EU on accession countries to harmonize their legislations with *acquis communataire* (the entire body of European laws). If

distinctions and contrasts can be made in the welfare regimes of Western Europe (see Esping-Andersen, 1990, 1996, for one influential model and, for a critique, Pringle, 1998a, 2002b), the historical trajectories of gender orders and state regimes in the countries of Central and Eastern Europe will need to be brought to the level of comparative analysis, together with research on how the ongoing gendering of these nation-states incorporates and transforms these trajectories.

A gender analysis of the constructed welfare regimes should be combined with a critique and greater attention to conscious gendering of men's practices and relations to the welfare regime developments by taking into account their interaction with dominant cultural, regional men's practices, and traditional views of men and masculinities. This challenge involves an emphasis on the relatively weak connection (or its absence) between gender research and statistical reporting on men's practices within the countries of Central and Eastern Europe—in contrast, for example, to such countries as Germany, Norway, and the United Kingdom. Moreover, gender as a category in statistical reporting and analysis is not used in Central and Eastern Europe to the extent to which the data can be used for research on men's practices as gendered process. This points emphatically to the shortage and even public and academic invisibility of feminist, women's, and gender studies in the countries of the region and the politically grounded transplantation of gender into mainstream academic language to neutralize the critical stance of this category of analysis.

Thus, in this chapter, we have not only demonstrated that the "re-creation" of the "New Europe" centrally involves gendered and gendering processes; we have suggested that these processes cannot be fully understood without consideration of the complex interaction of oppressive power relations operating between a dominant West (partly in the form of institutions such as the European Union and NATO) and the countries of Central and Eastern Europe. How far those power relations can be subverted in transformation by the rapidly changing societies of that part of Europe will be a crucial issue over the next decade for the well-being of those living there—especially women and children, but also men. In this context, it is to be hoped that those institutions that generate transnational research (such as the European Union) will develop further projects, such as the thematic research network from which the coauthors have drawn here, to carefully scrutinize these processes. Current indications, such as the recent publication of the European Commission Framework 6 Programme, are not necessarily encouraging.

NOTES

1. This network is funded by the European Commission (Contract Number HPSE-CT-1999-0008). The Web site for the network is http://www.cromenet.org.

2. The EU currently comprises 15 countries: Austria, Belgium, Denmark, Finland, France, Germany, Greece, Ireland, Italy, Luxembourg, the Netherlands, Portugal, Spain, Sweden, and the United Kingdom. At the time of writing (the very beginning of 2003), 10 more countries have been formally invited to join the EU by 2004, subject to positive outcomes in national referenda: Cyprus, the Czech Republic, Estonia, Hungary, Latvia, Lithuania, Malta, Poland, Slovakia, and Slovenia. In addition, it is projected that Bulgaria and Romania should be able to join by 2007. In addition, 12 of the 15 EU member states (all except Denmark, Sweden, and the United Kingdom) now have the same currency (the Euro), as part of the European Monetary Union.

3. The summary that follows, of current research on men's practices in Western Europe (including brief considerations of men at home and work, under conditions of social exclusion, men's violence, and men's health), draws heavily on the outcomes of the European Commission-funded thematic network mentioned earlier (see Hearn et al., 2002; Hearn & Pringle, 2001).

4. The notion of "abjection" as an explanation for oppression and discrimination is derived from Julia Kristeva's (1982) book *Powers of Horror: An Essay on Abjection*, in which she succinctly says, "The abject has only one quality of the object and that is being opposed to I." Kristeva's theory of abjection is concerned with figures that are in a state of transition or transformation. The abject is located in a liminal state that is on the margins of two positions; it has to do with "what disturbs identity, system, order. What does not respect borders, positions, rules" (Kristeva, 1982, p. 4).

REFERENCES

Acker, J. (1990). Hierarchies, jobs, bodies: A theory of gendered organizations. *Gender and Society, 4*(2), 139-158.

Aronson, A., & Kimmel, M. (2001). The saviors and the saved: Masculine redemption in contemporary films. In P. Lehman (Ed.), *Masculinity: Bodies, movies, culture* (pp. 43-50). New York: Routledge.

Bauman, Z. (1998). *Europe of strangers.* Retrieved December 31, 2003, from http://www.transcomm .ox.ac.uk/working%20papers/bauman.pdf

Blom, I., Hagemann, K., & Hall, C. (2002). Introduction. In I. Blom, K. Hagemann, & C. Hall (Eds.), *Gendered nations: Nationalism and gender order in the long nineteenth century* (pp. xv-xviii). Oxford: Berg.

Bourdieu, P. (2001). *Masculine domination.* Cambridge, England: Polity Press.

Brittan, A. (1989). *Masculinity and power.* Oxford, England: Blackwell.

Chernova, J. (2001). *Russia national report on statistical information on men's practices work-package 2.* Retrieved January 1, 2004, from http://www.cromenet.org/customers/crome/cro me.nsf/resources/A203BD5911CF9CB9C2256 A3B004F0A68/$file/Russia+WP2.rtf

Collinson, D. L., & Hearn, J. (1994). Naming men as men: Implications for work, organisations and management. *Gender, Work and Organization, 1*(1), 2-22.

Collinson, D. L., & Hearn, J. (Eds.). (1996). *Men as managers, managers as men: Critical perspectives on men, masculinities and managements.* London: Sage.

Connell, R. W. (1987). *Gender and power: Society, the person and sexual politics.* Stanford, CA: Stanford University Press.

Connell, R. W. (1991, June 7-8). *The big picture—a little sketch: Changing Western masculinities in the perspective of recent world history.* Paper presented at the Research and Masculinity and Men in Gender Relations Conference, Sydney.

Connell, R. W. (1995). *Masculinities.* Berkeley: University of California Press.

Connell, R. W. (1998). Masculinities and globalization. *Men and Masculinities, 1*(1), 3-23.

Connell, R. W. (2002). *Gender: An introduction.* Cambridge, England: Polity Press.

Cornwall, A., & Lindisfarne, N. (1994). Introduction. In A. Cornwall & N. Lindisfarne (Eds.), *Dislocating masculinity: Comparative ethnographies.* London: Routledge.

Eley, G. (1998). From welfare politics to welfare states: Women and the socialist question. In H. Gruber & P. Graves (Eds.), *Women and socialism, socialism and women: Europe between the two World Wars* (pp. 507-516). New York: Berghan Books.

Esping-Andersen, G. (1990). *The three worlds of welfare capitalism.* Cambridge, England: Polity Press.

Esping-Andersen, G. (Ed.). (1996). *Welfare states in transition: National adaptations in global economies*. London: Sage.

European Commission. (1994). *The way forward. . . .* Brussels: Author.

Ferguson, H. (2001). Men and masculinities in late-modern Ireland. In B. Pease & K. Pringle (Eds.). *A man's world: Changing men and masculinities in a globalized world* (pp. 118-134). London: Zed Books.

Ferguson, K. (1984). *The feminist case against bureaucracy*. Philadephia: Temple University Press.

Greig, A., Kimmel, M., & Lang, J. (2000, May). *Men, masculinities and development: Broadening our work towards gender equality* (UNDP Monograph Series No. 10). New York: United Nations Department of Publications.

Hearn, J. (1996). Deconstructing the dominant: Making the one(s) the other(s). *Organization, 3*(4), 611-626.

Hearn, J. (1998). *The violences of men*. London: Sage.

Hearn J. (2001). Nation, state and welfare: The cases of Finland and the UK. In B. Pease & K. Pringle (Eds.), *A man's world: Changing men and masculinities in a globalized world* (pp. 85-102). London: Zed Books.

Hearn, J., & Parkin, W. (1983). Gender and organizations: A selective review and a critique of a neglected area. *Organization Studies, 4*(3), 210-242.

Hearn, J., & Parkin, W. (1995). *"Sex" at "work": The power and paradox of organisation sexuality* (Rev. & Updated). Hemel Hempstead: Harvester Wheatsheaf/Prentice Hall.

Hearn, J., & Pringle, K., with network partners. (2001). Thematic network on the social problem and societal problematisation of men and masculinities (MEN). In L. Hantrais (Ed.). *Researching family and welfare from an international comparative perspective* (pp. 58-62). Brussels: European Commission.

Hearn, J., Pringle, K., Müller, U., Oleksy, E., Lattu, E., Chernova, J., Ferguson H., Holter, Ø. G., Kolga, V., Novikova, I., Ventimiglia, C., Olguik, E., & Tallberg, T. (2002). Critical studies on men in ten European countries: 1. The state of academic research. *Men and Masculinities, 4*(4), 380-408.

Heiskanen, M., & Piispa, M. (1998). *Usko, toivo, hakkaus: Kyselytutkimus miesten naisille tekemästä väkivallasta* [Faith, hope, battering: A survey of men's violence against women in Finland]. Helsinki: Tilastokeskus.

Holter, O. G. (1997). *Gender, patriarchy and capitalism: A social forms analysis*. Unpublished doctoral dissertation, Faculty of Social Science, University of Oslo, Oslo.

Hondagneu-Sotelo, P., & Messner, M. M. (1994). Gender displays and men's power: The "new man" and the Mexican immigrant man. In H. Brod & M. Kaufman (Eds.), *Theorizing masculinities* (pp. 200-218). Thousand Oaks, CA: Sage.

Jedlinki, J. (1990). The revolution of 1989: The unbearable burden of history. *Occasional Papers No. 29*. Washington, DC: The Wilson Center.

Kolga, V. (2001). *Estonia national report on statistical information on men's practices workpackage 2*. Retrieved January 1, 2004, from http://www.cromenet.org/customers/crome/crome.nsf/resources/982F16F67DD09DF4C2256A3B004DA7B4/$file/Estonia+WP2.doc

Kristeva, J. (1982). *Powers of horror: An essay on abjection* (L. S. Roudiez, Trans.). New York: Columbia University Press.

Kurti, L. (1997). Globalisation and the discourse of otherness in the "new" Eastern and Central Europe. In T. Modood and P. Werbner (Eds.), *The politics of multiculturalism in the new Europe: Racism, identity, and community* (pp. 29-53). London: Zed Books.

Lemons, G. (2001). Toward the end of "black macho" in the United States: Preface to *A (pro)womanist vision of black manhood*. In B. Pease & K. Pringle (Eds.), *A man's world: Changing men and masculinities in a globalized world* (pp. 150-162). London: Zed Books.

Lundgren, E., Heimer, G., Westerstrand, J., & Kalliokoski, A.-M. (2001). *Slagen dam: Man's vald mot kvinnor i jamstallda Sverige—en omfangsundersokning* [The captured queen: Men's violence against women in gender-equal Sweden. A prevalence survey]. Umea, Sweden: Crime Victim Compensation and Support Authority.

Maniokas, K., Starkeviciute, M., Dilba, R., Zalimiene, L., Poškute, V., Zelvys, R., et al. (2000). *Lithuanian Human Development Report 2000*. Retrieved January 1, 2004, from http://www.un.lt/HDR/2000/default.htm

Månsson, S.-A. (2001). Men's practices in prostitution: The case of Sweden. In B. Pease & K. Pringle (Eds.), *A man's world: Changing men and masculinities in a globalized world* (pp. 135-149). London: Zed Books.

Mills, A., & Tancred, P. (Eds.). (1992). *Gendering organizational analysis*. Newbury Park, CA: Sage.

Modood, T., & Werbner, P. (1997). *The politics of multiculturalism in the new Europe: Racism, identity and community*. London: Zed Books.

Mooney, J. (1993). *The hidden figure: Domestic violence in North London*. London: Centre for Criminology, Middlesex University.

Müller, U. (2000). *National report on men's practices for Germany: Workpackage 1* (Contract No. HPSE-CT-1999–0008). Bielefeld, Germany: University of Bielefeld.

Novikova, I. (2000). Soviet and post-Soviet masculinities: After men's wars in women's memories. In I. Breines, R. Connell, & I. Eide (Eds.), *Male roles, masculinities and violence: A culture of peace perspective* (pp. 117-129). Paris: Presses Universitaires de France.

Novikova, I., & Kambourov, D. (2003). *Men in the global world: Integrating post-socialist perspectives.* Helsinki: Kikimora.

Oleksy, E. (2001). *Poland national report on statistical information on men's practices workpackage 2.* Retrieved January 2, 2004, from http://www.cromenet.org/customers/crome/crome.nsf/resources/FA555552F4288EEDC2256A3B004E B7A0/$file/Poland+WP2.doc

Oushakine, S. (Ed.). (2002). *O muzhe(N)stvennosti* [On masculinity]. Moscow: Novoe Literaturnoe obozrenie.

Papic, Z. (2000, September). *Violence: Eastern Europe.* Paper presented at the first Helsinki Forum—Whose Europe?, Helsinki, Finland. Retrieved January 1, 2004, from http://www.mv.helsinki.fi/helsinkiforum/english/text/papic.html

Pease, B., & Pringle, K. (Eds.). (2001). *A man's world: Changing men and masculinities in a globalized world.* London: Zed Books.

Powell, G. (1988). *Women and men in management.* Newbury Park, CA: Sage.

Pringle, K. (1995). *Men, masculinities and social welfare.* London: UCL Press.

Pringle, K. (1998a). *Children and social welfare in Europe.* London: Open University Press.

Pringle, K. (1998b). Profeminist debates on men's practices and social welfare. *British Journal of Social Work, 8,* 623-633.

Pringle, K. (2001, June). *Some reflections on issues of racism and xenophobia in the European Union.* Paper presented at the International Seminar on Racism and Xenophobia, Uppsala Universitet, Uppsala, Sweden.

Pringle, K. (2002a, March). *Comparing perspectives on the Swedish child welfare system: Current and future challenges. Some initial reflections from a qualitative study.* Paper presented at a National Seminar on Swedish Child Welfare, Linköping Universitet, Linköping, Sweden.

Pringle, K. (2002b, September). *Risks in childhood: Processes leading to social exclusion.* Keynote address presented at the European Union Conference, Gender and Social Exclusion, Copenhagen, Denmark.

Pringle, K. (2002c, August). *Trouble in paradise? Comparing perspectives on gender and ethnicity in the Danish, Swedish and English child welfare systems.* Paper presented at the Nordic Sociological Congress "Nätverkssamhället— frihet eller fjättrar," University of Reykjavik, Reykjavik, Iceland.

Pringle, K., & Harder, M. (1999). *Through two pairs of eyes: A comparative study of Danish social policy and child welfare.* Aalborg, Denmark: Aalborg University Press.

Pringle, K., Hearn, J., Mueller, U., Oleksy, E., Chernova, J., Ferguson, H., et al. (2001). The European Research Network on Men in Europe: The social problem of men. *Journal of European Social Policy, 11*(2), 171-173.

Segal, L. (1990). *Slow motion: Changing masculinities, changing men.* New Brunswick, NJ: Rutgers University Press.

Smidova, I. (2002). *Men in the Czech Republic: A few questions and thoughts on studying (some) men.* Unpublished manuscript, Masaryk University, Brno, Czech Republic.

Smidova, I. (2003). Men in the Czech Republic: According to selected "different men." In I. Novikova & D. Kambourov (Eds.), *Men in the global world: Integrating post-socialist perspectives* (pp. 159-175). Helsinki: Kikimora.

Smidova, I. (2004). Czech Republic: Domination and silences. In J. Hearn et al. (Eds.), *Men and masculinities in Europe.* London: Whiting & Birch.

Tomlinson, J. (1999). *Globalization and culture.* Cambridge, England: Polity Press.

Watson, P. (1996). The rise of masculinism in Eastern Europe. In M. Threlfall (Ed.), *Mapping the women's movement: Feminist politics and social transformations in the North* (pp. 216-231). London: Verso.

Wenk, S. (2000). Gendered representations of the nation's past and future. In I. Blom, K. Hagemann, & C. Hall (Eds.), *Gendered nations: Nationalism and gender order in the long nineteenth century* (pp. 63-77). Oxford: Berg.

Whitehead, S. M. (2002). *Men and masculinities: Key themes and new directions.* Cambridge, England: Polity Press.

Yuval-Davis, N. (1997). *Gender and nation.* London: Sage.

PART III

STRUCTURES, INSTITUTIONS, AND PROCESSES

10

CLASS AND MASCULINITY

DAVID MORGAN

Students of gender tend only to see gender; class analysts tend only to see social classes. The research questions are often crudely put as being questions of gender or class instead of asking how gender and class interact in the lives of historically situated social groups.

—Marianne Gullestad (1992, p. 62)

Class is one of a number of social hierarchies or systems of social stratification that have represented core elements in sociological analysis. Other systems include slavery and caste and feudal systems, and these are usually seen as being distinct from class relationships in that they are associated with particular historical epochs or geographical areas. Class stratification is seen as the form most closely associated with industrial and capitalist societies, although elements of other systems may also be present. In addition, there are hierarchies that can overlap and coexist with any of these particular systems of stratification. These can include gender, age, and generation, as well as race and ethnicity; some more recent analyses would argue for the inclusion of hierarchies based on sexualities and forms of ability and disability.

All these sets of differences have some features in common. They are relational in that the various elements (working class, slave, women, black, etc.) cannot be considered apart from other, usually opposed, elements. They refer to some kind of hierarchical organization and inequalities of power. They are structured in that they, to a greater or lesser extent, exist outside individuals and persist over time. And they are, again to varying degrees, seen as significant distinctions in the societies in which they exist. Sociological analysis, until fairly recently, has tended to focus on class and class relationships, although there may be considerable variation in the ways in which these terms are understood. This is partly because of the influence of at least two of the discipline's "founding fathers," Marx and Weber, and partly because of sociology's central interest in the defining and distinctive characteristics of "modern" societies.

It should be noted at the outset that there is a particularly British or European focus in this chapter, although the chapter does not, as we shall see, exclude wider considerations. This is partly because of my own intellectual background as a British academic but also partly because many of the key debates and modes of analysis originated in Britain, although they made use of some of the key theories from other parts of Europe. Class has sometimes been seen as a particularly British obsession, and this in part relates to its historical position as the first industrial capitalist society, a point recognized by Marx and many of the early socialists. However, questions of origin are here less important in a chapter that is exploring the interrelationships between masculinities and class, and I hope that, in the course of this discussion, some general principles may be developed that may be found useful in analyzing a wide range of social and historical contexts.

Questions about the relationships between different social hierarchies developed in the last part of the 20th century, and one of the more heated sociological debates has revolved around issues of class and gender, more specifically about whether women have been marginalized in traditional class analysis. Joan Acker (1973), in an influential article, claimed that the relative invisibility of women in class analysis was a case of "intellectual sexism"; John Goldthorpe (1983) presented a vigorous defense of the traditional view. One important issue raised in the course of this debate was whether the individual or the "family" should be treated as the unit of class analysis (Crompton, 1993; Lee & Turner,1996; Morgan, 1996).

As was so often the case when gender was discussed, the focus was almost wholly on women and their marginal position within traditional class analysis. As such, the debate could be seen as part of the wider feminist critique of conventional social science and the way in which, whatever the topic, women were either marginalized or stereotyped. What was not explored in the course of the debate was the position of men within class analysis. Yet a moment's thought would seem to suggest that men and masculinity were heavily implicated in class analysis, where, in British iconography at least, the bowler hat of the upper middle class hangs between the cloth cap of the working man and the top hat of the traditional upper class. Was it simply an accident that led to men being presented as the key class actors, or were the connections between class and masculinity closer than might first have been suspected?

About the same time as the gender and class debate, there was another loosely associated debate concerning the centrality (or otherwise) of class analysis (Devine, 1997; Lee & Turner, 1996; Pakulski & Waters, 1996; Savage, 2000).

Toward the latter part of the 20th century, there appeared to be a general impression, at least within the United Kingdom, that class analysis no longer had a "promising future." This was in part a consequence of a recognition of other, at least equally important, social divisions, such as those of gender or race and ethnicity. Class analysis also appeared to be less relevant with the collapse of the Berlin Wall and the erosion of many communist societies. With a developing global perspective, many of the traditional, often eurocentric, class divisions seemed to be less able to explain social inequalities and conflicts all over the world. Class increasingly has global dimensions, and these do not necessarily link easily to categories developed in other times and under other conditions. Even within the countries where class analysis had originated, there was a growing suspicion that although inequalities clearly persisted, the old language of class was inadequate when it came to understanding these inequalities. The development of terms such as "underclass" and "social exclusion" seemed to bear witness to a diffuse sense of unease about traditional class categories. Finally, there was a growing popular perception that class divisions were old-fashioned and that the remaining remnants would be swept away in a fluid, increasingly open, postmodern society.

More recently, however, class analysis seems to have returned, albeit with some important modifications (Devine, 1997; Savage, 2000). One interesting question, however, remains. How far was this apparent erosion—or at least transformation—of class analysis linked to shifts in the gender order and the possible erosion of patriarchal structures? If, as the class and gender debates suggested, class had been fairly strongly linked to themes of men and masculinity, were there links between changes in the gender order and changes in the position of class within the analysis of social structures?

In this chapter, I shall enquire what it was about class, and class analysis, that seemed to encourage a particularly strong identification with men and masculinities. However, this identification was implied rather than explicit, latent rather than manifest. Part of the story is the way in which questions about the gendering of class were avoided or remained invisible for so long. I shall present a fairly closely integrated and relatively stable model closely linking the two and contrast this with a more fluid and open set of connections that may be said to be characteristic of late modern times. Before this, however, I shall need to consider what is meant by class and some differences in emphasis and approach within class analysis.

Definitions and Distinctions

Picture a first-year sociology class in, say, the 1980s or even later. The topic for discussion is what we mean by class. Is it income? But what about the rock star or a sports personality who may, at his peak, be earning more than the prime minister? Is it occupation? If so, on what basis do we say that one occupation ranks higher than another? Perhaps it is education. But does this not depend on income and occupation? Then, especially if the discussion is taking place in a British university, someone will raise questions of accent and how a person talks, arguing that you can place individuals as soon as they open their mouths.

Much of the discussion, you conclude, revolves around particularly British obsessions to do with relatively fine distinctions, snobbery, Oxbridge, and the old school tie. The concern seems to be more at the individual level, about how to place that individual in relation to another, rather than more abstract concerns about social structure. When British social critics refer to "outmoded" class distinctions, it is usually these distinctions, which are manifested at the interpersonal level, that are being referred to rather than wider structural differences associated with a capitalist society. But a little reflection on these debates might suggest that it is important to distinguish the particular historical experiences of any one particular society from understandings of class in a more general, structural sense.

In this chapter, I am less concerned with the differences between different theoretical traditions—notably the Marxist and the Weberian—and more concerned with some of the more common features of and issues within class analysis. Thus there will be general agreement that we are dealing with inequalities that are the products of social structure rather than the presence or absence of individual attributes, such as intelligence, physical strength, and so on. There is also a general agreement that in talking about class, we are talking about economic divisions and inequalities. A kind of more or less explicit Weberian analysis would seem to be at the heart of much empirical class analysis. This entails looking at the unequal distribution of life chances insofar as these deal with the ownership or nonownership of different forms of property and different levels of income. Weberians would argue that such a mode of analysis is more inclusive than a more strictly Marxist analysis in that Marxist class and class action remains a potentiality within Weber's categories, although not the only one.

Within class analysis, there are a range of qualifications and distinctions, some of which have a particular relevance when it comes to considering the relationships between masculinity and class:

- *Objective and subjective understandings of class.* This is the distinction between the categories that are established in class analysis and the way in which class is actually understood and experienced by individuals or, indeed, whether the term *class* has any meaning at all.
- *Class in itself and class for itself.* This well-known distinction, deriving from Marxist analysis, contrasts class as a category, a mode of distinguishing and classifying people and class as the basis for some form of collective action. This entails the development of some form of class consciousness, an awareness of some shared fate, and collective experiences, together with some understanding of the possibilities of challenging or even changing the class system.
- *Bipolar models of class and more complex hierarchical models.* This may refer to sociological accounts or social actors' own perceptions of the class structure. Bipolar models may be more or less simple descriptions (mental-manual) or imply some degree of class antagonism (bourgeoisie-proletariat) or fall somewhere in between (them-us). The more complex models see the class structure as a sort of ladder with three or more levels.
- *Class and status.* Although, strictly speaking, this takes us beyond class analysis, it is important, as several popular and social-scientific understandings of class contain elements of both. Roughly speaking, *class* in this instance refers to the unequal distribution of life chances; *status* refers to the social distribution of honor or prestige. It could be argued that the popular and widely used distinction between upper, middle, and working contains elements of both class and status.

- *Class as based on individuals and class as based on families or households.* This is a distinction with particular relevance for a gendered analysis of class (Curtis, 1986). Much class analysis takes individuals as the units and then aggregates them. However, several sociologists have argued that the family or the household should be the unit of analysis, although the matter becomes complex once one moves away from assuming that the class position of a household is determined by the class of the main (male) breadwinner (Morgan, 1996).

- One final distinction deals with the *historical location of the idea of class.* The Communist Manifesto famously begins with the words "the history of all hitherto existing society is the history of class struggles" (McLellan, 1988, p. 21). Much of its actual focus, however, is on classes under capitalism. Sociological analysis has tended, explicitly or implicitly, to limit the idea of class to capitalism and postcapitalism. Thus there is a distinction between an almost timeless notion of class divisions, popularly outlined in terms of the "haves" and the "have nots," and one that is much more historically situated and identified with modernity.

What I have presented here is a highly simplified version of some complex debates. Their relevance for the exploration of the relationships between class and masculinity will, I hope, emerge in the subsequent discussion. One final set of issues remains for clarification. In common with much current discussion, reflected elsewhere in this volume, I shall henceforth write of masculinities rather than masculinity, although I recognize that there are some difficult issues associated with this move. Within this framework, as will appear later, the idea of hegemonic masculinity is important. These ideas are discussed at greater length elsewhere in this volume.

THE MASCULINITIES OF CLASS

There is one further distinction that should be made before continuing with the analysis. We may see, as has already been suggested, men as holders of class power. Thus men will be found disproportionately located in the highest levels of political, economic, educational, and cultural organizations. In this respect, we may see men as centrally involved in class practices, as individual or collective class actors. But we may also see men involved in the central discourses about class power. Many of the key theorists of class have been men, and it is reasonable to suppose that their location in gender hierarchies is as important in shaping, if not in determining, their worldviews as their locations within a class system. Of course, in reality, this distinction becomes a little blurred, as discourses and practices are always closely related. Put another way, modes of understanding and researching class may reflect gendered perspectives just as the class practices themselves will also be gendered.

We may see these issues below the surface of the gender-class debate already mentioned. Goldthorpe's (1983) defense of the "conventional view" of class claimed that he was representing the world as it was rather than the world as we might like it to be. If that world be male dominated or patriarchal, then, to simplify considerably, that is how we should represent it. Up to a point, Goldthorpe's argument was correct in its generality, if not in its particularities. In everyday as well as in social science discourse there does seem to be something particularly masculine about the idea of class. And class practices, although much more open to variation, might seem to reflect these discourses, at least for much of what we describe as modern times. Put simply, class is gendered, and men have assumed, or have been allocated, the role of class agents.

How has this identification, albeit often submerged, between men and class come about? There are several overlapping reasons.

If we return to the key elements in the (broadly Weberian) model of class, we find strong connections between property, occupation, and masculinities. In the case of property, we find, historically, strong identifications between ownership of different kinds of property, family and family name, and inheritance and the male line. In the case of occupation, the connections are perhaps less strong, although it can be argued that most occupational titles have strong masculine connotations. Some occupational titles (e.g., policeman) are explicitly gendered, and popular speech still talks of sending for a "man" to come round and repair the central heating or the dishwasher. Other titles have strong historical and symbolic associations with prized masculine characteristics such as physical strength or group solidarity, coal mining and steel working, for example. Even less physical occupations, clerical workers for example, or bank clerks, initially were associated with "respectable" men until these occupations became feminized (Lockwood, 1958). The same is true for a whole range of professions, and many of these occupational boundaries were often fiercely defended against the incursions of women through the practices of trade unions and professional associations (Walby, 1986). We can say, therefore, that occupational titles and occupational boundaries were policed by the practices of men and that, insofar as occupation became a key indicator of social class, the identification of masculinities and class can be seen as having deep historical roots. The same is also true in terms of property, the other basis of class distinctions, where the links between property, class, and masculinity were often given legal underpinnings. This is not to say that women did not have occupations or property but that male property and male occupations became the more dominant.

Another set of distinctions reinforced the masculine character of class: those between the public and the private. Conventionally, the terrain of class and class struggle is located in the public sphere, the sphere of employment, where the deployment of wealth and property and politics is easily seen. The public sphere was also the sphere dominated by men as they engaged in employment or class and political action. Women might be seen as backstage or "behind-the-scenes workers" in class struggles, their own class position reflecting that of their husbands (Porter, 1983). In some cases, they provided very obvious and significant support, but this was usually defined as "support," secondary to the main action. Only rarely, in the public imagination, did women appear as class actors in their own right.

Drawing together the two last points, we have the development of the idea of "the breadwinner" and "the family wage." Conventionally, or so it emerged from the early 19th century, the head of the household was a man, and he constituted the main or sole provider for his wife and children. It was on this basis that claims were made in terms of "the family wage." In practice, the reality was much more complicated, but the idea of the man as "provider" remains remarkably persistent in a wide range of

modern cultures, right up to the present day (e.g., for Warin, Solomon, Lewis, & Langford, 1999; also, Hobson, 2002). It can be argued, in fact, that the idea of the provider is a major element in the construction of masculine identity; it is a moral as well as an economic category. Hence the devastating personal effects of unemployment that have been documented by many researchers over many years.

In a somewhat more abstract vein, we may consider the contribution of the ideological construction, which sees men, in contrast to women, as effective actors. This is partly because the public sphere, as outlined earlier, is not simply different from the private sphere but is also seen as being, in many ways, more significant than the private sphere. The elevation of the economy and the spheres of war and politics are accompanied by the downgrading of the domestic. Thus public statues celebrate warriors and statesmen, and the large-scale heroic canvas is given greater significance than the miniature or the still life. On the one side there is risk and danger, the possibilities for heroic achievement or spectacular downfalls; on the other side there is the routine and the everyday (see Morgan, 2003). The very word "actor" (which has been taken over into sociological analysis) still has some masculine connotations. Wherever the "action" is, it is not in the home. *Action* and *actor* merge with *active*, which in its turn contrasts with *passive*.

Finally we need to emphasize the distinction between production and reproduction, which some writers see to as a key to understanding the masculinization of class. O'Brien (1981), in particular, recognized the contribution to class analysis made by Marx and Engels, but she also demonstrated how the Marxist tradition tended to focus on labor and production and played down reproduction. Indeed, it could be argued that, within Marxism, reproduction tended to be seen in more metaphorical terms (stressing the reproduction of class relationships) rather than as something to do with gendered relationships (O'Brien, 1981).

It can also be argued that class contributed to both a unified sense of masculinity and more diffused, perhaps more conflictual, models of masculinities. On the one hand, we have the identification of men, all men, with the public sphere, the sphere of production, which contained those areas in society where the action was. Many men, whatever the amount or source of their income, could identify with the provider role and the sense of moral responsibility that this implied. But at the same time, class experiences and practices pointed to different ways of being men, different ways of being constituted as effective social actors. These differences (which will be explored in more detail later) could be polarized between "them" and "us" or become embodied in a range of finer distinctions, such as those between "mental" and "manual," "skilled" and "unskilled," or even workers in different departments or offices. Other masculine themes that might be woven into class analysis are notions of collective solidarity (traditionally associated with the working class) and individual achievement and risk taking, associated with the classic bourgeoisie, or the middle classes. Yet again, we can contrast a sense of masculinity that derives from having authority or control over others and the solidarities of the shop floor or the coal face.

Representations of class struggle and class differences traditionally drew from masculine imagery. Although the rhetoric might refer to "working people," the representations of the working class frequently included masculine symbols (such as the hammer or clenched fists) and emphasized collective solidarity. At the very least, such representations of solidarity dissolved gender differences in a large class identity and frequently went further than this to convey collective, embodied masculinity. The language was the language of struggle, of class war and conflict. Representations of the opposition also deployed masculine, if negatively valued, images of wealth and luxury.

Media representations of industrial disputes in the latter part of the 20th century frequently seemed to play on these understandings. On the one hand, we have the raised arms of the mass meeting; on the other, we have men in suits, more individualized, leaving or entering cars or making public statements in an abstract language of rationality (Philo, 1995). Here, in contrast to the working class images, workers were presented as sheep who were easily led by politically motivated leaders or group pressure. Management, on the other hand, was presented as dealing with some of the key issues in the national economy. However valued, both sets of representations drew on different strands in the construction of masculinities, and it could be said that the class struggle was represented in terms of these contrasting versions.

Within the writings on men and masculinities, class and gender converge in the concept of "hegemonic masculinity" (Connell, 1995). The main argument here is that the recognition of a diversity of masculinities should not obscure the fact that in a particular social formation, certain masculinities are more dominant, more valued, or more persuasive than others. In part, these refer to characteristics that have little directly to do with class, such as heterosexuality or responsibility. But in part, they also have strong connections with class. A good example of this is the idea of rationality. However defined (and this is clearly a complex, multistranded concept), rationality is associated with the practices of men and, increasingly, with the public life and with those most visibly or actively involved in public life. It is associated with the abstract logic of the market, the dominant principles of bureaucratic organization, and the general conduct of private life. The idea of rationality is an ideological theme that brings together both class and gender, forming a core feature of modern hegemonic masculinity.

THE CLASS OF MASCULINITY

One of the earliest books in the recent flood of texts on men and masculinities specifically placed class and class differences at the center of its analysis (Tolson, 1977). To a large extent, Tolson takes it for granted that class provides a major framework within which masculine experiences and contradictions may be explored. Thus he begins a section titled "Working-class masculinity" with these words: "The paradox of masculinity at work is most apparent within the experience of manual labor" (p. 58).

A later section within the same chapter focuses on the distinctive features of middle class masculinity. As already noted, we can see two contrasting ways of "doing" masculinity, and these are easily recognized within certain constructions of social class. The one is collective, physical and embodied, and oppositional. The other is individualistic, rational, and relatively disembodied. These can be broadly described as working class and middle class masculinities, respectively. Of course, more detailed probing will reveal complexities and ambiguities. There are, for example, the middle class (and often embodied) solidarities of clubs, sports teams, public schools, and so on. And there are working class individualities represented in popular social types such as "Jack the lad," "the cheeky chappie," and "the hard man." It is, indeed, difficult to come to terms with some of the contradictions within constructions of masculinity without taking on board some sense of class distinction. Masculinities are both solidaristic and individualistic, both embodied and disembodied. An understanding of class and of historically constructed class differences helps us to explore some of the tensions and ambiguities of masculinity.

Up to now, we have tended to focus on a bipolar, largely oppositional model of class, and it may be argued that this focus on struggle or opposition conforms to one influential model of masculinity. However, there are other models of class and class differences that point to three or more classes. Clearly, the very notion of the "middle" class implies at least three classes, although much sociological analysis that uses class classifications tends to leave out the upper class, largely because the numbers involved are assumed to be too small to influence analysis of, say, health or voting patterns. However, more structural analysis should include the upper class (or power elite or any alternative term), as it is clearly highly influential, if numerically small. Moreover, such a class is both constructed by and has a major role in constructing dominant or hegemonic notions of masculinity to do with control, the exercise of power, rationality, and so on. C. Wright Mills's (1959) *The Power Elite*, for example, can be read as a study of masculinities.

Once we move beyond the bipolar model, a range of possibilities become open to us. There is, first, the possibility of three or more classes, usually based on some classification of occupations. Occupations are implicated, in different ways, in the classifications developed by the British Registrar General, Goldthorpe, and Erik Olin Wright (see, e.g., Marshall, Rose, Newby, & Vogler, 1989, pp. 13-62). The trouble with many of these classifications is that they do not necessarily map easily into class experiences; the fact that certain occupations may be grouped together for the purposes of analysis does not necessarily mean that the individuals so grouped will understand their commonalities in class terms. Class, once we move from bipolar

models, comes to be seen as something that is played out in different sites that do not necessarily have much to do with each other. Divisions at the workplace, in terms of skills, pay, privileges, and so on, do not necessarily carry over into the areas where these individuals live their family lives or enjoy their leisure activities. Class as experience needs to be filtered through particular agencies, such as housing, residential area, educational experience, and so on. Further, although masculinities may be shaped by or play a part in shaping these differences, this is by no means inevitable. Some divisions, indeed, such as the divisions between the "rough" and the "respectable" working class or the fine gradations recorded by Robert Roberts (1971) in his account of *The Classic Slum* may be as much maintained by the work of women as by the occupational status of men.

Further, one of the key features of a class system, as opposed to feudalism or a caste system, is its relative openness and the degree of mobility, both social and geographical, that is allowed. Recognizing the possibilities of social and geographical mobility does open up the possibility for more complex masculinities and their relationship to class. Here we have the "failed" masculinity of the downwardly mobile individual whose failure in class terms may be read as an indication of a weakness of character, which might also be gendered (lack of ambition, alcoholism, etc.). Here we have the defensive and uneasy masculinity of the recent arrival into middle class occupations, localities, or lifestyles. This may contrast with the apparently more stable masculinities of those who have managed the easier passage from the middle class family, through school and university, into a middle class occupation and a lifestyle enhanced by an appropriate marriage and the "right" location. This may also contrast with the, probably dwindling, traditional working class communities that provide another basis for the reaffirmation of masculinities through shared experiences and lifestyles. Geographical mobility (with or without social mobility) may also play its part in blurring or sharpening masculine identities. Community studies have explored differences between the "established" and the "outsiders" that, to some extent, cut across class divisions (Elias & Scotson, 1994).

Watson developed the useful term "spiralist" to describe those who are both geographically and socially mobile (Watson, 1964). Such mobilities may now, increasingly, take on a global dimension. Whether such complexities contribute to an overall eroding of hegemonic masculinity or whether they open up the possibilities for a much wider range of masculine practices is a matter for further investigation.

It might also be argued that the experience and practice of mobility itself is related to the construction of masculinity in opposition to femininity and the experiences of women. Thompson (1997), using more qualitative oral historical material, argues (in the British context) that the generation of men born in the 1930s and 1940s experienced some modest improvements in the course of their life. This was not the case with the women in the sample. For women, marriage often has a depressing effect on social status. Thompson argues for the importance of considering the interplays between family, occupation, and gender in exploring the processes of social mobility and the numerous, often unrecognized or unacknowledged ways in which women assist in men's experiences of upward mobility.

We may reach an interim conclusion at this point. We have seen a two-way interaction between class and gender, with particular reference to masculinities. Masculinity remains a relatively underexplored aspect in the examination of class practices. Yet the position that class analysis plays, or at least has played, in sociological analysis as a whole and the continuing importance of class as a social division may in part derive from this close but largely unrecognized masculine character of class. Conversely, one of the reasons why it has been found necessary to pluralize "masculinities" is that ways of doing masculinity are always mediated through other social divisions, of which class remains one of the most important. The connection between class and masculinity is an intimate one. When I see a middle class man, I do not see someone who is middle class and then someone who is a man, or vice versa. I see both at the same time. The major social divisions—class, gender, ethnicity, age, and so on—may be likened to primary colors, which are more often seen in their many combinations than individually.

Up to now I have suggested a relatively close association between class and masculinity, although the last few paragraphs have pointed to some possible complexities. In very broad

terms, a relatively tight association between class and masculinity may be characteristic of modern or capitalist societies (for a historical analysis, see Davidoff & Hall, 1987). Some of the relevant features of these societies are relatively clear distinctions between home and work, clear and relatively stable occupational titles, the dominance of a male breadwinner model, and the continuing importance of heavy and manufacturing industry. With a return to more blurred distinctions between home and work, the decline of clear occupational titles and jobs or careers for life, the decline of the male breadwinner model, and the growth of a service economy, we may also have a weakening of the relationship between masculinity and class. This will be explored in the next section.

Masculinity and Class in Late Modernity

The last three decades has seen a subtle reworking of the relationship between class, masculinity and the individual.

Mike Savage (2000, p. xi)

Probably one of the most significant influences on the changing relationship between class and masculinity has been the decline of the male breadwinner model in practice and, although perhaps to a lesser extent, in ideology. In the past, it might be argued, men were more strongly "classed" than women because they had closer associations to the key practices and institutions that maintained class. For many men, of course, this might be an illusion; nevertheless it might be possible for the more weakly "classed" men (perhaps because of unemployment, disability, or simply having a wife who was the main breadwinner) to continue to derive some class identity from their more fortunate brothers. Hence there was some partial justification for the traditional practice of locating a household in terms of the class of its head and for women to be allocated class positions on the basis of their husbands' or fathers' class positions. With a weakening of men's attachment to the labor market and a strengthening of women's attachment, some revision was clearly necessary.

As has already been noted, two analytical strategies emerged in response to the growing involvement of married women in the labor market and the related decline in relevance (but not always in ideological importance) of the male breadwinner model. The first was to state clearly that the unit of class was the individual rather than the household. Various consequences followed. Both men and women could be seen as units within the class structure, although men tended to occupy higher class positions than women. It is also likely that the issues around which everyday class struggles were fought became more various. Notions of "the family wage" became less important and issues to do with working conditions, hours of work, parental leave, and so on came more and more to the fore. It would not be true to say that class itself became feminized, but it could certainly be argued that it became less masculine.

The other strategy was to take seriously the idea of the household as a unit and to explore the consequences of this. However, there were also shifts in the idea of the household as a unit so that new models no longer treated the household as an undifferentiated "black box" and came to take account of differences within the household. For example, an interest in "cross-class marriages" (in which husbands and wives were, in terms of occupation, of different classes) developed, and the consequences of these differences were explored in a variety of ways (McRae, 1986). Particular attention was paid, as might be expected, to those households wherein the wife was of a higher social class than her husband. One might argue that this might further lead to the weakening of the association between class and masculinity or serve to remind us that, in interactional terms, the impact of class and the elaboration of class-based identities might vary according to the different sites within which an individual was involved. Thus a working class man married to a middle class women might have a different sense of class at home than at work, where some of the more traditional solidarities might still be relevant.

Such conclusions, however, may be premature. For one thing, the class differences within many cross-class households were relatively small and were based on occupational criteria that might not necessarily be of any relevance, certainly outside the workplace. In short, the objective measures of class might not necessarily translate into more subjective processes of class experiences and identities. However, the presence of cross-class households constituted one piece of a larger jigsaw that, when completed, would show a much more complicated relationship between class and gender.

One relatively underexplored theme might be mentioned. Classically, class (based on economic criteria) was distinguished from status, where issues of prestige and esteem were central. However, as both were aspects of social stratification, it was frequently the case that the distinctions became blurred. Status considerations could reinforce class distinctions (as in cases where we get a merging of economic and cultural capital) or could cut across them and, presumably, weaken their political effectiveness. In the male breadwinner model, it could almost be said that class and status frequently overlapped and, further, that the distinction between them was gendered. Thus men tended to be to the fore in matters of class and class struggle, and women were involved in maintaining and reproducing everyday status distinctions through their domestic labor, their parenting, their organization of consumption, and their general moral demeanor within the local community. Partly as a result of the changes already discussed, men come to be more involved in status work and women in class work, and the distinction between the two modes of stratification, always difficult to maintain in practice, becomes even less easy to maintain.

It is likely, in fact, that the tensions between class and status have always been present and that a gendered understanding of stratification, especially one that takes masculinities seriously, might highlight some of these. Thus it can be argued that different ways of doing masculinity or of "being a man" can themselves constitute status divisions. This, indeed, is one of the consequences of thinking about hegemonic masculinities. One complex set of examples may be derived from considering issues of sexualities. Studies of young men, in particular, have shown how a notion of aggressive heterosexuality may be the basis of positive and negative status (Mac an Ghaill, 1994). However, sexual status hierarchies might not necessarily correspond to conventional notions of heterosexuality or homosexuality, as Lancaster's (2002) study of Nicaraguan men indicates that what is often more important is a distinction between taking the active or passive role rather than the gender of the sexual partner. Clearly, such distinctions take place within conventional class divisions, although they do not necessarily undermine them.

What of the alleged decline in the centrality of class and its possible impact on hegemonic masculinity or patriarchy? Speaking very generally, it is possible to talk about a late-modern development whereby class and class divisions became less central and more complex. Alternatively, we may talk of a late-modern development in which class has become more simplified. In terms of the first, the lines of argument have already been indicated. This includes a decline in the overall salience of class (especially as related to occupation); a growing emphasis on other social divisions; a fragmentation of class divisions, identities, and the sites where class work is performed; and a blurring of the distinction between class and status. This last reflects a context within which consumption and leisure assume greater importance. We may also note organizational changes; for example, the development of "flatter" hierarchical structures, which might be seen as having the consequence of a reduction of class and status divisions at the place of work. These factors, in combination, might contribute to a weakening of patriarchal structures in general but will certainly undermine the masculinity of class. However, these finer, more complex class and status divisions might still be important in exploring the varieties of masculinities present in a late modern society.

A more simplified model, however, emerges if we take the idea of "life chances" seriously. Here we look at different combinations of economic and cultural capital and assess the consequences of these for the life chances of individuals. Theoretically, a large number of combinations may be possible, but in practice, we may talk of three major divisions. At the highest level, we have those with considerable amounts of cultural and economic capital and who are at the highest level of private organizations and state bureaucracies. This is clearly a minority, but also, increasingly, a global minority. For the most part, we are talking about men so that there are clear interactions between masculinities and class and status situations. One only has to look at the photographs of international top-level gatherings to become aware that we are dealing with the practices of men and the reproduction of hegemonic masculinities.

At the lowest level, we have those with relatively little economic and cultural capital (certainly little economic capital!) and with highly uncertain life chances. Terms such as *underclass* or *the socially excluded* have been developed to capture this group, although both terms have their problems. Thus Devine (1997, pp. 220-221) concludes, along with numerous other commentators, that the idea of an "underclass" is flawed, although it is possible to recognize the growth of a sizable minority (sometimes estimated as around 20%) of people in poverty in both the United States and the United Kingdom. This is, clearly, not an exclusively masculine group, and, indeed, it is often the case that the burdens rest more heavily on women, whether as single parents or as workers in low-paid, uncertain jobs. The dominant characteristics of this "class" become magnified when seen through a global lens.

It is doubtful whether there is a single masculinity that can be identified with the socially excluded, although certain public representations are highly gendered. Thus media representations stress themes of masculine violence, either collective (as in rioting) or more individualistic. Or there are themes that concern absent fathers and the lack of a stable adult male role model. Dominant themes are those to do with either a failed masculinity, the lack of opportunity to live up to what is expected in terms of being a provider, or stigmatized forms of masculinity. Thus Savage (2000) writes, "working-class work has been constructed as 'servile' work, which no longer bestows mastery or autonomy on its incumbent" (p. 153). However, even attempts to live up to hegemonic models of masculinity (as in the case of asylum seekers who might otherwise be characterized as heroic individuals) also become stigmatized.

Between these two extremes, there is the more fluid class situation characterized by different mixes of economic and cultural capital and different life chances. The middle group (which is not the same as some theoretical notion of "the middle class") may, for example, be ranged in terms of relative stability, and certainty of life chances, from the very stable or predictable at the top to the highly uncertain at the bottom. It is here that the links between masculinities and class are becoming more various or more fluid. Although there are considerable differences within this broad middle category, whether these differences coalesce into class differences is a little more difficult to determine. Clearly, there are some occupations that are still shaped around strong constructions of masculinity; on both sides of the Atlantic, firefighters constitute one such occupational identity (Baigent, 2001). But whether members of such occupations construct themselves in terms of wider class identities remains open to question. The same might also be said of some newer occupational identities, such as "bouncers" or doormen, associated with developing leisure industries.

Up to now, apart from a few passing references, the analysis has been based largely in material and theories developed in the United Kingdom and, to a lesser extent, the United States. In terms of traditional class analysis, there might be some justification for this, as has already been argued. However, there are good reasons to doubt whether such an analysis can be straightforwardly transplanted to countries outside Europe and Anglophone nations. For example, Scott (1996) argues for a variety of capitalist classes and suggests that the variations such as the "Latin" model might be shaped by familistic and kinship ties to a greater degree than late-modern models in the West. Such models of the capitalist class also deploy different constructions of masculinity. Bertaux (1997) argues that most studies of social mobility (the kinds that have proliferated in Britain and the United States) tend to assume a relatively stable political order, within which such class movements take place. However, notions of mobility become much more problematic for those countries (such as the formerly communist nations of Eastern Europe) that experienced revolutionary upheavals that challenged notions of privilege and inequalities. The gendered implications of these major transformations have not been explored to any large extent.

A further challenge emerges when we abandon the implicit assumption that the nation-state is our unit of analysis and, instead, begin to explore flows and movements on a global scale (Urry, 2000). It remains an open question as to whether the class models, developed from the core writings of Marx and Weber and reflecting very particular historical events, can simply be translated to this more global framework. Similarly, it is doubtful whether a simple upgrading of the class struggle from the national to the global arena can be anything more than a first approximation of what is an increasingly complex situation. Thus Waters (1995), in a useful survey of globalization theories, argues against the strong model for the development of transnational classes. There are, however, an increasing variety of transnational class experiences (which also have relevance for the constructions of masculinities). A more fruitful line of analysis would seem to be to explore the different interpenetrations of the global and the local and the ways in which these shape and are shaped by classed and gendered experiences. For example, Waters notes how processes of consumption and production mingle in global cities: "Under globalization, migration has brought the third world back to the global cities where its exploitation becomes ever more apparent" (p. 93). Such meetings do not necessarily undermine the close associations between masculinities and other social divisions; indeed, they may well intensify them.

CONCLUSION

This chapter has argued that there has been a relatively underexplored theme in the analysis of social class; namely, its association with the construction of masculinity. Very broadly, it could be argued that in the early stages of industrial capitalism and up until the late 20th century, there was a relatively strong association between class and class practices and masculinities. As we move close to our own times, these connections have, in some cases, perhaps become more apparent, although in other cases, the links have become more obscure. The growing uncertainty in class analysis perhaps reflects and has an impact on what is sometimes, rather too loosely, called the crisis of masculinity.

This is not the place to elaborate on the problematic idea of that "crisis," which is discussed elsewhere in this volume. However, very simply, we may identify a model of stable masculinity against which any sense of crisis might be measured. Such a model would include a relatively high degree of congruence between public discourses about masculinity and the public and private practices of masculinity. For individual men, there would be a sense of ontological security—a relatively stable sense of "being in the world." Even where a man may feel that he has fallen short of his responsibilities as a man (reflected, perhaps, in notions of dishonor or unmanliness), the standard by which he is seen to have fallen short remains relatively clear.

Such an ideal, typical model of masculinity could clearly accommodate and interact with hierarchies based in social class. Class divisions may have underlined the fact that there were different ways of "doing" masculinity (collective versus individual, hands versus brains, and so on), and these different modes of masculinity were reinforced by clear distinctions at work and between communities. To some extent, however, these differences might be seen as variations on a theme; the "respectable" breadwinning working man and the sober, rational member of the bourgeoisie might have a lot in common in terms of a sense of what it is to be a man, despite the large differences and oppositions in class terms. Put another way, class might be seen as a problem in terms of Marxist contradictions or more liberal notions of citizenship and social justice, but masculinity was not seen in this light. Hence class analysis remained ungendered for a long period of time, and it has been only in relatively recent times that any discussions of gender and class have come to focus on the practices of men rather than on those of women.

It is part of the argument of this chapter that the undermining of a relatively stable sense of masculinity (at least in its more public discourses) was associated with growing uncertainty about the nature and significance of class. Thus, the growing "presence" of women in all areas of social, political, and economic life presented a problem for conventional class analysis, just as it presented a problem for established or hegemonic masculinities. Both class and gender became challenged by the recognitions of other social divisions, such as race and ethnicity, age, sexualities, disabilities, and abilities. A great sense of fluidity in social life, brought about by flexibilities in working practices and the various complex strands of postmodernity and globalization, provided yet further challenges to both class and gender. More detailed historical and social analysis will be required to unravel the connections between class and masculinities, but it is hoped that this chapter makes clear that such a program would be worthwhile.

REFERENCES

Acker, J. (1973). Women and social stratification: A case of intellectual sexism. *American Journal of Sociology, 78*(4), 936-945.

Baigent, D. (2001). *One more last working class hero: A cultural audit of the UK fire service.* Cambridge, England: Fire Service Research and Training Unit, Anglia Polytechnic University.

Bertaux, D. (1997). Transmission in extreme situations: Russian females expropriated by the October Revolution. In D. Bertaux & P. Thompson (Eds.), *Pathways to social class: A qualitative approach to social mobility* (pp. 230-258). Oxford, England: Clarendon Press.

Connell, R. W. (1995). *Masculinities.* Berkeley: University of California Press.

Crompton, R. (1993). *Class and stratification.* Cambridge, England: Polity Press.

Curtis, R. E. (1986). Household and family in theory on inequality. *American Sociological Review, 51*, 168-183.

Davidoff, L., & Hall, C. (1987). *Family fortunes.* London: Hutchinson.

Devine, F. (1997). *Social class in America and Britain.* Edinburgh, Scotland: Edinburgh University Press.

Elias, N., & Scotson, J. L. (1994). *The established and the outsiders* (2nd ed.). London: Sage.

Goldthorpe, J. H. (1983). Women in class analysis: In defence of the conventional view. *Sociology, 17*, 466-488.

Gullestad, M. (1992). *The art of social relations: Essays on culture, social action and everyday life in modern Norway.* Oslo, Norway: Scandinavian University Press.

Hobson, B. (Ed.). (2002). *Making men into fathers: Men, masculinities and the social politics of fatherhood.* Cambridge, England: Cambridge University Press.

Lancaster, R. (2002). Subject honor, object shame. In R. Adams & D. Savran (Eds.), *The masculinity studies reader* (pp. 41-68). Oxford, England: Blackwell.

Lee, D. J., & Turner, B. S. (Eds.). (1996). *Conflicts about class: Debating inequality in late industrialism.* Harlow, England: Longman.

Lockwood, D. (1958). *The black-coated worker.* London: Allen & Unwin.

Mac an Ghaill, M. (1994). *The making of men: Masculinities, sexualities and schooling.* Buckingham, England: Open University Press.

McRae, S. (1986). *Cross-class families: A study of wives' occupational superiority.* Oxford, England: Clarendon Press.

Marshall, G., Rose, D., Newby, H., & Vogler, C. (1989). *Social class in modern Britain.* London: Unwin Hyman.

McLellan, D. (Ed.). (1988). *Marxism: Essential writings.* Oxford, England: Oxford University Press.

Mills, C. W. (1959). *The power elite.* New York: Galaxy Books.

Morgan, D. H. J. (1996). *Family connections: An introduction to family studies.* Cambridge, England: Polity Press.

Morgan, D. H. J. (2003). Everyday life and family practices. In E. B. Silva & T. Bennett (Eds.), *Contemporary culture and everyday life.* Durham, NC: Sociologypress.

O'Brien, M. (1981). *The politics of reproduction.* London: Routledge & Kegan Paul.

Pakulski, J., & Waters, M. (1996). *The death of class.* London: Sage.

Philo, G. (Ed.). (1995). *Glasgow Media Group reader* (Vol. 2). London: Routledge.

Porter, M. (1983). *Home and work and class consciousness.* Manchester, England: Manchester University Press.

Roberts, R. (1971). *The classic slum.* Manchester, England: Manchester University Press.

Savage, M. (2000). *Class analysis and social transformation.* Buckingham, England: Open University Press.

Scott, J. (1996). Patterns of capitalist development. In D. J. Lee & B. S. Turner (Eds.), *Conflicts about class: Debating inequality in late industrialism* (pp. 159-170). Harlow, England: Longman.

Thompson, P. (1997). Women, men and trans-generational family influence in social mobility. In D. Bertaux & P. Thompson (Eds.), *Pathways to social class: A qualitative approach to social mobility* (pp. 32-61). Oxford, England: Clarendon Press.

Tolson, A. (1977). *The limits of masculinity.* London: Tavistock.

Urry, J. (2000). *Sociology beyond societies: Mobilities for the twenty-first century.* London: Routledge.

Walby, S. (1986). *Patriarchy at work.* Cambridge, England: Polity Press.

Warin, J., Solomon, Y., Lewis, C., & Langford, W. (1999). *Fathers, work and family life.* London: Joseph Rowntree Foundation/Family Policy Studies Centre.

Waters, M. (1995). *Globalization.* London: Routledge.

Watson, W. (1964). Social mobility and social class in industrial communities. In M. Gluckman (Ed.), *Closed systems and open minds: The limits of naivety in social anthropology* (pp. 129-157). Edinburgh, Scotland: Oliver & Boyd.

11

MALE SEXUALITIES

KEN PLUMMER

I want to fuck. I need to fuck. I've always needed and wanted to fuck. From my teenage years I've always longed after fucking.

—A male friend speaking to social psychologist Wendy Hollway (1996)

Men have an overwhelming desire to relieve themselves upon a woman's body.

—Roger Scruton (1986)

I just like screwing. I can remember going back when I was six, seven, eight, nine, ten, we had a pub in [country town]. Saturday, Sunday morning, I'd lay in bed and flip myself ten or twelve times, and get the thrill of not being able to ejaculate. I've always been highly sexed.

—Barney, a gay man, speaking to Gary Dowsett (1996)

For a man, sex instinctively is a testosterone drive towards the ultimate release of climax. When he becomes aroused, he automatically seeks release. His fulfillment in sex is mainly associated with the release of tension leading to and including the orgasm.

—John Gray (1998, May 8)

I have started this chapter with these quite provocative quotes because they capture the very common and very simple story that is most frequently told of male sexuality. It is powerful, natural, driven; it is uncontrollable; it is penis centered; it seeks to achieve orgasm whenever it can. The truth of this is often not very nice. After all, as we have seen depicted and been told many times, it is overwhelmingly men who rape, who buy pornography, who develop sexual fetishes, who engage in sexual violence of all kinds, and who become the serial killers. It is men who are driven to seek sex in all its diversities. They are the assertors, the insertors, and the predators. Of course, some women—perhaps a growing number—do these

Author's note: I would like to acknowledge here the thoughtful and helpful comments of Jeff Hearn and Bob Connell on an earlier draft.

things. But overall, sex is seen to have a much more *driven* quality for men. They are pressured to have sex as some intense inner need and, in turn, they may well pressure others into it.[1]

Thus, men are much more likely than women to become *sexual consumers:* They will pay for sex in all its varieties—prostitution, pornography, striptease, sex tourism, massage, lap dancing, telephone sex, fetish sales. They are much more likely to feel that they can assert themselves to *take* sex when they want it, not just in obvious rape situations, but more routinely, with their wives (wife rape), girlfriends (date rape), children (son or daughter rape), and other men (homosexual rape). They are much more likely than women to feel they have a *specific turn-on*—a little out of the ordinary—which must be met. Where are all the women who "must" steal male underwear, who must expose their genitals to men passing by in the street, who must make obscene phone calls to unknown men? "Perversion," says Robert Stoller (a leading psychiatrist of sexual diversity), "is far more common in men than in women; women practice almost none of the official diagnoses" (Stoller, 1976, p. 34). Men are much more likely than women to be driven to break the sex laws and become sex offenders; male sex offenders overwhelmingly outnumber female sex offenders in all areas except one—prostitution—and although women may commit crimes of passion, they are not the same as the so-called lust murders of men (Caputi, 1988). Most recently, with the creation of the new so-called diseases of "sexual addiction" and "sexual compulsion," it is again overwhelmingly men who identify with this category and seek help through compulsive anonymous groups. Patrick Carnes, the guru of sexual addiction theory, has described the seemingly extraordinary lengths to which some men will go to get their sex (Carnes, 1984). Many become "sex addicts." Again, only a minority of men may be involved in all of these, but it seems that many, many fewer women are.

HEGEMONIC SEXUALITY: THE PENIS-CENTERED MODEL OF SEX

At the center of this image of male sexuality, both physically and symbolically, lies the penis. As feminists so clearly know, ours is a phallocentric culture. Not only is the penis the source of the male's erotic pleasures—a feature that even young boys can learn, and one that can make masturbation such a prominent feature of male sexuality—but it is also an enormously *potent* symbol. Engorged and erect, it is a sign of male power, assertion, and achievement, a gun to conquer the world. But flaccid, it is also a sign. It has become "weak, soft (or semi-soft), less active; it has no stamina, no control. It cannot perform 'like a man'" (Potts, 2002, p. 142). At its worst, it is a sign of impotence, and, as Paul Hoch (1979) once remarked, "absolutely the worst thing a man can be is impotent" (p. 65). In the microcosm of an erotic encounter, a man seems always to have to worry over the performance of his penis, and this—combined with the pleasure goal—gives a significance to the penis that is hard to ignore (Hoch, 1979).[2]

All this connects to another version of male sexuality that is a seemingly rather sadder story—the flip side of the coin, but a perhaps more tragic vision. Male sexualities are also signs of weakness and vulnerability. Many accounts of male sexualities start from a sense of man's insecurity and fear. Most commonly, the issue of the penis is raised. The penis in itself is a rather poor appendage of the male body. It is "fragile, squashy, delicate . . . even when erect the penis is spongy, seldom straight, and rounded at the tip, while the testicles are imperfect spheres, always vulnerable, never still" (Dyer, 1985, p. 30). The phallus (the erect penis), however, is a different story. As Richard Dyer (1982) once said, "The fact is the penis isn't a patch on the phallus" (p. 71). The point is that although the penis communicates messages of sexualities, it is immensely symbolic as well as physical. Thus the need to conceal an erection at certain times or to have and maintain an erection at others is crucial. The penis can betray the man, and it has to become socialized and able to perform in the right ways at the right moments (Tieffer, 1995). As Reynaud (1981) has argued, "Man's misfortune is that his penis, the symbol of power, is in fact one of the most fragile and vulnerable organs of his body" (p. 36).

Men's sexuality so frequently seems to come to focus on the penis (physical) and the phallus (symbolic): Both can bring problems. Thus there are worries of size when it is flaccid, worries of it not getting erect quickly enough, worries of it being too erect too often, worries of it not staying erect long enough, and severe worries of it not getting erect at all. Then there are problems of ejaculation—of coming too soon, too late, or not at all. Often, all of this is significant because men let it—or make it—define their masculinity. Sexuality, it has been argued, is "the mainstay of male identity" (Person, 1980, p. 605). As the psychoanalytic theorist Ethel Person (1980) once famously argued, "There is a wealth of evidence to suggest that in this culture, genital sexual activity is a prominent feature in the maintenance of masculine gender, while it is a variable feature in feminine gender. . . . In men, gender appears to lean on sexuality" (p. 619).

All this may seem obvious to many students of male sexualities. True, this is the common-sense story, and it is mirrored a thousand times by more scientific stories. Indeed, while writing this chapter, I was persistently drawn to it. Yet, obvious as it may seem to many, I kept thinking that sexuality is not really like this at all for *all* men at *all* times. To argue so would be to fall into the trap of essentialism and, worse, to see male sexuality as overdetermined. If male sexuality were really just like this, we surely would find even more problems concerning it than we do. We can, indeed, find enough problems around it to make some feminists argue that this is precisely their point: Sexuality is male, and it is trouble.

In the face of a wave of research and writing that I have come to call the "new theories of sexualities,"[3] we can now see that men change (just like women) across time, space, and contexts. Sexualities are never simple biological facts, however much some people protest that they are. Indeed, for some commentators, "Sexuality is so diverse, confusing and culturally informed that perhaps it is beyond any real understanding" (Whitehead, 2002, p. 162).

In this view, *human sexualities are complex historical actions, relations, and practices performed through metaphors and languages, shaped by social divisions, lodged in political processes, and always open to change.* Recent work shows very definitely that sexualities are patterned by cultures; they are shaped by class, gender, and age; they are negotiated through institutions of family, religion, education, and economy; they shift across the life space and cycle; and they are enmeshed in all manner of power relations. More generally, as Lynne Segal (1997b) comments,

Male sexuality is most certainly not any single shared experience for men. It is not any single or simple thing at all—but the site of any number of emotions of weakness and strength, pleasure and pain, anxiety, conflict, tension and struggle, none of them mapped out in such a way as to make the obliteration of the agency of women in heterosexual engagements inevitable. Male sexuality cannot be reduced to the most popular meanings of sex acts, let alone to sex acts themselves. It becomes intelligible only if placed within actual histories of men's intimate relationships with others—or the lack of them. (p. 215)

I think Lynne Segal is correct, but you would not really know this from the spate of studies that support the view I have outlined. Indeed, what we may have here is a case of *hegemonic male sexuality,*[4] buttressed by a series of scientific and cultural props pointing in the same direction and telling us what men are really like. Hegemony expresses the privileged positions of dominant groups and establishes "the fund of self evident descriptions of social reality that normally go without saying" (Fraser, 1992, p. 179). Hegemonic male sexuality works to essentialize the male sexualities of some men into the sexualities of all, as well as reinforcing assumptions about a bipolar feminine essential sexuality.

In this chapter, I look a little at these hegemonic stories; there is no doubt that they are very common, but they are not definitive. I will look at the persistent reinforcement of this hegemonic model in nearly all directions, and then turn to changes that suggest that the sexualities of men may well not be as unified or as simple as commonly outlined. Focusing on hegemony is important, but it fails to take into account the fact that human beings are agents and actors who resist and transform hegemonies (Connell, 1995). This will take me into what may be called the "new sexualities studies" and into contemporary social changes that some identify as queer postmodernism. A sense of some of the new male sexualities that challenge and fracture the hegemony will be highlighted.

STORIES OF HEGEMONIC MALE SEXUALITY

In what follows, I plan to quickly raid a sample of stories. They all point toward a major narrative of an essential male sexuality, mirroring what I have located so far. In various ways, they help to assemble the resources through which male sexuality comes to be seen as given and normal. Any one account on its own would not stand, but I hope to show that there is a massive convergence into a particular version of what it is to be a sexual male.

Evolution and the Biological Story

Perhaps the major contemporary account of male sexuality to display this story line has grown from biology and evolutionary theory. For many, it mirrors common sense so perfectly that its validity seems almost irrefutable and inevitable. Although there are many variations on the theme, the core position is that gender differences in regard to sexuality are striking and given "in nature." In one version, the presence of testosterone in the male is seen as a prime driver of sexuality (e.g., Goldberg, 1973). In another, the biological significance of a single sperm and a single egg are seen to differ dramatically. Thus, a physically adult man releases hundreds of millions of sperm in a single ejaculation and then makes more, whereas a newborn female's ovaries contain her entire lifetime allotment of follicles or immature eggs; a woman commonly releases a single mature egg cell from her ovaries each month. Thus, although a man is biologically capable of fathering thousands of offspring, a woman is able to bear only a relatively small number of children. It is but a short step from this biologically based difference to argue that each sex is well served in long-term evolutionary adaptations by distinctively different "reproductive strategies." From a strictly biological perspective, a man reproduces his genes most efficiently by being promiscuous—that is, readily engaging in sex with many partners. This scheme, however, opposes the reproductive interests of a woman, whose relatively few pregnancies demand that she carry the child for 9 months, give birth, and care for the infant for some time afterward. Thus, efficient reproduction on the part of the woman depends on carefully selecting a mate whose qualities (beginning with the likelihood that he will simply stay around) will contribute to their child's survival and successful reproduction. For reproductive potentials to be fulfilled and humans to satisfactorily reproduce themselves, there is an evolutionary necessity for men to have sexual intercourse with as many

women as they can; for women, the task is to find the best man and the best seed.

This popular argument of evolutionary psychology hence argues that men are much more sexual and that this serves evolutionary adaptive needs. The male is seen as more sexual and more likely than the female to desire sex with a variety of partners. Of course, this theory may also be seen as a major device to legitimize these behavioral patterns in men and women: They are natural, adaptive, and, hence, necessary. In more extreme versions, they can even come to legitimize phenomena such as rape and sexual violence. One example of this new evolutionary thinking is the controversial study of rape by sociobiologists Randy Thornhill and Craig Palmer (2000). Drawing on the evolutionary theory of sex, they claim that rape is a necessary part of the evolutionary process. They see it as completely congruent and compatible with the development of sex differences. In this view, rape becomes a device in which men can have sex no matter what. Male rape "arises from men's evolved machinery for obtaining a high number of mates in an environment where females choose mates" (Thornhill & Palmer, 2000, p. 190). Sociobiology suggests that cultural patterns of reproduction, promiscuity, the double standard, and, indeed, rape, like many other patterns, have an underlying biologic. Simply put, male sexualities have developed around the world because women and men everywhere tend toward distinctive reproductive strategies that reinforce hegemonic sexuality. It is seen as an evolutionary necessity.

Conventional Sociological Stories

A quick version of hegemonic masculinity may also be found in one of the earliest sociological statements of men's studies (David & Brannon, 1976; see pp. 11-35). This study is organized around four key dimensions of the male sex role, and although these are stereotypes, and knowledge has moved beyond them as the world of their existence has changed, they may well serve as a useful starting point when applied to sexuality. David and Brannon suggest that men in general are bound into the following expectations (and here they can also be seen to embody their sexualities more particularly):

"No sissy stuff"—the stigma of anything vaguely feminine. The implication here is that sexuality for men must not involve anything remotely feminine (emotional, passive, etc.). It hints at the way in which homophobia (the fear of homosexuality) may serve to partially structure male sexuality, and it also suggests that men's sexuality must indeed be different from that of women.

The "big wheel"—success, status, and the need to be looked up to. The implication here is that sexuality for men must involve being seen to be successful, that a man must be looked up to for his sexual competence. And, as suggested earlier, for men, sexual competence may well have a lot to do with the effective working of their well-socialized penises: getting it up and getting to ejaculate.

The "sturdy oak"—a manly air of toughness, confidence, and self-reliance. The implication here is that sexuality for men must be assertive. Men should not have any self-doubt about their sexuality.

"Give 'em hell"—the aura of aggression, violence, and daring. The implication here is that sexuality for men must conform to that most worrying of expectations—rough and violent sex. For some this may mean that coercive sex (from rape to harassment) may be felt as a central feature of good sex.

Each of these broad themes, then, can be seen to characterize aspects of hegemonic male sexuality. Men must not be like women in any way; must succeed in sex; must exude a manly sexuality; and must be forceful, assertive, and aggressive.[5]

Feminist Stories

Although it is well recognized that there are many contrasting feminist positions, at the heart of many accounts of male sexuality, of whatever persuasion, lies a description of men that is hardly flattering—one that is likely to arouse considerable discomfort, if not outright anger, in men. In the 1970s, for example, Phyllis Chessler (1979) almost groans with pity for us:

What demon do men run from? What enemy hovers behind them, what enemy waits to envelop them from within, if they pause a bit in the taking—if not the giving—of sexual pleasure? Is this style the inevitable conclusion of a childhood in which boys spend years trying to hide their erection, years of trying to masturbate in the dark—as quickly, as silently as they can, in order

to avoid discovery? Is it such prolonged childhood silence that leads men into valuing loud noises, yelling out "dirty words," or into a dependency on repetitious, visually exaggerated, closely detailed pornographic displays? (pp. 224-225)

Certain themes consistently reappear in feminist discussions of male sexuality, and accounts of male sexuality as prone to violence, pressure, coercion, and objectification abound. For some, sexuality is almost defined as male; for others, it is seen as a major device through which men maintain their positions of power and keep women under a constant state of threat. One group of English feminists, writing in the 1980s, captured such themes succinctly under seven headings. Asking themselves what male sexuality was like, they concluded that it was about *power, aggression, penis orientation, the separation of sex from loving emotion, objectification, fetishism, and uncontrollability* (Coveney, Jackson, Jeffreys, Kay, & Mahony, 1984). There is no doubt from their discussions that they saw each of these features not only as male but also as very damaging and destructive to women, creating the composite stereotype of the traditional macho man: an emotionally crippled, sex-obsessed, aggressive dominator. Taken together, many of these attributes could highlight a whole structure of fear and violence imposed on women by men—of sexual slavery, sexual exploitation, and sexual terrorism. The theoretical analyses and the empirical evidence brought to focus on male sexuality led to an inexorable logic: *Sexuality is male*. Once women recognized this, they had only a few options: Attack sexuality with all their might, for "we are fighting for our lives; we are dealing with a life and death situation" (Dworkin, 1981, p. 26); retreat entirely from it, leaving men to their sexuality and women to establish alternative worlds; or both. In any event, a woman-identified world—without men—became the goal (Dworkin, 1981; Leidholdt & Raymond, 1990; Vance, 1984). As Andrea Dworkin (1981) remarks,

Man fetishizes [the woman's] body as a whole and in its parts. He exiles her from every realm of expression outside the strictly male-defined sexual or male-defined maternal. He forces her to become that thing that causes erection, then holds himself helpless and powerless when he is aroused by her. His fury when she is not that thing, when she is either more or less than that thing, is intense and punishing. (p. 1)

More nuanced readings still agree that men are the problem, but they also highlight the linked problems of women's sexuality and, sometimes, the role of women in mothering men. In a gentler form, Dorothy Dinnerstein says that "a central rule under a strikingly widespread set of conditions is, first, that men act sexually more possessive than women, and second that women act less free than men to seek 'selfish sexual pleasure'" (cited in Williams & Stein, 2002, p. 5). Even here, in this weaker form, male sexuality is more possessive and selfish than female sexuality.

Research Stories:
The Clinical Therapy Tradition

Another tradition for looking at sexuality takes it increasingly into the realm of the clinical and therapeutic. This is a deeply normative and prescriptive view of the world. It establishes broad, normative models of what human sexuality is really like, identifies problems people experience because they do not fit the model, and then proceeds to assist people to follow that model. In the early days, much of therapy concerned issues of object choice (the "clinical disorder" of homosexuality, for example), but since the 1960s, a major sex therapy "industry" has grown up that maps out the proper routes for male and female sexualities. The work of Masters and Johnson (1966) was most famous for its "discovery" of a sexual response cycle: excitement, plateau, orgasm, and resolution. This model is almost entirely focused on a sequencing of arousal and orgasm—establishing, in effect, that whenever a firm erection is not possible, or orgasms do not take place, there is sexual dysfunction. Although on an individual level, therapy may be able to provide support and change, on a wider public level, it has the consequence of reinforcing what male and female sexualities should be like. It is highly normative and prescriptive.

The ideological functions of sex research have been much discussed. Janice Irvine's (1990) study *Disorders of Desire* is a fine account of just how coercive much sexology and sex research has been over the past century. Indeed, much contemporary therapy and sexology continues in the same vein today, with the help of new technologies, all usually bringing potential reinforcement to the hegemonic model. Viagra is a clear case of this. Hitting the headlines during the 1990s, it signposted what was a hitherto unknown sexual problem, but one that now appeared on a massive scale. The problem was impotence. If sales of Viagra are any indication (nearly 200,000 prescriptions are filled each week, and some 17 million Americans use the drug), then it could flag a new (even global!) social problem for men—and women, too. *Erectile dysfunction* now becomes the issue. This also suggests a model of dysfunction for the aging male, with Viagra and medicalization as the solution.[6]

Both Leonore Tiefer (2000) and Barbara Marshall (2002) suggest that the story of Viagra and, indeed, medical interventionism over the "science" of sexual dysfunction is a wholly mechanical way of looking at sexual issues, and one that most of the world had not even dreamt of before its arrival in the mid-1990s. At its heart, it deflects attention from all the political and cultural concerns of sexuality and works to make cultural expectations of gender become more rigid (Marshall, 2002).

Research Stories:
The Empirical Tradition

Much research during the 20th century has catalogued the differences between male and female sexuality. The mammoth volumes produced by Kinsey and his colleagues (Kinsey, Pomeroy, & Martin, 1948; Kinsey, Pomeroy, Martin, & Gebhard, 1953) provide a mound of data based on some 12,000 (nonrandom) North Americans living in the 1930s and 1940s, and in *Sexual Behavior in the Human Female* (Kinsey et al., 1953), some key contrasts are brought out in Part 3.

Another major example can be found in the studies of Shere Hite (1981), conducted in the 1970s and early 1980s and providing one of the largest surveys of male sexuality ever produced. Although it is very detailed—7,239 men returned a 13-page questionnaire, and this was turned into a 1,000-page book composed of their comments—it has been much criticized on scientific (and political) grounds. Nevertheless, it does contain a wealth of detail from men willing to write about their sex lives. At the heart of the study, once again, is the idea that sex is very important to men. They like intercourse because of the physical pleasure, because of psychological and emotional support, and because in part it is a validation of their masculinity (p. 333). They have a fear of impotence or loss of erection (p. 340). Hite claims that a traditional model of sex—foreplay, intercourse, male orgasm in the vagina—is "far and away the most usual type of sex" (p. 414) and, indeed, suggests that for men, the male orgasm is "the point of sex and intercourse" (p. 454;. although they have their strongest orgasms in masturbation [p. 431], and nearly everyone in the study masturbated [a mere 1% did not]). Often sex was accompanied by guilt (p. 486). "Love" was important but often painful; marriage, even when difficult, was liked (p. 206) because there was someone to care for them and because of the stability, domestic warmth, and regularity of home life (p. 209). It was common to have sex outside of marriage, unknown to their wives; many had little guilt about it and even felt it had enhanced their marriage (p. 142).

In a slightly different vein, research stories from young people suggest these differences appear at an early age. James Messerschmidt (1993), in a review of many contemporary studies of young men across class and ethnicity, suggests that "normative heterosexuality is constructed as a practice that helps to reproduce the subordination of young women and to produce age specific heterosexual styles of masculinity, a masculinity centering on an uncontrollable and unlimited sexual appetite" (p. 90). "Natural sex" serves as a routine resource in accomplishing and reinforcing young men's emerging manliness.[7]

Likewise, in an influential U.K. study, Holland, Ramazanoglu, Sharpe, and Thomson (1998) found that "many of the young men implicitly concur with the absence of subordination of female desire in the very commonly expressed view that while men want sex, women want love and relationships" (p. 124). Some boys' voices from the study make this clear:

Most boys can have sex without any feelings, whereas a girl has to have feelings. It's totally different. It's much deeper for a girl than it is for a boy. (young male, middle class, AC,[8] 18 years old)

Sometimes I just want to have sex, and I am going to have sex, but it is only going to be for me. (young male, working class, ESW, 19 years old)

The interviewer asks one young man: "and did the girls enjoy it?" and the response comes:

I don't know. I didn't really ask. As long as I enjoyed it I weren't bothered. I am now, but then I didn't know, I just thought it was their duty. I was a bit sexist. (young male, working class, A, 17 years old)

Likewise, in New Zealand, Louisa Allen (2003), studying some 500 young people, found that the major discourses among the young replicated classic positions. Her article is even called "Girls Want Sex, Boys Want Love," and in one focus group, we hear the following:

Michael: Guys are basically always ready.

Anabella: I heard some statistics . . . and guys supposedly think of sex six times an hour on average.

Darren: Oh it's heaps more than that. (all laugh)

Tim: If I wanted to ejaculate, I could probably do so in less than a minute. . . .

Chris: . . . a guy is sort of almost guaranteed to feel good (having sex you know, feel the same in the end anyway so. . . .)

Darren: Guys have got a lot to prove. There's a lot . . . there's a lot for guys to live up to like uhm gotta be all macho and gotta be cool and all this sort of stuff, gotta score nice chicks or if you have got one chick, you have got to score often. . . .

But they do go on to suggest a change in the making:

Peter: Sex is good. It's nice but its not essential. I'd still love her . . . I'd still want to be with her. So you know it's nice but I mean if it had to stop then it would, and I would still go out with her. . . . (p. 227)

"Pop Narratives"

Then there are the immensely popular cultural texts, such as John Gray's (1992) *Men Are From Mars, Women Are From Venus.* Here men and women are seen as being so very different that they might as well come from different planets, and their lives are lives of inevitable conflicts. Thus Gray's task is to act as an omniscient interpreter of all this and to help show what the differences are and what can be done about them. "Great sex," as he calls it, involves connecting up these differences. Great sex connects the core selves of men and women. Graphically, he says, "He is trying to empty out while she is trying to be filled up" (p. 27). He is force and active—she wants it. Women are told that "sex is the direct line to a man's heart" (p. 18); men have a need for "quickies" or "fast food sex" (pp. 77, 82, *passim*); and women should be patient; because men become aroused very quickly (indeed, it is "as easy as shaking a can of beer and then letting it pop") (Gray, 1992, 1995, 1998, and as discussed in Potts, 1998).

Bernie Zilbergeld's (1999) best seller, *The New Male Sexuality*, provides a guide that is much more cautious than Gray's.[9] Although in this book he starts by suggesting that most men are engulfed in a "Fantasy Model of Sex" (for which the claim is, "It's Two Feet Long, Hard as Steel, and Will Knock Your Socks Off," p. 15), the main message of the book is that this fantasy model is breaking down, and a new openness is starting to appear. At the start of the book he is at pains to suggest some of the myths that surround men's sexuality. In a sense, they do constitute some elements of the main male story line of sex, and so they are worth repeating here—not so much as myths, but as key plots that often shape the workings of male sexuality. Slightly abridged, they include the following:

- A real man isn't into sissy stuff like feelings and communicating.
- All touching is sexual or should lead to sex.
- A man is always interested in and always ready for sex.
- A real man performs in sex.
- Sex is centered on a hard penis and what's done with it.
- If your penis isn't up to snuff, we have a pill that will take care of everything.
- Sex equals intercourse.
- A man should make the earth move for his partner or at the very least knock her socks off.
- Good sex is spontaneous with no planning and no talking. (Chapter 2)

We have been here before. The list rehearses most of the features we have already encountered.[10]

Gay Male Sexual Stories

Gay male sexuality poses a curious series of questions for the hegemonic model. By definition, hegemonic male sexuality is defined through heterosexuality, and gay relations are ostensibly excluded. And yet there is one major strand of "gay" analysis in the gay male community which suggests that gay male sexuality takes us closer to what "true" male sexuality is all about. In the 1980s, for instance, there was a notorious debate with certain feminists over whether gay men were more phallic centered and more male in their sexualities than heterosexual men—who at least had their sexualities (partially) regulated by (some) women. Liz Stanley (1982), an English lesbian sociologist, could remark that

> gay men, perhaps more than any other men ally themselves with the activities and products of sexism. More than any other men they choose to act and construe themselves and each other in ways dominated by phallocentric ideologies and activities. (pp. 210-211)

But there are also those within the gay movement who see that sex is the core of the gay male experience and is too often sanitized and demeaned. Gay sex is revolutionary sex. Repeatedly, gay men rehearse the idea that

> gay sensibility is truly subversive because it insists on the primacy of sexuality beneath its adoration of the civilized. While ostensibly it is concerned with disseminating new ideas about culture, its real concern is the dissemination of sexual knowledge, with which it is obsessed. . . . Gay sensibility sexualizes the world. (Kleinberg, 1980, pp. 62-63)

In a recent and very engaging history of gay culture, Michael Bronski (1998) suggests that it is male sexuality that heralds gay radicalism. For him, gays signpost a very positive but very threatening pleasure class that embodies "the possibility of freedom of pleasure for its own sake" (p. 214). And because, he says, "our most fundamental experience of pleasure is essentially sexual in nature" (p. 213), gay men provide the means for us to reconnect our bodies to our minds, to experience wholeness, to avoid splitting. It is a lot to ask from "sexuality"—and gay men.

Much research on the sexualities of gay men documents the sheer quantity and range of sexual experiences that many gay men have and how they have built sexualized communities and institutions to embody them: car parks, woods and parks, toilets and beaches, parties, bathhouses and clubs become colonized for male desires (Delph, 1978). One recent study finds just how central a sense of masculinity may be for gay male sexuality:

> I was just thinking how incredibly hot it was to have this stud sort of fucking me. . . . That he was inside me and giving himself to me and so on. And in that sense he represented all the, you know, . . . all the masculinity and that strength and so on that I, you know, wanted it up inside me. . . .
>
> And it's like . . . it's almost like this man in injecting some of his masculinity into me . . . giving me some of that. And so I find it [receptive anal sex] a very augmenting experience as opposed to a diminishing experience. . . . In a sense it's like me sort of taking something from him. . . .
>
> It was quite a sexual thrill to do something dangerous. It is going beyond the boundaries, that is what sex is all about . . . about breaking the taboos. . . . It was an incredible thrill. . . . (Ridge, 2004)

For some (but by no means all or even most) gay men, then, this meant the creation of a macho culture of sleaze and leather, where the notion of desire or lust took precedent over other concerns. Male pleasure is closely linked to male fetishism and male power. The pleasure of the penis takes over—a gay phallocentric culture is invented. The gay male culture of sleaze and leather can be seen as a model of truly liberated lust—sex for pleasure's sake, uncontaminated by bourgeois notions of intimacy and relationships. One example of political pornography put it like this:

> *Meat* may be the most moral book ever assembled; a morality of participants in which being "good" is giving a good blow or rim job, being "good" is being hot and hard, being good is letting it all come out: sweat, shit, piss, spit, scum; being good is being able to take it all, take it all the way. . . . Story after story in *Meat* expresses the sheer joy and exuberance—the wild pleasure in licking assholes, eating shit, drinking piss—taking it all. . . . The truth is the biggest turn on. (Gay Sunshine Press, 1981, pp. 6-7)

So here is a curious paradox. Gay male sexuality may be the key to heterosexual male sexuality—it may suggest the routes that most men would take if they were not shaped by relations with women. Gay men become the champions of the pleasure principle. And yet, once again, although this may be a feature of some parts of the gay world, I would worry if this were presumed to characterize it all. Once again, we are on the verge of a sexualized essentialism that will need challenging.[11]

Research on HIV/AIDS

One last comment. Since the 1980s and the growth of the worldwide pandemic of HIV/AIDS, there has been a growing industry of research into sexual behavior. Most of this suggests just how driven male sexualities are, more or less across the world. Whether this drivenness is biological or cultural is largely beside the point. In AIDs prevention work, over and over again, men talk of how it is their right to have sex; to have unprotected sex, which is more natural; that they have the need for outlets; that if their partners will not give them sex, they have to take it. As a global Panos report indicates,

> Thais of both sexes say men "have strong sexual desire and need some outlet"; South African miners claim that regular intercourse is essential for a man's good health; and in Indian society "it is considered natural for men to be 'lustful.'" This viewpoint appears universal. (Panos, 1999, p. 17)

DISMANTLING THE HEGEMONY? TRANSFORMING WESTERN MEN'S SEXUALITIES

From the snapshots I have displayed, there would almost seem to be a universal convergence on the nature of male sexuality, from many different perspectives. There would seem to be a *hegemonic male sexuality*. And yet, this is far too generalized a picture. An essentializing narrative has taken hold that portrays men as driven by sex; focused on their penises; in persistent need of orgasm; and often as borderline, if not actual, rapists. This may be the hegemony, but I for one am not really happy with this. True, I can see many signs of all this in many men in many contexts, including myself, as I move through my daily round. Yet it is a very dark picture, and there is something worryingly inaccurate about it.

What, then, is to be made of all this? Certainly not that all men are like this and no women are: The first key thing to notice is that there are significant overlaps between male and female sexualities, overlaps that may even be increasing for some. Indeed, sociologists Pepper Schwartz and Virginia Rutter (1998) have made a surprising claim—based largely on research evidence. They suggest that there is a bell curve continuum of women's and men's sexuality. As they say,

> A large proportion of both female and male populations share much of the middle ground . . . sexual experience isn't all that different for men and women, but perhaps like us you wonder what causes men and women at one end of the continuum to be so different from other men and women. (pp. 37-38)

It is these differences at the ends of the continuum that seem to be highlighted in research. Given the evidence shown earlier, there is surely a general contrast that may be unmistakable at the ends of these bell curves, but to focus exclusively on this is to miss vast areas of overlap.

Another key thing to notice is that the sexualities of men are decidedly not all cut from the same cloth. Indeed, many of the studies cited earlier, although giving prominence to what we call the hegemonic model, also show that male sexualities do vary according to class backgrounds, positions in the age cycle, ethnicities, relationships with peers, wider cultures, and personalities. Men are manifestly not all the same. Many men, then, are decidedly not like the conventional portrait. Just as Connell (1995) recognizes that this is not the full story for men in general (there are many "masculinities"), so, too, we may be sure that there are many male sexualities. We need only look around to see that many of the men we know do not (at least on the surface) seem to follow the standard model. Despite the popular adages, all men are not rapists; all men are not demons. Following Connell's line of arguing, there may be many different responses to hegemonic male sexualities. Some may be complicit (different from hegemonic but in support of them, e.g., in marriage); some may be subordinated (practices that expel some men, such as gays, from a "circle of legitimacy" [Connell, 1995, p. 79]); some can be very different—emphasizing femininity, or homosexuality, or

being highly resistant to gender; and others may be marginalized (e.g., those patterns outside of authorization).

Third, we do need to realize that human sexualities are forms of social actions. That is, people compose their sexual lives—their feelings, actions, talk, identities, even body work—out of the social resources at hand. Sexualities are messy and ambiguous social practices, not fixed and straightforward "drive releases." It is true that the hegemony can provide guidelines for many men across the world, centrally, because it enhances their power, but it is never just a straightforward matter; it always has to be worked at. This means that much sexual action will take different pathways from that of the hegemonic model.[12]

THE NEW THEORIES OF SEXUALITIES

All this is to enter what has been called "the new theories of sexualities" (Plummer, 2002). When sociologists, historians, feminists, and anthropologists started to study human sexuality, they soon realized that it was often profoundly unlike that found in other animals. Of course there is a biological substratum that connects us to all animal life, but what is distinctive about human sexuality is that it is both (a) symbolic and meaningful and (b) linked to power. In all of this, we see that the simple study of sex as sex, of sex sui generis, has gone from the agenda. Human sexuality is always conducted at an angle: It is never "just sex." There is no straightforward (male) drive pressing for release; sex is not a simple property of people (or men); it does not exist in a social vacuum but is flooded with the social. Human sexualities are interactive, relational, structural, embodied, and organized within a broad template of power relations. They connect to identities, interactions, and institutions. They are fashioned by patriarchal relations, sex negativism, homophobia, and heterosexism, as well as by continuums of sexual violence. People "do" sexualities as well as telling stories about them. As such, human sexualities are far from biologically fixed. These are the wisdoms of the new sexualities theories (although the theories themselves come in many forms). A key feature of much of this new theoretical work is to locate sexualities within frameworks of scripts, discourses, stories, and male power (e.g., Foucault, 1976; Gagnon & Simon, 1973; Jackson, 1999; Plummer, 1995).

In general, these new social accounts offer up more modest accounts of sexualities than those found in the sexological world. They throw into doubt any "grand narratives" of sexuality (such as that of an essential male sexuality) that have haunted much of the modern world's analysis of sexuality. "Sex" is no longer the source of a truth, as it was for the moderns with their strong belief in science. Instead, human sexualities have become destabilized, decentered, and de-essentialized: The sexual life is no longer seen as harboring an essential unitary core locatable within a clear framework (such as the nuclear family), with an essential truth waiting to be discovered. There are only fragments. There is an affinity here with some versions of postmodernism, and links can be made to the growing interest in queer theory. One of the key tenets of a postmodern approach to the world is to highlight the dissolution of any one grand account, narrative, or story of the world. In effect, this means that much of what has been presumed about sexuality, or gender, or intimacy in the past simply no longer holds. The "grand story" of male sexuality—that hegemonic male sexuality described in the opening sections of this chapter—does, of course, continue. But it is now challenged from many sides. The idea of any fixed, essential, or dominant version of men and their sexualities becomes weakened, fragmented, and deconstructed, and we are left with multiple tellings and more fluid patterns (Halberstam, 1998). Of course, this also means that what it is to do sexualities at the start of the 21st century is altogether less clear, and this brings anxieties with it. This is also what queer theory aims to do: It seeks to persistently subvert and deconstruct commonly held polarities, categories, and ideas about sexuality and gender. Postmodern and queer thinking seek both to find new ways of thinking about sexual categories (and hence male sexuality) and to recognize that a new kind of society may be in the making in which new patterns of sexuality may be starting to emerge (and, hence, changing forms of male sexualities) (Simon, 1996).

Some researchers have already suggested an array of discourses or scripts that help fashion sexualities. Wendy Hollway (1996) saw three gendered sexualities discourses. Apart from the hegemonic male sexual drive discourse, she also saw a "have-hold" discourse (linked to monogamy, partnership, and family life, within which women are more likely to experience sex as a lack and move on to mothering and emotional bonding) and a permissive discourse (within which women are more likely to be coopted into the male drive model). Although there is a clear recognition that "the male sex drive discourse" is dominant and hegemonic (Hollway, 1996, p. 85), there is also space for other patterns of sexualities to emerge for women. In contrast, Matt Mutchler (2000), in his study of young gay men, sees a wider range of scripting for men. Four dominant gendered sexual scripts among young gay men are highlighted: romantic love, erotic adventure, safer sex, and sexual coercion. These are hybrid models, as, traditionally, romantic love is seen as the main script for women and erotic adventure as the main script for men, but young gay men navigate their way through a mix of both.[13]

Although recently there has been a great deal of talk about "New Men" and "masculinity in crisis," much of this can be seen as backlash against women in general and feminism in particular, and much of it is not even new (Whitehead, 2002, pp. 54-59). Much of it sees women and feminism as a threat and proceeds to assert some kind of new essential man as a response to it. My view, however, is that simultaneously (maybe more slowly than some suggest), we are moving into a new set of relationships in what might be called postmodern times (for some at least), where certain worlds are becoming less sure of themselves, more fragmented and shifting, pluralistic, and so on. It is a world I have described elsewhere, of postmodern intimacies, which brings a whole array of new conflicts and problems (Plummer, 2000, 2003). It touches on shifts in gender, bodies, relationships, eroticism, identities, and families. In its wake, it brings massive anxieties: As a 44-year-old client of the therapist Zibergeld puts it,

The one sure thing I know about life right now is that it's bewildering. It's not clear what it means to be a man or a woman, how to have a relationship, or even how to act in bed. I see lots of people trying to get clear by reading John Gray's books, but I don't think it helps. Things are in flux; there are no answers. While I know that's the truth, I wish it were otherwise. It's so much hassle the way it is. ("Z," in Zilbergeld, 1999, p. x)

For Zilbergeld, the traditional or fantasy model of sex is being replaced by a "new model of sex" (p. xiv) that is no longer focused on a pressurized male performance but instead focuses on "pleasure, closeness, and self and partner enhancement rather than performance and scoring" (p. xiv). He suggests there are now "whole menus of choices." I think he is right. What we are seeing is a progressive post-modernization of sex that brings an array of new sexual stories, new options for living, and a series of continuing dialogues, all of which are likely to change the workings of male sexualities in the future, possibly rendering them more diverse and less open to hegemonic male sexuality. I stress that they are dialogues rather than monologic assertions. They harbor conflicts and potentials for disagreements through which new sexualities will be negotiated. Thus, for example, we have the growing impact of newish forms of cybersexualities on our lives, and we have the increasing linkages between sexualities and other spheres of life—from consumption to work (Hearn & Parkin, 2001). To briefly conclude, let me suggest just a few of these new, storied dialogues that are now opening up.

NEW STORIED DIALOGUES FOR RETHINKING MALE SEXUALITIES

The Family-Heterosexuality Dialogue

The traditional order of family life is changing as we enter a period of postmodern families and "families of choice" (Weeks, Donovan, & Heaphy, 2001; Weston, 1990). In the recent past, families have been predominantly heterosexual and so have child rearers. But now, even as many elect to stay with traditional patterns, there are large numbers exploring many newer forms of living together and child raising: assisted conception, cohabitation, living alone, single parenting, same-sex partnerships, divorce, stepparenting, serial relationships, polyamory—and all the new patterns of relationships that these bring. Words have not yet even been invented for some of these new "familial" roles, and they pose challenges for conventional ways of thinking about sexualities and gender. But as the new stories of these ways of living come more and more to the forefront

and are placed in dialogues with other stories, so the possibility of shifts in male sexualities starts to be extended.

The Deconstructive-Renarrating Dialogue

One of the ways in which radical dialogues over the nature of sexualities have been proceeding in recent years can be found in the stories of deconstruction that pit themselves against the idea of language as a natural reflection of sexual life and of sexuality as a given, unchanging essence. In his telling study of male sexual language, for example, Peter Francis Murphy (2002) shows that male sexuality is often trapped in a discourse of machines, sports, and bodies that work to make sexuality for men appear more driven. Once we become aware of these linguistic strategies that "assemble" male sexualities, the possibilities of changing them and creating new ones can become more possible. Another study, by Annie Potts (2002), draws together much of this deconstructive work to show how male-female heterosexualities are drenched in a language that gives priority to orgasm and the penis, an outer world of men and an inner world of women. She argues the case for "deprioritizing coital sex" as the cornerstone of sexuality and suggests this may have positive impacts:

> A cultural deprioritization of penile vaginal sex would profoundly alter the relevance of contemporary constructions of male and female so-called sexual problems. . . . Men may no longer have to conform to a phallic ideal, and women's bodies may no longer be the targets of their penetration. (Potts, 2002, pp. 260-261)

She also argues (as many recently have) for a challenging of the masculine (active)–feminine (passive) dichotomy and for a search for alternative versions of sexuality from women (which, by implication, will start to rewrite the scripts of male sexualities as well).[14] What is required is a concern with the building of new narratives of sexuality that are much more open, pluralistic, diverse, and hence that may create the possibility for future change.

One way of sensing this change and working with it is to listen to what may be called the "deep, thick stories" of sexualities. Elsewhere,

I have made a number of claims about the importance of story work in both understanding sexualities and in bringing about political change (Plummer, 1995, 2001). I see deep stories as a little like Geertz's (1973) "thick description"—they are the very rich, deep, extended stories people tell of their sexual lives. They contrast with shallow, brief, quick, linear stories. Deep storytelling is encouraged in a postmodern or queer world and enables us to see more clearly that lives are not simply straightforward in their genders, bodies, sexualities, or relationships. We may dwell in simple polar categorizations, but lives are usually much messier than this. To get at a person's sexual story requires burrowing deep down. The stories men tell of their sexualities may look straightforwardly hegemonic, but men may also negotiate with their stories, resist them, or even transgress them in multiple ways (Geertz, 1973).[15]

The Women's Sexuality Dialogue

There has been a striking attempt to break down the representations of what it means to be a woman, and under this guise now many women appear to be at least as sexual as men. Watch any "reality show" that has anything to do with relationships (usually youthful), and you will see women behaving in ways that mirror the male hegemonic model: They are assertive, objectificatory, lustful—not only do they want to have fun, they also want to fuck. Likewise, the whole issue of women's agency—of their acting sexually in the world and of having rights to sexuality—has been placed on the agenda in ways it was not before the latter part of the 20th century. Of course, it is always true that some women (often on the margins) have "liked to fuck" (Vance, 1984), but the idea that women have gone actively in pursuit of their men (or women) without stigma or shame seems somewhat recent. It is part of what Ehrenreich, Hess, and Jacobs (1984) have dubbed "the feminization of sex" in their account of this change during the mid-1980s. In all, women are repositioning themselves in relation to power and being under control, and this, in turn, pushes the definitions of male sexualities (often rendering them less sure and stable).

Sexual Violence and New Men's Groups Dialogue

Although it is true that there are few signs of any decrease in violent male sexualities across the world, it is likely that there has been a growing awareness of them and of what needs to be done. Not only have laws and policies changed, giving credence to the need for hegemonic male sexualities to change (debates over rape in marriage, sexual harassment, date rape, child abuse, and hate crimes, all linked to the rise in the number of women's shelters, rape hot lines, and the like), so too has there been a heightened awareness of the role of media representations of masculinities of this kind. It has made some men very aware of the problematic nature of their sexualities vis-à-vis women, and men's groups have consequently been set up that work to challenge the hegemony.[16] Thus we have Men Against Pornography, Men Against Rape, and the broader men's Anti-Sexism Movement. At its most extreme, perhaps, are the men like John Stoltenberg (1990), who argue the case for a sexuality that is consensual, mutual, and respectful—one not shaped by the images of pornography, not molded by drugs, and not "fixated on fucking" (pp. 36-39).

The Gay Dialogue

Gay men also raise issues about sexualities and men. At one extreme is the situation in which gay men have friendships and relate to each other in nonsexual ways (Nardi, 1999).[17] At the other, as we have seen, gay men parade the importance of sex—and not just sex, but wide-ranging sexualities that can range from anal sex to what might best be called "sleazy sex." For many, there is a pure delight in unconstrained bodily lust. One of Dowsett's (1996) respondents has 10,000 partners, and many have a parade of partners each night. Often they lose themselves to kinds of sex that take over their whole body: Men in this situation may want to turn themselves into sex objects, gear themselves into being desired rather than simply desiring. Indeed, Leo Bersani (1988) accuses gay male sexuality and writings about it of being too frequently merely conventional, whereas he himself looks for the "redemptive reinvention of sex" (p. 215). In this he seeks the radical potential that actually comes from being fucked (with the loss of a presumed manhood, the loss of self, the engulfment). Gay male sexualities may have potential for transgressing the male hegemony in major ways.[18]

The Identity Dialogue

Social identities designate the ways we define ourselves, and they change a lot over time (both historically and biographically). In the past, identities were often just given and taken for granted; they were unproblematic. In the modern world, they become more self-conscious and worked—less taken for granted than invented. In the postmodern–late modern world, identities proliferate and have become much less stable and coherent. Identities mark out a past; create boundaries in the contemporary world of who we are and who we are not; and anticipate a future, laying guidelines down of how we should behave to be consistent with our self-created identities.

The model of male hegemonic sexuality tends to presume the idea of a male heterosexual identity. This, in turn, implies some sense of sameness, commonality, and continuity. If not actually present, the search is nevertheless at least on for an identity—a project of knowing who one is as a *man*. The category behind the identity is presumed and is often stridently clear. Being a man often means adopting the hegemonic identity; a man's identity may be defined though his sexuality. Postmodern queer theory suggests that this world of presumed and clear sexual identities (invented during the 19th and 20th centuries [Foucault, 1976]) is being challenged and is starting to break down. The categories and narratives of the modernist era are under threat in postmodern times. As grand stories of sexual lives break down, identities now become unsettled, destabilized, and open to flux and change. Indeed, queer theorists often suggest that sexual identities are becoming permanently unsettled, destabilized, under provisional construction, very much a project and never a thing. This renders the whole idea of male sexualities much less clear and sure. (Although even in this most extreme form it may well have to continue to recognize the need for and the power of categories and boundaries in the organization of the social. It is just that these continuities and samenesses are much more pluralized, shifting, and fragmented than they were previously thought to be.)

Past thinking on sexual identities has depended on a rather crude binary system, but this is starting to change. At the very least, in the modern Western world, new identities may be starting to appear: the "S&M," the fetishist (e.g., foot fetishist, underwear fetishist, armpit fetishist), the macho gay, the passive gay, the chubby gay, the "buff" gay, the queer, the vanilla gay, the hypersexual, the man who is not really interested in sex, the sex crazed, the "chicken hawk," the "bear," the jock, the good husband, the voyeur, the heavy pornography user, the masturbator, sugar daddies, rent boys, the polyamorous—to name only a few. Start to put adjectives in front—sexy, unsexy, attractive, unattractive, rough, tender, insatiable, dysfunctional, impotent, normal, abnormal, assertive, expressive, caring, single, philandering, serial killer, aging, married—and a further world of proliferating sexual identities opens up. Use the world "sexual" to identify the kind of body you have—beautiful, macho, thin, sick, fragile—and whole new embodied sexual identities appear. Put them alongside other categories—man, woman, Asian, Chicano, African American, Japanese—and another world of "hyphenated" sexual identities starts to appear. New dialogues work to splinter and fragment any one unitary model of the male sexuality.

In Conclusion: An Agenda for Queering Male Sexualities

Hegemonic male sexuality is, by definition, pervasive and dominant. It has a long history and wide support. Some new developments—from Viagra to evolutionary psychology—may well reinforce the immutability of male desires. At the same time, we are also entering a (postmodern) era in which a plethora of new possibilities are opening up. Hegemonic sexuality may continue to dominate or be negotiated (as it often has in the past), but it may also be increasingly resisted and even transgressed. Taking seriously the view that people are not just regulated by hegemony but are also actors who transform their social worlds, the second half of this chapter has looked at a few of the dialogues in the making that suggest changes from a penis-centered model of male sexuality.

Thus we have seen, inter alia, attempts to make male sexualities less penis centered and to weaken the link between sex and orgasms. We have seen analyses of the connection between masculinities and sexual violence and how possibly the enhanced understanding of this may lead to changes. We have sensed the growing awareness of the diversities of male sexualities across cultures, classes, ages, ethnicities, and so on. We have seen how queer theory and feminism work to challenge the polarities and dualities of men-women, gay-straight, and others. We can increasingly appreciate how male insecurities, especially in adolescence and early manhood, can harden hegemonic male sexuality. And most of all, we have seen how it is in the creation of new stories, narratives, and dialogues regarding men's different sexual lives that we can start to glimpse the potential for changing the hegemony.

NOTES

1. There are a number of studies on male sexuality, but many of them, such as Larry Morris's (1997) *The Male Heterosexual*, have a tendency to depict the sexuality of men as unproblematic and to see it passing through various key stages: from early acts of penetrative sex through marriage, fatherhood, and divorce. My article treats the whole idea as deeply problematic.

2. There have been a number of histories of the power of the penis and the phallus across society. See, for example, Klaus Theweleit (1987, 1989). It poses for me the interesting question: Could male sexuality exist without the penis?

3. There is not space to review all the new writing usually associated with names such as Foucault, Butler, Weeks, and others. For some overviews and samples, see Lancaster and di Leonardo (1997), Jackson and Scott (1996), Parker and Aggleton (1999), Williams and Stein (2002), and Plummer (2002).

4. The recent use of the term derives, of course, from Gramsci. Blye Frank introduced the idea of "hegemonic heterosexual masculinity" in 1987. The work of Bob Connell takes it further.

5. Although David and Brannon's listing is old, has become more nuanced, and links to a rather old-fashioned role theory, it still serves well as an opening set of images of hegemonic male sexuality.

6. In a recent but already classic study, McKinlay and Feldman (1994) report on 1,290 men from 40 to 70 years old: 17% found themselves "minimally impotent," 25.2% "moderately impotent," and 9.6% "completely impotent." At the same time, it should be noted that the "men in their sixties reported levels of satisfaction with their sex life and partners at about the same level as younger men in their forties" (p. 272).

7. A good ethnography to look partially at this is Elijah Anderson's (1999) *Code of the Street* (see Chapter 4).

8. Initials indicate the ethnic location. AC means African Caribbean; ESW, English, Scottish, Welsh; A, African.

9. Zilbergeld's (1999) model is entirely heterosexual—he does not discuss gay sex, gay relations, or the homophobia that underpins much male sexuality. Missing out on this is a serious weakness for a book called *The New Male Sexuality*!

10. Even though the work of Duncombe and Marsden (1996) suggests that many women find it unfulfilling.

11. During the 1970s, at least one pronounced sector of gay culture came to organize itself around "lust" and "desire," which became graphically portrayed in novels such as Larry Kramer's *Faggots* (1989), nonfiction such as Rechy's (1977) *The Sexual Outlaw* and White's (1980) *States of Desire*, in films such as *Taxi Zum Klo* (Ripploh, 1981), and in more "academic" texts, such as Lee's (1978) *Getting Sex* or Delph's (1978) *The Silent Community*. A set of locales and spaces emerged where sex became the central rationale, and in these locales, thousands of men would gather for millions of sexual excitements. In the bathhouse, the back room, the club, or the cruising ground, a large number of men could be found who had organized themselves around their desires.

12. This is, of course, part of the famous debate in sociology between action and structure: The most recent discussants of this include Anthony Giddens, Margaret Archer, and Rob Stones. This is not the place to consider this debate, except to say that there is room to develop some of these ideas in the field of sexuality—a task I start in a minimal way in the introduction to *Sexualities: Critical Assessments* (Plummer, 2002).

13. Michelle Fine (1988) also suggests four main discourses: those of "silence, danger, desire, and victimization." Much of this is fully supportive, however, of what I am calling hegemonic male sexuality and does not anticipate radical changes.

14. Likewise, Philaretou and Allen (2001) have shown how an essentialist or masculine scripting is at work that "signifies the beginning of the heterosexual act with male erection and its end with ejaculation" (p. 303). As I have suggested earlier, much research and thinking reinforces this masculinist model of a natural sexuality.

15. A small sample of 55 stories by men of their different sexualities can be found in Kay, Nagle, and Gould (2000).

16. Kenneth Clatterbaugh (1997) has outlined a spectrum of positions of the Men's Movement—not all are sympathetic to the critique of hegemonic male sexuality.

17. Peter Nardi has provided the most comprehensive discussion of gay men's friendships and how they usually do not intersect with sex. He discusses many possible permutations (Nardi, 1999, p. 80; see his Figure 4.1). Although for many, sex is off the agenda, for those who do have sex with a close friend, it seems to be a quick sexual fling that then gets defined into a friendship. It is widely perceived that sex complicates things too much—even if there is little actual evidence for this!

18. John Alan Lee (1979) suggests that in general, "sex is an artificially scarce resource in our society" but that one group of people—modern male homosexuals—have been able to develop gay connections through an urban gay community that enable them to enjoy "considerable sexual opportunities at any hour of the day or night." They are usually "inexpensive or free," "convenient and accessible" (p. 175).

19. A useful bibliography on male sexuality, "The Men's Bibliography: A Comprehensive Bibliography of Writing on Men, Masculinities, Gender, and Sexualities," compiled and recently updated by Michael Flood, is available on the Internet at http://www.xyonline.net/mensbiblio/

References[19]

Allen, L. (2003, May). Girls want sex, boys want love: Resisting dominant discourses of (hetero) sexuality. *Sexualities, 6*(2), 215-236.

Anderson, E. (1999). *Code of the street: Decency, violence and the moral life of the inner city.* New York: W. W. Norton.

Bersani, L. (1988). Is the rectum a grave? In D. Crimp (Ed.), *AIDS: Cultural analysis/cultural activism* (pp. 197-222). Cambridge, MA: MIT Press.

Bronski, M. (1998). *The pleasure principle: Sex, backlash and the struggle for gay freedom.* New York: St. Martin's Press.

Caputi, J. (1988). *The age of sex crime.* London: Women's Press.

Carnes, P. (1984). *The sexual addiction.* Minneapolis, MN: Compcare.

Chessler, P. (1979). *About men.* New York: Women's Press.

Clatterbaugh, K. (1997). *Contemporary perspectives on masculinity* (2nd ed.). Westview Press.

Connell, R. W. (1995). *Masculinities.* Cambridge, England: Polity Press.

Coveney, L., Jackson, M., Jeffreys, S., Kay, L., & Mahony, P. (1984). *The sexuality papers: Male sexuality and the social control of women.* London: Hutchinson.

David, D. S., & Brannon, R. (Eds.). (1976). *The forty-nine percent majority: The male sex role.* London: Addison-Wesley.

Delph, E. W. (1978). *The silent community: Public homosexual encounters.* London: Sage.

Dowsett, G. W. (1996). *Practicing desire: Homosexual sex in the era of AIDS.* Stanford, CA: University of Stanford Press.

Duncombe, J., & Marsden, D. (1996). Whose orgasm is this anyway? In J. Weeks & J. Holland (Eds.), *Sexual cultures.* London: Macmillan/Palgrave.

Dworkin, A. (1981). *Pornography: Men possessing women.* London: Women's Press.

Dyer, R. (1982, September/October). Don't look now: The male pin up. *Screen, 23*(3/4), 61-73.

Dyer, R. (1985). Male sexuality in the media. In A. Metcalf & M. Humphries (Eds.), *The sexuality of men* (pp. 28-42). London: Pluto Press.

Ehrenreich, B., Hess, E., & Jacobs, G. (1984). *Re-making love: The feminization of sexuality.* New York: Anchor.

Fine, M. (1988). Sexuality, schooling and adolescent females: The missing discourse of desire. *Harvard Educational Review, 58*, 29-53.

Foucault, M. (1976). *The history of sexuality: Vol. 1. An introduction* (R. Hurley, Trans.). London: Penguin Books.

Frank, B. (1987, autumn). Hegemonic heterosexual masculinity. *Studies in Political Economy, 24*, 159-170.

Fraser, N. (1992). The uses and abuse of French discourse theories for feminist politics. In N. Fraser & S. L. Bartky (Eds.), *Revaluing French feminism: Critical essays on difference, agency and culture* (pp. 177-194). Bloomington: Indiana University Press.

Gagnon, J. H., & Simon, W. (1973). *Sexual conduct: The social sources of human sexuality.* London: Hutchinson.

Gay Sunshine Press. (1981). *Meat: How men look, act, walk, talk, dress, undress, taste and smell. True homosexual experiences from STH.* San Francisco: Author.

Geertz, C. (1973). *The interpretation of cultures.* New York: Basic Books.

Goldberg, S. (1973). *The inevitability of patriarchy.* New York: Morrow.

Gray, J. (1992). *Men are from Mars, women are from Venus.* London: Thorson.

Gray, J. (1995). *Mars and Venus in the bedroom.* New York: Harper Collins.

Gray, J. (1998). *Men are from Mars, women are from Venus. The book of days: 365 inspirations to enrich your relationships.* New York: Harper Collins.

Halberstam, J. (1998). *Female masculinity.* Durham, NC: Duke University Press.

Hearn, J., & Parkin, W. (2001). *Gender, sexuality and violence in organisations.* London: Sage.

Hite, S. (1981). *The Hite report on male sexuality.* London: MacDonald.

Hoch, P. (1979). *White hero, black beast: Racism, sexism and the mask of masculinity.* London: Pluto Press.

Holland, J., Ramazanoglu, C., Sharpe, S., & Thomson, R. (1998). *The male in the head: Young people, heterosexuality and power.* London: Tufnell Press.

Hollway, W. (1996). Gender difference and the production of subjectivity. In S. Jackson & S. Scott (Eds.), *Feminism and sexuality: A reader* (pp. 84-100). Edinburgh, Scotland: University of Edinburgh Press.

Irvine, J. (1990). *Disorders of desire.* Philadelphia, PA: Temple University Press.

Jackson, S. (1999). *Heterosexuality in question.* London: Sage.

Jackson, S., & Scott, S. (Eds.). (1996). *Feminism and sexuality: A reader.* Edinburgh, Scotland: University of Edinburgh Press.

Kay, K., Nagle, J., & Gould, B. (Eds.). (2000). *Male lust: Pleasure, power and transformations.* New York: Harrington Park Press.

Kinsey, A. C., Pomeroy, W. B., & Martin, C. E. (1948). *Sexual behavior in the human male.* Philadelphia, PA: W. B. Saunders.

Kinsey, A. C., Pomeroy, W. B., Martin, C. E., & Gebhard, P. H. (1953). *Sexual behavior in the human female.* Philadelphia, PA: W. B. Saunders.

Kleinberg, S. (Ed.). (1980). *Alienated affections: Being gay in America.* New York: Warner.

Kramer, L. (1989). *Faggots.* New York: New American Library.

Lancaster, R. N., & di Leonardo, M. (Eds.). (1997). *The gender/sexuality reader.* London: Routledge.

Lee, J. A. (1978). *Getting sex.* Toronto: General.

Lee, J. A. (1979). The gay connection. *Urban Life, 8*(2), 175-198.

Leidholdt, D., & Raymond, J. M. (Eds.). (1990). *The sexual liberals and the attack on feminism.* New York: Pergamon Press.

Marshall, B. (2002, May). Hard science: Gendered constructions of sexual dysfunction in the "Viagra age." *Sexualities, 5*(2), 131-158.

Masters, W., & Johnson, V. (1966). *Human sexual response.* New York: Bantam Books.

McKinlay, J. B., & Feldman, H. A. (1994). Age related variation in sexual activity and interests in normal men: Results from the Massachusetts Male Aging Study. In A. Rossi (Ed.), *Sexuality across the life course* (pp. 261-285). Chicago: University of Chicago Press.

Messerschmidt, J. W. (1993). *Masculinities and crime: Critique and reconceptualization of theory.* Lanham, MD: Rowman and Littlefield.

Morris, L. (1997). *The male heterosexual.* London: Sage.

Murphy, P. F. (2002). *Studs, tools and the family jewels: Metaphors men live by.* Madison: University of Wisconsin Press.

Mutchler, M. (2000). Young gay men's stories in the States: Scripts, sex and safety in the time of AIDS. *Sexualities, 3*(1), 31-54.

Nardi, P. M. (1999). *Gay men's friendships: Invincible communities.* Chicago: University of Chicago Press.

Panos. (1999). *AIDS and men: Taking risks or responsibilities.* London: Author.

Parker, R., & Aggleton, P. (Eds.). (1999). *Culture, society and sexuality: A reader.* London: UCL Press.

Person, E. (1980). Sexuality as the mainstay of male identity. *Signs, 9,* 605-630.

Philaretou, A. G., & Allen, K. R. (2001, spring). Reconstructing masculinity and sexuality. *Journal of Men's Studies, 9*(3), 301-321.

Plummer, K. (1995). *Telling sexual stories.* London: Routledge.

Plummer, K. (2000). Intimate choices. In G. Browning, A. Halcli, & F. Webster (Eds.), *Theory and society: Understanding the present.* London: Sage.

Plummer, K. (2001). *Documents of life: 2. An invitation to a critical humanism.* London: Sage.

Plummer, K. (Ed.). (2002). *Sexualities: Critical assessments.* London: Routledge.

Plummer, K. (2003). *Intimate citizenship: Private decisions and public dialogues.* Seattle: University of Washington Press.

Potts, A. (1998). The science/fiction of sex: John Gray's *Mars and Venus in the bedroom. Sexualities, 1*(2), 153-174.

Potts, A. (2002). *The science/fiction of sex: Feminist deconstruction and the vocabularies of heterosex.* London: Routledge.

Rechy, J. (1977). *The sexual outlaw: A documentary.* New York: Grove Press.

Reynaud, E. (1981). *Holy virility: The social construction of masculinity.* London: Pluto.

Ridge, D. (2004, February). "It was an incredible thrill": The social meanings and dynamics of younger gay men's experiences of unprotected anal sex in Melbourne, Australia. *Sexualities, 7*(1).

Ripploh, F. (Writer/Director). (1981). *Taxi zum klo* [Taxi to the toilet] [Motion picture]. Wien, Germany: Cinevista.

Schwartz, P., & Rutter, V. (1998). *The gender of sexuality.* London: Sage.

Scruton, R. (1986). *Sexual desire.* London: Weidenfeld and Nicolson.

Segal, L. (Ed.). (1997a). *New sexual agendas.* London: Macmillan.

Segal, L. (1997b). *Slow motion: Changing masculinities, changing men* (2nd ed.). London: Virago.

Simon, W. (1996). *Postmodern sexualities.* London: Routledge.

Stanley, L. (1982). Male needs: The problems of working with gay men. In S. Friedman & E. Sarah (Eds.), *On the problems of men* (pp. 190-213). London: Women's Press.

Stoller, R. (1976). *Perversion: The erotic form of hatred.* New York: Pantheon.

Stoltenberg, J. (1990). *Refusing to be a man.* New York: Meridian/Penguin.

Theweleit, K. (1987). *Male fantasies* (Vol. 1). Cambridge, England: Polity Press.

Theweleit, K. (1989). *Male fantasies* (Vol. 2). Cambridge, England: Polity Press.

Thornhill, R., & Palmer, C. T. (2000). *A natural history of rape: Biological bases of sexual coercion.* Cambridge, MA: MIT Press.

Tiefer, L. (1995). *Sex is not a natural act and other essays.* Boulder, CO: Westview Press.

Tiefer, L. (2000, August). Sexology and the pharmaceutical industry: The threat of co-optation. *Journal of Sex Research, 37*(3), 273-283.

Vance, C. S. (Ed.). (1984). *Pleasure and danger.* London: Routledge.

Weeks, J., Donovan, C., & Heaphy, B. (2001). *Same sex intimacies: Families of choice and other life experiments.* London: Routledge.

Weston, K. (1990). *Families of choice.* New York: Columbia University Press.

White, E. (1980). *States of desire: Travels in gay America.* New York: Dutton.

Whitehead, S. M. (2002). *Men and masculinities.* Oxford, England: Polity Press.

Whitehead, S. M., & Barrett, F. J. (Eds.). (2001). *The masculinities reader.* Cambridge, England: Polity Press.

Williams, C., & Stein, A. (Eds.). (2002). *Sexuality and gender.* Oxford, England: Blackwell.

Zilbergeld, B. (1999). *The new male sexuality* (Rev. ed.). New York: Bantam Books.

12

MEN, MASCULINITIES, AND CRIME

JAMES W. MESSERSCHMIDT

In recent years, there has emerged a new and growing interest in the relationship among men, masculinities, and crime. Since the early 1990s, numerous works have been published, from individually authored books (Collier, 1998; Hobbs, 1995; Messerschmidt, 1993, 1997, 2000; Polk, 1994; Winlow, 2001), to edited volumes (Bowker, 1998; Newburn & Stanko, 1994; Sabo, Kupers, & London, 2001), to special issues of academic journals (Carlen & Jefferson, 1996). This is not the first time criminologists have been interested in masculinity and its relationship to crime. Such luminaries as Edwin Sutherland and Albert Cohen can be credited with actually placing masculinity on the criminological agenda by perceiving the theoretical importance of the gendered nature of crime. Yet these criminologists understood gender through a biologically based sex-role theory, the weaknesses of which are now well understood: It provides no grasp of gendered power, human agency, and the varieties of masculinities and femininities constructed historically, cross-culturally, in a given society, and throughout the life course (Connell, 1987). Moreover, the social and historical context in which Sutherland and Cohen wrote embodied a relative absence of feminist theorizing and politics and a presumed natural difference between women and men (Messerschmidt, 1993).

The social situation today is dramatically different. Second-wave feminism—originating in the 1960s—challenged the masculinist nature of academia by illuminating the patterns of gendered power that to that point social theory had all but ignored. In particular, feminism secured a permanent role for sexual politics in popular culture and moved analysis of gendered power to the forefront of much social thought. Moreover, feminist research—within and without criminology—spotlighted the nature and pervasiveness of violence against women. Since the mid-1970s, feminist scholars have examined girls' and women's crime, the social control of girls and women, and women working in the criminal justice system (see Daly & Chesney-Lind, 1988; Naffine, 1995). The importance of this feminist work is enormous. It has contributed significantly to the discipline of criminology and has made a lasting impact. Not only is the importance of gender to understanding crime more broadly acknowledged within the discipline, but it has led, logically, to the critical study of masculinity and crime. Boys and men are no longer seen as the "normal subjects"; rather, the social construction of masculinities has come under careful criminological scrutiny.

Feminism has exerted a major impact on my life personally, and academically it has influenced me to concentrate my work on masculinities and crime. Two issues were critical in my decision. First, as R. W. Connell taught us, when we think about gender in terms of power relations, as with any structure of power and inequality (such as race and class), it becomes necessary to study the powerful (men!). It is particularly important if we are committed to constructing a more equal society. Indeed, we must examine the advantaged, analyze how they act to reproduce that advantage, and probe what interest they may have in changing. Thus one reason for studying differences among men and diversity of masculinities is to promote possibilities for change.

Additionally, the gendered practices of men and boys raise significant questions about crime. Men and boys dominate crime. Arrest, self-report, and victimization data reflect that men and boys perpetrate more of the conventional crimes, including the more serious of these crimes, than do women and girls. Moreover, men have a virtual monopoly on the commission of syndicated, corporate, and political crime. Indeed, gender has been advanced consistently by criminologists as the strongest predictor of criminal involvement. Consequently, studying masculinities provides insights into understanding the highly gendered ratio of crime in industrialized societies and, perhaps, how to achieve a more equal society.

What follows is a "progress report" on current criminological thinking about men, masculinities, and crime. I begin with a brief outline of my initial approach to masculinities and crime and then critically examine several new directions in the criminological literature.

MASCULINITIES AND CRIME AS STRUCTURED ACTION

In *Masculinities and Crime* (Messerschmidt, 1993), I combined the theoretical work of Connell (1987), West and Zimmerman (1987), and Giddens (1981) to achieve a perspective that emphasized both the meaningful actions of individual agents and the structural features of social settings. Following West and Zimmerman (1987), I argued that gender is a situated, social and interactional accomplishment that grows out of social practices in specific settings and serves to inform such practices in reciprocal relation— we coordinate our activities to "do" gender in situational ways. Crucial to this conceptualization of gender as situated accomplishment is West and Zimmerman's (1987) notion of "accountability." Because individuals realize that they may be held accountable to others for their behavior, they configure and orchestrate their actions in relation to how these might be interpreted by others in the particular social context in which they occur. Within social interaction, then, we facilitate the ongoing task of accountability by demonstrating that we are male or female through concocted behaviors that may be interpreted accordingly. Consequently, we do gender differently depending on the social situation and the social circumstances we encounter. "Doing gender," then, renders us accountable for our social action in terms of normative conceptions, attitudes, and activities appropriate to one's sex in the specific social situation in which one acts (West & Zimmerman, 1987).

Nevertheless, "doing gender" does not occur in a vacuum but is influenced by the social-structural constraints we experience. Social structures are regular and patterned forms of interaction over time that constrain and enable behavior in specific ways; therefore, social structures "exist as the reproduced conduct of situated actors" (Giddens, 1976, p. 127). Following Connell (1987) and Giddens (1976), I pointed out that these social structures are neither external to social actors nor simply and solely constraining; on the contrary, structure is realized only through social action, and social action requires structure as its condition. Thus, as people do gender, they reproduce and sometimes change social structures. Not only, then, are there many ways of doing gender—we must speak of masculinities and femininities—gender must be viewed as *structured action,* or what people do under specific social-structural constraints.

In this way, gender relations link each of us to others in a common relationship: We share structural space. Consequently, shared blocks of gendered knowledge evolve through interaction in which specific gender ideals and activities play a part. Through this interaction, masculinity is institutionalized, permitting men to draw on such existing, but previously formed, masculine ways of thinking and acting to construct a masculinity for specific settings. The particular criteria of masculinity are embedded in the social situations and recurrent practices whereby social relations are structured (Giddens, 1989).

Accordingly, men are positioned differently throughout society, and socially organized power relations among men are constructed historically on the basis of class, race, and sexual orientation. That is, in specific contexts, some men enjoy greater power than do other men. In this sense, masculinity can be understood only as a relational construct. Connell's (1987) notion of "hegemonic masculinity" is crucial to understanding the power relations among men. Hegemonic masculinity is the culturally idealized form of masculinity in a given historical and social setting. It is culturally honored, glorified, and extolled situationally—such as at the broader societal level (e.g., through the mass media) and at the institutional level (e.g., in school)—and is constructed in relation to "subordinated masculinities" (e.g., homosexuality) and in relation to women. Hegemonic masculinity influences, but does not determine, masculine behavior— the cultural ideals of hegemonic masculinity do not correspond to the actual identities of most men (Connell, 1987, pp. 184-185). Thus, masculinity is based on a social construct that reflects unique circumstances and relationships— a social construction that is renegotiated in each particular context. In this way, men construct varieties of masculinities through specific practices as they simultaneously reproduce, and sometimes change, social structures.

Following this approach, I conceptualized masculinity and crime in new ways—ways that enabled criminologists to explore how and in what respect masculinity is constituted in certain settings at certain times, and how that construct relates to crime (Messerschmidt, 1993). I have argued that one crucial way (not the only way) to understand the "making of crime" by men is to analyze "the making of masculinities." Of course, men's resources for accomplishing masculinity vary depending on position within class, race, age, and gender relations. These differences are reflected in the salience of particular crimes available as resources for accomplishing masculinity. Accordingly, different crimes are chosen as means for doing masculinity and for distinguishing masculinities from each other in different social settings. My work not only criticized traditional criminological theory and radical and socialist feminism but explained class and race differences in male adolescent crimes and in a variety of adult male crimes, from domestic violence to corporate crime (Messerschmidt, 1993).

Recently, two new directions in masculinities and crime literature have emerged: (a) psychoanalysis and (b) difference, the body, and crime. I discuss each of these directions in turn.

PSYCHOANALYSIS

Tony Jefferson (1996b, p. 340) noted 8 years ago that contemporary work on masculinity and crime fails to address a crucial criminological question: "why only particular men from a given class or race background (usually only a minority) come to identify with the crime option, while others identify with other resources to accomplish their masculinity" (p. 341). More recently, John Hood-Williams (2001, p. 43) echoed Jefferson by observing that most crime is not committed by men but, rather, by a "highly specific sub-group of the category 'men'"—even though the group's members do not form a unified subgroup. Thus he asks this question: Why is it that "only a minority of men need to produce masculinity through crime rather than through other, non-criminal, means?" (p. 44). Both are fair and provocative questions. Hood-Williams did not offer an argument to resolve these questions, but Jefferson, in sketchy form, has advanced what he calls a "psychosocial theory." Let us then scrutinize Jefferson's perspective.

Jefferson combines the postmodernist notion of discourse with such psychoanalytic concepts as anxiety and the alleged unconscious defenses of "splitting" and "projection" to understand the discursive positions adopted by individuals.[1] Jefferson (1996b, p. 341) argues that social structures are "dissolved into a plethora of discourses" and criticizes postmodernism for making the individual an effect of discourse, as this simply reproduces the determinism of structuralism. In contrast, Jefferson contends that to break from this "deterministic impasse," criminology must conceptualize how individuals position themselves in relation to the discursive choices facing them and how they come to adopt particular positions and not others: "how people become invested in, motivated by, or identified with particular [discursive] positions" (p. 341).

A return to psychoanalysis, Jefferson maintains, would allow such an understanding of the relationship among subjects, discourses, masculinity, and crime. Jefferson turns to the work of the Austrian child psychoanalyst Melanie Klein (1882-1960) on how behavior allegedly is related to unconscious defenses against anxiety. Following Klein, Jefferson argues that the key to understanding the discursive choices made by individuals—which are choices that collectively constitute a person's "identity"—is "to be found in the defensive attempts people make to ward off anxiety, to avoid feelings of powerlessness" (Jefferson, 1996a, p. 158). Application of this perspective has involved deconstructions of various journalistic accounts of sensational crimes, as well as interviews with men and women on the fear of crime, highlighting how anxieties result from feelings of powerlessness and, thus, how individuals choose masculine "subject positions" that permit them to gain sufficient power over other people to protect their anxiety-driven, insecure selves.

The world heavyweight boxing champion Mike Tyson, and his involvement in crime as a young boy, is a case in point. In a number of papers, Jefferson (1996a, 1996c, 1997b, 1998) examined the life of Tyson from a "little fairy boy" to "the complete destroyer." Although Jefferson provides an account of Tyson's life from childhood to boxing career, our interest here is his analysis of Tyson's eventual involvement in youth crime. Thus what follows is a brief synopsis of Jefferson's account of Tyson "becoming delinquent."

Jefferson (1996a) reports that as a child, Tyson experienced chronic poverty, emotional malnourishment (his father was absent and his mother drank, fought with her boyfriend, and eventually could not cope), "and a genetic endowment that gave him a body and a head too big and bulky for either his years or his soft, lisping voice, the kind of combination that made him a constant target of bullying" (p. 155). It is not surprising that for most of his childhood, Tyson was passive and withdrew into a less-threatening "inner world," but that withdrawal did not save him from continued peer abuse. One particular bullying incident was a turning point in Tyson's life. One day an older local bully assumed Tyson was a safe target for abuse because of his reputation for passivity and, consequently, the bully proceeded to rip the head off one of Tyson's beloved pigeons (which he kept as pets). In this specific situation, Tyson did not remain docile as he had in the past; not only did he choose to fight back, he was successful in

physically defeating the older bully. From that time on, Tyson no longer was compliant and reserved in interaction with his peers, and he eventually became a "badass" member of the Jolly Stompers, a Brooklyn street gang. How does Jefferson explain this movement from "little fairy boy" to "badass" gang member? Because Tyson now embraced a "tough guy" discourse that denoted the ability to survive on the street through the capacity to meet and resist physical challenges. Not explaining why Tyson at this particular time chose to favor this specific discourse—nor if the endorsement of this discourse was prior to or after the successful assault of the bully—Jefferson (1996c, p. 102) does argue that, given Tyson's powerless position, based on his own unique biography, such a discourse offered Tyson an attractive masculine subject position because it protected him from the anxiety of powerlessness and vulnerability. As Jefferson (1996c) notes, Tyson's childhood experiences were "symptomatic of an unhealthy level of anxiety for a young child" (p. 94). Consequently, these "anxiety-inducing" discourses became the object of splitting and projection. In other words, the "little fairy boy" is

> split off and projected outwards, onto the new victims who then become despised (hence legitimate victims) for "possessing" the bad, weak parts which had become too painful for Tyson to accommodate in himself. This bullying, and the accompanying crime, took Tyson from the ghetto to the reformatory and, we can assume, new anxieties. But, rather than "own" these, his recidivism and growing reputation as a hardcore delinquent suggests a continuation of the splitting. (p. 102)

In sum, Tyson experienced a specific set of social and psychic consequences that "add up to a compelling satisfaction in or desire to inflict punishment and thereby triumph over the threat of having it inflicted" (Jefferson, 1998, p. 94).

Jefferson's psychosocial theory of masculinity and crime clearly has intuitive appeal and is a provocative contribution to the literature. Nevertheless, serious problems seem inherent in his perspective. Let me highlight a few.

Although Jefferson (1997b) acknowledges that "the social world is traversed by relations of power (class, gender, race, etc.)" (p. 286), such power relations quickly vanish from Jefferson's analysis because allegedly they "can only signify, and hence be understood by individual subjects, through available discourses." Consequently, in Jefferson's theory of masculinity and crime, there is scant discussion of gendered power relations (either between men and women or among men) and how such power is connected to race and class and, eventually, crime.

Because of this lack of theoretical attention to power, Jefferson argues that social meaning is only and always the product of available discourses, not social structures. Indeed, for Jefferson, social structures disappear into an overabundance of discourses. Jefferson is interested in how individuals allegedly position themselves in relation to all of the so-called discursive choices facing them—that is, how they come to adopt particular "subject positions" and not others. The problem with this theoretical beginning is that we never learn from where all these alleged discourses come and, therefore, never learn of all the so-called available subject positions. In other words, what is the empirical base of discourse? In the Tyson example, where did the "tough guy" discourse originate? Jefferson ignores the fact that discourse is constructed through practice, is structurally connected with other practices, and has much in common with other forms of practice (Connell, 1987). Jefferson's perspective seems unable to demonstrate—indeed, is glaringly uninterested in—the source of the discourse in relation to which individuals allegedly position themselves. This is a major difficulty, because without such empirical verification, literally anything could be defined as discourse, depending on how the theorist chooses to interpret it.

Even within individual case studies such as that of Tyson, we do not learn specifically *how* the particular individual becomes "invested in" or "identified with" a certain discourse but not others or *when* that investment or identification takes place. What does it actually mean to become invested in or identified with a particular discourse? How does this investment or identification actually occur? What is the particular process? Because Tyson is part of the "specific sub-group of the category 'men'" that engages in crime, it seems imperative to grasp the various discourses available to the adolescent Tyson and why, when, and how he chose the "tough guy" discourse and rejected others. However, there is nothing built into Jefferson's perspective that permits selection among the various possibilities

of discourse in a particular social situation or when or how the subject invests or identifies with such discourses.

I agree that it is important to explain why particular men identify with the crime option and other men, from similar milieux, do not. Given Jefferson's parallel concern with this issue, one would expect this to be a priority in his research agenda. Surprisingly, he makes no attempt to address this topic. Other than his efforts at theory construction (e.g., Jefferson, 1994), in all of his published work to date, we are simply provided with individual case studies of boys' or men's involvement in crime, specifically, interpersonal violence. Consequently, Jefferson is unable to explain why individuals with very similar backgrounds—that is, positioned similarly with regard to available discursive choices and suffering similar anxieties—chose not to engage in crime. In other words, following the logic of Jefferson's perspective, it is not sufficient to point out that Tyson, for example, is anxiety driven and chose to adopt the "tough guy" discourse—it is necessary to specify why people in the same milieu as Tyson responded to similar anxieties in *noncriminal* ways. Fortunately, the vast majority of male youth in the ghetto who suffer similar biographical powerlessness and emotional malnourishment do not join gangs or engage in violence. Why don't they? What discourse do they adopt, and why did Tyson not adopt that alternative discourse? In short, Jefferson fails to investigate the effects of childhood powerlessness and emotional malnourishment on nonviolent boys and men, and he simultaneously ignores the range of masculine paths in Tyson's childhood milieu and the interconnections among these differing masculinities. Indeed, masculinity can only be understood in relation to the variety of masculinities in each social situation.

An additional problem is the psychoanalytic angle Jefferson attaches to discourse. As with his conception of discourse, he does not subject the "unconscious" process by which individuals allegedly split and project to empirical verification; he simply infers it. How then do we know that such splitting and projection take place? The only possible answer is that Jefferson says so. Arguably, such so-called psychic processes as the "unconscious," "splitting," and "projection" can never be the objects of direct observation. Therefore, these concepts can be constructed only by Jefferson, who, by giving a name and form to them (following Klein), does not discover them but simply creates them. Thus, as with most psychoanalytic theories, the alleged psychic processes can, for Jefferson, only be hypothetical and speculative, and therefore their validity is highly questionable. It is Jefferson who imagines (and thus contrives) what the empirical evidence cannot supply: that anxious individuals—like Mike Tyson—"unconsciously split and project." In short, Jefferson's identified psychoanalytic terms are nonmeasureable, and, consequently, his theory is nonfalsifiable.

Moreover, because (according to Jefferson) anxieties result from feelings of powerlessness, it should not be surprising to find that when he discusses men, he examines only those who at some point in their lives experienced extreme masculine powerlessness and subsequently became involved in interpersonal violence rather than those who experienced feelings of powerfulness and subsequently became involved in interpersonal violence. Because Jefferson concentrates on powerlessness (but, as stated earlier, ignores a reciprocal conception of power), his perspective is unable to account for boys and men who do not fit this stereotype—the powerful male who is full of self-confidence (and does not "feel" powerlessness) yet also engages in violence. Research shows that certain forms of violence may be associated with, for example, threatened egotism: "highly favorable views of self that are disputed by some person or circumstance" (Baumeister, Smart, & Boden, 1996, p. 5). When individuals who regard themselves as "superior beings" are challenged in some way, they may respond with physical violence. As Baumeister and colleagues (1996) have shown,

> Aggression emerges from a particular discrepancy between two views of self: a favorable self appraisal and an external appraisal that is much less favorable. That is, people turn aggressive when they receive feedback that contradicts their favorable views of themselves and implies that they should adopt less favorable views. More to the point, it is mainly people who refuse to lower their self-appraisals who become violent. (p. 8)

Consequently, although perhaps unintentionally, Jefferson's work reads as though no such self-confident males exist and therefore appears to assume that only certain males are "deviantly" anxiety driven, and that it is "those guys" who commit violence. Jefferson asks us to assume that all crimes committed by boys and men result from splitting and projection because of anxious powerlessness. In doing so, he reifies masculinity by arguing that it results from anxious powerlessness common to all violent men. Clearly, a satisfactory theory requires a more thoroughgoing appreciation of the varieties of masculinities and their relation to violence.

Moreover, Jefferson's concentration exclusively on interpersonal violence is problematic. Other crimes that are predominantly "male"—such as robbery, burglary, syndicated crime, and the varieties of corporate and political crimes—are underrepresented and therefore undertheorized in Jefferson's work. Thus, one is left with the impression that masculinity (and thus gender) matters only in crimes involving interpersonal violence. Or are we to assume that boys and men involved in crimes other than those involving interpersonal violence similarly experience anxious powerlessness and subsequently split and project prior to committing such crimes?

In addition, Jefferson only speaks of men and masculinity, ignoring the reality that women and girls sometimes do masculinity (as well as violence). As Hood-Williams (2001) asks, "Are we to believe that the genders really do constitute coherent, uniform categories whose social and psychic consequence is a perfect, homogenous binary?" (p. 39). In other words, there is nothing built into Jefferson's perspective that allows for the conceptualization of women, girls, masculinities, and crime. Consequently, his perspective reifies gender difference.

Finally, although Jefferson attempts a psychoanalytic interpretation of masculinity, the concepts he uses to analyze "unconscious" psychic processes—anxiety, splitting, and projection—have nothing to do with gender (Hood-Williams, 2001). As Hood-Williams points out, there is "nothing in the character or structuring of the psyche that explains sexual difference. That must come from elsewhere" (p. 52). And that elsewhere is, according to Hood-Williams, found in the social realm: Masculinity "does not express an inner, psychic core" but is the "performative work of acts, gestures, enactments" and, consequently, "this means recognizing that masculinity must be understood phenomenologically" (p. 53).

Jefferson (2001) most recently recognized that the Kleinian concepts he employs are gender-neutral terms, and, as he states, this forces him "into the realm of the social to explain sexual difference, but without denying the (irreducible) significance of the psyche" (p. 11). To connect psychic processes with the performance of masculinity (which means, for Jefferson, masculine practices by men, *not* by women), Jefferson initially turns to the work of Nancy Chodorow (1978) on the differential significance of maternal separation for boys and girls. Chodorow argues that because women typically are the primary caretakers of children—because of the unequal gender division of labor in child care—both boys and girls develop early, intense relations with the mother. When the time comes to separate from her, however, this separation process occurs in different ways for boys and girls. According to Chodorow, girls remain closer to the mother than do boys and, therefore, girls do not experience a sharp break from Mom. Consequently, girls achieve femininity by being like their mothers and internalize "feminine" characteristics, such as a capacity for empathy with, and dependence on, others—first their mother, later their spouse. For boys, becoming masculine requires their becoming different from mother and separating completely from her by repudiating all that is feminine. Consequently, boys fail to learn empathy for others and become fearful of intimacy and dependence. Boys' psyches, then, are well suited to being achievement oriented; girls' psyches are well adapted to emotional work. In this way, the gender division of labor in parenting is reproduced as boys become the breadwinners and girls become the primary caretakers of children. The unequal gender division of labor in parenting is reproduced in the psyches of individuals, and masculine dominance is reinforced.

Feminists have criticized Chodorow's thesis for being ahistorical, for falsely universalizing childhood experience, for ignoring differences of race and class, and for being incomplete as a theory of women's subordination because it does not explain how the gender division of labor in parenting emerged (Jaggar, 1983). In addition, Connell (1998, p. 457) points out that the reasons for the reproduction of this specific division of labor probably have little to do with psychology; more likely, they involve the economic costs to families from the loss of a man's wage. Connell goes on to point out—as has Chodorow (1994, 1999)—that a gender division of labor in parenting does not necessarily produce dichotomous gender patterns in later life.

It is perplexing why Jefferson now suddenly supports Chodorow's thesis. As is evident, Chodorow's work is a theory of the reproduction of a specific *social structure* and has nothing to say about *discourse.* This is particularly problematic because Jefferson, as stated earlier, argues that social structures disappear into an overabundance of discourses. Additionally, Jefferson (1998, p. 92) had previously rejected Chodorow's position as a much too general and sociological account of gender formation even though it retained psychoanalytic terminology. Although Jefferson (2001) more recently agreed that Chodorow's thesis is reductive and generalizing, he nevertheless feels that as "an internal process early psychic separation provides the (psychic) preconditions for entry into the (social) world of male domination" (p. 12). In an attempt to save his theory by overcoming the reductive character of Chodorow's perspective, unexpectedly, Jefferson turns to the work of Jessica Benjamin (1998) rather than Chodorow's (1999) most recent reformulation of her thesis.[2]

Benjamin (1998) argues that separation from mother into masculine dominance is but one path the boy may take, and it must be supplemented by an account of the father and the child's identification with him: "This redefines the preoedipal position as one characterized by multiple identifications with both mother and father (or substitutes) and what they symbolize" (Jefferson, 2001, p. 13). The universal task of the child now is not one-dimensional, but rather involves

> separating from a particular mother (and her particular relationship to gender) and learning to share her with a particular father (and his particular relationship to gender) against a backdrop of managing the inevitable excitement and anxiety generated by loving attachments, both the desire for (object love) and the desire to be like (identificatory love). The timing and management of these universal tasks will determine how any particular individual relates to questions of sexual difference. (p. 13)

Curiously, Jefferson's perspective abruptly ends here without showing how such "timing and management" of the so-called "universal tasks" result in different types of masculinity and how such masculinities eventually are related to crime. Moreover, Jefferson seems to assume a unilateral influence from individual parental figures in childhood to specific constructions of gender without providing any theoretical space for influences outside the family context—such as peers and teachers—or what agency the infant has in this interaction. Indeed, Jefferson neglects research on agency that specifically shows how infants are born into a world populated by self-regulating participants in the interactional achievement of masculinities and femininities. For example, this research suggests that through interaction with others, infants are exposed to gender "contingencies of reinforcement" and, as a result, infants exhibit specific but differentiated patterns of gendered behavior (Cahill, 1986, p. 170). In other words, for some time, research has explained early gender development in infancy not through separation anxiety but as a reflexive process between the infant and others' (parents', children's, and adults') mutual reinforcement.

Consequently, Jefferson's psychosocial theory begs the question: Does a psychoanalytic dimension add a necessary explanatory level to our understanding of masculinities and crime? Because of its sketchy and incomplete nature, as well as the numerous inherent problems associated with his perspective, as outlined, we can only conclude that it does not. (Indeed, Jefferson's [2003] most recent statement of his theory ignores gender altogether.) Instead, a satisfactory theory of masculinities and crime requires an understanding of the meanings boys and men attach to their social actions and how these actions are related to conscious choice and specific social structures in particular settings. It is to the latter that we now turn our attention.

DIFFERENCE, THE BODY, AND CRIME

Despite the problems inherent in psychoanalysis, Jefferson raises an important limitation of past masculinity and crime research: the failure to inquire why some boys and men engage in crime and other boys and men from the same milieu do not, and why those who do engage in crime commit different types of crimes. In addition, Collier (1998) pointed to a second oversight: the importance of the body

and its relation to crime. To these beneficial criticisms, it should be added that earlier work on masculinities and crime has not addressed adequately the relationship among masculinities, race, and class. In other words, to understand crime, we must comprehend how gender, race, and class relations are part of all social existence and not view each relation as extrinsic to the others. Because crime operates through a complex series of gender, race, and class practices, crime usually is more than a single activity. In this final section, then, I discuss some recent criminological work that has begun to address these criticisms.

For some time, criminologists have been attempting to conceptualize the "intersection" of gender, race, class, and crime. For example, 8 years ago, an edited volume by Schwartz and Milovanovic (1996) examined, as the title suggests, *Race, Gender, and Class in Criminology: The Intersection*. As well, Marino Bruce's (1997) work on youth crime specifically investigated the interrelation of race and class with the construction of masculinities by delinquent lower working class boys. Similarly, Mark Lettiere's (1997) ethnographic study of masculinities among African American, white, and Latino men in a homeless heroin-addict community showed how "doing begging" and "doing crime" are resources for "doing" different racialized masculinities and thus for constructing a power hierarchy among these men. Most recently, Barak, Flavin, and Leighton (2001) show how gender, race, and class affect the nature and functioning of the criminal justice system, and Jurik and Martin (2001) demonstrate historically how gender, race, class, and sexuality frame and organize work, specifically in policing and corrections. One of the difficulties criminological theorists have experienced is conceptualizing how gender, race, and class are linked or how they actually intersect. The attraction of Jurik and Martin's (2001) work is that they have shown conclusively how workplace social interaction constructs and reaffirms gender, race, and class differences.

A specific method for connecting social interaction with gender, race, class, and crime is the life history. The life history is an important qualitative method because it necessitates a close consideration of the meaning of social life for those who enact it as a way of revealing their experiences, choices, practices, and social world. No other social science method provides as much detail about social development and change as does a life-history study of practices over time.

In *Crime as Structured Action* (Messerschmidt, 1997), I explore, for example, the changes in Malcolm X's masculinities within a range of race and class social contexts: a childhood in which he constantly battled for acceptance as a young man; a zoot-suit culture that embraced him without stigma as a "hipster" and "hustler"; and a spiritual and political movement that celebrated him as father, husband, and national spokesperson. Across these sites and through shifting currencies of his sense of gender, race, and class, Malcolm X moved in and out of crime. Malcolm X simply appropriated crime as a resource for doing masculinity at a specific moment in his life, a period when gender, race, and class relations were equally significant. In this way, the life-history method provides data not only about why people engage in crime at certain stages of their lives but how that engagement relates to the salience of various combinations of gender, race, and class.[3]

My most recent research involves life-history interviews of violent and nonviolent boys and addresses the following questions: Why is it that some boys engage in violence and some boys do not? and Why do the boys who engage in violence commit different types of violence? (Messerschmidt, 2000). The goal of each interview was an attempt to reflect the situational accomplishment of masculinities and the eventual use of violence (or nonviolence) as an outcome of specific choices in a subject's personal life history.

Because of space constraints, I cannot discuss all of the life stories. However, for a taste of the data, I present the life stories of two of the boys interviewed—Hugh and Zack—who simultaneously lived in the same working class neighborhood and attended the same high school, yet took different paths: One became a sex offender and the other an assaultive offender. These two cases, then, are juxtaposed nicely because they report data as to why boys from the same social milieu come to engage in different types of violence. What follows is a brief outline of their life stories and how their differing forms of violence are related to their body, structured action, and masculinity.

Both boys grew up in working class homes that articulated for them a practiced definition of masculine power. In their separate families, Hugh and Zack found themselves in milieux in which they were attached to an adult male—Hugh to his grandfather and Zack to his uncle—who both emphasized hegemonic masculinity through practice. This attachment led both boys consciously to undertake to practice what was being preached and represented. Connell (1995) defines this proactive adoption of "family values" (such as manual and athletic skills and male power and control of others) as the "moment of engagement" with hegemonic masculinity, "the moment at which the boy takes up the project of hegemonic masculinity as his own" (p. 122). Although constructed in different ways, such moments of engagement occurred in both boys' lives through interaction—junctures when the individual boys consciously chose to engineer a newly professed masculinity. Moreover, for both Hugh and Zack, an important part of this engagement with hegemonic masculinity entailed a commitment to the "family value" that use of physical violence is an appropriate means to solve interpersonal problems. In other words, both boys chose to embrace the practice (constructed within their families and the school attended) that physical violence is the fitting and well-chosen masculine response to threat—a "real man" was obligated to respond in this fashion.[4] Although both boys were similar in the sense of accepting that the legitimate response to threat is physical retaliation, the differences between them surfaced during interactions at school.

We begin our examination of these differences with the case of Hugh, an assaultive, tall, and well-built 15-year-old. Hugh was rewarded with favorable appraisal from others for his physicality—at home from his grandfather, at school from other kids, and from his peers in the gang he joined. Consider the following dialogue about Hugh's fighting ability at school:

Q. What did the other kids think about you fighting?

A. Since I was a good fighter, everybody my age looked up to me, you know. I wasn't afraid to fight. I liked it. I was the only one my age who fought the older kids.

Q. How did that make you feel?

A. Better than the others.

Q. Why?

A. Always, ever since I can remember, I'd say I wasn't going to let anybody push me around. I was going to be like Gramps—a force in this world.

Q. Did you want to be like Gramps? Was he a force?

A. Yeah. He didn't let people push him around.

Q. Did the other kids think of you as a force?

A. They looked up to me, as I said. Because it wasn't about beating the older kids up or them beating me up. It was that I held my own. I didn't let people walk all over me. And they thought that was cool.

Q. Did you develop a reputation?

A. Yeah. I became that force, you know. In the back of kids' minds it would always be like, "Man, is this kid going to hit me?" So they didn't mess with me. I was strong and good with my fists, you know. (Messerschmidt, 2000, p. 53)

This dialogue discloses the intricate interplay of Hugh's body with the social processes of becoming a "force" at school. The social requirement to validate one as a masculine force—that is, physically fighting—is an embodied practice that connects specific bodily skill and competence ("good with my fists") with a predictable consequence to that practice ("they looked up to me" and "they thought that was cool"). Hugh consciously responded to masculinity challenges by constructing a bodily presence in school ("I held my own") that was revered by his classmates.

This construction of being a "force" eventually led Hugh to attacking teachers physically. Hugh expressed to me that the physical power he exerted on the playground gave him the confidence to challenge a teacher's power in the classroom under certain conditions. I asked Hugh for an example of when such violence might occur:

The teacher told me to do my work and I'd say: "I don't want to do my work." And then the teacher would say I had to, and then I'd throw my desk at him. I couldn't stay in class and do what I had to do. I was always getting in trouble. I was the one getting detention and stuff. I'd throw my desk and walk out, sayin' "Fuck you." (Messerschmidt, 2000, p. 54)

When I asked Hugh how it made him feel to respond that way, he stated,

It felt good. It was a sense of retaliation, you know. I was doing something about it. And after I got out of the principal, kids would pat me on the back. They all wanted to be my friend, you know. I had a reputation of not being pushed around by teachers, and I liked that. So I did it more. (Messerschmidt, 2000, p. 54)

Being tall and muscular for his age, Hugh's bodily resources empowered him to implement physically confrontational practices when he encountered masculinity challenges. His body served, in part, as agent and resource in his practice of embodied force; thus, Hugh embodied power at school through a calculated effort to present his body in a specific way.

For Hugh, then, his body *facilitated* masculine agency. In the face of masculinity challenges from other students and teachers, he successfully constructed himself as a "tough guy" who was "superior" to his victims—his assaultive acts enforced and shaped masculine boundaries. Indeed, his physical ability to fight when provoked convinced him of his own eminent masculine self-worth. His bodily resources empowered him to implement a physically confrontational masculinity, permitted him to resist the school physically, and enabled him to construct specific behavior patterns—acting out in class, bullying other students, and assaulting students and teachers. Thus, within the social setting of the school, Hugh's body became his primary resource for masculine power and esteem and simultaneously constructed his victims as subordinate.

In certain ways, Hugh was following the bodily dictates of the school social structure in which he was embedded. Research shows that in junior high and high school, the tallest and strongest boys are usually the most popular, admired by peers (and parents and teachers) for their size and athletic prowess (Thorne, 1993). In the context of school, a boy's height and musculature increase self-esteem and prestige, thus creating a more positive body image (Thorne, 1993). Research on male adolescent development reveals that boys are acutely aware of the changes in themselves during puberty, as well as other people's responses to those changes (Petersen, 1988). Boys who participate in sports, for example, state that "they take pleasure in their agency and their bodies simultaneously. They feel like they accomplish things in their bodies and in their lives" (Martin, 1996, p. 55).

As the testimonial indicates, Hugh had a very similar response to his embodied practices. Most of the time, Hugh's attention did not focus on his own embodiment; it was simply taken for granted. However, in times of verbally antagonistic and physically confrontational interactions at home and school—that is, during masculinity challenges—the body now became the central aspect of Hugh's attention and experience. Indeed, for Hugh, the body seized center stage and acted—because of its physical size, shape, and skill—according to his chosen masculine goal of being a force in the world. In other words, during these interactions entailing masculinity challenges, both gender and body were highly salient—they became the object of his practice. Moreover, his body facilitated masculine social action—it was a successful masculine resource—by creating boundaries between Hugh and his numerous victims.

Additionally, the embodied practices of Hugh show that such practices are intersubjective. That is, the space in which Hugh's assaultive actions occurred was occupied by others; and it is these others, in part, toward whom the assaultive actions were intended. As Crossley (1995) argues, embodied social action is "other oriented" and derives its sense or meaning from its participation in shared situations: Embodied action is "not only acting-towards-others; it is acting-towards-others in a way that is acceptable to others (in general) by virtue of its reliance upon commonly held rules and resources, and its observance of ritual considerations" (pp. 141-142). Hugh's assaultive actions, then, were accomplished in accordance with a shared masculine subjectivity of others who populated the same school and home space where the assaultive actions occurred.

But boys unlike Hugh—specifically, boys who do not possess the appropriate body shape and size and thus are unable to use their bodies in the physical ways proposed by the school social structure—frequently experience distress (Petersen, 1988). In the teen world, bodies are subject increasingly to inspection and surveillance by peers; and less muscular, nonathletic boys are often labeled "wimps" and "fags"

(Kindlon & Thompson, 1999). In junior high and high school, masculine social hierarchies develop in relation to somatic type. Such somatic differentiation affirms inequality among boys, and in this way, diverse masculinities are constructed in relation to biological development (Canaan, 1998; Connell, 1987, 1995; Thorne, 1993). The relationship among these masculinities forms a specific social structure within the social setting of the school. For example, in most secondary schools, we are likely to find power relations between hegemonic masculinities (i.e., "cool guys," "tough guys," and "jocks") and subordinated masculinities (i.e., gay boys, "wimps," and "nerds"). Ethnographies of secondary education in Britain, Australia, and the United Sates consistently report such masculine power relationships, which construct a specific social structure in secondary schools (see Connell, 1996, for a review). In short, today the body increasingly has become crucial to self-image, especially among teenage youth. Through interaction at school, adolescents make bodies matter by constructing some bodies as more masculine than other bodies; thus, social structures are embodied.

Although Hugh's embodied practices represent hegemonic or exemplary masculinities at school, I found subordinate school masculinities in several of the adolescent male sex offenders I interviewed. Consider the case of Zack, who was 15 years old when I interviewed him. When he was in third grade, he gained a considerable amount of weight, and other students considered him "fat," as did he. The "cool guys" at school consistently verbally and physically abused Zack: "They'd call me 'fatty,' 'chubby cheeks,' 'wimp,' and stuff like that. I got pushed down a lot and stuff. I got beat up a lot in the schoolyard" (Messerschmidt, 2000, p. 42). The abuse for being overweight and the constant physical assault extended through grade school and middle school. Unlike some other kids at school, Zack chose not to respond physically to these masculinity challenges because he felt he would be "beat up." As Zack stated,

> I felt like I was a "wimp" 'cause I couldn't do what other boys did. I never could in my life. I couldn't do anything. Other people always told me what to do, I never told anybody. I felt pretty crappy about myself. (Messerschmidt, 2000, p. 43)

Consequently, the peer abuse at school exerted a masculinity challenge, and, subsequently, Zack attempted to invalidate his status as a "wimp" by joining the junior high football team. As Zack stated, "It would make me feel like I was actually worth something, like other guys, you know" (Messerschmidt, 2000, p. 43). However, during the summer, between fifth and sixth grades, Zack broke his wrist while attempting to "get in shape." He remained overweight, and although he tried out for the team in his sixth grade year, he was soon cut.

Also during his sixth grade year, Zack developed a sexual interest in girls. He learned this not from the adults in his life but through interaction at school. Because of the frequent "sex talk" at school, Zack wanted to experience sex to be like the other boys. Because Zack had never been able to arrange a date, he felt extremely "left out" and identified himself as a "virgin." The continual rejection by girls made Zack feel discontented: "I didn't really like myself 'cause girls didn't like me. I was fat and I just didn't seem to fit in. Like I'm the only virgin in the school."

Q.   Did you want to fit in?

A.   Yeah. And I tried really hard. I tried to play football so the popular guys would like me. I tried to dress differently, dress like they [popular kids] did. I tried going on diets. I tried to get girls. (Messerschmidt, 2000, p. 45)

Prior to the masculinity challenges he faced at school, Zack did not think much about his body. However, Zack's body became *much more a part of* his lived experience. This resulted in his body becoming a site of intersubjective disdain through interaction at school that led inevitably to his negative self-conceptualization. In turn, Zack made the conscious choice—to help fulfill his goal to be masculine—to attempt to "fit in" by reconstructing his body: He tried to get into shape to play football, dress "cool at school," and go on diets. In other words, Zack's body became an object of his practice as a result of its socially constructed subordinated presence. Zack actively worked on his body in an attempt to mold it into an "appropriate" gendered body for the particular school setting. Thus, his physical sense of masculinity was in part derived from his attempt to transform his body through social practices (Connell, 1987).

In addition to this disciplined management of his body, Zack consciously attempted to obtain heterosexual dates. In all such attempts, however, he failed miserably.

Unable to be masculine like the "cool guys," the masculinity challenges exerted greater pressure on Zack, and he eventually turned to expressing control and power over his youngest female cousin through sex. During his sixth grade year—a time when he experienced the distressing events just described and "discovered" heterosexuality—Zack consciously chose to seek out his cousin: "I wanted to experience sex, like what other boys were doing. I wanted to do what they were talking about but I was rejected by girls at school" (Messerschmidt, 2000, p. 46). Zack sexually assaulted (fondling and oral penetration) his youngest cousin over a 3-year period by using a variety of seemingly nonviolent manipulative strategies. I asked Zack how it made him feel when he manipulated his cousin, and he stated, "It made me feel real good. I just felt like finally I was in control over somebody. I forgot about being fat and ugly. She was someone looking up to me, you know. If I needed sexual contact, then I had it. I wasn't a virgin anymore" (Messerschmidt, 2000, p. 47).

Zack saw himself as not "measuring up" physically to the school view of the ideal masculine body. Consequently, his body was a *restraint* on his agency—he could not do the masculine practices the "cool guys" were doing, including "fighting back" when bullied and engaging in sex with peers. Moreover, his immediate situation at school was seen by him as a dangerous place, as he inhabited the most subordinate position in the masculine power social structure of the school. Consequently, the embodied practices activated by the contextual interactions at school could be directed only outside the school situation. Zack's body became party to a surrogate practice that directed him toward a course of social action that was physically and sexually realizable. For Zack, then, the dominant masculine practices in school were not rejected. Rather, physical and sexual subordination directed Zack toward consciously fixating not only on his body, but on a specific site (the home) and a particular form of embodied conduct (sexual violence) where such masculine practices could be realized. Given that Zack was removed from any type of recognized masculine bodily status in school, the available sexual "outlet" at home was especially seductive and captivating, became an obsession, and was a powerful and pleasurable means of being masculine. In attempting to masculinize and heterosexualize his body within the captivating conceptualization of "cool guy" masculinity, Zack engendered a powerful sense of self by consciously "taking charge" at home and conquering his cousin's body through sexual violence. The choice to be sexually violent, then, was a situational masculine resource in which Zack could be dominant, powerful, and heterosexual through bodily practice. Thus, it was in this way that Zack's body shared in his social agency by shaping and generating his course of action toward sexual violence.

For Zack, then, the peer abuse and inability to "be a man" according to the social structure of the school brought about an absolute split between his subordinate masculinity and the masculinity of other boys—in particular, the "cool guys"—at school. Such, however, is not the case for Hugh. Although engaging in assaultive violence—as Hugh did—placed the body at center stage, it did not disrupt his masculine reality but rather confirmed it; his body was a superordinate masculine presence at school. Indeed, within the social context of Hugh's and Zack's school, such practices as physically fighting are experienced as part of masculine life, not placed outside it. Consequently, these acts maintain intentional links with other boys and reproduce the masculine school social structure of power—their success at assaultive actions enforced the boundary between hegemonic and subordinate masculinities. In contrast, Zack's habitual masculine world was disrupted and correlated with a new relation to his body—it now became a subordinate masculine presence at school. Thus, although Hugh's embodied violent actions are interwoven with others in a common masculine project, Zack constituted embodied subordination in the masculine power hierarchy at school. The result is that Zack experienced social isolation and a telic demand to be free from his subordinate masculine situation— which he "satisfied" through sexual violence.

In short, the interactions experienced by Hugh and Zack at school were situational moments marked by masculinity challenges in which each boy was defined as a rival to other boys, entailing a socially distant, hostile, and power relationship among them. For Zack, however, heterosexual meanings added to the power divide among boys. Yet in the brief, illusory moment of each sexually violent incident—in which the sex offender practiced spatial and physical dominance over his cousin—Zack was a "cool guy"; the subordinate was now the dominant.

CONCLUSION

Psychoanalysis provides little help in understanding these life stories and embodied practices. The goal for both Hugh and Zack was hegemonic masculinity and being a "cool guy" who could solve problems through interpersonal violence. In Sartre's (1956) words, this was their "fundamental choice," or the gendered attitude they took toward the world. Accordingly, both boys engaged in a *conscious choice* to pursue hegemonic masculinity (defined by the practices in their particular milieu of home and school) as their project, or the fundamental mode by which they chose to relate to the world and express themselves in it. Hugh and Zack's behavior, then, is best understood from the point of view of their socially structured, consciously chosen project rather than from some alleged yet spurious "unconscious" motivation. To appreciate why Hugh and Zack engaged in violence, we must first discover the planned project for both. This is the basic difference between the method employed here and that of Jefferson. Jefferson attempts to comprehend the person in light of "unconscious" antecedents; following Sartre (1956, 1963), I understand the person in light of his conscious choices—in particular, social situations—as he pursues future-oriented projects.

Additionally, the case studies of Hugh and Zack demonstrate that the materiality of bodies often matters in the pursuit of a project. Bodies participate in social action by delineating courses of social conduct: "Bodies in their materiality have both limits and capacities which are always in play in social processes" (Connell, 1998a, p. 6). Indeed, our bodies constrain or facilitate social action and therefore mediate and influence social practices. It is not surprising that it was through masculinity challenges—that is, when both body and gender became highly salient as organizing principles of interaction—and subsequent bodily and sexual subordination (Zack) or superordination (Hugh) that choice and behavior became focused in the specific direction of sexual violence (Zack) or assaultive violence (Hugh). The masculine social structure of the school each boy attended defined both physical and sexual performance as essential criteria for "doing masculinity." Thus, these dominant criteria—within the context of a body either able or unable to construct such criteria—directed the boys' ultimate choices of a specific type of violence and victimization. Nevertheless, both boys viewed their bodies as instruments—weapons in the service of a desire to dominate and control another body through a particular type of interpersonal violence. Accordingly, these two case studies help us understand the relationship among the body, masculinities, and differing types of violence.

Although not generalizable, these two case studies provide additional justification for structured action theory. It was the social structural power relations among differing masculinities at school that made the masculinity challenges and differing forms of violence possible, but not necessarily inevitable. The agency of Hugh and Zack, their interactions within that structure, and their ultimate conscious choices made the masculinity challenges and interpersonal violence happen—which, in turn, reproduced that masculine power social structure. Indeed, one way gender is built into institutions—such as schools—is through hierarchical divisions of masculine power. This particular power hierarchy was a regular and patterned form of interaction that constrained and channeled how the two boys conceptualized and chose to practice masculinity. The school masculine power relations became a constitutive principle of their masculine "identity" through being adopted as a personal project. Thus, the masculine personality of Hugh and Zack existed only as social actions fashioned in accordance with the school power hierarchy. Hugh reproduced a specific form of hegemonic masculinity through assaultive violence. Zack, although choosing to passively maintain his subordinate status within the confines of the school, actively attempted to invalidate that status for himself through sexual violence at home.

In closing, let me suggest some avenues for future research.

First, the current movement in criminology toward conceptualizing the interrelationship among gender, race, class, sexualities, and crime is an important direction for future research. Structured action theory provides *one* way to examine that interrelationship. Others will emerge. Moreover, we need a variety of methodological approaches, from historical and documentary research to ethnographies and life histories, to examine how gender, race, class, and sexuality differently affect crime.

Second, I do not suggest that the body is always salient to the commission of crime. Thus, we should investigate empirically when the body becomes salient to crime and when it does not. In other words, an important question for future research is, What is the relationship among the body, masculinities, and crime?

Third, because Connell (2000) correctly notes that "gender is social practice that constantly refers to bodies and what bodies do, it is not social practice reduced to the body" (p. 27), it follows that masculinities occasionally are enacted by girls and women. Consequently, an important research direction is the relationship between masculinities and crime by girls and women. Indeed, Jody Miller's (2001) important book *One of the Guys* points in this direction by showing how some gang girls consider the gang a "masculine enterprise" in which they participate in practices similar to those of the boys.[5]

Fourth, a new area of criminological study is globalization and crime. Criminological research on gender can contribute to this subject matter by examining how masculinities are related to crime in different societies and how they are linked to historical and contemporary conditions of globalization. Moreover, understanding masculinities and crime in industrialized societies (such as the United States) can be enhanced through a conceptualization of how globalization affects social conditions and thus crime in such societies. Simon Winlow's (2001) book, *Badfellas*, which examines the changes in masculinities and crime in the northeast of England since the 1880s and how those changes are related to globalization, has initiated the research in this area.

Fifth, how gender is constructed by criminal justice personnel is essential to understanding social control in industrialized societies. Jurik and Martin (2001), for example, have been prominent in this regard by showing specifically how the transformation of policing and corrections into professional occupations evinces a modification of hegemonic masculinity from being interpersonally and physically aggressive to wielding control through technical expertise. Moreover, in the important new book *Prison Masculinities,* Sabo et al. (2001) demonstrate, through the words of prisoners and academics, the varieties of masculinities constructed within that closed social setting.

Sixth, postmodern feminist criminologists have disclosed the importance of discourse analysis to the understanding of cultural conceptions of gender and crime (Collier, 1998; Young, 1996). The results of these researches are important, but it is essential to recognize, as stated earlier, that discourse is the result of practice. The work of Gray Cavender (1999) is prominent in this regard. For example, in "Detecting Masculinity," Cavender (1999) shows how masculinities are constructed differently in feature films by reason of historical context—1940s versus 1980s—and discourses that male actors practice as "detectives" in each of the films. We need more research that is similarly sensitive to how practice in particular social settings constructs discourse.

Finally, it is important to examine why some people engage in crime and others do not. A significant task, then, for future research is to discover what type of masculinity people construct who do not commit crime and how it is different from the gender of those who do commit crime.

In short, I recommend these as the chief areas of focus for those working in the area of masculinities and crime. All such studies seek to engage the demanding empirical inquiries that confidently will lead to theoretical reappraisal and, inevitably, to advances in theory.

NOTES

1. For a postmodern position on masculinities and crime, see Collier (1998). For a critique of this position, see Messerschmidt (1999).

2. Either Jefferson does not know about this work or he rejects it simply because Chodorow is critical of discourse analysis.

3. *Crime as Structured Action* discusses numerous cases in which race, class, and masculinities affect crime. Additionally, the chapter on "lynchers" is unique in criminology through its examination of the role "whiteness" may play in crime.

4. "Violence to solve problems" clearly is a discourse but is rooted—for Hugh and Zack—in the structured actions of home and school.

5. See Messerschmidt (2004) for an examination of the similarities and differences of violent and nonviolent masculinities by both boys and girls.

REFERENCES

Barak, G., Flavin, J. M., & Leighton, P. S. (2001). *Class, race, gender, and crime: Social realities of justice in America.* Los Angeles: Roxbury.

Baumeister, R. F., Smart, L., & Boden, J. M. (1996). Relation of threatened egotism to violence and aggression: The dark side of high self-esteem. *Psychological Review, 103*(1), 5-33.

Benjamin, J. (1998). *Shadow of the other: Intersubjectivity and gender in psychoanalysis.* New York: Routledge.

Bowker, L. (Ed.). (1998). *Masculinities and violence.* Thousand Oaks, CA: Sage.

Bruce, M. (1997, November). *Party animals and badasses: Evidence of the gender, race and class nexus.* Presented at the Annual Meeting of the American Society of Criminology, San Diego, CA.

Cahill, S. E. (1986). Childhood socialization as a recruitment process: Some lessons from the study of gender development. In P. A. Adler & P. Adler (Eds.), *Sociological studies of child development* (pp. 163-186). Greenwich, CT: JAI Press.

Canaan, J. (1998). Is "doing nothing" just boys' play? Integrating feminist and cultural studies: Perspectives on working-class young men's masculinity. In K. Daly & L. Maher (Eds.), *Criminology at the crossroads: Feminist readings in crime and justice* (pp. 172-187). New York: Oxford University Press.

Carlen, P., & Jefferson, T. (1996). (Eds.). Masculinities and crime. *British Journal of Criminology, 33*(6, Special issue).

Cavender, G. (1999). Detecting masculinity. In J. Ferrell & N. Websdale (Eds.), *Making trouble: Cultural constructions of crime, deviance, and control* (pp. 157-175). New York: Aldine de Gruyter.

Chodorow, N. J. (1978). *The reproduction of mothering.* Berkeley: University of California Press.

Chodorow, N. J. (1994). *Femininities, masculinities, sexualities: Freud and beyond.* Lexington: University of Kentucky Press.

Chodorow, N. J. (1999). *The power of feelings: Personal meaning in psychoanalysis, gender, and culture.* New Haven, CT: Yale University Press.

Collier, R. (1998). *Masculinities, crime and criminology: Men, heterosexuality and the criminal(ised) other.* London: Sage.

Connell, R. W. (1987). *Gender and power: Society, the person, and sexual politics.* Stanford, CA: Stanford University Press.

Connell, R. W. (1995). *Masculinities.* Berkeley: University of California Press.

Connell, R. W. (1996). Teaching the boys: New research on masculinity and gender strategies for schools. *Teachers College Record, 98*(2), 206-235.

Connell, R. W. (1998a). *Bodies, intellectuals, and world society.* Plenary address to British Sociological Association and Annual Conference, Edinburgh, Scotland

Connell, R. W. (2000). *The men and the boys.* Sydney: Allen & Unwin.

Crossley, N. (1995). Body techniques, agency and intercorporeality: On Goffman's *Relations in Public. Sociology, 29*(1), 133-149.

Daly, K., & Chesney-Lind, M. (1988). Feminism and criminology. *Justice Quarterly, 5*(4), 497-538.

Giddens, A. (1976). *New rules of sociological method: A positive critique of interpretive sociologies.* New York: Basic Books.

Giddens, A. (1981). Agency, institution, and time-space analysis. In K. Knorr-Cetina & A. V. Cicourel (Eds.), *Advances in social theory and methodology: Toward an integration of micro- and macro-sociologies* (pp. 161-174). Boston, MA: Routledge.

Giddens, A. (1989). A reply to my critics. In D. Held & J. B. Thompson (Eds.), *Social theories of modern societies: Anthony Giddens and his critics* (pp. 249-301). New York: Cambridge University Press.

Hobbs, D. (1995). *Bad business: Professional crime in modern Britain.* New York: Oxford University Press.

Hood-Williams, J. (2001). Gender, masculinities and crime: From structures to psyches. *Theoretical Criminology, 5*(1), 37-60.

Jaggar, A. (1983). *Feminist politics and human nature.* Totowa, NJ: Rowman and Allanheld.

Jefferson, T. (1994). Theorizing masculine subjectivity. In T. Newburn & E. A. Stanko (Eds.), *Just boys doing business? Men, masculinities and crime* (pp. 10-31). New York: Routledge.

Jefferson, T. (1996a). From "little fairy boy" to "the complete destroyer": Subjectivity and transformation in the biography of Mike Tyson. In M. Mac an Ghaill (Ed.), *Understanding masculinities* (pp. 153-167). Philadelphia, PA: Open University Press.

Jefferson, T. (1996b). Introduction. *British Journal of Criminology, 36*(6), 337-347.

Jefferson, T. (1996c). "Tougher than the rest": Mike Tyson and the destructive desires of masculinity. *ARENA Journal, 6*, 89-105.

Jefferson, T. (1997a). Masculinities and crime. In M. Maguire, R. Morgan, & R. Reiner (Eds.), *The Oxford handbook of criminology* (pp. 535-557). Oxford, England: Clarendon Press.

Jefferson, T. (1997b). The Tyson rape trial: The law, feminism and emotional "truth." *Social and Legal Studies, 6*(2), 281-301.

Jefferson, T. (1998). "Muscle," "hard men," and "iron" Mike Tyson: Reflections on desire, anxiety, and the embodiment of masculinity. *Body and Society, 4*(1), 77-98.

Jefferson, T. (2001, January). *Subordinating hegemonic masculinity.* Keynote address presented at the Australian and New Zealand Annual Criminology Conference, Melbourne, Australia.

Jefferson, T. (2003). For a psychosocial criminology. In K. Carrington & R. Hogg (Eds.), *Critical criminology: Issues, debates, challenges* (pp. 145-167). London: Willan.

Jurik, N. C., & Martin, S. E. (2001). Femininities, masculinities, and organizational conflict: Women in criminal justice occupations. In C. M. Renzetti & L. Goodstein (Eds.), *Women, crime and criminal justice: Original feminist readings* (pp. 264-281). Los Angeles: Roxbury.

Kindlon, D., & Thompson, M. (1999). *Raising Cain: Protecting the emotional life of boys.* New York: Ballantine.

Lettiere, M. (1997, November). *"I'm gettin' a lick 'cus I ain't no white bitch": Racialized masculinities and crime among San Francisco's homeless heroin addicts.* Paper presented at the Annual Meeting of the American Society of Criminology, San Diego, CA.

Martin, K. A. (1996). *Puberty, sexuality, and the self: Boys and girls at adolescence.* New York: Routledge.

Messerschmidt, J. W. (1993). *Masculinities and crime: Critique and reconceptualization of theory.* Lanham, MD: Rowman & Littlefield.

Messerschmidt, J. W. (1997). *Crime as structured action: Gender, race, class, and crime in the making.* Thousand Oaks, CA: Sage.

Messerschmidt, J. W. (1999). *Masculinities, Crime and Criminology* by Richard Collier (Review). *Theoretical Criminology, 3*(2), 246-249.

Messerschmidt, J. W. (2000). *Nine lives: Adolescent masculinities, the body, and violence.* Boulder, CO: Westview.

Messerschmidt, J. W. (2004). *Embodied masculinities, embodied violence: Boys, girls, the body, and assault.* Lanham, MD: Rowman & Littlefield.

Miller, J. (2001). *One of the guys: Girls, gangs, and gender.* New York: Oxford University Press.

Naffine, N. (Ed.). (1995). *Gender, crime, and feminism.* Brookfield, MA: Dartmouth University Press.

Newburn, T., & Stanko, E. A. (1994). *Just boys doing business? Men, masculinities and crime.* London: Routledge.

Petersen, A. C. (1988). Adolescent development. *Annual Review of Psychology, 39*, 583-607.

Polk, K. (1994). *When men kill: Scenarios of masculine violence.* New York: Cambridge University Press.

Sabo, D., Kupers, T. A., & London, W. (Eds.). (2001). *Prison masculinities.* Philadelphia, PA: Temple University Press.

Sartre, J. P. (1956). *Being and nothingness.* New York: Washington Square Press.

Sartre, J. P. (1963). *Search for a method.* New York: Alfred A. Knopf.

Schwartz, M. D., & Milovanovic, D. (Eds.). (1996). *Race, gender, and class in criminology: The intersection.* New York: Garland.

Thorne, B. (1993). *Gender play: Girls and boys in school.* New Brunswick, NJ: Rutgers University Press.

West, C., & Zimmerman, D. H. (1987). Doing gender. *Gender and Society, 1*(2), 125-151.

Winlow, S. (2001). *Badfellas: Crime, tradition and new masculinities.* New York: Berg.

Young, A. (1996). *Imagining crime: Textual outlaws and criminal conversations.* Thousand Oaks, CA: Sage.

13

MASCULINITIES IN EDUCATION

JON SWAIN

Boys negotiate and perform different versions of masculinity in a range of social and cultural situations, such as families, neighborhoods, schools, sport, popular media and culture, commodified style cultures, labor markets, and so on, and each of these sites offers boys ways of constructing appropriate ways of being male and possibilities for forming views of themselves and relations with others. The meanings, ideas, attitudes, and beliefs that are generated in each area interrelate and are carried over to the others, but this chapter sets out to consider the education system and, in particular, how school processes and the meanings and practices found within the school setting contribute to, and help form, young boys' masculinities. Many researchers writing on adolescent boys in secondary school have played down the role of schooling in the formation of masculinities for men (see, for example, Connell, 1989; Walker, 1988). Indeed, for Connell (1989), the "childhood family, the adult workplace or sexual relationships (including marriage)" (p. 301) are more important influences, but, as Skelton (2001) persuasively points out, these last two areas have far less immediate relevance for younger children, and so it is possible to conclude that the school plays a relatively more prominent role in the construction of identity for boys in primary and early secondary schooling.

This chapter argues that schooling affords boys a number of different opportunities to construct different masculinities that draw on the localized resources and strategies available. I examine current theories of masculinities and the powerful influence of boys' peer groups and discuss issues of subordination and homophobia, boys' relations with girls, and the place of the body in the enactment of masculinity.

The English public schools of the early 19th century were set up with the express intention of teaching boys about how to be male and how to become a (Christian) man (Connell, 2000; Heward, 1988). Until the last 50 years or so, these schools were unconcerned with meritocracy or academic qualifications and saw their main function as the preparation of a high proportion of their pupils for the armed services or the financial world of the city. Schooling in formerly British colonies has also been profoundly influenced by English models. In countries such as Australia, New Zealand, Canada, the United States, India, and South Africa, systems of schooling (at least for the elite) were consciously based on the English public school design, and this produced boys in the image of the metropolitan gentlemen with all the failings of misogyny, homophobia, and emotional repression (Epstein, 1998a; Morrell, 1994). Mass systems of schooling for the indigenous or colonized people were also modeled on metropolitan designs. In some places, educational experiences (such as the "Bantu Education" introduced in South Africa in 1955) were unfulfilling and violent, with an authoritarian pedagogy underwritten with corporal punishment. This produced patterns of masculinity that promoted toughness, gender inequality, and repression (Hyslop, 1999; Morrell, 2001).

Despite the fact that schooling has, historically, been connected with gender, the issue of gender in schools was largely ignored until the second wave of feminism in the 1980s (Rendel, 1985), when it came onto the agenda as an equity issue. Skelton (2001) points out that early studies of boys and schooling in the late 1970s tended to emphasize gender as difference *between* girls and boys, and it has only been since the late 1980s that researchers have begun to focus on the multiple differences *within* each gender group.[1] Since then, there has been a growing body of research into the effects and impact of masculinities in educational settings across both phases of schooling,[2] although the majority of these studies tends to focus on adolescent males in secondary schools. These texts provide us with a series of well-argued theoretical frameworks that allow us to both understand and explore how masculinities suffuse school regimes and recognize how schooling not only *reproduces* but also *produces* gender identities, although not always in ways that are either straightforward or transparent. Some writers describe schools as a "masculinity factory" (Heward, 1996, p. 39), or as "masculinity-making devices" (Connell, 1989, p. 291; Haywood & Mac an Ghaill, 1996, p. 59), where boys learn that there are a number of different, and often competing, ways of being a boy and that some of these are more cherished and prestigious, and therefore more powerful, than others (Kenway & Willis, 1998).

We live in an unequal society, and schooling is a political issue that plays a role in wider social developments. Schools exist, of course, within their own structural contexts, including the structure of their national education system, and these pressures have a profound influence on schools' policies and organizations, as "macro" interactions are enacted on the "micro" stage. For instance, in poorer countries, many schools are severely underresourced, access can be limited, and absenteeism high. Schooling is rarely free, making it difficult for lower income

groups to attain competitive levels of education, and it is also gender biased in the sense that boys are likely to get more schooling, and be educated to higher levels, than girls (Pong, 1999). In 1999, 120 million primary school–age children were not in school, 53% of them girls and 47% of them boys (UNICEF, 2001, p. 10). Schools may also have a curriculum hostile to local knowledge and culture, and the labor market has a greater purchase on what is taught and on how the schools function. Indeed, in many developing countries (and in some industrialized countries as well), child labor is a serious problem that severely limits children's educational opportunities.[3]

DISCURSIVE FIELDS IN U.K. EDUCATION

In the case of the United Kingdom, the central tenet of the postwar educational consensus was that the function of the education system was for the development of economic growth, to regulate and maintain the status quo, and to produce citizens fit to take their place in society; but there has also been a movement that emphasizes schooling for the purpose of delivering emancipation and producing social change toward a fairer, more equitable society (see Gordon, Holland, & Lahelma, 2000; Haywood & Mac an Ghaill, 1996). These expectations can overlap and be contradictory, but in recent years, there has been a fundamental restructuring of U.K. state schooling; in the New Right agenda that came to the fore in the early 1980s, the school has found itself located in and incorporated into a competitive marketplace (Power & Whitty, 1999).[4] When I came into teaching in 1979, my first school was still dominated by the child-centered discourses popular in the late 1960s through the late 1970s. There was an ideological language that Alexander (1988) refers to as "primaryspeak" (p. 148), and it was used as a power base for heads and advisers. It exerted a subtle but irresistible pressure, and you needed to learn and use its slogans and shibboleths to gain legitimacy and, dare I say, promotion. Some of the most salient pedagogic terms were (in alphabetical order) activities, apprenticeship, choice, cooperation, curiosity, developmental, display, facilitator, fascination, flexibility, freedom, group work, growth, in depth, integrated day,[5] natural, nurturing, Piaget, potential, progress, quality, stage of development, understanding, and workshop.

Twenty years later and schools are now pervaded by an alternative and powerful discourse of competitive corporate management. The dominant educational phrases of the late 1990s through the early 21st century are "school effectiveness" and "raising school standards" (Weiner, Arnot, & David, 1997). Again, it may be interesting to examine more closely some of the other terms and phrases that have infiltrated the language of education and schooling, taking note of the "bellicose" language and imagery (Raphael Reed, 1998). For example (and again in alphabetical order), achievement, accountability, action zones, assessment, attainment, best practice, boys' underachievement, comparisons, competition, effectiveness, evaluations, examinations, hit squads, improvement, inspection, learning opportunities, learning outcomes, measurement, monitoring, National Curriculum, OFSTED,[6] outcomes, performance, performance-related pay, planning, results, rigorous, SATs,[7] setting, shame and blame, standards, streaming, target setting, testing, 3 Rs,[8] whole-class teaching, whole-school approach, and zero tolerance.[9]

Under the current discourses of "school effectiveness" and "raising standards," Pollard and Filer (1999) point out that the assumption is that if standards are to rise, the curriculum must be taught more effectively, and there is little attempt to engage with pupils as learners per se. All the talk is of "better teaching" and a "better delivery of the curriculum," and in this account, the pupil is like a commodity with a relative value. Pollard and Filer (1999) contend that "education . . . is something which is done *to* children, not *with* children, and still less *by* children" (p. 21).

SCHOOLS AS INSTITUTIONS

Hansot and Tyack (1998) maintain that to understand gender in school, we need to "think institutionally" (see also Salisbury & Jackson, 1996). For Connell (1996), "gender is embedded in the institutional arrangements by which a school functions" (p. 213), which Kessler, Ashenden, Connell, and Dowsett (1985) refer to as the school's *gender regime:*

> This may be defined as the pattern of practices that constructs various kinds of masculinity and

femininity among staff and students, orders them in terms of prestige and power, and constructs a sexual division of labor within the institution. The gender regime is a state of play rather than a permanent condition. It can be changed deliberately or otherwise, but is no less powerful in its effects on pupils for that. It confronts them as a social fact, which they have to come to terms with somehow. (p. 42)

Schools are invariably hierarchical and create and sustain relations of domination and subordination; each orders certain practices in terms of power and prestige as it defines its own distinct gender regime. Although schools are located and shaped by specific sociocultural, politicoeconomic, and historical conditions, individual personnel, reproduced rules, routines and expectations, and the school's own use of resources and space will all have a profound impact on (and can make a substantive difference in) the way in which young boys (and girls) live and experience their lives at school. This means that there are different options and opportunities to perform different types of masculinity in each school; in other words, there are different alternatives, or possibilities, of *doing boy* that are contingent to each school setting, using the meanings and practices available. Some of these ways will be easier (or more open) to achieve than others, some less easy (or more restricted), and others almost impossible to access (closed). For example, sporty types of masculinity will be easier to achieve and perform in a school that sanctions competitive sport than in a school that bans, say, football; the opportunity of accruing prowess through wearing the latest training shoes will be virtually eliminated in a school that enforces a strict uniform policy.

MASCULINIZING PRACTICES

To understand the range of processes and practices involving the ways that boys are able to construct their masculine identities, some researchers have identified and differentiated between the official or formal and the unofficial or informal cultures of the school (see, for example, Connell, Ashenden, Kessler, & Dowsett, 1982; Gordon et al., 2000; Pollard, 1985), although they define them in slightly different ways. These two layers are intertwined in everyday school life and are not fixed but, rather, messy and shifting. The formal school culture is laid out in documents of the school and state and includes the teaching and learning; the pedagogy; the disciplinary apparatus; and the policy, organizational, and administrative structures. The informal school culture is not intended to be in binary opposition, for it is different from, rather than a reaction to, and is in continual negotiation with, the formal school culture. Although it also has its own particular hierarchy, rules, and criteria of evaluation and judgement, and many of its parameters are set by the formal regime, it has a whole life and meaning all its own: It includes not only the relations and interactions between the pupils, but the informal relations between pupils and teachers outside of the instructional relationship and relations between teacher and teacher and between pupils, teachers, and other groups in the school, such as support staff of various types and descriptions.

We also need to examine how particular sets of practices and the available story lines within schools are articulated and related to gender relations, and we will find that some are more obvious and conspicuous than others. Between them, Connell (1996) and Gilbert and Gilbert (1998) identify four key areas of "masculinising practices," which are concentrated at particular sites and include management, policy, and organizational practices (including discipline); the curriculum; sport and games; and teacher-and-pupil relations. Perhaps we should also add pupil-to-pupil relations, as the closed cultural circle of the peer group has become increasingly recognized as a key area of influence in masculinity making.

School policies and organization, and the management practices that constitute them, are a key part of the gender regime and are visible in such practices as academic competition and hierarchy, constant testing, team games, a strict code of dress or uniform, divisions of labor, patterns of authority, a strict discipline (often from male teachers), and so on. In many countries, schools still rely on harsh, authoritarian systems of discipline, which undoubtedly influence constructions of masculinity. For instance, an attempt in 1996 to ban corporal punishment in South Africa failed to end its use in all schools. Although there are signs that more consensual models of discipline are being introduced,

corporal punishment continues to be widely used in the township schools, particularly among male learners, where its use in the home gives it legitimacy (Morrell, 2001).

The relations between teachers and pupils have been thoroughly documented: Teachers make gender distinction a central element of pupil identity, and it has been shown how they are similar to parents in that they tend to treat boys and girls according to gendered stereotypes (see Alloway, 1995). There is a tendency for the questions they ask, the manner of their responses, and the systems they use for rewards and sanctions to be influenced by assumptions about gender differences. For instance, Walkerdine (1989) shows how teachers are more likely to attribute boys' academic success to their natural ability but girls' to hard work, and Cohen (1998) has traced the history of this predilection back to the 17th century. Moreover, as Haywood and Mac an Ghaill (1996) point out, styles of teaching are also affected by connections of masculinity with power, authority, and competence, and they argue that "signs of weakness" are often associated with femininity.

The curriculum itself is the product of particular political developments, which need to be located historically and with regard to particular interest groups and ideologies. Many writers (see, for example, Connell, 1996; Gilbert & Gilbert, 1998; Gordon et al., 2000; Haywood & Mac an Ghaill, 1996; Salisbury & Jackson, 1996) have pointed out that the curriculum can be seen as an area of strategic importance in the production of masculinities. With its institutionalized patterns of knowledge, the curriculum is associated with the Foucauldian disciplinary techniques of hierarchical (academic) classification, normalizing judgments, and the examination, and masculinities emerge through the pupils' relationship with it. The curriculum offers boys a resource to use in developing particular patterns of masculinity through a range of responses to it (Haywood & Mac an Ghaill, 1996), and although many are able to use it to establish status through teacher approval and test results, some boys actively resist school learning and expectations and look for alternative resources of prestige to validate their masculine identities (Connell, 1989). Practices of "setting" and "streaming" also produce explicit divisions between pupils, thereby creating different types of masculinity, and so the ways in which the pupils are organized in relation to the curriculum are at least as important as, if not more important than, the curriculum content itself (Skelton, 2001).

Another site is sport and games, and even though there has recently been a general reduction in the amount of school time given to sport and games in the United Kingdom, they still have a great significance in the cultural life of many schools, engaging the school population as a whole in the "celebration and reproduction of the dominant codes of gender" (Connell, 1996, p. 217). School sport is not meant to be some kind of innocent pastime but is used to create a "top dog" model of masculinity that many boys try to aim for and live up to (Salisbury & Jackson, 1996, p. 205). Typically, top sporty boys have a higher status, particularly in the informal peer group. Sport is also inextricably connected with the body. Boys learn about the need to exert bodily power and the necessity of hardening their bodies to prepare them for physical challenges and confrontations. School sport embodies violent practices, and the language is often connected to the language and metaphor of war (Gilbert & Gilbert, 1998; Salisbury & Jackson, 1996).

Thus we can see that the school's role in the formation of masculinity needs to be understood in two ways, for as well as providing the setting and physical space in which the embodied actions and agencies of pupils and adults take place, its own structures and practices are involved as *institutional agents* that produce these "masculinizing practices." In some ways, the coeducational system makes the differences between gender even more conspicuous than in single-sex schooling, and these differences can be seen in terms of segregated toilets and changing facilities, school uniforms or codes of dress, practices such as lining boys and girls up separately, designated seating arrangements in class, and so on. However, we should not forget that many educational practices actually ameliorate gender differences, and many are as much a force for gender *equity* as they are for *in*equity. By restricting pupils' choice, the National Curriculum has helped reduce gender differentiation: Boys and girls share the same timetable in the same classroom, and they follow the same daily routines. As Connell (2000) says, "schools may be having a gender *effect* without producing gender *difference*" (p. 152).

THE POWER OF THE PEER GROUP

Some of the most important contributions to the understandings of masculinity in schools have come from a series of ethnographic studies of boys' own cultures and their interpersonal relations at the micro level. The boys' peer group is one of the most important features of school as a social setting, for peer-group cultures are also agents in the making of masculinities; they have a fundamental influence on the construction of masculine identities, and there are constant pressures on individuals to perform and behave to the expected group norms (see, for example, Adler & Adler, 1998; Connell, 2000; Connolly, 1998; Gilbert & Gilbert, 1998; Harris, 1998; Kenway, 1997; Mac an Ghaill, 1994; Pollard, 1985; Walker, 1988; Woods, 1990). Each peer group has its own cultural identity, which can be said to refer to a "way of life" (Dubbs & Whitney, 1980, p. 27) with shared values and interests, providing boys with a series of collective meanings of what it is to be a boy. Harris (1998) argues that the peer group actually has more influence on children than their parents in the formation of their identity, of who they are now, and who they will become and is the main conduit by which cultures are passed from one generation to another. Thus the construction of masculinity is, primarily, a collective enterprise, and it is the peer group that is the main bearer of gender definitions, rather than individual boys (Connell, 2000; Lesko, 2000). This may help to explain why some boys, who may be disruptive and troublesome when part of a group, are sensitive and amenable when on their own.

For many pupils, the safest position to aim for in the formal school culture is to be "average," for although, in some schools, boys have to be careful not to show they are working too hard, they do not want to be thought of as dupes, and this can require careful negotiation. In the informal pupil culture, the aim is to be the "same as the others," for this provides a certain protection from teasing and, perhaps, even subordination (Gordon et al., 2000). In fact, it is a paradox that although pupils attempt to construct their own individual identity, no one aspires to be, or can afford to be, too different, and they are conscious that they need to be "normal" and "ordinary" within the strict codes set by their own peer group.

One of the most urgent dimensions of school life for boys is the need to gain popularity and, in particular, status (see Adler & Adler, 1998; Corsaro, 1979; Weber, 1946): Indeed, the search to achieve status is also the search to achieve an acceptable form of masculinity. Boys' notion of status comes from having a certain position within the peer group hierarchy that becomes relevant when it is seen in relation to others. It is not something that is given but is often the outcome of intricate and intense maneuvering and has to be earned through negotiation and sustained through performance, sometimes on an almost daily basis. Ultimately, a boy's position in the peer group is determined by the array of social, cultural, physical, intellectual, and economic resources that he is able to draw on and accumulate.

Although some of the most esteemed resources will generally be an embodied form of physicality (sportiness, toughness, etc.), others may also be intellectual (general academic capability and achievement), economic (money), social and linguistic (interpersonal), or cultural (in touch with the latest fashions, music, TV programs, computer expertise, etc.). Of course, ultimately, these resources are all symbolic in that their power and influence derives from their effect and from what they are perceived to mean and stand for. These resources will also always exist within determinate historical and spatial conditions; moreover, the resources that are available will vary within different settings, and some may be easier to draw on than others at particular times and in particular places. This means that the boys who use a set of resources and interactional skills to establish high status in the dominant pupil hierarchy in one school will not necessarily be able to sustain this position in another.

LEARNING TO BE A SCHOOLBOY

In many parts of the world, pupils' experience of school is unfulfilling, inhospitable, and unremitting. Far from being safe places of learning, schools can be sites of bullying, sexual harassment, abuse, and homophobia, and, with institutional, sanctioned violence in the form of corporal punishment, boys' masculinity can often reflect this experience (Hyslop, 1999; Morrell, 2001).[10]

However, wherever children go to school, they will learn how to become "pupils," and this involves acquiring a considerable variety of skills. These include understanding the basic features of the pedagogic process, the hierarchical relations within the school, and the appropriate rules and conventions outside as well as inside the classroom. Pollard (1985) maintains that the two major sources of support for pupils come from their peers and their teachers, and to enjoy their time at school, pupils need to negotiate and manage skillfully "a satisfactory balance between the expectations of these two sources" (Pollard & Filer, 1996, p. 309), which often exert contradictory pressures. Many boys experience a tension between what the teachers (representing the school) expect from them as pupils and the expectations that they have themselves about what they think it means to be a boy. Woods (1990, p. 131) points out that this can involve a delicate balance of affiliation or "knife-edging" as boys learn to become school-*boys,* but boys' (and girls') options and strategies in their relations to the formal school authority are actually quite restricted: They can either conform and comply, challenge and resist, or, like the majority, they can pragmatically negotiate a path that best satisfies their interests (see, for example, Connell et al., 1982; Gilbert & Gilbert, 1998; Pollard, 1985; Pollard & Filer, 1996; Woods, 1990).

Most boys will actually employ more than one strategy at different times and in different contexts, especially when they are with different teachers, and the majority forms a pragmatic accommodation with the formal regime (Gilbert & Gilbert, 1998), negotiating what Pollard (1985) refers to as a "viable *modus vivendi*" (p. 194). Although boys tend to tell researchers that they go to school to have a good time and to be with their friends, many are aware that, ultimately, school means doing schoolwork, and they are able to balance these two commitments most of the time. Certainly, my own research into 10- and 11-year-old boys during their last year of primary school (Swain, 2001) revealed that many boys understood that good teacher reports and examination success were a desirable requirement for secondary school and future careers. Although many of the boys told me that they enjoyed most of their classwork, the great majority said that they worked hard for instrumental reasons:

They wanted to get on and do well in their SATs and recognized that there was a link between good qualifications and job and career prospects with their material remuneration. In other words, they had a utilitarian view of school and used it as a resource that provided a means to an end.

Some boys told me that they did not derive any enjoyment from their work, although in this next interchange there is also a hint of the parental influence on their superficial conformity:

JS: Do you think you need to pass exams to get a good job?

Vinny: Yeah.

Hussein: Yeah, definitely.

Vinny: It will go on your record. . . .

Hussein: If you get 2, 2, 2 [levels in the SATs] and you get expelled after, you end up being a rubbish man or unemployed.

Vinny: That's what my mum says.

JS: So you really need to work? How much of the work do you do because you have to pass the SATs and how much do you do because you enjoy it?

Hussein: Basically we don't enjoy any of it, we just get it because we're going to get somewhere with it in life. . . . We're going to get a job, earn a living. (Swain, 2001, p. 212)

Although it can be possible (depending on the school culture) for boys to work hard and gain academic success without damaging their masculine status in primary school, it seems harder to achieve this balance when they move on to secondary school, where constructions of masculinity and femininity become increasingly polarized around sport and work (Frosh, Phoenix, & Pattman, 2002). Although learning at primary school is also often feminized and equated with being a sissy, this becomes far more pronounced between 11 and 16 years old, at which point some boys' constructions as "real lads" are formed in relation to the feminized world of schoolwork and are characterized by toughness, sporty prowess, and resistance to teachers and education (Frosh et al., 2002; Jackson, 1998; see also Connell, 1989; Mac an Ghaill, 1994; Martino, 1999). Although some boys manage their academic careers carefully,

avoiding an open commitment to work and often being able to negotiate a "cool cleverness" that allows them to work without being teased and victimized (Bleach, 1996), in general, securing male esteem and being attentive to schoolwork are regarded as fundamentally incompatible.

Of course, this is hardly a new phenomenon, and, indeed, those boys who resist schoolwork and reject school values are the most studied group of masculinities in schools (Delamont, 2000). See, for example, Willis (1977) with the "lads," Kessler et al. (1985) with the "bloods," Walker (1988) with the "footballers" and the "competitors," Mac an Ghaill (1994) with the "macho lads," Parker (1996a) with the "hard boys," and Sewell (1997) with the "rebels." Although some of these groups are less hostile to school than others, they all pursue a continuous, belligerent and recalcitrant style of conduct. One of the most comprehensive pictures of this type of masculinity is Willis's (1977) study, and, indeed, Gilbert and Gilbert (1998) argue that it has acted as a prototype for others.[11] The "lads" renounced the mental for the manual, and the teachers, who had little knowledge of the world the boys respected, were dismissed as "wankers." Nearly 20 years later, Mac an Ghaill's (1994) influential study saw a group of boys that he called the "macho lads" who felt dominated, alienated, and belittled and consequently consciously decided to reject the school system (the curriculum, rules, and regulations) in favor of being tough and "hard," which for them involved "fighting, fucking, and football."

We also need to be aware that lying behind these masculine identities is the powerful variable of social class. The middle classes have long recognized the link between examination success and improved career opportunities and generally have higher expectations of accomplishment.[12] Parental dispositions to education are important, and these are evident in a generally more calculative attitude toward long-term career goals from boys in middle class schools, who also tend to show greater levels of support of the school authority. Indeed, the inequality of attainment between social classes is one of the longest established trends in education: Put simply, on average, the higher a child's social class, the greater his or her attainments are likely to be (Gillborn & Mirza, 2000, p. 18).

SOCIAL THEORIES OF MASCULINITY

In every setting, such as a school, there will be a hierarchy of masculinities, and each will generally have its own dominant, or hegemonic, form of masculinity, which gains ascendance over and above others; it becomes "culturally exalted" (Connell, 1995) and personifies what it means to be a "real" boy. Many academic papers and empirical studies use the concept of hegemonic masculinity (Carrigan, Connell, & Lee, 1985), and within the last decade it has emerged as a central reference point for understanding masculinity and male dominance;[13] indeed, Kerfoot and Whitehead (1998) argue that the concept has gained such an ascendancy in academic writings that it has come to represent its own hegemony. However, the inherent weaknesses and limitations of the notion of hegemonic masculinity have been raised by a number of writers (see, for example, Donaldson, 1993; Edley & Wetherell, 1995; Haywood & Mac an Ghaill, 1996; Kerfoot & Whitehead, 1998; MacInnes, 1998; Whitehead, 1999). Whitehead (1999) argues that hegemonic masculinity can only explain so much, that its own legitimacy becomes weakened once the multiplicity of masculinities and identities are stressed, and that it is unable to reveal "the complex patterns of inculcation and resistance which constitute everyday social action" (Whitehead, 1999, p. 58).[14]

Nevertheless, and despite Connell's recontextualization of hegemony from macro class relations into the micro interpersonal relations in the school, I still find many of his arguments on hegemonic masculinity highly persuasive and regard it as a major analytical device, useful in conceptualizing masculine hierarchies. The hegemonic masculine form is not necessarily the most common type on view, and may be contested, but although it is often underwritten by the threat of violence, it generally exerts its influence by being able to define "the norm," and many boys find that they have to fit into, and conform to, its demands. Most significantly, it prefers to work by implicit *consent,* for, after all, the easiest way to exercise power and to gain advantage over others is for the dominated to be unaware of, and therefore be complicit in, their subordination. In many ways, the less resistance, the more effective the hegemony. The hegemonic form may differ in each school, and, depending on the features of the formal culture, it may be either more stable or unstable, more visible or invisible, more passive or violent, more conformist or resistant to the formal school authority, and, although some forms may be created by school practices, others will be invented by the boys themselves. However, despite not being a "fixed character type" (in the sense of character being impervious to change), the hegemonic form generally mobilizes around a number of sociocultural constructs such as physical and athletic skill, strength, fitness, control, competitiveness, culturally acclaimed knowledge, discipline, courage, self-reliance, and adventurousness. These attributes are also indicative of a masculinity that is associated with, or implicated with, violence (Hearn, 1998; Mills, 2001). Indeed, in many settings, the features of the hegemonic form are actually quite narrow, and this can be a problem for boys wishing to construct alternative forms. In fact, the dominant patterns of masculinity are often linked to the physical capital of the body, and for many boys, the physical performative aspect of masculinity is seen as the most acceptable and desirable way of being male (Gilbert & Gilbert, 1998). I will return to a discussion on embodiment later in the chapter.

Of course, there will also be other patterns of masculinity that are actually produced at the same time as the dominant or hegemonic form (Connell, 2000). The number of boys actually able to practice the hegemonic pattern containing every feature is usually quite small, and there will often be other aspirant forms of masculinity that are peripheral, or liminal, and are confined to the margins. The boys who represent this form would like to be like the leading boys but lack a sufficient number of resources to be fully accepted. Indeed, in my own research, the boys that I have classified exhibiting this form could often be seen hanging around the edges of the dominant group watching the action; in the term used by Adler and Adler (1998), they were "wannabes." There are also other boys who join in with, and are closely connected to, the boys in the top group; they embody many of the qualities and traits of the "idealized" form without ever quite being one of the "frontline troops" (Connell, 1995, p. 79). Unlike the wannabes, not all of these boys want to be leaders, but they are complicit with the dominant form and content to benefit from many of the advantages that stem from it, or, in Connell's (1995) term, its "patriarchal dividend" (p. 79).

However, just because there is a culturally authoritative form of masculinity within each setting, it does not automatically follow that all boys (or men) will attempt to engage with, aspire to, or wish to challenge it. Some, of course, are simply unable to do so. For example, they may have a deficit of the necessary physical attributes and resources (in terms of body coordination, shape, strength, force, speed, etc.). However, this does not necessarily mean that these boys (or men) are inevitably subordinated, or that they have any desire to subordinate others. These alternative masculine ways of being a boy coexist alongside the dominant form and have been recognized and described by other researchers as being "softer" and more "transgressive" (see Frosh et al., 2002; Pattman, Frosh, & Phoenix, 1998); I have classified them as "personalized" (Swain, 2001). In one of the schools in my own research (an independent, private school), the hegemonic form was constructed around the ideal of the top sporty boy. However, I found that the majority of the boys had formed themselves into a series of small, well-established friendship networks with boys who had an array of similar interests, such as in computer games; they were popular within their own peer cliques and were generally nonexclusive and egalitarian, without any clearly defined leader. Although they may have been pathologized by a few of the top sporty boys and even, at least implicitly, by the formal school culture, they posed no threat to the hegemonic regime and so were generally accepted and not picked on by any of their peers. Although their nonopposition can be seen as an expression of consent to the hegemonic form, in many ways, they coexisted alongside the hegemonic form. I found no evidence that they had any feelings of envy toward the sporty boys, and they appeared to have no desire to challenge them. In many ways, these personalized groups seemed to have a high degree of social security and regarded themselves as different rather than inferior. They were not complicit in any subordination; nor did they, in general, feel an imperative to subordinate anyone else. If, at this school, top sporty boy equated with "real" boy, these other boys seemed to feel no less "real" for not being able to demonstrate sporting excellence.

SUBORDINATION

In direct contrast to hegemonic masculinity are subordinate modes of masculinity, which are positioned outside the legitimate forms of maleness as represented in the hegemonic form and which are controlled, oppressed, and subjugated. As all forms of masculinities are constructed in contrast to being feminine, those that are positioned at the bottom of the masculine hierarchy will be symbolically assimilated to femininity and tend to have much in common with feminine forms (Gilbert & Gilbert, 1998). The various strategies of subordination used in schools are generally constructed under the two generic headings of *difference* and *deficit* (or *deficient*). Being different from the majority is often an unenviable position for boys (and girls) to be in. The powerful pressures to conformity that characterize peer group cultures mean that a boy has only to look, and be, *slightly* different from the norm to be accorded inferior status. Under the rubric of difference, boys can be subordinated for associating too closely with the formal school regime (such as by working too hard, being too compliant or overpolite, by speaking too formally or correctly or being "too posh," or by looking different—aberrant physical appearances and differences in body language are keenly scrutinized and commented on. The major material bodily difference often comes from the impression of being overweight, and the data from my own study are littered with disparaging references directed to boys and girls being "a big fat blob," "fat boy," "too fat," "so fat," "really fat," and so on. It is a serious handicap to boys' (or girls') attempts to establish peer group status, and boys need to use other strategies and resources to compensate for it.

As we have already seen, boys have to work hard at learning the appropriate peer group norms, and to be included, they have to be what Thornton (1997) calls "in the know": that is, they need to be able to talk about the right subjects, use the right speech (using the same style and vocabulary), wear the right clothes, play the right playground games, and move (sit, walk, run, catch, throw, kick, hit, etc.) in the "right" way, the way that being a boy demands.

Under the heading of deficit, subordination can come through perceived exhibitions of immature and babyish behavior (doing "silly" things, playing infantile games, or associating too closely with younger children); displaying a deficit or deficiency of toughness (such as crying, showing fear, not sticking up for yourself, or acting "soft"); being too passive and generally not active enough during both school sports and informal playground games; and showing a deficit, or lack, of effort (usually connected to a sporting context). Boys are also subordinated for the perception that they are deficient in certain culturally acclaimed traits, particularly with embodied forms of physicality and athleticism (such as skill, strength, fitness, speed, etc.) and in areas of locally defined class norms of academic achievement (which may include pupils on the school's register for "special" educational needs). Subordination can also accrue from deficiency in locally celebrated knowledge—for example, in the latest culturally hot topics, such as a TV program; in the technical language of football; or in unfamiliarity with the latest computer games—and this can render a boy silent and be used as a marker of difference. It is also important for a boy to be able to show a commitment to his adolescent future by being "in the know" regarding the meaning of certain swear words and matters of sexuality. Some of these themes are illustrated in the following exchange, taken from my own study, in which two boys are explaining to me why they have been calling another boy, Timothy, a girl.

Sinclair: He doesn't like football, he doesn't like any sports apart from golf . . .

Calvin: He's different from everyone else.

JS: Yeah, but—

Derek: He's just one person . . .

Calvin: And he likes to be by himself very often.

JS: What do you mean, he's like a girl?

Sinclair: Well . . .

Calvin: Well he does everything—

Derek: Well he doesn't really act like a boy. . . . He's quite scared of stuff as well, like scared of the ball in rugby—

Sinclair: Yeah I remember in football, there were two people running for the ball and Timmy sort of like backed away.

Derek: And when the ball is coming at him [in rugby] he just drops it and . . .

Sinclair: Yeah he can't kick it you know . . . it was painful to watch yesterday.

Calvin: He's like a boy yeah, he's like. . .

Sinclair: He's a boy but he, like, wants to be a girl.

Calvin: Well he doesn't want to be, I think like, he backs away from everything, and he's like . . . if someone has a go at us . . . if someone pushes us we'll push them back, this is a simple way of saying it: if someone pushes us, we'll push them back. (Swain, 2001, p. 328)

HOMOPHOBIA

Some of the main defamatory aspersions used to equate too close a conformity with the formal school regime include "goody-goody," "teacher's pet," "boff," and "swot." "Wimp," "sissy," and particularly "girl" and "gay" are frequently used interchangeably to confirm hegemonic masculinity as exclusively heterosexual and to position boys as different and attack their identity. Research has shown that homophobia is an enduring constituent of the peer group culture at school; in fact, the word *gay* is probably the most common word of abuse and is used to describe anything from not very good to absolute rubbish. Many researchers (see, for example, Connell, 1992; Epstein, 1996; Epstein & Johnson, 1998; Gilbert & Gilbert, 1998; Johnson, 1996; Mason, 1996; Redman, 1996) argue that dominant masculinity sees homosexuality as a threat and so attempts to distance itself by vilifying and oppressing it through homophobia. By doing so, boys are making the point that their own sexualities are entirely "straight" and unfeminine in every way, and "in a doubly defining moment the homophobic performance consolidate[s] the heterosexual masculinity of Self and the homosexual femininity of Other" (Kehily & Nayak, 1997, p. 82). Hence it can also be argued that by subordinating alternative masculinities or sexualities, these performances also, by default, subordinate femininities— which, therefore, include all girls.

Epstein (1996) maintains that homophobia also plays a fundamental role in regulating and constructing heterosexual masculinities in schools: Masculinity and heterosexuality are entwined, and thus to be a "real" boy (or girl) is to be heterosexual. Parker (1996a) asserts that these homophobic insults should be conceptualized, at least implicitly, "in terms of *gender* as opposed to *sexuality*" (p. 149, my italics), and that they therefore imply being "nonmasculine" and "effeminate" rather than homosexual. However, the essential point is that homophobia is used to police and control the general behavior of boys *and* their sexuality and is used as a strategy to position boys at the bottom of the masculine hierarchy.

RELATIONS WITH GIRLS

Difference from girls is an integral component in the construction of dominant masculinity, for although the experiences of gender for boys can be complicated, and these experiences change between settings, masculinity is always constructed in relation to a dominant image of gender difference and ultimately defines itself as what femininity is not. Indeed, it can be argued that the boys' construction of girls as "other" is a way of expelling femininity from within themselves (Mac an Ghaill, 1994). Thorne (1993) calls the interactions between boys and girls on the playground "border work," although she emphasizes that this often highlights and reinforces gender differences just as much as it reduces them. From an early age, boys learn that they risk derogation if they associate too closely with girls, and they have to work hard to prove that they have the right masculine credentials as heterosexual boys. In one of the interviews from my research, a boy whom I called Fred told me of a conversation he had had with Jinesh (one of the class leaders) that had arisen after some of the boys had been calling him "Barbie" (after the Barbie doll). This had happened because he was perceived to be fraternizing too closely with the girls. The following quotation shows Jinesh clearly defining the normative boundaries.

Fred: I mean, [I said to him] "It's nice to be popular with girls, like with the boys," and he [Jinesh] went, "No it isn't, I like to play with the boys, and if you're a boy you're like a sissy if you play with the girls." (Swain, 2001, p. 240)

This knowledge regulates and prevents boys from associating too closely with girls (or,

indeed, any "other"); in other words, the "other" is always present and acts to control boys' behaviors even when the real other is not there. Given the choice, few boys or girls ever choose to sit next to each other, and most try hard to avoid it. However, this is not to say that all boys feel the need to secure their sense of maleness by traducing all things feminine and female, especially when they feel that their masculine foundations are relatively stable and secure. Although boys construct girls as different, they do not necessarily categorize them as being oppositional, and often the most common feeling is one of disinterest.

There has recently been a growing number of studies considering the heterosexual positions of boyfriend and girlfriend, particularly at the upper end of the primary school around the ages of 9 through 11 years old (see, for example, Adler & Adler, 1998; Epstein, 1997; Renold, 2000; Thorne, 1993; Thorne & Luria, 1986), although Connolly (1998) found that 5- to 7-year-old boys were also able to gain a significant level of status by having a girlfriend. Some researchers, such as Renold (2000), find that "having a girlfriend" is a common occurrence in boys' peer group culture and creates an "acceptable and assumptive" status (p. 319) that emanates from the need to reinforce dominant versions of heterosexual masculinities. However, in the vast majority of cases, boys want to do little more than *possess* a girl like a trophy, to use as a status symbol, and it is the ability to be able to *claim* the relationship that is the main objective. In secondary schools, Frosh et al. (2002) found that boys evaluate different aspects of femininity differently at different times and differentiate girls by liking and desiring some and not others. As boys get older, more are able to take the risk of crossing the gender divide, although many are still wary of being seen spending too much time with girls. Boys also begin to look to have physical relationships with girls, although few boys actually have a girlfriend, and it is unusual for boys to want girlfriends as "friends."

THE BODY

Masculinity does not exist as an ontological given but comes into existence as people act (Connell, 2000). That is, the social and material practices through which, and by which, boys' masculine identities are defined are generally described in terms of what boys do with or to their bodies, and a number of writers have embraced the concept of embodiment (see, for, example, Crossley, 1996; Light & Kirk, 2000; Lyon & Barbalet, 1994; Shilling, 1993; Synnott, 1993; Turner, 2000). Although there are a number of ways of defining embodiment, it needs to be understood as a social process (Elias, 1978). Although bodies are located in particular social, historical structures and spaces, boys are viewed as embodied social agents, for they do not merely have a passive body that is inscribed and acted upon; they are actively involved in the development of their bodies throughout their school life (and, indeed, for their entire life span). Thus, as Connell (1995) argues, we should see bodies as both the "objects and agents of practice, with the practice itself forming the structures within which bodies are appropriated and defined," and he calls this "body-reflexive practice" (p. 61). Boys experience themselves simultaneously *in* and *as* their bodies (Lyon & Barbalet, 1994, p. 54), and in this respect, *they are bodies* (Turner, 2000). They can be seen being consciously concerned about the maintenance and appearance of their bodies; they can be seen learning to control their bodies, acquiring and mastering a number of techniques, such as walking, running, sitting, catching, hitting, kicking, and so forth; and they can be seen using them in the appropriate ways that being a boy demands. Moreover, they are aware of the body's significance, both as a personal (but unfinished) resource and as a social symbol, which communicates signs and messages about their self-identity.

Foucault (1977) gives us the useful notion of "biopower," which he sees as a form of social control that focuses on the body. In schools, institutionalized practices involve knowledge of, and power over, individual gestures, movements, and locations: these can be used to produce (or attempt to produce) "docile" bodies through techniques of discipline, surveillance, classification, and normalization (Foucault, 1977) that can be regulated and controlled and that are generally acceptable to adults. School rules and regulations prescribe what is and what is not allowed in school, which includes how bodies are to behave and how they are allowed move and act in space (Nespor, 1997).

Bodies in schools can be seen collectively or individually, but the school tries to control and train both. However, a body that can be trained can also be contested. All schools contain relations of (teacher) control and (pupil) resistance (Epstein & Johnson, 1998), and there is the ongoing tension between the body as object and as agent, which, in many ways, is about the struggle for the control of the boy's body. In fact, boys' bodies are often far away from the "docile," passive bodies that the school attempts to produce; they are full of energy and action, and, especially in the context of playground games and activities, boys' bodies become bodies in motion, literally and metaphorically. As in Connell's (1995) conception, they are both the objects and agents in the performances and practices in which their bodies and identities became defined and appropriated by others as "skillful," "fast," "tough," "hard," and so on.

For much of the time, boys define their masculinity through action, and, as I have already stated, the most esteemed and prevalent resources that boys draw on to establish status are physicality and athleticism, which are inextricably linked to the body in the form of strength, toughness, power, skill, fitness, and speed. Boys are classified and divided by their physicality by both formal and (their own) informal school cultures, where the other bodies around them provide them with a differential reference point for their own bodily sense of self. Sport provides a way of measuring boys' masculine accomplishment not only against each other, but also against the wider world of men. Sporting success (particularly in football) is a key signifier of successful masculinity, and has been recognized by a number of writers:[15] Typically, high performance in sport and games (both on the field and in the playground) is the single most effective way of gaining popularity and status in the male peer group.

Calvin:	If you're not good at football you're not friends with anybody who's good at football, all the people who are good at football are the best people, like the most—
Josh:	Popular.
Calvin:	Yeah, popular.
JS:	[To Josh and Patrick] True?
Josh:	Very true!

Patrick: Yeah.

Josh: We're sporty people.

Calvin: And the sporty people are much preferred than the people who are much more brainy. (Swain, 2001, p. 257)

Gilbert and Gilbert (1998) maintain that most boys realize that they are either good or incompetent at sport by the time they are 9 or 10 years old, and I would suggest that this actually happens a good a deal earlier. I wish to argue, therefore, that, although bodies have agency, many of the opportunities to achieve peer group status in boyhood (and also in later life) are largely conditioned by the shape and physical attributes of the body.

CONCLUSIONS

The journey from boy to man is unpredictable, disorderly, and frequently hazardous, with multiple pathways shaped by social class, ethnicity, and sexuality. This chapter has shown that the educational setting furnishes boys with a number of different ways of *doing* boy and that there is diversity not just *between* settings but *within* settings. To understand how masculinities are made in the school setting, I have needed to examine the school as an institution, to look at its gender regime, and to differentiate between the layers of the formal and informal peer group cultures. Both the individual school and the boys themselves are agents in the production of masculinities, and identities are constructed using the localized resources and strategies available. Formal school policies and practices can either open, restrict, or close down opportunities, but it is the peer group that is the greatest influence on the formation of masculinities, for much of the information about how to be like a boy (and future man) comes from being with other boys in groups. Rather than the passive one-way process of learning the norms, as suggested by sex-role and socialization theories, the construction of masculinity is the result of active, skillful negotiation and manipulation. The body is a key signifier of how boys understand themselves as gendered and is entwined with the performative nature of masculinity. Boys use a variety of strategies and draw on a series of resources

to gain status, but although the resources of physicality and athleticism are generally the principle material symbols of successful masculinity, they may be articulated in different ways within each school context. Although hegemonic modes of masculinity in school have a tendency to be rather narrow and restrictive, it is important to remember that, as masculinity is constructed and socially situated, it is also open to change. This provides opportunities for schools to identify the dominant images of masculinity (often containing associations with violence, misogyny, and homophobia) operating in their own setting and then introduce specific programs of intervention offering alternative forms.

NOTES

1. Many of these theories are feminist or feminist inspired and are influenced by poststructuralism.

2. See, for example, Askew and Ross (1988); Heward (1988); Walker (1988); Connell (1989, 1996); Davies (1989); Woods (1990); Holland, Ramazanoglu, and Sharpe (1993); Thorne (1993); Mac an Ghaill (1994); Jordan (1995); Haywood and Mac an Ghaill (1996); Salisbury and Jackson (1996); Kehily and Nayak (1997); Warren (1997); Epstein (1997, 1998b, 1998c); Skelton (1996, 1997, 2000); Renold (1997, 1999, 2000); Adler and Adler (1998); Benjamin (1998, 2001); Connolly (1998); Gilbert and Gilbert (1998); Lingard and Douglas (1999); Martino (1999); Francis (1998, 2000); Gordon, Holland, and Lahelma (2000); Lesko (2000); Swain (2000, 2002a, 2002b); Frosh, Phoenix, and Pattman (2002).

3. The International Labour Organisation's Bureau of Statistics estimates that the number of working children between 5 and 14 years old is at least 120 million (cited in Mansurov, 2001, p. 149).

4. Similar changes have also occurred in the rest of Europe, the United States, Australia, and New Zealand (Francis, 2000). Moreover, Skelton (2001) points out that the discourses of management and marketization have been so powerful and effective that, despite changes in government, many of the policies and practices of the New Right have been incorporated by the new governments in these countries.

5. An "integrated day" is one in which pupils are working on more than one curriculum area at any one time.

6. OFSTED is the Office for Standards in Education, officially the Office of Her Majesty's Chief Inspector of Schools in England. It was set up in 1992 and is a nonministerial government department.

7. SATs are Standard Assessment Tasks (tests), which pupils take in English, mathematics, and science when they are 7, 11, and 14 years old.

8. The expression "3 Rs" dates back to the 19th century and refers to the traditional core subjects of reading, writing, and arithmetic.

9. "Zero tolerance" means that no concessions for failure will be permitted.

10. An underresearched area is the effect that HIV/AIDS will have on schooling in the Third World, particularly in Africa. For instance, in South Africa (using 1990 estimates), almost a quarter of the population is infected, and children are being infected at the rate of 50,000 a year (McGreal, 2000). As yet, we do not know how this might affect gender relations and masculinity, but there are already some indications that resulting deaths and loss will shape constructions of gender identity (Morell, Unterhalter, Moletsane, & Epstein, 2001).

11. However, it should be noted that at the time, Willis saw the main focus of his study as class, hence the title (alluding to "working class kids"); it is in retrospect that he and other writers have recognized it to be about masculinity.

12. Connell (2000) points out that middle class masculinities also tend to emphasize the acquisition of knowledge and expertise.

13. See, for example, Benjamin (1998, 2001); Brown (1999); Connell (1990); Connolly (1998); Fitzclarence and Hickey (2001); Gilbert and Gilbert (1998); Kenway and Fitzclarence (1997); Lee (2000); Light and Kirk (2000); Mac an Ghaill (1994); Martino (1999); Parker (1996a); Renold (1997, 1999, 2001); Skelton (1997), Swain (2000).

14. Skelton (2001, p. 52), however, also points out that much of the criticism directed against hegemony is caused by writers' lack of understanding and loose application of the concept.

15. See, for example, Kessler et al. (1985); Messner and Sabo (1990); Whitson (1990); Mac an Ghaill (1994); Connell (1995, 1996, 2000); Parker (1996a, 1996b); Bromley (1997); Renold (1997); Fitzclarence and Hickey (1998); Gilbert and Gilbert (1998); Lingard and Douglas (1999); Martino (1999); Skelton (2000); Swain (2000).

References

Adler, A., & Adler, P. (1998). *Peer power: Preadolescent culture and identity.* London: Rutgers University Press.

Alexander, R. (1988). "Garden or jungle?" Teacher development and informal primary education. In A. Blyth (Ed.), *Informal primary education today* (pp. 148-188). London: Falmer Press.

Alloway, N. (1995). *Foundation stones: The construction of gender in early childhood.* Carlton, Australia: Curriculum Corporation.

Askew, S., & Ross, C. (1988). *Boys don't cry: Boys and sexism in education.* Milton Keynes, PA: Open University Press.

Benjamin, S. (1998). Fantasy football league: Boys learning to "do boy" in a special (SEN) school classroom. In G. Walford & A. Massey (Eds.), *Children learning in context* (pp. 115-136). London: Jai Press.

Benjamin, S. (2001). Challenging masculinities: Disability and achievement in testing times. *Gender and Education, 13,* 39-55.

Bleach, K. (1996). *What difference does it make? An investigation of factors influencing the motivation and performance of year 8 boys in a West Midlands comprehensive school.* Wolverhampton, England: University of Wolverhampton, Educational Research Unit.

Bromley, R. (1997). The body language: The meaning of modern sport. *Body & Society, 3,* 109-118.

Brown, D. H. (1999). Complicity and reproduction in teaching physical education. *Sport, Education and Society, 4,* 143-159.

Carrigan, T., Connell, R. W., & Lee, J. (1985). Towards a new sociology of masculinity. *Theory and Society, 5,* 551-602.

Cohen, M. (1998). "A habit of healthy idleness": Boys' underachievement in historical perspective. In D. Epstein, J. Elwood, V. Hey, & J. Maw (Eds.), *Failing boys? Issues in gender and achievement* (pp. 19-34). Buckingham, England: Open University Press.

Connell, R. W. (1989). "Cool guys, swots and wimps": The interplay of masculinity and education. *Oxford Review of Education, 15,* 291-303.

Connell, R. W. (1990). An iron man: The body and some contradictions of hegemonic masculinity. In M. A. Messner & D. F. Sabo (Eds.), *Sport, men and the gender order: Critical feminist perspectives* (pp. 83-95). Champaign, IL: Human Kinetics.

Connell, R. W. (1992). "A very straight gay": Masculinity, homosexual experience, and the dynamics of gender. *American Sociological Review, 57,* 735-751.

Connell, R. W. (1995). *Masculinities.* Cambridge, England: Polity Press.

Connell, R. W. (1996). "Teaching the boys": New research on masculinity and gender strategies for schools. *Teachers College Record, 98,* 206-235.

Connell, R. W. (2000). *The men and the boys.* Cambridge, England: Polity Press.

Connell, R. W., Ashenden, D. J., Kessler, S., & Dowsett, D. W. (1982) *Making the difference: Schools, families and social division.* Sydney: Allen and Unwin.

Connolly, P. (1998). *Racism, gender identities and young children: Social relations in a multi-ethnic, inner-city primary school.* London: Routledge.

Corsaro, W. A. (1979). Young children's conceptions of status and role. *Sociology of Education, 52,* 46-59.

Crossley, N. (1996). Body-subject/body-power: Agency, inscription and control in Foucault and Merleau-Ponty, *Body and Society, 2,* 99-116.

Davies, B. (1989). *Frogs and snails and feminist tails: Pre-school children and gender.* Sydney: Allen & Unwin.

Delamont, S. (2000). The anomalous beasts: Hooligans and the sociology of education. *Sociology, 34,* 95-111.

Donaldson, M. (1993). What is hegemonic masculinity? *Theory and Society, 22,* 643-657.

Dubbs, P. J., & Whitney, D. D. (1980). *Cultural contexts: Making anthropology personal.* Boston: Allyn & Bacon.

Edley, N., & Wetherell, M. (1995). *Men in perspective: Practice, power and identity.* London: Prentice Hall.

Elias, N. (1978). *The history of manners: The civilising process* (Vol. 1). Oxford, England: Basil Blackwell.

Epstein, D. (1996). Keeping them in their place: Hetero/sexist harassment, gender and the enforcement of heterosexuality. In J. Holland & L. Adkins (Eds.), *Sex, sensibility and the gendered body* (pp. 202-221). London: Macmillan.

Epstein, D. (1997). Boyz own stories: Masculinities and sexualities in schools. *Gender and Education, 9,* 105-115.

Epstein, D. (1998a). Marked men: Whiteness and masculinity. *Agenda, 37,* 49-59.

Epstein, D. (1998b). "Real boys don't work": Underachievement, masculinity, and the harassment of "sissies." In D. Epstein, J. Elwood, V. Hey, & J. Maw (Eds.), *Failing boys? Issues in gender and achievement* (pp. 96-108). Buckingham, England: Open University Press.

Epstein, D. (1998c, August 28-30). *"Stranger in the mirror": Gender, sexuality, ethnicity and nation in education.* Keynote address presented at the Nordic Research Symposium [Norfa], "Multiple Marginalities: Gender, Citizenship and Nationality in Education," Helsinki, Finland.

Epstein, D., & Johnson, R. (1998). *Schooling sexualities.* Buckingham, England: Open University Press.

Fitzclarence, L., & Hickey, C. (1998). Learning to rationalise abusive behaviour through football. In L. Fitzclarence, C. Hickey, & R. Matthews (Eds.), *Where the boys are: Masculinity, sport and education* (pp. 67-81). Geelong, Australia: Deakin Centre for Education and Change.

Fitzclarence, L., & Hickey, C. (2001). Real footballers don't eat quiche: Old narratives in new times. *Men and Masculinities, 4*(2), 118-139.

Foucault, M. (1977). *Discipline and punish: The birth of the prison.* London: Penguin Books.

Francis, B. (1998). *Power plays.* Stoke-on-Trent, England: Trentham.

Francis, B. (2000). *Boys, girls and achievement: Addressing the classroom issues.* London: Routledge/Falmer.

Frosh, S., Phoenix, A., & Pattman, R. (2002). *Young masculinities: Understanding boys in contemporary society.* London: Palgrave.

Gilbert, R., & Gilbert, P. (1998). *Masculinity goes to school.* London: Routledge.

Gillborn, D., & Mirza, H. S. (2000). *Educational inequality: Mapping race, class and gender. A synthesis of research evidence.* London: OFSTED.

Gordon, T., Holland, J., & Lahelma, E. (2000). *Making spaces: Citizenship and differences in schools.* Basingstoke, England: Macmillan Press.

Hansot, E., & Tyack, D. (1998). Gender in public schools: Thinking institutionally. *Signs, 13,* 741-760.

Harris, J. R. (1998). *The nurture assumption: Why children turn out the way they do.* London: Bloomsbury.

Haywood, C., & Mac an Ghaill, M. (1996). Schooling masculinities. In M. Mac an Ghaill (Ed.), *Understanding masculinities* (pp. 50-60). Buckingham, England: Open University Press.

Hearn, J. (1998). *The violences of men: How men talk about and how agencies respond to men's violence to women.* London: Sage.

Heward, C. (1988). *Making a man of him: Parents and their sons' careers at an English public school 1929-1950.* London: Routledge.

Heward, C. (1996). Masculinities and families. In M. Mac an Ghaill (Ed.), *Understanding masculinities* (pp. 35-49). Buckingham, England: Open University Press.

Holland, J., Ramazanoglu, C., & Sharpe, S. (1993). *Wimp or gladiator: Contradictions in acquiring masculine sexuality.* London: Tufnell Press.

Hyslop, J. (1999). *The classroom struggle: Policy and resistance in South Africa 1940-1990.* Pietermaritzburg, South Africa: University of Natal Press.

Jackson, D. (1998). Breaking out of the binary trap: Boys' underachievement, schooling and gender relations. In D. Epstein, J. Elwood, V. Hey, & J. Maw (Eds.), *Failing boys? Issues in gender and achievement* (pp. 77-95). Buckingham, England: Open University Press.

Johnson, R. (1996). Sexual dissonances: Or the "impossibility" of sexuality education. *Curriculum Studies, 4*(Special issue), 163-189.

Jordan, E. (1995). Fighting boys and fantasy play: The construction of masculinity in the early years of schooling. *Gender and Education, 7*, 69-86.

Kehily, M. J., & Nayak, A. (1997). Lads and laughter: Humour and the production of heterosexual hierarchies. *Gender and Education, 9*, 69-87.

Kenway, J. (1997). Boys' education, masculinity and gender reform: Some introductory remarks. In J. Kenway (Ed.), *Will boys be boys? Boys' education in the context of gender reform.* Deakin, Australia: Australian Curriculum Studies Association.

Kenway, J., & Fitzclarence, L. (1997). Masculinity, violence and schooling: Challenging poisonous pedagogies. *Gender and Education, 9*, 117-133.

Kenway, J., & Willis, S., with Blackmore, J., & Rennie, L. (1998). *Answering back: Girls, boys and feminism in schools.* London: Routledge.

Kerfoot, D., & Whitehead, S. (1998, September 11-13). *W(h)ither hegemonic masculinity?* Paper presented at the International Conference "Gendering the Millennium," University of Dundee, Scotland.

Kessler, S., Ashenden, D. J., Connell, R. W., & Dowsett, G. W. (1985). Gender relations in secondary schooling. *Sociology of Education, 58*, 34-48.

Lee, D. (2000). Hegemonic masculinity and male feminisation: The sexual harassment of men at work. *Journal of Gender Studies, 9*(2), 141-155.

Lesko, N. (Ed.). (2000). *Masculinities at school.* London: Sage.

Light, R., & Kirk, D. (2000). High school rugby, the body and the reproduction of "hegemonic" masculinity. *Sport, Education and Society, 5*(2), 163-176.

Lingard, B., & Douglas, D. (1999). *Men engaging feminisms.* Buckingham, England: Open University Press.

Lyon, M. L., & Barbalet, J. M. (1994). Society's body: Emotion and the "somatization" of social theory. In T. J. Csordas (Ed.), *Embodiment and experience: The existential ground of culture and self* (pp. 48-66). Cambridge, England: Cambridge University Press.

Mac an Ghaill, M. (1994). *The making of men: Masculinities, sexualities and schooling.* Buckingham, England: Open University Press.

MacInnes, J. (1998). *The end of masculinity?* Buckingham, England: Open University Press.

Mansurov, V. (2001). Child labour in Russia. In P. Mizen, C. Pole, & A. Bolton (Eds.), *Hidden hands: International perspectives on children's work and labour* (pp. 149-166). London: RoutledgeFalmer.

Martino, W. (1999). "Cool boys," "party animals," "squids" and "poofters": Interrogating the dynamics and politics of adolescent masculinities in school. *British Journal of Sociology of Education, 20*, 239-263.

Mason, G. (1996). Violence against lesbian and gay men. In K. Healey (Ed.), *A culture of violence? Issues for the nineties.* Balmain, NSW: Spinney Press.

McGreal, C. (2000, November 30). AIDS: South Africa's new apartheid. *Guardian.* Retrieved January 28, 2004, from http://www.guardian.co .uk/international/story/0,3604,404738,00.html

Messner, M. A., & Sabo, D. F. (1990). *Sport, men, and the gender order: Critical feminist perspectives.* Champaign, IL: Human Kinetics Books.

Mills, M. (2001). *Challenging violence in schools: An issue of masculinities.* Buckingham, England: Open University Press.

Morrell, R. (1994). Masculinity and white boys' boarding schools of Natal, 1880-1930. *Perspectives in Education, 15*(1), 27-52.

Morrell, R. (2001). Corporal punishment and masculinity in South African schools. *Men and Masculinities, 4*(2), 140-157.

Morrell, R., Unterhalter, E., Moletsane, L., & Epstein, D. (2001). Missing the message: HIV/AIDS interventions and learners in South African schools. *Canadian Women's Studies, 21*(2), 90-95.

Nespor, J. (1997). *Tangled up in school: Politics, space, bodies, and signs in the educational process.* London: Lawrence Erlbaum Associates.

Parker, A. (1996a). The construction of masculinity within boys' physical education. *Gender and Education, 8*, 141-157.

Parker, A. (1996b). Sporting masculinities: Gender relations and the body. In M. Mac An Ghaill (Ed.), *Understanding masculinities* (pp. 126-138). Buckingham, England: Open University Press.

Pattman, R., Frosh, S., & Phoenix, A. (1998). Lads, machos and others: Developing "boy-centred" research. *Journal of Youth Studies, 1*(2), 125-142.

Pollard, A. (1985). *The social world of the primary school.* London: Cassell.

Pollard, A., & Filer, A. (1996). *The social world of children's learning: Case studies of pupils from four to seven.* London: Cassell.

Pollard, A., & Filer, A. (1999). *The social world of pupil career: Strategic biographies through primary school.* London: Cassell.

Pong, S.-L. (1999). Gender inequality in educational attainment in Peninsular Malaysia. In C. Heward & S. Bunwaree (Eds.), *Gender, education and development: Beyond access to empowerment* (pp. 155-170). Trowbridge, England: Redwood Books.

Power, S., & Whitty, G. (1999). Market forces and school cultures. In J. Prosser (Ed.), *School culture* (pp. 15-29). London: Sage.

Raphael Reed, L. R. (1998). "Zero tolerance": Gender performance and school failure. In

D. Epstein, E. Elwood, V. Hey, & J. Maw (Eds.), *Failing boys? Issues in gender and achievement* (pp. 56-76). Buckingham, England: Open University Press.

Redman, P. (1996). Curtis loves Ranjit: Heterosexual masculinities, schooling and pupils, sexual cultures. *Educational Review, 48*, 175-182.

Rendel, M. (1985). The winning of the Sex Discrimination Act. In M. Arnot (Ed.), *Race and gender: Equal opportunities policies in education* (pp. 81-95). Oxford, England: Pergamon Press.

Renold, E. (1997). "All they've got on their brains is football": Sport, masculinity and the gendered practices of playground relations. *Sport, Education and Society, 2*, 5-23.

Renold, E. (1999). *"Presumed innocence": An ethnographic exploration into the construction of gender and sexual identities in the primary school.* Unpublished doctoral dissertation, University of Cardiff, Wales.

Renold, E. (2000). "Coming out": Gender, (hetero)sexuality and the primary school. *Gender and Education, 12*, 309-326.

Renold, E. (2001). Learning the "hard" way: Boys, hegemonic masculinity and the negotiation of learner identities in the primary school. *British Journal of Sociology of Education, 22*(3), 369-385.

Salisbury, J., & Jackson, D. (1996). *Challenging macho values: Practical ways of working with adolescent boys.* London: Falmer Press.

Sewell, T. (1997). *Black masculinities and schooling: How black boys survive modern schooling.* Stoke-on-Trent, England: Trentham Books.

Shilling, C. (1993). *The body and social theory.* London: Sage Publications.

Skelton, C. (1996). Learning to be "tough": The fostering of maleness in one primary school. *Gender and Education, 8*, 185-197.

Skelton, C. (1997). Primary boys and hegemonic masculinities. *British Journal of Sociology of Education, 18*, 349-369.

Skelton, C. (2000). "A passion for football": Dominant masculinities and primary schooling. *Sport, Education and Society, 5*(1), 5-18.

Skelton, C. (2001). *Schooling the boys: Masculinities and primary education.* Buckingham, England: Open University Press.

Swain, J. (2000). "The money's good, the fame's good, the girls are good": The role of playground football in the construction of young boys' masculinity in a junior school. *British Journal of Sociology of Education, 21*, 95-109.

Swain, J. (2001). *An ethnographic study into the construction of masculinity of 10-11 year old boys in three junior schools.* Unpublished doctoral dissertation, Institute of Education, University of London.

Swain, J. (2002a). The resources and strategies boys use to establish status in a junior school without competitive sport. *Discourse, 23*(1), 91-107.

Swain, J. (2002b). The right stuff: Fashioning an identity through clothing in a junior school. *Gender and Education, 14*(1), 53-69.

Synnott, A. (1993). *The body social: Symbolism, self and society.* London: Routledge.

Thorne, B. (1993). *Gender play: Girls and boys in school.* New Brunswick, NJ: Rutgers University Press.

Thorne, B., & Luria, Z. (1986). Sexuality and gender in children's daily worlds. *Social Problems, 33*, 176-190.

Thornton, S. (1997). The social logic of subcultural capital. In K. Gelder & S. Thornton (Eds.), *The subcultures reader* (pp. 200-209). London: Routledge.

Turner, B. S. (2000). An outline of a general sociology of the body. In B. S. Turner (Ed.), *The Blackwell companion to social theory* (2nd ed., pp. 481-501). Oxford, England: Blackwell.

UNICEF. (2001, September). *Progress since the World Summit for Children: A statistical review.* Retrieved January 16, 2004, from http://www .unicef.org/publications/pub_wethechildren_ stats_en.pdf

Walker, J. (1988). *Louts and legends.* Sydney: Allen and Unwin.

Walkerdine, V. (1989). Femininity as performance. *Oxford Review of Education, 15*, 267-279.

Warren, S. (1997). Who do these boys think they are? An investigation into the construction of masculinities in a primary classroom. *International Journal of Inclusive Education, 1*(2), 207-222.

Weber, M. (1946). Class, status and party. In H. Gerth & C. W. Mills (Eds. & Trans.), *From Max Weber* (pp. 180-195). New York: Oxford University Press.

Weiner, G., Arnot, M., & David, M. (1997). "Is the future female?" Female success, male disadvantage and changing gender patterns in education. In A. Halsey, H. Lauder, P. Brown, & A. S. Wells (Eds.), *Education: Culture, economy and society* (pp. 620-630). Oxford, England: Oxford University Press.

Whitehead, S. (1999). Hegemonic masculinity revisited (Review). *Gender, Work and Organization, 6*(1), 58-62.

Whitson, D. (1990). Sport in the social construction of masculinity. In M. A. Messner & D. F. Sabo (Eds.), *Sport, men and the gender order: Critical feminist perspectives* (pp. 19-29). Champaign, IL: Human Kinetics Books.

Willis, P. (1977). *Learning to labour: How working class kids get working class jobs.* Farnborough, England: Saxon House.

Woods, P. (1990). *The happiest days?* London: Falmer.

14

BOYS AND MEN IN FAMILIES

The Domestic Production of Gender, Power, and Privilege

MICHELE ADAMS

SCOTT COLTRANE

The title of this chapter suggests a troubling contradiction: Whereas boys and men "come from" or "have" families, they often experience profound difficulties being "in" them, insofar as they typically seem incapable of offering the emotional intimacy or providing the personal care that have become the hallmarks of modern family life. Popular culture tends to assume that families need fathers and that men and boys need families, but when we look closely at ideals about expressing boyhood or achieving manhood, it is clear that notions of masculinity have much less to do with everyday life in domestic settings than they do with accomplishments in extrafamilial arenas such as business, sports, or politics. In this chapter, we explore how putatively separate public (i.e., work or politics) and private (i.e., family) spheres reflect and reproduce gender differences and perpetuate gender inequality. To illustrate, we review scholarship on the social construction of gender in families, with special attention to the trials and tribulations of boys in the United States during the late 20th century. We also discuss how patterns of courtship, sexuality, marriage, divorce, housework, parenting, and family violence mirror gender inequities in the larger society and set up dilemmas for men, who are rarely equipped to be full participants in everyday family life. Finally, we suggest that structural and social constructionist theories of gender and society offer the best prospects for understanding how and why men and boys maintain ambivalent connections to families.

INTERROGATING "FAMILY" AND "MASCULINITY"

Ideas like "family" or "masculinity" are social constructions because they make sense only in

Authors' note: A portion of an earlier version of the first half of this chapter was published in Scott Coltrane's *Families and Society: Classic and Contemporary Readings* (Adams & Coltrane, 2004).

terms of historically and culturally specific shared understandings (Coltrane, 1998). Social constructionist approaches to studying culture and society have a long and varied history within philosophy, sociology, anthropology, and social psychology (e.g., Berger & Luckmann, 1966; Blumer, 1969; Garfinkel, 1967; Geertz, 1973; Goffman, 1967; Mead, 1934; Schutz, 1970). Using a social constructionist approach to study boys and men in families allows us to explore how these concepts and the relations among them have changed and are likely to continue to change. Combining a social constructionist perspective with a sociological, or social structural, approach enables us to show how strong economic and institutional forces also shape people's lives. Only by looking at the structural constraints people face—things like access to education or jobs—can we understand how and why cultural definitions and practices governing men inside and outside families have developed. And only by combining a social constructionist approach with a social structural approach can we evaluate the prospects for patterns of family life changing in the future (Coltrane, 1998).

Most people take for granted what "family" means, but it is not a term with a definite or stable meaning (Gubrium & Holstein, 1990; Levin & Trost, 1992; Stacey, 1996). The word "family" (or its equivalent) has meant different things in different times and places. In ancient Greece, "family" (*oikos*) referred to the household economy—including the land, house, and servants belonging to the household head. In medieval Europe, peasants who lived on feudal estates were considered part of the lord's "family," and the lord was called their "father" (*pater*) even though they were not related to him by blood (Collins, 1986). In many countries, such as Mexico, godparents (*compadres*) are treated as family members and act as coparents toward the children, disciplining them and providing financial or emotional support, even though they have no direct biological relationship to them (Griswold del Castillo, 1984). Similarly, in contemporary Native American families, the terms used to describe family relationships are more encompassing than narrow English usage would imply: A "grandmother" may actually be a child's aunt or grand-aunt, and "cousin" may have variable meanings not necessarily based on birth and marriage

(Yellowbird & Snipp, 1994). To understand families and the specific social relations they represent, we must therefore recognize that the term and the idea are socially constructed; that is, the meaning of "family" changes in response to a wide variety of social, economic, political, cultural, and personal conditions (Coltrane, 1998). Just as there is no stable definition of family, the definition of masculinity is also variable (Connell, 1995; Hearn, 1992; Kimmel, 1996; Lorber, 1994; West & Zimmerman, 1987). Treating masculinity as socially constructed leads us to focus on the social conditions that promote different versions of it, as well as implying that change in masculinity is possible and desirable. In this chapter, we focus on changes in family practices and ideals of masculinity that have the potential to affect social reproduction (Laslett & Brenner, 1989) across many generations.

THE CULTURAL IDEAL OF SEPARATE SPHERES

According to the ideal of separate spheres that emerged during the Victorian era, men and women are part of diverse social worlds: Men inhabit the public sphere, and women, the private (see Bose, 1987, and Hearn, 1992, for critiques of the "dual spheres" perspective). Nineteenth-century biological derivatives of this social scheme assumed that male and female reproductive capacity substantiated this division and illuminated supposed inherent psychological differences between the sexes: The "FEMALE detaches genetic cells that remain more or less stationary, while the MALE detaches cells that go more or less at large" (Searcy, 1895, as cited in Hughes, 1990, p. 53). Thus, according to popular cultural ideals that emerged at about this time, males were active and independent, whereas females were passive and were dependent on males for completion. Moreover, these highly differentiated reproductive and psychological competencies supposedly propelled men "to excel in competitive, aggressive life" and women to become skilled in "home duties and not in competitive and aggressive life" (Searcy, 1895, as cited in Hughes, 1990, p. 53). Although subsequent economic and social changes thrust women into the paid labor force, gutting the reality of separate spheres, and advances in biological understandings of reproduction gave females a more pro-active role than Dr. Searcy's comments would allow, the ideology of separate spheres has remained resistant to change. Indeed, social theorist Jeff Hearn (1992) stresses the continuing need to question the accuracy of the concept, noting that "an important aspect of the power of the public domains and of public men is the normalization, rather than problematization, of the public/private divisions" (p. 7).

Nevertheless, despite evidence to the contrary, most societies continue to subscribe to the notion that men and women have distinctly different, and generally opposite, psychological and behavioral tendencies. And although cross-cultural variation in the actual content of gender roles is enormous, families generally teach us that women and men should occupy different places in the social order. Relying on the ideology of separate spheres, families continue to raise children "to be" masculine or feminine based on the reproductive equipment with which they are born. Furthermore, the ideology of separate spheres has been elevated to the very structure of society, where its gender prescriptions and proscriptions organize schools, workplaces, laws, religions, and other social institutions, making it difficult, if not impossible, to escape. By institutionalizing gender differences, we have also institutionalized gender hierarchy and the power of men, who have historically shaped institutions to reflect their own interests. "In a world dominated by men," according to Michael Kaufman, "the world of men is, by definition, a world of power" (1999, p. 75). As the chapters of this handbook attest, that world is shaped by, and in turn shapes, what it means to be masculine. However, as Kaufman further suggests (1999), men's power is also tainted, reflecting "a strange combination of power and privilege, pain and powerlessness" (p. 75). As we discuss below, these contradictory experiences play out in men's ambivalent relations to family life.

The combination of male power and power-lessness is reflected in the fact that we don't quite know what to do about the problems created (for girls, women, boys, and men) when we privilege the masculine ideal of independence over connection. As we raise boys to be masculine men, we often end up with troubled boys. Snips, snails, and puppy dog tails, little boys are noisier, more active, more competitive, and more aggressive than little girls, according to research and popular cultural stereotypes. They reject (as they are taught) their mothers, their families, and adults in general. Sometimes they grow up to join gangs, assault young women, attack other young men, or commit suicide. At some (often indeterminate) point, they cross the cultural boundary between boyhood and manhood and become men who are unemotional, withdrawn from their families, aggressive, or violent. The trouble with boys is that they learn the lesson well and assume the cultural mantle of masculinity. "The trouble with boys," according to one British researcher, "is that they must become men" (Phillips, 1994, p. 270).

In this chapter, we look at how boys become men within the context of the family, and how, as part of that process, gender inequality is sustained and reproduced. We first examine how the cultural concept of masculinity is based on a pro-scription against being feminine. Noting how boys and girls are raised differently from the beginning of their lives, we observe how masculine ideals project boys out of and away from the family, whereas feminine ideals enmesh girls within it. We also point out the troubles faced by boys as they attempt to become men by incorporating ideals of dominant masculinity into their own gender schema. We then follow these boys-turned-men as they confront problems feeling "at home" in family environments. Here we see that the dilemmas men face reconciling their ideals of masculinity with their positions as husbands and fathers are part of a larger set of social problems that stem from separate spheres ideology and structural gender inequality in the society at large. We conclude by suggesting social and individual changes that might help attenuate the alienation that appears to be the plight of men living in today's families.

IDEALS OF MASCULINITY AND FEMININITY

Ideals of masculinity and femininity, passed down from 19th-century notions of separate spheres, assume that boys and girls are intrinsically and unalterably different in terms of personality and, therefore, behavior. Men, oriented to the public sphere, are understood to be active, strong, independent, powerful, dominant, and aggressive, with masculinity signifying "being in control" (Kaufman, 1993). Women, associated with the private sphere, are seen as passive, weak, dependent, powerless, subordinate, and nurturing. While social, economic, demographic, and cultural contexts have changed since the 19th century, idealized perceptions of masculinity and femininity have remained remarkably consistent. Even today, the notion of separate spheres and attendant sex differences in temperament are invoked to substantiate gender stratification institutionally (see, for instance, Bose, 1987; also Brush, 1999), as well as to privilege male power and interests in the home (Jones, 2000; Kimmel, 2000). Besides their prescriptive elements, these idealized gender differences in temperament are proscriptive as well, for "an essential element in becoming masculine is becoming not-feminine" (Maccoby, 1998, p. 52). Taken as a whole, the mandate for boys to be not-feminine, unlike (and in direct opposition to) the mandate for girls *to be* feminine, is a mandate that drives them away from family relations, particularly relations with their mothers (Silverstein & Rashbaum, 1994). Although assumed to be a baseline requirement for boys' achievement of manhood, this cultural mandate can cause problems for them when they mature into men. As men, they will have little ideological precedent for living harmoniously in a family environment, especially one that is increasingly predicated on ideals of democratic sharing. By continuing to follow the dictates of separate spheres, we may be creating manly men, but we are also crippling men emotionally and creating husbands and fathers who are destined to be outsiders or despots in their own families.

Socialization: Boys (and Girls) in Families

Society can work only if its members "organize their experience and behavior in terms of shared rules of interpretation and conduct" (Cahill, 1986, p. 163). All societies socialize children to internalize the shared rules and norms that drive collective behavior, thereby allowing them to become self-regulating participants in society. More formally, socialization is the process through which "we learn the ways of a given society or social group so that we can function within it" (Elkin & Handel, 1989, p. 2); whereas older notions of socialization suggested that the process began and ended in childhood, according to more recent theories, it is a lifelong process that allows us to move in and out of various social groups our entire lives. Part of this process involves gender socialization; that is, learning society's gender rules and regulations (typically dichotomized as either masculine or feminine) and becoming adept at behaving in accordance with the socially accepted gender patterns associated with our sex (male or female). Gender, that is to say, is not the same thing as sex, which generally groups people into categories based on their biologically given reproductive equipment. Gender, on the other hand, is a social construction, emergent, dynamic, variable within and across cultures, and historically situated, but also reflecting certain patterns within a given society (Coltrane, 1998; Connell, 1987). According to sociologists Candace West and Donald Zimmerman (1987), we "do gender" by acting out our culture's perception of those patterns that reflect what it is to be a man or a woman.

The family typically is considered the main institution for both production and reproduction of polarized gender values. Although individuals are socialized in many different contexts throughout their lives (school, neighborhood, community, peer group, workplace, church, polity), family tends to be the primary initial socialization agent, acting as a microcosm of society and providing a child's first exposure to interaction with others. It is generally in the family that children first acquire enduring personality characteristics, interpersonal skills, and social values (Maccoby, 1992). It is also in the family that children get their first look at what gender means, to them and to others, as they interact in daily life (Coltrane & Adams, 1997; Connell, 1987; Hearn, 1992). Specifically, it is in the family that boys first come to understand their privileged status and the ways in which male privilege equates to power. Finally, it is often in the family that these boys, grown into men, later come to understand the contradictions inherent in that power (Coltrane, 1996; Kaufman, 1999).

Early Gender Differentiation

Gendered parents transmit gender-laden assumptions and values to their children, starting before the children are born. Procedures such as amniocentesis and sonograms allow parents to find out the sex of their unborn child so that they might plan early for gender-appropriate nurseries and infant wardrobes, as fashion- (and gender-) conscious parents would be loathe, for instance, to bring their newborn son home in a pink or flowered cozy. Knowing the sex of an infant before birth can have other more sinister effects. In some countries, such as India and China, the traditional bias toward males is reflected in a prevalence of sex-selective abortions, as well as female neglect and infanticide after birth (Balakrishnan, 1994; Chunkath & Athreya, 1997; George, Rajaratnam, & Miller, 1992; Weiss, 1995). In rural Bangladesh, traditional son preference drives the use of contraceptives by women in their childbearing years (Nosaka, 2000). Furthermore, research has shown that more family resources, such as food and medicine, are allocated to sons, whose rate of survival is, thus, higher than that of daughters (Bhuiya & Streatfield, 1991; Chen, Huq, & D'Souza, 1981). These gender preference practices, some more extreme than others, are part of patriarchal societies where the notion prevails that sons have more value than daughters. Even in societies such as the United States and Canada, where disappointment over the birth of a girl may be more reserved, technologies allowing for "prenatal discrimination" are becoming more widely accepted (Bozinoff & Turcotte, 1993). In industrialized societies, as well as in less developed ones, notation of difference between boys and girls before birth signals the privilege and power that boys, and later, men, will experience in their lives.

Once the baby arrives, new parents advertise the sex of their infant so that no mistake can be made as to its traits or prospects for success: Is it a future president or a future wife and mother? Announcements and banners proclaim "It's a boy" or "It's a girl," giving admirers the gender context to remark on the baby's characteristics and potential. Mothers attach cute little pink bows to the bald heads of baby girls to set them apart from the supposedly rough-and-tumble boy babies (who, it turns out, are not only visually indistinguishable from girl babies but also slightly more fragile medically). The baby boy is housed in a nursery painted in bold colors of blue or red and outfitted with sports and adventure paraphernalia; the infant girl is treated to a pink boudoir with plenty of dolls and soft things to cuddle (Pomerleau, Bolduc, Malcuit, & Cossette, 1990). If a boy, the newborn is dressed in blue and is given gifts of tiny jeans and bold-colored outfits; if a girl, she is outfitted in pink and receives ruffled, pastel ensembles (Fagot & Leinbach, 1993). Moreover, research shows that based on what they are told the newborn's sex is, people (including strangers and especially children) tend to characterize infants, seeing those they are told are boys as stronger, bigger, noisier, and (sometimes) smarter than girls, even when the same baby is represented as male to some observers and female to others (Coltrane, 1998; Cowan & Hoffman, 1986; Stern & Karraker, 1989). That is, people draw on a cultural overlay of gender stereotypes to make their first assessment of a baby's personality and potential. Parents also use gender stereotypes when assessing the behavior and characteristics of their newborns (Rubin, Provenzano, & Luria, 1974) and interact with them based on these stereotyped preconceptions. For instance, parents (particularly fathers) tend to react to their infant boys by encouraging activity and more whole-body stimulation and to their girls with more verbalization, interpersonal stimulation, and nurturance (Fagot & Leinbach, 1993; Stern & Karraker, 1989).

Fathers tend to enforce gender stereotypes more than mothers, especially in sons. This tendency extends across activities and domains, including toy preferences, play styles, chores, discipline, interaction, and personality assessments (Caldera, Huston, & O'Brien, 1989; Fagot & Leinbach, 1993; Lytton & Romney, 1991). Although both boys and girls receive gender messages from their parents, boys are encouraged to conform to culturally valued masculine ideals more than girls are encouraged to conform to lower-status feminine ideals. Boys also receive more rewards for gender conformity (Wood, 1994). Because society places greater emphasis on men's gender identity than on women's, there is a tendency for more attention to be paid to boys, reflecting an androcentric cultural bias that values masculine traits over feminine characteristics (Bem, 1993; Lorber, 1994).

Paradoxically, masculine gender identity is also considered to be more fragile than feminine gender identity (Bem, 1993; Chodorow, 1978; Dinnerstein, 1976; Mead, 1949), and it takes more psychic effort to maintain because it requires suppressing human feelings of vulnerability and denying emotional connection (Chodorow, 1978; Maccoby & Jacklin, 1974). Boys, therefore, are given less gender latitude than girls, and fathers are more intent than mothers on making sure that their sons do not become sissies. Later, as a result, these boys-turned-men will be predisposed to spend considerable amounts of time and energy maintaining gender boundaries and denigrating women and gays (Connell, 1995; Kimmel & Messner, 1998). Nonetheless, fathers' role in sustaining gender difference is neither fixed nor inevitable. Mothers' relatively lax enforcement of gender stereotypes relates to the amount of time they spend with children. Because they perform most of the child care, mothers tend to be more pragmatic about the similarities and dissimilarities between children, and their perceptions of an individual child's abilities are somewhat less likely to be influenced by preconceived gender stereotypes. Similarly, when men are single parents or actively coparent, they behave more like conventional "mothers" than standard "fathers" (Coltrane, 1996; Risman, 1989). Involved fathers, like most mothers, encourage sons and daughters equally, utilizing similar interaction and play styles for both. They also tend to avoid both rigid gender stereotypes and the single-minded emphasis on rough-and-tumble play customary among traditional fathers (Coltrane, 1989; Parke, 1996). As a result, when fathers exhibit close, nurturing ongoing relationships with children, those children develop less stereotyped gender attitudes as teenagers and young adults (Hardesty, Wenk, & Morgan, 1995; Williams, Radin, & Allegro, 1992).

Different treatment of newborn boys and girls, based on their sex, is a product of the behavior of gendered adults (family members and strangers) and institutionalized expectations about gender derived from society as a whole (Coltrane & Adams, 1997). According to psychologist Sandra Bem (1983), gender is not something that is naturally produced in the mind of the child but instead reflects the gender polarization prevalent in the larger culture. Moreover, gender-differentiated treatment continues as the child grows up; gender-appropriateness is reinforced through toys (trucks, sports equipment, and toy guns for boys; dolls, tea sets, and toy stoves for girls), as well as expectations for

behavior that result in praise and reinforcement for "correct" (gender-appropriate) behavior and reprimand and punishment for "incorrect" (gender-inappropriate) behavior. For instance, taking into account the masculine imperative for emotional distance, studies analyzing a number of northern European countries, as well as the United States, find that parents tend to actively discourage displays of emotion in boys by pressuring them not to cry or otherwise express their feelings (Block, 1978, as cited in Maccoby, 1998, p. 139). Girls, in contrast, are not only encouraged to express their emotions but also are taught to pay attention to the feelings of others.

It is not just birth parents and stepparents who socialize children with gendered expectations, but also grandparents, extended family members, fictive kin, teachers, and other adults who are part of children's lives. Although research on such relationships is still rare, most studies find that grandparents, uncles, and other adult men are more likely to relate to boys than to girls, and to demand more gender conformity from children than do their female counterparts (grandmothers, aunts, etc.).

The result of this indoctrination is that, as they become developmentally able, boys and girls incorporate the gendered messages and scripts that parents, grandparents, and other significant adults have communicated to them into their own version of an age-appropriate gender schema (Bem, 1983). A gender schema is a cognitive way of organizing information, a sort of "network of associations" that "functions as an anticipatory structure" ready to "search for and to assimilate incoming information" in terms of relevant schematized categories (Bem, 1983, p. 603). A kind of perceptual lens, a gender schema predisposes a person to see the world in terms of two clearly defined "opposites"— male and female, masculine and feminine. Accordingly, children develop gender schemata without even realizing that the culture in which they live is stereotyped according to gender. Developing networks of associations that guide their perceptions, children come to see the world in gender-polarized ways and live out the gender polarization that they have learned to make their own. Children then go about re-creating, according to their own developmental ability, a world in which boys/men and girls/women are not just different but polar opposites, and where boys/men are generally powerful and privileged. As they grow up, moreover, they come to understand that although most men are more powerful than most women, not all men are equally powerful, and that some (hegemonic) masculinities entail more privilege than other (subordinated) masculinities (Connell, 1987, 1995, 2000; Hearn, 1992).

Children's Agency and the Construction of Gendered Behavior

We see evidence of the ways that children create their own gendered worlds in the fact that, from the time they are about 3 years old, they begin to associate consistently with same-sex playmates, generally without direct provocation or instigation from adult caretakers (Howes & Philipsen, 1992; Maccoby, 1998; Thorne, 1993). In this way, children begin to institute at an early age the gender segregation that traverses adult society. Noting this tendency, sociologist William Corsaro (1997) sees children as "active, creative social agents who produce their own unique children's cultures while simultaneously contributing to the production of adult societies" (p. 4). Moreover, forays into cross-gender territory generally herald advances toward a heterosexual romantic culture rather than enduring friendships that cross gender lines (Adler & Adler, 1998; Eder, 1995; Thorne, 1993). As these social scientists suggest, romantic "crossings" (Thorne, 1993) strengthen traditional gender boundaries and behaviors while reinforcing the gender segregation evident in same-sex friendship groupings.

Boys' play groups and girls' play groups exhibit distinctive styles of play. One significant difference between them is that boys appear to be more separated from the world of adults (Maccoby, 1998), a tradition that begins in the family when boys, between 24 and 36 months of age, begin to invite less contact from their mothers (Clarke-Stewart & Hevey, 1981; Maccoby, 1998; Minton, Kagan, & Levine, 1971). What is unclear about this "separation" is exactly how much is initiated by the child, and how much is initiated by the child's mother or parents, who feel that "too much" mothering can be dangerous to a boy's masculinity (Silverstein & Rashbaum, 1994). This impulse also conforms to the cultural mythology of "mother-blaming,"

reminding us (in movies, on television, and in novels) of the overinvolved, domineering mother who emasculates her son, makes him into a "sissy," and leaves him unfit and unable to take his place in the patriarchal scheme of oppression (Silverstein & Rashbaum, 1994). This separation from the adult world takes the form of increased mischievousness at home, in direct opposition to maternal direction (Minton et al., 1971), and less sensitivity to teachers (Fagot, 1985). Boys also play more roughly than girls, with their interaction frequently bordering on aggression, if not outright violence (Maccoby, 1998). Boys' rough-and-tumble play appears to be designed to create a dominance hierarchy and to mitigate a presumption of weakness (Jordan & Cowan, 1995; Maccoby, 1998; Petit, Bakshi, Dodge, & Coie, 1990); girls, on the other hand, do select leaders, but they draw on leadership qualities other than physical dominance (Charlesworth & Dzur, 1987; Maccoby, 1998). There is even a difference in styles of discourse, with girls negotiating to keep interaction going, while boys simply command and demand, thus stopping effective interaction (Maccoby, 1998, p. 49). Finally, boys' play groups involve more competition than girls', with boys spending much more time playing competitive games and girls focusing on recreation that entails taking turns (Crombie & Desjardins, 1993).

That these tendencies of boys in their same-sex play groups reflect parentally encouraged and socially approved masculine ideals is apparent, as boys display masculinity by withdrawing from adults (mothers, in particular) and by being dominant, competitive, aggressive, and (over)active. Because we take for granted that masculinity is a positive cultural and institutional ideal, we don't tend to view masculinity per se as a negative factor that can cause problems for boys as they negotiate their gender performance against a backdrop of broader principles of social order. Most of the time, when boys' behavior runs counter to social norms, we chuckle that "boys will be boys." When that behavior reaches beyond the acceptable, however, we begin to acknowledge that living up to masculine ideals can, indeed, cause trouble.

Boyhood Troubles

The way we raise boys in our society not only reinforces masculine personality ideals but also encourages behavior that reflects those ideals. We valorize manhood and start, from the beginning of their lives, to transmit that valorization to our children. Children realize, early on, that if they are fortunate enough to be born with the legitimating penis, then they are likely to receive the rewards, rights, privileges, and entitlements that come along with it, although the amount of those rewards is premised on other social factors as well. On the other hand, if they are female, they realize that they are destined to help provide those rewards to their more privileged brothers. That is, children begin to incorporate these ideals into their own perceptions and behaviors and begin to "act out" the gender scripts that they have learned.

Moreover, as gendered parents and grandparents, we expect and encourage boys to pursue our cultural ideals of masculinity. From early in their youth, we teach them (through, for instance, toys and sports) to symbolically correlate competition, violence, power, and domination with masculinity. Finally, we actively insist on their separation from mothers (in effect, their separation from anything feminine that might sully their budding masculinity). In short, by defining masculinity as "anything not feminine" and by defining femininity in conjunction with the family and domesticity, we are, in effect, defining boys and men away from the family and outside it. When the proscription against feminine behavior is translated into behavior attenuated by developmental stage, boys often end up in trouble—overactive and inattentive in school (the class clown), competitive and aggressive, even violent. Studies show that elementary school–aged boys are up to four times as likely as girls to be sent to child psychologists, twice as likely to be considered "learning disabled," and much more likely (up to 10 times) to be diagnosed with emotional maladies such as attention deficit disorder (Kimmel, 2000, p. 160; Pollack, 1998). Studies also show that "problem behaviors" of adolescent boys (including school suspension, drinking, use of street drugs, police detainment, sexual activity, number of heterosexual partners, and forcing someone to have sex) are associated with traditional masculine ideology (Christopher & Sprecher, 2000; Hearn, 1990; Pleck, Sonenstein, & Ku, 1994; Schwartz & Rutter, 1998).

Aggression has become a touchstone for American adolescent boys, and violence among them is epidemic. Kaufman (1998) noted that men construct their masculinity amid a triad of violence: men against women, men against men, and men against themselves. Hearn (1990) added another dimension to this triad, pointing out how men's normalized, institutionalized power and violence (reflected, for example, in business, sports, and even the historical "social relations of paternity") not only contribute to but also become child abuse and exploitation. Thus, men's violence applies even to adolescent boys, and it results, at least in part, from their internalizing the masculine ideal and attempting to live up to its precepts; as Hearn (1990, p. 85) points out, the problem lies not in "dangerous men" but in the "state of 'normal masculinity.'" Normal masculinity is evident in young men's violence against women, which Kaufman (1998, p. 4) suggests represents both an individual "acting out" of power relations and an individual's enactment of social power relations (sexism); it plays out in instances of rape (acquaintance and stranger) and sexual harassment, and it is perpetrated in all-male enclaves such as fraternities (Lefkowitz, 1997; Sanday, 1990) and athletic teams (Benedict, 1997). Research analyzing rape figures between 1979 and 1987 shows that youths 20 years old and younger accounted for 18% of single-offender and 30% of multiple-offender rapes (Kershner, 1996); the FBI reports, moreover, that adolescent males accounted for the greatest increase in arrested rape perpetrators in the United States during the early 1990s (Ingrassia, 1993; see also Kershner, 1996).

Male youth violence against other males is extensive, creating battlefields out of city parks and school playgrounds. Gangs of all racial and ethnic groups flourish in urban areas as adolescent boys attempt to create "family" with tools honed to incorporate ideals of manhood. In 1997, it was estimated that there were 30,500 youth gangs and 815,896 gang members active in the United States (National Youth Gang Center, 1999). Among youth, teenaged boys tend to be both the most frequent perpetrators of violent crimes and, as a group, the most frequent victims of such crimes. Although preteen boys and girls are equally as likely to be homicide victims, once children reach their teen years, boys are significantly more likely than girls to be murdered (Snyder & Sickmund, 1999). They are also more murderous than young women, representing 93% of known juvenile homicide offenders between 1980 and 1997. During the same time period fewer than 10 juvenile homicide offenders per year were age 10 or younger, and 88% of these offenders were also male (Snyder & Sickmund, 1999, pp. 53-54).

Of late, young men's violence has spilled over into more traditionally "safe," institutionalized space. In the United States, the school shootings of the 1990s (carried out overwhelmingly by boys, most of whom were from "good" [i.e., unbroken] homes) further attest to the lack of fit between how boys are learning to be men and the men that society wants. Disturbingly, a number of these rampages were orchestrated by boys who were seen by their peers not as bullies (the masculine ideal) but as bullied (the feminine counterpart), thus highlighting the desperate actions sometimes undertaken by young men to prove their "normal" masculinity against the public threat of being viewed as feminine.

Men's violence against themselves also can manifest itself in adolescence. One of the ways men do violence against themselves is by "stuffing" their emotions, in pursuit of a traditionally masculine ideal that reflects dread of feminine hyperemotionality. Young men are encouraged to avoid displays of emotion, as are young boys; we even tend to "see" male newborns as less emotional than their female counterparts, reading onto them the expectations of masculine non-emotionality. As boys grow up, they "often fail to learn the language with which they could describe their feelings, and without language it is hard for anyone to make sense of what he feels" (Phillips, 1994, p. 67). One articulation of this problem is the preponderance of suicide committed by male adolescents. In 1996, for example, 2,119 suicides in the United States involved youth under the age of 19, 80% of whom were male (Snyder & Sickmund, 1999, p. 24). Male youth suicide is a trend that extends beyond the United States: A Finnish study of adolescent males who committed suicide, for instance, showed that, compared with those with psychiatric disorders, those suicides with no diagnosable psychiatric disorders (that is, the "normal" boys) came from less disturbed families, were less antisocial, and used health care and social services less often (Marttunen et al., 1998, p. 669). Moreover, they had communicated intent to commit suicide for the first time shortly before actually taking their own lives,

suggesting a lack of emotional communication to those who might otherwise have provided help to them (Marttunen et al., 1998).

Boys Into Men:
Preparation for Family Life

Just as boys are expected to reject their mothers and leave their families (physically and emotionally) in order to achieve manhood, so, too, they are expected to return to family life after a period of time to create and lead families of their own. By the end of adolescence, these young men have been socialized into, and have internalized, the norms, values, and entitlements of the masculine ideal on a personal level, largely through interaction with gender-conscious parents and kin, as well as through involvement with same-sex school peer groups. As they leave adolescence, in the interim between being banished from and returning to family life, however, boys-becoming-men are often subjected to a higher level of initiation into manhood involving male bonding and solidification of the collective practice of masculinity; these initiation rites tap into interests that extend, moreover, to corporate, state, and even global levels (Connell, 1987, 1990, 1998, 2000; Hearn, 1990, 1992; Kimmel, 1996) and affect the ways men later interact in families. If athletic, young men join male-only football, basketball, or baseball teams; at college they are encouraged to belong to all-male fraternities; in the army, navy, marines, or air force, they are enlisted in the ranks of a group that, if not all-male, is overwhelmingly so; and in the workplace, they enter sex-stratified occupational organizations. Each of these male-dominated associations has its own rituals that involve strengthening masculine ideals and notions of entitlement, already internalized at a personal level, at an abstract level that makes them appear to be, more than ever, part of the "natural" gender order. Full initiation into such groups usually involves some type of woman- and/or gay-bashing activity that accentuates the boundary between male and not male, masculinity and femininity, heterosexuality and homosexuality. These activities entail a "link between personal experience and power relations" (Connell, 1990, p. 507), or, more specifically, *collective* male experiences and power. Through such fratriarchal (Remy, 1990) activities as college fraternity pranks (Lyman, 1998), collective condoning of gang or individual rape (Lefkowitz, 1997; Sanday, 1990), corporate victimization (Szockyj & Fox, 1996), and sexual harassment of women and homosexuals (Connell, 1992, 1995; Morris, 1994), these organizations inaugurate boys into "real" manhood at a social level (Hearn, 1992). With inauguration into the collective production of oppression, men become participants in and supporters of, to a greater or lesser extent based on cross-cutting issues of race and class, social institutions of inequality such as sexism, racism, classism, and homosexism (Hearn, 1990).

Historically, war also has been a fertile initiation ground for the collective practice of manhood; as sociologist Michael Kimmel (1996) noted, "All wars . . . are meditations on masculinity" (p. 72). As traditionally masculine enterprises, wars tend to institutionalize certain hegemonic ideals of masculinity, "distinguish[ing] 'more manly' from 'less manly' groups" (Connell, 1998, p. 13). For example, the recent "war on terrorism" has reinvigorated a certain image of "real" men as "[b]rawny, heroic, manly" (Brown, 2001, p. 5), at the same time connecting those images to gendered sex roles: "In contrast to past eras of touchy-feeliness (Alan Alda) and the vaguely feminized, rakish man-child of the 1990s (Leonardo DiCaprio), the notion of physical prowess in the service of patriotic duty is firmly back on the pedestal" (Brown, 2001, p. 5). State-sanctioned violence and aggression are once again being linked to masculinity through wartime imagery and discourse, for "without war, he [the male citizen warrior] would not know who he was or what the world was about" (Gibson, 1994, p. 308; see also Miedzian, 1991). Generally speaking, then, the collective practice of masculinity serves, both directly and indirectly, the interests of the state (and its corporate arm), which needs men who are aggressive, prone to violence, unemotional, patriotic, competitive, and somewhat distanced from family. Theoretically, the interests of the state (as the "general patriarch" [Mies, 1986, p. 26]) can also be seen as supporting the interests of the husband (as the "individual patriarch" [Connell, 1990, p. 507]), a collaboration apparent, for instance, in the lack of concern historically displayed by the state in intruding on a husband's "right" to batter or rape his wife (Caulfield & Wonders, 1993; Hearn, 1990; Mies, 1986).

MEN'S PRIVILEGED STATUS IN FAMILIES

Eventually, the boys that their families have socialized to be unemotional, violent, self-centered manly men tend to make their way back into families. Having internalized personal interpretations of masculine ideals and subsequently experienced valorization and reinforcement of those ideals in institutionalized settings, young men are expected to (re)turn to the family setting to prove their maturity (Ehrenreich, 1983) and enact what they have learned about being men. Although their social status changes at marriage, young men's personalized gender regimes (Connell, 1987) do not, and they often find themselves "force-fitting" their masculine ideals into the domestic sphere, a setting that is, by definition, feminine. Thus, rather than participating in families through caring, nurturing, and serving, men generally try instead to mold families to conform to their own sense of masculine entitlement, expecting that family members, particularly their wives, will care for and serve them. Historically, getting married signaled becoming a "respectable family man" and was "set against and constructed in relation to what were perceived to be the extra-familial and 'dangerous' masculinities of the undomesticated male" (Collier, 1995, p. 220). Scholars have documented how industrialization and urbanization undermined traditional social controls in society at large, raising fears among the growing middle class about the licentious sexuality and violence of lower-class men and recent immigrants. Hearn (1992), Collier (1995), Connell (1990), Kimmel (1996), and others have shown how the bifurcation between the dangerous and the familial emerged as Victorian ideals of separate spheres institutionalized new forms of public masculinities. Hearn (1992, pp. 81-82) suggested that in complex and historically specific ways, public domains were constructed by men to secure power from women. Men's separation from the birth process, and from the emotional care and child rearing that became associated with private families, in conjunction with the growth of industrial capitalism and more complex states, drove them to establish new forms of patriarchy. Fraternal recreation and social organizations, fratriarchal dominance of public space, and continued sexual exploitation of marginalized women coexisted with newer forms of masculine power and control, including a special form of technical rationality associated with corporations and bureaucracies. Inside families, men continued to exercise power and control over women sexually, socially, and physically, though often under the name of a religiously sanctioned paternal authority. Feminist theorists have long suggested that both public and private forms of patriarchy were developed by men so that they might control women's reproductive power (e.g., Hearn, 1987; O'Brien, 1981; Rubin, 1975; Sanday, 1981).

Marriage and family laws (until recently developed solely by men) generally encouraged continuity of male privilege between the public sphere and the home (see Collier, 1995; also Grossberg, 1990). For example, the common-law doctrine of coverture, which essentially made the wife not only the property but also the person of the husband, was *officially* abandoned only in the mid-19th century (Grossberg, 1985). The ideal of a wife giving up her identity to her husband continues to pervade the symbolic meaning of marriage, illustrated by women adopting the surname of their husband when they marry (Goodman, 2001; Johnson & Scheuble, 1995). Moreover, the traditional (albeit unwritten) marriage contract making the husband the head of, and responsible party for, the household and making the wife responsible for domestic services and child care (Weitzman, 1981) continues to provide ideological support for maintenance of a traditional man-as-provider, woman-as-family-caretaker model of family life. This ideological (and legal) model, in turn, allows a husband to be cared for and nurtured, even while sustaining his image of himself as independent and autonomous, that is, masculine.

This traditional family picture may work for a man as long as he has a traditional wife willing both to care for him and to deny that she is doing so, thus shoring up his fragile masculine image that revolves around "resist[ing] the regressive wish to be cared for" (Nock, 1998, p. 47). Some researchers suggest that "normative" family life is good for men; according to sociologist Steven Nock (1998), married men "earn more, work more, and have better jobs" (p. 82) than their nonmarried counterparts. Men also tend to benefit more from marriage than do women (Bernard, 1972; Fowers, 1991), reporting greater marital satisfaction and rating their marriages more positively in terms of finances, parenting, family, friends, and their partner's personality (Fowers, 1991). Finally, married men are less depressed and have lower rates of mental disorder than do married women (Busfield, 1996; Horwitz, White, & Howell-White, 1996; Marks, 1996). In short, traditional marriage appears to be a good deal for men.

The Gendered Domestic Division of Labor

One of the main reasons men benefit from marriage is the unequal and taken-for-granted division of domestic labor. Research shows that women historically have shouldered the overwhelming bulk of responsibility for doing household labor, spending three times the amount of time as men doing routine everyday household tasks (for a review, see Coltrane, 2000). Moreover, even though in recent decades women have increasingly entered the paid labor force and share, more than ever, the burden of providing financially for the family, men continue to do significantly less than their equal share of housework, claiming disinterest, disinclination, or general lack of aptitude (Deutsch, 1999). Along this line, doing household labor has been equated with doing gender; women do it and men don't, and disruptions in this pattern can be threatening to a family's gender order.

Proving that housework is not *inherently* gendered, studies show that men do more housework before they are married than they do after. Once married, however, they have the opportunity to denote most domestic chores as "women's work" and turn them over to their (less powerful) wives. Research does show that, overall, American men have begun to do a greater share of housework in recent decades, although much of this gain is the result of women doing less (Robinson & Godbey, 1999). In general, married men tend to create the need for more housework than they perform (Coltrane, 2000). Although some social scientists hail the relatively slight increase in men's housework performance as highly significant, others suggest that this small change "should be better understood in terms of a largely successful male resistance" (McMahon, 1999, p. 7). Why are men resisting? The short (and short-term) answer is that it is in men's interest to do so (Goode, 1992; McMahon, 1999), because it reinforces a separation of spheres that underpins masculine ideals and perpetuates a gender order privileging (some) men over women and over (some) other men. On the whole, we raise boys to expect mothers to wait on them and nurture them, and we raise girls to help their mothers perform the endless family work that is necessary for maintaining homes and raising children. It is no surprise that after being propelled away from families for a time, most young men come back to family life with a sense of masculine entitlement, expecting to be served by women and not noticing the myriad details of family life that demand someone's attention (Pyke & Coltrane, 1996).

Although family living has been found to be a protective factor for men with respect to some risky behaviors (Nock, 1998), attempting to live up to masculine ideals can put men at risk inside families as well as outside them. The psychological and emotional energy exerted to be in control, unemotional, independent, and uninvolved affects men's relations with their wives and children, as well as having deleterious medical consequences for the men themselves (Sabo, 1998). One of the most consistent problems identified by women with respect to marriage is their husbands' lack of communication and emotional expression (Coltrane, 1998; L. B. Rubin, 1983). This gender-stereotyped division of emotional labor even pervades men's friendships with women: One woman in L. B. Rubin's (1985) study of friendship commented, "I have one man friend I love very much, but I don't relate to him like I do to a woman. I can't talk to him the same way, and when I try, I'm disappointed. Either we're talking about him and his problems and I'm sort of like a mother or big sister, or it's all so heady and intellectualized that it's boring" (p. 160). Finally, men's relationships with their children suffer to the extent that they adopt emotionally remote and inexpressive styles of masculinity. A typical response to an emotionally absent father comes from one 17-year-old, interviewed by clinical psychologist William Pollack: "[M]y father is like his own father. He's not very communicative. I don't care if he coaches my soccer team for nine years in a row; I would rather he just talked to me once in a while" (Pollack, 2000, p. 238).

The shortcomings of men in families are not limited to inattention or emotional remoteness. Aided by governmental neglect and protected by the privacy of their homes, men have long

been expected to "keep women and children in their place" with the threat and use of physical force; moreover, to the extent that this expectation is normalized as a symbol of masculinity, violence and the threat of violence become one and the same (see Hearn, 1990). In the United States alone, estimates range up to 4 million women per year who are physically abused by their male partners (Greenfeld et al., 1998). Far too many women and children will continue to be the victims of domestic terror; as Kaufman (1993) noted, "all women, directly or indirectly, experience at least the *potential* of domination, violence, coercion and harassment at the hands of men" (p. 44).

MEN IN TRADITIONAL FAMILIES—A CATCH-22

For a number of reasons, men's experiences in families have been problematized within the last several decades, primarily at the instigation of the second wave of the women's rights movement, which started in earnest in the late 1960s. Feminism began largely as a movement about families and about the need for change in families; much of that need revolved around men's involvement (or lack of involvement) in those families. As women became more committed to breadwinning, they began to see themselves as more than "helpmates" for men; they began to envision a public life of their own and, as a result, a larger, more involved role in family for their male partners. While the relational aspects of traditional notions of gender demanded that a man could "only be a 'real man' if someone is around being a 'real woman'" (Kaufman, 1993, p. 47), it became clear that many women no longer had the time or the inclination to be "real women" in that sense, shielding their husbands from the contradictions of power and helplessness inherent in masculine ideals.

Women's new roles and self-images as family providers made them less inclined to play at "fascinating womanhood" (Andelin, 1974), living only for and through "their men." As women's collective consciousness was raised, men began to find themselves face-to-face with their own alienation from families. More important, feminism gave men a new vantage point from which to view their position in the family. As feminists introduced the politics of the personal, men came to see home as more than their castle and as, instead, a place where their children were growing up under their noses and without their involvement. Men in families, or more appropriately, outside families, began to recognize the emotional costs of chasing masculine ideals.

Economic structural shifts also affected men's sense of family involvement. The global and national economic transition from industry to service, "or from production to consumption, is symbolically a move from the traditional masculine to the traditional feminine" (Faludi, 1999, p. 38). As heavy manufacturing was replaced by the information economy, men began to find their masculine ideals less serviceable. Women's workforce participation and associated wages have increased gradually over the decades, whereas men's wages and job stability have stabilized or declined (Coltrane & Collins, 2001). As men have been economically "downsized" and as their wives have taken their own places as family providers, it has become harder to justify masculine entitlement.

Although these are not the only precipitating factors, they certainly have helped to problematize men's place in families and caused them to reexamine their taken-for-granted assumptions regarding the benefits of living up to a hegemonic ideal of masculinity. Structurally, psychologically, and relationally, these issues point to the tensions present for men in family life, tensions exacerbated by the felt need to live up to certain ideals of manhood that make them outsiders to the family. On one hand, hegemonic masculine ideals have provided them with power and privilege, in the home and in society at large. On the other hand, men have begun to realize the cost of their alienation from family life. In many ways, this tension represents a "line of fault" or "rupture in consciousness" (Smith, 1987, p. 52) between the ideals of masculinity and the experience of family life that is expressed in "feminized" terms of nurturance, caring, self-sacrifice, and dependence. This fault line has been articulated as a crisis of masculinity (Connell, 1995; Messner, 1997).

Attempts at Resolution

Various social and personal attempts have been made to resolve the rupture between men's experience in families and their masculine ideals, but most have failed because they continue to advocate for a masculinity that is defined in opposition to femininity. The 1980s ushered in the mythopoetic men's movement, which promoted a drum-beating, chest-thumping return to wildness in an attempt to reclaim the "'the deep masculine parts' of themselves that they believed had been lost" (Messner, 1997, p. 17). Far from being a radical departure from the status quo, this movement championed the search for some mythical quintessential masculinity that could overcome the "mother-son conspiracy" that was evicting fathers and feminizing sons, making them "soft males" (Bly, 1990, pp. 2, 18).

The 1990s brought the neoconservative, religiously oriented Promise Keepers, filling football stadiums across the United States (and other parts of the world) with "born-again Christians who interpret the bible literally and believe that men are ordained to serve God and lead their families" (Coltrane, 2001, p. 403). Promising to be better husbands and fathers, these men commit to being "servant leaders" in the home and to bond emotionally with other men in support of this goal; their wives, on the other hand, are encouraged to make a sort of "patriarchal bargain" (Anderson & Messner, 1997; also see Kandiyoti, 1988) and graciously submit to their husband's leadership in the home in exchange for his being a better family man. Other religiously based marriage proponents have joined political forces with conservative think tanks and communitarian social scientists to forge a public relations campaign promoting marriage and "responsible fatherhood" in the United States. These "family values" movements reflect the patriarchal ideal of separate spheres by insisting that fathers are the natural "head" of the family and rejecting the notion that women and men should participate equally in housework, child care, and economic provision.

Finally, many men have simply opted out of family life. Barbara Ehrenreich (1983) attributes men's lack of family commitment to a breakdown in the breadwinner ethic; encouraged to work and earn a "family wage," many men simply have chosen not to share that wage with a family. Other fathers will, after divorce, make monetary support payments but essentially disappear from their families' lives, abstaining from involvement with their children that requires a direct investment of their time; still others contribute neither financial nor nonfinancial support (Goldscheider, 2000, p. 532; Teachman, 1992). Even when contact is maintained initially, children's involvement with nonresident fathers tends to decline over time, especially for children whose fathers left when they were quite young. Although organizations promoting fathers' rights have had some success in promoting joint custody in divorce cases involving children, the rate of postdivorce father-child contact has been increasing very slowly (Bertoia & Drakich, 1993; Coltrane & Hickman, 1992). Despite massive efforts to increase child support payments from absent fathers, recent improvements in the amount collected have been modest (Coltrane & Collins, 2001). These various attempts to deal with men's alienation from families only tend to reinforce aspects of masculinity that contributed to men being family outsiders in the first place. The men involved in these movements generally fail to embrace and incorporate ideals of nurturing, emotionality, and service to others that might help resolve some of the contradictions they face as family members.

RESOLVING THE LINE OF FAULT

Our discussion has focused on the ways that the social construction of separate spheres and public masculinities in the 19th and 20th centuries has created dilemmas for boys and men in families. Our account draws on a historical understanding of developments in the United States and, to a lesser extent, England and other capitalist industrial countries (see, for example, Hearn, 1992). The broad outlines of our thesis, however, may apply more broadly. Research on nonindustrial societies suggests that if men and women share domestic tasks, they are also more likely to share wealth, property, and political decision making (Coltrane, 1989, 1992; Johnson, 1988; Sanday, 1981). There is a direct correspondence between sharing power in more public domains and sharing the care and drudgery of domestic life in the family domain.

We have argued that men's exercise of authority in public realms through the institution of social patriarchy both enables and undermines men's family experiences. Private

patriarchy, or the power and authority that men exercise within family settings, is both enhanced and subverted by social patriarchy. Women's entry into paid labor, along with their modest gains in terms of career mobility and earnings potential, has weakened social patriarchy, causing new tensions to emerge in families. Whereas women previously were dependent on marriage for economic security, they may now survive apart from men. Men are no longer afforded the unpaid services of a wife in return for being an economic provider. This makes marriage more optional and contingent for both women and men. We are currently witnessing emergent forms of marital negotiation and sharing not contingent on the economic and political dominance of men. To be sure, men still enjoy earnings and career advantages, and cultural and political arenas still tend to privilege men's needs over women's. Nevertheless, men increasingly are being challenged to share in the nurturing and emotional labor that is essential in the raising of children and the maintenance of family life. Men are resisting, but some are learning how to share in the everyday tasks of cooking and cleaning, and many are developing the emotional capacities and understandings that enable them to share in the upbringing of the next generation. More sharing in the family (however limited) mirrors more sharing in the public realms of politics and occupations.

When families work well, they provide security, a sense of self, a heightened understanding of others, and an atmosphere of caring, loving, and nurturing. Social animals that we are, families provide the first, and most basic, social grouping for our survival and can sustain us in our darker moments of solitude. But families are changing. The end of the 20th century witnessed a remarkable increase in family diversity as families took on more and different forms and functions. Along with the proliferation of diverse types of families, we have been introduced into new ways of "doing family" (Gubrium & Holstein, 1990), with the older traditional ways becoming harder and harder to sustain, both physically and psychologically. We can't go back to the separate spheres ideal of the Victorian era or the nostalgic Ozzie and Harriet family of the 1950s where "men were men" and "women were women," and never the twain would meet (Coontz, 1992, 1997). Nor should we want to go back. Promoting family life where men hang onto stereotypes of manhood that leave them distant and unattached outsiders or dominating patriarchs has proven to be both uncomfortable and unworkable. In such families, "masculinized" men find themselves "missing something" as human beings. Women find themselves struggling with the "second shift" of housework and child care. Both find themselves losing out on the emotional connections that companionate marriage ideals have promised, and children find themselves with fathers who are absent emotionally, even when physically present.

In this chapter, we have examined how we push boys, both interpersonally and institutionally, to follow an abstract dominant ideal of masculinity that instructs them that, in order to be masculine, they must avoid the feminine. We also have seen how living up to masculine ideals can result in men's contradictory experiences of entitlement and alienation, privilege and pain, which in turn causes problems for women and children. How can this dilemma be resolved? As optimists, we believe that feminism has given men the tools to resolve this disjuncture between ideals and experience, entitlement and alienation, but to do so requires getting rid of the assumption that masculinity is the antithesis of femininity, and that to be a man, one has to prove that he is not a woman. Without the burden of this supposition, boys would no longer need to be torn from their mothers and families in order to make them "real men." They could then incorporate the virtues of nurturing, caring, service, and emotional involvement that provide the underpinnings for successful family functioning. Without laboring under the abstraction of dominant masculinity, men would be freed to become family insiders and full participants, rather than outsiders and tyrants. Such changes will not be easy, nor will they be welcomed by those who feel more comfortable with separate gender spheres. But the structural and cultural forces promoting more egalitarian gender relations undoubtedly will increase some men's participation in family life and will continue to promote diversity in forms of cohabitation, marriage, and child rearing. These developments will create further pressures for change in masculine ideals throughout society. We wonder, however, if such pressures will grow strong enough to overcome long-standing military,

economic, political, and psychological interests in creating men who conform to and reproduce patriarchal masculinities. We can only raise the question here; the answer, however, could change the world.

REFERENCES

Adams, M., & Coltrane, S. (2004). Boys and men in families. In S. Coltrane (Ed.), *Families and society: Classic and contemporary readings* (pp.189-198). Belmont, CA: Wadsworth/Thomson Learning.

Adler, P. A., & Adler, P. (1998). *Peer power: Preadolescent culture and identity.* New Brunswick, NJ: Rutgers University Press.

Andelin, H. B. (1974). *Fascinating womanhood.* Santa Barbara, CA: Pacific Press Santa Barbara.

Anderson, C., & Messner, M. A. (1997, April). *The political is personal: Masculinity therapy and patriarchal bargains among the Promise Keepers.* Paper presented at the annual meeting of the Pacific Sociological Association, San Francisco, CA.

Balakrishnan, R. (1994). The social context of sex selection and the politics of abortion in India. In G. Sen & R. C. Snow (Eds.), *Power and decision: The social control of reproduction* (pp. 267-286). Cambridge, MA: Harvard School of Public Health.

Bem, S. L. (1983). Gender schema theory and its implications for child development: Raising gender-aschematic children in a gender-schematic society. *Signs, 8,* 598-616.

Bem, S. L. (1993). *The lenses of gender: Transforming the debate on sexual inequality.* New Haven, CT: Yale University Press.

Benedict, J. (1997). *Public heroes, private felons: Athletes and crimes against women.* Boston: Northeastern University Press.

Berger, P., & Luckmann, T. (1966). *The social construction of reality: A treatise on the sociology of knowledge.* Garden City, NY: Doubleday.

Bernard, J. S. (1972). *The future of marriage.* New York: The World Publishing Co.

Bertoia, C., & Drakich, J. (1993). The fathers' rights movement: Contradictions in rhetoric and practice. *Journal of Family Issues, 14*(4), 592-615.

Bhuiya, A., & Streatfield, K. (1991). Mothers' education and survival of female children in a rural area of Bangladesh. *Population Studies, 45,* 253-264.

Blumer, H. (1969). *Symbolic interactionism: Perspective and method.* Berkeley: University of California Press.

Bly, R. (1990). *Iron John: A book about men.* Reading, MA: Addison-Wesley.

Bose, C. E. (1987). Dual spheres. In B. B. Hess & M. M. Ferree (Eds.), *Analyzing gender: A handbook of social science research* (pp. 267-285). Newbury Park, CA: Sage.

Bozinoff, L., & Turcotte, A. (1993, May 10). Canadians are perplexed about choosing child's sex. *Gallup Report,* pp. 1-2.

Brown, P. L. (2001, October 28). Heavy lifting required: The return of manly men. *New York Times,* p. 5.

Brush, L. D. (1999). Gender, work, who cares?! In M. M. Ferree, J. Lorder, & B. B. Hess (Eds.), *Revisioning gender* (pp. 161-189). Thousand Oaks, CA: Sage.

Busfield, J. (1996). *Men, women, and madness: Understanding gender and mental disorder.* New York: New York University Press.

Cahill, S. E. (1986). Childhood socialization as a recruitment process: Some lessons from the study of gender development. *Sociological Studies of Child Development, 1,* 163-186.

Caldera, Y. M., Huston, A. C., & O'Brien, M. (1989). Social interactions and play patterns of parents and toddlers with feminine, masculine, and neutral toys. *Child Development, 60,* 70-76.

Caulfield, S. L., & Wonders, N. A. (1993). Personal AND political: Violence against women and the role of the state. In K. D. Tunnell (Ed.), *Political crime in contemporary America: A critical approach* (pp. 79-100). New York: Garland.

Charlesworth, W. R., & Dzur, C. (1987). Gender comparisons of preschoolers' behavior and resource utilization in group problem-solving. *Child Development, 58,* 191-200.

Chen, L. C., Huq, E., & D'Souza, S. (1981). Sex bias in the family allocation of food and health care in rural Bangladesh. *Population and Development Review, 7,* 55-57.

Chodorow, N. J. (1978). *The reproduction of mothering.* Berkeley: University of California Press.

Christopher, F. S., & Sprecher, S. (2000). Sexuality in marriage, dating, and other relationships: A decade review. *Journal of Marriage and the Family, 62*(4), 999-1017.

Chunkath, S. R., & Athreya, V. B. (1997). Female infanticide in Tamil Nadu: Some evidence. *Economic and Political Weekly, 32*(17), 21-28.

Clarke-Stewart, K. A., & Hevey, C. M. (1981). Longitudinal relations in repeated observations of mother-child interaction from 1 to 1½ years. *Developmental Psychology, 17*(2), 127-145.

Collier, R. (1995). *Masculinity, law and the family.* London: Routledge.

Collins, R. (1986). Courtly politics and the status of women. In *Weberian sociological theory* (pp. 297-321). New York: Cambridge University Press.

Coltrane, S. (1989). Household labor and the routine production of gender. *Social Problems, 36,* 473-490.

Coltrane, S. (1992). The micropolitics of gender in nonindustrial societies. *Gender and Society, 6,* 86-107.

Coltrane, S. (1996). *Family man: Fatherhood, housework, and gender equity.* New York: Oxford University Press.

Coltrane, S. (1998). *Gender and families.* Thousand Oaks, CA: Pine Forge Press.

Coltrane, S. (2000). Research on household labor: Modeling and measuring the social embeddedness of routine family work. *Journal of Marriage and the Family, 62,* 1208-1233.

Coltrane, S. (2001). Marketing the marriage "solution": Misplaced simplicity in the politics of fatherhood. *Sociological Perspectives, 44*(4), 387-418.

Coltrane, S., & Adams, M. (1997). Children and gender. In T. Arendell (Ed.), *Contemporary parenting: Challenges and issues* (pp. 219-253). Thousand Oaks, CA: Sage.

Coltrane, S., & Collins, R. (2001). *Sociology of marriage and the family: Gender, love, and property* (5th ed.). Belmont, CA: Wadsworth/ Thomson Learning.

Coltrane, S., & Hickman, N. (1992). The rhetoric of rights and needs: Moral discourse in the reform of child custody and child support laws. *Social Problems, 39*(4), 400-420.

Connell, R. W. (1987). *Gender and power: Society, the person, and sexual politics.* Stanford, CA: Stanford University Press.

Connell, R. W. (1990). The state, gender and sexual politics. *Theory and Society, 19*(5), 507-544.

Connell, R. W. (1992). A very straight gay: Masculinity, homosexual experience, and the dynamics of gender. *American Sociological Review, 57*(6), 735-751.

Connell, R. W. (1995). *Masculinities.* Berkeley: University of California Press.

Connell, R. W. (1998). Masculinities and globalization. *Men and Masculinities, 1*(1), 3-23.

Connell, R. W. (2000). *The men and the boys.* Berkeley: University of California Press.

Coontz, S. (1992). *The way we never were: American families and the nostalgia trap.* New York: Basic Books.

Coontz, S. (1997). *The way we really are: Coming to terms with America's changing families.* New York: Basic Books.

Corsaro, W. A. (1997). *The sociology of childhood.* Thousand Oaks, CA: Pine Forge Press.

Cowan, G., & Hoffman, C. (1986). Gender stereotyping in young children: Evidence to support a concept-learning model. *Sex Roles, 14,* 211-224.

Crombie, G., & Desjardins, M. J. (1993, March). *Predictors of gender: The relative importance of children's play, games and personality characteristics.* Paper presented at the biennial meeting of the Society for Research in Child Development, New Orleans.

Deutsch, F. M. (1999). *Halving it all: How equally shared parenting works.* Cambridge, MA: Harvard University Press.

Dinnerstein, D. (1976). *The mermaid and the minotaur: Sexual arrangements and sexual malaise.* New York: Harper & Row.

Eder, D., with Evans, C. C., & Parker, S. (1995). *School talk: Gender and adolescent culture.* New Brunswick, NJ: Rutgers University Press.

Ehrenreich, B. (1983). *The hearts of men: American dreams and the flight from commitment.* New York: Anchor Press.

Elkin, F., & Handel, G. (1989). *The child and society: The process of socialization.* New York: McGraw-Hill.

Fagot, B. I. (1985). Beyond the reinforcement principle: Another step toward understanding sex-role development. *Developmental Psychology, 21,* 1097-1104.

Fagot, B. I., & Leinbach, M. D. (1993). Gender role development in young children: From discrimination to labeling. *Developmental Review, 13,* 205-224.

Faludi, S. (1999). *Stiffed: The betrayal of the American man.* New York: William Morrow and Company.

Fowers, B. J. (1991). His and her marriage: A multivariate study of gender and marital satisfaction. *Sex Roles, 24*(3/4), 209-222.

Garfinkel, H. (1967). *Studies in ethnomethodology.* Englewood Cliffs, NJ: Prentice Hall.

Geertz, C. (1973). *The interpretation of cultures.* New York: Basic Books.

George, S., Rajaratnam, A., & Miller, B. D. (1992, May 10). Female infanticide in rural South India. *Economic and Political Weekly,* pp. 1153-1156.

Gibson, J. W. (1994). *Warrior dreams: Violence and manhood in post-Vietnam America.* New York: Hill and Wang.

Goffman, E. (1967). *Interaction ritual.* New York: Doubleday.

Goldscheider, F. K. (2000). Men, children and the future of the family in the third millennium. *Futures, 32,* 525-538.

Goode, W. (1992). Why men resist. In B. Thorne & M. Yalom (Eds.), *Rethinking the family: Some feminist questions* (Rev. ed., pp. 287-310). Boston: Northeastern University Press.

Goodman, E. (2001, September 4). Marriage name game is still being played. *Riverside Press Enterprise,* p. A10.

Greenfeld, L. A., Rand, M. R., Craven, D., Klaus, P. A., Perkins, C. A., Ringel, C., et al. (1998). *Violence by intimates: Analysis of data on crimes by current or former spouses, boyfriends, and girlfriends.* Washington, DC: U.S. Department of Justice. Retrieved from http://www.ojp.usdoj.gov/bjs/pub/pdf/vi.pdf

Griswold del Castillo, R. (1984). *La Familia* [The Family]. Notre Dame, IN: University of Notre Dame Press.

Grossberg, M. (1985). *Governing the hearth: Law and the family in nineteenth-century America.* Chapel Hill: University of North Carolina Press.

Grossberg, M. (1990). Institutionalizing masculinity: The law as a masculine profession. In M. C. Carnes & C. Griffen (Eds.), *Meanings for manhood: Constructions of masculinity in Victorian America* (pp. 133-151). Chicago: The University of Chicago Press.

Gubrium, J. F., & Holstein, J. A. (1990). *What is family?* Mountain View, CA: Mayfield.

Hardesty, C., Wenk, D., & Morgan, C. S. (1995). Paternal involvement and the development of gender expectations in sons and daughters. *Youth & Society, 26*(3), 283-297.

Hearn, J. (1987). *The gender of oppression: Men, masculinity, and the critique of Marxism.* Brighton: Wheatsheaf.

Hearn, J. (1990). "Child abuse" and men's violence. In The Violence Against Children Study Group, *Taking child abuse seriously: Contemporary issues in child protection theory and practice* (pp. 63-85). London: Unwin Hyman.

Hearn, J. (1992). *Men in the public eye: The construction and deconstruction of public men and public patriarchies.* London: Routledge.

Horwitz, A. V., White, H. R., & Howell-White, S. (1996). Becoming married and mental health: A longitudinal study of a cohort of young adults. *Journal of Marriage and the Family, 58,* 895-907.

Howes, C., & Philipsen, L. (1992). Gender and friendship: Relationships within peer groups of young children. *Social Development, 1*(3), 230-242.

Hughes, J. S. (1990). The madness of separate spheres: Insanity and masculinity in Victorian Alabama. In M. C. Carnes & C. Griffen (Eds.), *Meanings for manhood: Constructions of masculinity in Victorian America* (pp. 53-66). Chicago: The University of Chicago Press.

Ingrassia, M., with Annin, P., Biddle, N. A., & Miller, S. (1993, July 19). Life means nothing. *Newsweek,* pp. 16-17.

Johnson, D. R., & Scheuble, L. K. (1995). Women's marital naming in two generations: A national study. *Journal of Marriage and the Family, 57*(3), 724-732.

Johnson, M. M. (1988). *Strong mothers, weak wives: The search for gender equality.* Berkeley: University of California Press.

Jones, A. (2000). *Next time she'll be dead: Battering and how to stop it.* Boston: Beacon.

Jordan, E., & Cowan, A. (1995). Warrior narratives in the kindergarten classroom: Renegotiating the social contract? *Gender and Society, 9*(6), 727-743.

Kandiyoti, D. (1988). Bargaining with patriarchy. *Gender and Society, 2,* 274-289.

Kaufman, M. (1993). *Cracking the armour: Power, pain and the lives of men.* Toronto: Viking.

Kaufman, M. (1998). The construction of masculinity and the triad of men's violence. In M. S. Kimmel & M. A. Messner (Eds.), *Men's lives* (pp. 4-17). Boston: Allyn & Bacon.

Kaufman, M. (1999). Men, feminism and men's contradictory experiences of power. In J. A. Kuypers (Ed.), *Men and power* (pp. 75-103). Amherst, NY: Prometheus Books.

Kershner, R. (1996). Adolescent attitudes about rape. *Adolescence, 31*(121), 29-33.

Kimmel, M. (1996). *Manhood in America: A cultural history.* New York: Free Press.

Kimmel, M. S. (2000). *The gendered society.* New York: Oxford University Press.

Kimmel, M., & Messner, M. (Eds.). (1998). *Men's lives* (4th ed.). Boston: Allyn & Bacon.

Laslett, B., & Brenner, J. (1989). Gender and social reproduction: Historical perspectives. *Annual Review of Sociology, 15,* 381-404.

Lefkowitz, B. (1997). *Our guys: The Glen Ridge rape and the secret life of the perfect suburb.* Berkeley: University of California Press.

Levin, I., & Trost, J. (1992). Understanding the concept of family. *Family Relations, 41*(3), 348-351.

Lorber, J. (1994). *Paradoxes of gender.* New Haven, CT: Yale University Press.

Lyman, P. (1998). The fraternal bond as a joking relationship: A case study of the role of sexist jokes in male group bonding. In M. S. Kimmel & M. A. Messner (Eds.), *Men's lives* (4th ed., pp. 171-181). Boston: Allyn & Bacon.

Lytton, H., & Romney, D. M. (1991). Parents' differential socialization of boys and girls: A meta-analysis. *Psychological Bulletin, 109*(2), 267-296.

Maccoby, E. E. (1992). The role of parents in the socialization of children: An historical overview. *Developmental Psychology, 28,* 1006-1017.

Maccoby, E. E. (1998). *The two sexes: Growing up apart, coming together.* Cambridge, MA: The Belknap Press of Harvard University Press.

Maccoby, E. E., & Jacklin, C. N. (1974). *The psychology of sex differences.* Stanford, CA: Stanford University Press.

Marks, N. F. (1996). Flying solo at midlife: Gender, marital status, and psychological well-being. *Journal of Marriage and the Family, 58,* 917-932.

Marttunen, M. J., Henriksson, M. M., Isometsa, E. T., Heikkinen, M. E., Aro, H. M., & Lonnqvist, J. K. (1998). Completed suicide among adolescents with no diagnosable psychiatric disorder. *Adolescence, 33*(131), 669-681.

McMahon, A. (1999). *Taking care of men: Sexual politics in the public mind.* Cambridge, UK: Cambridge University Press.

Mead, G. H. (1934). *Mind, self, and society.* Chicago: University of Chicago Press.

Mead, M. (1949). *Male and female.* New York: William Morrow.

Messner, M. A. (1997). *Politics of masculinities: Men in movements.* Thousand Oaks, CA: Sage.

Miedzian, M. (1991). *Boys will be boys: Breaking the link between masculinity and violence.* New York: Anchor Books.

Mies, M. (1986). *Patriarchy and accumulation on a world scale: Women in the international division of labor.* Atlantic Highlands, NJ: Zed Books.

Minton, C., Kagan, J., & Levine, J. A. (1971). Maternal control and obedience in the two-year-old. *Child Development, 42,* 1873-1894.

Morris, C. (1994). *Bearing witness: Sexual harassment and beyond—everywoman's story.* Boston: Little, Brown and Company.

National Youth Gang Center. (1999). *1997 National youth gang survey.* Washington, DC: Office of Juvenile Justice and Delinquency Prevention.

Nock, S. L. (1998). *Marriage in men's life.* New York: Oxford University Press.

Nosaka, A. (2000). Effects of child gender preference on contraceptive use in rural Bangladesh. *Journal of Comparative Family Studies, 31*(4), 485-501.

O'Brien, M. (1981). *The politics of reproduction.* Boston: Routledge and Kegan Paul.

Parke, R. D. (1996). *Fatherhood.* Cambridge, MA: Harvard University Press.

Petit, G. S., Bakshi, A., Dodge, K. A., & Coie, J. D. (1990). The emergence of social dominance in young boys' play groups: Developmental differences and behavioral correlates. *Developmental Psychology, 26,* 1017-1025.

Phillips, A. (1994). *The trouble with boys: A wise and sympathetic guide to the risky business of raising sons.* New York: Basic Books.

Pleck, J. H., Sonenstein, F. L., & Ku, L. C. (1994). Problem behaviors and masculinity ideology in adolescent males. In R. D. Ketterlinus & M. E. Lamb (Eds.), *Adolescent problem behaviors: Issues and research* (pp. 165-186). Hillsdale, NJ: Lawrence Erlbaum Associates.

Pollack, W. (1998). *Real boys: Rescuing our sons from the myths of boyhood.* New York: Henry Holt and Company.

Pollack, W. S., with Shuster, T. (2000). *Real boys' voices.* New York: Random House.

Pomerleau, A., Bolduc, D., Malcuit, G., & Cossette, L. (1990). Pink or blue: Environmental gender stereotypes in the first two years of life. *Sex Roles: A Journal of Research, 22*(5-6), 359-367.

Pyke, K., & Coltrane, S. (1996). Entitlement, obligation, and gratitude in family work. *Journal of Family Issues, 17*(1), 60-82.

Remy, J. (1990). Patriarchy and fratriarchy as forms of androcracy. In J. Hearn & D. H. J. Morgan (Eds.), *Men, masculinities and social theory* (pp. 43-54). London: Unwin Hyman.

Risman, B. (1989). Can men "Mother"? Life as a single father. In B. J. Risman & P. Schwartz (Eds.), *Gender in intimate relationships: A microstructural approach* (pp. 155-164). Belmont, CA: Wadsworth.

Robinson, J. P., & Godbey, G. (1999). *Time for life: The surprising ways Americans use their time* (2nd ed.). University Park: Pennsylvania State University Press.

Rubin, G. (1975). The traffic in women: Notes on the "political economy" of sex. In R. Reiter (Ed.), *Toward an anthropology of women* (pp. 157-210). New York: Monthly Review Press.

Rubin, J., Provenzano, R., & Luria, Z. (1974). The eye of the beholder: Parents' views on sex of newborns. *American Journal of Orthopsychiatry, 44,* 512-519.

Rubin, L. B. (1983). *Intimate strangers: Men and women together.* New York: Harper & Row.

Rubin, L. B. (1985). *Just friends: The role of friendship in our lives.* New York: Harper & Row.

Sabo, D. (1998). Masculinities and men's health: Moving toward post-Superman era prevention. In M. S. Kimmel & M. A. Messner (Eds.), *Men's lives* (4th ed., pp. 347-361). Boston: Allyn & Bacon.

Sanday, P. R. (1981). *Female power and male dominance: On the origins of sexual inequality.* Cambridge, UK: Cambridge University Press.

Sanday, P. R. (1990). *Fraternity gang rape: Sex, brotherhood, and privilege on campus.* New York: New York University Press.

Schutz, A. (1970). *On phenomenology and social relations.* Chicago: University of Chicago Press.

Schwartz, P., & Rutter, V. (1998). *The gender of sexuality.* Thousand Oaks, CA: Pine Forge Press.

Silverstein, O., & Rashbaum, B. (1994). *The courage to raise good men.* New York: Penguin.

Smith, D. E. (1987). *The everyday world as problematic: A feminist sociology.* Boston: Northeastern University Press.

Snyder, H. N., & Sickmund, M. (1999). *Juvenile offenders and victims: 1999 national report.* Washington, DC: Office of Juvenile Justice and Delinquency Prevention.

Stacey, J. (1996). *In the name of the family: Rethinking family values in the postmodern age.* Boston: Beacon.

Stern, M., & Karraker, K. H. (1989). Sex stereotyping of infants: A review of gender labeling studies. *Sex Roles, 20,* 501-522.

Szockyj, E., & Fox, J. G. (1996). *Corporate victimization of women.* Boston: Northeastern University Press.

Teachman, J. D. (1992). Intergenerational resource transfers across disrupted households: Absent fathers' contributions to the well-being of their children. In S. J. South & S. E. Tolnay (Eds.), *The changing American family: Sociological and demographic perspectives* (pp. 224-246). Boulder, CO: Westview.

Thorne, B. (1993). *Gender play: Girls and boys in school.* New Brunswick, NJ: Rutgers University Press.

Weiss, G. (1995). Sex-selective abortion: A relational approach. *Hypatia, 10*(1), 202-217.

Weitzman, L. (1981). *The marriage contract: Spouses, lovers, and the law.* New York: Free Press.

West, C., & Zimmerman, D. (1987). Doing gender. *Gender and Society, 1,* 125-151.

Williams, E., Radin, N., & Allegro, T. (1992). Sex role attitudes of adolescents reared primarily by their fathers: An 11-year follow-up. *Merrill-Palmer Quarterly, 38,* 457-476.

Wood, J. (1994). *Gendered lives: Communication, gender, and culture.* Belmont, CA: Wadsworth.

Yellowbird, M., & Snipp, C. M. (1994). American Indian families. In R. L. Taylor (Ed.), *Minority families in the United States: A multicultural perspective* (pp. 179-201). Englewood Cliffs, NJ: Prentice Hall.

15

FATHERHOOD AND MASCULINITIES

WILLIAM MARSIGLIO

JOSEPH H. PLECK

Much has been learned about the various dimensions of fatherhood during the past few decades, as is documented in several recent and expansive reviews (Lamb, 1997; Marsiglio, Amato, Day, & Lamb, 2000; Parke, 2002; J. H. Pleck, 1997). These diverse emotional, psychological, and behavioral dimensions involve men's attitudes about and experiences with being fathers prior to conception, during pregnancy, and throughout their children's lives (with behavior often being referred to as involvement or investment). Most of this scholarship has focused on fathers living in various Western industrialized countries (Hobson, 2002; Lamb, 1987), although researchers have studied fathering in Asian cultures such as China (Ho, 1987; Jankowiak, 1992) and Japan (Ishii-Kuntz, 1992, 1993, 1994; Shwalb, Imaizumi, & Nakazawa, 1987) as well as numerous nonindustrialized societies around the world (Coltrane, 1988; Engle & Breaux, 1998; Hewlett, 1992, 2000; Tripp-Reimer & Wilson, 1991). Another noteworthy comparative study examined fathering behaviors in a diverse mix of 18 countries (Mackey, 1985).

Students of gender also may be interested in historical analyses of fathering that go beyond the scope of our review (Griswold, 1993; LaRossa, 1997; LaRossa & Reitzes, 1995; E. H. Pleck & Pleck, 1997).

Our primary aim in this review is to examine scholarship on fatherhood from a gendered and critical perspective. Although the literature that specifically addresses the relationship between masculinities and fatherhood is sparse, it is sufficient in scope to warrant a review and to allow us to propose a forward-looking research agenda. We supplement our review by incorporating literature that may not be informed explicitly by a critical gender perspective, but which still contributes to a gendered understanding of fatherhood. Our scope, however, does not allow us to discuss recent work on cultural representations of fatherhood in entertainment media and social marketing promoted by organizations with interests in fatherhood, and how gender displays are intertwined with the messages being conveyed (Coltrane & Allan, 1994; LaRossa, Gadgil, & Wynn, 2000; Lupton & Barclay, 1997).

Authors' note: Part of the work reported here was supported by the Cooperative State Research, Education and Extension Service, U.S. Department of Agriculture, under Project No. ILLU-45–0329 to Joseph H. Pleck.

At the outset, we focus on debates about whether men as fathers can uniquely affect their children. We then consider how the style of men's fathering contributes to gendered social inequalities within and outside families/households. At numerous points, we accentuate how men's participation in systems of gendered social relations—both between and within genders—shapes their fathering opportunities, attitudes, and behavior. Next, we underscore how fathering occurs in various settings where circumstances associated with age, race/ethnicity, socioeconomic status, and sexual orientation come into play. When viewed through a gender lens, we can see how these contexts create different opportunities and struggles for men as they think about and attempt to act as male parents. We conclude by suggesting avenues for future research that would advance our understanding of fatherhood from a critical gendered perspective.

As we take stock of the relevant literature, we emphasize several themes. Most important, we highlight the intersection among the main structures of social inequality—gender, race/ethnicity, and social class—while clarifying how these three factors affect the social construction of fatherhood images and the way men experience their lives as fathers. Consistent with recent theoretical work in the area of men and gender (Connell, 1995, 2000), fathering can be studied in connection to hegemonic masculinity as well as alternative constructions of masculinities that give meaning to men's everyday lives in diverse situations.

Just as it is critical to acknowledge the implications of multiple masculinities, we pay particular attention to the dual concerns of men as breadwinners and nurturing parents while focusing on the initial phases of the fathering life course. Fathers and their children typically spend three to six overlapping decades in their respective roles, but most fatherhood scholarship is restricted to the first 18 years of this joint father-child experience (but see Pillemer & McCartney, 1991; also Pfiefer & Sussman, 1991). Our review emphasizes fathering during these early years, although we suggest how future research can address a wider range of issues across the fathering life course.

Efforts to study fatherhood and promote father-relevant social policies have gone global in recent decades. Capturing the full breadth and depth of these initiatives is beyond our limited scope here. While we selectively review and integrate cross-cultural materials from industrialized and nonindustrialized societies into our assessment of the literature, much of what we cover is most salient to a U.S. context. In broad terms, the cross-cultural literature teaches us that there is considerable variation in how men act as fathers, that children can flourish in societies where different types of paternal models and expectations of children exist, and that gender as a social organizing principle is implicated in various ways throughout the world in structuring the opportunities for fathers to interact with and invest in their children. Hearn (2002) provides a useful review of men, fathers, and the state within an international context while advancing a critical perspective on studying men.

Finally, our review accentuates how knowledge about fathering is produced, disseminated, and evaluated. We take our cue from Stacey and Biblarz (2001), who showed how the production of knowledge can be assessed in a controversial area like sexual orientation and parenting. Being attentive to the social construction of knowledge about fathering is vital because, as those working closely in the field know, there are several hotly contested research and policy issues that challenge individuals to navigate the waters that muddle theory, research, and propaganda. Those debates that are most contentious focus on whether (and how) fathers matter to their children in unique and meaningful ways, the presumed positive value of marriage in fathers' lives, nonresident fathers' financial and interpersonal commitments to their children, and the potential danger that stepfathers may pose for their stepchildren. Not surprisingly, those who research and/or debate these issues often practice gender politics and swear allegiance to various brands of feminism, family and/or religious values, theoretical perspectives, or modes of scientific inquiry (Blankenhorn, 1995; Daniels, 1998; Dowd, 2000; Popenoe, 1996; Silverstein, 1996). Those stakeholders who are most effective in framing the key issues and paradigms in the minds of the research community, the general public, and policymakers can in various ways influence what is generally "known" about how fathers feel, think, and act. They do this by shaping the types of questions that researchers ask, the way research is conducted, and how research is presented, interpreted, and used by researchers, policymakers, social service professionals, and the general public alike. A critical review of the field, then, should pay attention not only to how fathering experiences are influenced by and shape gendered social structures and relations. It must also draw attention to the gender-related and ideological struggles among the knowledge producers that can confound research and political agendas within the field itself.

IS FATHERING "ESSENTIALLY" DIFFERENT FROM MOTHERING?

One highly politicized issue central to a discussion linking fathering and masculinities revolves around the debate whether fathers, as men, are uniquely equipped with characteristics that differentiate their parenting styles and contributions to children from those of mothers. This debate is often couched in terms of essentialist (Silverstein & Auerbach, 1999) and social constructionist approaches (Brandth & Kvande, 1998, Lupton & Barclay, 1997; Marsiglio, 1995, 1998) to fatherhood. These discussions gain political and theoretical visibility because they are often associated with the illusive and controversial concept of "fatherlessness" (Blankenhorn, 1995) and the championing of evolutionary psychological approaches to understanding parenting (Popenoe, 1996).

In gender studies, the critique of "essentialism" has been an important recent theoretical development (Coltrane, 1994; Hare-Mustin & Marecek, 1990). Essentialism provides a conceptual rubric under which to discuss several aspects of fatherhood that are fundamental to consider from a gender perspective. Silverstein and Auerbach (1999) identified and critically analyzed three component beliefs in an implicit "essentialist paradigm for fatherhood": (a) gender differences in parenting are universal and biologically based; (b) fathers' uniquely masculine form of parenting significantly improves developmental outcomes for children, especially for sons; and (c) the context in which fathers are most likely to provide for and nurture young children is heterosexual marriage. Their analysis caused quite a stir and was vigorously challenged in the popular press (Chavez, 1999; Horn, 1999).

As Silverstein and Auerbach noted, the essentialist view of fatherhood, particularly as

expressed by Blankenhorn (1995) and Popenoe (1996), underlies recent neoconservative policy initiatives to promote marriage. This view also is reflected in organizations such as the Promise Keepers (Brickner, 1999; Claussen, 2000) and the National Fatherhood Initiative (Horn, 1995). The enormous empirical and theoretical literature relevant to these three beliefs is beyond the scope of this chapter to review in any depth. Thus, we will discuss only selected issues, especially ones Silverstein and Auerbach did not address and those that enable us to highlight the larger context within which knowledge in this area is socially constructed.

THE UNIVERSALITY AND BIOLOGICAL BASIS OF GENDER DIFFERENCES IN PARENTING

The hypothetical universality of gender-differentiated parental rearing of the young—that is, fathers being less involved—has been considered both across nonhuman primate species and cross-culturally among human societies. For the former, both Lamb, Pleck, Charnov, and Levine's (1985) and Silverstein and Auerbach's reviews suggest that gender-differentiated parental rearing of the young is far less universal than is popularly believed. Smuts and Gubernick (1992) provided evidence that this interspecies variation can be explained by a "reciprocity hypothesis," holding that fathers invest more in the young when females have more to offer fathers. For example, in species with multimale family groups, in which females therefore choose which males to copulate with, fathers invest more in the young than in species with one-male groups (Silverstein, 1993; see Belsky, 1993, for a critique). Though provocative, inferences to human populations based on these findings should be made cautiously.

Mackey (1985), drawing on his extensive observational and comparative work on human fathers in 18 countries, concluded that it is harder to stimulate men to be caregivers for children. Mackey noted, however, that once fathers begin to respond, they do so in a manner similar to women. Mackey additionally noted that when two or more men are in an all-male group, it is harder to motivate simultaneous caregiving responses from them than is the case when two or more women are in an all-female gathering. Scholars also agree that there is actually significant variation across the world societies studied by anthropologists in fathers' level of involvement relative to mothers' (Hewlett, 1992; Mackey, 1985; Silverstein & Auerbach, 1999), a finding inconsistent with the essentialism perspective. Silverstein and Auerbach argued that this cross-cultural variation can be explained by the reciprocity hypothesis.

Those who conduct naturalistic observations of fathers living in nonindustrialized societies conceptualize fathers' behavior in terms of parental "investment," referring to activities that promote their offspring's survival. This construct is rooted in evolutionary and biosocial frameworks that emphasize ties between biology, gender, and reproductive strategies. These approaches recognize biology's role in shaping paternal behavior while attempting to explain diversities and commonalities in paternal experience between different societies. Although the anthropologists who use these frameworks tend not to refer explicitly to "essentialism," their models are consistent with at least some essentialist thinking. Many anthropologists, though reluctant to use these models, still view gender as a significant factor affecting paternal behavior because of its role in how cultures are modified to create various types of parenting opportunities and expectations. Without explicitly invoking the essentialist paradigm, Hewlett (1992) reviewed research based on naturalistic observation and concluded,

> While cross-cultural studies question some of the European and American research, this does not mean that all aspects of fathers' role are culturally relative. Fathers in all parts of the world do share certain characteristics: fathers provide less direct caregiving than mothers (but there may be some fathers within a culture that take on primary caregiving), fathers are expected to provide at least some economic support for their children, and fathers are expected to support the mother economically and/or emotionally. (p. xii)

He goes on to add that it is assumed that "fathers from all parts of the world are likely to have similar concerns about the safety, health, and tradeoffs between spending time with their children and doing things that attract and keep women (e.g., working to increase status, prestige or wealth)" (p. xv).

FATHERS' UNIQUE CONTRIBUTIONS TO CHILD DEVELOPMENT

Central to the essentialist conception of fatherhood is the proposition that fathers, as men, contribute to the development of their children in a unique way. This idea has generated contentious controversy, informed by research on the consequences for children of "father absence" (or growing up in a single-parent female-headed family) as well as research about the effects on children of variation in fathers' characteristics and behavior in families with fathers present. The scholarly disagreements over the meaning of the research are considerable. Widespread social concern about the large and perhaps growing number of fathers who are disconnected from their children has led to a broader, highly politicized public debate about father absence and father involvement. Different stakeholders—conservatives, feminists, fathers' rights groups, policymakers concerned with teen pregnancy and other issues, and researchers of different persuasions—advance radically conflicting positions.

Father "absence." In discussions of father absence, several issues have emerged as particularly important. First, the concept is ill-defined both conceptually and operationally. The obvious, but deceptively simple, approach focuses on whether the child's father lives in the household or not. Because fathers' potential residence or nonresidence occurs from birth to late adolescence, the length of time the father lives or does not live with the child should of course be taken into account. But exactly how long does there need to be no father in the household for a child to be "father absent"? Does absence occurring for any reason count, or only for some reasons? Should a father's being away from home for a year because of military reserve service, or his being away from home 2 weeks out of 3 because he is a long-distance trucker or a sales representative, be considered father absence? How do we classify the child who lives with her father every other weekend and 2 summer months out of 3, and with her mother the rest of the time? What about the child of a teen father who lives nearby, visits his child frequently, and contributes economically to her upbringing? And is it only the residence or nonresidence of the *biological* father that is important?

In research, respondents usually will provide an answer when asked whether they grew up in a two-parent or single-parent family. However, this does not mean their answers correspond to something that can be clearly defined or reliably measured. Readers of Blankenhorn's (1995), Horn's (1995), and Popenoe's (1996) compendiums of the negative outcomes occurring more frequently among children of absent fathers may be impressed by the length of their lists, but they may not ask how meaningful it really is to reduce the diversity of children's living arrangements over time to the simple dichotomy of father presence or absence. If one broadens the concept from physical to psychological father absence, it becomes even more difficult to define and measure reliably.

Even if these difficulties could be set aside, the results of existing research on father absence do not unequivocally establish the detrimental effects often claimed. The context in which father absence occurs can be critically important. There is evidence, for example, that the outcomes associated with father absence in the children of adult single mothers often are markedly more positive than those occurring for children of teen single mothers, who tend to have less human capital (Edelman, 1986). The potential problems of father absence in the context of teen parenthood are, nonetheless, inappropriately generalized to father absence in all circumstances. Other scholars have noted that the consequences of father absence depend on whether social supports are present or absent (Wilson, 1989).

In addition, father absence typically co-occurs with, and its effects are thus confounded by, other circumstances such as teen parenthood, divorce, and in particular low income. Simply comparing father-absent and father-present groups can thus be misleading. An analogy is that university-affiliated teaching hospitals have markedly higher rates of cesarean sections than community hospitals, but when risk factors (e.g., poor health) are controlled for, university hospitals' rate of C-sections is no higher. In many studies, similarly, controlling for family income and other factors markedly reduces the apparent negative correlates of father absence. Blankenhorn (1995), Horn (1995), and Popenoe (1996) make their case entirely with simple comparisons between father-present and -absent groups, without controlling for or acknowledging the potential confounding effects of other differences between the two groups.

Among more sophisticated analyses, McLanahan and Sandefeur's (1994) *Growing Up With a Single Parent* is the recent large-scale empirical study of father absence most widely cited. Using data from four different national surveys, these authors found, with race, maternal education, and number of children in the family included in their statistical models, that father absence has marked negative effects on educational outcomes, early childbearing, and employment. Although family income is controlled in other studies, it is not controlled here. McLanahan and Sandefeur hold that potential confounding variables should be controlled only when they represent "selection" factors for father absence (i.e., factors helping explain why father absence occurs, but which cannot be "caused" by father absence, like race and low maternal education). They argue that conditions potentially caused by father absence, such as low income, should not be controlled; doing so would underestimate the extent to which father absence actually leads to negative child outcomes. Given the difficulties in creating policies to provide adequate incomes to single-parent mothers, their argument has some pragmatic merit—and McLanahan and Sandefeur's focus clearly is on the social policy implications of father absence, not on evaluating the essentialist argument that fathers have a unique positive effect on child development. However, the essentialist position implies that father absence should have negative consequences even when the lower family income associated with it is taken into account. The supporting evidence for this claim is weak.

Fathering in two-parent families. Other relevant research concerns the effects on children resulting from variation in fathers' characteristics and behavior in families with fathers present. Considerable research in the 1950s and 1960s examined how paternal characteristics such as "sex typing" (the degree to which fathers have "masculine" personality characteristics, for example, ambitious, dominant, self-reliant), warmth, and control were related to children's gender identity, school achievement, and psychological adjustment. The influence of fathers' sex typing was of particular interest because fathers were thought to be crucial in promoting the development of children's, and especially sons', gender identities (J. H. Pleck, 1981). These studies generally find that a father's masculinity is much less important than his warmth and closeness with his child. In addition, the same characteristics in mothers are associated with positive outcomes in children. Thus, although this research finds that positive development is correlated with father behaviors, it does not suggest that development is associated with behaviors in fathers that are unique to male parents (Lamb, 1987).

More recent research focuses on the consequences for children of fathers' degree of contact with their children, more broadly termed "involvement" by Lamb, Pleck, Charnov, and Levine (1985, 1987; J. H. Pleck, Lamb, & Levine, 1985). Involvement is defined as "the amount of time spent in activities involving the child" (Lamb et al., 1985, p. 884) and includes three components: (a) engagement with the child (in the form of caretaking, or play or leisure), (b) accessibility to the child, and (c) responsibility for the care of the child, as distinct from the performance of care. Although Palkovitz (1997) has criticized Lamb et al. for assuming that father involvement must have positive effects on children, Lamb et al. explicitly argued that involvement might have positive effects on children only in specific contexts; for example, both mother and father want the father to be involved.

More recent work on the consequences of paternal involvement has shifted focus from simply the amount of involvement, implicitly "content-free," to the nature and quality of the involvement. In most research that finds a relationship between involvement and positive child outcomes, the involvement measures actually emphasize positive forms of interaction such as shared activities and helping children learn. Consequently, J. H. Pleck (1997) concluded that the concept of father involvement should be replaced by the concept of *positive* father involvement, as defined from the child's perspective. Amato and Rivera's (1999; see also Marsiglio et al., 2000) documentation of good childhood outcomes linked to positive paternal involvement illustrates two additional methodological improvements. Because paternal and maternal involvement may correlate, maternal involvement needs to be controlled for when testing relationships between father involvement and child outcomes. In addition, for associations

between involvement and child outcomes to be convincing, the two variables should be assessed by different observers, rather than relying on fathers' reports of both. In relationships between children and nonresident fathers as well, fathers' feelings of closeness to their child and authoritative parenting (defined as the combination of clear discipline, monitoring, and emotional support), but not simply amount of contact, are positively related to children's grades and negatively associated with children's externalizing and internalizing symptoms (Amato & Gilbreth, 1999). Other recent research suggests positive effects associated with fathers' breadwinning (Amato, 1998). These effects, however, are modest in magnitude.

The essentialist argument holds that fathers' positive effects on children are independent of mothers', which this research supports. However, the essentialist argument also requires that fathers' effects be gendered, specifically male effects. The finding that the dimensions of paternal and maternal behavior that influence children positively are the same seems inconsistent with this premise (Lamb, 1986; Amato & Rivera, 1999). The comparison between children raised in mother-father families and those growing up with two lesbian parents provides another kind of evidence. This research provides little indication that those children whose two parents include a male are better off in terms of psychological or social adjustment than those whose two parents are both females. In fact, Stacey and Biblarz (2001) argue that researchers have defensively downplayed the evidence in these studies that the children of lesbian parents are better off. As we show later, some research suggests that compared with heterosexual fathers, gay fathers are more likely to be nurturing and less likely to be traditional in their parental style.

Most contemporary developmental researchers are skeptical of the idea that fathering (or any other single factor) is "essential," in the literal sense, to human development, as assessed by outcomes such as school performance and good social relationships. Their view is that development is impaired by "cumulative" risk, not by any one risk factor. A good illustration is Sameroff, Seifer, Barocas, Zax, and Greenspan's (1987) study of the association between risk factors such as low birth weight, poverty, having a single parent, poor schools, and the like, and adolescent

IQ. Rather than focusing on specific factors, the researchers simply tabulated the total number of risk factors each individual experienced. Little difference was found in average IQ among children who experienced only one or two of these risk factors, compared with those who had none. For each additional risk factor beyond two, however, average IQ was 7 to 12 points lower. The general principle here is that the impact of any one factor, positive or negative, depends on the other factors present. This principle makes it more understandable why research generally finds that positive father involvement has only modest beneficial effects and that measures of father absence have only limited negative statistical effects.

MARRIAGE AND OTHER RELATIONSHIP CONTEXTS FOR FATHERING

When considering the essentialist view on fathering, the question of whether heterosexual marriage is the "best" context for fathers to rear children typically is asked in terms of children's well-being (see Amato & Gilbreth, 1999, Marsiglio et al., 2000, and Stacey & Biblarz, 2001, for relevant reviews). Recent research has begun to explore whether biological (particularly married, coresidential) fathers interact with and contribute to their children differently from men who act as father figures in other types of contexts (Anderson, Kaplan, & Lancaster, 1999; Buchanan, Maccoby, & Dornbusch, 1996; Hofferth & Anderson, 2003) and whether there are differences in how stepfathers and nonresident fathers affect their children (White & Gilbreth, 2001). Although this research tends to support the assumption that children fare better on average when they live with a mother and biological, resident father, stepfathers (including cohabiting fathers in some cases) also can make meaningful contributions to children's well-being.

A related question, one more central to our review, is whether men reap positive benefits by being fathers (Nock, 1998) or by increasing their involvement with their children (Lamb, Pleck, & Levine, 1986), especially in a marital context. Numerous commentators have argued that marriage and having children helps to civilize and/or give meaning to men's lives, thereby

affording children and men their best option for experiencing positive outcomes. Snarey (1993, p. 98) suggests that fathers are more likely to express their capacity for "establishing, guiding, or caring for the next generation" in the community at large, separate from their own children. Men's transition to parenting and active involvement with their children can help many men develop more nurturing personality traits (Hawkins & Belsky, 1989). Finally, although some studies show that positive paternal involvement can lead men to experience conflict, stress, and a lower self-esteem (especially with sons), these patterns do not appear to affect men's satisfaction with fathering (J. H. Pleck, 1997). Unfortunately, answers to these questions based on solid research are more difficult to come by than some persons either anticipate or are willing to admit.

One of the most widely discussed and politicized issues within the U.S. context involves nonresident fathers' financial and interpersonal commitments to their children (Griswold, 1993; see also Seltzer, 1998). Feminists, members of fathers' rights groups, persons who espouse traditional family ideologies, and others have weighed in on child support and visitation issues. Because the vast majority of nonresident parents are fathers, much of the debate about nonresident parents' responsibilities and rights has evolved around the issues of gender equity within a male-dominated economic system. Many believe that nonresident fathers in large numbers have reneged on their paternal breadwinning responsibilities. Other scholars, though, have struggled to refocus and sharpen the debate while raising public awareness about what they perceive to be a pervasive and distorted stereotypical image of "deadbeat dads" (Braver & O'Connell, 1998; Braver et al., 1993; Nielsen, 1999; Parke & Brott, 1999). These commentators are quick to stress mothers' gatekeeping roles; they suggest that many nonresident fathers are pushed away and often kept away from being involved with their children while being pressured to fulfill a detached breadwinner role.

Another controversial issue involves assertions about nonbiological fathers' treatment of their partners' children. It has become commonplace to assert that "stepfathers" and boyfriends are more likely to abuse the children of their romantic partners physically and sexually than are the children's biological fathers (Blankenhorn, 1995; Booth, Carver, & Granger, 2000; Daly & Wilson, 1998). Some go so far as to say that "stepfathers are far more likely than [biological] fathers to do so [sexually molest children]" (Blankenhorn, 1995, p. 40). Although it appears that a majority of studies find that stepchildren are at greater risk of abuse (Giles-Sims, 1997), various researchers have challenged the validity of these claims (Malkin & Lamb, 1994; Sedlak & Broadhurst, 1996; see also Silverstein & Auerbach, 1999). The scientific jury is still out as to whether stepfathers' hypothesized lower incentive to invest in their nonbiological children, according to an evolutionary perspective, explains any of the possible differences between biological and nonbiological fathers' abuse patterns in a societal context where men's involvement with children generally is not valued. This is one area where less rhetoric and more careful analysis and sober discussion clearly are needed. Exuberant ideological support of heterosexual marriage is misleading when based on muddled findings regarding nonbiological fathers' mistreatment of children. At the very least, such an argument overlooks the reality that domestic violence and sexual abuse would be higher if women and their children were encouraged to stay in "bad" or abusive marriages.

Turning to outcomes for men, Nock (1998) recently analyzed U.S. national survey data to examine the relationship between different features of a prevailing normative conception of marriage and men's public achievements. Consistent with Gilmore's (1990) cross-cultural anthropological work on the culture of manhood, Nock suggested that adult men are expected to achieve their masculinity by being fathers to their wives' children, providers for their families, and protectors of their wives and children. According to Nock, his analyses support Gilmore's thesis because they show that married men fare better than their nonmarried counterparts when assessed on the basis of what he calls three traditional definitions of adult male achievement (income, weeks worked, and occupational prestige). He found that becoming a father in a marital context was associated with a slight increase in men's income levels with no additional changes due to subsequent children, an increase of 2 additional weeks of work (only for the first child), and a small increase in occupational prestige, with a slight decline when men have four or more children. An alternative reading of these data suggests that the changes are so slight as to be negligible, and they are open to other interpretations. For example, the small increase in income probably is more than offset by the additional expenses associated with having children. Furthermore, his analyses ignore the complex and alternative expressions of masculinity that have existed in U.S. culture in recent decades and have influenced growing numbers of men's and others' perceptions of manhood and success (Ehrenreich, 1983).

Fatherhood and Gender Inequality

The critical analysis of gender views families as an important locus in which gender inequality is created and maintained (Fox & Murry, 2000; Thompson & Walker, 1995). When fatherhood is viewed through the lens of gender, the most important question about it is "How is fatherhood linked to gender inequality?" We consider this question in two contexts: within marriage and cohabitation, and outside co-resident relationships where strong romantic commitments are less likely (divorce, unmarried parenthood).

Marriage and Cohabiting Relationships

Feminist analyses of families identify men's limited performance of domestic family responsibilities relative to women's as a manifestation of broader gender inequality (Coltrane, 1996; Ferree, 1990; McMahon, 1999; Osmond & Thorne, 1993). The extent to which married men do less in the family has been documented in "time diary" and other time-use studies beginning in the 1960s (J. H. Pleck, 1985). In addition to showing that married men perform substantially less housework and child care than married women, they demonstrated that married men also did no more of these family tasks if their wives were employed than if their wives were not employed. In addition, in two-earner families, wives' time in these family activities and paid work combined was considerably greater than their husbands', a phenomenon sometimes called employed wives' "second shift" (Hochschild, 1989).

Focusing more specifically on gender inequality and fathering (implicitly in the context of two-parent families), Polatnick (1973-1974) argued that because women are the rearers of children, they are powerless vis-à-vis men, and because women are powerless, they are rearers of children. As a result of men doing so little in the family, some wives do not take paid employment, and those who are employed tend to give their family responsibilities higher priority. This contributes to the barriers preventing women from advancing occupationally and from getting the benefits potentially accruing from employment in terms of economic independence, pension rights, social valuation, and self-worth. In addition, because fathers encourage masculine behaviors in sons and feminine behaviors in daughters more than do mothers (Crouter, McHale, & Bartko, 1993; Lytton & Romney, 1991), the way that fathers socialize their children may reproduce gender inequality. Thus, fatherhood is a key element in the "gender politics of family time" (Daly, 1996).

Recent work relevant to fatherhood and gender inequality in two-parent families makes evident several developments. Lamb et al.'s (1985) construct of paternal involvement has become a dominant concept used in describing what fathers do compared to mothers. Scholars have contested the level of fathers' involvement and the extent to which it is changing in married-parent families. Some researchers find that fathers' time spent with their children is not trivial and is greater than often thought. Averaging across 13 national or smaller-scale studies between the mid-1980s and the late 1990s, and expressing fathers' time as a proportion of mothers' time, married U.S. fathers averaged 44% of mothers' engagement time and 66% of mothers' accessibility time (J. H. Pleck, 1997). In children's time diaries in a 1997 national study, fathers were engaged with their 3- to 5-year-old children an average of 79 minutes per day on weekdays and 215 minutes on weekend days; fathers were accessible an additional 68 minutes per weekday and 184 minutes per weekend day. Corresponding averages for younger children were higher, and for older children only slightly lower (Yeung, Sandberg, Davis-Kean, & Hofferth, 2001).

Some evidence also suggests that married U.S. fathers' engagement and accessibility have increased in recent decades. For example, in 11 time-use studies conducted between the mid-1960s and the mid-1980s, fathers averaged about one third of mothers' engagement and half

of their accessibility, both lower than the 44% and 66% noted above for the mid-1980s to the late 1990s (J. H. Pleck, 1997). Fathers' time with children also has increased in absolute terms (J. H. Pleck, 1997). Yeung et al. (2001) hold that because other factors besides gender influence paternal involvement, "a simple gender inequality theory is not sufficient in explaining the dynamics of household division of labor in today's American families" (p. 136).

Other scholars contest these interpretations. Hochschild's (1989, p. 4) report that time diary research showed that the average U.S. father spent only 12 minutes per day with his children received great play in the mass media (e.g., Skow, 1989), although this figure actually concerned fathers' time only on weekdays and was derived from 1965 data (J. H. Pleck, 1997). LaRossa (1988) evaluated the evidence for fathers' increased involvement as unconvincing, as did McMahon (1999), who went further to argue that this claim is complicit in maintaining male privilege.

Yet other scholars have assessed the construct of paternal involvement to be limited because, they argue, it is rooted in feminist-derived gender equity assumptions (Hawkins, Christiansen, Sargent, & Hill, 1993). These critics hold that involvement is defined implicitly as the way that mothers are involved with children, implying a "deficit perspective" for fathers (Palkovitz, 1997; see J. H. Pleck & Stueve, 2001, for a response). Taking a cross-cultural perspective, others observe that viewing fathers' involvement as a critical social indicator of gender equality is highly subject to cultural context, in effect assuming a Western/industrialized perspective (Hewlett, 1991). Clearly, father involvement in relation to gender inequality is subject to multiple interpretations.

Finally, research relevant to fathering and gender inequality has expanded its focus beyond married biological fathers to include both stepfathers and cohabiting biological fathers. Data on whether stepfathers are less involved than biological married fathers are at present somewhat inconsistent (Cooksey & Fondell, 1996; Hofferth, Pleck, Stueve, Bianchi, & Sayer, 2002; Marsiglio, 1991). As part of the growing recognition of "families formed outside of marriage" (Seltzer, 2000; Smock, 2000), cohabiting fathers (i.e., unmarried biological fathers residing with child and mother) are also beginning to receive attention. In the limited data available, cohabiting U.S. fathers show lower average levels of engagement with their children than do married biological fathers, but cohabiting fathers are similarly accessible (Hofferth et al., 2002). If these findings are replicated, they raise the possibility that cohabitation accentuates parental gender inequity, consistent with other feminist concerns about cohabitation.

Fathering Outside Co-Resident Relationships

Divorced fathers. Divorce and its aftermath represent an important arena in which fathers' behavior potentially both reflects and contributes to gender inequality, one explored in numerous qualitative and other studies (e.g., Arendell, 1992, 1995; Braver & O'Connell, 1998; Braver, Wolchik, et al., 1993; Catlett & McKenry, in press; Emery, 1999; Maccoby & Mnookin, 1992; see Griswold, 1993, pp. 260-265 for a historical perspective). In the last two decades, joint *legal* custody has become the statistical norm. In 9,500 divorce settlements in Wisconsin, it rose from 18% in 1980 to 81% in 1992, with about half the latter being 50/50 splits and the remainder ranging from 30/70 to 49/51. However, joint *physical* custody increased over this period from 2% to only 14%. Divorced fathers' rate of sole legal and physical custody has remained stable at about 10% (Melli, Brown, & Cancian, 1997). Some researchers, noting that when custody is contested, it is resolved in favor of the father between one third and one half of the time, have concluded that fathers have a gender-based advantage in getting custody (Polikoff, 1983). However, these statistics pertain to the small subset of divorces in which custody is contested, which overrepresents situations where the father has a good "case." As court-mandated mediation has become increasingly common in divorce, debate also has arisen about the extent to which it might privilege fathers (Okin, 1989). At the same time, mediation is associated with greater father contact as long as 9 years postdivorce (Dillon & Emery, 1996).

The majority of U.S. divorced fathers have relatively little contact with their children. Data from the 1981 National Survey of Children showed that half of all children from divorced families had not seen their father in the past year, and only one child in six saw their father once a week or more (Furstenberg & Cherlin, 1991). More recent data, from the 1992-1994 National Survey of Families and Households, based on nonresident fathers' reports and not controlling for whether the father had been married to the child's mother, revealed that 24% had been with their child only once or not at all in the last year, and 23% saw the child at least weekly (Manning & Smock, 1999). There is vehement debate about the extent to which these low average rates of contact result from mothers' "gatekeeping" versus fathers' own loss of interest (Braver & O'Connell, 1998; Braver et al., 1993; Doherty, Kouneski, & Erickson, 1998; Ihinger-Tallman, Pasley, & Buehler, 1993; Walker & McGraw, 2000). One factor is fathers' formal visitation rights. According to a 1996 federal survey of a national sample of custodial mothers (including never-married as well as divorced mothers), one in four fathers had no legal right to see their children (joint legal or physical custody, or visitation privileges). Among those with joint custody, 85% saw their children in the last year, and among those with visitation rights, 75% did (U.S. Bureau of the Census, 1999). In addition, about one third of nonresident fathers have children in new families.

Fathers' payment or nonpayment of child support has profound implications for gender equality. Unfortunately, data on child support compliance often are summarized without distinguishing between divorced fathers and nonmarried fathers. Detailed tabulations from the 1996 federal survey indicate that among divorced fathers subject to support awards, 73% paid some child support in that year (Graham & Beller, 2002; U.S. Bureau of the Census, 1999), and this percentage has risen slowly but steadily. However, only 68% of divorced fathers were required to pay support. Taking this into account, 48% of all divorced mothers received any child support. Among divorced mothers receiving any support, the average amount received was relatively low, $4,046. Some assume that if all fathers paid the full child support they are ordered by the court to pay, the proportion of single-parent female-headed families living in poverty would be reduced dramatically; however, this may not be the case. As Krause (1989) put it, "while very impressive progress in child support collection from absent parents has been made, the very progress seems to have led us to overestimate, and consequently overemphasize, the financial support that can be obtained from absent parents" (p. 398).

Unmarried, nonresident fathers. In the United States over the last two decades, there has been heightened concern about the rising numbers of unmarried mothers. Although an increasing percentage of these mothers are adults, social concern focuses predominantly on *teenage* mothers raising children on their own (Luker, 1996). The fathers of the children of teenage mothers have less contact with their children and pay less child support than other nonresident fathers (Graham & Beller, 2002). These patterns may contribute to higher levels of gender inequality in these situations.

Lerman and Ooms (1993) and others use the term "young unwed fathers" rather than "teen fathers" to describe the procreating partners of teenage mothers because in a high proportion of cases, these men are 20 years of age or older. From a critical gender perspective, this finding raises an important question: When the father is older than the teenage mother, how often is sexual coercion involved? Although the answer to that question is unclear, the data do reveal that the average age difference is small and only a small proportion of these relationships involve persons who are more than 2 years apart in age (Darroch, Landry, & Oslak, 1999; Lindberg, Sonenstein, Ku, & Martinez, 1997).

GENDERED FATHERING CONTEXTS

When men conceptualize fatherhood, become fathers, and act as fathers, they do so within larger social and cultural contexts, many of which intersect with systems of gender relations. These specific settings are influenced by men's human capital and personal characteristics as well as others' interpretations of them. In this section, we briefly review how fathering experiences are connected to factors such as age, race/ethnicity, economic standing, and sexual orientation. These factors can affect men's opportunities to achieve particular masculine ideals associated with fathering.

Being "Too" Young

Many males who become fathers as teenagers or young adult men come face to face with their

inability to live up to being a family breadwinner, a crucial component for most models of adult masculinity (Marsiglio & Cohan, 1997). Those with limited education and work experience often struggle with feeling disconnected from their father identities and children because of their poor economic prospects for the foreseeable future (Achatz & MacAllum, 1994; Kiselica, 1995). This pattern is exacerbated for African American and Hispanic young males, whose educational credentials and employment opportunities tend to be less promising than those for whites in the U.S. context. Males tend to feel more inadequate when their children's mothers and maternal grandparents voice their dissatisfaction with their meager financial child support (Furstenberg, 1995). Adolescents who become young fathers also quickly discover that their current masculinity assets (e.g., physical appearance and prowess) are of little use as they make the transition to the adultlike status associated with being a father.

In addition, as young men they are unlikely to possess many of the parental and interpersonal skills, such as "emotional literacy," that would enable them to confront successfully the challenges of caring for their children and managing their relationships with their partners (Brody, 1985; Goodey, 1997). Although the culture of boyhood for the most part does not encourage males to develop parental skills and effective interaction styles for their romantic relationships, some boys and young men are still able to develop these skills and incorporate them into how they treat their children and partners. Several small-scale studies have shown that some young fathers are clearly committed to being involved with their children in positive ways (Allen & Doherty, 1996; Christmon, 1990; Rivara, Sweeney, & Henderson, 1986).

Although some research finds that a small percentage of young men see paternity as an emblem of masculinity (Sonenstein, Stewart, Lindberg, Pernas, & Williams, 1997), many young men apparently recognize that being a "man" involves more than siring a child. For example, one qualitative study reported that young men who were 16 to 30 years of age were often quick to assert that any man can make a baby, but males who really want to demonstrate their manhood do so by assuming financial responsibilities for their children and are involved in their everyday lives (Marsiglio & Hutchinson, 2002).

MEN OF COLOR

Circumstances associated with race and ethnicity in the United States may affect how men view fatherhood and are involved with their children, although rigorous research in this area is rather limited and the confounding of socioeconomic status and race/ethnic variables is a common shortcoming within this research area (Mirandé, 1991). Cochran (1997) suggests that "fatherhood for African American men cannot be separated from their shared culture and sociohistorical background, institutional racism, and the marginal status of African American males" (p. 343). Meanwhile, during the past several decades the stereotypical image of machismo has been advanced and challenged as an important factor affecting Latino men's involvement in family life (Carroll, 1980; Mirandé, 1991; Zambrana, 1995). Research exploring the possible connections between other race/ethnic categories and fathering within the United States is sparse.

Viewed through a gender lens, perhaps the most significant contextual issue for understanding African American men's approach to fatherhood is that black men, on average, represent a relatively disadvantaged subpopulation. Proportionately speaking, they are more likely to be unemployed, be imprisoned, have poor access to health care and a shorter life expectancy, be victims of fatal crimes, and have less education than their white and Latino counterparts (Majors & Gordon, 1994). Because African American men are disproportionately disadvantaged, with fewer opportunities to achieve and display their manhood using mainstream strategies, they are more likely than their white counterparts to rely on risk-taking behaviors and the "cool pose" (Majors & Billson, 1992) to express their male identities. The difficulties they encounter in fulfilling the family provider role are related in complex ways to assuming full-time parenting roles (Hamer & Marchioro, 2002) and psychosocial functioning problems (Bowman & Sanders, 1998). The strategies they adopt to confront their role strain may shift across the life course. Though less pronounced, relatively similar patterns and dynamics may be a part of Latino men's lives (Mirandé, 1997). Not surprisingly, some men of color who feel marginalized within society see creating children as one of the few legal ways they can achieve an adult masculine status (Majors & Billson, 1992).

Available research does not allow us to say definitively whether men of color interact with their children in unique ways that are truly independent of their socioeconomic status and family structure circumstances. It does seem apparent, though, that men of color have unique opportunities to mentor their children into a social word tainted with prejudice, a world, for example, where being young, African American, and male is often associated with negative stereotypes and suspicion. Thus, men's paternal role as teacher of race/ethnic relations may be especially salient to fathers' interactions with their sons. Educating sons on what it means to be a black or Latino man in a white society where hegemonic forms of masculinity reign is an experience that speaks to how fathers' experiences can be affected directly by their race/ethnic identity. Unfortunately, this question has not received systematic, scholarly attention.

Social Class

Most research on fathering that addresses some aspect of social class deals with men who are financially disadvantaged, although several studies have attempted to show how other facets of social class may be related to men's lives as fathers (Erickson & Gecas, 1991). As we've alluded to above, when men are unemployed or underemployed, they often find it difficult to feel good about themselves as fathers because the provider role continues to be an important feature of hegemonic images of masculinity and men's fathering experience (Bowman & Sanders, 1998; Christiansen & Palkovitz, 2000). Although poverty issues disproportionately influence men of color and are therefore intertwined with subcultural issues, numerous white fathers also deal with feelings of inadequacy as breadwinners.

Having money is important not only for those fathers who are living with their children; men's socioeconomic standing also can influence how fathers negotiate and manage their fathering experience during those times when they live apart from their children. Money begets power, and those men fortunate enough to have adequate incomes are better positioned to orchestrate their paternal identities, fathering activities, and family arrangements so they can display their masculinity vis-à-vis their contributions to family life. For example, in their qualitative study of divorced fathers, Catlett and McKenry (in press) found that those men with the highest incomes were best equipped to achieve the often conflicting outcomes of being an adequate provider and a nurturing caregiver. Maintaining these dual roles was essentially impossible for the poorest fathers and quite difficult for the middle-income fathers as well. Middle-income fathers may actually experience more tension postdivorce than low-income fathers because the former experience a steeper decline in their ability to perform the provider role postdivorce.

Along a somewhat different line, Cooper (2000) provided an intriguing qualitative analysis of what she termed a "nerd masculinity" that has recently emerged in connection to the work styles found within the Silicon Valley economy. To achieve this new type of gendered subjectivity,

> men must be technically brilliant and devoted to work. They must be tough guys who get the job done no matter what. Fathers so identify with these qualities that their desire to work all the time is experienced by them as emanating from their own personality traits rather than from co-worker or management expectations. (p. 403)

Her analysis shows that this new masculinity operates as a "key mechanism of control in high-tech workplaces that rely on identity-based forms of control and that the enactment of this new masculinity impacts the way fathers think about, experience, and manage their work and family lives" (p. 379). In practical terms, fathers who embrace this nerd masculinity adopt work-family practices in which they do not talk about work-family conflicts in order to give the impression—not always the reality—that work is their top priority. Fathers also allow their worker mentality as a "go-to guy" to influence the way they think about and experience their lives at home. This can be seen in "their use of market language to make sense of their personal relationships as well as their desire to fit family needs within a capitalist paradigm" (p. 403).

BEING GAY

Given the centrality of heterosexuality to hegemonic masculinity, public perceptions of fatherhood typically emphasize a heterosexual bias as well. A fundamental challenge to this mainstream conception of masculinity is instigated by biological fathers who self-identify as gay. Similarly, anecdotal evidence of how gay step- and adoptive fathers are viewed by the general public suggests that these men are performing roles inconsistent with mainstream notions that masculinity can be achieved through fatherhood.

The largest category of gay fathers includes men who have had children within marriages but are now divorced (Green & Bozett, 1991). However, a growing percentage of gay men appear to be pursuing parenthood after they have already established their gay identities (Patterson, 2000). This latter trend implies that as the social stigma associated with same-gender partnerships continues to lessen, future cohorts of gay men may be less inclined to pursue the marital emblem of masculinity, and some will still want to experience fatherhood. Given the financial costs and practical hurdles that unmarried gay men will encounter in trying to achieve biological fatherhood, the overall proportion of gay biological fathers may actually decline over time (Stacey & Biblarz, 2001).

Patterson and Chan's (1997) recent review of the gay fatherhood literature shows that research in this area is rather sparse and largely based on highly restricted samples of white, well-educated, affluent men living in large cities. Interpreting these studies' findings must occur in full view of the complex reality that "sexual desires, acts, meanings, and identities are not expressed in fixed or predictable packages" (Stacey & Biblarz, 2001, p. 165). Unfortunately, little of this research focuses directly on masculinity themes. The research that does have implications for gender research tends to consider whether gay fathers treat their children differently than either heterosexual fathers or lesbians, and whether children's attitudes and behaviors related to gender are affected. One underlying question guiding this research is this: To what extent and in what ways does gender and sexual orientation affect how gay men parent?

Although the limited research has not found drastic differences in the ways heterosexual fathers and gay fathers "do fathering," some research suggests that gay fathers may be more nurturing and less traditional in their parenting in general (Bigner & Jacobsen, 1989, 1992; Scallen, 1982, cited in Flaks, 1994). In light of these tentative findings, Patterson and Chan (1997) speculated that gay fathers may have parenting styles that are more consistent with authoritative parenting. In one study comparing gay and lesbian parents, gay fathers were more likely to encourage their children to play with sex-typed toys (Harris & Turner, 1985/1986).

Although most research focuses on biological gay fathers, Crosbie-Burnett & Helmbrecht (1993) studied 48 gay stepfamilies that included the father, his male lover or partner, and at least one child who cohabited or visited the household. These researchers found that whereas 96% of gay fathers indicated that they were open about their sexual orientation with heterosexual friends, only 46% of their adolescent children reported that their heterosexual friends knew about their father's sexual orientation. Some children have shown concern that they will be perceived to be homosexual if others know about their fathers' sexual identities (Bozett, 1980, 1987). The limited research from small-scale studies attempting to show whether living in gay fathers' households influences children's sexual orientation does not suggest any clear-cut pattern (Bailey, Bobrow, Wolfe, & Mikach, 1995).

AVENUES FOR FUTURE RESEARCH

Other publications (see the citations in the opening paragraph) outline extensive agendas for future fatherhood research. Thus, we comment here on issues directly involving a gendered approach to fathering, while accentuating fathers' diverse circumstances. We stress the need to examine if and how fathers uniquely influence their children, how fathering affects gender equity inside and outside families, and how men's fathering is influenced by contextual factors. Future research, informed by theoretical discussions in the fields of "men and masculinities" and "fatherhood," needs to explore more fully the complex ways that gender intersects with age, race, class, and sexual orientation to form the social landscape upon which fathers navigate. In several places, we have highlighted how processes associated with the production of knowledge have influenced research on fathering; similar concerns are vital to keep in mind when proposing new research.

Scholars interested in understanding fathers should realize that within the field of family

studies, "new theoretical models conceptualize families as systems affected by, and effecting change in, reciprocal influences among social, behavioral, and biological processes" (Booth et al., 2000, p. 1018). Recent technological advances allow researchers to examine in more rigorous ways these complex processes, including fathers' potentially unique ways of interacting with children. Many social constructionists and feminists are content to emphasize cultural forces inside and outside the home, downplaying possible biologically based differences in men's and women's behaviors and information processing. Some fear that paradigms emphasizing either behavioral endocrinology, behavior genetics, or evolutionary psychology will be used to justify a deterministic or "essentialist" model of parenting and gender relations. They assume that such a model would provide the groundwork for a conservative political philosophy toward gender inequities. In our view, studying social and cultural forces will provide deeper and broader insights about men's complex experiences as fathers; however, researchers would be remiss to discourage explorations of the "possible" biosocial dimensions of fathering (parenting).

Recent heated debates about whether fathers provide unique or essential contributions to their children's development focus on possible parenting differences between men and women. These debates also draw attention to comparisons between men within and outside the United States. Research on U.S. fathers shows that they tend to play differently with their children than mothers; however, we do not yet understand precisely why this happens. We do know that culture plays a major role in shaping parenting styles that vary by gender. For example, compared with fathers in the United States, fathers in some countries are discouraged from playing with their children or do so in ways in which they are less aggressive and encourage less risking (Hewlett, 1992).

One important research issue is identifying why some males are more likely than others to move beyond traditional forms of gender socialization and become involved with their children and partners in ways that embrace the "nurturant" father model. Likewise, additional research is needed to better understand how changing structural, cultural, social, and psychological factors influence how men and women negotiate their contributions to parenting and domestic labor as well as their "agreements" about child custody, support, and visitation. These negotiations have implications for gender equity within the diverse romantic relationships, families, and household arrangements relevant to children's well-being. Given the controversial nature of these value-laden issues, interested parties must be vigilant in monitoring how knowledge in these areas is produced, disseminated, and interpreted.

Drawing on a sociological perspective, one fruitful area of inquiry could focus on how fathers' interactions with their children are shaped by their involvement in different gendered organizational and social contexts. A number of these settings have been and will continue to be affected by the debates and activities of the Fatherhood Responsibility Movement (Gavanas, 2002). Prime sites for such research include several social movements including Promise Keepers (Silverstein, Auerbach, Grieco, & Dunkel, 1999) and fathers' rights groups (Bertoia & Drakich, 1993) in which gendered ideologies of family life are featured prominently. Another intriguing site includes group counseling sessions for violent men (Fox, Sayers, & Bruce, 2001). Research on other settings flavored by a distinctive masculine culture (e.g., the military, law enforcement, prison) could provide valuable insights. We need to learn more about how fathers, as men, manage their impressions to others inside various organizational and social settings that transcend the typical family/household setting (Marsiglio & Cohan, 2000). Viewed in this light, father involvement can be examined as a socially constructed performance that implicates how the gender order both supports and discourages fathers' involvement with their children.

Paternity leave policies (and parental leave policies more generally) are an important aspect of the gender order that should generate policy-oriented research in various industrialized countries (Haas & Hwang, 1995; Hobson, 2002). Policymakers in the various European countries, the United States, and elsewhere have shown some interest in recent years in providing options for both mothers and fathers to leave their jobs temporarily to care for their newborn or sick children. Researchers should be concerned with what people think about these policies as they relate to fathers, what factors influence fathers' use, and the consequences for men's, women's and children's lives when

men take advantage of them (J. H. Pleck, 1993; Wisensale, 2001).

Future research targeting fathers from a gender perspective should be enhanced as the amount, type, and quality of survey data continues to improve (Day & Lamb, 2004; Federal Interagency Forum and Child and Family Statistics, 1998) and scholars advance their knowledge about how to conduct qualitative research with men as men (Schwalbe & Wolkomir, 2002) and with men as fathers (Marsiglio, 2004a; Marsiglio & Cohan, 2000). Collecting data that can inform a critical gender analysis of fathering will require researchers to sharpen their understanding of how men's potential interests in presenting a "masculine self" can influence the research process. Researchers need to explore ways of collecting more accurate and richer data about paternity, nonresident fathering, child support, stepfathering, child abuse, breadwinning, and other issues that challenge male research participants to confront their vulnerabilities. For example, survey researchers should conduct methodological experiments on how men respond to using CASI (computer-assisted survey interview) technology. Does its use alter fathers' willingness to report more accurately their attitudes, feelings, and behaviors related to fathering? Qualitative researchers who interview (or observe) fathers and men who are thinking about having children can also advance their respective methods for studying these populations by sharing their self-critiques of their research process (Marsiglio, 2004b; Marsiglio & Hutchinson, 2002).

Researchers must also address the complex realities of contemporary men's lives. These realities include the diverse and dynamic ways men move in and out of both relationships and households involving children; how gendered social structures (e.g., work, prison) and processes (e.g., negotiating child care or visitation) within and outside a family context influence how men are involved with their children; and how fathers' resources, perceptions, and ways of interacting with their children may change over the duration of fathers' and children's shared life course. These realities call for researchers to develop meaningful ways of capturing men's presence and involvement in children's lives that ensure confidence that research findings have not been tainted by ideological or political motives.

Ultimately, if gender scholars collectively wish to study men's lives as fathers in a comprehensive fashion, they should expand their vision of fatherhood. Men need to be studied not just as fathers of minor children but also as gendered beings capable of imagining and creating human life. Similarly, men interact with, care for, and are provided care by their adult children. Thus, focusing on how gender affects the evolution of men's lives as persons capable of procreation and fathering places fathers' lives squarely within developmental and life-course perspectives. Those who use these perspectives need to be sensitive to the ways that context matters. Of course, the immediacy of certain social policy concerns about child outcomes, as well as the selective availability of funding, will inspire most researchers to study the types of issues that have been examined most frequently. Family and gender scholars should be encouraged, though, to expand their vision of fatherhood and venture beyond these traditional agendas.

REFERENCES

Achatz, M., & MacAllum, C. A. (1994). *The young unwed fathers demonstration project: A status report*. Philadelphia: Public/Private Ventures.

Allen, W. D., & Doherty, W. J. (1996). The responsibilities of fatherhood as perceived by African American teenage fathers. *Families in Society: The Journal of Contemporary Human Services, 77*, 142-155.

Amato, P. (1998). More than money? Men's contribution to their children's lives. In A. Booth & A. C. Crouter (Eds.), *Men in families: When do they get involved? What differences does it make?* (pp. 242-278). Mahwah, NJ: Erlbaum.

Amato, P., & Gilbreth, J. G. (1999). Nonresident fathers and children's well-being: A meta-analysis. *Journal of Marriage and the Family, 61*, 557-573.

Amato, P., & Rivera, F. (1999). Paternal involvement and children's problem behaviors. *Journal of Marriage and the Family, 61*, 375-384.

Anderson, K. G., Kaplan, H., & Lancaster, J. (1999). Paternal care by genetic fathers and stepfathers I: Reports from Albuquerque men. *Evolution and Human Behavior, 20*, 405-431.

Arendell, T. (1992). Father absence: Investigations into divorce. *Gender & Society, 6*, 562-586.

Arendell, T. (1995). *Fathers and divorce*. Thousand Oak, CA: Sage.

Bailey, J. M., Bobrow, D., Wolfe, M., & Mikach, S. (1995). Sexual orientation of adult sons of gay fathers. *Developmental Psychology, 31*, 124-129.

Belsky, J. (1993). Promoting father involvement—An analysis and critique: Comment on Silverstein. *Journal of Family Psychology, 7*, 287-292.

Bertoia, C., & Drakich, J. (1993). The fathers' rights movement: Contradictions in rhetoric and practice. *Journal of Family Issues, 14*, 592-615.

Bigner, J. J., & Jacobsen, R. B. (1989). Parenting behaviors of homosexual and heterosexual fathers. In F. W. Bozett (Ed.), *Homosexuality and the family* (pp. 173-186). New York: Harrington Park.

Bigner, J. J., & Jacobsen, R. B. (1992). Adult responses to child behavior and attitudes toward fathering: Gay and nongay fathers. *Journal of Homosexuality, 23*, 99-112.

Blankenhorn, D. (1995). *Fatherless America: Confronting our most urgent social problem*. New York: Basic Books.

Booth, A., Carver, K., & Granger, D. A. (2000). Biosocial perspectives on the family. *Journal of Marriage and the Family, 62*, 1018-1034.

Bowman, P. J., & Sanders, R. (1998). Unmarried African American fathers: A comparative life span analysis. *Journal of Comparative Family Studies, 29*, 39-56.

Bozett, F. W. (1980). Gay fathers: How and why they disclose their homosexuality to their children. *Family Relations, 29*, 173-179.

Bozett, F. W. (1987). Children of gay fathers. In F. W. Bozett (Ed.), *Gay and lesbian parents* (pp. 39-57). New York: Praeger.

Brandth, B., & Kvande, E. (1998). Masculinity and child care: The reconstruction of fathering. *The Sociological Review, 46*, 293-313.

Braver, S. L., & O'Connell, D. (1998). *Divorced dads: Shattering the myths*. New York: Tarcher/Putnam.

Braver, S. L., Wolchik, S. A., Sandler, I. N., Sheets, V., Fogas, B., & Bay, R. C. (1993). A longitudinal study of noncustodial parents: Parents without children. *Journal of Family Psychology, 7*, 9-23.

Brickner, B. W. (1999). *The Promise Keepers: Politics and promises*. Lanham, MD: Lexington Books.

Brody, L. R. (1985). Gender differences in emotional development: A review of theories and research. *Journal of Personality, 53*, 102-149.

Buchanan, C. M., Maccoby, E. E., & Dornbusch, S. M. (1996). *Adolescents after divorce*. Cambridge, MA: Harvard University Press.

Carroll, J. C. (1980). A cultural consistency theory of family violence in Mexican-American and Jewish-ethnic groups. In M. A. Strauss & G. T. Hotaling (Eds.), *The social causes of husband-wife violence* (pp. 68-81). Minneapolis: University of Minnesota Press.

Catlett, B. S., & McKenry, P. C. (in press). Class-based masculinities: Divorce, fatherhood, and the hegemonic ideal. *Fathering: A Journal of theory, research, and practice about men as fathers.*

Chavez, L. (1999, July 22). Fatherhood going to the apes—literally. *Jewish World Review.* Retrieved from http://www.jewishworldreview.com

Christiansen, S. L., & Palkovitz, R. (2000). Why the "good provider" role still matters: Providing as a form of paternal involvement. *Journal of Family Issues, 22,* 84-106.

Christmon, K. (1990). Parental responsibility of African-American unwed adolescent fathers. *Adolescence, 25,* 645-653.

Claussen, D. S. (2000). *The Promise Keepers: Essays on masculinity and Christianity.* Jefferson, NC: McFarland & Co.

Cochran, D. L. (1997). African American fathers: A decade review of the literature. *Families in Society: The Journal of Contemporary Human Services, 78,* 340-350.

Coltrane, S. (1988). Father-child relationships and the status of women: A cross-cultural study. *American Journal of Sociology, 93,* 1060-1095.

Coltrane, S. (1994). Theorizing masculinities in contemporary social science. In H. Brod & M. Kaufman (Eds.), *Theorizing masculinities* (pp. 39–60). Thousand Oaks, CA: Sage.

Coltrane, S. (1996). *Family man: Fatherhood, housework, and gender equity.* New York: Oxford University Press.

Coltrane, S., & Allan, K. (1994). "New" fathers and old stereotypes: Representations of masculinity in 1980s television advertising. *Masculinities, 2,* 1-25.

Connell, R. W. (1995). *Masculinities.* Berkeley: University of California Press.

Connell, R. W. (2000). *The men and the boys.* Berkeley: University of California Press.

Cooksey, E. C., & Fondell, M. M. (1996). Spending time with his kids: Effects of family structure on fathers' and children's lives. *Journal of Marriage and the Family, 58,* 693-707.

Cooper, M. (2000). Being the "go-to-guy": Fatherhood, masculinity, and the organization of work in the Silicon Valley. *Qualitative Sociology, 23,* 379-405.

Crosbie-Burnett, M., & Helmbrecht, L. (1993). A descriptive empirical study of gay male stepfamilies. *Family Relations, 42,* 256-262.

Crouter, A. C., McHale, S. H., & Bartko, W. T. (1993). Gender as an organizing feature in parent-child relationships. *Journal of Social Issues, 49,* 161-174.

Daly, K. (1996). Spending time with the kids: Meanings of family time for fathers. *Family Relations, 45,* 466-476.

Daly, M., & Wilson, M. (1998). *The truth about Cinderella: A Darwinian view of parental love.* New Haven, CT: Yale University Press.

Daniels, C. R. (1998). *Lost fathers: The politics of fatherlessness in America.* New York: St. Martin's.

Darroch, J. E., Landry, D. J., & Oslak, S. (1999). Age differences between sexual partners in the United States. *Family Planning Perspectives, 31*(4), 160-167.

Day, R. D., & Lamb, M. E. (2004). *Conceptualizing and measuring fathering involvement.* Mahwah, NJ: Lawrence Erlbaum.

Dillon, P., & Emery, R. E. (1996). Divorce mediation and resolution of child custody disputes: Long-term effects. *American Journal of Orthopsychiatry, 66,* 131-140.

Doherty, W. J., Kouneski, E. F., & Erickson, M. F. (1998). Responsible fathering: An overview and conceptual framework. *Journal of Marriage and the Family, 60,* 277-292.

Dowd, N. E. (2000). *Redefining fatherhood.* New York: New York University Press.

Edelman, M. W. (1986). *Families in peril: An agenda for social change.* Cambridge, MA: Harvard University Press.

Ehrenreich, B. (1983). *The hearts of men: American dreams and the flight from commitment.* New York: Anchor.

Emery, R. E. (1999). *Marriage, divorce, and children's adjustment* (2nd ed.). Thousand Oaks, CA: Sage.

Engle, P. L., & Breaux, C. (1998). Fathers' involvement with children: Perspectives from developing countries. *Social Policy Report, 12*(1), 1-23.

Erickson, R. J., & Gecas, V. (1991). Social class and fatherhood. In F. W. Bozett & S. M. H. Hanson (Eds.), *Fatherhood and families in cultural context* (pp. 114-137). New York: Springer.

Federal Interagency Forum and Child and Family Statistics. (1998). *Nurturing fatherhood: Improving data and research on male fertility, family formation, and fatherhood.* Washington, DC: Author.

Ferree, M. M. (1990). Beyond separate spheres: Feminism and family research. *Journal of Marriage and the Family, 52,* 866-884.

Flaks, D. (1994). Gay and lesbian families: Judicial assumptions, scientific realities. *William and Mary Bill of Rights Journal, 3,* 345-372.

Fox, G. L., & Murry, M. V. (2000). Gender and families: Feminist perspectives and family research. *Journal of Marriage and the Family, 62,* 1160-1172.

Fox, G. L., Sayers, J., & Bruce, C. (2001). *Beyond bravado: Redemption and rehabilitation in the fathering accounts of men who batter.* Unpublished manuscript, Department of Child and Family Studies, University of Tennessee, Knoxville.

Furstenberg, F. F. (1995). Fathering in the inner city: Paternal participation and public policy. In W. Marsiglio (Ed.), *Fatherhood: Contemporary theory, research, and social policy* (pp. 119-147). Thousand Oaks, CA: Sage.

Furstenberg, F. F., & Cherlin, A. J. (1991). *Divided families: What happens to children when parents part.* Cambridge, MA: Harvard University Press.

Gavanas, A. (2002). The fatherhood responsibility movement: The centrality of marriage, work and male sexuality in reconstructions of masculinity and fatherhood. In B. Hobson (Ed.), *Making men into fathers: Men, masculinities and the social politics of fatherhood* (pp. 213-242). Cambridge, UK: Cambridge University Press.

Giles-Sims, J. (1997). Current knowledge about child abuse in stepfamilies. *Marriage & Family Review, 26,* 215-230.

Gilmore, D. D. (1990). *Manhood in the making: Cultural concepts of masculinity.* New Haven, CT: Yale University Press.

Goodey, J. (1997). Boys don't cry: Masculinities, fear of crime, and fearlessness. *British Journal of Criminology, 37,* 401-418.

Graham, J. W., & Beller, A. H. (2002). Nonresident fathers and their children: Child support and visitation from an economic perspective. In C. S. Tamis-LeMonda & N. Cabrera (Eds.), *Handbook of father involvement: Multidisciplinary perspectives* (pp. 431-453). Mahwah, NJ: Erlbaum.

Green, G. D., & Bozett, F. W. (1991). Lesbian mothers and gay fathers. In J. C. Gonsiorek & J. D. Weinrick (Eds.), *Homosexuality: Research implications for public policy* (pp. 197-214). Thousand Oaks, CA: Sage.

Griswold, R. L. (1993). *Fatherhood in America: A history.* New York: Basic Books.

Gutmann, M. C. (1996). *The meanings of macho: Being a man in Mexico City.* Berkeley: University of California Press.

Haas, L., & Hwang, P. (1995). Company culture and men's usage of family leave benefits in Sweden. *Family Relations, 44,* 28-36.

Hamer, J., & Marchioro, K. (2002). Becoming custodial dads: Exploring parenting among low-income and working-class African American fathers. *Journal of Marriage and the Family, 64,* 116-129.

Hare-Mustin, R. T., & Marecek, J. (1990). *Making a difference: Psychology and the construction of gender.* New Haven, CT: Yale University Press.

Harris, M. B., & Turner, P. H. (1985/1986). Gay and lesbian parents. *Journal of Homosexuality, 12,* 101-113.

Hawkins, A. J., & Belsky, J. (1989). The role of father involvement in personality change in men across the transition to parenthood. *Family Relations, 38,* 378-384.

Hawkins, A. J., Christiansen, S. L., Sargent, K. P., & Hill, E. J. (1993). Rethinking fathers' involvement in child care. *Journal of Family Issues, 14,* 531-549.

Hearn, J. (2002). Men, fathers and the state: National and global relations. In B. Hobson (Ed.), *Making men into fathers: Men, masculinities, and the social politics of fatherhood* (pp. 245-272). Cambridge, UK: Cambridge University Press.

Hewlett, B. S. (1991). *Intimate fathers: The nature and context of the Alka Pygmy paternal infant care.* Ann Arbor: University of Michigan Press.

Hewlett, B. S. (1992). *Father-child relations: Cultural and biosocial contexts.* New York: Aldine de Gruyter.

Hewlett, B. S. (2000). Culture, history, and sex: Anthropological contributions to conceptualizing fathering involvement. *Marriage & Family Review, 29,* 59-73.

Ho, D. Y. F. (1987). Fatherhood in Chinese culture. In M. E. Lamb (Ed.), *The father's role: Cross-cultural perspectives* (pp. 227-245). Hillsdale, NJ: Lawrence Erlbaum.

Hobson, B. (2002). *Making men into fathers: Men, masculinities and the social politics of fatherhood.* Cambridge, UK: Cambridge University Press.

Hochschild, A. (1989). *The second shift: Working parents and the revolution at home.* New York: Viking.

Hofferth, S. L., & Anderson, K. G. (2003). Are all dads equal? Biology versus marriage as a basis for parental investment. *Journal of Marriage and the Family, 65,* 213-232.

Hofferth, S. L., Pleck, J. H., Stueve, J. L., Bianchi, S., & Sayer, L. (2002). The demography of fathers: What fathers do. In C. S. Tamis-LeMonda & N. Cabrera (Eds.), *Handbook of father involvement: Multidisciplinary perspectives* (pp. 63-90). Mahwah, NJ: Erlbaum.

Horn, W. (1995). *Father facts 2* (Rev. ed.). Lancaster, PA: National Fatherhood Initiative.

Horn, W. (1999, July 7). Lunacy 101: Questioning the need for fathers. *Jewish World Review.* Retrieved from http://www.jewishworldreview.com

Ihinger-Tallman, M., Pasley, K., & Buehler, C. (1993). Developing a middle-range theory of father involvement postdivorce. *Journal of Family Issues, 14,* 550-571.

Ishii-Kuntz, M. (1992). Are Japanese families "fatherless"? *Sociology and Social Research, 76,* 105-110.

Ishii-Kuntz, M. (1993). Japanese families: Work demands and family roles. In J. C. Hood (Ed.),

Men, work, and family (pp. 45-67). Newbury Park, CA: Sage.

Ishii-Kuntz, M. (1994). Paternal involvement and perception toward fathers' roles: A comparison between Japan and the United States. *Journal of Family Issues, 15,* 30-48.

Jankowiak, W. (1992). Father-child relations in urban China. In B. S. Hewlett (Ed.), *Father-child relations: Cultural and biosocial contexts* (pp. 345-363). New York: Aldine de Gruyter.

Kiselica, M. A. (1995). *Multicultural counseling with teenage fathers: A practical guide.* Thousand Oaks, CA: Sage.

Krause, H. D. (1989). Child support reassessed: Limits of private responsibility and the public interest. *University of Illinois Law Review, 1989,* 367-398.

Lamb, M. E. (1986). The changing roles of fathers. In M. E. Lamb (Ed.), *The father's role: Applied perspectives* (pp. 3-27). New York: Wiley.

Lamb, M. E. (Ed.). (1987). *The father's role: Cross-cultural perspectives.* Hillsdale, NJ: Lawrence Erlbaum.

Lamb, M. E. (Ed.). (1997). *The role of the father in child development* (3rd ed.). New York. Wiley.

Lamb, M. E., Pleck, J. H., Charnov, E. L., & Levine, J. A. (1985). Paternal behavior in humans. *American Zoologist, 25,* 883-894.

Lamb, M. E., Pleck, J. H., Charnov, E. L., & Levine, J. A. (1987). A biosocial perspective on paternal behavior and involvement. In J. B. Lancaster, J. Altmann, A. S. Rossi, & L. R. Sherrod (Eds.), *Parenting across the life span: Biosocial perspectives* (pp. 111-142). Hawthorne, NY: Aldine.

Lamb, M. E., Pleck, J., & Levine, R. (1986). Effects of increased paternal involvement on fathers and mothers. In C. Lewis & M. O'Brien (Eds.), *Reassessing fatherhood* (pp. 108-125). London: Sage.

LaRossa, R. (1988). Fatherhood and social change. *Family Relations, 37,* 451-458.

LaRossa, R. (1997). *The modernization of fatherhood: A social and political history.* Chicago: University of Chicago Press.

LaRossa, R., Gadgil, J. M., & Wynn, G. R. (2000). The changing culture of fatherhood in comic strip families: A six-decade analysis. *Journal of Marriage and the Family, 62,* 375-387.

LaRossa, R., & Reitzes, D. C. (1995). Gendered perceptions of father involvement in early 20th century America. *Journal of Marriage and the Family, 57,* 223-229.

Lerman, R. I., & Ooms, T. J. (1993). *Young unwed fathers: Changing roles and emerging policies.* Philadelphia: Temple University Press.

Lindberg, L. D., Sonenstein, F. L., Ku, L. T., & Martinez, G. (1997). Age differences between minors who give birth and their adult partners. *Family Planning Perspectives, 29*(2), 61-66.

Luker, K. (1996). *Dubious conceptions: The politics of teenage pregnancy.* Cambridge, MA: Harvard University Press.

Lupton, D., & Barclay, L. (1997). *Constructing fatherhood: Discourses and experiences.* Thousand Oaks, CA: Sage.

Lytton, H., & Romney, D. M. (1991). Parents' differential socialization of boys and girls: A meta-analysis. *Psychological Bulletin, 109,* 267-296.

Maccoby, E. E., & Mnookin, R. H. (1992). *Dividing the child: Social and legal dilemmas of custody.* Cambridge, MA: Harvard University Press.

Mackey, W. C. (1985). *Fathering behaviors: The dynamics of the man-child bond.* New York: Plenum.

Majors, R. G., & Billson, J. M. (1992). *Cool pose: The dilemmas of black manhood in America.* New York: Lexington Books.

Majors, R. G., & Gordon, J. U. (1994). *The American black male: His present status and his future.* Chicago: Nelson-Hall.

Malkin, C. M., & Lamb, M. E. (1994). Child maltreatment: A test of sociobiological theory. *Journal of Comparative Family Studies, 25,* 121-134.

Manning, W. D., & Smock, P. J. (1999). New families and nonresident father-child visitation. *Social Forces, 78,* 87-116.

Marecek, J. (1995). Gender, politics, and psychology's ways of knowing. *American Psychologist, 50,* 162-163.

Marsiglio, W. (1991). Paternal engagement activities with minor children. *Journal of Marriage and the Family, 53,* 973-986.

Marsiglio, W. (1995). Fathers' diverse life course patterns and roles: Theory and social interventions. In W. Marsiglio (Ed.), *Fatherhood: Contemporary theory, research, and social policy* (pp. 78-101). Thousand Oaks, CA: Sage.

Marsiglio, W. (1998). *Procreative man.* New York: New York University Press.

Marsiglio, W. (2004a). Studying fathering trajectories: In-depth interviewing and sensitizing concepts. In R. D. Day & M. E. Lamb (Eds.), *Conceptualizing and measuring fathering involvement* (pp. 61-82). Mahwah, NJ: Lawrence Erlbaum.

Marsiglio, W. (2004b). *Stepdads: Stories of love, hope, and repair.* Boulder, Co: Rowan & Littlefield.

Marsiglio, W., Amato, P., Day, R. D., & Lamb, M. (2000). Scholarship on fatherhood in the 1990s and beyond. *Journal of Marriage and the Family, 62,* 1173-1191.

Marsiglio, W., & Cohan, M. (1997). Young fathers and child development. In M. E. Lamb (Ed.), *The role of the father in child development* (3rd ed., pp. 227-244, 373-376). New York: Wiley.

Marsiglio, W., & Cohan, M. (2000). Contextualizing father involvement and paternal influence: Sociological and qualitative themes. *Marriage & Family Review, 29,* 75-95.

Marsiglio, W., & Hutchinson, S. (2002). *Sex, men, and babies: Stories of awareness and responsibility.* New York: New York University Press.

McLanahan, S., & Sandefeur, G. (1994). *Growing up with a single parent: What hurts, what helps.* Cambridge, MA: Harvard University Press.

McMahon, A. (1999). *Taking care of men: Sexual politics in the public mind.* Cambridge, UK: Cambridge University Press.

Melli, M. S., Brown, P. R., & Cancian, M. (1997). Child custody in a changing world: A study of postdivorce arrangements in Wisconsin. *University of Illinois Law Review, 49,* 773-800.

Mirandé, A. (1991). Ethnicity and fatherhood. In F. W. Bozett & S. M. H. Hanson (Eds.), *Fatherhood and families in cultural context* (pp. 53-82). New York: Springer.

Mirandé, A. (1997). *Hombres y machos: Masculinity and Latino culture.* Boulder, CO: Westview.

Nielsen, L. (1999). Demeaning, demoralizing, and disenfranchising divorced dads: A review of the literature. *Journal of Divorce & Remarriage, 31,* 139-177.

Nock, S. L. (1998). *Marriage in men's lives.* New York: Oxford University Press.

Okin, S. M. (1989). *Justice, gender, and the family.* New York: Basic Books.

Osmond, M. W., & Thorne, B. (1993). Feminist theories: The social construction of gender in families and society. In P. G. Boss, W. H. Doherty, R. LaRossa, W. R. Schumm, & S. K. Steinmetz (Eds.). *Sourcebook of family theories and methods: A contextual approach* (pp. 591-625). New York: Plenum.

Palkovitz, R. (1997). Reconstructing "involvement": Expanding conceptualizations of men's caring in contemporary families. In A. J. Hawkins & D. C. Dollahite (Eds.), *Generative fathering: Beyond deficit perspectives* (pp. 200-216). Thousand Oaks, CA: Sage.

Parke, R. D. (2002). Fathers and families. In M. Bornstein (Ed.), *Handbook of parenting* (2nd ed., pp. 27-73). Hillsdale, NJ: Lawrence Erlbaum.

Parke, R. D., & Brott, A. (1999). *Throwaway dads: The myths and barriers that keep men from being the fathers they want to be.* Boston: Houghton Mifflin.

Patterson, C. J. (2000). Family relationships of lesbian and gay men. *Journal of Marriage and the Family, 62,* 1052-1069.

Patterson, C. J., & Chan, R. W. (1997). Gay fathers. In M. E. Lamb (Ed.), *The role of the father in child development* (3rd ed., pp. 245-260). New York: Wiley.

Pfiefer, S. K., & Sussman, M. B. (Eds.). (1991). *Families: Intergenerational and generational connections.* Binghamton, NY: Haworth Press.

Pillemer, K., & McCartney, K. (1991). *Parent-child relations throughout life.* Hillsdale, NJ: Erlbaum.

Pleck, E. H., & Pleck, J. H. (1997). Fatherhood ideals in the United States: Historical dimensions. In M. E. Lamb (Ed.), *The role of the father in child development* (pp. 33-48). New York: Wiley.

Pleck, J. H. (1981). *The myth of masculinity.* Cambridge, MA: MIT Press.

Pleck, J. H. (1985). *Working wives/working husbands.* Beverly Hills, CA: Sage.

Pleck, J. H. (1993). Are "family-supportive" employer policies relevant to men? In J. C. Hood (Ed.), *Men, work, and family* (pp. 217-237). Newbury Park, CA: Sage.

Pleck, J. H. (1997). Paternal involvement: Levels, sources, and consequences. In M. E. Lamb (Ed.), *The role of the father in child development* (3rd ed., pp. 66-103, 325-332). New York: Wiley.

Pleck, J. H., Lamb, M. E., & Levine, J. A. (1985). Epilog: Facilitating future change in men's family roles. *Marriage and Family Review, 9,* 11-16.

Pleck, J. H., & Stueve, J. L. (2001). Time and paternal involvement. In K. Daly (Ed.), *Minding the time in family experience: Emerging perspectives and issues* (pp. 205-226). Oxford, UK: Elsevier Science.

Polatnick, M. (1973-1974). Why men don't rear children: A power analysis. *Berkeley Journal of Sociology, 18,* 45-86.

Polikoff, N. (1983). Gender and child-custody determinations: Exploding the myths. In I. Diamond (Ed.), *Families, politics, and public policy: A feminist dialogue on women and the state* (pp. 183-202). New York: Longman.

Popenoe, D. (1996). *Life without father.* New York: Free Press.

Rivara, F., Sweeney, P., & Henderson, B. (1986). Black teenage fathers: What happens when the child is born? *Pediatrics, 78,* 151-158.

Sameroff, A., Seifer, R., Barocas, R., Zax, M., & Greenspan, S. (1987). Intelligence quotient scores of 4-year-old children: Social-environmental risk factors. *Pediatrics, 79,* 343-350.

Schwalbe, M. L., & Wolkomir, M. (2002). Interviewing men. In J. F. Gubrium & J. A. Holstein (Eds.), *Handbook of interview research: Context & method* (pp. 203-219). Thousand Oaks, CA: Sage.

Sedlak, A. J., & Broadhurst, D. D. (1996). *Third national incidence study of child abuse and neglect.* Washington, DC: National Center on

Child Abuse and Neglect, U.S. Department of Health and Human Services.

Seltzer, J. A. (1998). Father by law: Effects of joint legal custody on nonresident fathers' involvement with children. *Demography, 35,* 135-146.

Seltzer, J. A. (2000). Families formed outside of marriage. *Journal of Marriage and the Family, 62,* 1247-1268.

Shwalb, D. W., Imaizumi, N., & Nakazawa, J. (1987). The modern Japanese father: Roles and problems in a changing society. In M. E. Lamb (Ed.), *The father's role: Cross-cultural perspectives* (pp. 247-269). Hillsdale, NJ: Lawrence Erlbaum.

Silverstein, L. B. (1993). Primate research, family politics, and social policy: Transforming "cads" into "dads." *Journal of Family Psychology, 7,* 267-282.

Silverstein, L. B. (1996). Fathering is a feminist issue. *Psychology of Women Quarterly, 20,* 3-37.

Silverstein, L. B., & Auerbach, C. F. (1999). Deconstructing the essential father. *American Psychologist, 6,* 397-407.

Silverstein, L. B., Auerbach, C. F., Grieco, L., & Dunkel, F. (1999). Do Promise Keepers dream of feminist sheep? *Sex Roles, 40,* 665-688.

Skow, J. (1989, August 7). The myth of male housework. *Time,* 62.

Smock, P. J. (2000). Cohabitation in the United States: An appraisal of research themes, findings and implications. *Annual Review of Sociology, 26,* 1-20.

Smuts, B. B., & Gubernick, D. J. (1992). Male-infant relationships in nonhuman primates: Paternal investment or mating effort? In B. S. Hewlett (Ed.), *Father-child relations: Cultural and biosocial contexts* (pp. 1-30). New York: Aldine de Gruyter.

Snarey, J. (1993). *How fathers care for the next generation: A four-decade study.* Cambridge, MA: Harvard University Press.

Sonenstein, F. L., Stewart, K., Lindberg, L. D., Pernas, M., & Williams, S. (1997). *Involving males in preventing teen pregnancy: A guide for program planners.* Washington, DC: The Urban Institute.

Stacey, J., & Biblarz, T. J. (2001). (How) does the sexual orientation of parents matter? *American Sociological Review, 66,* 159-183.

Thompson, L., & Walker, A. (1995). The place of feminism in family studies. *Journal of Marriage and the Family, 57,* 847-865.

Tripp-Reimer, T., & Wilson, S. E. (1991). Cross-cultural perspectives on fatherhood. In F. W. Bozett & S. M. H. Hanson (Eds.), *Fatherhood and families in cultural context* (pp. 1-27). New York: Springer.

U.S. Bureau of the Census. (1999). *Child support for custodial mothers and fathers: 1995* [Current Population Reports, Series P-60, No. 196]. Washington, DC: Government Printing Office.

Walker, A. J., & McGraw, L. A. (2000). Who is responsible for responsible fathering? *Journal of Marriage and the Family, 62,* 563-569.

White, L., & Gilbreth, J. G. (2001). When children have two fathers: Effects of relationships with stepfathers and noncustodial fathers on adolescent outcomes. *Journal of Marriage and the Family, 63,* 155-167.

Wilson, M. N. (1989). Child development in the context of the black extended family. *American Psychologist, 44,* 380-385.

Wisensale, S. K. (2001). *Family leave policy: The political economy of family and work in America.* New York: M. E. Sharpe.

Yeung, W. J., Sandberg, J. F., Davis-Kean, P. E., & Hofferth, S. L. (2001). Children's time with fathers in intact families. *Journal of Marriage and the Family, 63,* 136-154.

Zambrana, R. E. (1995). *Understanding Latino families.* Thousand Oaks, CA: Sage.

16

"GENTLEMEN, THE LUNCHBOX HAS LANDED"

Representations of Masculinities and Men's Bodies in the Popular Media

JIM McKAY

JANINE MIKOSZA

BRETT HUTCHINS

Muscles are the sign of masculinity.

—Glassner (1988, p. 168)

In an article titled "Invisible Masculinity," Kimmel (1993) made the seemingly contradictory comment that men had no history. Kimmel was referring to the paradoxical situation whereby (hegemonic) men have been conspicuous as athletes, politicians, scientists, and soldiers but largely indiscernible *as men*. As Kimmel (1993) noted, this veiled status is one of the principal ingredients of men's power and privilege:

> The very processes that confer privilege to one group and not to another are often invisible to those upon whom that privilege is conferred . . . men have come to think of themselves as genderless, in

part because they can afford the luxury of ignoring the centrality of gender. . . . Invisibility reproduces inequality. And the invisibility of gender to those privileged by it reproduces the inequalities that are circumscribed by gender. (p. 30)

Men's concealed and privileged status is particularly evident with respect to research on representations of men's bodies in the media. For instance, Witz (2000, p. 11) maintains that in sociological research, men's bodies have inhabited an "ambiguous" and "liminal space," [a] "borderland between female corporeality and male sociality that, for a fleeting conceptual moment, male bodies appear, only to disappear immediately." Witz argues that sociologists have constructed men as inherently social and women as essentially corporeal/natural, thus granting men the status of what Shilling (1993) terms the "absent-presence." However, sociologists are not the only scholars who have been implicated in dissembling research on men's bodies. Until fairly recently, intellectuals in the humanities and social sciences in general have been reluctant to engage with such an apparently biological phenomenon as men's bodies. Representations of men's bodies have also received little attention from some intellectuals because of their disdain for popular cultural forms, such as magazines, film, TV, and sport. A related version of this "opiate of the masses" thesis is the belief by some scholars that studying discursive phenomena deflects our attention away from the material inequalities of gender relations.

In addition to being marginalized by academics, hegemonic men's bodies have been positioned by the discourse of "compulsory heterosexuality" that governs the media. Whereas the passive, seminude, and naked bodies of heterosexual women have been constructed as objects for the pleasurable gaze of heterosexual male viewers, there has been a strong taboo against portraying men's bodies in similar ways, as this would pose a threat to the visual power of heterosexual men. This dichotomy is evident in a scene from the popular film *The Full Monty*, from which we have taken the title of this chapter. Early in the narrative, Guy, who is auditioning for a part in a male striptease ensemble, is chosen after dropping his trousers and revealing his large penis to the selection panel. However, we never actually *see* Guy's penis; we are privy only to the astonished reactions of the judges, followed by their leader Gaz's pronouncement, "Gentlemen, the lunchbox has landed."

These factors have meant that research on representations of men's bodies has received significantly less attention from scholars than topics such as sexuality, violence, work, family life, education, and health. For example, it is rare for material on either men's bodies or men and the mass media to appear in some of the widely used academic texts on men and masculinities (see Table 16.1) or the two leading men's studies journals (see Table 16.2). Moreover, most analyses in these forums have either approached the media atheoretically or simplistically via topics such as role models or the effects of consuming the mass media on violent behavior; in the same way, most treatments of men's bodies have been perfunctory. The specialist journal *Body & Society* has published very few articles on either men's bodies or men and the media (see Table 16.3), and just one article on men's bodies and two on masculinities have been published in recent volumes of the prestigious *Media, Culture & Society* (see Table 16.4).

Table 16.1   Coverage of Men's Bodies and the Mass Media in Some Widely Used Academic Texts on Masculinity and Men's Studies

Text	*Entry for Bodies in Index?*	*Separate Chapter on Men's Bodies?*	*Entry for Mass Media in Index?*	*Separate Chapter on the Mass Media?*
Kilmartin (2000)	No	No	Yes	No
Clatterbaugh (1997)	No	No	Yes	No
Hearn (1992)	Yes	No	Yes	No
Seidler (1991)	Yes	No	Yes	No
Hearn and Morgan (1990)	Yes	No	No	No
Doyle (1995)	No	No	Yes	No
Connell (1983)	Yes	Yes	No	No
Kimmel and Messner (1995)	No index	Yes	No index	Yes

Table 16.2 Number of Articles in *Journal of Men's Studies* and *Men and Masculinities* With Media-Related[a] and Body-Related[b] Terms in the Title, Abstract, or Key Words

Journal	Total Articles	Body-Related Term	Media-Related Term	Both Body- and Media-Related Terms
Men and Masculinities (1998–2001)	57	5	9	1
Journal of Men's Studies (1997–2001)	94	4	12	0

a. Includes film, magazine, and Internet.

b. Includes body, bodies, embodiment, and physical.

Table 16.3 Number of Articles Published in *Body & Society* That Included Media-Related and Masculinity-Related Terms as Key Words or in the Title

Total Number of Articles Published in Body & Society *(1997–2001)*	Number of Articles That Included a Media-Related Term	Number of Articles That Included a Masculinity-Related Term	Number of Articles That Included Both Body- and Media-Related Terms
94	9	3	0

Table 16.4 Number of Articles Recently Published in *Media, Culture & Society* That Included Body-Related and Masculinity-Related Terms as Key Words or in the Title

Total Number of Articles Published in Media, Culture & Society *(1997-2001)*	Number of Articles That Included a Body-Related Term	Number of Articles That Included a Masculinity-Related Term	Number of Articles That Included Both Body- and Media-Related Terms
141	1	2	0

A SELECTIVE OVERVIEW OF RECENT RESEARCH ON THE MASS MEDIA AND MEN'S BODIES

Although a few items on men and the mass media were published in the 1980s (Dyer, 1982, 1986; Fiske, 1987; Neale, 1983), the first substantial collection of research did not appear until Craig's volume in 1992. Craig's social constructionist framework posed a challenge to the psychologically reductionist, static, and sometimes apolitical aspects of research on men that had resulted from a miscellany of functionalist sociology, psychoanalysis, sex-role socialization theory, content analysis, and "media effects" research. Likewise, although some seminal pieces on men's bodies appeared in the 1980s and early 1990s (Connell, 1983, 1991; Fiske, 1987; Messner, 1990; Neale, 1983; Theweleit, 1987), Goldstein's (1994) book was the first extensive compilation of research on this topic.

Despite this traditional lack of scholarly enthusiasm for analyzing relationships between men's bodies and the mass media, a sizable amount of research has started to appear in recent years. In reviewing this research, we need to issue the usual caveat that we had to be selective in our analysis. In sketching a general overview of this literature, we focused on the substantive topics that have been studied and the theoretical and methodological perspectives

Table 16.5 Number of Articles Retrieved From a Search of *Sociological Abstracts* and *Humanities Index Abstract of Journal Articles*, 1999-2001, Containing Terms Relevant to the Media and Men's Bodies

Search Terms (Boolean)	Results
(men or male or masculine or masculinity or masculinities) and (body or bodies or corporeal) and media	19
(men or male or masculine or masculinity or masculinities) and media	145
(men or male or masculine or masculinity or masculinities) and (body or bodies or corporeal)	190

that have been employed. In order to keep our synopsis manageable, we concentrated on articles that were published in major academic journals over the past 3 years. Our rationale is that these outlets serve as the most up-to-date forum for research. By using a combination of terms that included variations on the descriptors "men," "male," "masculinity," "masculinities," "body," "bodies," "corporeal," and "media," we conducted searches of two major databases in the humanities and social sciences: *Sociological Abstracts* (which covers approximately 2,500 journals) and *Humanities Index* (which includes 345 journals). We are aware that these databases do not exhaust the literature and also contain a strong Eurocentric bias. However, they have the advantage of sensitizing us to some general trends in the most recent publications.

The results of these searches appear in Table 16.5. However, the figures are inflated, because a search under a term like "body" occasionally yielded irrelevant "hits" such as "body of literature" or "organizational body." Our searches yielded a kaleidoscope of disciplines, theories, and methods across a variety of (mainly Western) national contexts: psychoanalysis, textual analysis, semiotics, surveys, interviews, discourse analysis, content analysis, queer theory, Foucauldian analysis, genealogy, history, communication studies, men's studies, women's studies, gender studies, cultural studies, poststructuralism, postcolonialism, and postmodernism. Indeed, simply categorizing the articles into topics, disciplines, and methods presented us with the difficult task of multidirectional and occasionally arbitrary cross-referencing. Perhaps this complex scenario is to be expected in an era that is frequently understood through the lenses

of hybridity, bricolage, intertextuality, liminality, postcolonialism, and postmodernism. Despite the diverse and fragmented nature of the research, we were able to discern some dominant features. For example, there was a distinct theoretical divide between psychoanalysts and social constructionists, and textual analysis was the most widely used method. The topics ranged through alcohol, commodification, health, men's movements, the "new man," pornography, rurality, sport, sexuality, race, ethnicity, disability, violence, and myriad forms of electronic and print media. Because an exhaustive overview of the articles is impossible, we will now provide a brief and selective account of some of the more easily categorized ones. For analytical purposes, we have divided our analysis according to whether an article was *predominantly* either on the media or men's bodies, even though it was not always easy to make this distinction.

MEN AND THE MASS MEDIA

Researchers who have studied men and the mass media have used a variety of methodological and theoretical frameworks to explore masculinity in TV, advertising, magazines, comics, and film. One of the foremost perspectives is social constructionism, in which popular texts and images are seen to be closely connected with wider relations of domination and subordination both among men and between men and women. We now turn to a selective overview of two of the substantive topics that typify this social constructionist approach: sexuality and race.

Sexuality

Dworkin and Wachs (1998) analyzed how American newspapers covered the disclosures by multiple-Olympic champion diver Greg Louganis (an out gay man), professional basketball superstar Magic Johnson, and professional boxer Tommy Morrison (the latter both self-avowed straight men) that they were HIV-positive. Using a combination of Foucault's model of the confessional and a sin-and-redemption narrative framework, they reported that the three athletes were constructed in markedly differently ways. Johnson was hailed for his sporting achievements, cast sympathetically for allegedly being infected by one of the legion of sexually predatory women whom he had unselfishly "accommodated," and lionized for accepting his HIV-positive status so graciously and raising public awareness about AIDS, especially among African American men. Thus, Johnson was redeemed as an "undeserving victim" of HIV/AIDS and seldom criticized for his sexually "promiscuous" behavior. Morrison also was depicted as a tragic victim of sexually voracious women. Louganis, by contrast, received little recognition for his athletic accomplishments and was positioned as an irresponsible "carrier" who posed a risk to heterosexuals. Dworkin and Wachs also illustrated how the three men were positioned by their ethnic, racial, and social class backgrounds.

King (2000) analyzed media coverage of Canadian male figure skaters who died of AIDS-related illnesses, in the context of health policy in Canada. King maintained that although compassion and tolerance toward the skaters was evident, this response also reinscribed commonsense ideas about "at-risk" populations by enabling the public to identify with the skaters' families rather than the athletes themselves. According to King, the media's reaction could be read as an attempt to construct Canada as a more compassionate and tolerant nation than the United States. King also argued that the media coverage exonerated the Canadian government's abysmal response to people living with HIV/AIDS.

McKee (2000) conducted semistructured interviews with a small group of gay Australian men in order to investigate their memories of TV representations. Although most of the interviewees recalled seeing only a few gay men

on screen, they reported that these instances generated strongly positive feelings about themselves. McKee concluded that TV programming can be important in overcoming gay men's sense of isolation and promoting their self-esteem, thereby contributing to a decrease in the disproportionately high rates of suicide and attempted suicide among young gay men. Brickell (2000) analyzed electronic and print media coverage of gay and lesbian pride parades and reported that a "discursive inversion" constructed gays and lesbians as invaders of unmarked, heterosexual public space.

Race

Coltrane and Messineo (2000) conducted a content analysis of nearly 1,700 commercials on American TV during 1992-1994. They found that despite commonsense notions that market segmentation and narrowcasting have made TV more inclusive, racist and sexist stereotypes persisted: Whites were shown more frequently than African Americans, Asians, and Latino/as; whites were shown more frequently than people of color in authoritative occupations; women were much more likely than men to be depicted as sex objects; African American men tended to be depicted as aggressive and menacing; and Latinos were virtually nonexistent. Coltrane and Messineo argued that rather than portraying the diversity of American society, the "fantasy" of TV advertising served to essentialize gender and racial differences.

Brown (1999) outlined how racist discourses that construct Africans as having bodies but not minds have had specific consequences for African American men who have been constituted as physical and sexual threats, despite being denied access to patriarchal power under slavery and also locked out of the white power structure. This paradoxical status of being emasculated but also feared, while living in cultures that value them primarily for their physical prowess, has resulted in African American men being channeled into the sport and entertainment industries. Brown noted that as a response to this racist regime, African American men have often adopted hypermasculine practices that unintentionally reinforce the very racist stereotypes that oppress them. Brown used semiotic analysis and opportunistic interviews with fans to investigate how masculinity was represented in comic books that feature African American male superheroes. This is an interesting question, given that "superhero comics are one of our culture's clearest illustrations of hypermasculinity and male duality premised on the fear of the unmasculine" (Brown, 1999, p. 31). Brown disagrees with the common criticism that the comics simply articulate a "chocolate-dip Superman." Although Brown recognized that any superhero comic book will contain elements of hegemonic masculinity, he also argued that the narratives constituted an alternative to African American hypermasculinity, in that they "put the mind back in the body" (Brown, 1999, p. 35) by depicting African American male heroes as valuing intelligence.

Adams (1999) examined the white "soft" masculine body in the American film *Copland* by locating the white male body in a nexus of race, politics, and masculinity. Adams also explored aspects of spatial and racial segregation in the film: the black city versus the white suburbs, with the borders of the white suburbs (and thus the white male body) always being open to infiltration. She argued that the politics of former U.S. president Bill Clinton (friendly, diplomatic, and thus a shift from the "hard body" and brute force of the Reagan era) were reflected in the soft white body of the film's male star, Sylvester Stallone. Although the film did not explicitly valorize the male body, Adams noted that we still see a white man whose masculinity is restored through the search for justice. She concluded that "new" forms of masculinity (as typified by Clinton) are not necessarily progressive, as they do not automatically entail *institutional* shifts. Thus, Adams argued that masculinity is pliable and changes in ways that reinforce the status quo.

MEN'S BODIES

The bulk of the research on men's bodies, especially the body image literature, tends to be theoretically unsophisticated, uncritical, and essentialist, using frameworks such as sex role "theory" and role models or explaining the effects of the media on men's attitudes and behavior in crude ways. The literature on bodies and technology is more sophisticated and critical, even though it tends to ignore the important feminist work on posthuman bodies and cyborgs (Hables Gray, Figueroa-Sarriera, Mentor, & Haraway, 1996; Haraway, 1997; Kirkup, Janes, & Woodward, 1999; Willis, 1997). We now examine two of the topics in this area: body image and technology.

Body Image

Using a combination of Barthes's concept of myth and postmodern feminism, Pinfold (2000) argued that both the gay and feminist movements have destabilized the traditional function of facial hair as a signifier of masculinity. Wienke (1998) discussed the centrality of muscularity in defining hegemonic masculinity in American popular culture. Wienke used a narrative interpretation and conducted in-depth interviews with 20 young American men in order to investigate how they viewed their bodies in relation to this muscular ideal. Wienke reported that almost all of his participants desired a mesomorphic body type. Within this overall context, the men had organized their bodily practices in three main ways: reliance, reformulation, and rejection. The majority of the respondents had adopted a strategy of reliance, meaning that they identified with and attempted to attain the active, muscular, and powerful bodies associated with hegemonic masculinity. The reformulators also identified with the hegemonic male body but realized they could not achieve it, so developed alternative practices that enabled them to embody authority, strength, and self-control. Some men had rejected the muscular ideal of masculinity, seeing it as driven by unrealistic or outdated expectations.

Leit, Pope, and Gray (2001) analyzed depictions of male models' bodies in *Playgirl* magazine between 1973 and 1997. Using height and weight information in the magazines, the authors found that norms of the ideal male body had placed increasing emphasis on muscularity. Milkin, Wornian, and Chrisler (1999) examined the covers of 21 women's and men's magazines and reported that the former focused on improving physical appearance, whereas the latter emphasized entertainment, expanding knowledge, and hobbies. Demarest and Allen (2000) surveyed 120 male and female college students in order to ascertain which types of bodies were perceived to be the most attractive. Men and women misjudged which shapes the opposite sex rated as most attractive. African American women had the most accurate perceptions of what men found to be attractive, whereas Caucasian women had particularly distorted views. Men also predicted that women would prefer bulkier shapes than they actually did. The authors argued that these findings had implications for the lower incidence of eating disorders among African American women compared with their Caucasian counterparts. Strong, Singh, and Randall (2000) surveyed an ethnically diverse group of homosexual and heterosexual men and reported that gay males had a lower level of satisfaction with their bodies. They suggested that gay men's childhood socialization practices contributed to dissatisfactions with their bodies in adulthood. Oberg and Tornstam (1999) surveyed more than 2,000 Swedes aged 15 to 95 years about body image and found that some assumptions about aging and bodies that pervade consumer culture were not matched by people's individual experiences of their own bodies.

Technology

Clarsen (2000) analyzed relationships among gender, bodies, and technology in early-20th-century popular narratives of automobiles in Australia and the United States. She argued that although some narratives certainly could be read as articulating sexual difference, for example, by using images of Samson and Tarzan delivering technological benefits to incompetent women drivers, they also contained elements of (middle-class) female technical competence. Clarsen also demonstrated how relations among gender, bodies, and technology intersected with divisions of race and social class.

Poggi (1997) analyzed representations of men's and women's bodies in the sculptures, paintings, novels and poems of early-20th-century, male Italian futurists. Poggi argued that the aesthetics of this avant-garde group displayed a "system of oppositions and substitutions," with men's bodies envisioned in Nietzschean-like ways—as omnipotent, passionless, militaristic cyborgs that conquer nature—and women's bodies positioned by maternal, misogynistic, and erotic motifs. Poggi also drew some parallels with Theweleit's (1987) classic work on the psychological and corporeal boundaries of Fascist German soldiers.

McCormack (1999) applied a blend of cultural geography, Foucault's concept of governmentality, and the insights of postmodern feminists to analyze the representational politics of fitness associated with NordicTrack, an American-manufactured home fitness machine that is targeted at the affluent segment of the market. McCormack showed that among a welter of discourses—biomedical, scientific, and engineering expertise; consumerism; sexual difference; occupational flexibilization; self-discipline; and individuation—the NordicTrack aesthetic constructed a cyborg that was located within a "white, masculinist myth of the Nordic superman." Like Poggi, McCormack alluded to the Nietzschean themes that pervaded the NordicTrack text. A useful aspect of McCormack's conclusion is that the "geography of fitness" connected with NordicTrack both destabilizes *and* rescripts conventional dualisms such as male/female, nature/culture, and human/nonhuman.

UNDERSTUDIED AND NEGLECTED TOPICS

We noticed that many topics had been understudied or neglected. Again, we have only enough space to single out a few topics for special attention.

Cyberbodies in Cyberspace

The exponential spread of new global communication technologies, with features such as "bodyless selves" and "cybersex" (Stratton, 1997, pp. 30-32), has been the focus of some fascinating studies of bodies and the media. Kibby and Costello (1999) found that heterosexual adult video conferencing partially destabilized conventional discourses of sexual display and voyeurism by allowing women to watch erotic images of men engaging in sexual exhibitionism. Nevertheless, some dominant codes still prevailed: Men generally were depicted in active roles, rarely showed their faces and genitals concurrently, and used nicknames that conveyed archetypal phallic size and power. Similar themes emerged in Slater's (1999) ethnography of how "sexpics" were traded on heterosexual Internet Relay Chat (IRC). Despite appearing to be transgressive and libertarian, exchanges on the sites followed traditional heterosexual and homophobic scripts. Despite the disembodied context of IRC, real bodies still needed to be authenticated by people who used the sites for various purposes:

> [The IRC] world looks post-war rather than post-human, with constant talk of fidelity and cheating, true love, and American high school romance language of dating and going steady. . . . One suspects that the IRC sexpics scene is a strange halfway house, a place where anything is possible but little is realized because, although the malleability of the body allows any identity to be performed, no identity can be taken seriously, trusted or even properly inhabited without the ethical weight—persistence in time over time and location in space—that dependable bodies are believed to provide. (Slater, 1999, p. 116)

Further research like this is required because both academic and popular claims about the alleged revolutionary effects of new communication technologies usually neglect how they are usually embedded in established gender tropes.

Subordinated and Marginalized Masculinities

Some scholars have conducted insightful research by analyzing interactions among hegemonic, subordinated, marginalized, and complicit masculinities in several contexts. Turning first to studies of rural masculinities, Bell (2000) argued that films such as *Deliverance* and *Pulp Fiction* construct a binary divide between fashionable "metrosexuality" and unsophisticated rural homosexuality. Homosexual acts by the protagonists in these films fetishize the "rustic sodomite," presenting rural men as sexually driven and socially primitive. Rural men—"hard hitting, hard riding ranchmen, cattle men, prospectors, lumbermen"— have been represented as being interested in sex without affection or affectation, with such displays associated with "sissy" urban gay men (Bell, 2000, p. 551). In this context, sex between men has been represented as a senseless and perfunctory act.

Brandt and Haugen (2000) tracked changes in the representation of masculinities in the Norwegian forestry press over a 20-year period and observed a shift away from the traditional "macho man" toward the technically and professionally proficient "organizational" or "management man." They noted that despite this change, conventional signifiers of "real" masculinity, such as physical competence, strength, and toughness, remained: "the most respected men seemed to be the ones who can display masculinities at both the forestry and managerial sites, men for whom both the power-saw and the time manager are important symbols" (Brandt & Haugen, 2000, p. 352). Liepins (2000) used Foucauldian insights to study rural masculinities in Australia and New Zealand. Like Brandt and Haugen, Liepins found that the "organizational man" had emerged in recent years. The media produced by farming organizations in these two countries valorized elements of strength and struggle against both nature and the organizational and political hierarchies that regulated rural industries: the rugged and active man with muscles and testosterone who could "carry the fight" to make a "better deal for farmers" represented the "true" farmer. Contributions like these are important on two counts: First, they challenge the implicit naturalization of urbanized masculinities as the norm; second, they provide useful examples of the importance of spatial and cultural contexts in understanding gender relations. More research like this is needed in order to understand constructions of rural and urban masculinities, particularly in nations with rich frontier mythologies like Australia, Canada, New Zealand, South Africa, and the United States.

Regarding masculinities in urban contexts, both Farrell (2003) and Pearce (2000) argued that *The Full Monty* begins by embodying the gendered economy of deindustrializing societies, with the marginal working-class men unable to cope with unemployment and disenfranchisement and the women responding in a resilient manner. However, they also claimed that the film ends by reasserting the status quo: "Masculinity has been shored up once more, to the exclusion of the women, who have been returned to their proper place. . . . Men are once more the powerful sex, their bodies once more the (albeit unlikely) instruments of this power" (Pearce, 2000, p. 235). Farrell (2003) and Goddard (2000) maintained that the alleged "reversal" in the film actually reinforces hegemonic gender relations, and Farrell also showed how issues of social class were omitted from the script. These investigations show

how even subordinated and marginalized masculinities can reinforce hegemonic representations of gender and conceal exploitative class relations among men.

At the other end of the social class spectrum, Kendall (1999) drew on Connell's concepts of hegemonic, subordinated, marginalized, and complicit masculinities to analyze representations of "nerds" in American films, magazines, and newspapers, and on the Internet. She found that depictions of this once "liminal masculine identity" had been partially incorporated into hegemonic masculinity and also served to perpetuate racial stereotypes. A valuable aspect of Kendall's investigation was that she located her texts in the economic processes by which global capitalism has reconstituted the cultural and economic capital associated with information technology work. Chan (2000) also employed the concepts of hegemonic, complicit, subordinated, and marginalized masculinities to explore Chinese American masculinity in Bruce Lee films. Chan argued that Asian American men generally are excluded, stereotyped, and desexualized in the media.

Non-Western Contexts

Chan's work reminds us that most of the research on the media and men's bodies relates to advanced capitalist societies. A notable exception is Derne's (1999) examination of Hindi films and their audiences via a combination of content analysis, participant observation, and interviews. Derne argued that the eroticization of violence against women by male heroes in the films facilitated both the creation of unfriendly social spaces for women—the cinema halls—and a broader culture of harassment and violence. Although Derne expressed reservations about a cause-and-effect relationship between the films and wider patterns of violence, the extreme popularity of the films is compelling (some unmarried men attend the cinema 20-30 times a month). Further studies of this type are needed in other non-Western contexts in order to shed light on the relationships among gender, the media, and bodies.

Local/Global Articulations

Although the above studies have provided valuable insights about men and masculinities at numerous micro levels, Connell (2000, pp. 8-9, 39) has noted that it is vital to connect local circumstances with global processes. The media are fertile sites for studying local/global links because their images and texts circulate within the global "traffic" of cultural commodities. However, except for sex tourism (Altman, 2001; Clift & Carter, 2000; Kempadoo, 1999; Ryan & Hall, 2001), most of the literature we examined showed little sensitivity to articulations between local and global situations. Consequently, insufficient attention has been paid to the important issue of global ownership and control of the media, at a time when some of the biggest financial transactions in history have occurred via corporate mergers among multinational media conglomerates. Virtually all the moguls who have signed these deals and consequently exert enormous power over the global media industries are privileged, able-bodied, and white middle-aged men. At the level of production, we suggest that researchers should be interrogating the interests of this narrow group of men who own and control the global media industries. It is imperative to emphasize that this is not simply an "economic" question. As du Gay (1997, p. 4) argued, "The economic . . . too is thoroughly saturated with culture . . . [and] . . . 'Economic' practices and processes . . . depend on meaning for their effects and particular 'conditions of existence.'" So rather than seeing "economic processes and practices as 'things in themselves,'" we should be analyzing the "'cultural' dimensions of economic activities—the meanings and values these activities hold for people" (du Gay, 1997, p. 3). We will revisit these links between cultural and economic processes later in our analysis of magazines.

WHERE TO FROM HERE?

Our selective overview shows that research across a range of disciplines and topics is a strong point of research on both the media and men's bodies. It also is clear that research has been fragmented and that there has been little cross-fertilization among scholars working in different paradigms. Thus, analyses of the specific articulations among masculinities, media, and men's bodies are extremely rare. On the few occasions that dialogues do occur, they either tend to be confined to the theoretical level or rely on a restricted theoretical and/or methodological perspective. An example of the former is Hanke's (1998) excellent overview of some of the major developments in research on the relationships among bodies, masculinity, and the mass media. An illustration of the latter is the research on film and TV that has analyzed many important topics but has done so mainly through the perspective of psychoanalytic theory and the method of textual analysis (Bell, 2000; MacMurraugh-Kavanagh, 1999; McEachern, 1999; Reiser, 2001; Thomas, 1999). It worth noting that we found only three articles that either mentioned both the mass media and men's bodies in the title, abstract, or key words and/or included them in the research design (Adams, 1999; Grindstaff & McCaughey, 1998; Krenske & McKay, 2000). We now suggest a framework that we believe might help scholars to study representations of men's bodies in a more nuanced way.

Methods

As noted, most studies of men and the mass media have relied heavily on content analysis or semiotics. Although these techniques will continue to be indispensable for research in the area, they fail to account for how audiences decode discourses about masculinity. Since publication of the highly influential work of Hall (1980) on encoding-decoding practices and Morley (1980) on audience receptions, it has been axiomatic in the field of media studies that although messages are always relatively "fixed," consumers can interpret them in ways that were unintended during the encoding process. Hence, there has been a plethora of intriguing studies showing how audiences "read" messages differently on the basis of gender, race, and social class (Ruddock, 2001). Thus, Ang (1996, p. 110), one of the most influential exponents of audience ethnographies, has correctly called for research that writes men, and especially gender as a relational phenomenon, back into studies of the mass media. Pertinent to our interest is the research that has demonstrated how women readers of women's magazines and romance novels use these texts in a multiplicity of ways that were unintended by the authors and editors (Hermes, 1995; McCracken, 1993; Radway, 1984; Sheridan, 1995). This "ethnographic turn," however, seems to have bypassed

researchers who have analyzed men and the media. For instance, we found only six journal articles that used audiences in their research design (Derne, 1999; Harrison & Cantor, 1997; Hetsroni, 2000; May, 1999; Rutherdale, 1999). Jackson, Stevenson, and Brooks's (2001) use of focus groups with men who read men's magazines is a welcome step in this direction; their industry-text-audience nexus is also a useful template, although they did not focus specifically on bodies.

Theory

Male bodies are there if we look for them.

—Witz (2000, p. 19)

At an abstract level, we propose that research on representations of men's bodies could be analyzed much more productively through the cultural studies model proposed by du Gay and his colleagues (du Gay, 1997; du Gay, Hall, Janes, Mackay, & Negus, 1997; Hall, 1997). Du Gay et al. (1997) view culture as a *circuit* of meaning-making that "does not end at a pre-ordained place" (p. 185). According to du Gay, the key recursive and interrelated social practices through which meanings are constructed are

- *Production:* how cultural objects are "encoded" from both technical and cultural viewpoints
- *Representation:* the signs and symbols that selectively construct commonsense meanings about cultural objects
- *Identification:* the emotional investments that consumers have in cultural artifacts
- *Consumption:* the diverse ways in which people actually use cultural objects
- *Regulation:* the cultural, economic, and social technologies that determine how cultural objects are both created and transformed

Although these elements can be separated into discrete entities for analytical purposes, "in the real world they continually overlap and intertwine in complex and contingent ways" (du Gay et al., 1997, p. 4). So, even though it is often useful to isolate a single component, the others all inform one another—often in contradictory ways. We will return to this abstract framework with a concrete example of "men's magazines" below.

In approaching bodies through this model, we need to "look" for male bodies—to make them *visible*. Therefore, studies of men's bodies have much to learn from the "corporeal turn" in women's studies. The task here, as Witz (2000) noted, is to write men *in* without writing women *out*. Drawing on the work of Shilling (1993), Witz suggested that by asking "Whose body?," researchers can focus on how men's and women's bodies are differently stigmatized, celebrated, and ignored. We suggest that Fiske's (1987) idea of *inscription/exscription* and Barthes's (1973) concept of *exnomination* are particularly useful in this regard, at least at the textual level of analysis. Both of these terms refer to how the power of hegemonic groups is mythologized and naturalized, on one hand, and the wants and needs of subaltern groups are marginalized and pathologized, on the other. For example, in a case study of Australian sport, McKay and Middlemiss (1995) used a relational perspective to show how a constellation of media metaphors, metonyms, and images simultaneously exnominated and valorized men's bodies according to scripts associated with hegemonic masculinity, while inscribing women's bodies in terms of the passive, supportive, and sexually objectified tropes of emphasized femininity. In a similar way, Rowe, McKay, and Miller (2000) highlighted how the media glorified men's bodies and pathologized those of women in "body panics" surrounding HIV/AIDS in sport.

An Application: Men's Bodies/"Men's Magazines"

In order to illustrate how this "circuit of culture" paradigm can be applied to a concrete context, we now analyze how the bodies of the "new man" and the "new lad" have been constructed in popular "men's magazines." Magazines serve as both reflectors and shapers of social relations, and they "demonstrate the potential for significant change in gender relations and identities, while simultaneously reinscribing traditional forms of masculinity" (Jackson et al., 2001, p. 157). Because these publications are driven by the advertising imperatives of keeping up with both shifting marketing trends and social tastes, a comparison between "new man" and "new lad" magazines illustrates the complex

and contradictory ways in which the media both stabilize and disrupt representations of men's bodies. The five elements of the "circuit of culture" come into play here as we touch upon the interrelated vectors of production, consumption, regulation, representation, and identity.

Men's Bodies in Postmodern Culture

Traditionally, the imperative of "compulsory heterosexuality" has compelled media personnel to differentiate men from women by showing the former with bodies that are authoritative and powerful in the public sphere, and portraying the latter with bodies that denote nurturance, domesticity, passivity, narcissism, and sexual pleasure for male onlookers. Any hint that this binary code has been breached still invokes homophobic or misogynist moral panics in the media (Miller, McKay, & Martin, 1999). However, in postmodern contexts human bodies have become an increasingly visible locus of the highly personal needs and desires that have accompanied the institutionalization of consumer capitalism. For instance, Featherstone (1982, p. 27) posited that traditionally ascribed body characteristics have become more malleable and "a new relationship between body and self has developed": the "performing self" has emerged, "which places greater emphasis on 'appearance, display and the management of impressions.'" Featherstone (1982, p. 18) asserted that our inner and outer bodies are, in fact, "conjoined" in consumer culture, with the aim of inner body maintenance being the improvement of outer body appearance and the cultivation of "a more marketable self." Thus, bodies now have an important exchange value: high if they signify ideals associated with youth, health, fitness, and beauty; low if they denote lack of control or laziness (Featherstone, 1982, pp. 23-24). Featherstone (1982) suggested that the body has been redefined as "a vehicle of pleasure and self-expression" (p. 18) and is "the passport to all that is good in life" (p. 26). Moreover, men increasingly have been regulated by this emphasis on corporeal presentation and monitoring (Nixon, 1996, 2000). However, as Wernick (1991, p. 66) warned over a decade ago, the interpellation of man-as-narcissist by the mass media merely signals that the archetypal "possessive individual," who was at the center of early capitalism and liberal contract theory, has metamorphosed into the "promotional individual":

> The equalization of gender status which is beginning to occur in the sphere of consumption is not in the least the equality we might dream of: the equality of free and self-determining beings in a free and self-determining association with another. It is the equality, rather, of self-absorbed, and emotionally anxious, personalities for sale. With the makeup mirror dangled invitingly before them, men, like women, are being encouraged to focus their energies not on realizing themselves as self-activating subjects, but on realizing themselves as circulating tokens of exchange. (Wernick, 1991, p. 66)

Constructing the "New Man"

In this postmodern scenario, the mass media are faced with the problem of how to sell "soft" products and lifestyles to men without simultaneously threatening the traditional bases of hegemonic masculinity. One archetype the media created in order to solve this conundrum was the "new man," which was framed in terms of classic postmodern motifs (e.g., sensitivity, self-care), as well as by essentialist messages about needing to "get in touch with his inner self." Thus, during the 1990s, films, TV, and magazines were replete with images of men cuddling their babies, playing with their children, grooming themselves, exercising their bodies, and embracing other (heterosexual) men during "weekend warrior" retreats. Mort (1996) noted that the British (and we would argue the Australian) conceptions of the "new man" were different from the American one, as the latter market responded to the women's movement, whereas the former did not. This was due to the British publishers' perception that the women's movement was not interested in the operations of the marketplace and "in contrast [to the United States], the project for masculinity championed in [magazines] was overwhelmingly commercial" (Mort, 1996, p. 44). The emergence of the "new man" coincided with a shift toward lifestyle advertising with its attendant techniques of market research (Chapman, 1988, p. 229). Thus, men were increasingly being sold images (of fashion, health, fatherhood) by which they were "stimulated to look at themselves—and other men—as objects of consumer desire" (Mort, 1988, p. 194).

Lifestyle magazines targeted at men have functions similar to those of long-established women's magazines, in that masculinity is framed as a problem (sometimes even depicted as being "in crisis") that requires self-regulation and improvement. Thus, these magazines include instructions on how to exercise, groom, buy clothes, and perform sex. One outcome of heterosexual men increasingly coming under the gaze was a qualitative change in how their bodies were framed, often represented passively, a pose that is very different from traditional representations of the "active man." The shift to grooming and health also disrupted the image of the conventional "breadwinner" image. An important precursor to this discourse was *Playboy*, which advocated a hedonistic lifestyle that was free from marriage and children, and also made the personal consumption of mass-produced commodities legitimate for men (Conekin, 2001; Osgerby, 2001). However, as McMahon (1999, p. 110) pointed out, amid this ostensible feminization of masculinity in consumer culture, the media still have to find ways of maintaining sexual difference. In advertising, this frequently is achieved by encoding commodities such as fragrances with terms such as "strong," "powerful," or "bold" and in "masculine" colors like gray or blue. Another way sexual convergence is nullified is through the marketing of technological products such as computers and DVDs that rarely appear in comparable women's magazines such as *Cosmopolitan*.

Some critics dismissed the "new man" as an insincere "yuppie" who simply knew how to *appear* to be sensitive (Jackson et al., 2001, p. 35). McMahon (1999) argued that the "new man" was an artifact of the media, and despite all the focus on "sensitive" masculinity, men's self-interests were still being served via the sexual division of domestic labor. As Moore (1989) wryly put it, "Did anyone seriously think that a few skincare products were going to cause the collapse of patriarchy?" (p. 47). Moreover, representations of this "new masculinity" were overwhelmingly restricted to affluent, white, able-bodied heterosexual men and underpinned by essentialist discourses about gender identities and relations (McKay & Ogilvie, 1999). Thus, this allegedly "new man" constituted no real threat to the traditional gender order:

[I]mages of the "New Man" in the media and advertising suggest men can be caring and sensitive without "losing" their masculinity. But far from reversing institutionalized male domination in marriage and the household, these "new" ideas can be seen as facilitating the conditions within which individual men can come to acquire a few more masculine "brownie points" in the struggle to differentiate themselves from other men, and from women. Rather than overturning the unequal power relations between the sexes in relation to domestic work or childcare, the New Man image arguably opens up legitimate space for the colonization and appropriation of those aspects of childcare, which are the most rewarding and which offer immediate creative statement, couched in the language of enhancing men's masculinity and social prowess. (Kerfoot & Knights, 1993, p. 669)

Jackson et al. (2001, p. 12) pointed out, however, that a rather judgmental tone is apparent in the research and critiques of the new forms of masculinity, much of which views the "new man" as purely marketing hype or blatant pretence. They concur with Mort (1988, pp. 218-219) that there are some positive outcomes of these representations, especially the differing profiles of masculinity, with various outcomes reflecting and constituting new identities. Young men are now carving out new spaces, representing themselves in different ways and living out fractured identities. In any event, just as the "new man" had become the flavor of the month, editors and journalists turned their attention to the "new lad."

MEN BEHAVING BADLY: CONSTRUCTING THE "NEW LAD"

When fears over male narcissism and incorporation of the feminine had receded, the media began to reinscribe conventional modes of masculinity (McMahon, 1999, p. 119). This move was enhanced by the criticism that the "new man" was dishonest and hypocritical. Thus, by the mid-1990s, the Australian and British media had switched their attention to the "new lad," who unapologetically symbolized the traits associated with hegemonic masculinity: drinking with his mates, taking risks, telling dirty jokes, and, most of all, looking at skimpily dressed women. Nixon (1996) argued that "new

lad" magazines marked a return to established masculine heterosexual scripts (of the "hard" sexist "traditional man") that were located in soft pornography magazines during the 1970s. This was because no new masculine repertoires were articulated in representations in the "new man" magazines, so there was the opportunity for traditional tropes to reemerge. Magazines like *Loaded* (U.K.), *Ralph* (Australia), and *FHM* (For Him Magazine, Australia), which targeted young, heterosexual men, epitomized this "new laddism." This genre of masculinity was based on biological assumptions (nurturing is for women/risk-taking is for men) and also enunciated what it meant to be an "authentic" male (Jackson et al., 2001, p. 85), which was not to be intimidated by other men or, especially, by women.

The "men's magazine" market, especially in Australia, has always been highly contested, as manifested in the demise of publications like *Max* and *GQ*. The two most successful "men's magazines" in the Australian market are *FHM* and *Ralph*. (Two homologous sport-related publications, *Inside Sport* and *Tracks*, are also popular; see Jefferson Lenskyj, 1998, and Henderson, 1999.) The "new lad" magazines are more akin to a male version of *Cosmopolitan* than a soft-core pornography magazine such as *Playboy* (Mikosza, 2003, p. 135). In fact, the Australian version of *Playboy* has folded due to falling circulation and advertisers shifting to the "new lad" magazines (Dale, 2000). The traditional meaning of soft-core pornography magazines for men has been reinscribed by the meanings and images associated with the "new lad" in these magazines, which are highly desirable to advertisers, with their mixture of sex, sport, alcohol, the public world, and "carefully managed" fashion for a heterosexual male readership (Bonner, 2002, p. 194). If meanings are "always made in usage" (du Gay et al., 1997, p. 85), then these magazines have come to signify hedonism, risk-taking, consumerism, and voyeurism, as well as what it is to be a young man in Australian culture.

In terms of form and content, the glossy "new lad" magazines usually are classified as either "men's interests" or "general lifestyle," even though they almost always have a woman in a bikini on the cover and *FHM* contains elements that are commonly found in soft porn publications. They are, however, also given a

"G" (general) rating and are policed through the appropriate national censor. They are also regulated in the community: Some issues of *FHM* have been banned from sale in local supermarket chains for being too sexually explicit. However, cultural regulation of the magazines also exists at the level of production and consumption, with the editors self-censoring/regulating in different ways. An example is the exclusion of sexually explicit information on the cover that women's magazines often incorporate. To a lesser degree, readers also write letters to the editors about their likes and dislikes of the magazines, which occasionally affect subsequent content.

The content of these magazines ranges through health, grooming, exercise, alcohol, "boys' toys," advertisements for myriad commodities, and, most prominent, images of women, who are there to be looked at even if the copy also subjects men to the gaze. The magazines sell products similar to those in "new men" magazines while adroitly distancing themselves from the feminine and preempting criticism by invoking an ironic, self-deprecating, and tongue-in-cheek style of humor. Hence, Schirato and Yell (1999) noted that the editors and journalists of these magazines appeal to media-savvy readers' "knowing sexism"—an awareness of feminism and gay rights that is fused with an enjoyment of conventional representations of women in revealing swimsuits. (*Loaded* carries the sardonic subtitle "For guys who should know better.") Schirato and Yell claimed that women are active in the magazines and not simply there to display their passive bodies for men to look at. For example, *Ralph* magazine has a two- or three-page photo and text spread titled "Babes behaving badly," in which three or more women discuss their likes and dislikes regarding men and sex; thus, these women are "in on the joke" about men. Using Butler's concept of gender performance, Schirato and Yell analyzed a story from *Ralph* magazine and concluded that the enactment of "stereotypical" masculinity in the magazines was a "self-conscious" act that recognized that sexist masculinity was obsolete. We argue, however, that the representations continue to be defined quite rigidly by conventional gender dualisms, with women mainly contained in passive settings. So, when women are depicted as "agents," as in the story above, they are invariably young, single, and positioned as providers

of tips to men on how to pick up women. The bodies of the women are also posed in similar ways to the bikini shots in other parts of the magazine. These representations are in line with the magazines' general narratives, which are informed by an appeal to voracious male heterosexuality.

Men's bodies are present in various guises in "new lad" magazines, usually in a muscular form. Whereas the eponymous *Men's Health* focuses on improving men's well-being (Toerien & Durrheim, 2001), *FHM* and *Ralph* concentrate on risk-taking behavior. Although these magazines do construct men in "feminized" ways (e.g., via male models or images of men exercising or grooming their bodies), predictable masculine discourses also are present. For instance, men's bodies are almost always depicted as active, and even when posed in fashion shoots, are in some way involved in a bonding activity with other men (e.g., playing sports or doing business), or positioned with women in ways that assure the (assumed male heterosexual) readers of their heterosexuality.

Men's bodies are also constructed in "new lad" magazines as instruments that need to be managed through contradictory regimes of exercise, sex, and sometimes-dangerous practices (e.g., drinking, driving fast cars). Jackson et al. (2001, p. 94) argued that the function of health advice sections in these magazines is to prevent anxiety and insecurity surrounding the declining and aging male body. Thus, magazines such as *FHM* also have sections on bodily care, health, and grooming. So, in a similar way to the contradictory nature of women's magazines (with stories on being happy about your body shape positioned next to a feature on a new diet), the magazine constructs a paradoxical framework of men's interests. In summary, the media, and especially "men's magazines," position themselves for various audiences; as Gauntlett (2002, p. 255) notes, the media

> are far more interested in generating "surprise" than in maintaining coherence and consistency. Contradictions are an inevitable by-product of the drive for multiple points of excitement, so they rarely bother today's media makers, or indeed their audiences.

We are not suggesting that this circuit-of-culture model can or should be applied mechanistically to every research site. We argue, however, that it is a useful theoretical and methodological "toolbox" for conducting research on the links between men's bodies and the media. First, it alerts us to the fact that the media both reinforce *and* destabilize everyday understandings of men's bodies in multifarious and paradoxical ways. Thus, the media can create contradictory images about "lads" while simultaneously breathing new life into the "new man." The most recent rearticulation of the latter archetype is the "metrosexual," epitomized by soccer player David Beckham, whose status as a globally recognized sports star traditionally has been associated with "the frontline troops of patriarchy" (Connell, 1995, p. 79) rather than the "new man" (Cashmore & Parker, 2003; Simpson, 2002; Whannel, 2001). Second, it sensitizes us to the close connections among gender and the *cultural economy* of the global entertainment, advertising, and marketing industries. For instance, *FHM* can now be purchased in 16 countries, meaning that it is important to investigate how local practices articulate with the generic formula (e.g., in some countries, women's nipples are not allowed to be shown through swimsuits, so are airbrushed out). Third, it underscores the need for *relational* research on gender. For instance, the magazines we analyzed ostensibly are *about* and *for* men, but women also are involved as executives, producers, photographers, journalists, and consumers, and little is known about their roles in this gender regime. Moreover, there are several admirable analyses of men's *or* women's magazines, but no one has conducted a comparative study of men's *and* women's magazines. Finally, it allows researchers to study the various "moments" of the circuit of meaning-making, as well as illuminating how production, consumption, regulation, representation, and identity are mutually constitutive of one another.

SUMMARY AND CONCLUSIONS

Whatever happened to Gary Cooper, the strong, silent type? That was an American. He wasn't in touch with his feelings. He just did what he had to do. See, what they didn't know is that once they got Gary Cooper in touch with his feelings, they couldn't get him to shut up. It's dysfunction this, dysfunction that.

—Mafia boss Tony Soprano to his female psychiatrist in the first episode of the critically acclaimed *The Sopranos*

Heterosexuality and homophobia are the bedrock of hegemonic masculinity.

—Donaldson (1993, p. 645)

The politics surrounding representations of men's bodies is of particular importance to gender studies scholars and activists because the media are deeply implicated in literally embodying hegemonic forms of masculinity, albeit in selective, uneven, and contradictory ways. At the beginning of a new millennium, the intricate nexus of desires, pleasures, and power surrounding men's bodies in the mass media is undoubtedly much more intricate than, say, in the 1950s, when, as Pomerance (2001, p. 7) put it, Hollywood films did "describe and reflect the social world" in a relatively seamless fashion. As the spectacle of a corpulent mob boss in therapy on a popular TV program indicates, the sheer plurality of representations of men's bodies that circulate in the contemporary mass media means that hegemonic masculinity is less culturally secure than hitherto. Nevertheless, it is important not to overemphasize or romanticize the subversive potential of alternative representations, on one hand, and to underestimate the resilience of hegemonic modes of masculinity, on the other. As Hall (1985) emphasized, social texts, identities, and practices are always relatively anchored. In the case of gender, we argue that although hegemonic masculinity is not as rigid as it once was, given the fragmented and contradictory representations of masculinities in the contemporary media, it remains powerful (both materially and symbolically) through the interdependent and mutually reinforcing structures of heterosexism and homophobia alluded to above by Donaldson. Tony Soprano might be a caring family man who is in therapy, but reminiscent of how the hypermasculine Arnold Schwarzenegger was reconstituted in *Terminator 2*, he also is "softened and sensitized into a man who can both kill *and* care" (Pfeil, 1995, p. 53).

Thus, at one level, we would agree with both Bordo (1998) and Pearce (2000) that *The Full Monty* destabilizes the stereotypical *mise-en-scène* whereby women take off their clothes for the pleasure of heterosexual male viewers, as well as posing an alternative to the violent, spectacular, and mesomorphic bodies of Arnold Schwarznegger, Bruce Lee, and Wesley Snipes that traditionally have been valorized in the cinema. After all, who can forget the film's denouement, where Gaz and his troupe of embattled working class men with mainly unimposing bodies throw their hats into the audience, thereby appearing fully naked? Yet, in keeping with the strong taboo on exposing the penis that was also evident in the scene with Guy we alluded to earlier, it is instructive to note that we see their naked bodies only from *behind*. As film historian Peter Lehman commented on the film, "It is still a moment of shockingly great significance when they show the penis. They can't just show it in a casual manner, and that is still quite different from the manner in which the female body is commonly shown" (quoted in Lehigh, 2000, p. 13S). In summary, the time when we see a front-on pan of a row of "full Monties" in the popular media is still some way off.

REFERENCES

Adams, R. (1999). Fat man walking: Masculinity and racial geographies in James Mangold's *Copland*. *Camera Obscura, 42,* 4-29.

Altman, D. (2001). *Global sex*. Chicago: University of Chicago Press.

Ang, I. (1996). *Living room wars*. London: Routledge.

Barthes, R. (1973). *Mythologies* (A. Lavers, Trans.). London: Paladin.

Bell, D. (2000). Farm boys and wild men: Rurality, masculinity, and homosexuality. *Rural Sociology, 65*(4), 547-561.

Bonner, F. (2002). Magazines. In S. Cunningham & G. Turner (Eds.), *The media & communications in Australia*. Crows Nest: Allen & Unwin.

Bordo, S. (1998). Pills and power tools. *Men and Masculinities, 1*(1), 88-90.

Brandt, B., & Haugen, M. S. (2000). From lumberjack to business manager: Masculinity in the Norwegian forestry press. *Journal of Rural Studies, 16*(3), 343-355.

Brickell, C. (2000). Heroes and invaders: Gay and lesbian pride parades and the public/private distinction in New Zealand media accounts. *Gender, Place and Culture, 7*(2), 163-178.

Brown, J. A. (1999). Comic book masculinity and the new black superhero. *African American Review, 33*(1), 25-42.

Cashmore, E., & Parker, A. (2003). One David Beckham? Celebrity, masculinity, and the soccerati. *Sociology of Sport Journal, 20,* 214-231.

Chan, J. (2000). Bruce Lee's fictional models of masculinity. *Men and Masculinities, 2*(4), 371-387.

Chapman, R. (1988). The great pretender: Variations on the new man theme. In R. Chapman & J. Rutherford (Eds.), *Male order: Unwrapping masculinity*. London: Lawrence & Wishart.

Clarsen, G. (2000). The "dainty female toe" and the "brawny male arm": Conceptions of bodies and power in automobile technology. *Australian Feminist Studies, 15*(32), 153-163.

Clatterbaugh, K. (1997). *Contemporary perspectives on masculinity: Men, women, and politics in modern society* (2nd ed.). Boulder, CO: Westview.

Clift, S., & Carter, S. (Eds.). (2000). *Tourism and sex: Culture, commerce, and coercion*. New York: Continuum International Publishing Group.

Coltrane, S., & Messineo, M. (2000). The perpetuation of subtle prejudice: Race and gender imagery in 1990s television. *Sex Roles, 5*(6), 363-389.

Conekin, B. (2001). Fashioning the playboy: Messages of style and masculinity in the pages of *Playboy* magazine, 1953-1963. *Fashion Theory: The Journal of Dress, Body and Culture, 4*(4), 447-466.

Connell, R. W. (1983). Men's bodies. In *Which way is up? Essays on sex, class, and culture*. Sydney: Allen & Unwin.

Connell, R. W. (1991). An iron man: The body and some contradictions of hegemonic masculinity. In M. Messner & D. Sabo (Eds.), *Sport, men, and the gender order: Critical feminist perspectives*. Champaign, IL: Human Kinetics Press.

Connell, R. W. (1995). *Masculinities*. Sydney Allen & Unwin.

Connell, R. W. (2000). *The men and the boys*. St. Leonards: Allen & Unwin.

Craig, S. (Ed.). (1992). *Men, masculinity and the media*. Newbury Park, CA: Sage.

Dale, D. (2000, February 19). I only buy it for the articles . . . *The Sydney Morning Herald*, p. 40.

Demarest, J., & Allen, R. (2000). Body image: Gender, ethnic, and age differences. *The Journal of Social Psychology, 140*(4), 465-472.

Derne, S. (1999). Making sex violent: Love as force in recent Hindi films. *Violence Against Women, 5*(5), 548-575.

Donaldson, M. (1993). What is hegemonic masculinity? *Theory & Society, 22,* 643-657.

Doyle, J. A. (1995). *The male experience* (3rd ed.). New York: McGraw-Hill.

du Gay, P. (1997). Introduction. In P. du Gay (Ed.), *Production of culture/cultures of production*. London: Sage/The Open University.

du Gay, P., Hall, S., Janes, S., Mackay, L., & Negus, K. (1997). *Doing cultural studies: The story of the Sony Walkman.* London: Sage/The Open University.

Dworkin, S., & Wachs, F. L. (1998). "Disciplining the body": HIV-positive males, media surveillance and the policing of sexuality. *Sociology of Sport Journal, 15,* 1-20.

Dyer, R. (1982). Don't look now—the male pin-up. *Screen, 23*(3-4), 61-73.

Dyer, R. (1986). *Heavenly bodies: Film stars and society.* New York: St. Martin's.

Easthope, A. (1992). *What a man's gotta do: The masculine myth in popular culture.* New York: Routledge.

Farrell, K. (2003). Naked nation. *The Full Monty,* working-class masculinity, and the British image. *Men and Masculinities, 6*(2), 119-135.

Featherstone, M. (1982). The body in consumer culture. *Theory, Culture & Society, 1*(2), 18-32.

Fiske, J. (1987). *Television culture.* London: Routledge.

Gauntlett, D. (2002). *Media, gender and identity: An introduction.* London: Routledge.

Glassner, B. (1988). *Bodies: Why we look the way we do (and how we feel about it).* New York: Putnam.

Goddard, K. (2000). "Looks maketh the man": The female gaze and the construction of masculinity. *The Journal of Men's Studies, 9,* 23-39.

Goldstein, L. (Ed.). (1994). *The male body: Features, destinies, exposures.* Ann Arbor: University of Michigan Press.

Grindstaff, L., & McCaughey, M. (1998). Feminism, psychoanalysis, and (male) hysteria over John Bobbitt's missing manhood. *Men and Masculinities, 1*(2), 173-192.

Hables Gray, C., Figueroa-Sarriera, H. J., Mentor, S., & Haraway, D. (Eds.). (1996). *The cyborg handbook.* New York: Routledge.

Hall, S. (1980). Encoding and decoding. In S. Hall, D. Hobson, D. Lowe, & P. Willis (Eds.), *Culture, media, language.* London: Hutchinson.

Hall, S. (1985). Signification, representation, ideology: Althusser and the post-structuralist debates. *Critical Studies in Mass Communication, 2*(2), 91-114.

Hall, S. (Ed.). (1997). *Representation: Cultural representations and signifying practices.* London: Sage/The Open University.

Hanke, R. (1998). Theorizing masculinity with/in the media. *Communication Theory, 8*(2), 183-203.

Haraway, D. (1997). *Modest_witness@second_millenium.femaleman©_meets_oncoMouse™: Feminism and Technoscience.* New York: Routledge.

Harrison, K., & Cantor, J. (1997). The relationship between media consumption and eating disorders. *Journal of Communication, 47*(1), 40-67.

Hearn, J. (1992). *Men in the public eye: The construction and deconstruction of public men and public patriarchies.* London: Routledge.

Hearn, J., & Morgan, D. (Eds.). (1990). *Men, masculinities and social theory.* London: Unwin Hyman.

Henderson, M. (1999). Some tales of two mags: Sports magazines as glossy reservoirs of male fantasy. *Journal of Australian Studies, 62,* 64-75.

Hermes, J. (1995). *Reading women's magazines.* Cambridge, MA: Polity.

Hetsroni, A. (2000). Choosing a mate in television dating games: The influence of setting, culture, and gender. *Sex Roles, 42*(1-2), 83-106.

Jackson, P., Stevenson, N., & Brooks, K. (2001). *Making sense of men's magazines.* Cambridge, MA: Polity.

Jefferson Lenskyj, H. (1998). "Inside Sport" or "On the Margins"? Australian women and the sport media. *International Review for the Sociology of Sport, 33*(1), 19-32.

Kempadoo, K. (Ed.). (1999). *Sun, sex, and gold: Tourism and sex work in the Caribbean.* Lanham, MD: Rowman & Littlefield.

Kendall, L. (1999). Nerd nation. Images of nerds in US popular culture. *International Journal of Cultural Studies, 2*(2), 260-283.

Kerfoot, D., & Knights, D. (1993). Management, masculinity and manipulation: From paternalism to corporate strategy in financial services in Britain. *Journal of Management Studies, 30,* 660-677.

Kibby, M., & Costello, B. (1999). Displaying the phallus. *Men and Masculinities, 1*(4), 352-364.

Kilmartin, C. T. (2000). *The masculine self* (2nd ed.). New York: McGraw-Hill.

Kimmel, M. (1993, September/October). Invisible masculinity. *Society,* 28-35.

Kimmel, M., & Messner, M. (Eds.). (1995). *Men's lives* (3rd ed.). Boston: Allyn & Bacon.

King, S. (2000). AIDS, figure skating, and Canadian identity. *Journal of Sport & Social Issues, 24*(2), 148-175.

Kirkup, G., Janes, L., & Woodward, K. (Eds.). (1999). *The gendered cyborg: A reader.* New York: Routledge.

Krenske, L., & McKay, J. (2000). "Hard and heavy": Gender and power in a heavy metal music subculture. *Gender, Place and Culture, 7*(3), 287-304.

Lehigh, S. (2000, February 26). Come on boys, grin and bear it. *The Sydney Morning Herald,* p. 13S.

Leit, R. A., Pope, H. G., & Gray, J. J. (2001). Cultural expectations of muscularity in men: The evolution of Playgirl centerfolds. *International Journal of Eating Disorders, 29*(1), 90-93.

Liepins, R. (2000). Making men: The construction and representation of agriculture-based masculinities in Australia and New Zealand. *Rural Sociology, 65*(4), 605-620.

MacMurraugh-Kavanagh, M. K. (1999). Boys on top: Gender and authorship on the BBC Wednesday Play, 1964-1970. *Media, Culture and Society, 21,* 409-425.

May, R. A. B. (1999). Tavern culture and television viewing: The influence of local viewing culture on patrons' reception of television programs. *Journal of Contemporary Ethnography, 28*(1), 69-99.

McCormack, D. (1999). Body shopping: Reconfiguring geographies of fitness. *Gender, Place and Culture, 6*(2), 155-177.

McCracken, E. (1993). *Decoding women's magazines: From Mademoiselle to Ms.* New York: St. Martin's.

McEachern, C. (1999). Comic interventions: Passion and the men's movement in the situation comedy *Home Improvement. Journal of Gender Studies, 8*(1), 5-18.

McKay, J., & Middlemiss, I. (1995). "Mate against mate, state against state": A case study of media constructions of hegemonic masculinity in Australian sport. *Masculinities, 3*(3), 38-47.

McKay, J., & Ogilvie, E. (1999). New Age—same old men: Constructing the "new man" in the Australian media. *Mattoid, 54,* 18-35.

McKee, A. (2000). Images of gay men in the media and the development of self-esteem. *Australian Journal of Communication, 27*(7), 81-98.

McMahon, A. (1999). *Taking care of men: Sexual politics in the public mind.* Cambridge, UK: Cambridge University Press.

Messner, M. A. (1990). When bodies are weapons: Masculinity and violence in sport. *International Review for the Sociology of Sport, 25,* 203-219.

Mikosza, J. (2003). In search of the "mysterious" Australian male: Editorial practices in men's lifestyle magazines. *Media International Australia/Culture and Policy, 107,* 134-144.

Milkin, A. R., Wornian, K., & Chrisler, J. C. (1999). Women and weight: Gendered messages on magazine covers. *Sex Roles, 40*(7/8), 647-655.

Miller, T., McKay, J., & Martin, R. (1999). Courting lesbianism. *Women and Performance: A Journal of Feminist Theory, 11*(1), 211-234.

Moore, S. (1989, March 2). The year of the post-man. *New Statesman & Society, 2,* 47.

Morley, D. (1980). *The Nationwide audience: Structure and decoding.* London: British Film Institute.

Mort, F. (1988). Boys own? Masculinity, style and popular culture. In R. Chapman & J. Rutherford (Eds.), *Male order: Unwrapping masculinity.* London: Lawrence & Wishart.

Mort, F. (1996). *Cultures of consumption: Masculinities and social space in late twentieth-century Britain.* London: Routledge.

Neale, S. (1983). Masculinity as spectacle. *Screen, 24*(6), 2-17.

Nixon, S. (1996). *Hard looks: Masculinities, spectatorship and contemporary consumption.* London: UCL Press.

Nixon, S. (2000). Exhibiting masculinity. In S. Hall (Ed.), *Representation: Cultural representations and signifying practices.* London: Sage/The Open University.

Nolan, J. M., & Ryan, G. W. (2000). Fear and loathing at the cineplex: Gender differences in descriptions and perceptions of slasher films. *Sex Roles, 42*(1-2), 39-56.

Oberg, P., & Tornstam, L. (1999). Body images among men and women of different ages. *Ageing and Society, 19,* 629-644.

Osgerby, B. (2001). *Playboys in paradise: Masculinity, youth and leisure-style in modern America.* London: Berg.

Pearce, S. (2000). Performance anxiety: The interaction of gender and power in *The Full Monty. Australian Feminist Studies, 15*(32), 227-236.

Pfeil, F. (1995). *White guys: Studies in postmodern domination and difference.* London: Verso.

Pinfold, J. (2000). I'm sick of shaving every morning: Or, the cultural implications of "male" facial presentation. *Journal of Mundane Behavior, 1*(1). Retrieved from www.mundanebehavior.org/index

Poggi, C. (1997). Dreams of metallized flesh: Futurism and the masculine body. *Modernism/Modernity, 4*(3), 19-43.

Pomerance, M. (Ed.). (2001). *Ladies and gentlemen, boys and girls: Gender in film at the end of the twentieth century.* Albany: State University of New York Press.

Radway, J. (1984). *Reading the romance: Feminism and the representation of women in popular culture.* Chapel Hill: University of North Carolina Press.

Reiser, K. (2001). Masculinity and monstrosity: Characterizations and identification in the slasher film. *Men and Masculinities, 3*(4), 370-392.

Rowe, D., McKay, J., & Miller, T. (2000). Sports and postmodern bodies. In J. McKay, M. Messner, & D. Sabo (Eds.), *Men, masculinities, and sport.* Thousand Oaks, CA: Sage.

Ruddock, A. (2001). *Understanding audiences: Theory and method.* Thousand Oaks, CA: Sage.

Rutherdale, R. (1999). Fatherhood, masculinity, and the good life during Canada's baby boom, 1945-1965. *Journal of Family History, 24*(3), 351-373.

Ryan, C., & Hall, M. (2001). *Sex tourism: Marginal peoples and liminalities.* London: Taylor & Francis.

Schirato, T., & Yell, S. (1999). The "new" men's magazines and the performance of masculinity. *Media International Australia: Culture and Policy, 92*, 81-90.

Seidler, V. (1991). *Recreating sexual politics: Men, feminism, and politics.* London: Routledge.

Sheridan, S. (1995). Reading the *Women's Weekly:* Feminism, femininity and popular culture. In B. Caine & R. Pringle (Eds.), *Transitions: New Australian feminisms.* St. Leonards: Allen & Unwin.

Shilling, C. (1993). *The body and social theory.* London: Sage.

Simpson, M. (2002). *Meet the metrosexual.* Retrieved from http://archive.salon.com/ent/feature/2002/07/22/metrosexual/

Slater, D. (1999). Trading sexpics on IRC: Embodiment and authenticity on the Internet. *Body & Society, 4*(4), 91-117.

Stratton, J. (1997). Not really desiring bodies: The rise and fall of Email affairs. *Media International Australia, 84*, 28-38.

Strong, S. M., Singh, D., & Randall, P. K. (2000). Childhood gender nonconformity and body dissatisfaction in gay and heterosexual men. *Sex Roles, 43*(7/8), 427-439.

Theweleit, K. (1987). *Male fantasies* (S. Conway, in collaboration with E. Carter and C. Turner, Trans.). Cambridge, MA: Polity.

Thomas, C. (1999). Last laughs: Batman, masculinity and the technology of abjection. *Men and Masculinities, 2*(1), 26-46.

Toerien, M., & Durrheim, K. (2001). Power through knowledge: Ignorance and the "real man." *Feminism & Psychology, 11*(1), 37-54.

Wernick, A. (1991). *Promotional culture: Advertising, ideology, and symbolic expression.* London: Sage.

Whannel, G. (2001). Punishment, redemption and celebration in the popular press: The case of David Beckham. In D. L. Andrews & S. J. Jackson (Eds.), *Sport stars: The cultural politics of sporting celebrity.* London: Routledge.

Wienke, C. (1998). Negotiating the male body: Men, masculinity, and cultural ideals. *The Journal of Men's Studies, 6*(3), 255-282.

Willis, S. (1997). *High contrast: Race and gender in contemporary Hollywood film.* Durham, NC: Duke University Press.

Witz, A. (2000). Whose body matters? Sociology and the corporeal turn in sociology and feminism. *Body & Society, 6*(2), 1-24.

17

MEN AND MASCULINITIES IN WORK, ORGANIZATIONS, AND MANAGEMENT

DAVID L. COLLINSON

JEFF HEARN

Drawing on the important insights of second wave feminism, the field of critical studies of men and masculinities is now well established, and it has become so in the relatively short span of time of the last 20 years or so. Yet, within this field, men's relations to work, organizations, and management have not generally been very prominent. Despite the fact that these relations provide some of the most obvious sources of men's individual and collective power, there has been something of an avoidance of these issues even within the general critical field. Often informed primarily by social theory rather than organizational theory, studies of masculinity have tended to underestimate or even to neglect the significance of organizations as sites for the reproduction of men's power and masculinities. This is even though key workplace issues such as organizational power, control, decision making, remuneration, cultures, and structure typically reflect and reinforce masculine material discursive practices in complex ways.

It is as if the very obvious associations of men with work, organizations, and management, at both the material and ideological levels, have meant that a "fresh start" has had to be attempted. This might be seen as a reversal of the now well-drawn tendency to explain men's behavior with reference to job, occupational, and organizational positions, in contrast with explanations of women's behavior in relation to the family (Feldberg & Glenn, 1979). Thus, this "fresh start" might involve seeing men in terms of family, friends, health, body, emotions, sexuality, violence, and so on. Important though these and other long-neglected aspects are, work, organizations, and management continue to be major forces in the construction of men, masculinities, and men's power.

With these considerations in mind, here we present a "return to work," specifically the organizational workplace, but in a rather different way from those simple, usually implicit associations of men and "work" that often have been dominant in both substantive social milieux and academic studies. Here we seek to make the connections between men, work, workplaces, organizations, and management more explicitly gendered, and thus subject to more critical analysis. This chapter reviews recent developments in the critical study of men and masculinities, in relation to work, organizations, and management, including the strengths and weaknesses of some major concepts that have influenced the literature.

The chapter comprises three main sections. It begins by considering the meaning of work, organization, and management. This focus on the multiple meanings of terms like "work," "organization," and "management" then leads into a consideration of "multiple masculinities," a conceptual framework that has been highly influential within debates on critical studies of men and masculinities. Despite its valuable contribution, this approach contains various conceptual difficulties. The third main section therefore critically evaluates a number of these recent concerns (and also challenges some of the critics). The chapter concludes by discussing likely future analytical directions, including transnational organizations, and the impact of new information and communication technologies, as in the development of virtual organizations.

WHAT ARE WORK, ORGANIZATIONS, AND MANAGEMENT?

Work

In the light of this initial discussion, it is important to ask what is meant by the basic concepts of work, organizations, and management.

First, "work" is a socially contextualized phenomenon. The meaning and naming of work is heavily linked to broad societal organization. It does not only mean organizational, paid, employed work in formal organizations in the public sphere. Feminist studies have been highly influential in naming domestic labor as work. They have highlighted the importance of unpaid domestic labor as an important site of gendered "work" and of men's domination of women. Indeed, the home is still often not seen as a workplace at all. For women, this is one of the many ways in which they and their work remain less visible and undervalued. In many societies, women are mainly or solely responsible for three

quarters of all housework; there are also major differences between the kinds of domestic tasks performed by men and women. The former tend to "specialize" in putting children to bed, taking out and playing with children, waste disposal, household repairs, and do-it-yourself projects. Such tasks generally are preferred by men over the much more time-consuming, supposedly mundane, and indeed socially subordinated tasks of cleaning, daily shopping, washing, ironing, cooking, and the routine care of infants and children (Oakley, 1985).

There is now a good deal of evidence to show that, on average, women work much longer hours than men when the full allocation of both paid and unpaid work is taken into account. In a sample of eight developing countries, 34% of females' time was spent on SNA work (System of National Accounts) and 66% on non-SNA work, compared with 76% of males' time on SNA work and 24% on non-SNA work (53% of total performed by males and 47% of total by females). In a sample of seven industrial countries, the equivalent figures were 34% and 66% for females, and 66% and 34% for males (51% of total performed by males and 49% by females) (United Nations Development Programme, 1996). This remarkable persistence of global inequality in gendered distributions of paid and nonpaid work and time use sits alongside the material differences between the more and less wealthy parts of the world.

Hence, "work" also encompasses domestic, unpaid, nonemployed labor outside formal organizations in the private sphere. It includes what have come to be called reproductive labor (Hearn, 1983, 1987; O'Brien, 1981, 1986), carework (Beams, 1979), sexual work/labor (Hearn & Parkin, 1995), people work (Goffman, 1961), emotion work (Fineman, 1993; Hochschild, 1983), childwork (Hearn, 1983), solidary work (Lynch, 1989), and unspoken work (Reis, 2002), as well as other often unrecognized forms of labor. O'Brien (1981) in particular provides an exemplary political philosophy of reproductive labor, inverting the Marxist placing of reproduction as superstructure upon the base of production (also see Hearn, 1987). Furthermore, work is organized across these boundaries of public and private, paid and unpaid, within what has been called the total social organization of work (Glucksmann, 1995). This is most clear in the organization of work within socioeconomic systems that are characterized by the blurring of the public-private divide, such as household production systems and family businesses. Work clearly is not only a matter of labor under capitalist systems; it also includes work under slavery, feudalism, socialism, communism, and various other hybrid economic systems.

Work is socially, indeed societally, organized, according to what generally has come to be called the sexual division of labor, although the term "gender division of labor" probably is more accurate. It has often been argued that in many societies, there is a tendency for men more often to do strenuous, dangerous manual work (Murdock, 1937). However, things are not always what they seem. Even Murdock's classic survey of 224 tribes from around the world found that there was an even distribution between those societies where agriculture tended to be defined as "women's work," as against those where it tended to be defined as "men's work." An excellent critical review of this kind of literature, problematizing many of these basic assumptions both theoretically and empirically, was produced by Margrit Eichler (1980).

The gender division and distribution of labor has real, societally variable, effects on women and men. Brettell and Sargent (2000) observe that women's status is highest in societies in which the public and domestic spheres are only weakly differentiated. Thus, the most egalitarian societies are those where men participate in the domestic sphere (Pease & Pringle, 2001, p. 6). This matches well with Coltrane's (1996, 1998) analysis of "premodern" societies in Africa, Asia, the Middle East, and the South Pacific. He concludes that more gender-balanced parenting was related to greater gender equality in other areas of life and in social power. Other connections might be made, more generally still, between the gender division of labor and patterns of violence. For example, Howell and Willis (1980) found that in those societies where men were permitted to acknowledge fear (as is more likely when, for example, men specialize in fighting, killing, and dangerous work), levels of violence were low (Kimmel, 2001, p. 35) (also see Sanday, 1981).

In such ways, constructions, definitions, and understandings of work are themselves both material and ideological. What "work" is considered to be—both in practical everyday life and in research—is itself gendered and contested. In this chapter, we focus on work in organizational workplaces, while also seeking to be aware of the interconnections of work in organizations and in the home. Work in the family is discussed in other chapters in this volume (especially Chapter 14, by Adams and Coltrane, and Chapter 15, by Marsiglio and Pleck).

Organizations

The notion of organization is complex, problematic, and gendered. Feminist analyses have significantly extended understandings of the meaning of organization. Organizations may appear to be neutral obvious ways of organizing, but they are historical, variable, and usually premised on other, often unpaid, unrecognized, invisible labor elsewhere—in the home, in families, in other parts of the world, in "non-organizations," by unknown others. Organizations are those *particular* social collectivities that result from those acts and processes, but organizations are not to be thought of as mere static outcomes. Instead, they should be understood as shifting social processes that are in a state of becoming something else.

At its simplest, the notion of an organization conjures up the highly tangible picture of a church, a factory, an office, a prison, a state apparatus, or even a university—something that can be seen, something that appears to function within four walls. But such an idea of an organization is increasingly a fantasy. Although it is probably misguided to search for the origins of (an) "organization," there are many strong contenders from the growth of religious, monarchic, and state organizations, whether in their ancient or medieval forms (see Burrell, 1997; Ezzamel & Hoskin, 2002). More recently, much of the ideal-typical picture of the visible organization does not even come from the heyday of the Industrial Revolution; it stems if anywhere from the 18th century, with the relatively isolated industrial mill that could be *seen*. It was with the passing of this organizational form to the multiple-unit "organization" that could not be fully seen that, rather paradoxically, the idea of the organization, and thus organization theory, became constituted and more popularly available. By the height of the 19th-century Industrial Revolution, the isolated organization was already to a considerable extent decomposing and anachronistic. Its decomposition was accompanied by its diffusion and expansion.

As organizations grew in size and became more consolidated, and indeed more powerful concentrations of resources, they also became more diffuse and less concentrated at particular times and places. Part of the reason for this was the mode of expansion of some organizations. Their expansion was not just upward and outward on the same site (within four walls or expanding those four walls); it was also through horizontal and vertical *connection* and *integration*, and above all geographical and temporal expansion and diffusion. The organization was no longer a simple place—or indeed a simple time. The notion of organizations has thus become progressively more complex. It still refers to the individual organization, but it also encompasses conglomerations of organizations, as in multi-organizations, such as the state and transnational corporations. Within each organization (within such multi-organizations) there are, of course, further smaller subunits that might often reasonably be called organizations too. The number of virtual organizations and cyberorganizations also is increasing, a topic to which we return in our concluding discussion.

Thus organizations, and indeed actions within organizations, are always embodied in social contexts. This context-embeddedness means that it is necessary in conceptualizing, analyzing, and writing about organizations to bear in mind that attempts to characterize organizations are limited and provisional. One complication is that organizations are both *social places* of organizing and *social structurings* of social relations and practices whose interrelations are historically dynamic and shifting. Another is that organizations are not collectivities formed simply by the individual, intentional action of their founders and members. Rather, organizations occur in the context of preexisting (organizational) social relations. The search for any *tabula rasa* is in vain. To paraphrase Marx and Engels (1970), "organizations make history but not in the conditions of their own choosing" (Hearn & Parkin, 2001, p. 2).

In many societies, the form organizations take is intimately bound up with the relation of the public and domestic spheres. As David Morgan (1992, 2001) has shown, there are complex historical interconnections between "work" and "home" both before and since the Industrial Revolution. The relations of men to home and work have shifted through traditional, early modern, late modern, and postmodern historical periods. These various changes produced different meanings around the family/workplace nexus for men and masculinities (D. L. Collinson, 1998). Indeed, in many ways organizations and organizational workplaces are built upon the unpaid labor of the domestic sphere (Hearn, 1987). Gender domination within organizations often is paralleled by the dominant gendered valuing of the public sphere over the domestic sphere; hence, we may recognize a dual-gendered domination in the construction of organizations.

All these complex historical changes have had major implications for men and constructions of masculinity. Men and masculinities have been formed and constructed in workplace processes of, for example, control, collaboration, innovation, competition, conformity, resistance, and contradiction. Equally, particular groups of men have been prominent in the formation, development, and transformation of (different forms of) organizations. As entrepreneurs, innovators, leaders, owners, board members, managers, supervisors, team leaders, administrators, manual workers, and even unemployed workers, men have crucially shaped the trajectory and nature of organizational progress, especially since the Industrial Revolution and the complex elaboration of public patriarchies.

Management

The notion of "management" also raises a number of conceptual challenges. It refers either to those people who work as managers or to those aspects of organizational structuring and processes that are significantly involved in the management—that is, the control and coordination—of organizations. The "elite" and dominant conception of management typically includes several different hierarchical layers of the authority structure (from junior to executive boardroom levels) and various specialties (e.g., production, service, accounting, human resources management, and marketing). "Professional" managers within these specialties are employed to make decisions, create workplace structures and cultures, and solve organizational problems using "scientific" and "rational-analytical" practices. A wider and more social conception of management (D. L. Collinson, 1992) recognizes that "all human beings are managers too; people struggling to cope, to manage, to shape their destinies" (Watson, 1994, p. 12). Although this alternative view raises important issues, for the purposes of the current analysis, we adhere to the dominant "elite" conception of the professional management function.

Typically, it is with the managerial function that organizational power formally resides, and decision making is a key aspect of managerial authority. In most contemporary organizations, managerial prerogative in "strategic" decisions remains the taken-for-granted norm. Yet, as we elaborate below, this assertion of managerial prerogative, and the managerial power and authority that it reflects and reinforces, tends to be not only hierarchical but also gendered. In most organizations, industries, and countries, it is still men who predominate in senior managerial positions (D. L. Collinson & Hearn, 1996a). This is clear with the growth of the historical development of the management function within military and paramilitary organizations, for example, in the concept of the military general staffs (Gooch, 1974; Hearn, 1992b) and other military innovations (Hoskin & Macve, 1988, 1994).

Similarly within capitalist organizations, facilitated by the separation of ownership and control (Berle & Means, 1932), the growth of management as a professional, elite occupation has been one of the most significant features of large-scale modern organizations (Chandler, 1977). More recently, the strict separation of ownership and control has become problematized in some organizational forms. The emergence of management as the central organizational activity of 20th-century corporations is reflected in the huge literature that explores the function's assumptions, responsibilities, and practices (e.g., Drucker, 1979; M. Reed, 1989; Stewart, 1986). Yet despite, and possibly even because of, the frequently pervasive association between men, power, and authority in organizations, the literature on management has consistently failed to question its gendered nature.

Many studies of managers and management, ranging from textbooks (e.g., Rosenfeld & Wilson, 1999) to detailed empirical studies (e.g., Watson, 1994) to biographies of famous managers (e.g., Geneen, 1985; Iacocca, 1984), can be re-read as implicit accounts of men, men's practices, and their masculinities. This ungendered tendency can also be seen in the

development of management theory, from scientific management to human relations, systems and contingency theories, and, more recently, population ecology and institutional perspectives. For example, Mintzberg (1989) examined the political alliances and strategies played out by managers in their search for power, influence, and organizational security. His accounts do not seem to recognize that within, between, and across managerial and organizational hierarchies, masculine discourses and practices are often crucial bases for alliances and conflicts between men in senior positions. Although critical studies examine management's overriding concern with the control of labor and the extraction of profit (Alvesson & Willmott, 1996), even these rarely attend to the continued predominance of men in managerial positions and the gendered processes, networks, and assumptions through which women are intentionally and unintentionally excluded, subordinated, or both.

So, whether they adopt prescriptive, descriptive, or critical perspectives, most studies of management have failed to question the highly masculine images that typically characterize their representations of middle and senior managers.

MULTIPLE GENDERINGS OF MEN AND MASCULINITIES IN THE WORKPLACE

Many studies of work, organizations, and management, as well as those on related areas such as leadership, industrial relations, the state, and politics, have long assumed that their subject is both male and neutral. Men often have been studied without realizing that this was the case, or men have been studied without attending to the gendering of the men in question in any critical detail. This is so in a number of classic studies, such as *Men Who Manage* (Dalton, 1959), *The Organization Man* (Whyte, 1956), and *The Man on the Assembly Line* (Walker & Guest, 1952). However, in great swaths of studies and researches—in business studies, management theory, international business, industrial economics, marketing, and so on—there is not even the beginning of recognition of the relevance of these things. A blissful ignorance remains. While most mainstream fields studying organizations and management continue to be neglectful, a small number of critical textbooks do address workplace gender relations (for example, Fulop & Linstead, 2000).

Recent years have seen the growth of a wide range of studies that seek to make explicit the gendering of men and masculinities in work, organizations, and management. In some ways, this development can be understood as consonant with the move to more differentiated, historically specific analyses of patriarchy (Hearn, 1987, 1992b; Walby, 1986, 1990). Emphasizing the importance of paid work as a central source of men's identity, status, and power, feminist organizational studies (e.g., Cockburn, 1991; Pringle, 1989) have demonstrated how "most organizations are saturated with masculine values" (Burton, 1991, p. 3). They have critically analyzed the continued centrality of the masculine model of lifetime, full-time, continuous employment and revealed the embeddedness of masculine values and assumptions in organizational structures, cultures, and practices. For many men, employment provides interrelated economic resources and symbolic benefits that mutually reinforce their position of power, authority, and discretion both at "work" and at "home." Men have been shown to exercise workplace control over women in many ways; for example, through job segregation, sex discrimination, "the breadwinner wage"/pay inequities, and sexual harassment.

Initially, most critical empirical research on men and masculinities in organizations concentrated on those in subordinate positions generally and manual workers in particular. A number of U.K. studies revealed how workplace power relations can be crucially shaped by masculinities. Willis (1977) described how working class lads constructed countercultures that "celebrated" masculinity and the so-called "freedom" and "independence" of manual work, only to realize the reality of class subordination once they reached the factory with no educational qualifications and little chance of escape. Cockburn's (1983) study of printers illustrated how skilled manual work could be defined by men as their exclusive province (also see Gray, 1987; Tolson, 1977). D. L. Collinson (1992, 2000) showed how male manual workers construct organizational countercultures and working class masculine identities based on the negation of "others" such as management, office workers, and women.

Together, these studies revealed the symbolic and material significance for (male) manual workers of specific forms of masculine practices and identity work for making sense of their (relatively subordinated) lives. They graphically demonstrated that informal shopfloor interaction between male manual workers is often deeply masculine, being highly aggressive, sexist and derogatory, humorous yet insulting, and playful but degrading (Ackroyd & Thompson, 1999). New members can be teased incessantly and tested to see whether they are "man enough" to take the insults couched in the humor of "piss taking" and the embarrassment of highly explicit sexual references (D. L. Collinson, 1988; Hearn, 1985). Such studies of working class life are usefully read alongside others focusing on men's family relations, including those that highlight the impact of uncertain employment and unemployment on women and children (for example, Clarke & Popay, 1998; Waddington, Critcher, & Dicks, 1998). Equally, these working class masculinities are increasingly vulnerable to challenge and change with the coming of global economic restructuring and other transformations (Blum, 2000).

The analytical importance of multiplicity has been particularly evident in these recent studies and debates on men in organizations. This follows well-established pluralist and Weberian traditions in industrial sociology and industrial relations. However, in some ways, more radically, poststructuralist feminism has increasingly recognized men's and women's diverse, fragmented, and contradictory lives in and around organizations. Attention has focused on gendered subjectivities and their ambiguous, discontinuous, and multiple character within asymmetrical relations (Henriques, Hollway, Urwin, Venn, & Walkerdine, 1984; Kondo, 1990). Informed by these ideas, the concept of "multiple masculinities" (Carrigan, Connell, & Lee, 1985) has become one of the most influential terms in analyzing men at work and in organizations and management over the past few years. It has been used to represent the various ways that specific forms of masculinity may be constructed and persist in relation both to femininity and to other forms of masculinity. Masculinity or masculinities can be understood as those combinations of signs that say and show someone is a man. Difference and the social construction of difference (such as that which differentiates men and masculinities according to religion, age, size, class, sexuality, ethnicity, occupation, and so on) are important bases through which gendered asymmetrical power between men, and between men and women, are often constructed and reproduced.

This growing interest in "masculinities" has facilitated new ways of understanding workplace power relations. Within these debates, an important distinction has been made between hegemonic, complicit, and subordinated masculinities (Connell, 1995). It has been argued that some masculinities (for example, white, middle-class, middle-aged, heterosexual/homophobic, Anglo-Saxon, Christian, Western, able-bodied) often dominate others (for example, working class and gay). These former masculinities tend to predominate, at least at the level of ideology, in powerful organizational positions such as middle and senior management, while other masculinities (for example, black, working class, and homosexual) are relatively subordinated. On the other hand, the U.K. Gay and Lesbian Census (ID Research, 2001) found that although 15% of lesbians and gay men in the workplace who responded believe their sexuality has hindered their job prospects, a surprisingly large proportion—43%—have managerial roles. These figures are not fully representative, as they do not take account of individuals who are not "out" in the workplace.

In rejecting sex-role theory with its emphasis on masculinity in the singular, critical writers have argued that these material and symbolic multiplicities and differences are very important in explaining the reproduction and shifting nature of gendered power asymmetries. As Connell (1995) argues, masculinities are not fixed, but may shift over time and place. They are historically, culturally, and temporally contingent. This focus on multiple masculinities (Carrigan et al., 1985; Connell, 2000) has been particularly helpful in naming and examining the shifting nature of (asymmetrical) power relations not only between men and women, but also between men, in organizational workplaces and management. It also begins to recognize that gendered power relations can simultaneously both change (in character) yet remain broadly the same (in structure).

The multiplicity and diversity of masculinities is also partly shaped by the different forms and locations of workplaces—the sites of work and of masculinity (D. L. Collinson & Hearn, 1996b). These sites are likely to vary, for example, according to occupation, industry, culture, class, and type of organization. Accordingly, the dominant masculinities evident in small and family-run businesses may be significantly different from those that pervade large multinational corporations. Multiple masculinities are likely to interconnect with multiple sites such as the home, the shop floor, the office, and the outlet or branch. Barrett's (2001) study of U.S. male Navy officers illustrates how multiple masculinities can coexist in an organization. He found that aviators emphasized their masculinity in terms of risk taking, surface warfare officers prioritized their endurance, and supply officers prided themselves on their technical rationality. Barrett's study also identifies some of the similarities that characterize these multiple masculinities. He shows how the Navy reproduces a dominant masculinity taking multiple forms that value physical toughness, perseverance, aggressiveness, a rugged heterosexuality, unemotional logic, and a stoic refusal to complain. This military culture of masculinity constructs itself in opposition to that which it is not, namely women and gay men, who are deemed to be physically weak and unable to do what (heterosexual) men do. They serve as the differentiated others, against which heterosexual men construct, project, and display a gendered identity. Barrett shows how Navy officers attach themselves to one of these hegemonic masculinities as a means of self-differentiation and elevation from colleagues.

Multiple workplace masculinities may also be shaped by different national cultures (Hofstede, 1980). For example, Woodward (1996) reveals how international organizations like the European Commission are also gendered bureaucracies in which the "male" norm is dominant and masculine practices of resistance to female leadership persist. In the light of changing forms and practices of management worldwide, interrelations of men, masculinities, and management in contemporary organizations are likely to become even more important. Connell (1998) has spelled out the form of transnational business masculinity that, he argues, is increasingly hegemonic and is directly connected to the patterns of world trade and communication that are dominated by the North. This is a dominant masculinity marked by egocentrism, highly precarious and conditional forms of loyalty, and a declining sense of responsibility (also see Hearn, 1996a). This "fast-capitalist entrepreneur" is also increasingly libertarian in regard to sexuality, staying in hotels around the world that provide businessmen with pornographic videos and even well-developed prostitution networks.

Recently, there has been growing interest in the analysis of men and masculinities in management and leadership. This increasing interest sheds new light on the analysis of workplace power relations (D. L. Collinson & Hearn, 2000a). Relevant studies include those on the historical development and association of men and management (Hollway, 1996); the place of men and management in reproducing patriarchy (or patriarchies) (Hearn, 1992b); transformations in forms of managerial masculinities (Roper, 1991, 1994); the relationship of bureaucracy, men, and masculinities (Bologh, 1990; D.H.J. Morgan, 1996; Sheppard, 1989); the continuing numerical dominance of men, especially at the highest levels; the reconceptualization of management-labor relations in terms of interrelations of masculinities (D. L. Collinson, 1992); the actions and reactions of men in both male-dominated and "female-concentrated" organizations (Lupton, 2002, Nordberg, 2002); processes of managerial identity formation (Kerfoot & Knights, 1993); and the use of masculine models, stereotypes, and symbols in management.

As noted earlier, men continue to dominate business management, constituting about 95% of senior management in the United Kingdom and the United States. This is especially so at the very top and more highly paid levels of the business sector, where men compose as much as 98% of top managers. Davidson and Burke (2000) reported that "in the European Union countries fewer than 5 per cent of women are in senior management roles and this percentage has barely changed since the early 1990s" (p. 2). Men's domination is even more pronounced in the boards of directors of large companies. The 1998 UK Institute of Management survey found that 3.6% of directors were women (Institute of Management/Remuneration Economics, 1998; also see D. L. Collinson & Hearn, 1996a). This compares with a figure of 17% of directors who were women on the 114 Finnish stock exchange–listed companies in 1995 (Veikkola, Hänninen-Salmelin, & Sinkkonen, 1997, pp. 83-84). Two of these

companies had women CEOs. More recently, a survey of the largest 100 Finnish corporations showed that overall, there is 1 woman on the board for every 9 men, and in top management the ratio is 1 woman for every 9.4 men (Hearn, Kovalainen, & Tallberg, 2002). There is some evidence of increases in women in middle management and small business ownership, and thus management overall (Davidson & Burke, 2000; Vinnicombe, 2000). However, at the highest executive levels and for directorships, the numbers may actually be declining, static, or increasing very slowly indeed (Institute of Management/Remuneration Economics, 1998; Veikkola et al., 1997).[1]

Although various masculinities frequently shape managerial practices, managerial practices also can affect the emergence of specific masculinities. For example, pervasive and dominant managerial masculinities might take the form of different workplace control practices such as authoritarianism, careerism, paternalism, and entrepreneurialism (D. L. Collinson & Hearn, 1994, 1996b). Roper (1991, 1994) describes how British male managers in the postwar era frequently identified strongly with machinery and products. Undervaluing the role of labor in the manufacture of products, male managers tended to fetishize the masculine self through the idolization of products. Kerfoot and Knights (1993) contended that paternalism and strategic management are concrete manifestations of historically shifting forms of masculinity. Arguing that these managerial approaches both reflect and reinforce "discourses of masculinism," they suggested that "paternalistic masculinity" and "competitive masculinity" have the effect of privileging men vis-à- vis women, ranking some men above others, and maintaining as dominant certain forms and practices of masculinity. Managerial masculinities might thus be understood as form(s) of (different) hegemonic masculinities.

In our own work, we have examined the ways that (men) managers can routinely discriminate against women in selection (D. L. Collinson, Knights, & Collinson, 1990, Hearn & Collinson, 1998; also P. Y. Martin, 1996, 2001) and can mismanage cases of sexuality and sexual harassment (D. L. Collinson & Collinson, 1989, 1992; M. Collinson & Collinson, 1996). In addition, we have considered the ways that men managers as (working) fathers can frequently "distance" themselves from children and family responsibilities (D. L. Collinson & Hearn, 1994, 2000b). Within organizations, such "distancing" strategies are often seen as evidence of commitment to the company, yet these kinds of pressures can significantly reinforce stresses, gendered stresses, within families, which have their own gendered power relations (D. L. Collinson & Collinson, 1997). The potential development of men's nonoppressive, even profeminist management and leadership also has been explored (Hearn, 1989, 1992a, 1994).

There are also innumerable ways in which the authority and status of managers can signify "men" and, indeed, vice versa, just as there are many signs that can simultaneously signify the power of both "manager" and "men." These cultural processes of signification include the size and position of personal offices; office furniture and the display of pictures, paintings, and plants; the use or control of computers and other technological equipment; and, of course, the choice of clothing. Although business suits appear to have a transnational significance, their particular style, cut, and cost are also important, not least as a means of managing impressions through "power dressing" (Collier, 1998; Feldman & Klich, 1991). The color and style of shirts, braces, shoes, and socks, as well as the size and pattern of ties (see Gibbings, 1990), can carry totally embodied and context-specific meanings for both managers and men that may reflect and reinforce their organizational hegemony.

Managerial masculinities are also hegemonic within organizations in the sense that those in senior positions enjoy comparatively high salaries and ancillary remuneration packages through secretarial support, share options, company cars, pensions, extensive holiday entitlements, and other material and symbolic benefits. Even when they are dismissed, managers may receive substantial "golden handshakes," and poor performance does not seem to prevent reemployment in other lucrative, high-status managerial positions (Pahl, 1995). On the other hand, there is also some movement toward a "proletarianization" and reduced security for some managers, as in delayering and business process reengineering. This is an important trend that might signal a fundamental historical shift in the class and gender relations of both nonmanagers and managers, especially those at the less senior levels.

Kanter (1977, 1993) used the term "homosocial reproduction" to describe the processes by which senior male managers selected other male managers in ways that reproduced an all-male managerial elite. Typically, men were appointed to managerial positions because they were perceived to be more reliable, committed, and predictable, as well as free from conflicting loyalties between home and work. Although Kanter's study usefully describes how elitist practices can characterize management, it is less valuable in analyzing the gendered nature of these persistent interrelations and networks (see also Acker, 1989; Pringle, 1989; Witz & Savage, 1992). Kanter contended that what appear to be differences between men and women in organizations are related not to gender, but to work position and the structure of opportunity. In seeking to deny difference, she failed to recognize fully how organizational power relations are frequently heavily gendered. Her concern to separate "sex" from "power" inevitably neglects the way that particular masculinities may be embedded in and help to reproduce and legitimize managerial power and authority (see D. L. Collinson & Hearn, 1995).

In organizations where the manager is also the owner, power relations can be especially asymmetrical and gendered. The ways in which the ownership of many businesses is still passed on from one generation to the next constitutes a vivid example of "patriarchy in action." In the majority of these cases, it is the son who inherits the firm from his father, thus ensuring the reproduction of patriarchal authority, both in the workplace and at home. Highlighting the gendered nature of the so-called "self-made man," R. Reed (1996) contrasted the lives of David Syme (1827-1908), the Scottish-born Australian publisher of *The Age* newspaper, and Rupert Murdoch, the contemporary Australian-born international media entrepreneur. Whereas Syme conformed to the Weberian image of the sober, self-made modern capitalist who adopted a paternalistic and dutiful approach to management, Murdoch's style is adventurist and more akin to premodern forms of capitalism and management. Studies of entrepreneurialism also reveal the interdependence between men's organizational power and the family. For example, Mulholland (1996) conducted research on 70 of the richest entrepreneurial families in a Midlands county of England. She found that although men consistently claimed the credit for their business success, in practice their capital accumulation was highly dependent on the hidden household (and workplace) services provided by wives/women. Other studies report similar dynamics whereby men's careers are constructed through the invisible support of women as secretaries and wives (for example, Finch, 1984; Grey, 1994; Reis, 2004).

There is a growing interest in leadership development as the "solution" to many contemporary organizational problems (Deal & Kennedy, 2000). In the United Kingdom, "heroic," "strategic," and "visionary" leaders are still often seen as the key to organizational success in both the private and public sectors. Charismatic leadership was also a key theme in the 1980s discourses on corporate culture. Psychologists (e.g., Schein, 1985) and management consultants (e.g., Peters & Waterman, 1982) emphasized corporate leaders' responsibility for "managing meaning" (G. Morgan, 1997) and establishing strong organizational cultures (Deal & Kennedy, 1982). Writers such as Peters and Austin (1985) presented long taxonomies of prescriptions on how to be a visionary leader who, above all else, can and must manage and manipulate organizational culture. Such charismatic leadership styles are deeply masculine in their assumptions and images (Hearn & Parkin, 1988). The popular emphasis on the power and impact of individual "great men," especially CEOs, stands in contrast to the current broader research-based, though virtually always ungendered, focus on upper echelon management and management teams (Goines, 2002; Hay Group, 2001; Surowiecki, 2002; Weisbach & Hermalin, 2000).

In sum, the term "multiple masculinities" has emerged as an important concept that helps to demonstrate the pervasive, diverse, and shifting character of men's hegemonic power, culture, and identity in contemporary organizations. Certain masculinities usually predominate and are privileged in organizations and management, but they can take different forms at different times in different organizations and within different strata of an organization. The term "multiple masculinities" helps to illustrate how organizational and gendered power relations can shift in detail while simultaneously remaining asymmetrical in overall structure. It begins to address the ways that men's power, cultures, and identities can change yet remain ascendant in contemporary organizations. This is an important, apparent paradox. On one hand, gender relations are changing; women and men are apparently changing. Yet on the other hand, there is an intractability and tenacity in men's dominant organizational position. Indeed, one of the key issues to address is the paradoxical and contradictory ways in which asymmetrical power relations simultaneously change yet remain broadly similar. Analyses need to address the flexible, shifting, and often ambiguous nature of gendered power relations in general and men's power, cultures, and identities in particular.

THE LIMITS OF HEGEMONY AND MULTIPLICITY

As the foregoing discussion suggests, there have been significant developments in the analysis of hegemony and multiplicity in relation to men and masculinities within organizational workplaces and management. Recently, however, there also have been a number of concerns expressed about these key concepts within critical studies on men. Among other recent critiques, it has been argued that masculinities, as a theoretical concept, is (a) unclear in meaning, (b) too descriptive, (c) overly negative, (d) obsolescent, and (e) oversimplifying in its construction of power relations. We now turn to these debates and discuss each of these criticisms in turn, emphasizing their implications for the analysis of men in work, organizations, and management.

Meaning?

First, it has been argued that although the term is now well established, the meaning of "hegemonic masculinity/multiple masculinities" (HM/MM) remains somewhat unclear, vague, and imprecise, lacking in definition (Donaldson, 1993). Does "masculinity" in this context refer to men's behaviors, identities, relationships, experiences, appearances, images, discourses, or practices in workplaces? If it includes all of these, precisely how does it do so? If one means men's work practices, both collective and individual, then it would be simplest to say so. Also, if there is hegemonic masculinity, it would be reasonable to look for resistance to hegemonic masculinity, in organizations and management, as elsewhere (Donaldson, 1993). Equally, if the term can also be used to describe some women's behavior, then its meaning becomes even more flexible, vague, and difficult to specify.[2]

Other related criticisms include its possible ethnocentrism, lack of historical/spatial/cultural specificity, and false causality (Hearn, 1996b). Wetherell and Edley (1999) showed that the term "masculinities" is rather vague, sketchy, and imprecise, especially when one researches at the micro level of talk and conversation. More broadly still, the focus on masculinities may facilitate a possible psychologism (McMahon, 1993), and thus neglect asymmetrical gender structural relations, within patriarchy or patriarchies (Hearn, 1992b). A growing number of studies in this area have emphasized the discursive, ideological, and symbolic aspects of hegemonic masculinity, thereby rejecting essentialist or deterministic perspectives. A minority have also focused on the material and economic dimensions of men's power and identity in organizations. An adequate account needs to examine both the material and discursive features of masculinity, within the context of patriarchal social relations (D. L. Collinson, 1992; Hearn, 1992b).

Some writers have been unwilling to provide a single definition of masculinity/ies. Connell (1995), for example, is reluctant to offer such a definition because he wants to emphasize the shifting and contingent character of masculinity. Others, however, have tried to define the central meanings of "masculinity" and/or "hegemonic masculinities." For example, Kerfoot and Knights (1996, 1998) examined the privileged form of masculine identity associated with dominant management practice—abstract, rational, calculating, highly instrumental, controlling of its object, future-oriented, strategic, and, above all, masculine and wholly disembodied. These masculine managerial subjectivities typically are expressed in aggressive and competitive practices concerned to succeed, master, and dominate. Kerfoot (2001) argued that contemporary managerialist masculinity is characterized by the instrumental search for control, the elimination of uncertainty, and the intense goal-driven pursuit of "performance" and "success." For managerial masculinities, noninstrumental

forms of relationship—especially those involving spontaneity, ambiguity, and intimacy—are to be avoided because they involve "letting go" of the barriers of predictable scripts and revealing vulnerability. Whitehead (2001) argued that gender change will occur only when men adopt a more self-reflexive approach to their own gendered identity. Based on his research in the further education sector, he contends that many men remain "the invisible gendered subject," unable to understand the gendered realities surrounding them.

Bird (1996) argued that through male homosocial, heterosexual interactions, hegemonic masculinity is maintained as the norm to which men are held accountable. For Bird, male homosociality (conceptualized as the nonsexual attractions held by men) is about emotional detachment, being highly competitive, and viewing women as sexual objects. These interrelated values perpetuate hegemonic masculinity, suppress subordinate masculinity, and reproduce a pecking order among men. Similarly, Kimmel (1994) contended that dominant masculinity is best understood as "homophobia," that men's fear of other men is the "animating condition of the dominant definition of masculinity in America" (p. 135). He is particularly concerned with "marketplace masculinity," which he describes as the normative definition of U.S. masculinity. This includes the characteristics of aggression, competition, and anxiety. The (work-related) "marketplace" is the arena in which manhood is tested and proved. This definition of "hegemonic masculinity" sets the standard against which all men are measured and against which other forms of manhood are evaluated, a notion of manhood that is equated with being strong, successful, capable, reliable, and in control. Kimmel argues that masculinity is "a defence against the perceived threat of humiliation and emasculation in the eyes of other men" (p. 135). In this sense, dominant cultural definitions of masculinity are strongly related to the place of men and men's practices in work, employment, and organizations, and thus in some cases management. The economic "marketplace" is held to produce the cultural.

Hence, there has been a revitalized search to conceptualize masculinity, to focus on the shared commonalities and gendered features that define or encapsulate contemporary "manhood." These concerns are partly related to growing interest in the ways that subjectivities interact with power relations, a development which we see as productive and valuable. This approach is informed in particular by recent poststructuralist developments in studies of both management and gender that emphasize the need to recognize that workplace power relations are multiple, ambiguous, and frequently characterized by contradictory outcomes. Poststructuralist analyses are keen to avoid the essentialism that tended to characterize earlier attempts at defining masculinity.

Descriptive?

Second, the term "multiple masculinities" has been criticized for being merely descriptive and documenting various differences and "types." It is indeed possible that a focus on difference could collapse into a taxonomy of masculinities and a list of objectified categories of men. A more sophisticated critique might also observe that constructing typologies may itself constitute a masculine and/or managerial preoccupation with the control of the world and the meanings in it; a totalizing exercise intended to achieve a kind of closure. Work and organizations provide clear opportunities for such evaluative, hierarchizing processes. Categorization fails to address either men's lived social experience "as men" or the fluidity, shifting, and changing character of all social relations, identities, and practices, as examined by Kondo (1990) at work. It may also pose difficulties in acknowledging the sheer complexity of the very large number of possible permutations and interrelations of types of men in organizations. The numerical combinations are themselves complicated by the diversity of ways, at work and elsewhere, in which interrelations can exist and develop.

In our view, the emphasis on multiple masculinities is much less about categorizing differences between men than about critically examining power differences between men as well as between women and men. Studies that highlight the diversity of men's workplace power, status, and domination seek to analyze the multiple, shifting, but tenacious nature of gendered power regimes. This approach has the potential to examine and understand the often contradictory organizational relations through which men's differences and similarities are reproduced and transformed in particular practices and power asymmetries. For example, just as a major issue within feminism has been the relation of commonalities and differences between women, so men can be analyzed usefully in terms of commonalities and differences, within the context of patriarchy. In organizations, there are often tensions between the collective power of men and the differentiations between them (D. L. Collinson & Hearn, 1994, 2000b).

Men's power is maintained partly through their commonalities with each other. Typically, men are bound together, not necessarily consciously, by shared interests and meanings (for example, sport), dominant sexuality, socio-economic-political power, and representational privileging. Men's collective power persists partly through the assumption of hegemonic forms of men and masculinities—often white, heterosexual, and able-bodied—as the primary form, to the relative exclusion of subordinated men and masculinities. Different men, dominant or otherwise, are reproduced in relation to other social divisions. Indeed, in many social arenas there are tensions between the collective power of men/masculinities and differentiations among masculinities, defined through other social divisions such as age, class, family, status, generation, race, and sexuality (Hearn & Collinson, 1994).

Within critical studies on men and masculinities, there is often an unresolved tension between the analysis, on one hand, of multiplicity and diversity, and on the other, of men's structured domination, their shared economic and symbolic vested interests and sense of unity. We refer to this somewhat polarized debate as the unities and differences between men and masculinities (Hearn & Collinson, 1994). Here, a particularly important question is whether the unities or differences should be attributed analytical primacy. Furthermore, how are they to be related? We argue for the need to examine both the unities and the differences between men and masculinities as well as their interrelations. By examining these processes simultaneously, we can develop a deeper understanding of the gendered power relations of organization; the conditions, processes, and consequences of their reproduction; and how they could be resisted and transformed. It is important to take account of both the unities and the differences between men and masculinities as well as the ways that these may overlap in specific organizational processes. The increasing emphasis on multiplicity and differentiation needs to be combined with a consideration of men's unities and their interrelations. This approach can contribute important insights into the conditions, processes, and consequences of gendered power relations in organizations and the ways that these may be reproduced, rationalized, and/or resisted.

Negative?

A third criticism of HM/MM is that it presents an overly negative orientation toward men in the workplace. For example, the recurrent message from a recent book by Alvesson and Due Billing (1997) is that established theories of gender and organizations are rather exaggerated and too critical (*sic*) of men and masculinity. These writers question the perspectives of radical feminists and "masochistic" (p. 32) men that, in their view, construct a world of "innocent" (p. 200) and "good" (p. 203) women and "nasty" (p. 200), "evil" (p. 30), and "bad" (p. 203) men. Alvesson and Due Billing are highly critical of what they see as "gender oversensitivity," referring to a tendency to use gender as a totalizing explanation, treating it as relevant and decisive everywhere. For them, many feminist studies exaggerate the importance and asymmetry of gender in organizations and focus on "misery stories." Alvesson and Due Billing argue that gender patterns are complex, often ambiguous, and contradictory, and are likely to vary in rich and crucial ways over time and space.

We agree with Alvesson and Due Billing that organizational life cannot be reduced exclusively to processes of gender, and indeed, we previously have written to that effect (D. L. Collinson & Hearn 1996a, 1996b). Equally, we accept that there can be important positive aspects of some men's masculine identities. While we can be highly questioning of many "heroic" ideologies that elevate corporate leaders, there is a need to recognize that acts of male altruism, heroism, care, and courage certainly do occur and that these can be informed by traditional masculine values and priorities. Masculine identities can indeed inform acts of great sacrifice for others. For example, Baigent (2001) critically examined the ways in which firefighters construct and reproduce specific masculine cultures and

identities, and their multiple motives in fire fighting. They were concerned to "get in" to extinguish fires; uphold their professional/ humanitarian ethos in efficient and effective service for the public (for example, to be calm under pressure, brave but modest); experience the "adrenaline rush" of successfully undertaking dangerous, life-saving work; and maintain an identity as a "good firefighter."

However, Alvesson and Due Billing failed to locate the studies they criticized in their context, and they did not always read very carefully those that they critiqued. Many of the studies they criticized were written against the backdrop of both mainstream and critical literatures that have treated gender as largely irrelevant. Equally, men's exercise of power and authority can in certain times and places have seriously negative effects not only for women and children, but also for other men and for men themselves. In their concern to highlight negativity and oversensitivity, Alvesson and Due Billing tended to underestimate the potential detrimental processes and consequences of dominant masculinities in the workplace, including the effects on women, both at home and in organizations. For example, the *Challenger* space shuttle disaster illustrates the potentially disastrous consequences that hegemonic masculinities can have on key managerial decisions where high-risk decisions are informed by managers "doing masculinity" by suppressing doubt, fear, and uncertainty (Maier & Messerschmidt, 1998; Messerschmidt, 1996).

Obsolescent?

A fourth, and in some ways related, critique of this literature has been outlined by MacInnes (1998, 2001), who contends that we are witnessing "the end of masculinity." For him, masculinity is not only limited as a term but also actually becoming obsolete as a way of describing contemporary social structures and processes, including in work and organizations. Masculinity can be seen as "the last ideological defence of male supremacy in a world that has already conceded that men and women are equal" (2001, p. 326). Accordingly, he suggests that critical studies of masculinity, or what he terms "the politics of identity approach to masculinity" (2001, p. 323), which focus on men's "emotional inarticulacy," are misleading. He suggests that they assume that only men can be masculine and that masculinity can become "a general term for anything we don't like" (2001, p. 324). He argues that if gender is socially constructed, then we must accept that women also can be masculine. Equally, MacInnes argues that such studies of masculinity tend to present a psychological focus on masculine identity to the extent that the impact of social structures, including work and organizational structures, is underestimated or neglected. In his view, this approach confuses symptom and cause, such that the term masculinity "obscures the analysis of social relations between the sexes" (2001, p. 327). Consequently, he rejects the interest in critiquing and transforming masculinity as a way of struggling for greater gender equity in favor of a shift toward the pursuit of equal rights for women and men.

In our view, MacInnes is too hasty in suggesting that masculinity has outlived its relevance. His account also tends to dismiss issues of subjectivity entirely in precisely the way that he complains that those interested in masculinity neglect social structure. By contrast, an interest in subjectivities *in relation to power asymmetries* does not *necessarily* constitute a collapse into psychologism and the neglect of structure in the ways that MacInnes suggests. Rather, it can significantly enhance the analysis of workplace power relations by illuminating the processes through which structures are negotiated, reproduced, and resisted. For an understanding of masculinity, we believe that it is important to examine the interplay and the interconnections between social (and work and organizational) structures and subjectivities. The analysis of subjectivities can assist understanding of how organizational structures are reproduced and maintained in particular practices. More specifically, an awareness of the multiple sources of identity (and the ways that these may be in tension) can assist the identification of the crosscutting nature of workplace power relations and thereby produce more complex accounts of "hegemonic/multiple masculinities" that recognize ambiguity, simultaneity, and contradiction, as we discuss below.

Oversimplification?

A final area of concern is the issue of workplace power relations. "Hegemonic" and "multiple masculinity/ies" can be criticized for oversimplifying workplace power relations and for neglecting their simultaneous, countervailing, and potentially contradictory character. For example, men managers' power is not only about gender but also about hierarchy, bureaucracy, class, age, ethnicity, payment systems, and so on. Rarely, if ever, is it possible to reduce complex organizational processes and power relations exclusively to issues of gender and/ or masculinity. Teasing out the relationship between masculinities and other key features of organizations and, in particular, other social divisions and inequalities requires further attention. Managerial control and labor resistance, for example, might in certain cases be shaped by specific masculinities, but they will not be totally determined by them. To focus only on gender or men and masculinity may not provide a complete account of these complex processes. Equally, though, their neglect often renders critical analyses of power relations fundamentally flawed.

In emphasizing HM/MM, there is a danger of excluding other social divisions and power inequalities in organizations and of failing to appreciate the interrelations of these divisions and inequalities. On one hand, it is important to acknowledge the way in which masculinities can change over time; be shaped by underlying ambiguities and uncertainties; differ according to class, age, culture, ethnicity, and similar factors; and also be central to the reproduction of other social divisions. On the other hand, this emphasis on hegemony and multiplicity ought not to degenerate into a diversified pluralism that gives insufficient attention to structured patterns of gendered power, control, and inequality. As Cockburn (1991) wrote, a focus on multiple masculinities should not "deflect attention from the consistency in men's domination of women at systemic and organizational levels, from the continuation of materials, structured inequalities and power imbalances between the sexes" (p. 225). She argues that this increasing emphasis on plurality and multiplicity needs to retain a focus on the structured asymmetrical relations of power between men and women.

Different social divisions can cut across asymmetrical power relations in multiple, mutually reinforcing or counterposing ways. So, for example, white, male-dominated shopfloor masculinities may be hegemonic in terms of gender, ethnicity, or sexuality but simultaneously subordinated with regard to class, hierarchy, and workplace status (D. L. Collinson, 1992). Men's control and authority as managers may be more contradictory, precarious, and heterogeneous than often it at first appears. For example, the recent delayering and intensification of managerial work, particularly through measurement and evaluation, significantly problematizes the view that management constitutes the most clear-cut form of hegemonic masculinity (D. L. Collinson & Collinson, 1997). The hierarchical and gendered power of male managers is by no means homogeneous, monolithic, or inevitable. Power relations are complex and shifting (Kondo, 1990), sometimes mutually reinforcing but on other occasions crosscutting, with countervailing and contradictory effects.

Hence, when we try to apply notions of "hegemonic" or "multiple" masculinities to *organizational* issues, their meanings are not always obvious. Masculinities (for example, white, gay masculinities or black, middle-class masculinities) can carry internal contradictions between elements confirming or undermining power and identity. Indeed, it may be difficult to address these contrary processes through the notion of "hegemonic masculinities." Other concepts, such as manliness, maleness, and manhood, may be more appropriate in different historical and cultural contexts. On one hand, men often seem to collaborate, cooperate, and identify with one another in ways that reinforce a shared unity between them. On the other hand, these same masculinities also can be characterized simultaneously by conflict, competition, and self-differentiation in ways that highlight and intensify the differences and divisions between men. Accordingly, the unities that exist between men should not be overstated. They are often precarious, shifting, and highly instrumental. Herein may lie the seeds of change, as illustrated in the classic Marxist account of class conflict, class struggle, and the "fundamental contradiction" of capital and labor, and feminist accounts of the contradictions, and hence dynamics of change, of patriarchy. Indeed, classic Marxist, many neo-Marxist, and many other accounts of class struggle and economic class relations can themselves be reformulated as gendered accounts, privileging men and certain masculinities (see Morgan, Chapter 10, this volume).

An important contradictory feature of hegemonic and multiple masculinities in organizations is the intense competition that typically characterizes relations between men. The highly competitive nature within and between hegemonic and multiple masculinities appears to be fueled by a concern to display dominance and validate identity. Yet, the competitive practices of other men may actually render the search for dominance at best highly precarious and at worst an impossible long-term goal, by reinforcing the very insecurity competition was intended to overcome. Competitive workplace cultures may therefore reproduce the material (for example, wages, job security) and symbolic (status, reputation, and identity) insecurities that individuals seek to overcome through competing successfully.

Men frequently invest their identities in particularly individualized, competitive workplace projects, such as the search to validate masculine identity through career progress that inevitably intensifies competition within organizations. A "successful" career may be an important medium through which men seek to establish masculine identities in the workplace. Upward mobility can be a key objective in the search to secure a stable, middle-class masculine identity and to embellish the male ego. For those who are promoted into management, such identities are reinforced by the remuneration, status, and perks of most senior positions. Competitive career strategies often reflect the way in which men are still, in many cultures, positioned as the privatized breadwinners whose primary purpose is to "provide" for their families. Yet, particularly in the current conditions of "delayering," widespread redundancies, and extensive career bottlenecks, there are considerable contradictions associated with such orientations. Committed to upward progress, men often feel compelled to work longer hours, meet tight deadlines, travel extensively, participate in residential training courses, and move house at the behest of the company. These work demands are likely to be incompatible with domestic responsibilities and can contribute to the breakdown of marriages. Equally, as men grow older, they are likely to slow down and thus be less able to compete effectively with their younger, more "hungry" and aggressive male colleagues. Hence, in the short and/or long term, career competitiveness is unlikely to achieve the kind of security at work for which men often strive.

Given the socially constructed, multiple, and shifting character of identities and power asymmetries, these attempts may actually reinforce the very uncertainty and ambiguity they are intended to overcome (D. L. Collinson & Hearn, 1994, 2000b). Equally, men's masculine identities can be further threatened by social and economic forces such as increasing female employment, new technology, unemployment, feminism/equal opportunity initiatives, and domestic and marriage relations, as well as by class and status divisions. Men's search to construct masculine identities in the eyes of colleagues (and themselves) appears to be an ongoing, never-ending project that can be characterized by ambiguity and contradiction. Like all identities, masculine selves constantly have to be constructed, negotiated, and achieved both in the workplace and elsewhere through simultaneous processes of identification and differentiation. Barrett (2001) argues that masculine identities in the U.S. Navy are constructed by differentiating the self through outperforming, discounting, and negating others. Underpinning these concerns, he suggests, is an enduring sense of subjective insecurity that is not resolved but reinforced by these processes. Accordingly, these masculine identity strategies reproduce insecurity and competition, which in turn reinforce the perceived need for identity-protection strategies.

Such men's gender identities are constructed, compared, and evaluated by the self and others according to a whole variety of criteria indicating personal "success" in the workplace. This tendency to become preoccupied with seeking to define coherent identities through identification and differentiation may further reinforce, rather than resolve, the very sense of insecurity these strategies were intended to overcome (D. L. Collinson, 1992). The dual experience of "self" and "other" is a central and highly ambiguous feature of human subjectivity, often reinforced by the multiple nature of identities and the asymmetrical nature of conventional gendered power relations. When attempts to construct and sustain particular identities try to deny this ambiguity and uncertainty, they are likely to be unsuccessful.

To summarize, this section has considered a number of issues in relation to hegemonic and multiple masculinities; two interrelated and central concepts in the literature on critical studies of men. While recognizing the validity of several of these concerns, we have also challenged those writers who appear to reject the concern to develop a critical approach to understanding men and masculinities in organizations. Rather than try to deny the significance of a critical approach to men and masculinity/ies, we view the primary and pressing issue as the need to develop more sophisticated understandings of these very important concerns that have impacts in many, if not all, organizational and social settings.

CONCLUDING DISCUSSION

This chapter has overviewed recent debates in the critical literature that seeks to make explicit the gendering of men and masculinities in work, organizations, and management. The emphasis in recent critical studies on "hegemonic" and "multiple" masculinities raises important questions regarding the contemporary analysis of workplace power relations as well as the practices through which they are reproduced and contested. Many of the more or less critical studies of "men"/"masculinities" and "work"/ "organization"/"management," discussed in this chapter, are part of the general deconstruction of the unified, rational, transcendent subject of men. This critical approach facilitates a challenge to men's taken-for-granted dominant masculinities. This, in turn, could facilitate the emergence of less coercive and divisive organizational structures, cultures, and practices; a fundamental rethinking of the social organization of the domestic division of labor; and a transformation of "men at work."

Although hegemonic masculinity and multiple masculinities are useful concepts in the critical analysis of gender relations in the workplace, more theoretical and empirical work is necessary to develop these ideas. Several conceptual and theoretical problems remain unresolved (see also D. L. Collinson & Hearn, 1994, 2000b; Hearn, 1996b). First, the conceptualization of "masculinity/ies" requires further clarification. For example, how do the ideological/discursive and symbolic features of masculinities interrelate with economic, material, and physical aspects? Second, the ways in which masculinities relate to other elements of power, culture, and subjectivity in organizations need greater consideration. For example, in what ways and with what consequences are multiple masculinities embedded and interwoven in other workplace practices, such as control, consent, compliance, and resistance? There needs to be greater focus on the interconnections, tensions, and contradictions within and between these different aspects of workplace power, culture, and subjectivity. Third, while recognizing a multiplicity of possible masculinities and workplace sites, analyses also need to retain a focus on the structured asymmetries of gendered power relations.

Finally, there is a need, both theoretically and empirically, to take regard of the changing shape of organizations and managements. Whereas previously most organizations could be relatively isolated geographically, this is increasingly becoming problematic, as organizations are reorganized across time, space, and even cyberspace and cybertime. The place of the notion of organization in relation to transnationalism, globalization, glocalization (Robertson, 1995), and the impact of new information and communication technologies is becoming progressively more complex. This means that the rather rapid change in the relationship of time and space makes it increasingly necessary to question the equation of organization, work, and *place* (see Hearn & Parkin, 2001; Connell, Chapter 5, this volume).

The nation-state is no longer necessarily the most important economic or political unit. The dominance of local and national organizations and nation-states is problematized by the growth of transnational organizations and corporations, as part of globalizing processes. Transnational corporations constitute collective social actors that may transcend the nation, being in some cases larger in size than individual nations. Their growing importance stems particularly from their operation across national boundaries, rather than simply within one or a few nations, and their recent overall expansion. The GNP of some nation-states is exceeded by the assets of many supranational corporations. Of the 100 largest economies, half are corporations and half are countries. The world's 500 largest industrial corporations, which employ only 0.05% of the world's population, control 25% of global economic output and 42% of the world's wealth (Korten, 1996, 1998, p. 4).

Moreover, changes in internal structures of transnational corporations and organizations have implications for gender relations therein. Relations between companies within larger transnational corporations may have further impacts, depending on whether they are highly integrated and strongly centralized globally, or local networks. Strongly centralized transnational corporations contrast with polycentric transnational corporations, with looser guidelines for subsidiaries on, for example, corporate equal opportunities policies. Centralized transnational corporations may be more likely to develop consistency in such policies, even if their local impact is variable. Decentralized transnational corporations may be more likely to develop more autonomous, variable structures in local or functional units.

Organizations—that is, gendered organizations—need to be understood as a shorthand for a wide range of social connected structures and processes, including multi-organizations, transnational organizations, interorganizational relations, network organizations, Internet organizations, and virtual organizations. These changing historical conditions, in turn, create many more possible positions of power, hegemony, and multiplicity for men and masculinities, and hence many more ways for men, organizations, and managements to be reciprocally formed, in this late modern, glocalizing world (Hearn, 1996a; Connell, 1998). Such possible power positions are themselves still made possible by the organization of unpaid work and the total social organization of labor (Glucksmann, 1995).

NOTES

1. Studies of women managers' coping strategies also reveal the persistence of "hegemonic" managerial masculinities. For example, J. Martin (1990) showed how senior men expected women managers to organize cesarean operations to fit in with the launch of new products. Sheppard (1989) found that women managers' strategies of resisting or trying to blend in to the dominant male culture were both ineffective (see also Scase & Goffee, 1989). Frequently experiencing a "no-win" situation (Cockburn, 1991), women managers may decide to resign, possibly to become self-employed (Kanter, 1993). This was the case in Marshall's research (1995), in which women managers frequently felt isolated, excluded, and

continuously tested on masculine criteria of success such as toughness, political skill, and total commitment. Pierce (1996) argued that in the U.S. courtroom, with its adversarial model of dispute resolution, male lawyers act as "Rambo litigators" seeking to dominate through intimidation and "strategic friendliness." She found that those women litigators who adopted similar strategies were denigrated, whereas women who were more supportive were seen as "too soft" and compliant. In the United Kingdom, Wajcman (1998) found that the very few women in her study who "made it" into senior management felt compelled to "manage like a man," working long hours, being totally committed to the organization, and being "tough," "hard," and at times aggressive. Although female managers had to abandon aspects of their femininity to develop attributes more typically associated with male executives, systematic gender inequalities ensured that women's experience in management could not be the same as that of men. Wajcman concluded that, because these female managers are in most respects indistinguishable from their male counterparts, there is no such thing as a "female" management style (also see Boulgarides, 1984; Eagly & Johannesen-Schmidt, 2001; Powell, 1993).

2. Indeed, another area of critique follows from the question of whether masculinities are irreducibly related to men or instead are discourses in which women can also invest. It could be argued that women in organizations behave in similar ways to men, invest in equivalent discourses, and engage in analogous strategies of power and identity (Wajcman, 1998). On all-female shop floors, for example, research suggests that women often swear and participate in aggressive and sexualized forms of behavior (e.g., Pollert, 1981; Westwood, 1984). Such practices do indeed display similarities to those of men in all-male shopfloor settings. Because issues of gender are by no means exhaustive of the social relations and practices in which they are embedded, it seems reasonable to assume that certain commonalities may exist between men's and women's experience of and response to subordination, for example in relation to class and control. Yet, these femininities are also likely to be shaped by the gender division of labor both at home and in organizations, and by the gendered nature of specific workplace cultures.

REFERENCES

Acker, J. (1989). The problem with patriarchy. *Sociology, 23*(2), 235-240.

Ackroyd, S., & Thompson, P. (1999). *Organizational misbehaviour.* London: Sage.

Alvesson, M., & Due Billing, Y. (1997). *Understanding gender and organizations.* London: Sage.

Alvesson, M., & Willmott, H. (1996). *Making sense of management.* London: Sage.

Baigent, D. (2001). *Gender relations, masculinities and the fire service.* Unpublished doctoral thesis, Anglia Polytechnic University, Cambridge, UK.

Barrett, F. (2001). The organizational construction of hegemonic masculinity: The case of the U.S. Navy. In S. Whitehead & F. Barrett (Eds.), *The masculinities reader* (pp. 77-99). Cambridge, MA: Polity.

Beams, M. (1979). One woman's work is another woman's daughter: A contribution to the sociology of childbirth. *Women's Studies International Quarterly, 2,* 57-67.

Berle, A. A., & Means, G. C. (1932). *The modern corporation and private property.* New York: Macmillan.

Bird, S. (1996). Welcome to the men's club: Homosociality and the maintenance of hegemonic masculinity. *Gender and Society, 10,* 120-132.

Blum, J. A. (2000). Degradation without deskilling: Twenty-five years in the San Francisco shipyards. In M. Burawoy et al. (Eds.), *Global ethnography* (pp. 106-136). Berkeley: University of California Press.

Bologh, R.W. (1990). *Love or greatness? Max Weber and masculine thinking—a feminist inquiry.* London: Unwin Hyman.

Boulgarides, J. D. (1984). A comparison of male and female business managers. *Leadership and Organisational Development Journal, 5*(5), 27-31.

Brettell, C., & Sargent, C. (Eds.). (2000). *Gender in cross-cultural perspective* (3rd ed.). Englewood Cliffs, NJ: Prentice Hall.

Burrell, G. (1997). *Pandemonium: Towards a retro-organization theory.* London: Sage.

Burton, C. (1991). *The promise and the price.* Sydney: Allen and Unwin.

Carrigan, T., Connell, R. W., & Lee, J. (1985). Toward a new sociology of masculinity. *Theory and Society, 14*(5), 551-604.

Chandler, A. D. (1977). *The visible hand: The managerial revolution in American business.* Cambridge, MA: Harvard University Press.

Clarke, S., & Popay, J. (1998). "I'm just a bloke who's had kids": Men and women on parenthood. In J. Popay, J. Hearn, & J. Edwards (Eds.), *Men, gender divisions and welfare* (pp. 196-230). London: Routledge.

Cockburn, C. (1983). *Brothers.* London: Pluto.

Cockburn, C. (1991). *In the way of women: Men's resistance to sex equality in organizations.* London: Macmillan.

Collier, R. (1998). "Nutty professors," "men in suits" and "new entrepreneurs": Corporeality, subjectivity and change in the law school and legal practice. *Social & Legal Studies, 7*(1), 27-53.

Collinson, D. L. (1992). *Managing the shopfloor: Subjectivity, masculinity and workplace culture.* Berlin: Walter de Gruyter.

Collinson, D. L. (1988). "Shift-ing lives": Work-home pressures in the North Sea oil industry. *Canadian Review of Sociology and Anthropology, 35*(3), 301-324.

Collinson, D. L. (2000). Strategies of resistance: Power, knowledge and subjectivity in the workplace. In K. Grint (Ed.), *Work and society: A reader* (pp. 163-198). Cambridge, MA: Polity.

Collinson, D. L., & Collinson, M. (1989). Sexuality in the workplace: The domination of men's sexuality. In J. Hearn, D. Sheppard, P. Tancred-Sheriff, & G. Burrell (Eds.), *The sexuality of organization* (pp. 91-109). London: Sage.

Collinson, D. L., & Collinson, M. (1992). Mismanaging sexual harassment: Blaming the victim and protecting the perpetrator. *Women in Management Review, 7*(7), 11-17.

Collinson, D. L., & Collinson, M. (1997). Delayering managers: Time-space surveillance and its gendered effects. *Organization, 4*(3), 373-405.

Collinson, D. L., & Hearn, J. (1994). Naming men as men: Implications for work, organization and management. *Gender, Work and Organization, 1*(1), 2-22.

Collinson, D. L., & Hearn, J. (1995). Men managing leadership? *Men and Women of the Corporation* revisited. *International Review of Women and Leadership, 1*(2), 1-24.

Collinson, D. L., & Hearn, J. (Eds.). (1996a). *Men as managers, managers as men.* London: Sage.

Collinson, D. L., & Hearn, J. (1996b). "Men" at "work": Multiple masculinities in multiple workplaces. In M. Mac an Ghaill (Ed.), *Understanding masculinities: Social relations and cultural areas* (pp. 61-76). Buckingham, UK: Open University Press.

Collinson, D. L., & Hearn, J. (2000a). Critical studies on men, masculinities and managements. In M. Davidson & R. Burke (Eds.), *Women in management, current research issues* (Vol. 2, pp. 263-278). London: Sage.

Collinson, D. L., & Hearn, J. (2000b). Naming men as men: Implications for work, organization and management. In S. Whitehead & F. Barrett (Eds.), *The masculinities reader* (pp. 144-169). Cambridge, MA: Polity.

Collinson, D. L., Knights, D., & Collinson, M. (1990). *Managing to discriminate.* London: Routledge.

Collinson, M., & Collinson, D. L. (1996). It's only Dick: The sexual harassment of women managers in insurance. *Work, Employment and Society, 10*(1), 29-56.

Coltrane, S. (1996). *Family man: Fatherhood, housework, and gender equity.* New York: Oxford University Press.

Coltrane, S. (1998). *Gender and families.* Thousand Oaks, CA: Pine Forge Press.

Connell, R. W. (1995). *Masculinities.* Cambridge, MA: Polity.

Connell, R. W. (1998). Globalization and masculinities. *Men and Masculinities, 1*(1), 3-23.

Connell, R.W. (2000). *The men and the boys.* Cambridge, MA: Polity.

Dalton, M. (1959). *Men who manage: Fusions of feeling and theory in administration.* New York: Wiley.

Davidson, M., & Burke, R. (Eds.). (2000). *Women in management: Current research issues* (Vol. 2). London: Sage.

Deal, T. E., & Kennedy, A. A. (1982). *Corporate culture: The rites and rituals of corporate life.* Reading, MA: Addison-Wesley.

Deal, T. E., & Kennedy, A. A. (2000). *The new corporate cultures.* London: Texere.

Donaldson, M. (1993). What is hegemonic masculinity? *Theory and Society, 22*(5), 643-657.

Drucker, P. (1979). *The practice of management.* London: Heinemann.

Eagly, A. H., & Johannesen-Schmidt, M. C. (2001). The leadership styles of women and men. *Journal of Social Issues, 57*(4), 781-797.

Eichler, M. (1980). *The double standard: A feminist critique of feminist social science.* London: Croom Helm.

Ezzamel, M., & Hoskin, K. (2002). Retheorizing accounting, writing and money with evidence from Mesopotamia and Ancient Egypt. *Critical Perspectives on Accounting, 13,* 333-367.

Feldberg, R. L., & Glenn, E. N. (1979). Male and female: Job versus gender models in the sociology of work. *Social Problems, 26*(5), 524-538.

Feldman, D., & Klich, N. (1991). Impression management and career strategies. In R. Giacalone & P. Rosenfeld (Eds.), *Applied impression management* (pp. 67-80). Newbury Park, CA: Sage.

Finch, J. (1984). *Married to the job: Wives' incorporation in men's work.* London: Allen and Unwin.

Fineman, S. (Ed.). (1993). *Emotion in organizations.* London: Sage.

Fulop, L., & Linstead, S. (2000). *Management: A critical text.* London: Macmillan.

Geneen, H. S. (1985). *Managing.* London: Collins.

Gibbings, S. (1990). *The tie: Trends and traditions.* London: Studio Editions.

Glucksmann, M. (1995). Why "work"? Gender and the "total social organization of labour." *Gender, Work and Organization, 2*(2), 63-75.

Goffman, E. (1961). *Encounters.* Harmondsworth, UK: Penguin.

Goines, J. T. (2002, April). *Management teams' experience, working relationships and turnover: Implications on performance.* Paper presented at the Midwest Academy of Management 45th conference, Indianapolis. Available at www.cobweb.creighton.edu/MAM/papers/Goines.doc

Gooch, J. (1974). *The plans of war: The general staff and British military strategy c. 1900–1916.* London: Routledge and Kegan Paul.

Gray, S. (1987). Sharing the shopfloor. In M. Kaufman (Ed.), *Beyond patriarchy: Essays by men on pleasure, power, and change* (pp. 216-234). New York: Oxford University Press.

Grey, C. (1994). Career as a project of the self and labour process discipline. *Sociology, 28*(2), 479-498.

Hay Group. (2001). *Top teams: Why some work and some do not.* Philadelphia: Hay Group. Available at www.haygroup.co.uk/downloads/TopTeamsBooklet.pdf

Hearn, J. (1983). *Birth and afterbirth: A materialist account.* London: Achilles Heel.

Hearn, J. (1985). Men's sexuality at work. In A. Metcalf & M. Humphries (Eds.), *The sexuality of men* (pp. 110-128). London: Pluto.

Hearn, J. (1987). *The gender of oppression: Men, masculinity, and the critique of Marxism.* New York: St. Martin's.

Hearn, J. (Ed.). (1989). Men, masculinities and leadership: Changing patterns and new initiatives [Special issue]. *Equal Opportunities International, 8*(1).

Hearn, J. (1992a). Changing men and changing managements: A review of issues and actions. *Women in Management Review and Abstracts, 7*(1), 3-8.

Hearn, J. (1992b). *Men in the public eye: The construction and deconstruction of public men and public patriarchies.* London: Routledge.

Hearn, J. (1994). Changing men and changing managements: Social change, social research and social action. In M. J. Davidson & R. Burke (Eds.), *Women in management—current research issues* (pp. 192-209). London: Paul Chapman.

Hearn, J. (1996a). Deconstructing the dominant: Making the one(s) the other(s). *Organization: The Interdisciplinary Journal of Organization, Theory and Society, 3*(4), 611-626.

Hearn, J. (1996b). Is masculinity dead? A critique of the concept of masculinity/masculinities. In M. Mac an Ghaill (Ed.), *Understanding masculinities: Social relations and cultural arenas* (pp. 202-217). Buckingham, UK: Open University Press.

Hearn, J., & Collinson, D. L. (1994). Theorizing unities and differences between men and between masculinities. In H. Brod & M. Kaufman (Eds.), *Theorizing masculinities* (pp. 97-118). Newbury Park, CA: Sage.

Hearn, J., & Collinson, D. L. (1998). Men, masculinities, managements and organisational culture. *Zeitschrift für Personal Forschung, 12*(1), 210-222.

Hearn, J., Kovalainen, A., & Tallberg, T. (2002). *Gender divisions and gender policies in top Finnish corporations* (Research Report 57). Helsinki: Swedish School of Economics and Business Administration.

Hearn, J., & Parkin, W. (1988). Women, men and leadership: A critical review of assumptions, practices and change in the industrialized nations. In N. J. Adler & D. Izraeli (Eds.), *Women in management worldwide* (pp. 17-40). New York: M. E. Sharpe.

Hearn, J., & Parkin, W. (1995). *"Sex" at "work": The power and paradox of organisation sexuality* (Rev. and updated). New York: St. Martin's.

Hearn, J., & Parkin, W. (2001). *Gender, sexuality and violence in organizations: The unspoken forces of organization violations.* London: Sage.

Henriques, J., Hollway, W., Urwin, C., Venn, C., & Walkerdine, V. (1984). *Changing the subject.* London: Methuen.

Hochschild, A. R. (1983). *The managed heart: Commercialization of human feeling.* Berkeley: University of California Press.

Hofstede, G. (1980). *Culture's consequences: International differences in work-related values.* London: Sage.

Hollway, W. (1996). Masters and men. In D. L. Collinson & J. Hearn (Eds.), *Men as managers, managers as men* (pp. 25-42). London: Sage.

Hoskin, K., & Macve, R. (1988). The genesis of accountability: The West Point connections. *Accounting, Organizations and Society, 13*(1), 37-73.

Hoskin, K., & Macve, R. (1994). Reappraising the genesis of managerialism: A re-examination of the role of accounting at the Springfield Armory, 1815–1845. *Accounting, Auditing and Accountability Journal, 7*(2), 2-29.

Howell, D., & Willis, R. (Eds.). (1980). *Societies at peace.* New York: Routledge.

Iacocca, L. (1984). *Iacocca: An autobiography.* New York: Bantam.

ID Research. (2001). *Gay and lesbian census.* London: ID Research.

Institute of Management/Remuneration Economics. (1998). *UK national management survey.* London: Institute of Management.

Kanter, R. M. (1977). *Men and women of the corporation.* New York: Basic Books.

Kanter, R. M. (1993). *Men and women of the corporation* (2nd ed.). New York: Basic Books.

Kerfoot, D. (2001). The organization of intimacy: Managerialism, masculinity and the masculine subject. In S. Whitehead & F. Barrett (Eds.), *The masculinities reader* (pp. 233-252). Cambridge, MA: Polity.

Kerfoot, D., & Knights, D. (1993). Management, masculinity and manipulation: From paternalism to corporate strategy in financial services in Britain. *Journal of Management Studies, 30*(4), 659-679.

Kerfoot, D., & Knights, D. (1996). "The best is yet to come?" The quest for embodiment in managerial work. In D. L. Collinson & J. Hearn (Eds.), *Men as managers, managers as men* (pp. 78-98). London: Sage.

Kerfoot, D., & Knights, D. (1998). Managing masculinity in contemporary organizational life: A "man"agerial project. *Organization, 5*(1), 7-26.

Kimmel, M. S. (1994). Masculinity as homophobia: Fear, shame, and silence in the construction of gender identity. In H. Brod & M. Kaufman (Eds.), *Theorizing masculinities* (pp. 119-141). Thousand Oaks, CA: Sage.

Kimmel, M. S. (2001). Global masculinities. In B. Pease & K. Pringle (Eds.), *A man's world: Changing men's practices in a globalized world* (pp. 21-37). London: Zed Books.

Kondo, D. (1990). *Crafting selves: Power, gender and discourses of identity in a Japanese workplace.* Chicago: University of Chicago Press.

Korten, D. (1996). *When corporations rule the world.* London: Earthscan Publications.

Korten, D. (1998). *Taming the giants.* Retrieved from www.geocities.com/RainForest/3621/KORTEN.HTM

Lupton, B. (2002). *"What kind of man are you?" Masculinity, social-class and men who work in female-concentrated occupations.* Unpublished doctoral thesis, Manchester Metro University.

Lynch, K. (1989). Solidary labour: Its nature and marginalisation. *Sociological Review, 37*(1), 1-14.

MacInnes, J. (1998). *The end of masculinity.* Buckingham, UK: Open University Press.

MacInnes, J. (2001). The crisis of masculinity and the politics of identity. In S. Whitehead & F. Barrett (Eds.), *The masculinities reader* (pp. 311-329). Cambridge, MA: Polity.

Maier, M., & Messerschmidt, J. (1998). Commonalities, conflicts and contradictions in organizational masculinities: Exploring the gendered genesis of the Challenger disaster. *Canadian Review of Sociology and Anthropology, 35*(3), 325-344.

Marshall, J. (1995). *Women managers moving on.* London: Routledge.

Martin, J. (1990). Deconstructing organizational taboos: The suppression of gender conflict in organizations. *Organizational Science, 1*(4), 339-359.

Martin, P. Y. (1996). Gendering and evaluating dynamics: Men, masculinities and managements. In D. L. Collinson & J. Hearn (Eds.), *Men as managers, managers as men* (pp. 186-209). London: Sage.

Martin, P. Y. (2001). "Mobilizing masculinities": Women's experiences of men at work. *Organization, 8*(4), 587-618.

Marx, K., & Engels, F. (1970). *The German ideology.* London: Lawrence and Wishart.

McMahon, A. (1993). Male readings of feminist theory: The psychologization of sexual politics in the masculinity literature. *Theory and Society, 22,* 675-695.

Messerschmidt, J. (1996). Managing to kill: Masculinities and the space shuttle Challenger explosion. In C. Cheng (Ed.), *Masculinities in organizations* (pp. 29-53). Thousand Oaks, CA: Sage.

Mintzberg, H. (1989). *Mintzberg on management.* New York: Macmillan.

Morgan, D. H. J. (1992). *Discovering men.* London: Unwin Hyman/Routledge.

Morgan, D. H. J. (1996). The gender of bureaucracy. In D. L. Collinson & J. Hearn (Eds.), *Men as managers, managers as men* (pp. 29-53). London: Sage.

Morgan, D. H. J. (2001). Family, gender and masculinities. In S. Whitehead & F. Barrett (Eds.), *The masculinities reader* (pp. 223-232). Cambridge, MA: Polity.

Morgan, G. (1997). *Images of organization.* London: Sage.

Mulholland, K. (1996). Entrepreneurialism, masculinities and the self-made man. In D. L. Collinson & J. Hearn (Eds.), *Men as managers, managers as men* (pp. 123-149). London: Sage.

Murdock, G. P. (1937). Comparative data on the division of labor by sex. *Social Forces, 15*(4), 551–553.

Nordberg, M. (2002). Constructing masculinity in women's worlds: Men working as pre-school teachers and hairdressers. *NORA: The Nordic Journal of Women's Studies, 10*(1), 26-37.

Oakley, A. (1985). *Sex, gender and society.* Aldershot, UK: Ashgate.

O'Brien, M. (1981). *The politics of reproduction.* London: Routledge and Kegan Paul.

O'Brien, M. (1986). *Reproducing the world.* Boulder, CO: Westview.

Pahl, R. (1995). *After success: Fin-de-siecle anxiety and identity.* Cambridge, MA: Polity.

Pease, B., & Pringle, K. (2001). Introduction: Studying men's practices and gender relations in a global context. In B. Pease & K. Pringle (Eds.), *A man's world: Changing men's practices in a globalized world* (pp. 1-17). London: Zed.

Peters, T. J., & Austin, N. K. (1985). *A passion for excellence: The leadership difference.* New York: Random House.

Peters, T. J., & Waterman, R. H. (1982). *In search of excellence.* New York: Harper and Row.

Pierce, J. (1996). Rambo litigators: Emotional labour in a male dominated organization. In C. Cheng (Ed.), *Masculinities in organizations* (pp. 1-28). Thousand Oaks, CA: Sage.

Pollert, A. (1981). *Girls, wives, factory lives.* London: Macmillan.

Powell, G. (1993). *Women and men in management.* Newbury Park, CA: Sage.

Pringle, R. (1989). *Secretaries talk.* London: Verso.

Reed, M. (1989). *The sociology of management.* London: Harvester Wheatsheaf.

Reed, R. (1996). Entrepreneurialism and paternalism in Australian management: A gender critique of the self-made man. In D. L. Collinson & J. Hearn (Eds.), *Men as managers, managers as men* (pp. 99-122). London: Sage.

Reis, C. (2004). *Men managers in a European multinational company.* Mering & München, Germany: Rainer Humpp Verlog.

Robertson, R. (1995). Glocalization: Time-space and homogeneity-heterogeneity. In M. Featherstone, S. Lash, & R. Robertson (Eds.), *Global modernity* (pp. 25-44). London: Sage.

Roper, M. R. (1991). Yesterday's model: Product fetishism and the British company men 1945-85. In M. R. Roper & J. Tosh (Eds.), *Manful assertions: Masculinities in Britain since 1800* (pp. 190-211). London: Routledge.

Roper, M. R. (1994). *Masculinity and the British organization man since 1945.* Oxford, UK: Oxford University Press.

Rosenfeld, R., & Wilson, D. (1999). *Managing organizations: Texts, readings and cases* (2nd ed.). Maidenhead: McGraw-Hill.

Sanday, P. R. (1981). *Female power and male dominance: On the origins of sexual inequality.* New York: Cambridge University Press.

Scase, R., & Goffee, R. (1989). *Reluctant managers.* London: Unwin Hyman.

Schein, E. (1985). *Organizational culture and leadership.* San Francisco: Jossey-Bass.

Sheppard, D. (1989). Organizations, power and sexuality: The image and self-image of women managers. In J. Hearn, D. Sheppard, P. Tancred-Sheriff, & G. Burrell (Eds.), *The sexuality of organization* (pp. 139-158). London: Sage.

Stewart, R. (1986). *The reality of management.* London: Heinemann.

Surowiecki, J. (2002, July 23). Did Iacocca ruin American business? *The Guardian.* Retrieved December 29, 2003, from www.guardian.co.uk/worldcom/story/0,12167,761721,00.html

Tolson, A. (1977). *The limits of masculinity.* London: Routledge.

United Nations Development Programme. (1996). *UN human development report.* New York: Oxford University Press for the United Nations Development Programme.

Veikkola, E.-S., Hänninen-Salmelin, E., & Sinkkonen, S. (1997). Is the forecast for wind or calm? In E.-S. Veikkola (Ed.), *Women and men at the top: A study of women and men as leaders in the private sector* (pp. 82-87). Helsinki: Statistics Finland.

Vinnicombe, S. (2000). The position of women in management in Europe. In M. Davidson & R. Burke (Eds.), *Women in management, current research issues* (Vol. 2, pp. 9-25). London: Sage.

Waddington, D., Critcher, C., & Dicks, B. (1998). "All jumbled up": Employed women with unemployed husbands. In J. Popay, J. Hearn, & J. Edwards (Eds.), *Men, gender divisions and welfare* (pp. 231-256). London: Routledge.

Wajcman, J. (1998). *Managing like a man.* Cambridge, MA: Polity.

Walby, S. (1986). *Patriarchy at work.* Cambridge, MA: Polity.

Walby, S. (1990). *Theorizing patriarchy.* Oxford, UK: Basil Blackwell.

Walker, C. R., & Guest, R. H. (1952). *The man on the assembly line.* Cambridge, MA: Harvard University Press.

Watson, T. (1994). *In search of management.* London: Routledge.

Weisbach, M. S., & Hermalin, B. E. (2000). *Boards of directors as an endogenously determined institution: A survey of the economic literature* (NBER Working Paper 8161). Cambridge, MA: National Bureau of Economic Research. Available at http://papers.ssrn.com/sol3/delivery.cfm/000619306.pdf?abstractid=233111

Westwood, S. (1984). *All day, every day: Factory and family in the making of women's lives.* London: Pluto.

Wetherell, M., & Edley, N. (1999). Negotiating hegemonic masculinity: Imaginary positions and psycho-discursive practices. *Feminism & Psychology, 9*(3), 335-356.

Whitehead, S. (2001). Man: The invisible gendered subject? In S. Whitehead & F. Barrett (Eds.), *The masculinities reader* (pp. 351-368). Cambridge, MA: Polity.

Whyte, W. H. (1956). *The organization man.* New York: Simon and Schuster.

Willis, P. (1977). *Learning to labour.* London: Saxon House.

Witz, A., & Savage, M. (1992). The gender of organizations. In M. Savage & A. Witz (Eds.), *Gender and bureaucracy* (pp. 3-62). Oxford, UK: Blackwell.

Woodward, A. E. (1996). Multinational masculinities and European bureaucracies. In D. L. Collinson & J. Hearn (Eds.), *Men as managers, managers as men* (pp. 167-185). London: Sage.

PART IV

BODIES, SELVES, DISCOURSES

18

STILL A MAN'S WORLD?

Studying Masculinities and Sport

MICHAEL A. MESSNER

Recently, two sports events stirred enough controversy to spill the stories off the sports pages and into wider public discussion and debate. First, in 2002-2003, the U.S. Secretary of Education formed a commission to evaluate Title IX, the popular 30-year-old law that is credited by women's sports activists as a primary force behind the dramatic growth of girls' and women's sports. By almost any measure, men's sports still receive far more money, scholarships, attention, and adulation than do women's sports, yet critics blame Title IX for a kind of "reverse discrimination" that they claim has threatened or eliminated athletic opportunities for boys and men. Around the time of the commission's hearings, emotional and sometimes vitriolic public hearings were held; editorials were written; and letter-writing campaigns to the White House were organized.

The second recent event that made a large media splash occurred in 2003, when pro golfer Annika Sorenstam was invited to compete in a Professional Golfers' Association (PGA) event. That Sorenstam would become the first woman to play head-to-head in a major tournament against the men since Babe Didrikson Zaharias, more than half a century earlier, was big news. It also was controversial: Some male golfers, led by Vijay Singh, snarled at her inclusion, implying that it insulted the integrity of the game to include a woman. Other male golfers were openly supportive of her inclusion. Similarly, some media pundits criticized her inclusion as "inadequate" and "awful," while others wrote in admiration of Sorenstam's skill and courage. Sorenstam's inclusion in the PGA event became—at least for a few weeks—one of the main topics of discussion on talk radio, letters to the editor, and around office watercoolers.

These two events—debates over Title IX in school sports and debates about including a woman in a men's pro sports event—are salient because they echo continuing controversies at the heart of gender and sports. Should sport, as a social institution that is an integral part of schools and universities, offer equal opportunities? Should boys and girls, and women and men, play sports together? Do coed sports reveal how similar we are, or do they unveil essential differences between women and men? These debates don't go away or get "resolved," and that is because sport continues to be more than a place to play and recreate. Sport is a key terrain of contest for gender (and race, class, sexual, and global) relations. It is a highly visible forum in which male and female bodies are literally "built," their limitations displayed, their capacities debated. As such, it is a key site for ideological contest over the meanings of "masculinity," as well as "femininity."

Both the opposition to Title IX and some of the more vitriolic opposition to Annika Sorenstam's competing in the PGA reprise an argument that goes back well over a hundred years. Men, we learn from the historical and social scientific literature on sport, created modern sport as an institution that affirms the categorical superiority of male bodies over female bodies, as well as men's centrality in public life. The idea of sex equity in sports, as well as the reality of a woman athlete successfully competing with top male athletes, directly threatens the ideology of male superiority, and thus men's positions of centrality. Fortunately, over the past 30 years or so, scholars of sport, gender, and masculinity have built a rich foundation of research that now can be drawn upon to inform these public debates. In this essay, I will give an overview of this work and point to some current challenges and new directions in research on sport and gender.

Sport as a Contested Terrain

In the wake of the second wave of feminism, and often inspired by the nascent "men's liberation movement," a trickle of essays about men, masculinity, and sport began to emerge in the 1970s (e.g., Farrell, 1974; Naison, 1972; Schafer, 1975). The best of these works were collected in Sabo and Runfola's groundbreaking 1980 book, *Jock: Sports and Male Identity.* These works contained the kernel of what other scholars later would develop into more sophisticated critiques of the sexism, homophobia, violence, and militarism at the heart of men's sports. Many of these works, however, were journalistic, anecdotal, and/or personal critiques of sport. There were two reasons for this. First, there was as yet no systematic and theoretically sophisticated analysis of men and masculinities in gender studies. Most scholarly studies of men were still mired in the largely ahistorical, static, and categorical language of sex role theory. Related to this first limitation was a second: In the 1970s, feminist studies of

women and sport were still in their infancy, and they were also for the most part limited to analysis of sex roles.

This changed rapidly in the 1980s, as the foundation was laid for the development of a broader and deeper scholarly study of men and sport. One layer of this foundation was built on the increasingly sophisticated works by feminist scholars studying women and sport (e.g., Birrell, 1984; Hall, 1984; Theberge, 1981). Second, in 1985, Don Sabo systematically laid out the first programmatic statement of what a profeminist research agenda on the topic of men and sport could look like (Sabo, 1985). Sabo sketched out an array of specific research topics and questions on boys' socialization through sport, competition and success, bodies, emotions, pain and injury, aggression and violence, sexuality, male athletes' devaluation of women, and the possibilities for sport to develop in progressive, profeminist directions (including questions about "cross-sex sport"). Over the next decade, Sabo and other scholars took up most of these questions.

Third, scholars in the late 1980s increasingly drew ideas from R. W. Connell's emergent theorization of masculinities (Connell, 1987). Connell supplied sport studies scholars with a conceptual toolbox with which to examine the complexities of gender dynamics in men's sports, without falling into the traps and limitations of sex role theory. Scholars could see that sport is an institutional realm in which men construct and affirm their separation from, and domination over, women. But sport does not operate seamlessly to reproduce men's power over women; sport also has been a realm in which men of dominant groups (in the United States, white, heterosexual, middle- and upper-class men) have affirmed their dominance and superiority over other men. Connell's concepts of hegemonic, marginalized, and subordinated masculinities gave conceptual form to the emergent idea of gender as multiple. These concepts gave scholars a language with which to speak about seemingly paradoxical gender dynamics: Hegemonic masculinity, the currently dominant and ascendant form of masculinity, is constructed as not-feminine, but also simultaneously as not-gay, not-black, not-working class, and not-immigrant. This idea is fundamental to many of the chapters in the first scholarly collection of works on men, masculinities, and sport. In *Sport,*

Men, and the Gender Order: Critical Feminist Perspectives (Messner & Sabo, 1990), scholars critically examined the ways that sport affirms men's power over women, as well as the fissures and contradictions (especially along lines of race, social class, and sexualities) within and between masculinities.

Historical scholarship also informed the 1980s work on men and sport. Sport in industrializing societies developed as a "male preserve" separate from women's spheres of life (Dunning, 1986). Sport also served to differentiate ruling men from subordinated men. In the 19th and early 20th centuries, the British consciously developed sport in their public schools as a means of preparing boys to administer the British Empire (Mangan, 1986). The British eventually extended their schooling system, along with sports like cricket, to the middle classes of the colonized nations, in hopes that these middle-class men would adopt British morality, ethics, and values and thus help to solidify colonial control. It didn't always work that way. Historian and social analyst C. R. L. James (1983), in his brilliant book on cricket in the colonial West Indies of the 1920s and 1930s, shows that the British sporting ethic tended to cut both ways. On one hand, public schools—and especially cricket—taught middle-class mulatto (mixed race) West Indian boys and young men the values of "Puritanism" and "moral restraint," as well as the "general superiority of British culture" (James, 1983, p. 72). But because teams were strictly segregated by race as well as nationality (British vs. colonized), the game provided a context in which the contradictions of racism and colonial domination were laid bare. For James and others, then, the cricket field often became an important arena for symbolic resistance against racism and British domination.

In the United States, modern men's sport was formed during industrialization and urbanization, in a time of shifting work and family dynamics for women and men, at the tail end of the first wave of feminism, and amid racist fears of immigration (Crosset, 1990; Kimmel, 1990). At this time, sport bolstered faltering ideologies of white middle-class masculine superiority over women, and over race- and class-subordinated men. But throughout the 20th century, sport was a contested terrain—contested by working class women and men, by women and men of color, and by feminists (Bryson, 1987; Messner, 1988; Whitson, 1990; Willis, 1983).

Based on this foundational work in gender studies and in feminist sport studies, scholars since the early 1990s have contributed to an explosion of studies of men, masculinities, and sport. Critical analyses of masculinities were fundamental to empirical studies of gay male athletes (Anderson, 2002; Pronger, 1990); the lives of male athletes of different social classes and racial/ethnic groups (Messner, 1992); African American males' "cool pose" and sport (Majors, 1990); sexual and gender paradoxes in the lives of male bodybuilders (Klein, 1993); the sporting culture of Australia (McKay, 1991, 1997); how masculinities mesh with class politics in Canadian hockey (Gruneau & Whitson, 1994); the production of masculinities in Mexican baseball (Klein, 2000); and the production, imagery, and consumption of the *Sports Illustrated* "swimsuit issue" (Davis, 1997).

The idea that sport is, on one hand, a modern bastion of patriarchal power, and on the other hand, a terrain that has been contested continually by women and by marginalized men, has been foundational in studies of sport and gender. Over the past two decades, concrete studies of gender and sport have repeatedly demonstrated how the once unquestioned bastion of powerful, competitive, hierarchical, and often violent heterosexual masculinity is not a seamless patriarchal institution. Rather, the very heart of the gender regime of men's sport is contested and wrought with contradiction and paradox (Messner, 2002). These contradictions and paradoxes have been explored within a number of thematic areas, three of which I will next briefly discuss: bodies, health, and violence.

Bodies

A key ideological outcome of sport has been to create the illusion that masculinity naturally coheres to male bodies, and femininity to female bodies, and that these binary categories of male/masculinity vs. female/femininity are naturally and categorically different (Dworkin & Messner, 1999). However, as Connell (1987) has noted, if the differences between men and women are so natural, then why do people put so much work and effort into creating, marking, and defending these differences? Indeed, empirical research into the construction of male bodies in sport lays bare the profoundly social basis of categorical and essentialist gender ideology. Rather than revealing something about human "nature," research illuminates sport as a collective practice that constructs masculinity. Connell's (1990) life history study of an Australian "Iron Man" athlete illustrates how the mental, emotional, and physical training regime involved in becoming a top competitive athlete encourages a man to block or ignore fears, anxieties, or other inconvenient emotions, while mentally controlling his body to perform its prescribed tasks. "The decisive triumph," Connell concludes, "is over oneself, and specifically over one's body. The magnificent machine of [the iron man's] physique has meaning only when subordinated to the will to win" (Connell, 1990, p. 95). Similarly, Klein's (1993) ethnographic study of male bodybuilders illustrates not only the quite literal construction of hard male bodies but also the emotional insecurities, health costs, sexual anxieties, and contradictions that lie beneath the layers of muscle. Athletic careers construct masculine bodies as machines or tools, often in the process alienating men from their health, feelings, and relationships with others (Messner, 1992). But athletic male bodies are not shaped only by gender; race, social class, sexual orientation, and national origin also help to shape particular embodiments of masculinity in sport. For instance, gay male athletes may embody an "ironic" masculinity (Pronger, 1990), black male athletes often embody a "cool pose" (Majors, 1990), and Mexican baseball players may embody a combination of "toughness and tenderness" that is antithetical to simplistic stereotypes of the "macho" Latino male (Klein, 2000).

If studies of men's sports began to reveal both the constructedness of masculine bodies and their limits, the growing body of literature on women's sports further shattered simplistic essentialist thinking about differences between women and men. What sport illustrates, Judith Lorber (1996) concluded, is not natural categorical difference but social construction of such. Gendered institutions (like sport) create binary sex categories, not the opposite. Indeed, in a highly influential article, Mary Jo Kane (1995) argued that the more we observe girls and boys or men and women running, swimming, jumping, and playing competitive sports, the more

we must conclude that variation among bodies exists along a "continuum of difference." Differences between male and female bodies tend to be average, not categorical, and there are far greater differences among men's bodies than there are average differences between women and men. Many women are faster, stronger, and more agile than many men. Those committed to categorical thinking might have seen Annika Sorenstam's "failure" in 2003 to make the cut in the PGA event that she played in as "proof" that men are better players than women. Armed with the idea of a "continuum of difference," we might instead observe that Sorenstam finished with a poorer score than a number of men, but she also finished with a better score than several other men. In addition, she's clearly a better golfer than more than 99% of women and men who play golf throughout the world.

Men's Health

Scholarly research on men and sport has pointed to another paradox concerning bodies. Popular wisdom tends to see sport as healthy activity, and sporting bodies as paragons of fitness and health. But research reveals that men's sport activity is often associated with unhealthy practices, drug and alcohol abuse, pain, injury, and (in some sports) low life expectancy (White, Young, & McTeer, 1995; Young & White, 2000). In an often-reprinted article that drew on his experience as a college football player, Don Sabo (1994) argued that boys and men were subject to a highly authoritarian system of control that taught them to conform to what he called "the pain principle." To become successful athletes, Sabo argued, male athletes tend to

> adopt the visions and values that coaches are offering: to take orders, to "take out" opponents, to take the game seriously, to take women, and to take their place on the team. And if they can't take it, then the rewards of athletic camaraderie, prestige, scholarships, pro contracts, and community recognition are not forthcoming. (p. 87)

This system of rewards and punishments is backed up by a lifetime of group-based socialization that teaches boys to "shake it off," ignore their own pain, and treat their bodies as instruments to be used—and used up—to get a job done. Boys learn early on that if they don't conform to the pain principle, they may lose their position on the team, or they may be labeled as "women," "fags," or "pussies" for not being manly enough to play hurt. The world of sport clearly is one in which homophobia polices the boundaries of acceptable masculine practices, and nowhere is this more clear than in the ways boys learn to be manly through risk taking. Through this social process, it eventually comes to seem "natural" for boys and men to decide to play hurt—perhaps with the aid of painkilling drugs—thus risking their long-term health (Messner, 1992).

Scholars view the mantra of "no pain, no gain" as paradigmatic of the health costs paid by boys and men who were socialized to narrow, instrumental goal orientations through sport (McKay, 1991). But male athletes' acceptance of pain and injury, as well as their instrumental goal orientation concerning their bodies, is not a phenomenon that is particular to the world of sport. Similar, for instance, are the "workaholics" in the professional and corporate world and the nonathlete high school boys who take anabolic steroids mostly for cosmetic reasons. It may be, in fact, that athletic male bodies are merely amplified versions of the more general ways that boys and men are encouraged to engage the world in their bodies. Thus, research on men and sport may serve as a useful window for scholars who are interested in developing a more general study of men's health (Sabo & Gordon, 1995). This may be especially true of studies that explore the structured channeling of disproportionate numbers of men of subordinate social classes and racial/ethnic groups into the more risky and violent sports. These men's experiences tend to mirror and reinforce the kinds of health risks that marginalized groups of men face more generally in the workforce, the military, the street, or prisons (Sabo, 2001).

Violence

One of the most fruitful research trajectories to develop from scholarly research on men and sport has focused on male athletes' violence against women (Brackenridge, 1997; Young, 2002). Research suggests that far from being an aberration perpetrated by some marginal deviants, male athletes' off-the-field violence is generated from the normal, everyday dynamics

at the center of male athletic culture (Burstyn, 1999). A number of studies of men's college athletics in recent years have pointed to statistically significant relationships between athletic participation and sexual aggression (Benedict & Klein, 1997; Boeringer, 1996; Fritner & Rubinson, 1993; Koss & Gaines, 1993). Todd Crosset and his colleagues surveyed 20 universities with Division 1 athletic programs and found that male athletes, who in 1995 constituted 3.7% of the student population, were 19% of those reported to campus Judicial Affairs Offices for sexual assault (Crosset, Benedict, & McDonald, 1995; Crosset, Ptacek, McDonald, & Benedict, 1996). In a subsequent article, Crosset (2000) argued that researchers have been using too broad a brush in looking generally at the relationship of "men's sports" to violence against women. Studies that have compared across various sports have found important differences: The vast majority of reported assaults were perpetrated by athletes in "revenue producing contact sports" like basketball, football, and ice hockey. These data, according to Crosset, should warn us of the dangers of "clumping all sport environments together under the rubric of athletic affiliation" (p. 152).

Perhaps fearing that pointing the finger at high-profile athletes will reinforce oppressive stereotypes of African American males (who make up about 80% of the National Basketball Association [NBA], for instance) as violent sexual predators, activists like Donald McPherson (2002) prefer instead to pull male athletes into positions of responsibility to educate peers to prevent violence against women. This question of how antisexist organizing against men's violence against women might fan the flames of racism is a real concern to researchers in this field. As the media frenzy surrounding the trials of Mike Tyson and O. J. Simpson (for rape and for murder, respectively) illustrated, American culture seems especially obsessed with images of what Stuart Alan Clarke (1991) called "black men misbehaving"—especially if the alleged misbehaviors involve a combination of sex and violence. Racist stereotypes of black men as violent sexual predators have historically served as a foundation for institutional and personal violence perpetrated against African Americans. So, when data reveal that college athletes in revenue-producing sports have higher rates of sexual assaults against women, there is a very real danger that the term "athletes in revenue-producing sports" will smuggle in racist stereotypes as a thinly veiled code word for *black male athletes* (Berry & Smith, 2000).

Evidence suggests that the apparent overrepresentation of black male athletes charged with sexual assault in college is due to their dramatic overrepresentation in the central team sports of football and basketball. When we look at high schools, where white males are more evenly represented in the student athlete population, we see that white male athletes perpetrated many of the most egregious examples of sexual assaults. When we look at Canada, where white men dominate the central sport, ice hockey, we see that white males commit the vast majority of sexual assaults by athletes (Robinson, 1998). Following this logic, we can hypothesize that the more salient variable is not male athletes' race or ethnicity, but their *positions at the center of athletics*, that makes some male athletes more likely to engage in sexual assault than others.

Researchers have increasingly focused on the group interactions that underlie male athletes' violence against women. Studies of boys in sports have revealed the early development of group-based dominance bonding, grounded in aggressive, homophobic, and misogynist talk and banter (Eveslage & Delaney, 1998; Fine, 1987; Hasbrook & Harris, 2000). Studies of the competitive and sexually aggressive interactions in men's locker rooms (Curry, 1991; Kane & Disch, 1993), and of college men's sexual and violent dynamics in a sports bar (Curry, 2000), have been especially illuminating in this regard. There is no single factor that explains how male athletes come to assault women (or other men, in some cases). Rather, a combination of several group-based factors create a context that makes violence likely: misogynist and homophobic dominance bonding, a learned suppression of empathy for others, a "culture of silence" within the group, and an institutional environment that valorizes and rewards the successful utilization of violence against others (Messner, 2002). Intervention strategies that aim to educate coaches and athletes about sexual assault, or to reform men's sports, attempt to confront and change these group dynamics (Messner & Stevens, 2002).

NEW DIRECTIONS IN RESEARCH ON MEN, GENDER, AND SPORT

The first wave of studies on masculinities and sport in the late 1980s and early 1990s focused mostly on illuminating men's experiences within the homosocial "sportsworld." There have been two interrelated shifts away from this focus in recent years. First, many scholars are conducting studies that explore women's and men's relational constructions of gender in sport. Second, many scholars are challenging and stretching the conventional conceptualization of "the sportsworld" as an object of study. At the heart of this challenge is a strong move toward greater interdisciplinarity. For the most part, the idea of race/class/gender/sexual orientation "intersectionality" is built into these new directions in research.

Gender as Relational

Because sport historically has been organized as extremely sex segregated, it should not surprise us that the first wave of studies of sport tended to focus either on "men's sports" *or* on "women's sports." In the past decade, facilitated by the increasing growth and integration of girls' and women's sports in communities, schools, and universities, scholars have shifted their focus toward studies of boys *and* girls, men *and* women. These studies have the advantage of illustrating the *relational* construction of gender (and often, race, social class, and sexuality as well). To be sure, this shift is a matter of degree: The best of the earlier studies always examined men's or women's homosocial sport experiences within the context of sophisticated relational theories of gender, race, and class. Today, we see an increasing commitment to *empirical studies of gender relations* in sport.

Inspired partly by Thorne's (1993) pioneering work on children's construction of gender in schools, scholars of sport have increasingly turned their attention to relational studies of children, gender, and sport (Hasbrook, 1999). For instance, Hasbrook and Harris's (2000) study of inner-city first- and second-graders illustrated how athletic bodies facilitate the construction of race- and class-based masculinities and femininities in grade schools. Messner (2000) used an observation of a group interaction between 4- and 5-year-old girls' and boys' soccer teams to illuminate the structural and symbolic context of gendered interactions. Shakib and Dunbar (2002) compared boys and girls in high school basketball, while Laberge and Albert (2000) studied the social class implications in adolescent girls' and boys' interpretations of boys' "gender transgressions."

Sport has also entered public discussions of how to prevent youth crime and deviance. For instance, in the early 1990s, there was a public debate about creating "midnight basketball" in inner cities to keep young males off the streets, and busy with what were perceived to be positive activities (Hartmann, 2001). But research indicates that social reformers who see sport as a way to prevent youth crime should be aware of the limitations of what sport activities can offer children. Initiatives like midnight basketball also reveal the tendency to view racialized categories of "at-risk" youth (especially African American boys) as potential social problems who might be rescued from criminality by sports (Coakley, 2002).

The growth of relational studies of children and youth in sport has been mirrored by the emergence of relational studies of adults. In what is probably the most sophisticated empirical application of Connell's theory of gender, McKay (1997) compared the political and institutional dynamics of affirmative action policies in sport in Australia, New Zealand, and Canada. The ways that women's "invisible labor" often props up men's leisure and sport activities has been the topic of two excellent studies. Shona Thompson's (1999) book *Mother's Taxi* illuminates how women's labor facilitates children's and men's sport and leisure. Similarly, Boyle and McKay (1995) studied the exploitation of older women's labor in men's recreational sport.

Relational studies have also begun to reflect on health and fitness. Dworkin (2003) observed how the gendered geography of gyms contributes to a "glass ceiling" on women's musculature. In addition, recent studies that draw on national survey data shed new light on differences and similarities among various groups of high school athletes and nonathletes in terms of health outcomes and risks among teen athletes (K. E. Miller, Sabo, Melnick, Farrell, & Barnes, 2000), gender and race patterns in athletic participation and self esteem (Tracy & Erkut, 2002), anabolic steroid use among adolescent male and female athletes (K. E. Miller, Barnes,

Sabo, Melnick, & Farrell, 2002), and educational outcomes among various groups of boys and girls who play high school sports (Videon, 2002). All these studies challenge simplistic categorical assumptions about boys, girls, and sports, and suggest new questions for future research.

Relational studies of emergent sport formations are also contributing to the broadening of the field. Wheaton and Tomlinson (1998) observed that gendered patterns among windsurfers do not conform to those in dominant institutional sports that most sport studies scholars have studied. This raises the question, they suggested, of whether marginal or emergent sports might provide space for different—even oppositional—constructions of gender. Research on BMX bicyclists suggests further complexities: Perhaps rather than providing a space for the development of more egalitarian relations, some "extreme sports" are expressions of a backlash by white males who feel that their positions of centrality have been threatened by the ascendancy of girls and women, and by men of color (Kusz, 2003). Studies of coed sports point to additional paradoxes: When women and men play sports together, there are highly visible moments of gender transgression that challenge gender ideologies. However, the formal rules of coed sports, as well as the ways that players "do gender," tend to reaffirm gender boundaries and ideologies of natural difference (Henry & Comeaux, 1999; Wachs, 2002, 2003).

FROM SPORTSWORLD TO SPORTS IN THE WORLD

Recent scholars of sport, men, and gender have increasingly connected their analysis of sport to other (nonsport) institutional and cultural forms. This shift is a matter of degree. Sport studies scholars have long pointed to ways that sport connects to, reflects, and reinforces cultural values and power relations in nonsport institutional spheres of life. But earlier works tended to focus more on life inside "the sportsworld," and this may have contributed to a ghettoization of sport studies. In recent years, the study of sport and gender has become more integrated with other scholarly fields. Scholars increasingly frame their object of study not as "the sportsworld," but instead as "sports in the world." In particular, we see the integration of the study of sport within broader cultural studies approaches to the mass media and consumption (McKay & Rowe, 1997; T. Miller, 2001), general cultural critiques of race relations (Boyd, 1997; Carrington, 1998), and examinations of the gendered division of labor and leisure in families (Boyle & McKay, 1995).

One of the most fruitful dimensions of this interdisciplinary "cultural turn" in studies of gender and sport concerns studies of media imagery (Whannel, 2002). Drawing from the critical cultural studies tradition, scholars have analyzed the cultural meanings of race and gender in media coverage and broader cultural productions of sport. For instance, Cole and King (1998) presented a fascinating analysis of the ways that the popular documentary film *Hoop Dreams* expresses cultural tensions about race and gender in a postindustrial, post-Fordist and postfeminist America. Other studies have focused on the contradictory meanings of popular star athletes like U.S. baseball player Nolan Ryan (Trujillo, 1991), and U.S. pro basketball player and MTV star Dennis Rodman (Dunbar, 2000). In this same vein, a recent collection includes fascinating case studies of athletes like basketball star and "postmodern celebrity" Michael Jordan (McDonald & Andrews, 2001), Generation X icon of white masculinity Andre Agassi (Kusz, 2001), and British football celebrity Ian Wright's role as "the most visible postmodern black cultural icon in Britain today" (Carrington, 2001, p. 103). This genre of research is increasingly global in its scope. It also tends to challenge some of the assumptions of liberalism that underlie many conventional sociological studies of sport. For instance, Brian Pronger (2000) examined the suppression of the erotic and the narrowing of the concept of masculinity that has occurred in mainstream "gay sports" and asked a critical question—"Who's winning?"—when gay men embrace the very cultural forms (like mainstream sport) that have been so much a part of their historic oppression.

An important backdrop for these cultural analyses of sport is a continuing core of studies that document the asymmetrical quality and quantity of coverage of women's and men's sports in the mass media (e.g., Curry, Arriagada, & Cornwell, 2002; Eastman & Billings, 2001; Messner, Duncan, & Cooky, 2003; Messner, Duncan, & Wachs, 1996). One study of the

televised sports that boys and men watch concluded that the multimillion-dollar "sports-media-commercial complex" supplies boys and men with a consistent set of images, which the authors call "the televised sports manhood formula" (Messner, Dunbar, & Hunt, 2000). This formula is an ideological package of messages that encourage boys and men to value risk taking and violence, to tolerate pain and injury, and to treat girls and women either as peripheral to men's activities, or as sexualized objects of consumption. In a world of rapidly changing gender relations, the televised sports manhood formula appears as a stabilizing force for conventional, asymmetrical, and unequal relations between women and men. It also continually tweaks the insecurities of boys and men, and it offers them pseudo-empowerment through consumption of beer, snack foods, and auto-related products (Messner, 2002).

The "cultural turn" in sport studies meshes well with the turn toward relational studies of gender: Men's homosocial "sportsworld" does not exist in isolation—men's relations within sport, and the images of masculinity projected by the sports media, are integral parts of boys' and men's relations with each other, and with girls and women, in schools, families, and workplaces. One important area in which scholars are beginning to explore these connections concerns the connection between sports violence on and off the field. McDonald (1999) explored the gender and race dynamics in media coverage of well-known male figures in sport who were accused of domestic violence. In an innovative study, Sabo, Gray, and Moore (2000) interviewed women who had been physically abused by their male partners during or shortly after the men watched televised sports. This kind of study begins to give researchers and activists a handle on what the links might be between a man's act of violence against a woman partner and his acts of viewing violent sports, drinking alcohol, and gambling on sports. Similarly, Wenner's (1998) and Curry's (2000) studies of sports bars begin to show the construction of (sometimes violent) masculinities within the context of an institution that thrives on men's consumption of televised sports and alcohol.

Studies of media treatment of "sexual deviance" by big-name male athletes have been especially useful in illuminating the intersections of gender with race and sexual orientation. For instance, McKay (1993) reflected critically on the ways that the media responded to basketball star Earvin "Magic" Johnson's revelation that he was HIV-positive by projecting Johnson's sexual promiscuity onto "wanton women." And Dworkin and Wachs's (1998, 2000) comparison of mass media treatment of three stories of HIV-positive male athletes showed the ways that social class, race, and sexual orientation came into play in the media's very different framings of these three stories.

Although interpersonal sexual violence perpetrated by male athletes has received a great deal of attention from researchers, the role of sport in constituting or legitimizing institutionalized, often state-sponsored violence has received far less attention. There are stirrings, though, of a focus on how gender and sport are integral to emergent global formations (T. Miller, McKay, Lawrence, & Rowe, 2001). In particular, researchers have examined the symbiotic blurring of the language of sport with the gendered language and relations of warfare (Bairner, 2000; Malszecki & Cavar, 2001; Sabo & Jansen, 1994; Trujillo, 1995). These kinds of transnational analyses of sport and militarism should become increasingly important in this era of apparently permanent warfare.

CONCLUSION

In this chapter, I have sketched out my understanding of the trajectory of the past 30 years of research on men, gender, and sport. My points of emphasis, as well as my blind spots, are undoubtedly influenced by my own interests, political perspective, and limited standpoint as a U.S. sociologist. However, the main points that I have sketched out may be of help to current scholars' thinking about where the next fruitful directions in research might be. In particular, I hope that the underlying question of dynamic power relations between women and men, and among various groups of men, will remain foundational in studies of sport and gender. The extent to which sport continues to be contested and changed by women and by marginal groups of men, and the extent to which sport is "still a man's game" (Rowe & McKay, 1998), should provide plenty of interesting questions for future researchers.

REFERENCES

Anderson, E. (2002). Openly gay athletes: Contesting hegemonic masculinity in a homophobic environment. *Gender & Society, 16,* 860-877.

Bairner, A. (2000). After the war? Soccer, masculinity, and violence in Northern Ireland. In J. McKay, M. A. Messner, & D. F. Sabo (Eds.), *Masculinities, gender relations, and sport* (pp. 176-194). Thousand Oaks, CA: Sage.

Benedict, J., & Klein, A. (1997). Arrest and conviction rates for athletes accused of sexual assault. *Sociology of Sport Journal, 14,* 73-85.

Berry, B., & Smith, E. (2000). Race, sport, and crime: The misrepresentation of African Americans in team sports and crime. *Sociology of Sport Journal, 17,* 171-197.

Birrell, S. (1984). Studying gender and sport: A feminist perspective. In N. Theberge & P. Donnelly (Eds.), *Sport and the sociological imagination* (pp. 125-135). Fort Worth: Texas Christian University Press.

Boeringer, S. D. (1996). Influences of fraternity membership, athletics and male living arrangements on sexual aggression. *Violence Against Women, 2,* 134-147.

Boyd, T. (1997). *Am I black enough for you? Popular culture from the 'hood and beyond.* Bloomington: Indiana University Press.

Boyle, M., & McKay, J. (1995). "You leave your troubles at the gate": A case study of the exploitation of older women's labor and "leisure" in sport. *Gender & Society, 9,* 556-576.

Brackenridge, C. (1997). "He owned me basically . . .": Women's experience of sexual abuse in sport. *International Review for the Sociology of Sport, 32,* 115-130.

Bryson, L. (1987). Sport and the maintenance of masculine hegemony. *Women's Studies International Forum, 10,* 349-360.

Burstyn, V. (1999). *The rites of men: Manhood, politics and the culture of sport.* Toronto: University of Toronto Press.

Carrington, B. (1998). Sport, masculinity, and black cultural resistance. *Journal of Sport and Social Issues, 22,* 275-298.

Carrington, B. (2001). Postmodern Blackness and the celebrity sports star: Ian Wright, "race" and English identity. In D. L. Andrews & S. J. Jackson (Eds.), *Sport stars: The cultural politics of sporting celebrity* (pp. 102-123). London: Routledge.

Clarke, S. A. (1991). Fear of a black planet. *Socialist Review, 21,* 37-59.

Coakley, J. (2002). Using sports to control deviance and violence among youths: Let's be cautious and critical. In M. Gatz, M. A. Messner, & S. Ball-Rokeach (Eds.), *Paradoxes of youth and sport* (pp. 13-61). Albany: State University of New York Press.

Cole, C. L., & King, S. (1998). Representing black masculinity and urban possibilities: Racism, realism, and hoop dreams. In G. Rail (Ed.), *Sport and postmodern times* (pp. 49-86). Albany: State University of New York Press.

Connell, R. W. (1987). *Gender and power.* Stanford, CA: Stanford University Press.

Connell, R. W. (1990). An iron man: The body and some contradictions of hegemonic masculinity. In M. A. Messner & D. F. Sabo (Eds.), *Sport, men, and the gender order: Critical feminist perspectives* (pp. 83-96). Champaign, IL: Human Kinetics.

Crosset, T. (1990). Masculinity, sexuality, and the development of early modern sport. In M. A. Messner & D. F. Sabo (Eds.), *Sport, men, and the gender order: Critical feminist perspectives* (pp. 45-54). Champaign, IL: Human Kinetics.

Crosset, T. (2000). Athletic affiliation and violence against women: Toward a structural prevention project. In J. McKay, M. A. Messner, & D. F. Sabo (Eds.), *Masculinities, gender relations, and sport* (pp. 147-161). Thousand Oaks, CA: Sage.

Crosset, T. W., Benedict, J. R., & McDonald, M. (1995). Male student athletes reported for sexual assault: A survey of campus police departments and judicial affairs offices. *Journal of Sport and Social Issues, 19,* 126-140.

Crosset, T., Ptacek, J., McDonald, M., & Benedict, J. (1996). Male student athletes and violence against women: A survey of campus judicial affairs offices. *Violence Against Women, 2,* 163-179.

Curry, T. (1991). Fraternal bonding in the locker room: Pro-feminist analysis of talk about competition and women. *Sociology of Sport Journal, 8,* 119-135.

Curry, T. (2000). Booze and bar fights: A journey to the dark side of college athletics. In J. McKay, M. A. Messner, & D. F. Sabo (Eds.), *Masculinities, gender relations, and sport* (pp. 162-175). Thousand Oaks, CA: Sage.

Curry, T. J., Arriagada, P., & Cornwell, B. (2002). Images of sport in popular nonsport magazines: Power and performance versus pleasure and participation. *Sociological Perspectives, 45,* 397-415.

Davis, L. L. (1997). *The swimsuit issue and sport: Hegemonic masculinity in Sports Illustrated.* Albany: State University of New York Press.

Dunbar, M. D. (2000). Dennis Rodman—Do you feel feminine yet? Black masculinity, gender transgression, and reproductive rebellion on MTV. In J. McKay, M. A. Messner, & D. F. Sabo (Eds.), *Masculinities, gender relations, and sport* (pp. 263-285). Thousand Oaks, CA: Sage.

Dunning, E. (1986). Sport as a male preserve: Notes on the social sources of masculine identity and its transformation. *Theory, Culture & Society, 3,* 79-90.

Dworkin, S. L. (2003). A woman's place is in the ... cardiovascular room?? Gender relations, the body, and the gym. In A. Bolin & J. Granskog (Eds.), *Athletic intruders: Ethnographic research on women, culture, and exercise* (pp. 131-158). Albany: State University of New York Press.

Dworkin, S. L., & Messner, M. A. (1999). Just do ... what? Sport, bodies, gender. In J. Lorber, M. M. Ferree, & B. Hess (Eds.), *Revisioning gender* (pp. 341-361). Thousand Oaks, CA: Sage.

Dworkin, S. L., & Wachs, F. L. (1998). Disciplining the body: HIV positive athletes, media surveillance, and the policing of sexuality. *Sociology of Sport Journal, 15,* 1-20.

Dworkin, S. L., & Wachs, F. L. (2000). The morality/manhood paradox: Masculinity, sport, and the media. In J. McKay, M. A. Messner, & D. F. Sabo (Eds.), *Masculinities, gender relations, and sport* (pp. 47-66). Thousand Oaks, CA: Sage.

Eastman, S. T., & Billings, A. C. (2001). Sportscasting and sports reporting: The power of gender bias. *Journal of Sport and Social Issues, 24,* 192-213.

Eveslage, S., & Delaney, K. (1998). Trash talkin' at Hardwick High: A case study of insult talk on a boys' basketball team. *International Review for the Sociology of Sport, 33,* 239-253.

Farrell, W. (1974). *The liberated man.* New York: Random House.

Fine, G. A. (1987). *With the boys: Little League baseball and preadolescent culture.* Chicago: University of Chicago Press.

Fritner, M. P., & Rubinson, L. (1993). Acquaintance rape: The influence of alcohol, fraternity membership and sports team membership. *Journal of Sex Education and Therapy, 19,* 272-284.

Gruneau, R., & Whitson, D. (1994). *Hockey night in Canada: Sport, identities, and cultural politics.* Toronto: Garamond.

Hall, M. A. (1984). Towards a feminist analysis of gender inequality in sport. In N. Theberge & P. Donnelly (Eds.), *Sport and the sociological imagination.* Fort Worth: Texas Christian University Press.

Hartmann, D. (2001). Notes on midnight basketball and the cultural politics of recreation, race, and at-risk urban youth. *Journal of Sport and Social Issues, 25,* 339-371.

Hasbrook, C. (1999). Young children's social constructions of physicality and gender. In J. Coakley & P. Donnelly (Eds.), *Inside sports* (pp. 7-16). London: Routledge.

Hasbrook, C. A., & Harris, O. (2000). Wrestling with gender: Physicality and masculinities among inner-city first and second graders. In J. McKay, M. A. Messner, & D. F. Sabo (Eds.), *Masculinities, gender relations, and sport* (pp. 13-30). Thousand Oaks, CA: Sage.

Henry, J., & Comeaux, H. (1999). Gender egalitarianism in coed sport: A case study of American soccer. *International Review for the Sociology of Sport, 34,* 277-290.

James, C. R. L. (1983). *Beyond a boundary.* New York: Pantheon.

Kane, M. J. (1995). Resistance/transformation of the oppositional binary: Exposing sport as a continuum. *Journal of Sport and Social Issues, 19,* 191-218.

Kane, M. J., & Disch, L. J. (1993). Sexual violence and the reproduction of male power in the locker room: The "Lisa Olsen incident." *Sociology of Sport Journal, 10,* 331-352.

Kimmel, M. S. (1990). Baseball and the reconstitution of American masculinity, 1880-1920. In M. A. Messner & D. F. Sabo (Eds.), *Sport, men, and the gender order: Critical feminist perspectives* (pp. 55-66). Champaign, IL: Human Kinetics.

Klein, A. (1993). *Little big men: Bodybuilding subculture and gender construction.* Albany: State University of New York Press.

Klein, A. (2000). Dueling machos: Masculinity and sport in Mexican baseball. In J. McKay, M. A. Messner, & D. F. Sabo (Eds.), *Masculinities, gender relations, and sport* (pp. 67-85). Thousand Oaks, CA: Sage.

Koss, M., & Gaines, J. (1993). The prediction of sexual aggression by alcohol use, athletic participation and fraternity affiliation. *Journal of Interpersonal Violence, 8,* 94-108.

Kusz, K. (2001). Andre Agassi and Generation X: Reading white masculinity in 1990s America. In D. L. Andrews & S. J. Jackson (Eds.), *Sport stars: The cultural politics of sporting celebrity* (pp. 51-69). London: Routledge.

Kusz, K. (2003). BMX, extreme sports, and the white male backlash. In R. E. Rinehart & S. Sydnor (Eds.), *To the extreme: Alternative sport, inside and out* (pp. 153-175). Albany: State University of New York Press.

Laberge, S., & Albert, M. (2000). Conceptions of masculinity and gender transgressions in sport among adolescent boys: Hegemony, contestation, and the social class dynamic. In J. McKay, M. A. Messner, & D. F. Sabo (Eds.), *Masculinities, gender relations, and sport* (pp. 195-221). Thousand Oaks, CA: Sage.

Lorber, J. (1996). Beyond the binaries: Depolarizing the categories of sex, sexuality, and gender. *Sociological Inquiry, 66,* 143-159.

Majors, R. (1990). Cool pose: Black masculinity in sports. In M. A. Messner & D. Sabo (Eds.), *Sport, men, and the gender order: Critical feminist perspectives* (pp. 109-114). Champaign, IL: Human Kinetics.

Malszecki, G., & Cavar, T. (2001). Men, masculinities, war, and sport. In N. Mandell (Ed.), *Feminist issues: Race, class, and sexuality* (3rd ed., pp. 166-192). Toronto: Pearson Education Canada.

Mangan, J. A. (1986). *The games ethic and imperialism: Aspects of the diffusion of an ideal.* New York: Viking Penguin.

McDonald, M. G. (1999). Unnecessary roughness: Gender and racial politics in domestic violence media events. *Sociology of Sport Journal, 16,* 111-133.

McDonald, M. G., & Andrews, D. L. (2001). Michael Jordan: Corporate sport and postmodern celebrityhood. In D. L. Andrews & S. J. Jackson (Eds.), *Sports stars: The cultural politics of sporting celebrity* (pp. 20-35). London: Routledge.

McKay, J. (1991). *No pain, no gain: Sport in Australian culture.* Englewood Cliffs, NJ: Prentice-Hall.

McKay, J. (1993). "Marked men" and "wanton women": The politics of naming sexual "deviance" in sport. *Journal of Men's Studies, 2,* 69-87.

McKay, J. (1997). *Managing gender: Affirmative action and organizational power in Australian, Canadian, and New Zealand sport.* Albany: State University of New York Press.

McKay, J., & Rowe, D. (1997). Field of soaps: Rupert vs. Kerry as masculine melodrama. *Social Text, 50,* 69-86.

McPherson, D. G. (2002). Sport, youth, violence and the media: An activist athlete's perspective. In M. Gatz, M. A. Messner, & S. Ball-Rokeach (Eds.), *Paradoxes of youth and sport* (pp. 241-247). Albany: State University of New York Press.

Messner, M. A. (1988). Sports and male domination: The female athlete as contested ideological terrain. *Sociology of Sport Journal, 5,* 197-211.

Messner, M. A. (1992). *Power at play: Sports and the problem of masculinity.* Boston: Beacon.

Messner, M. A. (2000). Barbie girls vs. sea monsters: Children constructing gender. *Gender & Society, 14,* 765-784.

Messner, M. A. (2002). *Taking the field: Women, men, and sports.* Minneapolis: University of Minnesota Press.

Messner, M. A., Dunbar, M., & Hunt, D. (2000). The televised sports manhood formula. *Journal of Sport and Social Issues, 24,* 380-394.

Messner, M. A., Duncan, M. C., & Cooky, C. (2003). Silence, sports bras, and wrestling porn: The treatment of women in televised sports news and highlights. *Journal of Sport and Social Issues, 27,* 38-51.

Messner, M. A., Duncan, M. C., & Wachs, F. L. (1996). The gender of audience-building: Televised coverage of men's and women's NCAA basketball. *Sociological Inquiry, 66,* 422-439.

Messner, M. A., & Sabo, D. F. (Eds.). (1990). *Sport, men, and the gender order: Critical feminist perspectives.* Champaign, IL: Human Kinetics.

Messner, M. A., & Stevens, M. (2002). Confronting male athletes' sexual violence against women. In M. Gatz, M. A. Messner, & S. Ball-Rokeach (Eds.), *Paradoxes of youth and sport* (pp. 225-240). Albany: State University of New York Press.

Miller, K. E., Barnes, G. M., Sabo, D. F., Melnick, M. J., & Farrell, M. P. (2002). Anabolic-androgenic steroid use and other adolescent problem behaviors: Rethinking the male athlete assumption. *Sociological Perspectives, 45,* 467-490.

Miller, K. E., Sabo, D. F., Melnick, M. J., Farrell, M. P., & Barnes, G. M. (2000). *The Women's Sports Foundation report: Health risks and the teen athlete.* East Meadow, NY: Women's Sports Foundation.

Miller, T. (2001). *Sportsex.* Philadelphia: Temple University Press.

Miller, T., McKay, J., Lawrence, G., & Rowe, D. (2001). *Globalization and sport: Playing the world.* Thousand Oaks, CA: Sage.

Naison, M. (1972, July/August). Sports and the American empire. *Radical America,* 95-96, 107-110.

Pronger, B. (1990). *The arena of masculinity: Sports, homosexuality, and the meaning of sex.* New York: St. Martin's.

Pronger, B. (2000). Homosexuality and sport: Who's winning? In J. McKay, M. A. Messner, & D. F. Sabo (Eds.), *Masculinities, gender relations, and sport* (pp. 222-244). Thousand Oaks, CA: Sage.

Robinson, L. (1998). *Crossing the line: Violence and sexual assault in Canada's national sport.* Toronto: McClelland & Stewart.

Rowe, D., & McKay, J. (1998). Sport: Still a man's game. *Journal of Interdisciplinary Gender Studies, 3,* 113-128.

Sabo, D. (1985). Sport, patriarchy, and male identity: New questions about men and sport. *Arena Review, 9,* 1-30.

Sabo, D. (1994). Pigskin, patriarchy and pain. In M. A. Messner & D. F. Sabo, *Sex, violence and power in sport: Rethinking masculinity* (pp. 82-88). Freedom, CA: Crossing Press.

Sabo, D. (2001). Doing time, doing masculinity: Sports in prison. In D. Sabo, T. Kupers, & W. London (Eds.), *Prison masculinities* (pp. 61-66). Philadelphia: Temple University Press.

Sabo, D., & Gordon, D. F. (Eds.). (1995). *Men's health and illness: Gender, power, and the body.* Thousand Oaks, CA: Sage.

Sabo, D., Gray, P., & Moore, L. (2000). Domestic violence and televised athletic events: "It's a man thing." In J. McKay, M. A. Messner, & D. F. Sabo (Eds.), *Masculinities, gender relations, and sport* (pp. 127-146). Thousand Oaks, CA: Sage.

Sabo, D., & Jansen, S. C. (1994). Seen but not heard: Images of black men in sports media. In M. A. Messner & D. F. Sabo, *Sex, violence and power in sports: Rethinking masculinity.* Freedom, CA: Crossing Press.

Sabo, D. F., & Runfola, R. (1980). *Jock: Sports and male identity.* Englewood Cliffs, NJ: Prentice-Hall.

Schafer, W. S. (1975). Sport and male sex role socialization. *Sport Sociology Bulletin, 4,* 47-54.

Shakib, S., & Dunbar, M. D. (2002). The social construction of female and male high school basketball participation: Reproducing the gender order through a two-tiered sporting institution. *Sociological Perspectives, 45,* 353-379.

Theberge, N. (1981). A critique of critiques: Radical and feminist writings on sport. *Social Forces, 60,* 341-353.

Thompson, S. (1999). *Mother's taxi: Sport and women's labor.* Albany: State University of New York Press.

Thorne, B. (1993). *Gender play: Girls and boys in school.* New Brunswick, NJ: Rutgers University Press.

Tracy, A. J., & Erkut, S. (2002). Gender and race patterns in the pathways from sports participation to self-esteem. *Sociological Perspectives, 45,* 445-466.

Trujillo, N. (1991). Hegemonic masculinity on the mound: Media representations of Nolan Ryan and American sports culture. *Critical Studies in Mass Communication, 8,* 290-309.

Trujillo, N. (1995). Machines, missiles, and men: Images of the male body on ABC's *Monday Night Football. Sociology of Sport Journal, 12,* 403-423.

Videon, T. M. (2002). Who plays and who benefits: Gender, interscholastic athletics, and academic outcomes. *Sociological Perspectives, 45,* 415-444.

Wachs, F. L. (2002). Leveling the playing field: Negotiating gendered rules in coed softball. *Journal of Sport and Social Issues, 26,* 300-316.

Wachs, F. L. (2003). "I was there . . .": Gendered limitations, expectations, and strategic assumptions in the world of co-ed softball. In A. Bolin & J. Granskog (Eds.), *Athletic intruders: Ethnographic research on women, culture, and exercise* (pp. 177-200). Albany: State University of New York Press.

Wenner, L. A. (1998). In search of the sports bar: Masculinity, alcohol, sports, and the mediation of public space. In G. Rail (Ed.), *Sport and postmodern times* (pp. 303-332). Albany: State University of New York Press.

Whannel, G. (2002). *Media sports stars: Masculinities and moralities.* New York: Routledge.

Wheaton, B., & Tomlinson, A. (1998). The changing gender order in sport? The case of windsurfing subcultures. *Journal of Sport and Social Issues, 22,* 252-274.

White, P. G., Young, K., & McTeer, W. G. (1995). Sport, masculinity, and the injured body. In D. Sabo & D. F. Gordon (Eds.), *Men's health and illness: Gender, power, and the body* (pp. 158-182). Thousand Oaks, CA: Sage.

Whitson, D. (1990). Sport in the social construction of masculinity. In M. A. Messner & D. F. Sabo (Eds.), *Sport, men, and the gender order: Critical feminist perspectives* (pp. 19-30). Champaign, IL: Human Kinetics.

Willis, P. (1983). Women in sport in ideology. In J. Hargreaves (Ed.), *Sport, culture, and ideology* (pp. 117-135). London: Routledge & Kegan Paul.

Young, K. (2002). From "sports violence" to "sports crime": Aspects of violence, law, and gender in the sports process. In M. Gatz, M. A. Messner, & S. Ball-Rokeach (Eds.), *Paradoxes of youth and sport* (pp. 207-224). Albany: State University of New York Press.

Young, K., & White, P. (2000). Researching sports injury: Reconstructing dangerous masculinities. In J. McKay, M. A. Messner, & D. F. Sabo (Eds.), *Masculinities, gender relations, and sport* (pp. 108-126). Thousand Oaks, CA: Sage.

19

THE STUDY OF MASCULINITIES AND MEN'S HEALTH

An Overview

DON SABO

S cholars and researchers have begun to study the influences of gender on men's health and illness (Courtenay & Keeling, 2000; Sabo & Gordon, 1995; Schofield, Connell, Walker, Wood, & Butland, 2000). The growth of women's health movements in the 1960s and 1970s fueled systematic and interdisciplinary studies of gender and health, and by the mid-1980s, the focus on gender had become a recognizable aspect of epidemiology, medical sociology, and interdisciplinary studies of psychosocial aspects of illness (Lorber, 1997; Stillion, 1985; Verbrugge, 1985; Waldron, 1983). However, most of this early work on gender and health revolved almost exclusively around women. For some men, the reconceptualization of gender that was initiated by feminist scholars and activists became the inspiration for the emergence of "men's studies" in the 1970s and 1980s. As the new men's studies took shape in men's minds and politics, so too did some of these early male scholars begin to explore how conformity to traditional masculinity sometimes increased men's physical health risks and impoverished their emotional lives. The theory

in men's health studies generally followed the conceptual trajectory of interdisciplinary gender studies and, more particularly, the study of men and multiple masculinities (Connell, 2000; Courtenay, 2000; Sabo, 1998).

Today, the study of men's health has expanded from a handful of isolated scholars and activists to an international array of researchers, health promoters, health educators, and specialists working in world health organizations, government programs, health care delivery systems, academia, public health offices, and community-based organizations. In academia, a nascent yet recognizable subfield within gender studies has taken shape. There is a growing awareness in social scientific and biomedical circles that males share specific health risks and needs; for example, a nurse working in a prostate cancer clinic thinks in terms of "men's health" as well as "women's health," and a reproductive health educator in Toronto, Canada, develops a program to teach adolescent males about safe sex. "Gender-specific health" is becoming a biomedical specialty (Legato, 2000b). Most recently, men's health professionals and scholars have begun to think about their work within global frameworks, communicating and networking across national and cultural boundaries (Courtenay, 2002). This global network is more a vision than a reality, but men's health studies promise to expand in future decades.

This chapter renders an overview of the history and development of the study of men's health, along with providing a discussion of key theoretical models and some of men's gender-specific health issues. Several groups of boys and men with unique health needs are identified, and finally, some global frameworks for understanding men's health are presented. This overview is incomplete because the subfield of men's health studies has gotten too large, complex, and global for any one person to fully monitor, so my primary focus on North American issues and developments is evident.

Origins and History

North American research and writing on men's health during the 1960s generally collapsed men and masculinity into a demographic category. Biomedical researchers reported variations in morbidity and mortality "by sex," and disease rates between "the sexes" were compared and contrasted. A historical irony had unfolded. The bulk of academic scientific medical research after World War II had focused mainly on men because most physicians were men, men dominated medical research, and it was men and not women who were selected as research subjects for most studies (Legato, 2000a, 2000b). Not only did the patriarchal biases of male medical researchers produce myopic and sexist views of women, but they also reduced the personal and cultural aspects of men's lives to biological and statistical categories. The gendered aspects of *both* women's and men's health behaviors and outcomes were not discerned.

The growth of women's health movements during the 1970s challenged the patriarchal status quo. Second Wave feminists made many researchers and health practitioners acutely aware of gender relations. They decried men's domination of health care delivery systems, exposed sexism in the diagnosis and treatment of women, and explored how women's adoption of certain feminine traits and behaviors negatively affected physical and mental health. Women's

pioneering analysis of the links between gender and health, however, did not include critical scrutiny of men's health, and only a few *male* writers in the early "men's liberation" movement alluded to men's health issues (Nichols, 1975; Snodgrass, 1977). Some prominent writers focused on men's health issues such as the risks imposed by violence and overinvestment in work and career (Farrell, 1975; Feigen-Fasteau, 1974; Goldberg, 1976, 1979). Sabo (2000) described the thinking around men's health in the 1970s as "exploratory," that is, "tangentially informed by feminist theory and politics, and conceptually organized around the general premise that men's conformity to traditional masculinity produce certain health deficits" (p. 134).

During the 1980s, male scholars elaborated the deficit model of men's health with greater zeal and detail. The emergence of profeminist men's movements, the growth of the "new men's studies" (Brod, 1987) and research on "men and masculinity," and the rapid growth of sex role theory in mainline social sciences formed a conceptual framework for explaining how conformity to traditional masculinity elevated health risks. Bravado in boys was linked to fighting and physical injury, drinking, and automobile accidents, while the "demands of the male role," stress, and symptom denial were tied to men's risk for coronary heart disease (Harrison, Chin, & Ficcarrotto, 1992). Stillion (1985) explored differences in the ways females and males perceived sickness and death. Sabo, Brown, and Smith (1986) documented how men's adherence to the traditional husband-provider role shaped their experiences with a female partner's breast cancer and mastectomy. Jackson's (1990) critical autobiography explored how his masculine identity suffused his experiences of being diagnosed and treated for heart disease. The growth of gay rights activism in the 1980s also fueled public health initiatives and educational efforts regarding gay and bisexual men. There were protests against governmental and homophobic indifference to the health needs of gay and bisexual men, and community-based awareness grew concerning the need for safe sex and the dangers of HIV transmission. In contrast, very little research or health initiatives focused on the health needs of poor men or men of color.

During the 1990s, the study of men's health grew rapidly, integrating clinical and epidemiological research findings into progressively interdisciplinary conceptual frameworks that highlighted the workings of gender (Courtenay, 2002). Analyses of men's health closely followed theoretical developments in what in various scholarly circles were called men's studies, the new men's studies, or critical studies of men and masculinity. The use of critical feminist perspectives to analyze men, masculinity, and health emerged as "men's health studies" (Sabo & Gordon, 1995). Building on critiques of sex role theory's narrow focus on gender identity, socialization, and conformity to role expectations, critical feminist thinkers argued that men's health is profoundly affected by power differences that shape relationships between men and women, women and women, and men and men (Courtenay, 2000). Connell's (1987, 1995) concept of "hegemonic masculinity" forged a conceptualization of men's gender identity as actively worked out, revamped, and maintained by individuals who are situated in socially and historically constructed webs of power relations—and it is amid these myriad webs that health processes and outcomes were understood to take shape. Critical analyses of men's health increasingly recognized the "plurality of masculinities" and the intersections among gender, class, race/ethnicity, and sexual orientation. Men's health behaviors unfolded within multiple hierarchies composed of rich and poor men, First World and Third World men, straight and gay men, and professional men and those who labored in factories or on farms.

Most recently, relational theories of gender and health have emerged that recognize that men's and women's health outcomes are intricately interconnected (Sabo, 1999; Schofield et al., 2000). Most scholars have focused on health and illness *within* each sex rather than *between* the sexes. As Schofield et al. (2000) stated it, "A gender relations approach is one which proposes that men's and women's interactions with each other, and the circumstances under which they interact, contribute significantly to health opportunities and constraints" (p. 251). Sabo (1999) has developed a model for assessing the health impacts of various relationships between the sexes. He argues that a "positive gendered health synergy" exists where the pattern of gender relations promotes favorable health processes or outcomes for both sexes; for example, a husband-father's contributions to child care and domestic work free up the wife-mother to pursue a fitness agenda. In contrast, a "negative gendered health synergy"

occurs where the pattern of gender relations is associated with unfavorable health processes or outcomes for one or both sexes; for example, a depressed male batters his wife, triggering physical injury and emotional trauma.

Courtenay (2002) extends the vision of relational models this way:

> These models would take into account the dynamic intersection of various health determinants, such as those among biological functioning, environmental pollution, psychological well-being, social and cultural norms, genetic predisposition, institutional policies, political climates, and economic disparities. (p. 9)

Such "relationships," he argues, cover a challenging span of human interactions and social structures, including relations between men and women, men and men, individuals and institutional structures, cultures, and nations around the world. (More is said about globalization and men's health later in this chapter.)

SIFTING THROUGH DEMOGRAPHICS OF DIFFERENCE

Ashley Montagu (1953) long ago observed the marked differences in the mortality rates between males and females. Because males died earlier than females throughout the entire human life span, from conception to old age, he argued that men were biologically inferior to women. Epidemiological data show, for example, that males in the United States are about 12% more likely than females to experience prenatal death and about 130% more likely to die during the first three months of life. Table 19.1 illustrates the disparities between male and female infant mortality rates (i.e., death during the first year of life) across a 50-year span of the 20th century. Men's greater mortality rates persist through the "age 85" subgroup and, as Table 19.2 shows, male death rates are higher than female rates for 12 of the 15 leading causes of death in the United States (National Center for Health Statistics, 2002).

Whereas biological differences between the sexes probably influence the variation in mortality rates, social and cultural processes are also at play. For example, women's relative advantage over men in life expectancy was rather small in

Table 19.1   Gender and Infant Mortality Rates for the United States, 1940-1989

Year	Both Sexes	Males	Females
1940	47.0	52.5	41.3
1950	29.2	32.8	25.5
1960	26.0	29.3	22.6
1970	20.0	22.4	17.5
1980	12.6	13.9	11.2
1989	9.8	10.8	8.8

SOURCE: Adapted from Centers for Disease Control and Prevention, *Monthly Vital Statistics Report*, 40(8, Suppl. 2), p. 41.

NOTE: Rates are for infant (under 1 year) deaths per 1,000 live births for all races.

Table 19.2   Ratio of Male to Female Age-Adjusted Death Rates, for the 15 Leading Causes of Death for the Total U.S. Population in 2002

Rank	Cause of Death	Number of Total Deaths	Percentage	Male to Female Ratio
1	Diseases of heart	710,760	29.6	1.4
2	Malignant neoplasms	553,091	23.0	1.5
3	Cerebrovascular diseases	167,661	7.0	1.0
4	Chronic lower respiratory diseases	122,009	5.1	1.4
5	Accidents (unintentional injuries)	97,900	4.1	2.2
6	Diabetes mellitus	69,301	2.9	1.2
7	Influenza and pneumonia	65,313	2.7	1.3
8	Alzheimer's disease	49,558	2.1	0.8
9	Nephritis, nephritic syndrome, nephrosis	37,251	1.5	1.4
10	Septicemia	31,224	1.3	1.2
11	Intentional harm (suicide)	29,350	1.2	4.5
12	Chronic liver disease and cirrhosis	26,552	1.1	2.2
13	Essential hypertension and hypertensive renal disease	18,073	0.8	1.0
14	Assault (homicide)	16,765	0.7	3.3
15	Pneumonitis due to solids and liquids	16,636	0.7	1.8

SOURCE: Adapted from National Center for Health Statistics, *National Vital Statistics Report*, 50(15), September 16, 2002, Table C.

the early 20th century (Verbrugge & Winegard, 1987; Waldron, 1995). As the century progressed, female mortality declined faster than male mortality, thus widening the gender gap in life expectancy. While women benefited from decreased maternal mortality, the rise in men's life expectancy was slowed by higher rates of heart disease and lung cancer, which, in turn, were owed mainly to increased smoking among males. In recent decades, the differences between men's and women's mortality rates have narrowed, partly because women have increasingly taken up smoking and other risk behaviors that elevated their rates of heart disease and certain cancers. The historical variations in gender differences in life expectancy in the United States, Canada, and other post-industrial nations suggest that both biology and sociocultural processes shape men's and women's mortality. Waldron (1983) speculated that gender-related behaviors contribute more than biogenic factors to the variations in mortality between the sexes.

Although females generally outlive males, they report higher rates of acute illnesses such as respiratory conditions, infective and parasitic conditions, and digestive system disorders than males do. In contrast, males report higher rates of injuries than females, with injuries related to socialization and lifestyle differences, such as working in manufacturing jobs, involvement with contact sports, and risky occupations (Cypress, 1981; Dawson & Adams, 1987; Givens, 1979). Cockerham (1995) wondered if women really do experience more sickness than men, or whether men are less likely than women to report symptoms and seek medical care. He stated, "The best evidence indicates that the overall differences in morbidity are real" and, further, that they are due to a mixture of biological, psychological, and social influences (p. 42).

Understanding the disparate morbidity and mortality rates between men and women is further complicated by the emphasis on gender differences, which, ironically, has been part of traditional patriarchal beliefs *and* much Second Wave feminist thought. Whereas patriarchal culture exaggerated differences between men and women, and masculinity and femininity, Second Wave feminists theorized a "presumed oppositionality" between men and women, and masculinity and femininity (Digby, 1998). Epidemiologically, however, the emphasis on differences can sometimes hide similarities. For example, MacIntyre, Hunt, and Sweeting (1996) questioned the conventional wisdom that in industrialized countries men die earlier than women, and that women get sick more often than men. They studied health data sets from both Scotland and the United Kingdom and found that, after controlling for age, statistically significant differences between many of men's and women's self-reported psychological and physical symptoms disappeared. They concluded that *both* differences and similarities in men's and women's health exist and, furthermore, that changes in gender roles during recent decades "may produce changes in men's and women's experiences of health and illness" (p. 623).

In summary, although some gender differences in mortality and morbidity are associated with biological or genetic processes, or with reproductive biology (e.g., testicular or prostate cancer), it is increasingly evident that the largest variations in men's and women's health are related to shifting social, economic, cultural, and behavioral factors (Courtenay, McCreary, & Merighi, 2002; Kandrack, Grant, & Segall, 1991). For this reason, Schofield et al. (2000) critiqued the prevailing "men's health discourse," which too often equates "men's health" to the delivery of biomedical services to men, or to private sector marketing services or products designed to enhance "men's health." They reject lumping "all men" into statistical comparisons between men's and women's health outcomes because, mainly, it is disadvantaged men (e.g., poor men, men of color, uninsured men, gay men) who disproportionately contribute to men's collective higher mortality and morbidity rates in comparison to women. As Keeling (2000) writes, "So it is that there is no single, unitary men's health—instead, sexual orientation, race, socioeconomic status, and culture all intervene to affect the overall health status of each man and of men of various classes or groups" (p. 101).

CURRENT MEN'S HEALTH ISSUES

A variety of health issues have received particular attention from researchers and men's health advocates. Some issues that have received particular attention in North America are discussed below.

Alcohol Use

Although social and medical problems stemming from alcohol abuse involve both sexes, males constitute the largest segment of alcohol abusers. Some researchers observe connections between the traditional male role and alcohol abuse. Isenhart and Silversmith (1994) showed how, in a variety of occupational contexts, expectations surrounding masculinity encourage heavy drinking while working or socializing during after-work or off-duty hours. Some predominantly male occupational groups are known to engage in high rates of alcohol consumption, such as longshoremen (Hitz, 1973), salesmen (Cosper, 1979), and military personnel (Pursch, 1976).

Findings from a Harvard School of Public Health (Wechler, Davenport, Dowdell, Moeykens, & Castillo, 1994) survey of 17,600 students at 140 colleges found that 44% engaged in "binge drinking," defined as drinking five drinks in rapid succession for males and 4 drinks for females. Males were more apt to report binge drinking during the past 2 weeks than females—50% and 39%, respectively. Sixty percent of the males who binge-drank three or more times in the past 2 weeks reported driving after drinking, compared with 49% of their female counterparts, thus increasing their risk for accident, injury, and death. Compared with non-binge drinkers, binge drinkers were seven times more likely to engage in unprotected sex, thus elevating the risk for unwanted pregnancy and sexually transmitted disease.

Binge drinking among all adults in the United States increased 17% between 1993 and 2001, with a steeper 56% incline among 18- to 20-year-olds. Whereas males averaged 12.5 bingeing episodes in 2001, females averaged 2.7 episodes (Centers for Disease Control and Prevention [CDC], 2002b). Alcohol use is a primary factor in car crashes among males (Wilcox & Marks, 1994), which contributed to 78% of fatal injuries among younger males in 1995 (Maternal and Child Health Bureau, 1997). Worldwide, tens of thousands of people die and are seriously injured annually in highway accidents (Roberts & Mohan, 2002). Breen (2002) indicated that road crashes are the leading cause of death in persons under 45 years old in the European Union. It may be that males are more apt than females to equate risk taking with manliness, to combine alcohol use with sensation seeking, or simply to travel more often after drinking. For all U.S. males, the age-adjusted death rate from automobile accidents in 1998 was 29.3/100,000 for African American males and 26/100,000 for Caucasian males, compared with 9.4/100,000 for African American females and 10.7/100,000 for Caucasian females (U.S. Census Bureau, 2001).

The efforts of public health advocates to promote sobriety among male adolescents and responsible drinking among adult males can be complicated by cultural equations between manhood and alcohol consumption. Mass media often sensationalize and glorify links between booze and male bravado. Postman, Nystrom, Strate, and Weingartner (1987) studied the thematic content of 40 beer commercials and identified a variety of stereotypical portrayals of the male role that were used to promote beer drinking, among them reward for a job well done; manly activities that feature strength, risk, and daring; male friendship and esprit de vcorps; and romantic success with women. The researchers estimated that, between the ages of 2 and 18, children view about 100,000 beer commercials.

Anabolic Steroid Use

Some males use anabolic steroids to build muscle mass, to augment strength, to enhance athletic performance, and/or to engage in extreme dietary practices. Users are at risk of side effects that can include acne, liver disease, cardiovascular disease, atrophy of the testicles, depression, and increased aggression. About 5% to 10% of U.S. male adolescents (and about 2.5% of female adolescents) have indicated they use anabolic steroids (American Academy of Pediatrics, 1997). An estimated 375,000 males and 175,000 females were using anabolic steroids in 1995 (Yesalis, Barsukiewicz, Kopstein, & Bahrke, 1997). Although it is common to portray anabolic steroid use among adolescents as mainly a problem for male athletes, about 40% of steroid users do not play sports, and approximately 29% are female (Miller, Barnes, Sabo, Melnick, & Farrell, 2002a). Whether they are athletes or not, male adolescents who use anabolic steroids also have greater risks for other problem behaviors such as illicit drug use, alcohol use, aggression, suicidal ideation/behavior, and pathogenic weight-loss behavior (Miller, Barnes, Sabo, Melnick, & Farrell, 2002b).

Klein (1993, 1995) studied the links between anabolic steroid use, overtraining, and muscularity in the bodybuilding subculture, where masculinity is equated to muscle and where the psychosocial drive to be big and powerful is prominent. Bodybuilders often put their personal health at risk in pursuit of ideal masculinity (Glassner, 1989; Messner & Sabo, 1994).

Erectile Disorders

Erectile Dysfunction Disorder (EDD), also known as impotence, occurs when a man is unable to sustain an erection sufficiently firm enough for intercourse or through to orgasm. In the past, the issue of male impotence was either joked about or cloaked by cultural silence. However, the recent introduction of Viagra to the medical marketplace has spurred discussion about erectile disorders, which, according to some estimates, afflict between 10 and 30 million U.S. men (Krane, Goldstein, & Saenz de Tejada, 1989; National Institutes of Health, 1993). One nationwide study of noninstitutionalized, healthy American men between the ages of 40 and 70 years found that 52% reported minimal, moderate, or complete impotence; the prevalence of erectile disorders increased with age, and 9% of respondents reported complete impotence (Feldman, Goldstein, Hatzichristou, Krane, & McKinlay, 1994). Ayta, McKinlay, and Krane (1995) used data from the Massachusetts Male Aging Study and the United Nations to estimate that 322 million men worldwide will suffer from EDD in the year 2025.

Although erectile disorders may result from masculine inadequacy or lack of psychological well-being, the causes of impotence are now believed to stem mainly from physiological rather than emotional factors (Zilbergeld, 1999). EDD is often tied to other physiological disorders such as hypertension, heart disease, diabetes, and excessive alcohol use (Fedele et al., 2001). Today, diagnosis and treatment of erectile disorders typically combines psychological and medical assessment (Ackerman & Carey, 1995).

HIV/AIDS

Human immunodeficiency virus (HIV) infection became a leading cause of death among North American males in the 1980s. By 1990, HIV infection was the second leading cause of death among men aged 25 to 44, compared with the sixth leading cause of death among same-age women ("Update: Mortality Attributable to HIV Infection/AIDS," 1993). Among reported cases of acquired immunodeficiency syndrome (AIDS) for adolescent and adult men in 2000, more than half were men who had sex with other men, 25% were intravenous drug users, and about 14% were exposed through heterosexual sexual contact. For cases of AIDS among adolescent and adult women in 2000, 33% were intravenous drug users and 64% were infected through heterosexual sexual contact (CDC, 2002a).

Perceptions of the AIDS epidemic in the United States and its victims have been tinctured by sexual attitudes, homophobia, and the stigma associated with illicit drug use. Thoughts and feelings about men with AIDS are also influenced by attitudes toward race, ethnicity, and poverty. Just as men and women of color are overrepresented in poverty, so also are they overrepresented with regard to HIV/AIDS prevalence. In the United States, HIV/AIDS is most prevalent among poor persons, and the 1995 incidence of AIDS was 6.5 times greater for African Americans and 4.0 times greater for Hispanics than it was for whites (Garrett, 1994). (Also see Table 19.3 for comparisons.) HIV/AIDS has erroneously been dubbed a "minority disease," yet it is not racial biology that confers risk for HIV/AIDS, but rather behavioral adaptations to cultural and economic circumstances that include community disintegration, unemployment, homelessness, eroding urban tax bases, mental illness, substance use, and criminalization (R. Wallace, 1991; Zierler & Krieger, 1997). For example, males (who composed the majority of homeless persons in New York City during the 1980s) were prone to drug addiction, which in turn was linked to HIV infection (Ron & Rogers, 1989; Torres, Mani, Altholz, & Brickner, 1990).

Pain and Symptom Denial

Studies done in the United States revealed differences between the ways men and women experience and perceive pain. Generally, boys are taught not to express their pain, to be tough and deny pain, whereas girls are encouraged to be vulnerable to pain and to be openly emotional in the midst of pain (Hoffmann & Tarzian, 2001). Adults often respond more to girls' pain than boys' pain, and girls begin to have more pain episodes than boys at very young ages (Keefe et al., 2000). There is some evidence that men with more masculine traits tend to have higher pain thresholds than those who are less masculine (M. Robinson, Riley, & Myers, 2000; Wise, Price, Myers, Heft, & Robinson, 2002). Whereas women's coping strategies around pain

Table 19.3   AIDS Cases Reported in 2000 and Estimated 2000 Population, by Race/Ethnicity, United States

Race/Ethnicity	Percentage of AIDS Cases Reported	Percentage of the U.S. Population
Asian/Pacific Islander	1	4
American Indian/Alaska Native	1	1
Black, not Hispanic	47	12
Hispanic	19	13
White, not Hispanic	32	71

Total AIDS cases $N = 42,156$
Total population $N = 285,863,000$

SOURCE: Centers for Disease Control and Prevention. Retrieved June 4, 2002, from http://www.cdc.gov/hiv/graphics/images/1178/1178-12.htm

NOTE: Includes 117 persons with unknown race/ethnicity.

revolve more around emotions, men often deny pain, suppress the emotional aspects of pain, and take an action-oriented approach to coping with pain (Keough & Herdenfeldt, 2002).

Prostate Cancer

As men pass through middle age, they are apt to experience benign prostatic hyperplasia, an enlargement of the prostate gland that is associated with symptoms such as dribbling after urination, frequent urination, or incontinence. Others may develop infections (prostatitis) or malignant prostatic hyperplasia (prostate cancer). On average, one in three U.S. males will develop prostate cancer in his lifetime, and it is the second leading cause of cancer deaths in American men (Mayo Clinic, 2003). Prostate cancer is more common than lung cancer (Martin, 1990). One in 10 men develop this cancer by age 85, with African American males showing a higher prevalence rate than their Caucasian counterparts (Greco & Blank, 1993). Lack of economic resources and reduced access to health care lead many African American males to delay seeking treatment for prostate symptoms, which in turn increases their mortality rates compared with Caucasian males (Cooley & Jennings-Dozier, 1998; Freedman, 1998).

Treatments for prostate problems depend on the specific diagnosis and may range from medication to radiation and surgery. Some invasive surgical treatments for prostate cancer can produce incontinence and impotence. Researchers have begun to explore men's psychosocial reactions and adjustments to treatments for prostate cancer (Gray, Fitch, Phillips, Labrecque, & Fergus, 2000; Stanford et al., 2000). Support groups, established in many North American cities, provide male survivors with information, camaraderie, and emotional connection (Gray, 2003).

Suicide

It is estimated that 80% of suicide completers in the United States are male (Moscicki, 1994). Suicide is the third leading cause of death among Americans aged 15 to 24, with boys incurring higher rates of completion than girls (Portner, 2001; Stillion, 1995). One explanation for boys' higher rates of lethality from suicide attempts is that males adopt more traditionally "masculine" methods (e.g., use of guns or knives) and psychological postures (e.g., aggression, goal directedness, passion to succeed, and denial of feelings) when attempting to kill themselves (Canetto, 1995). Traditionally, males also have been more attracted to guns than females. Indeed, Groholt, Ekeberg, Wichstrom, and Haldorsen (2000) suggested that gender differences in the suicide methods used by Norwegian adolescents have become less marked in recent decades due to the greater availability of firearms to both sexes. On this point, Johnson, Krug, and Potter's (2000) cross-cultural study of 34 countries found a significant association between number of firearms and firearm-related suicide rates. Finally, a study of 10 European nations documented higher rates of suicide for males than for females (Hearn et al., 2002a, 2002b).

The links between gender and suicide risk also vary across racial and ethnic groups, subcultures, and age-groups. Among poor and marginalized boys of color, self-destructive behaviors such as intravenous drug use and weapons carrying may indirectly express suicidal inclinations (Staples, 1995). Family breakdown, poverty and despair, and illicit drug use contribute to suicide risk among Native Americans (L. J. Wallace, Calhoun, Powell, O'Neil, & James, 1996). Suicide among young African Americans increased 114% from 1980 to 1995 (from 2.1 to 4.5 deaths per 100,000 persons) (CDC, 1998). In contrast, adolescent male athletes show lower risk for suicidal ideation and attempts than their nonathletic counterparts (Ferron, Narring, Cauderay, & Michaud, 1999; Sabo, Miller, Melnick, Farrell, & Barnes, 2002; Tomori & Zalar, 2000).

Elderly males in North America commit suicide significantly more often than elderly females. Whereas Caucasian women's lethal suicide rate peaks at age 50, Caucasian men 60 and older have the highest rate of lethal suicide, even surpassing the rate for young males (Manton, Blazer, & Woodbury, 1987). Canetto (1992) suggested that elderly men's higher suicide mortality is chiefly owed to their limited coping skills and flexibility to meet changes that come with aging.

Finally, some data suggest that gay and bisexual males (especially among adolescents) are at greater risk for suicide than heterosexual males. However, research in this area is sparse and fraught with methodological difficulties, among them lack of valid self-reports on sexual orientation, underreporting on medical records, and confusion about sexual orientation (Garofalo & Katz, 2001). In one study of a population-based sample of U.S. adolescents, Remafedi, French, Story, Resnick, and Blum (1998) found that among gay or bisexual males, 28% reported a past suicide attempt, compared with 4% of the heterosexual males. Fergusson, Horwood, and Beautrais (1999) conducted a 21-year longitudinal study of a birth cohort of 1,007 New Zealand youth and found that, by ages 18 to 21, gay and bisexual males (and females) had higher rates of psychiatric disorders and suicide attempts. Yet researchers also caution that sexual orientation alone does not predict suicide risk as much as other mediating factors such as depression, hopelessness, substance abuse, family dysfunction, social support, interpersonal conflicts related to sexual orientation, and nondisclosure of sexual orientation to others (D'Augelli, Hershberger, & Pilkington, 2001; Rutter & Soucar, 2002).

Testicular Cancer

Though relatively rare in the general U.S. population, testicular cancer is the fourth most common cause of death among 15- to 34-year-old males (Devesa et al., 1999). It is the most common form of cancer affecting 20- to 34-year-old white males. The incidence of testicular cancer has been increasing since the 1950s in both the United States (Pharris-Ciurej, Cook, & Weiss, 1999) and Canada (Ries et al., 1999). An estimated 7,200 new U.S. diagnoses were made in 2001 (American Cancer Society, 2001). If detected early, the survival rates are high, whereas delayed diagnosis is life-threatening (Kinkade, 1999). Regular testicular self-examination (TSE), therefore, is a potentially effective preventive means for ensuring early detection and successful treatment. Regretfully, however, few physicians teach TSE (Rudolf & Quinn, 1988), and most males do not practice TSE. One study of United Kingdom young men found that only 22% practiced TSE (R. A. Moore & Topping, 1999).

Denial may influence men's perceptions of testicular cancer and TSE (Blesch, 1986). Studies show that most males are not aware of testicular cancer and, even among those who are aware, many are reluctant to examine their testicles as a preventive measure. Even when symptoms are recognized, men sometimes postpone seeking treatment. Moreover, men who are taught TSE are often initially receptive, but the practice of TSE decreases over time. Men's resistance to TSE has been linked to awkwardness about touching themselves, associating touching genitals with homosexuality or masturbation, or the idea that TSE is not a manly behavior. Finally, men's individual reluctance to discuss testicular cancer may derive in part from the widespread cultural silence that envelops it. The penis is a cultural symbol of male power, authority, and sexual domination. Its symbolic efficacy in traditional, male-dominated gender relations, therefore, would be eroded or neutralized by the realities of testicular cancer.

Although testicular cancer rates are increasing in many countries, mortality rates have declined in the European Union, Eastern Europe, Japan, the United States, and Canada (Levi, LaVecchia, Boyle, Lucchini, & Negri, 2001). Declining mortality is likely owed to advances in medical diagnosis and treatment, early detection, TSE, and greater educational awareness among males. Finally, survivors of testicular cancer generally go on to have physically and emotionally healthy lives (Gordon, 1995; Rudberg, Nilsson, & Wikblad, 2000).

VIOLENCE

Men's violence is a major public health problem. Hearn et al. (2002a, 2002b) analyzed public health data in 10 European nations and found that "men are strongly overrepresented among those who use violence, especially heavy violence including homicide, sexual violence, racial violence, robberies, grievous bodily harm, and drug offences" (2002a, p. 23). They also documented widespread violence of men against women, which has been found in most other nations.

Cultural prescriptions for traditional masculinity can evoke aggression and toughness in boys and men (Kuypers, 1992). Emerging research on children in elementary school shows that aggressive boys are more popular among their peers and that bullies use aggression to secure resources from lesser-status children (Pellegrini & Long, 2002). Aggressive behavior is used by some males to separate themselves from women and femininity, and to pursue status in male hierarchies. Male violence at any age is both personal and institutional, moored in personality but channeled by group relations and cultural practices (Connell, 2000). Males can use the threat or application of violence to exert their personal will and to maintain political and economic advantage over women and lesser-status men. Kaufman (1998) has shown how the "triad of men's violence" (men's violence against other men, women, and themselves) negatively affects public health.

Homicide is the second leading cause of death among 15- to 19-year-old males. Males aged 15 to 34 years were almost half (49%, $N = 13,122$) of U.S. homicide victims in 1991. In the United States during 2001, men were 89% of persons arrested for murder and nonnegligent manslaughter, 99% of those arrested for forcible rape, 90% of those arrested for robbery, and 80% of those arrested for aggravated assault (U.S. Department of Justice, 2001).

Women are often victimized by men's anger and violence in the forms of rape, date rape, wife beating, assault, sexual harassment on the job, and verbal harassment (Thorne-Finch, 1992). However, men's violence also exacts a heavy toll on men themselves in the forms of fighting, gang clashes, hazing, gay bashing, injury, homicide, suicide, and organized warfare. In the United States, for example, men were 90% of all murderers in 2001, as well as 77% of murder victims (U.S. Department of Justice, 2001).

War and Guns

Paleontological evidence suggests that the institutions of war and patriarchy emerged during the same phase of social evolution about 12,000 to 14,000 years ago (Eisler, 1988). War has always been a predominantly male activity (Connell, 1989; Malszecki & Carver, 2001) that, historically, has exacted high rates of morbidity and mortality among the men who fight in battles. Warriors were taught to conform to a type of hegemonic masculinity that embodies violence-proneness, toughness, and obedience to male authority. The negative health consequences of war for both sexes are painfully evident. Many boys and men, who are disproportionately enlisted to fight in wars, are killed or physically and psychologically maimed, whereas elite male groups may profit or solidify political power through warfare. Men's violence on the patriarchal battlefields also often spills over into civilian populations, where women and children are victimized (Brownmiller, 1975; Chang, 1997). As Sen (1997) observed, "Historically, wars between nations, classes, castes, races, have been fought on the battlefield on the bodies of men, and off the battlefield on the bodies of women" (p. 12). Recent expressions of the militarization of men's violence, partly inspired and fueled by hegemonic masculinities, can be found in the Taliban of Afghanistan, Irish Republican Army of Ireland (Bairner, 2000), terrorist movements, and the U.S./Iraqi war of 2003.

Guns and masculinity go hand in hand in many cultures. Disarmament and peacemaking efforts in Afghanistan, for example, have been partially thwarted by the masculine symbolism that males invest in owning and carrying guns. In the United States, hunting and marksmanship have been mainly male cultural activities, with gun ownership being four times higher among men than among women (Smith & Smith, 1994). Evidence indicates that gun ownership elevates risk for morbidity and mortality. About 30,000 persons are killed with firearms each year in the United States, almost as many deaths as accrue from motor vehicle accidents (Siebel, 2000). Contrary to common beliefs, most gun-related deaths are the result of accidents and not criminal activity (Price & Oden, 1999). Gun ownership is also linked to suicide risk, and one cross-cultural study of 34 countries found a significant association between number of firearms and firearm-related suicide rates (Johnson et al., 2000).

Finally, although there may be some biological impetus for men's higher levels of aggression compared with women's, we also know that male aggression varies a great deal across cultures, individuals, and historical settings. To the extent that masculinity is culturally defined and malleable, therefore, health promoters can encourage the development of more cooperative and peaceful forms of masculinity.

MALE GROUPS
WITH SPECIAL HEALTH NEEDS

There is no such thing as masculinity; there are only masculinities (Sabo & Gordon, 1995), and the view of "all men" as a single, large category in relation to "all women" is misleading (Connell, 1987). The fact is that men are not all alike, and various male groups face different conditions in the gender order. At any given historical moment, there are competing masculinities—some dominant, some marginalized, and some stigmatized— each with their respective structural, psychosocial, and cultural moorings that, in turn, influence variations in men's health. Men's health researchers have begun to study a wide range of male groups; some are discussed below.

Adolescent Males

Researchers and public health advocates identified adolescent health as a major priority during the 1990s (Schoen et al., 1997; Schoen, Davis, DesRoches, & Shehkdar, 1998). A comparative analysis by the Centers for Disease Control and Prevention showed mixed trends in the health risks of high school students between 1991 and 1999 (CDC, 2000b). Fewer teenagers reported having sex, and rates of condom use and seatbelt use increased during the past decade. But cigarette smoking and use of marijuana and cocaine increased, as did the percentage of high school students who attempted suicide (CDC, 2000b).

Pleck, Sonenstein, and Ku (1992) researched the problem behaviors and health among a national sample of adolescent, never-married males aged 15 to 19, surveying and interviewing their participants in 1980 and 1988. Hypothesis tests were geared to assessing whether "masculine ideology" (which measured the presence of traditional male role attitudes) put boys at risk for an array of problem behaviors. The researchers found a significant, independent association with 7 of 10 problem behaviors. Specifically, traditionally masculine attitudes were associated with being suspended from school, drinking and use of street drugs, frequency of being picked up by the police, being sexually active, the number of heterosexual partners in the last year, and tricking or forcing someone to have sex. These kinds of behaviors, which are in part expressions of the pursuit of traditional masculinity, elevate boys' risk for sexually transmitted diseases, HIV transmission, and early death by accident or homicide. At the same time, however, these same behaviors can also encourage victimization of women through men's violence, sexual assault, unwanted teenage pregnancy, and sexually transmitted diseases.

Obesity in adolescence increases lifelong risk for a variety of diseases such as coronary heart disease, diabetes mellitus, joint disease, and certain cancers. Obesity among *both* boys and girls has been increasing; for example, the percentage of overweight children aged 12 to 19 moved from 5% in 1970 to 14% in 1999 (National Health and Nutrition Examination Survey [NHANES], 2003). Between 1988 and 1994, about 11.3% of all boys in this age-group were overweight compared with 9.7% of all girls. Adolescents from racial/ethnic minorities were especially likely to be overweight. Among non-Hispanic blacks, 10.7% of boys and 16.3% of girls were overweight, and among Mexican Americans, the corresponding proportions were 14.1% for boys and 13.5% for girls (NHANES, 2003).

Males are also a majority of the estimated 1.3 million teenagers who run away from home each year in the United States. For both boys and girls, living on the streets raises the risks for poor nutrition, homicide, alcoholism, drug abuse, and AIDS. Young adults in their 20s constitute about 20% of new AIDS cases and, when the lengthy latency period is calculated, it is evident that they are being infected in their teenage years. Runaways are also more likely to be victims of crime and sexual exploitation (Hull, 1994).

Boys With ADHD

Attention deficit/hyperactivity disorder (ADHD) has become a common chronic condition among school-aged children. About 1.6 million elementary school-aged children in the United States have been diagnosed with ADHD, with boys being three times as likely as girls to be diagnosed (CDC, 2002b). The symptoms are mainly behavioral and include impulsivity, hyperactivity, poor impulse control, short attention span, distractibility, irritability, and mood changes. Many boys and parents have been caught up in the ongoing debate about whether ADHD is a genuine medical problem that should be treated with medications and other therapies, or instead is an example of the medicalization of undesirable behaviors in children.

Gay and Bisexual Men

Lifestyle and sexual practices place gay and bisexual males at risk for diseases and behaviors tied to sexual behaviors. When HIV infection became a leading cause of death among gay and bisexual men in North America during the 1980s, health educators (both straight and gay) pushed for more health promotion and services. Workshops and educational materials were created that addressed mental and physical health, safe sex practices, and HIV prevention. Such efforts to enhance the health of gay and bisexual men were thwarted by homophobia, discrimination, and governmental and public indifference. The links between masculinity and gay men's health risks, however, did not receive much attention (Kimmel & Levine, 1989).

Although rates of sexually transmitted disease declined in the 1980s among American men who had sex with men (MSM), data gathered in some cities indicate a resurgent trend toward increased prevalence rates since 1993 (CDC, 1999; Fox et al., 2001). These latter data may mean that more MSM are engaging in sexual behaviors that elevate risk for contagion, such as unprotected anal and oral sex. Other researchers suggest that some risky sexual behaviors among MSM are related to polysubstance abuse. An American Medical Association council report (1996) estimated the prevalence of substance abuse among gay men and lesbians at 28% to 35%, compared with a 10% to 21% rate for heterosexuals. Some studies of gay communities have found higher rates of substance use (e.g., heavy drinking, amphetamines, heroin, and Ecstasy) than among heterosexual males (Crosby, Stall, Paul, & Barrett, 1998; Klitzman, Pope, & Hudson, 2000; Stall & Wiley, 1998).

Sometimes gay and bisexual boys and men become targets for ridicule and gay bashing. Bias against sexual orientation was involved with 14.3% of the hate crimes perpetrated in the United States during 2000 (U.S. Department of Justice, 2001).

Infertile Men

About 5.3 million American couples experience difficulty conceiving a pregnancy (American Society for Reproductive Medicine, 1995). Although factors related to infertility can be found in both sexes, the bulk of extant research focuses on the psychosocial aspects of women's experiences with involuntary childlessness and in vitro fertilization (Daniluk, 1997; Nachtigall, Becker, & Wozny, 1992). In one of the few studies of men's experiences, Webb and Daniluk (1999) interviewed men who had never biologically fathered a child and were the sole cause of the infertility in their marriages. They found that men experienced a "tremendous blow to their masculine identities" (p. 21), profound grief and loss, loss of control, personal inadequacy, isolation, a sense of foreboding, and desire to overcome and survive. They recommend that both "infertile men and women receive compassionate support when faced with negotiating this challenging life transition" (p. 23).

Male Athletes

The linkages between athletic participation and health are complex and often paradoxical. On one hand, sports activities are associated with

338 • BODIES, SELVES, DISCOURSES

building cardiovascular endurance, muscular development, and emotional health. On the other hand, certain sports elevate men's risk for head injury and neuropsychological deficit (boxing, soccer, and football), pathogenic weight loss behavior (wrestling, horse racing), knee injuries (basketball, football), and erectile disorders (cycling).

Injuries are basically unavoidable in sports but, in traditional men's sports, there has been a tendency to glorify pain and injury, to inflict injury on others, and to sacrifice one's body in order to "win at all costs." The "no pain, no gain" philosophy, which is rooted in traditional cultural equations between masculinity and sports, can jeopardize the health of athletes who conform to its ethos (Sabo, 2003). Many male athletes believe that the endurance of pain will help them achieve upward mobility, yet only a handful ultimately make it to elite levels of successful competition (Sabo, 2003). Sometimes parents, especially fathers, push their sons into "physically abusive sports to harden them for a competitive world and to eliminate any effeminate qualities" (p. 177).

The connections between sport, masculinity, and health are also evident in Klein's (1993, 1995) study of bodybuilders, who often use anabolic steroids, overtrain, and engage in extreme dietary practices. In the bodybuilding subculture, masculinity is equated to maximum muscularity, and men's striving for bigness and physical strength hides emotional insecurity and low self-esteem. The links between masculinity and muscle mass are currently embodied by the G. I. Joe action figures that possess gigantic biceps and quadriceps, as well as by the overmuscled stars of the World Wrestling Federation. Klein lays bare a tragic irony in American culture; that is, that the powerful male athlete, a symbol of strength and health, has often sacrificed his health in pursuit of ideal masculinity (Messner & Sabo, 1994).

Some evidence suggests that the ill health impacts from youthful sports participation may emerge later in life. The National Institute for Occupational Safety and Health, for example, conducted a retrospective study of former National Football League players who played between 1959 and 1988. The data showed that both offensive and defensive linemen had a 52% greater risk for death from a heart attack than the general population. The physically largest players were six times as likely as lesser-sized players to develop heart disease (Freeman & Villarosa, 2002). Despite the prevalence and visibility of sports injury, however, such longitudinal studies on the health impacts of participation in predominantly male sports such as rugby, ice hockey, football, wrestling, and boxing are rare. Researchers can only speculate about how many athletes end up broken, battered, drugged, and in varying states of chronic pain (Sabo, 2003). The parents of athletes, school officials, or public health planners have little evidence available to assess the long-range health risks of athletes.

Male Caregivers

Life expectancy is increasing in postindustrial societies and, as more elderly men and women develop chronic illnesses, they are apt to be cared for by family members in home settings. Contrary to stereotypes that equate caregiving to femininity, many males are caregivers for their loved ones. For example, an estimated 36% of the caregivers for persons with Alzheimer's disease in the United States are men (Kramer, 1997). A Commonwealth Fund (1992) survey found comparable numbers of men and women age 55 and over (28% and 29%, respectively) were caring for a sick or disabled friend, relative, parent, or spouse.

The research findings on male caregivers are mixed. Although they experience varying levels of stress, depression, and physical fatigue, they also derive emotional benefits (Kaye & Applegate, 1995). One study of men caring for persons with Alzheimer's disease showed that although they rated their own health from "fair" to "excellent," their symptoms of physical illness increased by one third since taking on the caregiver role (Shanks-McElroy & Strobino, 2001). In summary, the experiences of male caregivers are a key research area for men's health studies.

Male Victims of Sexual Assault

Sexual violence typically involves a male perpetrator and female victim. Whereas researchers and public health advocates began to recognize the sexual victimization of women in Western countries during the late 1960s, it was not until the latter 1990s that the sexual abuse of males began to receive systematic scrutiny from human service professionals and gender researchers (O'Leary, 2001). Recognition of the issue in Canada was spurred by media coverage of the sexual abuse of youth hockey players by their coaches (L. Robinson, 1998). Prison reformers have recently decried man-on-man rape in North American prisons (Sabo, Kupers, & London, 2001). The alleged cover-ups by Catholic bishops in the United States, in relation to some priests' pedophilic exploitation of boys, and the activism and litigation of victims have expanded public awareness of the problem. Despite growing public recognition, research in this area is rare, and little is know about the prevalence of sexual abuse of boys and its psychosocial effects (Dhaliwal, Gauzas, Antonowicz, & Ross, 1996). Some studies show that males who suffer sexual victimization as children experience lasting self-blame, feelings of powerlessness and stigmatiza-tion, suspicion of others, and confusion about sexual identity, and some eventually repeat the cycle by victimizing others as adolescents and adults (Mendel, 1995; Messerschmidt, 2000; O'Leary, 2001).

Men of Color

Variations in health and illness among men of color in the United States are best understood against the historical and social context of eco-nomic inequality. Generally, African Americans, Hispanics, and Native Americans are dispropor-tionately poor; they are more likely to work in low-paying and dangerous occupations, live in polluted environments, be exposed to toxic substances, experience the threat and reality of crime, and worry about meeting basic needs. Prejudice and cultural barriers can also compli-cate their access to available health care. Poverty is correlated with lower educational attainment, which in turn mitigates against adoption of pre-ventive health behaviors. Economic disadvan-tages, lower access to preventive care, racism, and underutilization of health care services put many men of color at greater risk for illness and death. Data for both sexes show that, compared with whites, African Americans experience twice as much infant mortality, are twice as likely to die from diabetes-related complications, have 80% more strokes, have 20% to 40% higher rates of cancer, and have 5 to 7 years less life expectancy (Burrus, Liburd, & Burroughs, 1998; Chin,

Zhang, & Merrell, 1998; Straub, 1994; Wingo et al., 1996). Black women outlive black men by an average of 7 years (U.S. Department of Health and Human Services [DHHS], 2000). The age-adjusted death rate is greater for men in all racial/ethnic groups: 1.7 times greater among African Americans, 1.8 times greater among Asians, and 1.5 times greater among Latinos/Hispanics (Collins, Hall, & Neuhaus, 1999; Courtenay et al., 2002).

The neglect of public health in the United States is particularly pronounced in relation to African Americans (Polych & Sabo, 1995, 2001). In Harlem of the early 1990s, for example, where 96% of the inhabitants were African American and 41% lived below the poverty line, the survival curve beyond the age of 40 for men was lower than that for men living in Bangladesh (McCord & Freedman, 1990). Whereas accidents are the leading cause of death among white males age 15 to 19, homi-cide is the leading cause among their same-age African American counterparts (National Vital Statistics, 2000, as cited by Franklin, 2002). Indeed, the number of young African American male homicide victims in 1977 ($N = 5,734$) was higher than the number killed in the Vietnam War between 1963 and 1972 ($N = 5,640$) (Gibbs, 1988, p. 258).

African American men have higher rates of alcoholism, infectious diseases, and drug-related conditions. In 1993, the AIDS rate for African American males aged 13 and older was almost five times as high as the rate for Caucasian males (CDC, 1994). More than 36% of urban African American males are drug and alcohol abusers (Staples, 1995). Poor black males are less likely to receive health care, and when they do, they are more likely to receive inferior care (Bullard, 1992; Gibbs, 1988; Staples, 1995). Recent data show black males are falling behind black females in upward social mobility, For example, black males are less likely than black females to hold profes-sional jobs, more likely to drop out of high school (17% versus 13.5%), and less likely to go to college (25% versus 35%) (Close, 2003). For these reasons, young African American males have been described as an "endangered species" (Gibbs, 1988), while Boyd-Franklin and Franklin (2000) assert that the major priority of African American parents is to keep their sons alive past the age of 25.

A similarly bleak health profile is found with Native Americans and Native Canadians. Alcohol is the number one killer of Native Americans between the ages of 14 and 44 (May, 1986), with 42% of Native American male adolescents problem drinkers, compared with 34% of same-age Caucasian males (Lamarine, 1988). Native Americans (10–18 years of age) constitute 34% of in-patient admissions to adolescent detoxification programs (D. Moore, 1988). Compared with the "all race" population, Native American youth exhibit more serious problems in the areas of depression, suicide, anxiety, substance use, and general health status (Blum, Harman, Harris, Bergeissen, & Restrick, 1992). The rates of morbidity, mortality from injury, and AIDS are also higher (Metler, Conway, & Stehr-Green, 1991; Sugarman, Soderberg, Gordon, & Rivera, 1993). Similarly, Connell (2000) has observed an "exceptionally serious range of health problems" among Australian indigenous men when compared with the population as a whole (p. 182). These health problems are correlates of poverty and social marginalization such as school dropout, hopelessness, the experience of prejudice, poor nutrition, and lack of regular health care.

Prisoners

Rates of imprisonment vary around the world. Nearly 1.6 million persons are imprisoned in the United States (600/100,000), compared with 1.2 million in China (103/100,000) and 1 million in Russia (690/100,000). Prison populations tend to be disproportionately male, economically impoverished, and, in some nations, mainly racial and ethnic minorities. In the United States, the state and federal prison population expanded from 200,000 in 1970 to 1,324,465 by the end of the year 2001, with about 6.6 million Americans currently incarcerated or on parole or probation (Sentencing Project, 2003). Blacks constituted 46% of the male prison population, and Hispanics another 16% (Mauer, 1999). One in seven black males (13.4%) aged 25 to 29 is in prison, compared with 1 in 24 Hispanic men and 1 in 55 white men (Sentencing Project, 2003).

Prisons are also gendered institutions exhibiting earmarks of patriarchal institutions such as sex segregation, hierarchical relationships, and social control through aggression and violence (Sabo et al., 2001). The gendering of prison life is also evident in the constructions of masculinity among prisoners that revolve around a male code for acting tough, being prepared to fight, avoiding intimacy, minding one's own business, and avoiding feminine behaviors (Kupers, 1999; Newton, 1994). Traditional masculinity is also evoked by politicians who call for harsher punishments of prisoners and less rehabilitative approaches (Levit, 2001).

Epidemiologically, the North American corrections system acts as a whirlpool of risk for many men who, upon arrest, reside in structurally disadvantaged communities where poverty, unemployment, and racial oppression already yield higher morbidity and mortality rates (e.g., tuberculosis, hepatitis, and AIDS) (Polych & Sabo, 2001). Because of unhealthy prison conditions, they are yet again exposed to heightened risk for illness (Bellin, Fletcher, & Safyer, 1993; Kupers, 1999; Toepell, 1992). For example, the incidence of active tuberculosis among New York State prisoners went from 15/100,000 in the 1970s to 139/100,000 in 1993, while 58% of new tuberculosis (TB) infections among medical personnel working with these inmates were attributed to occupational exposure (Steenland, Levine, Sieber, Schulte, & Aziz, 1997). A study of New York City jails, where the average inmate stay is 65 days, found that 1 year of jail time doubled the probability of contracting TB. The authors expressed concerns that, should a multidrug-resistant strain of TB enter the jail system, the resulting infection would be rapidly transmitted to the wider urban population as inmates returned to their homes (Bellin et al., 1993). In addition, despite the realities of man-on-man sexual relations (both consensual sex and rape) and intravenous drug use in prisons, inmates are rarely provided with condoms or clean needle works, thus elevating risk for contagious disease (Expert Committee, 1994).

The failure of correctional institutions to provide health education and effective treatment interventions is putting prisoners, as well as the public at large, at greater risk for disease (Courtenay & Sabo, 2001; Polych & Sabo, 1995). Prisons are not sealed off from their surrounding communities, and men constantly move in and out of the corrections system, oftentimes carrying physical or mental illness with them. The average prison sentence in the United States is less than 5 years, and about 95% of all prisoners are eventually released, despite the trends toward longer sentences (Kupers, 1999). Upon release, many infected male prisoners return to communities in which poor and racially oppressed populations of *both* males and females already exhibit disproportionately higher rates of HIV infection and AIDS (Zierler & Krieger, 1997). The cycles of risk and infection grind forward.

Despite the World Health Organization's call for greater therapeutic and rehabilitative corrections practices, prison policies in various nations continue to emphasize punishment and endanger the public health. Two recent studies examine the interplay between masculinities and men's health in Scotland (de Viggiani, 2004) and Norway (Johnsen, 2001). Furthermore, negative gendered health synergies are set into motion through which punitive, predominantly male prison administrators maintain policies and conditions that jeopardize the health of male prisoners and corrections staff, and concomitantly, the women and children in their lives.

GLOBALIZATION, GENDER, AND HEALTH

Globalization generally refers to the growing interdependence among the world's societies. The idea of interdependence does not necessarily connote international harmony or global community, but rather the recognition that what happens in any single society is increasingly influenced by its interactions with the many other societies on the globe. For example, international cooperation among health organizations now makes early detection, control, and prevention of pandemics more effective; local droughts or natural catastrophes are often met by worldwide relief campaigns. But global interdependence also reflects and reproduces exploitative relations between nations, fueling economic and social inequalities that, in turn, can increase morbidity and mortality. For example, Farmer (1999) showed how the global tourist industry influenced the historical development of HIV/AIDS in Haiti. Harsh living conditions in Haiti's marginalized economy helped prostitution to take hold, and the influx of tourists in search of a tropical climate and cheap goods and services accelerated the spread of HIV/AIDS among both Haitians and tourists.

Global economic inequalities profoundly affect men's and women's life chances in poorer nations. Whereas mortality from infectious disease is generally not a pressing health issue in First World nations, for example, diseases such as acute respiratory infections, diarrheal diseases, tuberculosis, malaria, and meningitis are major killers in Third World countries (Platt, 1996; Robbins, 2002). Geopolitical struggles can also produce marked shifts in men's and women's health. The end of the Cold War and the disintegration of the Soviet Union in the early 1990s profoundly affected the public health. Whereas Russian boys born in 1972 had a life expectancy of 65 years, the figure plummeted to 56 years for boys born in December of 1998 (Garrett, 2000). A representative from the Russian Academy of Medical Sciences predicted in the mid-1990s that, if the health crisis continued, "only 54 percent of the sixteen-year-olds (males) will live to pension age" (quoted in Garrett, 2000, p. 127). Alcoholism rates soared, with some estimates at 80% of all Russian men, and the alcohol poisoning rate approached 200 times that of the rate of American males (Eberstadt, 1999). The hike in male alcoholism rates was accompanied by rising rates of physical abuse and rape of women and male suicide (Garrett, 2000).

The Dawn of Global Awareness

In First World countries, most men's health scholars and advocates have not stretched their analytic purview beyond local or national boundaries. Many are doing good work. Examples include those doing group work with prostate cancer patients in Toronto, Canada; coordinating a network of support groups for men recovering from heart disease in Rochester, New York; counseling poor, urban boys in Canberra, Australia, to reduce their risk for violence; teaching San Francisco teenagers about condom use and risk for HIV transmission; conducting research on male caregivers in Norway; and giving a workshop to men in the U.S. armed services on men's violence against women. Despite the growth of men's health studies since its "birth" in the 1970s, however, global awareness has been minimal.

Connell (1998) was the first to entreat those studying men and masculinities to think more about "men's gender practices in terms of the global structure and dynamics of gender" (p. 7). His concept of the "world gender order" is painted against the historical backdrop of post-colonialism and neoliberalism. He argued that new forms of hegemonic masculinity are ascending within the interdependent global matrices of transnational corporations, world markets, and capital and information flows. He created bridging concepts to foster a global analysis. The concept of "transnational business masculinity" described a form of hegemonic masculinity common among businessmen and political executives who dominate these emerging global institutions, a masculinity typified by "increasing egocentrism, very conditional loyalties (even to the corporation), and a declining sense of responsibility to others (except for purposes of image making)" (p. 16). Furthermore, when a pattern of masculinity begins to become institutionalized beyond the confines of specific nations, it becomes a "globalizing masculinity" competing for hegemony within the world gender order (Connell, 1998, p. 12).

Connell's vision has helped to steer the study of men and masculinities toward a global analysis, and men's health scholars have begun to heed the message. The *International Journal of Men's Health* was established in 2002, and its editor, Will Courtenay, called for "comprehensive international and relational models of men's health (that) would address micro and macro health determinants at international, national, community, and individual levels" (Courtenay, 2002, p. 12). Two leading periodicals that focus on research on men and masculinities, the *Journal of Men's Studies* and *Men and Masculinities*, have become more internationally inclusive and more likely to publish health-related works.

Probably the most ambitious research and public health policy initiative in men's health studies to date is flowing from the European Research Network on Men in Europe project (Hearn et al., 2002a, 2002b). An international network of researchers has been gathering and analyzing data from 10 European nations in four key areas, including health. The chief aim of the project is "to develop empirical, theoretical, and policy outcomes on the gendering of men and masculinities in Europe" (Hearn et al., 2002a, p. 6). Their comparative analysis of cross-national descriptive data is being developed with a critical, relational, and global framework that is intended to inform policy development that will favorably affect the health of both men and women.

The Global Sex Industry: A Case Study

An analysis of the global sex industry can illustrate how the shifting patterns of gender relations that are linked to globalization are producing negative impacts on men's and women's health. Transnational business masculinity is also earmarked by "increasingly libertarian sexuality, with a growing tendency to commodify relations with women" (Connell, 1998, p. 16). Transnational business masculinity is becoming a globalizing masculinity within the emerging global sex industry. Elements of this globalizing masculinity are bound up with a variety of emerging gendered health synergies within a variety of national settings.

Some of the institutional and cultural tentacles of the global sex industry should be outlined before we point toward their gendered health impacts. Businessmen sometimes entertain themselves or their associates in sex clubs or nude dancing establishments. Some arrange for prostitutes to "service" clients. In one case, mining industry executives drove a visiting New York City lawyer in a stretch limousine through the impoverished streets of a Peruvian city, en route to a "girly club" in which women performed as totally nude table dancers. He was shocked and dismayed by the total indifference of his male hosts to the suffering of the people on the streets and the dehumanization of the women dancers, who also functioned as prostitutes (John Larkin, personal communication, October 19, 1998).

Men's sexual transactions within the global sex industry can be direct or indirect. In Thailand, Brazil, or Haiti, foreign men with money may directly purchase sex from indigenous sex workers, or indirectly, these sex workers may be paid to pose naked or perform in pornographic videos that are subsequently marketed and exported to men in First World countries. For example, a hardcore porn video such as *The Girls of Thailand* may be sold by mail-order companies, shown by hotels that cater to businessmen, or pictorially excerpted for "men's magazines" that are sold openly in airports or drugstores. There is also a growing market among Western males for pornography featuring "exotic" foreign females (e.g., Asian, Latin American, or African women). The sexual "tastes" of many Western men are also focusing on younger females, and the global sex industry appears to be recruiting younger girls into the ranks of its sex workers, models, and video performers.

Pornography is also rife in cyberspace, and the Internet has become the major marketing and distribution vehicle for the proliferating global sex industry. For example, the combined entry of the search terms "teen," "sex," and "Asian" will yield hundreds of millions of Web sites. The fascination of many men for young girls, in part amplified and normalized by global pornography flows, is related to reports of thousands of girls and younger women being recruited, abducted, or sold into forced prostitution (Human Rights Watch, 1995, p. 196; Moreau, 1997).

The production and consumption of sex and pornography by Western men is also linked to the operations of the global sex industry in Second and Third World nations. The expanding demand for sex and pornography among First World males provides economic incentives for the sexual exploitation of sex workers in Second and Third World economies. Local emissaries of the global sex industry are often linked to criminal organizations within specific nations or urban centers. The controlling agents of local sex industrial organizations (e.g., sex clubs, prostitution rings, or porn video production companies), as well as their supportive criminal organizations, are likely to be men. Messerschmidt (1987) has examined how males use crime as a resource for constructing masculinity and, consistent with West and Zimmerman's (1987) concept of "doing gender," he argues that males actively use crime in a variety of situations in order to make statements about their status and identity as men. The social construction of hegemonic masculinity in various institutional sectors of the global sex industry reflects, supports, and actively cultivates criminal forms of male behavior that foster the exploitation and health risks of many females and males.

The growth and institutionalization of the global sex industry are linked *both* to economic inequalities across and within First, Second, and Third World nations and to gender inequalities within respective gender orders. Sen (1997) argued that a "central feature of globalization is the extent to which it draws upon and uses women's labour flexibly" (p. 11). The displacement of many women from more secure niches within local and global economies means that some will take jobs within the growing sex industry. As Sen (1997) wrote,

> Women across the world are under enormous pressure to earn incomes, just as social security systems are crumbling and public provisioning for household work is becoming less and less secure. The failure to provide adequately for the resources, labour time, and emotional needs that bearing, raising, and caring for human beings require is one of the major in-built flaws of capitalism. . . . (p. 11)

And so Russian girls are taking to the streets as prostitutes amid economic collapse, and East African women are emigrating to become sex workers in the red light district of Amsterdam, catering to male tourists from around the world. Similarly, in the streets of New York City, São Paulo, or Bangkok, economically marginalized boys and men are also being drawn into and exploited at lower ranks of the sex industry as sex workers, actors, and petty drug pushers or users. Sex work and life within the sexual underground bring with them elevated risk for disease, victimization by violence, and early mortality.

Finally, Sen (1997) observed that the "growing hegemony of tastes, consumption patterns, and aspirations, as well as an objectification of women's bodies and female sexuality, have been made possible by globalization of media and new communications technology" (p. 12). Her observation is especially salient in relation to the global sex industry, where the emerging cultural template for human relationships being generated can be said to objectify men's bodies and male sexuality in ways that erode men's capacity to empathize and care for women (or for male partners). One result may be that men's motivations to enter into long-standing intimate relationships, to form and maintain stable family relationships, are being stunted.

The resulting health impacts flowing from the growth of the global sex industry include elevated risk for HIV infection, STDs, victimization from men's violence, drug abuse, and crime. There is clearly a risk for early mortality for *both* female and male workers within the sex industry and, to a lesser extent, the predominantly male consumers of sexual services and products. Finally, there is mounting risk for the wider population of citizens, especially women, who may have little or no contact with the global sex industry but who nonetheless are at increasing risk for contagion and crime that are being generated by the global sex industry. Within the emerging world gender order, it is no longer absurd to ponder the probability of a faithful wife and mother of three residing in the American Midwest contracting the HIV virus or a drug-resistant form of hepatitis C from a businessman husband who, in the pursuit of hegemonic masculinity, had unprotected sex with a prostitute in Santiago, Chile.

CONCLUSION: THEORY, GENDER HEALTH EQUITY, AND ADVOCACY

Garcia-Moreno (1998) argued that the purpose of gender analysis is to unravel the ways that inequalities arise as a result of unequal power relations between the sexes and how one's life chances are influenced by being a member of one sex or another. Consonant with this goal, advocates for gender health equity have generally sought to improve the health of women, to ensure that the sexes receive similar levels and quality of health care services, to foster research on women's health and program evaluation, and to secure comparable resource allocation to meet women's health needs (Whitehead, 1992). Proponents of gender health equity call for more "gender aware" policies, but their messages are not always heard by the males who predominate in the leadership and planning circles of national and international health governance organizations (Pfannenschmidt & McKay, 1997).

In recent years, some men in international health organizations have pointed to women's greater longevity compared with men's in countries such as Sri Lanka, Russia, and Pakistan (Evans, 1998). When viewed simply as an outcome measure, data showing greater longevity for women seem to confound or undermine women's call for prioritizing women's health initiatives. The surface question becomes whether the appeals for increased resources for women's health should be heeded in light of men's greater mortality. This type of thinking, however, can foster a tendency to see issues of gender equity in categorical and binary terms, that is, as men versus women.

When concerns about men's greater mortality rates enter the dialogue around gender health

equity, women's health advocates sometimes infer that a focus on men's health could undermine the rationale for gender health equity; for example, a heightened concern for men's health might detract from women's efforts to secure greater awareness and resource allocation for women's health needs. Scientifically, the basic question is how the study of men's health can be integrated into a theory of women's health or gender and health. Or, as Sabo and Gordon (1995) asked, "How can men's health studies position itself in relation to women's health studies, women's studies, gender studies, or the feminist paradigm?" (p. 16). Politically, the issues generally revolve around finding a place for men within feminist theory and practice, and more specifically, mapping out men's roles in relation to women's health movements.

More research on men's health is issuing from around the globe, from the streets of North American cities to Central African villages. Public health policymakers are beginning to draw on the emerging research and theory on masculinities and health in their work, and progress is being made on the theoretical front, most recently through the work of Jonathan Watson (2000). He discusses several dominant perspectives that shape men's health, including the biomedical paradigm, sociostructural theories, epidemiology and risk discourse, feminist perspectives, and critical studies of men and masculinities. Without falling prey to reductionism, he shows how embodiment is the "personal ground of culture" (p. 146), linking everyday behaviors and lay knowledge to the wider worlds of marriage, family, work, and economic conditions. Watson's critical analysis unearths the limitations of both neoliberal approaches to health promotion (i.e., it's up to individuals to manage risk) and new public health agendas that presume that mainly socioeconomic conditions shape health outcomes.

The development of relational and global models of gender and health promises to address the important issues of gender health equity. Some Latin American scholars, for example, have begun to question "the exclusive emphasis on women in reproductive health research, seeking instead to examine men's influence on women's health and on reproductive decisions in general" (Viveros Vigoya, 2001, p. 251). While they critique and problematize men's adoption of destructive forms of traditional masculinity, they also reveal how men's and women's health behaviors and outcomes are interrelated when it comes to negotiations around contraceptive use, decisions about abortion, and parenting (Tolbert, Morris, & Romero, 1994; Viveros & Gomez, 1998), thus opening a conceptual and policy door that has the potential to enhance both men's and women's health and make gender health equity more of a reality in Latin America and elsewhere.

REFERENCES

Ackerman, M. D., & Carey, P. C. (1995). Psychology's role in the assessment of erectile dysfunction: Historical precedents, current knowledge and methods. *Journal of Counseling & Clinical Psychology, 63*(6), 862-876.

American Academy of Pediatrics, Committee on Sports Medicine and Fitness. (1997). Adolescents and anabolic steroids: A subject review. *Pediatrics, 99*(6), 904-908.

American Cancer Society. (2001). *Prevention and early detection*. Atlanta: Author (available at www.cancer.org)

American Medical Association. (1996). Health care needs of gay men and lesbians in the United States. *Journal of the American Medical Association, 275*, 1354–1359.

American Society for Reproductive Medicine. (1995). Gender's role in response to infertility. *Psychology of Women Quarterly, 15*, 295-314.

Bairner, A. (2000). After the war? Soccer, masculinity, and violence in Northern Ireland. In J. McKay, M. A. Messner, & D. Sabo (Eds.), *Masculinities, gender relations, and sport* (pp. 176-194). Thousand Oaks, CA: Sage.

Bellin, E. Y., Fletcher, D. D., & Safyer, S. M. (1993). Association of tuberculosis infection with increased time in or admission to the New York City jail system. *Journal of the American Medical Association, 269*(18), 2228-2231.

Blesch, K. (1986). Health beliefs about testicular cancer and self-examination among professional men. *Oncology Nursing Forum, 13*(1), 29-33.

Blum, R., Harman, B., Harris, L., Bergeissen, L., & Restrick, M. (1992). American Indian-Alaska Native youth health. *Journal of the American Medical Association, 267*(12), 1637-1644.

Boyd-Franklin, N., & Franklin, A. J. (2000). *Boys into men: Our African American teenage sons.* New York: Dutton.

Breen, J. (2002). Protecting pedestrians. *British Medical Journal, 324*, 1109-1110.

Brod, H. (Ed.). (1987). *The making of masculinities: The new men's studies*. Boston: Allen & Unwin.

Brownmiller, S. (1975). *Against our will: Men, women, and rape*. New York: Simon and Schuster.

Bullard, R. D. (1992). Urban infrastructure: Social, environmental, and health risks to African-Americans. In B. J. Tidwell (Ed.), *The State of Black America 1992* (pp. 183-196). New York: National Urban League.

Burrus, B. B., Liburd, L. C., & Burroughs, A. (1998). Maximizing participation by Black Americans in population-based diabetes research: The Project Direct pilot experience. *Journal of Community Health, 23*, 15-37.

Canetto, S. S. (1992). Gender and suicide in the elderly. *Suicide and Life-Threatening Behavior, 22*(1), 80-97.

Canetto, S. S. (1995). Men who survive a suicidal act: Successful coping or failed masculinity? In D. Sabo & D. F. Gordon (Eds.), *Men's health and illness: Gender, power, and the body* (pp. 292-304). Thousand Oaks, CA: Sage.

Centers for Disease Control and Prevention. (1992, January 7). *Monthly Vital Statistics Report, 40*(8, Suppl. 2).

Centers for Disease Control and Prevention. (1994). AIDS among racial/ethnic minorities—United States, 1993. *Morbidity and Mortality Weekly Report, 43*(35), 644-651.

Centers for Disease Control and Prevention. (1998, March 20). Fact sheets. Hyattsville, MD: Office of Communication Media Relations, National Center for Health Statistics. Retrieved from www.cdc.gov/nchs/releases.htm

Centers for Disease Control and Prevention. (1999). Youth risk behavior surveillance—United States, 1999. *Mortality and Morbidity Weekly Report, 49*, 1.

Centers for Disease Control and Prevention. (2000a). Outbreak of syphilis among men who have sex with men—Southern California, 2000. *Morbidity and Mortality Weekly Report, 50*, 117-120.

Centers for Disease Control and Prevention. (2000b). Youth risk behavior surveillance—United States, 1999. *Morbidity and Mortality Weekly Report, 49*(SS-5), 1.

Centers for Disease Control and Prevention. (2002a). *HIV/AIDS surveillance—General epidemiology, L178 slide series through 2000*. Retrieved January 30, 2004, from www.cdc.gov/hiv/graphics/surveill.htm

Centers for Disease Control and Prevention. (2002b). New CDC report looks at Attention-Deficit/Hyperactivity Disorder. Retrieved from www.cdc.gov/nchs/releases/02news/attendefic.htm

Chang, I. (1997). *The rape of Nanking: The forgotten holocaust of World War II*. New York: Penguin Books.

Chin, M. H., Zhang, J. X., & Merrell, K. (1998). Diabetes in the African-American Medicare population. *Diabetes Care, 21,* 1090-1095.

Close, E. (2003, March 3). The Black gender gap. *Newsweek*, pp. 46-51.

Cockerham, D. (1995). *Medical sociology.* Englewood Cliffs, NJ: Prentice-Hall.

Collins, K. S., Hall, A., & Neuhaus, C. (1999). *US minority health: A chartbook.* New York: The Commonwealth Fund.

Commonwealth Fund Americans Over 55 at Work Program. (1992). *The nation's great overlooked resource: The contributions of Americans 55+.* New York: Commonwealth Fund.

Connell, R. W. (1987). *Gender and power: Society, the person, and sexual politics.* Stanford, CA: Stanford University Press.

Connell, R. W. (1989). Masculinity, violence and war. In M. S. Kimmel & M. A. Messner (Eds.), *Men's lives* (pp. 194-200). New York: Macmillan.

Connell, R. W. (1995). *Masculinities.* Cambridge, MA: Polity Press.

Connell, R. W. (1998). Masculinities and globalization. *Men and Masculinities, 1*(1), 3-23.

Connell, R. W. (2000). *The men and the boys.* Berkeley: University of California Press.

Cooley, M. E., & Jennings-Dozier, K. (1998). Cultural assessment of Black American men treated for prostate cancer: Clinical case studies. *Oncology Nursing Forum, 25,* 1729-1736.

Cosper, R. (1979). Drinking as conformity: A critique of sociological literature on occupational differences in drinking. *Journal of Studies on Alcoholism, 40,* 868-891.

Courtenay, W. H. (2000). Constructions of masculinity and their influence on men's well-being: A theory of gender and health. *Social Science and Medicine, 50*(10), 1385-1401.

Courtenay, W. H. (2002). A global perspective on the field of men's health: An editorial. *International Journal of Men's Health, 1*(1), 1-13.

Courtenay, W. H., McCreary, D. R., & Merighi, J. R. (2002). Gender and ethnic differences in health beliefs and behaviors. *Journal of Health Psychology, 7*(3), 219-231.

Courtenay, W. H., & Sabo, D. (2001). Preventive health strategies for men in prison. In D. Sabo, T. Kupers, & W. London (Eds.), *Prison masculinities* (pp. 157-172). Philadelphia: Temple University Press.

Crosby, G. M., Stall, R. D., Paul, J. P., & Barrett, D. C. (1998). Alcohol and drug use patterns have declined between generations of younger gay-bisexual men in San Francisco. *Drug and Alcohol Dependence, 52,* 177-182.

Cypress, B. K. (1981). *Patients' reasons for visiting physicians: National ambulatory medical care survey, U.S. 1977–78* (DHHS Publication No. [PHS] 82-1717, Series 13, No. 56). Hyattsville, MD: National Center for Health Statistics.

Daniluk, J. C. (1997). Gender and infertility. In S. R. Leiblum (Ed.), *Infertility: Psychological issues and counseling strategies* (pp. 103-125). New York: Wiley.

D'Augelli, A. R., Hershberger, S. L., & Pilkington, N. W. (2001). Suicidality patterns and sexual orientation—Related factors among lesbian, gay, and bisexual youth. *Suicide and Life-Threatening Behavior, 31*(3), 250-264.

Dawson, D. A., & Adams, P. F. (1987). *Current estimates from the national health interview survey: U.S. 1986* (Vital Health Statistics Series, Series 10, No. 164; DHHS Publication No. [PHS] 87-1592). Washington, DC: Government Printing Office.

Devesa, S. S., Grauman, D. G., Blot, W. J., Pennello, G., Hoover, R. N., & Fraumeni, J. F. (1999). *Atlas of cancer mortality in the United States, 1950–94* (NIH Publication No. NIH 99-3464). Washington, DC: Government Printing Office.

De Viggiani, N. (2004). *(Un)healthy masculinities: Theorising men's health in prisons.* Unpublished doctoral dissertation submitted to the University of Bristol, Faculty of Social Sciences, School for Policy Studies.

Dhaliwal, G. K., Gauzas, L., Antonowicz, D. H., & Ross, R. R. (1996). Adult male survivors of childhood sexual abuse: Prevalence, sexual abuse characteristics, and long-term effects. *Clinical Psychology Review, 16*(7), 616-639.

Digby, T. (Ed.). (1998). *Men doing feminism.* New York: Routledge.

Eberstadt, N. (1999, June). Russia: Too sick to matter? *Foreign Affairs,* pp. 3-24.

Eisler, R. (1988). *The chalice and the blade: Our history, our future.* San Francisco: HarperSanFrancisco.

Evans, T. (1998, May). *Introduction.* Presented at the Gender and Health Equity Workshop: Global Health Equity Initiative, Cambridge, MA.

Expert Committee on AIDS. (1994). *HIV/AIDS in prisons: Final report of the Expert Committee on AIDS* (Ministry of Supply and Services Canada Catalogue No. JS82-68/I-1994E). Ottawa: Correctional Service of Canada.

Farmer, P. (1999). *Infections and inequality: The modern plagues.* Berkeley: University of California Press.

Farrell, W. (1975). *The liberated man.* New York: Random House.

Fedele, D., Coscelli, C., Cucinotta, D., Forti, G., Santeusanio, F., Biaggi, S., et al. (2001). Incidence of erectile dysfunctions in Italian men with diabetes. *Journal of Urology, 166*(4), 1368-1371.

Feigen-Fasteau, M. (1974). *The male machine.* New York: McGraw-Hill.

Feldman, H. A., Goldstein, I., Hatzichristou, D. G., Krane, R. J., & McKinlay, J. B. (1994). Impotence and its medical and psychosocial correlates: Results of the Massachusetts Male Aging Study. *Journal of Urology, 151,* 54-61.

Fergusson, D. M., Horwood, L. J., & Beautrais, A. L. (1999). Is sexual orientation related to mental health problems and suicidality in young people? *Archives of General Psychiatry, 56*(10), 878-880.

Ferron, C., Narring, F., Cauderay, M., & Michaud, P. A. (1999). Sport activity in adolescence: Associations with health perceptions and experimental behaviours. *Health Education Research, 14,* 225-233.

Fox, K. K., del Rio, C., Holmes, K. K., Hook, E. W., III, Judson, F. N., Knapp, J. S., et al. (2001). Gonorrhea in the HIV era: A reversal in trends among men who have sex with men. *American Journal of Public Health, 91,* 959-964.

Franklin, A. J. (2002, October). *Raising African-American boys into men: Research and clinical findings.* Paper presented at the American Family Therapy Academy conference, Niagara on the Lake, Ontario, Canada.

Freedman, T. G. (1998). "Why don't they come to Pike Street and ask us?" Black American women's health concerns. *Social Science and Medicine, 47,* 941-947.

Freeman, M., & Villarosa, L. (2002, September 26). The perils of pro football follow some into retirement. *New York Times,* p. D1.

Garcia-Moreno, C. (1998). *Gender and health* (Technical paper). Geneva: World Health Organization.

Garofalo, R., & Katz, E. (2001). Health care issues of gay and lesbian youth. *Current Opinion in Pediatrics, 13*(4), 298-302.

Garrett, L. (1994). *The coming plague.* New York: Farrar, Straus and Giroux.

Garrett, L. (2000). *Betrayal of trust: The collapse of global public health.* New York: Hyperion.

Gibbs, J. T. (Ed.). (1988). *Young, black, and male in America: An endangered species.* Dover, MA: Auburn House.

Givens, J. (1979). *Current estimates from the health interview survey: U.S. 1978* (DHHS Publication No. [PHS] 80-1551, Series 10, No. 130). Hyattsville, MD: Office of Health Research Statistics.

Glassner, B. (1989). Men and muscles. In M. S. Kimmel & M. A. Messner (Eds.), *Men's lives* (pp. 287-298). New York: Macmillan.

Goldberg, H. (1976). *The hazards of being male: Surviving the myth of male privilege.* New York: New American Library.

Goldberg, H. (1979). *The new male: From self-destruction to self-care.* New York: New American Library.

Gordon, D. F. (1995). Testicular cancer and masculinity. In D. Sabo & D. F. Gordon (Eds.), *Men's health and illness: Gender, power, and the body* (pp. 246-265). Thousand Oaks, CA: Sage.

Gray, R. (2003). *Prostate tales: Men's experiences with prostate cancer.* Harriman, TN: Men's Studies Press.

Gray, R. E., Fitch, M., Phillips, C., Labrecque, M., & Fergus, K. (2000). Managing the impact of illness: The experiences of men with prostate cancer and their spouses. *Journal of Health Psychology, 5,* 531-548.

Greco, K. E., & Blank, B. (1993). Prostate-specific antigen: The new early detection test for prostate cancer. *Nurse Practitioner, 18*(5), 30-38.

Groholt, B., Ekeberg, O., Wichstrom, L., & Haldorsen, T. (2000). Young suicide attempters: A comparison between a clinical and an epidemiological sample. *Journal of the American Academy of Child and Adolescent Psychiatry, 39,* 868-875.

Harrison, J., Chin, J., & Ficcarrotto, T. (1992). Warning: Masculinity may be dangerous to your health. In M. S. Kimmel & M. A. Messner (Eds.), *Men's lives* (pp. 271-285). New York: Macmillan.

Hearn, J., Pringle, K., Müller, U., Oleksy, E., Lattu, E., Chernova, J., et al. (2002a). Critical studies on men in ten European countries: 2. The state of statistical information. *Men and Masculinities, 5*(1), 5-31.

Hearn, J., Pringle, K., Müller, U., Oleksy, E., Lattu, E., Chernova, J., et al. (2002b). Critical studies on men in ten European countries: 3. The state of law and policy. *Men and Masculinities, 5*(2), 192-219.

Hitz, D. (1973). Drunken sailors and others: Drinking problems in specific occupations. *Quarterly Journal of Studies on Alcohol, 34,* 495-505.

Hoffmann, D., & Tarzian, A. (2001). The girl who cried pain: A bias against women in the treatment of pain. *Journal of Law, Medicine & Ethics, 29*(1), 13-27.

Hull, J. D. (1994, November 21). Running scared. *Time,* pp. 93-99.

Human Rights Watch. (1995). *Trafficking of women and girls into forced prostitution and coerced marriage.* New York: Human Rights Watch.

Isenhart, C. E., & Silversmith, D. J. (1994). The influence of the traditional male role on alcohol abuse and the therapeutic process. *Journal of Men's Studies, 3*(2), 127-135.

Jackson, D. (1990). *Unmasking masculinity: A critical autobiography.* London: Unwin Hyman.

Johnsen, B. (2001). *Sport, masculinities, and power relations in prison.* Dissertation submitted to the Norwegian University of Sport and Physical Education, Oslo, Norway. (ISBN 82-502-0359-3)

Johnson, G. R., Krug, E. G., & Potter, L. B. (2000). Suicide among adolescents and young adults: A cross-national comparison of 34 countries. *Suicide and Life-Threatening Behavior, 30*(1), 74-82.

Kandrack, M., Grant, K. R., & Segall, A. (1991). Gender differences in health related behavior: Some unanswered questions. *Social Science & Medicine, 32*(5), 579-590.

Kaufman, M. (1998). The construction of masculinity and the triad of men's violence. In M. S. Kimmel & M. A. Messner (Eds.), *Men's lives* (pp. 4-17). Boston: Allyn & Bacon.

Kaye, L. W., & Applegate, J. S. (1995). Men's style of nurturing elders. In D. Sabo & D. F. Gordon (Eds.), *Men's health and illness: Gender, power, and the body* (pp. 205-221). Thousand Oaks, CA: Sage.

Keefe, F., Lefebvre, J., Egert, J., Affleck, G., Sullivan, M., & Caldwell, D. (2000). The relationship of gender to pain, pain behavior, and disability in osteoarthritis patients: The role of catastrophizing. *Pain, 87,* 325-334.

Keeling, R. R. (2000). College health: Biomedical and beyond. *Journal of American College Health, 49,* 101-104.

Keough, E., & Herdenfeldt, M. (2002). Gender coping and the perception of pain. *Pain, 97,* 195-201.

Kimmel, M. S., & Levine, M. P. (1989). Men and AIDS. In M. S. Kimmel & M. A. Messner (Eds.), *Men's lives* (pp. 344-354). New York: Macmillan.

Kinkade, S. (1999). Testicular cancer. *American Family Physician, 59,* 2539-2544.

Klein, A. M. (1993). *Little big men: Bodybuilding subculture and gender construction.* Albany: State University of New York Press.

Klein, A. M. (1995). Life's too short to die small: Steroid use among male bodybuilders. In D. Sabo & D. F. Gordon (Eds.), *Men's health and illness: Gender, power, and the body* (pp. 105-120). Thousand Oaks, CA: Sage.

Klitzman, R., Pope, H., & Hudson, J. (2000). Ecstasy abuse and high risk sexual behaviors among 169 gay and bisexual men. *American Journal of Psychiatry, 157,* 1162-1164.

Kramer, B. J. (1997). Differential predictors of strain and gain among husbands caring for wives with dementia. *Gerontologist, 37,* 239-249.

Krane, R. J., Goldstein, I., & Saenz de Tejada, I. (1989). Impotence. *New England Journal of Medicine, 321,* 1648-1659.

Kupers, T. (1999). *Prison madness: The mental health crisis behind bars and what we must do about it.* San Francisco: Jossey-Bass.

Kuypers, J. A. (1992). *Man's will to hurt: Investigating the causes, supports and varieties of his violence.* Halifax, Canada: Fernwood.

Lamarine, R. (1988). Alcohol abuse among Native Americans. *Journal of Community Health, 13*(3), 143-153.

Legato, M. J. (2000a). Gender and the heart: Sex-specific differences in normal anatomy and physiology. *Journal of Gender Specific Medicine, 3*(7), 15-18.

Legato, M. J. (2000b). Is there a role for gender-specific medicine in today's health care systems? *Journal of Gender Specific Medicine, 3*(3), 12-21.

Levi, F., LaVecchia, C., Boyle, P., Lucchini, F., & Negri, E. (2001). Western and Eastern European trends in testicular cancer mortality. *Lancet, 357,* 1853-1854.

Levit, N. (2001). Male prisoners: Privacy, suffering, and the legal construction of masculinity. In D. Sabo, T. Kupers, & W. London (Eds.), *Prison masculinities* (pp. 93-102). Philadelphia: Temple University Press.

Lorber, J. (1997). *Gender and the social construction of illness.* Thousand Oaks, CA: Sage.

MacIntyre, S., Hunt, K., & Sweeting, H. (1996). Gender differences in health: Are things really as simple as they seem? *Social Science of Medicine, 42*(2), 617-624.

Malszecki, G., & Carver, T. (2001). Men, masculinities, war, and sport. In N. Mandell (Ed.), *Feminist issues: Race, class, and sexuality* (pp. 166-192). Toronto: Pearson Education Canada.

Manton, K. G., Blazer, D. G., & Woodbury, M. A. (1987). Suicide in middle age and later life: Sex and race specific life table and cohort analyses. *Journal of Gerontology, 42,* 219-227.

Martin, M. (1990). Male cancer awareness: Impact of an employee education program. *Oncology Nursing Forum, 17*(1), 59-64.

Maternal and Child Health Bureau. (1997). *U.S. Department of Health and Human Services. Child health USA 1996–97* (DHHS Pub. No. HRSA-M-DSEA-97-98). Washington, DC: Government Printing Office.

Mauer, M. (1999). *Race to incarcerate.* New York: New Press.

May, P. (1986). Alcohol and drug misuse prevention programs for American Indians: Needs and opportunities. *Journal of Studies of Alcohol, 47*(3), 187-195.

Mayo Clinic. (2003). *Prostate cancer.* Retrieved January 7, 2004, from http://www.mayoclinic.com/index.cfm

McCord, C., & Freedman, H. P. (1990). Excess mortality in Harlem. *New England Journal of Medicine, 1322*(22), 1606-1607.

Mendel, M. P. (1995). *The male survivor: The impact of sexual abuse.* London: Sage.

Messerschmidt, J. W. (1987). *Masculinities and crime: Critique and reconceptualization of theory.* Lanham, MD: Rowman & Littlefield.

Messerschmidt, J. W. (2000). *Nine lives: Adolescent masculinities, the body, and violence.* Boulder, CO: Westview.

Messner, M. A., & Sabo, D. (1994). *Sex, violence & power in sports: Rethinking masculinity.* Freedom, CA: Crossing Press.

Metler, R., Conway, G., & Stehr-Green, J. (1991). AIDS surveillance among American Indians and Alaska natives. *American Journal of Public Health, 81*(11), 1469-1471.

Miller, K., Barnes, G., Sabo, D., Melnick, M., & Farrell, M. (2002a). Anabolic-androgenic steroid use and other adolescent problem behaviors: Rethinking the male athlete assumption. *Sociological Perspectives, 45*(4), 467-489.

Miller, K., Barnes, G., Sabo, D., Melnick, M., & Farrell, M. (2002b). A comparison of health risk behavior in adolescent users of anabolic-androgenic steroids, by gender and athlete status. *Sociology of Sport Journal, 19,* 385-402.

Montagu, A. (1953). *The natural superiority of women.* New York: Macmillan.

Moore, D. (1988). Reducing alcohol and other drug use among Native American youth. *Alcohol Drug Abuse and Mental Health, 15*(6), 2-3.

Moore, R. A., & Topping, A. (1999). Young men's knowledge of testicular cancer and testicular self-examination: A lost opportunity? *European Journal of Cancer Care, 8,* 137-142.

Moreau, R. (1997, July 20). Sex and death in Thailand. *Newsweek,* pp. 50-51.

Moscicki, E. K. (1994). Gender differences in completed and attempted suicides. *Annals of Epidemiology, 4*(2), 152-158.

Nachtigall, R. D., Becker, G., & Wozny, M. (1992). The effects of gender-specific diagnosis on men's and women's response to infertility. *Fertility and Sterility, 57,* 113-121.

National Center for Health Statistics. (2002, September 16). *National Vital Statistics Report, 50*(15), Table C.

National Health and Nutrition Examination Survey (NHANES). (2003). *Overweight among U.S. children and adolescents.* Hyattsville, MD: Department of Health and Human Services, Centers for Disease Control and Prevention. Retrieved from www.cdc.gov/nchs/nhanes.htm.

National Institutes of Health. (1993). Consensus development panel on impotence. *Journal of the American Medical Association, 270,* 83-90.

Newton, C. (1994). Gender theory and prison sociology: Using theories of masculinities to interpret the sociology of prisons for men. *Howard Journal of Criminal Justice, 33*(3), 193-202.

Nichols, J. (1975). *Men's liberation: A new definition of masculinity.* New York: Penguin.

O'Leary, P. (2001). Working with males who have experienced childhood sexual abuse. In B. Pease & P. Camilleri (Eds.), *Working with men in the human services* (pp. 80-92). New South Wales, Australia: Allen & Unwin.

Pellegrini, A. D., & Long, J. D. (2002). A longitudinal study of bullying, dominance, and victimization during the transition from primary school to secondary school. *British Journal of Developmental Psychology, 20,* 259-280.

Pfannenschmidt, S., & McKay, A. (1997). *Through a gender lens: Resources for population, health and nutrition projects.* Research Triangle Park, NC: Women's Studies Project, Family Health International, the Gender Working Group, Population, Health and Nutrition Center, U.S. Agency for International Development.

Pharris-Ciurej, N. D., Cook, L. S., & Weiss, N. S. (1999). Incidence of testicular cancer in the United States: Has the epidemic begun to abate? *American Journal of Epidemiology, 150,* 45-46.

Platt, A. E. (1996). *Infecting ourselves: How environmental and social disruption trigger disease.* Washington, DC: Worldwatch Institute.

Pleck, J., Sonenstein, F. L., & Ku, L. C. (1992). Problem behaviors and masculinity ideology in adolescent males. In R. Ketterlinus & M. E. Lamb (Eds.), *Adolescent problem behaviors* (pp. 133-144). Hillsdale, NJ: Lawrence Erlbaum.

Polych, C., & Sabo, D. (1995). Gender politics, pain, and illness: The AIDS epidemic in North American prisons. In D. Sabo & D. F. Gordon (Eds.), *Men's health and illness: Gender, power, and the body* (pp. 139-157). Thousand Oaks, CA: Sage.

Polych, C., & Sabo, D. (2001). Sentence—Death by lethal infection: IV-drug use and infectious disease transmission in North American prisons. In D. Sabo, T. Kupers, & W. London (Eds.), *Prison masculinities* (pp. 173-183). Philadelphia: Temple University Press.

Portner, J. (2001). *One in thirteen: The silent epidemic of teen suicide.* Beltsville, MD: Gryphon House.

Postman, N., Nystrom, C., Strate, L., & Weingartner, C. (1987). *Myths, men and beer: An analysis of beer commercials on broadcast television.* Falls Church, VA: Foundation for Traffic Safety.

Price, J. H., & Oden, L. (1999). Reducing firearm injuries: The role of local public health departments. *Public Health Reports, 114,* 533-539.

Pursch, J. A. (1976). From quonset hut to naval hospital: The story of an alcoholism rehabilitation service. *Journal of Studies on Alcohol, 37,* 1655-1666.

Remafedi, G., French, S., Story, M., Resnick, M. D., & Blum, R. (1998). The relationship between suicide risk and sexual orientation: Results of a population-based study. *American Journal of Public Health, 88*(1), 57-60.

Ries, L. A. G., Kosary, C. L., Hankey, B. F., Miller, B. A., Clegg, L., & Edwards, B. K. (Eds.). (1999). *SEER cancer statistics review, 1973-1996.* Bethesda, MD: National Cancer Institute.

Robbins, R. H. (2002). *Global problems and the culture of capitalism.* Boston: Allyn & Bacon.

Roberts, I., & Mohan, D. (2002). War on the roads. *British Medical Journal, 324,* 1107-1108.

Robinson, L. (1998). *Crossing the line: Violence and sexual assault in Canada's national sport.* Toronto: McClelland and Stewart.

Robinson, M., Riley, J., & Myers, C. (2000). Psychosocial contributions to sex-related differences in pain responses. In R. B. Fillingim (Ed.), *Sex, gender, and pain* (pp. 41-70). Seattle, WA: IASP Press.

Ron, A., & Rogers, D. E. (1989). AIDS in New York City: The role of intravenous drug users. *Bulletin of the New York Academy of Medicine, 65*(7), 787-800.

Rudberg, L., Nilsson, S., & Wikblad, K. (2000). Health-related quality of life in survivors of testicular cancer 3 to 13 years after treatment. *Journal of Psychosocial Oncology, 18,* 19-31.

Rudolf, V., & Quinn, K. (1988). The practice of TSE among college men: Effectiveness of an educational program. *Oncology Nursing Forum, 15*(1), 45-48.

Rutter, P. A., & Soucar, E. (2002). Youth suicide risk and sexual orientation. *Adolescence, 37*(146), 289-299.

Sabo, D. (1999). *Understanding men's health: A relational and gender sensitive approach* (Working paper series number 99.14.1999). Cambridge, MA: Harvard Center for Population and Development Studies Global Health Equity Initiative Project.

Sabo, D. (2000). Men's health studies: Origins and trends. *Journal of American College Health, 49*(3), 133-142.

Sabo, D. (in press). The politics of sports injury: Hierarchy, power, and the pain principle. In K. Young (Ed.), *Sporting bodies, damaged selves: Sociological studies of sports-related injury.* London: Elsevier Science.

Sabo, D., Brown, J., & Smith, C. (1986). The male role and mastectomy: Support groups and men's adjustment. *Journal of Psychosocial Oncology, 3*(2), 19-31.

Sabo, D., & Gordon, D. F. (Eds.). (1995). *Men's health and illness: Gender, power, and the body.* Thousand Oaks, CA: Sage.

Sabo, D., Kupers, T. A., & London, W. (Eds.). (2001). *Prison masculinities.* Philadelphia: Temple University Press.

Sabo, D., Miller, K., Melnick, M., Farrell, M., & Barnes, G. (2002). Athletic participation and the health risks of adolescent males: A national study. *International Journal of Men's Health, 1*(2), 173-194.

Schoen, C., Davis, K., Collins, K. S. L., Greenberg, L., DesRoches, C., & Abrams, M. (1997). *The Commonwealth Fund survey of the health of adolescent girls.* New York: The Commonwealth Fund.

Schoen, C., Davis, K., DesRoches, C., & Shehkdar, A. (1998). *The Commonwealth Fund survey of the health of adolescent boys.* New York: The Commonwealth Fund.

Schofield, T., Connell, R. W., Walker, L., Wood, J. F., & Butland, D. L. (2000). Understanding men's health and illness: A gender relations approach to policy, research and practice. *Journal of American College Health, 48*(6), 247-256.

Sen, G. (1997, June). *Globalization in the 21st century: Challenges for civil society.* The UVA Development Lecture, delivered at the University of Amsterdam.

Sentencing Project. (2003). *Facts about prisons and prisoners.* Washington, DC: Author.

Shanks-McElroy, H. A., & Strobino, J. (2001). Male caregivers of spouses with Alzheimer's disease: Risk factors and health status. *American Journal of Alzheimer's Disease and Other Dementias, 16*(3), 167-175.

Siebel, B. J. (2000). The case against the gun industry. *Public Health Reports, 115,* 410-418.

Smith, T. W., & Smith, R. J. (1994). *Changes in firearm ownership among women, 1980–1994.* Paper presented to the American Society of Criminology, Miami.

Snodgrass, J. (1977). *For men against sexism.* Albion, CA: Times Change Press.

Stall, R., & Wiley, J. (1998). A comparison of alcohol and drug use patterns of homosexual and heterosexual men: The San Francisco men's health study. *Drug and Alcohol Dependence, 22,* 63-73.

Stanford, J. L., Feng, Z., Hamilton, A. S., Billiland, F. D., Stephenson, R. A., Eley, J. W., et al. (2000). Urinary and sexual function after radical prostatectomy for clinically localized prostate cancer: The prostate cancer outcomes study. *Journal of the American Medical Association, 283,* 354-360.

Staples, R. (1995). Health among Afro-American males. In D. Sabo & D. F. Gordon (Eds.), *Men's health and illness: Gender, power, and the body* (pp. 121-138). Thousand Oaks, CA: Sage.

Steenland, K., Levine, A. J., Sieber, K., Schulte, P., & Aziz, D. (1997). Incidence of tuberculosis infection among New York State prison employees. *American Journal of Public Health, 87*(12), 2012-2013.

Stillion, J. M. (1985). *Death and the sexes: An examination of differential longevity, attitudes, behaviors, and coping skills.* New York: Hemisphere.

Stillion, J. M. (1995). Premature death among males. In D. Sabo & D. F. Gordon (Eds.), *Men's health and illness: Gender, power, and the body* (pp. 46-67). Thousand Oaks, CA: Sage.

Straub, N. R. (1994, Winter). African Americans: Their health and the health care system. *The Pharos*, pp. 18-20.

Sugarman, J., Soderberg, R., Gordon, J., & Rivera, F. (1993). Racial misclassification of American Indians: Its effects on injury rates in Oregon, 1989–1990. *American Journal of Public Health, 83*(5), 681-684.

Thorne-Finch, R. (1992). *Ending the silence: The origins and treatment of male violence against women.* Toronto: University of Toronto Press.

Toepell, A. R. (1992). *Prisoners and AIDS: AIDS education needs assessment.* Toronto, Canada: John Howard Society of Metropolitan Toronto.

Tolbert, K., Morris, K., & Romero, M. (1994). *Los hombres y el proceso de decision respecto al aborto: Hacia un modelo de relaciones de genero y el aborto.* Paper presented at Encuentro de Investigadores Sobre Aborto Inducido en America Latina y el Caribe, Bogata, Colombia.

Tomori, M., & Zalar, B. (2000). Sport and physical activity as possible protective factors in relation to adolescent suicide attempts. *International Journal of Sport Psychology, 31,* 405-413.

Torres, R. A., Mani, S. Altholz, J., & Brickner, P. W. (1990). HIV infection among homeless men in a New York City shelter. *Archives of Internal Medicine, 150,* 2030-2036.

Update: Mortality attributable to HIV infection/AIDS among persons aged 25-44 years—United States, 1990-91. (1993). *Morbidity and Mortality Weekly Report, 42*(25), 481-486.

U.S. Census Bureau. (2001). *Statistical abstract of the United States, 2001* (121st ed.). Washington, DC: Author.

U.S. Department of Health and Human Services. (2000). *Deaths: Final data for 1998* (DHHS Publication No. [PHS] 2000-1120; *National Vital Statistics Reports, 48*[11]). Hyattsville, MD: National Center for Health Statistics.

U.S. Department of Justice, Federal Bureau of Investigation. (2001). *Crime in the United States, 2001.* Washington, DC: Government Printing Office.

Verbrugge, L. M. (1985). Gender and health: An update on hypotheses and evidence. *Journal of Health and Social Behavior, 17,*1107-1123.

Verbrugge, L. M., & Winegard, W. C. (1987). Sex differences in health and mortality. *Women's Health, 12,* 103-145.

Viveros, M., & Gomez, F. (1998). La eleccion de la esterilizacion masculine: Alianzas, arbitrajes y desencuentros conyugales. In L. G. Arango (Ed.), *Muyeres, hombres y conbio social en Bogata* (pp. 85-133). Bogata, Colombia: Universidad Nacional de Colombia.

Viveros Vigoya, M. (2001). Contemporary Latin American perspectives on masculinity. *Men and Masculinities, 3*(3), 237-260.

Waldron, I. (1983). Sex differences in illness incidence, prognosis and mortality. *Social Science and Medicine, 17,* 1107-1123.

Waldron, I. (1995). Contributions of changing gender differences in behavior and social roles to changing gender differences in mortality. In D. Sabo & D. F. Gordon (Eds.), *Men's health and illness: Gender, power and the body* (pp. 22-45). Thousand Oaks, CA: Sage.

Wallace, L. J., Calhoun, A. D., Powell, K. E., O'Neil, J., & James, S. P. (1996). *Homicide and suicide among Native Americans, 1979-1992* (Violence Surveillance Summary Series, No. 2). Atlanta: Centers for Disease Control and Prevention, National Center for Injury Prevention and Control.

Wallace, R. (1991). Traveling waves of HIV infection on a low "sociogeographical" network. *Social Science Medicine, 32*(7), 847-852.

Webb, R. E., & Daniluk, J. C. (1999). The end of the line: Infertile men's experiences of being unable to produce a child. *Men and Masculinities, 2*(1), 6-25.

Wechler, H., Davenport, A., Dowdell, G., Moeykens, B., & Castillo, S. (1994). Health and behavioral consequences of binge drinking in college: A national survey of students at 140 campuses. *Journal of the American Medical Association, 272*(21), 1672-1677.

West, C., & Zimmerman, D. (1987). Doing gender. *Gender and Society, 1,* 125-151.

Whitehead, M. (1992). The concepts and principles of equity and health. *International Journal of Health Services, 22*(3), 429-445.

Wilcox, L. S., & Marks, J. S. (Eds.). (1994). *From data to action: CDC's public health surveillance for women, infants, and children.* Atlanta: Centers for Disease Control and Prevention.

Wingo, P. A., Bolden, S., Tong, T., Parker, S. L., Martin, L. M., & Heath, C. W. (1996). Cancer statistics for African Americans, 1996. *CA: A Cancer Journal for Clinicians, 46,* 113-125.

Wise, E., Price, D., Myers, C., Heft, M., & Robinson, M. (2002). Gender role expectations of pain: Relationship to experimental pain perception. *Pain, 96,* 335-342.

Yesalis, C. E., Barsukiewicz, A. N., Kopstein, A. N., & Bahrke, M. S. (1997). Trends in anabolic-androgenic steroid use among adolescents.

Archives of Pediatric and Adolescent Medicine, 151, 1197-1206.

Zierler, S., & Krieger, N. (1997). Reframing women's risk: Social inequalities and HIV infection. *Annual Review of Public Health, 18*(1), 401-436.

Zilbergeld, B. (1999). *The new male sexuality.* New York: Bantam.

20

MASCULINITIES AND INTERPERSONAL VIOLENCE

WALTER S. DEKESEREDY

MARTIN D. SCHWARTZ

Choose a form of violence and examine international statistics on the gender of its perpetrators. You will always find a severely unbalanced sex ratio, generally with 90% to 100% of the violence being perpetrated by men and less than 10% being perpetrated by women. From time to time, a small number of violent acts committed by women gain newspaper headlines and perhaps even a few scholarly articles on the rise in female crime. The reality behind this is that female violent crime rate is so rare that some states and provinces have managed to survive for a century without any prison for women. The few female criminals who needed to be incarcerated were shipped off to larger adjacent states and paid for via a per diem rate.

—Bowker (1998a, p. xiv)

THE GOOD AND BAD OF MEN

There are few fields in which men around the globe are not making outstanding contributions every day: technology, medicine, education, science, entertainment, and sports are just a few. Among these areas of male accomplishment, profeminist men are playing a vital role in the ongoing struggle to end violence against women, engaging in activities such as protesting pornography, supporting and participating in woman abuse awareness programs, and protesting against racist practices and discourses (DeKeseredy, Schwartz, & Alvi, 2000; Johnson, 1997; Thorne-Finch, 1992). Despite all of this good, however, much of what is bad in the world,

from genocide to terrorism, and including interpersonal violence, is essentially the product of men and some of their masculinities. A large social science literature shows that men, especially those who adhere to the ideology of familial patriarchy,[1] perpetrate the bulk of the violence in intimate heterosexual relationships throughout the world (DeKeseredy & MacLeod, 1997; Renzetti, Edleson, & Kennedy Bergen, 2001).

Similarly, men "have a virtual monopoly" on the commission of crimes of the powerful, such as price-fixing and the illegal dumping of toxic waste (Messerschmidt, 1997). We would be hard-pressed to find more than a handful of women who are involved in acts of state terrorism,[2] such as the one below, described by a man

353

who resided in one of Argentina's brutal detention centers in the mid-1970s:

> [T]hey would use the "submarino" (holding our heads under water), hang us up by our feet, hit us on the sexual organs, beat us with chains, put salt on our wounds and use any other method that occurred to them. They would also apply 220-volt direct current to us, and we know that sometimes, as in the case of Irma Necich—they used what they called the "piripipi," a type of noise torture. (Cited in Herman, 1982, p. 114)

How often do we hear about women participating in mass killings like the one at Columbine High School on April 20, 1999? How many women took part in the plot to fly planes into the World Trade Center and the Pentagon on September 11, 2001? At the risk of belaboring the issue, the most important point to consider is that data sets generated by a variety of scientific means all show that men's involvement in all types of violent crime greatly exceeds that of women (Kimmel, 2000).

What accounts for this glaring difference? One argument is that most men are not violent, and thus those who beat, rob, kill, torture, rape, or behave in other injurious ways are deviant members of an otherwise harmonious society (Websdale & Chesney-Lind, 1998). There is a kernel of truth to this statement. For example, serial killers like John Wayne Gacy are very rare, committing less than 1% of all U.S. homicides (Fox & Levin, 1999; Jenkins, 1994).

Yet male violence itself is not particularly rare. Just as one example of male violence, each year at least 11% of North American women in marital/cohabiting relationships are physically abused by their male partners. Similar figures have been reported in a variety of other English-speaking countries. Violence is endemic to our society (DeKeseredy & MacLeod, 1997; Gordon, 1988). In a Canadian national representative sample survey of undergraduate students, about 28% of the females said that they had been sexually assaulted in some manner *in the past year alone* by a male boyfriend or dating partner, while 11% of the men admitted to such sexual violence in the past year (DeKeseredy & Kelly, 1993).[3] This does not include physical, unadmitted, economic, or psychological violence.

Such data call into question popular notions that men who harm female intimates are "different," "deviant," or "sick." Who are these violent men? They are not generally men who suffer from mental illness. Of course, *some* abusive men have clinical pathologies (Aldarondo & Mederos, 2002a), but generally no more than 10% of all incidents of intimate violence can be blamed on mental disorders, which means that theories stressing this causal factor cannot account for at least 90% of the events (Gelles & Straus, 1988; Pagelow, 1993). In fact, in another setting we suggested that woman abuse on campus is so rampant that an argument might be made that men who *do not* engage in woman abuse could be seen as the deviants (Godenzi, Schwartz, & DeKeseredy, 2001).

Mental illness is not the only possible explanation for the pervasiveness of male violence. Others include such biological arguments as high testosterone levels and evolutionary male competition for sexual access to women.[4] These perspectives are, like some neoconservative theories of poverty (e.g., Herrnstein & Murray, 1994),[5] little more than ideologies "dressed up in . . . scientific regalia" (Devine & Wright, 1993, p. 125). Men are not naturally aggressive. As Katz and Chambliss (1991) discovered through an in-depth review of the research on the relationship between biology and crime,

> An individual learns to be aggressive in the same manner that he or she learns to inhibit aggression. One is not a natural state, and the other culturally imposed: both are within our biological potential. . . . Violence, sexism and racism are biological only in the sense that they are within the range of possible human attitudes and behaviors. But nonviolence, equality and justice are also biologically possible. (p. 270)

British psychotherapist Roger Hottocks (1994) made the bridging argument that although the above is true, certain societies are much more likely to teach violence to men than others. "Therefore I insist: it is not men who are intrinsically violent, but certain societies which are violent and warlike and genocidal" (p. 136).

There are other theories about male violence. Evolutionary theorists (e.g., Daly & Wilson, 1988) claim that male violence is the result of competition for sexual access to women. Yet men kill not only men but also women. Why do so many men beat, rape, or kill female intimates? As Kimmel (2000) reminds us, "To murder or assault the person you are trying to inseminate is a particularly unwise reproductive strategy" (p. 244). Another challenge to evolutionary theory is that many societies have much lower rates of male violence than those of the United States. So if "boys will be boys," they "will be so differently" (Kimmel, 2000), depending on where they live, their peer groups, social class position and race, and a host of other factors (Messerschmidt, 1993).

Missing in the above brief review of theories and in most media accounts of the causes of male violence (e.g., drugs, video games) is any discussion of the role of masculinities in contemporary society (Messerschmidt, 2000). The main objective of this chapter is to review and critique the extant sociological literature on the relationship between this important factor and variations in interpersonal violence across different social class and racial/ethnic backgrounds. Before doing so, however, it is first necessary to define interpersonal violence and explain why masculinities studies provide a rich social scientific understanding of this problem.

Understanding Interpersonal Violence: The Contribution of Masculinities Studies

Although the definition of interpersonal violence has been much debated, here it means "the threat, attempt, or use of physical force by one or more persons that results in physical or non-physical harm to one or more persons" (Weiner, Zahn, & Sagi, 1990, p. xiii). More specifically, the behaviors examined in this chapter are non-lethal forms of male-to-female physical and sexual assaults (e.g., wife beating and rape), homicide, and youth gang violence, which we chose to examine because these harms have thus far garnered the most empirical and theoretical attention by social scientists interested in masculinities and crime. This is not to say, however, that we do not also view other highly injurious behaviors as interpersonal violence.

Part of the problem in defining interpersonal violence is that there are many behaviors that may seem extremely violent but nevertheless are not viewed that way by many or most people (Bessant & Cook, 2001). Certainly, killing the enemy in warfare is violent, but that is grounds for being awarded a medal. Sports often provide our most ambiguous area, where exceptional

levels of very harmful behavior are often seen as "just part of the game." It is relatively common for events to "occur in the name of sport, which, if they were perpetrated under any other banner short of open warfare, would be roundly condemned as crimes against humanity" (Atyeo, 1979, p. 11). Here are two professional ice hockey examples:

• Boston's "Terrible" Ted Green and Wayne Maki of St. Louis engaged in a stick duel during an exhibition game in Ottawa. Green was struck on the head by a full-swinging blow. His skull fractured, he almost died.

• Boston's Dave Forbes and Minnesota's Henry Boucha engaged in a minor altercation for which both were penalized. Forbes threatened Boucha from the penalty box; then, leaving the box at the expiration of the penalties, he lunged at Boucha from behind, striking him near the right eye with the butt end of his stick. Boucha fell to his knees, hands over face; Forbes jumped on his back, punching until pulled off by another player. Boucha was taken to a hospital, where he received 25 stitches and the first of several eye operations (Smith, 1983, pp. 15-16).

Unfortunately, cases such as these are not isolated incidents. It is exacerbated because serious violence is widely regarded as a legitimate or acceptable part of many contact sports. Further, it is not difficult to identify many other injurious behaviors that sizable numbers of people do not regard as violent, and to find that the number of people who regard them as violent differs radically from society to society (Newman, 1976). For example, although a broad range of health workers and parents in North America regard such behavior as abusive and violent, and it has been found to be unacceptable by the Committee of Ministers of the Council of Europe,[6] many North Americans not only see nothing wrong with slapping or spanking a child, but they also may regard such behavior as necessary, normal, and good (Straus, 1991).

Nevertheless, there is considerable agreement about the seriousness of the violent behaviors discussed in this chapter. In other words, they are "consensus crimes." This means that most citizens share norms and values that legally prohibit these forms of conduct, and impose penalties on those who violate laws relating to them.

Of course, it is also important to note that although men commit most violent crimes and that although such violence is widespread, this still does not mean that all men are violent (Connell, 2000). For example, homicide is an infrequent violent crime, and thus "we are not talking about a tendency that is either universal or inevitable" (Newburn & Stanko, 1994a, p. 4). Further, there is no simple standard of being a man that guides all male behavior, including violence (Messerschmidt, 1993; Polk, 2003). In fact, although society functions in many ways to promote male violence, there remain in any situation other means of expressing one's masculinity (Connell, 2000).

For example, we noted earlier that professional hockey players can be exceptionally violent. They live in an atmosphere heavily influenced by hegemonic masculinity (Connell, 1995), and they learn through pressure from owners, sportswriters, coaches, teammates, fans, and parents to be aggressive, carry the capacity for violence, strive for achievement and status, avoid all things feminine and particularly emotions deemed feminine (e.g., crying), and actively engage in homophobia (Connell, 1990; Levant, 1994). Official statistics are kept on penalty minutes, and executives and sports magazines talk approvingly about how teams need to hire "enforcers" who may have no talent for ice skating or hockey but can intimidate others through the use of violence. To pick one isolated but not unusual example, one of Detroit's mainstream newspapers "ran a picture of bleeding Colorado goalie Patrick Roy under the huge headline, BLOODY GOOD" (Reilly, 2003, p. 24). What this leads to is a sport where fights are very common.

Yet, some hockey players will not engage in fighting with an opponent because they can "do masculinity" in other ways. A prime example is Wayne Gretzky, who recently ended his stellar career holding the record for most goals scored in the National Hockey League (NHL). Gretzky rarely fought. His amazing abilities to score goals and help his teams win games and championships were key resources at his disposal to demonstrate that he was "manly." Those lacking his skills, but under intense pressure from employers, teammates, and spectators to fight those who challenge them, commonly feel that they would be derided as "of doubtful moral worth" and "relatively useless to the team"

(Smith, 1983, p. 42) if they walked away from violent "honor contests" (Polk, 2003).

Similarly, why are corporate executives unlikely to participate in street fights? The issue can be more complex for some African American athletes, rap artists, and entertainers who attempt to derive their credibility ("cred") among fans from their willingness to engage in violence. Yet, although most skilled athletes of color are not likely to commit violent acts on the street, such violence is a resource that can be used by poor men of color who lack other resources for "accomplishing masculinity" (Messerschmidt, 1993).

Obviously, more will be said about masculinities and violence in the rest of this chapter, but it must be emphasized that masculinities studies demonstrate the fallacy of relying on essentialist explanations such as those briefly reviewed earlier. Further, masculinities studies show that although men are encouraged to live up to the ideals of hegemonic masculinity and can be sanctioned for not doing so, violence is just one of many ways of "doing gender" in a culturally specific way (Sinclair, 2002; West & Zimmerman, 1987). Moreover, masculinities studies show us that the decision to be violent is affected by class and race relations that structure the resources available to accomplish what men feel provides their masculine identities (Messerschmidt, 1997; Schwartz & DeKeseredy, 1997).

Hegemonic masculine discourses and practices, including violence, are learned through personal and impersonal interactions with significant others such as teachers, journalists, parents, entertainers, and politicians (Connell, 1995). However, the all-male patriarchal subculture is one of the most important agents of socialization (Bowker, 1983; DeKeseredy & Schwartz, 2002; Sinclair, 2002). As described in the next section, membership in such a peer group, regardless of its social class composition, promotes and legitimates the physical and sexual victimization of female intimates.

Violence Against Women in Intimate Heterosexual Relationships

There is no question that many women are victimized by men within intimate relationships each year, including the physical or sexual assault of about 10% of those in marital/cohabiting relationships (DeKeseredy & MacLeod, 1997) and the physical or sexual assault of women when they try to leave or have left their spouses or live-in lovers.[7] University/college dating relationships are also marked by high numbers of physical and sexual assaults (DeKeseredy & Schwartz, 1998b; Koss, Gidycz, & Wisniewski, 1987). Why do these assaults take place? Although there seem to be several key reasons, many quantitative and qualitative studies have found that one of the most important is *male peer support,* "the attachments to male peers and the resources that these men provide which encourage and legitimate woman abuse" (DeKeseredy, 1990, p. 130).

The relationship between male peer support and various forms of violence against women varies across different social classes and settings. For example, in universities and colleges across North America, the identified sexual abusers typically are white middle-class men, especially if they belong to the "hypererotic" subcultures that exist on most campuses (Godenzi et al., 2001). As Kanin (1985) found, these all-male homosocial cohorts produce high or exaggerated levels of sexual aspiration, and members expect to engage in a very high level of consensual sexual intercourse, or what is to them sexual conquest. Of course, for most men, these goals are impossible to achieve. When they fall short of what they see as their friends' high expectations, and perhaps short of what they believe their friends are actually achieving, some of these men experience relative deprivation. This sexual frustration caused by a "reference-group-anchored sex drive" can result in predatory sexual conduct (Kanin, 1967, p. 433). These men are highly frustrated not because they are deprived of sex in some objective sense, but because they feel inadequate in their attempts to get what their peers have defined as the proper amount of sex to establish their heterosexual masculinity. Hence, sexual assaults committed by socially and economically privileged white male undergraduates are largely functions of a fear of appearing to be a "misfit" or of being "left out" (Messerschmidt, 2000).

Like the more affluent college students, impoverished men also form "specialized relationships with one another" (Messerschmidt, 1993, p. 110). Such close bonds, under certain conditions, also promote violence against women as a means of meeting "masculinity challenges," although these challenges are different from those encountered by members of hypererotic subcultures (Messerschmidt, 2000). For example, men in public housing are significantly more likely to physically assault their female partners than those who live in middle- and upper-class communities (DeKeseredy, Alvi, Schwartz, & Perry, 1999). To explain this problem, DeKeseredy and Schwartz (2002) offered an empirically informed Economic Exclusion/Male Peer Support Model, described in Figure 20.1.[8]

Briefly, DeKeseredy and Schwartz (2002) contended that recent major economic transformations (e.g., the shift from a manufacturing to a service-based economy) displace working-class men and women, who often end up in urban public housing or other "clusters of poverty" (Sernau, 2001).[9] Unable to support their families economically and live up to the culturally defined masculine role as breadwinner, socially and economically excluded men experience high levels of life-events stress because their "normal paths for personal power and prestige have been cut off" (Raphael, 2001b, p. 703). For example, because they cannot afford to look after both their partners and their children, some women evict male intimates or "invert patriarchy" in other ways by making decisions for the household and having the lease and car in their names (Edin, 2000). Such actions often are perceived by patriarchal men as "dramatic assaults" on their "sense of masculine dignity" (Bourgois, 1995, p. 215).

Some men deal with stress caused by their partners' inversions of patriarchy by leaving them, while others use violence as a means of sabotaging women's attempts to gain economic independence (Bourgois, 1995; Raphael, 2001a). Other men, however, turn to their male peers for advice and guidance on how to alleviate stress caused by female challenges to patriarchal authority. Large numbers of socially and economically excluded male peers in and around public housing view wife beating as a legitimate means of repairing "damaged patriarchal masculinity" (Messerschmidt, 1993; Raphael, 2001b), and they often serve as role models because many of them beat their own intimate partners (DeKeseredy, Alvi, Schwartz, & Tomaszewski, 2003).

In sum, male physical and sexual violence against women is very much a function of men's

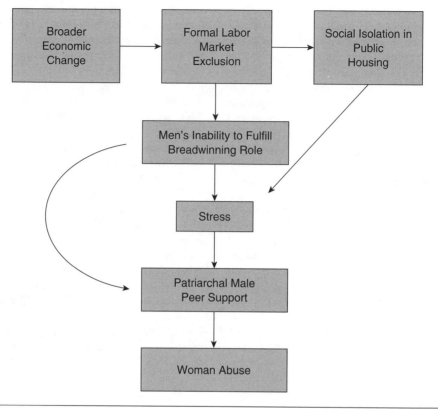

Figure 20.1   Economic Exclusion/Male Peer Support Model

deep-rooted concern with "presenting an image of themselves as men within their social networks" (Sinclair, 2002, p. 20), although patriarchal peer groups' definitions of what it means to be a man vary across social class categories. Similarly, there are variations in motives for different types of homicide, determined by the structure and location of one's peer group.

HOMICIDE

Stanko (1994) makes it clear that although men are violent to women, they are in fact much more violent to each other. Any discussion of male violence must include some understanding of how men experience violence, both as perpetrators and as victims. Not only can't we fully explore the nature of violence in men's lives here, but we can't even describe all the various scenarios of the form of violence we choose to center on here: homicide. Instead, we focus on a few subthemes of two common ones identified

by Polk (1994): (a) homicide in the context of sexual intimacy and (b) confrontational homicide. Although Polk studied Australian men, many masculinities scholars argue that his findings are just as relevant to the discussion of men in other countries.

Male proprietariness is closely related to sexual intimacy homicide, especially during the stages of separation or divorce. M. Wilson and Daly (1992) define it as "the tendency [of men] to think of women as sexual and reproductive 'property' they can own and exchange" (p. 85). More generally, proprietariness refers to "not just the emotional force of [the male's] own feelings of entitlement but to a more pervasive attitude [of ownership and control] toward social relationships [with intimate female partners]" (M. Wilson & Daly, 1992, p. 85). Jealousy also plays a major role in a man's decision to kill a woman who threatens his power and control by seeking to leave or actually leaving him. As Polk (2003, p. 134) pointed out, "[T]ime and time again the phrase 'if I can't have you, no one will' echoes through the data" on homicide in the context of sexual intimacy.

However, although intimate homicide is one of the most common types of murder committed by men, it is a relatively rare crime. If we live in a patriarchal society that promotes male proprietariness, why then do only some men kill their estranged female partners? Certainly there are variations in male proprietariness (DeKeseredy & Schwartz, 1998b; Smith, 1990), which means that female challenges through attempts or successful departures from a relationship, like all single factors, cannot account for estrangement homicide (DeKeseredy, Rogness, & Schwartz, in press). This is why it is necessary to focus simultaneously on all-male subcultural dynamics when attempting to explain the linkage between masculinities and homicides. For example, as stated previously, many patriarchal men have male friends with similar beliefs and values, and these peers reinforce the notion that women's exiting is a threat to a man's masculinity (DeKeseredy & Schwartz, 2002). Again, patriarchal male peer support contributes to the perception of damaged masculinity and motivates possessive men to "lash out against the women . . . they can no longer control" (Bourgois, 1995, p. 214). Another point to consider is that if a patriarchal man's peers see him as a failure with women because his partner wants to leave or has left him, he is likely to be ridiculed because he "can't control his woman."

Peers can also directly or indirectly influence Polk's (1994) second type: male-to-male confrontational homicides, which account for more than 50% of all murders. Such killings are similar to "interpersonal disputes," which, according to Wallace (1986):

> formed the basis of the majority of killings outside the domestic sphere. A large number of these quarrels were unpremeditated events that erupted between strangers or acquaintances, usually while socializing in or around a club or hotel, or in the home of either victim or offender. The content of the disputes in these circumstances may be less important than the male context in which they occurred. (p. 155)

A common variant of confrontational homicide involves a "pub fight," an event Polk (2003) referred to as an "honor contest." Typically committed by young working-class men who are under the influence of alcohol and who have histories of violence, such murders are triggered by a perceived challenge to their masculinity or honor. This challenge may involve an insult, a "minor jostle," a comment to a girlfriend or wife, or "challenging eye contact" (Polk, 2003, p. 135). Honor contest participants do not intend to kill each other. Rather, their main goal is to fight, and male peers often serve as bystanders in these tragic events. Consider the following scenario described by Polk (1994). Anthony and his friends were returning from a local Octoberfest when they met up with another group that included Don and Peter, who, it turns out, were armed with broken pool cues and knives. A confrontation grew out of a young woman in Anthony's group who wanted to ride a bike belonging to Peter. Insults and challenges were traded back and forth. Polk (1994) describes what happened next:

> The exchanges escalated into pushing and shoving. Anthony said: "If you want to have a go, I'll have a go back." Don then threw a punch at Anthony, and the fight was on. At first it was a general group scuffle, and at one point Anthony broke a beer stein (obtained at Octoberfest) over the head of a member of Don's group.
>
> The main group conflict began to simmer down, but Anthony and Don sought each other out and continued their personal dispute. At first Don was armed with the broken pool cue, but Anthony was able to take it off him. Peter then handed Don a knife. Witnesses agree that at this point, Anthony kept repeating to Don: "I'll kill you, I'll kill you." Don was able to come in close to Anthony, however, and slashed out with his knife, stabbing Anthony in the left thigh, right hand, and finally the left side of his chest. By now all eyes of the group were on the two. They say Anthony staggered, and he began to bleed profusely. The two groups broke off the fight, each going their separate ways. . . . Don had no idea of the seriousness of the injuries he had caused, and was said by his friends to be "shocked" when he was informed the next day of Anthony's death. (pp. 60-61)

Sometimes, male peers function in more ways than as a social audience. Above, Peter handed Don a knife during an honor contest. Although other scenarios of homicide do not involve male peers, even when perpetrators act alone, peer influence should not be ruled out as a causal factor. Many men and male youths commit violent crimes in anticipation of the status they will gain (or lose) from friends, who may not be present at the scene (Warr, 2002).

YOUTH GANG VIOLENCE

Before explaining how male adolescent involvement in gang violence is a means of accomplishing masculinity, it is first necessary to define the term "gang." Many use this term loosely to refer to groups of young men who "hang around" street corners, malls, or other public places (Schissel, 1997). However, don't adults "hang out" in public places too? Why aren't they also defined as gang members?

Not surprisingly, many social scientists sharply oppose popular stereotypes of male youth gangs, and they do not view all groups of unsupervised young men interacting on the street as members of deviant or criminal cohorts (Short, 1997). Still, there is much debate among sociologists and criminologists about what constitutes a gang.[10] However, most researchers agree with Warr's (2002) assertion that "gangs constitute only a small fraction of delinquent groups, and that a ganglike structure is not a prerequisite for delinquent behavior" (p. 5). Thus, following Curry and Spergel (1988, p. 383), we define a violent youth gang as "a group or collectivity of persons engaged in significant illegitimate or criminal activities, mainly threatening and violent." Of course, as much as they engage in these activities, most violent gang members spend much of their time engaging in conformist activities such as listening to music, playing video games, and watching television (Jackson, 1989; Shakur, 1994).

Just because young men with similar social backgrounds associate with each other does not mean that they are gang members or that they are violent. In fact, it is normal and healthy for young men to want to interact with their peers (Huff, 1993). Benefits derived from strong peer interactions include the following:

- They help facilitate a successful transition from childhood to adulthood.
- Peers are important sources of emotional support during a time in young men's lives in which many rapid changes are occurring (e.g., puberty, physical maturation, and the transition to higher levels of education).
- Interactions with peers help adolescents learn about the norms of work, dating, sex, and life in general (Warr, 2002, pp. 23-25).

Most serious crime by young men (e.g., violence) is committed in groups (Bursik & Grasmick, 2001; Zimring, 1998), but the vast majority of young men who "flock together" do not belong to violent gangs, are not perpetrators of serious crimes, and do not see themselves as part of a gang. Thus, many popular perceptions of male youth street gangs are shaped by stereotypes (Shelden et al., 2001). These observations are hardly trivial because they contribute to an ongoing moral panic about "kids out of control," and they target and scapegoat visible minorities (Schissel, 1997).

For example, newspapers often feature headlines such as "Asian gang members responsible for violent attack." Unfortunately, such racial references are common in the popular media. One is not likely to find headlines referring to "white youth offenders" or "European American gangs" (Schissel, 1997). Racism is part and parcel of much of the popular discourse on violent youth gangs, and average white citizens respond differently to three or four young men of color mingling together on the street than they do to groups of white youths doing so (Shelden et al., 2001).

To summarize all the rapidly growing literature on how masculinities influence young men's involvement in violent gang activities in a short section of a chapter is a daunting, if not impossible, task.[11] Instead, we address key themes that emerge from this body of knowledge. The first and perhaps most important one is status frustration caused by economically and socially marginalized young men's inability to accomplish masculinity at school through academic achievement, participation in sports, and involvement in extracurricular activities (Cohen, 1955; Messerschmidt, 1993). This problem plagues both whites and minorities. As Cohen (1955) pointed out decades ago, some youths try to deal with this problem by seeking extra help from their teachers, while others quit school and come into contact with other "dropouts" who share their frustration. A subculture soon emerges that grants members status based on accomplishing gender through violence and other illegitimate means. However, some dropouts avoid gang participation because they construct their masculinity through such behaviors as legitimate working.

Still, for many young men living in inner-city or rural communities damaged by deindustrialization, the frustration spawned by the inability to accomplish masculinity in the school setting is exacerbated by their failure to find a steady well-paying job, which is another important theme that emerges from the extant literature on masculinities and gangs. These young men are hit with a "double whammy" that puts them at even greater risk of teaming up with others to create a subculture that promotes, expresses, and validates masculinity through violent means (Hagedorn, 1988; Messerschmidt, 1993). In communities damaged by deindustrialization, there is also "a greater proportion of peer groups that subscribe to violent macho ideals" (Schwendinger & Schwendinger, 1983, p. 205).

Then there are young men who are hit with a "triple whammy." They are not only failures in school and unable to find a job, but also people of color who face institutional racism on a daily basis (Perkins, 1987; Shelden et al., 2001), especially if they live in public housing complexes. An example of how public housing contributes to social and economic isolation is provided below by a Chicago-based employer interviewed by W. J. Wilson (1996, p. 116). He felt that people who lived in public housing would jeopardize his financial status:

> I necessarily can't tell from looking at an address whether someone's from Cabrini Green or not, but if I could tell, I don't think that I'd want to hire them. Because it reflects on your credibility. If you came here with this survey, and you were from one of those neighborhoods, I don't know if I'd want to answer your questions. I'd wonder about your credibility.

In sum, then, many inner-city African American young men are denied masculine status in three ways: through the inability to succeed in school, a lack of meaningful jobs, and the racism and stereotypes of their neighborhoods. Many Hispanic and Asian young men experience similar problems. Thus, it is not surprising that members of these socially marginalized ethnic groups compose most of the street gangs in the United States (Klein, 2002). Nevertheless, it cannot be emphasized enough that social factors—not skin color or biological makeup—contribute to a higher concentration of these people in violent youth gangs. These are young men who are most likely to go to schools that lack adequate financial and human resources, who live in neighborhoods plagued by concentrated urban poverty, and who are unable to find jobs in a society brutalized by major structural transformations, such as the shift from a manufacturing to a service-based economy (DeKeseredy, Alvi, Schwartz, & Tomaszewski, 2003; Kazemipur & Halli, 2000; W. J. Wilson, 1996; Zielenbach, 2000).

Unfortunately, for many of the young men facing the problems described here, the only way of gaining masculine status, a reputation, and self-respect is through youth gang violence (Shakur, 1994). Moreover, "the prospects for the future are not very good" (Shelden et al., 2001, p. 266). For example, at the time of writing this chapter, U.S. companies were in the process of cutting many jobs. The sad reality is that as of May 2003, 7.45 million American adults were officially unemployed, not to mention those who are not counted by government agencies because they had simply given up looking for work (Reich, 2003).[12] Not only is work continuing to disappear, but schools also are facing massive cuts to their budgets, which precludes teachers from effectively reaching out to socially and economically marginalized young men who have special needs. Racial segregation in poor inner cities also is a major problem (Massey & Denton, 1993; W. J. Wilson, 1996). For these and other reasons, we assert that there will be a major increase in the number of male youths lacking legitimate or conventional resources to communicate their masculinity to significant others and to society at large. Some support for our argument is provided by data showing that Los Angeles gang wars culminated in 20 murders during a 1-week period near the end of 2002 (KNBC.COM, 2002).

OTHER FORMS OF MALE VIOLENCE

In a short chapter, it has been possible to go into depth in only three specific areas of men's interpersonal violence. Needless to say, there are many more arenas in which masculinities play a role in facilitating men's violence. In fact, as Australians Connell (1995) and Hatty (2000) have pointed out, there are various forms of masculinities, which helps to explain the wide range of responses to the contemporary crises facing men.

Among these other arenas is child discipline. We mentioned earlier in this context of discipline that many people see slapping or spanking a child as violent behavior. An entire field of child abuse is devoted to the physical abuse of children outside the confines of mild disciplinary actions. Similarly, although we discuss youth violence in the context of gang behavior, there is a great deal of interpersonal violence, especially in the United States, outside the context of youth gangs.

Barbara Perry (2003), following Connell (1987), has argued that a great deal of racist violence and homophobic violence ("gay bashing") can be traced to the desire of white men to assert their superiority and dominance as well as to the desire to "prove the very essence of their masculinity: heterosexuality" (p. 158). She argued that many men do not view such violence as breaking a cultural norm (on violence) as much as affirming "a culturally approved hegemonic masculinity: aggression, domination, and heterosexuality" (p. 158). Of course, men engage in masculinist discourse to justify and allow their own violence in many other areas.

POLICY AND PRACTICE

Thus far, there have not been many programs that have been exceptionally successful in reducing men's violence. In fact, as Hearn (1996) noted, although there was tremendous attention from a variety of sources to the development of a new field of men's studies, such studies have "generally not explored the question of men's violence to any large extent" (p. 22). However, a broad number of forces in many countries are now working in many different arenas to deal specifically with men's interpersonal violence in intimate relationships. As mentioned earlier, for example, profeminist men's groups are engaging in a wide variety of practices to protest racism and sexism, and to try to promote men's awareness (DeKeseredy, Schwartz, & Alvi, 2000). Unsurprisingly, at least in North America the most active of these are taking place on university campuses (e.g., Moynihan, 2003). However, a wide variety of groups are dealing with a very different population, attempting to work with men who batter women. These programs had their beginnings in the United States, often at the instigation of shelter houses and with the strong support of lower court judges who did not wish to allow batterers to be released on probation without at least sentencing them into "treatment." Although widely called "treatment" programs, their efforts are most commonly short awareness programs that are more properly termed intervention programs (for extensive discussions, see Aldarondo & Mederos, 2002b). Such programs are now found in a variety of European countries and Australia, although the theoretical underpinnings may be very different (Hearn, 1998). Even though male peer support studies have made it clear that men with social support for violence are more likely to be violent (DeKeseredy & Schwartz, 2002), the hope for such programs is that it is also possible that the right kind of male social support can help a man to stop being violent (Hearn, 1998).

CONCLUSIONS

There are many theories that attempt to lay out which offender characteristics best predict interpersonal violence, but the single best determinant of who commits beatings, homicide, rapes, and so on is whether the offender is male (Schwartz & Hatty, 2003). Why are most violent offenders men? As stated before, it has little to do with their biological makeup or with factors identified by evolutionary psychologists. The best answer is provided by masculinities studies and research on how masculinities conducive to violence are shaped by male subcultural dynamics. Clearly, for many men, violence is, under certain situations, the only perceived available technique of expressing and validating masculinity, and male peer support strongly encourages and legitimates such aggression. Broader patriarchal forces alone do not motivate people to kill, rape, or rob others.

Still, the accounts of the three harms examined here, like other explanations of the connection between masculinities and violence, require more in-depth analyses of complex factors related to race/ethnicity. For example, so far, to the best of our knowledge, not one systematic study on how masculinities contribute to date rape among the African American community has been conducted.[13] Similarly, Messerschmidt (1997, p. 117) appears to be the only researcher guided by the work of masculinities theorists who has examined "the historical and/or contemporary constructions of varieties of whiteness and their relation to crime."[14] Furthermore, the contribution of technological developments, such as the Internet, require in-depth examination (DeKeseredy & Schwartz, 1998a). Today, many males are developing friendships via electronic mail, "chat rooms," and other electronic means. It is necessary to determine whether these homosocial cohorts, referred to by Warr (2002) as "virtual peer groups," present men with new or reconstituted masculinity challenges that spawn violence. Chances are that virtual peer groups simply reinforce existing hegemonic masculine discourses and practices, but only among males who can afford or have access to computers. However, as Warr (2002, p. 87) pointed out, there is no evidence that virtual peer groups, regardless of whether they promote violence, have "replaced or supplanted real ones."

Additional new directions in empirical and theoretical work could easily be suggested and will be taken in the near future, because there is a growing interest in the relationship between masculinities and crime, as demonstrated by a series of important books published since the early 1990s (Bowker, 1998b; Hatty, 2000; Messerschmidt, 1993, 1997; Newburn & Stanko, 1994b; Polk, 1994). Even so, as Connell (2000, p. 82) reminds us, "masculinities are not the whole story about violence." Obviously, there are many other sources of crimes covered in this chapter and elsewhere. Nevertheless, violence and its reduction cannot be adequately understood without an in-depth understanding of masculinities.

NOTES

1. This is a subsystem of social patriarchy, and it refers to male control in domestic or intimate settings (Barrett, 1980; Ursel, 1986).

2. Barak (2003) defines state terrorism as "the type of governmental abuse and terror perpetrated by traditional dictatorships, from Europe to Central and South America" (p. 129).

3. See DeKeseredy and Schwartz (1998b) for more information on the methods used in this study and the data generated by it.

4. See Kimmel (2000) for a more in-depth review of these perspectives.

5. Herrnstein and Murray (1994) contended that broader social forces, such as class, gender, and ethnic inequality, do not cause poverty. Rather, based on their analysis of highly questionable "scientific data" generated by the Armed Forces Qualifications Test (AFQT), they argue that low intelligence or "cognitive ability" is the main cause of poverty and other social problems such as crime.

6. See *The Protection of Women Against Violence*, Recommendation Rec(2002)5 of the Committee of Ministers to member states on the protection of women against violence adopted on April 30, 2002, and Explanatory Memorandum, Council of Europe, Strasbourg.

7. For example, Mahoney and Williams (1998) estimated that at least 1 in 10 married women experience marital rape. Two thirds of the women in Finkelhor and Yllo's (1985) interview sample ($N = 50$) were raped in the last days of a relationship, either after previous separations or when they were trying to leave a relationship.

8. This model is a modified version of Sernau's (2001, p. 24) Web of Exclusion Model and is heavily informed by sociological perspectives offered by him, DeKeseredy and Schwartz (1993), W. J. Wilson (1996), and Young (1999).

9. A recent analysis of 2000 Census Bureau data (see Jargowsky, 2003), however, shows that the poor are becoming less concentrated in urban areas than they were prior to the 1990s. Still, in Washington, D.C., Los Angeles, and San Diego, the percentage of people in high-poverty areas increased during this time period.

10. See Shelden, Tracy, and Brown (2001) for an in-depth overview of conflicting social scientific definitions of gangs.

11. See Messerschmidt (1993) for an in-depth overview of the literature on violent youth gang activity and its relationship to masculinities.

12. In the United States, to be counted as unemployed, one has to be actively looking for paid work.

13. There is, however, a recent study of dating violence, including sexual assault, among African American youth (West & Rose, 2000). Further, some researchers (e.g., Bell & Mattis, 2000) have examined the linkage between African American manhood and violence against women.

14. In Chapter 1 of his 1997 book, he argues that "during reconstruction and its immediate aftermath, lynching was a response to the perceived erosion of white male dominance and was an attempt to recreate what white supremacist men imagined to be a lost status of unchallenged white masculine supremacy" (p. 16).

REFERENCES

Aldarondo, E., & Mederos, F. (2002a). Common practitioners' concerns abut abusive men. In E. A. Aldarondo & F. Mederos (Eds.), *Programs for men who batter: Intervention and prevention strategies in a diverse society* (pp. 2-1-2-17). Kingston, NJ: Civic Research Institute.

Aldarondo, E., & Mederos, F. (Eds.). (2002b). *Programs for men who batter: Intervention and prevention strategies in a diverse society.* Kingston, NJ: Civic Research Institute.

Atyeo, D. (1979). *Blood and guts: Violence in sports.* New York: Paddington.

Barak, G. (2003). *Violence and nonviolence: Pathways to understanding.* Thousand Oaks, CA: Sage.

Barrett, M. (1980). *Women's oppression today: Problems in Marxist feminist analysis.* London: Thetford.

Bell, C. C., & Mattis, J. (2000). The importance of cultural competence in ministering to African American victims of domestic violence. *Violence Against Women, 6,* 515-532.

Bessant, J., & Cook, S. (2001). Understanding violence against women: Universal human rights and international law. In C. M. Renzetti & L. Goodstein (Eds.) *Women, crime, and criminal justice* (pp. 176-187). Los Angeles: Roxbury.

Bourgois, P. (1995). *In search of respect: Selling crack in El Barrio.* New York: Cambridge University Press.

Bowker, L. H. (1983). *Beating wife-beating.* Lexington, MA: Lexington Books.

Bowker, L. H. (1998a). Introduction. In L. H. Bowker (Ed.), *Masculinities and violence* (pp. xi-xviii). Thousand Oaks, CA: Sage.

Bowker, L. H. (Ed.). (1998b). *Masculinities and violence.* Thousand Oaks, CA: Sage.

Bursik, R. J., & Grasmick, H. G. (2001). Defining gangs and gang behavior. In M. W. Klein, C. L. Maxon, & J. Miller (Eds.), *The modern gang reader* (2nd ed., pp. 2-14). Los Angeles: Roxbury.

Cohen, A. (1955). *Delinquent boys: The culture of the gang.* New York: Free Press.

Connell, R. W. (1987). *Gender and power.* Stanford, CA: Stanford University Press.

Connell, R. W. (1990). An iron man: The body and some contradictions of hegemonic masculinity. In M. A. Messner & D. F. Sabo (Eds.), *Sport, men, and the gender order: Critical feminist perspectives* (pp. 83-96). Chicago: Human Kinetics.

Connell, R. W. (1995). *Masculinities.* Sydney: Allen and Unwin.

Connell, R. W. (2000). Masculinity and violence in world perspective? In A. Godenzi (Ed.), *Frieden, kultur und geschlecht* (pp. 65-84). Fribourg, Switzerland: University of Fribourg Press.

Curry, G. D., & Spergel, I. A. (1988). Gang homicide, delinquency, and community. *Criminology, 26,* 381-405.

Daly, M., & Wilson, M. (1988). *Homicide.* Hawthorne, NY: Aldine de Gruyter.

DeKeseredy, W. S. (1990). Male peer support and woman abuse: The current state of knowledge. *Sociological Focus, 23,* 129-139.

DeKeseredy, W. S., Alvi, S., Schwartz, M. D., & Perry, B. (1999). Violence against and the harassment of women in Canadian public housing. *Canadian Review of Sociology and Anthropology, 36,* 499-516.

DeKeseredy, W. S., Alvi, S., Schwartz, M. D., & Tomaszewski, E. A. (2003). *Under siege: Poverty and crime in a public housing community.* Lanham, MD: Lexington Books.

DeKeseredy, W. S., & Kelly, K. (1993). The incidence and prevalence of woman abuse in Canadian university and college dating relationships. *Canadian Journal of Sociology, 18,* 137-159.

DeKeseredy, W. S., & MacLeod, L. (1997). *Woman abuse: A sociological story.* Toronto: Harcourt Brace.

DeKeseredy, W. S., Rogness, M., & Schwartz, M. D. (in press). Separation/divorce sexual assault: The current state of social scientific knowledge. *Aggression and Violent Behavior.*

DeKeseredy, W. S., & Schwartz, M. D. (1993). Male peer support and woman abuse: An expansion of DeKeseredy's model. *Sociological Spectrum, 13,* 393-413.

DeKeseredy, W. S., & Schwartz, M. D. (1998a). Male peer support and woman abuse in postsecondary school courtship: Suggestions for new directions in sociological research. In R. Kennedy Bergen (Ed.), *Issues in intimate violence* (pp. 83-96). Thousand Oaks, CA: Sage.

DeKeseredy, W. S., & Schwartz, M. D. (1998b). *Woman abuse on campus: Results from the Canadian national survey.* Thousand Oaks, CA: Sage.

DeKeseredy, W. S., & Schwartz, M. D. (2002). Theorizing public housing woman abuse as a function of economic exclusion and male peer support. *Women's Health and Urban Life, 1,* 26-45.

DeKeseredy, W. S., Schwartz, M. D., & Alvi, S. (2000). The role of profeminist men in dealing with woman abuse on the Canadian college campus. *Violence Against Women, 6,* 918-935.

Devine, J. A., & Wright, J. D. (1993). *The greatest of evils: Urban poverty and the American underclass.* New York: Aldine de Gruyter.

Edin, K. (2000). What do low-income single mothers say about marriage? *Social Problems, 47,* 112-133.

Finkelhor, D., & Yllo, K. (1985). *License to rape: Sexual abuse of wives.* New York: Holt, Rinehart and Winston.

Fox, J. A., & Levin, J. (1999). Serial murder: Myths and realities. In M. D. Smith & M. A. Zahn (Eds.), *Studying and preventing homicide: Issues and challenges* (pp. 79-96). Thousand Oaks, CA: Sage.

Gelles, R. J., & Straus, M. A. (1988). *Intimate violence: The causes and consequences of abuse in the American family*. New York: Simon & Schuster.

Godenzi, A., Schwartz, M. D., & DeKeseredy, W. S. (2001). Toward a gendered social bond/male peer support theory of university woman abuse. *Critical Criminology, 10,* 1-16.

Gordon, L. (1988). *Heroes of their own lives: The politics and history of family violence*. New York: Penguin.

Hagedorn, J. M. (1988). *People and folks: Gangs, crime and the underclass in a rustbelt city*. Chicago: Lake View Press.

Hatty, S. E. (2000). *Masculinities, violence, and culture*. Thousand Oaks, CA: Sage.

Hearn, J. (1996). Men's violence to known women: Historical, everyday and theoretical constructions by men. In B. Fawcett, B. Featherstone, J. Hearn, & C. Toft (Eds.), *Violence and gender relations: Theories and interventions* (pp. 22-37). London: Sage.

Hearn, J. (1998). *The violences of men*. London: Sage.

Herman, E. S. (1982). *The real terror network: Terrorism in fact and propaganda*. Montreal: Black Rose Books.

Herrnstein, R. J., & Murray, C. (1994). *The bell curve: Intelligence and class structure in American life*. New York: Free Press.

Hottocks, R. (1994). *Masculinity in crisis*. New York: St. Martin's.

Huff, C. R. (1993). Gangs in the United States. In A. P. Goldstein & C. R. Huff (Eds.), *The gang intervention handbook* (pp. 3-20). Champaign, IL: Research Press.

Jackson, P. G. (1989, June). Theories and findings about youth gangs. *Criminal Justice Abstracts*, 313-329.

Jargowsky, P. A. (2003). *Stunning progress, hidden problems: The dramatic decline of concentrated poverty in the 1990s*. Washington, DC: The Brookings Institution.

Jenkins, P. (1994). *Using murder: The social construction of serial homicide*. New York: Aldine de Gruyter.

Johnson, A. G. (1997). *The gender knot: Unraveling our patriarchal legacy*. Philadelphia: Temple University Press.

Kanin, E. J. (1967). An examination of sexual aggression as a response to sexual frustration. *Journal of Marriage and the Family, 29,* 428-433.

Kanin, E. J. (1985). Date rapists: Differential sexual socialization and relative deprivation. *Archives of Sexual Behavior, 14,* 219-231.

Katz, J., & Chambliss, W. J. (1991). Biology and crime. In J. F. Sheley (Ed.), *Criminology: A contemporary handbook* (pp. 245-271). Belmont, CA: Wadsworth.

Kazemipur, A., & Halli, S. S. (2000). *The new poverty in Canada: Ethnic groups and ghetto neighbourhoods*. Toronto: Thompson Educational Publishing.

Kimmel, M. S. (2000). *The gendered society*. New York: Oxford University Press.

Klein, M. W. (2002). Street gangs: A cross-national perspective. In C. R. Huff (Ed.), *Gangs in America III* (pp. 237-256). Thousand Oaks, CA: Sage.

KNBC.COM. (2002, November 24). *Los Angeles' gang warfare has claimed 20 lives in the past week*. Retrieved from www.streetgangs.com/topics/2002/112402capital.html

Koss, M. P., Gidycz, C. A., & Wisniewski, W. (1987). The scope of rape: Incidence and prevalence of sexual aggression and victimization in a national sample of higher education students. *Journal of Consulting and Clinical Psychology, 55,* 162-170.

Levant, R. (1994). *Male violence against female partners: Roots in male socialization and development*. Paper presented at the American Psychological Association meetings, Los Angeles.

Mahoney, P., & Williams, L. M. (1998). Sexual assault in marriage: Prevalence, consequences, and treatment of wife rape. In J. L. Jasinski & L. M. Williams (Eds.), *Partner violence: A comprehensive review of 20 years of research* (pp. 113-162). Thousand Oaks, CA: Sage.

Massey, D., & Denton, N. (1993). *American apartheid: Segregation and the making of the underclass*. Cambridge, MA: Harvard University Press.

Messerschmidt, J. W. (1993). *Masculinities and crime: Critique and reconceptualization*. Lanham, MD: Roman & Littlefield.

Messerschmidt, J. W. (1997). *Crime as structured action: Gender, race, class, and crime in the making*. Thousand Oaks, CA: Sage.

Messerschmidt, J. W. (2000). *Nine lives: Adolescent masculinities, the body, and violence*. Boulder: Westview.

Moynihan, M. (2003, July). *Establishing a community of responsibility*. Paper presented at the Annual Conference on Criminal Justice Research and Evaluation, U.S. National Institute of Justice, Washington, DC.

Newburn, T., & Stanko, E. A. (1994a). Introduction: Men, masculinities and crime. In T. Newburn & E. A. Stanko (Eds.), *Just boys doing business?: Men, masculinities and crime* (pp. 1-9). London: Routledge.

Newburn, T., & Stanko, E. A. (Eds.). (1994b). *Just boys doing business?: Men, masculinities and crime*. London: Routledge.

Newman, G. (1976). *Comparative deviance: Perception and law in six cultures*. New York: Elsevier.

Pagelow, M. (1993). Response to Hamberger's comments. *Journal of Interpersonal Violence, 8,* 137-139.

Perkins, U. E. (1987). *Explosion of Chicago's black street gangs: 1900 to the present.* Chicago: Third World Press.

Perry, B. (2003). Accounting for hate crime. In M. D. Schwartz & S. E. Hatty (Eds.), *Controversies in critical criminology* (pp.147-160). Cincinnati: Anderson.

Polk, K. (1994). *When men kill: Scenarios of masculine violence.* New York: Cambridge University Press.

Polk, K. (2003). Masculinities, femininities and homicide: Competing explanations for male violence. In M. D. Schwartz & S. E. Hatty (Eds.), *Controversies in critical criminology* (pp.133-146). Cincinnati: Anderson.

Raphael, J. (2001a). Domestic violence as a welfare-to-work barrier: Research and theoretical issues. In C. M. Renzetti, J. L. Edleson, & R. Kennedy Bergen (Eds.), *Sourcebook on violence against women* (pp. 443-456). Thousand Oaks, CA: Sage.

Raphael, J. (2001b). Public housing and domestic violence. *Violence Against Women, 7,* 699-706.

Reich, R. B. (2003, May 1). The economy is on the move – downward. *Los Angeles Times,* p.B15.

Reilly, R. (2003). *The life of Reilly.* New York: Sports Illustrated Books.

Renzetti, C. M., Edleson, J. L., & Kennedy Bergen, R. (Eds.). (2001). *Sourcebook on violence against women.* Thousand Oaks, CA: Sage.

Schissel, B. (1997). *Blaming children: Youth crime, moral panics and the politics of hate.* Halifax: Fernwood.

Schwartz, M. D., & DeKeseredy, W. S. (1997). *Sexual assault on the college campus: The role of male peer support.* Thousand Oaks, CA: Sage.

Schwartz, M. D., & Hatty, S. E. (2003). Introduction. In M. D. Schwartz & S. E. Hatty (Eds.), *Controversies in critical criminology* (pp. ix-xvii). Cincinnati: Anderson.

Schwendinger, J., & Schwendinger, H. (1983). *Rape and inequality.* Beverly Hills, CA: Sage.

Sernau, S. (2001). *Worlds apart: Social inequalities in a new century.* Thousand Oaks, CA: Pine Forge Press.

Shakur, S. (1994). *Monster: The autobiography of an L.A. gang member.* New York: Penguin.

Shelden, R. G., Tracy, S. K., & Brown, W. B. (2001). *Youth gangs in American society* (2nd ed.). Belmont, CA: Wadsworth.

Short, J. F. (1997). *Poverty, ethnicity, and violent crime.* Boulder, CO: Westview.

Sinclair, R. L. (2002). *Male peer support and male-to-female dating abuse committed by socially displaced male youth: An exploratory study.* Unpublished doctoral dissertation, Carleton University.

Smith, M. D. (1983). *Violence and sport.* Toronto: Butterworths.

Smith, M. D. (1990). Patriarchal ideology and wife beating: A test of a feminist hypothesis. *Violence and Victims, 5,* 257-273.

Stanko, E. A. (1994). Challenging the problem of men's individual violence. In T. Newburn & E. A. Stanko (Eds.), *Just boys doing business? Men, masculinities and crime* (pp.32-45). London: Routledge.

Straus, M. A. (1991). Discipline and deviance: Physical punishment of children and violence and other crime in childhood. *Social Problems, 38,* 133-154.

Thorne-Finch, R. (1992). *Ending the silence: The origins and treatment of male violence against women.* Toronto: University of Toronto Press.

Ursel, E. (1986). The state and the maintenance of patriarchy: A case study of family labor and welfare legislation. In J. Dickinson & B. Russell (Eds.), *Family, economy and state* (pp.150-191). Toronto: Garamond.

Wallace, A. (1986). *Homicide: The social reality.* Sydney: New South Wales Bureau of Crime Statistics and Research.

Warr, M. (2002). *Companions in crime: The social aspects of criminal conduct.* New York: Cambridge University Press.

Websdale, N., & Chesney-Lind, M. (1998). Doing violence to women: Research synthesis on the victimization of women. In L. H. Bowker (Ed.), *Masculinities and violence* (pp.55-81). Thousand Oaks, CA: Sage.

Weiner, N. A., Zahn, M. A., & Sagi, R. J. (1990). Introduction. In N. A. Weiner, M. A. Zahn, & R. J. Sagi (Eds.), *Violence: Patterns, causes, public policy.* San Diego: Harcourt, Brace, Jovanovich.

West, C. M., & Rose, S. (2000). Dating aggression among low income African American youth: An examination of gender differences and antagonistic beliefs. *Violence Against Women, 6,* 470-494.

West, C., & Zimmerman, D. H. (1987). Doing gender. *Gender and Society, 1,* 125-151.

Wilson, M., & Daly, M. (1992). Till death do us part. In J. Radford & D.E.H. Russell (Eds.), *Femicide: The politics of woman killing* (pp. 83-98). New York: Twayne.

Wilson, W. J. (1996). *When work disappears: The world of the new urban poor.* New York: Knopf.

Young, J. (1999). *The exclusive society.* London: Sage.

Zielenbach, S. (2000). *The art of revitalization: Improving conditions in distressed inner-city neighborhoods.* New York: Garland.

Zimring, F. E. (1998). *American youth violence.* New York: Oxford University Press.

21

Masculinity and Degrees of Bodily Normativity in Western Culture

Thomas J. Gerschick

What makes someone male or a man? Are people born with an unalterable sex, or can it be changed at will? If one is assigned to the sex category "male," must he always remain there? If one thinks of oneself as a man, is one? Must one have a penis in order to be a man? To what degree are sex and gender physical characteristics based in one's genetic code, the brain, and the body, and to what degree are they psychological, cultural, or social constructions? Do the answers to the above questions differ as historical, cultural, and structural contexts change? These questions concerning the relationship between the body, sex, and gender continue to be debated by scholars and activists in law, medicine, social sciences, humanities, and natural sciences. None, however, questions the central role of the body in social life.

Over the past 30 years, scholarship about the body spanning the natural sciences, humanities, and social sciences has exploded. Consequently, the study of the body is highly interdisciplinary. The literature reflects many different academic interest areas including cultural studies, health and illness, disability, women's/men's/gender studies, technology, sports, media studies, and medical sociology. The literature also addresses a wide range of subjects, including the relationship between agency and constraint; identity and structure; power, privilege, and inequality; surveillance and self-regulation; and similarities and differences by race, class, and sexuality, ability, and disability (Dworkin, 2001).

Some of this scholarship is biographical or empirical; some is more interpretive or theoretical. Much of the writing on the body has focused on females' bodies, largely because feminist scholarship arose as a critique of the androcentric nature of much of the previous scholarship. Because feminism focuses on inequality and emancipation, feminist scholarship detailed the various arenas in which women have historically been oppressed, including

Author's note: I would like to thank Bob Broad for his insights and many suggestions as he read multiple copies of this chapter. Additionally, I would like to thank the book editors and the copy editor for their patience, support, and advice, without which this chapter would not have been completed.

through their bodies. Examples of such topics of inquiry include body image (Bordo, 1995), eating disorders (B. W. Thompson, 1992), illness (Lorber, 1997), disability (Fine & Asch, 1988), cosmetic surgery (Davis, 1995), physical and sexual violence (Bart & Moran, 1993), self-defense (McCaughey, 1997), reproductive rights (Roberts, 1998), and sexuality (Collins, 2000).

There is increasing recognition that the diversity of human bodies does not fit neatly into Western culture's two sex/body categories. As a consequence, there is a burgeoning literature in what loosely might be called transgender/queer studies (Stryker, 1998).[1] Examples of the topics explored in this literature include intersexuality (Kessler, 1998), transsexuality and transgression (Bornstein, 1995), cross-dressing (Garber, 1993), gender blurring (Devor, 1989), and multigendered societies (W. L. Williams, 1986).

The development of the Disability Rights Movement in the late 1960s led to an upsurge of interest in disability studies among people with disabilities, academics, and researchers throughout the world (Barnes, Barton, & Oliver, 2002). This has generated an increasingly expansive multidisciplinary literature spanning cultural studies, the humanities, and social sciences (Barnes et al., 2002). Comprising a combination of personal accounts and scholarly works, this literature has shifted researchers' thinking about disability away from medical conditions requiring pity and intervention to an understanding of the social conditions that create and reinforce disability (Monaghan, 1998). Hence, the emphasis is on the cultural, attitudinal, and structural barriers that people with disabilities face rather than on their physical limitations. This movement has increasingly become institutionalized. In the United States, for instance, Temple University's Institute on Disabilities recently celebrated its 30th anniversary. The Society for Disability Studies was founded in 1982 and shortly thereafter began publishing the *Disability Studies Quarterly*, and the University of Illinois at Chicago created the first PhD program in disability studies in the United States in 1998.

Building on a literature dating to the 1970s that focused on men's health issues, masculinity and sports, and men's sexuality and violence, there has been a steady growth of interest in male bodies and their relation to social life (Bordo, 2000; Connell, 1983, 1995; Goldstein, 1995; Kimmel, 1994). Increasing attention has been paid to the male body in sports (Dworkin & Messner, 1999; Messner, 1992) and disability (Gerschick, 2000; Gerschick & Miller, 1995; Shakespeare, Gillespie-Sells, & Davies, 1996), health and illness (Sabo & Gordon, 1995), globalization (Connell, 1998), and sexuality (Connell, 1990). Race and ethnicity, class, and the male body are relatively unexplored topics. (Some notable exceptions include Almaguer, 1991, and Stodder, 1979.)

This chapter discusses a range of biographical, empirical, and theoretical literature on masculinities and the body, with particular attention to men with less-normative bodies, especially men with disabilities.[2] It summarizes and analyzes key questions, themes, and debates in this literature and concludes with suggestions for future research. The lives of men with less-normative bodies, such as those with disabilities, provide an instructive arena in which to study the intersection of bodies and masculinity.

Depending on the degree of their deviation, men with less-normative bodies contravene many of the beliefs associated with being a man. Yet little has been written about the intersection of less-normative bodies and masculinity. Studying their circumstances provides valuable insight into the struggles that all men experience in this realm. Men with less-normative bodies also occupy unique subject positions in what Patricia Hill Collins (2000) calls the matrix of domination and privilege. These men have gender privilege by virtue of being men, yet this privilege is eroded to differing degrees by their less-normative bodies, which leaves them subject to a range of possible sanctions. Their positions in the gender stratification hierarchy provide insight that is obscured from those with more conventional bodies (Janeway, 1980).

APPROACHES TO THE BODY

To what degree are bodies shaped by natural and social/cultural influences? Are the differences among and between female and male bodies largely due to biology, therefore legitimizing sex and gender stratification? Or are they largely socially constructed to benefit some men at other men's and women's expense? To what degree are our thoughts, behaviors, emotions, and physical bodies shaped by the genes we inherit versus our life experiences? At the heart of these questions are assumptions, theories, and debates over the definition of the body and what shapes it.

Bodies mean different things to different theorists depending on the questions they ask, the assumptions they make, and the methods they utilize. When one synthesizes the various approaches to studying the body and the resulting conclusions, the accumulated knowledge demonstrates that "the body is simultaneously a physical, biological entity and a symbolic cultural artifact" (Johnston, 2001, p. xv). That adherents of these different views of the body tend to ignore other perspectives and thereby talk past one another makes it more difficult to improve the existing theories about the body. It is probably most appropriate, then, to think of the literature on the body as multifaceted, with little overlap or integration.

Bodies are simultaneously created, maintained, and changed through a constant and enduring interplay of biological and social forces. Bodies are both internal subjective environments and objects for others to observe, evaluate, and project upon (Johnston, 2001). Bodies and the resulting bodily practices are at once individual and collective entities. Humans actively engage the physical and social worlds through the medium of their bodies (Toombs, 2001). Bodies and bodily expectations vary widely across time and space. They are shaped by social factors including race, class, gender, and disability. People are self-reflexive and agentic as they negotiate their way through cultural values, rules, and regulations of social life. Bodies thus incorporate and live cultural tensions and paradoxes. This brief synthesis is not a claim of consensus; multiple perspectives exist regarding what constitutes bodies.

Biologically Based Explanations

The recent, contentious debate between sociologist J. R. Udry (2000, 2001) and his critics (Kennelly, Merz, & Lorber, 2001; Miller & Costello, 2001; Risman, 2001) published in the flagship journal of the American Sociological Association demonstrates that the debate over biological causes of gender behavior continues to rage. Although the biological perspective has some high-profile adherents such as E. O. Wilson, accounts of how popular it is and among whom vary. Some commentators (Kimmel,

2000) maintain it is pervasive among biologists, whereas others (O'Brien, 1999, p. 37) maintain that most natural and social scientists agree that human behavior, including gendered behavior, is a complex combination of genetic tendencies and environmental influences.

Defining the biological perspective is difficult for a number of reasons. First, it shares at least three names—biological essentialism, sociobiology, and evolutionary psychology—thereby causing undue confusion. Second, a range of viewpoints occurs along a continuum within this perspective; the viewpoints depend on the emphasis that adherents place on biological factors and the degree to which they acknowledge social influences on human bodies, behavior, and psychologies, if at all. Third, it is clouded by politics because of the implications of the theory. Critics of sociobiology maintain that it unjustly rationalizes sexual and gender inequality.

Representing one end of the continuum, biological essentialism, at its core, is a belief in the primacy of genes. That is, genes determine and control the human body and brain, and consequently behavior and psychology. The 23 pairs of human chromosomes are thought to carry between 80,000 and 100,000 genes that regulate the expression of all physical, psychological, and behavioral characteristics and traits. At various points in a human's life, these genes instruct when and in what amounts "male" or "masculinizing" hormones such as androgen and testosterone or "female" or "feminizing" hormones such as progesterone and estrogen are released.

The differences in hormones are then presumed to be responsible for seemingly natural and pervasive bodily, psychological, and behavioral differences between women and men. Specifically, hormonal processes are thought to be responsible for bodily differences such as brain structure and the use of the brain, verbal abilities, and math and science abilities. Hormones also are thought to be responsible for differences in interests, occupational preferences and achievement, sexuality, and parenting styles. Although adherents to this perspective recognize that some overlap exists between the sexes, they think of them as largely dichotomous, as demonstrated by the bodily, psychological, and behavioral differences that are thought to complement one another. This is codified in the English language through such phrases as "the opposite sex."

These differences are thought to be the result of evolutionary adaptation to natural environments that became embedded in humans' genetic structures over long periods of time. "Survival of the fittest" selects for success: Beings with traits that promote survival or reproduction pass on their genes, and others die out. Examples include explanations for males' typically higher scores in math and science, females' sexual selectiveness, and males' promiscuity, and rape. For instance, biologist Randy Thornhill and anthropologist Craig T. Palmer (2000) suggested that rape could be an alternative reproduction strategy resulting from natural selection. Evolutionarily, rape may have increased men's chances of successfully transmitting their genes. Genetics, then, are thought to determine human bodies and the psychologies, abilities, and behaviors that emanate from them. The focus in the biological perspective consequently is much more on differences between the sexes and genders and the similarities within them. Because they are both rooted in biology, sex and gender are thought to be essentially the same thing, and the terms are generally used interchangeably.

According to this perspective, then, the body plays two key roles. First, it houses hormones and genes. Second, it represents the behavioral, psychological, and physical expression of those genes. Consequently, bodies are simultaneously perceived to be both the source of sex differences and the physiological, psychological, and behavioral evidence of them. Because these differences are presumed to be rooted in nature and largely static and immutable, attempts to change them will lead to serious social problems (Udry, 2001).

More recently, some researchers have exhibited a greater appreciation of and interest in interactions between biology and social and environmental forces, along with the effects of these interactions on the body and behavior. Although it may be impossible to unravel completely the connections among these, increasingly the consensus is that biology provides human potential that in turn is nurtured and/or constrained by culture. Researchers pursuing this line of thought seek to end what Natalie Angier (2003) characterized as a "false yet obdurate" dichotomy between nature and nurture.

For instance, psychologist David Reiss and his colleagues studied 720 pairs of adolescents with different degrees of genetic relatedness, from identical twins to step siblings. Their research (Reiss, Plomin, Neiderhiser, & Hetherington, 2003) suggests that genetic tendencies are encouraged or stifled by specific parental responses. "To have any effect, genes must be activated. Whether, and how strongly, genes that underlie complex behaviors are turned on, or 'expressed,'" noted Reiss, "depends on the interactions and relationships a child has with the important people in his or her life" (quoted in Begley, 2000, p. 64). Thus, genetic factors influence development, but social processes are critical for shaping those influences (Begley, 2000). How this interactive effect works remains a subject of much speculation and research.

This new wave of research demonstrates that biological and social explanations for anatomical, behavioral, and psychological differences among humans are not necessarily incompatible, although they are frequently pitted against one another (O'Brien, 1999). Unfortunately, integrative thinking is in its infancy and is only beginning to extend to the relationship between the body and gender (Fausto-Sterling, 2000).

Social Constructionist Perspectives[3]

> The realness of social forces, whether one accepts them uncritically or wrestles them continually, can be seen written across the body. (O'Brien, 1999, p. 64)

Counter to biological theorists, social constructionists stress bodily sex similarities while focusing on the social processes through which gender differences are created, maintained, and changed. Social constructionists acknowledge that males and females have highly differentiated reproductive systems, but they maintain that there are only minor physical differences between the sexes and great overlaps in physique and capacity between them (Connell, 1999, p. 450). These minor differences are socially nurtured throughout the life course to the point that very different sexual beings are created. Consequently, social constructionists attend to the social, cultural, and psychological processes involved in the creation of gendered bodies, behaviors, and practices.

One of the most profound decisions that is ever made for a human being occurs at birth, or in some cases in utero via a sonogram. That decision is the assignment to a dichotomous sex category via a cursory look at the genitals. This assignment sets in motion a powerful set of social practices that strongly shape, but do not determine, the trajectory of an individual's life. Once an infant is bodily assigned to a sex category, she or he is then assigned to the associated gender category: feminine or masculine. On the basis of this, human beings then expect different things from these "different" infants. These expectations vary according to the historical, cultural, structural, and global contexts.

Yet, as a brief look around the United Nations or the Olympics reveals, bodies vary tremendously; they do not fit neatly into dichotomous categories. Biology partially accounts for this. Basic genetic variation accounts for some. In other cases, missing, fragmented, or extra sex chromosomes and exposure to toxins contribute to this variation, as reflected in hermaphrodites and pseudo-hermaphrodites. Yet, social constructionists maintain that social processes are the primary factor in bodily and gender differentiation. Thus, for social constructionists, bodies physically exist along a continuum rather than as a dichotomy.

The social differentiation and disciplining of bodies assigned to the sex categories of female and male is reinforced throughout one's lifetime via social institutions such as school, families, medicine, and the law. For instance, from birth, girls and boys are taught to use their bodies very differently. Karin Martin's (1998) research on the hidden curriculum of preschools demonstrates how boys are encouraged to be expansive in the use of their bodies whereas girls are taught to be reserved. These differential bodily practices, taught covertly, reinforce the belief that boys and girls are "naturally" different. It is through this training and reinforcement that masculinity becomes internalized in boys' bodies. Practices become habits. As these become more deeply internalized, males become increasingly self-monitoring (S. J. Williams & Bendelow, 1998). Social constructionists, then, are interested in how meanings, practices, and identities consolidate consciously and unconsciously in the body and the ramifications of this for men and women. Thus, they are interested in the interplay between agency and structure.

Definitions of masculinity and masculine bodies vary within different historical, structural, and cultural contexts: There are likely few, if any, transhistorical or cross-cultural ideals; what is considered normative varies across time and space (Burton, 2001; Kimmel, 2000). Kimmel (1994), for instance, tracked the arc of masculinities and their relation to bodies in the United States between 1832 and 1920. As work increasingly became bureaucratized, men turned to the gym, athletics, and the outdoors as the foundation of their masculinity. They read self-improvement books and quaffed elixirs and tonics. They grew beards and moustaches and developed their muscles, all as ways of distinguishing themselves from the feminine. Manly countenances and physiques demonstrated masculinity. "The body did not contain the man," Kimmel (1994, p. 26) concluded; "it was the man."

Similarly representing the centrality of the body to masculinity, but utilizing very different standards, the Wodabe men of the Sahara utilize physical beauty as the foundation of their masculinity. "To be ugly," a Wodabe proverb goes, "is to be unforgiven" (Knickmeyer, 2003, p. A10). One of the first items entrusted to a boy is a mirror. Lifelong attention to appearance culminates in a series of beauty pageants in which adult males compete to win prestigious brides. Competitors and their families go to great lengths to prepare for these pageants. Families may spend up to a year fashioning the young men's costumes, bedecking them with embroidery, dangling earrings, and a profusion of necklaces. A young man will travel for days to find the right ingredients to make his face paint (Knickmeyer, 2003). Accounts like these are rare; there is much we do not know about cross-cultural and transhistorical bodily standards. Our task is becoming more complex as conceptions of masculinity and masculine bodies increasingly become more global, and this occurs as the media and multinational corporations penetrate the remotest regions of the planet (Connell, 1998). Consequently, this is a key area for future research.

Because of the large amount of human variation across time and space and the array of expectations and contexts, it makes sense when discussing the body to discuss degrees of normativeness—from more normative to less. There are many ways in which a body can be less normative. Characteristics such as race, ethnicity, class, age, physique, weight, height, ability, disability, appearance, and skin color predominate. People can be less normative by being too light, too dark, too fat or too skinny, too poor, too young or too old, too tall, too short, too awkward, or too uncoordinated. The degree to which one is bodily normative matters considerably because it helps place one in the stratification order (Connell, 1983; Shakespeare et al., 1996). The treatment one experiences, then, depends on the degree of normativeness, one's resources, and the particular historical, cultural, and structural contexts. People are privileged by the degree to which they approximate cultural ideals (Gerschick, 1998).

The degree to which bodily and gender variation has been accepted has varied across time and culture. Although the number of sex and gender categories has varied historically and culturally, in the West and increasingly across the globe, societies are committed to two, and only two, sex and gender categories. For instance, in the contemporary West, when there is both sexual ambiguity (resulting from chromosomal problems, for instance) and access to technology, surgeons seek to create bodies that more neatly fit into cultural categories. In other places and times, especially where surgical technology does not exist, there has been greater acceptance of sexual and gender diversity, although individuals outside the norms have been assigned to special categories. Anthropologist Walter Williams (1986), for example, has documented a range of genders occupied by Native American men called berdache and the resulting social relations that occurred prior to European colonization. Unfortunately, colonization largely ended these practices among indigenous people in the Americas, demonstrating the early power of globalization.

Bodies are symbolic. One's body serves as a type of social currency that signifies one's worth. Consequently, people with less-normative bodies are vulnerable to being denied social recognition and validation.[4] People respond to one another's bodies, which initiates social processes such as validation and the assignment of status (Goffman, 1963). Thus, to have a less-normative body is not only a physical condition; it is also a social and stigmatized one (Goffman, 1963; Zola, 1982).

This stigma is embodied in the popular stereotypes of people whose bodies are less normative. People with disabilities, for instance, are perceived to be weak, passive, and dependent (Shapiro, 1993). Our language exemplifies this stigmatization; people with disabilities are de-formed, dis-eased, dis-abled, dis-ordered, ab-normal, and in-valid (Zola, 1982, p. 206).

Asian men in the West are perceived either to be shrewd and cunning or effeminate, neutered, and weak; either martial arts masters and evil sadistic soldiers or houseboys, laundrymen, computer nerds, and faceless salarymen (Espiritu, 1997; Iwata, 1991).

This stigma is embedded in daily interactions among people. People are evaluated in terms of normative expectations and are, because of their bodies, frequently found wanting. As demonstrated by the social responses to people with disabilities, people with less-normative bodies are avoided, ignored, and marginalized (Fine & Asch, 1988; Shapiro, 1993). They experience a range of reactions from subtle indignities and slights to overt hostility and outright cruelty. This treatment creates subtle but formidable physical, economic, psychological, architectural, and social obstacles to their participation in all aspects of social life. For example, writing about Asian American men in the United States, Asian American journalist Edward Iwata (1991, p. 52) observed the following (note how central the body is to his description of these dynamics):

> by others and by ourselves, we're rendered impotent. I wasn't a limp lover. But outside my home or bedroom, I felt powerless—desexed like a baby chick. It was as if I didn't exist. Employers didn't acknowledge my work. Professors in college rebuffed my remarks in the classroom. Maitre d's ignored my presence in restaurants. I felt voiceless, faceless. (1991, p. 129)

Having a less-normative body can also become a primary identity that overshadows almost all other aspects of one's identity.

The type of less-normative body—its visibility, the severity of it, whether it is physical or mental in origin, and the contexts—mediate the degree to which a person with a less-normative body is socially compromised (Gerschick, 2000). For instance, a severe case of the Epstein-Barr virus can disable someone, thereby creating a less-normative body; however, typically the condition is not readily apparent and as a consequence does not automatically trigger stigmatization and devaluation. Conversely, having quadriplegia and utilizing a wheelchair for mobility is highly visual, is perceived to be severe, and frequently elicits invalidation. One of the challenges facing researchers is to develop a systematic theory to address the degrees of non-normativity and the circumstances that lead to different levels of stigmatization and marginalization and how these differ for women and for men.

The degree to which one's body is devalued is also affected by other social characteristics including social class, sexual orientation, age, and race and ethnicity. For instance, Hearn (1995) notes that although a paradoxical and frequently contradictory range of images of older men exists in the West, those images are dominated by marginalization, redundancy, and obsolescence. Older men are not depicted or treated as hegemonic men in the United States, but rather as diminished (E. H. Thompson, 1994). Like age, race also factors into the valuation of bodies. For the 40 years between 1932 and 1972, the United States Public Health Service conducted a study of the effects of late-stage untreated syphilis on 399 poor black men in Alabama (Jones, 1993, p. 1). According to the press, at least 28 and perhaps as many as 100 men died as the direct result of complications caused by the treatable syphilis. Others developed other serious conditions that may have contributed to their deaths (Jones, 1993, p. 2). The study was roundly criticized for callously not treating the men, actively preventing them from getting treatment, and keeping knowledge of the disease from them in order to indulge scientists' curiosity (Jones, 1993). This follows a long history in the United States and globally of abusing black males' bodies with impunity. Thus, a hierarchy of bodies exists in any particular historical, cultural, structural, and global context.

People with less-normative bodies are engaged in an asymmetrical power relationship with their more-normative-bodied counterparts, who have the power to validate their bodies and their gender. In order to accomplish gender, each person in a social situation needs to be recognized by others as appropriately masculine or feminine. Those with whom we interact continuously assess our gender performance and decide whether we are "doing gender" appropriately in that situation. Our "audience" or interaction partners then hold us accountable and sanction us in a variety of ways in order to encourage compliance (West & Zimmerman, 1987). Our need for social approval and validation as gendered beings further encourages conformity. Much is at stake in this process because one's sense of self rests precariously upon the audience's decision to validate or reject one's

gender performance. Successful enactment bestows status and acceptance; failure invites embarrassment and humiliation (West & Zimmerman, 1987).

Consequently, bodies are central to achieving social recognition as appropriately gendered beings. In the contemporary West, men's gender performance tends to be judged using the standard of hegemonic masculinity, which represents the optimal attributes, activities, behaviors, and values expected of men in a culture (Connell, 1983, 1990). Social scientists have identified career orientation, activeness, athleticism, sexual desirability and virility, independence, and self-reliance as exalted masculine attributes in Western culture/society (Connell, 1983, 1995; Ervø & Johansson, 2003; Gerschick & Miller, 1995; Kimmel, 1994). In the developing world, anthropological accounts suggest that toughness, the ability to endure pain and drink to excess, willingness to take risks, and sexual performance are all central to achieving masculinity (Gilmore, 1990). Thus, men whose bodies allow them to evidence the identified characteristics are differentially rewarded over those who cannot. Despite the fact that attaining these attributes is often unrealistic and more based in fantasy than in reality, men continue to internalize them as ideals and strive to demonstrate them as well as judge themselves and other men using them. Women also tend to judge men using these standards. Successfully creating and maintaining self-satisfactory masculine gender identities under these circumstances is an almost Sisyphean task. Consequently, masculinity is threatened when corporeal appearance and performance are discordant with hegemonic expectations, such as in the case of having a having a less-normative body (Connell, 1983, 1995; Ervø & Johansson, 2003; Gerschick & Miller, 1995).

Because of the tremendous pressures to conform and the perceived rewards associated with doing so, people will go to great lengths to make their bodies appear more normatively masculine. How and what they do is influenced by gender expectations and financial, technological, and cultural resources available to them. A range of possible bodily modification practices exists, from relatively low-tech procedures such as exercise/body building, tattoos, dieting, piercings, and cutting/scarring to more technologically sophisticated forms of cosmetic surgery such as hair transplants and rhinoplasty. Klein (1993), for instance, introduced readers to the importance of musculature in establishing and maintaining masculinity in the United States. Among the Karo of Ethiopia, where technology is relatively undeveloped, men use elaborate hair designs, body painting, and piercings as trademarks of their masculinity. Scarification of the chest and wearing of gray or ochre-colored hair buns are reserved for men who have proven their masculinity by killing an enemy or a dangerous animal (Burton, 2001, p. 60d). In the developed world, using surgical techniques is more common. For instance, Iwata (1991, p. 52) underwent cosmetic surgery to replace his Asian facial features with Caucasian:

> It is a taboo subject, but true. Many people of color have, at some point in their youths, imagined themselves as Caucasian, the Nordic or Western European ideal. Hop Sing meets Rock Hudson. Michael Jackson magically transformed into Robert Redford. For myself, an eye and nose job—or blepharoplasty and rhinoplasty in surgeons' tongue—would bring me the gift of acceptance. The flick of a scalpel would buy me respect. . . . I felt compelled to measure up to a cultural ideal in a culture that had never asked me what my ideal was.

Bodies, then, largely are not fixed biologically but rather are significantly malleable, fluid, and plastic and are greatly influenced by context-specific gender expectations. Physical construction of bodies, then, is intimately linked to social construction.

In addition to disciplining their own bodies, people will go to great lengths to discipline others' to ensure that they are more normative too. A premier example is the treatment of intersexed bodies in the United States. ABC News' *Primetime Live* (1997) aired a segment on children with ambiguous or damaged genitals. In one of the two cases highlighted, a genetically male child was born without any genitals. In the other case, a boy's penis was destroyed in a circumcision accident. Following medical professionals' advice that the boys could never have normally functioning penises, in both cases the parents authorized sex reassignment surgery to raise the children as girls. Without a functioning penis, the doctors maintained that they could not be either male or a man. In one case, the doctors were quoted as saying that without the surgery,

"He will have to recognize that he is incomplete, physically defective, and that he must live apart" (Colapinto, 2000, p. 16).

As the above examples indicate, penises are particularly tangible symbols of masculinity. Circumcision, for instance, is a popular masculine rite of passage in many cultures. Among the Xhosa and Basotho in Africa, male circumcision initiates one into manhood (Cauvin, 2001). Historically, the ritual was performed as boys were preparing to search for paid work, typically in their early twenties. However, economic changes, urbanization, industrialization, and peer pressure have led to a decrease in ages, typically closer to 18 and increasingly younger than that. In cities and universities, uncircumcised teens are increasingly shunned or derided. As a result, boys pursue circumcision and manhood at an increasing risk. In 2001, at least 35 boys died from infections caused by botched procedures, and hundreds more were mutilated (Cauvin, 2001). This demonstrates just one of the ways that masculinity can be injurious to one's health. Anticircumcision activists in the United States maintain that circumcision is a masculine form of genital mutilation. Some "cut men," as they refer to themselves, resort to weights or tape to stretch their penile skin back over the glans; others undergo surgery to restore the foreskin/prepuce (Newman, 1991; Whipple, 1987).

Like penis shape, penis size has long been a preoccupation of men in the West in regard to their masculinity. Perry (1992), describing himself as "hung like a hamster," details his constant vigilance regarding his "manhood." He faked taking showers after gym class by using toilet water to slick his hair, quit the swim team in high school because the suits were too revealing, and pledged a particular fraternity solely because it had individual toilets and shower stalls. He explicated years of feeling inadequate, impotent, cheated, and humiliated because of his small size.

In some cultures, relief from such predicaments is available. In the United States, there are doctors who specialize in penile enlargement. Whether or not penis size can be dramatically improved remains a topic of debate, but it is known that there are limitations to technological intervention. Presently, surgical techniques are not advanced enough to create a functional or normative appearing penis. Consequently, many female-to-male transsexuals elect not to have the "surgery down there" and leave their vaginas intact. Although they typically have radical mastectomies to reduce their breasts and adopt a public persona of being male and masculine, their bodies are not completely in concert with their new identity. Whether or not and under what conditions the "partial operative" transsexuals might represent challenges to the gender order is a matter of debate (Cram & Schermerhorn, 1997).

It is not just how bodies look that secures the label of masculine, but also how they move and what they do. Bodies operate kinesthetically as a key mechanism through which men perform and achieve gender. Kimmel (1994, pp. 37-38) observed that males' bodies are "the ultimate testing ground for identity in a world in which collective solutions to the problem of identity seem all but discredited." For instance, on Truk Island, a tiny atoll in the Pacific, men historically have associated masculinity with daring and risk. They chanced their health and their lives by undertaking long fishing expeditions in shark-infested waters with little thought to safety. Drinking to excess, fighting, and seeking sexual conquest were all elements of their quest to be recognized as males (Marshall, 1979, cited in Gilmore, 1990). Among the rural cultivating Amhara tribe of Ethiopia, manliness was demonstrated via participation in bloody whipping matches in which faces frequently were lacerated. Any sign of pain or weakness resulted in mockery and taunts of being effeminate. Boys also would burn their arms with hot embers to demonstrate their masculinity (Reminick, 1982, cited in Gilmore, 1990).

In a far different context, Stodder (1979) detailed the abuse he took as a roughneck (oil rig worker) as men continually tested each other's masculinity by challenging their bodies. This involved subjecting each other to very dangerous pranks, such as dropping men suspended by a tether 100 feet as if the safety device failed, only to stop them short of crashing onto the oil rig floor. Threats of anal rape were frequent and sometimes involved going so far as tying and stripping the potential victim and threatening him with a tarred implement. Despite the constant challenges to his masculinity and sexuality, Stodder also described the sense of accomplishment he experienced from earning his place in this particular men's club. By working at

breakneck and dangerous speeds and surviving the constant challenges to his masculinity, he proved himself a man while simultaneously enriching his employer. In this latter way, his body and the bodies of men like him can be understood as instrumental commodities to be sacrificed to capitalism.

In addition to what they represent, what they look like, and what they physically do, bodies also contain minds—the locus of cognition where people create meaning about gender. Historically, some philosophers conceived of the mind as masculine and distinct from the body. Men's minds represented rationality and logic. Conversely, women were thought to represent and be governed by the body. They were earthly, irrational, and wanton (S. J. Williams & Bendelow, 1998). Despite many attempts, the relationship of the body to the brain and to the mind has yet to be satisfactorily theorized. Poet Kenny Fries (1997, p. 220), who was born with a disability affecting his legs, asked, for instance, "Can anyone comprehend how the mind reacts to what the body remembers?" People experience their worlds through their bodies; that experience is simultaneously physical and cognitive, but the relationship of these components is not yet understood. Consequently, this represents another promising avenue of research. As the following example demonstrates, we have much to think about.

For some men in some cultures, the foundation of their masculinity is not in their physical bodies but rather in their minds. For instance, the traditional emphasis on literacy and love of learning in Jewish culture confers dignity and masculinity. In the United States, however, intellectualism is a cultural liability (Kimmel, 1988). Because of this, Jewish men in many areas of the Diaspora are often considered effeminate and unathletic, that is, as less than men. "The historical consequences of centuries of laws against Jews, of anti-Semitic oppression," Kimmel (1988, p. 154) argues, "are a cultural identity and even a self-perception of being 'less than men,' who are too weak, too fragile, too frightened to care for our own."

NOTES

1. Stryker (1998) described in detail how scholars wrangle over terms and definitions. No

universal language exists to reflect the diversity of less-normative bodies, sexes, and genders.

2. Wherever possible, I draw on examples from different time periods and across the globe. However, most of the extant literature focuses on men in the West (Ervø & Johannson, 2003), and consequently this is reflected in the examples that I utilize throughout this chapter. Within this literature, the United States is grossly overrepresented; this chapter reflects that overrepresentation. Addressing this limitation is a fruitful area for future research.

3. Although the focus of this chapter is masculinity and the body, the social and bodily dynamics articulated below generally hold for both men and women. Consequently, they are presented as such. Given the allotted space, it is beyond the scope of this chapter to explore the ways in which these dynamics vary for women and men.

4. The next several pages draw on and extend my previous research. Insights in this section are drawn from an in-depth interview study of 10 men in southeast Michigan, United States (Gerschick, 1998; Gerschick & Miller, 1995) and synthesis of a diverse body of literature focusing on the intersection of gender and disability (Gerschick, 2000).

REFERENCES

Almaguer, T. (1991). Chicano men: A cartography of homosexual identity and behavior. *Differences, 3*(2), 75-100.

Angier, N. (2003, February 5). Not just genes: Moving beyond nature vs. nurture. *New York Times,* p. F1.

Barnes, C., Barton, L., & Oliver, M. (2002). *Disability studies today.* Cambridge, UK: Polity.

Bart, P. B., & Moran, E. G. (Eds.). (1993). *Violence against women: The bloody footprints.* Newbury Park, CA: Sage.

Begley, S. (2000, March 27). The nature of nurturing. *Newsweek,* p. 64.

Beisser, A. (1989). *Flying without wings: Personal reflections on being disabled.* New York: Doubleday.

Bordo, S. (1995). *Unbearable weight: Feminism, Western culture, and the body* (Reprint ed.). Berkeley: University of California Press.

Bordo, S. (2000). *The male body : A new look at men in public and in private.* New York: Farrar Straus & Giroux.

Bornstein, K. (1995). *Gender outlaw: On men, women, and the rest of us.* New York: Vintage Books.

Burton, J. M. (2001). *Culture and the human body: An anthropological perspective.* Prospect Heights, IL: Waveland Press.

Cauvin, H. E. (2001, August 6). How rush to manhood scars young Africans. *New York Times,* p. A6.

Colapinto, J. (2000). *As nature made him.* New York: HarperCollins.

Collins, P. H. (2000). *Black feminist thought: Knowledge, consciousness, and the politics of empowerment* (2nd ed.). New York: Routledge.

Connell, R. W. (1983). *Which way is up? Essays on sex, class, and culture.* Sydney: George Allen & Unwin.

Connell, R. W. (1990). An iron man: The body and some contradictions of hegemonic masculinity. In M. Messner & D. Sabo (Eds.), *Sport, men, and the gender order* (pp. 83-96). Champaign, IL: Human Kinetics.

Connell, R. W. (1995). *Masculinities.* Berkeley: University of California Press.

Connell, R. W. (1998). Masculinities and globalization. *Men and Masculinities, 1*(1), 3-23.

Connell, R. W. (1999). Making gendered people: Bodies, identities, sexualities. In M. M. Ferree, J. Lorber, & B. B. Hess (Eds.), *Revisioning gender* (pp. 449-471). Thousand Oaks, CA: Sage.

Cram, B., & Schermerhorn, C. (1997). *You don't know Dick: Courageous hearts of transgendered men* [Video]. Berkeley: University of California Extension Center for Media and Independent Learning.

Davis, K. (1995). *Reshaping the female body: The dilemma of cosmetic surgery.* New York: Routledge.

Devor, H. (1989). *Gender blending: Confronting the limits of duality.* Bloomington: Indiana University Press.

Dworkin, S. (2001, March). Sex and gender matters in the "sociology of the body." *American Sociological Association Sex and Gender News,* p. 2.

Dworkin, S. L., & Messner, M. A. (1999). Just do . . . what? Sports, bodies, gender. In M. M. Ferree, J. Lorber, & B. B. Hess (Eds.), *Revisioning gender* (pp. 341-361). Thousand Oaks, CA: Sage.

Ervø, S., & Johansson, T. (2003). *Bending bodies: Moulding masculinities* (Vol. 2). Aldershot, UK: Ashgate.

Espiritu, Y. L. (1997). *Asian American women and men.* Thousand Oaks, CA: Sage.

Fausto-Sterling, A. (2000). *Sexing the body: Gender politics and the construction of sexuality.* New York: Basic Books.

Fine, M., & Asch, A. (Eds.). (1988). *Women with disabilities: Essays in psychology, culture, and politics.* Philadelphia: Temple University Press.

Fries, K. (1997). *Body, remember.* New York: Dutton.

Garber, M. B. (1993). *Vested interests: Cross-dressing and cultural anxiety.* New York: HarperPerennial.

Gerschick, T. J. (1998). Sisyphus in a wheelchair: Men with physical disabilities confront gender domination. In J. O'Brien & J. Howard (Eds.), *Everyday inequalities: Critical inquiries* (pp. 189-211). Oxford, England: Blackwell.

Gerschick, T. J. (2000). Toward a theory of disability and gender. *Signs, 25*(4), 1263-1268.

Gerschick, T. J., & Miller, A. S. (1995). Coming to terms: Masculinity and physical disability. In D. Sabo & D. F. Gordon (Eds.), *Men's health and illness: Gender, power, and the body* (pp. 183-204). Thousand Oaks, CA: Sage.

Gilmore, D. D. (1990). *Manhood in the making: Cultural concepts of masculinity*. New Haven, CT: Yale University Press.

Goffman, E. (1963). *Stigma: Notes on the management of spoiled identity*. New York: Simon and Schuster.

Goldstein, L. (Ed.). (1995). *The male body: Features, destinies, exposures*. Ann Arbor: University of Michigan Press.

Hearn, J. (1995). Imaging the aging of men. In M. Featherstone & A. Wernick (Eds.), *Images of aging: Cultural representations of later life* (pp. 97-115). London: Routledge.

Iwata, E. (1991, May). Race without face. *San Francisco Focus*, pp. 50-53, 129-132.

Janeway, E. (1980). *Powers of the weak*. New York: Alfred A. Knopf.

Johnston, J. R. (Ed.). (2001). *The American body in context: An anthology*. Wilmington, DE: Scholarly Resources.

Jones, J. H. (1993). *Bad blood: The Tuskegee syphilis experiment*. New York: Free Press.

Kennelly, I., Merz, S. M., & Lorber, J. (2001). Comment: What is gender? *American Sociological Review, 66*(4), 598-604.

Kessler, S. J. (1998). *Lessons from the intersexed*. New Brunswick, NJ: Rutgers University Press.

Kimmel, M. (1988). Judaism, masculinity and feminism. In H. Brod (Ed.), *A mensch among men: Explorations in Jewish masculinity* (pp. 153-156). Freedom, CA: The Crossing Press.

Kimmel, M. S. (1994). Consuming manhood: The feminization of American culture and the recreation of the male body, 1832-1920. In L. Goldstein (Ed.), *The male body* (pp. 12-41). Ann Arbor: University of Michigan Press.

Kimmel, M. S. (2000). *The gendered society*. New York: Oxford University Press.

Klein, A. M. (1993). *Little big men: Bodybuilding subculture and gender construction*. Albany: State University of New York Press.

Knickmeyer, E. (2003, December 26). Men compete for wives in pageant. *Pantagraph*, p. A10.

Lorber, J. (1997). *Gender and the social construction of illness*. Thousand Oaks, CA: Sage.

Martin, K. A. (1998). Becoming a gendered body: Practices of preschools. *American Sociological Review, 63*, 494-511.

McCaughey, M. (1997). *Real knockouts: The physical feminism of women's self-defense*. New York: New York University Press.

Messner, M. A. (1992). *Power at play: Sports and the problem of masculinity*. Boston: Beacon.

Miller, E. M., & Costello, C. Y. (2001). Comment: The limits of biological determinism. *American Sociological Review, 66*(4), 592-597.

Monaghan, P. (1998, January 23). Pioneering field of disability studies challenges approaches and attitudes. *Chronicle of Higher Education*, p. A15.

Murphy, R. F. (1990). *The body silent*. New York: Norton.

Newman, R. (1991, Fall/Winter). Circumcision: The false initiation. *Changing Men*, 19-21.

O'Brien, J. (1999). *Social prisms*. Thousand Oaks, CA: Pine Forge.

Perry, G. (1992). Hung like a hamster: The heavy weight of a small penis. In C. Harding (Ed.), *Wingspan: Journal of the male spirit* (pp. 41-42). New York: St. Martin's.

Primetime Live. (September 3, 1997). *Boy or girl? What happens when doctors choose your child's sex* [television show]. New York: American Broadcasting Corporation.

Reiss, D., Plomin, R., Neiderhiser, J., & Hetherington, E. M. (2003). *The relationship code: Deciphering genetic and social influences on adolescent development*. Cambridge, MA: Harvard University Press.

Risman, B. J. (2001). Comment: Calling the bluff of value-free science. *American Sociological Review, 66*(4), 605-610.

Roberts, D. E. (1998). The future of reproductive choice for poor women and women of color. In R. Weitz (Ed.), *The politics of women's bodies: Sexuality, appearance and behavior* (pp. 287-302). New York: Oxford University Press.

Sabo, D., & Gordon, F. (1995). *Men's health and illness: Gender, power and the body*. Thousand Oaks, CA: Sage.

Shakespeare, T., Gillespie-Sells, K., & Davies, D. (1996). *The sexual politics of disability: Untold desires*. London: Cassell.

Shapiro, J. P. (1993). *No pity: People with disabilities forging a new civil rights movement*. New York: Random House.

Stodder, J. (1979). Confessions of a candy-ass roughneck. In E. Shapiro & B. Shapiro (Eds.), *The women say, the men say* (pp. 40-44). New York: Delacorte.

Stryker, S. (1998). The transgender issue: An introduction. *GLQ: A journal of lesbian and gay studies, 4*(2), 145-158.

Thompson, B. W. (1992). "A way outa no way": Eating problems among African-American, Latina, and white women. *Gender & Society, 6*(4), 546-561.

Thompson, E. H. (1994). Older men as invisible men in contemporary society. In E. H. Thompson

(Ed.), *Older men's lives* (pp. 1-21). Thousand Oaks, CA: Sage.

Thornhill, R., & Palmer, C. T. (2000). *A natural history of rape: Biological bases of sexual coercion.* Cambridge, MA: The MIT Press.

Toombs, S. K. (2001). The lived experience of disability. In J. R. Johnston (Ed.), *The American body in context* (pp. 31-48). Wilmington, DE: Scholarly Resources Books.

Udry, J. R. (2000). Biological limits of gender construction. *American Sociological Review, 65*(3), 443-457.

Udry, J. R. (2001). Reply: Feminist critics uncover determinism, positivism, and antiquated theory. *American Sociological Review, 66*(4), 611-618.

West, C., & Zimmerman, D. H. (1987). Doing gender. *Gender & Society, 1*, 125-151.

Whipple, J. (1987). Circumcision: A conspiracy of silence. In F. Abbott (Ed.), *New men, new minds: Breaking male tradition* (pp. 110-113). Freedom, CA: The Crossing Press.

Williams, S. J., & Bendelow, G. (1998). *The lived body: Sociological themes, embodied issues.* London: Routledge.

Williams, W. L. (1986). *The spirit and the flesh: Sexual diversity in American Indian culture.* Boston: Beacon.

Zola, I. K. (1982). *Missing pieces: A chronicle of living with a disability.* Philadelphia: Temple University Press.

22

TRANSGENDERING, MEN, AND MASCULINITIES

RICHARD EKINS

DAVE KING

In 1961 Lou Sullivan was a 10-year-old girl living in the suburbs of Milwaukee, Wisconsin; in 1991 he was a gay man dying of AIDS in San Francisco.

—Stryker (1999, p. 62)

As I grew older my conflict became more explicit to me, and I began to feel that I was living a falsehood. I was in masquerade, my female reality, which I had no words to define, clothed in a male pretence.

—Morris (1974, p. 16)

"For every woman who burned her bra, there is a man ready to wear one," says Veronica Vera, who founded Miss Vera's Finishing School for Boys Who Want to Be Girls in 1992 as a resource for the estimated three to five percent of the adult male population that feels the need, at least occasionally, to dress in women's clothing.

—*Miss Vera's Finishing School for Boys Who Want to Be Girls* (n.d., 2)

"Have you ever wanted to dress as a man, try on a male guise and enter the male domain?" asks Torr in the ads for her "Drag King For A Day" workshops. A stream of housewives, artists, straight, lesbian, young and old, sign up for Torr's classes. The first thing Torr tells them, is to "stop apologising," then over one afternoon they learn how to construct a penis, bind their breasts, sit with their legs open and "take up space." They then have to go to a bar to put it all into practice.

—Cooper (1998)

These fragments, chosen fairly randomly, illustrate a little (but only a very little) of the complex and diverse nature of the human experiences that today are considered together under the heading of "transgender." Although this term has been used in other ways (Ekins & King, 1999, p. 581), transgender is most commonly used today in the extensive sense of Thom and More (1998): to encompass "the community of all self identified cross gender people whether intersex, transsexual men and women, cross dressers, drag kings and drag queens, transgenderists, androgynous, bi-gendered, third gendered or as yet unnamed gender gifted people" (p. 3). Until recently, a sharp distinction was made between transvestites, transsexuals, and others whose bodies appeared to be consonant with their assigned sex, and those people who were born with intersexed bodies. Now people with intersexed bodies, as in the encompassing definition of Thom and More (1998), are often included—and sometimes include themselves—under the umbrella term of transgender, especially where the term "transgender" has a transgressive connotation.

In addition to emphasizing diversity, the concept of "transgender," emerging out of the transgender community itself, has avoided assumptions of pathology inherent in the discourse of transvestism, transsexualism, gender identity disorder, and gender dysphoria generated by the medical profession. It also allows consideration of a range of transgender phenomena that have not been subjected to the medical gaze.

We prefer the gerund "transgendering" because of its focus not on *types* of people but on social *process*. Transgendering refers to the idea of moving across (transferring) from one preexisting gender category to the other (either temporarily or permanently), to the idea of living in between genders, and to the idea of transcending or living "beyond gender" altogether (Ekins & King, 1999, 2001b). In the context of this book, it is most usefully viewed as a social process in which males *renounce* or *suspend* the masculinity that is expected of them and females (unexpectedly) *embrace* it.

In the mid-1970s, when we began to research this area, the literature was comparatively small and we could be reasonably confident that we were at least aware of it all. The relevant sections in Bullough, Dorr Legg, Elcano, and Kepner's bibliography (1976) contain about 450 references. More recent bibliographies demonstrate the growth in the literature since that time. Demeyere's (1992) bibliography, particularly strong on anthropological material, and Denny's (1994) bibliography, particularly strong on medical and psychological literature, each include more than 5,000 entries. The growth in the literature since 1994 has been rapid.

Not only has the literature increased in size, but it also now ranges across a large number of disciplines and fields of study. In the mid-1970s,

the bulk of the literature came from medicine and psychology. Now, although these disciplines are still dominant, much can also be found coming from sociology (Devor, 1997; Ekins, 1997; King, 1993), social anthropology (Ramet, 1996), social history (Meyerowitz, 2002), law (Sharpe, 2002), lesbian and gay studies (Prosser, 1997), women's studies (Maitland, 1986), and (especially in recent years) cultural studies (Garber, 1992). In addition, transgender topics appear regularly in the popular media, on television, in the cinema, in the press, and, of course, on the Internet. There are transgender plays and novels, there is transgender photography, and there is transgender art and transgender pornography. Trans people themselves have written their autobiographies, formed organizations, and produced magazines, bulletins, and guides to and celebrations of the topic. During the 1990s, in particular, a number of openly trans people made significant contributions to the academic literature (e.g., More & Whittle, 1999).

In all this material, concepts of masculinity and femininity and what it means to be a man or woman are omnipresent but usually taken for granted. Often, the transgender literature makes sense only against an implicit backdrop composed of prevailing stereotypes of masculinity and femininity and related conceptions of what it means to be a man or woman. Only sometimes is the searchlight turned onto this backdrop. Similarly, although there are occasional references to transgender in the masculinity literature (Connell, 1995; Petersen, 1998), this latter literature has largely ignored the area of transgender.

It is not possible in a single chapter to cover all aspects of transgendering, and here our focus is on transgenderism in contemporary Western societies, which has been the focus of the bulk of the academic literature. It is within this literature that the conceptual apparatus of transvestite, transsexual, and transgender has originated. A small but growing literature does, however, exist on "transgender"-related phenomena in non-Western cultures. Most of this has focused on North American indigenous cultures (see Fulton & Anderson, 1992; Jacobs, Thomas, & Lang, 1997; Whitehead, 1981), although there is work on other cultures (Nanda, 1988; Ramet, 1996; Totman, 2003; Wikan, 1977; Young, 2000). Recently, there has been a surge of anthropological interest in transgender, principally in Southeast Asia (Jackson & Sullivan, 1999;

Johnson, 1997) and in South America (Kulick, 1998a, 1998b). Western medicine assumes that, in its conceptualizations of gender disorders, it is discovering the "truth" of such phenomena, and it has tended to use the anthropological literature to illustrate the universality of the "conditions" (e.g., Steiner, 1985). Recent transgender theorists (e.g., Cromwell, 1999; Feinberg, 1996) have used the same literature to emphasize the diversity and cultural specificity of gender categories, an approach that is more in keeping with the anthropological literature itself, which has often focused on the idea of an institutionalized "third" gender or liminal gender space, anticipating in many ways some of the concepts common in contemporary transgender theory. Nevertheless, it is also evident that Western discourses of transgenderism have been exported to many parts of the world and are usurping or are heavily influencing more traditional notions of gender and "transgender" phenomena (Teh, 2001; Winter, 2002; Winter & Udomsak, 2002).

In this chapter, we have chosen to take a historical and chronological approach and focus on four very influential perspectives on the topic and discuss their conceptions of and implications for masculinity (and usually of and for femininity, too). The first of these perspectives to emerge, and the one that in many ways is still dominant, is that of medicine, although it is not articulated only by those who are medically qualified. The second perspective was first articulated by self-identified "transvestites" as they sought to provide their own voice for their own experiences and began to form their own subcultural groupings. The third perspective, articulated by a number of feminist gender theorists, consisted of major critiques of both the medicalization of gender roles and what they saw as the male-to-female transsexuals' and transvestites' "masculinist" appropriation of "femaleness" and "femininity." Finally, we look at the emergence, at the end of the 20th century, of a late modern/postmodern approach within which emphasis is placed on transgender diversity, fluidity, and moving beyond the rigidities of the binary gender divide, to celebrate new combinations of masculinity and femininity. Here, the predominant voice is that of activists who identify as transgendered.

The theme of the relationship of masculinity and femininity to male and female runs throughout the history of these four perspectives. All forms of transgendering potentially raise

questions about the fundamental cultural assumptions (a) that "normal" men do (and should) have male bodies, and do (and should) display an appropriate amount of masculinity; and (b) that "normal" women do (and should) have female bodies, and do (and should) display an appropriate amount of femininity. Masculinity or femininity without the appropriate "accompaniments" is then often depicted as "not real." Another theme is that of identity. Throughout the history of the phenomenon of transgender, the paramount concern has been "What am I?" or "What is he/she?" in gender terms. In our review of the four major approaches, we will highlight these themes.

MEDICAL DISCOURSE, PATHOLOGY, AND "RENOUNCING" MASCULINITY

The original emphasis within this approach is on male-to-female, as opposed to female-to-male, transgender. This has remained so until recently. The dominant voice within this perspective came to be on males who wish to "renounce" their masculinity and "embrace" femininity permanently. In the period prior to technologies that enabled "sex change" reassignment, the focus was on a medical discourse that considered the "reality" of men's appropriation of femininity. Could a "real" man embrace the "feminine"? From the 1950s onward, when "sex change" surgery became a practical possibility, the focus shifted to enabling—in selected cases—the renouncing of male bodies, along with such manliness and masculinity that "transsexuals" may have acquired. The "real reality" of what now came to be conceptualized as psychological sex—"gender identity"—was privileged over the "apparent reality" of the body—morphological sex. The modern "transsexual" was "invented."

Although it is possible to cite examples of the phenomenon of transgender throughout human history, the roots of our modern conception of transgenderism are to be found in the latter half of the 19th century. This period saw the beginning of what Foucault terms the "medicalisation of the sexually peculiar" (Foucault, 1979, p. 44). It was during this period that psychiatrists and other medical practitioners began to puzzle over the nature of people who reported that they felt like/dressed as/behaved like a person of the "opposite sex."

Early manifestations of what later came to be seen as transgenderism were first seen as variations of homosexuality. "Real" men were masculine and heterosexual. Men who were homosexual were not "real men" and often were conceptualized as feminine souls in male bodies. Men who enjoyed behaving and dressing as women or, indeed, wished to be women, simply took the whole business much further! It was Hirschfeld (1910/1991) who coined the term "transvestite" for this latter group. In doing so, he argued that the transvestites' love of the feminine did not make them women. Rather, they were men who enjoyed expressing femininity. Hirschfeld redefined the link between being a man and masculinity. He argued that men (and women) are variously masculine and feminine:

> There are men with the gentle emotions of a Marie Baskiertschew, with feminine loyalty and modesty, with predominant reproductive gifts, with an almost unconquerable tendency to feminine preoccupations such as cleaning and cooking, also such ones who leave women behind in vanity, coquetry, love of gossip, and cowardice, and there are women who greatly outweigh the average man in energy and generosity, such as Christine of Sweden, in being abstract and having depth, such as Sonja Kowalewska, as many modern women in the women's movement in activity and ambition, who prefer men's games, such as gymnastics and hunting, and surpass the average man in toughness, crudeness, and rashness. There are women who are more suited to a public life; men more to a domestic life. There is not one specific characteristic of a woman that you would not also occasionally find in a man, no manly characteristic not also in a woman. (Hirschfeld, 1910/1991, pp. 222-223)

By implication, male "transvestites" are no less "men." In a similar way, Hirschfeld argued that renouncing masculinity did not necessarily involve homosexuality: "one has to extend the sentence 'not all homosexuals are effeminate' to include 'and not all effeminate men are homosexual'" (1910/1991, p. 148). Later, he wrote that "today we are in a position to say that transvestism is a condition that occurs independently and must be considered separately from any other sexual anomaly" (Hirschfeld, 1938, pp. 188-189). Havelock Ellis also saw what he preferred to call eonism (Ellis, 1928) as separate from homosexuality, although he had a more conventional belief than Hirschfeld in the biologically given and fundamentally different (but complementary) natures of men and women (Ellis, 1914).

Both Hirschfeld and Ellis were broadly supportive of those who would later be distinguished as transvestites and transsexuals (they did not employ the then fashionable language of degeneracy or perversion), but they nevertheless viewed such people as anomalies to be explained within a medical framework. Not surprisingly, given the then "expected" congruity between sex, gender, and heterosexuality, both surmised that the explanation could only be biological.

Ellis's and Hirschfeld's views were not without their critics. Onetime psychoanalyst Stekel (1934), for example, disagreed with the separation from homosexuality and also argued for a psychological explanation.

The implications of these contrasting views became more apparent when, around the middle of the 20th century, a number of technological developments came together that made it possible, by altering the body in more or less limited ways, to grant the wishes of some people to "change sex." The term "transsexual" began to make its appearance in medical and popular vocabularies, and the question of whether (and if so, on what grounds) men should be allowed to renounce and be assisted in renouncing their male bodies (and, to a lesser extent, women their female bodies) came to the fore.

In brief, the arguments have revolved around the perceived "authenticity" or otherwise of the transsexual's masculinity or femininity. On the assumption that authentic masculinity and femininity are rooted in the body, claims of biological origins have been and are used to prove the transsexual's entitlement to renounce his or her assigned sex. Claims of psychopathology have been used to deny any such entitlement.

During the 1950s, a new conception began to develop that provided a somewhat different argument in favor of bodily intervention. This was the separation of sex from gender. Stoller (1968) put it in this way:

> *Gender* is a term that has psychological or cultural rather than biological connotations. If the proper terms for sex are "male" and "female," the corresponding terms for gender are "masculine" and "feminine"; these latter may be quite independent of (biological) sex. (p. 9)

In addition to stressing the independence of sex and gender, the writings of Money (1973), Stoller, and others also stressed the immutability of the latter when conceptualized as "gender identity." What became referred to as "core gender identity" (Stoller, 1977) was regarded as unalterable after the age of 2 or 3, thus attaining a degree of "reality" comparable to that of the body. On this conception, therefore, it became possible to be both a male and a man in terms of the body and a female and a woman in terms of the psyche or, indeed, vice versa. Thus, Benjamin gave his male-to-female transsexual patients a certificate that contained the following sentences: "Their anatomical sex, that is to say, the body, is male. Their psychological sex, that is to say, the mind, is female" (Benjamin, 1966, p. 66). Despite the separation, there was still an assumption that, as Stoller put it, "masculinity fits well with maleness and femininity goes with femaleness" (1977, p. 173) so that if a "fully differentiated gender identity" is immutable, it makes sense to achieve harmony by altering the body to the extent that technological developments allow. Money and Tucker write of the transsexual as

> a person whose sex organs differentiated as male and whose gender identity differentiated as female. Medical science has found ways to reduce the incompatibility by modifying anatomy to help that person achieve unity as a member of a sex ... but medical science has not yet found a way to modify a fully differentiated gender identity. (Money & Tucker, 1977, pp. 69-70)

Although not entirely without controversy, the hormonal and surgical renunciation of maleness and masculinity and femaleness and femininity has become accepted in many Western countries, and elsewhere it no longer seems to require continual justification. Although gender identity has continued to take priority over morphological sex, the search is still on for what is assumed will be a biological determinant of the sexed brain. A document titled *Transsexualism: The Current Medical Viewpoint*, written for the main United Kingdom campaigning organization by a group of medical specialists, claims that

> the weight of current scientific evidence suggests a biologically-based, multifactoral aetiology for transsexualism. Most recently, for example, a study identified a region in the hypothalamus of

the brain which is markedly smaller in women than in men. The brains of transsexual women examined in this study show a similar brain development to that of other women. (Press for Change, 1996, "Aetiology")

Opponents of bodily modification have tended to argue that the transsexual does not have an "opposite gender identity" but instead is suffering from some form of psychic disturbance. This argument is orthodox among those many psychoanalysts, for instance, who consider that "healthy" development leads toward "mature" heterosexual relationships that presuppose two members of the "opposite" sex who each manifest "healthy" degrees of "masculinity" and "femininity," respectively. Socarides, for instance, is a vociferous exponent of this view:

> The fact that the transsexual cannot accept his sex as anatomically outlined ... is a sign of the intense emotional and mental disturbance which exists within him. It is the emotional disturbance which must be attacked through suitable means by psychotherapy which provides alleviation of anxiety and psychological retraining rather than amputation or surgery. (Socarides, 1969, p. 1424)

According to this view, the gender identity and role that is seen to be at variance with biological sex must be a sham, an imitation of the "real thing." Socarides (1975), for example, wrote of "behaviour imitative of that of the opposite sex" (p. 131) and a "caricature of femininity" (p. 134). Like the supporters of surgery, its opponents tend to employ traditional stereotypes of gender identity and roles. Ostow argued that in the case described by Hamburger, Stürup, and Dahl-Iversen (1953), there was "no desire for sexual relations with men" and "no evidence of any maternal interest" (Ostow, 1953, p. 1553). Meyer and Hoopes (1974) have similarly argued that

> a true feminine identification, for instance, would result in warm and continued relationships with men, a sense of maternity, interest in caring for children, and the capacity to work productively and continuously in female occupations. ... The adult "transsexual" reaches accommodation with a simulated femininity or masculinity at a sacrifice in total personality. (p. 447)

The medical approach has facilitated some degree of migration (Ekins & King, 1999) from one sex (body) to the other, but it retains a view of sex, sexuality, and gender as binary and has, on the whole, accepted existing stereotypes of what constitutes masculinity and femininity and their linkages to male and female bodies. Thus, in the absence of a "test" that will unequivocally demonstrate that a person is a transsexual, suitability for hormone and (especially) surgical "sex change" is determined by the extent to which the candidate "passes" or demonstrates sufficient masculinity or femininity, as the case may be. Some critics (and some of the candidates themselves) have complained that the conceptions of masculinity and femininity that the medical profession has employed in this respect have become outmoded and are out of step with notions of masculinity and femininity in "the real world."

The second approach that we consider in the following section also makes use of traditional stereotypes, but it loosens the linkage between sex and gender to a greater extent than the medical approach. As with the bulk of the medical literature on transsexuality, there tends to be a downplaying of the details of transgender sexuality (eroticism) and the relations between "masculine" and "feminine" sexuality, as opposed to the details of sex (the body) and gender (both as identity and as the social and cultural accompaniments of sex).

THE TRANSGENDER COMMUNITY, VIRGINIA PRINCE, "FULL PERSONALITY EXPRESSION," AND "SUSPENDING" MASCULINITY

From the early 1960s onward, the voices of transgendered people, themselves, began to be heard outside the medical case histories. The dominant voice within this, our second approach, was of those who sought to avoid medicalization and develop a view of their identities and behaviors in terms of their "suspending" aspects of masculinity for various periods of time, while not renouncing it entirely. Although self-identified transsexual "renouncers" tended to articulate themselves within the developing medical discourse, the "suspenders" sought to develop their own perspective and accompanying concepts of what it meant to be male/masculine and female/feminine. Here, the work of Virginia Prince was particularly influential, and her view that men should

express "the girl within" gained a following in "transvestite" groups throughout the world. For Prince, being a male with a fully developed personality expression entailed embracing "femininity" in various modes, for varying periods of time, and in various spaces and places. Prince was, it may be said, man enough to be a woman. Although Prince, herself, eventually came to live full-time as what she termed a "transgenderist" (a male woman without sex reassignment surgery), her main influence has been in articulating a "transvestite" lifestyle in which males "oscillate" (Ekins & King, 1999, 2001b) between the expression of masculinity and of femininity in the service of "full personality expression."

Although Hirschfeld coined the term "transsexualism" in 1923 (Hirschfeld, 1923; Ekins & King, 2001a), it was not widely used until the 1950s and, at least in the English-speaking world, the term "transvestism" (which he had coined earlier, in 1910) was employed in a very broad sense to denote a diverse range of transgender practices, from what he termed "name transvestism" (the adoption of an opposite-sex name) to full "sex changes." With massive media attention focused on cases of the latter in the early 1950s, medical attention focused on transsexualism, which, as we have seen, achieved a degree of respectability in some quarters.

There was much less interest in the other main transgender practice (transvestism) to come to the notice of the medical profession. This was that of (mainly) men who did not wish to renounce their masculinity permanently but who would sometimes suspend it by cross-dressing and behaving "in a feminine fashion," usually in private but sometimes in public. This compulsion (as it was often experienced) was sometimes troubling enough for some men to seek a "cure." The term "transvestism" came to refer principally to compulsive and sexually arousing cross-dressing, usually by biological males. Because no "cure" was available (despite a brief flurry of interest in the use of aversion therapy in the 1960s), and because (despite the anguish of some transvestites and sometimes their partners) cross-dressing was seen as a relatively harmless "perversion," transvestism was of little interest to most of the medical profession.

So it was left to transvestites themselves to fashion an identity and a script that was more tenable than that on offer by the medical profession. Central to this was Virginia Prince, who, after struggling to find a cure for her cross-dressing, was encouraged by a psychiatrist to "stop fighting it." Prince went on to fashion a new identity depicting a certain type of cross-dressing supported by an explanatory and justificatory philosophy with which she sought to educate the medical profession and transvestites themselves. In doing so, she provided the basis for the beginnings of what we now call the transgender community.

Prince (1957, p. 82) distinguished between three types of males who may share "the desire to wear feminine attire." These were the homosexual, the transvestite, and the transsexual. Prince then distinguished the homosexual and the transsexual from what she called the "true transvestite" (Prince, 1957, p. 84). The true transvestites are "exclusively heterosexual . . . frequently married and often fathers" (Prince, 1957, p. 84). "They value their male organs and enjoy using them and do not wish them to be removed" (p. 84).

In 1960, Prince published a magazine called *Transvestia* that was sold by subscription and through adult bookshops. The message on the inside cover read: "*Transvestia* is dedicated to the needs of those heterosexual persons who have become aware of their 'other side' and seek to express it." Gradually, Prince developed an organization called the Foundation for Full Personality Expression (FPE or Phi Pi Epsilon) that was clearly aimed at those cross-dressers who, like Prince (at that time), were heterosexual and married—homosexuals and transsexuals were not admitted. This organization was immensely successful and spread to many parts of the world.

By 1967, Prince (writing under the pseudonym "Bruce," 1967) was evidently familiar with the gender terminology and concepts that are taken for granted today. Sex, she points out, is anatomical and physiological; gender is psychosocial. Transvestism, for Prince, is very firmly about gender. She argues that sex, the division into male and female, is something we share with other animals. Gender, the division of masculine and feminine, is, on the other hand, "a human invention" and "not the inevitable result of biological necessity" (Bruce, 1967, p. 129). But in their socialization, children are pushed in one or the other gender direction and, consequently, anything associated with the other

gender has to be suppressed, particularly in the case of males. Transvestism is the expression of this suppressed femininity.

Prince's views on the nature of masculinity and femininity are particularly apparent in her publications aimed at instructing transvestites themselves on how to dress and behave in order to express the woman within. *How to Be a Woman Though Male* (Prince, 1971) is a practical guide for males who wish to be women, and this involves Prince in presenting what looks like a very dated, traditional view of women and men, even for its time. To be masculine is to be active, competitive, strong, logical, and so on; to be feminine is to be the opposite—passive, cooperative, weak, and emotional (Prince, 1971, pp. 115-116). However, she is aware that she is presenting a stereotype of womanhood and writes that she agrees with the feminist criticism of some aspects of it, but she argues that this is how things are, not as they should be, and this is what it takes to be a woman in our culture (Prince, 1971, p. 116).

It is also, we should note, a very middle-class stereotype of femininity: Prince tells her readers, "if you are going to appear in society as a woman, don't just be a woman, be a lady" (Prince, 1971, p. 135); and

> it is the best in womanhood that the [transvestite] seeks to emulate, not the common. Be the LADY in the crowd if you are going to be a woman at all, not the scrubwoman or a clerk. It is the beauty, delicacy, grace, loveliness, charm and freedom of expression of the feminine world that you are seeking to experience and enjoy, so "live it up"— be as pretty, charming and graceful as you can . . . (Prince, 1971, p. 136)

Prince's views are important in this context for her insistence on breaking the link between femininity and femaleness, and (implicitly, for she has little to say about this) between masculinity and maleness. The conception of the woman within the man (and presumably the man within the woman) gave a more serious edge to the emerging identity of the transvestite, and the notion of whole persons, both masculine and feminine, does strike a chord with some of the visions of the past 30 or so years.

However, Prince's apparent recognition of the cultural relativity of masculinity and femininity seems at odds with the notion of them emerging "from within" and, ultimately, Prince herself seems to have found it hard to retain the separation of sex and gender. She wrote in 1979 that "I have had my beard removed by electrolysis and . . . as a result of a course of hormone therapy I now possess a nice pair of 38B breasts" (Prince, 1979, p. 172).

FEMINISM, THE "TRANSSEXUAL EMPIRE," AND "REJECTING" MASCULINITY

From the late 1960s, with the emergence of the gay and women's movements, there arose an interest in the political significance of transgendering and its relationship to forms of sexual and gender oppression. From one point of view, "transvestites" and "transsexuals" (the terms in use at the time) were seen as politically conservative, reinforcing gender stereotypes by performing hyperfemininity, for instance. From an alternative standpoint, however, insofar as they broke the congruity between sex and gender, they were seen by some to be radical (e.g., Brake, 1976). However, by far the most influential single political critique of what she termed "the transsexual empire" was that put forward by Janice Raymond. Raymond (1980) argued that the creation by the male medical profession of transsexualism and its "treatment" by means of sex change surgery obscures the political and social sources of the "transsexual's" suffering. This, then, was the period of influence of feminist transgender theory disposed to "rejecting" men and masculinity. The male-to-female transsexual's claim to womanhood and femininity was rejected, as well as that medical discourse and practice which sought to aid the transsexual's "renouncing" of his masculinity. Raymond saw female-to-male transsexuals as merely "tokens" who had no significance for her argument. In this sense, too, females who wished to "embrace" the masculinity attendant on their sex reassignment surgery were rejected from her considerations.

As we have seen, some medical approaches have accepted the authenticity of a masculine or feminine identity at variance with the body and have given priority to the identity over the body. Prince and the organizations influenced by her philosophy have also recognized an authentic femininity within a male body and presumably would allow an authentic masculinity within a female body. Other approaches from within the medical profession have seen transvestism and transsexualism unequivocally as psychopathologies and have denied the reality of a gender identity at variance with the evidence of the body.

Although some of these approaches have noted the culturally contingent nature of masculinity and femininity, they have not questioned the content of these categories and have shown little awareness of gender inequality. Yet, in the late 1960s, when sex change surgery had gained a degree of legitimacy as the treatment of choice for those who claimed a gender identity other than that suggested by their bodies and who displayed the appropriate masculinity or femininity, the emerging women's movement was beginning to question just what was appropriate about these categories. The problem that transsexuals posed for the women's movement was this: Who qualifies as a woman?

As the transgender activist Wilchins (1997) was to put it later,

> Feminist politics begins with the rather common sense notion that there exists a group of people understood as women whose needs can be politically represented and whose objectives sought through unified action. A movement for women—what could be simpler? But implicit in this is the basic idea that we know who comprises this group since it is their political goals we will articulate. What if this ostensibly simple assumption isn't true? (p. 81)

Although it is not the only feminist position on transsexualism, that of Janice Raymond (1980) is probably the best known. Although it has been subjected to considerable criticism (e.g., Califia, 1997; Riddell, 1996; Wilchins, 1997), its influence can still be found in the work of some writers, such as Jeffreys (1996, 2003). At the heart of Raymond's position is the denial of the legitimacy of the transsexual's "chosen" gender. What she calls "male-to-constructed-females" can never be women because of their lack of both female biology and female life experiences. Raymond asserts:

> it is biologically impossible to change chromosomal sex. If chromosomal sex is taken to be the fundamental basis for maleness and femaleness, the male who undergoes sex conversion surgery is *not* female . . . Transsexuals are *not* women. They are *deviant males*. (1980, pp. 10, 183)

Raymond argued that transsexualism is not an individual condition, a personal problem for which changing sex is merely a neutral, technical method of treatment, but instead is a social and political phenomenon. According to her, "transsexuals" are among the victims of patriarchal society and its definitions of masculinity and femininity. By creating transsexualism and treating it by means of sex change, the political and social sources of the "transsexuals'" suffering are obscured. Instead, it is conceptualized as an individual problem for which an individual solution is devised.

Raymond argues that by means of this illegitimate medicalization, the "real" problem remains unaddressed. Medicalization also serves to defuse the revolutionary potential of transsexuals, who are "deprived of an alternative framework in which to view the problem" (1980, p. 124).

She argues that not only does transsexualism reflect the nature of patriarchal society, but it is also ultimately caused by it:

> The First Cause, that which sets other causes of transsexualism in motion . . . is a patriarchal society, which generates norms of masculinity and femininity. Uniquely restricted by patriarchy's definitions of masculinity and femininity, the transsexual becomes body-bound by them and merely rejects one and gravitates toward the other. (Raymond, 1980, p. 70)

Thus, we have a circular process by which patriarchy creates, via the family and other structures, problems for individuals that are then dealt with as transsexualism, thus reinforcing the conditions out of which the problems arose.

However, this is primarily a one-way movement, for Raymond sees transsexualism as primarily a male movement. Female-to-male transsexuals are mere tokens created to maintain the illusion that it is a "condition" that affects both sexes. The reason why it is primarily a male problem, says Raymond (1980), is because men are seeking to possess

> the power that women have by virtue of female biology. This power, which is evident in giving birth, cannot be reduced to procreation. Rather birthing is only representative of the many levels of creativity that women have exercised in the history of civilization. Transsexualism may be one way by which men attempt to possess female

creative energies, by possessing artifactual female organs. (p. xvi)

In addition, Raymond (1980) sees the creation of transsexualism and sex change surgery as an attempt to replace biological women (p. 140) and argues that "gender identity clinics" where transsexuals are "treated" are prototypical "sex-role control centers" (p. 136). Thus, transsexualism is not merely another example of the pervasive effects of patriarchal attitudes; it actually constitutes an attack on women. "Transsexualism constitutes a sociopolitical program that is undercutting the movement to eradicate sex role stereotyping and oppression in this culture" (p. 5).

Apart from measures directed at the "first cause" itself (patriarchy), Raymond advocates restrictions on "sex change" surgery; the presentation of other, less favorable, views of its consequences in the media; and nonsexist counseling and consciousness-raising groups for transsexuals themselves to enable them to realize their radical potential (1980, appendix).

How much acceptance Raymond's thesis has had is difficult to tell, but it clearly has been widely read and discussed. Stone (1991) writes of Raymond's book that "here in 1991, on the twelfth anniversary of its publication, it is still the definitive statement on transsexualism by a genetic female academic" (p. 281). The position of Raymond and other feminist academics was not merely "academic." In the middle and late 1970s, as Carol Riddell explains (personal communication, 1994),

> a small but very active section of the feminist movement, the "Revolutionary Feminists," were taking over some positions in the radical subcultures of extreme feminism. They owed a little intellectually to Mary Daly and her ex-student Janice Raymond, from whose doctoral thesis *The Transsexual Empire* was written. There were reports of threats to transsexuals in London, and I myself was threatened with violence when I attended a Bi-sexuality conference there.

The position was much the same two decades later, when members of the New York City chapter of the activist Transexual Menace confronted Janice Raymond at the launch of her 1994 edition of *The Transsexual Empire*. Wilchins (1997) has written eloquently of the struggles for male-to-female transsexuals to gain admittance to "womyn-born womyn only" spaces and the harassment they have suffered at events that ban "nongenetic women" (Wilchins, 1997, p. 110).

POSTMODERNITY, "TRANSCENDING," AND BREAKING THE LINK BETWEEN MALES AND MASCULINITY

Finally, we look at the emergence, at the end of the 20th century, of a postmodern approach: the coming of age of transgenderism. Now the emphasis is on transgender diversity, fluidity, and moving beyond the rigidities of the binary gender divide. New combinations of masculinity and femininity are celebrated. Particularly significant, from the standpoint of masculinity, is the concept of female masculinity put forward by Judith "Jack" Halberstam (1998). Whereas the vast majority of the men and masculinities literature concerns itself with variants of masculinity considered in relation to males, Halberstam breaks that link. Furthermore, in a postmodern age, medical technology becomes something to call upon for the purposes of "optional" body modification, as opposed to "diagnosis," treatment, or management of pathology or disorder.

Virginia Prince notwithstanding, the voices of transgendered people themselves were largely missing from the earlier approaches that we have looked at; they appeared largely as cases in the medical literature or as dupes of the medical profession in the dominant feminist discourses. This was to change radically in the 1990s as a new discourse emerged, constituting a major paradigm shift. A key work in this new approach was Sandy Stone's "The *Empire* Strikes Back" (1991), in which she argued that "the people who have no voice in this theorizing are the transsexuals themselves. As with males theorizing about women from the beginning of time, theorists of gender have seen transsexuals as possessing something less than agency" (1991, p. 294).

Stone also pointed out that transsexuals had failed to develop a counterdiscourse. It is easy to see why, because the main "traditional" transgender identities have "worked" only to the extent that they have been covert and temporary. The male transvestite who suspends his masculinity for varying amounts of time most usually does not want to be "read" as such. Except within a small subcultural setting, he wishes to be seen as a "normal" man or (to the extent that he is able to suspend his masculinity in public) as a "normal" woman. Similarly, the male transsexual who is renouncing his masculinity permanently, like the female transsexual who is seeking to embrace it, are also seeking to be read as a woman and a man, respectively. Both identities are also temporary ones; the transvestite oscillates (Ekins & King, 1999, 2001b) between masculinity and femininity; the transsexual passes through a trans phase on the way to a permanent masculine or feminine identity.

Where these identities have become open and/or permanent, they have been seen as pathological and/or problematic. In other words, no permanent "in-between" identity was allowed for. To the extent that the transvestite or transsexual passes as a person of the other gender, and to the extent that the transgendering remains hidden, the "fact" of two invariant genders remains unquestioned. As Stone (1991) put it, "authentic experience is replaced by a particular kind of story, one that supports the old constructed positions" (p. 295). In consequence, Stone argued that transsexuals can develop their own discourse only by recognizing their unique gender position:

> For a transsexual, as a transsexual, to generate a true, effective and representational counterdiscourse is to speak from outside the boundaries of gender, beyond the constructed oppositional nodes which have been predefined as the only positions from which discourse is possible. (1991, p. 295)

Stone contended that the dominant binary model of gender and its employment in the category of transsexuality has obscured the diversity of the transsexual experience. It "foreclosed the possibility of analyzing desire and motivational complexity in a manner which adequately describes the multiple contradictions of individual lived experience" (1991, p. 297). What began to happen, in fact, during the 1990s was the recognition of the vast diversity of transgender experiences. Some people did begin questioning "the necessity of passing for typically gendered people" and began to develop new gender identities. For some people, "the experience of crossed or transposed gender is a strong part of their gender identity; being out of the closet is part of that expression" (Nataf, 1996, p. 16).

The following quotation from Denny (1995) underscores the point of diversity:

> With the new way of looking at things, suddenly all sorts of options have opened up for transgendered people: living full-time without genital surgery, recreating in one gender role while working in another, identifying as neither gender, or both, blending . . . characteristics of different genders in new and creative ways, identifying as genders and sexes heretofore undreamed of—even designer genitals do not seem beyond reason. (p. 1)

The 1995 International Bill of Gender Rights (reprinted in Feinberg, 1996, pp. 171-175) claims that "all human beings have the right to define their own gender identity" . . . "to free expression of their self-defined gender identity," and to change "their bodies cosmetically, chemically, or surgically, so as to express a self-defined gender identity" (pp. 172-173). Califia (1997), too, writes of the "individual's right to own his or her own body, and [to] make whatever temporary or permanent changes to that body the individual pleases. . . . A new sort of transgendered person has emerged, one who approaches sex reassignment with the same mindset that they would obtaining a piercing or a tattoo" (p. 224).

However, at the same time as there is an acknowledgment of diversity, there has also developed a greater sense of unity. Writers now comment on the "transgender community," and this is sometimes seen to extend into the gay community (Mackenzie, 1994; Whittle, 1996). Parts of this community have been working more vociferously and more effectively than ever before to end discrimination toward, and claim what are described as the rights of, transgendered people. The emphasis has shifted to the rights of transgendered people *as* transgendered, and not as members of their "new" gender. A particular focus of this activism has been the advocacy of the right of "gender expression" subversive of masculine/feminine dichotomies as linked to "male" and "female" bodies.

Stone's (1991) chapter can also be seen to provide the starting point for the emergence of transgender theory, which is now seen by some to be at the very cutting edge of debates about sex, sexuality, and gender and has achieved a position of prominence in a number of recent contributions to cultural studies and "queer theory." Stone's image of transsexuals as "outside the boundaries of gender" chimed in well with many of the themes in cultural studies and queer theory and provided a motif that has been much developed since.

This idea points to the position of trans people as located somewhere outside the spaces customarily offered to men and women, as people who are beyond the laws of gender. So the assumption that there are only two (opposite) genders, with their corresponding "masculinities" and "femininities," is opened up to scrutiny. Instead, it is suggested that there is the possibility of a "third" space outside the gender dichotomy. This idea refers not simply to the addition of another category; it is conceived as "a space for society to articulate and make sense of all its various gendered identities" (Nataf, 1996, p. 57), or, as Herdt (1994) put it, "the third is emblematic of other possible combinations that transcend dimorphism" (p. 20).

Within this approach, the idea of permanent core identities and the idea of gender itself disappear. The emphasis is on transience, fluidity, and performance. Kate Bornstein, for instance, talks about "the ability to freely and knowingly become one or many of a limitless number of genders for any length of time, at any rate of change" (Bornstein, 1994, p. 52). In that gender fluidity recognizes no borders or "laws" of gender, the claim is to live "outside of gender" (Whittle, 1996) as "gender outlaws" (Bornstein, 1994).

Writing at the beginning of the 1990s, Rubin pointed out that "transsexual demographics are changing. FTMs [female-to-males] still comprise a fraction of the transsexual population, but their numbers are growing and awareness of their presence is increasing" (1992, p. 475). Conveniently written off as "tokens" by Raymond, female-to-male transsexuals or, more accurately, female-bodied trans persons, indeed had become a more visible feature of the transgender community by the end of the 20th century and leading into the 21st century. In fact, they have come to play key roles within that community and within transgender politics, and they have been prominent in the emergence of transgender theory (e.g., Cromwell, 1999; Prosser, 1998; Whittle, 1996). More specifically, it is trans men who have led the way in linking transgender to revolutionary socialism (Feinberg, 1996), to radical lesbianism (Nataf, 1996), to radical body configurations and pansexualism (Volcano, 2000), and to the beginnings of a hitherto neglected transgender approach to class, race, and masculinity (Volcano & Halberstam, 1999). In the main, followers of Raymond such as Jeffreys (1996) have continued to turn a blind eye to the significance of FTMs within the transgender community.

Notably, it is Judith "Jack" Halberstam who has turned the spotlight onto "female masculinity" or "masculinity" without men (Halberstam, 1998), thus avoiding the limitations of seeing masculinity as "a synonym for men and maleness" (Halberstam, 1998, p. 13). Halberstam's main aims are to demonstrate that women historically have contributed to the construction of contemporary masculinity and to underline the diversity of female masculinity, which has been obscured because it challenges "mainstream definitions of male masculinity as nonperformative" (Halberstam, 1998, p. 234).

Concluding Comments

The "lessons" of transgender for masculinity (and femininity) are complex and often contradictory. They revolve around the nature of and the relationships between sex, gender, and sexuality. The neat binary divisions in each of these areas has given way to diversity, and the simple linkages between them have given way to complexity. Not surprisingly, much academic and popular discussion has been focused on the most dramatic aspect of transgender, that of transsexualism. Against a backdrop of the assumed correlation of sex, gender, and heterosexuality, radical refashioning of the body has been conventionally sanctioned by the medical profession after the demonstration by the "applicant" that the applicant's body is "out of sync" with the applicant's gender and sexuality, thereby restoring harmony. Recent thinking has upset that harmony.

The early attempts by Hirschfeld and Ellis to distinguish transvestism or eonism from homosexuality and Prince's insistence on the gendered nature of transvestism led to an underplaying of the significance of transgendered sexuality. The diversity of transgender sexual experiences evident in the early medical literature was gradually replaced by a "heteronormative" perspective in which those transsexuals who took steps to change their bodies to match their perceived identity on the "opposite" side of the binary divide, and who took up a heterosexual position from the vantage point of this "opposite" side, were privileged over transgendered people who evidenced other forms of transgender experience. This heteronormative position that privileges heterosexuality, as set within a binary male and female gender divide, over other forms of sexual and gender expression, may be illustrated by Benjamin's (1968) statement:

> Transsexuals are attracted only to members of their own anatomical sex; however, they cannot be called homosexual because they feel they belong to the sex opposite to that of the chosen partner. The transsexual man loves another man as a woman does, in spite of his phenotype and in spite of his genital apparatus which he feels he must change. The transsexual woman woos another woman as a man would, feeling herself to be a man regardless of her anatomical structure. (p. 429)

It was not until 1984 that Dorothy Clare coined the term "transhomosexuality" (Clare, 1984) in recognition of the fact that the "transsexual's" renouncing masculinity did not necessarily mean renouncing sexual attraction to women and that embracing masculinity did not necessarily entail embracing women as sexual partners (see also Feinbloom, Fleming, Kijewski, & Schulter, 1976). More recently, through the popularization of the writings of Ray Blanchard (e.g., 1989) by Anne Lawrence (1999) and Michael Bailey (2003) (see Ekins & King, 2001c), the recognition of a sexual motivation for sex reassignment has occurred. This literature highlights the complex interrelations between "masculine" and "feminine" transgendered sexuality insofar as many self-identified male-to-female transsexuals are committed to renouncing many elements of their masculinity, but paradoxically this desire for permanent renunciation derives from a sexuality that is in important respects stereotypically masculine. Significantly, Lawrence (1999) refers to such male-to-female transsexuals as "Men Trapped in Men's Bodies." The key concept here is "autogynephilia" (love of oneself as a woman). As Lawrence puts it (personal communication, 2001), "I renounced a masculine sexed body and for the most part renounced masculine gender behavior, in an attempt to both express and control my (masculine) autogynephilic sexuality. Paradoxically, the control aspect also involved a renunciation of masculine sexuality, at least in part."

Similarly, the straightforward dichotomy of male and female bodies is also breached by recent developments. Transvestites altered their bodies only in temporary or reversible ways; transsexuals were either pre- or post-op, and post-op meant that the body had been reconfigured to resemble as closely as possible the "normal" body that "fitted" the gender identity. The only limits were those imposed by cost or technical limitations. Now some people are not going "all the way" and are choosing to reconfigure their bodies in ways that are not "standard" male or female. Virginia Prince, radical in some ways and clearly ahead of her time, might not be happy with the sexual implications in the following quotation, but she would otherwise, we feel, approve:

> If a man says he loves me, he'd better love all of me. Ain't no part of me that ain't me. Ain't no part of me that's bad. I am an African American heterosexual woman who is transgendered with a penis. . . . A man either love all of me or none of me. And I mean ALL of me. (quoted in Griggs, 1998, p. 93)

Another example of body diversity is that of those people born with intersexed bodies who have been (and often still are) surgically and hormonally fitted into one or the other category as early in their lives as possible. Now, increasingly, people with intersexed bodies who were neither aware of nor able to control such surgical and hormonal intervention are questioning those practices and demanding the right to determine whether, when, and how their bodies should be altered (Chase, 1998; Kessler, 1998).

As we explained earlier, it was the primacy given to gender and specifically gender identity that gave legitimacy to the efforts of the medical profession to change the sex of those seeking to change. By and large, only two gender identities were "allowed": masculine and feminine. Again the dichotomy is being questioned, as there is emerging a diversity of identities "in between" or even "outside" the conventional parameters.

Members of the medical profession—health professionals and therapists, too—have begun to look at their patients or clients in less dichotomous ways. Bockting and Coleman, for example, wrote that their clients "often have a more ambiguous gender identity and are more ambivalent about a gender role transition than they initially admit" (1992, p. 143). Their

treatment program allows their clients, they say, to "discover and express their unique identity" (1992, p. 143) and "allows for individuals to identify as neither man nor woman, but as someone whose identity transcends the culturally sanctioned dichotomy" (1992, p. 144).

We leave the penultimate word to Jason Cromwell, who expresses the idea clearly when he says that "there is more to gender diversity than being transvestite or transsexual . . . there are more than two sexes or genders" (Cromwell, 1999, p. 6). By the same token, there is more to Men and Masculinities Studies than men and masculinities. Therein lies the particular contribution of transgendering to the field.

REFERENCES

Bailey, J. M. (2003). *The man who would be queen: The science of gender-bending and transsexualism.* Washington, DC: John Henry Press.

Benjamin, H. (1966). *The transsexual phenomenon.* New York: Julian Press.

Benjamin, H. (1968). The transsexual phenomenon. *Transactions of the New York Academy of Sciences, 29*(4), 428-430.

Blanchard, R. (1989). The concept of autogynephilia and the typology of male gender dysphoria. *Journal of Nervous and Mental Disease, 177,* 616-623.

Bockting, W. O., & Coleman, E. (1992). A comprehensive approach to the treatment of gender dysphoria. In W. O. Bockting & E. Coleman (Eds.), *Gender dysphoria: Interdisciplinary approaches to clinical management* (pp. 131-155). New York: Haworth.

Bornstein, K. (1994). *Gender outlaw: On men, women and the rest of us.* London: Routledge.

Brake, M. (1976). I may be a queer, but at least I am a man. In D. L. Barker & S. Allen (Eds.), *Sexual divisions and society: Process and change* (pp. 174-198). London: Tavistock.

Bruce, V. (1967). The expression of femininity in the male. *Journal of Sex Research, 3*(2), 129-139.

Bullough, V. L., Dorr Legg, W., Elcano, B. W., & Kepner, J. (1976). *An annotated bibliography of homosexuality* (Vol. 2). London: Garland.

Califia, P. (1997). *Sex changes: The politics of transgenderism.* San Francisco: Cleis Press.

Chase, C. (1998). Hermaphrodites with attitude: Mapping the emergence of intersex political activism. *GLQ A Journal of Lesbian and Gay Studies, 4*(2), 189-211.

Clare, D. (1984). Transhomosexuality [Abstract]. In *Proceedings of the Annual Conference of the*

British Psychological Society (p. 6). Warwick, UK: University of Warwick.

Connell, R. W. (1995). *Masculinities.* Sydney: Allen and Unwin.

Cooper, V. (1998). Female camp? Drag and the politics of parody and "queer" performance. *Cultural Studies from Birmingham, 2*(1). Retrieved January 16, 2004, from http://artsweb.bham.ac.uk/bccsr/issue1/cooper.htm

Cromwell, J. (1999). *Transmen and FTMs: Identities, bodies, genders, and sexualities.* Urbana: University of Illinois Press.

Demeyere, G. (1992). *Transvestism and its wider context: A working bibliography.* (Available from G. Demeyere, Turnhoutsebaan 588, B2110 Wijnegem, Belgium)

Denny, D. (1994). *Gender dysphoria: A guide to research.* New York: Garland.

Denny, D. (1995). The paradigm shift is here! *Aegis News, 4,* 1.

Devor, H. (1997). *Female-to-male transsexuals in society.* Bloomington: Indiana University Press.

Ekins, R. (1997). *Male femaling: A grounded theory approach to cross-dressing and sex-changing.* London: Routledge.

Ekins, R., & King, D. (1999). Towards a sociology of transgendered bodies. *Sociological Review, 47*(3), 580-602.

Ekins, R., & King, D. (2001a). Pioneers of transgendering: The popular sexology of David O. Cauldwell. *International Journal of Transgenderism, 5*(3). Retrieved January 23, 2004, from www.symposion.com/ijt/cauldwell/cauldwell_01.htm

Ekins, R., & King, D. (2001b). Tales of the unexpected: Exploring transgender diversity through personal narrative. In F. Haynes & T. McKenna (Eds.), *Unseen genders: Beyond the binaries* (pp. 123-142). New York: Peter Lang.

Ekins, R., & King, D. (2001c). Transgendering, migrating and love of oneself as a woman: A contribution to a sociology of autogynephilia. *International Journal of Transgenderism, 5*(3). Retrieved January 23, 2004, from www.symposion.com/ijt/ijtvo05no03_01.htm

Ellis, H. H. (1914). *Man and woman* (5th ed.). London: Walter Scott.

Ellis, H. H. (1928). *Studies in the psychology of sex* (Vol. 7). Philadelphia: F. A. Davies.

Feinberg, L. (1996). *Transgender warriors: Making history from Joan of Arc to Dennis Rodman.* Boston: Beacon.

Feinbloom, D. H., Fleming, M., Kijewski, V., & Schulter, M. P. (1976). Lesbian/feminist orientation among male-to-female transsexuals. *Journal of Homosexuality, 2*(1), 59-71.

Foucault, M. (1979). *The history of sexuality* (Vol. 1). London: Allen Lane.

Fulton, R., & Anderson, S. W. (1992). The Amerindian "man-woman": Gender liminality and cultural continuity. *Current Anthropology, 33*(5), 603-610.

Garber, M. (1992). *Vested interests: Cross-dressing and cultural anxiety.* New York: Routledge.

Griggs, C. (1998). *S/he: Changing sex and changing clothes.* Oxford, UK: Berg.

Halberstam, J. (1998). *Female masculinity.* Durham, NC: Duke University Press.

Hamburger, C., Stürup, G. K., & Dahl-Iversen, E. (1953). Transvestism: Hormonal, psychiatric, and surgical treatment. *Journal of the American Medical Association, 152*(5), 391-396.

Herdt, G. (1994). Preface. In G. Herdt (Ed.), *Third sex, third gender: Beyond sexual dimorphism in culture and history* (pp. 11-20). New York: Zone Books.

Hirschfeld, M. (1923). Die intersexuelle Konstitution. *Jahrbuch für Sexuelle Zwischenstufen, 23,* 3-27.

Hirschfeld, M. (1938). *Sexual anomalies and perversions.* London: Encylopaedic Press.

Hirschfeld, M. (1991). Transvestites: The erotic drive to cross-dress. New York: Prometheus. (Original work published 1910)

Jackson, P. A., & Sullivan, G. (Eds.). (1999). *Lady boys, tom boys, rent boys: Male and female homosexualities in contemporary Thailand.* New York: Harrington Park Press.

Jacobs, S., Thomas, W., & Lang, S. (Eds.). (1997). *Two-spirit people: Native American gender identity, sexuality, and spirituality.* Urbana: University of Illinois Press.

Jeffreys, S. (1996). Heterosexuality and the desire for gender. In D. Richardson (Ed.), *Theorising heterosexuality: Telling it straight* (pp. 75-90). Buckingham, UK: Open University Press.

Jeffreys, S. (2003). *Unpacking queer politics.* Cambridge, MA: Polity.

Johnson, M. (1997). *Beauty and power: Transgendering and cultural transformation in the southern Philippines.* Oxford, UK: Berg.

Kessler, S. J. (1998). *Lessons from the intersexed.* New Brunswick, NJ: Rutgers University Press.

King, D. (1993). *The transvestite and the transsexual: Public categories and private identities.* Aldershot, UK: Avebury.

Kulick, D. (Ed.). (1998a). Transgender in Latin America [Special issue]. *Sexualities, 1*(3).

Kulick, D. (1998b). *Travesti: Sex, gender, and culture among Brazilian transgendered prostitutes.* Chicago: University of Chicago Press.

Lawrence, A. (1999, August). *Men trapped in men's bodies: Autogynephilic eroticism as a motive for seeking sex reassignment.* Paper presented at the 16th Harry Benjamin International Gender Dysphoria Association Symposium, London.

Mackenzie, G. O. (1994). *Transgender nation.* Bowling Green, OH: Bowling Green University Popular Press.

Maitland, S. (1986). *Vesta tilley.* London: Virago Press.

Meyer, J. K., & Hoopes, J. E. (1974). The gender dysphoria syndromes: A position statement on so-called transsexualism. *Plastic and Reconstructive Surgery, 54*(4), 444-451.

Meyerowitz, J. (2002). *How sex changed: A history of transsexuality in the United States.* Cambridge, MA: Harvard University Press.

Miss Vera's Finishing School for Boys Who Want to Be Girls. (n.d.). Retrieved January 16, 2004, from www.missvera.com/book-1.html

Money, J. (1973). Gender role, gender identity, core gender identity: Usage and definition of terms. *Journal of the American Academy of Psychoanalysis, 1*(4), 397-403.

Money, J., & Tucker, P. (1977). *Sexual signatures: On being a man or a woman.* London: Abacus.

More, K., & Whittle, S. (Eds.). (1999). *Reclaiming genders: Transsexual grammars at the fin de siècle.* London: Cassell.

Morris, J. (1974). *Conundrum.* London: Faber and Faber.

Nanda, S. (1988). *Neither man nor woman: The Hirjas of India.* Belmont, CA: Wadsworth.

Nataf, Z. I. (1996). *Lesbians talk transgender.* London: Scarlet Press.

Ostow, M. (1953). Transvestism. *Journal of the American Medical Association, 152*(16), 1553.

Petersen, A. (1998). *Unmasking the masculine: "Men" and "identity" in a sceptical age.* London: Sage.

Press for Change. (1996). *Transsexualism: The current medical viewpoint.* Retrieved January 16, 2004, from www.pfc.org.uk/medical/mediview

Prince, C. V. (1957). Homosexuality, transvestism and transsexualism: Reflections on their etiology and differentiation. *American Journal of Psychotherapy, 11,* 80-85.

Prince, V. (1971). *How to be a woman though male.* Los Angeles: Chevalier.

Prince, V. (1979). Charles to Virginia: Sex research as a personal experience. In V. L. Bullough (Ed.), *The frontiers of sex research* (pp. 167-175). New York: Prometheus.

Prosser, J. (1997). Transgender. In M. Medhurst & S. Munt (Eds.), *Lesbian and gay studies: A critical introduction* (pp. 309-327). London: Cassell.

Prosser, J. (1998). *Second skins: The body narratives of transsexuality.* New York: Columbia University Press.

Ramet, S. (1996). *Gender reversals and gender cultures.* London: Routledge.

Raymond, J. (1980). *The transsexual empire.* London: The Women's Press.

Raymond, J. (1994). *The transsexual empire* (2nd ed.). New York: The Teachers Press.

Riddell, C. (1996). Divided sisterhood: A critical review of Janice Raymond's *The Transsexual Empire.* In R. Ekins & D. King (Eds.), *Blending genders: Social aspects of cross-dressing and sex-changing* (pp. 171-189). London: Routledge.

Rubin, G. (1992). Of catamites and kings: Reflections on butch, gender and boundaries. In J. Nestle (Ed.), *The persistent desire: A femme-butch reader* (pp. 466-482). Boston: Alyson.

Sharpe, A. (2002). *Transgender jurisprudence: Dysphoric bodies of law.* London: Cavendish.

Socarides, C. (1969). The desire for sexual transformation: A psychiatric evaluation of transsexualism. *American Journal of Psychiatry, 125*(10), 1419-1425.

Socarides, C. (1975). *Beyond sexual freedom.* New York: Quadrangle.

Steiner, B. W. (Ed.). (1985). *Gender dysphoria: Development, research, management.* New York: Plenum.

Stekel, W. (1934). *Bi-sexual love.* New York: Physicians and Surgeons Book Co.

Stoller, R. J. (1968). *Sex and gender: Vol. 1. The development of masculinity and femininity.* New York: Science House.

Stoller, R. J. (1977). Gender identity. In B. B. Wolman (Ed.), *International encyclopedia of psychiatry, psychology, psychoanalysis and neurology* (Vol. 5, pp. 173-177). New York: Van Nostrand for Aesculapius.

Stone, S. (1991). The *empire* strikes back: A post-transsexual manifesto. In K. Straub & J. Epstein (Eds.), *Body guards: The cultural politics of gender ambiguity* (pp. 280-304). New York: Routledge.

Stryker, S. (1999). Portrait of a transfag drag hag as a young man: The activist career of Louis G. Sullivan. In K. More & S. Whittle (Eds.), *Reclaiming genders: Transsexual grammars at the fin de siècle* (pp. 62-82). London: Cassell.

Teh, Y. K. (2001). Mak nyahs (male transsexuals) in Malaysia: The influence of culture and religion on their identity. *International Journal of Transgenderism, 5*(3). Retrieved January 23, 2004, from www.symposion.com/ijt/ijtvo05no 03_04.htm

Thom, B., & More, K. (1998). Welcome to the festival. In *The second international transgender film and video festival.* London: Alchemy.

Totman, R. (2003). *The third sex: Kathoey—Thailand's ladyboys.* London: Souvenir Press.

Volcano, D. (2000). *Sublime mutations.* Tübingen: Konkursbuch.

Volcano, D., & Halberstam, J. (1999). *The drag king book.* London: Serpent's Tale.

Whitehead, H. (1981). The bow and the burden strap: A new look at institutionalised homosexuality in native North America. In S. B. Ortner & H. Whitehead (Eds.), *Sexual meanings* (pp. 80-115). Cambridge, UK: Cambridge University Press.

Whittle, S. (1996). Gender fucking or fucking gender? Current cultural contributions to theories of gender blending. In R. Ekins & D. King (Eds.), *Blending genders: Social aspects of cross-dressing and sex-changing* (pp. 196-214). London: Routledge.

Wikan, U. (1977). Man becomes woman: Transsexualism in Oman as a key to gender roles. *Man, 12*(2), 304-319.

Wilchins, R. (1997). *Read my lips: Sexual subversion and the end of gender.* Ithaca, NY: Firebrand Books.

Winter, S. (2002). *Why are there so many Kathoey in Thailand?* Unpublished manuscript. Retrieved January 23, 2004, from http://web.hku.hk/~sjwinter/TransgenderASIA/paper_why_are_there_so_many_kathoey_htm

Winter, S., & Udomsak, N. (2002). Male, female and transgender: Stereotypes and self in Thailand. *International Journal of Transgenderism, 6*(1). Retrieved January 23, 2004, from www.symposion.com/ijt/ijtvo06no01_04.htm

Young, A. (2000). *Women who become men: Albanian sworn virgins.* Oxford, UK: Berg.

PART V

POLITICS

23

NATION

JOANE NAGEL

"It is no secret," James Messerschmidt argues in *Masculinities and Crime*, "who commits the vast majority of crime. Arrest, self-report, and victimization data all reflect that men and boys both perpetrate more conventional crimes and the more serious of those crimes than do women and girls" (1993, p. 1; see also Messerschmidt, 2000). Likewise, it is also no secret who commits the vast majority of war crimes, or who sits at the helms of national governments and movements around the world, or who articulates the ideologies and dominates the ruling structures of nations and states. Men organize, run, and "man" the machinery of government; they set policy, and they make war; men occupy the vast majority of positions of power and influence in nations in the global system.

This is not to say that women do not have roles to play in the making and unmaking of states and nations: as citizens, as members of the nation, as activists, as leaders. It is to say that the scripts in which these roles are embedded are written primarily by men, for men, and about men, and that women are, by design, supporting actors. If nations and states are gendered institutions, as much recent scholarship asserts (Brown, 1988, 1992; Davis, Leijenaar, & Oldersma, 1991; Eisenstein, 1985; Enloe, 1990, 1993; Hooper, 2001; MacKinnon, 1989; Walby, 1989), then to limit the examination of gender in

politics to an investigation of women only, as much contemporary research has tended to do, is to miss a major, perhaps *the* major, way in which gender shapes politics—through men and their interests, their notions of manliness, and the articulation of masculine micro (everyday) and macro (political) cultures. For instance, in her study of gender, race, and sexuality in colonialism, *Imperial Leather*, McClintock (1995, pp. 356-357) notes the "gendered discourse" of nationalism, commenting that "if male theorists are typically indifferent to the gendering of nations, feminist analyses of nationalism have been lamentably few and far between. White feminists, in particular, have been slow to recognize nationalism as a feminist issue." The intimate historical and modern connection between manhood and nationhood is forged through the construction of patriotic manhood and exalted motherhood as icons of nationalist ideology—in which the nation is a family with men as its defenders and women as the defended embodiment of home and hearth; through the designation of gendered "places" for men and women in the nation and national politics—where men are seen as rightly concerned with such manly activities as all things military and international, and where women are seen as properly concerned with such womanly things as family and domestic issues; through the institutionalization of masculine interests and ideology in nationalist movements—by which the convergence of masculinism and nationalism operates to keep men in charge and women in their place; through the tight fit between masculine microcultures and nationalist ideology—by which the congruence of masculinism and nationalism is reflected in the embeddedness in nationalist ideology of such masculine preoccupations as honor, cowardice, strength, face-saving, and manliness on playgrounds and battlefields, as well as in sports arenas and international affairs; through the militarization of [hetero]sexuality in nationalist conflicts—by which heterosexuality is enlisted in the service of defending the nation, and "enemy" men and women are sexually constructed as simultaneously oversexed and undersexed Other men and promiscuous Other women; and through the mobilized, sometimes frantic defense of masculine, racial, and heterosexual privilege in male-dominated national and nationalistic arenas—in which the "purity" of traditions and institutions of hegemonic masculinity, such as military schools, armed forces, and combat theatres, is sanctified and segregated. The following incident from 19th-century U.S. history illustrates the powerful brotherhood of masculinities even in cases where competing manhoods and nationhoods confront one another in battle.

A CLASH OF MANHOODS

In 1931, Hunkpapa Lakota, Moving Robe Woman, recounted a battle that took place on June 24, 1876, at Peji Sla Wakapa (Greasy Grass), an event remembered by most Americans today as the "Battle of Little Bighorn":

> I was born seventy-seven winters ago, near Grand River, South Dakota. . . . I belonged to Sitting Bull's band. They were great fighters. . . . I am going to tell you of the greatest battle. This was a fight against Pehin Hanska (General Custer). . . . Several of us Indian girls were digging wild turnips . . . [and we] looked toward camp and saw a warrior ride swiftly, shouting that the soldiers were only a few miles away. . . . I heard Hawk Man shout: "Hoka He! Hoka He!" (Charge! Charge!). . . . Someone said that another body of soldiers was attacking the lower end of the village. I heard afterwards that these soldiers were under the command of Long Hair (Custer). With my father and other youthful warriors I rode in that direction. . . . The valley was dense with powder

smoke. I never heard such whooping and shouting. "There is never a better time to die!" shouted Red Horse. Long Hair's troopers were trapped in an enclosure. There were Indians everywhere. . . . It was not a massacre, but a hotly contested battle between two armed forces. (Hardorff, 1997, pp. 91-95)

The battle at Peji Sla Wakapa was between troops of the U.S. Seventh Cavalry led by General George Armstrong Custer and warriors from the Lakota, Northern Cheyenne, and Arapaho nations led by Sitting Bull, Crazy Horse, and Two Moons, among others.[1] Custer's forces were caught between groups of native warriors and were killed in the cross fire. Historians identify a number of events leading up to the Indian victory at Little Bighorn that constitute a familiar 19th-century scenario (Gray, 1976, 1991; Hedren, 1991; Leckie, 1993, p. 201; Michno, 1997; Utley, 1984b; Viola, 1999), but to this day Custer's defeat remains a source of immense controversy among scholars and intense interest among hobbyists. Custer and Little Bighorn remain stuck in the collective American craw. The attention given to—some might argue, obsession with—Custer's defeat generated several official and military inquiries, hundreds of scholarly monographs and articles, numerous popular books and films, dozens of newsletters and enactment groups, countless Internet Web sites and links, and even Little Bighorn trading cards.[2]

Moving Robe Woman's words quoted above provide considerable insight into the enduring preoccupation with Custer and the Battle of Little Bighorn in the American scholarly and popular imagination: "It was . . . a hotly contested battle." What was contested in the Battle of Little Bighorn was not simply the land and who would control it, though that political economic contest was and remains central to understanding the history of indigenous-settler relations in America and around the world. The "hotly contested battle between two armed forces" was a gendered conflict, a confrontation of masculinities that played itself out on the U.S. northern plains in 1876 and in the years to follow. It was a battle not only over land and resources; it was a struggle over the definition and boundaries of manhood and nationhood, a contest to determine the shape and content of American national identity and—I will argue in this chapter, its constant companion—American masculine identity.

Figure 23.1   Custer's Last Dodge

SOURCE: From www.savedge.com/pinhole/images/civilwar/custer.jpg. Reprinted with permission of Billie Anne Wright.

The commentary of Wooden Leg, a Cheyenne fighter in the battle, articulates the gendered character of this battle for native men as well:

> Our war cries and war songs were mingled with many jeering calls, such as: "You are only boys. You ought not to be fighting. We whipped you on the Rosebud. You should have brought more Crows or Shoshones with you to do your fighting." Little Bird and I were after one certain soldier. Little Bird was wearing a trailing warbonnet. He was at the right and I was at the left of the fleeing man. We were lashing him and his horse with our pony whips. It seemed not brave to shoot him. Besides, I did not want to waste my bullets. (Nabokov, 1979, pp. 136-137)

Wooden Leg's contempt for Custer and his "boys" is one articulation of a much larger discourse of masculinities sizing up one another, sometimes conflicting and sometimes collaborating in the construction of nations and nationalities. The interplay between indigenous and settler manhoods throughout history is complex and contradictory. U.S. Indian-white relations were and are enacted as part of a gendered drama in which white men "play Indian" by dressing in feathers and beating on drums to consume fetishized native manly arts and power (Deloria, 1998; Huhndorf, 1997; Nelson, 1998; Schwalbe, 1995), and in which Indian men participate in the spectacle of American manhood by serving in the U.S. military and in honoring veterans for their service to recuperate vanquished manhoods and nationhoods (Fowler, 1987; Whitehorse, 1988).

This gendered reading of Custer's last stand and the continuing anxieties associated with its place in the American nationalist imaginary serve as my first illustration of the link between manhood and nationhood (see also Clark & Nagel, 2001). The remainder of this chapter explicates and explores further the intimate relationship between men and nations in a variety of national settings during the past century.

CONSTRUCTING MEN AND NATIONS

In her evocative book *Bananas, Beaches, and Bases*, Cynthia Enloe (1990, p. 45) observes that "nationalism has typically sprung from masculinized memory, masculinized humiliation and masculinized hope." She argues that women are relegated to minor, often symbolic, roles in nationalist movements and conflicts, either as icons of nationhood, to be elevated and defended, or as the booty or spoils of war, to be denigrated and disgraced. In either case, the real actors are men who are defending their freedom, their honor, their homeland, and their women. Enloe's insight about the connection between manhood and nationhood raises definitional questions about each: What do we mean by "masculinity," and what do we mean by "nationalism"? Because much of this volume is dedicated to a discussion of masculinity in theory and practice, I will limit my discussion of that concept to two observations.

First, historical studies of masculinity in the United States and Europe argue that contemporary patterns of U.S. middle-class masculinity arose out of a crisis and renaissance of manliness in the late 19th and early 20th centuries (Carnes, 1989; Leverenz, 1989; Trachtenberg, 1982). Scholars document a resurgent preoccupation with masculine ideals of physique and behavior around the turn of the century that became institutionalized into such organizations and institutions as the modern Olympic movement, which began in 1896 (MacAloon, 1981, 1984); Theodore Roosevelt's "Rough Riders" unit, which fought in the Spanish American War in 1898 (Morris, 1979; Rotundo, 1993); a variety of boys' and men's lodges and fraternal organizations, such as the Knights of Columbus and the Improved Order of Red Men, which were established or expanded in the late 19th century (Kauffman, 1982; Orr, 1994; Preuss, 1924); and the Boy Scouts of America, which were founded in 1910, 2 years after the publication of R.S.S. Baden-Powell's influential *Scouting for Boys* (MacKenzie, 1987; Warren, 1986, 1987). These organizations embodied U.S. and European male codes of honor (Nye, 1993), which stressed a number of "manly virtues" described by Mosse (1996) as "normative masculinity"; these included willpower, honor, courage, discipline, competitiveness, quiet strength, stoicism, sangfroid, persistence, adventurousness, independence, sexual virility tempered with restraint, and dignity, and they reflected masculine ideals such as liberty, equality, and fraternity.

Second, despite debates about the racial, class, sexual, historical, or comparative limits of various definitions and depictions of masculinity, or about the extent to which U.S. or Western European cultures of masculinity typify manhoods around the world, most scholars argue that at any time, in any place, there is an identifiable "normative" or "hegemonic" masculinity that sets the standards for male demeanor, thinking, and action (Connell, 2000; Gilmore, 1990). Hegemonic masculinity is more than an "ideal"; it is assumptive, it is widely held, and it has the quality of appearing to be "natural" (Donaldson, 1993; Morgan, 1992). Whether current U.S. hegemonic masculinity is derived from a 19th-century renaissance of manliness or is rooted in earlier historical cultural conceptions of manhood, it is certainly identifiable as the dominant form among several racial, sexual, and class-based masculinities in contemporary U.S. society (see Kimmel, 1996; Kimmel & Messner, 1995; Pfeil, 1995). The same can be said for other countries as well—in Europe, Latin America, Africa, Asia, or the Middle East. For instance, whether the manly attitudes and rules for behavior for Arab men described by T. E. Lawrence in *Seven Pillars of Wisdom* (1926) set the current standards of manliness for men in the modern Arab world is not so much the question, as whether some current set of masculine standards exists and can be identified as hegemonic. The answer to that question is, most certainly, yes (see Kandiyoti, 1991; Massad, 1995; Mehdid, 1996).

NATIONALISM

Max Weber defines a nation as a community of sentiment that would adequately manifest itself in a state and that holds notions of common descent, though not necessarily common blood (Gerth & Mills, 1948, pp. 172-179). Layoun (1991, pp. 410-411) concurs: Nationalism "constructs and proffers a narrative of the 'nation' and of its relation to an already existing or potential state." By these definitions, nationalism is both a goal (to achieve statehood) and a belief (in collective commonality). Nationalists seek to accomplish both statehood and nationhood. The goal of sovereign statehood—"state-building"—often takes the form of revolutionary or anticolonial warfare. The maintenance and exercise of statehood vis-à-vis other nation-states often takes the form of armed conflict. As a result, nationalism and militarism seem to go hand in hand.

The goal of nationhood—"nation-building"—often involves "imagining" a national past and present (Anderson, 1991), inventing traditions (Hobsbawm & Ranger, 1983), and symbolically constructing community (Cohen, 1985). As Gellner (1983) argues, "it is nationalism that engenders nations, and not the other way around" (p. 49). The tasks of defining community, of setting boundaries, and of articulating national character, history, and a vision for the future tend to emphasize both unity and "otherness." The project of establishing national identity and cultural boundaries tends to foster nationalist ethnocentrism. As a result, nationalism and chauvinism seem to go hand in hand. Chauvinistic nationalism is often confined to the ideational realm in the form of attitudes and beliefs about national superiority. During periods of nationalist conflict or expansion, however, such ethnocentrism becomes animated. The result in modern world history has been for nationalism to display an intolerant, sometimes murderous face. Nairn (1977) refers to the nation as "the modern Janus" to contrast nationalism's two sides: a regressive, jingoistic, militaristic "warfare state" visage versus a progressive, community-building "welfare state" countenance—guns versus butter (see Hernes, 1987).

The distinction between ideology and action characterizes most discussions of the definition and operation of nationalism. Nationalist ideology (i.e., beliefs about the nation—who we are, what we represent) becomes the basis and justification for national actions (i.e., activities of state- and nation-building—the fight for independence, the creation of a political and legal order, the exclusion or inclusion of various categories of members, the relations with other nations). Whether nationalism is manifested in action or ideology, most scholars identify the 19th century as the origin of nationalism as a way of understanding and organizing local and global politics. Nairn (1977) argued that "nationalism in its most general sense is determined by certain features of the world political economy in the era between the French and Industrial Revolutions and the present day" (p. 333). These features include a "new and heightened significance accorded to factors of nationality, ethnic inheritance, customs, and speech" and "the creation of a national market economy and a viable national bourgeois class" (p. 333). Similarly, Seton-Watson identifies the late 1700s as the dividing line between "old" and "new" nations in Europe, where the old nations, such as the English, Scots, Danes, French, and Swedes, enjoyed relative autonomy, and the new nations, basically the rest of the world, mobilized in the form of national movements to achieve independence, either from monarchies or from colonialism, articulating a form of nationalism designed to "implant in [their constituents] a national consciousness and a desire for political action" (Seton-Watson, 1977, p. 9).

MEN'S AND WOMEN'S PLACES IN THE NATION

By definition, nationalism is political and closely linked to the state and its institutions. Like the military, most state institutions have been historically and remain dominated by men. It is therefore no surprise that the culture and ideology of hegemonic masculinity go hand in hand with the culture and ideology of hegemonic nationalism. Masculinity and nationalism articulate well with one another, and the modern form of Western masculinity emerged at about the same time and place as modern nationalism. Mosse (1996, p. 7) notes that nationalism "was a movement which began and evolved parallel to modern masculinity" in the West about a century ago. He describes modern masculinity as a centerpiece of all varieties of nationalist movements:

> The masculine stereotype was not bound to any one of the powerful political ideologies of the previous century. It supported not only conservative movements . . . but the workers' movement as well; even Bolshevik man was said to be "firm as an oak." Modern masculinity from the very first was co-opted by the new nationalist movements of the nineteenth century. (Mosse, 1996, p. 7)

Other political ideologies of that time, in particular colonialism and imperialism, also resonated with contemporary standards of masculinity (see Bologh, 1990; Walvin, 1987). Many scholars link the renaissance in manliness in Europe to the institutions and ideology of empire (Hobsbawm, 1990; Koven, 1991; Sinha, 1995). Springhall (1987, p. 52) describes the middle-class English ideal of Christian manliness, "muscular Christianity," with its emphasis on sport—the "cult of games" in the public schools. He outlines how, through organizations such as the "Boys' Brigades," these middle-class values were communicated to "less privileged, board school–educated, working-class boys in the nation's large urban centres." Boys from both classes served throughout the Empire in British imperial armies.

Contemporary nationalist politics remains a major venue for "accomplishing" masculinity (Connell, 1987) for several reasons. First, as noted above, the national state is essentially a masculine institution. Feminist scholars point out its hierarchical authority structure, the male domination of decision-making positions, the male superordinate/female subordinate internal division of labor, and the male legal regulation of female rights, labor, and sexuality (Connell, 1995; Franzway, Court, & Connell, 1989; Grant & Tancred, 1992).

Second, the culture of nationalism is constructed to emphasize and resonate with masculine cultural themes. Terms such as honor, patriotism, cowardice, bravery, and duty are hard to distinguish as either nationalistic or masculine because they seem so thoroughly tied both to the nation and to manhood. My point here is that the "microculture" of masculinity in everyday life articulates very well with the demands of nationalism, particularly its militaristic side. When, over the years, I have asked my undergraduate students to write down on a piece of paper their answer to the question "What is the worst name you can be called?," the gender difference in their responses has been striking. The vast majority of women have responded "slut" (or its equivalent), with "bitch" a rather distant second; a vaster majority of men have responded "wimp" or "coward" or "pussy." Only cowards shirk the call to duty; real men are not cowards.

Patriotism is a siren call few men can resist, particularly in the midst of a political "crisis"; if they do, they risk the disdain or worse of their communities and families, sometimes including their mothers. Counter to the common stereotype of mothers attempting to hold back their sons as they march off to war, Boulding (1977, p. 167) reports that many mothers of conscientious objectors during World War II opposed their sons' pacifism, and she argues that women play a clear role in preparing "children and men for life-long combat, whether in the occupation sphere, the civic arena, or the military battlefield" (see also Vickers, 1993, pp. 43-45; Adams, 1990, pp. 131-132). The disdain of men for pacifists is considerably greater, as Karlen (1971) recounts in *Sexuality and Homosexuality:*

> In 1968 pacifists set up coffee houses to spread their word near military bases. A Special Force NCO said to a *Newsweek* reporter, "We aren't fighting and dying so these goddam pansies can sit around drinking coffee. (p. 508)

Fear of accusations of cowardice is not the only magnet that pulls men toward patriotism, nationalism, or militarism. There is also the masculine allure of adventure. Men's accountings of their enlistment in wars often describe their anticipation and excitement, their sense of embarking on a great adventure, their desire not to be "left behind" or "left out" of the grand quest that the war represents.

> I felt the thrill of it—even I, a hard-boiled soldier of fortune—a man who was not supposed to have the slightest trace of nerves. I felt my throat tighten and several time the scene of marching columns swam in oddly elliptical circles. By God, I was shedding tears. (Adams, 1990, p. vii; see also Green, 1993)

Finally, women are the foils against which men are defined and made. Women occupy a distinct, symbolic role in nationalist culture, discourse, and collective action. The restriction of women to a more "private" sphere of action in nationalist arenas reflects a gender division of nationalism that parallels the gender division of labor in the larger society. Anthias and Yuval-Davis have identified five ways in which women have tended to participate in ethnic, national, and state processes and practices:

(a) as biological producers of members of ethnic collectivities;

(b) as reproducers of the (normative) boundaries of ethnic/national groups (by enacting proper feminine behavior);

(c) as participating centrally in the ideological reproduction of the collectivity and as transmitters of its culture;

(d) as signifiers of ethnic/national differences; and

(e) as participants in national, economic, political, and military struggles (Yuval-Davis & Anthias, 1989, pp. 7-8)

Although some of these roles involve action—women participating in nationalist struggles—Anthias and Yuval-Davis (1992), Walby (1989), Tohidi (1991), and Jayawardena (1986), among others, note the pressure felt by women nationalists to remain in supportive, symbolic, and traditional roles. Thus, women's place as national symbols tends to limit their interest in or ability to assume active, public roles. There are, of course, exceptions to this (i.e., women leaders of nationalist movements, resistance movements, and states), but the list is short, and the same names are heard again and again. As Horrocks (1994) notes, when discussing male dominance in public life, "The exception—Margaret Thatcher—proves the rule" (p. 25).

Some scholars argue that "woman nationalist" is an oxymoron reflecting the historic contradiction between the goals and needs of women and those of nationalists (see Enloe, 1990, 2000; McClintock, 1995). Feminists often find themselves attempting to negotiate the difficult—some would say impossible—terrain that lies between the interests of women and the interests of nationalists. Discussing Hindu and Muslim nationalism in Indian politics, Hasan (1994) notes the tension between feminist principles and communal solidarity: "Forging community identities does not imply or guarantee that women will always identify themselves with or adhere to prevailing religious doctrines which legitimise their subordination" (p. xv). The goals of feminists and nationalists, particularly "retraditionalizing" (Nagel, 1996, p. 193) nationalists (which many are), are often at odds. This is because men in many national communities have an interest in regulating the activities and appearance of women as the bearers of the nation's culture, honor, and future.

Sometimes women attempt to enact nationalism through traditional roles assigned to them by nationalists—by supporting their husbands, raising their (the nation's) children, and serving as symbols of national honor. In these cases, women can exploit patriarchal views of women's roles in order to participate in nationalist struggles. For instance, in situations of military occupation, male nationalists seen on the street alone or in groups can be targets of arrest or detention. Women are less likely to be seen as dangerous or "up to something," and so can serve as escorts for men or messengers for men who are sequestered inside houses. Similarly, women are often more successful at recruiting support for nationalist efforts because they are seen as less threatening and militant (Mukarker, 1993; Sayigh & Peteet, 1987). Edgerton (1987) describes Northern Irish Catholic women's use of traditional female housekeeping roles as a warning system against British army raids; the practice was called "bin [trash can] lid bashing":

> When troops entered an area, local women would begin banging their bin lids on the pavement; the noise would carry throughout the area and alert others to follow suit. . . . At the sound of the bin lids, scores of women would emerge armed with dusters and mops for a hasty spring clean. (Edgerton, 1987, p. 65)

In addition to brandishing these "weapons of the weak" (Hart, 1991; Scott, 1985), women also have participated more directly in various nationalist movements and conflicts. Sometimes, women's participation has been in support of male nationalist efforts, and at other times, women have been involved themselves in cadres and military units (Helie-Lucas, 1988; Nategh, 1987; Sayigh & Peteet, 1987; Urdang, 1989). Despite their bravery, sometimes marked by taking on traditional male military roles, and despite the centrality of their contribution to many nationalist struggles, it is often the case that feminist nationalists find themselves once again under the thumb of institutionalized patriarchy once national independence is won. A nationalist movement that encourages women's participation in the name of national liberation often balks at feminist demands for gender equality with arguments that national needs must come first.

Enloe (1990) argues that waiting is a dangerous strategy for feminists because "every time women succumb to the pressures to hold their tongues about problems they are having with men in nationalist organizations, nationalism becomes that much more masculinized" (p. 60). Women who press their case face challenges to their loyalty, their sexuality, or their ethnic or national authenticity: They are either "carrying water" for colonial oppressors, or they are lesbians, or they are unduly influenced by Western feminism. Third World feminists are quite aware of these charges and share some concerns about the need for an indigenous feminist analysis and agenda. As Delia Aguilar, a Filipino nationalist feminist, comments:

when feminist solidarity networks are today proposed and extended globally, without a firm sense of identity—national, racial and class—we are likely to yield to feminist models designed by and for white, middle-class women in the industrial West and uncritically adopt these as our own. (in Enloe, 1990, p. 64)

Despite efforts to build an indigenous feminism into nationalist movements, many women in these movements and states fail to achieve gender equality. Indeed, patriarchal, masculinist notions of men's and women's roles often become more entrenched during nationalist mobilizations and after independence. There are some exceptions to this. For instance, in the many socialist revolutions in the Second and Third Worlds, women were granted constitutionally equal rights, though in practice this complete de jure gender equality generally fell short of the mark. Nonetheless, the legal challenges to patriarchal customary and official law brought about by socialist gender policies often represented quite a radical break with tradition, though this radicalism was sometimes short-lived. For instance, Shen (2003) reports that women's legal and social gains in mainland China have begun to erode as the country shifts from a centrally planned to a market economy.

In Afghanistan, nationalist struggles during the past two decades often have involved control not only over geographical territory, but also over the gendered terrain of women's and men's bodies. In the 1980s, competing Afghani nationalisms pitted relatively egalitarian socialism against patriarchal traditionalism. In that decade, international superpower competition led to U.S. support of Afghan rural, traditionalist, clan-based and Mujahideen rebels who opposed the Soviet-backed Kabul regime's policies of "expanding economic and educational opportunities for Afghanistan's women" (Enloe, 1990, p. 57). Although at the time, the United States criticized the neighboring Islamic regime in Iran's repression of women, the U.S. policy of supporting Pashtu traditionalists in Afghanistan continued despite a resulting "militarized purdah" in clan-controlled regions where women were kept in tight seclusion and where, for instance, girls' enrollments in U.N. schools numbered 7,800 compared with 104,600 for boys in 1988 (Enloe, 1990; see also Moghadam, 1991). In 1996, U.S.- and Pakistani-backed politicized Muslim conservatism took over the capital city,

Kabul, when the Taliban movement ascended to power, prohibited the education of girls and the employment of women outside the home, and strictly enforced complete Islamic dress and a rigid code of conduct for women. The consequences of this sequence of events is, as they say, history. The Taliban's Afghanistan became a training ground and refuge for international militant Islam, and it allegedly was the financial, ideological, and strategic base from which the September 11, 2001, attacks on the World Trade Center in New York City and the Pentagon in Washington, D.C., were launched (Goodwin & Neuwirth, 2001; Rashid, 2000).

It is important to note that the relationship between masculinity and nationalism is an organizing and hegemonic one not only for Islamic societies, but for most others as well. Religious nationalism—indeed, all nationalism—tends to be conservative, and "conservative" often means "patriarchal" (Lievesley, 1996; Manning, 1999; Waylen, 1996). This is partly due to the tendency of nationalists to embrace tradition as a legitimating basis for nation-building and cultural renewal. These traditions—real or invented—are often patriarchal. The "feminism lost" or losing ground in nationalist movements in many states—whether in Afghanistan or Algeria or Russia or India or Hungary or Tanzania or any number of modern states—points out the entrenched nature of masculine privilege and the intimate link between masculinity and nationalism (see Lutz, Phoenix, & Yuval-Davis, 1995; Mayer, 2000; Steinfels, 1995; Twine & Blee, 2001; Williams, 1996). The quickness with which nationalists put women in their traditional places not only reveals the relatively greater power of men but also suggests that very powerful hegemonic forces are at work in nationalism. Masculinity is one such hegemonic force.

FEMININE SHAME AND MASCULINE HONOR IN THE NATIONAL FAMILY

Many theorists of nationalism have noted the tendency of nationalists to liken the nation to a family (McClintock, 1991; Skurski, 1994; van den Berghe, 1978); it is a male-headed household in which both men and women have "natural" roles to play. Although women may be subordinated politically in nationalist movements and politics, as we have seen asserted above, they occupy an important symbolic place as the mothers of the nation. As exalted "mothers in the fatherland" (Koonz, 1987), their purity must be impeccable, so nationalists often have a special interest in the sexuality and sexual behavior of their women. Although traditionalist men may be defenders of the family and the nation, women are thought by traditionalists to embody family and national honor; women's shame is the family's shame, the nation's shame, the man's shame (see Thomas, 1992).

In his analysis of ethnicity and caste in Ethiopia, Quirin (1992) notes the rigid seclusion and sexual restrictions placed on "Falasha" or "Beta Israel" (Jewish) women. She concludes that "gender may often be used as a marker of ethnic differentiation . . . [since] the Beta Israel considered their more rigid treatment of women as an indication of a higher level of moral purity than existed in Abyssinian society" (p. 209). Sapiro (1993) comments on the general tendency for nationalists to be preoccupied with women's appearance and behavior:

> Perhaps one of the most obvious illustrations of a merging of the significance of gender and cultural or national membership is the history of political control over women's dress and demeanor. . . . [That] ethnic or religious communities often identify themselves with physical markers—sometimes in clothing, sometimes hair styles, and sometimes in bodily alteration—is clear, but . . . in the politics of dress and demeanor women and men are rarely treated similarly. Despite the support of Westernization of male dress in Korea in the 1890s, women who adopted Western hairstyles and dress were attacked. (Sapiro, 1993, pp. 44-45)

The politicization of women's bodies and the politics of the veil in Islamic societies is yet another often-cited example of male nationalists asserting both manhood and nationhood through the control of women's bodies (see Augustin, 1993; Berberi, 1993; Shirazi, 2001; Tohidi, 1991).

Women's sexuality often turns out to be a matter of prime national interest for at least two reasons. First, women as mothers are exalted icons of nationalism. In their discussion of Afrikaner nationalism in South Africa, Gaitskell and Unterhalter (1989) argue that Afrikaner women appear regularly in the rhetoric and imagery of the Afrikaner "volk" (people) and

that "they have figured overwhelmingly as mothers" (p. 60). As Theweleit (1987, p. 294) summarizes, "woman is an infinite untrodden territory of desire which at every stage of historical deterritorialization, men in search of material for utopias have inundated with their desires." Second, women's sexuality is of concern to nationalists because women as wives and daughters are bearers of masculine honor. For instance, ethnographers report that Afghani Muslim nationalists' conception of resource control—particularly of labor, land, and women—is defined as a matter of honor; "purdah is a key element in the protection of the family's pride and honor" (Moghadam, 1991, p. 433). El-Solh and Mabro (1994, p. 8) further refine the connection between men's and family honor and women's sexual respectability as a situation in which honor is men's to gain and women's to lose: "honour is seen more as men's responsibility and shame as women's . . . honour is seen as actively achieved while shame is seen as passively defended."

It is not only Third World men whose honor is tied to their women's sexuality, respectability, and shame. Whereas female fecundity is valued in the mothers of the nation, unruly female sexuality threatens to discredit the nation. Mosse (1985) describes this duality in depiction of women in European nationalist history: On one hand, "female embodiments of the nation stood for eternal forces . . . [and] suggested innocence and chastity" (p. 98) and most of all respectability, but on the other hand, the right women needed to be sexually available to the right men: "the maiden with the shield, the spirit that awaits a masculine leader" (p. 101) to facilitate "the enjoyment of peace achieved by male warriors" (p. 98). These images of acceptable female sexuality stood in contrast to female "decadents" (prostitutes or lesbians) who were seen as "unpatriotic, weakening the nation" (Mosse, 1985, p. 109) and dishonoring the nation's men. Both willing and unwilling sexual encounters between national women and "alien" men can create a crisis of honor and can precipitate vengeful violence. Saunders (1995) describes the outrage of Australian men (white and aborigine) about voluntary sexual liaisons between African American servicemen and Australian women during World War II, which escalated to such a high level of "racial and sexual hysteria" that six black GIs were executed for allegedly raping two white nurses in New Guinea (see also Luszki, 1991; Nagel, 2003).

MILITARIZED HETEROSEXUALITY

Concerns about the sexual purity and activities of women are not the only way that sexuality arises as an issue in masculinity and nationalism. Enloe (1990, p. 56) argues that "when a nationalist movement becomes militarized . . . male privilege in the community usually becomes more entrenched." She is referring to the highly masculine nature of things military. The military, it turns out, is also highly sexual. I am referring here to several (masculine hetero)sexualized aspects of military institutions and activities.

First is the sexualized nature of warfare. Hartsock (1983, 1984) argues that all forms of political power, including military power, have an erotic component. She points particularly to a masculine eroticism embedded in notions of military strength and valor. Classical history is replete with references linking strength and valor on the battlefield with masculine sexual virility, hence Julius Caesar's (1951) admonition to men to avoid sexual intercourse before a battle (or, in more modern times, before that social equivalent of war, sport) so as not to sap their strength. Mosse (1985, p. 34) discusses debates in Germany about masturbation and homosexuality as sexual practices that endangered national military strength, and describes war as an "invitation to manliness," exemplified in the following poem used to introduce a nationalistic play about a military battle (at Langemarck):

> A naked sword grows out of my hand,
> The earnestness of the hour flows
> through me hard as steel.
> Here I stand alone, proud and tall,
> Intoxicated that I have now become a
> man. (Mosse, 1990, p. 166)

A second way that military institutions and actions are sexualized centers on the depiction of the "enemy" in conflicts. Accounts of many wars and nationalist conflicts include portrayals of enemy men either as sexual demons, bent on raping nationalist women, or as sexual eunuchs, incapable of manly virility. Bederman's (1995) analysis of Theodore Roosevelt's nationalist discourse provides examples of both. In *African Game Trails,* Roosevelt adopts a colonialist's superior, indulgent attitude toward "childlike" African men, whom he describes as "strong, patient, good-humored . . . with something childlike about them that makes one really fond of them. . . . Of course, like all savages and most children, they have their limits" (quoted in Bederman, 1995, p. 210). Roosevelt's assessment of Native Americans was less patronizingly benevolent, because Indians represented a military threat to the white man who was

> not taking part in a war against a civilized foe; he was fighting in a contest where women and children suffered the fate of the strong men. . . . His sweetheart or wife had been carried off, ravished, and was at the moment the slave and concubine of some dirty and brutal Indian warrior. (Bederman, 1995, p. 181)

Mosse (1985, p. 127) describes portrayals of women on the battlefield as victims of sexual aggression or exploitation along the lines depicted above. He notes, however, that "women haunted soldiers' dreams and fantasies" in other roles as well, either as "objects of sexual desire or as pure, self-sacrificing Madonnas, in other words, the field prostitute or the battlefield nurse" (p. 128). Enemy women are more uniformly characterized as sexually promiscuous and available: sluts, whores, or legitimate targets of rape. The accounts of virtually all wars are replete with references to and discussions of the rape, sexual enslavement, or sexual exploitation of women not only by individuals or small groups of men, but also by army high commands and as part of state-run national policies (see Brownmiller, 1975; Sturdevant & Stoltzfus, 1992).

A third sexualized aspect of militarized conflict is the use of the masculine imagery of rape, penetration, and sexual conquest to depict military weaponry and offensives. A commonly reported phrase alleged to have been written on U.S. missiles targeted on Iraq during the 1990 Gulf War was "Bend over, Saddam" (Cohn, 1993, p. 236). There is a tendency in national defense discourse to personify and sexually characterize the actions of states and armies. Cohn reports that one "well-known academic security advisor was quoted as saying that 'under Jimmy Carter the United States is spreading its legs for the Soviet Union'" (Cohn, 1993, p. 236). She reports similar sexualized depictions by a U.S. defense analyst of former West German politicians who were concerned about popular opposition to the deployment of nuclear Euromissiles in the 1980s: "Those Krauts are a bunch of limp-dicked wimps" (p. 236). Such sexualized military discourse is very much from a heterosexual standpoint, as is clear when we consider the imagery of rape during the 1990 Gulf War: Attacks that needed to be defended or retaliated against were cast as heterosexual rapes of women ("the rape of Kuwait"); attacks that were offensive against the Iraqi enemy were phrased as homosexual rapes of men ("bend over, Saddam") (see also Cohn, 1987, 1990).

CONCLUSION

What does this exploration of masculinity and nationalism tell us? For one thing, understanding the extensive nature of the links between nationalism, patriotism, militarism, imperialism, and masculinity helps to make sense of some puzzling items in the news. It has always seemed a mystery to me why the men in the military and paramilitary institutions—men concerned with manly demeanor and strength of character—seemed to get so agitated by, seemed to be so afraid of the entry of, first blacks, then (still) women, and now homosexuals into military institutions and organizations. This unseemly, sometimes hysterical resistance to a diversity that clearly exists outside military boundaries makes more sense when it is understood that these men are not only defending tradition but also defending a particular racial, gendered, and sexual conception of self—a white, male, heterosexual notion of masculine identity loaded with all the burdens and privileges that go along with hegemonic masculinity. Understanding that their reactions reflect not only a defense of male privilege but also a defense of male culture and identity makes it clearer that there are very fundamental issues at stake here for men who are committed to these masculinist and nationalist institutions and lifeways.

Another puzzling issue that this study of masculinity and nationalism has illuminated for me is the question of why men are so much more likely to advocate war and go to war than are women. This not to say that all men or all women respond in the same way to "a call to arms." Many women are patriotic, concerned about honor, and mobilizable; many men are critical of hegemonic masculinity and nationalism, and are not mobilizable. And there are historical moments when hegemony wavers—the widespread resistance to the U.S. war in Vietnam in the 1970s was one such moment. Further, masculinist and nationalist ideology can affect women as well as men. Take the epithet "wimp." I argued above that this is among men's most dreaded insults but that for women it or an equivalent is either not on their list or is nowhere near the top of the list. Carol Cohn (1993) was called a wimp while participating in a RAND Corporation war simulation. She reported being "stung" by the name-calling despite the fact that she was "a woman and a feminist, not only contemptuous of the mentality that measures human beings by their degree of so-called wimpishness, but also someone for whom the term *wimp* does not have a deeply resonant personal meaning" (p. 237). Cohn's explanation for her reaction centers on the power of group membership and reality-defining social context. While she was a participant in the simulation, she became "a participant in a discourse, a shared set of words, concepts, symbols that constituted not only the linguistic possibilities available to us but also constituted *me* in that situation" (pp. 237-238). In other words, Cohn became "masculinized."

But why don't women who participate in masculine organizations or situations "feminize" those institutions and settings, rather than becoming, however momentarily, masculinized themselves? Do women who join the military become "men"? Or if enough women join the military, will they "feminize" it? Is there a critical mass—a point at which women cease to become masculinized in masculine institutions and begin to transform the institutions according to the feminine interests and culture they bring with them to that setting? I wonder, is the gender makeup of governments why nationalism is more associated with preparing for and waging war than with building schools, museums, hospitals and health care systems, social security systems, public transportation, arts and entertainment complexes, and nature preserves? While states concern themselves with these things, they never seem to become the "moral equivalent of war."

The answer to this question of women becoming masculinized or masculine institutions becoming feminized is an important one for making sense of national and international politics. As women enter the political realm in greater numbers around the world, will we see a shifting of state agendas and a decoupling of nationalism from masculinity? Enloe (1990, p. 64) is skeptical. She notes the limited change that has resulted from the many nationalist independence movements around the world, and she observes that in many post–World War II states it is "business as usual" with indigenous masculinity replacing colonialist masculinity at the helms of states.

There is one final puzzle that this exploration of masculinity and nationalism has begun to solve for me—that is, the different way that I, as a woman, may be experiencing my citizenship compared with the citizenship experience of men. According to a Southern African Tswana proverb, "a woman has no tribe" (Young, 1993, p. 26). I wonder whether it might not also be true that a woman has no nation, or that for many women, the nation does not "feel" the same as it does to many men. We are not expected to defend our country, run our country, or represent our country. Of course, many women do these things, but our presence in the masculine institutions of state—the government and the military—seems unwelcome unless we occupy the familiar supporting roles—secretary, lover, wife. We are more adrift from the nation, less likely to be called to "important" and recognized public duty, and our contributions are more likely to be seen as "private," as linked only to "women's issues," and as such, less valued and acknowledged. Given this difference in men's and women's connection to and conception of the nation and the state, it is not surprising that there is a "gender gap" dividing men and women on so many political issues.

The terrorist attacks on the U.S. in September 2001 narrowed somewhat the U.S. gender gap. When asking about public support for the U.S. war in Afghanistan following the attacks, opinion pollsters found a much smaller than usual discrepancy between men's and women's support for the war. In November 2001, U.S. pollsters asked American women and men where they stood on the war in Afghanistan. They reported that 79% of men and 72% of women responded "Support Strongly."[3] This narrowing of the U.S. gender gap over issues of military action had begun to widen again in polls

taken 2 months after the 2003 U.S. invasion of Iraq, when 52% of women and 62% of men reported supporting the war (Raasch, 2003). The relatively closer agreement between men and women on these two conflicts can be understood, in part, from the way the attacks were perceived and defined by the public, politicians, and the media. That collective definition was reflected in the title of the new cabinet-level post created immediately following the attacks: Secretary of Homeland Security. The joining of these two differently gendered domains, "homeland" and "security," reflects a wedding of the traditional interests of women and of men into one U.S. agency, and it suggests that there are historical moments when cultures of masculinity and femininity can combine into national gender alliances.

NOTES

1. This narrative of the Little Bighorn battle is drawn from several historical sources: Hardorff (1997, 1998, 1999), Utley (1973/1984a, 1984b, 1988), Gray (1976, 1991), and Viola (1999). There is some controversy regarding the actual number of native warriors whom Custer and his approximately 500 men faced that June morning in 1876. Estimates range from a few hundred to several thousand; see Utley (1984a), Michno (1997), Eastman (1900), and Means (1995).

2. The most famous court of inquiry was the 1879 Reno Court of Inquiry that exonerated Major Reno (see Graham, 1954); see also Dippie (1994), the Web site of the Little Big Horn Associates (www .lbha.org/newsletter/), and the Old West Legacy site, which sells Little Big Horn Trading Cards (www .helenamontana.com/LBH/).

3. A Washington Post/ABC News poll conducted by telephone on November 5-6, 2001, among a national sample of 756 randomly selected adults; see www.washingtonpost.com/wp-srv/politics/polls/ vault/stories/data112801.htm.

REFERENCES

Adams, M. C. C. (1990). *The great adventure: Male desire and the coming of World War I.* Bloomington: Indiana University Press.

Anderson, B. (1991). *Imagined communities.* London: Verso.

Anthias, F., & Yuval-Davis, N. (1992). *Racial boundaries: Race, nation, gender, colour and class and the anti-racist struggle.* London: Routledge.

Augustin, E. (Ed.). (1993). *Palestinian women: Identity and experience.* London: Zed Books.

Bederman, G. (1995). *Manliness and civilization: A cultural history of gender and race in the United States, 1880-1917.* Chicago: University of Chicago Press.

Berberi, Y. (1993). Active in politics and women's affairs in Gaza. In E. Augustin (Ed.), *Palestinian women: Identity and experience* (pp. 43-54). London: Zed Books.

Bologh, R. W. (1990). *Love or greatness: Max Weber and masculine thinking—A feminist inquiry.* London: Unwin Hyman.

Boulding, E. (1977). *Women in the twentieth century world.* Beverly Hills, CA: Sage.

Brown, W. (1988). *Manhood and politics: A feminist reading in political theory.* Totowa, NJ: Rowman and Littlefield.

Brown, W. (1992). Finding the man in the state. *Feminist Studies, 18,* 7-34.

Brownmiller, S. (1975). *Against our will: Men, women, and rape.* New York: Bantam Books.

Caesar, J. (1951). *The conquest of Gaul.* Baltimore: Penguin.

Carnes, M. C. (1989). *Secret ritual and manhood in Victorian America.* New Haven, CT: Yale University Press.

Clark, D. A. T., & Nagel, J. (2001). White men, red masks: Appropriations of "Indian" manhood in imagined Wests. In M. Basso, L. McCall, & D. Garceau (Eds.), *Across the Great Divide: Cultures of manhood in the American West* (pp. 109-130). New York: Routledge.

Cohen, A. (1985). *The symbolic construction of community.* New York: Tavistock.

Cohn, C. (1987). Sex and death in the rational world of defense intellectuals. *Signs, 12,* 687-718.

Cohn, C. (1990). "Clean bombs" and clean language. In J. B. Elshtain & S. Tobias (Eds.), *Women, militarism, and war: Essays in history, politics, and social theory* (pp. 33-55). Savage, MD: Rowman and Littlefield.

Cohn, C. (1993). Wars, wimps, and women: Talking gender and thinking war. In M. Cooke & A. Woollacott (Eds.), *Gendering war talk* (pp. 227-246). Princeton, NJ: Princeton University Press.

Connell, R. W. (1987). *Gender and power: Society, the person and sexual politics.* Stanford, CA: Stanford University Press.

Connell, R. W. (1995). *Masculinities.* Berkeley: University of California Press.

Connell, R. W. (2000). *The men and the boys.* Berkeley: University of California Press.

Davis, K., Leijenaar, M., & Oldersma, J. (1991). *The gender of power.* Newbury Park, CA: Sage.

Deloria, P. J. (1998). *Playing Indian.* New Haven, CT: Yale University Press.

Dippie, B. W. (1994). *Custer's last stand: The anatomy of an American myth.* Lincoln: University of Nebraska Press.

Donaldson, M. (1993). What is hegemonic masculinity? *Theory and Society, 22,* 643-657.

Eastman, C. A. (1900). The story of the Little Bighorn (told from the Indian standpoint by one of their race). *The Chataquan, 31,* 353-358.

Edgerton, L. (1987). Public protest, domestic acquiescence: Women in Northern Ireland. In R. Ridd & H. Callaway (Eds.), *Women and political conflict* (pp. 61-83). New York: New York University Press.

Eisenstein, H. (1985). The gender of bureaucracy: Reflections on feminism and the state. In J. Goodnow & C. Pateman (Eds.), *Women: Social science and public policy* (pp. 104-115). Sydney: Allen and Unwin.

El-Solh, C. F., & Mabro, J. (1994). Introduction: Islam and Muslim women. In C. F. El-Solh & J. Mabro (Eds.), *Muslim women's choices: Religious belief and social reality* (pp. 1-32). Providence, RI: Berg.

Enloe, C. (1990). *Bananas, beaches, and bases: Making feminist sense of international politics.* Berkeley: University of California Press.

Enloe, C. (1993). *The morning after: Sexual politics at the end of the Cold War.* Berkeley: University of California Press.

Enloe, C. (2000). *Maneuvers: The international politics of militarizing women's lives.* Berkeley: University of California Press.

Fowler, L. (1987). *Shared symbols, contested meanings: Gros Ventre culture and history, 1778-1984.* Ithaca, NY: Cornell University Press.

Franzway, S., Court, D., & Connell, R. W. (1989). *Staking a claim: Feminism, bureaucracy, and the state.* Cambridge, MA: Polity.

Gaitskell, D., & Unterhalter, E. (1989). Mothers of the nation: A comparative analysis of nation, race, and motherhood in Afrikaner nationalism and the African National Congress. In N. Yuval-Davis & F. Anthias (Eds.), *Woman-nation-state* (pp. 58-78). New York: St. Martin's Press.

Gellner, E. (1983). *Nations and nationalism.* Oxford, UK: Blackwell.

Gerth, H. H., & Mills, C. W. (1948). *From Max Weber: Essays in sociology.* London: Routledge and Kegan Paul.

Gilmore, D. D. (1990). *Manhood in the making: Cultural concepts of masculinity.* New Haven, CT: Yale University Press.

Goodwin, J., & Neuwirth, J. (2001, October 19). The rifle and the veil. *New York Times.* Retrieved October 9, 2001, from http://www.nytimes.com/

Graham, W. A. (1954). *Abstract of the official record of the Reno Court of Inquiry.* Harrisburg, PA: Stackpole.

Grant, J., & Tancred, P. (1992). A feminist perspective on state bureaucracy. In A. J. Mills & P. Tancred (Eds.), *Gendering organizational analysis* (pp. 112-128). Newbury Park, CA: Sage.

Gray, J. S. (1976). *Centennial campaign: The Sioux War of 1876*. Fort Collins, CO: Old Army Press.

Gray, J. S. (1991). *Custer's last campaign: Mitch Boyer and the Little Bighorn reconstructed.* Lincoln: University of Nebraska Press.

Green, M. (1993). *The adventurous male: Chapters in the history of the white male mind.* University Park: Pennsylvania State University Press.

Hardorff, R. C. (1997). *Lakota recollections of the Custer fight: New sources of Indian military history.* Lincoln: University of Nebraska Press.

Hardorff, R. C. (1998). *Cheyenne memories of the Custer fight.* Lincoln: University of Nebraska Press.

Hardorff, R. C. (1999). *Hokahey! A good day to die! The Indian casualties of the Custer fight.* Lincoln: University of Nebraska Press.

Hart, G. (1991). Engendering everyday resistance: Gender, patronage, and production in politics in rural Malaysia. *Journal of Peasant Studies, 19,* 93-121.

Hartsock, N. (1983). *Money, sex, and power: Toward a feminist historical materialism.* New York: Longman.

Hartsock, N. (1984). Prologue to a feminist critique of war and politics. In J. H. Stiehm (Ed.), *Women's views of the political world of men* (pp. 123-150). Dobbs Ferry, NY: Transnational Publishers.

Hasan, Z. (1994). Introduction: Contextualising gender and identity in contemporary India. In Z. Hasan (Ed.), *Forging identities: Gender, communities and state in India* (pp. viii-xxiv). Boulder, CO: Westview.

Hedren, P. L. (Ed.). (1991). *The great Sioux war, 1876-77.* Helena: Montana Historical Society Press.

Helie-Lucas, M.-A. (1988). The role of women during the Algerian liberation struggle and after: Nationalism as a concept and as a practice towards both the power of the army and the militarization of the people. In T. E. Isaksson (Ed.), *Women and the military system* (pp. 171-189). New York: St. Martin's Press.

Hernes, H. M. (1987). *Welfare state and woman power: Essays in state feminism.* New York: Oxford University Press.

Hobsbawm, E. (1990). *Nations and nationalism since 1780.* Cambridge, UK: Cambridge University Press.

Hobsbawm, E., & Ranger, T. (1983). *The invention of tradition.* Cambridge, UK: Cambridge University Press.

Hooper, C. (2001). *Manly states: Masculinities, international relations, and gender politics.* New York: Columbia University Press.

Horrocks, R. (1994). *Masculinity in crisis: Myths, fantasies, and realities.* New York: St. Martin's Press.

Huhndorf, S. (1997). From the turn of the century to the new age: Playing Indian, past and present. In W. S. Penn (Ed.), *As we are now: Mixblood essays on race and identity* (pp. 181-198). Berkeley: University of California Press.

Jayawardena, K. (1986). *Feminism and nationalism in the Third World.* London: Zed Books.

Kandiyoti, D. (1991). *Women, Islam, and the state.* Philadelphia: Temple University Press.

Karlen, A. (1971). *Sexuality and homosexuality: A new view.* New York: W. W. Norton.

Kauffman, C. J. (1982). *Faith and fraternalism: The history of the Knights of Columbus, 1882-1982.* New York: Harper and Row.

Kimmel, M. S. (1996). *Manhood in America: A cultural history.* New York: Basic Books.

Kimmel, M. S., & Messner, M. A. (Eds.). (1995). *Men's lives.* New York: Allyn and Bacon.

Koonz, C. (1987). *Mothers in the Fatherland: Women, the family, and Nazi politics.* New York: St. Martin's Press.

Koven, S. (1991). From rough lads to hooligans: Boy life, national culture, and social reform. In A. Parker, M. Russo, D. Sommer, & P. Yaeger (Eds.), *Nationalisms and sexualities* (pp. 365-391). New York: Routledge.

Lawrence, T. E. (1926). *Seven pillars of wisdom: A triumph.* New York: Doubleday.

Layoun, M. (1991). Telling spaces: Palestinian women and the engendering of national narratives. In A. Parker, M. Russo, D. Sommer, & P. Yaeger (Eds.), *Nationalisms and sexualities* (pp. 407-423). New York: Routledge.

Leckie, S. A. (1993). *Elizabeth Bacon Custer and the making of a myth.* Norman: University of Oklahoma Press.

Leverenz, D. (1989). *Manhood and the American Renaissance.* Ithaca, NY: Cornell University Press.

Lievesley, G. (1996). Stages of growth? Women dealing with the state and each other in Peru. In S. M. Rai & G. Lievesley (Eds.), *Women and the state: International perspectives* (pp. 45-60). London: Taylor and Francis.

Luszki, W. (1991). *A rape of justice: MacArthur and the New Guinea hangings.* Lanhan, NC: Madison Books.

Lutz, H., Phoenix, A., & Yuval-Davis, N. (1995). *Crossfires: Nationalism, racism, and gender in Europe.* East Haven, CT: Pluto Press for the European Forum of Left Feminists.

MacAloon, J. J. (1981). *This great symbol: Pierre de Coubertin and the origins of the modern*

Olympic Games. Chicago: University of Chicago Press.

MacAloon, J. J. (1984). Olympic Games and the theory of spectacle in modern societies. In J. J. MacAloon (Ed.), *Rite, drama, festival, spectacle: Rehearsals toward a theory of cultural performances* (pp. 241-280). Philadelphia: Institute for the Study of Human Issues.

MacKenzie, J. M. (1987). The imperial pioneer and hunter and the British masculine stereotype in late Victorian and Edwardian times. In J. A. Mangan & J. Walvin (Eds.), *Manliness and morality: Middle-class masculinity in Britain and America, 1800–1940* (pp. 176-198). Manchester, UK: Manchester University Press.

MacKinnon, C. (1989). *Toward a feminist theory of the state.* Cambridge, MA: Harvard University Press.

Manning, C. J. (1999). *God gave us the right: Conservative Catholic, Evangelical Protestant, and Orthodox Jewish women grapple with feminism.* New Brunswick, NJ: Rutgers University Press.

Massad, J. (1995). Conceiving the masculine: Gender and Palestinian nationalism. *Middle East Journal, 49,* 467-483.

Mayer, T. (2000). *Gender ironies of nationalism: Sexing the nation.* New York: Routledge.

McClintock, A. (1991). "No longer in a future heaven": Woman and nationalism in South Africa. *Transition, 51,* 104-123.

McClintock, A. (1995). *Imperial leather: Race, gender and sexuality in the colonial contest.* London: Routledge.

Means, R. (1995). *Where white men fear to tread: Autobiography of Russell Means.* New York: St. Martin's.

Mehdid, M. (1996). En-gendering the nation-state: Woman, patriarchy and politics in Algeria. In S. M. Rai & G. Lievesley (Eds.), *Women and the state: International perspectives* (pp. 78-102). London: Taylor and Francis.

Messerschmidt, J. (1993). *Masculinities and crime.* Lanham, MD: Rowman and Littlefield.

Messerschmidt, J. (2000). *Nine lives: Adolescent masculinities, the body, and violence.* Boulder, CO: Westview.

Michno, G. (1997). *Lakota noon: The Indian narrative of Custer's defeat.* Missoula, MT: Mountain Press.

Moghadam, V. M. (1991). Revolution, Islam, and women: Sexual politics in Iran and Afghanistan. In A. Parker, M. Russo, D. Sommer, & P. Yaeger (Eds.), *Nationalisms and sexualities* (pp. 424-446). New York: Routledge.

Morgan, D. (1992). *Discovering men.* London: Routledge.

Morris, E. (1979). *The rise of Theodore Roosevelt.* New York: Ballantine.

Mosse, G. L. (1985). *Nationalism and sexuality: Middle-class morality and sexual norms in modern Europe.* Madison: University of Wisconsin Press.

Mosse, G. L. (1990). *Fallen soldiers: Reshaping the memory of the world wars.* New York: Oxford University Press.

Mosse, G. L. (1996). *The image of man: The creation of modern masculinity.* New York: Oxford University Press.

Mukarker, F. (1993). Life between Palestine and Germany: Two cultures, two lives. In E. Augustin (Ed.), *Palestinian women: Identity and experience* (pp. 93-107). London: Zed Books.

Nabokov, P. (1979). *Native American testimony: An anthology of Indian and white relations: First encounter to dispossession.* New York: Harper-Colophon Books.

Nagel, J. (1996). *American Indian ethnic renewal: Red Power and the resurgence of identity and culture.* New York: Oxford University Press.

Nagel, J. (2003). *Race, ethnicity, and sexuality: Intimate intersections, forbidden frontiers.* New York: Oxford University Press.

Nairn, T. (1977). *The break-up of Britain: Crisis and neo-nationalism.* London: New Left Books.

Nategh, H. (1987). Women: Damned of the Iranian revolution. In R. Ridd & H. Callaway (Eds.), *Women and political conflict* (pp. 45-60). New York: New York University Press.

Nelson, D. D. (1998). *National manhood: Capitalist citizenship and the imagined fraternity of white men.* Durham, NC: Duke University Press.

Nye, R. A. (1993). *Masculinity and male codes of honor in modern France.* New York: Oxford University Press.

Orr, J. (1994, March). *Masculinity in trouble: A comparison of the primitive masculinity movement of the late 19th century and the modern mythopoetic men's movement.* Paper presented at the annual meeting of the Midwest Sociological Society, St. Louis.

Pfeil, F. (1995). *White guys: Studies in postmodern domination and difference.* London: Verso.

Preuss, A. (1924). *A dictionary of secret and other societies.* St. Louis: B. Herder Book Company.

Quirin, J. (1992). *The evolution of the Ethiopian Jews: A history of the Beta Israel (Falasha) to 1920.* Philadelphia: University of Pennsylvania Press.

Raasch, C. (2003, May 8). Capture of September 11 mastermind encouraging but doesn't signal end of terrorism war. *USA Today.* Retrieved January 20, 2004, from www.usatoday.com/news/opinion/columnist/raasch/2003-05-08-0306-raasch_x.htm

Rashid, A. (2000). *Taliban: Militant Islam, oil and fundamentalism in Central Asia*. New Haven, CT: Yale University Press.

Rotundo, A. (1993). *American manhood: Transformations in masculinity from the Revolution to the modern era*. New York: Basic Books.

Sapiro, V. (1993). Engendering cultural differences. In M. C. Young (Ed.), *The rising tide of cultural pluralism: The nation state at bay?* (pp. 36-54). Madison: University of Wisconsin Press.

Saunders, K. (1995). In a cloud of lust: Black GIs and sex in World War II. In J. Damousi & M. Lake (Eds.), *Gender and war: Australians at war in the twentieth century* (pp. 178-190). Cambridge, UK: Cambridge University Press.

Sayigh, R., & Peteet, J. (1987). Between two fires: Palestinian women in Lebanon. In R. Ridd & H. Callaway (Eds.), *Women and political conflict* (pp. 106-137). New York: New York University Press.

Schwalbe, M. (1995). *Unlocking the iron cage: A critical appreciation of mythopoetic men's work*. New York: Oxford University Press.

Scott, J. (1985). *Weapons of the weak: Everyday forms of peasant resistance*. New Haven, CT: Yale University Press.

Seton-Watson, H. (1977). *From nations to states*. Boulder, CO: Westview.

Shen, H. (2003). *Crossing the Taiwan Strait: Global disjunctures and multiple hegemonies of class, politics, gender, and sexuality*. Unpublished doctoral dissertation, University of Kansas.

Shirazi, F. (2001). *The veil unveiled: The hijab in modern culture*. Gainesville: University of Florida Press.

Sinha, M. (1995). *Colonial masculinity: The "manly Englishman" and the "effeminate Bengali" in the late nineteenth century*. Manchester, UK: Manchester University Press.

Skurski, J. (1994). The ambiguities of authenticity: *Dona Barbara* and the construction of national identity. *Poetics Today, 15*, 605-642.

Springhall, J. (1987). Building character in the British boy: The attempt to extend Christian manliness to working-class adolescents, 1880-1940. In J. A. Mangan & J. Walvin (Eds.), *Manliness and morality: Middle-class masculinity in Britain and America, 1800-1940* (pp. 52-74). Manchester, UK: Manchester University Press.

Steinfels, P. (1995, July 1). In Algeria, women are caught in the cross-fire of men's religious and ideological wars. *New York Times*, pp. 8, 10.

Sturdevant, S. P., & Stoltzfus, B. (1992). *Let the good times roll: Prostitution and the U.S. military in Asia*. New York: The New Press.

Theweleit, K. (1987). *Male fantasies* (Vol. 1, Stephen Conway, Trans.). Minneapolis: University of Minnesota Press.

Thomas, D. Q. (1992). *Criminal injustice: Violence against women in Brazil—An Americas Watch report*. New York: Human Rights Watch.

Tohidi, N. (1991). Gender and Islamic fundamentalism: Feminist politics in Iran. In C. T. Mohanty, A. Russo, & L. Torres (Eds.), *Third World women and the politics of feminism* (pp. 251-265). Bloomington: Indiana University Press.

Trachtenberg, A. (1982). *The incorporation of America: Culture and society in the gilded age*. New York: Hill and Wang.

Twine, F. W., & Blee, K. M. (2001). *Feminism and antiracism: International struggles for justice*. New York: New York University Press.

Urdang, S. (1989). *And still they dance: Women, war, and the struggle for change in Mozambique*. New York: Monthly Review Press.

Utley, R. M. (1984a). *Frontier regulars: The United States Army and the Indian, 1866-1891*. Lincoln: University of Nebraska Press. (Original work published 1973)

Utley, R. M. (1984b). *The Indian frontier of the American West, 1846-1890*. Albuquerque: University of New Mexico Press.

Utley, R. M. (1988). *Custer battlefield: A history and guide to the Battle of the Little Bighorn*. Washington, DC: U.S. Department of the Interior.

van den Berghe, P. (1978). Race and ethnicity: A sociobiological perspective. *Racial and Ethnic Studies, 1*, 402-411.

Vickers, J. (1993). *Women and war*. London: Zed Books.

Viola, H. J. (1999). *Little Bighorn remembered: The untold Indian story of Custer's Last Stand*. New York: Times Books.

Walby, S. (1989). Woman and nation. In A. D. Smith (Ed.), *Ethnicity and nationalism* (pp. 81-99). New York: E. J. Brill.

Walvin, J. (1987). Symbols of moral superiority: Slavery, sport and the changing world order, 1900-1940. In J. A. Mangan & J. Walvin (Eds.), *Manliness and morality: Middle-class masculinity in Britain and America, 1800-1940* (pp. 242-260). Manchester, UK: Manchester University Press.

Warren, A. (1986). Citizens of the empire, Baden-Powell, scouts, guides, and an imperial ideal. In J. M. MacKenzie (Ed.), *Imperialism and popular culture* (pp. 232-256). Manchester, UK: Manchester University Press.

Warren, A. (1987). Popular manliness: Baden-Powell, scouting, and the development of manly character. In J. A. Mangan & J. Walvin (Eds.), *Manliness and morality: Middle-class masculinity in Britain and America, 1800-1940* (pp. 199-219). Manchester, UK: Manchester University Press.

Waylen, G. (1996). Democratization, feminism, and the state in Chile: The establishment of SER-NAM. In S. M. Rai & G. Lievesley (Eds.), *Women and the State: International perspectives* (pp. 103-117). London: Taylor and Francis.

Whitehorse, D. (1988). *Pow-wow: The contemporary pan-Indian celebration* (Publications in American Indian Studies, No. 5). San Diego: San Diego State University.

Williams, B. F. (1996). *Women out of place: The gender of agency and the race of nationality.* New York: Routledge.

Young, C. (1993). *The rising tide of cultural pluralism: The nation-state at bay?* Madison: University of Wisconsin Press.

Yuval-Davis, N., & Anthias, F. (Eds.). (1989). *Woman-nation-state.* London: Macmillan.

24

GLOBALIZATION AND ITS MAL(E)CONTENTS

The Gendered Moral and Political Economy of Terrorism

MICHAEL S. KIMMEL

The chief social basis of radicalism has been the peasants and the smaller artisans in the towns. From these facts one may conclude that the wellsprings of human freedom lie not where Marx saw them, in the aspirations of classes about to take power, but perhaps even more in the dying wail of a class over whom the wave of progress is about to roll.

—Barrington Moore (1966, p. 505)

Globalization changes masculinities, reshaping the arena in which national and local masculinities are articulated, and transforming the shape of men's lives. Globalization disrupts and reconfigures traditional, neocolonial, or other national, regional, or local economic, political, and cultural arrangements. In so doing, globalization transforms local articulations of both domestic and public patriarchy (see Connell, 1998). Globalization includes the gradual proletarianization of local peasantries, as market criteria replace subsistence and survival. Local small craft producers, small farmers, and independent peasants traditionally stake their definitions of masculinity in ownership of land and economic autonomy in their work; these are increasingly transferred upward in the class hierarchy and outward to transnational corporations. Proletarianization also leads to massive labor migrations—typically migrations of *male* workers—who leave their homes and populate migrant enclaves, squatter camps, and labor camps.

Globalization thus presents another level at which hegemonic and local masculinities are constructed. Globalization was always a gendered process. As Andre Gunder Frank pointed out several decades ago in his studies of economic development, development and underdevelopment were not simply stages through which all countries pass, and there was no single continuum along which individual nations might be positioned. Rather, he argued, there was a relationship between development and

Author's note: The author has made every effort to obtain written permission for use of the cartoons appearing in this chapter.

underdevelopment, that, in fact, the development of some countries implied the specific and deliberate underdevelopment of others. The creation of the metropole was simultaneous and coordinated with the creation of the periphery.

As with economic development, so too with gender—the historical constructions of the meanings of masculinity. As the hegemonic ideal was being created, it was created against a screen of "others" whose masculinity was thus problematized and devalued. Hegemonic and subaltern emerged in mutual but unequal interaction in a gendered social and economic order. Colonial administrations often problematized the masculinity of the colonized. For example, in British India, Bengali men were perceived as weak and effeminate, though Pathans and Sikhs were perceived as hypermasculine—violent and uncontrolled (see Sinha, 1995). Similar distinctions were made in South Africa between Hottentots and Zulus, and in North America between Navaho or Algonquin on one hand, and Sioux, Apache, and Cheyenne on the other (see Connell, 1998, p. 14). In many colonial situations, the colonized men were called "boys" by the colonizers.

Today, although they appear to be gender-neutral, the institutional arrangements of global society are equally gendered. The marketplace, multinational corporations, and transnational geopolitical institutions (World Court, United Nations, European Union) and their attendant ideological principles (economic rationality, liberal individualism) express a gendered logic. The "increasingly unregulated power of transnational corporations places strategic power in the hands of particular groups of men," while the language of globalization remains gender neutral so that "the 'individual' of neoliberal theory has in general the attributes and interests of a male entrepreneur" (Connell, 1998, p. 15).

As a result, the impact of global economic and political restructuring is greater on women. At the national and global levels, the world gender order privileges men in a variety of ways, such as unequal wages, unequal labor force participation, unequal structures of ownership and control of property, unequal control over one's body, and cultural and sexual privileges. What's more, in the economic South, for example, aid programs disproportionately target women (as in population planning programs that involve only women), while in the metropole, attacks on the welfare state generally weaken the position of women, domestically and publicly. These effects, however, are less the result of bad policies or even less the results of bad—inept or evil—policymakers, and more the results of the gendered logic of these institutions and processes themselves (Connell, 1998; Enloe, 1990).

HEGEMONIC MASCULINITY AND ITS DISCONTENTS

In addition, the patterns of masculinity embedded within these gendered institutions also are rapidly becoming the dominant global hegemonic model of masculinity, against which all local, regional, and national masculinities are played out and to which they increasingly refer. The emergent global hegemonic version of masculinity is readily identifiable: You can see him sitting in first-class waiting rooms in airports, or in elegant business hotels the world over, wearing a designer business suit, speaking English, eating "continental" cuisine, talking on his cell phone, his laptop computer plugged into any electrical outlet, while he watches CNN International on television. Temperamentally, he is increasingly cosmopolitan, with liberal tastes in consumption (and sexuality) and conservative political ideas of limited government control of the economy. This has the additional effect of increasing the power of the hegemonic countries within the global political and economic arena because everyone, no matter where they are from, talks and acts as he does.

The processes of globalization and the emergence of a global hegemonic masculinity have the ironic effect of increasingly "gendering" local, regional, and national resistance to incorporation into the global arena as subordinated entities. Scholars have pointed out the ways in which religious fundamentalism and ethnic nationalism use local cultural symbols to express regional resistance to incorporation (see especially Barber, 1995, and Juergensmeyer, 1995, 2000). However, these religious and ethnic expressions are often manifest as gender revolts, and they often include a virulent resurgence of domestic patriarchy (as in the militant misogyny of Iran or Afghanistan), the problematization of global masculinities or neighboring masculinities (as in the former Yugoslavia), and the overt symbolic efforts to claim a distinct "manhood" along religious or ethnic lines to which others do not have access and which will restore manhood to the formerly privileged (white militias in the United States and skinhead racists in Europe).

Thus, gender becomes one of the chief organizing principles of local, regional, and national resistance to globalization, whether expressed in religious or secular, ethnic or national terms. These processes involve flattening or eliminating local or regional distinctions, along with cultural homogenization as citizens and social heterogenization as new ethnic groups move to new countries in labor migration efforts. Movements thus tap racialist and nativist sentiments at the same time as they can tap local and regional protectionism and isolationism. They become gendered as oppositional movements also tap into a vague masculine resentment of the economic displacement, loss of autonomy, and collapse of domestic patriarchy that accompany further integration into the global economy. Efforts to reclaim economic autonomy, to reassert political control, and to revive traditional domestic dominance thus take on the veneer of restoring manhood.

To illustrate these themes, one could consider several political movements of men, in North America or elsewhere. Indeed, Promise Keepers, men's rights, and fathers' rights groups all respond to the perceived erosion of public patriarchy with an attempted restoration of some version of domestic patriarchy. The mythopoetic men's movement responds instead to a perceived erosion of domestic patriarchy with assertions of separate mythic or natural space for men to experience their power—because they can no longer experience it in either the public or private spheres. (For more on these men's movements in the United States, see Kimmel, 1996a, 1996b, and Messner, 1998.)

In this chapter, I will examine the ways in which masculinities and globalization are embedded in the emergence of extremist groups on the far right in Europe and the United States, with a final discussion of the Islamic world. Specifically, I will discuss the ways in which globalization reconfigures certain political tendencies among different class fractions. In the economic North, the members of the far right white supremacists in the United States and Scandinavia tend to be from a declining lower middle class—traditionally the class basis of totalitarian political solutions like socialism or fascism. They are movements of the far right. It is the lower middle class—those strata of

independent farmers, small shopkeepers, craft and highly skilled workers, and small-scale entrepreneurs—who have been hit hardest by the processes of globalization. "Western industry has displaced traditional crafts—female as well as male—and large-scale multinational-controlled agriculture has downgraded the independent farmer to the status of hired hand" (Ehrenreich, 2001). This has resulted in massive and uneven male displacement—migration, downward mobility. It has been felt the most not by the adult men who were the tradesmen, shopkeepers, and skilled workers, but by their sons, by the young men whose inheritance has been seemingly stolen from them. They feel entitled and deprived—and furious.

In the economic South, however, the sons of the rising middle classes, whose upward mobility is thwarted by globalization, join the downwardly mobile sons of the lower middle classes. The terrorists of Al Qaeda, or other Middle East terrorist organizations like Hezbollah, tend to be highly educated young men, trained for professional jobs that have been choked off by global economic shifts. Historically, this rising middle class, as Barrington Moore noted, were the backbone of the bourgeois revolutions; today, the rising middle class is no longer rising, and in its descent, the young men who trained for upward mobility seek enemies upon whom to heap their rage, as well as alternate strategies of mobility (see, for example, Barro, 2002; Kristof, 2002a, 2002b). These are movements of the ultra-left. Both of these groups of angry young men are the foot soldiers of the armies of resentment that have sprung up around the world. They are joined in the new ways in which masculine entitlement has become gendered rage.

In this essay, I will discuss white supremacist youth in both the United States and Scandinavia as my two primary case studies, and I conclude with a brief comparative discussion of the terrorists of Al Qaeda who were responsible for the heinous acts of September 11, 2001.[1] All use a variety of ideological and political resources to reestablish and reassert domestic and public patriarchies. All deploy "masculinity" as a symbolic capital (a) as an ideological resource to understand and explicate their plight, (b) as a rhetorical device to problematize the identities of those against whom they believe themselves fighting, and (c) as a recruitment device to entice other, similarly situated young men to join them. These movements look backward, nostalgically, to a time when they—native-born white men, Muslim men in a pre-global era— were able to assume the places in society to which they believe themselves entitled. They seek to restore that unquestioned entitlement, both in the domestic sphere and in the public sphere. They are movements not of revolution, but of restoration.

Types of Patriarchies

In this chapter, I describe the transformation of two forms of patriarchy. It is important to note that patriarchy is both a system of domination by which men dominate women and a system by which some men (older men; fathers, in the classic definition of the term) dominate other men.

Public patriarchy refers to the institutional arrangements of a society, the predominance of males in all power positions within the economy and polity, both locally and nationally, as well as the "gendering" of those institutions themselves (by which the criteria for promotion, for example, appear to be gender-neutral but actually reproduce the gender order).

Domestic patriarchy refers to the emotional and familial arrangements in a society, the ways in which men's power in the public arena is reproduced at the level of private life. This includes male-female relationships as well as family life, child socialization, and the like.

Both public patriarchy and domestic patriarchy are held together by the threat, implicit or explicit, of violence. Public patriarchy, of course, includes the military and police apparatus of society, which are also explicitly gendered institutions (revealed in their increased opposition to women's entry). In the aggregate, rape and domestic violence help sustain domestic patriarchy (see Hearn, 1992, 1998).

These two expressions of men's power over women and other men are neither uniform nor monolithic; they vary enormously and are constantly in flux. Equally, they are not coincident, so that increases or decreases in one invariably produce increases or decreases in the other. Nor are they so directly linked that a decrease in one automatically produces an increase in the other, although there will be pressures in that direction. Thus, women's entry into the workforce or increased representation in legislatures undermines public patriarchy and will likely produce

both backlash efforts to reinforce domestic patriarchy (covenant marriage, tightening divorce laws to restrain women's exit from the home, increased domestic assault) or even a virulent resurgence of domestic patriarchy (the Taliban). At the same time, women's increased public presence will also undermine domestic patriarchy, by pressing men into domestic duties they had previously avoided (such as housework and parenting).

All these movements exhibit what Connell (1995, pp. 109-112) calls "protest masculinity"— a combination of stereotypical male norms with often unconventional attitudes about women. Exaggerated claims of potency are accompanied by violent resistance to authority, school, and work, accompanied by engagement with crime and heavy drinking. In such a model, the "growing boy puts together a tense, freaky façade, making a claim to power where there are no real resources for power," Connell writes (1995, p. 109). "There is a lot of concern with face, a lot of work keeping up a front." However, those groups in the economic North claim to support women's equality (in varying degrees), whereas those in the Islamic world have made women's complete resubordination a central pillar of the edifice of their rule.

By examining extreme right white supremacists in the United States and their counterparts in Scandinavia, we can see the ways in which masculinity politics may be mobilized among some groups of men in the economic North; while looking at the social origins of the Al Qaeda terrorists, we might merely sketch how they might work out in Islamic countries. Although such a comparison in no way effaces the many differences that exist among these movements, especially between the movements in the economic South and North, a comparison of their similarities enables us to explore the political mobilization of masculinities and to map the ways in which masculinities are likely to be put into political play in the coming decades.

RIGHT-WING MILITIAS: RACISM, SEXISM, AND ANTI-SEMITISM AS MASCULINE REASSERTION[2]

In an illustration in *W.A.R.*, the magazine of the White Aryan Resistance, for 1987, a working-class white man, in hard hat and flak jacket, stands proudly before a suspension bridge while a jet plane soars overhead. "White Men *Built* This nation!!" reads the text. "White Men *Are* This nation!!!"

Illustration 24.1   *W.A.R.* Cartoon

SOURCE: Copyright © 2000 White Aryan Resistance. Used by permission of Tom Metzger.

Most observers immediately see its racist intent, but rarely do we see the deeply gendered meaning of the statement. Here is a moment of fusion of racial and gendered discourses, when both race and gender are made visible. "This nation," we now understand, "is" neither white women nor nonwhite.

The White Aryan Resistance that produced this illustration is situated on a continuum of the far right that runs from older organizations such as the John Birch Society, the Ku Klux Klan, and the American Nazi Party, to Holocaust deniers, neo-Nazi or racist skinheads, White Power groups like Posse Comitatus and White Aryan Resistance, and radical militias like the Wisconsin Militia or the Militia of Montana. The Southern Poverty Law Center cites 676 active hate groups in the United States, including 109 Klan centers 209 neo-Nazi groups, 43 racist skinheads groups, and 124 neo-Confederate groups, and more than 400 U.S.-based Web sites ("Maps of White Supremacist Organizations," 2002).

These fringe groups of the far right are composed of young white men, the sons of independent farmers and small shopkeepers. Estimates of their numbers range from an "improbably modest" 10,000 to an "improbably cautionary" 100,000 (Kramer, 2002, p. 24), while the number of far-right extremists and Patriots of any sort is estimated to run to between three and four million who "believe themselves victims, real or intended, of an international plot to destroy their freedom and their faith and pollute their blood" (Kramer, 2002, p. 30; see also Jipson & Becker, 2000). Buffeted by the global political and economic forces that have produced global hegemonic masculinities, they have responded to the erosion of public patriarchy (displacement in the political arena) and of domestic patriarchy (their wives now work away from the farm) with a renewal of their sense of masculine entitlement to restore patriarchy in both arenas. Ideologically, what characterizes these scions of small-town rural America—both the fathers and the sons—is (a) their ideological vision of producerism, threatened by economic transformation; (b) their sense of small-town democratic community, an inclusive community that was based on the exclusion of broad segments of the population; and (c) a sense of entitlement to economic, social, and political and even military power.

(It is, of course, true that women play an important role in many of these groups, ranging from a Ladies' Auxiliary to active participants as violent skinheads [see Blee, 2002, and Kimmel, 2002]. Yet although their activities may range from holding a Klan bake sale, using Aryan cookbooks, and helping their children with their racist coloring books to active physical violence and participation in hate crimes against immigrants, blacks, Jews, and gays, their gender ideology remains firmly planted in notions of unchallenged domestic patriarchy.)

To cast the middle class straight white man simply as the hegemonic holder of power in the United States would be to fully miss the daily experience of these straight white men. They believe themselves to be *entitled* to power—by a combination of historical legacy, religious fiat, biological destiny, and moral legitimacy—but they believe they do not have power. That power has been both surrendered by white men (their fathers) and stolen from them by a federal government controlled and staffed by legions of the newly enfranchised minorities, women, and immigrants, all in service to the omnipotent Jews who control international economic and political life. "Heaven help the God-fearing, law-abiding Caucasian middle class," explained Charlton Heston to a recent Christian Coalition convention, especially

> Protestant or even worse evangelical Christian, Midwest or Southern or even worse rural, apparently straight or even worse admittedly [heterosexual], gun-owning or even worse NRA card-carrying average working stiff, or even worst of all, male working stiff. Because not only don't you count, you're a downright obstacle to social progress. (quoted in Citizens Project, p. 3)

Downwardly mobile rural white men—those who lost the family farms and those who expected to take them over—are squeezed between the omnivorous jaws of capital concentration and a federal bureaucracy that is at best indifferent to their plight and at worst facilitates their further demise. What they want, says one, is to "take back what is rightfully ours" (in Dobratz & Shanks-Meile, 2001, p. 10).

In many respects, the militias' ideology reflects the ideologies of other fringe groups on the far right from whose ranks they typically recruit, especially racism, homophobia, nativism, sexism, and anti-Semitism. These discourses of hate provide an explanation for the feelings of entitlement thwarted, fixing the blame squarely on "others" whom the state must now serve at the expense of white men. The unifying theme of these discourses, which traditionally have formed the rhetorical package Richard Hofstadter labeled "paranoid politics," is *gender*. Specifically, it is by framing state policies as emasculating and problematizing the masculinity of these various "others" that rural white militia members seek to restore their own masculinity.

Contemporary American white supremacists tap into a general malaise among American men who seek some explanations for the contemporary "crisis" of masculinity. Like the Sons of Liberty who threw off the British yoke of tyranny in 1776, these contemporary Sons of Liberty see "R-2," the Second American Revolution, as restorative—a means of retrieving and refounding traditional masculinity by the exclusion of others. The entire rhetorical apparatus that serves this purpose is saturated

with gendered readings—of the problematized masculinity of the "others," of the emasculating policies of the state, and of the rightful masculine entitlement of white men. As sociologist Lillian Rubin puts it:

> It's this confluence of forces—the racial and cultural diversity of our new immigrant population; the claims on the resources of the nation now being made by those minorities who, for generations, have called America their home; the failure of some of our basic institutions to serve the needs of our people; the contracting economy, which threatens the mobility aspirations of working class families—all these have come together to leave white workers feeling as if everyone else is getting a piece of the action while they get nothing. (Rubin, 1994, p. 186)

One issue of *The Truth at Last* put it this way:

> Immigrants are flooding into our nation willing to work for the minimum wage (or less). Super-rich corporate executives are flying all over the world in search of cheaper and cheaper labor so that they can "lay off" their American employees. . . . Many young White families have no future! They are not going to receive any appreciable wage increases due to job competition from immigrants . . . (cited in Dobratz & Shanks-Meile, 2001, p. 115)

White supremacists see themselves as squeezed between global capital and an emasculated state that supports voracious global profiteering. In a song, "No Crime Being White," Day of the Sword, a popular racist skinhead band, confronts the greedy class:

> The birthplace is the death of our race.
> Our brothers being laid off is a truth
> we have to face.
> Take my job, it's equal opportunity
> The least I can do, you were so
> oppressed by me
> I've only put in twenty years now.
> Suddenly my country favors gooks and
> spicks and queers.
> Fuck you, then, boy I hope you're
> happy when your new employees are
> the reason why your business ends.
> (cited in Dobratz & Shanks-Meile,
> 2001, p. 271)

The North American Free Trade Agreement (NAFTA) took away American jobs; the eroding job base in urban centers also led many African

Americans to move to formerly all-white suburbs to find work. As a result, what youngsters now see as the "Burger King" economy leaves no room at the top so many "see themselves as being forced to compete with nonwhites for the available minimum wage, service economy jobs that have replaced their parents' unionized industry opportunities" (Coplon, 1989, p. 84).

That such ardent patriots as militia members are so passionately antigovernment might strike the observer as contradictory. After all, are these not the same men who served their country in Vietnam or in the Gulf War? Are these not the same men who believe so passionately in the American dream? Are they not the backbone of the Reagan Revolution? Indeed they are. Militia members face the difficult theoretical task of maintaining their faith in America and in capitalism, and simultaneously providing an analysis of an indifferent state, at best, or an actively interventionist one, at worst, coupled with a contemporary articulation of corporate capitalist logic that leaves them, often literally, out in the cold—homeless, jobless, hopeless.

It is through a decidedly gendered and sexualized rhetoric of masculinity that this contradiction between loving the nation and hating its government, loving capitalism and hating its corporate iterations, is resolved. First, like others on the far right, militia members believe that the state has been captured by evil, even Satanic forces; the original virtue of the American political regime deeply and irretrievably corrupted. "The enemy is the system—the system of international world dominance," according to the Florida Interklan Report (in Dobratz & Shanks-Meile, 2001, p. 160). Environmental regulations, state policies dictated by urban and northern interests, the Internal Revenue Service—all are the outcomes of a state now utterly controlled by feminists, environmentalists, blacks, and Jews.

In their foreboding futuristic vision, communalism, feminism, multiculturalism, homosexuality, and Christian-bashing are all tied together, part and parcel of the New World Order. Multicultural textbooks, women in government, and legalized abortion can individually be taken as signs of the impending New World Order. Increased opportunities for women can only lead to the oppression of men. Tex Marrs proclaims, "In the New Order, woman is finally on top. She is not a mere equal. *She is Goddess*" (Marrs,

1993, p. 28). In fact, she has ceased to be a "real" woman—the feminist now represents the confusion of gender boundaries and the demasculinization of men, symbolizing a future where men are not allowed to be real men.

The "Nanny State" no longer acts in the interests of "true" American men but is, instead, an engine of gender inversion, feminizing men, while feminism masculinizes women. White men not involved in the movement are often referred to as "sheeple," while feminist women, it turns out, are more masculine than men are. Not only does this call the masculinity of white men into question, but it also uses gender as the rhetorical vehicle for criticizing "other" men. Typically, problematizing the masculinity of these others takes two forms simultaneously: Other men are both "too masculine" and "not masculine enough," both hypermasculine—violent rapacious beasts incapable of self-control—and hypomasculine—weak, helpless, effete, incapable of supporting a family.

Thus, in the logic of militias and other white supremacist organizations, gay men are both promiscuously carnal and sexually voracious and effete fops who do to men what men should only have done to them by women. Black men are seen both as violent hypersexual beasts, possessed of an "irresponsible sexuality," seeking white women to rape (*W.A.R., 8*(2), 1989, p. 11; cited in Ferber, 1998, p. 81) and less than fully manly, "weak, stupid, lazy" (*NS Mobilizer*, cited in Ferber, 1998, p. 81). In *The Turner Diaries,* the apocalyptic novel that served as the blueprint for the Oklahoma City bombing and is widely read and peddled by militias, author William Pierce depicts a nightmarish world where white women and girls are constantly threatened and raped by "gangs of Black thugs" (Pierce, 1978, p. 58). Blacks are primal nature—untamed, cannibalistic, uncontrolled, but also stupid and lazy—and whites are the driving force of civilization. "America and all civilized society are the exclusive products of White man's mind and muscle" is how *The Thunderbolt* put it (cited in Ferber, 1998, p. 76). "[T]he White race is the Master race of the earth . . . the Master Builders, the Master Minds, and the Master warriors of civilization." What can a black man do but "clumsily shuffle off, scratching his wooley head, to search for shoebrush and mop" (in *New Order,* cited in Ferber, 1998, p. 91).

Most interesting is the portrait of the Jew. On one hand, the Jew is a greedy, cunning, conniving, omnivorous predator; on the other, the Jew is small, beady-eyed, and incapable of masculine virtue. By asserting the hypermasculine power of the Jew, the far right can support capitalism as a system while decrying the actions of capitalists and their corporations. According to militia logic, it's not the capitalist corporations that have turned the government against them, but the international cartel of Jewish bankers and financiers, media moguls, and intellectuals who have already taken over the U.S. state and turned it into ZOG (Zionist Occupied Government). The United States is called the "Jewnited States," and Jews are blamed for orchestrating the demise of the once-proud Aryan man.[3]

In white supremacist ideology, the Jew is the archetypal villain, both hypermasculine—greedy, omnivorous, sexually predatory, capable of the destruction of the Aryan way of life—and hypomasculine, small, effete, homosexual, pernicious, weasely. A cartoon in *Racial Loyalty* from 1991 illustrates this simultaneous position.

Illustration 24.2   *Racial Loyalty* Cartoon

SOURCE: *Racial Loyalty, 71* (June 1991). Copyright © 1991 by *Racial Loyalty*.

In the militia cosmology, Jews are both hypermasculine and effeminate. Hypermasculinity is expressed in the Jewish domination of the

world's media and financial institutions, and especially Hollywood. They're sexually omnivorous, but calling them "rabid, sex-perverted" is not a compliment. *The Thunderbolt* (#301, p. 6; cited in Ferber, 1998, p. 140) claims that 90% of pornographers are Jewish. At the same time, Jewish men are seen as wimpish, small, nerdy, and utterly unmasculine—likely, in fact, to be homosexual. It's Jewish *women* who are seen as "real men"—strong, large, and hairy.

In lieu of their brawn power, Jewish men have harnessed their brainpower in their quest for world domination. Jews are seen as the masterminds behind the other social groups who are seen as dispossessing rural American men of their birthright. Toward that end, they have co-opted blacks, women, gays, and brainwashed and cowardly white men to do their bidding. In a remarkable passage from *The New Order*, white supremacists cast the economic plight of white workers as being squeezed between nonwhite workers and Jewish owners:

> It is our RACE we must preserve, not just one class . . . White Power means a permanent end to unemployment because with the non-Whites gone, the labor market will no longer be over-crowded with unproductive niggers, spics and other racial low-life. It means an end to inflation eating up a man's paycheck faster than he can raise it because OUR economy will not be run by a criminal pack of international Jewish bankers, bent on using the White worker's tax money in selfish and even destructive schemes. (*The New* Order, March 1979, p. 8; cited in Ferber, 1998, p. 140)

Because Jews are incapable of acting like real men—strong, hardy, virtuous manual workers and farmers—a central axiom of the international Jewish conspiracy for world domination is their plan to "feminize White men and to masculinize White women" (*Racial Loyalty, 72,* 1991, p. 3; cited in Ferber, 1998, p. 141). *The Turner Diaries* describes the "Jewish-liberal-democratic-equalitarian" perspective as "an essentially feminine, submissive worldview" (Pierce, 1978, p. 42). *W.A.R.* echoes this theme: "One of the characteristics of nations which are controlled by the Jews is the gradual eradication of masculine influence and power and the transfer of influence into feminine forms" (cited in Ferber, 1998, pp. 125-126).

Embedded in this anti-Semitic slander is a critique of white American manhood as soft, feminized, weakened—indeed, emasculated. Article after article decries "the whimpering collapse of the blond male," as if white men have surrendered to the plot (in Ferber, 1998, p. 127). According to *The Turner Diaries,* American men have lost the right to be free; slavery "is the just and proper state for a people who have gown soft" (Pierce, 1978, p. 33). The militias simultaneously offer white men an analysis of their present situation and a political strategy for retrieving their manhood. As *National Vanguard* puts it,

> As Northern males have continued to become more wimpish, the result of the media-created image of the "new male"—more pacifist, less authoritarian, more "sensitive," less competitive, more androgynous, less possessive—the controlled media, the homosexual lobby and the feminist movement have cheered . . . the number of effeminate males has increased greatly . . . legions of sissies and weaklings, of flabby, limp-wristed, non-aggressive, non-physical, indecisive, slack-jawed, fearful males who, while still heterosexual in theory and practice, have not even a vestige of the old macho spirit, so deprecated today, left in them. (cited in Ferber, 1998, p. 136)

It is through participation in these movements that American manhood can be restored and revived—a manhood in which individual white men control the fruits of their own labor and are not subject to the emasculation of Jewish-owned finance capital or a black- and feminist-controlled welfare state. It is a fantasy of "the Viking warrior who comes to rescue his people from the 'evil Jews and subhuman mongrels,'" a militarized manhood of the heroic John Rambo—a manhood that celebrates their God-sanctioned right to band together in armed militias if anyone—or any governmental agency—tries to take it away from them (see Blazak, 2001, p. 991). If the state and capital emasculate them, and if the masculinity of the "others" is problematic, then only real white men can rescue this American Eden from a feminized, multicultural androgynous melting pot. "The world is in trouble now only because the White man is divided, confused, and misled," we read in *The New Order.* "Once he is united, inspired by a great ideal and led by real men, his world will again become livable, safe, and happy" (in Ferber, 1998, p. 139). The movements of the far right seek to reclaim their manhood gloriously, violently.

Perhaps this is best illustrated with another cartoon from *W.A.R.,* the magazine of the White Aryan Resistance. In this deliberate parody of countless Charles Atlas advertisements, the timid white 97-pound weakling finds his power, his strength as a man, through racial hatred. In the ideology of the white supremacist movement and its organized militia allies, it is racism that will again enable white men to reclaim their manhood. The amorphous groups of white supremacists, skinheads, and neo-Nazis may be the symbolic shock troops of this movement, but the rural militias are its well-organized and highly regimented infantry.

White Supremacists in Scandinavia

While significantly fewer in number than their American counterparts, white supremacists in the Nordic countries have also made a significant impact on those normally tolerant social democracies. Norwegian groups such as Bootboys, NUNS 88, the Norsk Arisk Ungdomsfron (NAUF), Varg, and the Vikings; the Green Jacket Movement (Gronjakkerne) in Denmark; and the Vitt Ariskt Motstand (VAM, or White Aryan Resistance), Kreatrivistens Kyrka (Church of the Creator, COTC), and Riksfronten (National Front) in Sweden have exerted an impact beyond their modest numbers. Norwegian groups number a few hundred, and Swedish groups may barely top 1,000 adherents, with perhaps double that number as supporters and general sympathizers.

Their opposition seems to come precisely from the relative prosperity of their homelands, a prosperity that has made the Nordic countries attractive to ethnic immigrants from the economic South. Most come from lower-middle-class families; their fathers are painters, carpenters, tillers, bricklayers, and road maintenance workers. Some come from small family farms. Several fathers own one-man businesses and are small capitalists or self-employed tradesmen (Fangen, 1999, p. 360). In her life-history analysis of four young Norwegian participants, Katherine Fangen (1999, pp. 359-363) found that only one claimed a working-class identity, and his father owned his own business; another's father owned a small printing company, another was a carpenter, and the fourth came from a family of independent fishermen.

Illustration 24.3 *W.A.R.* Cartoon

SOURCE: Copyright © 2000 White Aryan Resistance. Used by permission of Tom Metzger.

All the sons are downwardly mobile; they work sporadically, they have little or no control over their own labor or workplace, and none owns his own business. Almost all members are between 16 and 20 years of age (Fangen, 1999, p. 360). Youth unemployment has spiked, especially in Sweden, just as the numbers of asylum seekers has spiked, and with them

attacks on centers for asylum seekers. They struggle, Fangen notes, to recover a class identity "that no longer has a material basis" (2003, p. 2). Danish Aryans have few assets and "few prospects for a better future" (Bjorgo, 1997, p. 104; see also Bjorgo, 1998).

This downward mobility marks these racist skinheads from their British counterparts, who have been embedded within working class culture. These young Nordic lower-middle-class boys do not participate in a violent, racist counterculture as preparation for their working lives on the shop floor (see, for example, Willis, 1981). Rather, like their American counterparts, they see *no* future in the labor market. They do not yearn nostalgically for the collective solidarity of the shop floor; for them, that life was already gone.

Like the American white supremacists, Scandinavian Aryans understand their plight in terms of masculine entitlement, which is eroded by state immigration policies, international Zionist power, and globalization. All desire a return to a racially and ethnically homogeneous society, seeing themselves, as one put it, as a "front against alienation, and the mixing of cultures" (Fangen, 1998, p. 214).

Antigay sentiments also unite these white supremacists. "Words are no use; only action will help in the fight against homosexuals," says a Swedish magazine, *Siege.* "With violence and terror as our weapons we must beat back the wave of homosexual terror and stinking perversion whose stench is washing over our country" (cited in Bjorgo, 1997, p. 127). Almost all have embraced anti-Semitism, casting the Jews as the culprits for immigration and homosexuality. According to a Swedish group, Vitt Ariskt Motstand, the Jew represents a corrupt society that "poisons the white race through the immigration of racially inferior elements, homosexuality, and moral disorder" (in Loow, 1998a, p. 86). As *Storm,* the magazine of the Swedish White Aryan Resistance, put it,

> In our resistance struggle for . . . the survival of the white race . . . we must wield the battle axe against our common enemy—the Zionist Occupation Government (ZOG) and the liberal race traitors, the keen servants of the hook noses who are demolishing our country piece by piece. (cited in Bjorgo, 1997, p. 219)[4]

Anti-Semitism, however, also has inhibited alliances across the various national groups in Scandinavia. Danish and Norwegian Aryans recall the resistance against the Nazis, and they often cast themselves as heirs to the resistance struggle against foreign invasion. Some Swedish groups, on the other hand, openly embrace Nazism and Nazi symbols. To maintain harmony among these different national factions of the Nordic Aryan movement, the Danish groups have begun to use Confederate flags and other symbols of the racist U.S. South, which all sides can agree signifies the Ku Klux Klan and the "struggle against Negroes, communists, homosexuals and Jews" (in Bjorgo, 1997, p. 99).

Another unifying set of symbols includes constant references to the Vikings. Vikings are admired because they lived in a closed community, were fierce warriors, and were feared and hated by those they conquered (Fangen, 2003, p. 36). Vikings also represent an untrammeled masculinity, an "armed brotherhood" of heroes and martyrs (Bjorgo, 1997, p. 136).

Masculinity figures heavily in white supremacist rhetoric and recruitment. Young recruits are routinely savagely beaten in a "baptism of fire." Among Danes, status is achieved "by daring to do something others don't. You are a hell of a guy if you go to 'work' at night and come home the next day with 85,000 crowns [about US$10,000]" (cited in Bjorgo, 1997, p. 104). One Norwegian racist recounted in court how his friends had dared him to blow up a store owned by a Pakistani in Brumunddal. He said he felt a lot of pressure, that they were making fun of him, and he wanted to prove to them that he was a man after all. After he blew up the shop, he said, the others slapped his back and cheered him. Finally, he felt accepted (Fangen, 1999, p. 371). A former Swedish skinhead recounted his experience of masculine transformation as he joined up:

> When I was 14, I had been bullied a lot by classmates and others. By coincidence, I got to know an older guy who was a skinhead. He was really cool, so I decided to become a skinhead myself, cutting off my hair, and donning a black Bomber jacket and Doc Martens boots. The next morning, I turned up at school in my new outfit. In the gate, I met one of my worst tormentors. When he saw me, he was stunned, pressing his back against the wall, with fear shining out of his eyes. I was stunned as well— by the powerful effect my new image had on him and others. Being that intimidating—boy, that was a great feeling! (cited in Bjorgo, 1997, p. 234)

Like their American counterparts, Scandinavian white supremacists also exhibit the other side of what Connell calls "protest

Illustration 24.4   *Vigrid* Cartoon

masculinity"—a combination of stereotypical male norms with often rather untraditional attitudes that include respecting women. All these Nordic groups experience significant support from young women because the males campaign on issues that are of significance to them; that is, they campaign against prostitution, abortion, and pornography because these are seen as degrading to women (see Durham, 1997). On the other hand, many of these same women soon become disaffected when they feel mistreated by their brethren, "unjustly subordinated" by them, or just seen as "mattresses" (in Fangen, 1999, p. 365; see also Durham, 1997).

In another illustration, the hypocrisy of the Norwegian state and culture is ridiculed. One man confronts another who is shouting in favor of censorship. "Are you against freedom of speech?" he asks. Then he gets angry and accuses the first man of being anti-democratic. "You should be ashamed of your undemocratic behavior!" he says. However, when the first man informs him that he's protesting the Nazis, the second man abandons his principles and joins right in.

Often, sexualized images of women are used to recruit men. In one comic strip for *Vigrid*'s newspaper, a topless woman with exaggerated breasts is hawking the newspaper on the streets. "Norway for Norwegians!" she shouts. She's arrested by the police for "selling material based on race discrimination"; meanwhile, caricatures of blacks and Pakistanis burn the city and loot a liquor store.

Illustration 24.5 *Vigrid* Cartoon

One significant difference between the American and the Scandinavian Aryan movements concerns their view of the environment. Whereas American Aryans support right-wing and conservative Republican efforts to discard environmental protection in the name of job creation in extractive industries, and are more than likely meat-eating survivalists, Nordic white supremacists are strong supporters of a sort of nostalgic and conservative environmentalism. Many are vegetarians, some vegan. Each group might maintain that its policies flow directly from its political stance. The Nordic groups claims that the modern state is "impure," "perverted," and full of "decay and decadence" and that their environmentalism is a means to cleanse it. As Matti Sundquist, singer in the Swedish skinhead group Svastika, puts it (in Loow, 1998b, p. 134),

> Well, it's the most important thing, almost, because we must have a functioning environment in order to have a functioning world . . . and it's almost too late to save the earth, there just be some radical changes if we are to stand a chance.[5]

THE RESTORATION OF ISLAMIC MASCULINITY AMONG AL QAEDA

Although too little is yet known to develop as full a portrait of the terrorists of Al Qaeda, certain common features warrant brief comment. For one thing, the class origins of the Al Qaeda terrorists appear to be similar to those of these other groups. Virtually all the young men who participated in the hijackings on 9/11 were under 25 and well educated. Some were lower middle class, downwardly mobile; others were sons of middle-class fathers whose upward mobility was blocked.

Other terrorist groups in the Middle East appear to have appealed to similar young men, although they were also organized by theology professors—whose professions also were threatened by continued secularization and westernization. For example, Jamiat-I-Islami, formed in 1972, was begun by Burhannudin Rabbani, a lecturer in theology at Kabul University. (Another leader, Ahmed Shah Masoud, was an engineering student at Kabul University.) Hisb-e-Islami, which split off in 1979 from Jamiat, was organized by Gulbuddin Hekmatyar, also an

engineering student at Kabul University. This group appealed particularly to relatively well-educated radical students, most of whom were studying engineering. Ittihad-I-Islami was formed by Abdul Rasoul Sayyaf, former theology lecturer at Kabul University (see Marsden, 2002, pp. 29-31; see also Waldman, 2002). One study of 129 Lebanese members of Hezbollah found them to be better educated and far less impoverished than the Lebanese population of comparable age (see Barro, 2002). Another study of 149 suicide bombers offers a fascinating portrait. More than two thirds (67.1%) were between 17 and 23 years of age; almost all the rest were between 24 and 30. More than one third (37.6%) had a high school education, and another 35.6% had at least some college. Nearly nine of ten were single ("Who They Are," 2002, p. 25).

Of course, it is well-known that several of the leaders of Al Qaeda are quite wealthy. Ayman al-Zawahiri, the 50-year-old doctor who was the closest adviser to Osama bin Laden in 2001, was from a fashionable suburb of Cairo; his father was dean of the pharmacy school at the university there. Osama bin Laden himself was a multimillionaire. By contrast, many of the September 11 hijackers were engineering students, for whom job opportunities had been dwindling dramatically. (From the minimal information I have found, about one fourth of the hijackers had studied engineering.) Kamel Daoudi studied computer science at a university in Paris, and Zacarias Moussaoui, the first man to be formally charged with a crime in the United States for the events of September 11, took a degree at London's South Bank University. Marwan al-Shehhi, a chubby, bespectacled 23-year-old from the United Arab Emirates, was an engineering student, and Ziad Jarrah, a 26-year-old Lebanese, had studied aircraft design.

The politics of many of these Islamic radical organizations appear to be similar. All oppose globalization and the spread of Western values; all oppose what they perceive as corrupt regimes in several Arab states (notably Saudi Arabia and Egypt), which they see as merely puppets of U.S. domination. Central to their political ideology is the recovery of manhood from the devastatingly emasculating politics of globalization. Over and over, Nasra Hassan writes, she heard the refrain "The Israelis humiliate us. They occupy our land, and deny our history"

(2001, p. 38). The Taliban saw the Soviet invasion and Westernization as humiliations. Osama bin Laden's October 7, 2001, videotape (shown on CNN News on October 8, 2001, and elsewhere) describes the "humiliation and disgrace" that Islam has suffered for "more than eighty years." Even more telling is his comment to the Arab television network Al Jazeera in December 1998, in which the masculinity of the American is set against that of the Muslim:

> Our brothers who fought in Somalia saw wonders about the weakness, feebleness and cowardliness of the U.S. soldier. We believe that we are men, Muslim men who must have the honor of defending [Mecca]—We do not want American women soldiers defending [it]. The rulers in that region have been deprived of their manhood and they think that the people are women. By God, Muslim women refuse to be defended by these American and Jewish prostitutes. (cited in Judt, 2001)

This fusion of antiglobalization politics, convoluted Islamic theology, and virulent misogyny has been the subject of much speculation. Viewing these through a gender lens, though, enables us to understand the connections better. The collapse of certain public patriarchal entitlements led to a virulent and violent effort to replace them with others, for example in the reassertion of domestic patriarchal power. "This is the class that is most hostile to women," said the scholar Fouad Ajami (Crossette, 2001, p. 1). But why? Journalist Barbara Ehrenreich explains that whereas "males have lost their traditional status as farmers and breadwinners, women have been entering the market economy and gaining the marginal independence conferred even by a paltry wage." As a result, "the man who can no longer make a living, who has to depend on his wife's earnings, can watch Hollywood sexpots on pirated videos and begin to think the world has been turned upside down" (Ehrenreich, 2001, p. 37).

When these groups have gained some political power, as has the Taliban, they have moved quickly to enact deliberately gendered policies, designed both to remasculinize men and to refeminize women. "The rigidity of the Taliban gender policies could be seen as a desperate attempt to keep out that other world, and to protect Afghan women from influences that could weaken the society from within" (Marsden, 2002, p. 99). Thus, not only were policies of the

Afghani republic that made female education compulsory immediately abandoned, but women also were prohibited from appearing in public unescorted by men, from revealing any part of their body, or from going to school or holding a job. Men were required to grow their beards, in accordance with religious images of Mohammed—but also because wearing beards has always been associated with men's response to women's increased equality in the public sphere. Beards especially symbolically reaffirm biological natural differences between women and men, even as they are collapsing in the public sphere. Such policies removed women as competitors and also shored up masculinity because they enabled men to triumph over the humiliations of globalization, as well as to triumph over their own savage, predatory, and violently sexual urges that would be unleashed in the presence of uncovered women.

Perhaps this can be best seen paradigmatically in the story of Mohammed Atta, apparently the mastermind of the entire September 11 operation and the pilot of the first plane to crash into the World Trade Center tower. The youngest child of an ambitious lawyer father and pampering mother, Atta grew up a shy and polite boy. "He was so gentle," his father said. "I used to tell him 'Toughen up, boy!'" (in *New York Times Magazine,* October 7). Atta spent his youth in a relatively shoddy Cairo neighborhood. Both his sisters are professionals—one is a professor, the other a doctor.

Atta decided to become an engineer, but his "degree meant little in a country where thousands of college graduates were unable to find good jobs."[6] His father had told him he "needed to hear the word 'doctor' in front of his name. We told him your sisters are doctors and their husbands are doctors and you are the man of the family." After he failed to find employment in Egypt, he went to Hamburg, Germany, to study to become an architect. He was "meticulous, disciplined and highly intelligent," yet an "ordinary student, a quiet friendly guy who was totally focused on his studies," according to another student in Hamburg.

But his ambitions were constantly thwarted. His only hope for a good job in Egypt was to be hired by an international firm. He applied and was constantly rejected. He found work as a draftsman—highly humiliating for someone with engineering and architectural credentials and an imperious and demanding father—for a German firm involved with razing lower-income Cairo neighborhoods to provide more scenic vistas for luxury tourist hotels.

Defeated, humiliated, emasculated, a disappointment to his father and a failed rival to his sisters, Atta drifted into an increasingly militant Islamic theology. By the time he assumed control of American Airlines Flight 11, he evinced a gendered hysteria about women. In the message he left in his abandoned rental car, he made clear what really mattered to him in the end. "I don't want pregnant women or a person who is not clean to come and say good-bye to me," he wrote. "I don't want women to go to my funeral or later to my grave" (CNN, October 2, 2001).

Masculine Entitlement and the Future of Terrorism

Of course, such fantasies are the fevered imagination of hysteria; Atta's body was without doubt instantly incinerated, and no funeral would be likely. But the terrors of emasculation experienced by the lower middle classes all over the world will no doubt continue to resound for these young men whose world seems to have been turned upside down, their entitlements snatched from them, their rightful position in their world suddenly up for grabs. And they may continue to articulate with a seething resentment against women, "outsiders," or any other "others" perceived as stealing their rightful place at the table.

The common origins and common complaints of the terrorists of 9/11 and their American "comrades" were not lost on American white supremacists. In their response to the events of 9/11, American Aryans said they admired the terrorists' courage, and they took the opportunity to chastise their own compatriots. Bill Roper of the National Alliance publicly wished his members had as much "testicular fortitude" ("Reaping the Whirlwind," 2001). "It's a disgrace that in a population of at least 150 million White/Aryan Americans, we provide so few that are willing to do the same," bemoaned Rocky Suhayda, Nazi Party chairman from Eastpointe, Michigan. "A bunch of towel head/sand niggers put our great White Movement to shame" (in Ridgeway, 2001, p. 14). It is from that gendered shame that mass murderers are made.

NOTES

1. Let me make clear that I explore here only the terrorism of social movements, such as Al Qaeda, and not the systematic terrorism of states, where terror is a matter of political strategy or military opportunity. My analysis, however, may well apply to social movements in the former Yugoslavia, as well as to other cases. An earlier version of this chapter was published in *International Sociology, 18*(3), September 2003. It is part of a larger research project on "angry white men." I have benefited from comments from my coeditors as well as many colleagues and friends, notably Amy Aronson, Abby Ferber, Michael Kaufman, and Lillian Rubin.

2. This section is based on collaborative work with Abby Ferber and appears in Kimmel and Ferber (2000). I recognize that the illustrations may be offensive to some. I offer them as emblematic of the ways in which discourses of masculinity offen saturate political hate speech.

3. Of course, there is a well-developed literature on the "gendered" elements of Nazism that underlies my work here. See especially Theweleit (1987-1989).

4. Interestingly, Loow (1994, p. 21) found that the localities with the highest numbers of attacks on asylum seekers in the early 1990s had the highest concentrations of national socialist or racist organizations in the 1920s through the 1940s.

5. In that sense, these groups are similar to British groups such as Blood and Soil, and the Patriotic Vegetarian and Vegan Society.

6. All unattributed quotations come from a fascinating portrait of Atta (Yardley, 2001).

REFERENCES

Barber, B. (1995). *Jihad vs. McWorld: How globalization and tribalism are reshaping the world.* New York: Ballantine.

Barro, R. (2002, June 10). The myth that poverty breeds terrorism. *Business Week,* p. 26.

Bjorgo, T. (1997). *Racist and right-wing violence in Scandinavia: Patterns, perpetrators, and responses.* Leiden, The Netherlands: University of Leiden.

Bjorgo, T. (1998). Entry, bridge-burning, and exit options: What happens to young people who join racist groups—and want to leave? In J. Kaplan & T. Bjorgo (Eds.), *Nation and race: The developing Euro-American racist subculture* (pp. 231-258). Boston: Northeastern University Press.

Blazak, R. (2001). White boys to terrorist men: Target recruitment of Nazi skinheads. *American Behavioral Scientist, 44*(6), 982-1000.

Blee, K. (2002). *Inside organized racism: Women in the hate movement.* Berkeley: University of California Press.

Connell, R. W. (1995). *Masculinities.* Berkeley: University of California Press.

Connell, R. W. (1998). Masculinities and globalization. *Men and Masculinities, 1*(1), 3-23.

Coplon, J. (1989, May/June). The roots of skinhead violence: Dim economic prospects for young men. *Utne Reader,* pp. 89-90.

Crossette, B. (2001, October 4). Living in a world without women. *New York Times.* Retrieved January 30, 2004, from www.changemakers.net/library/nytimes110401.cfm

Dobratz, B., & Shanks-Meile, S. (2001). *The white separatist movement in the United States: White power! White pride!* Baltimore: Johns Hopkins University Press.

Durham, M. (1997). Women and the extreme right: A comment. *Terrorism and Political Violence, 9,* 165-168.

Ehrenreich, B. (2001, November 4). Veiled threat. *Los Angeles Times,* p. 37.

Enloe, C. (1990). *Bananas, beaches and bases: Making feminist sense of international politics.* Berkeley: University of California Press.

Fangen, K. (1998). Living out our ethnic instincts: Ideological beliefs among rightist activists in Norway. In J. Kaplan & T. Bjorgo (Eds.), *Nation and race: The developing Euro-American racist subculture* (pp. 202-230). Boston: Northeastern University Press.

Fangen, K. (1999). On the margins of life: Life stories of radical nationalists. *Acta Sociologica, 42,* 357-373.

Fangen, K. (2003). Death mask of masculinity. In S. Ervo (Ed.), *Images of masculinities: Moulding masculinities.* London: Ashgate.

Ferber, A. L. (1998). *White man falling: Race, gender and white supremacy.* Lanham, MD: Rowman and Littlefield.

Hassan, N. (2001, November 19). An arsenal of believers. *The New Yorker,* pp. 31-40.

Hearn, J. (1992). *Men in the public eye.* London: Routledge.

Hearn, J. (1998). *The violences of men.* London: Sage.

Jipson, A., & Becker, P. (Eds.). (2000). White supremacy and hate crimes [Special issue]. *Sociological Focus, 33*(2).

Judt, T. (2001, November 15). America and the war. *New York Review of Books, 48*(18). Retrieved January 28, 2004, from www.nybooks.com/articles/14760

Juergensmeyer, M. (1995). *The new Cold War? Religious nationalism confronts the secular state.* Berkeley: University of California Press.

Juergensmeyer, M. (2000). *Terror in the mind of God: The global rise of religious violence.* Berkeley: University of California Press.

Kimmel, M. (1996a). *Manhood in America: A cultural history.* New York: Free Press.

Kimmel, M. (Ed.). (1996b). *The politics of manhood.* Philadelphia: Temple University Press.

Kimmel, M. (2002). [Review of the book *Inside organized racism*]. *Contexts, 1*(3), 60-61.

Kimmel, M., & Ferber, A. (2000). "White men are this nation": Right wing militias and the restoration of rural American masculinity. *Rural Sociology, 65*(4), 582-604.

Kramer, J. (2002, May 6). The patriot. *The New Yorker,* pp. 23-30.

Kristof, N. (2002a, June 7). All-American Osamas. *New York Times,* p. A27.

Kristof, N. (2002b, May 8). What does and doesn't fuel terrorism. *International Herald Tribune,* p. 13.

Loow, H. (1994, July). *"Wir sind wieder da"—From National Socialism to militant race ideology: The Swedish racist underground in a historical context.* Paper presented to the XIII World Congress of Sociology, Bielefeld.

Loow, H. (1998a). Racist youth culture in Sweden: Ideology, mythology, and lifestyle. In C. Westin (Ed.), *Racism, ideology and political organisation* (pp. 77-98). Stockholm: CEIFO Publications, University of Stockholm.

Loow, H. (1998b). White power rock and roll: A growing industry. In J. Kaplan & T. Bjorgo (Eds.), *Nation and race: The developing Euro-American racist subculture* (pp. 126-147). Boston: Northeastern University Press.

Maps of white supremacist organizations and patriot militias. (2002, Spring). *Intelligence Report.* Available at www.intelligenceproject.org

Marrs, T. (1993). *Big sister is watching you: Hillary Clinton and the White House feminists who now control America—and tell the President what to do.* Austin, TX: Living Truth Publishers.

Marsden, P. (2002). *The Taliban: War and religion in Afghanistan.* London: Zed.

Messner, M. (1998). *Politics of masculinities: Men and movements.* Newbury Park, CA: Pine Forge Press.

Moore, B. (1966). *The social origins of dictatorship and democracy: Lord and peasant in the making of the modern world.* Boston: Beacon.

Pierce, W. (1978). *The Turner diaries.* Hillsboro, VA: National Vanguard Books.

Reaping the Whirlwind. (2001, Winter). *Intelligence Report, 104.* Available at www.splcenter.org/intel/intelreport/article.jsp?aid=158

Ridgeway, J. (2001, November 6). Osama's new recruits. *Village Voice,* p. 14.

Rubin, L. (1994). *Families on the fault line.* New York: HarperCollins.

Sinha, M. (1995). *Colonial masculinity: The manly Englishman and the effeminate Bengali in the late nineteenth century.* Manchester, UK: Manchester University Press.

Theweleit, K. (1987-1989). *Male fantasies* (Vols. 1 and 2) (S. Conway, E. Carter, & C. Turner, Trans.). Minneapolis: University of Minnesota Press.

Waldman, A. (2002, April 24). How in a little English town jihad found young converts. *New York Times*, pp. 1, 24.

Who they are. (2002, April 15). *Newsweek,* pp. 25-27.

Willis, P. (1981). *Learning to labor*. New York: Columbia University Press.

Yardley, J. (2001, October 10). A portrait of the terrorist: From shy child to single-minded killer. *New York Times*, p. 22.

25

WAR, MILITARISM, AND MASCULINITIES

PAUL HIGATE

JOHN HOPTON

The nexus linking war, militarism, and masculinities has remained an enduring and consistent feature of societies and their cultures across time. Despite these close linkages, it is surprising that scholars have tended to overlook the masculinist dimensions of the military; in so doing, they have unwittingly preserved the naturalized dimension of military masculinity. This chapter's focus on the British military, an institution characterized by its unique role in the acquisition and maintenance of a global empire, aims to explore the connections between the armed forces and their masculinist culture.

According to one source, British defense spending is currently in the region of £36.9 billion ($60 billion), with a further £3 billion being set aside for the 2003 war in Iraq (£50 per head for U.K. citizens) and an extra £330 million being spent on domestic counterterrorism measures. This would mean that military spending currently accounts for 6% of the total U.K. budget (White & Norton-Taylor, 2002). An alternative source suggests that "British defense spending

has declined more than 30 percent to a current level of 2.7 percent of Gross Domestic Product" (National Center for Policy Analysis, 2002). Worldwide,

> military expenditure, which has been increasing since 1998, accelerated sharply in 2002, by 6% in real terms to $794 billion in current prices. It accounted for 2.5% of world GDP. . . . The current level of world military expenditure is 14% higher in real terms than it was at the post-cold war low of 1998, but is still 16% below its 1988 level, when world military expenditure was close to its cold war peak.
>
> The increase in 2002 is dominated by a 10% real terms increase by the USA, accounting for almost three-quarters of the global increase, in response to the events of 11 September 2001. . . . The USA now accounts for 43% of world military expenditure, when currencies are converted at market exchange rates, as is the SIPRI practice in this Yearbook. The top five spenders—the USA, Japan, the UK, France and China—account for 62% of total world military expenditure. (Stockholm International Peace Research Institute, n.d.)

Author's note: This chapter is a synthesis of two previously published chapters (Higate, 2003a; Hopton, 2003) from *Military Masculinities: Identity and the State* (Higate, 2003b). We are grateful to Praeger for allowing to reproduce these texts in this form.

These figures give some sense of the centrality of the armed forces to government spending priorities and provide a context for the subsequent discussion.

The British military's development might be considered somewhat unique: nevertheless, the examples drawn on throughout the chapter have a strong resonance with the universal feature of armed forces more widely. The chapter begins with a historical overview of the structural and ideological links between masculine and military cultures. This is followed by discussion suggesting that the 1990s represented a change in the relationship between women and the military, in terms of both the military role in the postmodern world and the role of the women within the military. Finally, we attempt to evaluate how deep this apparent "feminization" of the military runs in reality and to speculate how the military may change again in the coming decades.

Throughout history, there are examples of women assuming male military dress to join armed forces or to fight in specific battles or campaigns. For example, there is the historical example of the Ancient Briton Boudicca/Boadicea fighting the Romans, and there are many stories of women dressing as men in the 18th and 19th centuries in order to enlist on fighting ships or in armies (Wheelwright, 1989), as well as examples of women taking up arms in various locations in the Americas and Africa between the 16th and 19th centuries and even during World War II. Similarly, in the late 20th century, women sometimes played key roles within "liberation"/terrorist movements, and some countries at various times attempted integration of women into their armed services, including the assumption of some combat roles (Klein, 2003; Kovitz, 2003; R. Morgan, 1989).

Nevertheless, throughout modernity, one of the enduring characteristics of military organization has been a gendered division of labor (Connell, 2000; Enloe, 2000; Kovitz, 2003). Although there have been some indications in recent years that this division of labor is becoming more fluid, barriers remain in place that exclude women from certain forms of military service. For example, in Britain women are still excluded from service on submarines and in elite airborne and commando units. Thus, at the time of writing, it is still possible to see explicit links between militarism and ideologies of masculinity, although the effects of the opening up of more opportunities to women in the military require further consideration.

MILITARISM AND THE INSTITUTIONALIZATION OF MASCULINITY

Writers who have developed critiques of masculinity (e.g., Connell, 1987; Harris, 1995; Hearn, 1996; MacInnes, 1998; Miedzian, 1992) suggest that there is a form of masculine identity (hegemonic masculinity) to which boys and men are generally encouraged to aspire. This form of masculinity is characterized by the interrelationship of stoicism, phallocentricity, and the domination of weaker individuals (Brittan, 1989; Rogers, 1988; Stanley & Wise, 1987; Stoltenberg, 1990), competitiveness, and heroic achievement (Brittan, 1989; Harris, 1995; Miedzian, 1992). Thus, men who exemplify this model of masculinity tend to be accorded a higher social status than those who do not (Connell, 1987). By publicly demonstrating that he has at least the potential to conform to this model of masculinity, a boy or man may have his masculinity affirmed. Military organizations, military successes, military pageantry, and rituals such as the "passing out" parades for successful recruits to the armed forces represent the public endorsement of such values and their institutionalization in national culture (Dawson, 1994). Certainly, there are other manifestations of this process of celebrating masculinity, but uniquely the exploits of the military are always openly and aggressively celebrated in the public sphere (Hockey, 2003; McGregor, 2003). Indeed, there are echoes of militarism in everyday language. For example, in the United Kingdom the term "Dunkirk spirit" (a reference to Britain fighting on after the humiliating defeat at Dunkirk early in World War II) is used as a shorthand for expressing admiration for someone's unwillingness to accept defeat; and someone who is finally defeated after a lengthy struggle may still be said to have "met their Waterloo" (a reference to Wellington's final defeat of Napoleon Bonaparte nearly 200 years ago). Furthermore, boys encounter many militarist influences during their childhood and adolescence (Dawson, 1994).

Although there are exceptions to the rule (such as the Woodcraft folk, an explicitly pacifist British organization that has always accepted both boys and girls), uniformed youth organizations that were originally only for boys tend to explicitly reflect military culture. For example, the organization, uniforms, and culture of the Boy Scout movement reflect the military background of its founder, Robert Baden-Powell. Similarly, from its very beginning, military-style drilling was a core activity of the Boys' Brigade to the extent that its founder, William Smith, originally introduced wooden dummy rifles into these activities. Although the use of wooden rifles was abandoned relatively early on in the Boys' Brigade's history, drilling remained a core activity, and a military structure of brigade, battalions, and companies together with a quasi-military hierarchy of officers and noncommissioned officers has been retained to this day (McFarlan, 1983). More explicitly, the various army, air, and sea cadet forces in Britain (which were originally boys-only organizations), which offer young people opportunities to participate in many adventure activities and sports at low cost, have been supported by the Ministry of Defence (MoD). These and other similar organizations have played a key role in "exporting" a culture equating masculinity and militarism from the elite British privately funded schools such as Eton and Harrow to boys from the middle and working classes (Brod, 1987; Weeks, 1981). Although not all boys and men will ever have any connection with uniformed youth organizations such as the Boy Scouts or the Boys' Brigade, most adult males are aware of the cultural values promoted by such organizations and will have been exposed to such influences via their peers. Thus, a shared understanding of masculinity will be influenced by the values promoted by such organizations.

This valorization of military values is reflected in other ways as well. One of the most commonly cited examples is the kinds of toys that boys traditionally have been encouraged to play with by their peers and/or their parents. Typically, these may include toy tanks, toy guns, toy warplanes, and toy soldiers (Dawson, 1994). Indeed, even many of the fantasy figure–type toys that have become popular over the last 20 years are armed with what clearly are meant to be lethal weapons (Goldstein, 2001, p. 238). Links between militarism and masculinity also are evident in printed matter and other media aimed at the youth market (Gibson, 1994, p. 111). For example, during the 1960s, British boys' comics such as *The Valiant* and *The Victor*, whose very titles reflected military culture, celebrated the heroic exploits of both fictional and nonfictional soldiers. In the 1980s, television series such as *The A-Team*, *Airwolf*, and *Magnum, PI* (some of which were aimed at adults as much as children) attributed the astuteness, strength, self-reliance, and sexual attractiveness of the central male characters to their military backgrounds, while during the 1990s many video and computer games featured violence or had explicitly militarist themes (Goldstein, 2001, pp. 294-296). Such cultural influences are a powerful influence on how children and young people interpret the world around them and their place within it, and these influences may lead to them equating manliness with military ideals.

THE RECIPROCAL RELATIONSHIP BETWEEN MILITARISM AND MASCULINITY

Historically, there has been a reciprocal relationship between militarism and masculinity. On one hand, politicians have utilized ideologies of idealized masculinity that valorize the notion of strong active males collectively risking their personal safety for the greater good of the wider community (see Barnett, 1982; Platt, 1992; Segal, 1990) to gain support for the use of violence by the state (such as wars in the international arena and aggressive policing in the domestic situation). On the other hand, militarism feeds into ideologies of masculinity through the eroticization of stoicism, risk-taking, and even lethal violence (Goldstein, 2001). This can be detected in populist fictional and nonfictional books about war and weapons as well as in newspaper coverage of military actions (Newsinger, 1997; Shepherd, 1989).

The reciprocal relationship between militarism and masculinity can be illustrated using World War I as an example. In the earlier part of the 1914-1918 war, recruitment of volunteer soldiers owed much to Victorian ideologies that defined masculinity in terms of strength, courage, determination, and patriotism. In turn, this image of masculinity was reinforced by wartime propaganda that glamorized military culture and military success and that tacitly encouraged brutality toward war resisters and those males (such as Jewish refugees from Eastern Europe) who were ineligible for military service (Showalter, 1987; Taylor & Young, 1987).

In the British context, a more recent example of this process is the media obsession with the Special Air Service (SAS), an obsession that began with the Iranian Embassy Siege of 1980 (e.g., Geraghty, 1980; Warner, 1983, pp. 271-273). Geraghty, himself a journalist, neatly encapsulated the media image of the SAS trooper as the epitome of socially constructed masculinity.

The deployment of the SAS in situations that might (arguably) have been more appropriately handled by the civil police, and the subsequent media coverage of such events, is particularly interesting in the context of the relationship between masculinity and militarism. Whether the victims of such intervention are Iranian or Irish "terrorists" or protesting prisoners (J. Jenkins, 1989; Scraton, Sim, & Skidmore, 1991; Warner, 1983, pp. 271-273), the message is the same: Although the dissidents are displaying the masculinist virtues of aggression, domination, and endurance, glory and respect (see Bibbings, 2003, and Stanko, 1990) can belong only to the fighting men whose aggression is controlled and regulated by the State and used to uphold the authority of the State. Segal has shown how, in addition to celebrating "heroic" exploits of aggression and competitiveness, the ideology that links maleness with rugged individualism may also play a role in promoting intensely conservative politics and values (Segal, 1990, p. 20).

However, the link between militarism and masculinity reaches beyond the eroticization of masculinism through the glamorization of military culture and military actions; it can be detected in the law-and-order policies of British governments during the 1980s and 1990s. The most obvious manifestation of this is the increase in the use of paramilitary tactics by the police (see Jefferson, 1990), and it also can be seen in penal policy. The use of police cavalry charges and similar paramilitary approaches to "riot control" throughout the 1980s and 1990s (e.g., Coulter, Miller, & Walker, 1984; Hillyard & Percy-Smith, 1988; "Tony," 1990) have been extensively documented. Taken in isolation, such policies do not seem to have a direct bearing on the politics of sexuality. However, if the main purpose of such actions is taken to be the suppression of dissent (Hillyard & Percy-Smith, 1988), they may be interpreted as being a public spectacle wherein the forces of law and order appropriate the symbols and ritualized behavior of eroticized masculinity (military language, helmets, combat dress, special weapons and tactics) (see Stoltenberg, 1990, pp. 117 and following, and Macnair, 1989) to enforce the authority of a government that systematically reinforced ideologies of the patriarchal family (Lister, 1990; Millar & Glendinning, 1989) and attacked alternative sexualities (Shepherd & Wallis, 1989). The sexual-political undertones here are that these masculinist symbols and ritualized behaviors are associated in "commonsense" assumptions with the exercising of legitimate power and authority.

Within the penal system, militarism from time to time has been reflected in ideas about the rehabilitation of young offenders. For example, young offenders' institutions have adopted regimes based on military drill and army-style physical training in the belief that this will prepare young male offenders for law-abiding manhood (Muncie, 1990). Here, the motive seems to be to deny the possibility that young men's "crimes" may represent political protest or reaction to social disadvantage, and instead to view their "antisocial" behavior as arising from destructive biological urges (e.g., Brittan, 1989, pp. 78-82) that military-style discipline will enable them to control. Such policies seem to be rooted in an ideology that regards militarism as the ultimate form of disciplined masculinity (Brittan, 1989, pp. 74-75) and ignores the contradiction that militarism is in fact a celebration of the most extreme forms of violence (Harrison, 2003).

If the reciprocal relationship between masculinity and militarism is being in some sense weakened, so too is the power of the state to manipulate public support for its right to use violence to pursue its policies at home and abroad, and to encourage young men to join the armed forces. Thus, the state has a vested interest in maintaining strong ideological links between militarism and masculinity.

1991: A TURNING POINT

The 1991 Gulf War seems to represent a turning point in the relationship between militarism and masculinity. On one hand, the traditional relationship between masculinity and militarism was clearly evident in the political rhetoric that was used to justify the war. On the other hand, a weakening of the link between the traditional preoccupations of hegemonic masculinity and militarism also is evident in the buildup to the war, the defeat of Iraq, and the aftermath of the war. First, notwithstanding the contradictory attitudes sometimes shown toward such women, female armed services personnel involved in the war were given a high profile. Second, as the war reached its conclusion, notions of a "new world order" and new forms of military intervention began to emerge, although these also were contradictory.

It has been argued that the 1991 war against Iraq was an avoidable event that was deliberately created by Western governments—principally those of the United States and the United Kingdom—that previously had ignored Iraq's poor record on human rights (Cale, 1991; Cockburn & Cohen, 1991; Farry, 1991; Melichar, 1991). In this context, the rhetoric of the "new world order" that accompanied the promotion of the war may be interpreted as an attempt by (mostly male) politicians in the West to capitalize on the political changes in Eastern Europe (and the resultant demise of the Warsaw Pact military alliance, which might otherwise have kept their ambitions in check) to justify the further pursuit of militaristic policies and to act out the masculinist fantasy of becoming "heroes-hunters-competitors-conquerors" (Brittan, 1989) on a global scale.

Nevertheless, the presence of 40,000 female personnel among the American military force in Saudi Arabia during the war (Douglas, 1991) appeared to represent a change in the relationship between women and the military. Historically, the militarization of women's lives has tended to involve the regulation and control of women serving the needs of male military personnel. This has been manifested in the roles traditionally ascribed to women in patriarchal societies: wives, cooks, laundresses, prostitutes, secretaries, and so on (Enloe, 1988). During the 1991 Gulf War, though, women were serving as soldiers, marines, air force personnel, and sailors in support units close to and within combat zones (Ellicott, 1991). Although, on a superficial level, this seems to signal a radical change in the relationship between militarism and social constructions of femininity, this new relationship was contradictory.

Press coverage of the Gulf War referring to female personnel tended to highlight those female soldiers who were also mothers of young children (e.g., Ellicott, 1991; this story was accompanied by a picture of Captain Jo Ann Conley in full combat dress with a photograph of her 2-year-old daughter fixed to her helmet). Such imagery implicitly challenges the view that the violence of war is inextricably linked to men's violence against women. However, when a female soldier was captured by the Iraqis, fears were expressed openly that she might be raped by her captors, or that female soldiers who were mothers might be killed, and that this might adversely affect the morale of male troops (Muir, 1991). Thus, although a clear message was given that war and other military interventions were no longer to be strictly gendered activities, there was also tacit recognition that the casual misogyny that pervades military culture may lead to male sexual violence against women becoming an integral part of war (see Enloe, 1988; McGowan & Hands, 1983; Mladjenovic, 1993; Smith, 1989; Theweleit, 1987).

Nevertheless, during the period between the 1991 Gulf War and the events of September 11, 2001, the pace of change to women's service in the British armed forces increased. For example, between 1992 and 1994, the (British) Women's Royal Army Corps, Women's Royal Naval Service, and Women's Royal Air Force became fully integrated with, respectively, the British Army, the Royal Navy, and the Royal Air Force; in 1995, the first woman qualified as an RAF combat-ready Tornado bomber pilot (Cooke, 1995). Although these developments appear to signal a material change in the nexus linking women with military service, questions remain over the extent to which the increasing presence of women in the armed forces will affect the nature of its masculinist culture.

THE CONTEMPORARY MILITARIZATION OF WOMEN

To summarize, militarism is the major means by which the values and beliefs associated with ideologies of hegemonic masculinity are eroticized and institutionalized. Although there are alternative contexts in which traditional masculine virtues are valorized and eroticized, they lack the potential to link masculinity with the political concerns of the state. This is not to say that women are innately pacifist. Indeed, both male and female pacifists have been known to renounce pacifism when faced with brutal political regimes or genocidal armies (Kuzmanic et al., 1994; Oldfield, 1989). Furthermore, throughout history, women have participated actively in military life in a variety of roles (Wheelwright, 1989).

The willingness of some women to join the armed forces and even assume combat roles may be used to refute an essentialist position in relation to feminist pacifism (see Segal, 1990). Nevertheless, militarism has tended to work against the interests of women, often in ways that directly benefit men. For example, both Wheelwright (1989) and Rogers (1988) have shown how military organizations that openly incorporate women have sometimes contrived to prevent them from enjoying equal benefits, privileges, and advantages with the men in those organizations. Furthermore, Brittain (1953) and Enloe (1988) have documented the role of the military throughout modern history with regard to the regulation and control of the sexuality, social roles, and labor of women in the interests of patriarchal states.

Since the early 1990s, there has been increased emphasis on developing policies that give female armed forces personnel equal rights with their male counterparts; for example, allowing women to take maternity leave (whereas previously mothers would not be allowed to continue their careers) and resurrecting debates about their potential to be fully combatant. Although this might simply reflect growing concern to genuinely promote equal opportunities and diversity and/or change the culture within the armed forces, there may be alternative explanations. For example, the emergence of a view of masculinity that refuses to equate militarism with manliness (Stoltenberg, 1990) has presented the masculinist-militarist power elites with a potential labor shortage that could be offset in part by allowing an expansion of the role of women in the armed forces (Dandeker, 2000).

Overall, however, women remain a thorny issue in debates about gender integration in the armed forces, with (military) men tending to remain invisible and unchallenged in their privileged positions. In relation to a review of the literature examining the Canadian military in respect to gender integration, for example, Donna Winslow and Justin Dunn highlight the domain of combat. Although women have been allowed to enter the combat arms since 1989, they still face many barriers that are rooted in the negative attitudes of their male peers who believe that combat should remain a male bastion (Winslow & Dunn, 2001, p. 50). Canada might be considered to have one of the more enlightened armed forces with regard to equal opportunities and diversity initiatives, and although recent integration trials have not gone as far as some would prefer, nevertheless it has been argued that a base has been established for further progress. Whatever the rationale behind these developments, though, the relationship between militarism and masculinity appears to be shifting. The question is whether the *essence* of militarism has been transformed by the sexual politics of the last 30 years, or whether an increased presence of women in the armed services has just modified its superficial appearance.

CHANGING THE GENDERED CULTURE?

Will the presence of more women, particularly at the heart of the male bastion of face-to-face combat, affect the nature of the combat masculine warrior ethic? Assumptions of this sort may rely on naturalist discourses of sex and gender, and they implicitly view femininity in a homogeneous way, a point that ignores the extent of self-selection. Said one female West Point graduate:

> Women who are in military training to be an officer are not the girl next door or your mother . . . they were among the top athletes in college. Military women are just like men who become airborne—he is not your average guy—he's in the top five percent. (Skaine, 1999, p. 202)

The influence of increased proportions of women in the military is yet to be assessed conclusively, though some have suggested that it may shape the behavior of male colleagues in positive ways suggested by experiences in the British police force (Martin, 1996, p. 523). Similar "civilizing" effects also have been documented within the context of particular missions, including Peace Support Operations (PSO) (see Olsson, Ukabiala, Blondle, Kampungu, & Wallensteen, 1999, pp. 1-24). In addition, accessibility to local civilian communities that have suffered at the hands of militarized men might be improved by the greater inclusion of civilian and military women. Here, masculinized gender ideologies can be challenged and less aggressive responses to volatile situations implemented.

However, there are numerous parallels between the pace of change effected by diversity and equal opportunity strategies in professions dominated by men, on one hand, and the extent of transformation of gendered culture in the military, on the other. Countless uniformed masculinist organizations, including the fire service, for example, have been slow to develop (Baigent, 2001). A further masculinist sphere of employment that has received rather less scholarly attention is that of the British construction industry. This gendered sphere is similarly masculinist, traditional, hierarchical, and resistant to change. In using this example, it is possible to highlight the more universal aspects of gendered culture that serve to maintain the status quo with respect to cultural shift around the acceptance of women at both the formal and informal levels. Clara Greed's work on the British construction industry has considerable generalizability and has particular resonance with the military. She states that

[C]ritical mass . . . is one of the most frequently used terms in the [construction] industry when discussing equal opportunities . . . [it] is highly optimistic and over-simplistic if used as a predictive social concept *without acknowledging the immense cultural and structural obstacles present.* (Greed, 2000, p. 183, emphasis added)

The approach currently taken by the British MoD is to stress the opening up of posts. Women may well be "accepted"—but will they be accepted as equal? How would we know if the negative aspects of military masculine culture—in particular, those that serve to marginalize women—had been neutralized? What does an organization of equal opportunities and diversity look like? As Pringle (1989) asks, might not the influx of women into certain military jobs result in the feminization and decline in status of particular specialties where women come to be concentrated? The fuller integration of women into the armed forces necessarily has to take place within a framework of formalized and wide-ranging equal opportunities. Issues that must be addressed if the military is to more fully integrate women could concern the following:

Questions concerning the granting of maternity leave and career progress,

Dual service marriages,

The availability of child care and single-parent households,

The posting of women away from families, and

Overall family support policies in times of increasing pressure on resources. (Winslow & Dunn, 2001, p. 50)

Although it is possible to point to degrees of incremental structural change with respect to women in the armed forces, cultural and structural obstacles to their integration remain. However, might this institutional resistance become diluted in the face of the alleged emergence of masculinities that have appropriated more feminized ways of being? Commentary concerning the ascendancy of the so-called "New Man" could be of significance here, as the associated ways of "doing masculinity" are argued to be gaining both legitimacy and popularity, and they may, over time, shape the more traditional masculinist culture of the military via the importation of recruit values. However, the term "New Man" is often taken for granted. One way in which to make sense of the phrase is suggested by Hondagneu-Sotelo and Messner (1994), who state:

[W]hen analysed within a structure of power, the gender displays of the New Man might best be seen as strategies to reconstruct hegemonic masculinity by projecting aggression, domination and misogyny onto subordinate groups of men. (p. 215)

In any case, debates about New Men may be less than relevant to the divergence of military from civilian culture, particularly when the extent of self-selection among young male enlistees is taken into account. A number of these individuals may import hypermasculine values, perhaps linked to their earlier experiences of growing up in deprived areas where frequent exposure to and the use of physical aggression could represent part-component of the motivation to enlist (Higate, 2002). The degree to which recruits "self-select" is unlikely to change as long as these masculine subcultures persist and the combat masculine warrior ethic is linked to the armed forces in the minds of the wider public and potential recruits.

The Future Military: Two Scenarios

Given recent and current trends, what might we expect gendered military culture to look like in 2020? A hypothetical all-volunteer British armed forces of the year 2020 could take the form of a culturally homogeneous single service organization. In theory at least, it could differ from today's armed forces by virtue of representative levels of gender, sexual orientation, and ethnic minority integration across all military occupations (however, see Mason and Dandeker, 2001, for discussion of the MoD's inconsistent thinking on women and ethnic minorities). Service people in this future organization may be held in high public esteem and enhance, rather than degrade, certain elements of the local civilian communities in which they work and live. To these ends, there would be no sign of "camp following" sex workers sustained by servicemen (Enloe, 2000; Moon, 1997) and no evidence of violence in drinking establishments within garrison towns—circumstances that may arise from a "spilling over" of the combat masculine warrior ethic. Indeed, future service personnel would be perceived as well-remunerated professional "technocratic warriors" carrying out risky and challenging work on behalf of the state.

In the second scenario, we note little difference to the British armed forces seen today. The three services would retain their discrete identities, together with the continued underrepresentation of women, gay personnel, and ethnic minorities. Although public opinion would remain high in terms of perceptions of the armed forces generally (Dandeker, 2000), service personnel would continue to be involved in occasional high-profile violent incidents in and around garrison towns, and they would be implicated in disproportionate incidences of domestic violence in military communities and sexual harassment in the military workplace; the ambivalent label of "squaddie" would remain.

Both of these hypothetical organizations would be smaller in size when compared with today's tri-service armed forces, and they would be configured to respond rapidly to global "hot spots," Peace Support Operations, and assisting the civil powers in antiterrorism, drug enforcement, and illegal immigration (Dandeker, 1999). One possibility might be that missions would come to be mainly "euro-national" in composition within the context of growing debates about the future role of the North Atlantic Treaty Organization (NATO). Considerable advances in technology might come to supplant individual troop differences in terms of physical and mental capability, and there would be a greater reliance on quickly mobilized reserve forces.

LOCATING THE CONTEMPORARY MILITARY

It has been argued that the military is a microcosm of society (Chamallas, 1998, p. 307). Framing the military in this way provides the key point of departure when thinking through how the organization might transform, as we cannot ignore future economic, political, and social change across the host society and beyond, into the global context. If the armed forces truly have become "postmodern," as some have suggested (Moskos, Williams, & Segal, 2000), then we might expect to see the celebration of diversity, as it is asserted to represent a key dimension of the postmodern condition. It has been suggested, however, that a "postmodern" military might mean no military at all, as uniformity remains the key philosophy on which military culture turns (Booth, Kestnbaum, & Segal, 2001).

Current and future political climates at the national level are likely to have significant impacts on the gendered characteristics of military cultures, with a continuum ranging from "traditional" (conservative) through to "detraditional" (liberal) signposting the extent to which diversity initiatives are prioritized (Dandeker, 1999, p. 64). The armed forces are likely to be buttressed by an increasing number of reservists and civilians, many of whom we might imagine would be more tolerant of homosexuals and women in the workplace, a situation that has evolved more fully in civilian life (Dandeker, 1999, p. 31). A further trend suggesting convergence between civilian and military cultures is signaled by the development of an occupational or "civilianized" attitude to working life in the armed forces. The apparent decline in institutional attitude, traditionally informed by a strong public service ethos to military service, has received considerable attention over the years (Moskos, 1988). Might there be a correlation between occupational/civilian attitudes to military service and positive perceptions of the drive to increase diversity in the military organization as institutional/military affiliations are noted to weaken? Other developments in the military include the decreasing tolerance of physical brutality directed toward military recruits by their training instructors. If physical brutality were to be considered an accepted and previously unquestioned component of (military) masculine ideology, then changes to basic army training through which recruits are more "empowered" (rendering them less open to physical and mental assault from instructors) represents a further important development (Dandeker, 1999, p. 36; Skaine, 1999, p. 138). Career structures in the armed forces also have changed dramatically over the last 20 years, with shorter engagements becoming the norm (Dandeker, 1999, p. 40). It seems likely that this trend will continue and that more "flexible" working conditions will further align the organization with developments in civilian labor markets and in so doing have the potential to give relatively greater opportunities to women who wish to take career breaks to raise families. An intensifying trend in contemporary militaries, frequently discussed within the context of the execution of "clinical" wars, is the appropriation of and fascination with technological developments. To what extent does this increasing reliance on technology serve to weaken the arguments of those who highlight the relative physical shortcomings of women?

TECHNOLOGY AND GENDER

Morris Janowitz suggested that changes in technology influence both organizational behavior and the characteristics of combat within the military (Winslow & Dunn, 2001). Given that overall, technological developments have tended to erode the significance of physical strength and aggression, we might expect women to be more accepted in the role of "closing with the enemy." However, it is the embodied elements of their combat effectiveness that constantly have been questioned, frequently within an ideological context (Cohn, 2000). It is claimed that the "blurring" of the "cyborg" soldier's gender (Hables-Gray, 1997, p. 247) is likely to intensify as technology develops. As Hables-Gray states (1997), "It seems the female soldier's identity is beginning to collapse into

the archetype soldier persona creating a basically male vaguely female mechanical image" (p. 175), though we would argue that this view exaggerates developments thus far. A vision of the future in these somewhat idealized "postmodern" terms could take technological transformations to their end point, where combatant women would come to be considered as wholly interchangeable with male soldiers. More significantly, technological developments themselves are likely to continue to be masculinized, and women's role within them considered somewhat peripheral. Computer systems are one important example of vital future (and current) military technology:

> They are "masculine," in the full ideological sense of that word which includes, integrally, soldiering, and violence. There is nothing far-fetched in the suggestion that much AI [artificial intelligence] research reflects a social relationship: "intelligent" behavior means the instrumental power Western "man" has developed to an unprecedented extent under capitalism and which he has always wielded over woman. (Hables-Gray, 1997, p. 246)

The gendering of science and war as masculine looks unlikely to change in the near or distant future. Indeed, could an example of the alleged pinnacle of technological advance, the "missile defense system" proposed by George W. Bush, ever have been called the "daughter of Star Wars"? Here, we are dealing with discourses that tend to close off the technological arena from women, both structurally and culturally.

SEXUAL ORIENTATION AND MILITARY MASCULINE CULTURE— CURRENT AND FUTURE TRENDS

Mark Simpson and Steven Zeeland ironically illuminate the homoerotic and homosexual rather than the straightforwardly heterosexual elements of life in the armed forces in the case of both the British and United States' militaries (Simpson & Zeeland, 2001). Further, anecdotal evidence suggests that a "significant proportion" of the more senior of the female officers in the British army may be homosexual, although this label tells us little of their explicit views of and attitudes toward the organization and how they might evolve with respect to its gendered culture. David

Morgan's autobiographical writing about the British National Service includes reflection on an effeminate colleague who was presumed by some to be homosexual. He was described as a popular man whose camp and comical performances were celebrated rather than condemned (D. Morgan, 1987). The notion that there exists a uniform culture of (hetero)sexuality in the British military and those of other countries remains an area of some contestation. However, the inscription of heterosexuality into all aspects of culture ranging from language through to leisure activities remains deeply bound up with the combat masculine warrior ethic, ensuring that homosexuality is seen as deviant and likely to threaten unit cohesion.

Yet, what of the future scenario outlined above in which sexuality, like gender, is no longer an issue within the military environment? Might not the already present "inconsistencies" flagged above give way to greater toleration in the future as civilian society becomes more disposed to subvert the binaries of homo- and heterosexuality that frame the public face of the military? The MoD's statement on diversity represents the formal face of the organization and explicitly links "sexual orientation" with "tolerance." Although future catalysts for change may be rooted in both formal policy and human rights legislation, it is difficult to envisage the ways in which advances toward equality at the level of culture can be satisfactorily achieved. Given the oppressive and sometimes brutal approach taken toward the identification and removal of homosexuals from the armed forces in the very recent past, future enlightened developments will be slow in coming (Hall, 1995; Tatchell, 1995).

NATIONALITY AND MILITARY MASCULINE CULTURE

Military masculinities are embedded into discourses of nationalism (Bickford, 2003; Caplan, 2003; Dawson, 1994; Shaw, 1991). Constructions of "Englishness" or "Britishness," invoking past victories, and resonating with the imperial and colonial trajectories of the United Kingdom have remained tenacious for both the military and its host society. "Our boys" belong to us and not "the (foreign) other," and serviceperson identity is constructed around this

sharp dichotomy. The experience of being deployed overseas frequently amplifies this distinction, and expressions of nationality are refracted through military masculinity. In addition, we might note the ways in which social class structures these performances, with the more junior ranks embarking on high-profile "drinking binges" (Hockey, 2003) as a way in which to celebrate their nationality rowdily and mark themselves out from the local "foreigners." The reputation for "squaddies" to celebrate the masculinized ritual of high alcohol consumption is unlikely to disappear within the context of either a home posting or further afield, as particular elements of civilian society continue to reinforce "lad culture."

It has been argued that a future military located within rapidly changing situations, tasked with multirole missions, and able to cope with the scrutiny of the media will need to rely increasingly on the role of the soldier-scholar and the soldier-statesman to augment those involved with fighting wars (Dandeker, 1999, p. 36). These two roles are strongly gendered, and it is not clear how women might be easily assimilated into them. In terms of the first, the soldier-scholar, it is expected that technological and political conditions represent the central issues with which personnel would have to deal. Once again, these realms continue to be dominated by men (and, no doubt, these gendered processes are intensified within the context of the armed forces), and there would need to be considerable thought given to the ways in which they can be opened up to women, not just at the level of accessibility, but also in a cultural sense. In terms of the second, the soldier-statesman, there may be more acceptance of female service personnel from the perspective of commanders on account of their handling of "delicate missions" requiring diplomacy and sensitivity.

THE TENACITY OF MILITARY-MASCULINE CULTURE

In the years following the conclusion of the 1991 Gulf War, there were some significant changes in the politics of war, the role of the armed forces of the major world powers, and, in the case of some nation-states, the role of women within the armed forces. However, the observation by some commentators that the new world order that was emerging in the wake of the Gulf War heralded the retreat of militarism has proved to have been mistaken (Shaw, 1991). Nevertheless, between the end of the 1991 Gulf War and the events of September 11, 2001, there were changes in the politics of war, the nature of militarism, and the sexual politics of militarism. The most obvious change in the politics of war between the 1991 Gulf War and the destruction of the World Trade Center on September 11, 2001, was the tendency of Western governments to claim humanitarian motives for any military intervention beyond their own borders. Although similar arguments may be advanced to justify Britain's declaration of war against Nazi Germany in 1939, Western military interventions during the 1990s were inconsistent and ambiguous. For example, there was large-scale United Nations and NATO intervention in the Balkans, Somalia, and Iraq, but little attempt to intervene militarily in similar situations in Rwanda and other "Third World" countries (Friends Committee on National Legislation, 1993; Gittings, 1995; Richards, 1993). Notwithstanding such inconsistency, though, there was a steep increase in United Nations peacekeeping activities after 1991 "which in 1993 cost about $3bn. In 1994 almost 80,000 'Blue Helmets' were deployed around the world, most based in 'South' countries and without the consent of one or other of the parties in the conflicts" (Assie, 1995, p. 8). By the late 1990s, though, politicians were using the same logic they had used to justify the deployment of ground troops to protect humanitarian aid convoys or act as peacekeepers to justify aerial bombing raids on Iraq and Serbia (Chomsky, 1999; S. Jenkins, 1998; Swain, Campbell, Rhodes, et al., 1998; Wintour, 1999). Significantly, the politicians who sanctioned these bombing raids justified their action with a rhetoric of "determination," "courage," and euphemistic references to "diminishing and degrading" Saddam Hussein's nuclear and chemical weapon stocks or "attacking the heart of Slobodan Milosevic's security structure." Although it is clear that both Hussein and Milosevic were leaders whose regimes committed crimes against humanity, such rhetoric is reminiscent of traditional masculine-militaristic political posturing. Indeed, George W. Bush's declaration of a worldwide war against terrorism in the wake of the events of September 11, 2001, and subsequent wars in

Afghanistan and Iraq rather underline the point that traditional masculinist/militarist preoccupations have yet to disappear. Furthermore, the high profile given to press reports of an apparently risky operation to rescue the injured female American soldier Private Jessica Lynch from her Iraqi captors during the 2003 war against Iraq could be interpreted as a sign that female soldiers are valued differently from their male comrades (Hamilton & Charter, 2003). Leaving aside speculation that this operation may not have been as risky or as necessary as originally suggested, male soldiers were rescued alongside Private Lynch, and it is possible that the intelligence that led to the rescue mission presented the American forces with a unique opportunity. The facts remain, though, that this particular rescue mission was given more prominence in the news media than any other similar operations that might have taken place, and that the gender of Private Lynch was very much stressed in much of the media coverage.

A British Army recruiting advertisement in the late 1990s emphasized the integration of women in the Armed Forces and, significantly, linked this to the growth in the army's peacekeeping role. The film shows a woman cowering in the corner of a building as the commentary intones, "She's just been raped by soldiers. The same soldiers murdered her husband. The last thing she wants to see is another soldier—unless that soldier is woman." Then, as the advertisement concludes, an armed female soldier in full battledress enters the room. Thus, notwithstanding the persistence of militaristic posturing on the part of certain politicians, there are signs that the relationship between militarism and masculinity have begun to change (de Groot, 1999). If it is the case that "pure fighting functions will become of secondary importance" and that the tasks for the military after 2000 are to "protect, help and save" (Dandeker, 1999, p. 60), these changing doctrines seem to suggest that while a need for combat will remain, its significance and centrality may decline. Given that the combat masculine warrior ethic is derived from the military's unique purpose of conducting face-to-face violence, interesting questions might be raised about future military masculine cultures. Will any potential decline in the significance of combat result in a similar diminution in the "spillover" features of the combat masculine warrior ethic? Will violence in military and civilian communities, in military homes, and in the military workplace become increasingly rare as the culture evolves?

Peace Support Operations—A Model for the Future?

Given that Peace Support Operations function in postconflict environments in which women and girls have borne the brunt of war, we might expect the activities of the Blue Helmets toward this particularly vulnerable element of the population to be beyond question. We might even consider that Peace Support Operations could come to represent models of good practice within the context of gendered relations because their activities are informed by international agreements such as UN Resolution 1325 protecting the rights of women and children. Thus, it is difficult to escape from a sense of pessimism when considering the future of military-dominated institutions, their internal gendered culture, and their impact on wider gendered relations when seen against the backdrop of recent scandals involving male peacekeepers. A number of these military personnel have been implicated in trafficking in women for the purpose of sexual slavery (Rees, 2002) and the routine use of prostitutes in peacekeeping missions (Higate, in press; Rehn & Sirleaf, 2002). Although the "good news" stories about their positive impact on gendered relations is given considerably less attention by both the media and scholars working in the field, nevertheless, military masculinist culture has proved resistant to change, and a number of powerful and privileged male peacekeepers are routinely abusing women and girls in the postconflict setting. Finally, PSO have signally failed to mainstream gender successfully, with only a tiny percentage of their numbers being made up of female peacekeeping personnel (Lessons Learned Unit, 2000).

Conclusions

Traditionally, the casual sexism, competitiveness, and celebration of aggression and the domination of others that are characteristic of hegemonic masculinity have been explicitly and unambiguously reflected in military culture

(e.g., Hicklin, 1995; Jennings & Weale, 1996). Similarly, militarism (i.e., the celebration of military culture in national politics and popular culture) has represented an affirmation of the legitimacy of hegemonic masculinity. Conversely, men who reject militarism have often been portrayed as effeminate, naive, untrustworthy, or even politically dangerous (Taylor & Young, 1987). Thus, there are clear links between militaristic attitudes, male self-esteem, and sexual charisma (Bristow, 1989; Hicklin, 1995; Warner, 1982).

Although this established relationship was evident in the events leading up to, during, and immediately following the 1991 Gulf War, that war and its aftermath also appeared to represent a turning point in the relationship between militarism and masculinity. First, there was an expansion of the role of the women in the British armed services and full integration of separate women's services into the army, navy, and air force. Second, there was a shift in the political discourses concerning military intervention, away from traditional masculine preoccupations with power, dominance, and territoriality and toward issues of human rights and peacekeeping. On the other hand, some (male) politicians continued to behave in stereotypically masculinist-militarist fashion, pursuing overtly militaristic foreign policy and justifying their actions in language that reflected both traditional masculinist-militaristic concerns and a newer rhetoric of promoting human rights and political stability. Since the destruction of the World Trade Center on September 11, 2001, politicians have continued to imply that being prepared to sanction military intervention is a sign of moral courage, strong government, and commitment to establishing global security.

The armed forces continue to represent the exemplar masculinist institution in terms of their dominant values and gendered division of labor. These models of masculinity extend beyond the military and tend to shape hegemonic ideologies of what it is to be a man throughout many aspects of life. From the links between privately funded elite British schools, through children's toys to video games and other aspects of popular culture, military masculine culture continues to be valorized. The reciprocal relationship between militarism and masculinity functions at the level of identity as well as the state (Higate, 2003b). For example, aspects of the British criminal justice system are influenced by paramilitary symbols and practice as a way in which to legitimate particular forms of violence such as those used by the police force.

In light of the recent military action by the United States and allies against Iraq, there has been a regression to traditional gender roles, with men cast as the protectors and women as the protected. In looking to the future of the gendered culture of the British armed forces, we have made a number of speculative comments about potential areas of development. As wider social change intensifies, we might expect that the military would reflect these influences, given that it has been argued to be a microcosm of its host society. Yet, not only does military culture change slowly (Goldstein, 2001), but in addition, it has been argued that there exists a growing gulf between the military and civilian spheres, particularly politicians, few of whom have direct experience of military service (Dandeker, 2000). In this understanding, the military is argued to be unique and to have a "need to be different" (Dandeker, 2000); it should not, therefore, be treated as a social laboratory by "uninformed civilians."

We also commented on potential points of convergence and divergence concerning the permeable civilian-military interface. Here, the somewhat mythical New Man was invoked and disregarded in the face of the extent to which a number of young enlistees—particularly those drawn to the combat arms—may be disposed to activities deemed hypermasculine. Other developments, concerning the links between technology, nationality, sexuality, the so-called soldier-scholar, and the soldier statesman, were speculatively discussed. Throughout, we felt unable to identify areas that might ultimately serve to dilute either the spillover effects of military masculinist ideologies, beliefs, and practices, or those that offered unarguable and sustainable progress for military women.

Finally, within the context of Peace Support Operations, it was suggested that the recent sexual exploitation and abuse of local women in peacekeeping missions offers little hope for future developments, perhaps pointing to the universality of wider masculine culture. The links between hegemonic forms of masculinity and the military are surprisingly tenacious, and

in tracing many practices to the level of the state and more globally, it is clear that militarist values continue to have disproportionate influence on the ways in which hegemonic masculinity is both created and reproduced.

REFERENCES

Assie, F. (1995, Summer). United Nations. *Peace Matters, 10*, 6-9.

Baigent, D. (2001). *Gender relations, masculinities and the fire service: A qualitative study of firefighters' constructions of masculinity during firefighting and their social relations of work.* Unpublished doctoral thesis, Department of Sociology and Politics, Anglia Polytechnic University, Cambridge.

Barnett, A. (1982). *Iron Britannia.* London: Allison & Busby.

Bibbings, L. (2003). Conscientious objectors in the Great War: The consequences of rejecting military masculinities. In P. R. Higate (Ed.), *Military masculinities: Identity and the state.* Westport, CT: Praeger.

Bickford, A. (2003). The militarization of masculinity in the former German Democratic Republic. In P. R. Higate (Ed.), *Military masculinities: Identity and the state.* Westport, CT: Praeger.

Booth, B., Kestnbaum, M., & Segal, D. R. (2001). Are post-Cold War militaries postmodern? *Armed Forces and Society, 27*(3), 319-342.

Bristow, J. (1989). Homophobia/misogyny: Sexual fears and sexual definitions. In S. Shepherd & M. Wallis (Eds.), *Coming on strong.* London: Unwin Hyman.

Brittain, V. (1953). *Lady into woman.* London: Andrew Dakers.

Brittan, A. (1989). *Masculinity and power.* Oxford, UK: Basil Blackwell.

Brod, H. (Ed.). (1987). *The making of masculinities.* London: Allen & Unwin.

Cale, K. (1991). Kuwait was never the issue. *Living Marxism, 30*, 12-15.

Caplan, G. (2003). Militarism and masculinity as keys in the former German Democratic Republic. In P. R. Higate (Ed.), *Military masculinities: Identity and the state.* Westport, CT: Praeger.

Chamallas, M. (1998). The new gender panic: Reflections on sex scandals and the military. *The Minnesota Law Review, 83*(2), 305-375.

Chomsky, N. (1999). *The new military humanism: Lessons from Kosovo.* London: Pluto Press.

Cockburn, A., & Cohen, A. (1991). The unnecessary war. In V. Brittain (Ed.), *The gulf between us.* London: Virago.

Cohn, C. (2000). How can she claim equal rights when she doesn't have to do as many push-ups as I do? *Men and Masculinities, 3*(2), 131-151.

Connell, R. W. (1987). *Gender and power.* Cambridge, MA: Polity.

Connell, R. W. (2000). Arms and the man. In I. Breines, R. Connell, & I. Eide (Eds.), *Male roles, masculinities and violence.* Paris: UNESCO.

Cooke, R. (1995, February 26). Tired of women in fatigues. *Sunday Times* [London].

Coulter, J., Miller, S., & Walker, M. (1984). *State of siege.* London: Canary Press.

Dandeker, C. (1999). *Facing uncertainty: Flexible forces for the twenty-first century.* Karlstad, Sweden: National Defence College.

Dandeker, C. (2000). The United Kingdom: The overstretched military. In C. Moskos, J. A. Williams, & D. R. Segal (Eds.), *The postmodern military.* Oxford, UK: Oxford University Press.

Dawson, G. (1994). *Soldier heroes.* London: Routledge.

de Groot, G. J. (1999, June 14). Women: A force for change. *Guardian* [London], p. 5.

Douglas, C. A. (1991). Dear Ms Woolf, We are returning your guineas. *Trouble and Strife, 21,* 21-22.

Ellicott, S. (1991, December 1). America faces dilemma over female role. *Times* [London].

Enloe, C. (1988). *Does khaki become you?* London: Pandora.

Enloe, C. (2000). *Maneuvers.* Berkeley: University of California Press.

Farry, M. (1991). Iraqi Women's League speak out. *Spare Rib, 223,* 14-17.

Friends Committee on National Legislation. (1993, January). Somalia: Not just drought, famine and war. *Peace News, 2362,* 8-9.

Geraghty, T. (1980). *Who dares wins.* Glasgow: Fontana/Collins.

Gibson, J. W. (1994). *Warrior dreams.* New York: Hill and Wang.

Gittings, J. (1995, February). UN intervention: Too little, too late. *Red Pepper, 9,* 20-21.

Goldstein, J. (2001). *War and gender.* Cambridge, UK: Cambridge University Press.

Greed, C. (2000). Women in the construction professions: Achieving critical mass. *Gender, Work and Organisation, 7*(3), 181-196.

Hables-Gray, C. (1997). *Postmodern war: The new politics of conflict.* London: Routledge.

Hall, E. (1995). *We can't even march straight.* London: Vintage.

Hamilton, A., & Charter, D. (2003, April 3). Saving Private Jessica. *Times* [London], p. 3.

Harris, I. M. (1995). *Messages men hear.* London: Taylor & Francis.

Harrison, D. (2003). Violence in the military community. In P. R. Higate (Ed.), *Military masculinities: Identity and the state.* Westport, CT: Praeger.

Hearn, J. (1996). A critique of the concept of masculinity/masculinities. In M. Mac an Ghaill (Ed.), *Understanding masculinities.* Buckingham, UK: Open University Press.

Hicklin, A. (1995). *Boy soldiers.* Edinburgh: Mainstream.

Higate, P. (2002). Traditional gendered identities: National service and the all volunteer force. *Comparative Social Research, 20,* 229-236.

Higate, P. (2003a). Concluding thoughts: Looking to the future. In P. Higate (Ed.), *Military masculinities: Identity and the state* (pp. 201-216). Westport, CT: Praeger.

Higate, P. (Ed.). (2003b). *Military masculinities: Identity and the state.* Westport, CT: Praeger.

Higate, P. (in press). *Peacekeeping and gendered relations in the Republic of Congo and Sierra Leone.* Pretoria, South Africa: Institute for Security Studies.

Hillyard, P., & Percy-Smith, J. (1988). *The coercive state.* London: Fontana.

Hockey, J. (2003). No more heroes: Masculinity in the infantry. In P. R. Higate (Ed.), *Military masculinities: Identity and the state.* Westport, CT: Praeger.

Hondagneu-Sotelu, P., & Messner, M. A. (1994). Gender displays and men's power. In H. Brod & M. Kaufman (Eds.), *Theorizing masculinities.* London: Sage.

Hopton, J. (2003). The state and military masculinity. In P. Higate (Ed.), *Military masculinities: Identity and the state* (pp. 111-124). Westport, CT: Praeger.

Jefferson, T. (1990). *The case against paramilitary policing.* Milton Keynes, UK: Open University Press.

Jenkins, J. (1989, January 27). Truth on the rocks. *New Statesman and Society, 2*(34), 10-11.

Jenkins, S. (1998, December 18). Stone age strategy. *Times* [London], p. 22.

Jennings, C., & Weale, A. (1996). *Green-eyed boys.* London: HarperCollins.

Klein, U. (2003). The military and masculinities in Israeli society. In P. R. Higate (Ed.), *Military masculinities: Identity and the state.* Westport, CT: Praeger.

Kovitz, M. (2003). The roots of military masculinity. In P. R. Higate (Ed.), *Military masculinities: Identity and the state.* Westport, CT: Praeger.

Kuzmanic, T., Ostric, Z., Uskovic, Z., Cuckova, T., Tomovski, M., Orascanin, V., et al. (1994, September). An open letter to peace movements. *Peace News* [London], 2382, 6.

Lessons Learned Unit. (2000). *Mainstreaming a gender perspective in multidimensional peace operations.* New York: Department of Peacekeeping Operations, United Nations.

Lister, R. (1990). Women, economic dependency and citizenship. *Journal of Social Policy, 19*(4), 445-467.

MacInnes, J. (1998). *The end of masculinity.* Buckingham, UK: Open University Press.

Macnair, M. (1989). The contradictory politics of SM. In S. Shepherd & M. Wallis (Eds.), *Coming on strong.* London: Unwin Hyman.

Martin, C. (1996). The impact of equal opportunities policies on the day-to-day experiences of women constables. *British Journal of Criminology, 36*(4), 510-528.

Mason, D., & Dandeker, C. (2001). The British armed services and the participation of minority ethnic communities: From equal opportunities to diversity? *The Sociological Review, 49*(2), 219-235.

McFarlan, D. M. (1983). *First for boys: The story of the Boys' Brigade 1883-1983.* London: Boys' Brigade.

McGowan, R., & Hands, J. (1983). *Don't cry for me sergeant-major.* London: Futura.

McGregor, R. (2003). The popular press and the creation of military masculinities in Georgian Britain. In P. R. Higate (Ed.), *Military masculinities: Identity and the state.* Westport, CT: Praeger.

Melichar, J. (1991). Indecent and indelicate. *The Pacifist, 29*(4), 3.

Miedzian, M. (1992). *Boys will be boys.* London: Virago.

Millar, J., & Glendinning, C. (1989). Gender and poverty. *Journal of Social Policy, 18*(3), 363-381.

Mladjenovic, L. (1993, March). Universal soldier: Rape in war. *Peace News* [London], 2364, 6.

Moon, C. (1997). *Sex among allies.* New York: Columbia University Press.

Morgan, D. (1987). *It will make a man of you: Notes on National Service, masculinity and autobiography* (Studies in Sexual Politics 17). Manchester, UK: University of Manchester Department of Sociology.

Morgan, R. (1989). *The demon lover.* London: Mandarin.

Moskos, C. (1988). *The military: Just another job?* London: Brasseys.

Moskos, C., Williams, J. A., & Segal, D. R. (Eds.). (2000). *The postmodern military.* Oxford, UK: Oxford University Press.

Muir, K. (1991, February 5). Bridging the gender gulf. *Times* [London].

Muncie, J. (1990). Failure never matters: Detention centres and the politics of deterrence. *Critical Social Policy, 10,* 53-64.

National Center for Policy Analysis. (2002, March 29). Privatized British military more efficient. *Daily Policy Digest.* Retrieved January 23, 2004, from www.ncpa.org/iss/pri/2002/pd032902a .html

Newsinger, J. (1997). *Dangerous men.* London: Pluto Press.

Oldfield, S. (1989). *Women against the iron fist.* Oxford, UK: Basil Blackwell.

Olsson, L., Ukabiala, Blondle, Y. I., Kampungu, L., & Wallensteen, P. (1999). *Mainstreaming a gender perspective in multidimensional peace keeping operations.* Uppsala, Sweden: Uppsala University, Department of Peace and Conflict.

Platt, S. (1992). Casualties of war. *New Statesman & Society, 4*(139), 12-13.

Pringle, R. (1989). *Secretaries talk: Sexuality, power and work.* London: Verso.

Rees, M. (2002). International intervention into Bosnia-Herzegovina: The cost of ignoring gender. In C. Cockburn & D. Zarkov (Eds.), *The postwar moment.* London: Lawrence and Wishart.

Rehn, E., & Sirleaf, E. J. (2002). *Women, war and peace: The independent experts' assessment on the impact of armed conflict on women and women's role in peace-building.* New York: UNIFEM.

Richards, F. (1993, February). Behind the West's humanitarian mask. *Living Marxism, 52,* 18-22.

Rogers, B. (1988). *Men only.* London: Pandora.

Scraton, P., Sim, J., & Skidmore, P. (1991). *Prisons under protest.* Milton Keynes, UK: Open University Press.

Segal, L. (1990). *Slow motion.* London: Virago.

Shaw, M. (1991). *Post-military society.* Cambridge, MA: Polity.

Shepherd, S. (1989). Gay sex spy orgy. In S. Shepherd & M. Wallis (Eds.), *Coming on strong.* London: Unwin Hyman.

Shepherd, S., & Wallis, M. (Eds.). (1989). *Coming on strong.* London: Unwin Hyman.

Showalter, E. (1987). *The female malady.* London: Virago.

Simpson, M., & Zeeland, S. (2001). *The queen is dead.* London: Arcadia Books.

Skaine, R. (1999). *Women at war: Gender issues of Americans in combat.* Jefferson, NC: McFarland & Company.

Smith, J. (1989). *Misogynies.* London: Faber & Faber.

Stanko, E. (1990). *Everyday violence.* London: Pandora.

Stanley, L., & Wise, S. (1987). *Georgie Porgie.* London: Pandora.

Stockholm International Peace Research Institute. (n.d.). *Recent trends in military expenditure.* Retrieved February 2, 2004, from http://projects .sipri.se/milex/mex_trends.html

Stoltenberg, J. (1990). *Refusing to be a man.* New York: Meridian.

Swain, J., Campbell, M., Rhodes, T., et al. (1998, December 20). War and impeachment. *Sunday Times* [London], p. 15.

Tatchell, P. (1995). *We don't want to march straight.* London: Listen Up!

Taylor, R., & Young, N. (1987). *Campaigns for peace.* Manchester, UK: Manchester University Press.

Theweleit, K. (1987). *Male fantasies.* Cambridge, MA: Polity.

"Tony." (1990). Sticks and stones. *New Statesman & Society, 3,* 95.

Warner, P. (1982). *Auchinleck: The lonely soldier.* London: Sphere.

Warner, P. (1983). *The SAS: The official history.* London: Sphere.

Weeks, J. (1981). *Sex, politics and society.* London: Longman.

Wheelwright, J. (1989). *Amazons and military maids.* London: Pandora.

White, M., & Norton-Taylor, R. (2002, July 5). 1bn rise in defence spending. *Guardian.* Retrieved February 2, 2004, from www.guardian.co.uk/guardianpolitics/story/0,3605,749735,00.html

Winslow, D., & Dunn, J. (2001). Women in the Canadian Forces. In G. Kummel (Ed.), *The challenging continuity of change and the military: Female soldiers, conflict resolution, South America.* Strausberg: Sozial Wisenschaftliches Institut der Bunderswehr.

Wintour, P. (1999, April 4). War in the Balkans: The home front. *Observer* [London], p. 20.

26

ISLAMIST MASCULINITY AND MUSLIM MASCULINITIES

SHAHIN GERAMI

The terrible conflicts that herd people under falsely unifying rubrics like "America," "The West" or "Islam" and invent collective identities for large numbers of individuals who are actually quite diverse, cannot remain as potent as they are, and must be opposed. We still have at our disposal the rational interpretive skills that are the legacy of humanistic education, not as a sentimental piety enjoining us to return to traditional values or the classics but as the active practice of worldly secular rational discourse.

—Edward Said (2003, p. 23)

INTRODUCTION

It has become a common mantra to acknowledge the incredible diversity of Islamic cultures, identities, and interpretations. Having said that, we then proceed to identify and analyze commonalities and even offer generalizations. Following Edward Said and borrowing from Bayat, I will distinguish between Islamist identity as an abstract construct applied by others, on one hand, and Muslim identities as "concrete, contested, and differentiated" identities created through individual or group agency, on the other. Bayat reminds us that "'Islamic society' becomes a totalizing notion" that is undifferentiated, while "'Muslim societies'

are never monolithic as such, never religious by definition, nor are their cultures simply reducible to mere religion" (2003, p. 5).

Accepting this dynamic and self-conscious process of cultural construction within Muslim societies, it is then more plausible to conceive of gender identities not merely reducible to Islamic femininity or Islamic feminist; nor are masculinities reducible to one dimension of Islamic masculinity. In this chapter, I will explore the prototype of Islamist masculinity and Muslim masculinities. The former is more of a category recognized by others; the latter is more representative of construction of masculinities within Muslim countries.

Author's note: I would like to thank Doris Ewing and Michael Kimmel for their insightful comments and suggestions. I am indebted to Sondra Cogswell for her untiring assistance in preparing various versions of this chapter.

Gender discourses in Muslim cultures have a double life. Similar to other gender dichotomies, gender identities have indigenous faces and external stereotypes. The indigenous women's identities are multifaceted and are becoming more visible and diverse. The men's discourse is visible as a standard and the norm. It is the Western cultural references of these roles that are very visible and stereotypical.

Exploring Muslim masculinity has found its cultural context not in the Islamic societies but in the post–September 11 context of Western cultures. The Western popular cultures have seen their demons, and they are Muslim men (Ratnesar & Zabriskis, 2004). Their universally recognized prototypes are bearded, gun-toting, bandanna-wearing men, in long robes or military fatigues of some Islamist (read terrorist) organization or country.

Analysis of masculinities is another new Western discourse that may eventually spread to other cultures. Kimmel and Messner (2001) maintain that masculinity studies in the United States are influenced by feminist studies, race and class studies, queer theory, and poststructuralisms. Because masculinity studies—like their predecessor, women's studies—come from the West, they are constructed within Western gender dichotomies. The major premises of these studies indicate that (a) gender is socially constructed, and thus, gender identities are acquired; (b) power differential is societal and not natural; (c) the intersection of race, class, gender, and other social distinctions makes some categories of women privileged as compared with others; (d) gender privileges of masculinities must be made visible and thus challenged; (e) human biology is defined by the linguistic tools of a culture, and thus, biological hierarchies of race and gender are open to interpretations; and finally, (f) heterosexuality is a given culturally privileged sexuality. Masculinities studies have borrowed from all of the above, proposing plural construction of masculinities (Duroche, 1990; Edwards, 1990; Kegan Gardiner, 2000; Pleck & Sawyer, 1974). Of the above premises, the first three have been accepted in the academic and intellectual gender discourses in many Muslim countries; the others, especially sexuality as socially constructed, has a long way to go.

There is a nascent literature in the North analyzing lived experiences of Muslim men, focusing on the Middle Eastern/North African countries (MENA). Among them, some articles in Sinclair-Webb's (2000) volume explore individual agency and group construction of masculinities in this region. Articles in a special issue of the journal *Men and Masculinities* (2003) deliver additional perspectives on masculinity discourse in this region. Nevertheless, the emphasis has remained on Arab cultures and Middle Eastern and North African societies. Because the Western notions of Muslim men are driven from the stereotypes of Middle Eastern cultures, I will focus on Muslim Middle Eastern and North African societies as well. The vast diversities of Central and South Asian countries and Muslim cultures of European and North American societies will not be covered. This will be a historical extraction of masculine modalities in this region since the colonial domination.

In the remainder of this chapter, I will explore the role of global hegemonic masculinity and the emergence of national masculinity figures out of the independence movements and nation-building process in MENA societies. Later, I will examine the postindependence and Cold War period when we witness varied representations of Muslim masculinities on the national scene in the region. In the last three decades, we have witnessed the arrival of Islamist masculinity from Islamic and fundamentalist movements. Finally, I will attempt to make plural Muslim masculinities visible.

GLOBAL HEGEMONIC MASCULINITY

Is there a hegemonic masculinity universally recognized? Inevitably, one leads to the media-projected images of Western masculinity broadcast around the globe. This hegemonic masculinity is invariably white, Christian, heterosexual, and dominant. Its virtual presentations are on movie screens and Internet sites. Its real-life representatives are Western political and military leaders peering from front pages of newspapers and TV screens. In the era of CNN, even in small villages there are a few satellite dishes that project these images.

The appearance of global hegemonic masculinity dates back to colonial expansion. Previous invasions of the motherland or its rape and pillage were more regional and by groups that were culturally and physically somewhat similar to the victims. None had the magnitude of colonial domination by a different race and culture. This invasion also intensified the language of rape of motherland by a penetrating foreign force (Ahmed, 1992). In Muslim societies, as in many other colonized cultures, the colonial domination raised serious challenges to the local masculinities across the region. Men's honor was threatened, and they were called upon to protect it. This catapulted women's veil to the national and political scene as the symbol of men's honor. No longer was women's honor particular to a clan, a tribe, or a man; it became symbolic of the national honor. Female symbolisms figure strongly in independence movements from Egypt to the Indian subcontinent (Abdel Kader, 1987; Gerami, 1996).

What hampers the recognition of masculinity studies in the South is the marginal attention given to the colonized masculinities as opposed to the Western hegemonic masculinity. Feminist studies have overcome this by both acknowledgment of Western feminist scholars and the rich literature appearing both from and by the feminists of the South. In contrast, when colonized masculinities are considered, they are hyphenated ethnic masculinities of Western societies. This is less a failure of Western gender studies than a result of the cultural context of gender debate in the South. The Islamic societies are grappling with crosscurrents of globalization, cultural liberalization, Islamic fundamentalism, and democracy, to name a few. In this context, the gender discourse for the foreseeable future will revolve around women's rights and roles.

Whereas women's studies are emerging and even thriving in many parts of the South, masculinity issues remain un-organic. Needless to say, the privileged position of gender discourse in the West calls for consideration of colonized masculinities, in the hope that when the time comes, organic studies of masculinities will emerge from within gender studies of the South.

NATIONAL CONSTRUCTION OF MASCULINITY

The pervasiveness of hegemonic masculinity overshadows the national and cultural masculinities in most Muslim societies. Needless to say, national masculinity figures are present and visible; and in some cases they are omnipresent, as in Egypt, Iraq, Pakistan, and Iran, among other countries (Saghieh, 2000). Although a national masculinity dominates the social scene, it remains secondary to global masculinity.

During the nation-building period, strong national leaders emerged and overshadowed tribal or ethnic ideals of masculinities. Heroic models like Mustafa Kemal Ataturk in Turkey, Jamaal Abdul Nasser in Egypt, Iran's Reza Shah, and Pakistan's Jinnah became the counterparts to the Western hegemonic masculinity. With the ideal of nationhood and a centralized state came the ideal of one national leader subsuming regional or ethnic masculinities. As these leaders each forcefully forged a nation-state, he also forged a national masculinity by subduing other contending masculine figures. For example, Reza Shah in Iran, following the example of Ataturk in Turkey, not only banned women's veil but also barred men from wearing ethnic, religious, or tribal clothing. Men's public appearance was made to comply in both countries with Western codes of suit and tie.

Cold War Masculinities

The postwar, postindependence situation of the Muslim countries was dominated by the Cold War of the two superpowers; therefore, each national leader was subservient to another hegemonic male figure. For example, Egyptian Nasser was under the protection of the Soviets' Nikita Khrushchev, just as the Iranian Shah and Pakistani Butu were under the patronage of various American presidents from Dwight D. Eisenhower to Richard Nixon. The closer a country was to a dominant core, the more present and dominating the hegemonic masculinity was in the peripheral country. While Eisenhower was present in the subtext of Iranian politics, he was less visible and perhaps less influential in Turkish national discourse, as Turkey was less of a client state of the United States than was Iran.

The postcolonial period offered a hierarchy of nation-states accompanied by a hierarchy of masculine modalities. A global hegemonic masculinity was followed by national masculinity figures born with their nation-states. The national masculinity of the independence movements became more diffused and more penetrating. The Cold War and the détente period offered a respite allowing diffusion of cultural discourses, among them gender narratives spreading to the mainstream of Western cultures. From this appeared varied representations of plural masculinities in the core and peripheral countries.

Cultural Masculinities

As variations of Western masculinities, particularly in terms of ethnicity and racial diversity, became visible, so did Muslim masculinities witness some diversions. Postindependence Muslim men in the MENA region experienced some freedom of expression that was allowed the hegemonic man of the Western cultures. Masculinities in Muslim societies came full circle by starting from the diffused ethnic, tribal, rural, and urban masculinities of precolonialism to a national masculinity of independence movements, and then to diverse masculinities of postindependence and the Cold War era.

The dominant prototype remained the strong nationalistic—as opposed to ethnic—Muslim leader; however, mass media provided for alternative masculinities. These were never too far from the prototype, but less austere and more representative of the class and ethnic diversity of a society. Weak men or funny figures were allowed and made fun of to teach a lesson in proper masculinity. The national media, especially the visual media, experimented with variations in terms of ethnic, working class, peasant, and even criminal masculinities.

The national cinema in countries such as Egypt, Iran, and Turkey had typecasts representing these masculinities. They were virile men, physically and morally strong. They could be simple or rural, as opposed to the cunning urban men. They defended the good woman's honor and sometimes saved a woman from turning in vile and corrupt ways (Armbrust, 2000; Leaman, 2001).

These prototypes, whether a strong leader, working class hero, or historical figure, usually were secular but committed to Islamic moralities. The religious subtext informed all moral dimensions of personalities and identities, female or male. The wrongdoers and evil masculinites departed from the right path of Islamic moral codes, and heroes adhering to them saved the day.

In addition to the indigenous portrait of Islamic masculinities, Western examples of masculinity resembling John Wayne and company provided potent models. I remember that many of the prime-time characters of American television, such as Dr. Kildare, Western cowboys, and even Perry Mason were duplicated and imitated in Iranian TV productions or in radio shows. The same happened in the Egyptian or Turkish genre of TV production.

The Iranian Contributions of the Warrior and the Shahid

Being Shiite, the Iranian heroes had the masculine attributes of Ali and Hussein; the prophet's son-in-law and grandson. Shiites believe that before his death, the Prophet had designated his son-in law, Ali, and his descendants to be his true successors. But after the Prophet's death, the community elders elected his father-in-law, Abu Baker, as the first caliph. Ali eventually became the fourth caliph and ruled for 5 years that ended with his assassination by a militant group. In 680 C.E., his second son, Hussein, tried to regain the power from caliph Yazid to restore the true Islamic society. In the Battle of Karbala, he was defeated, and he and many members of his small entourage were killed.

These two ideals of righteousness have colored the notion of justice and morality as well as gender ideals of masculinity in Shiite communities. Ali and Hussein reflect different types of masculinities in the Shiite construction-of-masculinity package. Ali's manly persona of "the Warrior" has been replicated in Shiite cultures from Pakistan to Lebanon, from poetry to cinema. Hussein represents another type of masculinity, that of "the *shahid*," a martyr. Hussein's model became the essence of injustice and denied rights in the Iranian consciousness (Hegland, 1995). He is praised and mourned every year in Shiite communities of the region in street plays (*tazieh*). Whereas the Iranian cinema seized on Ali's myth to present new folk heroes, Hussein's persona as a *shahid* became the essence of the street play and later was integrated into the construction of Islamist masculinity.

ISLAMIST MASCULINITY

Here I distinguish between Islamist masculinity and plural Muslim masculinities. The former is a product of fundamentalist resistance movements and Western media. The latter are the gender identities of real men formed across boundaries of nationality, ethnicity, and class.

During the 1970s, Middle Eastern experimentations with Western models of development such as capitalism, socialism, or even a mixed economy were showing signs of fissure. The Islamic Revolution in Iran marked the first reaction to the failure of the experiments and, in hindsight, the future of the Cold War policies. The Iranian revolution marks the beginning of Islamic fundamentalism as a solution to the problems of Muslim nations and as a political base for the state. In the late 20th century, fundamentalist movements spread across the region and contributed to the prominence of one particular image of masculinity. It became a response to the hegemonic global masculinity and its various national duplicates. Fundamentalist movements in many Muslim societies share elements of a retroactive ideology to reinstate the earlier "pure" Islamic society. Therefore, their gender ideologies dictate religiously ordained places for each sex. There is a rich literature documenting Islamic fundamentalisms' doctrinal mandates and policies for women (Afshar, 1998; Gerami & Safiri, in press; Mir-Hosseini, 1999; Shehadeh, 2003). Men's ideals within these ideologies are receiving some attention (Gerami, 2003a). Kurzman (2002) provides a concise summary of characteristics of Islamic fundamentalism and the socioeconomic background of some famous Islamist men. Peteet (2000) contributes to our understanding of the construction of Islamist masculinity in the occupied territories. Indirectly, the growing body of work on Islamic precepts, jihad, and the hermeneutics of Quran further the discourse on Muslim identity and Muslim men (Esposito, 2003; Lawrence, 1998; Soroush, 2000).

The Islamist masculinity is the product of this era. Two major narratives inform the prototype of Islamist masculinity discourse across the world: *jihad* and *shahadat*. The majority of Muslims, regardless of their orientation, distinguish between "the greater *jihad*, the personal, spiritual struggle, and the lesser, warfare form of *jihad*" (Esposito, 2003, p. 38). It is the warfare *jihad* that is known by non-Muslims and forms the narrative of this Islamist masculinity.

Equally, the *shahadat* (martyrdom) narrative also occupies a personal and a public level of engagement (Gerami, 2003b, p. 266). When Muslims take witness that "there is no God but Allah and Mohammad is the Prophet of Allah," they take witness to strive against desires of flesh, polytheism, and concerns for worldly possessions. The public aspect of *shahadat* is the act of sacrificing one's life in a *jihad* to protect Islam or an Islamic nation. Needless to say, these personal levels have been subsumed under the public aspects of the narratives to deliver the Islamist masculinity of today.

The invasion of Iran by Iraqi forces in 1980 created the perfect context for the coming together of the above narratives. The Islamic ideology of the revolution and charismatic force of the Ayatollah Khomeini had already created a fertile ground to move beyond the personal aspects of *jihad* and *shahadat* to the public arena of a social movement. These narratives further evolved in the context of the Iraqi invasion and the ensuing 8-year war. Thus the modern myth of the *shahid* was born. Although the ideal of *shahadat* was used by the Afghani mujahideens against the Soviet Union, or the Palestinian resistance against the occupation, none had the force and prominence of the Iran/Iraq war.

The Iranian resistance institutionalized and internationalized *shahadat* and its masculinity prototypes. *Shahids* are poster men (boys) of Islamist masculinity. They are young men, pure and innocent (virgin), who battle the forces of the infidel while taking witness to their faith.

There are cultural variations to this masculinity script but no major deviation from its essence of maleness, purity, and faith. The real-life examples of Islamist masculinity may have none of the above, but they claim admission to the rank of *shohada* (plural of *shahid*) by virtue of their sacrifice. In the Iran/Iraq war, this hero worship prompted many boys to join the ranks of *bosiji* (volunteers). To the outside world, they were child soldiers or human cannonballs. To the Islamist discourse, they were martyrs. This ideal of martyrdom later engulfed the region. In Egypt, various uprisings were attributed to the Muslim Brotherhood (*Al-ikvans al-muslimun*). Among their heroes is President Anwar Sadat's murderer. All the hijackers of September 11, 2001, have the characteristics of this prototype, and for many in the region they fit the *shahid* persona.

Warrior rites in the past and soldiering rituals of modern armies mark the transition of the child into manhood. In cultures with a siege component, military aspects of masculinity signal the arrival and inclusion of the "man" as venerated citizen (Arkin & Dobrofsky, 1978; Sinclair-Webb, 2000). Kaplan (2000) and Peteet (2000) illustrate how masculinities are forged through daily violent confrontations between Israeli soldiers and stone-throwing Palestinian youth. Soldiers and the youth obtain their venerated manhood through acts of sacrifice in the name of faith, land, and honor.

Kaplan maintains that military service in Israel confers "recognized and legitimate themes identified with hegemonic masculinity" (2000, p. 136) within the Zionist enterprise. This masculinity is then poised and ready to battle the enemy's masculinity. Therefore, as the ritualized battles confer hegemonic masculinity to the young Israeli men, the beatings by these soldiers and imprisonment confer militant manhood upon the Palestinian boys (Peteet, 2000). According to Sahmmas (quoted by Peteet, 2000, p. 106), the Israeli military does not use the Hebrew word for "children" when referring to Palestinian boys; rather, it will report that a young man of 10 was shot dead by soldiers. The military initiation that turns the Israeli youth into hegemonic men, by beating, turns Palestinian youth into freedom fighters, and maybe martyrs. The Palestinian youth then has deference and respect bestowed upon him by his community, upon release from prison. These daily examples of violence inflicted upon boys are used to confer status and mark recognition to manhood.

Islamist masculinity is one player in this global guerrilla warfare of hegemonic masculinities. *Shahid* as a category is abstract and fails to encompass the diversity of the participants, including women ("Hamas Woman Bomber Kills Israelis," 2004). Kimmel points out that gender, "their masculinity, their sense of masculine entitlement, and their thwarted ambitions" (2004, p. 82), is the commonality that bonds Timothy McVeigh, Adolf Hitler, and Atta together. He and others have also pointed to the shared middle- and lower-middle-class background of the participants in this brand of masculinity (Gerami, 2003b; Wickham, 2002; Wiktorowicz, 2001).

MUSLIM MASCULINITIES

Young urban men are the majority of men in the MENA countries. They are under the age of 30 years, born to middle- or lower-class urban parents. The majority of this population has a high school education, with some having a few years of postsecondary schooling. Regardless, they are poorly trained for limited, desirable jobs in technology. Their families' expectations deem manual jobs undesirable, leaving them with limited prospects of employment. This large group is in the center of two major countercurrents: Islamic fundamentalism and cultural liberalization. The ideal of a prosperous nuclear family is out of reach for most members of this group. Islamic fundamentalism provides the answer for some segment of this population; however, its strict mandates of austere lifestyle do not have wide appeal, contrary to the media views in the West.

The older generations of urban middle-class men have their own unyielding problems to tame. These groups, who have moved to cities or were born there, have some secondary education. Most are small merchants or civil service employees. With families to support, they face the exorbitant cost of housing and the demands of supporting large families, usually of more than four. Inflation, unresponsive governments, corruption, and obligations of extended family create counterpressures (Salehi Esfahani & Taheripour, 2002). This group may welcome Islamic fundamentalisms' restrictions on women, as they allows them to better control their women in the cities. They then pay for the stay-at-home wife and daughters who cannot contribute to the family income. Additionally, they have to deal with their adolescent children's demands for new consumer goods.

The lower-income urban and rural men are further frustrated by the above-mentioned pressures. Disappointed with the poor employment prospects of rural areas and small towns, they are the first to migrate to larger cities of the region. There, they swell the ranks of the under- and unemployed and contribute to increased crime. The demand for manual labor in cities is limited to construction and some service work. These jobs, when available, offer little savings to be sent to the family left behind or for wedding expenses. Islamist organizations offer some of these young men an answer but cannot offer employment or pay for the expenses of large masses of recruits.

The professional upper-middle-class men have the advantages of a life of consumerism and meaningful work. They are more secure financially and can support their children's dreams. Despite their contribution to the system, they remain the technocrats in most governments and face blocked avenues of political participation. They have the continuous anxiety of their children's future. Most universities cannot meet the demands of a large pool of young applicants, leaving men of this class and their families searching for a better future for their children. For many, this better future lies in the long lines of visa applicants at Western consulates (Gerami, 2003a).

Interestingly, as in the United States, higher education in many Muslim countries records more female than male students. Countries such as Egypt, Iran, and Turkey report more female than male students passing the Herculean entrance exams and entering universities (Sachs, 2000; UNESCO, 2000-2001). Several factors have contributed to this gender reversal, among them the increase in urban mothers who have a high school education and approve higher education for their daughters. It is more acceptable for young men to travel abroad for education than for single women, and thus more scholarships are guaranteed to men for study abroad. Indeed, some countries, such as Saudi Arabia, require that an adult supervise a young women's travel abroad. The high cost of living has led to postponement of marriage for both sexes, and the young families need the woman's income to maintain their middle-class standard or even to achieve it.

For men, higher education as a means toward the "global good life" has failed to deliver. Women with more education are making some men feel insecure and are challenging their sense of male entitlement. In addition, the responsibility of being the male provider may have contributed to young men's disdain of a higher education that does not guarantee return. Thus, some young men look for innovative approaches (Merton, 1968) to obtain the good life for themselves and their families.

Muslim masculinities are produced within these structural and cultural currents (Lubeck, 2000). Islamic fundamentalisms, with their associated vigilance against Western hegemony; relaxation of traditional gender roles; and a strong desire for cultural authenticity, demand a conservative approach. Economic globalization has reduced micro agricultural production and the demand for farm labor while failing to produce living-wage manufacturing jobs in cities (Coes, 1995; Onis & Webb, 1994). Unresponsive governments that are run by a single family or stratum lack flexibility to respond to these forces. Additionally, for the majority of Muslims, the Palestinians' suffering has turned into a chronic feeling of guilt and shame, regardless of ethnic identity (Kurd, Arab, or Iranian) or religious orientation (Armenians, Druz, etc.). The Middle Eastern/Islamic psyche aches with the pain and humiliation of the Palestinians, sometimes leading to desperate measures.

There are other currents worthy of note, such as the influx of information through the Internet, international migration and heightened awareness of the promised land of the West, and women's movements of various strength. Additionally, the Muslim population worldwide is very young, with the median age in the MENA region about 21 years old (United Nations Population Division, 2002). The demographics alone promises reconstruction of gender roles for the next millennium. More than ever, this large population will form their masculine identity influenced by economic and cultural forces of a hegemonic global system. Their responses vary by their socioeconomic background and their perception of available opportunities.

For example, in the Cape Town ghettos in South Africa, urban youth combine machismo and vigilantism to fight drug dealers and take back their neighborhood in the name of Islam (Bangstad, 2002, p. 10). In France, second-generation "reconvert" youth walk the cities inside or outside the country to spread Islam. "They are between 18 and 36 years of age and live essentially in the French suburbs, where the cumulated difficulties of unemployment, exclusion and racism are predominant" (Khedimellah, 2002, p. 20).

Liberal Masculinities

Muslim masculinities are also responding to the positive aspects of globalization, namely cultural tolerance and political liberalization. As I am finishing this chapter the Iranian experiment of adjusting democracy to Islam is struggling with liberalization. The Iranian electorates are gearing for the Majles (parliamentary) election in February of 2004. The Guardian Council, a constitutional body of mostly conservative clerics, is responsible for checking every bill and every law to guarantee compatibility with the Islamic mandates. The Council is also responsible for vetting candidates for the parliament or presidency by reviewing their credentials for their Islamic worthiness. For the current elections, the Council has rejected about 3,000 candidates, among them most of the current representatives.

The Islamic Republic is an experimental model of negotiating between Islam and modernity. Individual civil liberties, secularism, organizational separation of faith and state apparatus, universal definition of citizenship free from gender, and ethnicity or religious restrictions all are being debated.

Children of the revolution, born at the end of the war, call themselves "generation 3" and are at the forefront of this debate. Their middle-class urban parents believed in small families and lavished on their offspring what they had desired for themselves, especially on education. Now this generation has arrived, and they are impatient, young, technology-savvy children of global expectations. They face another group of children of the revolution from their own generation, mostly from the lower strata of urban areas; they are more inclined toward Islamic organizations and are loyal to the regime and the revolution.

Families are siding with their children too. Families of the *shahids* or those of the veterans of the war are vigilant to keep the spirit of the revolution and Islam alive and present. These families have a lot to lose, both psychologically and financially. The pain of giving a son for a cause when the memories are cherished is more bearable than when the son is forgotten or his memories are diminished. These families receive tangible benefits from the giant Shahid Foundation in terms of pension, material goods, and favorable quotas in employment and university admission.

The university students are the countertrends to the *shahids*. These young, clean-shaven, urban youth are for liberalized education, free access to civil liberties, and privatization of religious institutions and practices. They want to mix and socialize with the opposite sex freely, and they find mandatory dress and behavior codes humiliating and oppressive. They often organize in student protests, sit-ins, and media events to express their opinions on issues. Unlike the Islamists, who blame mostly the outsiders,

imperialists, or globalization, this group puts the blame at the door of the national leaders.

The Iranian liberal masculinities are in accordance with a nascent youth movement in Muslim societies. This is an anti-Islamist movement and anti-*shahid*. It is a product of, and contributes to, a new discourse on modernity that has gone beyond the old dichotomy of "the West and the Rest." It is an attempt not to modernize Islam, but rather to design an Islamized modernism compatible with pluralism, reformation (*ijtihad*), and dismantling of religious jurisprudence. The liberal Muslim men pioneering this narrative are writers such as Soroush, Mujtahid-Shabastari, Kadviar, or the Algerian opposition leader, Abbasi Madani. This new brand and their ideological leaders are against "ideologization of religion, which means turning it into an instrument of fanaticism and hatred" (Soroush, 2000, p. 21). The second-generation Western-born youth or Muslim converts in Europe (Allievi, 2002) echo the same sentiments. Progressive Muslim men of this brand are borrowing from the environmental and women's movements to reinterpret the Quran, and they espouse new constructions of Muslim identity (Esack, 2003). They are against exclusionary ideologies of fundamentalism and Wahabism and strive toward a discourse of tolerance and gender redefinition. This is a fine line, especially for Muslim men in the West. While they are striving for acceptance, they are being singled out by the public and profiled by the authorities. To the conservative Muslims, they lack ethnic authenticity and have sold out their true faith for the price of admission to the West. To the dominant group of their Western homes, they are suspects deserving to be watched.

POSTSCRIPT

My personal experiences have suggested that men's class position creates more commonalities than do their combined ethnic and religious background. During my first 2 years of college, I rented an apartment from an Armenian woman in a lower-middle-class neighborhood of old Tehran. My landlady, a businesswoman, covered her hair like her Muslim neighbors, though slightly differently. The majority of the shops and businesses belonged to ethnic Iranians. The prominent distinguishing feature of the community was not its religious plurality, but rather its rich language diversity. The men looked, acted, and treated their businesses and their families very similarly. The only way you knew their religious background was through their language. With each other, they spoke in Farsi; with their ethnic members, they broke into Armani, Turkish, and Kurdish, with a few sprinkles of Assyrian. As expected, they knew their customers' backgrounds and spoke appropriate languages. The class distinction bound men of my neighborhood from the lower middle class of the old city, to the middle class of suburbia, and later to the yuppie condos. Their diverse ideologies of Sunni and Shiia Islam, Christian Armenian, Kalimi Jewry, and later Marxism-Leninism, were secondary.

Men's social class and its associated life chances are the primary factors in their identity construction. Their ethnicity, rural or urban background, and religious orientations contribute to their agency in constructing masculinity out of opposing trends and pressures. Feminist men oppose the spread of Shari'at, for it can restrict women's civil rights. Contrary to expectations that Islamic states will increase men's advantages, in countries that have implemented Shari'at law, men are not faring better in terms of economic gains or life chances of health, education, or improved standards of living. If fundamentalist governments were to improve men's opportunities, Afghani men should have been at the forefront of Muslim masculinities.

Schacht and Ewing (1998) remind us of a feminist agenda of "creating nonoppressive realities" by challenging "the invisible ways patriarchal and corresponding gender assumptions have dominated our thinking" (p. 14). The current demonization of brown men in the Western media, particularly American, is harmful to all of us. The pervasiveness and the penetrating power of American media beckon us to challenge its continuous vilification of Muslim and Middle Eastern men. A study of Muslim masculinities is necessary, for it will aid women and gender studies in the Muslim societies, it will help Muslim men to understand and negotiate rapid social changes, and it will aid Western masculinity studies in going beyond self-absorption with sexuality and in further incorporating the discourse of imperialism into the mainstream of gender discourse and perhaps the popular culture. Finally, it will help to make real Muslim masculinities visible.

REFERENCES

Abdel Kader, S. (1987). *Egyptian women in a changing society, 1899-1987.* Boulder, CO: Lynne Rienner.

Afshar, H. (1998). *Islam and feminism: An Iranian case study.* New York: St. Martin's.

Ahmed, L. (1992). *Women and gender in Islam: Historical roots of the modern debate.* New Haven, CT: Yale University Press.

Allievi, S. (2002, December). Converts and the making of European Islam. *International Institute for the Study of Islam in the Modern World Newsletter, 11.* Retrieved February 10, 2004, from www.isim.nl/files/newsl_11.pdf

Arkin, W., & Dobrofsky, L. R. (1978). Military socialization and masculinity. In *Journal of Social Issues, 34*(1), 151-168.

Armbrust, W. (2000). Farid Shauqi: Tough guy, family man, and cinema star. In M. Ghoussoub & E. Sinclair-Webb (Eds.), *Imagined masculinities: Male identity and culture in the modern Middle East.* London: Saqi.

Bangstad, S. (2002, December). Revisiting PAGAD: Machoism or Islamism? *International Institute for the Study of Islam in the Modern World Newsletter, 11,* 10.

Bayat, A. (2003, December). The use and abuse of "Muslim Societies." *International Institute for the Study of Islam in the Modern World Newsletter, 13.* Retrieved February 10, 2004, from www.isim.nl/files/Newsl_13.pdf

Coes, D. V. (1995). *Macroeconomic crises, policies, and growth in Brazil, 1964-1990.* Washington, DC: World Bank.

Duroche, L. (1990). Male perception as social construction. In J. Hearn & D. Morgan (Eds.), *Men, masculinities and social theory.* London: Unwin Hyman.

Edwards, T. (1990). Beyond sex and gender: Masculinity, homosexuality and social theory. In J. Hearn & D. Morgan (Eds.), *Men, masculinities and social theory.* London: Unwin Hyman.

Esack, F. (2003). In search of progressive Islam beyond 9/11. In O. Safi (Ed.), *Progressive Muslims.* Oxford, UK: Oneworld.

Esposito, J. (2003). *Unholy war.* New York: Oxford University Press.

Gerami, S. (1996). *Women and fundamentalism: Islam and Christianity.* New York: Garland.

Gerami, S. (2003a). Men and immigration. In M. Kimmel & A. Aronson (Eds.), *Men and masculinities: A social, cultural, and historical encyclopedia.* Santa Barbara, CA: ABC-CLIO.

Gerami, S. (2003b). Mullahs, martyrs and *men*: Conceptualizing masculinity in the Islamic Republic of Iran. *Men and Masculinities, 5*(3), 257-295.

Gerami, S., & Safiri, M. (in press). Qur'an: Women and modern interpretations, late 1800 to the present. In S. Joseph & A. Najmabadi (Eds.), *Encyclopedia of women and Islamic cultures.* Thousand Oaks, CA: Sage.

Hamas woman bomber kills Israelis. (2004, January 14). *BBC News World Edition.* Retrieved from http://news.bbc.co.uk

Hegland, M. (1995). Shi'a women of Northwest Pakistan and agency through practice: Ritual, resistance, resilience. *Political and Legal Anthropology Review, 18,* 65-79.

Kaplan, D. (2000). The military as a second bar mitzvah: Combat service as initiation to Zionist masculinity. In M. Ghoussoub & E. Sinclair-Webb (Eds.), *Imagined masculinities: Male identity and culture in the modern Middle East.* London: Saqi.

Kegan Gardiner, J. (2000). Introduction. In J. Kegan Gardiner (Ed.), *Masculinity studies and feminist theory.* New York: Columbia University Press.

Khedimellah, M. (2002, December). Aesthetics and poetics of apostolic Islam in France. *International Institute for the Study of Islam in the Modern World Newsletter, 11,* 20.

Kimmel, M. (2004). Gender, class and terrorism. In M. Kimmel & M. Messner, *Men's lives* (6th ed.). Boston: Allyn and Bacon.

Kimmel, M., & Messner, M. (2001). *Men's lives* (5th ed.). Boston: Allyn and Bacon.

Kurzman, C. (2002, Fall/Winter). Bin Laden and other thoroughly modern Muslims. *Contexts,* 13-20.

Lawrence, B. (1998). *Shattering the myth: Islam beyond violence.* Princeton, NJ: Princeton University Press.

Leaman, O. (2001). *Companion encyclopedia of Middle Eastern and North African film.* London: Routledge.

Lubeck, P. (2000). The Islamic revival: Antinomies of Islamic movements under globalization. In R. Cohen & S. M. Rai (Eds.), *Global social movements.* New Brunswick, NJ: Athlone.

Merton, R. (1968). *Social theory and social structure.* New York: Free Press.

Mir-Hosseini, Z. (1999). *Islam and gender: The religious debate in contemporary Iran.* Princeton, NJ: Princeton University Press.

Onis, Z., & Webb, S. B. (1994). Turkey: Democratization and adjustment from above. In S. Haggard & S. B. Webb (Eds.), *Voting for reform.* Oxford, UK: Oxford University Press.

Peteet, J. (2000). Male gender and rituals of resistance in the Palestinian Intifada: A cultural politics of violence. In M. Ghoussoub & E. Sinclair-Webb (Eds.), *Imagined masculinities: Male identity and culture in the modern Middle East.* London: Saqi.

Pleck, J. H., & Sawyer, J. (Eds.). (1974). *Men and masculinity.* Englewood Cliffs, NJ: Prentice Hall.

Ratnesar, R., & Zabriskis, P. (2004, January 26). The rise of the *Jihadists. Time,* pp. 30-31.

Sachs, S. (2000, July 22). In Iran, more women leaving the nest for university. *New York Times.* Retrieved February 10, 2004, from www .library.cornell.edu/colldev/mideast/irnwmnz .htm

Saghieh, H. (2000). "That's how I am, world!": Saddam, manhood and monolithic image. In M. Ghoussoub & E. Sinclair-Webb (Eds.), *Imagined masculinities: Male identity and culture in the modern Middle East.* London: Saqi.

Said, E. (2003, August 4). *Orientalism* 25 years later. *CounterPunch.* Retrieved February 10, 2004, from www.counterpunch.org/said08052003.html

Salehi Esfahani, H., & Taheripour, F. (2002). Hidden public expenditures and the economy in Iran. *International Journal of Middle East Studies, 34,* 691-718.

Schacht, S. P., & Ewing, D. W. (Eds.). (1998). *Feminism and men: Reconstructing gender relations.* New York: New York University Press.

Shehadeh, L. R. (2003). *The idea of women in fundamentalist Islam.* Gainesville: University Press of Florida.

Sinclair-Webb, E. (2000). "Our bulent is now a commando": Military service and manhood in Turkey. In M. Ghoussoub & E. Sinclair-Webb (Eds.), *Imagined masculinities: Male identity and culture in the modern Middle East.* London: Saqi.

Soroush, A. (2000). *Reason, freedom and democracy in Islam* (M. Sadri & A. Sadri, Eds. and Trans.). Oxford, UK: Oxford University Press.

UNESCO Institute of Statistics. (2000-2001). *Statistical tables.* Retrieved from www.uis. unesco .org/TEMPLATE/html/Exceltables/education/ ger_tertiary.xls

United Nations Population Division. (2002). *Annex tables.* Retrieved from www.un.org/esa/population/ publications/wpp2002/wpp2002annextables. PDF

Wickham, C. (2002). *Mobilizing Islam: Religion, activism and political change in Egypt.* New York: Columbia University Press.

Wiktorowicz, Q. (2001). *The management of Islamic activism: Salafis, the Muslim brotherhood and state power in Jordan.* Albany: State University of New York Press.

27

MEN'S COLLECTIVE STRUGGLES FOR GENDER JUSTICE

The Case of Antiviolence Activism

MICHAEL FLOOD

Men's collective struggles for gender justice are an important aspect of contemporary contestations of gender. Groups and networks of men across the globe, often in collaboration with women, are engaged in public efforts in support of gender equality. Men's antiviolence activism is the most visible and well-developed aspect of such efforts. Among the range of groups and campaigns enacted by men in the name of progressive gender agendas over the last three decades, antiviolence work has been the most persistent focus, has attracted the largest involvements, and has achieved the greatest international participation. Men's antiviolence activism therefore is an important case study of male involvement in struggles for gender justice. What does this activism involve, why do men participate, and how do patriarchal inequalities shape both men's efforts and their reception?

Antisexist men's networks and campaigns are an instance of "masculinity politics"—"those mobilisations and struggles where the meaning of masculine gender is at issue, and, with it, men's position in gender relations" (Connell,

1995, p. 205). Four other forms of masculinity politics currently visible among men include gay men's movements, men's groups and networks focused on "men's liberation" or "masculinity therapy," mythopoetic men's groups, and men's rights and fathers' rights groups engaged in a defense of patriarchal masculinity. These diverse forms of gendered activity are both symptoms of and contributors to a wider problematization of men and men's practices (Hearn, 2001, p. 85). A range of terms has been used to describe male political and intellectual endeavors sympathetic to feminism, from antisexist and antipatriarchal to profeminist.

Men's collective and profeminist mobilizations on gender issues are a delicate form of political activity, as they involve the mobilization of members of a privileged group in order to undermine that same privilege. Most if not all contemporary societies are characterized by men's institutional privilege (Messner, 1997, p. 5), such that men in general receive a "patriarchal dividend" from gendered structures of inequality (Connell, 1995, pp. 79-82). The danger, therefore, is that by mobilizing men collectively as men and thus drawing on their shared interests, activists inadvertently will entrench gender privilege (Connell, 1995, pp. 234-238). This potential has been realized among men's rights and fathers' rights groups, which are energetically engaged in an antiwomen and antifeminist backlash (Flood, 1997, 1998).

However, men can be and are motivated by interests other than those associated with gender privilege. There are important resources in men's lives for the construction of nonviolent masculinities and forms of selfhood, such as men's concerns for children, intimacies with women, and ethical and political commitments. Furthermore, given the intersection of gender with other social divisions of race, class, sexuality, nation, and so on, men share very unequally in the fruits of gender privilege (Messner, 1997, p. 7), and men's material interests are multiple and complex. The argument that men have contradictory experiences of power, pioneered by Kaufman (1993), is influential in international discourses of male involvement in movements toward nonviolence and gender equality. Kaufman (2003, p. 14) argues that efforts to involve men in building gender equality must simultaneously challenge men's power and speak to men's pain.

The tension here between men's shared patriarchal interests and their interests in undermining patriarchy is one with which any men's activism for gender justice must reckon. This same tension is evident in the answers offered to the question "Why should men change?" There are two broad responses: Men ought to change, and it is in men's interests to change. First, given the fact of men's unjust privilege, there is an ethical obligation for men to act in support of the elimination of that privilege (Pease, 2002, pp. 167-168). The basis of profeminist men's politics is the moral imperative that men give up their unjust share of power (Brod, 1998, p. 199). Second, men themselves will benefit from supporting feminism and advancing toward gender equality. Although men's position brings power and status, it also involves burdens, such that men's self-interest can be served by supporting feminism (Kaufman, 2003, p. 13; Kilmartin, 2001, pp. 29-30; Pease, 2002, pp. 166-167).

This second reason is more contentious, as there are dangers of men asserting their interests at women's expense, denying male privilege and seeing themselves as victims. Yet to sustain their involvement, it is important for men to see their stake in feminist futures. As Brod (1998, p. 199) argues, "self-sacrificing altruism is insufficient as the basis for a political movement" and there is "a moral imperative to go beyond mere moral imperatives." It is therefore vital that antisexist men invite men to see beyond prevailing patriarchal constructions of men's interests and articulate nonpatriarchal notions of what Pease (2002, p. 173) calls men's "emancipatory interests" and Brod (1998, p. 199) calls men's "long-term enlightened self-interest."

ANTIVIOLENCE ACTIVISM

Men's violence against women has been a key focus of antisexist men's groups since they first emerged in the early 1970s in response to the second wave of feminism. Violence against women is widely identified as a central element in gender injustice, as both an expression of men's power over women and a way to maintain that power. Men's antiviolence activism therefore addresses a paradigmatic expression of patriarchal power. This activism has intensified and spread since the early 1990s. In many countries, both developing and developed, groups of men have emerged whose agenda is to end men's violence against women and children. They share the fundamental premise that men must take responsibility for stopping men's violence. Taking responsibility begins with individual men taking personal steps to minimize their use of violence (Funk, 1993, pp. 95-111; Kimmel, 1993; Madhubuti, 1993; Warshaw, 1988, pp. 161-167; Weinberg & Biernbaum, 1993). But it goes beyond this, to public and collective action. Antiviolence men's groups engage in community education; hold rallies and marches; work with violent men; facilitate workshops in schools, prisons, and workplaces; and act in alliance with women's groups and organizations. There are at least two other ways in which men have been involved in antiviolence efforts: as the participants in programs for perpetrators of violence and as the targets of public education campaigns that aim to increase men's understanding of and opposition to violence against women. The discussion in this chapter focuses largely on efforts by men that are community based and often voluntary.

The best known example of men's antiviolence activism is the White Ribbon Campaign, a grassroots education campaign that spans at least four continents and 35 countries. The White Ribbon Campaign is the largest collective effort in the world among men working to end men's violence against women. It began in 1991 on the second anniversary of one man's massacre of 14 women in Montreal, Canada, and it has spread to the United States, Europe, Africa, Latin America, Asia, and Australia. During White Ribbon Week, in November each year, men are encouraged to show their opposition to men's violence against women by purchasing and wearing a white ribbon. In pinning on the ribbon, men pledge themselves never to commit, condone, or remain silent about violence against women. The White Ribbon Campaign also involves year-round educational strategies, including advertising campaigns, concerts, fathers' walks, and fund-raising for women's organizations. Monies raised by the campaign go to services for the victims and survivors of violence and to women's advocacy programs. In Canada, close to 180,000 ribbons were distributed in 2002 and 250,000 in 2001.

Alongside this international campaign, there are men's groups in at least a dozen countries that share the goal of ending men's violence against women. In Mumbai, India, the Men Against Abuse and Violence is a volunteer organization focused on ending domestic violence (Greig, Kimmel, & Lang, 2000, p. 12). A substantial educational campaign in Central America aimed at men and tackling domestic violence began in 1999. In Nicaragua, Puntos de Encuentro (Meeting Points) and the Asociación de Hombres Contra la Violencia (Men Against Violence) ran a large-scale campaign encouraging men to respect their partners, resolve conflicts peacefully, and seek help to avoid domestic violence (Solórzano & Montoya, 2001). In Namibia, a National Conference on Men Against Violence Against Women was held in February 2000 (Odendaal, 2001, pp. 90-91), and men are involved in networks against gender-based violence in Malawi, Kenya, South Africa, and Zimbabwe (Wainana, 2002). In Australia, Men Against Sexual Assault (MASA) began in 1989, a national network of MASA groups was established over the period from 1989 to 1992, and at MASA's height, marches of 300 to 500 men were held in many capital cities (Fuller & Fisher, 1998, p. 3).

Men's antiviolence groups appear to be most well established in North America. There are more than 100 such groups in the United States, including Men Overcoming Violence (MOVE) in San Francisco, the Atlanta-based Men Stopping Violence, and the Men's Resource Centre in Massachusetts. Men Can Stop Rape in Washington, D.C., mobilizes young men across the United States to behave as allies to women in preventing rape and other forms of men's violence. Such groups share the belief that men must act to stop men's violence. As a full-page newspaper advertisement taken out by the Men's Resource Centre in November 1999 proclaimed, "We call on all men to reject the masculine culture of violence and to work with us to create a culture of connection, of cooperation and of safety for women, for men and for children" (*Daily Hampshire Gazette*, November 11, 1999, p. B7).

There is a growing international dialogue on men's involvement in stopping violence against women. From June to October 2002, 560 people from 46 countries participated in a Virtual Seminar Series on Men's Roles and Responsibilities in Ending Gender-Based Violence, hosted by the United Nations International Research and Training Institute for the Advancement of Women (INSTRAW). From May to July 2003, a similar online discussion series on "Building Partnerships to End Men's Violence" was sponsored by the United States–based Family Violence Prevention Fund.

Men's antiviolence groups and organizations have adopted strategies of both violence prevention and violence intervention. Prevention aims to lessen the likelihood of men using violence in the first place by undermining the beliefs, values, and discourses that support violence, challenging the patriarchal power relations that promote and are maintained by violence, and promoting alternative constructions of masculinity, gender, and selfhood that foster nonviolence and gender justice. A recent example is Men Can Stop Rape's campaign called "My strength is not for hurting." The Strength Campaign includes presentations to high schools, posters for schools and buses, a handbook for teachers and school staff, and a youth magazine. All address men's role as women's allies in ending violence in dating relationships by encouraging men to practice consent and respect in their sexual relations.

Violence intervention refers to strategies focused on those people who have committed acts of violence and those people who have been subject to violence. Some men's antiviolence groups work with male perpetrators of violence, including men who have volunteered to participate in counseling programs and men in court-mandated groups within the criminal justice system. Men's antiviolence activists share a commitment to the provision of appropriate resources and services for the victims and survivors of men's violence.

An important way in which antiviolence education has been conducted is to find examples of boys' and men's resistance to hegemonic and violent masculinities and evidence of their gender-equitable practice, then to foster communities of support with which to sustain and spread these. Among boys, an educator may identify already existing interests in and commitments to nonviolent relations with girls and women, find exceptions to dominant practices and narratives of masculinity, affirm and build on such histories, and identify significant others who can support them (Denborough, 1996). For example, in an action-research project in low-income settings in Rio de Janeiro, Brazil, young men who questioned prevailing violence-supportive views were trained as peer educators to foster gender-equitable relations in their communities (Barker, 2001).

Men's antiviolence work has involved a wide range of creative strategies, including the use of film in India to encourage men to reflect on their relations with women (Roy, 2001), "guerrilla theater" in South African bars to spark discussion, the distribution of pamphlets to men in community markets in Cambodia (Kaufman, 2003, p. 36), and a "Walk Across America" to raise community awareness about violence against women. Although men's antiviolence efforts often aim to shift men's attitudes in order to shift their behavior, some also work in the reverse direction. By inviting men to publicly commit to a course of action, such as by wearing a white ribbon or participating in an antirape rally, some strategies aim to increase men's private acceptance of the attitudes that support that behavior (Kilmartin, 2001, p. 70). Other strategies empower men to resist conformity to sexist peer norms. Men typically overestimate each other's comfort with coercive and derogatory comments about and behavior toward women, so that publicizing survey results documenting men's discomfort with other men's sexism can

undermine male approval of sexist behavior (Kilmartin, 2001, pp. 63-66).

Antirape education efforts directed at men have an increasing presence on university campuses, particularly in North America. Campus rape-prevention programs typically are conducted by male peer educators, among all-male groups, and address men's acceptance of violence-supportive myths and lack of empathy for victims of rape. Such efforts generally result in positive changes in men's attitudes and their intentions to commit rape and sexually coercive behavior (Earle, 1996; Foubert, 2000; Foubert & Marriott, 1997; Foubert & McEwen, 1998; Parrot, Cummings, & Marchell, 1994; Schewe & O'Donohue, 1993, 1996; Smith & Welchans, 2000).

Boys and young men in schools are a particularly important target group for antiviolence efforts. Many males come to university, paid work, and other adult settings with proabuse attitudes already firmly in place, having grown up in home, school, and peer contexts that foster tolerance for violence against women (DeKeseredy, Schwartz, & Alvi, 2000, pp. 925-926). In antiviolence education, "starting young" is vital, because adolescence is a crucial period in terms of women's and men's formation of healthy, nonviolent relationships later in life (National Campaign Against Violence and Crime, 1998, p. 23). Recognizing that the formal and informal processes of schools have a critical role in either discouraging or encouraging violence, both men's groups and government agencies have developed programs for boys and young men in school settings (Cameron, 2000; Gilbert & Gilbert, 1998, pp. 222-251; Kaufman, 2003, pp. 27-28).

What motivates the men who are active in struggles against men's violence against women? What inspires men to question sexist cultural values and patriarchal power relations? John Stoltenberg (1990) offers an account of how men come to join the struggle for women's equality, and its themes are pertinent ones for these questions. Some men come to antisexist involvements because their loyalty and closeness to a particular woman in their lives—a mother, a partner, a friend, a sister—has forged an intimate understanding of the injustices suffered by women and the need for men to take action. Some men's advocacy is grounded in other forms of principled political activism, such as pacifism, economic justice, green issues, or gay liberation. They have been exposed to feminist and related ideals through their political involvements, their workplaces, or their higher education. Others become involved through dealing with their own experience of sexual violence or sexual abuse from other men and sometimes women, perhaps as children or teenagers (Stoltenberg, 1990, pp. 11-12). Men's commitments to the movement against violence against women have blossomed in the same soil of deeply felt personal experiences; particular relationships, intimacies, and loyalties; and ethical and political involvements.

For Gender Justice

Men's antiviolence activism is significant in at least two ways. First, this activity symbolizes the growing recognition that violence against women will cease only when men join with women to put an end to it. Men are the overwhelming majority of the perpetrators of violence against women, a substantial minority of males accept violence-supportive attitudes and beliefs, and cultural constructions of masculinity inform men's use of physical and sexual violence against women. Profound changes in men's lives, gendered power relations, and the social construction of masculinity are necessary if violence against women is to be eliminated.

More widely, in working to transform the social structures, relationships, and ideologies on which gender inequality is based, it is vital to engage with men and boys (Kaufman, 2003, p. 1). Many men participate in sexist practices and the maintenance of unjust gender relations, men often play a crucial role as "gatekeepers" of the current gender order and as decision makers and community leaders, and men's own health and well-being are limited by contemporary constructions of manhood. Involving men in efforts toward achieving gender equality runs the risk of reinforcing men's existing power and jeopardizing resources and funding directed at women, so the goal of promoting gender justice must be central. Male participation is not a goal in itself, but a means to an end: healthy and non-violent relations for all.

The notion that it is desirable to involve men in the movements to stop violence against women and girls is rapidly becoming institutionalized in the philosophies and programs of international organizations. The Beijing Platform for Action in 1995 recognized that "men's groups mobilising against gender violence are necessary allies for change," and this was reaffirmed and extended in the follow-up meeting in 2000 (Hayward, 2001, p. 49). In 1997, at the regional meeting titled "Ending Violence Against Women and Girls in South Asia," sponsored by the United Nations International Children's Emergency Fund (UNICEF), the United Nations Development Fund for Women (UNIFEM), and the United Nations Development Programme (UNDP), the 100 or so men present added the following statement to the Katmandu Commitment, issued at the meeting: "We men, realizing that no sustainable change can take place unless we give up the entrenched ideas of male superiority, commit ourselves to devising new role models of masculinity" (UNICEF, 1998; cited in Hayward, 1999, p. 9). Also in 1997, the United Nations Educational, Scientific, and Cultural Organization (UNESCO) held an Expert Group Meeting in Oslo on "Male Roles and Masculinities in the Perspective of a Culture of Peace." Participants emphasized that the transformation from a culture of violence to a culture of peace depends on the development of more egalitarian and partnership-oriented forms of masculinity, as opposed to traditional forms premised on dominance, authority, control, and force (AVSC International and International Planned Parenthood Federation/Western Hemisphere Region, 1998, pp. 66-67).

Second, the existence of men's antiviolence activism demonstrates that men *can* take collective public action to oppose men's violence. The groups and campaigns I have described represent successful attempts to create among men, albeit sometimes small numbers of men, a public response to men's violence. More broadly, men can and do organize and agitate in support of gender justice. There are historical precedents in men's organized support for women's suffrage and equality in the 18th and 19th centuries (John & Eustance, 1997; Kimmel & Mosmiller, 1992; Strauss, 1982). In addition, contemporary men's antiviolence groups are one expression of a wider network of profeminist men's activism, represented for example by the National Organization of Men Against Sexism (NOMAS) in the United States, the European Profeminist Men's Network, the Men for Change Network in the United Kingdom, and emergent progressive men's networks in Africa and elsewhere. Thus, "it is not a question of whether men can take action but how" (Pease, 1997, p. 76).

PARTNERSHIPS ACROSS GENDER

Partnerships with women are central to men's antiviolence efforts. Most of the men's groups and organizations I have described conduct their efforts in alliance with women and women's groups involved in antiviolence campaigns or in services for the victims of violence. More radically, many profeminist men's groups position themselves as accountable to feminist constituencies: They consult with women's groups before initiating their campaigns, do not compete with women's groups for funding or other resources, and build strong lines of communication and trust (Funk, 1993, pp. 125-126, 132-134). There are debates over the processes through which accountability is established (Hall, 1994) and over *which* feminism one is accountable to, and given the diversity of feminisms, this is an ongoing issue.

Men's partnerships with antiviolence women's groups are critical. They enable men to learn from existing efforts and scholarship rather than "reinventing the wheel." They lessen the risk that men will collude in or comply with dominant and oppressive forms of masculinity. They are a powerful and practical demonstration of men's and women's shared interest in stopping violence. Men's partnerships with women are an inspiring example of cross-gender collaboration, a form of activism that reaches across and transforms gender inequalities.

Should men's efforts to end men's violence be linked to wider struggles for gender equality, social justice, and human rights? Michael Kaufman writes pragmatically that in order for large numbers of men to unite to end violence, they should put aside their differences over other issues of gender and justice such as abortion (Kaufman, 2000). Keith Pringle, on the other hand, firmly locates men's work against violence within a broader antioppressive practice. Men challenging violent masculinities must also address other dimensions of oppression that intersect with gendered domination (Pringle, 1995, p. 150). Support for Pringle's position comes from the scholarship on cross-cultural predictors of violence against women.

Levels of violence against women are higher in societies showing male economic and decision-making dominance in the family, and wife abuse is more likely in couples with a dominant husband and an economically dependent wife (Heise, 1998, pp. 270-271). Given that men's violence is fueled by and itself perpetuates gender inequalities (and other forms of injustice), antiviolence work should be situated within a broader project of gender justice.

Although men must take action in support of gender justice, this in no way means that women's groups and campaigns must include men. There continue to be reasons why "women's space," women-only, and women-focused campaigns are vital: to support those who are most disadvantaged by pervasive gender inequalities, to maintain women's solidarity and leadership, and to foster women's consciousness-raising and collective empowerment. Nor should growing attention to male involvement threaten resources for women and women's programs. At the same time, reaching men to reduce and prevent violence against women is, by definition, spending money to meet the interests and needs of women, and it will expand the financial and political support available to women's programs (Kaufman, 2003, p. 11).

Men's and mixed-sex antiviolence projects are important sites for the daily reconstruction of gender identities and relations. Antisexist men's consciousness-raising groups have been used since the early 1970s to facilitate a critical self-questioning of sexist practice, to build peer support for new ways of being, and to provide a basis for public activism. Antipatriarchal consciousness-raising can be effective in constructing profeminist subjectivities among men, and it is an important element in wider articulations of a collective profeminist politics (Pease, 2000, p. 55). For example, an American women's network that recruited male volunteers as antiviolence educators reports that it now has strong male allies, dedicated volunteers who are making a difference to its social change work (Mohan & Schultz, 2001, pp. 29-30). In another example, although men in a campus-based Men Against Violence network showed defensive homophobic responses to others' perceptions of gayness and effeminacy and espoused chivalric notions of themselves as protectors and defenders of women, they also engaged in a substantial rejection or reformulation of key constructions of stereotypical masculinity (Hong, 2000).

Men's collective efforts to undermine patriarchal inequalities are themselves shaped by those same inequalities. Although many men's participation in antiviolence movements is informed by their critical distance from hegemonic masculinity, they also may struggle with complicity in patriarchal behaviors and attitudes. Many men have carried an "invisible backpack" of privilege, a taken-for-granted set of unearned benefits and assets (McIntosh, 1989). It is understandable, therefore, that feminist women have been hesitant about men's participation in campaigns against violence (DeKeseredy et al., 2000, p. 922). The American women's network mentioned above also encountered sexism, lack of empathy for survivors, and stereotypical expectations of their roles as women (Mohan & Schultz, 2001). When women and men work together, gendered norms of male-female interaction can hinder egalitarian relationships and drain women's labor and emotional energies. In ways that mirror the patterns of traditional heterosexual relationships (Duncombe & Marsden, 1995, p. 246), men may expect nurturance and emotional support from women, and women may comply with unequal relations because of their internalized sexism.

The public reception of men's antiviolence work also is shaped by patriarchal privilege. First, men's groups receive greater media attention and interest than similar groups of women (Luxton, 1993, p. 368). This is partly the result of the former's novelty, but it is also a function of the status and cultural legitimacy granted to men's voices in general. Second, men acting for gender justice receive praise and credit (especially from women) that often is out of proportion to their efforts. Any positive action by men may be seen as gratifying in the face of other men's apathy about and complicity in violence against women. Third, men are able to draw on their and other men's institutional privilege to attract levels of support and funding rarely granted to women (Landsberg, 2000, p. 15). This can, of course, be turned to strategic advantage in pursuing an end to men's violence.

Profeminist men's public challenge to dominant masculinities also attracts the ridicule, contempt, and anger of men who consider them to be wimps and sissies, gay, or traitors (Luxton, 1993, p. 360). For example, in response to my articles on the profeminist Web site XYonline, one fathers' rights advocate wrote by e-mail that I was a "fucking faggot, feminazi pussy licker." This response, with its hostility toward and conflation of homosexuality and femininity, is typical of the coercive ways in which dominant constructions of masculinity are policed among boys and men in general. Homophobia is a key means of policing heterosexual masculinities (Epstein & Johnson, 1994, p. 204), and among adolescent boys, the term "gay" or other abusive synonyms is a "principal repository for unacceptable male 'otherness'" (Plummer, 1999, p. 81).

Men's collective activism is a vital element in the struggle to end violence against women. As with international efforts on other gender-related issues such as HIV/AIDS, sexual and reproductive health, poverty, and development, in working against violence it is critical to involve men. Men's participation must be guided by gender justice and gender partnership, as these principles are integral to men's ability to cultivate a lasting legacy of peace.

REFERENCES

AVSC International and International Planned Parenthood Federation (IPPF)/Western Hemisphere Region. (1998, October). *Literature review for the symposium on male participation in sexual and reproductive health: New paradigms.* Oaxaca, Mexico.

Barker, G. (2001). "Cool your head, man": Preventing gender based violence in favelas. *Development, 4*(3), 94-98.

Brod, H. (1998). To be a man, or not to be a man—that is the feminist question. In T. Digby (Ed.), *Men doing feminism* (pp. 197-212). New York: Routledge.

Cameron, M. (2000). *Young men and violence prevention* (Trends and Issues in Crime and Criminal Justice No. 154). Canberra: Australian Institute of Criminology.

Connell, R. W. (1995). *Masculinities.* Sydney: Allen & Unwin.

DeKeseredy, W. S., Schwartz, M. D., & Alvi, S. (2000). The role of profeminist men in dealing with woman abuse on the Canadian college campus. *Violence Against Women, 6*(9), 918-935.

Denborough, D. (1996). Step by step: Developing respectful and effective ways of working with young men to reduce violence. In C. McLean, M. Carey, & C. White (Eds.), *Men's ways of being* (pp. 91-115). Boulder, CO: Westview.

Duncombe, J., & Marsden, D. (1995). Can men love? "Reading," "staging" and "resisting" the romance. In L. Pearce & J. Stacey (Eds.), *Romance revisited* (pp. 238-250). London: Lawrence & Wishart.

Earle, J. P. (1996). Acquaintance rape workshops: Their effectiveness in changing the attitudes of first year college men. *National Association of Student Personnel Administrators, 34*(1), 2-18.

Epstein, D., & Johnson, R. (1994). On the straight and narrow: The heterosexual presumption, homophobias and schools. In D. Epstein (Ed.), *Challenging lesbian and gay inequalities in education* (pp. 197-230). Buckingham, UK: Open University Press.

Flood, M. (1997). Responding to men's rights. *XY: Men, Sex, Politics, 7*(2), 37-40.

Flood, M. (1998, June). Men's movements. *Community Quarterly, 46,* 62-71.

Foubert, J. D. (2000). The longitudinal effects of a rape-prevention program on fraternity men's attitudes, behavioral intent, and behavior. *Journal of American College Health, 48,* 158-163.

Foubert, J. D., & Marriott, K. A. (1997). Effects of a sexual assault peer education program on men's belief in rape myths. *Sex Roles, 36*(3/4), 259-268.

Foubert, J. D., & McEwen, M. K. (1998). An all-male rape prevention peer education program: Decreasing fraternity men's behavioral intent to rape. *Journal of College Student Development, 39*(6), 548-556.

Fuller, B., & Fisher, S. (1998, June). A decade of pro-feminist activism: A brief history of men against sexual assault. *Community Quarterly, 46,* 7.

Funk, R. E. (1993). *Stopping rape: A challenge for men.* Philadelphia: New Society Publishers.

Gilbert, R., & Gilbert, P. (1998). *Masculinity goes to school.* Sydney: Allen & Unwin.

Greig, A., Kimmel, M., & Lang, J. (2000). *Men, masculinities & development: Broadening our work towards gender equality* (Gender in Development Monograph Series No. 10). New York: United Nations Development Programme.

Hall, R. (1994). Partnership accountability. *Dulwich Centre Newsletter, 2/3,* 6-29.

Hayward, R. (1999, October). *Needed: A new model of masculinity to stop violence against girls and women.* Presented at the WHO Global Symposium on Violence and Health, Kobe, Japan.

Hayward, R. (2001). Needed: A culture of masculinity for the fulfilment of human rights. *Development, 4*(3), 48-53.

Hearn, J. (2001). Men stopping men's violence to women. *Development, 4*(3), 85-89.

Heise, L. L. (1998). Violence against women: An integrated, ecological framework. *Violence Against Women, 4*(3), 262-283.

Hong, L. (2000). Toward a transformed approach to prevention: Breaking the link between masculinity and violence. *Journal of American College Health, 48*(6), 269-279.

John, A. V., & Eustance, C. (Eds.). (1997). *The men's share? Masculinities, male support and women's suffrage in Britain, 1890–1920.* London: Routledge.

Kaufman, M. (1993). *Cracking the armour: Power, pain and the lives of men.* Toronto: Penguin.

Kaufman, M. (2000). Working with men and boys to challenge sexism and end men's violence. In I. Breines, R. Connell, & I. Eide (Eds.), *Male roles, masculinities and violence: A culture of peace perspective* (pp. 211-222). Paris: UNESCO Publishing.

Kaufman, M. (2003). *The AIM framework: Addressing and involving men and boys to promote gender equality and end gender discrimination and violence.* New York: UNICEF. Available at www.michaelkaufman.com

Kilmartin, C. T. (2001). *Sexual assault in context: Teaching college men about gender.* Holmes Beach, FL: Learning Publications.

Kimmel, M. S. (1993). Clarence, William, Iron Mike, Tailhook, Senator Packwood, Spur Posse, Magic . . . and us. In E. Buchwald, P. Fletcher, & M. Roth (Eds.), *Transforming a rape culture* (pp. 119-138). Minneapolis: Milkweed Editions.

Kimmel, M. S., & Mosmiller, T. E. (1992). *Against the tide: Pro-feminist men in the United States, 1776–1990.* Boston: Beacon.

Landsberg, M. (2000, Spring). Canadian feminists' uneasy alliance with men challenging violence. *Voice Male,* p. 15.

Luxton, M. (1993). Dreams and dilemmas: Feminist musings on "the man question." In T. Haddad (Ed.), *Men and masculinities: A critical anthology* (pp. 347-374). Toronto: Canadian Scholars' Press.

Madhubuti, H. R. (1993). On becoming anti-rapist. In E. Buchwald, P. Fletcher, & M. Roth (Eds.), *Transforming a rape culture* (pp. 165-178). Minneapolis: Milkweed Editions.

McIntosh, P. (1989, July/August). White privilege: Unpacking the invisible knapsack. *Peace and Freedom.* Retrieved January 30, 2004, from www.vanderbilt.edu/cft/resources/newsletters/vol2-2/mcintosh.htm

Messner, M. A. (1997). *Politics of masculinities: Men in movements.* Thousand Oaks, CA: Sage.

Mohan, L., & Schultz, A. (2001, October). Mauled by MAVEN: Our story of involving men in the movement. *Off Our Backs,* pp. 25-30.

National Campaign Against Violence and Crime. (1998). *Working with adolescents to prevent domestic violence.* Canberra, Australia: NCAVAC Unit, Attorney-General's Department.

Odendaal, W. (2001). The Men Against Violence Against Women movement in Namibia. *Development, 4*(3), 90-93.

Parrot, A., Cummings, N., & Marchell, T. (1994). *Rape 101: Sexual assault prevention for college athletes.* Holmes Beach, FL: Learning Publications.

Pease, B. (1997). *Men & sexual politics: Towards a profeminist practice.* Adelaide, Australia: Dulwich Centre Publications.

Pease, B. (2000). *Recreating men: Postmodern masculinity politics.* London: Sage.

Pease, B. (2002). (Re)constructing men's interests. *Men and Masculinities, 5*(2), 165-177.

Plummer, D. (1999). *One of the boys: Masculinity, homophobia, and modern manhood.* New York: Harrington Park Press.

Pringle, K. (1995). *Men, masculinities and social welfare.* London: UCL Press.

Roy, R. (2001). The eyes are silent . . . the heart desires to speak: Exploring masculinities in South Asia. *Development, 4*(3), 15-20.

Schewe, P. A., & O'Donohue, W. T. (1993). Sexual abuse prevention with high risk males: The roles of victim empathy and rape myths. *Violence and Victims, 8*(4), 339-351.

Schewe, P. A., & O'Donohue, W. T. (1996). Rape prevention with high-risk males: Short-term outcome of two interventions. *Archives of Sexual Behavior, 25,* 455-471.

Smith, P., & Welchans, S. (2000). Peer education: Does focusing on male responsibility change sexual assault attitudes? *Violence Against Women, 6*(11), 1255-1268.

Solórzano, I., & Montoya, O. (2001, January 8). *Men against marital violence: A Nicaraguan campaign.* Retrieved January 27, 2004, from www.id21.org/static/insights35art5.htm

Stoltenberg, J. (1990). *Refusing to be a man: Essays on sex and justice.* New York: Penguin.

Strauss, S. (1982). *"Traitors to the masculine cause": The men's campaigns for women's rights.* Westport, CT: Greenwood.

Wainana, N. (2002). *Men as partners in the struggle for gender equality: The FEMNET experience* (Seminar 2, Virtual Seminar Series on Men's Roles and Responsibilities in Ending Gender-Based Violence). New York: United Nations International Research and Training Institute for the Advancement of Women. Retrieved February 6, 2003, from www.un-instraw.org/en/research/mensroles/vss/vss_2_3

Warshaw, R. (1988). *I never called it rape.* New York: Harper & Row.

Weinberg, J., & Biernbaum, M. (1993). The conversations of consent: Sexual intimacy without sexual assault. In E. Buchwald, P. Fletcher, & M. Roth (Eds.), *Transforming a rape culture* (pp. 87-100). Minneapolis: Milkweed Editions.

INDEX

About the Editors

Michael S. Kimmel is Professor of Sociology at the State University of New York at Stony Brook. His books include *Changing Men* (1987), *Men Confront Pornography* (1990), *Men's Lives* (6th edition, 2003), *Against the Tide: Profeminist Men in the United States, 1776-1990* (1992), *The Politics of Manhood* (1996), *Manhood: A Cultural History* (1996), *The Gendered Society* (2nd edition, 2003), and the *Encyclopedia of Men and Masculinities* (2004). He edits *Men and Masculinities,* an interdisciplinary scholarly journal. He is the spokesperson for the National Organization for Men Against Sexism (NOMAS) and lectures extensively on campuses in the United States and abroad.

Jeff Hearn is Academy Fellow and Professor, Swedish School of Economics, Helsinki, Finland, and Research Professor, University of Huddersfield, United Kingdom. His authored and coauthored books include *The Gender of Oppression* (1987), *Men in the Public Eye* (1992), *"Sex" at "Work"* (1987/1995), *The Violences of Men* (1998), *Gender, Sexuality and Violence in Organizations* (2001), and *Gender Divisions and Gender Policies in Top Finnish Companies* (2002). Coedited books include *The Sexuality of Organization* (1989), *Men, Masculinities, and Social Theory* (1990), *Violence and Gender Relations* (1996), *Men as Managers, Managers as Men* (1996), *Men, Gender Divisions, and Welfare* (1998), *Consuming Cultures* (1999), *Transforming Politics* (1999), and *Hard Work in the Academy* (1999). He has just completed coediting *Information Society and the Workplace* (2004). He was Principal Contractor in the EU FP5 Research Network "The Social Problem of Men" (2000-2003) (www.cromenet .org) and is currently researching men, gender relations and transnational organizing, organizations, and management.

R. W. Connell, Professor of Education at the University of Sydney, formerly was at the University of California, Santa Cruz, and Macquarie University. A researcher on gender, masculinities, education, social class, intellectuals, and social theory, he is the author of *Gender* (2002), *The Men and the Boys* (2000), *Masculinities* (1995), and *Gender and Power* (1987), among other books.

ABOUT THE CONTRIBUTORS

Michele Adams is Assistant Professor at Tulane University. She has published in the areas of family and gender. Her present research examines the cultural impacts of marriage and the gender implications of the pro-marriage movement.

David L. Collinson is FME Professor of Strategic Learning and Leadership in the Department of Management Learning at Lancaster University Management School. Formerly at the Universities of Warwick, Manchester, St. Andrews, and South Florida, he was also Hallsworth Visiting Professor at Manchester Business School in 2001. Adopting a critical approach to management and organization studies, he has published on power, resistance, gender, subjectivity, safety, and humor. Throughout his career, he has been particularly concerned to examine the significance of men and masculinity in shaping workplace processes of control, opposition, and survival. His current research focuses on the development of critical approaches to leadership.

Scott Coltrane is Professor of Sociology at the University of California, Riverside; Associate Director of the UCR Center for Family Studies; recipient of the UCR Distinguished Teaching Award; and former President of the Pacific Sociological Association. He completed his undergraduate studies at Yale University and the University of California, Santa Cruz, and received MA and PhD degrees in sociology from the University of California, Santa Cruz. Coltrane studies gender equity and family functioning, with particular attention to the allocation of housework and child care. He has written about the interrelationships among fatherhood, motherhood, marriage, parenting, domestic labor, popular culture, ethnicity, and structural inequality. He is the author of *Family Man: Fatherhood, Housework, and Gender Equity* (1996; winner of the American Library Association CHOICE Outstanding Academic Book Award), *Gender and Families* (1998), and *Sociology of Marriage and the Family: Gender, Love, and Property* (5th edition, 2001, with Randall Collins), and editor of *Families and Society* (2004). His research has been published in various scholarly journals, including the *American Journal of Sociology*, *Social Problems*, *Sociological Perspectives*, *Journal of Marriage and the Family*, *Journal of Family Issues*, *Gender & Society*, *Sex Roles*, and *Masculinities*.

Critical Research on Men in Europe (CROME) consists of Irina Novikova, Director of the Center for Gender Studies, University of Latvia; Keith Pringle, Professor of Social Work, Aalborg University, Denmark, Honorary Professor, University of Warwick, United Kingdom, and Professor in Social Research, Malardalens Hogskola, Sweden; Jeff Hearn, Academy Fellow and Professor, Swedish School of Economics, Helsinki, Finland, and University of Huddersfield, United Kingdom; Ursula Müller, Professor of Sociology and Women's Studies and Director of the Interdisciplinary Women's Studies Center, University of Bielefeld, Germany; Elzbieta Oleksy, Professor of Humanities, University of Lodz and University of Warsaw; Emmi Lattu, doctoral researcher, Tampere University, Finland; Janna Chernova, Department of Political Science and Sociology, European University at St. Petersburg, Russia; Harry Ferguson, Professor of Social Work, University of West of England, Bristol, U.K.; Øystein Gullvåg Holter, Senior Researcher, Work Research Institute, Oslo, Norway; Voldemar Kolga, Professor of Personality and Developmental Psychology and Chair of the Women's Studies Center, University of Tallinn, Estonia; Carmine Ventimiglia, Professor of Family Sociology, University of Parma, Italy; Eivind Olsvik, formerly Nordic Co-ordinator for Critical Studies on Men, Nordic Institute of Women's Studies and Gender Research, Oslo, Norway; and Teemu Tallberg, doctoral researcher, Swedish School of Economics, Helsinki, Finland. The CROME Web site (including the European

Documentation Centre and Database on Men's Practices) may be found at www.cromenet.org

Walter S. DeKeseredy is Professor of Criminology at the University of Ontario Institute of Technology and recently served as Chair of the American Society of Criminology's Division on Critical Criminology. He and Katharine Kelly conducted the first Canadian national representative sample survey of woman abuse, including sexual assault, in university/college dating. For this work, he was given the Division's Critical Criminologist of the Year Award in 1995. DeKeseredy, who received his PhD in sociology from York University in Toronto, has also published dozens of scientific articles and book chapters on woman abuse, criminological theory, and crime in public housing. He is the author of *Woman Abuse in Dating Relationships: The Role of Male Peer Support* (1988) and is the coauthor of *Woman Abuse: Sociological Perspectives* (1991, with Ronald Hinch), the second edition of *The Wrong Stuff: An Introduction to the Sociological Study of Deviance* (1996, with Desmond Ellis), *Woman Abuse: A Sociological Story* (1997), *Sexual Assault on the College Campus: The Role of Male Peer Support* (1997, with Martin D. Schwartz), *Woman Abuse on Campus: Results From the Canadian National Survey* (1998, with Martin D. Schwartz), *Contemporary Criminology, Contemporary Social Problems in North American Society* (2000, with Shahid Alvi and Desmond Ellis), and *Under Siege: Poverty and Crime in a Public Housing Community* (2003, with Shahid Alvi, Martin D. Schwartz, and E. Andreas Tomaszewski).

Tim Edwards is Lecturer in sociology at the University of Leicester. He is currently writing a book on masculinities and cultural theory, is editing a collection on cultural theory, and holds an Economic and Social Research Council grant to research children's consumption of fashion. Major previous publications include *Contradictions of Consumption* (2000), *Men in the Mirror* (1997), and *Erotics & Politics* (1994).

Richard Ekins is a psychoanalyst in private practice and Reader in Cultural and Media Studies in the School of Media and Performing Arts at the University of Ulster at Coleraine, where he is Director of the Transgender Research Unit and Archive. He coedits the

International Journal of Transgenderism. His edited and authored books include *Centres and Peripheries of Psychoanalysis* (1994, with Ruth Freeman), *Blending Genders* (1996, with Dave King), *Male Femaling* (1997), *Selected Writings by Anna Freud* (1998, with Ruth Freeman), and *Unconscious Mental Life and Reality* (2002).

Michael Flood is Research Fellow at the Australia Institute, a public interest think tank. He has also held positions as a Lecturer in Women's and Gender Studies at the Australian National University, and as the Sexual Health Promotion Coordinator at Sexual Health and Family Planning ACT (Australian Capital Territory). His research interests include men and masculinities, sexualities and especially male sexuality and heterosexuality, interpersonal violence, sexual and reproductive health, and boys and youth cultures. He has been involved in profeminist men's activism since 1987.

Judith Kegan Gardiner is Professor of English and of Gender and Women's Studies as well as being Interim Director of the Center for Research on Women and Gender at the University of Illinois at Chicago. She is a member of the editorial collective of the interdisciplinary journal *Feminist Studies*. Her books include *Craftsmanship in Context: The Development of Ben Jonson's Poetry* (1975), *Rhys, Stead, Lessing, and the Politics of Empathy* (1989), and two edited volumes, *Provoking Agents: Gender and Agency in Theory and Practice* (1995) and *Masculinity Studies and Feminist Theory: New Directions* (2002). Currently she is coediting the *Routledge International Encyclopedia of Men and Masculinity*.

Shahin Gerami is Professor of Sociology and Gender Studies at Southwest Missouri State University. She is a native of Iran and has a law degree from the University of Tehran, as well as a master's and PhD in sociology from the University of Oklahoma. Her research interests focus on gender issues within the context of religious fundamentalism, economic development, and modernization. Her publications in these areas include the book *Women and Fundamentalism: Islam and Christianity* (1996); articles in *Gender and Society, Social Science Quarterly,* and *Early Child Development*; and chapters in books and encyclopedias.

Thomas J. Gerschick is Associate Professor of sociology at Illinois State University, where he teaches about social inequality. His research focuses on the intersection of gender and disability, especially how people with disabilities create self-satisfying gender identities. Outside of academia, he loves to build with Habitat for Humanity.

Matthew C. Gutmann is Associate Professor of Anthropology at Brown University, where he teaches classes on gender, ethnicity-race, health, and ethnography in the Americas. Among his publications are *The Meanings of Macho: Being a Man in Mexico City* (1996), *The Romance of Democracy: Compliant Defiance in Contemporary Mexico* (2002), *Mainstreaming Men Into Gender and Development: Debates, Reflections, and Experiences* (2000, with Sylvia Chant), and the edited volumes *Changing Men and Masculinities in Latin America* (2003) and *Perspectives on Las Americas: A Reader in Culture, History and Representation* (2003, with Felix Matos Rodriguez, Lynn Stephen, and Patricia Zavella).

Paul Higate is Lecturer in Social Policy at the School for Policy Studies at the University of Bristol, United Kingdom. He has a background in the British armed forces. His research interests have developed in recent years to focus on military masculinities within the context of peacekeeping operations. In Spring, 2003, he undertook a period of fieldwork in the Peace Support Missions in the Democratic Republic of Congo and Sierra Leone. He is editor of *Military Masculinities: Identity and the State* (2003) and a research monograph, *Men, Masculinities and Peacekeeping in Sub-Saharan Africa* (in press).

Øystein Gullvåg Holter, PhD in sociology, is Senior Researcher at the Work Research Institute, Oslo, Norway. His background is in gender research, work/family studies, and studies of men. He has worked as Nordic coordinator for studies of men at the University of Oslo. He has written extensively on gender, masculinities, and equality theory, and currently participates in several Nordic and European projects in this field.

John Hopton completed most of his primary and secondary education after moving to Slough in 1963. He originally pursued a career in mental health nursing and nurse education, undertaking higher education courses in the 1980s and completing an MA and PhD within the Centre for Crime and Social Justice, Edge Hill College, in the 1990s. He has been a social science lecturer at Manchester University since 1995 and has published extensively in a range of journals, mostly about mental health. His work in the field of gender studies includes work on masculinity and militarism, the links between hegemonic masculinity and managerialist ideologies, and an exploration of the predominantly masculine culture of the sport known as mixed martial arts or submission fighting.

Brett Hutchins is Lecturer in the School of Sociology and Social Work at the University of Tasmania, where he teaches media studies and social theory. He is currently researching the topic of regional media and globalization. He is the author of *Don Bradman: Challenging the Myth* (2002).

Dave King is Senior Lecturer in the Department of Sociology, Social Policy and Social Work Studies at the University of Liverpool. He has been researching and writing on the sociological aspects of transgender for a number of years. He coedits the *International Journal of Transgenderism*. In addition to several articles, he has written *The Transvestite and the Transsexual: Public Categories and Private Identities* (1993) and is the coeditor (with Richard Ekins) of *Blending Genders: Social Aspects of Cross-dressing and Sex-changing* (1996). He is currently interested in exploring issues and problems around aging and transgendering.

William Marsiglio is Professor of Sociology at the University of Florida. Much of his writing has focused on the social psychology of fatherhood, broadly defined. In addition to his numerous articles on various aspects of men's reproductive and fathering experiences, Marsiglio has written several books on these topics, including *Stepdads: Stories of Love, Hope, and Repair* (2004), *Sex, Men, and Babies: Stories of Awareness and Responsibility* (2002), and *Procreative Man* (1998). He also edited *Fatherhood: Contemporary Theory, Research, and Social Policy* (1995). He and his colleagues coauthored the decade review on fatherhood for the *Journal of Marriage and Family* (2000). He has served as a consultant for major national surveys on men and sexuality/fatherhood issues.

Jim McKay is Associate Professor in the School of Social Science at the University of Queensland, where he teaches courses on gender and popular culture. His most recent books are *Managing Gender: Affirmative Action and Organizational Power in Australian, Canadian, and New Zealand Sport* (1997), *Men, Masculinities, and Sport* (2000, with Michael Messner and Donald Sabo), and *Globalization and Sport* (2001, with Toby Miller, Geoffrey Lawrence, and David Rowe).

James W. Messerschmidt is Professor of Sociology in the Criminology Department at the University of Southern Maine. He is the author of numerous books and articles on men, masculinities, and crime, including *Masculinities and Crime* (1993), *Crime as Structured Action* (1995), and *Nine Lives* (2000). His current work involves life-history research on girls, gender, and violence and is published in his newest work, *Embodied Masculinities, Embodied Violence: Boys, Girls, the Body, and Assault* (2004).

Michael A. Messner is Professor of Sociology and Gender Studies at the University of Southern California, where he currently chairs the sociology department. His books include *Taking the Field: Women, Men, and Sports* (2002), *Paradoxes of Youth and Sport* (2002), and *Power at Play: Sports and the Problem of Masculinity* (1992). He has conducted several commissioned studies on gender and sports media, and he is a past President of the North American Society for the Sociology of Sport.

Janine Mikosza is a PhD candidate in the School of Social Science at the University of Queensland. Her thesis topic is the cultural production of men's magazines in Australia. She has authored various journal articles and book chapters on gender, the media, and the body.

David Morgan recently retired from the University of Manchester, where he taught sociology for more than 35 years. He currently has an emeritus professorship at Manchester and a part-time position as "Professor 2" at Norwegian Technological University, Trondheim. He is the author of a number of books and articles on gender and family, including *Discovering Men* (1992) and *Family Connections* (1996).

Robert Morrell is Professor of Education at the University of Natal. He is a historian by training but currently focuses his research on masculinities in South Africa and the continent more broadly and on the gendered dimensions of sexuality in a context of AIDS. He is the author of *From Boys to Gentlemen: Settler Masculinity in Colonial Natal, 1880-1920* (2001) and editor of *Changing Men in Southern Africa* (2001).

Joane Nagel is University Distinguished Professor of Sociology at the University of Kansas. She is author of *American Indian Ethnic Renewal* (1996) and *Race, Ethnicity, and Sexuality: Intimate Intersections, Forbidden Frontiers* (2003).

Joseph H. Pleck is Professor of Human Development and Family Studies at the University of Illinois at Urbana-Champaign. His books include *The Myth of Masculinity* (1981), *Working Wives, Working Husbands* (1985), and *The Impact of Work Schedules on the Family* (1985). He has also published numerous articles and chapters on adolescent male contraception, attitudes toward masculinity, and father involvement. His current work focuses on paternal identity in residential fathers and on the development of stable romantic unions in young adult men. He is Co-Principal Investigator of the National Survey of Adolescent Males program.

Ken Plummer is Professor of Sociology at the University of Essex, England. His main books are *Sexual Stigma* (1975), *Documents of Life* (1983), *Documents of Life-2* (2001), *Telling Sexual Stories* (1995), and *Intimate Citizenship* (2003); he also coauthored *Sociology: A Global Introduction* (2nd ed., 2002, with John Macionis). He has written numerous articles on sexuality, life stories, symbolic interactionism, and lesbian and gay studies. He is the founder and editor of the journal *Sexualities*.

Don Sabo is Professor of Sociology at D'Youville College in Buffalo, New York, and Director of the Center for Research on Physical Activity, Sport & Health (www.sporthealthresearch.org). He is a recognized expert on gender relations and has been writing and lecturing about issues including physical activity and health, gender equity in athletics, sport and masculinity, and men's violence since 1980. His research and writing also focus on linkages among gender, health, and illness, and he has spearheaded the development of "men's health studies." His latest book, *Prison Masculinities* (2001, coedited with T. A. Kupers and W. London), explores the ways that American prisons mirror the worst aspects of society-wide gender relations. He is an eye-to-eye scholar, an avid keynoter, and a public intellectual who is regularly quoted in the national media.

Martin D. Schwartz is Professor of Sociology and Presidential Research Scholar at Ohio University and is now Visiting Research Fellow at the National Institute of Justice, U.S. Department of Justice. He has written or edited 11 books, more than 60 refereed journal articles, and another 40 book chapters, government reports, and essays. A former officer of several organizations, he received the lifetime achievement award of the American Society of Criminology's Division on Critical Criminology and currently serves as coeditor of the journal *Criminal Justice: An International Journal of Policy and Practice.* He serves on or has served on the editorial boards or as deputy editor of 11 journals, including the top American criminology journals *Criminology* and *Justice Quarterly.* He has done manuscript reviews for 55 journals and publishers. At Ohio University, he has won a variety of teaching and service awards, including Graduate Professor of the Year and Best Arts and Sciences Professor (twice), while being the first social scientist to win the university's research achievement award, the title of Presidential Research Scholar. His PhD is from the University of Kentucky, where he was awarded the 2002 Thomas R. Ford Distinguished Alumni Award.

Jon Swain worked for 17 years as a primary school teacher in the United Kingdom before earning a PhD at the Institute of Education, University of London, with a thesis on the construction of boys' masculinities. His particular academic interests are gender, education, and identities. He is currently working as Research Fellow at King's College, London, on two projects concerning adult numeracy.

Sandra Swart is a socioenvironmental historian of southern Africa and lectures at the University of Stellenbosch. She received both her doctorate in history and a master's degree in environmental change and management from Oxford University. She has published on Afrikaner masculinity and on the socio-environmental history of the dog and horse in southern Africa.

Futoshi Taga is Associate Professor in the Faculty of Literature, Kurume University, Japan, where he teaches sociology, education, and gender studies. He was the first person in Japan to complete a PhD on a topic related to masculinities; his thesis was subsequently published as the book *Dansei no Jenda Keisei* (The Gender Formation of Men). He also has a chapter, "Rethinking Male Socialisation: Life Histories of Japanese Male Youth," in the collection *Asian Masculinities* (2003).

Mara Viveros Vigoya is Associate Professor of Anthropology at the Universidad Nacional de Colombia in Bogotá, where she also directs the master's program in cultural anthropology. She is the author of *Hombres e identidades de género: Investigaciones desde América Latina* (2001, with José Olavarría and Norma Fuller) and *De quebradores y cumplidores: Sobre hombres, masculinidades y relaciones de género en Colombia* (2002), as well as being the coeditor of *Mujeres de los Andes: Condiciones de vida y salud* (1992, with Anne-Claire Defossez and Didier Fassin), *Genero e identidad: Ensayos sobre lo femenino y lo masculino* (1995, with Luz Gabriela Arango and Magdalena León), and *Cuerpo, diferencias y desigualdades* (1999, with Gloria Garay).

Heavy Equipment

Heavy Equipment:

The World's Largest Machinery

John Carroll

CHARTWELL
BOOKS, INC.

A QUINTET BOOK

Published by Chartwell Books
A Division of Book Sales Inc.
114 Northfield Avenue
Edison, New Jersey 08837

This edition produced for sale in the U.S.A., its
territories and dependencies only.

ISBN 0-7858-0607-5

This book was designed and produced by
Quintet Publishing Limited
6 Blundell Street
London N7 9BH

Creative Director: Richard Dewing
Art Director: Silke Braun
Designer: Steve West
Project Editor: Clare Hubbard
Editor: Rosie Hankin
Picture Researcher: Penni Bickle

Typeset in Great Britain by
Central Southern Typesetters, Eastbourne
Manufactured in Bath, England
by DP Graphics
Printed in Singapore by
Star Standard Industries (Pte.) Ltd.

The author would like to acknowledge the help of
John Atherton of Alto Plant Services Ltd, Bardon (England) Ltd,
Ennemix Construction Materials, Tarmac Quarry Products
Eastern Ltd, and Ian Clegg.

Note
Tons (t) given in this book are US short tons. 1 ton = 2,000 pounds.
Metric tonnes (MT) are also provided. 1 metric ton = 2,204.6 pounds.

Contents

Introduction

One of the smaller steam excavators in the cut of the Manchester Ship Canal.

Introduction

As long as there has been any form of civilization, human beings have sought through civil engineering to modify the environment around them to enable them to live more easily. As early as 510 BC, Darius, the King of Persia, ordered a canal to be cut from the River Nile to the Red Sea, the Romans built canals in various parts of Europe, and the Chinese built a series of waterways including the 600-mile (965.58-kilometer) long Grand Canal which in the eighth century is recorded as having carried 2.24 million tons (2.03 million tonnes) of goods. From medieval times onward, canal building spread widely across Europe but it was the Industrial Revolution that heralded the beginnings of the age of major civil engineering, of mechanization, and the development of the machine which enabled the scale of what was possible to increase exponentially. For example Ch'iao Wei-Yo, a Chinese engineer, is known to have invented the pound or chamber lock in order to lift and lower boats between different levels of waterway and had one built in AD 984. The principle was established and later Leonardo da Vinci would build a series of such locks on the Naviglio Interno near Milan in fifteenth-century Italy but it was the developments of the Industrial Revolution that enabled the construction of locks big enough to carry ocean-going ships. These developments affected both the undertaking and scale of civil engineering projects and the way in which they could be accomplished. Steam would provide the power for ships and railroad locomotives. It would also deliver the power for the machines used in their construction; it would provide the means to extract the fossil fuel for the machines. The machines would be capable of extracting minerals for the making of steel and of quarrying stone for construction.

The history of machines for construction is intertwined with the economics of the labor market and economies of scale. The use of heavy machinery became widespread in the United States earlier than it did in Europe for reasons of economy: in the United States labor was scarce and expensive, so machines made economic sense, whereas in Europe labor was considerably more plentiful and cheaper. As a result much of the construction of the canal and, later, railroad systems in Europe was achieved through the efforts of countless laborers, known as "navvies" in Britain where many of their number were Irish. The Eastwick & Harrison Company from Philadelphia were amongst the pioneers of the mechanical excavator in the United States. Their limited-slew type Otis steam excavator was in use for railroad construction as early as 1838. By the 1930s the steam shovel was such an accepted part of American industry that mention of it by Woody Guthrie, the American Dust Bowl balladeer, would scarcely raise an eyebrow although his songs did: "...a dust storm buried her. She was a good girl; long, tall and stout. I had to get a steam shovel just to dig my darlin' out." ("Dust Bowl Blues").

Canal Development

One of the Ruston, Proctor & Co. Ltd Steam Navvies at work on the Manchester Ship Canal. Steam Navvies were named after the laborers who operated them.

Swift progress in engineering projects was made after the Industrial Revolution so that what was once only a dream soon became the achievable. An example is the Suez Canal that was designed as a short cut for ships between the Mediterranean and the Red Sea. The idea had been considered in as early as 1799 by Napoleon I of France but no progress was made for another six decades. Ferdinand de Lesseps was the man who provided much of the momentum behind the project and launched the International Suez Canal Company in 1858. The scale of the project was daunting, the line of the canal was 100 miles (161 kilometers) and it had to be wide and deep enough to carry ocean-going vessels. Despite British strategic concerns, work began in 1859 and was completed in November 1869.

One of the last canals constructed in Great Britain was the Manchester Ship Canal, a 36-mile (57.93-kilometer) ditch between the sea and the inland city of Manchester. It was opened in 1894. The project required at various times up to 17,000 laborers and tradesmen, and temporary railroads were laid to carry wagons used for removing the soil. This massive project also provided a hint of what was to come as a great deal of